PETRA GREAT TEMPLE

VOLUME III

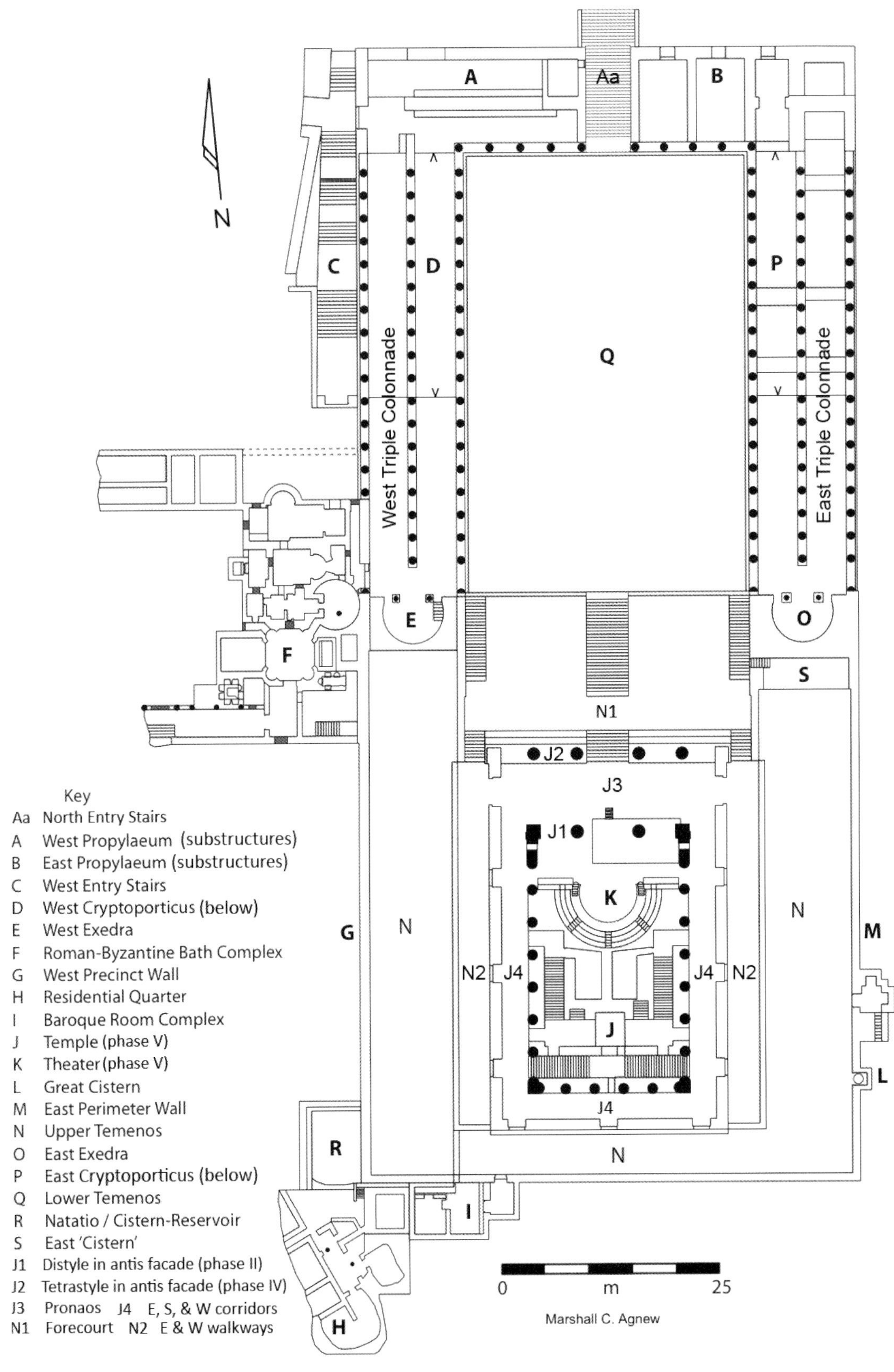
N
A
Aa
B
C
D
P
Q
West Triple Colonnade
East Triple Colonnade
E
O
F
S
N1
J2
J3
J1
K
G
N
N
M
N2
J4
J4
N2
J
L
J4
R
N
I
H
Key
Aa North Entry Stairs
A West Propylaeum (substructures)
B East Propylaeum (substructures)
C West Entry Stairs
D West Cryptoporticus (below)
E West Exedra
F Roman-Byzantine Bath Complex
G West Precinct Wall
H Residential Quarter
I Baroque Room Complex
J Temple (phase V)
K Theater (phase V)
L Great Cistern
M East Perimeter Wall
N Upper Temenos
O East Exedra
P East Cryptoporticus (below)
Q Lower Temenos
R Natatio / Cistern-Reservoir
S East 'Cistern'
J1 Distyle in antis facade (phase II)
J2 Tetrastyle in antis facade (phase IV)
J3 Pronaos J4 E, S, & W corridors
N1 Forecourt N2 E & W walkways
0 m 25
Marshall C. Agnew

PETRA GREAT TEMPLE

VOLUME III

Brown University Excavations 1993-2008
Architecture and Material Culture

Edited by

MARTHA SHARP JOUKOWSKY

with contributions by

Marshall C. Agnew, Etan Ayalon, Deirdre G. Barrett, Dávid Bartus, Joseph J. Basile, Ruby Cerón-Carrasco, Christian F. Cloke, Emily Catherine Egan, Rune Frederiksen, Traianos Gagos, Angela Murock Hussein, Fawwaz Rushdi Ishakat, Sarah Whitcher Kansa, Margaret O'Hea, Megan A. Perry, Francois Poplin, Eleanor A. Power, Shaher M. Rababeh, Shari S. Saunders, Donna Strahan, and Christopher A. Tuttle

with the financial assistance of

Brown University Petra Exploration Fund
Joukowsky Institute for Archaeology and the Ancient World
Brown University, Providence, Rhode Island

Oxford & Philadelphia

Published in the United Kingdom in 2017 by
OXBOW BOOKS
The Old Music Hall, 106–108 Cowley Road, Oxford OX4 1JE

and in the United States by
OXBOW BOOKS
1950 Lawrence Road, Havertown, PA 19083

Hardcover Edition: ISBN 978-1-78570-612-7
Digital Edition: ISBN 978-1-78570-613-4

A CIP record for this book is available from the British Library

Library of Congress Control Number: 2016955260

Layout: C. Corley
Printed in the Czech Republic by FINIDR, s.r.o.

For a complete list of Oxbow titles, please contact:

UNITED KINGDOM
Oxbow Books
Telephone (01865) 241249, Fax (01865) 794449
Email: oxbow@oxbowbooks.com
www.oxbowbooks.com

UNITED STATES OF AMERICA
Oxbow Books
Telephone (800) 791-9354, Fax (610) 853-9146
Email: queries@casemateacademic.com
www.casemateacademic.com/oxbow

Oxbow Books is part of the Casemate Group

Front cover image: View of The Great Temple in ancient city Petra, Jordan
(Nickolay Vinokurov/Shutterstock)

ADDRESSES OF CONTRIBUTORS

Marshall Agnew
4415 Eastern Ave N, Seattle, WA 98103
mcagnew@gmail.com

Etan Ayalon
Eretz Israel Museum, POB 17068, Tel Aviv 61170 Israel
etana@eretzmuseum.org.il

Deirdre Grace Barrett
Semitic Museum, Harvard University,
6 Divinity Ave., Cambridge, MA 02138
deirdre_barrett@icloud.com

Dávid Bartus
Department of Classical and Roman Archaeology,
Eötvös Loránd University of Budapest,
Múzeum krt. 4/B, 1088 Budapest, Hungary
bartusdavid@gmail.com

Joseph J. Basile
Maryland Institute College of Art,
1300 Mount Royale Ave., Baltimore, MD 21217
jbasile@mica.edu

G. W. Bowersock
Institute for Advanced Study,
Olden Lane, Princeton, NJ 08540
gwb@ias.edu

Dr Ruby N Ceron-Carrasco
Collections Unit
Historic Environment Scotland |
Àrainneachd Eachdraidheil Alba
Longmore House, Salisbury Place,
Edinburgh, EH9 1SH Scotland
ruby.ceron-carrasco@hes.scot

Christian F. Cloke
3333 University Blvd W Apt 606,
Kensington, MD 20895
Christian.Cloke@alumni.brown.edu

Emily Catherine Egan
Assistant Professor of Ancient Eastern
Mediterranean Art and Archaeology
University of Maryland,
Dept. of Art History and Archaeology
4216 Parren J. Mitchell Building,
3834 Campus Drive, College Park, MD 20742
ecegan@umd.edu

Rune Frederiksen
National Museum of Denmark, Prinsens Palais,
Ny Vestergade 10 1471 Copenhagen, Denmark
rufr@GLYPTOTEKET.DK

Angela Murock Hussein
Heuberger Tor Weg 17.4, Tübingen 72076 Germany
anginegypt@yahoo.com

Fawwaz Rushdi Ishakat
Queen Rania Institute of Tourism & Heritage,
The Hashemite University, P. O. Box 150459,
Zarqa, 13115 Jordan
anto.lepone@gmail.com

Martha Sharp Joukowsky
Joukowsky Institute for Archaeology and
the Ancient World, Brown University,
Box 1837, Providence, RI 02912
martha_joukowsky@brown.edu

Sarah Whitcher Kansa
The Alexandria Archive Institute,
125 El Verano Way, San Francisco, CA 94127
sarahkansa@gmail.com

Dr. Margaret O'Hea, FSA
Senior Lecturer in Archaeology in the
Dept. of Classics Archaeology and Ancient History,
Director of the Museum of Classical Archaeology,
School of Humanities,
The University of Adelaide, Australia 5005
margaret.ohea@adelaide.edu.au

François Poplin
Muséum National d'Histoire naturelle,
UMR 7209 du CNRS, 55 rue Buffon,
Paris, 75005 France
poplin@mnhn.fr

Elly Power
Santa Fe Institute, 1399 Hyde Park Rd.,
Santa Fe NM 87501
eleanorapower@gmail.com

Shaher M. Rababeh
Department of Conservation Sciences and
Department of Architecture,
The Hashemite University, P. O. Box 15049,
Zerqa, Jordan
srababeh@yahoo.com

Shari Saunders
507, 175 Hunter East Hamilton,
Ontario Canada L8N 4E7
shari_egypt@yahoo.com

Donna Strahan
Sherman Fairchild Center for Objects Conservation,
The Metropolitan Museum of Art,
1000 Fifth Avenue, New York, NY 10028

Christopher A. Tuttle , Ph.D.
Executive Director, Council of American Overseas
Research Centers (CAORC), PO Box 37012,
MRC 178, Washington, DC 20013-7012
tuttle.ca@caorc.org

Petra Great Temple, Volume III appears under the auspices of, and in collaboration with, the Joukowsky Institute for Archaeology and the Ancient World at Brown University, Providence, Rhode Island. The Joukowsky Institute also produces an ongoing series of books entitled *Joukowsky Institute Publications* (*JIP*), published and distributed by Oxbow Books. These volumes, under the General Editorship of Prof. John F. Cherry, have as their focus the dissemination of the results of conference and workshops held under the Institute's aegis, on fieldwork reports and other scholarly studies by faculty associated with the Institute, and on the publication of archaeological material in Brown University collections.

Joukowsky Institute Publications titles now available or forthcoming include:

JIP 1 *KOINE: Mediterranean Studies in Honor of R. Ross Holloway*, edited by Derek B. Counts and Anthony S. Tuck (2009)

JIP 2 *Re-Presenting the Past: Archaeology through Text and Image*, edited by Sheila Bonde and Stephen Houston. (2013)

JIP 3 *Locating the Sacred: Theoretical Approaches to the Emplacement of Religion*, edited by Claudia Moser and Cecelia Feldman (2014)

JIP 4 *Violence and Civilization: Studies of Social Violence in History and Prehistory*, edited by Roderick Campbell (2014)

JIP 5 *Of Rocks and Water: Towards and Archaeology of Place*, edited by Ömür Harmansah (2014)

JIP 6 *Archaeologies of Text: Archaeology, Technology, and Ethics*, edited by Matthew T. Rutz and Morag M. Kersel (2014)

JIP 7 *Archaeology for the People*, edited by John F. Cherry and Felipe Rojas (2015)

JIP 8 *Antiquarianisms: Contact, Conflict, Comparison*, edited by Benjamin Anderson and Felipe Rojas (forthcoming 2017)

JIP 9 *The Art of War: Imagery, Ideology, Impact*, edited by Laurel Bestock and Anne Hunnell Chen (forthcoming 2018)

TABLE OF CONTENTS

GENERAL ABBREVIATIONS

1. Previous volumes

Vol. 1	*Petra: The Great Temple, vol. I: Brown University excavations 1993-1997* (Brown University, Petra Exploration Fund 1998).
Vol. 2	*Petra Great Temple, vol. II: Archaeological contexts of the remains and excavations. Brown University Excavations in Jordan at the Petra Great Temple 1993-2007* (Brown University, Petra Exploration Fund 2007).

2. Journal abbreviations

AA	*Archäologische Anzeiger*
AAS	*Annales archéologiques de Syrie*
AASOR	*Annual of the American Schools of Oriental Research*
ACOR	American Center of Oriental Research, Amman
ACORN	*ACOR Newsletter*, American Center of Oriental Research, Amman
ADAJ	*Annual of the Department of Antiquities of Jordan, Amman*
AfO	*Archiv für Orientforschung*
AI	*Art International*
AIHV	*L'association internationale pour l'histoire du verre*
AJA	*American Journal of Archaeology*
ANRW	*Aufstieg und Niedergang der römischen Welt*
AnatSt	*Anatolian Studies*
ANSMN	*American Numismatic Society Museum Notes*
AntJ	*The Antiquaries Journal. The Journal of the Society of Antiquaries of London*
AntK	*Antike Kunst*
AOS	*American Oriental Society.*
ARAM	International Conference(s). The Nabataeans (Oxford)
BA	*The Biblical Archaeologist, American Schools of Oriental Research*
BAR	British Archaeological Reports
BAR-S	British Archaeological Reports, International Series
BASOR	*Bulletin of the American Schools of Oriental Research*
BJb	*Bonner Jahrbücher des Rheinischen Landesmuseums*
BMC	*British Museum catalogue of the Greek coins of Phoenicia*
BMCRE	*Coins of the Roman Empire in the British Museum (London 1923-)*
BMQ	*British Museum Quarterly*
BSRAA	*Bulletin de la Société royale d'archéologie d'Alexandrie*
BTS	*Bible et Terre Sainte*
CAH	*Cambridge Ancient History*
CahByrsa	*Cahiers de Byrsa*
CAJ	*Cambridge Archaeological Journal*
CIL	*Corpus Inscriptionum Latinarum*
CIS II	*Corpus Inscriptionum Semiticarum.* Pars II. Tomus II. Fasc. I. Sectio Secunda. *Inscriptiones Nabataeae* (Paris)
Corinth	*Corinth. Results of excavations conducted by the American School of Classical Studies at Athens*
CQ	*Classical Quarterly*
CRAI	*Comptes rendus de l'Académie des inscriptions et belles lettres*
CronPomp	*Cronache pompeiane*
DaM	*Damaszener Mitteilungen*
DarSag	C. Daremberg and E. Saglio, *Dictionnaire des antiquités grecques et romaines* (Paris 1875)
Das Altertum	*Das Altertum*
DossArch	*Les Dossiers d'archéologie*
DOP	*Dumbarton Oaks Papers*
EEF	Egypt Exploration Fund
EW	*East and West*
Expedition	*Expedition, Bulletin of the University Museum of the University of Pennsylvania*
FIFAO	*Fouilles de l'Institut français d'archéologie orientale*
IEJ	*Israel Exploration Journal*
IES	Israel Exploration Society
IFAPO	Institut français d'archéologie du Proche-Orient
IGLSyr	*Inscriptions grecques et latines de la Syrie*
ILN	*Illustrated London News*
IOS	*Israel Oriental Studies*
IstItMEO	Istituto italiano per il Medio ed Estremo Orient
JA	*Journal Asiatique*
JAOS	*Journal of the American Oriental Society*
JArchSci	*Journal of Archaeological Science*
JANES	*Journal of Ancient Near Eastern Society*

JEOL	*Jaarbericht Vooraziatisch-Egyptisch Gezelschap "Ex Oriente Lux"*
JGS	*Journal of Glass Studies*
JHS	*Journal of Hellenic Studies*
JNES	*Journal of Near Eastern Studies*
JQR	*Jewish Quarterly Review*
JRA	*Journal of Roman Archaeology*
JRGZM	*Jahrbuch des Römisch-Germanischen Zentralmuseums Mainz*
JRS	*Journal of Roman Studies*
JSOR	*Journal of the Society of Oriental Research*
KölnJb	*Kölner Jahrbuch für Vor- und Frühgeschichte*
LCL	Loeb Classical Library (texts quoted with name of editor[s] and translator[s])
LRBC	*Late Roman bronze coinage, A.D. 324-498* (2 vols., London)
MASCAJ	*MASCA Journal* (Museum Applied Science Center for Archaeology, University Museum, University of Pennsylvania)
MASCAP	*MASCA Research Papers in Science and Archaeology*
MMAJ	*Metropolitan Museum of Art Journal*
NC	*The Numismatic Chronicle*
NEA	*Near Eastern Archaeology* (American Schools of Oriental Research, Boston)
NomChron	*Nomismatika chronika*
OIP	Oriental Institute Publications, University of Chicago
OpArch	*Opuscula archaeologica*
PEFA	*Palestine Exploration Fund Annual*
PEQ	*Palestine Exploration Quarterly*
QDAP	*Quarterly of the Department of Antiquities in Palestine*
Qobes	*Qobes 'al-Yad* (Jewish Palestine Exploration Society, Jerusalem)
RA	*Revue archéologique*
RBibl	*Revue biblique*
RCRFActa	*Rei Cretariae Romanae Fautorum Acta*
RIC	*The Roman Imperial Coinage* (London 1923-)
SHAJ	*Studies in the History and Archaeology of Jordan*
SIMA	*Studies in Mediterranean Archaeology*
SNG ANS	*Sylloge Nummorum Graecorum. The collection of the America Numismatic Society, New York*
ZDPV	*Zeitschrift des Deutschen Palästina-Vereins*
ZfA	*Zeitschrift für Archäologie*

3. Other Abbreviations:

The Great Temple database systems use different abbreviations for encoding the Catalogue, Architectural Fragments, Coins, Lamps and Glass databases.
The Grosso Modo database has specific fields for part, function, shape, liquid and paint color, motif, plastic decoration and culture.

AB	abacus when encoding Grosso Modo stucco shape
AD	architectural decoration when encoding Grosso Modo stucco moldings for function
AF	architectural fragment when encoding Grosso Modo stucco
Arch. Frag.	Architectural Fragment, also AF(s)
a.s.l.	above sea level
-B-	in a catalogue number indicating the object is bone
BO	boss when encoding Grosso Modo stucco shape
b.s.l.	below sea level
c.	century
c.	*circa*
-C-	in a catalogue number indicating the object is a coin
Cat. no.	Catalogue Number of object in site registry
CD	column decoration when encoding Grosso Modo stucco for function
cf.	compare
-CO-	indicating stucco in a catalogue number
d.	depth
DFF	Daily field form
DL	dentil when encoding Grosso Modo stucco shape
DoA	Jordanian Department of Antiquities
DT	dart/tongue when encoding Grosso Modo stucco shape
ed./edd.	edited by, editor(s)
-ED-	egg and dart/tongue when encoding Grosso Modo stucco shape
edn.	edition
EG	egg when encoding Grosso Modo stucco shape
F	flat when encoding Grosso Modo stucco shape
-F-	in a catalogue number indicating the object is faïence
FL	floral when encoding Grosso Modo stucco shape
-G-	in a catalogue number indicating the object is glass
GM	Grosso Modo, database for multiple artifacts
INAA	instrumental neutron analysis
-L-	in a catalogue number indicating the object is a lamp
LF	leaf when encoding Grosso Modo stucco shape
Loc.	Locus
LT	Lower Temenos (area)
-M-	in a catalogue number indicating the object is metal
m.s.l.	mean sea level
Nazzal's	name for dig house used before Burckhardt Center
-OS-	other string course when encoding Grosso Modo stucco shape
P	Propylaeum (area)
-P-	in a catalogue number indicating the object is pottery
P/GT	Petra Great Temple
P/ST	Petra Southern Temple (used before 1995) and P/GT
RI	ribbed or fluted when encoding Grosso Modo stucco shape
RQ	Residential Quarter
-S-	in a catalogue number indicating the object is stone
Seq. No.	Excavation sequence
SF	Special Find (to go to the catalogue)
-Sh-	in a catalogue number indicating the object is shell
SH	in Grosso Modo indicating the object is shell
SP	Special Project sondage, probe
-ST-	stucco when encoding Grosso Modo material
T	Temple (area)
Tr.	Trench
UT	Upper Temenos (area)
-Veg-	in a catalogue number indicating the object is vegetable matter
VI	vine when encoding Grosso Modo stucco shape
VO	volute when encoding Grosso Modo stucco shape
vol.(s)	Volume(s)
WD	wall decoration when encoding Grosso Modo stucco for function

LIST OF FIGURES

CHAPTER 14: THE GLASS (1998-2006)

CHAPTER 15: COINS FROM THE GREAT TEMPLE EXCAVATIONS:AN OVERVIEW

LIST OF TABLES AND CHARTS

APPENDICES –TABLES

APPENDIX 1: GREAT TEMPLE LIST OF TRENCHES AND SPECIAL PROJECTS BY AREA

APPENDIX 3: DATABASE METHODOLOGY AND RESULTS

APPENDIX 4: GREAT TEMPLE CERAMICS

APPENDIX 5: GREAT TEMPLE ARCHITECTURAL FRAGMENTS

FOREWORD

When I first went to Petra almost fifty years ago and slept in the surprisingly hospitable cave known as Nazal's Camp, the site was no less unforgettable and magical than it was when John Lewis Burckhardt went there in 1812 or Edward Lear in 1858. It retains its magnificence today, thanks to the famously rose-red sandstone environment that nature provided for the Nabataean Arabs to construct their imposing tombs in the encompassing rock walls. The creation of a park at the site and the proliferation of tourist accommodations outside the ancient city have now greatly facilitated access to Petra's marvels.

Excavations over the years since my first visit have uncovered long buried structures, such as the Temple of the Winged Lions, opened up by Philip Hammond from Utah, and the Byzantine church, meticulously published by Jaakko Frôsén, Zbigniew Fiema, and their team at the Center of Excellence in Helsinki. Jordanian archaeologists have now dug down to the shrine that preceded the spectacular Khazneh that greets every visitor who walks into the city through its narrow rock-bound entrance known as the Siq. The Finns have rescued a cache of carbonized papyri from the sixth century AD that suddenly gave new life to a city that had been assumed moribund after an earthquake in the fourth century. Petra is as remarkable today as it always was, but the place itself, like its history, has become strikingly different from when I first saw it.

This change is due in no small measure to the stupendous excavations that Brown University launched in 1993 above the south side of the colonnaded street under the direction of Martha Sharp Joukowsky. On an elevation, approached by a grand staircase or propylaeum, to the east of the Temenos Gate on the street, lie the remains of a monumental complex that led Walter von Bachmann, Peter Parr, and others to name these ruins the Great Temple. It was to recover this monument with its propylaeum that the Brown archaeologists began the extensive excavations that occupied them for fifteen years. They continue to call their monument the Petra Great Temple, and for good reason. It is large, imposing, and centrally situated in the heart of the city, and although there has been considerable debate as to whether this was a sacred or secular space I now find it hard to believe that it can have been anything other than a temple, though used for more than cultic purposes. It has proven to be an architectural complex of astonishing originality, which propels its Nabataean builders well beyond their well deserved reputation for handsome rock-cut tombs. Its location and its splendor imply that it played a central role in both the religious and civic life of Petra. The small theater that was discovered inside it would seem to reflect its use for ceremonies and meetings as well as for religious rituals.

The Brown excavations have so far been described in two massive scholarly publications, beautifully composed and illustrated, the first in 1998 and the second in 2007. Now Professor Joukowsky has brought the immense work of publication to a triumphant conclusion with a third volume, which complements all that went before, with new analyses and new material. Some of the finds that have already made the Great Temple so renowned re-appear in fresh treatments, above all the elephant-head capitals that were such a surprise when they turned up twenty years ago, and the unexpected theater located inside the temple in what is by no means the only example of this phenomenon in the region. The temple's water systems become highly relevant to the adjacent Roman-Byzantine baths, to which the ninth chapter is devoted, as well as to the ornamental pool and garden (*paradeisos*) that was engineered to the east of the temple. The pool evokes the notorious aquatic entertainments of the Maiouma that are epigraphically documented for the large shallow pool that has now emerged at Aphrodisias in Turkey.

On a personal note, I am moved to signal the contribution to this volume from Traianos Gagos on the inscriptions from the Great Temple, because every passing year makes me realize what a superb scholar we have lost through his untimely death only a few years ago. And on another personal note I want to salute Martha Joukowsky for her dynamic leadership throughout the course of the Great Temple project. Her concern for the conservation, preservation, and presentation of her finds reflects the dedication that she and her husband, Artemis, have shown to the extraordinary antiquities of Jordan from the beginning. She and I first met through our friend Kenan Erim when she was working on his excavations at Aphrodisias, and I dare to believe that the two sites in the ancient Mediterranean world that mean the most to me, Aphrodisias and Petra, mean just as much to her.

G. W. BOWERSOCK
11 January 2016

Preface

Variety distinguishes Petra's natural environment. Deeply nestled in the rift valley, the site evokes a sense of geographic protection and isolation from the outside world. Scattered amongst 800 tombs and a number of freestanding structures such as the Great Temple, within the picturesque city are to be found rugged sandstone outcrops of bedrock, endless mazes of craggy weathered ridges, and dramatic hills and valleys. Created by crumbling sandstone, the soil is sandy and thin, with few trees, thorny shrubs, and oleander bushes blooming in summer. The landmarks of the Nabataean past blend into the present. This relationship of geography and metropolis did not just happen: it arose by nature's design and from the minds of those who lived there.

From the earliest days of the Nabataean era, nameless leaders brought together traditionally separate tribes into a single entity under the banner that we call 'Nabataean'. This integration, which must have required some time, became a manifestation of a single rule. The political ingenuity of the early leaders must have been to select active military men who knew well the rigors of the desert and the locations of its watering holes, men expert in the monitoring and defense of its trade routes. Within a few decades, selected among them was one who could guarantee their stability and trust, and he became their leader king.

Those who followed selected Petra to be the Nabataean capital of a nation state. With its sprawling development, Petra became a bustling city with exciting and distinctive architectural and artistic styles as the Petraeans determined what a resplendent capital with a burgeoning population and assured economic future should represent. These Nabataeans sought advantages through expansion of their kingdom and the trade and commerce that followed. They also wished to transform Petra, their capital showpiece, to be as grand as the other leading 1st-c. cities such as Pergamum, Antioch, Athens and Alexandria. Architects and artisans were sought whose flair and imagination would enhance the spectacular natural features of the site and its magical setting. What strikes us today are the conscious choices made over the years by the Nabataeans — the pride of their kings, public officials, city planners, architects and artisans, who must have believed that Petra was a covenant between the people and the exquisite natural setting. As will become clear from the chapters in this volume devoted to the Great Temple, a single precinct in the city, this was an individualized development process.

The book, describing the natural diversity at the Great Temple and revealing various facets of Nabataean material culture, arises from the questions we asked about the data from the Great Temple. It intends to expose a cross section of the material culture, from water-supply systems and architectural designs (including the distyle and tetrastyle temples and the Theater-in-Temple), to studies of artifacts (sculpture, ceramics, numismatics, metal and bone); we also offer a look at subsistence patterns at the site.

The book is divided into two main sections. Part I explores the principles of the temple layout and how it was built: Nabataean construction techniques, hydraulic systems, the use of plaster decoration and stucco revetments, pilaster relief sculptures, Nabataean-Corinthian capitals from the Great Temple, elephant-head capitals, the Theater-in-the-Temple, and the Roman-Byzantine Baths. Each of these features proves to be idiosyncratic to the Great Temple precinct.

Chapter 1 introduces the site and how our investigations unfolded. It serves as a blueprint for understanding the Great Temple by providing the archaeological context, including a discussion of the precinct's major features (Propylaeum, Lower Temenos, Upper Temenos and Temple[s]). Next, the chronology assigned to the 15 Site Phases based on the stratigraphic deposition and the dating of deposts is discussed. The phases from the Nabataean period through the Byzantine and Modern periods are then summarized, followed by a year-by-year summary of the excavations. The CAVE (Cave Automatic Virtual Environment), the first Virtual Reality 3D GIS application for ongoing fieldwork, is summarized before giving an overview of databases (including the catalogues).

Chapter 2 (M. C. Agnew and F. Rushdi Ishakat) is devoted to the Great Temple surveying systems. Agnew in particular has laboriously rendered and re-ordered the site plans for this volume. Ishakat stepped in as head surveyor in 2009. By the end of that season we had recovered and clarified years of surveying data. Ishakat was able to plug all the slices of existing data into a crystallized GPS scenario for a comprehensive strategy not only for Petra but for the Great Temple in particular and the chapter describes how this was accomplished. How did the Nabataeans build the Great Temple? In chapt. 3, S. M. Rababeh pays close attention to architectural detail to analyse the dynamic temple construction. The water supply of the Great Temple, a significant achievement of Nabataean hydraulic engineering, includes a complex system of water storage and distribution systems. The temple builders considerably changed the landscape to construct a massive subterranean drainage system. We began tracing the paths of these surface and subsurface features in 1995 using ground-penetrating radar (GPR), and chapt. 4 (C. F. Cloke) is a comprehensive concordance of the water systems of the Great Temple. His plotting of the systems allows an appreciation of their ingenious construction in a complex topographic setting. Having supervised excavation of the Great Cistern, Cloke presents the precinct's vast hydraulic systems, the bulk of which were put in place before the earliest distyle temple was built. The Great Cistern remains the largest known water depository in the central part of the city. The self-reliant Nabataean spirit transformed the hostile Petra environment by manipulating the available water resources, altering the landscape by re-routing and capturing supplies to suit the site's needs.

The Nabataeans also mastered fresco decoration. Some of the designs on the Great Temple's walls echo ones known from the Roman world. Much of this rich evidence has survived even if poorly preserved. In chapt. 5, E. C. Egan, who excavated the fresco-embellished South Corridor of the Temple, decodes these evanescent designs through careful observation of their design.

The sculpted pilaster reliefs (chapt. 6) are the focus of J. J. Basile, who has been involved with analysis of the Great Temple's sculpture since 1997 and published their characteristic representations in 2001, but this is the first systematic approach to the pilaster blocks. There seems to be a basic thematic unity with depiction of the Roman Fortuna (Greek Tyche), identified with fortune, luck and fate. The style and content of the pilaster relief figures are clearly Nabataean in date, demonstrating the eclectic adoption of earlier representational art while sculpting it in an individualistic Nabataean style.

Divided into two parts, chapter 7 presents the Nabataean sculptural vocabulary of the Great Temple's capitals. First, the Nabataean-Corinthian capitals decorating Phase II, the earliest distyle temple, are examined by A. Murock Hussein. These meticulously carved capitals are among the finest works of the Nabataean sculptural canon. Then comes an exploration of the elephant-head-capitals of Phase IV that adorned the Triple Colonnades of the Lower Temenos. Their particular value lies in the inventive creativity lavished on each elephant head. Many craft specialists must have been involved in view of their enormous scale of production. Instead of looking to the West, this inspiration originated in the East. The depiction of the Asian elephant in the Nabataean period is quite unexpected and remarkable. There must be other evidence for an exchange of ideas between Nabataea and India, but it is not yet clear what processes lay behind the surprising Nabataean adoption of the elephant as an icon.

One of the innovative landmarks of the Great Temple is the Theater-in-Temple. Chapter 8 reveals more clearly the building process and the theater in its setting as R. Frederiksen scrutinizes the design of this anomalous structure and sets its construction within the horizon of classicized theaters and temples of the time.

Chapter 9 is a description of the elegant Roman-Byzantine Baths by E. A. Power, who excavated and researched the baths in 2005, 2006 and 2008. Further clarification of the architecture came in 2009. Power grappled with enormous amounts of data which she has evaluated and incorporated into her analysis of this well-preserved 24-room system.

Part II is devoted to additional aspects of Nabataean material culture, each chapter reflecting the world to which the particular artifacts belonged. It includes the residue of the Great Temple finds amassed over the years, with chapters devoted to the site databases, ceramics and Nabataean potting traditions, lamps, figurines, glass, coins, faunal and worked bone analyses, metal objects, ballista balls, and miscellaneous sculpture.

Chapter 10 comprises a brief overview of the Catalogue of Objects by the registrar, D. G. Barrett. Chapter 11 addresses the ceramic and architectural database methodologies and presents a discussion of how we interpret these data. Other sites, particularly Ez Zantur on the hill above the Great Temple, share in the potting traditions of the Great Temple. Inter-site relationships are a vital component of a site report, and we are beginning to make links between excavated sequences.

In chapt. 11, S. Saunders, drawing on analogies of excavated material from Petra as a whole and other Nabataean sites, presents the results of fine- and plain-ware ceramic typologies based on the finds from the Upper Temenos Residential Quarter. Associations between lamp attributes not only help to date changes over time but also are fundamental for studying inter-site contact, and in chapt. 12 Barrett reviews how this artifact class developed and changed over time.

Nabataean conventions and choices on what to represent in their figurines are identified and discussed in chapt. 13 by C. A. Tuttle. Even if we are not well informed about symbolic meanings for the Nabataeans, we know that the manufacture of figurines was deliberate and important. His iconographic analysis of 79 recognizable examples from the Great Temple establishes a new typology for the Nabataean conventions. More importantly, he discusses and interprets which talismans people chose to collect.

Glass manufacturing developed long before the Nabataean period but in *c.*50 B.C. the Romans introduced glass blowing. To judge by several extraordinary pieces, delicate glass objects were prized by those who used the Great Temple throughout antiquity. M. O'Hea focuses her analysis (chapt. 14) on shape composition and relationships in production with Egypt and other areas.

Based on the rulers who issued them, coins can be used to date the phases when they are associated with closed contexts. In chapt. 15, C. F. Cloke uses local and imported coins to establish Petraean and inter-regional chronological links. By defining where the currency found in the Great Temple excavations originated, he indicates a broad spectrum of inter-regional contacts. In chapt. 16, the late T. Gagos interprets the marble inscriptions recovered.

Chapter 17 is in three parts. The first (by S. Whitcher Kansa) presents the animals exploited, processed and consumed at the Great Temple. The data (animal species, age, butchering techniques and other factors) allow for a better understanding of human exploitation of the animal populations and of relationships between them. As Petra lies 100 km from the Red and Mediterranean Seas, the fish remains, studied by R. Cerón-Carrasco, are of extraordinary interest. She makes us aware of the wide variety of fish food choices exploited by the Petraeans. The third part 17 C (by M. A. Perry) is devoted to the few human remains.

Chapter 18, also in three sections, treats worked bone objects. Although worked bone objects are few, of note is an assemblage of pins, spoons, rings, buttons, and decorative artifacts. Next, an extraordinary bone handle shaped in the form of a leg is presented, and lastly a fragmentary artifact made of hippopotamus tusk, probably imported from Egypt.

Metal artifacts had not been studied until 2008 when A. Murock Hussein undertook their analysis. Indeed, copper and bronze do not survive well in the acidic Petra soil. Hussein (chapt. 19) helps us assess the surviving nails, locks and other objects having specific uses, adding a report on their chemical content. She suggests that smelting may have taken place in the Upper Temenos.

Many ballista balls and arrows for use in siege warfare have been recovered from the Great Temple, and the ballista ball repertoire and their interpretation are presented in chapt. 20. Chapter 21 is a catalogue of the miscellaneous aniconic and representative sculpture found, including

Nabataean *nefesh* and *betyls*, with a compendium of assorted iconic sculpture, from heads of deities and a life-sized marble warrior torso to theater masks and a table support.

Concluding remarks are offered in chapt. 22 and the volume closes with Appendices, the objective of which is to provide the researcher with the details of our work, as well as the databases for the many kinds of artifacts. It includes charts with a list of trenches and special projects (excavation trenches of 1993-2008 in the Propylaeum, Lower Temenos, Upper Temenos, and Temple). Next comes a list of the dimensions and elevations of the Great Temple precinct. Further sections are devoted to the Grosso Modo Database and its coding and to distribution charts of pottery results by area, trench, vessel part, and site phase, along with an overarching discussion of ceramics by phase. Appendix 5 covers the architectural fragment database.

This is the third volume devoted to the Great Temple. Volume 1 (1998) was devoted to the first 5 years of excavation, and Volume II (2007) provided the archaeological contexts and stratigraphy from the 1993-2006 excavations. Our central goal in the present volume is to increase understanding of further aspects of Nabataean culture. The archaeological context and analysis of each and every artifact has its own contribution to make to a reconstruction of the Nabataean cultural sphere. The excavations have verified, unambiguously, the secular and/or sacred elements of the Great Temple, while also illuminating traditions in material culture during the first centuries of the present era. This evidence helped establish chronological parameters for the site.

The online *Open Context*[1] has been designed to assemble special research materials that could not be published here in print. For evaluating our results that are presented online, researchers using *Open Context* have the tools to perform their own analysis of the data. It would be surprising if some details in our databases did not lead to reconsideration of our authors' conclusions, and that is precisely why we created it and made it available.

Acknowledgements

This volume is a culmination of a 20-year commitment to the excavation of the Petra Great Temple. In addition to the three volumes, the project has generated or contributed to some 250 articles, a brochure/guide, and a film[2] by David and Michael Udris capturing the excavation progress and its stratigraphy.

Brown University team members 2007-2009

The complete list of team members from 1993 to 2006 was published in Volume II. Added to this list are Artemis W. Joukowsky and Süreya M. Köprülü in 2007, Artemis W. Joukowsky, Eleanor A. Power, Marshall Agnew, Rune Frederiksen, and Elizabeth Gebhard in 2008, and Artemis W. Joukowsky, Süreya M. Koprülü, Jane Silveira Joukowsky and Fawwaz R. Ishakat in 2009. In Providence I am grateful for the patience of David LaCroix, responsible from the outset for procuring our supplies and packing them for shipment to Jordan. I am also indebted to the indefatiguable Sarah Sharpe, Administrative Assistant of the Joukowsky Institute for Archaeology and the Ancient World, who kept the finances straight.

Jane Silveira Joukowsky filmed for our Great Temple documentary in 2009 and again in 2011. Special gratitude goes to Jane and my granddaughter, Süreya M. Köprülü and Badrilla Qublan who patiently served as assistants. We are also grateful for the expertise of Simone Zimmermann, Arne Drescher, Elke Stappert, and, most particularly, to David Barnum of Barnum Designs (New York) for his professionalism and creative energy in directing this project.

Brown University sponsors

We are grateful to our many sponsors/supporters who have helped over a 17-year period. Brown University presidents Christina Paxson and Ruth J. Simmons have given their wholehearted encouragement and general support, continuing in the tradition of Brown University Presidents Howard R. Swearer, Vartan Gregorian, and E. Gordon Gee. I also wish to express my gratitude to Provost David I. Kertzer for his

1 http://www.opencontext.org

2 Go online, type in *Open Context* and select Petra Great Temple. See also the specific *Open Context* listings after the site bibliography at the back of this book.

understanding of the lengthy process involved in archaeological research and publication. I appreciate the encouragement from my colleagues at the Brown University's Joukowsky Institute for Archaeology and the Ancient World (formerly Brown University's Center for Old World Archaeology and Art) under its director Susan E. Alcock.

Petra Expedition Fund

We are particularly grateful for the loyalty of several major sponsors, including several major foundations, without whom this great monument would not have been recovered and studied. We are especially grateful to Elizabeth Gebhard who continued the Luther I. Replogle Foundation's generous funding since 1996 for fieldwork and research. Contributions from the following have meant much to our work: Mr. and Mrs. Wuk Rai Cho, the Theo W. Bennett Charitable Income Trust, the CIGNA Foundation, Fidelity Charitable Gift Fund, Sarah T. Dowling, the Miriam and Arthur Diamond Charitable Trust, the Elbrun and Peter Kimmelman Foundation, the late Mr. Frederick Lippitt, The Luther I. Replogle Foundation, Dr. Ronald D. Margolin, Mr. and Mrs. Charles S. Rubinger, the Rezayat Trading Company Ltd., the late Mr. W. Chesley Worthington, the World Monuments Fund, the late Mrs. Julie Chrystie Webster, Mr. Richard F. Carolan, the late Mr. David A. Detrich, Mr. Charles M. Royce, Ms. Cynthia S. Miller, Mr. Richard R. Ballou, Mr. Gerard T. Lynch, Mr. Donald E. Besser, Dr. David S. Perloff, Mr. Peter A. Halmos, Mr. Norbert P. Donelly, Mr. Lee M. Cort, Dr. and Mrs. Michael Alderman, Mr. Paul R. Gebhard, the late Mr. Raymond H. Bittner, Mr. and Mrs. Thomas Bennett, Mr. Martin Granoff, Mr. Teymour Alireza, the late Mr. Nikita Romanoff, Iouri M. Samonov, Mr. Hidekasu Shibata and Mrs. Imsoo C. Shibata, Ms. Mary K. Ford, Mrs. Jill and Mr. Scott T. Ramsey, and Ms. Elizabeth Smolenski Warren. The above list cannot hope to be exhaustive, and there are many others whose help benefited our work through successive seasons. Further, all honoraria, film and book revenues were directed to the Petra Expedition Fund. I am pleased to acknowledge the Brown University Class of 1960 who directed funds towards the completion of this publication. All of the above have helped the present volume reach the light of day. Again, I gratefully acknowledge the generous financial assistance of Brown University and the above donors.

Site conservation

From 2000, the Joukowsky Family Foundation provided subventions for annual conservation expenses. Yearly conservation efforts also were made possible by two awards from The World Monuments Fund, a grant from the Samuel H. Kress Foundation, through an American Express Award from World Monuments Watch (1996 and 1998, respectively) a program of the World Monuments Fund, and the Joukowsky Family Foundation.

The SHAPE project

The S.H.A.P.E. (Shape, Archaeology. Photogrammetry, Entropy) Lab was formed with a 3-year, $1,250,000 grant, followed by a subsequent $2,000,000 grant from the National Science Foundation to several Brown University Departments (Center for Old World Archaeology and Art, and the Departments of Anthropology, Engineering, Applied Mathematics and Computer Science). This was a significant interdisciplinary effort to develop technical applications for archaeological methodology, analysis and research in conjunction with computer science and mathematical vision. The Great Temple site provided an excellent array of data for the project. I wish to thank my Brown University collaborators, the project's other principal investigators, David Cooper and Benjamin Kimia (Department of Engineering); David Laidlaw (Department of Computer Science), and David Mumford (Department of Applied Mathematics). Key researchers included post-graduate specialists Eileen L. Vote and Frederic Leymarie, a project leader in the Division of Engineering and specialist in computer vision problems. The team also included graduate students and undergraduates from the affiliated departments. The team focused on two main research goals: developing a system for a 3-D GIS, and automated pottery reconstruction. I am grateful to this dedicated team of research specialists who helped me view site data in creative ways through the virtual reality 3-D GIS system ("ARCHAVE"). In technical terms, it allowed us to view and interact with different types of artifacts and architectural finds *in situ*, in the context of a virtual room called a "CAVE" (Cave Automatic Virtual Environment). Within this virtual environment, we accessed life-size representations of the Great Temple site, its architecture, excavation trenches, trench loci, and 15 different types of artifacts represented with their find locations. As the Great Temple excavations covered 12,601 m^2, it was a large area to explore, with full mobility inside the environment. The project was designed to develop more descriptive and effective ways of using computers to model and make inferences about three-dimensional shapes and surfaces. The project's other major goals were to design more effective computer site models for unearthed artifacts and structures that would incorporate time, location, three-dimensional position and other data gleaned from object images. Using computers to construct three-dimensional models for re-assembling artifacts (including statues), columns and other structures from images, our challenge was to build a database of those fragments, and to use computers to recognize or infer artisan or artistic style from fragments of larger pieces. This helped determine who might have produced the objects, while also giving us the ability to relate to structures at other sites.

The Jordanian Department of Antiquities

Above all I am indebted to the Jordanian Department of Antiquities of the Ministry of Tourism as the beneficiary of its kindness. The Department has aided us in every way possible. A great part of the project's success can be ascribed to the Directors General of the Jordanian Department of Antiquities. Our work would not have been possible without the permission from and interest shown by the Directors of the Department of Antiquities: Safwan Tell (1993-94), Ghazi Bisheh (1995-97) and Fawwaz al-Kraysheh (1998-2009). For most of our field campaigns we were fortunate to be under the supervision of Suleiman Farajat and his assistant, Mohammad Abd-Al-Aziz Al-Marahleh as representatives of the Department. The Royal Air Force of the Hashemite Kingdom of Jordan aided us with aerial coverage.

Without the continued support of His Royal Highness, Prince Ra'ad bin Zeid Al-Hussein, and the friendship of Princess Majda and their family, the work would not have been as pleasant as it has been.

D. G. Barrett was responsible for transferring the artifacts to the Jordanian Department of Antiquities authorities at the Petra Museum for their final disposal. Some of the material culture from our excavations is now exhibited in the site museum in Petra and in the National Museum in Amman. Much of the material has been reburied on site or is stored in caves at the site under the jurisdiction of the Jordanian Department of Antiquities. As part of a generous 30-year loan to Brown University, a small collection of objects is on display at Brown University's Joukowsky Institute for Archaeology and the Ancient World.

The American Center of Oriental Research

We wholeheartedly thank Barbara Porter (Director) and Chris Tuttle (then Associate Director), as well as the staff of ACOR, for their assistance. They all provided invaluable help and advice. Our thanks go to Kathy Nimri, Nasreen Shaikh and Carmen Ayoubi for all they have done to facilitate our excavations.

Bedouin families in Petra

One of our greatest pleasures has been the friendship with the people of the valley, particularly those from Umm Sayhum. I express my grateful appreciation and respect in particular to Dakhilallah Qublan and his family for the countless valuable contributions they have made. He has been the site foreman and director of the conservation, consolidation and restoration measures. To the approximately 20 Bedouin workforce who contributed time, effort, experience and good humor, I offer my heartfelt thanks. In an effort to uphold the principles proposed by the International Council on Monuments and Sites, the International Committee on Archaeological Heritage Management (World Heritage Convention of 1972), the Venice Charter of 1966, the Hague Convention, and the tenets of the UNESCO Conventions of 1956, 1970 and 1985, we adhere to field treatments that prevent any harm to the site and are themselves reversible. Therefore architectural restoration at the Great Temple has not been undertaken in a true sense. With elements frequently lacking a clear basis for reconstruction, our measures were geared toward the immediate (though impermanent) preservation of the structural integrity of the precinct. When intact, original stones were reconstituted into temple masonry; in almost all cases original building materials were used. When necessary, original constructions were replaced by new stone fills quarried from the local bedrock. Our conservation preservation team has been on site since 1993.

Colleagues in Jordan

As Director of ACOR in Amman in 1992, Pierre Bikai first brought the Great Temple to my attention. The need for investigation of this vast, semi-visible site was apparent, although the task was daunting because of the enormous overburden and collapse. Yet ironically these conditions were in large part responsible for one of the best-preserved freestanding buildings of the classical Nabataean and Nabataean-Roman periods in Petra. Pierre and Patricia Bikai, both experts on Petra, have always provided invaluable comments on the progress of the excavations and have offered support of many kinds. A profitable dialogue has also been maintained with the architectural historian Judith S. McKenzie, always willing to share her encyclopaedic Nabataean art-historical knowledge. I also gratefully acknowledge Christian Augé who scrutinized our numismatic evidence, Laïla Nehmé, Stephan G. Schmid, John Oleson (who alerted me to fish capitals adorning the columns of the fish market on the Grand Canal in Venice), Elizabeth Gebhard, Mathew Dickie (who noted the connection between the cult of Dionysos and Alexander), Zbigniew T. Fiema, and Tali Erickson-Gini, who escorted us through Nabataean sites in the Negev. Staunch supporters over the years have been photographer Jane Taylor, and Karen, Mohammad and Jad Asfour, who have provided friendship and much welcome hospitality.

Technical preparations towards this volume

Drawings: Over the years, many hands have rendered our sections, plans and object drawings; they include Amy Grey, Ala H. Bedewy, Jean Blackburn, Simon Sullivan, John Philip Hagen, Emily Catherine Egan, Christian F. Cloke, The Maryland Institute College of Art, Joseph J. Basile and his documentation team including Katie O'Meara of the Institute's Department of Environmental design, and Lauren Braddock. The drawings of figurines in chapt. 13 are by Qeis Tweissi. I am most grateful for both Marshal C. Agnew's and Fawwaz R. Ishakat's commitment and skill in integrating the varied architectural components we have recovered over many years.

Databases: Since the beginning of our work our database designs have been superbly managed by Donna J. D'Agostino. These include the 'Grosso Modo', Architectural Fragments, the coin catalogue, and catalogue databases, all of which can be found on-line in *Open Context*. The glass, figurine, lamp, pottery, and coin databases are the creations of Margaret O'Hea, Christopher A. Tuttle, Deirdre G. Barrett, Shari L. Saunders, and Christian F. Cloke, respectively. These have been modified for on-line publication by the *Open Context* staff, headed by Sarah Whitcher Kansa, and Eric Kansa.

In Providence and St. Croix we have shared our progress with Sally and Joe Dowling, Richard Carolan, Marie J. Langlois and John Loerke, Beppie Huidekoper, Richard Ballou, Ronald Margolin, Patricia and Francis Scola, Sonya Hough, Steffen Larsen and Jan Mitchell, Joan and Peter Kumpitch, Eion Jackson, Francie Whittenberg, Connie Worthington and Terry Tullis, and Andries van Dam. They, among many others, have given generously of their time, knowledge, and encouragement.

The final work on this volume

Much of the architecture and many of the objects appeared in our earlier publications, but in the present volume the final architectural plans and the treatment of the artifacts have been revised and expanded. The present manuscripts were completed in 2010, after which I spent a year making changes to suit *JRA*'s requirements and format, which included combining the bibliographies from each chapter. From the beginning of 2011, Marshal C. Agnew patiently guided me through the process of redefining the photographs and site plans in order to bring out salient details. Tyler Parker corrected the knotty problems involved with photographs of artifacts. In October 2011 Steffen F. Larsen traveled to Petra and rephotographed the coins presented in chapt. 16. I wish to thank particularly Mohammad Al-Marahleh, Curator of the Petra Archaeological Museum, and Samia Flhat and Tahani Salhi for helping with the task of finding the coins in the storerooms. A few of our coins had been moved to the Jordan Museum in Amman where Faris Nimri, director, and Kharireh 'Amr welcomed us; it was Tammam Khasawneh who helped in finding the coins there and I am most grateful for his contribution.

Volume III was written in 2009-2011, and in 2010, it had been accepted for publication in the Supplementary Series of the prestigious *Journal of Roman Archaeology* by John H. Humphrey, General Editor. As the chapters arrived, I gave them a first edit and turned them over to John, who in his inimitable fashion, carefully scrutinized the text and made valuable suggestions. Thanks to the talented efforts of John's assistant, Claudine Corley, the layout was designed.

However, there were some chapters that remained to be edited, and in 2013 Russell Adams undertook this task, although illness precluded its timely completion. This two-year delay took its toll.

During this time, the remarkable John Humphrey, the driving force behind the *Journal of Roman Archaeology*, retired from publishing *JRA* supplements. Once again publication was held up. When John was alerted that the remaining chapters had been edited, he graciously hand-delivered the typeset chapters he had extensively edited. This decided the following course of action. We elected to keep the *JRA* format,[3] and to typeset the outstanding chapters. I turned to Joseph Gilbert of Gilbert Design, Pawtucket RI, who had designed *Petra Great Temple:* Volume II. I will always be grateful to Joe for coming to the rescue. We dusted ourselves off and dedicated ourselves to this volume. Joe coordinated bewildering technical details to bring this volume to press, and we will ever be grateful. Additionally our heartfelt thanks go to the most talented Anne-Marie Boerner for wrestling with the layout. She deserves a special note of appreciation.

Worthy of special acknowledgement are the scholars who offered to review various chapters and helped with the final editing. James Coulton facilitated the rewriting of Chapter 3; John Oleson assisted us with Chapters 4 and 9. Judith McKenzie prompted further development of Chapter 7A; and Theater expert, Frank Sear, was consulted for Chapter 8. Chapter 11was reviewed by S. G. Schmid. During the process of manuscript submission, we were profoundly saddened by the untimely death of the brilliant Trianos Gagos, who had submitted his Chapter 16 research on the bath inscriptions. Traianos was a dearest friend.

Chapter 18, worked bone, was extensively reviewed by Etan Ayalon, who offered so many useful suggestions that we asked him to co-author the chapter. Peter van Alfen reviewed Chapter 15, Coins, and T. M. Weber and Robert Wenning made many helpful suggestions for the sculpture presented in Chapter 21. We benefited enormously from the peer review of this volume and appreciate every reviewer's informed opinions, scholarship, enthusiasm and interest. I am indebted to these colleagues for their thoughtful suggestions

---

3 It is important to note that the bibliography reflects the JRA format and the authors' original submissions. The bibliography has not been updated since the author's submitted their manuscripts.

and advice. They helped us refine and strengthen the entries. To each and every reviewer, thank you for generously sharing your time and your candid thoughts with us.

Finally, each of our extraordinary authors has communicated the excitement of discovery and the relevance of their findings. I want to thank them for their patience and valuable ideas. Whatever flaws may be found in the text are my responsibility.

Glen Bowersock has attempted to save me and the contributors from errors. He read multiple chapters and shared his scholarship unreservedly, providing a myriad of assistances; I also thank him especially for contributing the Foreword. My thanks go to everyone at *JRA*, beginning with John Humphrey. Dan Davis was an indispensable ally through the early publication process. A special thanks to Claudine Corley for her further work on the images and for designing the layout, and to talented Christian Cloke who is responsible for the index.

Dedication of this volume

My husband of 60 years, Artemis W. Joukowsky, has been constant in his friendship, companionship, patience, and encouragement. As always I am indebted to him for his photographic expertise and for his drawing of walls. His keen eye behind the camera was instrumental in capturing the spirit of the site and its historic sense of place. I am also appreciative of my devoted daughter Nina, my sons Artemis and Misha and their children for providing the inspiration and support to complete the text.

Providence, November 2015

*TO DEAREST ARTIE, OUR CHILDREN, AND OUR GRANDCHILDREN,
AND TO OUR BEDOUIN FRIENDS IN UMM SAYHUM*

Fig. 1.1. The Great Temple in its setting, aerial view to the south (2008).

Fig. 1.2. The Great Temple, aerial view to the south (2006).

1
The Great Temple, 1993-2008: a brief review of the excavations, stratigraphy and phasing

Martha Sharp Joukowsky

The Petra valley, surrounded by precipitous mountains (300 m high) of Nubian sandstone, measures *c.*1.5 long by 1 km wide. Most of the city was constructed in the last quarter of the 1st c. B.C.; it remained independent until A.D. 106, when it was annexed by Rome. The Great Temple lies beyond the Siq, Treasury, Theater and Markets in the heart of the city (fig. 1.1), just before the visitor reaches the Temenos Gate of the Qasr al-Bint. Figure 1.2 reveals the enormity of the Great Temple complex, its monumental architecture and impressive topographic surroundings.[1] Brown University's excavation of the vast temple complex (7,560 m^2 or three-quarters of a hectare[2]) and adjoining areas (for a total of 12,601 m^2; fig. 1.3) began in 1993, and restoration continues to the present. A major architectural component of the city, the Great Temple is the largest freestanding building yet excavated. Lying south of the Roman Street and southeast of the Temenos Gate, its precinct is comprised of a Propylaeum (formal entry), a Lower Temenos (a sacred enclosure), and monumental East and West Stairways leading to the Upper Temenos, the sacred enclosure for the Temple proper. In general the temple precinct is oriented NE–SW, but, typically of Nabataean temples, the lack of a uniform alignment underscores a penchant for orientation according to the terrain, the designated area having to be manipulated. The necessity of placing the entrance on the street allowed the Nabataean architects to satisfy a desire to maintain an integral connection between the precincts, the major thoroughfare of the city center, and the Wadi Musa beyond. If the Great Temple stood 19 m high, as we presume, it would have stood *c.*34 m above the Colonnaded Street. Set on one of the city's high points, the Great Temple is like a citadel rising in a commanding position.

The major features

Each of the four areas (Propylaeum, Lower Temenos, Upper Temenos, Temple) has distinctive architectural components (see Appendix 6). Moving from north to south, we present a brief description of each area with its defining features.

Propylaeum

The northernmost component to the complex, the Propylaeum,[3] is set just south of the Roman Road, its W edge being 6.9 m east of the Qasr al-Bint Temenos Gate. Overall it measures *c.*55 m E-W x 12.5 m N-S (fig. 1.4). Extending across the front of the temple precinct, the Propylaeum is fronted by the Portico Wall, which in turn is divided by the Central Staircase into two equal E-W sections. At the north and running parallel to the street, the Portico Wall serves as the façade for the entire complex, separating the internal rooms of the Propylaeum from the sidewalk and street below. At the south, the structure is braced against the Propylaeum Retaining Wall into which are set the voussoirs of a vaulted cryptoporticus.

The chief features of the Propylaeum East are two rectangular rooms and a corridor with two more rooms on its E side, bordering the E edge of the precinct as a whole. These rooms, set perpendicular to the Roman Road, open onto its sidewalk.

---

1 Volume 2 provided reconstructions of the central city (figs. 1.1 and 1.2), with a topographic map (fig. 1.9). The site grid is illustrated in the present volume, fig. 2.3.

2 This excludes adjoining structures such as the Roman-Byzantine Baths, the 'Baroque Room', and Residential Quarter.

3 See vol. 2, 37-85 and fig. 2.1.

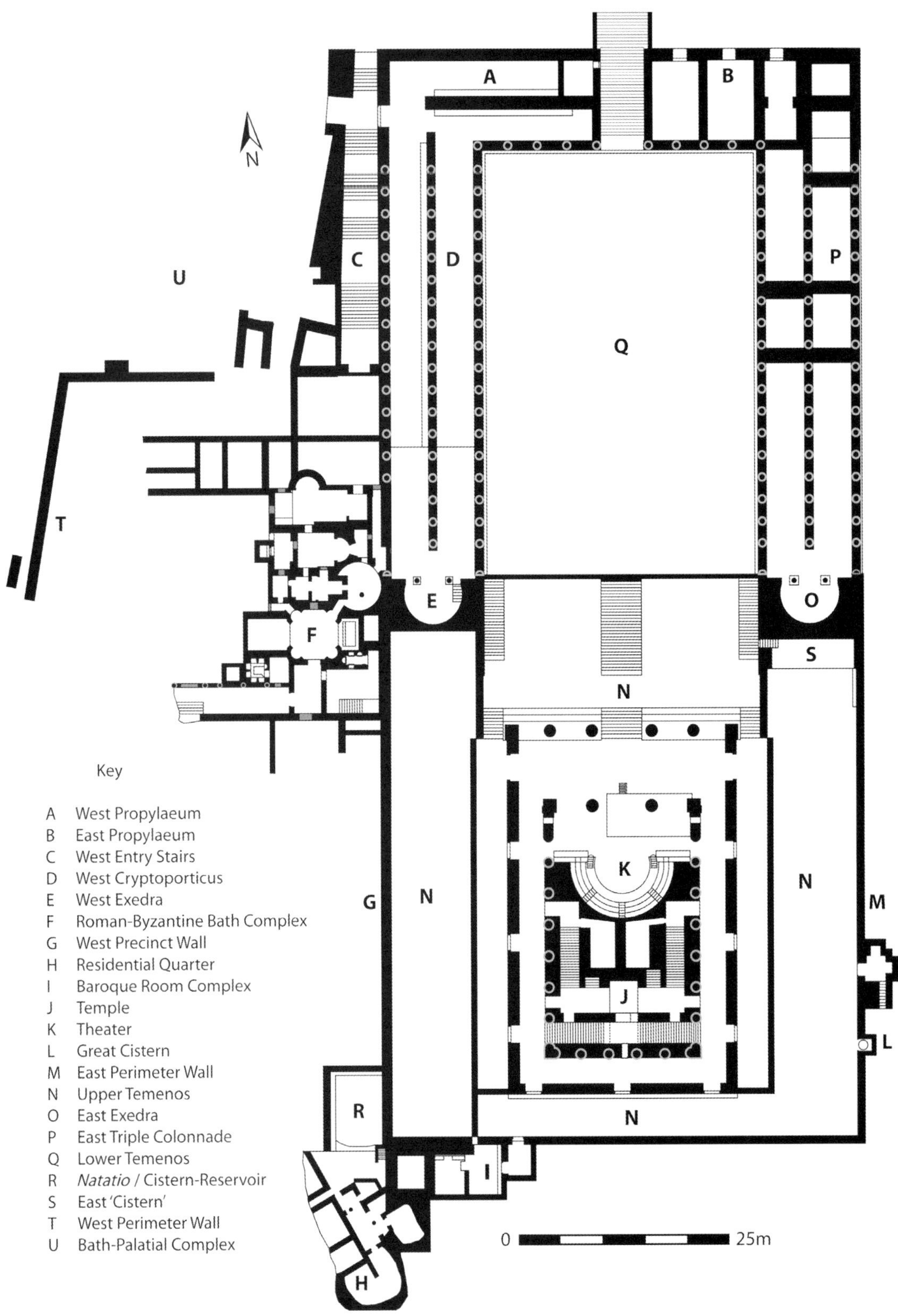
A
B
C
D
E
F
G
H
I
J
K
L
M
N
O
P
Q
R
S
T
U
N
0
25m
Key
A West Propylaeum
B East Propylaeum
C West Entry Stairs
D West Cryptoporticus
E West Exedra
F Roman-Byzantine Bath Complex
G West Precinct Wall
H Residential Quarter
I Baroque Room Complex
J Temple
K Theater
L Great Cistern
M East Perimeter Wall
N Upper Temenos
O East Exedra
P East Triple Colonnade
Q Lower Temenos
R Natatio / Cistern-Reservoir
S East 'Cistern'
T West Perimeter Wall
U Bath-Palatial Complex

Fig. 1.3. Great Temple, site plan (2008).

On the W side of the Central Stairs the Propylaeum is divided into two long E-W galleries running parallel to the Roman Road. They are separated by 'Wall K'.[4] The S gallery is framed on its N side with a bench that abuts the S face of that wall. Parallel to Wall K is the S wall of this gallery, termed the Propylaeum Retaining Wall. Entry to these galleries was by way of the West Entry Stairs.[5] On the E side of the N gallery lies Room 1 and a bench set against the N face of Wall K. A ceramic pavement once covered the floor of the N gallery. At the SW end of the N gallery is a niche where twin aniconic limestone *betyls* (standing libation stones signifying the god's presence) were found; below the niche is a bench for offerings. A limestone floor paves the area in front of the niche and offering bench. Found in the N gallery was a deposit of ballista balls, arrowheads, and helmet cheek-pieces, presumably a stockpile of weapons for defense or remains from an attack on the Great Temple (see chapt. 20 below).

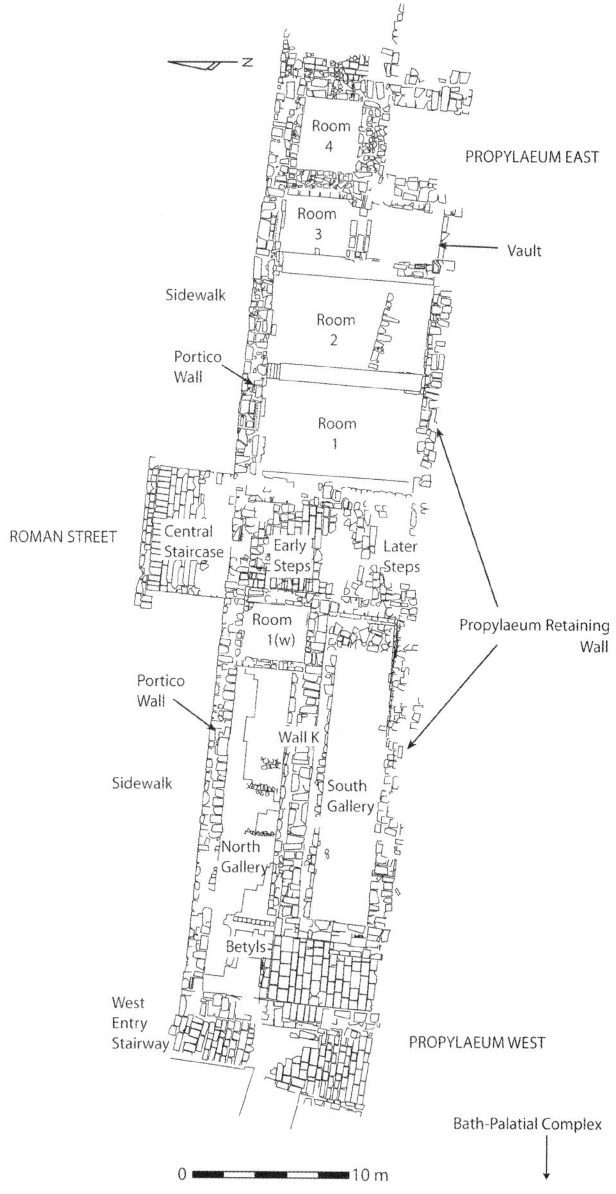

Fig. 1.4. Plan of Propylaeum.

Lower Temenos

Ascending the Central Stairs, the route leads into the Lower Temenos (fig. 1.5), set 8.5 m above the level of the Roman Road.[6] The Lower Temenos is an enormous plaza measuring *c.*49 m N-S by 56 m E-W, covered with large hexagonal flagstones of white limestone. It is flanked by E and W Triple Colonnades (50 m long, 12 m wide) with a total of 120 columns topped with elephant-head capitals. At the S end of these colonnades stand E and W semicircular exedrae. The triple colonnades are set on top of massive vaulted cryptoporticos. Beneath the hexagonal pavement is the main conduit for drainage (canalization). The massive Retaining Wall (28 m E-W, 2.76 m high) forms the S boundary of the Lower Temenos. It blocks an earlier main Central Staircase of the Upper Temenos but provides openings for lateral East and West Staircases which ascend from the Lower to the Upper Temenos and to the temple forecourt.

West Entry Stairway

The Stairway[7] at the extreme W side of the Lower Temenos follows the slope of the precinct. Entered from the Roman Road, it is composed of 5 flights of stairs interspersed with platforms. The stairs rise for 37 m and the uppermost platform is set 9.5 m above the Roman Road. The

4 Parr 1970, 351, fig. 1, and 353. At p. 370 he dates Wall K to later than the beginning of the reign of Aretas IV, or to some point in the 1st c. A.D. We place it some 60 years earlier in our Phase II, sometime in the mid-1st c. B.C.

5 The West Entry will be described with the features of the Lower Temenos.

6 See vol. 2, 89-133.

7 See vol. 2, fig. 3.5.

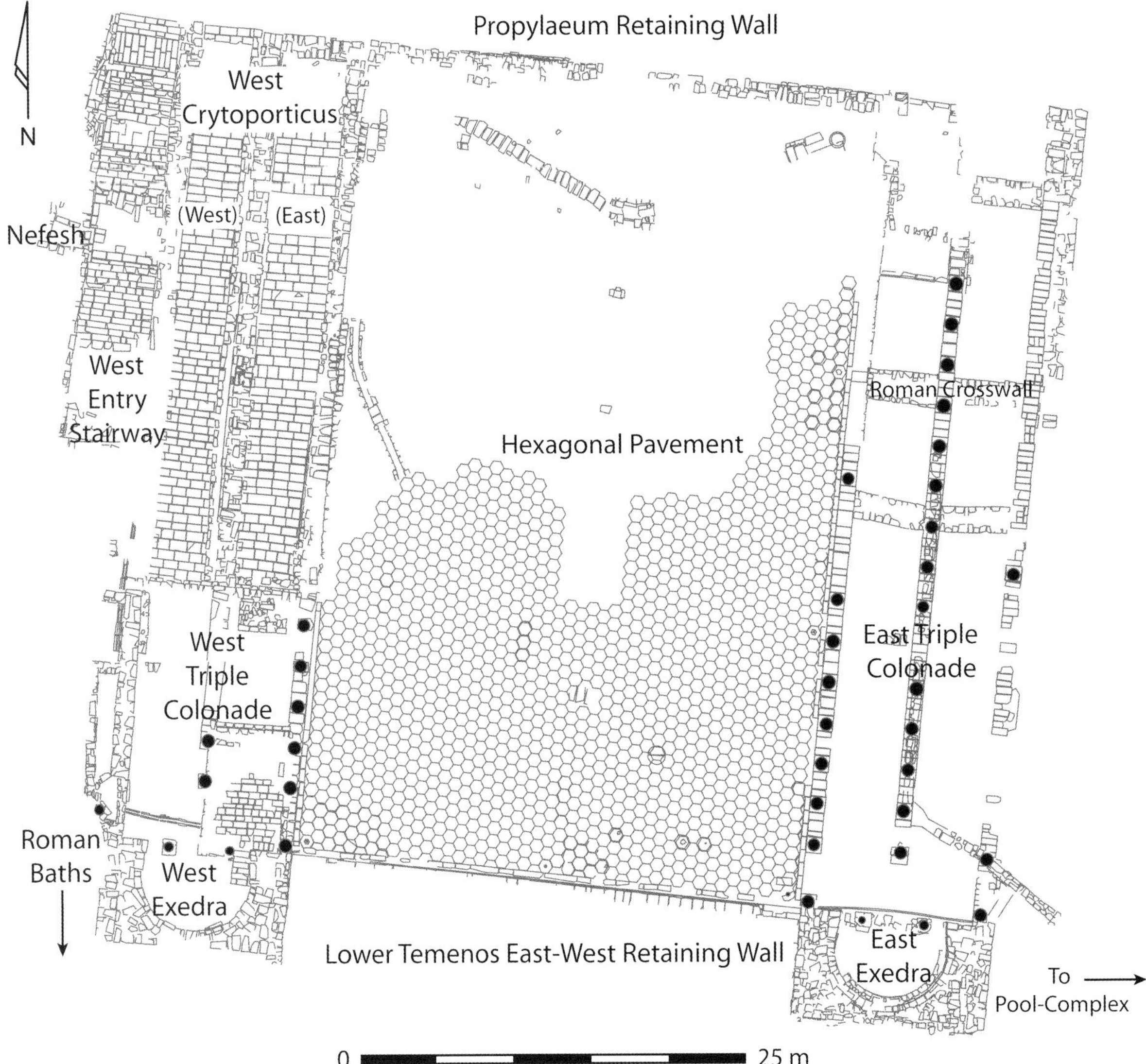

Fig. 1.5. Plan of Lower Temenos.

lowest landing provides entry to the West Propylaeum where twin betyls are set. Between the two uppermost flights of stairs as extant is a terraced landing on which was found a stele or *nefesh*,[8] accompanied by another *betyl*. The *nefesh* is an incised white lime- or sandstone block with an incised obelisk carved above a squared *betyl* block; it is accompanied by a separate *betyl* (freestanding).[9] The Lower Temenos is the findspot of many of the pilaster blocks and most elephant-head capitals.

Upper Temenos

Located on an elevated bedrock platform, the Upper Temenos (fig. 1.6) comprises a rectilinear area at the rear of the precinct surrounding the temple proper.[10] In the north the Upper Temenos is approached by two staircases on the E and W sides, each rising 6 m to connect the upper and lower

8 A Nabataean commemorative monument associating the essence of the deceased with a stone marker.

9 See vol. 2, figs. 3.57-58. For safekeeping the *nefesh* was removed from the site and a carved reproduction set up in its original position. The *betyl* originally had been affixed in the square with white mortar, part of which we removed for sampling. When the *betyl* was removed, it was found that the slab had been completely carved through and the *betyl* had been inserted into a 'window' of the *stele*.

10 See vol. 2, 137-213, figs. 4.1-2.

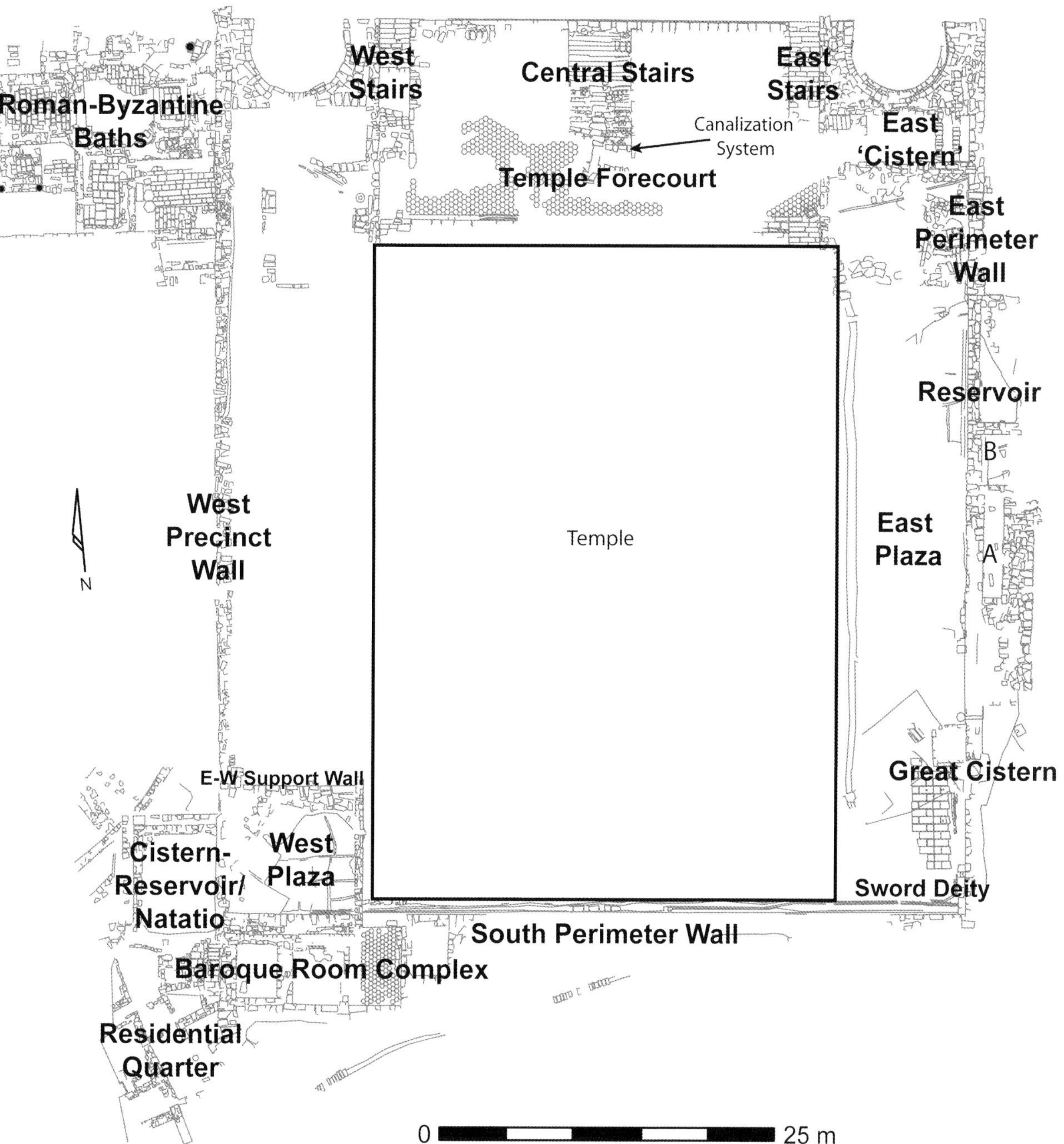

Fig. 1.6. Plan of Upper Temenos.

terraces of the temple precinct. An earlier staircase formed part of the original access to the temple, but it was blocked off in antiquity by the construction of the E–W Retaining Wall of the Lower Temenos. The Upper Temenos is enclosed by massive perimeter walls (the East Perimeter Wall is *c.*14 m in height).

To its east and south, the Upper Temenos contains a lavishly paved Temple Forecourt, broad paved plazas and passageways, and plastered cisterns above and below ground, including the 'Great Cistern' (measuring 8.5 x 7.8 m, with a depth of 5.17-5.88 m and a capacity of 327,640 litres). The latter lies adjacent to a series of vaulted rooms (A and B and the *Tabun* Room) set in the East Perimeter Wall. Further to the west is the 'Baroque Room Complex' with a settling tank, anteroom, shrine room and the 'Baroque Room' itself, so named because of the lavishly modeled plaster ceiling unearthed there in its collapsed state. Still further to the west is an extensive 11-room Residential

Quarter (15.48 x 9.22 m) with its caves and built rooms, and another massive Cistern Reservoir. To the northwest stand the well-preserved Roman-Byzantine Baths (32 x 28.4 m), equipped with a 'platform', *apodyterium*, *praefurnium*, 'splash pool', vestibule, *tepidarium*, service passage, several *caldaria*, *laconicum*, toilet, 'Well Room', and a colonnaded corridor surrounding a *palaestra*.

The temple proper, the focus of the vast precinct, is positioned on a high bedrock terrace immediately south of the extensive Lower Temenos. It is enclosed on the E, W, and S sides by the Upper Temenos. Expertly constructed from hewn sandstone and limestone, this composite structure exhibits elements of both its original and restructured designs. It will be presented in the following section under Chronology. Major reference elevations and distance measurements are given in Appendix 6.[11]

Chronology[12]

The Nabataean period[13] extends from the earliest reference to the Nabataeans in 312 B.C. by Diodorus Siculus to the Roman annexation in A.D. 106. The Roman period extends to A.D. 325. The earthquake of A.D. 551 marks all but the final devastation of the site; thereafter only localized activities occurred.

Stratigraphy, site phasing and dating of Great Temple deposits

The Great Temple deposits have been divided into 15 main periods (see Table 1.1 for a précis). A discussion of each of these phases with the major features was given in vol. 2 (22-36). The sequence (Pre-Site Phase I and Site Phases I-XIV) refers to various stages of the precinct's construction or its collapse and abandonment. Buildings and periods are divided up based on the context in which materials were found. A building's *terminus post quem* (earliest date after which it was completed) is judged by the latest artifact recovered from its substructure. But if a sculpture of the 2nd c. A.D. is found in the collapse of the West Perimeter Wall (constructed in Phase IV), it is placed in Phase IX because it was found mixed with other elements of the collapse of A.D. 363; thus artifacts are not phased with the architecture but with the fill with which they are associated. With a general lack of absolute dates, this does not permit more than a rather broad dating, but our phases do provide general benchmarks by which the architecture and artifacts can be assigned. The phasing charts placing every locus of each Trench and Special Project in one of the 15 site phases can be accessed in *Open Context*. Recent ^{14}C results have confirmed our general dating scheme.[14]

---

11 Detailed measurements of each area and its architectural features also are given in vol. 2, at 12, 14-18, 53, 55, 89-91, 137-40, 154, 200, and 212.

12 Generally for chronology we follow W. Rast's (1992, 45) overall periodization and dates: Early Hellenistic 332-198 B.C., Late Hellenistic 198-63 B.C., Early Roman 63 B.C.–A.D.135, Nabataea annexed by Rome in A.D. 106, Middle Roman A.D. 135-250, Late Roman A.D. 250-360, Early Byzantine A.D. 360-491, Late Byzantine A.D. 491-640, Islamic Umayyad Dynasty A.D. 661-750, Abbasid Dynasty A.D. 750-1258.

13 For relevant information on Nabataean history, see vol. 1, 15-31; vol. 2, 19-20.

14 Khaled al-Bashaireh (Department of Archaeology, Yarmouk University) took two samples of plaster and mortar from the Great Temple for analysis at the University of Arizona. He dated two samples from the Great Temple: a plaster (41) covering a column from the East Triple Colonnade in the Lower Temenos, and a grey-mortar bedding (39) from the latrine's anteroom at the Roman-Byzantine Bath complex. The date of sample 41 is 1921 ± 34 BP, calibrated A.D. 54-126. To show that the obtained date is reproducible, new powder of the same grain size was hydrolyzed and dated, and it yielded a similar date (1936 ± 56 BP, calibrated A.D. 4-128). A combined age of the two dates (i.e., 1925 ± 29 BP, calibrated A.D. 50-125) probably applies to the plastering of the column and to construction of the East Triple Colonnade. The second sample is dated 1619 ± 36 BP, calibrated A.D. 397-532, which agrees with the interpretation that reconstruction and repairs of specific areas took place in the 4th-5th c. Two further samples were also analysed: for the Winged Lions, the date resulting is A.D. 25-75, while for Qasr al Bint it is A.D. 5-55, which suggests that they were built and lined up at the same period.

TABLE 1.1.
SITE PHASES, DATES, AND MAJOR DEVELOPMENTS

Site phase	*Date*	*Major construction-destruction*
Pre-Site Phase-I	*c.* Pre-1st c. B.C.	Odd walls and cup marks in bedrock
Site Phase I	*c.* Early 1st c. B.C.	Bedrock preparation and canalization
Site Phase II	*c.* mid-1st c. B.C.	Construction of distyle *in antis* temple, portico wall; lowest steps of Propylaeum central steps
Site Phase III	*c.* mid- to late 1st c. B.C.–1st c. A.D.	Minor damage
Site Phase IV	*c.* 1st c. B.C.–1st c. A.D.	Grand design (expansion). Construction of tetrastyle *in antis* temple, full Propylaeum, West Entry stairway, *Nefesh*, Lower Temenos Triple Colonnades, exedrae, cryptoporticoes, Upper Temenos Great Cistern, East Perimeter Wall, Residential Quarter, 'Baroque Room'
Site Phase V	*c.* 1st c. A.D.	Nabataean redesign and repair, Theater added to Great Temple, *betyls* in Propylaeum
Site Phase VI	A.D. 106 and 113/114 earthquake	Roman takeover. Damage to Propylaeum West. Repairs to Lower Temenos, 'Baroque Room' collapse, Temple doorways and corridors narrowed, Bath complex initial construction
Site Phase VII	*c.* mid-2nd c. A.D.	Propylaeum repair, Wall K razed in east and rebuilt in west, West Propylaeum Room 1 constructed, Roman Street paved, East Propylaeum Rooms 1–3 constructed, East Exedra repair, Lower Temenos E-W cross walls in East Triple Colonnade, benches, temple doorways narrowed and walled-in, Theater stage constructed
Site Phase VIII	*c.* late 2nd c. A.D.	Damage, abandonment, collapse, dumping
Site Phase IX	A.D. 363 earthquake	Collapse of Propylaeum and Lower Temenos West Triple Colonnade, West Cryptoporticus collapse, Upper Temenos receives added features
Site Phase X	*c.* 4th-5th c. A.D.	Abandonment, fluvial deposit accumulates, Lower Temenos reconstruction of Triple Colonnade inter-columnar walls with re-used ashlars, domestic secondary re-use in all temple areas
Site Phase XI	Post-A.D. 551 earthquake	Further collapse, East Triple Colonnade collapse, West Entry Stairs collapse, Temple East Porch column collapse, baths go out of use
Site Phase XII	Late Byzantine A.D. 551-640	Abandonment and robbing
Site Phase XIII	Islamic period	Series of major collapses
Site Phase XIV	Modern period	Farming of Lower Temenos by Bedouin, dumping, construction of Bedouin walls, Brown University excavations

Summary of site phases

Pre-Phase I

Pre-Phase I is dated to the mid-1st c. B.C. Prior to the preparation of the site for the temple(s) there was an earlier settlement, but the new Nabataean builders erased its memory. The precinct was prepared for a monumental building in the following Site Phase I when beneath the entire complex a canalization system would be constructed, extending from the south escarpment in the rear of the temple to the Propylaeum.

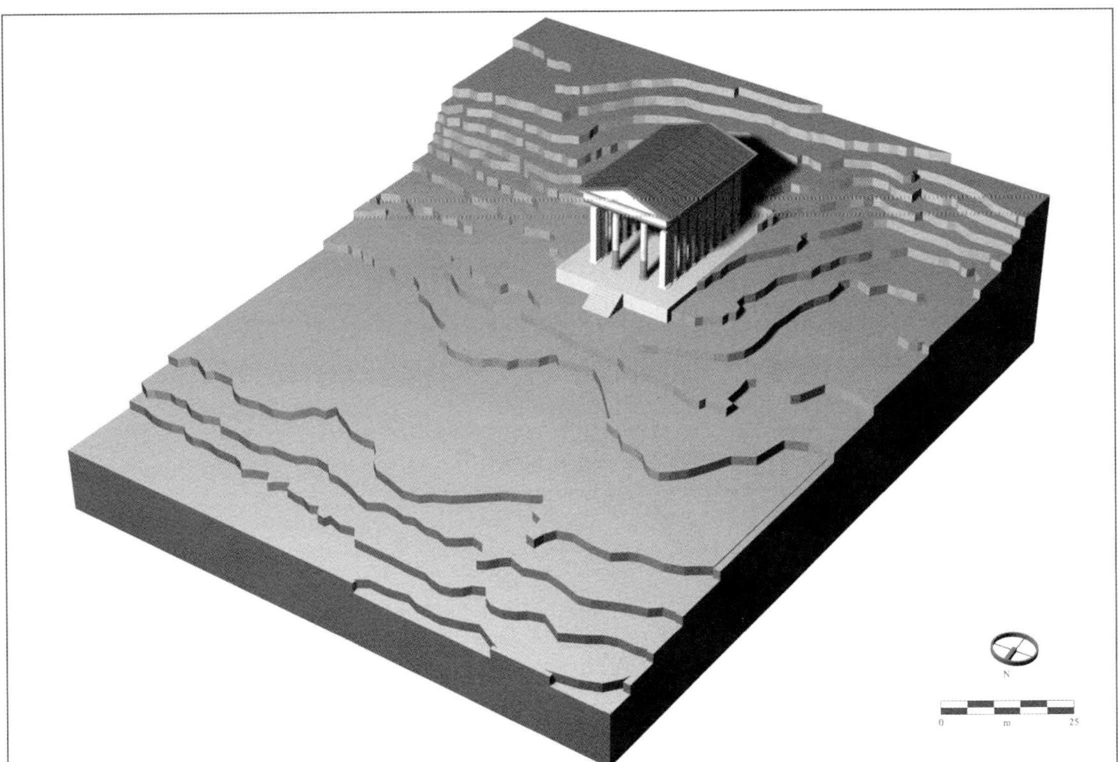

Fig. 1.7. Model of distyle temple (Phase II).

Phase I: site preparation

Phase I, roughly dated later than the mid-1st c. B.C., relates to the preparation of the precinct for the construction of the early prostyle distyle *in antis* temple. Over this half-century Nabataean masons chiselled away enormous amounts (*c.*12 m) of bedrock to set the early temple on a finely prepared and stable surface. The quarrying of bedrock, particularly on the E, W, and S sides for the terrace, as well as the introduction of fill for areas where the bedrock had fallen away, was essential to create a colossal terrace on which a massive temple would rise *c.*30 m above the central thoroughfare.

Phase II: the distyle in antis *temple*

The distyle temple (figs. 1.7-1.8) was erected in this phase.[15] Originally conceived as a distyle *in antis* building (30.07 m N–S x 18.36 m E–W), its central core was surrounded by brightly stuccoed columns with Nabataean Corinthian capitals and flanking *antae*; there were 8 plastered columns on the E and W sides, and 6 in the rear with heart-shaped columns at the SW and SW corners. Enclosing the

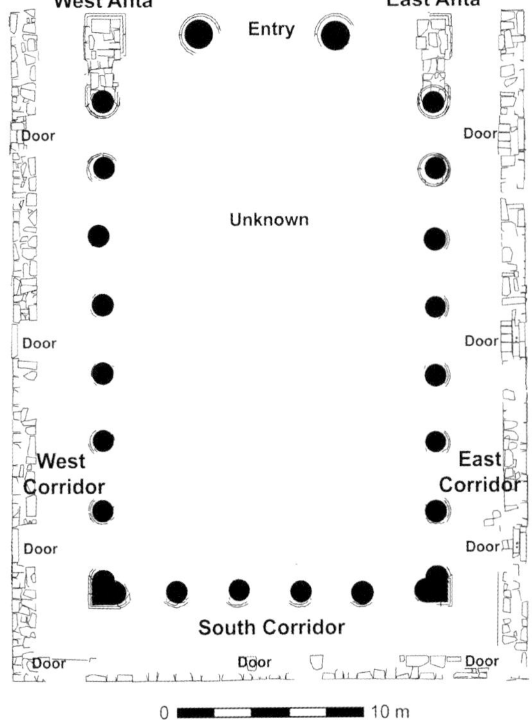

Fig. 1.8. Plan of distyle temple (Phase II).

15 See vol. 1, 147 and 219-22.

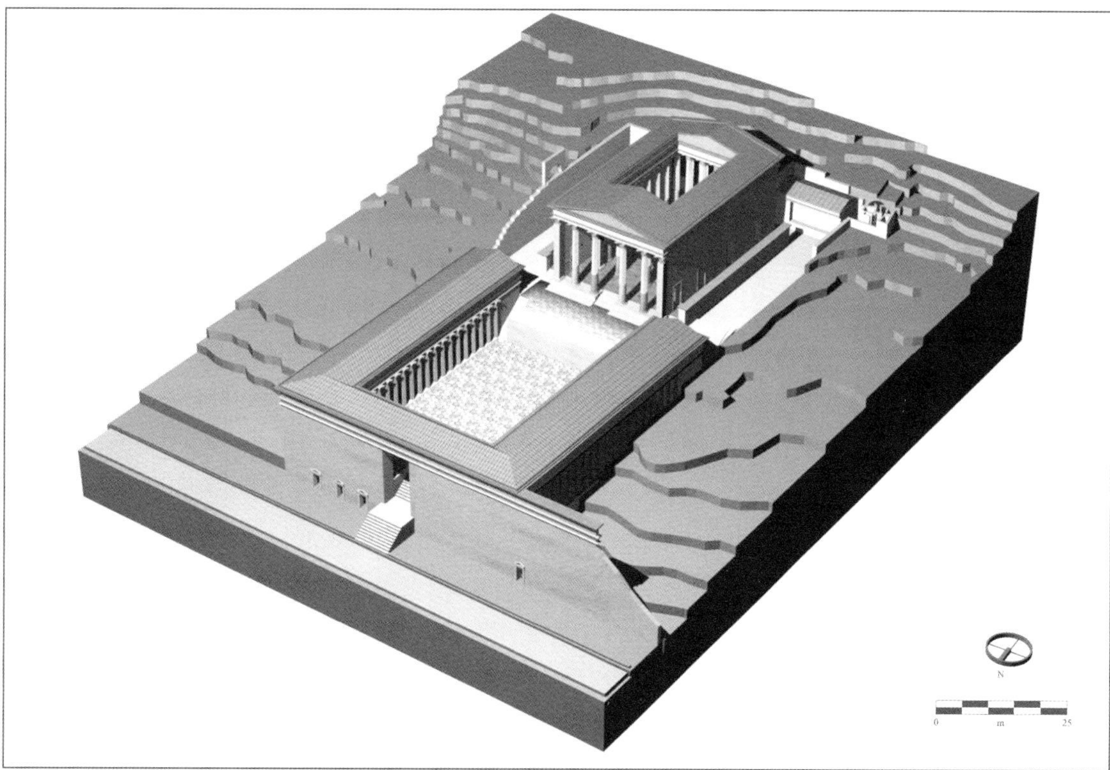

Fig. 1.9. Reconstruction of tetrastyle temple (Phase IV).

building on three sides are the East, West and South Corridors and their doorways decorated with colorfully frescoed walls resembling the Pompeian Second Style.

Phase III

In Phase III (mid- to late 1st c. B.C. to 1st c. A.D.) minor damage occurred. This half-century was a prelude to Phase IV and what we call the 'grand design', dated roughly from the last quarter of the 1st c. B.C. to the early years of the 1st c. A.D.

Phase IV: the tetrastyle in antis *temple*

In Phase IV the temple proper was expanded (42.5 m N–S x 35.5 m E–W) to include a renovated formal staircase connecting the small hexagonal forecourt pavement to the temple, itself now a new tetrastyle *in antis* structure (fig. 1.10). Figure 1.9 shows how the precinct developed at this time. The Pronaos (6.5 x 28 m) extended across the width of the building, and served as the formal access to the East or West Corridors (kept from the earlier phase).

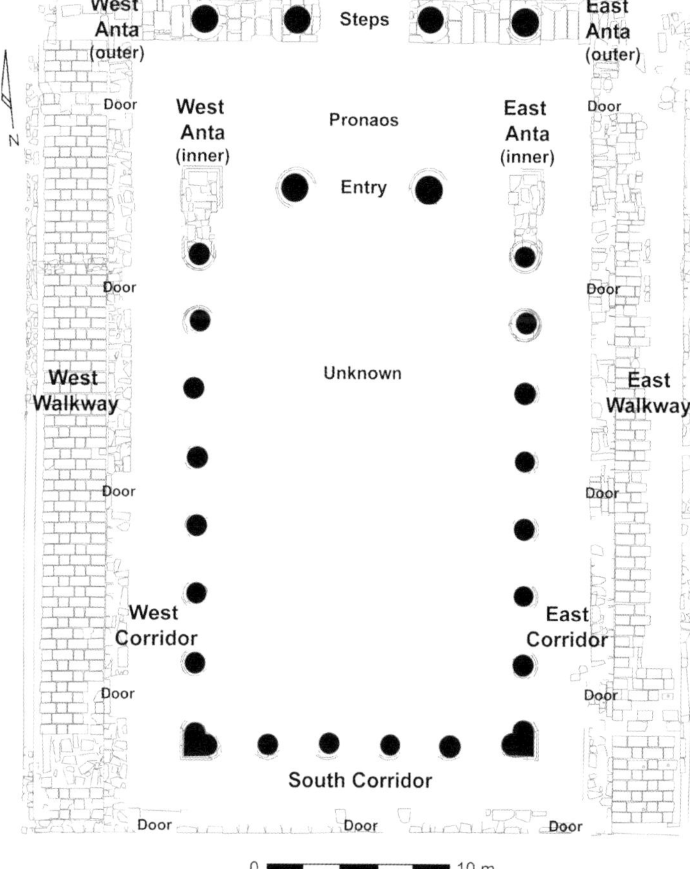

Fig. 1.10. Plan of tetrastyle temple (Phase IV).

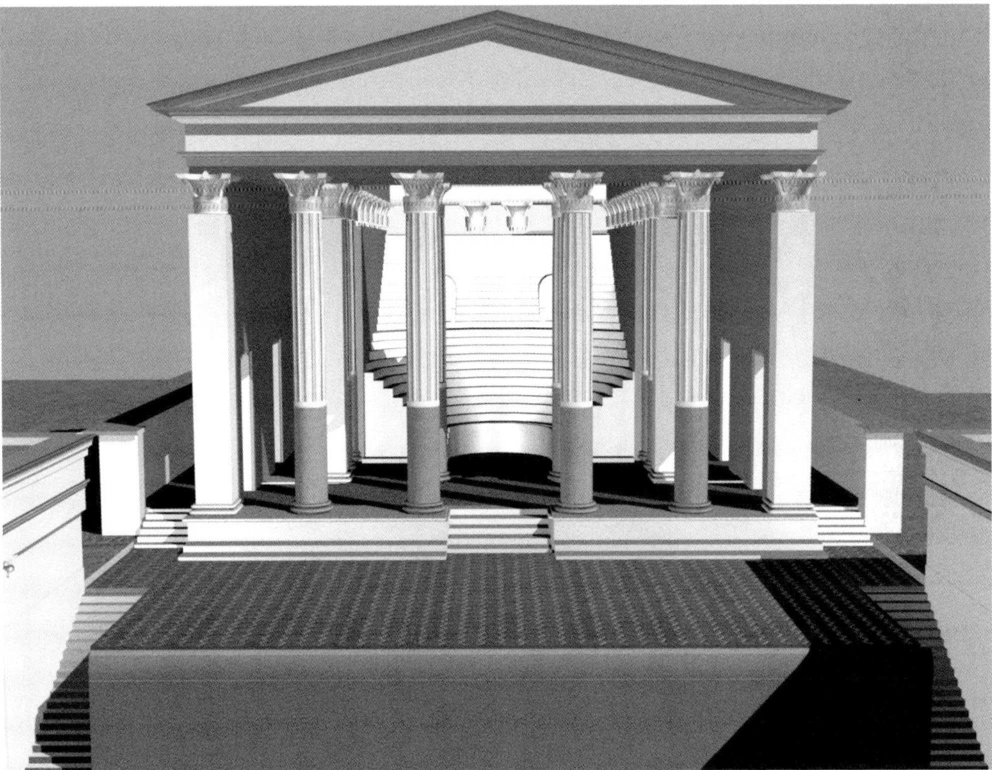

Fig. 1.11. Reconstruction of Theater-in-Temple (Phase V).

This expanded building also has perimeter East and West Walkways that flank and enclose the sides, enlarging the temple to the north, east and west. Between the corridor and walkway three broad doorways, fitted with fine limestone thresholds (2.1 m across on average) were inserted. These provided a direct entry from the walkways to the interior of the corridors. The structure was enlarged by the widened façade (Pronaos) added to the front of the earlier distyle temple, and by walkways flanking the original corridors on the E and W sides. The fine, deeply-carved pilasters of Fortuna with cornucopia and the other sculpted panels decorating the façade are placed in this phase.

In this phase the full architectural arrangement of the temple precinct is defined, embellished and enlarged. The four additional main areas of the precinct are what the visitor sees today: a monumental Propylaeum; an expansive Lower Temenos flanked by exedrae and triple colonnades adorned with elephant-head capitals; an Upper Temenos with a massive East Plaza; and, on the west, the 'Baroque Room Complex' (5.77 x 17.26 m) and Residential Quarter (15.48 x 9.22 m). In the center stands the massive tetrastyle Great Temple with a raised entry. The porch columns with the triangular pediment and entablature put the structure's height at a minimum of 19 m. All of these innovative features, constructed at the same time, exhibit decorative ideas borrowed from the wider Nabataean world.

Phase V: the Theater-in-Temple

A third major renovation brought the addition of a central Theater-in-Temple with 600-900 seats (diameter of orchestra floor 6.43 m), supported by a complex series of intercolumnar walls, a monumental central vault, internal staircases, platforms, and twin interior vaulted chambers; newly-built intercolumnar walls between the columns of the distyle colonnades provided a firm substructure for the new architectural elements, while staircases were built along the sides and two more across the rear, and platforms supported and gave access to the Theater-in-Temple from the rear of the complex (fig. 1.11). To the east and west, internal north and south staircases rose *c.*5 m

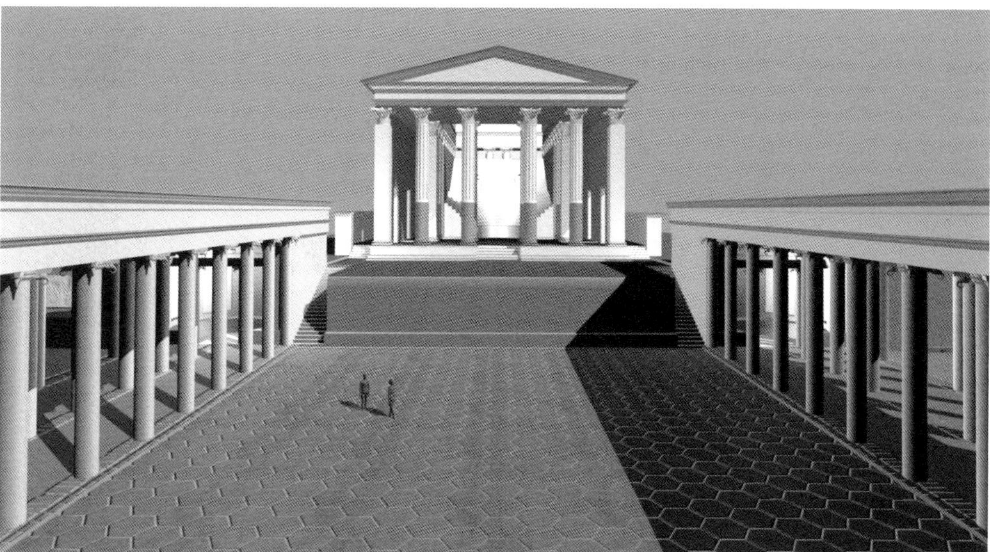

Fig. 1.12. Temple precinct (Phase V).

Fig. 1.13. Cross-section of the West Triple Colonnade and Theater-in-Temple.

above the temple floor to the second level of the building. Mirror images of each other, the East and West Internal Staircases measure *c.*2.4 m in width and 7 m in length, each constructed of 21 finely laid treads. Figure 1.12 illustrates the precinct in this phase with the Theater-in-Temple, while fig. 1.13 provides a cross section of the Lower Temenos Triple Colonnade and the East Exedra. Figure 1.14 gives an idea of how the precinct appeared with the addition of the Theater-in-Temple. Figure 1.16 shows the plan of the Theater-in-Temple in this phase,[16] a real innovation in Nabataean architecture.

16 The temple, its architectural features, and the dimensions of these features are discussed in detail in vol. 2, 214-77.

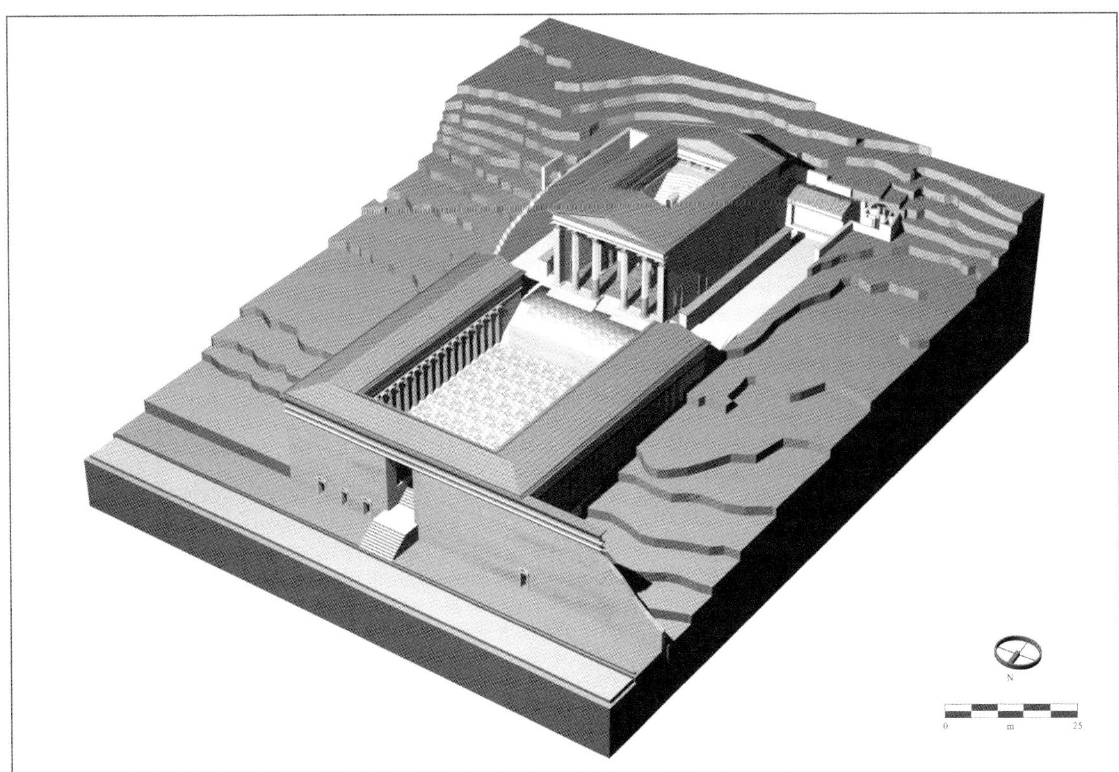

Fig. 1.14. Reconstruction of Great Temple precinct (Phase V).

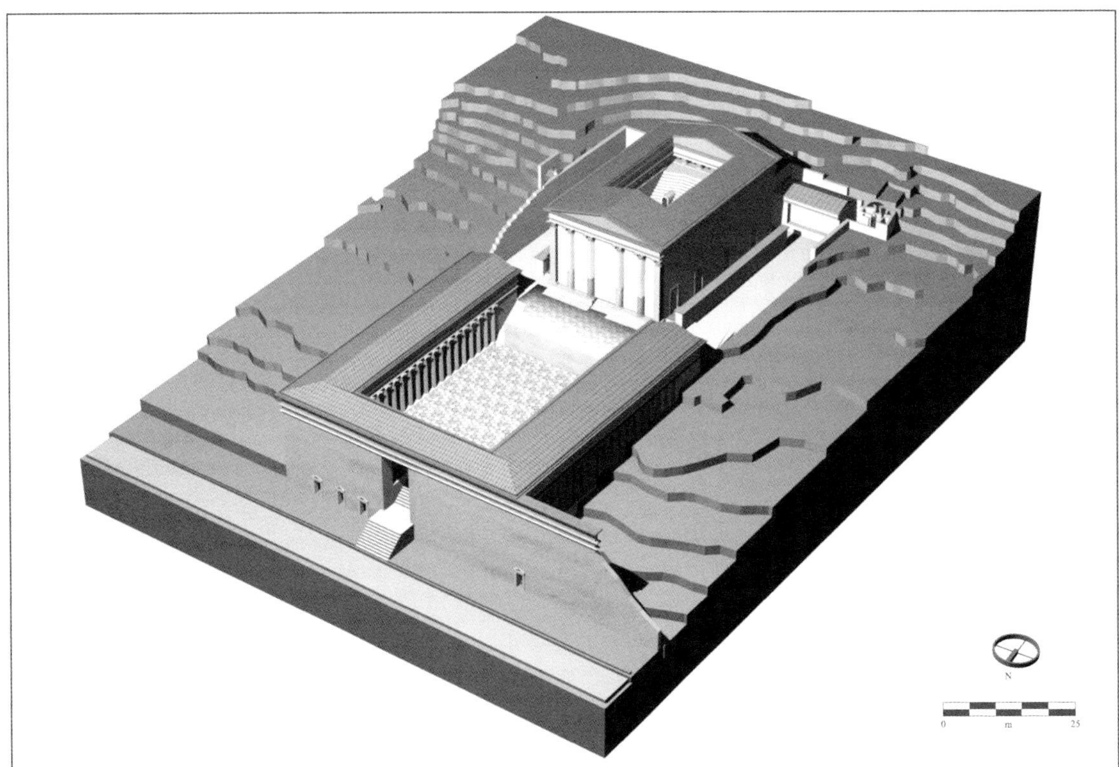

Fig. 1.15. Reconstruction showing walled-in temple (Phase VII).

Phase VI: the last Nabataean period and annexation by Rome

In Phase VI we believe a possible Roman attack took place *c.*A.D. 106 because of damage to the West Propylaeum walls and the recovery in the débris of some 423 ballista balls, 162 arrowheads, and armor. An earthquake in 113 or 114 brought architectural changes and modifications. The 'Baroque Room' collapsed and went out of use during this interval. During this same period the Baths were constructed in the W part of the temple precinct.

Phases VII-IX: Roman

Phase VII, dated to the mid-2nd c. A.D., was a time of repair, rebuilding and change, probably occasioned by the Roman occupation. The Propylaeum East was totally remodeled and reconfigured with a new plan. Metal bars were inserted in the doorways of the east rooms fronting the Roman Road. The Lower Temenos also shows extensive repairs and reconfigurations. In the temple, doorways are narrowed and walled up, effectively blocking off entry and closing the building; a stage building added to the Theater may be one reason for the walls being blocked off, or perhaps the Great Temple may have been converted into a defensive facility when each of the doorways in the corridor was closed with ashlars and walls were built between the porch columns (fig. 1.15). Perhaps there was a further earthquake, or some sort of conflict was anticipated.

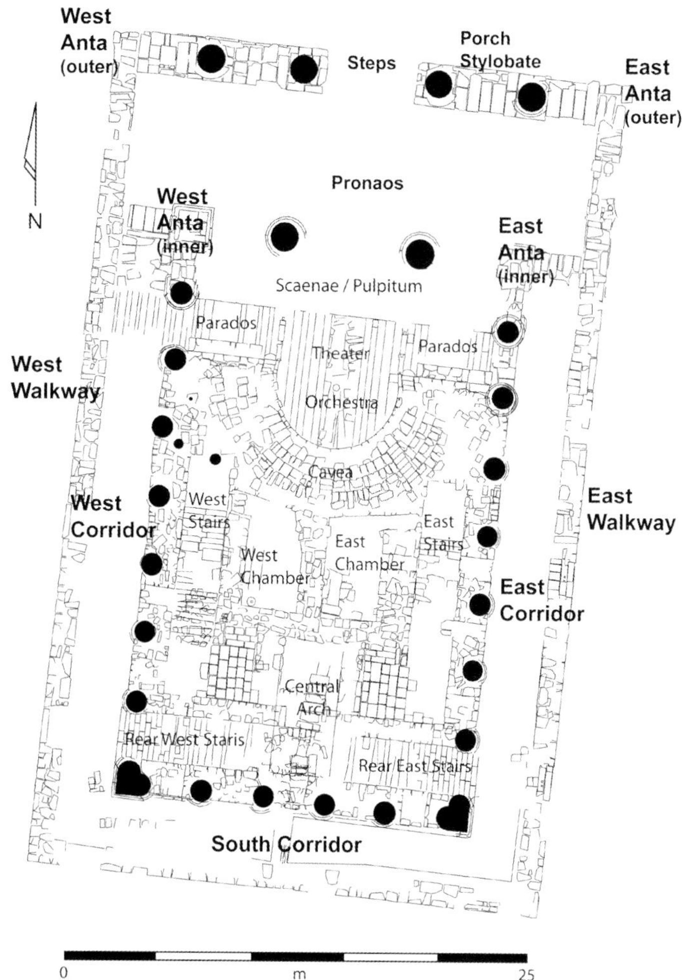

Fig. 1.16. Theater-in-Temple plan (Phase V).

Phase VIII is assigned to the late 2nd c. A.D. The range of material culture indicates that this was a period of damage, collapse, dumping, and abandonment. It saw the collapse of the colonnade[17] in the Propylaeum, and the Lower Temenos floor pavements and architectural elements were robbed. In the Great Temple there is evidence of localized conflagrations and the robbing of floor pavements, including those in the corridors and the upper treads of the interior staircases, the Residential Quarter, the East and West Vaulted Chambers, and the thresholds of the East and West Interior Staircases.

Phase IX is dated to the earthquake of May 363,[18] a cataclysmic event causing the collapse of the Propylaeum and the Lower Temenos cryptoporticoes, their vaults tumbling onto the floors and bringing down the West Triple Colonnade. The Upper Temenos saw the collapse of the West Perimeter Wall, the West Walkway and Precinct Walls, as well as the Cistern-Reservoir. This phase saw the final use of the Residential Quarter, unusually well preserved and, except for fill, showing

17 See vol. 2, fig. 2.40.

18 This is generally referred to by Near Eastern archaeologists as the start of the Early Byzantine period.

little post-depositional disturbance and thereby illuminating the lives of the inhabitants. Limited later use was made of the Roman-Byzantine Baths due to their partial collapse. The Porch columns in the W part of the Great Temple plummeted onto the Forecourt, pulverizing the hexagonal pavement, and other elements of the temple smashed and fell into the W part of the Upper Temenos and the Lower Temenos. Subsequent silting occurred with fluvial deposits and wash, and the intercolumnar wall in the West Colonnade buckled under the pressure of falling débris.

Phases X-XI: the Great Temple in the Early Byzantine period

In Phase X all the signs indicate an abandonment of the precinct, characterized by a fluvial deposit dated to about the 4th-5th c. Byzantine re-use of the Lower Temenos is evident in further destruction levels and the rebuilding of the Triple Colonnade's intercolumnar walls using pilaster reliefs from the temple as building elements. Industrial activities are taking place, including lime manufacture in the S part of the East Triple Colonnade and exedrae. Fallen architectural elements, including column drums, were used to build a platform in front of the West Exedra. The industrial re-use of several areas in some cases left significant quantities of burned ash. In the Upper Temenos the floors of the East Plaza were stripped, masonry walls are haphazardly constructed, drain-pipes clumsily installed, and shabby walls built. Multiple drainage systems are set in place. The most westerly Precinct Wall is rebuilt with an above-ground canalization system. Later in Phase X a kiln may have been installed in the baths over the remains of the southernmost *caldarium*. In the temple a clumsy attempt was made to rebuild the East and West Walkways. Scattered traces of secondary domestic use are found around the Theater-in-Temple stage, the Vaulted Chambers, Great Cistern, Central Arch, and in the East Corridor.

In Phase XI, a further collapse possibly postdates the 5th c. and may be due to the earthquake of 9 July, A.D. 551. Major collapses continue to occur in the Propylaeum. The Lower Temenos saw a continued accumulation of fill and the West Entry Stairs are no longer in use. The East Triple Colonnade collapsed along with the entablature of the East Exedra. The Upper Temenos is subject to further accumulation of fill following disuse of the drainage system. Modifications in the Roman-Byzantine Baths proceed its final collapse, after which the site of the baths is finally abandoned. By the late 6th/early 7th c., when Petra was experiencing a general decline, the East Porch columns of the temple collapse and fluvial deposits continue to accumulate. The earthquakes certainly contributed to a more impoverished community, finally bringing an end to the Baths and the Great Temple precinct.

Phases XII-XIV

Phase XII is a time of abandonment, robbing, and the accumulation of fluvial deposits. In Phase XIII there is again a series of major collapses. Phase XIV encompasses the modern era when the Lower Temenos is used for farming, marked by the division of the area into two fields separated by overturned column drums.[19] The Bedouin also constructed various makeshift walls in the Upper and Lower Temenoi. By the time our excavations began in 1993, the temple precinct was deeply buried beneath successive collapses and topsoil. The only visible components were the collapsed columns of the East Porch and the faint outline of temple walls, barely visible in aerial photographs.

Summary of the progress of the excavations

A summary of the annual excavations from 1993 to 2006 was published in vol. 2. Charts presenting the trenches and special projects by area are presented in Appendices 1-5 below. Figure 1.17 shows the Great Temple before our excavations began and the massive collapse of the columns of the East Porch. A brief summary of our work is as follows. In 1993 the temple façade was defined. From 1994 to 1996 excavations were undertaken in all areas of the precinct. Ground-penetrating

19 See vol. 2, fig. 3.18.

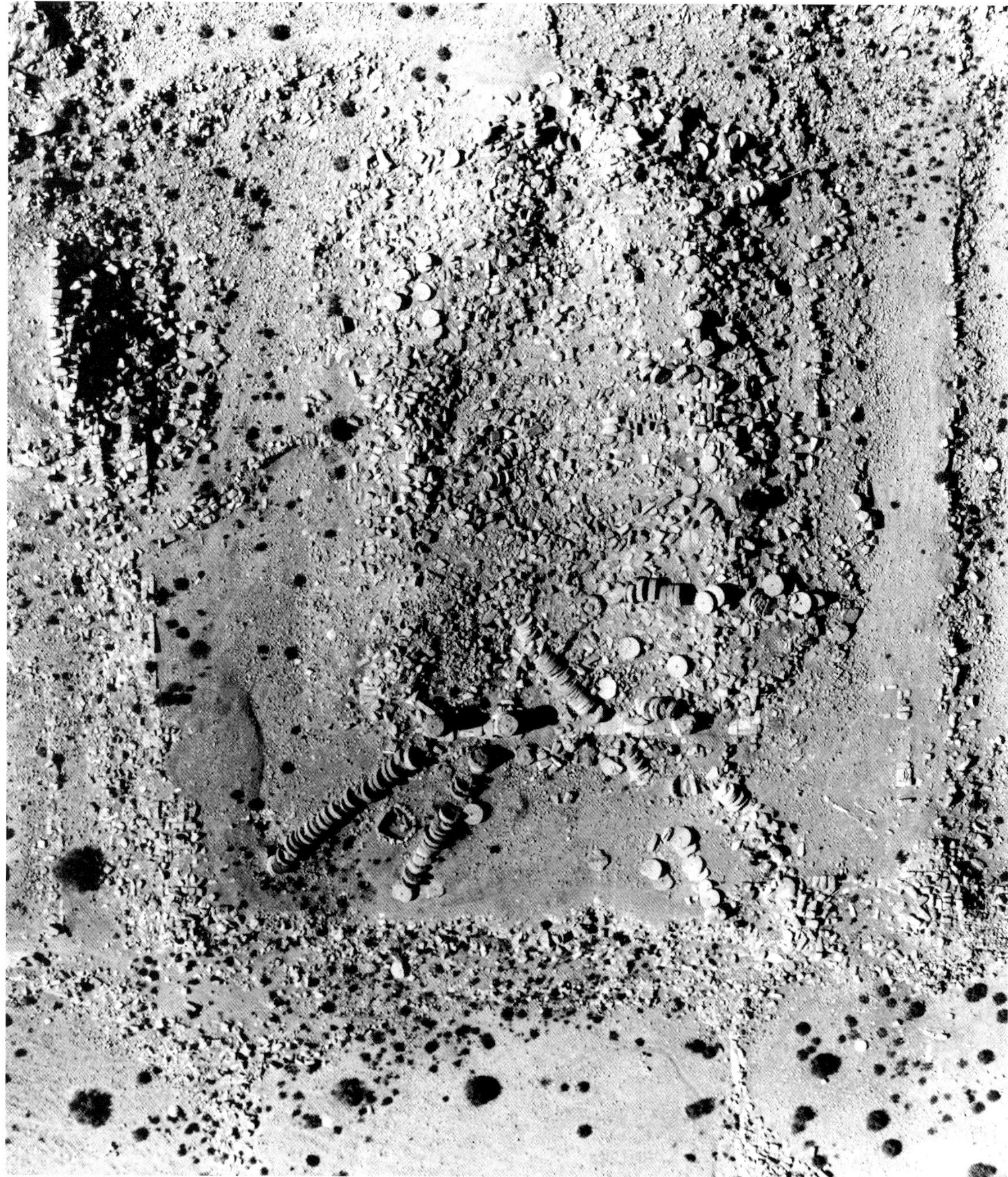

Fig. 1.17. Temple collapse, aerial view to the south (1993).

radar was employed in 1995 for the definition of the subterranean drainage system. The Theater-in-Temple was discovered in 1997 and excavations continued there in 1998. Figure 1.18, taken at the close of the 1998 campaign, shows the progress made in the various areas of the precinct. From 1999 to 2000 we defined many features in the precinct. In 2001 we found the Great Cistern. Adjacent to the Great Temple precinct was the Small Temple, a Roman imperial cult building, also excavated in 2000-1. In 2002 the Great Cistern was further explored. In the same year we found the 'Baroque Room Complex' with the remains of its brilliant gilded plaster ceiling. The aerial view taken in 2002 (fig. 1.19) shows the location of the Small Temple and clarification of the Great Temple deposits with the (then-incomplete) excavation of the West Cryptoporticus. In 2003 we concentrated on the survey and clearance of the Roman Road and the East Propylaeum, where three rooms were built perpendicular to this major artery. In 2004 several sondages were undertaken and excavation

Fig. 1.18. Temple precinct, view to the south (at close of 1998 season).

concentrated in the West Cryptoporticus, leading to the recovery of the West Propylaeum ballista ball assemblage. In 2005 several sondages tested the stratigraphy in the Pronaos of the temple and the orchestra of the theater. The West Entry Stairway was excavated. Exploration of the Roman-Byzantine Bath Complex was begun and continued into 2006 and 2008. In 2006 we removed two rows of Theater-in-Temple seats and excavated a sondage to a depth of 5 m, which showed that earlier structures were in place before the distyle temple was constructed. An aerial photograph taken at the conclusion of 2006 (fig. 1.20) defines progress in the clearance of the West Cryptoporticus galleries and in delineating the Baths. In 2007 we mounted 37 bilingual signs at different features on the site (fig. 1.21) and conducted our annual site conservation program.

In 2008 the goals were to define the limits of the Baths and better understand the deposits. In one of the rooms close to the West Entry Stairway of our Baths and adjacent to the West Palatial Baths (excavated by the Jordanian Department of Antiquuities in the 1960s), the excavators found a mound of rubbish which included sizeable numbers of discarded oyster shells, 5000 sea urchin spines (echinoderms), and a worked hippopotamus tusk (see chapt. 18C below). This rubbish had been dumped over a spiral stairway that probably led down to an as-yet-unexcavated floor level

Fig. 1.19. Temple precinct and the Small Temple excavations, view to the south (2002).

Fig. 1.20. Temple precinct, view to the south (at close of 2006 season).

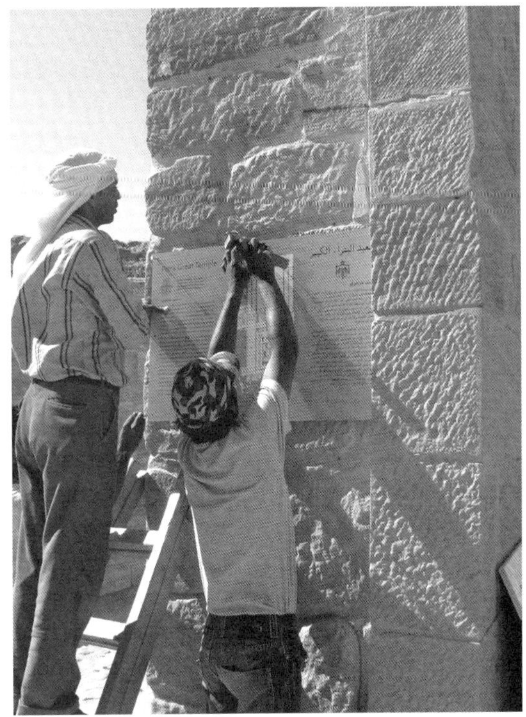

Fig. 1.21. Mounting signs at the Great Temple (2007).

in the West Palatial Baths. To the south, adjacent to the Colonnaded Corridor and aligned with and bonded to the South Corridor Wall, a suite of rooms was found. This series of walls appears to represent part of an adjoining complex but its function remains undefined. The 2008 excavations thus began to cast doubts upon the relationships between the sectors housing the Great Temple Baths and the West Palatial Baths, as well as the Great Temple baths themselves. Beyond the baths to the west, we unearthed a massive N-S West Perimeter Wall with a cryptoporticus beneath. The ashlar wall separates the Great Temple sector from the Small Temple district, forming the W boundary of the Great Temple precinct. The stratigraphy of this earlier wall, constructed in Phase IV, indicated that it preceded the construction of the baths; it continued in use through Phase IX, when it too suffered collapse in the A.D. 363 earthquake. Fallen from it in antiquity were a large sandstone horned altar, a marble head, and a distinctive marble warrior sculpture (see chapt. 22 below).

Following the 2008-9 restoration of the *caldarium*, in 2009 we were better able to define this elegant apsed structure originally appointed with heated pools in the west and south. The heating and water mechanics of the room were better understood, as is reflected by the plans and discussion in chapt. 9. In 2009 we also conducted interdisciplinary research into the conservation and preservation of the West Triple Colonnade. A shelter was built to protect the remains of the *caldarium*. An intensive topographic survey was undertaken of the area west of the Residential Quarter, as well as a comprehensive re-assessment of our GIS survey of all site data accumulated over the years (see chapt. 2).

In toto, within four areas[20] we excavated 125 trenches and 93 special projects.[21] While the archaeological investigations of the Great Temple structure and the majority of the precinct have been completed, further analysis of the remains (particularly the architecture and sculpture) should continue for some time to come.

Publications and other disseminations

In 1998, volume 1 covering the first five years of excavation (1993-97) was published with a CD-ROM. To date, some 230 further publications have become part of the public record, which can be found in the updated Great Temple Site Bibliography at the end of the present volume. Annual reports have appeared in the *Annual of the Department of Antiquities of Jordan* and in the *American Journal of Archaeology*. Our web page is at <http://www.brown.edu/Departments/joukowsky_institute/Petra/> and our databases, along with the phasing chart, trench and artifact drawings, pottery and glass typologies, coin catalogue, aerial photographs, annual trench and site plans, *ADAJ* annual reports, and trench and special project excavation reports, can be accessed on *Open*

20 The 4 main building areas were labelled P = Propylaeum, LT = Lower Temenos, UT = Upper Temenos, and T = Temple.

21 In the Propylaeum we made 15 trenches, in the Lower Temenos 38, in the Upper Temenos 35, and in the Temple 37. Of the Special Projects, 9 were in the Propylaeum, 24 in the Upper Temenos, 27 in the Temple, and 33 in the Lower Temenos (many Special Projects developed into full-fledged trenches).

Context. Volume 2, published in 2007, is devoted to the stratigraphy of each precinct area (Propylaeum, Lower Temenos, Upper Temenos and Temple proper), presenting our field research from 1993 to 2007. In chapts. 2-5 it included a comprehensive overview with a functional analysis of each area, in which the stratigraphy and phasing are presented so that the architectural changes within each part of the precinct can be appreciated. In chapt. 6, site preservation was discussed and various conservation measures undertaken annually were described. Chapter 7 contained a discussion of some of the issues the excavations have raised, including whether the Great Temple is a sacred or a secular monument.

In addition, we developed the CAVE (Cave Automatic Virtual Environment) and the first Virtual Reality three-dimensional GIS application for ongoing field archaeological research.[22] This system, with the name "ARCHAVE", allows users to view and interact with different types of artifacts and architectural finds, *in situ*, in the context of a virtual room in the CAVE.[23] For those who cannot travel to Petra, we have created a film about the site and a podcast (audiocast) that can be accessed through our web page cited in the previous paragraph.

Databases and catalogues

The artifact analysis first established classification systems for the most important artifacts and then examined these systems against the site phases in which artefacts were in use. We developed research models for artifact traits as a frame of reference, most importantly for the site itself and, whenever possible, for the Great Temple's relationships with other sites.[24] We used the FileMaker program so that data is converted to a relational format.[25] Nearly half a million artifacts have been

---

22 See Vote 2001.

23 The details of this project are outlined in Vol. 2, xxxix-xl.

24 One of our responsibilities was to develop a process to capture the incoming artifact repertoire and, in particular, to design how we would be selecting priorities, matching them with time constraints and ultimately implementing them. The goal of these efforts was to enhance all facets of the record of excavated artifacts. The strategic planning evolved from a set of recommendations made by a staff excavation committee in late 1992 and early 1993. These recommendations followed broad-based discussions amongst field supervisors and artifact specialists. The priorities as well as the analyses are summarized in our databases. We determined that it was essential to have comprehensive controls and to study all artifacts (pottery, stone, bone, metal, shell, stucco, vegetable matter) found in every part of the precinct, both those found on the surface and others recovered through excavation. The staff had to undertake the analysis during the excavation, a time-saving approach had to be developed, and a system had to be devised that would capture the basic provenance data as well as information about the different materials collected. Where possible, selected physical and functional characteristics would be recorded. Once the stratigraphic sequence had been established, the artifact repertoire was set against the site phasing.

25 Since 1996 D. D'Agostino has assisted in analyzing the data gathered in the field. After every field season the data are checked for accuracy, required fields are filled in, inconsistent labels corrected, and site phasing applied. The data from each year are then merged into one file. Simultaneously, the new relational applications are developed. A demonstration session for field personnel was held on site before the start of each season. An explanatory text key with codes was developed to make the system easier to 'translate' for users. We created a standard set of site abbreviations and developed a method for registering them. We also created a manual of field recording guidelines by which field supervisors were given explicit instructions on how to record. Through the normalization of a few aspects of the recording process, we attempted to improve the speed, accuracy and quality of the data collected, while maintaining as much consistency in reporting as possible. A number of reports have been produced to show the quantitative analysis of all materials grouped and sorted in various ways. All the Grosso Modo reports are available at http://www.opencontext.org. The goal was to determine if there was any significance in the numbers when grouped one way *versus* another. Scripts were developed to search, group, sort and summarize each combination of groupings; they were then added to a report menu on the ID file. Each report could generate up-to-date figures within seconds.

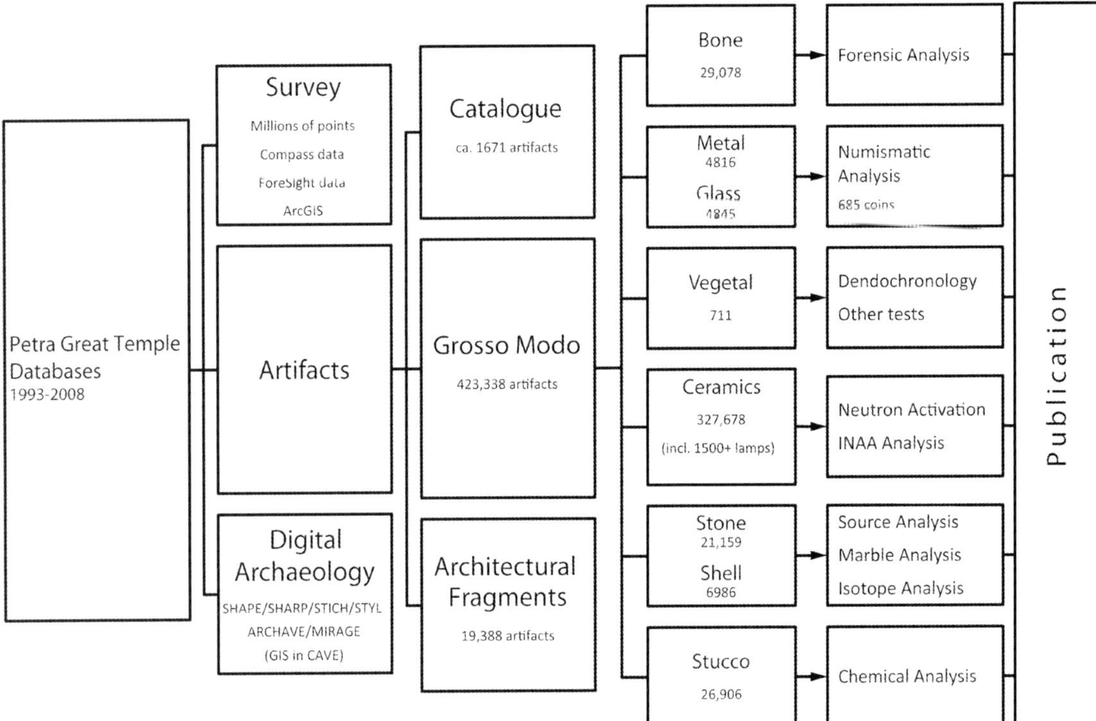

Fig. 1.22. 2008 Artifact distribution and databases.

classified in our databases.[26] As of 2008, 423,338 fragments have been registered in the overarching Grosso Modo database.[27] Ongoing are analyses by specialists of 6,809 glass fragments, 29,078 bones, more than 1500 lamps, and 327,678 ceramic fragments. Our database of architectural fragments now numbers 19,388 registered pieces, coins number 759, and the catalogue of small finds lists 1811 artifacts. Each of these registered artifacts in our databases has been assigned to a Site Phase. Figure 1.22 illustrates the 2008 flow chart of these elements. The archaeological information in each of our databases is well suited for electronic dissemination. The relevant databases accessible on *Open Context* are Grosso Modo and the Architectural Fragment databases. Also to be found are specific databases for the Great Temple glass, coins, figurines and lamps; the faunal database is also on-line.

The small finds catalogue was maintained as a separate database because special finds were turned over to the Jordanian Department of Antiquities at the end of each season. Those included all coins, worked bone pieces (bone needles, rings, and special objects like the bone knife-handle shaped like a leg), significant metal such as arrowheads, ceramics such as complete lamps, bowls and jugs, shell such as the dolphin pendant (fig. 10.7), stucco with inscriptions, and glass (including the delicate Roman head vases).

In future years archaeologists may explore the west Residential Quarter, and others will undoubtedly re-assess ideas and artifacts that we have published. One of the main goals of the project was to elucidate Nabataean civilization. We have attempted to address questions of Nabataean aesthetics, cultural inheritance and identity by studying their architecture, the iconography of their sculptural and stucco decoration, the animals they exploited, and the broad range of ideas they borrowed from the world around them.

---

26 The following figures exclude the databases developed at the Small Temple: Reid 2006.
27 Note that in Appendix 3 the Grosso Modo database accounted for 405,297 artifacts, but the numbers above refer to 2008 and include the 2007 and 2008 artifact recovery.

2

Surveying at the Great Temple, 1993-2009

Marshall C. Agnew and Fawwaz R. Ishakat

Fig. 2.1. E. A. Power and M. C. Agnew surveying the West Entry Stairway.

From the outset of the Great Temple project in 1993 it has been a primary goal to create a detailed and accurate plan of the site using modern surveying methods (fig. 2.1). In the nearly two decades since, an explosion in technology has led to rapid changes in surveying methodology. Our surveying team has adapted to incorporate the latest technologies for data collection, storage and presentation of the Great Temple. With a combination of global positioning systems (GPS), laser electronic distance measurement (EDM) surveys, computer-assisted design and drafting (CADD) software, low-altitude aerial photography, geo-referencing, and modern geographic information systems (GIS), the team has produced one of the most detailed and accurate site-specific maps available for Jordan.

A history of survey at the site

The earliest records of exploration of the temple site come from R. E. Brünnow and A. von Domaszewski in their 1904-9 project, *Die Provincia Arabia*, but W. von Bachmann was the first to postulate a 'Great Temple' on the hillside south of the colonnaded street in his revision of the Petra city plan.[1] The von Bachmann map was a fairly accurate depiction of central Petra along the Colonnaded Street (which is not colonnaded in front of the Great Temple precinct),[2] but most of the information it contains about the Great Temple was based on conjecture. A more comprehensive plan of central Petra was later drawn by P. J. Parr and published by J. S. McKenzie in 1990.[3] This plan outlined the Great Temple in its proper location, but it was based on an amalgamation of data from various periods and teams and thus not especially detailed or precise as far as the main features of the precinct were concerned. As we prepared for our excavations in 1993, it became clear that all previous maps of the site contained different and often conflicting information, resulting in our intent to create a detailed ground plan of the temple precinct. In 1992 and 1993, before excavation began, J. Wilson Myers and E. E. Myers conducted an aerial balloon survey of the site (fig. 2.2). With each successive excavation season we have continued to supplement survey data with low-altitude aerial photographs.

At the start of excavation in 1993, one of the first undertakings was to define master site plans and establish control points against which all site plans would be constructed. The surveying team (D. Pitney, L. P. Traxler and P. C. Zimmerman) selected three control point locations and tied them in to the known benchmarks on the Al-Katute ridge, using a Topcon laser survey unit. These three points, clearly marked and cemented in place, have served as the bases throughout the excavations. CP 103 lies on the East Precinct Wall (elevation 915.04), CP 104 lies south of the West Exedra wall (at 903.90), and CP 10 is at the top of the Propylaeum stairs (at 898.29 m). All elevations given in site

1 von Bachmann, Watzinger and Wiegand 1921, pl. 1: Ubersichtsplan des Stadtgebietes nach den Aufnahmen von 1916/17 "Der Korinthische Peripterale Podientempel," pp. 41-45.

2 See Zimmerman 2000.

3 McKenzie 1990, Map 7.

Fig. 2.2. Aerial overview (1992) before excavation began, with the temple precinct outlined.

reports over the years reference these points.[4] The surveying team then created a pre-excavation contour plan of the Great Temple precinct and its surroundings and a site grid in 10 m squares, roughly oriented N–S. The site grid provides a way to control, record and refer to architectural elements on the surface that are not associated with any specific trench. In 2006 the grid was expanded (fig. 2.3) as excavation moved beyond its original bounds.

The general approach has been to automate and integrate the collection of survey data as much as possible. Central to this goal was the early use of digital surveying methods for the collection, storage and presentation of data, as well as the periodic move to new and better technologies as they became available. For the first few years we used COMPASS, a survey data collection, storage and plotting software package developed by the University of Pennsylvania, and a CADD program (MiniCad 6) in conjunction with a Topcon laser surveying station. In 1996 the huge multi-year data files were updated and converted to a newer system called ForeSight, developed by P. C. Zimmerman, an early surveyor at our site. The conversion process was laborious and time-consuming, but the new system was more versatile, faster and easier to use. Thereafter the ForeSight system (along with its derivatives and updates) was used as the primary data collection and storage software through the 2006 season.[5]

GPS and geo-referencing at Petra was begun in 1997 by a US National Park Service test project led by D. C. Comer. This project established the first GPS coordinates for our site. In 1998 we

4 As discussed below, the conversion from a local coordinate system to a universal coordinate system in 1998 meant that the elevations for these points had to be updated in all the literature.

5 From 1997 to 2006 all surveying was done with Topcon laser total stations, ForeSight, and Vectorworks (a CADD program which succeeded MiniCad). In 2000, B. Brown took over from P. Zimmerman as Lead Surveyor; Brown was succeeded in 2004 by C. F. Cloke. In 2005 M. C. Agnew became Lead Surveyor and continued using the same systems through 2007.

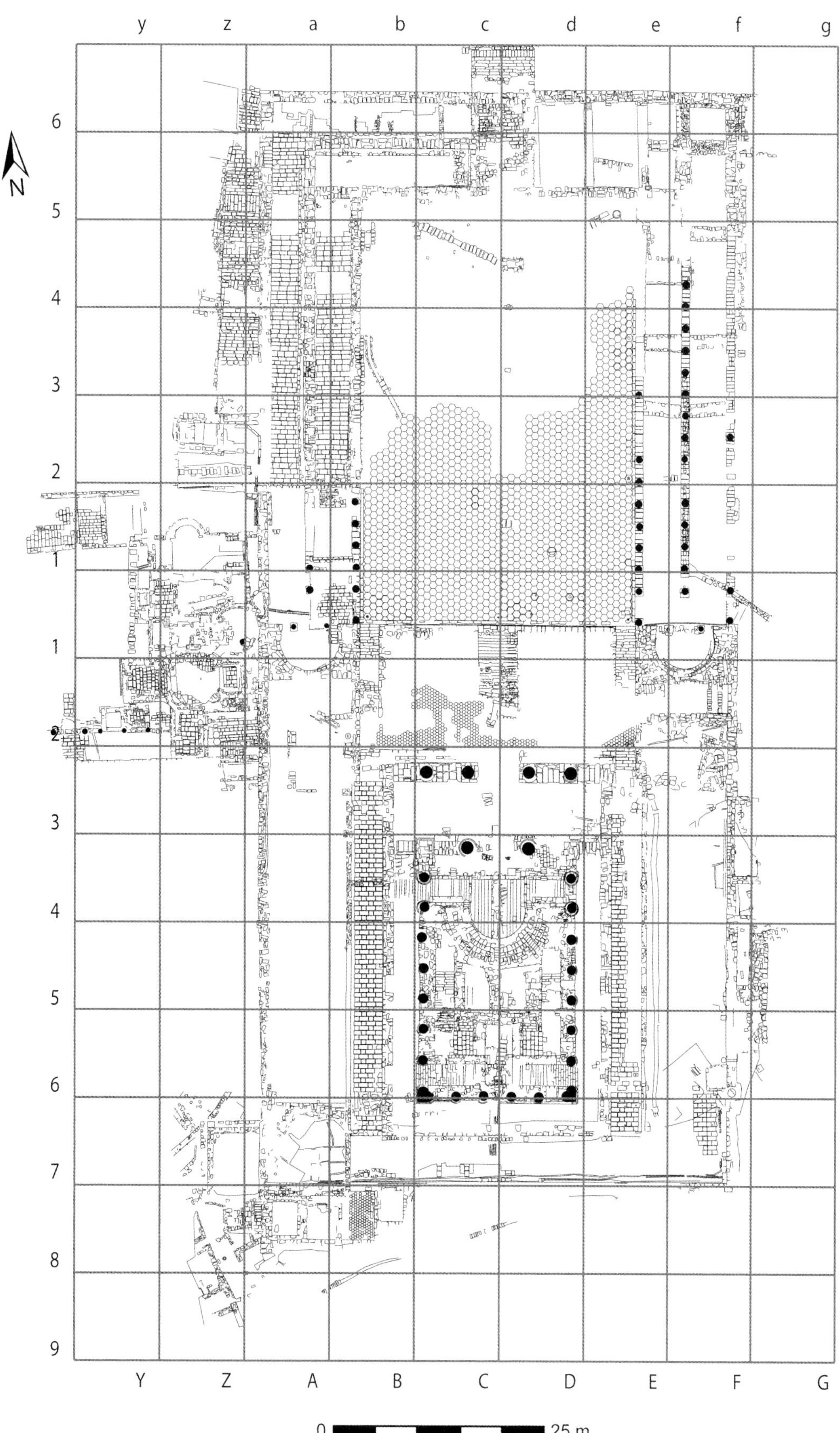

Fig. 2.3. Site-grid (2006) and overall survey plan.

had the opportunity to collaborate with the Petra Mapping Project (PMP), a joint venture between ACOR and the Hashemite University, which used much more accurate sub-centimeter GPS systems that allowed us to correlate our data with Universal Transverse Mercator (UTM) coordinate space, accurately positioning our plans in maps of the greater Petra area. In the efforts to update our data to UTM coordinates and using the more accurate GPS systems, we discovered that the coordinates for the three principal control points were off by nearly 20 m. Although our local coordinates were internally accurate, our data had to be updated in order to be tied in to the universal coordinates. All trench reports were changed to reflect the updated elevation values. Initially only the elevations were changed, leaving the absolute 2D coordinates of the plans incorrect until our major data conversion and update to all-UTM coordinates took place in 2008-9. Since our internal coordinates were not affected, our survey plans were accurate when presented individually and no harm seems to have been done. In 2008, when it had become clear that we should make another effort to modernize our data and collection systems, we enlisted the help of F. R. Ishakat, a GIS expert, to make the final switch to UTM coordinates and modern software. This change included moving to ArcGIS for data storage and display, converting all previously collected data to UTM coordinate space by tying in to the Greater Petra surveying network and moving to Real Time Kinematic Global Positioning System technology (RTK GPS) for future data collection. This is one of the most accurate and advanced stone-by-stone surveying methods available today. Our data should now be more versatile, more easily used and shared, and more consistent with other archaeological data sets. The widespread use of GPS instruments for various surveying projects has caused a major shift in professional surveying methods, and the standards of conventional measuring methods have been correspondingly revolutionized. Today, the GPS survey represents the most advanced surveying method. In many fields it has become a powerful tool, helping specialists grapple with mapping, GIS, and other surveying tasks in the field. Archaeology is one of these fields where the GPS survey is a great improvement over traditional surveying methods.

Establishing an accurate surveying network in Petra

The Jordanian government, together with foreign educational, governmental and non-governmental organizations, is engaged in protecting, conserving and restoring many of Petra's archaeological and cultural treasures. For many years these efforts confronted significant difficulties because of the lack of precise data and documentation. The idea of constructing a precise Surveying Network for Petra developed out of the need for a reliable and risk-free source of accurate information. To make all the necessary measurements for this advanced surveying network, Differential Global Positioning Systems, along with a modern reflectorless one-second-reading-accuracy Total Station, were employed. The effective design of such a network demands meticulous field reconnaissance and proper selection of surveying stations to form the vertices of the network. The network's chief objectives can be summarized as follows:

1. To replace all the local surveying coordinate systems by the universal coordinate system (Universal Transverse Mercator).
2. To establish a set of precise surveying control points that can be used for surveying activities at any time.

Network survey stations had to be carefully selected, the most accurate surveying equipment had to be employed, and a precise methodology had to be implemented. First, we obtained from the Royal Jordanian Geographic Centre a precise GPS reference point which was used to establish a local reference base-station. This station was permanently fixed over Dakhilallah Qublan's house in the village of Umm Sayhun, just above the ancient site. The point was carefully selected to serve all GPS measurements for present and future surveys. GPS in a static mode was used to obtain the final 3D coordinates for this point. The measured length of the baseline between the GPS reference point in the town of Ash-Shawbak and the reference station in Umm Sayhun was established at 19.2 km. The achieved accuracy of this distance position was 19 mm; the elevation was 32 mm.

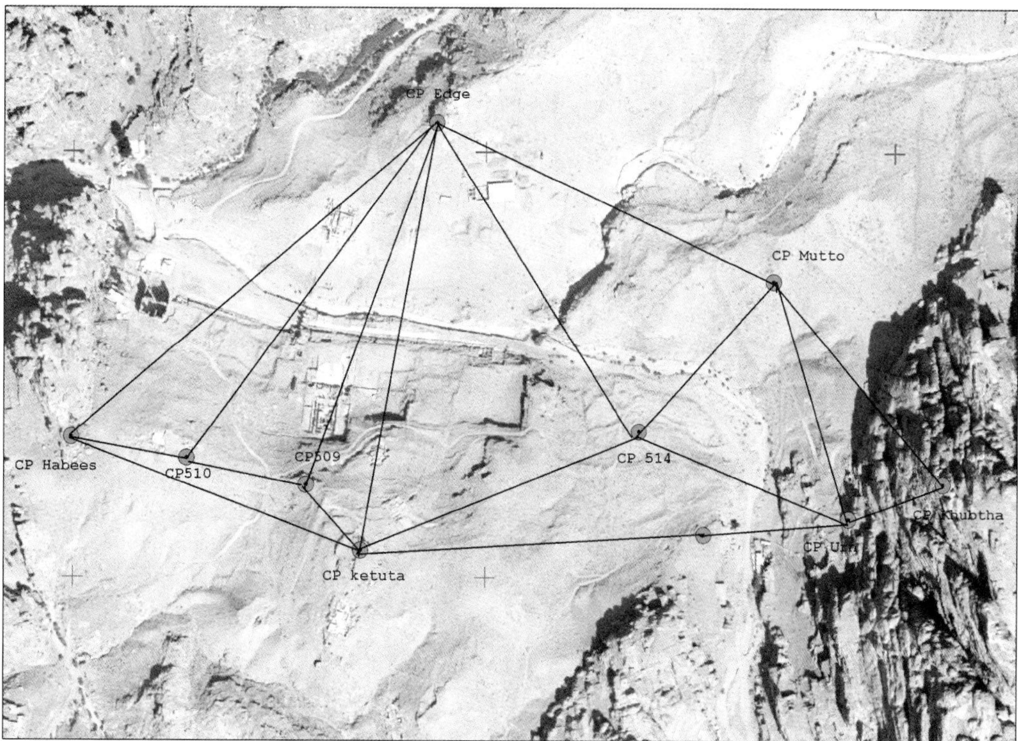

Fig. 2.4. The precise surveying network of Petra.

The main control points for the network were set in different locations in Petra (fig. 2.4) after taking into consideration the following factors:

1. Inter-visibility between the points: points were selected that could be used both as survey stations and for back sight.
2. Points were chosen to be accessible, so that surveyors could get to them easily with their heavy surveying equipment.
3. The points were carefully distributed to cover the central city of Petra.

All points were measured in static GPS mode, with an observation time up to 2 hours depending on the length of the baseline. Unlike typical surveying networks, we were unable to provide any adjustment because we had only two receivers; thus for each measured point we had only one base line. To ensure the precision of our network, in the field we verified the distance measurements and confirmed the angles of each triangle. In practical terms, both the verification of distances and the confirmation of angles were conducted using a one-second-reading electronic theodolite, the Leica T1800, for angular measurements and the Distomat Leica Dior 3002s for distance measurements. From a theoretical point of view, we had to return to some basics of analytical and trigonometric geometry in order to compute and analyze the measured data. This may be explained with reference to fig. 2.5. Suppose that the vertices of the triangle ABC represent the control points of our network. Using the coordinates of the end points, we computed the horizontal distance between each two points using a simple formula:

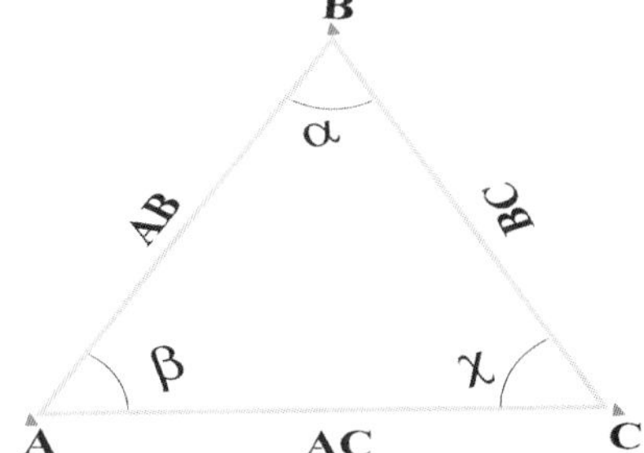

Fig. 2.5. Basic geometry being used to calculate distances and angles.

Equation 1: $\sqrt{(YB - YA)^2 - (XB - XA)^2}$ AB =

Where: AB is the distance to be computed;

(YB-YA) is the difference of Northing coordinates between the end points;

(XB-XA) is the difference of Easting coordinates between the endpoints.

For computing the angles we used the formula below:

Equation 2: α = Arc Cos (2*AB*BC)
Where: α is the angle to be computed;
AB, BC, AC are computed distances using Equation 1.

The distances as well as the angles were carefully and accurately measured. The errors in distance measurements were *c.* ±1 cm; for the angular measurements the accuracy was *c.* ±1 second. These extremely small errors confirm the accuracy and precision of the network. The results of the checks of distances and angles are shown in Tables 2.1-2.2 and fig. 2.6, respectively.

TABLE 2.1
CHART OF DISTANCES BETWEEN CONTROL POINTS OF THE PETRA NETWORK

Specific Distance	*Measured Distance (m)*	*Computed Distance (m)*	*Computed Error*
C.P. 509-C.P. 510	147.951	147.956	+0.005
C.P. Ridge-C.P. 510	454.235	454.221	-0.014
C.P. Ridge-C.P. 514	438.458	438.463	+0.005
C.P. Ridge-C.P. Ketuta	511.427	511.416	-0.011
C.P. 510-C.P. Ketuta	101.734	101.736	+0.002
C.P. 514-C.P. 510	409.052	409.069	+0.017
C.P. 514-C.P. Ketuta	365.941	365.943	+0.002
C.P. 509-C.P. Ketuta	237.083	237.070	-0.013
C.P. Mutto-C.P. Khubtha	316.391	316.388	-0.003
C.P. Khubtah-C.P. Habees	1063.758	1063.769	+0.011

TABLE 2.2
CHECK OF ANGLES OF THE PETRA NETWORK

Triangle	*Computed Inner Angles*			*Closure Error*	*Measured Inner Angles*			*Closure Error*	*True Error*
	inches	*feet*	*degrees*	*inches*	*inches*	*feet*	*degrees*	*inches*	*inches*
C.P. Ridge C.P. 514 C.P. Kututa	0.17	0	180	0.17	1.23	00	180	-1.23	+1.40
C.P. 514 C.P. Kututa C.P. 510	0	0	180	00	59.14	59	179	0.86	-0.86
C.P. Ridge C.P. Kututa C.P. 509	59.01	59	179	0.99	0.34	00	180	0.66	+0.33
C.P. Ridge C.P. Kututa C.P. 510	0	0	180	00	1.07	00	180	-1.07	+1.07
C.P. Ridge C.P. 509 C.P. 510	0	0	180	00	59.18	59	179	+0.82	-0.82

CP510 is the nearest network control point to the Great Temple and was used as a reference point to convert all the previous seasons' measurements into a new UTM coordinate system.

Using high-accuracy GPS surveying at the Great Temple

In 2009 we began using the RTK GPS technology. Before we began our stone-by-stone surveying, we had to adjust a shift of *c.*20 m (the result of never updating the original local coordinate spaces to UTM coordinates; see above). Going into the field with a printed copy of the plan showing all architectural details, we chose a number of identical points well distributed and easy to identify both on the ground and on the printed plan. Using RTK GPS technology, we measured

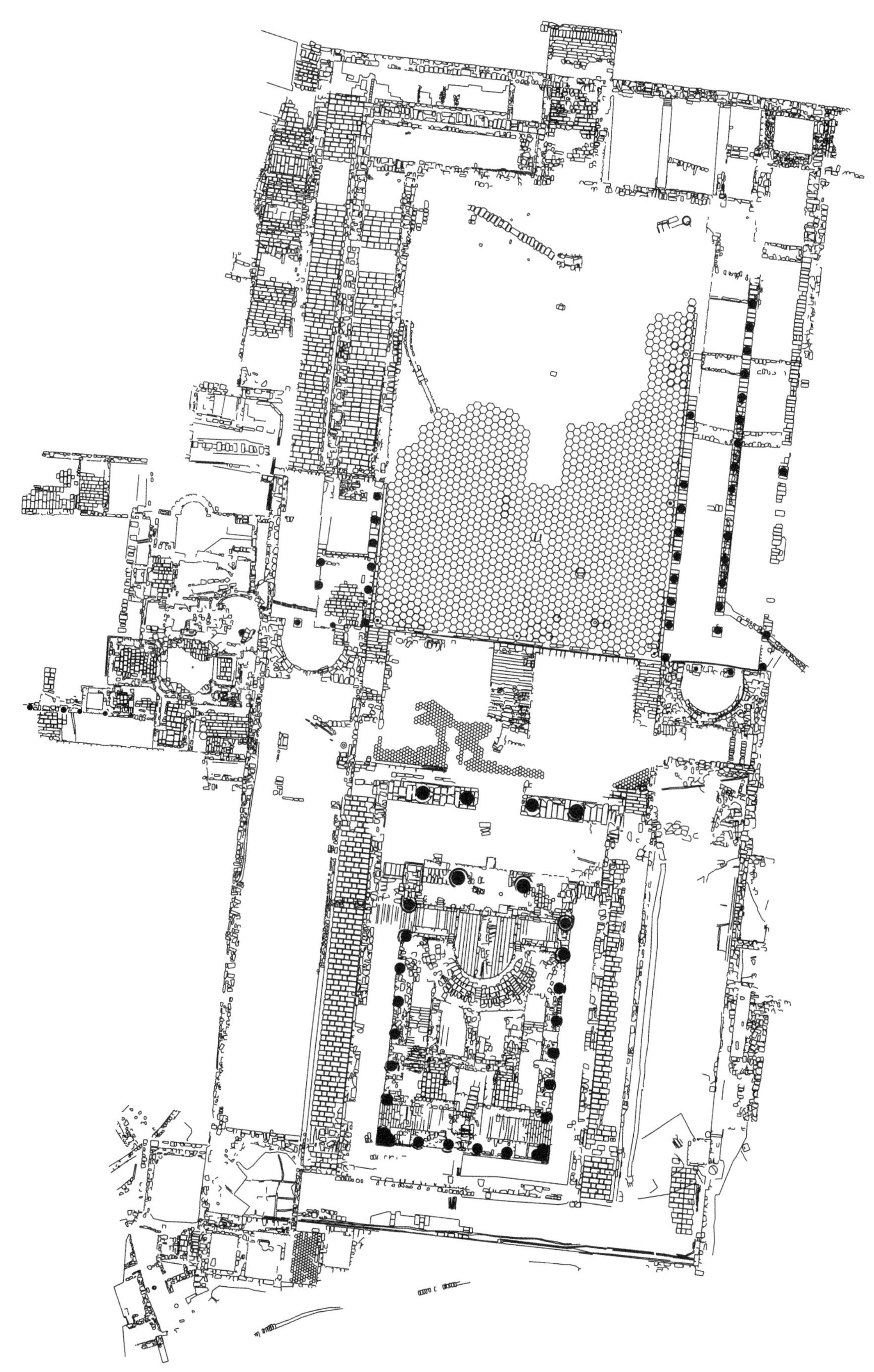

Fig. 2.6. Previous seasons' measurements transformed into UTM coordinate systems.

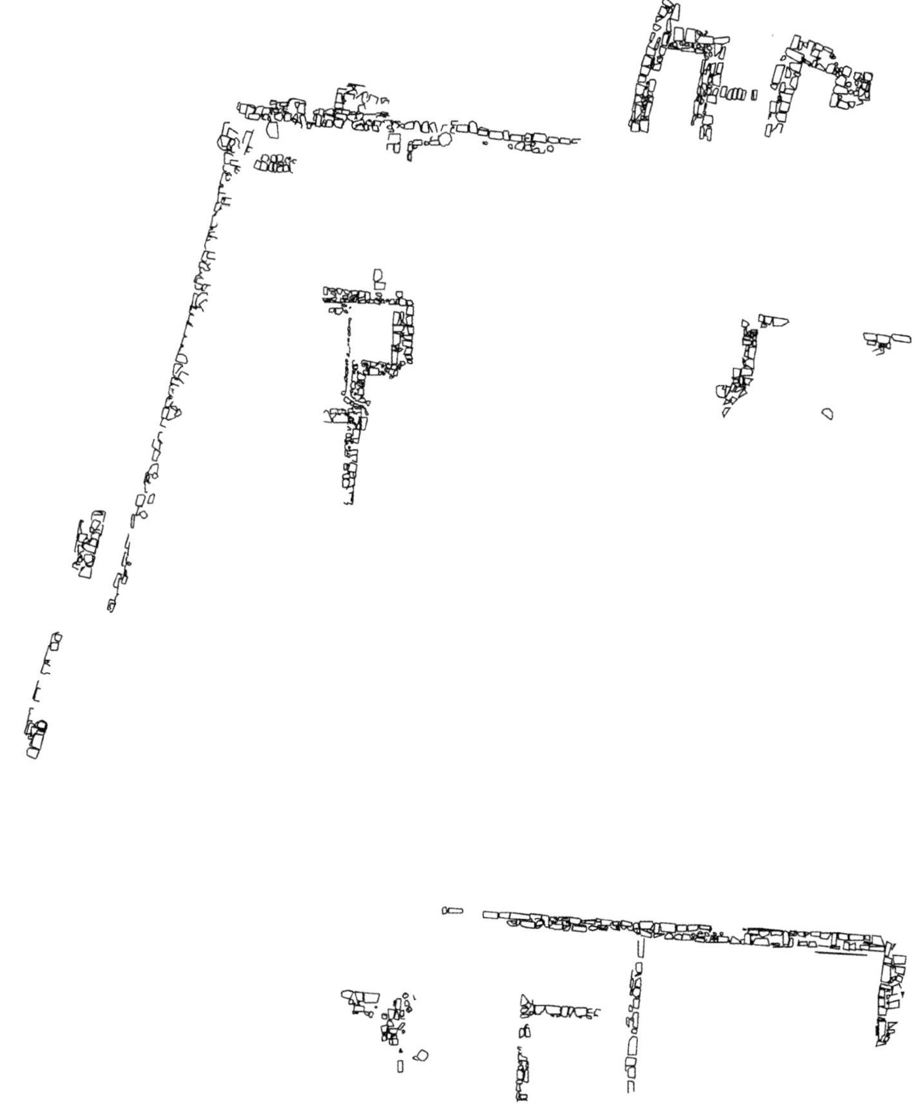

Fig. 2.7. RTK GPS stone-by-stone survey of the Great Temple in 2008.

all these points precisely, to within an accuracy of 1 cm. These points served as Ground Control Points for digital photogrammetry, but we employed them simply to transform the site's incorrect coordinates into the precise UTM coordinates. Using the software LISCAD (Leica Geosystems), we transformed these incorrect coordinates, and the accuracy of the transformation was verified (see the LISCAD report in the Appendix to this chapter). All prior seasons' measurements transformed into the UTM coordinate systems are shown in fig. 2.6. The 2008 season measurements were taken using the RTK GPS, when we performed a stone-by-stone survey of all the newly excavated architecture and other features. All measurements were conducted within an accuracy of 1-2 cm in the position and within 2-3 cm in elevation (fig. 2.7). When we merged the 2008 season (fig. 2.6) plan with the corrected drawing from prior seasons (fig. 2.7), they perfectly matched (fig. 2.8).

Our first use of the RTK GPS technology at the Great Temple demonstrated that we can rely on this new technology for any further measurements. It also offers a number of advantages over our previous systems:

1. It is quicker than the other conventional surveying methods and the accuracy achieved is very precise.
2. Unlike the other conventional surveying methods, it can operate at any time regardless of the weather conditions.

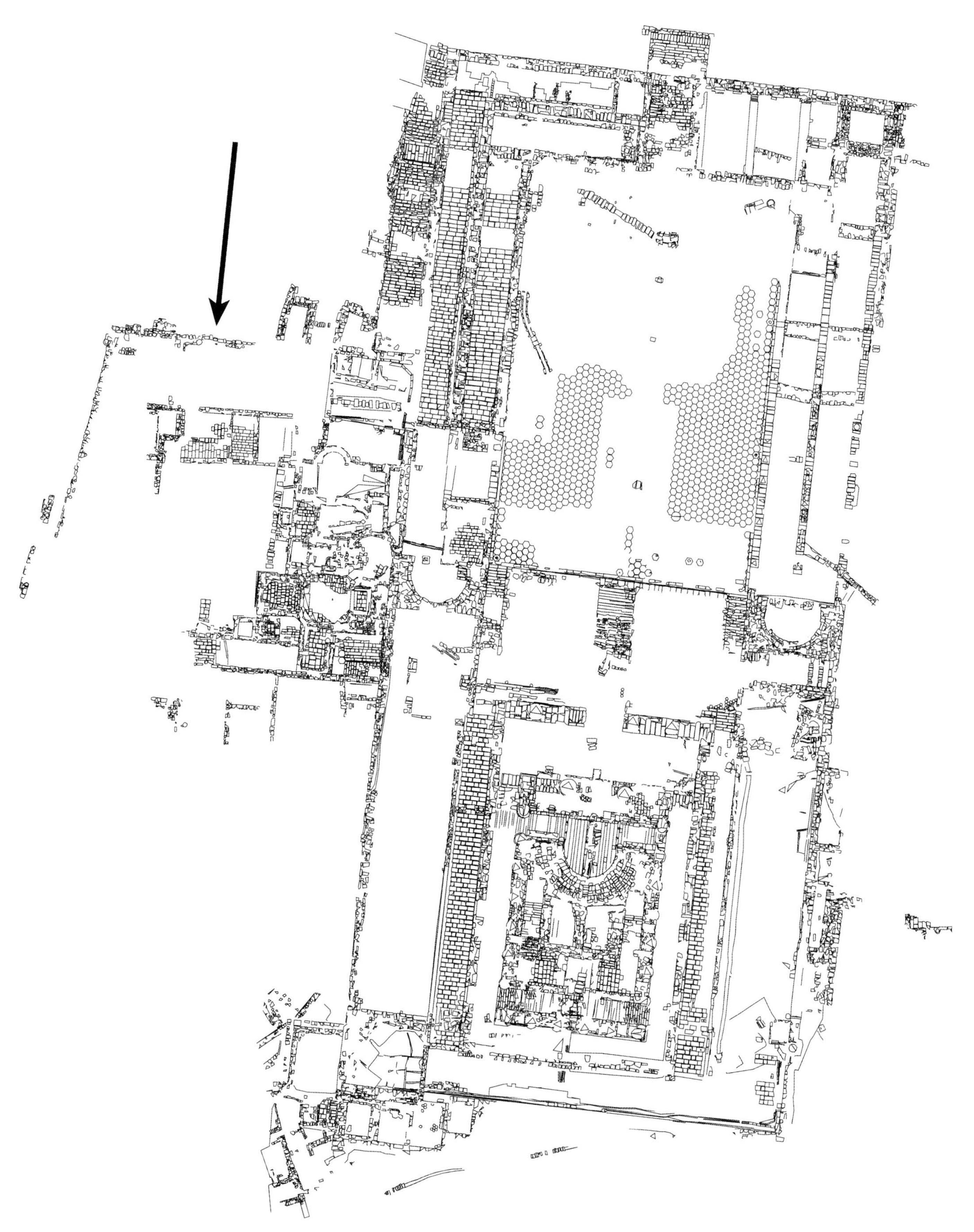

Fig. 2.8. Great Temple site plan covering seasons 1993-2009.

3. Inter-visibility between surveying stations is not necessary; just one station with known coordinates is sufficient to perform the surveying.

With the move to RTK GPS and use of an ArcGIS-based system, the Great Temple project remains on the cutting edge of archaeological surveying technology. We are now able to tie our data into UTM maps of Greater Petra and visualize data in more effective ways; we will also be able easily to share information with a wide range of other mapping projects and add to the dataset more quickly and effectively in coming years.

APPENDIX

LISCAD Report: Transformation Report 7/31/2009

Projection: Plane grid
Distance: Meters
Distance type: Grid
Transformation: Affine
X Axis Scale: 1.08120977
Y Axis Scale: 0.93778580
Deviation from Orthogonality: N1°23′52″E
Angle of Rotation: N3°13′24″E
X Translation: 147050.355
Y Translation: 158347.273

	East	*North*
ID: 90254		
Control	734765.400	3357649.030
Local	734748.120	3357665.732
Transformed	734765.416	3357648.999
Residual	0.016	-0.031
ID: 186367		
Control	734768.000	3357668.850
Local	734751.691	3357686.661
Transformed	734767.992	3357668.864
Residual	-0.008	0.014
ID: 186368		
Control	734768.850	3357668.790
Local	734752.471	3357686.535
Transformed	734768.841	3357668.805
Residual	-0.009	0.015
ID: 45433		
Control	734805.910	3357699.310
Local	734788.508	3357716.237
Transformed	734805.872	3357699.338
Residual	-0.038	0.028

	East	*North*
ID: 49715		
Control	734804.930	3357699.440
Local	734787.676	3357716.394
Transformed	734804.966	3357699.422
Residual	0.036	-0.018
ID: 51800		
Control	734811.400	3357787.680
Local	734798.912	3357809.762
Transformed	734811.398	3357787.691
Residual	-0.002	0.011
ID: 51712		
Control	734818.770	3357786.940
Local	734805.679	3357808.393
Transformed	734818.775	3357786.921
Residual	0.005	-0.019

3

Construction techniques of the Petra Great Temple: how the temple was reconstructed

Shaher M. Rababeh

Introduction

During World War I W. von Bachmann, C. Watzinger and T. Wiegand[1] originally mapped central Petra and named the structure on the south side of the Wadi Musa the Great Temple. They speculated that the temple was approached through a monumental Propylaeum with a grand staircase leading into a colonnaded terraced Lower Temenos. In 1993 Brown University's systematic investigations of the Great Temple began and now the excavations are essentially completed. Today the Great Temple and its precinct ranks among the most valued sites in Petra.

The purpose of this chapter is to synthesize the methods and techniques used by the Nabataeans in constructing the Great Temple precinct. Its well-restored state of provides the opportunity for a detailed study of the building techniques used, which in turn sheds light on the construction process. To achieve this objective emphasis is placed on the discussion and illustration of both structural and non-structural architectural components. We compare the technical features with other buildings in Petra and other Nabataean sites and offer comparisons with Greco-Roman sites revealing interactions between the Nabataeans and Greco-Roman cities.

Technical features including the specifics of bonding and jointing are documented and this evidence is then analyzed to determine why these features appeared and evolved. This is undertaken at the outset by surveying different building materials used by the Nabataean builders, all of which were recovered during the excavations. Fortunately most of these architectural elements still remain *in situ*.[2] We then turn to construction techniques used for building foundations, floors, and walls, including vaults and columns. Subsequently types of roofs are considered and the engineering used in their construction. Finally stucco decoration is examined in detail. Before turning to the analyses of materials, a précis of the site is offered.

Architectural background

The Petra Great Temple stratigraphy has been divided chronologically into 15 site phases by the Brown University excavators. This chapter will explore two of these phases, the Site Phase IV *tetrastyle In Antis*[3] dated from the last quarter of the 1st c. B.C. to the beginning of the 1st c. A.D., and the later Site Phase V dated to the 1st c. A.D. when there was a redesign of the architecture and a *theatron* or theater was inserted into the central fabric of the temple itself.

Although the functions of the 15 phases[4] are not yet known decisively, for convenience the nomenclature assigned by the excavators to the precinct areas—Propylaeum, Lower Temenos, Upper Temenos, and Temple—will be retained along with the published temple terminology.[5] Each area's characteristic features will be referred to as it relates to the architecture.

---

1 von Bachmann, C. Watzinger and T. Wiegand, 1921.

2 In their original contexts.

3 The façade with 4 columns between antae walls.

4 *Great Temple* vol. 2, 20-26, see also Table 1.1; Joukowsky divides the activities of the precinct into 15 phases. These include the architectural changes brought about by natural causes. In this chapter focus is on the two main site architectural phases, Site Phases IV and V.

5 Ibid.

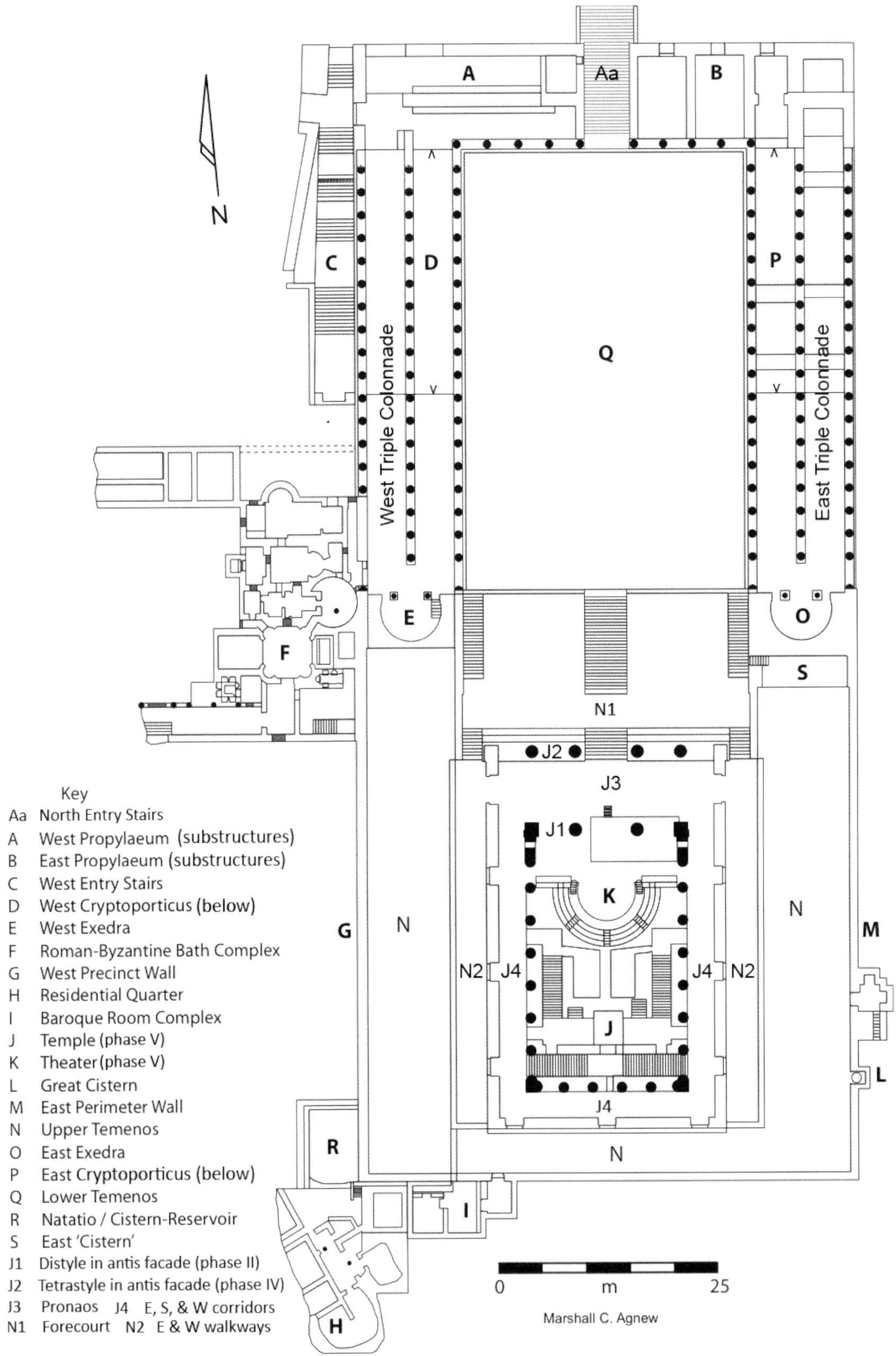
N
A
Aa
B
C
D
P
Q
West Triple Colonnade
East Triple Colonnade
E
O
F
S
N1
J2
J3
J1
K
N
N
G
M
N2
J4
J4
N2
J
L
J4
R
N
I
H
0
m
25
Marshall C. Agnew
Key
Aa North Entry Stairs
A West Propylaeum (substructures)
B East Propylaeum (substructures)
C West Entry Stairs
D West Cryptoporticus (below)
E West Exedra
F Roman-Byzantine Bath Complex
G West Precinct Wall
H Residential Quarter
I Baroque Room Complex
J Temple (phase V)
K Theater (phase V)
L Great Cistern
M East Perimeter Wall
N Upper Temenos
O East Exedra
P East Cryptoporticus (below)
Q Lower Temenos
R Natatio / Cistern-Reservoir
S East 'Cistern'
J1 Distyle in antis facade (phase II)
J2 Tetrastyle in antis facade (phase IV)
J3 Pronaos J4 E, S, & W corridors
N1 Forecourt N2 E & W walkways

Fig. 3.1. Petra Great Temple plan, 2006.

Site Phase IV, tetrastyle *structure*

During the Nabataean period, the Great Temple site underwent a rapid elaboration with a complete rebuilding of its precinct. Because of its renovated monumentality, the Site Phase IV precinct is identified by the excavators as the 'Grand Design' (fig. 3.1). At this time the Propylaeum is constructed and embellished with relief sculpture. The Lower Temenos, including the 5 stair flights of the 30 m to 40 m West Entry Stairway provides a main entry into the precinct. But focus is centered in the great open Lower Temenos plaza, 49 m N-S x 30 m E-W, with the sweep of the hexagonal pavement. Here are two-aisled Triple Colonnades with more than 120 columns adorned with elephant-headed capitals surrounding the plaza on three sides. These columns with elephant-headed capitals have a diameter ranging from 76 to 84 cm and are set 2.5 m apart. The overall width of each colonnade is 12.5 m and each aisle is c. 4.4 m.

Both Triple Colonnades terminate in exedras slightly greater than a half circle in plan (fig. 3.1). They measure 7.5 m in width across the center but are only 6.8 m in width at their openings and 5.5 m in depth. Each exedra is separated from the Triple Colonnades by a pair of sandstone columns 60 cm in diameter topped with smaller limestone elephant heads. During the excavations roof tiles are found in both exedras, but no voussoirs (or concrete) are reported.

Built below the Triple Colonnades are subterranean cryptoporticos measuring 28 m N-S x 4.30 m in E-W width. And linking the Lower Temenos to the Temple Forecourt are stairways with 30 steps, 9 m length x 2.70 m in width. Bordering the Lower Temenos to its south and linking the two exedrae, is the massive Lower Temenos Retaining Wall preserved to a 28 m length x 2.76 m height (fig. 3.2). The distance from the Propylaeum Retaining Wall to the Lower Temenos Retaining Wall is 49 m N-S x 56 m E-W.

During Site Phase IV facing north standing above the Lower Temenos is a monumental structure—a rectangular *tetrastyle* building measuring 42.50 m N-S x 27.1 m E-W. As can be seen in

Fig. 3.2. Great Temple aerial to south. Note the rear terrace where the bedrock is cut away. Here the Nabataeans extracted some of the blocks required for the building.

Fig. 3.1, it is built onto an earlier structure of Site Phase II, a smaller *distyle* structure with two columns between antae walls measuring 30.07 m N-S x 18.36 m E-W. The *tetrastyle* temple now consists of two parts: a broad Pronaos c. 6.50 m x 24.7 m, built onto the front of the earlier structure and a central hall or *naos*.[6] The Pronaos façade consists of 4 prostyle columns 1.5 m in diameter. The side columns are placed 5 m from each other, but the central two columns are set 7 m apart. Beyond these columns at either end of the façade are the antae walls, hypothetically embellished with pilaster reliefs.[7] Standing behind these massive front columns are the two columns from the earlier *distyle in antis* facade, each 1.5 m diameter with anta walls placed 4.5 m to either of their sides.

The central hall is surrounded by 8 side columns and 6 columns across the rear with heart shaped columns on each of the two southern corners. Each of these columns is topped with Corinthian-style capitals of the Nabataean type. Besides the heart-shaped double-engaged columns the side and rear columns are 1.2 m in diameter, and are placed from 3.27 m to 3.51 m apart. The clear span between the east and west row of columns (side colonnades) is approximately 16.0 m. This colonnade is enclosed with a wall 1.4 m in width[8] on the sides and the rear creating a 12 m long corridor x 3 m wide. Outside the corridors are East and West Walkways, 3.6 m in width x 41.5 m in length, adjacent and parallel to the East and West Corridors.[9] The external enclosure wall of the complex is 135 m N-S x 56 m E-W, and the overall area for the enormous temple precinct is 7560 m2.

Site Phase V

In Site Phase V dated to the 1st c. A.D.,[10] all the features of the earlier Site Phase IV temple complex continued in use but the main building is remodelled reflecting a dramatic architectural change. Inter-columnar walls 1.9 m in width are built between the columns of the central hall enclosing the columns—creating a clear span between the two side walls of 16 m. In addition, vaulted chambers, several interior vaulted stairways and landings, a theater *cavea*,[11] *orchestra*[12] and stage are built.[13] Up to this point the excavations have not recovered any traces of an altar.

While it is argued the precinct may have served another purpose, the excavated material and the evidence supported its identification as a Great Temple to the Brown University archaeologists[14] who followed von Bachmann's identification of the precinct as a temple. Joukowsky drew attention to several similar complexes in the Hellenistic and Roman worlds, such as the sanctuaries of Hercules Victor at Tivoli and of Fortuna Primigenia at Palestrina[15]. She concluded that the theater in Site Phase V had a sacred function and identified the building as a theater-temple complex. As central to her argument Joukowsky used the identification of the other theaters in Petra as ritual venues as proposed by Segal.[16]

---

6 The enclosed section of such a temple or cella.

7 The subject of Ch. 6 in this volume.

8 This wall is not visible in Netzer's plan (2003, fig. 95). However Site Phase IV had the wall around the *naos* as well. J. McKenzie, personal communication, 2004.

9 Netzer (2003, 77), reports that this walkway is poorly constructed and has been added to the temple in the Byzantine period.

10 *Great Temple* vol. 2, 22; Joukowsky and Basile (2001, 50) dated this phase to "a pre-Roman annexation or to the Nabataean period;" Schluntz (*Great Temple* vol. 1, 209).

11 The audience seating portion.

12 The space between the audience and the stage.

13 The Great Temple Theater and a description of these features is the subject of Ch. 8 in this volume.

14 *Great Temple* vol. 2; Joukowsky and Basile 2001, 52.

15 Sear 1982, fig. 12.

16 Segal 1995,16, 93.

In contrast Schluntz,[17] writing before the complete plan was uncovered, argued that the Great Temple, when compared to contemporary religious and secular architecture both in Petra and in the wider context of the eastern Mediterranean, could not support the interpretation of the site as a temple complex. She argued that the architecture, including the use of architectural sculpture, indicated that the complex was originally an audience hall for Nabataean kings in Site Phases IV-V. As a parallel she proposed the grand hall at the western end of the Herod's Third Winter Palace at Jericho as an example of an audience hall.[18] For Site Phase V, Schluntz suggested that after the Roman annexation in A.D. 106 the structure was converted to a *bouleuterion*[19] for the new Roman metropolis of Petra because the building appeared more like a council chamber or an odeion[20] rather than a temple.[21] She cited the Odeion at Epidauros as an example.[22] However, this author[23] found the architectural parallels Schluntz offered are not fronted with a pronaos or were built above a great Lower Temenos, unlike the Great Temple.

With these factors in mind let us turn to the some of the interesting building materials used in the construction of these features—sandstone, limestone, marble and mortar. We discuss their properties, availability and follow the discussion with a survey of architectural concepts utilized at the temple.

Building materials

Sandstone

Sandstone was the most readily available construction material for Nabataean masons. The Smooth, Tear, Honeycomb, and Disi sandstone quarries surround Petra's civic center—the vast main open area in the city.[24] The Great Temple builders took advantage of the readily available sandstone quarrying whatever they needed for monumental architectural purposes. Walls, most of the floors, and column drums were all quarried from the so-called Smooth, Tear, or the Honeycomb sandstones. The color of the fallen drums of the Great Temple Pronaos columns shows that they were extracted from the Umm Sayhun quarry,[25] and are similar to those found in the Temple of the Winged Lions.[26]

Supplementary material seems to have been quarried from the site itself by levelling it for further development, as is found in the adjacent Garden-Pool Complex[27] and the so-called "Middle

---

17 Schluntz 1999,135.
18 Ibid. 106-11, fig. 5. 9,10.
19 A building for members of the council chamber; an assembly hall for magistrates.
20 A small theater, often roofed, used for smaller entertainment venues such as performed music poetry readings, debates, or lectures.
21 Schluntz 1998a, 221; 1999, 135.
22 Schluntz 1999, 125, fig. 5.15.
23 Rababeh 2005, 210. Rababeh *et al.*2010a, 60-83.
24 Ibid. fig. 2.5.
25 Ibid. 49-50.
26 Rababeh (2005, 37) suggests the best time to perform this test is in wet weather when the natural colors are clearer. Pflüger (1995, 288) carried out the first step by using a variety of petrological and sedimentary characteristics to trace the blocks of the Qasr al-Bint to the Smooth sandstone, except for the orthostat blocks which he illustrated were extracted from Tear sandstone. Moreover, he showed that the flagstones of the procession road or Colonnaded Street west of the Temenos Gate were of Tear sandstone. These blocks can be traced to their stratigraphic origins through collaboration with other disciplines that specialize in chemical and geological materials.
27 Bedal, 2001, 24, suggested that the stone quarried was used in the front retaining wall of the pool and the Great Temple. Bedal (Ibid.) calculated the volume of extracted stone in the pool area as 33,280 m3, but by revising the calculations Rababeh 2005 found that she calculated the full height of the cliff without considering the natural slope of the hill, nor did she allow for a volume of waste. Rababeh's calculations making allowances for these points showed the quarried volume from the pool area to be approximately 8000 m3.

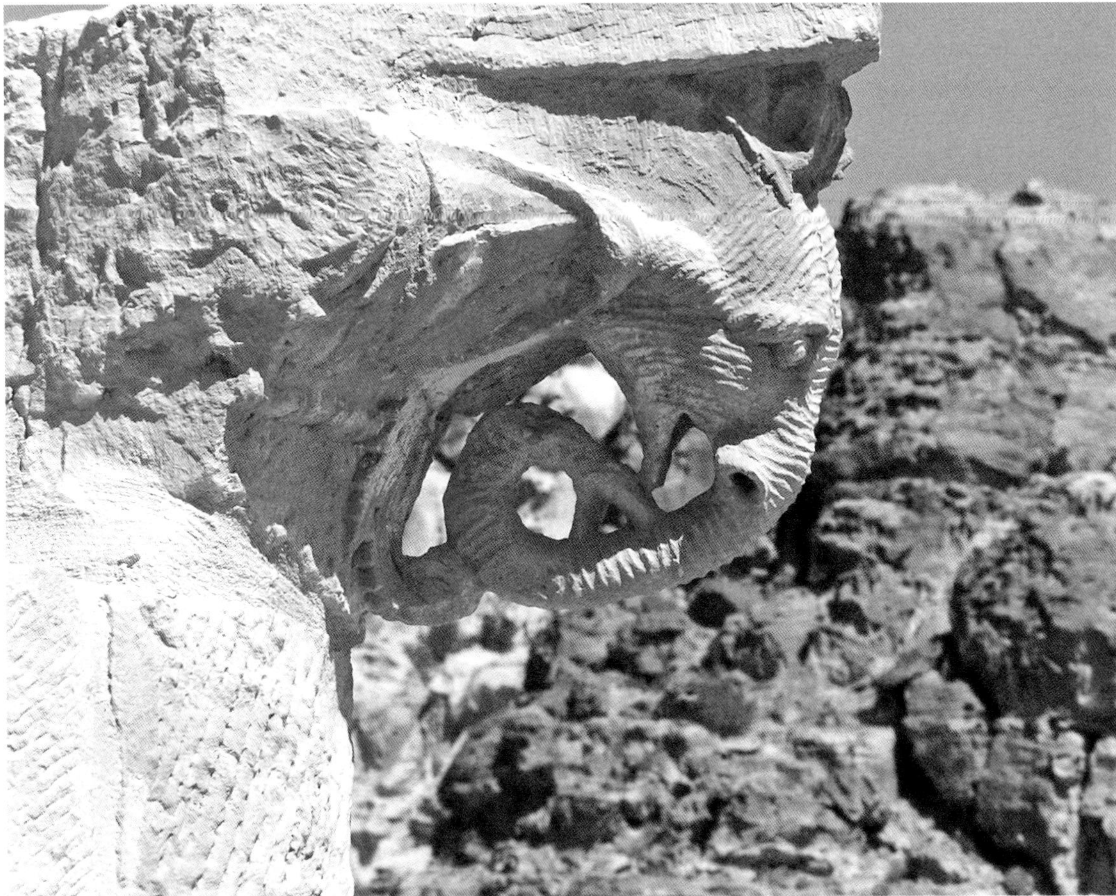

Fig. 3.3. A zoomorphic or elephant-headed Ionic capital from the Great Temple Lower Temenos.

and Upper Markets."[28] Similar activities can be seen in the Nabataean sites of the Negev, for example at Oboda where quarrying razed the site and the builders extracted large blocks of stone for construction.[29]

Limestone

While surveying building materials in the Great Temple, I[30] found that the Nabataeans used two different types of limestone for different purposes. One is a fine soft, yellowish white limestone and the other is a coarse white limestone. The fine soft limestone was used for column bases, floral capitals, but rarely for walls or stairs. The bases of the temple columns were fashioned from of this type of stone.[31] Limestone was also used for the floral capitals based on the Corinthian order and for thousands of other elaborate floral and vegetal fragments found in the Great Temple excavations.[32] The zoomorphic or elephant-headed Ionic capitals of the Great Temple (fig. 3.3) and two similar capitals found in the late 1950s east of the monumental gate of the Temenos of the

28 Kanellopoulos 2001, 11, 21, suggested that the stone extracted from the cliffs of the "Upper Market" was used in the construction of the Propylaeum (Rababeh 2005, 56).

29 Negev 1986, 49-50.

30 In order to differentiate between limestone and sandstone, Rababeh (2005, 39) used vinegar (CH3COOH). This, being an acid, reacts with limestone (CaCO3) to produce a salt plus water and carbon dioxide (CO2). The latter being a gas can be seen bubbling off the surface of limestone. Sandstone is basically composed of silica (SiO2) and shows no reaction to vinegar.

31 *Great Temple* vol.1, figs. 2.37, 5.41, 42.

32 Schluntz 1998a, 210; 1998b, 225).

Qasr al-Bint[33] (now known to belong to the Lower Temenos columns) and many other fragments found in the Great Temple Lower Temenos are all of this variety of limestone; similar are the type A floral capitals of the Temple of the Winged Lions. The use of this limestone for walls or stairs otherwise seems very rare in the building, but one exception is the two well-constructed staircases leading from the Lower Temenos to the Temple Forecourt. So too is the well-built limestone staircase leading down into the West Exedra which is probably late Roman or Byzantine in date.[34] Fine soft limestone also was used for the ring bases of the columns recovered in Room 19 of Ez Zantur.[35]

Coarse white limestone was used for decorative architectural elements and for paving the courtyards of the Great Temple 'Grand Design' of Site Phase IV.[36] The extensive pavement of the Lower Temenos (fig. 3.4) and the forecourt of the Upper Temenos were paved with hexagonal flagstones of this coarse limestone. In the southern portion of the West Colonnade a reused platform was paved by limestone slabs over a fill of sandstone column drums.[37] Similar hexagonal pavements were discovered in the floors of Nabataean and Roman houses at Ez Zantur as well as rectangular flagstones.[38] Another example is the West Entry Stairs landing leading from the Propylaeum of the Great Temple, which was paved by well-cut coarse limestone flagstones.[39] In addition to paving, the stylobates of the colonnades surrounding the court of the Great Temple Lower Temenos were fashioned from a similar limestone.

Fig. 3.4. The hexagonal pavement of the Great Temple Lower Temenos, measuring approximately 82 cm in width.

These aforementioned types of limestone are not technically from Petra. There is no limestone in Petra's rock formation;[40] it is found only in the modern town of Wadi Musa some 4 km to the east of Petra. Pflüger[41] suggests that limestone boulders were carried down the Wadi Musa by annual flash floods that reduced the efforts of quarrying and transport. On the contrary, I[42] posit that the quantity of boulders at any one time would not be sufficient and it is unlikely that the Nabataean builders could wait a number of years to collect enough material for such projects. The size of the boulders, averaging 90 cm x 60 cm x 40 cm, is sufficient for slabs but not for column bases or capitals like the zoomorphic capitals of the Great Temple or the floral capitals.[43] In the absence of further evidence it may be argued that this source possibly contributed to paving, but its product was sufficient neither in quantity nor in size to carve large capitals.

33 Schluntz 1998b, 232; Blagg 1990, 131-37 suggested that the two zoomorphic capitals came from nearby buildings, perhaps the Temple of the Winged Lions.

34 Basile 1998, 195, 203.

35 Kolb 2000, 356; Rababeh 2005, fig. 5.21.

36 *Great Temple* vol. 2, fig. 1.18.

37 Basile 1998, 198.

38 Schmid and Kolb 2000, 244-45, figs. 39, 41.

39 Basile 1998, figs. 5.3, 4.

40 Rababeh 2005, 39-40. Rababeh *et al.*2010a, 60-83.

41 Pflüger 1995, 290.

42 Rababeh 2005, 39-40. Rababeh *et al.*2010a, 60-83.

43 The size is approximately 1.8 m x 1.8 m x 1.5 m.

Marble

There are no marble deposits in Petra. However, in the East 'Cistern' of the Great Temple,[44] significant numbers of marble slabs and unfinished boulders were recovered, and it was suggested that the structure might have functioned as a repository for stone as it was stripped from the temple complex or other buildings nearby. These fragments suggest that this marble was used for veneers, not for capitals. Evidence for the local working of marble in Petra comes from the recent recovery of 1,000 pieces of marble in a marble workshop in the subterranean room in the Temple of the Winged Lions.[45] Marble of various colors was used in the floors of some buildings such as the *naos* floor and the altar platform of the Temple of the Winged Lions. Moreover rectangular marble slabs in the Qasr al-Bint still lie *in situ* southeast of the cella.[46]

Marble was most widely employed as veneer, however, no evidence for its use in the Great Temple was found. No plug holes are found to affix marble veneer to the walls like those recovered in other temples in Petra. The 1959 excavation of the northeast exterior of the Qasr al-Bint indicated the building originally stood on a podium over 2 m in height that had been faced with marble, one slab of which was still *in situ*.[47] In the Small Temple an extraordinary number of marble fragments, 4,669, show that these walls were covered with marble slabs, and two slabs still adorn its northeast corner. Marble veneer may have been fashioned in the Temple of the Winged Lions in front of the south wall of the cella. Multiple plug holes were found in the walls,[48] and similar remains for attachments were discovered in the interior wall of the Main Theatre.[49] Marble column bases are not found in the Great Temple, and they are rare in Petra—instead soft fine limestone was used. However, there is a unique example of marble bases carved in at least two separate pieces in the Temple of the Winged Lions. The colors of these bases range from banded beige, banded brown, and black with a white band.[50] Only one marble Corinthian capital has been found at Petra.[51] The lack of examples might reflect either that they are few in number originally or that they were later burnt for lime.[52]

Mortar

Mortar, in addition to its use as a core fill for the walls, was used in the Great Temple to bind the ashlar wall blocks. The exterior walls of the building are constructed of ashlar masonry, 1.9 m thick. The exterior blocks are closely fitted and horizontally coursed, however, the interior surfaces of the walls are not as finely finished, especially the interior face of the rear wall in which the thickness of the joints is about 12 cm. The thickness of the horizontal and vertical joints ranges from 2 cm to 12 cm. The thickness of mortar for joints varies considerably from one stretch of wall to another in the same wall or from wall to wall. This range may have been influenced by two factors.[53] The first was certainly the uneven dressing of the ashlars themselves. In such a case a bed of mortar was used to level the blocks or the surface. The second factor was probably the reliance of the builders on stucco wall decoration which concealed the irregular appearance of the joins between the stones. Variations in joint widths can be seen clearly on the interior faces of most buildings in Petra, whereas the joints between blocks in the external walls were regular. In the Qasr al-Bint, the wall facing blocks also consist of dressed ashlars on the exterior and rough ashlars on the interior walls that were hidden behind an overcoat of stucco. Thus mortared joints are less apparent on the

44 Basile 1998, 200.
45 Hammond 1987, 130-41; 1996, 50.
46 The inner room or sanctuary of a Roman temple where the statue of the god was located.
47 Parr 1960, Plates XXXIII A, B.
48 Hammond 1996, 55.
49 Hammond 1965, Plate XXII, 3.
50 Hammond 1996, Plates 9.2; 10.1; 13. 2-3.
51 McKenzie 1990, 95, Pl. 39c.
52 Rababeh 2005, 43.
53 Rababeh 2005, 47. Rababeh *et al.*2010b, 27-53.

exterior. The ashlar walls of the Temple of the Winged Lions[54] are left partially dressed on the interior and well finished on the exterior. This phenomenon is also reported in the walls at Mampsis.[55] Wright [56] notes that this feature is similar to an ancient Egyptian construction technique in which the walls appear almost dry-jointed externally, but are mortared internally.

Architectural elements

Now we turn to how the precinct was constructed from the ground up—from foundations to roofs. We cover the specifics of how the temple was built beginning with foundations followed by floors and walls. Moving up the structure we then look at vaults, doors and windows and then turn our attention to the columns and the complexities of roofing. After a description of decorative finishing with plaster/stucco, masons' marks are discussed.

Foundations

Examination of Petra's geological formation[57] shows that Petra has certain geological peculiarities that are not common to other cities. The rocky surface is solid and a suitable basis on which to build.[58] Therefore bedrock itself could be used and practically no foundations were necessary, however, the bedrock on which the building was to be constructed had to be levelled.[59]

The Great Temple was erected on the southern side of the Wadi Musa. The cella floor lies about 34 m above the Colonnaded Street. To connect the cella with the Colonnaded Street approximately 200 steps would have been necessary for access. This considerable number of steps resulted from the sizeable difference between the two elevations and forced the builders to cut away 12 m of bedrock and to use terraces to minimize the difference. Such a laborious adaptation of the site topography was a purposeful choice allowing for the precinct to dominate its urban context.[60]

Fig. 3.5. A partially intact example is visible in the Cryptoporticos with a 4.25 m span below the triple colonnades of the Lower Temenos. Some of the arches supporting sandstone slabs have been restored.

The builders divided the area into two levels (fig. 3.2). The most southerly consists of the central complex (Upper Temenos). The second to its north is of the lower court or Lower Temenos of the precinct. A group of subterranean rooms, cryptoporticoes are built beneath the lower court to build up the Lower Temenos (fig. 3.5), which resembles the technique used in the two-storied stoa in the agora at Pergamon.[61] The lower and upper levels are connected by stairs, similar to those in the Temple of the Winged Lions.

---

54 Hammond 1996, 24.
55 Negev 1988a, 51, 64-65, 77-78, 82, 163; 1988b, 35.
56 Wright 1961, 22.
57 Rababeh 2005, 31-36. Rababeh *et al.*2010a, 60-83.
58 Plommer 1956, 149.
59 Sometimes foundation trenches consist of a series of steps.
60 At the rear of the Great Temple where the bedrock slope was cut away, Nabataean architects extracted some of the blocks required for building.
61 Coulton 1977, 136; Lawrence 1996, 203.

It should be stressed that the lack of a podium in most Nabataean buildings is due to the use of terracing. It would be assumed that the upper terrace with its retaining wall could serve technically, visually and aesthetically as a high podium. This ascent to the temple was via a broad staircase.

It is evident that at the Great Temple, as elsewhere in Petra,[62] there are two common methods of constructing terrace foundations. The first is to build the foundations directly on the levelled bedrock, so the main axes of the foundations are perpendicular to the topographic contour lines and to the direction of the Wadi Musa. The position of the floor level is clearly indicated by a levelling course built above the bedrock. Its variable thickness, 10-15 cm, indicates that the bedrock was not perfectly levelled. The second type of the foundation is built parallel to the contour lines and the direction of the Wadi Musa flow. This type of foundation results in separate terraces serving as massive retaining walls.[63] This is exemplified by the massive retaining wall separating the Great Temple Lower and Upper Temene.

Floors

In Petra floor coverings could consist of clay, plaster, or stone. Clay and plaster floors were employed in the earlier phases of Nabataean buildings,[64] and pavements of thin stone slabs were employed from the early 1st c. B.C. onwards. These thin slabs were fashioned from marble, limestone, or sandstone to cover both unroofed and roofed structures. Floors were paved with different geometrically shaped flagstones—rectangular, hexagonal, and still others with elaborate *opus sectile*.[65] In the following discussion, pavements are classified according to the material used.

Marble or *opus sectile* pavements could have been used in the cellas of Nabataean temples either as a luxurious embellishment or for ritual purity similar to the halls of mortuary temples in Egypt,[66] which are paved with alabaster slabs. If this was the rule in Petra, it is reasonable to look at the floor of the Great Temple. What can be seen is a rectangular limestone pavement of Site Phase V. Perhaps the numerous slabs of marble recovered in the East 'Cistern'[67] had been removed from the cella of the Site Phase IV temple when the limestone pavement was later put in place. If so, the cella of the temple would have been paved with marble like other temples in the city.

Marble slabs embellished the main cella of the Temple of the Winged Lions. Rectangular flagstones were laid in straight east-west rows set in gray cement and grouted with white plaster to prevent water from penetrating through the joints.[68] Vitruvius[69] mentions the use of lime and oil to prevent water penetration between blocks. The flagstones on the west side of the Temple of the Winged Lions are slightly larger than those on its east side. The lengths of the flagstones vary from 0.29 m-1.20 m, and the widths range from 11 cm to 47 cm with a thickness of 2-3 cm.[70] The slabs are generally bevelled and trimmed to accommodate the bases of columns. The same features can be seen in the cella of the Qasr al-Bint and in the Small Temple,[71] but the pattern of flagstones in the Small Temple appears to have been regular because the flagstones were laid in straight east west rows parallel to each other.

62 Rababeh 2005, 113. Rababeh *et al.*2014a, 293-305.
63 Ibid., see figs. 5.2Dc; 4a. Rababeh 2011, 177-189; Rababeh *et al.*2014a, 293-305.
64 Kolb *et al.* 2000, 359.
65 Taylor 2003, 232. A technique where instead of individual tesserae, shapes are created from larger, especially cut pieces, usually of tile or stone.
66 Arnold 1991, 147.
67 Basile 1998, 200 considers the East 'Cistern' may have functioned as a storage room for marble slabs being stripped from other nearby buildings.
68 Hammond 1996, 37, pls. 9.2; 10.2.
69 Vitruvius 7.1,7.
70 This thickness is rather thin for a well-trafficked floor of a public place.
71 Reid 2002, 363-79.

Fig. 3.6. Smaller hexagonal pavers found in the Great Temple Forecourt.

In the Great Temple the pattern used for limestone slabs consists of two different sizes of hexagonal slabs. A coarser softer limestone than that used in the Colonnaded Street was used in both.[72] The first appears only in the Lower Temenos of the Great Temple.[73] Each side of the paving stones measures approximately 82 cm and their thickness varies from 10 to 12 cm (figs. 3.4, 6). The use of second smaller sized hexagonal slabs has been found in different places such as the Upper Temenos of the Great Temple (fig. 3.6), at el-Katute,[74] and in the Ez Zantur houses.[75] Similar slabs are recovered in the Nabataean temple at Wadi Ramm.[76] However, the sizes of this type vary from one building to another. Each side of the paving stones varies from 15 cm to 20 cm.

Fig. 3.7. The floor construction under the limestone pavements in the Great Temple Lower Temenos. The level of the bedrock is below the level required for the pavement; a sub-floor was made of compact layers of rubble.

The floor construction under the marble, limestone, and sandstone pavements is of two types.[77] When the level of the bedrock is below the level required for the pavement, a sub-floor is built up of compact layers of rubble, as seen clearly in the section of collapse in the Great Temple Lower Temenos (fig. 3.7). When the paved area was directly laid on the bedrock, as is found in rooms 6, and 7 in EZ IV at Ez Zantur,[78] a layer of mortar is placed on the levelled bedrock after which the paving slabs are

72 It is easy to recognise the difference between the soft and hard limestone. The latter is whiter especially in the wet season, while the softer limestone is yellowish, because it contains clay minerals.

73 Basile 1998, 193.

74 Khairy 1990, 3-6, Maps I–IV; Schmid and Kolb 2000, fig.15.

75 Schmid and Kolb 2000, 244-45, figs. 39, 41; Stucky 1995, 195.

76 Khairy 1990, 5.

77 Rababeh 2005,135. Rababeh *et al*.2010a, 60-83.

78 Kolb *et al*. 1998, 264.

laid. Vitruvius mentions the aids used to set floors—a ruler or straight piece of wood served as a guide against which lines of tesserae could be adjusted. A level, an A-shaped device with a plumb bob suspended from its apex, was used to ensure that the pavement was horizontal, and other implements such as set squares and compasses ensured the standardization of geometric shapes.

Walls

Wall courses in Petra buildings are neither isodomic nor pseudoisodomic. The joints of the courses are continuous along each stretch of wall, but the height varies on average of 40 cm to 60 cm, and the length of the ashlar blocks also varies from ca. 30 cm to c. 1.00 m. I identify this masonry[79] as either regularly coursed ashlar masonry, or, more appropriately, as 'irregularly coursed ashlar masonry.'

The Great Temple casemate walls are constructed of two rows of ashlars set parallel to one another. The space between the two rows is filled completely by small broken stones and mortar and there is little bonding between the inner and outer rows and the core. Characteristic of most Nabataean buildings, this category includes walls 0.7 m to 2.7 m in thickness with masonry and mortar cores. Vitruvius[80] describes this as "*emplecton*."[81] Examples of coursed ashlar masonry in Petra can be seen in most of its freestanding public buildings—the Temple of the Winged Lions[82] and the Qasr al-Bint. Walls with outer and inner rows of ashlars and a core are also found in the scaenae frons of the Main Theatre,[83] the Small Temple,[84] the Qasr al-Bint,[85] and in the Temenos Gate.[86] The courses vary from 40 cm to 60 cm in height. As the core is of rubble and mortar it recalls Roman concrete construction.[87]

In the Great Temple, in addition to the normal walls, 1.9 m in width, walls 1.3 m -1.8 m in width are built to carry the sloping vaults below the *cavea* seating. Moreover, curved casemate walls are used in the *exedrae* of the Lower Temenos constructed of well-cut Tear sandstone ashlars. The largest of these blocks, measuring 1.5 m in width follows the interior curvature of the apse.

String courses

One of the most important features of Nabataean construction is the extensive use of timber stringcourses and tie rods, presumably intended as a precaution against earthquakes. Recent excavations recovered the use of the same technique in the Great Temple (fig. 3.8). It is more likely that the original course was similar to those at the Qasr al-Bint.[88] A well- dated example of this technique is the superstructure of the Qasr al-Bint. Its survival is useful for understanding the structure's resistance during earthquakes. The cedar wooden beams, some of which have survived, are imbedded lengthwise along the walls. Rectangular in cross section two to three beams are set in one course. The beams (c. 15 cm x 20 cm in section) are positioned with a small 20 cm gap between them, which is filled up with rubble and mortar to form a stable course. Flat tie rods are placed at intervals across this course.[89]

---

79 Rababeh 2005, fig. 5.6e, d.
80 Vitruvius 2.8.7.
81 Masonry in which the outer faces of the wall are ashlars, the space between being filled with broken stone and mortar. He mentions its Italian form is a quickly built wall that builders rushed to complete. It differs from the Greek version of *emplecton*, where the wall completely is constructed of stone masonry without a core.
82 Hammond 1996, 22, calls this system "inplicton" or "weaving," ca. 70 cm in thickness.
83 1 m in width, Hammond 1965, 38.
84 1.5 m in width, Reid 2002, 363-79.
85 1.3-2.7 m in width; Wright 1961, McKenzie 1990, 132.
86 Wright 1961, 21-22; McKenzie 1990, 136.
87 Wright 1961, 128; McKenzie 1990, 132; Claridge *et al.*1998, 45.
88 Rababeh (2005), see the detail in fig. 6.41c and compare it with fig. 5.31a, b. Rababeh *et al.*2014b, 60-69.
89 When the wood has not survived it leaves a hollowed out line along the wall. Rababeh *et al.*2014b, 60-69.

Fig. 3.8. Timber string-courses in the East Corridor Wall, presumably intended as a precaution against earthquakes.

Similar devices have been found on most of the freestanding buildings at Petra. These include the massive arches of the "Liwan" in the southeast of the Temple of the Winged Lions,[90] the arches of the Qasr al-Bint compartments, the freestanding arches of the Urn Tomb, and the freestanding vault of the Palace Tomb. In all, the springing voussoirs rest on both mortared fill and wooden beams which in turn are supported by the tops of the columns. An example of this structural form is found in the Dome of the Rock in the wooden tie beams and the impost-block of the intermediate octagon.[91]

Vaults

The earliest roofs rest on barrel vaults. In Petra, vaulted recesses are cut inside the chambers of rock monuments perhaps to accommodate either graves or cult statues as seen in the rear walls of the Obelisk Tomb,[92] the Painted House,[93] the Tomb of the Roman Soldier,[94] the Urn Tomb,[95] and ed-Deir.[96]

Barrel vaults also were used to support the heavy weight of the seating of the *cavea* of the Great Temple Theater and they are found in the vaulted rooms below the *cavea*. These vaults were carried on unusually thick walls of 1.3 m-1.8 m. Two of the barrel vaults are sloping, and cover the staircases leading to the rear of the *cavea*. The slope of these vaults corresponds to both the slope of the stairs and the rising tiers of seats in the *cavea*. The use of vaults in the ceilings of earlier Greek theater passageways can be seen at Sikyon and the theater of Eretria, both dated to the early 3rd c. B.C.[97] A similar vaulted passage can be seen in the Temple of Apollo at Didyma dated to the first half of the 3rd c. B.C., and a sloping barrel vault covered a passageway, leading from the pronaos to the hypaethral adyton or the court.[98] This example is similar to typical theater vaults—in the Roman world, the Theatre of Marcellus in Rome. The most impressive example in the Roman East is the theater at Bosra built on level ground with its seating entirely supported by an artificial

90 Rababeh 2005, detailed in V.c.3, fig. 5.35a. Rababeh *et al.*2013, 118-130.
91 Detailed in Creswell 1989, fig. 8.
92 McKenzie 1990, pl.125a.
93 Ibid. pl. 113b.
94 Ibid. pl. 101a, b.
95 Ibid. pl. 94a.
96 Ibid. pl. 142b, 143a.
97 Boyd 1978, 84-85, fig. 2, ill.1.
98 Coulton 1977, 153-54, fig. 68; Boyd 1978, 86, fig. 4.

substructure consisting of radial vaults.[99] Elsewhere in the Roman East, as at Philadelphia (modern Amman), Gerasa, Pella, and Gadara, the *cavea* is partially or completely built on a hillside, but in all of these structures barrel vaults support the *summa cavea*.[100] Instead of sloping barrel vaults, stepped arches are used to support the *cavea* seating in the northern entrance of Gadara Theater and under the east section of the Hippodrome *cavea* in Gerasa.

Basically vault or arch structures carrying flat roofs involve separating the continuous roof into a number of shorter spans by arches constructed parallel to one another at fixed distances. Each arch is built in the casemate fashion with a rubble filling in between. The space between each pair of arches is spanned by using either horizontal stone slabs or wooden beams. The arches are resistant to compression, whereas the stone slabs or wooden beams are resistant to tension. At the Great Temple sandstone slabs between a series of arches were popular in a variety of contexts. First they appear in subterranean rooms. A partially intact example is visible in the cryptoporticus with a 4.25 m span below the triple colonnades of the Lower Temenos (fig. 3.5). Some of the arches supporting sandstone slabs have been restored. Other arches are intact only to the level of their lowest voussoirs. The arches spring directly from the 4th course of the lateral walls without any supporting pilasters. The distance between these arches ranges from 68 cm to 78 cm and the thickness of each arch is ca. 54 cm. Another application of arches supporting stone slabs, particularly common in Petra (although found elsewhere) is the roofing of cisterns. There are two arch-roofed cisterns at the Great Temple both measuring c. 4 m x 10 m. Two arches are still intact in the East 'Cistern.' The distance between the arches is 60 cm, and the thickness of each arch averages 50 cm.

A similar example can be seen in the shops of the Colonnaded Street. Some of these vaults/arches have been restored, but some of the original vaults are still intact. The vaults or arches spring directly from the walls and the height of arch springers from the floor is 2.2 m. The thickness of each vault is 50 cm and the distance between each pair of arches is 65 cm. This span certainly allows the use of arch slabs on top of the arches, a few of which were found in Shop 27.[101] A further example can be seen in the painters' workshop below the corridor on the west side and in front of the Pronaos podium of the Temple of the Winged Lions where 5 vaults, two of which survive intact, supported the corridor floor above. The width of the room is 2 m. The distance between the arches averages 92 cm with the thickness of each arch measuring 54 cm. In the metal workshop, the arches are spaced 1.1 m apart. Since a number of sandstone slabs have been recovered in the excavations, the interval of 1.1 m between the arches/vaults was spanned by slabs.

Another subterranean space with an arch-roof can be seen in Room 17 at Ez Zantur IV where sets of triple arches are bonded securely together. Above the center of each set of three arches stands a column.[102] The concentrated load of each column is distributed over the three bonded arches, not only on the central one. This configuration indicates advanced knowledge accumulated by Nabataean builders. Beneath the *proscenium*[103] of the Main Theater a series of arches support the floor above;[104] these arches are set 40 cm apart and are 50 cm in width. The intact arch spans 1.5 m and consists of 8 voussoirs. A special technical feature is the rock-cut imposts on which the arches rest that is similar to those used in rock-cut cisterns and in the eastern vault of the Main Theatre.

From the survey of different examples, I conclude[105] that where stone slabs are used the normal range of the size of the intervals between the arches is 40 cm to 80 cm, with a maximum of 1.1 m. Therefore the limit of the distance covered by the sandstone slab is 1.1 m and they overlap with the

99 Segal 1995, 8; Ward-Perkins 1981, 346. Rababeh 2011, 177-189; Rababeh *et al.*2014a, 293-305.
100 The highest tier of *cavea*, seating for less distinguished audience members.
101 Kanellopoulos 2001, 12.
102 B. Kolb, personal communication, 2003.
103 The stage of an ancient Greek or Roman theater.
104 Hammond 1965, folding Plate E.
105 Rababeh 2005, detailed in the table, fig. 6.37. Rababeh *et al.*2010a, 60-83.

arches on either side by 10 cm, thus giving the slabs a total length of approximately 1.3 m. Thicker slabs permit a longer span, but they would be heavier. In Petra the normal thickness of the slabs is 10 cm to 15 cm. These normal slabs were of similar size to those illustrated by Rababeh.[106] Evidence from Ez Zantur IV indicates that a 10-15 cm thick layer of small rubble is laid above the slabs and above this is a 5 cm thick layer of mortar.

Lintels, doors and windows

Generally, doorways and windows weaken load-bearing walls. The usual structural design for a lintel is to use a large horizontal block of stone or wood beam to span the opening. The lintel lower section structurally withstands the thrust of the tensile forces. Since sandstone is weak in resisting this kind of force, the Nabataeans used large stones of a suitable height. Several examples of these are preserved perfectly in Mampsis, such as the lintel of room 410 building XII, and room 354 in Building I.[107] In the latter, the lintel is comprised of one single limestone block (95 cm in width x 35 cm in height) spanning 65 cm. An interesting point to note at Mampsis is that hard limestone blocks similar to the lintel block are normally used for doorjambs, probably for aesthetic and structural reasons. The use of single lintel blocks is common also at Umm el-Jimal,[108] Bosra, and Gerasa.

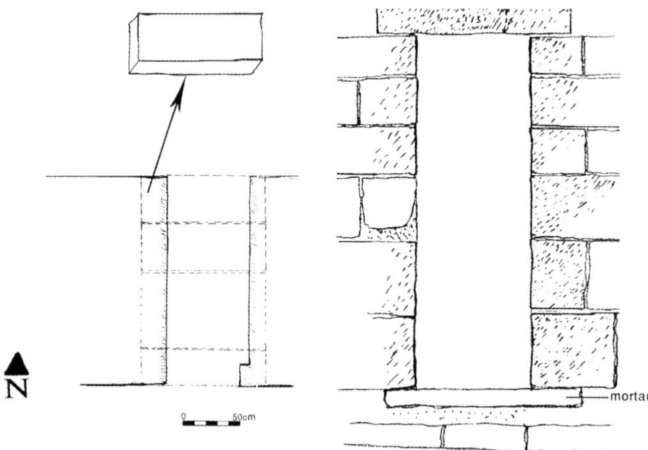

Figs. 3.9a. 3.9b. Doorway lintel in the rear façade of the Great Temple.

In Petra, Nabataean builders do not appear to have favored the use of large single blocks for the lintel. The only surviving example is the doorway lintel in the rear façade of the Great Temple (figs. 3.9a, 9b). The width of the doorway is 70 cm, and its depth is equal to the wall thickness, 1.75 m. The width of the slabs spanning it is less than the wall thickness, so a total of 5 slabs 14 cm in height are used. Technically this is similar to roofing by the use of slabs. Doorjambs and windows are fashioned from ashlars of the same quality as lintels and wall ashlars.

The quality of sandstone determined if the builders could use large single blocks horizontally. To my mind,[109] they considered the use of single lintel blocks in freestanding buildings unsatisfactory. Long rock-cut sandstone lintels and architraves are found in the rock-cut tomb facades, for example at Al-Khazna where the span of the main door is c. 4.35 m in length and the inter-columniations range from 2.75 m to 4.5 m, but

106 Ibid. fig. 6.63c.
107 Negev 1988a, 59, photo 19.
108 De Vries 1982, 16, fig. 7.
109 Rababeh 2005, 151.

they are carved out of the parent rock escarpment and are not built. The consistency of the rock is homogeneous, and structurally the architrave ends at the second storey (over 5 m), its strength originating from being carved from the parent rock.

Architraves

The architrave, the lowest element of an entablature, is normally the heaviest block in a classical building. In the Great Temple, as the case of other major freestanding buildings in Petra, no stone architrave blocks have been found. If they had been of stone the central architrave of the Qasr al-Bint for example would weigh c. 8 x 1 x 0.75 x 2.3 = 18 tons. Sandstone was not a suitable medium for the architrave—it is friable and cannot withstand high tensile forces.[110] This leads us to revise some of the reconstruction drawings for both the Great Temple and the Qasr al-Bint.

These blocks and column drums seem insignificant compared to those lifted in Assyrian, Egyptian, and Greek and Roman buildings.[111] But they are still too heavy and cumbersome to lift directly even by a number of labourers. A means of mechanical lifting would be needed to raise both the wall blocks and the column drums especially the extremely heavy drums of the Great Temple Pronaos, but no evidence for bosses survives in either wall blocks or column drums of the Great Temple. It is possible that the stonemasons removed them after lifting—however no such evidence has come to light.

As mentioned above, no securely identified architrave fragments have been found in any Petra excavation and the question of the technique and materials used by Nabataean builders to construct architraves is still unanswered. Such long blocks (if they existed) often were robbed later for reuse as lintels. One possibility is that the spans between the columns of *pronaoi*[112] of the temples and the Colonnaded Street[113] were bridged by wooden architraves supporting stone friezes and cornices. In early Greek architecture wooden architraves were used, as in the 7th c. B.C. temple of Apollo at Thermon.[114] But the architrave had no stone to support above. Once monumental architecture was widespread in the Greek world, wooden architraves were generally rejected.[115] The available stone in Greece is limestone or marble, not sandstone as at Petra. Moreover, wood is scarce in Petra, and even if the Nabataeans were able to import it, wooden architraves could not support the heavy load of stonework above. To solve this problem, it is probable that Nabataean builders used arches to span the columns of the *pronaoi* of the temples, as they did between the columns of the compartments and the main doorway of the Qasr al-Bint. Wood architraves could have been used for decorative elements in covering the opening of the arcades.

One problem for the builders was the protection of the lintel from the tremendous weight of the stone mass above it. A simple solution is the placement of a second lintel above the first with a few centimetres space between them. At Mampsis a number of lintels were built using this technique. One piece of limestone was laid to cover the door lintel and to reduce the load on it, and another stretcher was laid above it with a slightly concave shape at its base, apparently acting as relieving arch. Examples of this can be seen in Building XII rooms 417, 402.[116] I observed similar examples at Bosra and Kanawat (from the 2nd and 3rd c. A.D.) of basalt lintels slightly reduced in size in the second span.[117] This space was probably developed into in a flat arch.[118] An alternate method used

---

110 Ibid. 151-58.
111 To compare the loads of most of the Greek buildings see the table in Coulton 1974, 9-10, 14-15.
112 Plural of *pronaos*, the inner area of the portico of a Greek temple, leading to the *naos*.
113 Kanellopoulos 2001,19.
114 Orlandos 1966, 57-67, fig. 45.
115 A few later examples are found in Coulton 1976, 144.
116 Negev 1988a, 113-14, photos 89, 92.
117 Rababeh 2005, fig. 6.11a.
118 Ibid. fig. 6. 2b.

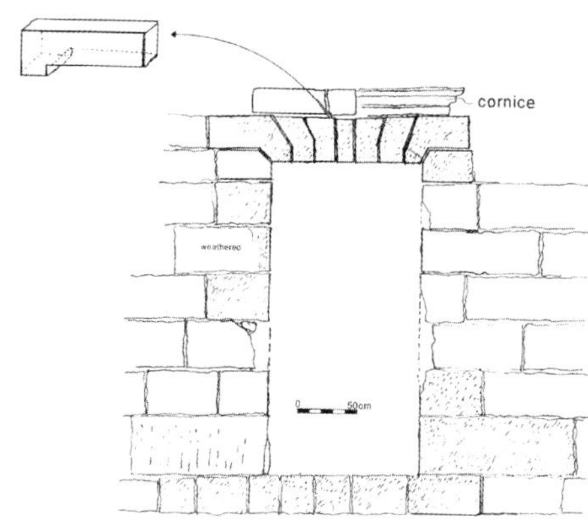

Figs. 3.10a, 3.10b, 3.10c. The flat arch of the East Perimeter Wall to Room A.

to reduce the span was to superimpose the lintel above the corbel blocks as seen at Kanawat. No example of this technique has been recovered in the Great Temple.

The flat arch is another solution. The most elaborate example can be seen in the rooms on the East Plaza of the Great Temple.[119] This flat arch (figs. 3.10a, 10b, 10c) consists of 7 wedge-shaped voussoirs and covers a span of 1.30 m. Additionally, the end voussoirs are especially shaped and hook over the course below creating a strong overlap and transmit the force and weight laterally across the adjacent voussoirs. Similar examples can be observed at Mampsis in the staircase-tower 351 of building I, where the first flight of stairs is entered with an opening covered by a flat arch.[120] In Roman buildings similar flat arches are commonly used for the lintels of buildings, for example the Peribolos of the Capitol at Sufetula,[121] the temple at Neha in Lebanon,[122] the Temple of Bacchus at Baalbek and the Cathedral south of the Nymphaeum in Gerasa.[123]

119 Rababeh 2005, figs. 6.3a, c; 4.
120 Negev 1988a, 71, photo 44.
121 Adam 1994, 69-72, fig. 410.
122 Taylor 1967, Pls. 6, 7, 8, 42, 43, 45.
123 Rababeh 2005, figs. 6.6; 5a. Rababeh 2011, 177-189; Rababeh *et al.*2014a, 293-305.

Figs. 3.11a, 3.11b. The west entrance of the Great Temple, illustrating another approach to the problem of spanning doorways with semi-circular arches.

Semi-circular vaults[124] were used widely in Petra. The western entrance of the Great Temple (figs. 3.11a, 11b) shows another approach to spanning doorways with semi-circular vaults, which allows the builder much greater freedom for the span of the lintel. This vault consists of 10 wedge-shaped voussoirs and spans 1.78 m. The western arch of the "Liwan" of the Temple of the Winged Lions consists of 6 voussoirs each of which was shaped to receive the adjacent block. The eastern arch consists of 7 voussoirs similarly arranged. The vault spans in the "Liwan" range from 1.5 m to 2.85 m. In the series of arches supporting the floor above the proscenium of the Main Theatre,[125] there is one intact arch which spans c. 1.5 m consisting of 8 voussoirs. These examples indicate that in Petra vaults and arches have both odd and even numbers of voussoirs and span openings up to 2.85 m. Whatever the number, there is the last voussoir to be laid, and this often has a special wedge-shaped form like a keystone.

Columns

Stone columns are extensively used in classical monumental architecture. Their shafts can be made of either one long block, the so-called monolithic shaft or by superimposing smaller blocks or drums on top of one another. The first method produces a strong and very stable column but it requires a hard compact stone. In Petra, the problems encountered include the availability of rock suitable for producing long blocks, and quarrying, transporting, and lifting the shafts.[126] Using drums presents an alternative solution to some of these technical problems, but raises new issues related to the bonding of the drums.

124 An arch is any part of a curved line in architecture, usually a curved member composed of wedge-shaped blocks. A vault is related to an arch in that a vault is an arched masonry structure that forms a ceiling or roof specifically engineered to support the weight above it.

125 Hammond 1965, Folding Plate E.

126 Rababeh 2005, 126. Rababeh 2015, 1023-1036.

In the Great Temple columns were made up of Smooth, Tear, and Honeycomb sandstone drums.[127] Drums had different diameters (figs. 3.12, 3.13) according to which they have been divided into two types, "Normal" and "Disc."[128] It is worth clarifying the reasons determining the diameter of the drum. Structurally speaking, the column had to be of sufficient diameter to carry the weight placed on it. Drums with large diameters were expected to carry heavier loads than those of smaller diameters. In theory this may be true but in classical practice diameter always relates to height and not directly to load bearing weight, so it is also a question of the scale of the order. In Petra, Disc Drums appear in the massive Great Temple Pronaos columns (fig. 3.13). These drums have diameters between 1.3 m-2 m and a height of c. 60 cm, whereas those of the Qasr al-Bint are 1 m in height. The difference between their diameter and height made the drums appear like huge discs. Examples of columns also can be seen in the Temple of the Winged Lions. These columns carry the heavy load of the

Fig. 3.12. Column drum from the Great Temple with a stucco overlay.

Fig. 3.13. Great Temple collapsed Pronaos drums, to west.

127 Except the Egyptian granite columns reused in the Blue Chapel, (Bikai 2002, 2).
128 Ibid.126.

entablature of the main façade and presumably the pediment. On the other hand, Normal Drums are proportionally higher/thicker because the columns have a smaller diameter (0.70 cm-1.00 m) but are of a similar height to the Disc Drums. Examples of columns made of Normal Drums appear in the Great Temple (fig. 3.12), the Colonnaded Street, the cella of the Temple of the Winged Lions, the Temenos Gate, the Baths, and in the houses of Ez Zantur. The Nabataeans constructed most of the Great Temple column shafts up with small disc-shaped drums, because the quarries would not easily yield larger blocks. The normal height of each drum was about 50 cm, but its diameter differed according to the size and the location of the column in the building. The drums found in the Pronaos of the Great Temple and the Temple of the Winged Lions have the same average height as the smaller type, but their average diameter is 1.50 m, so their average weight is 3.14 x 0.75 x 0.75 x 0.50 x 2300, or 2031.18 kg.

To accurately center the column-drums, the pin[129] technique was used.[130] Two forms of this technique are found in Petra. The first is seen only in Disc columns.[131] These have a shallow recessed square, 34 cm x 34 cm x 10 cm, with an internal circular hole 20 cm diameter and 15 cm deep, similar to those I observed in Qasr el-Abd.[132] This recessed square and the circle were carved in the center of the upper and lower surfaces of each drum. A hard wood plug would probably have been fitted into the circular hole that was carved out to receive a circular wooden pin.[133] The recessed square would have been filled with mortar after securing the pin and before positioning the upper drum over the protruding pin. The addition of mortar increased the strength of the fitting by making the pin inflexible so it could not be jostled out of position.[134] The second technique of centering column drums can be seen in the Normal Columns. These drums show a square hole, 10 x10 x c.15 cm.[135] A hard wood plug would have been fastened into this square hole and would have been carved to receive a circular wooden pin. The difference between the two forms can be traced back to the difference in drum sizes, to the load carried and column height.

Roofing

We now turn to analyze the methods and techniques the Nabataean architects used in solving the roofing problems in the Great Temple. The substructure was the dominant factor in choosing the shape of the roof and ceiling. Roofs and ceilings in antiquity can be classified into three types according to their resistance to specific types of stress.[136] The first type of roof is resistant largely to compressive forces. This usually involves the use of arches, vaults, or domes as structural shapes in which the stresses are compressive rather than tensile. In this case the basic material used is stone that can withstand significant pressure. The quality, size, and shape of the stone affect its durability. The second type of roof can be seen in the arch structures carrying a flat roof. Here arches are built over the space at fixed intervals and stone slabs or wooden beams are laid between them. Thus both compression and tension principles are utilized together. A third type of roof, resistant to tension, is where wooden beams are the basic material because of their ability to withstand tension owing largely to their fibrous composition. It makes no difference if wooden beams are used in flat or pitched roofs.

---

129 Usually called *empolion* in Greek architecture.

130 Dinsmoor 1975, 171-72; Martin 1965, 292-93; Orlandos 1968, 100-13.

131 Rababeh 2005, as detailed in fig. 5.26a, b. Rababeh 2015, 1023-1036.

132 Ibid. 5.26c.

133 Pins were normally made of wood, but in Greece these often were square plugs with round pins made as a set. Bronze pins were rarely used as in the Tholos at Delphi and Philon's porch at Eleusis. See Dinsmoor 1975, n.3, fig. 61.

134 In Greek examples, the jointing of drums was without mortar. The *anathyrosis* technique was employed to reduce the amount of surface that was actually in contact. See Dinsmoor 1975, 172, fig. 61; Martin 1965, pl. XXI; and Plommer 1956, 149. Rababeh 2015, 1023-1036.

135 Rababeh 2005, fig. 5.27a, b. Rababeh 2015, 1023-1036.

136 Rababeh, 2005, 149.

Fig. 3.14. Significant roof tile collapse were found immediately to the exterior of the South Corridor.

Roof tiles: The largest amount of roof tiles was found immediately on the outside of the colonnades, with fewer fragments found in the central area.[137] The tiles (fig. 3.14) have the same features as those found in the Temple of the Winged Lions and the Qasr el-Bint. Both are similar to the early type of Greek tile systems.[138] Their use is an indicator of pitched roofs in addition to the flat roof. However, the changes made to the Great Temple architectural plan suggest that a change in function may have caused some of confusion in understanding the function of each phase as well as difficulties in determining the roof system of each phase.

Joukowsky[139]reconstructed the roof of the corridors covered by pitched roofs and the exedras roofed with semi-domes. Basile[140] suggested that the exedras were partially roofed with tiles above the semi-domes and roofed with tiles where they joined the Triple Colonnaded porticoes. In this respect, Coulton[141] states, "circular buildings could not be roofed in the normal Greek way, for since a beam along any diameter of a circle must pass through its center, there could be only one bearer beam to serve the whole roof." From a reconsideration of the roof of the Arsinoeion at Samothrace, c. 285 BCE with a span of c. 16.80 m, he suggested a wigwam-like cone of rafters to roof circular buildings.[142] The exedras of the Great Temple Lower Temenos would have been much easier to roof, since they have a smaller diameter. Perhaps three quarter cones of rafters were set to meet the central north-south ridge beams of the Triple Colonnades.

In the preceding discussion we have concentrated largely on the structural methods used to roof smaller elements of the Great Temple, such as cisterns, subterranean rooms, and porticoes. How the builders managed to solve the technical roofing problems raised by the exceptionally large temple and hall requires some attention.

The function of the Great Temple may have implications for imagining the form of its roof. Two points can be made concerning the relationship between the functions of both Site Phases IV and V.

137 M. Joukowsky, personal communication, 2003. She mentioned more than 6000 roof tile fragments were collected here during the excavations.

138 Coulton 1977, 35, fig. 6.

139 Joukowsky and Basile 2001, fig. 6.

140 Basile 1998, 200.

141 Coulton 1977, 158.

142 Coulton (1976, 162, 295–296). For new reconstructions of the Arsenoeion roof, see McCredie *et al.* (1992, 27, fig. 18, Pls. LXX1, LXIII–LXXV).

If the building was a *bouleuterion* in Site Phase V, then it seems more likely that it served as a royal audience hall and not as a temple in the earlier phases. To remodel a sacred building and convert it to a council chamber seems improbable. However, there are no good parallels for audience halls of this kind with a Pronaos.[143] Alternatively, if the structure were a temple or shrine in Site Phases II-V it was probably a sacred building in Site Phase V and not a council chamber. No traces of an altar platform, which would be expected in a Nabataean temple have been found perhaps because it has not been possible to excavate under the seats where the altar platform would have stood.[144] We will not know the function unless the seats are excavated completely. Therefore, the evidence available is not decisive as to what the function of the building was, so I[145] have analyzed both secular and religious proposals in reconstructing the roof.

Let us[146] hypothesize that the building was a temple converted into a ritual theater. In the first phase, Netzer[147] reconstructed the cella covered entirely by one flat roof with the Pronaos covered with another roof at a higher level. He does not consider the question of the large span of the building, approximately 16.8 m E-W, which would have required wooden beams 80 cm or more in thickness and some 18 m in length. Such beams are difficult to obtain and to transport, and they would have been expensive. Clearly this is difficult but not impossible.

Owing to the lack of evidence in Site Phases IV-V, one cannot argue with absolute certainty whether the "temple" was left hypaethral or covered with either a flat roof or a pitched roof. The layout of the central colonnade is similar to that of Khirbet et-Tannur[148] where there was a colonnade along either side of the court. It is believed that the forecourt was unroofed because the excavators found drainage channels for rain water on the east forecourt inside the front wall.[149] The space there between the two rows of columns is about 16.7 m, which is approximately the same span between the side columns of the Great Temple. An example of a hypaethral *naos* can be seen in the Temple of Apollo at Didyma, in which a *naiskos* stood in an open courtyard with a pronaos in front.[150] Although occasionally found in the Hellenistic period (such as in the *Bouleuterion* at Miletos) and exceeded in Roman basilicas, 16.80 m is an unusually wide span for a roof. Therefore it is more likely that the "temple" in Site Phases IV-V had a covered Pronaos and surrounding portico,[151] but the central space of the *naos* was left unroofed. The altar would have been located at the rear of the open central area. The roof tile fragments found cannot be certainly attributed to this phase, and thus the Pronaos and Colonnaded Corridors of the *naos* may have been covered either by flat or pitched roofs. However, the parallels with the Qasr al-Bint and the Temple of the Winged Lions which are contemporary or slightly later,[152] suggest the use of a pitched roof over the pronaos[153] and a flat roof over the *naos* porticoes of the Great Temple. It is plausible that the same roofing technique was used in all three buildings.

---

143 Netzer 2003, 81, suggests that palace reception halls had a different layout and that they included guardrooms before one reached the king.

144 McKenzie 2003, personal communication.

145 Rababeh 2005, 214.

146 Ibid. 214.

147 Netzer, 2003, 77, fig.103, suggests that the entire core-structure was covered from the outset by a flat ceiling that rested on long wooden beams approximately 17 m in length, probably from date palms.

148 McKenzie 2003, figs. 175, 176.

149 Ibid. 172.

150 Akurgal 1969, 227.

151 This requires a wall missing in Netzer's plan.

152 McKenzie (1990, 51) suggests that the Qasr al-Bint and the Temple of the Winged Lions are contemporaries and belong to Group A. But on the basis of the capitals, she considered the latter was built later than the former. Hammond 1996 found a complete dedicatory inscription (not *in situ*) and dated the Temple of the Winged Lions to A.D. 26-27.

153 The inner area of the portico of a Greek temple, leading to the *naos*.

For Site Phase V, Netzer[154] reconstructed the theater entirely covered by a flat roof with the Pronaos roof at a higher level, similar to what he proposed for the Qasr al-Bint, the Temple of the Winged Lions and the earlier site phases of the Great Temple. But during this phase he considered the rear corridor to be covered by a roof of single pitch stretching from the rear wall of the theater to the rear wall of the corridor. Again he does not discuss the large span of the building (although it was reduced to 15.4 m in Site Phase V). Netzer's reconstruction is based on the number and position of the roof tile fragments found.

Joukowsky suggests the roof was pitched to the exterior and tiled over the corridors, like Netzer, but unlike him suggests theater was not roofed: "the evidence suggests that the center of the theater was hypaethral, but that roofing extended around the building between the corridors and the walkways."[155] The theaters in sanctuaries in Italy are unroofed, so she has no need to propose a roof existed. She also adopted this view because, as mentioned, she found massive amounts of roof tiles collapsed into the South Passageway and few in the central area. There was no need to change the roof of the central structure unless its function changed and the new function demanded it.[156] I have argued that it was unroofed in Site Phases IV-V, and that if it was a temple or shrine in Site Phase IV it was probably a sacred building in Site Phase V. If so, in both cases the center was unroofed. A parallel can be found at Khirbet et-Tannur.

On the other hand, if it was a meeting hall in Site Phase V, it was probably roofed like the council chambers of Miletos c. 170 B.C., and of Priene c. 200 B.C.[157] If so, in Site Phases I-V it would have been a secular building and was probably roofed. My observations of Site Phases IV-V are based on the Council Hall of Miletos, because this is a building not only with the most advanced structural system (with 15.9 m span), but it also offers so many points of resemblance in general layout and interior design to the Petra Great Temple of Site Phase V. The Council Chamber of Miletos was built as a donation by the king of Syria, Antiochus IV, 175-164 B.C. As he ruled the cedar forests of Lebanon,[158] it is probable that he provided the wooden beams. In addition, it is likely that the principle of the truss was known in Lebanon as it was an area rich in timber.[159] What are we to conclude? It seems probable that Nabataean builders not only imported wooden beams from Lebanon but also they borrowed the idea of the truss at the same time. We know cedar was imported to Petra for use in the stringcourses of the Qasr al-Bint. The technical problems posed by the lengthy span would have been solved by adopting the truss—it was used in similar contemporary buildings, particularly in the Miletos Council Chamber. This would allow the building to be used throughout the whole year whereas a hypaethral building's use would be restricted by sun in summer and rain in winter.[160]

In Great Temple Site Phase V, the clear span of the central area is 15.4 m which is approximately equal to the 15.90 m clear span of the Council Chamber at Miletos, and greater than the span in the Ekklesiasterion of Priene at 14.60 m.[161] This as Coulton states, "falls far short of Roman roof spans a century later, which could be over 25 m." The roof Basilica of Fano, described by Vitruvius[162] in the Augustan period spanned 17.8 m. Moreover, in the Odeion of Agrippa at Athens, ca. 15 B.C. had its

154 Netzer 2003, 75-76, fig. 100.

155 Joukowsky and Basile 2001, 49.

156 Rababeh 2005, 214.

157 Dinsmoor 1975, 296–297, fig. 108; Lawrence 1996, fig. 353; Gates, 2003, fig. 167, shows the trusses in the reconstruction interior.

158 Coulton 1976, 63, mentions that the east building of the South Market was probably built with funds supplied by Antiochos I before he became king; Coulton 1977, 158; Lawrence 1996, 202.

159 The skill of the Phoenician craftsmen in shipbuilding and their incorporation in the great building projects of Solomon and his successors is well known (Gates 2003, 178).

160 Netzer 2003, 81 suggests that both the hypaethral reception hall and the odeion could not have functioned under the sun or when it rained and a tent in such cases would have been preferable.

161 Coulton 1976, 157, fig. 51.

162 Vitruvius 5.1.6–9.

central hall with a span of 25 m covered by a truss while the lower roofs of a single pitch covered the walkways.[163] The Small Theatre (with a span of 26 m) at Pompeii was definitely roofed. These parallels suggest that a truss roof could have been employed to cover the Great Temple.

We now have the essential elements to reconstruct two possible models for the roofing of the Site Phase V of the Great Temple. Firstly, if it functioned as a "Theater-Temple" complex, the theater area could have been hypaethral with the walkway and Pronaos covered by a pitched roof, as Joukowsky suggests. Thus there would have been no change in roofing from Site Phases IV and V and the roof tiles found in the excavation can be attributed to either or both phases. Alternatively, if the building functioned as a political entity there would be two likely forms for the roof, both of which involve a truss roof. The first is similar to that found at Miletos in covering the central hall and the walkways with the truss on a single level, while the second is similar to the truss roof of the Odeion of Agrippa. In this second variant clerestory windows could have allowed light into the central area. There is no evidence at the Great Temple to support one model or the other.

Stucco coverings

The term "stucco" is used to refer to all relief decoration in plaster. Its composition was a mixture of white limestone and gypsum (CaSO42H2O). Enormous quantities of stucco were recovered in the Great Temple and most of the other monuments of Petra. Examples of these are cornices and other mouldings, panel fragments, frieze fragments, and other elements.[164] We should consider the weight and depth of some motifs, and determine the techniques used to fix them on walls.

Fig. 3.15. Stucco cable fluting overlay for the upper column drums.

The Great Temple, like other monuments in Petra and Hellenistic cities, were envisioned not only as architectural entities but also as vehicles for decorating with plaster, paint, and stucco patterns.[165] The extensive use of stucco on both rock-cut and free-standing structures is one of the most noteworthy revealing aspects of Nabataean art and architecture. Two methods were normally used to embellish the interior and the exterior surfaces. The first was veneer consisting of marble panels that was restricted to a few free-standing buildings.

Covering the drums by stucco cable fluting was a popular technique not only in the Great Temple (fig. 3.15) but also throughout Petra. The filets between flutes measure approximately 2 cm, and the flutes 6 cm to 8 cm, depending on the size of columns. The lower third of the columns was left unfluted and was normally painted red or yellow as can be seen in the well-preserved example in the Great Temple (fig. 3.16). Stucco fragments with egg-and-tongue and egg-and-dart motifs, vegetal elements, painted cornices, wall decoration (fig. 3.17), and two massive lion heads were recovered.[166]

163 Ward-Perkins 1981, 265-68.
164 Joukowsky 2003, 217; Zayadine 1987, 131-43; Lyttelton 1974, 67.
165 Ch. 5 in this volume.
166 Joukowsky 2003, 217.

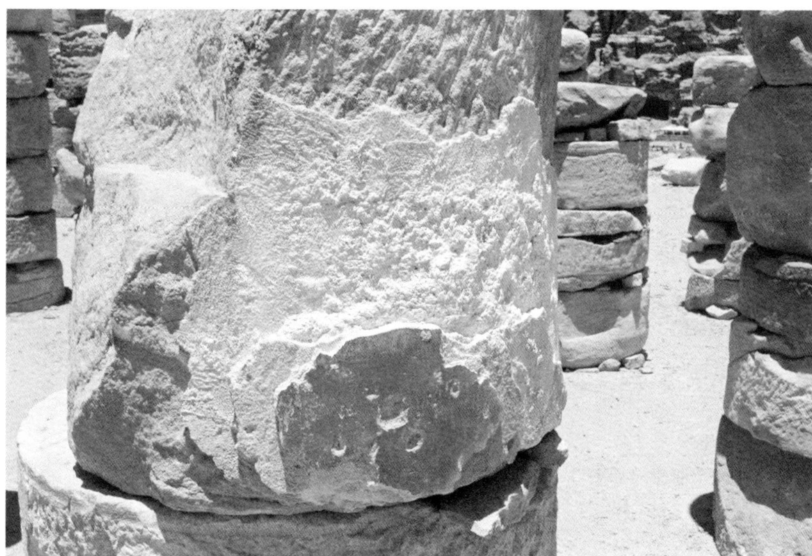

Fig. 3.16. Red plaster adhering to a lower temple column shaft.

Holes carved in the stone for lifting purposes would also help to secure the stucco. An example of this are the holes carved in the column shafts and pilasters of the Qasr al-Bint. They were used to secure the stucco decoration dividing them into drums of equal height.[167] There is no evidence for any wooden or metal plugs being used in the Great Temple to hold and affix the stucco to the drums. Both the diagonal dressing and the joints of the drums were effective in securing the stucco.[168]

Stucco cable fluting was a decorative element used whenever the carving of fluting in stone was considered to be difficult (fig. 3.15). Fluting in sandstone would be liable to damage; however, the method was frequently employed for limestone shafts in the Hellenistic period. Examples of this can be seen at Masada,[169] in Herod's Third Palace in Jericho,[170] and Pompeii,[171] but its use was not common to Petra. In addition to the limitations of sandstone as a material the Nabataeans aimed to save both time and expense with the use of stucco/plaster.

Fig. 3.17. Molding from the Great Temple South Corridor Wall. The Nabataeans used very thick stucco, the thickness varying from 10 cm to 15 cm.

It can be assumed that the Nabataean builders recognized the natural causes of destruction from experience rather than science.[172] They would have noticed that water and wind carrying sand affect the decay of most structural elements. Additionally frost damages masonry. Consequently, they plastered monumental facades meticulously aiming both to protect the surfaces against weathering and to achieve a pleasing decorative result. Plaster coverings

167 Zayadine *et al.* 2003, 114, fig. 48a.

168 Rababeh 2005, 126. Rababeh *et al.* 2010a, 60-83.

169 Foerster 1995, 80.

170 Netzer 2001a, 57.

171 De Franciscis 1978, 117, pl. 160.

172 Rababeh 2005, 121.

had a protective effect as they hindered the erosion from wind and rain. For the same reason, channels were cut in the rock above and on the sides of the facades in order to divert rainwater.[173] In extreme cases an entire drainage system was planned and constructed in conjunction with a building. In freestanding buildings damp rising through the walls was prevented through a damp-proof stone course and by ensuring the ground was well drained. A network of drains consisting of either built or rock-cut channels are found in and around many buildings and the Great Temple reveals a network of drains of various capacities, some principally for open courtyard areas and others to handle the water coming from the roofs. A similar network of drains can be seen in the Ez Zantur houses, the Temenos of the Qasr al-Bint, and the Temple of the Winged Lions. The channels led normally to subterranean cisterns beneath the ground floor. These cisterns were either built or cut into the sandstone bedrock.[174] The method of application was generally similar for all decorative plaster. The application of the stucco begins with a scratch coat, a first layer of mortar that is applied directly to the structure and allowed to slightly harden. Vitruvius[175] recommends 7 successive layers. A first rough layer, then three layers of mortar made with sand, and finally three layers of powdered marble mortar. Pliny[176] recommends only 5 layers instead of 7; three of mortar mixed with sand and two with mixed limestone and marble. But Adam[177] suggests that neither of these recommendations were applied to Roman monuments. He proposes three successive layers for the preparation of either external or internal surfaces corresponding to the evidence from Petra. Hammond[178] reports that the external and internal wall coverings in the Temple of the Winged Lions were made up of three successive layers.[179] Made of coarse plaster, the first two layers of lime and un-sifted sand were applied directly onto the surfaces and adhered well to the masonry walls. The thickness of these coats varied according to the smoothness and the vertical alignment of the wall masonry. The normal thickness varied from 5 cm to 15 cm. The final thin coat, the finest, was often made of lime plaster and it was keyed to the base coat by small copper or iron tacks.[180]

One problem present with a heavy wall coating is the weight of the plaster (fig. 3.17). The Nabataeans tended to use very thick stucco,[181] the thickness varying from10 cm to 15 cm, and because of its weight, unless the stucco was fixed firmly to the walls it would not have lasted very long during the building's use. Builders used different kinds of bonding agents. They used pegs to secure stucco panels on the walls and diagonal stone dressing and the roughness of the surfaces also were effective aids for holding the plaster in place. Two coats were also affixed to the wall ashlars by heavy iron nails driven between adjacent blocks and iron pegs were used to secure stucco in the Great Temple, although Schluntz[182] considered this to be uncommon in Petra. Recent excavations at the Ez Zantur houses in Area IV have recovered many stucco fragments supported by both wooden and metal pegs.[183] Iron pegs were certainly used in the Temple of the Winged Lions.[184] Additionally, some individual elements in the Temple of the Winged Lions have left empty holes leaving the impression of wooden pegs. Such holes can be seen elsewhere as well.[185]

173 I thank Suleiman Farajat for drawing this to my attention. See also Hammond 1995, 219; Kolb *et al.* 1993, 422; 1998, 267; 2000, 364-65.

174 Please refer to Ch. 4 for a discussion of water systems in this volume.

175 Vitruvius 7.3.5-6.

176 Cited by Adam 1994, 217.

177 Ibid. 217.

178 Hammond 1996, 61.

179 The plasterers in modern buildings in Jordan also build the plaster into three layers. The first is the coarsest, which they call "nail face," *i.e.*, the render coat. The second is the medium or the floating coat, and the final is the "finest base" which will be painted.

180 Hammond 1995, 219; 1996, 61.

181 Rababeh 2005, 121.

182 Schluntz 1998a, 213.

183 B. Kolb 2003, personal communication.

184 Hammond 1996, 62.

185 Rababeh 2005, figs. 5.4a; 5.7b; 6.40c; 42b-c, d; 43a-b.

Therefore, wooden pegs were commonly used at Petra to secure plaster and stucco decoration to the walls. In addition to those on the Qasr al-Bint, the use of wood pegs has been reported by Zayadine[186] in Tomb 813, Tomb 676 of the Nasara necropolis, the rear wall of the Tomb of Sextius Florentinus, Tombs in the 526 and 576 in the Mueisrah el-Wusta ridge, Tomb 808 in the western Khubtha cliff, in the eastern cliff face of el-Habis, and in the Baths-Palatial Complex.[187]

During the course of applying the stucco coverings Nabataean craftsmen used a variety of implements and tools. In the absence of the tools themselves, often paintings cast some light on the implements used and the process of the work. Examples are those reconstructed by Adam for Pompeii, and in the Musée de Sens in Gaul.[188] After examining these illustrations, the conclusion is that plastering, stucco, and painting started at the top of the wall with work proceeding downwards so as not to spoil the finished surface.[189] Because of the heights of the walls decorated in Petra one may safely assume the use of scaffolding. Plasterers certainly used trowels and painters usually used a cord, ruler, strings and compasses to draw the axes and the divisions of the circles of their wall paintings with different sized brushes. Presumably templates were used to check the accuracy of moldings.[190]

Masons' marks

Stonemasons marked symbols on the blocks to indicate their order in the building process. This technique was very common in Greek[191] and Roman architecture.[192] This author[193] noted inscribed drums and wall blocks among the artifacts collected from the Great Temple. The use of Nabataean letters is clear evidence that Nabataean masons themselves were master builders. Masons' marks appear on the drums in two forms, the first consists of Nabataean letters on the base of the drum (figs. 3.18a, 3.18b) and the second consists of numbers on the upper half of the side of the drum. Moreover, some blocks in the southwest corner of the West Walkway wall are inscribed with Nabataean letters.[194] The use of masons' marks also

Figs. 3.18a, 3.18b. Inscribed drums in the Great Temple. Masons' marks appear on the drums in two forms, consisting of Nabataean letters on the base and/or side of the drum.

186 Zayadine 1982, 374; 1987, 131-32.
187 al-Tell 1969, Pl.12.
188 Adam 1994, 222-23.
189 Rababeh 2005, 124.
190 Martin 1965, figs. 188, 189; Orlandos 1966, figs. 85, 88, 89.
191 Martin 1965, 225-31; Hellmann 2002, 88-91.
192 Adam 1994, 40.
193 Rababeh 2005, 91.
194 Ibid. 92.

is found in the west corridor of the Temple of the Winged Lions where there is a row of inscribed ashlars. Hammond[195] suggests that these blocks represent surplus materials left over from the original construction. Also there are masons' marks—letters and numbers—on the column drums of the Main Theatre.[196] Foerster[197] states that "the use of mason marks, probably for the assembly of the columns in this period is known from the Herodian sites like Jericho, but also from the Nabataean realm." Similarly, Hammond[198] states, "Such locational coding of drums is reported from Masada, where it is seen to be Nabataean in origin, although not done in Nabataean script." Hammond suggests that the Masada builders borrowed this marking system from the Nabataeans. However, apart from the alphabet used, both the Nabataean and the Masada systems are similar to the Greek system.

Discussion

The availability of building materials had a direct effect on the construction techniques used by the Nabataean builders of the Great Temple as is evident in foundations, masonry, and vaulting. It appears that the supply of the major building materials in bulk followed a logical economic model. Generally, the preference was for local resources, as the builders selected the most readily available and inexpensive supplies based on their location. Exceptions occurred when the building required special materials not found in the region, such as wood and marble.

The most readily available building material was sandstone. Petra sandstone is not a high quality construction material compared with limestone or granite, commonly used for classical monumental architecture elsewhere. This had a notable effect on the construction techniques used in the Great Temple. The advantages of sandstone were its local availability and its relative ease of cutting. However, its softness also made it quick to erode and it was weaker than limestone. Because the builders were aware of its weaknesses, they used coarse limestone for the paving of courts; the Upper and the Lower Temene, and softer fine limestone for bases and capitals of columns because it could be more finely carved (fig. 3.3). Marble slabs were probably used in paving the center of the temple, but not for column capitals. To modern eyes the color of sandstone is an attraction, but we have to remind ourselves that it was elegantly stuccoed (figs. 3.15, 3.16). In addition to its decorative use to add classical details,[199] stucco was also used extensively as a finish on the sandstone walls and column drums irregardless of the type of sandstone. It is unusual for claw chisel marks to be as visible as they are in the Great Temple ashlars and the other freestanding and rock cut monuments at Petra, this can be explained by their use as preparation for a stucco veneer.

The bedrock of the Great Temple, as the case of other buildings of Petra, offered a solid foundation for the building. The builders, as elsewhere, used terracing to minimize the amount of fill to be imported and to avoid constructing high retaining walls (fig. 3.2). The properties of sandstone influenced the size of blocks used for building both for the walls and the columns. In terms of size, wall blocks (average) measure c. 70 cm x 30 cm x 30 cm and weigh about c. 150 kg. The walls of the buildings were constructed using two normal methods: header and stretcher and/or casemate construction (fig. 3.8). No *opus reticulatum*;[200] has been found, unlike Herodian buildings dated to the end of 1st c. B.C. at Jericho. This indicates that the Nabataeans did not employ the Roman system of wall construction, nor were there Roman builders involved in Nabataean building projects at Petra. The Nabataeans certainly knew the technique of dowels and clamps, and the size of the cuttings for clamps recovered at Khirbet et-Tannur suggests Egyptian influence.[201] However Nabataean

195 Hammond 1996, 28, pls. 6, 7, 15. 2.
196 Hammond 1965, 13, 45-46, 49, 70-71, Pls. XXXIII.34, XLVII–L.
197 Foerster 1995, XIX.
198 Hammond 1996, 42.
199 Zayadine 1987, 131-43.
200 Claridge *et al.* 1998, 45.
201 Rababeh 2005, fig. 5.24.

builders at the Great Temple concentrated on the use of mortar and avoided the use of clamps. This was probably because clamps and dowels may have exerted a concentrated force on a small section of the sandstone ashlar blocks that would have been too stressful causing the stone to flake or chip. The unique use of clamps and dowels was in the limestone walls of Khirbet et-Tannur, but it is not found in sandstone walls of the Great Temple or other buildings in Petra. The Nabataeans selective use of techniques is related to the properties of the stone and their working knowledge of them.

The proportions the Nabataeans used for the Great Temple column drums were dependent on the properties of the sandstone. This caused the use of drums with a limited thickness. Consequently for large columns with a large diameter and a limited height make them appear like discs (0.7 m in h. x 1.5 m diam., fig. 3.13). Although their thickness is limited, the wooden pin technique was used for centering these discs which is also used for the Normal Drums of a smaller diameter. Alphabetic and numeric symbols were often incised in the bottoms and sides of the columns as in Greek architecture (figs. 3.18a, 3.18b). The weights of the column drums (Normal Drums 350 kg - 450 kg, Disk Drums two tons, and those of the Qasr al-Bint, 7 tons), and the weight of the wall blocks indicate that systems of simple and compound pulleys must have been used for lifting as elsewhere in Greco-Roman world. However, now no evidence has been found for the presence of bosses and slots on the sides of the column drums to indicate the use of lifting equipment. Notably the use of slots is unusual and could be related to the friability of the sandstone.

The types of material available and their properties were also the essential factors affecting the roofing techniques used in the Great Temple. On the basis of the technical features described, it has become clear that the lack of wood and the poor mechanical properties of sandstone were the main factors affecting roofing techniques. These presented a serious challenge to the Nabataean builders of the Great Temple which was solved by the use of local materials and the importation of others. Economical was the use of the readily available sandstone and it was modified using techniques paralleled in the Greco-Roman world.

In the Great Temple a series of vaults and arches with supporting arch slabs were used in roofing cisterns, rooms, lintels and basements (figs. 3.5, 3.11a-c). However Nabataean architects avoided using sandstone for large areas since it is friable and cannot withstand high tensile forces. When the builders could not use slabs to cover spans between the series of vaults they probably used local timber, such as juniper, olive, cypress or pine similar to what has been recovered at Mampsis. To solve the problem of spanning exceptionally large spaces the solution was to import timber.

The trading activities and the wealth of the Nabataeans made it possible to import wooden beams such as cedar with more than 5 m spans to roof the Great Temple. It is likely that the central authority supported these structures financially and ordered Nabataean architects and merchants to import wood. Along with the source of timber probably came the techniques for the construction of pitched roofs. Although not a local roofing technique, tiled roofs would have been more "classical" and prestigious.

In conclusion, the purpose of this chapter has been to explore the contribution that the Great Temple has made to our knowledge and understanding of the urban fabric in Petra in the Nabataean and Nabataean-Roman period. This chapter has focused on the surviving evidence concerning construction techniques used in the Great Temple. With reference to sites in Petra and the achievements of great cities in the region, we have explored a number of themes and issues of how the Great Temple was built. Data collected were used to provide the basis for a systematic study of the building materials to determine the specifications of the various types of Nabataean construction techniques applied to the Great Temple. Like the architecture, construction techniques reflect a combination of local and imported features. The source of the local features comes from available materials, and many of the construction techniques already were in use throughout the Greco-Roman world and were borrowed by Nabataean architects. The results reveal the Nabataeans used similar construction techniques in building the Great Temple as those found at Petra, other

Nabataean sites, and elsewhere beyond Nabataean borders in the Greco-Roman world. This chapter has presented the excavations and previously known sites as a basis for discussion, analyses, and elucidation of the architectural evidence. Within the 1st c. A.D. the Nabataeans were eclectic in the techniques they selected and mastered them to suit the properties of the locally available building materials—most notably sandstone.

4

The water systems of the Great Temple

Christian F. Cloke

Introduction

During the 1st c. B.C. and the 1st c. A.D. Nabataea's growing wealth from trade fostered the expansion of several major towns, including Petra. A focus on more permanent settlements in turn necessitated provisions for a reliable water supply in each town. To meet this demand the Nabataeans made great strides in water management, developing innovative strategies as well as adopting and adapting the methods employed in the major cities of the Greek East. Although Petra's inhabitants actively harvested water as early as the Iron Age (during the Edomite period), Nabataea's rise to prominence brought an unprecedented intensification and diversification of approaches to water management. Constructed during the same years of growth, the main design phases of the Great Temple (Site Phases I, II, and IV) incorporated a sophisticated array of features to collect, clean, store, and remove water along a substantial stretch of the urban center.

The archaeologists have uncovered an impressive array of underground channels leading either to storage facilities or out of the precinct. Built into the subterranean maze of winding stone-cut and masonry channels were a variety of cleverly designed and strategically positioned features such as settling basins and silt-collecting ledges to clean impurities and prevent blockages. Sections of ceramic and lead piping also traverse the precinct, demonstrating the longevity of the systems and their changing character, while the Roman Byzantine Baths[1] to the west of the Lower Temenos reflect profound differences in water use at the site following Arabia's annexation by Rome.

The myriad hydraulic features within the precinct were designed to perform several distinct functions. Drains were necessary in the Lower Temenos to divert excess rainwater from architecture and open spaces, while cisterns and purification features in the canalization attest to an equal concern for the storage and cleaning of water, and suggest that at least part of the supply was intended to be potable. The multi-purpose design of these systems, coupled with their location beneath a prominent civic structure, reflect the need for a reliable supply of water to the precinct and the care with which the Nabataeans harvested and preserved this essential commodity. The precint's stored stored supply could have been used for any number of purposes, although access was carefully guarded. As a major civic complex, it supplemented the water supply of the city from its own store.

Water flowed beneath the Great Temple from south to north, from the rear of the precinct to its entrance along Petra's main road. Water brought from natural springs to the south entered the precinct at its SW corner, passing east and then north through two large arteries, one directly through the center of the precinct, the other along its E edge, beneath the East Plaza and E side of the Lower Temenos (fig. 4.1). In the Lower Temenos, surface drains deposited rainwater into the same network of channels, and at several locations water was collected and stored in large quantities.

The following discussion traces the path of water through the precinct from south to north and from east to west, focuses on the working of the system as a whole, and highlights notable features within it. After the major components and their relationships have been discussed, attention will shift to features whose place within the overall water-management scheme was more peripheral. This system of subterranean canalization and pipes transported water nearly 135 m from south to north. While ceramic and lead pipes utilized pressure to move the water, gravity played a larger rôle at the inception of these systems. On the elevated hill south of the temple proper a length of canalization uncovered in Trench 77 lies at 914.702 m asl, constituting the highest water-related

1 See chapt. 9 below.

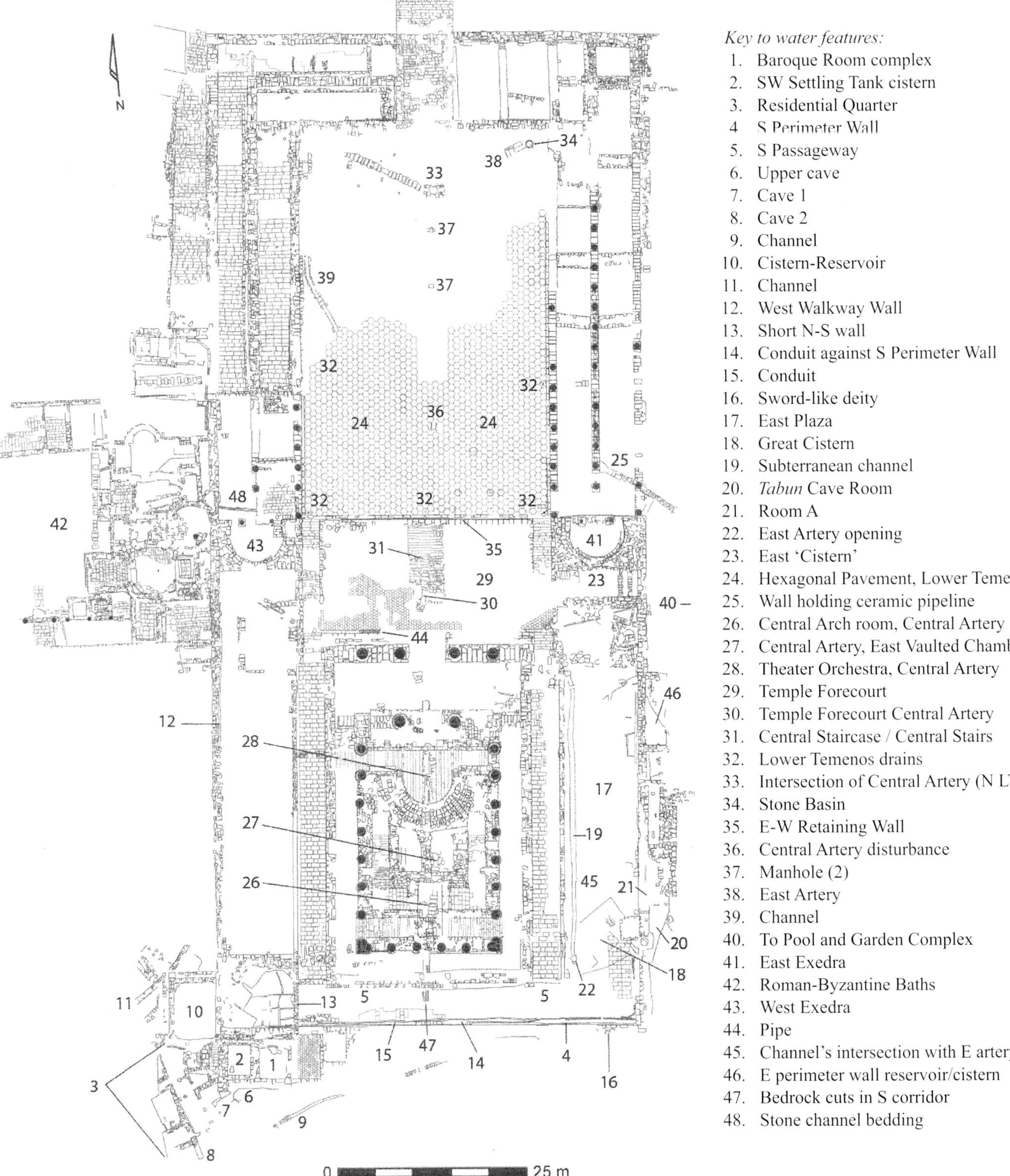

Fig. 4.1. Plan of the precinct showing the major water features.

feature in the precinct (fig. 4.1, no. 9). Beneath the forecourt to the temple, roughly halfway along the water's path, the capstones of the canalization have a top elevation of 903.846 m (fig. 4.1, no. 30). At the N side of the Lower Temenos the bedding of the canalization, exposed in 2002, drops to 896.459 m asl, which is 18.243 m lower than the highest canalization at the south (fig. 4.1, no. 33).

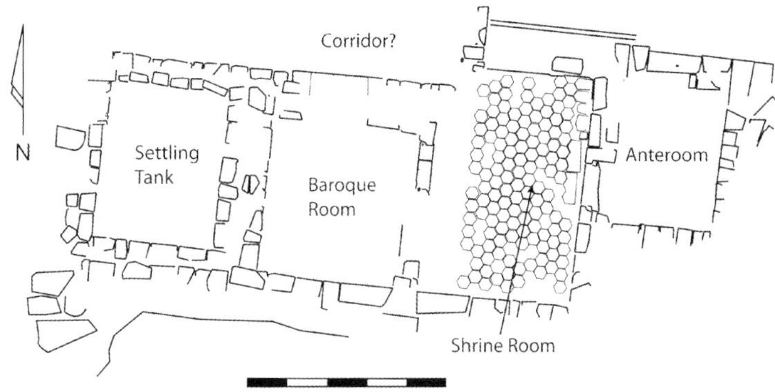

Fig. 4.2. The 'Baroque Room complex'.

The S part of the Great Temple precinct

Fig. 4.3. Hydraulic plaster lining of the settling tank.

At the far south of the precinct, above the South Perimeter Wall, are several channels, one of stone construction covered with square capstones, another made from ceramic pipe segments (fig. 4.1, no. 9). Running W–E (angled slightly toward the northeast), they brought water from groundwater springs[2] south of the temple for use within the precinct. Although the connection between the southern channels and the rest of the precinct's systems is no longer intact, the water was probably brought down through the South Perimeter Wall into the channels beneath the South Passageway pavement just inside (north of) this wall (fig. 4.1, nos. 14 and 15). Also in this general area was the SW Settling Tank, located between the Upper and Lower Caves and the Baroque Room Complex (with which it shares a wall) (fig. 4.1, no. 2). The SW Settling Tank (excavated fully in 2004) measured 5.39 m N-S by 4.82 m E-W and the interior was 1.46-1.96 m deep. It was lined with dark gray hydraulic mortar, 0.03 m thick (fig. 4.3). Emerging from the exterior of the N wall of the SW Settling Tank is a lead pipe (0.06-0.07 m in diameter, just under 0.5 cm in thickness), held in place by the same hydraulic mortar. This pipe, positioned 0.58 m above the pavement at the foot of the tank's N wall, allowed for release of the tank's water supply into the channels below. Although the SW Settling Tank was possibly a self-sufficient cistern, the arrangement of similar elements at sites such as Humayma rather suggests that this feature may have been a settling tank, albeit removed some distance from the larger cistern into which it fed (located on the other side of the precinct beneath the East Plaza).[3] Here the structure would have collected spring- and rain-water entering the precinct, allowing silt to settle to the bottom before the cleaned water flowed out through the lead pipe. This settling tank or cistern would have dispensed an easily controlled stream of clean water that then traveled through a series of pipes and channels to the much larger Great Cistern in the East Plaza, which constituted a more expansive and secure storage facility. Because the outlet pipe is of lead, there may once have been a valve or stopcock to modulate the outflow of water, although such a feature is more characteristic of Roman-era construction.[4] Nabataean Phase IIIb (*c.*A.D. 70/80-100) pottery found beneath a wall of this enclosure suggests that this feature was not built until the last

2 Other than rainwater, the most abundant known sources for the precinct were nearby 'Ain Musa and 'Ain Brak.

3 See Oleson 2010.

4 A bronze stopcock for controlling flow was added to a large public reservoir at Humayma during the Roman period: Oleson 2004, 357; id. 2010, 262-64 and 332-33.

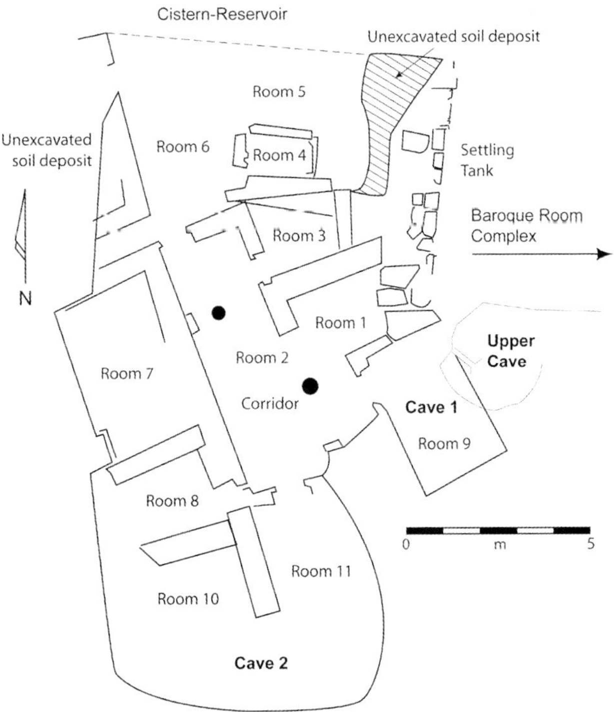

Fig. 4.4. The Residential Quarter.

quarter of the 1st c. A.D. at the earliest, and that it was in use primarily during phases IV and V.

Before the route of the water is traced farther, attention must be given to the domestic area found just southwest of the temple precinct. Two domestic caves excavated in 2002 to the rear and west of the Great Temple proper (fig. 4.1, nos. 6-8) contained a perplexing series of water channels and catchments. While this area's relationship with the Great Temple is not certain, it appears to have been in use simultaneously from Phase IV onwards and probably shared the same water resources. Rainwater from the hill behind the temple collected in a small upper cave (now open-fronted) just above and to the east of the domestic area. The floor of this small catchment had the typical dark gray, pebbly hydraulic mortar (fig. 4.3) found in water features in the temple complex, with an outlet (which may have held a ceramic pipe) directed toward the more easterly of the lower caves (Cave 1). A series of channels carried water beneath and through many of the walls dividing the area in front of the caves, eventually to reach the level of the pavement southwest of the temple, although the pattern of flow is not entirely clear. Most of the channels are cut into the bedrock and their covering is preserved in places. The discovery in 2005 of a monumental cistern-reservoir (dimensions 7.0 m N–S, 5.4 m E–W, average depth 1.96 m; capacity *c.*19,571 gallons or 74,084 liters) suggests that in Phases IV and V a large amount of water from the vicinity of the caves was collected above ground (fig. 4.1, no. 10). If unroofed, this enclosure may even have served as a *natatio* for swimming in connection with the Roman-Byzantine Baths to its north.

The South Passageway of the Temple

At the rear of the precinct one can follow the probable course of a channel carved into the bedrock, which runs E–W past the Southwest Cistern and the Baroque Room and continues beneath a short N-S wall aligned with the West Walkway Wall (fig. 4.1, no. 13). At the short wall's E face the rock-cut channel measures 0.09 m in height and 0.08 m in width. This area shows signs of repair and a redesign to the system. A ceramic pipe set in a bedding of hydraulic mortar runs parallel to the channel, *c.*0.11 m higher than the lip of the rock-cut channel and flush with the S Passageway pavement. On the W side it is blocked by the short N–S wall mentioned above, which cut off any access to water from a source beyond. The pipe's higher elevation and winding construction suggest that it was a later, unsuccessful attempt to solve a supply problem in this area. Instead, the builders retooled the existing rock-cut channel. The short N–S wall was the latest addition here, as shown by its construction atop 0.35 m of fill overlying the pavement. Both channels would have been in place together (the pipe being the later of the two) and one or both would have drawn water from the west. But a decision was made to modify or restrict movement to the rear of the temple in Phase VI and to close off the precinct from the domestic area to the west. The Settling Tank to the southwest, however, was too precious a source to eliminate, so the channel drawing from it was maintained and re-cut through the base of the new wall.

From the short N–S wall the two parallel conduits (pipe and channel), only centimeters apart, continue for 23.01 m to the east, before terminating midway along the South Passageway (fig. 4.1, nos. 14-15). At this point the bottom of the ceramic pipe forms a 90° angle pointed down into the mortar that holds it; an upper part presumably of similar shape would have created a square cross-section with an internal diameter of 0.11-0-12 m. The pipe's individual sections are simply laid end to end in their hydraulic mortar bedding (fig. 4.5) and not joined; these relatively crude additions probably belong to Phase VII. The rock-cut channel first built in Phase IV, however, continues to the E end of the South Perimeter Wall, though along the way it was blocked and its course altered. This important supply line, linking the SW Settling Tank to the Great Cistern of the East Plaza, evidently underwent several construction and rebuilding phases. A schematic sword-like deity is carved into the bedrock above,[5] just beneath a fissure that may have expelled water (fig. 4.1, no. 16). The carving may therefore betray a reverence toward the water supply of this area and the divine powers associated with its provision. Upon reaching the precinct's SE corner, the rock-cut channel below turns north to follow the side of the East Perimeter Wall where it is covered by rectangular pavers and is mirrored by an above-ground ceramic pipe (internal diam. 0.07-0.08 m) made of segments mortared to a stone bedding laid over the pavement. Both conduits continue north for *c.* 8.1 m before reaching a short channel flowing northwest, which once deposited water directly into the large cistern beneath the East Plaza. The presence of several channels and pipes in this area suggests that the massive cistern below was in use over a long period, during which its supply lines were occasionally modified and reconfigured.

Fig. 4.5. Parallel rock-cut channel and a ceramic pipe against the S Perimeter Wall.

The Great Cistern of the East Plaza

The Great Cistern (fig. 4.1, no. 18), part of the grand design of Phase IV (a Nabataean fineware juglet of the 1st c. B.C. was found in a silty layer at its bottom), was discovered in 2001 when the cylindrical shaft above its SE corner was opened and a test trench dug adjacent to its E interior wall to ascertain its depth. Attempts to locate another opening were helped when heavy rains during the following winter revealed a second shaft, more than 7 m southwest of the first, serving as the outlet (fig. 4.1, no. 22). In 2002 the SW exit shaft was cleared, and a trench was excavated in the W part of the cistern (figs. 4.6-4.7). The structure

Fig. 4.6. Main arch in the interior of the Great Cistern during excavation.

5 See vol. 2, 144-45, for a discussion of this carving.

Fig. 4.7. Bedrock pillar in the interior of the Great Cistern during excavation.

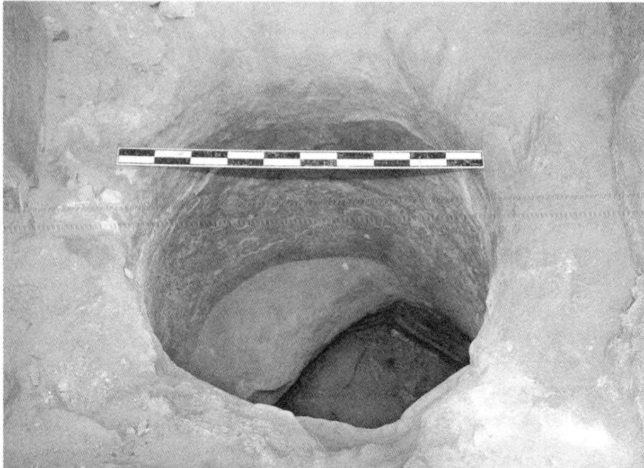

Fig. 4.8. Ledge of SE shaft of the Great Cistern.

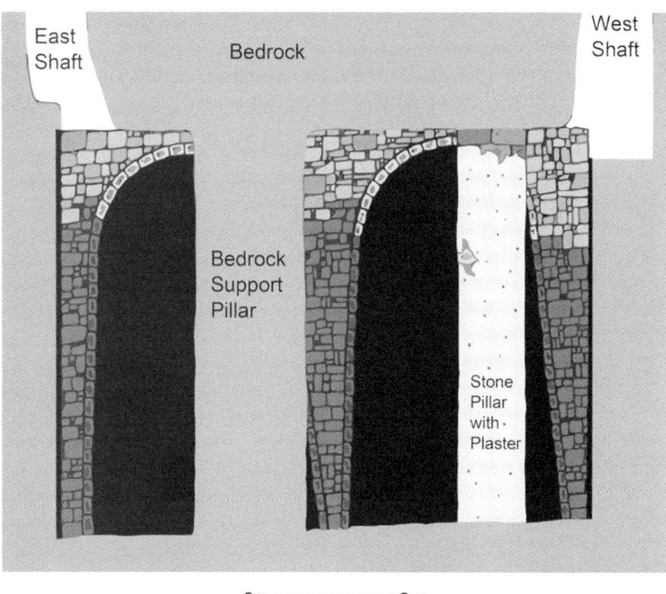

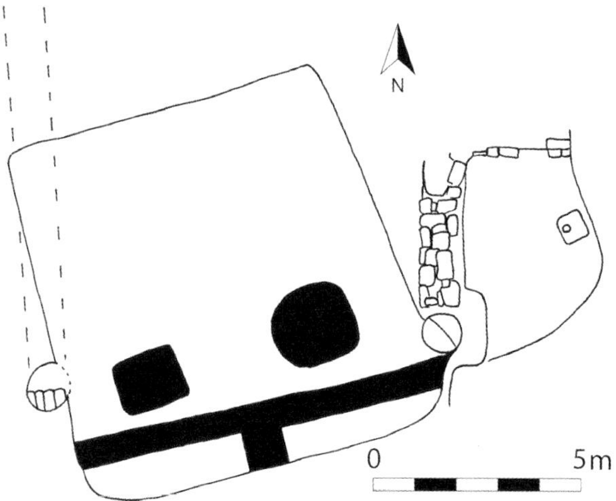

Fig. 4.9 a-b. Cross-section and plan of the Great Cistern.

combines Nabataean techniques for fashioning rock-cut water-storage chambers with strategies of masonry reinforcement found elsewhere in the eastern Greek world. The SE shaft measures 0.98 to 1.01 m in diameter at the top (elev. 905.164 m) and widens to 1.41 m at a depth of 1.64 m. On its E side (elev. 903.372) it has a semicircular ledge (1.41 m in length, 0.40 m in width), which probably facilitated access for repairs and cleaning (fig. 4.8). The cistern itself, which is roughly cubic in shape, was cut into and entirely surrounded by sandstone bedrock. In the area of the 2001 test trench the bottom descends to about elev. 897.382 m, which is 5.88 m below the ceiling (fig. 4.9). In our 2002 test trench on the west it descends to elev. 897.289 m, 5.17 m below the bedrock ceiling, which slopes down to the west. Thus the cistern is shallower at the west, which is the side intended as an outlet. The interior measures *c.*8.5 m N–S × 7.8 m E–W, with a capacity of *c.*327.64 m^3 (allowing for the space taken up by the architectural features discussed below, but excluding the area of the two shafts above ceiling level). A cistern of this size could have held *c.*86,553 gallons (327,638 liters) of water. It is the largest cistern yet documented in the city center, but the need for such a structure is clear. The necessity for stockpiling water was paramount, given the often drastic annual variation in rainfall:

> No [Nabataean] urban center could afford to concentrate on runoff water alone without building enormous reservoirs ... capable of holding a two-year supply.[6]

This type of mass storage space furnished a supply sufficient to meet even the greatest demands of the precinct and its neighbors, and at the same time kept water circulating in periods of abundance.[7] The Great Cistern, however, is only one part of a much larger storage network, which included other cisterns as well as a complex system of dams and channels throughout the Siq and the city.

Several internal supports provided stability for the large cubic void hewn out of the bedrock. On the E side is a column of solid bedrock (*c.*6.81 m in circumference) coated with the same plaster as the rest of the cistern (fig. 4.7). The cistern's walls were covered with three layers (*c.*0.05 m thick) of this coarse, porous hydraulic plaster (now coated in many places by crystalline calcification). On the W side is a rectangular pillar (its sides measuring 1.01-1.19 m) built of cobble-sized stones, also plastered, which spans 5.17 m from floor to celing (fig. 4.6, at right). The E column was carved from the bedrock during the cistern's initial construction to support the ceiling, while the masonry pillar was probably added slightly later, but before construction was completed and the whole cistern was plastered, since it is coated with the same plaster layers. A lamp of the late 1st c. A.D. was found between stones near the top of the feature. Architectural relationships suggest that the cistern itself belongs with the precinct's redesign during Phase IV (late 1st c. B.C. or early 1st c. A.D.). Because the masonry pillar appears original to the construction of the cistern, it seems likely that the lamp was deposited during repair work that occurred after a century or so. The pillar was clearly intended to support the bedrock ceiling in this area, which is cracked and less sound than it appears elsewhere. The bedrock column to the east, being far sturdier, provided sufficient support for the rest of the ceiling.

To the south, parallel to the S wall of the cistern, is a wall (7.3 m long, 0.60 m wide) built of cobble-sized stones and covered in waterproof plaster just like the stone-built pillar. Built into it are two arches reaching almost to the ceiling (fig. 4.6). It is abutted by a short wall (1.14 m) perpendicular to the S wall of the cistern, dividing the space behind into two chambers (one behind each arch). Because the space between the E-W wall and the stone-built pillar is very cramped, the wall must have been built first. The arches gave increased support without much compromising the internal capacity of the cistern. Single transverse arches are found in many Nabataean cisterns (e.g., at Humayma);[8] generally they feature in sturdy cross-walls that span the full width of masonry cisterns roofed with stone slabs. The precise combination of features used in the Great Cistern is less common. Rows of single-arched cross-walls bolstered many built cisterns in the vicinity of Petra, at Humayma and other sites of the Nabataean period, and they are common throughout the Hellenistic Eastern Mediterranean (e.g., on Delos), but the double-arched wall in the Great Cistern is atypical and the use of masonry architecture within a bedrock-enclosed cistern is unusual. While Humayma's large, public masonry cisterns may be viewed as the precursors of Petra's Great Cistern, the latter combines the arched support system with local techniques utilizing Petra's sound bedrock. Several of Humayma's large public cisterns, which employ adjoining settling tanks, display intake and outlet arrangements similar to that of the Great Cistern.[9] Bell- or bottle-shaped cisterns are the most common Nabataean type, and the Great Cistern mimics and elaborates upon these forms, particularly in its cylindrical entrance and exit shafts. Yet it differs from typical Nabataean structures in its internal support features, which made possible its larger size. While not altogether anomalous, the Great Cistern displays considerable innovation in combining and elaborating upon simpler contemporary designs.

---

6 Eadie and Oleson 1986, 71.
7 Nehmé 2003, 163.
8 See, e.g., Humayma Cistern 124 (Oleson 2010, 126-28).
9 Oleson 2010, 117-55.

Fig. 4.10. East Artery in the East Plaza.

The second cylindrical shaft in the cistern's SW corner (1.10-1.14 m in diameter at the top, 1.30-1.32 m in diameter at its lowest visible point, minimum depth 2.29 m; upper elevation 904.669) directed overflow into a subterranean channel flowing north along the W side of the East Plaza (fig. 4.1, no. 19). An E–W arch (0.99 long x 1.08 m wide, 0.26-0.30 m in height; top elevation 905.219 m) covers the opening. Longer sandstone archstones are set on either end and blocks half their length in between. The small keystones resting on the S side of the springers are 0.40-0.45 m long and 0.21-0.29 m wide. The stones of the arch were bossed on their undersides, which is of interest because this decoration would not have been seen except at the time of construction and during repair work being done in the cistern on its W side. Because of the cistern's presumed early date, it is unlikely that many readily re-usable architectural elements would have been available, and in any event the carefully cut stones of the arch seem to fit this feature too well to have been re-used.

Emerging from this shaft and heading north beneath the East Plaza is an enormous channel (35.4 m long, up to 1.5 m deep, up to 0.77 m wide) cut into bedrock (fig. 4.10), which carried overflow down toward the north and the front of the precinct. It also would have helped to alleviate pressure in the event that flooding threatened the cistern. The channel depositing water into the SE shaft also continued past this shaft, beneath the pavement of the East Plaza, to intersect with the large channel on the plaza's W side, *c.*9.5 m north of the SW shaft (fig. 4.1 no. 45; see the X on fig. 4.10). If the cistern was full, or if the SE shaft was intentionally blocked, this channel would have allowed water to bypass the cistern.

Access to water in the Great Cistern was achieved apparently via the *Tabun* Cave Room, located above the SE shaft. This room was hewn out of the bedrock and enclosed behind the East Perimeter Wall, which also arched above it into the hill above (fig. 4.1, no. 20). A large well shaft (1.94 x 0.87 m across, 2.88 m high), cut into the bedrock, connected the room to the cistern. The room had a small plaster-lined basin set in its floor, probably for water. The well shaft was originally blocked from the East Plaza by a wooden door or gate, indicated by a door jamb at the north (fig. 4.11). Drawing water up into the room could have been accomplished with a simple rope and bucket. At the time of excavation it was assumed that the basin in the Tabun Cave Room was a place for washing,

Fig. 4.11. *Tabun* Cave Room.

whether ritual or practical. Numerous cooking vessels and other domestic débris were found in the nearby Room A to the north (fig. 4.1, no. 21). This room, the well, and the SE shaft also formed the easiest access into the cistern for repair work, which suggests that the cistern was managed by individuals with access to the rooms behind the East Perimeter Wall. Not only was access to the well limited, but the cistern itself would have been invisible to those walking along the East Plaza. The rooms within the East Perimeter Wall constitute the sole, carefully-secured access point to the Great Cistern's store of water.

Providing access to the cistern may not have been the only function of the Tabun Cave Room, however. P. Zimmerman has postulated that the entire *Tabun* Cave Room could have served as a catchment for winter rainwater. While it is likely that an E–W arch springing from the top of the East Perimeter Wall covered it, an opening above the room would have been well situated for collecting winter rains from the slope just above. During the winter rainy season, the door opening onto a staircase towards Room A could have been securely closed, allowing rain water to collect and flow into the cistern. It seems likeliest, though, that this room was enclosed from above, restricting access to the cistern and protecting it from windblown débris. Moreover, broken pottery and a yellowish pebbly mortar on the floor suggest a build-up of occupational materials ill-suited to a room used for water catchment, although this build-up may date to a time after which the function of the room had changed from that of a water catchment. In addition, one would expect to find some vestiges of hydraulic mortar still adhering to the walls and floor of the room to prevent the porous sandstone from absorbing incoming water. Lastly, the E–W slope of the bedrock room seems insufficient to direct water towards the well and the cistern's opening. On balance then, it seems unlikely that the whole room was used to collect water unless later modifications have masked the evidence of such a function.

The East Plaza

Water exceeding the capacity of the Great Cistern rose up through the SW exit shaft and ran north beneath the East Plaza. The East Artery that transported water from the cistern was exposed for 35.30 m to the N end of the East Plaza, where it turns northwest toward the Lower Temenos. At the south, the channel's bottom elevation is 904.279 m and at the north 903.355; it has a

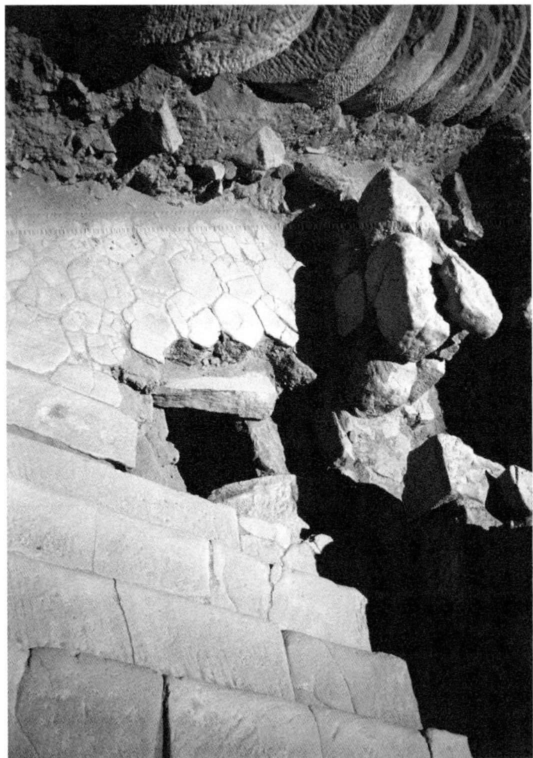

Fig. 4.12. East Artery opening beneath the Temple Forecourt (1995).

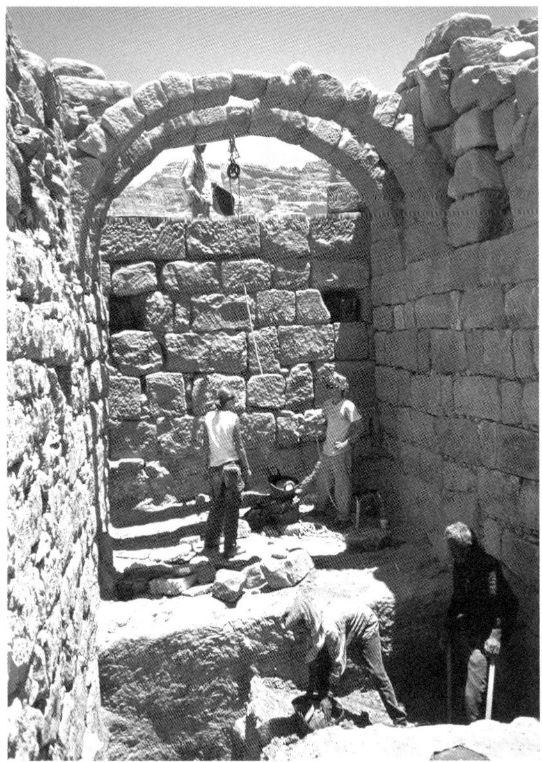

Fig. 4.13. East 'Cistern'.

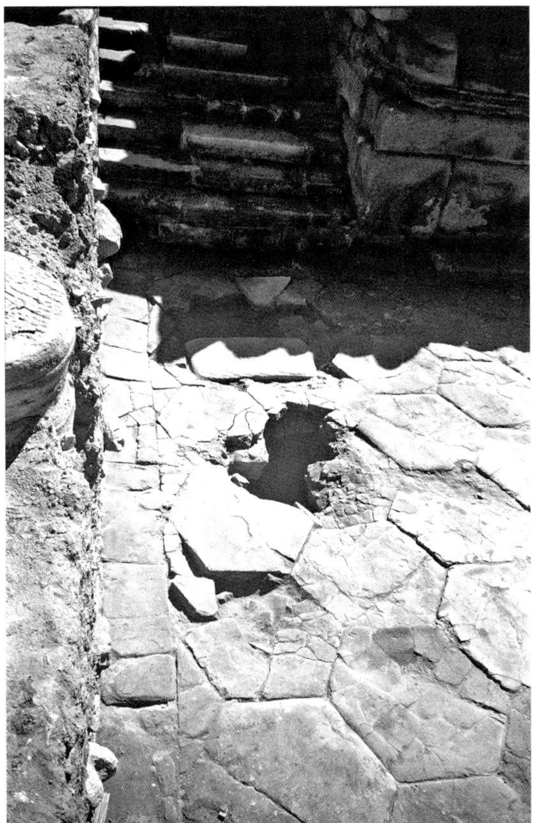

Fig. 4.14. Opening in the pavement where the East Artery emerges below the East Staircase of the Lower Temenos.

slight downward slope of 2.6°. The channel varies from 1 to 1.5 m in preserved depth and 0.26 to 0.77 m in width (it is wider at the top). It narrows at the N end of the East Plaza, and this would have increased the speed and momentum of the water into the Temple Forecourt and Lower Temenos. The channel was widened toward the middle of the East Plaza, near the junction with the channel bypassing the cistern, to accommodate additional flow. Because the channel was set well below the level of the East Plaza, it must once have been covered by a thick deposit of fill, which would have helped protect it. Midway across the East Plaza the walls of the channel dip to form a ledge on either side.[10] Here perhaps the capstones were designed to be removable, facilitating access for cleaning to ensure a smooth flow between the intersecting channels. Some 27 m north of the SW Great Cistern shaft, the bedrock from which the channel had thus far been cut falls away, necessitating walls built of irregular cobbles coated with hydraulic plaster (the channel here is 1.10 m deep, 0.54-0.58 m wide,

10 The ledges are marked by a drop in the bedrock wall of 0.57 m on the E and 0.45 m on the W side of the channel.

Fig. 4.15. Reservoir in the East Perimeter Wall.

and 8.4 m in length). A single capstone made of a limestone block survives in this section. At the far E side of the Temple Forecourt, where a further extent of the East Artery was explored, only a single capstone was missing (fig. 4.12). Here the plastering of the channel's masonry walls was discovered intact. Just beyond this point the channel passes below the East Staircase, leading down to the Lower Temenos, the treads of which have partially collapsed into the channel. In the E part of the Temple Forecourt, modifications to the Hexagonal Pavement suggest that significant repair or maintenance work was done to the channels beneath.[11] The East Artery then drops and enters the Lower Temenos, where a complicated series of channels collected water from it and from the Central Artery (see below), as well as rainwater deposited in drains around the edge of the Hexagonal Pavement (fig. 4.14; see fig. 4.1, no. 32). The parallel East and Central Arteries both directed water north beneath the Lower Temenos towards the Wadi Musa without seeming to intersect one another within the precinct.

One last feature in the Upper Temenos possibly related to these integrated elements is the reservoir or cistern (dimensions 9.2 x 3.1 m, max. preserved height of walls 1.3 m) built between the two sides of the casemate East Perimeter Wall near the N end of the East Plaza (fig. 4.15; fig 4.1, no. 46). Facing the East Plaza, a small lead pipe (diam. 0.07-0.09 m, length 0.74 m, 4 mm thick) belonging to this reservoir protrudes from the East Perimeter Wall. The pipe rests in a niche cut into the wall in antiquity. Inside the reservoir or cistern, a section of ceramic pipe is preserved where it forms a T-shaped junction with the lead pipe. The lower half of a ceramic pipe (diam. 0.08-0.09 m, length 0.33 m) survives within the S wall of the reservoir. The walls and floor of the reservoir are covered with a white chalky plaster to seal in water and prevent evaporation. Rainwater presumably filled the cistern through channels now lost or through pressurized pipes built into the East Perimeter Wall, but the intended destination and uses of this water are unknown.

---

11 Because the channel does not intersect with the East 'Cistern' (room) situated east of the East Staircase (fig. 4.1, no. 23: fig. 4.13), it seems that at the time the Great Cistern and East Artery were built, the so-called East 'Cistern' was not an active cistern connected to the precinct's main water systems. Although the lower portion of the room, resting on bedrock, may have been used to contain water at a very early phase, no connections to any other water systems are evident, nor is the fine painted plaster of the room typical of hydraulic installations.

The Great Temple proper

Beneath the Central Arch Room at the rear of the temple is the start of a second network of channels, termed the Central Artery (fig. 4.1, no. 26). A row of 16 capstones (total length 7.19 m within the Central Arch Room; widest visible capstone 1.19 m; average thickness *c.*0.30 m) mark the start of this artery. The main channel ran S–N and was joined on the southeast and southwest by two subsidiary channels. Several small grooves cut into a large stone slab were found above the capped west channel, but they cannot be followed past the south wall of the Central Arch Room and their function is not clear. Beneath the capstones the channel was seated on bedrock, its walls made of large sandstone blocks leveled off with small chinking stones. The walls of the channel were lined with the same dark gray (Munsell 5Y 3/1) hydraulic mortar seen in many other water features in the precinct.

The Central Artery clearly was designed to move a large volume of water north toward the front of the temple precinct, but the source of this water is a more complicated matter. The main artery apparently drew from channels on both the southeast and southwest, which meet it in a T-shaped junction, but it is unclear from where these two side channels emanated. Both extend toward the side walls of the Central Arch Room, beneath which they presumably continue. Probably the system drew water from the hill behind the temple, transporting it by gravity beneath the walls of the building. Another possibility, however, is that these concealed channels began at the base of drains (perhaps beneath gutters at the rear corners of the roof), to collect rainwater falling on the temple's tiled roof. The smaller stone-cut grooves cut into a block above the west feeder channel are still more difficult to understand. These 4 parallel channels (each 0.10-0.12 m wide) are cut for a length of *c.*0.58 m into a sandstone slab laid atop the large subterranean channel. They also show traces of the same dark gray hydraulic mortar. In the westernmost of the four channels were found remains of a lead pipe (diam. 0.06 m), set in thickly applied waterproof mortar. It seems that these four channels once housed pipes cut through the S Corridor wall, and may align with three small cuts (0.10-0.11 m wide, 0.09-0.11 m deep) in the South Corridor's bedrock, directly south of this room (fig. 4.1, no. 47). This network of cuts was set over earlier water features, indicating that it represents a modification of flow patterns beneath and through the temple proper, although this modified network ceased to function in phase VII. The cuts in the bedrock of the South Corridor must have gone out of use with the blocking of the South Corridor Wall's central doorway, up to which these cuts extend. This doorway's blocking, probably dated to the mid-2nd c. A.D., cut across the path of these channels, and the lead pipes within were removed for re-use. The lead pipes and their bedding had probably been installed during the late 1st or early 2nd c. (perhaps with the major rebuilding in Phase VI).

The Central Artery is next seen in the temple's East Vaulted Chamber, where excavation revealed 4 capstones (width 0.7-0.8 m) over a length of 2.0 m (fig. 4.1, no. 27). It passes 1.10 m east of the W wall in this small room, slightly offset from the wall's orientation. The walls rest over the capstone, however, showing that the canalization predates at least the temple's internal walls and the Theater. Thus the canalization was presumably laid out in Phase I, and it may belong with preparatory work for the initial distyle *in antis* building. A section of the Central Artery, covered by 5 capstones and with hydraulic plaster on its walls, was located in 2005 below the orchestra, oriented roughly S–N (fig. 4.1, no. 28). Farther north, the Central Artery re-appears beneath the Great Temple's Forecourt (fig. 4.1, no. 30).

The Temple Forecourt

The main intersection of the central artery with two side channels (fig. 4.16) can be found beneath the Temple Forecourt (fig. 4.1, no. 30). The side channels were built at the same time as the Central Artery, as is shown by their bonded corners, but upper courses of chinking stones point

Fig. 4.16. Main intersection of canalization beneath the central part of the Temple Forecourt.

to a repair or enlargement of the channels,[12] perhaps to accommodate an increased water flow at the time of the elaboration of the Great Temple and blocking of the Central Staircase (Phase IV). The Central Artery is 1.7-1.9 m high and 0.6-0.7 m wide with limestone capstones averaging 0.75 x 0.57 m across and 0.16 m thick, many of which show signs of cracking.[13] Above the capstones was a hard, densely packed layer (0.15 m thick) of sand and wadi pebbles. The layer of pink mortar bedding above, upon which the pavement was laid, is more claylike in consistency.[14] Covering subterranean channels before the pavement was put in place helped to seal and protect the channels from débris and damage.[15] The typical hydraulic mortar (10YR 3/1) was found bonded to the lower parts of the walls and floor of the channels.

For much of its extent the Central Artery declines gradually, but at a point 8.40 m south of the junction in the Temple Forecourt it takes a sharp dip, followed by another at its northernmost visible point, with a steep, stepped slope of 26°. As it approaches the Lower Temenos the Central Artery drops 6 m beneath the Central Stairs, the steps of which became the capstones of the channel in a clever feat of design (fig. 4.1, no. 31). This arrangement was especially convenient after the stairs were blocked and the surface level was raised, which provided the channel with additional separation from the surface.

The side channels feeding into the Central Artery are smaller (0.5 m wide, 1.1 high on the E side and 0.6 high on the W side). The E channel converges with the Central Artery farther to the north than does the W channel. There is an offset of 0.75 m between them, probably to allow the Central Artery to be spanned by a single capstone in each place.[16] Where the bedrock drops off, the side channels are built into the fill upon which the temple itself is constructed, [17] and so these channels were probably built in Phase II. They slope toward the Central Artery and must have collected water from the surface of the Hexagonal Pavement at the front of the Temple Forecourt, as

12 See Payne vol. 1, 171.
13 Ibid. 171 and 174.
14 Ibid. 173.
15 Ibid. 172.
16 Joukowsky and Schluntz 1995, 249.
17 Payne, vol. 1, 172.

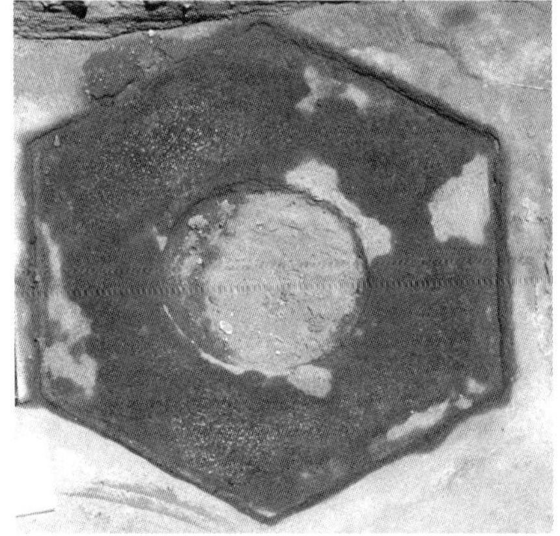

Fig. 4.17. Surface drain with bronze fitting in the SW Lower Temenos.

Fig. 4.18. Settling basin in the NE part of the Lower Temenos.

Fig. 4.19. 'Manhole' above central artery in the central part of the Lower Temenos.

is suggested by a drain discovered in the NW part of the forecourt, which leads into the W channel. The precinct's engineers thereby opted for at least two devices in this area to ensure adequate drainage and more efficient collection. Probably as a later addition, a pipe running E–W across the front of the temple drained into the subterranean Central Artery (fig. 4.1, no. 44).

The Lower Temenos

The Lower Temenos was furnished with at least 5 surface drains, one with its bronze fitting preserved *in situ* (figs. 4.17 and 4.1, no. 32), to feed rainwater run-off into the subterranean canalization of the East and Central Arteries. The array of channels and drains, which extended the full length and width of the Lower Temenos, gathered the area's water in the two main S–N conduits.

From the Temple Forecourt the Central Artery passes beneath the Central Stairway and follows a straight line for over 50 m to the N limit of the Lower Temenos. Several disturbances, one just north of the E–W Retaining Wall and another near the middle of the Lower Temenos, first exposed this canalization, which is 0.6 m wide and not less than 0.4 m deep (fig. 4.1, no. 36). Where the hexagonal pavement has collapsed can be seen the end of a capstone (1.17 m wide, 0.28 m thick) covering the Central Artery and set 0.96 m below the surface, separated from it by a thick pebble fill.

Near the center of the Lower Temenos are two small square shafts (elevation 898 m) directly above the path of the Central Artery (figs. 4.19 and 4.1, no. 37). The northernmost one, which falls within the bounds of Trench 66, measures 0.40 x 0.47 m on the inside of the opening and *c.*0.7 m in depth. A second opening of similar construction, which lies 6.90 m to the south, measures 0.39 x 0.55 m and has a depth of at least 1.17 m. Their sides are made of small, semi-coursed, well-cut slabs. The northern opening was capped with a re-used cornice block resting atop four stretchers of hewn limestone and sandstone blocks coated with waterproof plaster.[18] The shafts seem to be maintenance openings (manholes) into the Central Artery. A large intersection was found near the N end of the Lower Temenos between the Central Artery and two more side channels (fig. 4.1, no. 33). One of the channels was excavated to its NE terminus, a large stone basin where water collected and settled before flowing southwest toward the Central Artery (figs. 4.18 and 4.1, nos. 34 and 38). These systems were designed to collect and divert rainwater from the pavement while maintaining the northward march of water from the Upper Temenos to the street.

18 Joukowsky 1999, 2-3.

Fig. 4.20. Ledge in the Central Artery (2002).

The northernmost junction of channels is generally similar to the one beneath the Temple Forecourt except that a stone ledge (fig. 4.20), designed to remove silt and débris from flowing water, is set across the bottom of the Central Artery before it is met by the two side channels. The ledge is simply a rectangular slab (0.20 m high, 0.66 m wide, 0.12 m thick) extending from one wall of the channel to the other. Behind it was found a silty deposit, roughly 0.11 m thick.

Directly north of the junction a slight drop coincides with two stone door jambs built into the NE and NW corners of the intersection and projecting 0.16-0.18 m from the E wall and 0.20 m from the W wall. These jambs originally held a metal or wooden gate or grate designed to control the flow of water through this area and provide further filtration of the water supply. Perhaps this sluice could have been lowered or otherwise sealed to prevent water from exiting the precinct at times of shortage, or it may have been opened and closed to control the supply in case of flooding or back-up in the N part of the system. The main channel first widens from 0.66 to 0.98 m, then contracts to 0.60 m and drops by 0.20 m where water passed through the gate area. The narrowing would have increased the water pressure and speed, but the drop-off may have served instead to slow it. From these features it is clear that the precinct's designers and builders were careful to modulate the speed and volume of water in this area.

The whole intersection originally was probably covered by the same kind of capstones present throughout the temple precinct. A small N–S channel (0.09 m wide, 0.06 m deep) cut into the top of one corner wall seems to be a later modification, perhaps for siphoning off surface water following damage to the system. Just south of the East Propylaeum and in line with the east feeder channel is a settling basin (figs. 4.18 and 4.1, no. 34) for separating out sand and débris. The cylindrical basin (0.78 m across, internal depth 0.52-0.55 m, sides 0.11-0.14 m thick), cut from a single limestone block, was held in place by the fill used to level the area for the pavement, and retains traces of plaster. Water once entered the basin from a surface drain above or slightly to the east (now missing). The basin does not seem to have communicated with the East Artery. A thick slab rests over its south upper lip, blocking it from the direction of the East Artery, the alignment of which suggests it passed close by on the east. It may be that the East Artery terminated north and east of this basin, sending its water southwest where it would have swirled around before rising out to flow toward the Central Artery, leaving behind any accumulated silt and débris in the basin. The channel (0.43-0.44 m wide, 0.50-0.53 max. preserved height) exiting the basin is coated with three layers of waterproof mortar (fig. 4.1, no. 38). Nearby two of its capstones (0.66 x 0.94 m; 0.71 x 0.72 m and 0.17 m thick) remain *in situ*. The channel then disappears beneath Lower Temenos fill, but certainly once connected to the east feeder channel of the Central Artery.

The East Artery followed a trajectory similar to that of the Central Artery. After descending beneath the East Staircase, it entered the SE corner of the Lower Temenos below a surface drain (now missing). Its width here is 0.57 m, almost the same as at the N end of the East Plaza. The East Artery then continued north along the E side of the Lower Temenos. At some point the channel either turned west toward the Central Artery (possibly it once fed into the settling basin mentioned above) or it deposited its water elsewhere (i.e., into the Wadi Musa). Ground Penetrating Radar (GPR) seems to show a straight channel continuing all the way to the N end of the Lower Temenos, disappearing farther east than the basin. In the extreme northeast of the temple precinct some smaller stone-built channels found above the East Cryptoporticus, flowing SW-ENE, may represent one terminus of the East Artery, which could have turned to the east at the end of the Lower Temenos.

Ultimately all excavated channels continued to the N limits of the Lower Temenos before making another drop. The Central Artery continues beneath the main Propylaeum Staircase in a precipitous drop of *c*.7 m detected in 1995 by GPR. Somewhere in this vicinity there may have been a cistern or other storage feature. It is also likely that at least some of the water (perhaps the overflow) continued north through the Propylaeum and under the Colonnaded Street to empty into the Wadi Musa across the road,[19] but this cannot be said for certain without further invasive prospection.

Surface drains

Four intact surface drains remain around the edges of the Lower Temenos (they are visible at the SW corner, the south center, and on the E side), cut into hexagonal pavers (fig. 4.1, no. 32). Nearby subterranean channels confirm the presence of one of the drains on the W side, where it presumably fed the channel in the NW part of the Lower Temenos (fig. 4.1, no. 39). There originally would have been up to 9 or 10 such drains carrying rainwater into channels to the Central and East Arteries. The south-center (with a preserved opening 0.16 m in diameter) and inferred north-center drains would have deposited water directly into the Central Artery. The southernmost drain on the E side was presumably located above or just east of the East Artery where it emerges from the East Stairway. A channel from the second drain on the E side moved water laterally across the Lower Temenos in a NW direction. The corresponding channel on the W side heads east from the second drain (now crushed). Another channel must once have connected the SW surface drain to the Central Artery. A channel (now open) from the next drain north along the W side of the Lower Temenos is 0.80 m deep and 0.37-0.45 m wide; it is spanned by several capstones (one of which is a re-used cornice block, probably signalling a repair). A channel certainly led from the NW drain to feed into the Central artery at its northernmost intersection. The southernmost drain on the W side is the only one preserving its bronze drain fitting, which is hexagonal (33 cm corner to corner, 0.29 across side to side; diam. of opening 0.16 m) like the pavers among which it is set. It rests 15.28 m away from the south-center drain, while the distance between extant drains on the E side is 15.97 m, indicating fairly even spacing around the perimeter of the Lower Temenos. Each drain deposited water into an artery or a smaller tributary channel supplying an artery to create an interconnected system for all rainwater falling on the Lower Temenos; if one channel needed repairs or had become blocked, the others could pick up the slack and maintain the flow and removal of water.

The purpose of this system was to clear excess water accumulating on the surface while collecting and storing an ample supply of clean, potable water. Drains in the Temple Forecourt and Lower

---

19 Payne, vol. 1, 175.

Temenos might seem to have compromised the supply, but many steps were taken to cleanse the rainwater introduced to the system. In the eyes of the ancient Nabataeans, rainwater was clean, pure and free from pollutants. As A. T. Hodge once remarked, "All fresh water begins as rainfall, and ... as rainfall, all water is completely pure."[20] The Nabataean engineers took every step necessary to keep rainwater from becoming polluted, creating systems to filter out impurities as the water flowed. Where rainwater first entered the system in the Lower Temenos, we see an increased sensitivity to its cleanliness in the subterranean canalization system. Although the system was not sealed off from surface water, measures were taken to filter out impurities through settling basins and ledges. The removal of large amounts of winter rainwater from the surfaces of the precinct is one obvious benefit of the system, but that should not be construed as the sole justification for such a massive hydrological undertaking. First, significant rainfall would have occurred only in winter, making the elaborate system unnecessary for much of the year. Second, the flash floods that plagued Petra were of such a magnitude that the drains in the Lower Temenos would play only a small part in their diversion.[21] A larger network of hydrological features throughout the city assisted in minimizing the impact of winter flash floods, relegating localized drains like those in the precinct to the rôle of peripheral damage control. Years of lighter rainfall, on the other hand, demanded comprehensive collection and storage of rainwater. Thus the removal of water, although necessary for the stability of structures, was not the first priority of the Nabataean engineers and builders of the Great Temple. If the volume of water normally building up had been considered especially dangerous, the precinct's cistern would probably have been placed farther north, perhaps in the Lower Temenos, and not near the temple itself where flooding and backing up could occur. Instead, the primary goal of the engineers was to collect and store water for a "rainless day".

Other water features

Also visible throughout the precinct are several above-ground pipes, now preserved in unconnected segments. In the Lower Temenos a lead pipe (surviving segment 10.1 m long, external diam. 0.09-0.10 m, walls *c.*0.03 m thick) ran between the East and West Exedrae at the base of the East-West Retaining Wall (fig. 4.1, no. 35). The stone channel (at least 0.10 m deep, 0.10-0.18 m wide) into which it was set jogs to the north at the midpoint of the E-W Retaining Wall, suggesting that the Central Artery may have tapped its supply. This conduit originated to the east in the Pool and Garden Complex and once supplied water to the Roman-Byzantine Baths next to the West Exedra (fig. 4.1, no. 42). Drilled through the walls of the exedrae, the lead pipe is clearly a later addition of the 2nd c. A.D., contemporary with the construction of the baths.

In front (northeast) of the East Exedra, a segmented ceramic pipe (0.50 m long, diam. 0.08 m), set into a mortar bedding (0.23 m thick) is built into a wall that curves toward the north (fig. 4.1, no. 25). It heads west from the Pool and Garden Complex before turning northwest toward the Middle Stylobate of the East Cryptoporticus. It too probably channeled water west from the adjacent complex in phases VI-VII and perhaps later.

Both lead and ceramic pipes were added to the Pool and Garden Complex at the time of its re-design. The ceramic pipe in the East Cryptoporticus connects to a Roman ceramic pipe set in a long E-W wall transecting the Pool and Garden Complex.[22] This may well be contemporary with the lead piping, a common Roman addition at Petra; where lead pipes are found within the Great Temple precinct they always cut through earlier features. Replastering of the walls through which the lead pipe between the East and West Exedrae is drilled shows that, as modifications were made to the water-supply networks of the Great Temple precinct, great care was taken to preserve its aesthetic integrity.

---

20 A. T. Hodge 2000, 95.

21 Akasheh 2002.

22 Bedal 2002, 226; 2003, 72-76.

Lastly, a length (4.88 m) of stone-cut channel running E–W is visible directly north of the West Exedra (fig. 4.1, no. 48), in which is cut a plastered pipe bedding (0.06 m in diameter, sides 0.09 m high). The now-missing pipe perhaps drew water from the westward-flowing lead pipe between the East and West Exedrae. Slightly farther north several more segments of stone-cut channel are laid out in a S–N orientation, extending through several short walls in their path. The channels (0.27-0.37 m wide) are in 7 intact segments (an eighth is badly damaged), and the pipes set into them would have been between 0.05 and 0.10 m in diameter. They probably belonged to a late phase of modification intended to reroute water supplied by the E–W lead pipe in a northerly direction; no explicit connection to the baths is evident.

Conclusions

While some of the technology for capturing and storing water at Petra may have been borrowed from contemporary cities in the eastern Mediterranean, the limited rainfall and the difficult terrain facing the Nabataeans in their capital spurred them to achieve innovative hydrological feats of their own.[23] In implementing a complex and integrated system throughout the city, the inhabitants relied on built-in contingency plans to ensure the city would not go thirsty should a single component fail. Able to channel water from nearby and distant springs alike, while fastidiously collecting water from winter rains, the Nabataeans amassed a supply to last them through the year, and even longer in case of drought. The Great Cistern within the temple precinct exhibits great virtuosity and illustrates the considerable efforts exerted to store water. Wherever they settled, the Nabataeans were well-attuned to the practical needs of living cities in very dry climates, but at their capital they used their water supply in a variety of creative ways: waterfalls ornamented and cooled public areas, while a large Pool Complex displayed water in an equally breathtaking fashion, a manifestation of both reverence to the gods and exultation at human achievement. When Rome took over Petra, it found little lacking with the city's waterworks. Rome did not revamp or put its own stamp on the urban area to the extent it did at the northern provincial capital of Bostra;[24] rather, the chief results of a prolonged Roman presence at Petra were a nymphaeum (or perhaps two) on the newly paved main street and a bath adjacent to one of the major civic complexes.

The Great Temple's expansive system of hydrological features persisted through several centuries and served multiple functions. Drains did not simply remove run-off: they fed channels that transported clean potable water and stored it for the benefit of the Great Temple complex and other parts of the city center. The drains and channels of the Lower Temenos helped clear the area of excess water accumulation during heavy winter rainfall while also supplementing ground-water sources of fresh water. Painstakingly laid pipes and tightly covered and sealed channels show that the Nabataeans and their successors went to great lengths to safeguard their water from pollution and evaporation. Features in cisterns, settling basins, and ledges show that cleanliness was a priority when dealing both with rainwater and water drawn from springs (Ain Musa and Ain Brak to the south).The Great Cistern was a product of exhaustive efforts to preserve and store as much of this scarce commodity as possible.

Connections to the Pool and Garden Complex show that the temple precinct did not operate in a vacuum but was planned and modified with nearby structures in mind. The water collected and stored in neighboring complexes was used for a variety of purposes, which broadened in the Roman period to include social bathing. The systems were constantly evolving and being modified. A comprehensive and efficient system for the collection, diversion, and storage of water never went out of use during antiquity, even if its precise arrangements underwent periodic reconfiguration; where channels became damaged or blocked, they were repaired or abandoned, with other paths making up the shortfall.

---

23 Ortloff 2005, 108.

24 Dentzer, Blanc and Fournet 2002, 75-154.

5

Moulded elegance: analysis and interpretation of the stucco revetments from the Great Temple

Emily Catherine Egan

In connection with the rapid urbanization of the city center in the 1st c. B.C., surface plastering attained a new prominence in the ornamentation of religious and civic structures along Petra's main thoroughfare. Interior and exterior walls were embellished with delicately painted and intricately carved stucco veneers designed to appeal to the eye while simultaneously protecting the friable rose-red sandstone beneath from erosion.

The Great Temple showcases some of the city's best preserved examples of stucco decoration dating from the 1st c. B.C. to the 1st c. A.D., when the precinct underwent a series of substantial structural and decorative modifications. This chapter will survey the site's rich and diverse stucco corpus and offer interpretation of its place within, and contribution to, local and regional artistic canons.

East 'Cistern' behind the East Exedra

In 1998, excavations in the East 'Cistern' revealed the site's first substantial deposit of painted stucco fragments found mixed in among the lower débris layers. The fragments evidently were not part of the original decoration of the surrounding structure but part of a dump associated with one of the many periods of remodelling at the temple.[1] While some fragments were highly abraded, many retained traces of their original intricate decoration. Two preserve evidence of writing, the first a painted Nabataean inscription and the second an incised Greek graffito. A third fragment depicts part of a man's face, rendered in black outline on a reddish orange ground, with the iris of the eye tinted a pale blue (fig. 5.1).[2]

Fig. 5.1. Plaster painting of a face (cat. no. 98-CO-65, seq. no. 53086, trench 53, locus 2); l. 7.32 cm, w. 4.85 cm, th. 3.26 cm.

West Corridor of the temple

Also in 1998, a large deposit of collapsed plaster fragments was uncovered in the temple's West Corridor. In addition to brightly painted pieces of bead-and-reel, egg-and-tongue, dentils, rosettes, and S-curve mouldings, a large section (*c.*2.8 m long x 1.0 m high) of a plaster panel was discovered *in situ* on the E (interior) face of the W wall (fig. 5.2). The surviving section consists of large yellow and red painted zones embellished by a design in dark purple and green paint suggesting an architectural façade, doorway, or entrance surmounted by a curved lintel.[3]

1 Associated pottery from the East 'Cistern' suggests that the feature functioned as a dump as early as 100 B.C.: Joukowsky 1999, 212.

2 Vol. 2, 358-59.

3 Joukowsky 1999, 214; vol. 2, 359.

Fig. 5.2. *In situ* fresco from the West Corridor depicting an architectural façade (in green) with a curved lintel.

This *in situ* decorated panel generated interest in the materials and methods employed by the ancient artists. During excavation, it became clear that the interior courses of the West Corridor's walls were poorly aligned and the stones were dressed at random in order to create a rough surface into which a layer of foundation plaster (between 0.10 and 0.20 m thick) could be keyed. To strengthen the foundation layer, vegetal material was added to the wet plaster mixture, while dowels and nails lent additional support to large moulded attachments.[4] On top of the foundation plaster, two smooth thin layers of plaster (the first measuring 0.01-0.02 m thick, the second 0.005 m thick) were applied, to which the painted decoration was added as a final step.

Tests conducted by the Institut Canadien de Conservation on 8 fragments of flat stucco painted in hues of green, red, yellow, and blue determined the chemical composition of the plaster medium and pigments. In the laboratory, the samples were first placed in polyester resin and prepared as cross-sections. Next, using an electron microscope equipped with an x-ray energy spectrometer, the different colors on the stucco samples were analyzed for elemental content. Subsequently, the samples were examined by x-ray diffraction to identify the chemical components in both the support and pigment layers.[5] The analyses revealed that the foundation plaster, or support, was composed primarily of sand (quartz), with nominal amounts of calcite and gypsum. The pigments were identified as green earth, red earth, yellow earth, and Egyptian blue. Chemical analysis determined that the painted designs on the upper lime plaster layers were produced using the technique of true (*buon*) fresco, based on the fact that no binding medium (such as egg or plant gum) was detected.[6]

---

4 Dowel holes, fragmentary plastered dowels, and vegetal impressions were all extant in the fragments recovered from the collapse in the West Corridor (Joukowsky 1999, 214).

5 *Institut Canadien de Conservation ARL Report 3379* (1999) 1.

6 Ibid. 1-2.

Fig. 5.3. Proposed decorative program of the West Corridor Wall.

East and West Corridors of the temple

Following the initial discoveries of 1998, stucco fragments were found in 1999 in the central part of the Temple's East Corridor that closely resembled those found in the West Corridor. This suggests that both sides of the temple once featured similar decorative programs. Flat panels and mouldings painted in reds, greens, yellows, and blues were preserved *in situ* on the upper courses of the East Corridor wall, flanking the central doorway, while 147 stucco fragments with similar design and coloring were recovered from adjacent collapse deposits.

As excavations continued in the West Corridor, more of the *in situ* panel found in 1998 was revealed. This discovery allowed conservator U. Bellwald to reconstruct the wall's full decorative program (fig. 5.3). In Bellwald's rendering, the corridor's three exterior doorways are flanked by twin stucco pilasters each containing 6 raised cassettes and supported by a moulded Attic base. The color of the cassettes and their backgrounds alternates between blue and red, and each group of cassettes is contained within a vertical yellow panel. At the top of each pilaster Bellwald reconstructs an engaged Nabataean-Corinthian-style capital supporting a stucco frieze decorated with intertwining vines surmounted by a moulded cornice. The doorways below are framed in bands of green and red. In the wide spaces between the doorways are a series of decorative panels (*c.*2.0 m high) containing either one or three rectangular frames (façades), each crowned by an arched lintel. Above the frames are two horizontal mouldings spanning the distance between the pilasters at either side.

Stylistically, the design of the West Corridor's wall decoration combines elements of Roman stucco relief and trompe l'oeil painting (A. Mau's First and Second Styles).[7] At Petra, the latter style is most familiar from the Nabataean mansion (EZ IV) at Ez Zantur. There, the walls of Room 1 are

7 Mau 1902, 462-64. For more recent discussion of the styles of Roman wall-painting, see Ling 1991 and 1999.

embellished with a series of painted architectural façades that closely resemble the illusionistic wall decorations of Augustan Italy.[8] The visibly 'flatter' style of the paintings in the Great Temple West Corridor, however, is better compared with examples from a cave in Wadi Siyyagh featuring a low frieze of false doorways. This two-dimensional painting style, according to F. Zayadine,[9] is more characteristic of Hellenistic Egypt than Early Imperial Rome, which may suggest that the West Corridor paintings drew inspiration from artistic trends of the 3rd-2nd c. B.C.

In 2000, excavations in the West Corridor revealed additional fragments of moulded stucco cornices, including fragmentary bands of egg-and-tongue, acanthus leaves and vines, and polychrome border fragments.

South Corridor of the temple: panels in situ

Also in 2000, excavations in the temple's South Corridor revealed additional quantities of stucco fragments, including part of a moulded cassette with blue paint and fallen cornice fragments painted blue and white. Subsequently, in 2001, even more extraordinary finds came to light. The first of these were two large *in situ* stucco panels.[10] Located to either side of the central doorway on the N (interior) face of the South Corridor Wall, the panels preserved parts of moulded pilasters similar in design to the examples previously uncovered in the East and West Corridors. The better preserved panel (fig. 5.4), on the W side of the doorway, features three vertical red and dark blue bands, edged by a light blue *cyma reversa* moulding. West of the moulding is a raised flat panel decorated with a vertical vine design composed of connected black spirals on a white ground. West of this panel are a vertical thin white moulding, a black stripe, and a green moulding abutting a recessed dark-blue panel. Farther west again are two vertical mouldings spaced roughly 0.80 m apart that

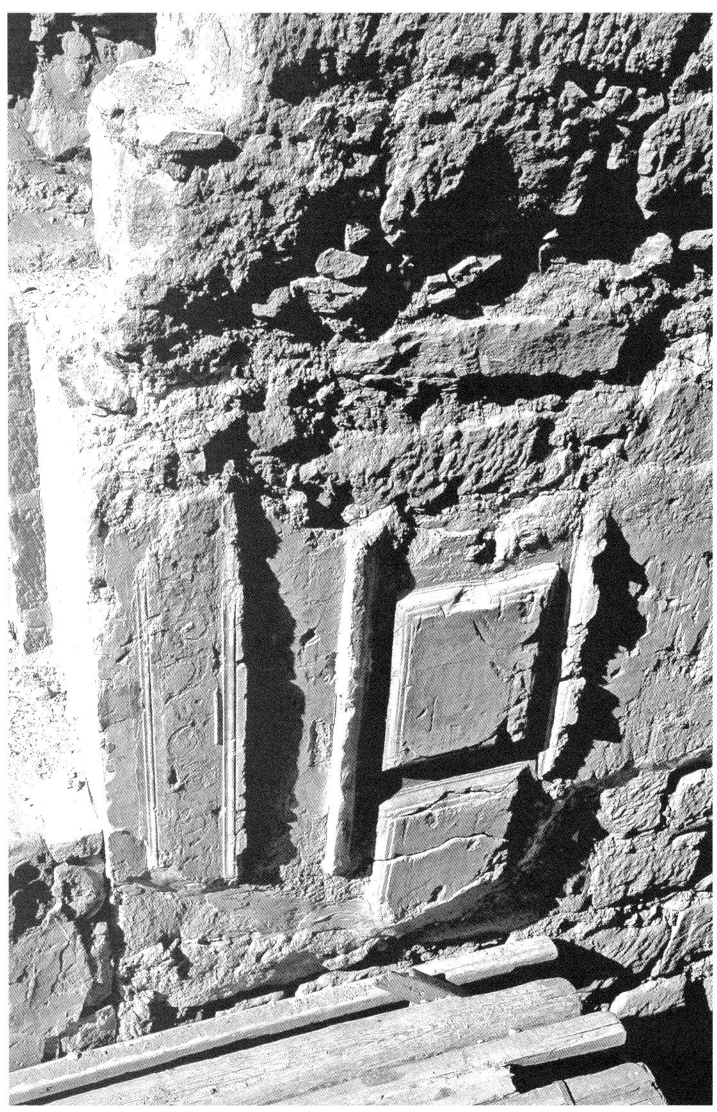

Fig. 5.4. Stucco decoration *in situ* on the South Corridor Wall, west of the central doorway.

8 Kolb 2003, 235-37. Based on ceramic analyses, Kolb and colleagues (2003, 234) assigned Room 1 a *terminus post quem* of A.D. 20.

9 Zayadine 1987, 140-41.

10 For additional discussion of these fragments, including a line drawing of the decoration in fig. 5.4, see Egan 2002, 348-51.

frame the remains of two stucco cassettes, stacked one above the other. The upper cassette (0.60 m wide, 0.72 m high), painted light blue and set in a red panel, is framed by a repeating border of nested black chevrons on a white ground. The center of the cassette has a red lozenge outlined by thin white and black bands, while the incomplete lower cassette, painted light blue and red and contained within a light blue panel, preserves no central decoration.

A number of the motifs in the preserved panels appear to be symbolic. The vine, for example, suggests fecundity. Associated with the Dionysian god Dushares and the Syrian vegetation goddess Atargatis, two primary deities of the Nabataean pantheon, the vine is common in both sacred and secular art, including fineware ceramics dating to the 1st c. A.D. At Siq el-Bared, a suburb of Petra, painted vines are visible in the ceiling decoration of the so-called "Painted House", dated by N. Glueck to the 1st or 2nd c. A.D.[11] Laden with grapes and flowers, these vines wind whimsically across the ceiling, creating a free-flowing tapestry effect. By contrast, the vine pattern in the South Corridor is unadorned and formalized, which seems to suggest a slightly earlier date or a greater influence of Nabataean artistic preferences, which, as argued by P. Hammond,[12] were dominated by the use of symmetry and stylization.

The shape, orientation, and position of the South Corridor's cassettes find close parallels in the reconstruction proposed by Bellwald for the stucco program in the West Corridor. If his design is correct, it is almost certain that the cassettes found in the South Corridor belong to the upper shafts of two pilasters that once framed the corridor's central doorway. In Nabataean architecture, pilasters were common alongside doorways. J. McKenzie[13] has observed that pilasters were a central element of Nabataean façade decoration, probably first reaching Petra during the Hellenistic period. Segmented stucco pilasters with alternating circular and octagonal mouldings are featured on the E and W *antae* of the Qasr al-Bint, constructed, according to Larché and F. Zayadine,[14] between the late 1st c. B.C. and early 1st c. A.D. Segmented pilasters are also visible in the Second-Style wall-paintings of the mansion at Ez Zantur, where in EZ IV, Room 1 *trompe l'oeil* pilasters are painted at the corners of Walls A and C, 'supporting' a painted cornice that extends around the room.[15] Although rendered in only two dimensions, the Ez Zantur pilasters, like the South Corridor examples, also feature large decorative lozenges. The excavators at Ez Zantur interpreted this and other geometric elements in Room 1 as painted imitations of *opus sectile*,[16] and the same may have been the intended effect of the decoration on the Great Temple's cassettes, the polychromy of which may have also simulated a variety of imported stones.

Stone (as opposed to stucco) pilasters also abound at Petra. The best parallels for the South Corridor examples can be found in a decorated niche at the rear of "Room 468" cut into the E face of Jebel ed-Deir during the first half of the 1st c. A.D.[17] This carving preserves 4 pilasters, two marking the edge of the outer façade and two flanking the interior niche.[18] The outer pilasters are segmented, each carved into a series of 6 raised cassettes set between two *cyma reversa* mouldings. The inner pilasters are smaller and deeper set, with no raised embellishment. Notably, the effect of this arrangement is also evident in the South Corridor, which features outer pilasters (segmented with cassettes and defined at either edge by the deep cyma reversa mouldings) as well as possible inner pilasters (smooth with a painted vine design and defined by two shallow cyma reversa mouldings). The sunken dark blue panel between the pilasters may be interpreted as a deliberate

11 Glueck 1956, 14-23.
12 Hammond 1973, 83.
13 McKenzie 1990, 88.
14 Larché and Zayadine 2003, 201.
15 Kolb 2003, fig. 260.
16 Ibid. 235 and fig. 259.
17 McKenzie 1990, 150-51, pls. 111-12.
18 Ibid. 1990, pl. 112.

depiction of negative space, as it serves to enhance the three-dimensional projection of the pilasters by visually depressing the area between them.[19]

Another comparison for the Great Temple's pilasters comes from Herod's Northern Palace at Masada. On the lowest terrace a large hall ("Banqueting Hall 1") of the late 1st c. B.C. is richly appointed with painted decoration.[20] The socle band, which wraps around the base of the wall, features large lozenges that match ours in color, framing, and orientation.[21]

In general, the South Corridor's decoration seems to be an amalgam of local and imported designs, but the precise mimicry of the lozenge motif suggests that the program is more Roman than Nabataean. Indeed, Herod's Northern Palace should be slightly earlier than the Great Temple in the 1st c. B.C., so there may be a direct (or indirect) Herodian or Roman influence on the decoration of the latter.[22] Alternatively, the South Corridor may have witnessed a thoroughly "Roman" redecoration. In the second half of the 1st c. A.D. the interior decoration of the nearby Temple of the Winged Lions was overhauled: Hellenistic motifs were replaced by appliqué floral motifs, and columns were embellished by red painted diamonds and blue and black lines.[23] Possibly, following increased Roman influence in the area, some painted motifs, including the lozenges and winding vine, may have been added over the unadorned Nabataean mouldings in the South Corridor. This could account for the differences in color scheme and the absence of the lozenge motif from the fragmentary moulded cassettes uncovered in the West Corridor and reconstructed by Bellwald.[24] The side passages, perhaps now less important because of new circulation patterns inside the temple, may not have been considered a priority for redecoration and as a result retained their original Nabataean design.

South Corridor of the temple: collapsed stucco revetments and cornices

In addition to the *in situ* panels, over 350 collapsed fragments of wall revetment were recovered from the Great Temple's South Corridor. Most are painted shades of blue, red, and purplish-black and have a smooth surface. Unpainted, amorphous fragments were also found in abundance: presumably, they represent coarse foundation plaster broken away from the fine, painted surface. Collectively, these fragments preserve a number of patterns from which larger decorative schemes can be inferred.

Eleven variations of cornice, differentiated primarily by color pattern and the precise arrangement of moulded components, are discernible among the stucco fragments.[25] Three main cornice types can be reconstructed:

1. A thin band of yellow egg-and-tongue, above three thin *cyma reversa* mouldings of white, red, and blue, over large square dentils, above a medium-sized band of egg-and-tongue, over a double unpainted *cyma reversa* moulding (fig. 5.5).

---

19 Ibid. 98-99, for further discussion of the use of blue paint in Alexandrian tombs and Second Style wall painting as a device to enhance perspective.

20 Foerster 1997, 68-71; 1995, xviii.

21 Yadin 1988, 49; Foerster 1995, 13-18 and col. pl. 10. For a recent discussion of Herodian painting styles and execution, with relevant bibliography, see Rozenberg 2009.

22 The possibility of a Herodian presence in Petra is also cited by Hammond (1996, 61), in reference to stylistic parallels between the First Style stucco decoration at the Temple of the Winged Lions and that seen in the Herodian repertoire.

23 Hammond (1996, 14 and 78) dates this remodeling at the Temple of the Winged Lions to early in the reign of Malichus II (A.D. 40-70), well past the beginning of formal Roman presence in the region in 64 B.C. Hammond suggests that the motivation behind the plaster redecoration was to "remove the more strictly Hellenistic ritualistic decoration and replace it with simple painted panels, indicating cultic or socio-political expressions," perhaps a sign of the influence of a new people such as the Romans.

24 During restoration of the West Corridor's stucco cassettes in 1999, work was also done on the South Corridor's W doorway, where Bellwald found sufficient evidence to restore the cassettes in the same manner as those in the West Corridor, again with the central lozenges absent.

25 For a detailed discussion of each of the 11 cornice styles, see Egan 2002, 352 (Table 1).

2. A wide band with decorative vegetal elements, above a thin egg-and-tongue band, over a smooth band that terminates in a drip cornice.

3. A simple egg-and-tongue band, above 4 smooth bands. This type is further differentiated by its unusual curvature. The largest fragment curves c.20° from vertical and may be part of what McKenzie[26] terms a semicircular arched "Syrian style" entablature.[27] Parallels for semicircular arched entablatures include the banded arch over the façade of Tomb 154 in Petra and the carved arch, decorated with an oversize egg-and-tongue pattern, of Tomb E17 at Medain Saleh.[28] Alternatively, the curved cornice may originally have been part of a "segmental" pediment, which McKenzie defines as one that involves "a curve which is a segment of a circle or a section of an ellipse, rather than a semicircle".[29] At Petra, rock-cut examples of such pediments with plain banded decoration are visible over the second doorway from the north of the Corinthian Tomb,[30] above the flanking niches on the lower orders of the Palace Tomb,[31] and crowning the Renaissance Tomb.[32] Segmental entablatures and pediments with carved dentils include those on the second order of the rock-cut façade of the Tomb of Sextius Florentinus (A.D. 129),[33] and on the plaster façade of the exterior S wall of the Qasr al-Bint.[34] At Medain Saleh, the entrances to tombs B19, C14 and A6, all dated to the 1st c. A.D., contain plain-carved segmental pediments (with no internal banding), supported at either end by carved pilasters.[35]

Fig. 5.5. Cornice fragment from South Corridor.

In order to integrate the three cornice types from the Great Temple's South Corridor into a single architectural program, the first two must be reconciled. Because the edges of the fragments are not finished, it would be possible to join the thin egg-and-tongue band at the top of the first type to the drip cornice at the base of the second type, yielding an immense triple egg-and-tongue cornice characteristic of eastern Ionic entablatures.[36] This reconstruction would also allow for the inclusion of the small, 5-petalled,[37] moulded yellow flowers which were found associated with the cornice elements in the débris. A versatile decorative motif, flowers have been documented widely at Petra; they are most prominently displayed in metope fields, such as those from the Doric frieze

26 McKenzie 1990, 184 and 193, diagram 18b.

27 For comparison, see the pediment drawn by C. S. Fisher of the E exterior façade of the Nabataean Temple at Khirbet Tannur, period III (Glueck 1965, Plan B). The temple is dated by Glueck (ibid. 138) to the first quarter of the 2nd c. A.D., probably contemporary with the Roman annexation of Petra. In his plan, Fisher places an arched stone cornice over the entrance, anchored at either end to a band cornice extending along the front of the temple.

28 McKenzie 1990, pls. 156b and c and 9d.

29 Ibid. 88-89.

30 Ibid. pl. 118b.

31 Ibid. pl. 145.

32 Ibid. pl. 154.

33 Ibid. pls. 151-52.

34 Larché and Zayadine 2003, 201, fig. 214.

35 McKenzie 1990, pls. 11c-d and 18c.

36 Ibid. 191.

37 This number is somewhat unusual in Petra, where 6-petalled flowers are preferred. Five-petal examples are known, however, in the decoration of the E façade at Khirbet Tannur and in the upper order of the Corinthian capitals of the colonnades of the Great Temple itself; see vol. 1, 227, fig. 5.44.

of the Qasr al-Bint,[38] but the small size and delicate nature of the examples from the South Corridor suggest that they were used instead to embellish the underside of the drip cornice.

An elaborate cornice with flowers and three tiers of egg-and-tongue would have been well-suited to the South Corridor, which served as a primary access point to shrines at the rear of the temple precinct. Such a massive moulding would also have been structurally feasible; most of the fragments are more than 0.15 m thick, enabling them to be anchored securely to the rough surface of the interior face of the wall. While no parallels exist in Nabataean architecture for a triple egg-and-tongue cornice, large and elaborate double egg-and-tongue cornices are common. Influenced by both Hellenistic and Roman models, the double egg-and-tongue style cornice is found on top of the central doorway of the vestibule of al-Khazna,[39] where egg-and-tongue bands are separated by a band of painted dentils drawn in the long, narrow style traditionally considered Hellenistic. A second cornice in this attenuated Hellenistic style is the pillar capital from the north arch of the Temenos Gate, which shows fully carved dentils.[40] By contrast, the dentils in the South Corridor are more squared, suggesting the use of Roman models.

Based on known comparanda, there seem to be three possibilities for the original placement of the cornice fragments within the South Corridor. The first is uninterrupted along the uppermost portion of the N face of the South Corridor Wall. This would coincide with Bellwald's reconstruction of the revetment in the West Corridor (fig. 5.3), which features a stucco cornice at the very top of the entablature supported by the pilasters. The second option is to split the cornice into two sections along the S wall, with one part extending between the east and center doorways and the other between the center and west doorways. In this arrangement, the two bands extending above the pilasters would have converged in the middle of the corridor, terminating in a semicircular arch over the central doorway like the one in the proposed façade of the Khirbet Tannur temple in period III. Although both of these scenarios are possible, the third and most likely position for the cornices in the South Corridor is over each of the three doorways (fig. 5.6). The strongest evidence for this reconstruction comes from the combined length of the recovered cornice fragments (3.23 m), which approximates the combined lengths of the east and central doorways (3.76 m) (the west doorway was outside the excavated trench). Comparanda for this arrangement include the Temenos Gate and al Khazna, both of which feature elaborately carved cornices prominently positioned over entryways.

The placement of the cornices over the South Corridor's doorways also works well in combination with the arched cornice fragment. While a curved entablature connecting the two halves of a split cornice is not difficult to imagine if one has the Khirbet Tannur temple reconstruction in mind, it is difficult to orient such a program around the South Corridor's pilasters. As illustrated by the Khirbet Tannur example, curved elements associated with split cornices typically extend a significant distance above the entablature.[41] If, however, the height of the South Corridor's S wall is identical to that restored for the West Corridor's W wall, there would not have been room for an arch in this position. Indeed, such an arrangement would have been possibly only if either:

A. The S wall of the temple was much higher than projected, possibly to support the rear of the theater structure; or

B. The 6 raised cassettes carved into the outer pilasters began at the base of the pilasters, rather than one-third of the way up the shaft (as they do in Bellwald's reconstruction), thereby diminishing the latter's height.

However, as there is no precedent for the pilasters to begin their carved decoration at floor level, and as it is unlikely that the rear wall of the temple was considerably higher than projected, instead

38 Larché and Zayadine 2003, 203, fig. 218.

39 McKenzie 1990, pl. 23d.

40 Ibid. pl. 37e.

41 Glueck 1965, Plan B.

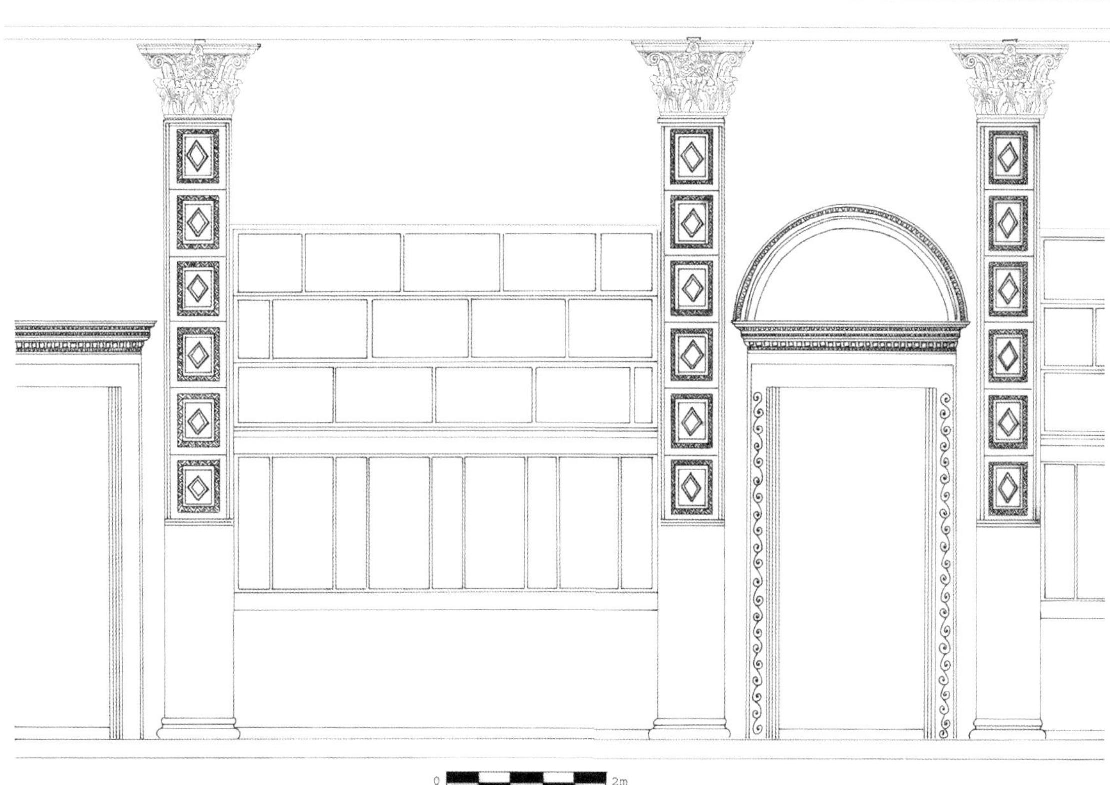

Fig. 5.6. Author's reconstruction of the decorative program of the South Corridor Wall, N face.

of extending over the tops of the segmented pilasters the arched cornice is most likely to have been placed over the central doorway, its ends resting on the cornice band and above the inner, vine-decorated pilasters (fig. 5.6).

South Corridor of the Temple: "marbled" fragments

Sizeable bits of smooth plaster painted to resemble blocks of cut stone were also recovered from the South Corridor. Two large joining fragments (fig. 5.7) best illustrate the marbling technique. They display a cloud-like vein pattern consisting of concentric purple rings edged in blue on a white background. The design is probably an imitation of the curved banding in alabaster, agate, or a type of veined marble. Wall-plaster, carved and painted to imitate stonework was common as an ancient decorative device, originating in Greece in the 4th c. and spreading around the Mediterranean world by the 2nd c. B.C.[42] Referred to generally as the "Masonry Style", this wall treatment traditionally consisted of stucco ashlar blocks modeled in low relief with "the margins of the blocks having been recessed in the manner of undressed, or 'drafted' masonry; colors are applied to suggest the use of different types of stone".[43] Such grooved margins are visible in a number of the South Corridor's marbled fragments, including the two noted above, which form part of a rectangular "block" measuring *c.*0.55 m in height.

In the Mediterranean, drafted stucco masonry typically falls into two stylistic categories: that used in the West (e.g., at Pompeii and Herculaneum) and that used in the East (e.g., on the Greek

42 Ling 1991, 12-22.

43 Ibid. 12. Examples of this type of stucco masonry are clearly visible in Rooms 2 and 3 of the Ez Zantur (EZ IV) mansion, which includes blocks painted in bright hues of red and yellow: Kolb 2003, 234-35 and figs. 257-58.

Fig. 5.7. Marbled plaster from the South Corridor wall.

islands and at sites in W Asia Minor and Egypt). As described by R. Ling, the eastern style, which is dated earlier than the western, is designed to resemble exterior masonry. In a rigid schema, the base of the wall consists of a narrow plinth. Above this are large square or rectangular panels under a thin string course, topped by a series of isodomic courses.[44] In addition to its structural realism, the eastern type adheres closely to natural coloration patterns, habitually tinting each course a single color in emulation of a known stone. Decorative marbling occurs frequently but is confined mainly to the string course and, less often, to the larger panels.[45] The western style (the "First Pompeian" Style) is more innovative. At the wall's base is a large, tall socle below a thin string course. Above this is a series of narrow vertical rectangular panels, then a thin frieze and a series of isodomic courses surmounted by an upper frieze. A moulded cornice often appears above both the lower and upper friezes.[46] The color scheme of the western style is erratic, and, unlike the monochromatic courses of the eastern style, it sees freer use of polychrome decoration. As Ling explains:

> Blocks in the same course can be painted in different colours, often apparently in quite random sequence, while the variegated effects of coloured marble or alabaster, confined in eastern versions principally to the orthostats and frieze-zone, are scattered through all levels of the decoration.[47]

Due to the paucity of large stucco panels from the South Corridor, it is difficult to tell whether the marbled fragments belong to the eastern or western tradition, or alternatively to some unique local schema. Some assistance, however, is offered by the fragments' archaeological context, which indicates their original position on the wall. Found in fill *c.*4 m above the floor, the marbled fragments would have rested at the level of either style's isodomic courses. Because the rigidity of the eastern style generally precludes the presence of a marbled panel in the upper isodomic courses, a western-style decorative program is more likely, and is the type represented in fig. 5.6. Intriguingly, this arrangement is also visible in the stucco decoration in Ez Zantur Room 3, which has *in situ* painted orthostat panels beneath an overlying string course and an isodomic band.[48]

South Corridor of the temple: moulded lions

Perhaps the most dramatic stucco elements from the Great Temple South Corridor are the fragments of moulded lions. The fragments, deriving from what seem to have been two sculpted lion

44 Ling 1991, 13.
45 Ibid. 13.
46 Ibid. 13-17.
47 Ibid. 16.
48 Kolb 2003, 234, fig. 257.

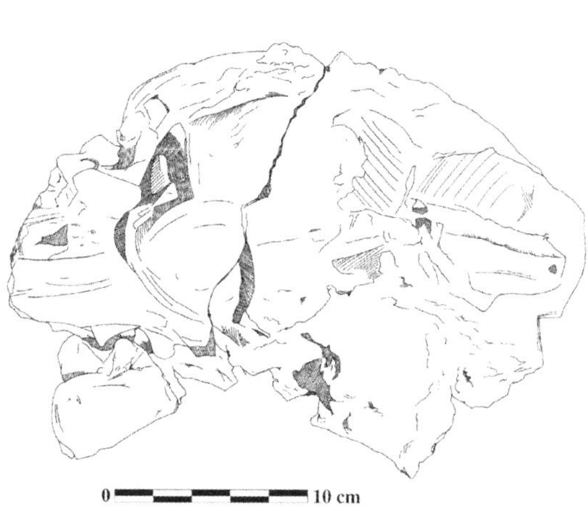

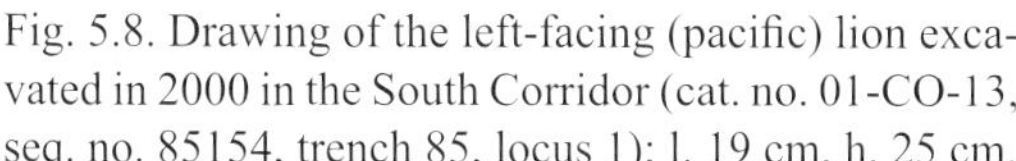

Fig. 5.8. Drawing of the left-facing (pacific) lion excavated in 2000 in the South Corridor (cat. no. 01-CO-13, seq. no. 85154, trench 85, locus 1); l. 19 cm, h. 25 cm.

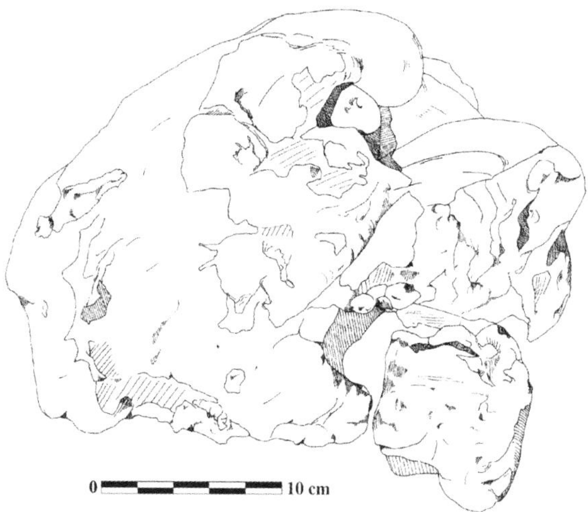

Fig. 5.9. Drawing of the right-facing (snarling) lion excavated in 2000 in the South Corridor (cat. no. 01-CO-12, seq. no. 85220, trench 85, locus 1); l. 34 cm, h. 24 cm.

Fig. 5.10a-b. Plaster lions' heads from the South Corridor, after cleaning.

protomes, include two heads (one facing left [fig. 5.8 and 5.10a], one facing right [fig. 5.9 and 5.10b]), two fragments of mane or fur, and a small paw carved almost fully in the round. To judge from the dowel holes in the backs of the head fragments, the lions were probably affixed to the N face of the South Corridor Wall, rather than being carved *in situ*. The high quality of the carving, particularly evident in the lions' facial features, shows the beasts' importance within the temple's decoration and is a testament to the craftsman's (or craftsmen's) skill. Physically, the two lion heads are very similar, and both of the animals' rounded jaws and fleshy noses (particularly evident on the right-facing lion) closely resemble the features of the lions affixed to the exterior cornices at Qasr Rabbah.[49] Each lion, however, has a distinctive personality. The left-facing lion appears to be the more pacific of the two and probably represents a female.[50] Carved in profile and broken into two pieces, this lion retains traces of blue paint on its eye, flecks of red on its bared tongue, and has two deep cuts at the back and base of its head where additional pieces of plaster (perhaps belonging to the beast's neck?) were attached. Impressions of reeds survive in the upper cut, indicating the use of vegetal matter to reinforce the plaster applied to the surface of the head. The eye of this lion is set deeply beneath a thin, arching brow and over a prominent, rounded cheek. The right-facing lion has a noticeably larger

49 Glueck 1965, pl. 164a-b.

50 I thank D. Qublan for this suggestion. It is equally possible, however, that the differences between the two lion heads are not indicative of the animals' sexes but reflect different artistic styles.

Fig. 5.11. Author's reconstruction of stucco lions on the South Corridor Wall, to either side of the central doorway.

face and seems to be a male. Its forehead arches upward and the eye is set deeply beneath a thick, rounded brow. While the left-facing lion is shown in direct profile, this lion is carved in a near three-quarters' view, with its head turned slightly outward. Its jaw, unlike the other lion's, is detached from the head and no paint is preserved on the tongue. Muzzle and forehead arch upward, as does the flesh of the mouth, curling around the nose in a half snarl. The rough, worn plaster at the back of the head suggests an original overlay of a mane or some other decorative attachment.

Judging from their position in the fill, the lion heads seem to have been placed prominently to either side of the central doorway (fig. 5.11). Flanking the doorway, the two lions may have been apotropaic. With open mouths and bared teeth, the animals may have provided symbolic protection for the temple, while simultaneously promoting a sense of power and majesty similar to that created by the elephant heads on the capitals of the temple's Triple Colonnades. Lions posed as guardians are seen predominantly in regional tomb architecture; they include the carved striding examples flanking the doorway to Petra's Lion *Triclinium*[51] and those sitting above the entablature of Tomb B17 at Medain Saleh.[52] Carved lion heads also appear in the form of gargoyles and fountain fixtures in high relief at Khirbet Tannur and Qasr Rabbah, where each beast bares its menacing fangs.[53] Alternatively, the South Corridor lions may have been representations of the consorts of the Syrian vegetation goddess, Atargatis,[54] who was commonly depicted in the company of such beasts in Hellenistic "Nabataean-Syrian-Parthian" cult iconography.[55] Clearer are the striking similarities in the physical characteristics and craftsmanship between the South Corridor lions and those carved on an Atargatis *stele* from Khirbet Tannur.[56] As described by N. Glueck, the latter lions, seated to either side of the enthroned deity, each possess a "low sloping forehead, deeply grooved eyes with protruding irises and perforated pupils, rounded cheeks, [and] flattened nose with flaring nostrils",[57] physical traits all readily visible in the Great Temple examples. Third, the use of lion-headed torques at Khirbet Tannur to adorn statues of deities may suggest that the South Corridor lions served as divine symbols. A twisted neck decoration perhaps borrowed by the Nabataeans from the Scythians, the torque appeared prominently around the neck of at least one statue of Zeus-Hadad, as well as on busts of Tyche and Atargatis.[58] Due to the ubiquity of the lion torque at Khirbet Tannur, Glueck reasoned that it was used as an "ornament of divine power rather than a symbol associated with a particular god".[59] This may be a more plausible reading of the South Corridor lions: they served to reinforce the sacred character of the rear of the temple without linking it exclusively to a single deity.

The "Baroque Room": stucco revetment

In 2002, excavations in a series of interconnected rooms at the SW corner of the temple precinct produced a second spectacular cache of stucco revetment. The most striking pieces came from the "Baroque Room" (4.50 x 3.67 m) built up against the bedrock at the temple's southern perimeter.[60] The fill of this room contained hundreds of fragments of brightly painted stucco in the form of moulded vegetal elements, cornices, and stacked modillions, all exquisitely rendered in fine detail (fig. 5.12). One larger fragment (almost 0.20 m in length) depicts the capital of an Ionic column (fig. 5.13). Painted in hues of red and light blue, the curved volutes and delicate flutes replicate the architectural detail characteristic of Second Style wall-painting.[61] A large number of solid-colored pieces accented by white lines were also recovered from the fill. Painted hues of red, yellow and deep blue, these fragments probably comprised a background field — the thin white lines serving to divide parts of the room's composition into panels.

Moulded elements may also have been applied to the surface of the wall-paintings, creating a multi-dimensional image. Such elements present in the collapse include cornices, egg-and-tongue bands, acanthus leaves, a cluster of grapes, and a miniature rounded column shaft and capital with

---

51 McKenzie 1990, pl. 135.

52 Ibid. pl. 10c.

53 Glueck 1965, 286, pls. 163b-c and 164a-b.

54 Glueck (ibid. 286) also mentions to the possibility that lions may represent the goddess Atargatis herself and not just her consorts. Due to the non-representational character of Nabataean art, animals or amorphous shapes often served as 'stand-ins' for the true forms of the gods or goddesses themselves.

55 Ibid. 207.

56 Ibid. pl. 161.

57 Ibid. 270.

58 Ibid. 206-7.

59 Ibid. 270.

60 Vol. 2, 185-91.

61 Parallels for the Ionic capital, with its drooping band connecting two curled volutes that abut the abacus, exist in *Cubiculum* 16 of the Villa of the Mysteries, *Cubiculum* M of the Villa of P. Fannius Sinistor at Boscoreale, and in Rooms 15 and 23 and *Triclinium* 14 at Oplontis.

Fig. 5.12. Collapsed stucco in the "Baroque Room", looking south

Fig. 5.13. Painted Ionic column in the "Baroque Room".

a decorative vine design.[62] The larger elements may have been arranged to replicate architectural façades, enhancing the effect of the painted Ionic column. One lavish section of moulding includes two adjacent bands of egg-and-tongue, one squared and one in the shape of a triangle. To judge from Pompeian parallels,[63] it was probably part of an ornamental border from either a wall panel or a ceiling coffer incorporated into the stuccowork as a framing element. The large, tiered cornices with stacked modillions were likely affixed to the uppermost portions of the walls, concealing the masonry seams between walls and ceiling and allowing the flow of moulded and frescoed designs to continue uninterrupted.

The "Baroque Room": ceiling medallion

Perhaps the most stunning stucco discovery at the Great Temple is an ornate circular (over 1.0 m diam.) ceiling medallion (fig. 5.14), discovered in the E part of the Baroque Room, right side up and resting on a substantial bed of earth. Based on the position of the fragments in the room's fill, it appears that in a relatively early period of destruction (probably the pre-106 A.D. destructions of Site Phase VI) the panel slid off the ceiling, dangled from the reeds or wires once supporting it, and flipped to land upright on the accumulated débris beneath.[64] Following its discovery, the collapsed medallion was carefully re-assembled by Bellwald (fig. 5.15), who affixed the individual fragments to a wire honeycomb

---

62 Vol. 2, 188, figs. 4.80-4.81.

63 See especially the moulded ceiling panels from the House of the Cryptoporticus: Ling 1999, 24-57.

64 Joukowsky 2003, 400.

Fig. 5.14. Reconstruction of central medallion in the "Baroque Room" (by U. Bellwald, restorer).

Fig. 5.15. Ceiling fragments of the "Baroque Room" during restoration.

frame using a water soluble plaster adhesive. At the center of the composition is an open-centered pomegranate (or possibly a blossoming poppy), surrounded by a ring of outward-curling acanthus leaves framed by an 8-pointed star composed of bands of egg-and-tongue, tongue alone, and smooth raised mouldings. Enclosing the star are concentric rings with similar moulded patterns. In between the pointed vertices and the innermost ring border are 8 lobe-shaped fields, each featuring bands of tongues wrapped around short stretches of egg-and-tongue. The medallion's moulded surface retains traces of red and blue paint, as well as gilding.

The medallion's compositional elements are well represented in the local artistic repertoire. The round, bulbous pomegranate or poppy at the center with its star-shaped opening and surrounding acanthus blossom is a familiar symbol of fecundity. In Nabataean art the pomegranate and acanthus feature prominently in decorative vegetal fields, including that behind the head of Atargatis on a semicircular panel from the temple at Khirbet Tannur,[65] as well as in the capitals and friezes of the Great Temple's Corinthian order. The bands of egg-and-tongue, tongue alone, and smooth raised mouldings enclosing the central field are also prominent motifs in the stucco cornices of the South Corridor, but the bands of the Baroque Room medallion are far more elaborate, intersecting to create fields that overflow with moulded decoration. Extravagant in its overall effect, this arrangement, best represented by its interlocking tongue designs and star-shaped octagonal framing, contrasts sharply with the more conventional patterns found inside the walls of the temple proper. While local comparanda for the individual features of the medallion abound, the overall composition remains stylistically unique.[66] Instead, it finds its closest parallels in Roman art of the late 1st c. B.C. At Pompeii, circular medallions similar in style and execution are found on the vaulted ceilings of the baths in the House of the Cryptoporticus, where excavators unearthed a circular medallion containing an 8-pointed star composed of bands of egg-and-tongue. The fields surrounding the star are embellished with acanthus flowers, and the entire composition is ringed by a band of moulded tongues.[67]

Conclusions

Collectively, the many fragments of stucco revetment found both *in situ* on the walls and collapsed in the fill of the Great Temple create a vivid picture of the grand edifice they once adorned. Drawing upon a wide range of local and foreign influences, painted and moulded components including pilasters, cornices, lions, and pomegranates provide a deeper understanding of the values and aesthetic preferences of local patrons, highlight the talents of local artisans, and serve as a further testament to the building's innovative spirit.

65 Glueck 1965, 143.

66 In the Nabataean canon, raised circular forms appear on building façades as Doric frieze decorations (e.g., the plain ones carved in the metopes of the ed-Deir monument, the Urn Tomb, the Obelisk Tomb, the Tomb of the Roman Soldier, and smaller tombs at Beidha and Medain Saleh), but the use of circles as medallions complete with interior embellishment is much less common (McKenzie 1990, pls. 138, 40b, 119b and 98b). Moulded plaster circles decorate the pilasters of the N, E and W façades of the Qasr al-Bint, but they lack decoration in their central fields (ibid. pls. 67a-b).

67 Ling 1999, 30-33, pl. XIb. In the Roman East, similar mouldings have been found at the Herodian palace at Jericho: Rozenberg 1996, 126 and figs. 21-23.

6

Sculpted relief panels from the Great Temple

Joseph J. Basile

The Great Temple and its various subordinate structures were richly decorated with sculpture both in relief and in-the-round, frescoes, moulded plaster, and tessellated pavements. These embellishments were added to and altered in the various redesign phases of the complex. Some of them, such as the elephant-head capitals of the Lower Temenos courtyard, the moulded and painted plaster decorating the interior passageways of the Great Temple and the small rooms to the south of it, or the free-standing *betyls* recovered from a niche in the NE corner of the cryptoportico of the Lower Temenos, number among the most accomplished examples of architectural decoration from Hellenistic and Roman Jordan; so too are fragments from a number of monumental panels of limestone and sandstone, worked in low relief.[1] These panels, depicting male and female figures as well as objects such as triumphal wreaths, form an important element in the overall decorative scheme. This chapter will briefly describe the various panel fragments and the circumstances of their recovery before reconsidering how, when, and why Nabataeans decorated the Great Temple, using information based upon a re-examination and documentation of the panels undertaken in 2006 by the author and a team from the Maryland Institute College of Art.[2]

The group

The relief fragments exhibit a variety of characteristics but several can be placed in a single group based on the material, style of execution, and circumstances of recovery. Specifically, nine relief sculpture fragments recovered from the Great Temple site and one that had been placed alongside the Colonnaded Street just below the Lower Temenos seem to have been part of the same decorative program. All are of the same material (a medium-to fine-grained limestone) and are worked in a similar low-relief technique, and most can be reconstructed as having originally been approximately the same size. Most share key characteristics such as a *cyma reversa* frame with fillet. Most depict human figures (both male and female) while one well-preserved panel and one fragment depict wreaths of leaves. Several of the figural reliefs preserve slots cut to insert the head, made in a separate piece (and perhaps executed in a different material, such as marble). They depict male and female forms in a heavy but naturalistic style. The iconography seems classicizing, as is the costume. All exhibit weathering and damage, and some seem to have been cut down into square blocks or "strips" from original dimensions of perhaps *c.*85-90 cm in width and *c.*60-65 cm in height. Almost all were recovered from the eastern part of the Lower Temenos, where several were re-used in later installations in the East Triple Colonnade and East Exedra. The panels will be considered in the order of their recovery.

1 (figs. 6.1-6.2). 86 cm wide, 24 cm high, 52 cm thick. Excavated in 1997 by the author in late fill of the Lower Temenos courtyard, just north of the East-West Retaining (terrace) Wall.[3] It had been sawn or chiseled widthwise into a narrow strip, probably for re-use, but it preserves almost its full original width (*cyma reversa* borders remain at both the right and left edges).

Upper portion of a nude male torso, with heavy, almost pendulous, pectoral muscles and rounded shoulders. A strap or baldric, sculpted as a raised band against the surface of the torso, runs diagonally between the pectorals from over the proper right shoulder to beneath the left breast. Between the pectorals, at what is now the lower edge, is a damaged cylindrical element, with a bump or

1 These objects and other artifactual material from the Great Temple are amply published in annual excavation reports in *ADAJ* by M. S. Joukowsky, as well as in vol. 2; Joukowsky 1998b, 133-48; Basile 2002b, 255-58; and at <www.brown.edu/Departments/joukowsky_institute/Petra>

2 Previously the most complete publication was Basile 2002a.

3 Schluntz, vol. 1, 231-32; Joukowsky 1998b, 298, fig. 8; Schluntz 1999, 69-72; Basile 2002a, 331-33, figs. 1-2.

Figs. 6.1-6.2. Nude male torso with *chlamys* and baldric.

knob at the top, which may represent the pommel and part of the grip of a sword/dagger or the top of a staff/wand.[4] Hung over the proper left shoulder is a bunched garment with deeply-cut folds, perhaps a riding cloak (*chlamys*). Too little is preserved to be certain of the identification.[5]

---

4 Wenning 2004, 166.

5 If the figural panels depict deities, personifications and/or mythological figures, the iconography might perhaps suggest one of the Dioskouroi, Apollo, Ares or Hermes. However, Wenning (ibid. 165-66) is highly critical of a number of conclusions in Basile 2002a, including identifications of panel subjects, although the author was careful to state (p. 333) that identifications were tentative and in most cases impossible to

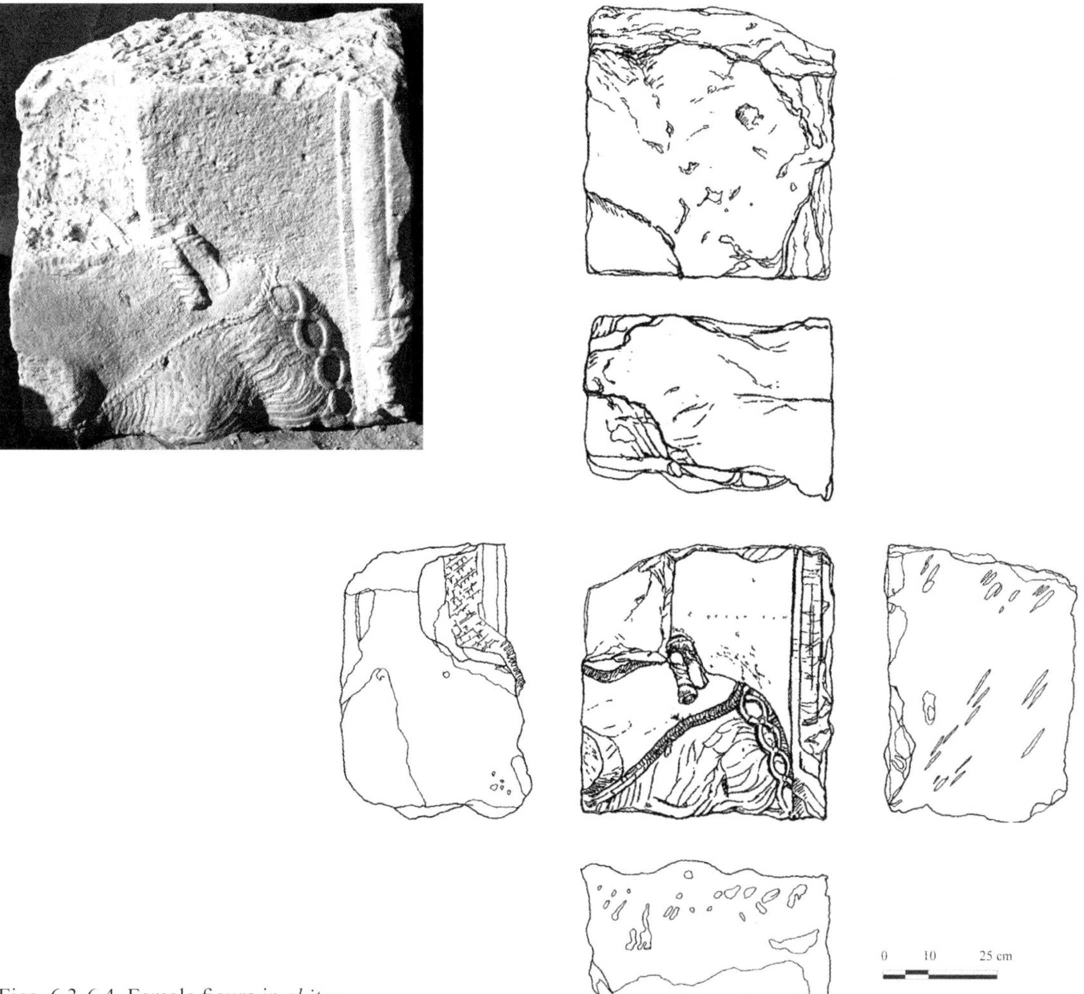

Figs. 6.3-6.4. Female figure in *chiton*.

2 (figs. 6.3-6.4). 53 cm wide, 49 cm high, 21 cm thick. Excavated in 1997 by E. Schluntz and D. Qublan from within a rough, probably Late Roman, wall (which included a number of re-used architectural fragments and evidence of re-plastering) built between the columns of the middle row of the East Triple Colonnade of the Lower Temenos (fig. 6.5). It had been sawn or chiselled into a square shape for re-use.[6]

Proper left side of a female figure, clad in an elaborately depicted *chiton, vel sim.* Neckline has

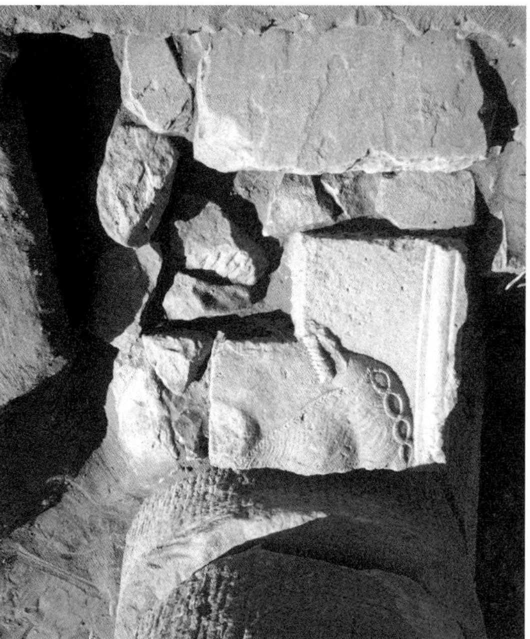

Fig. 6.5. Female figure in *chiton*, still *in situ*.

verify due to problems of preservation. Still, it is true that captions to illustrations assigned "types" (e.g., "Aphrodite/Amazon/Maenad type") to the relief panels for the sake of brevity, which would lead the reader to think that they had been conclusively identified. That mistake is corrected in the present treatment. Except for the Tyche/Fortuna type with preserved *cornucopia*, no identifications of the figural relief panels can be considered certain at this time.

6 Joukowsky 1999, 209, figs. 13-14; Schluntz 1999, 69, n.8 and 72, n.12; Basile 2002a, 333-34, figs. 3-5.

Fig. 6.6. Bust of "Tyche/Fortuna".

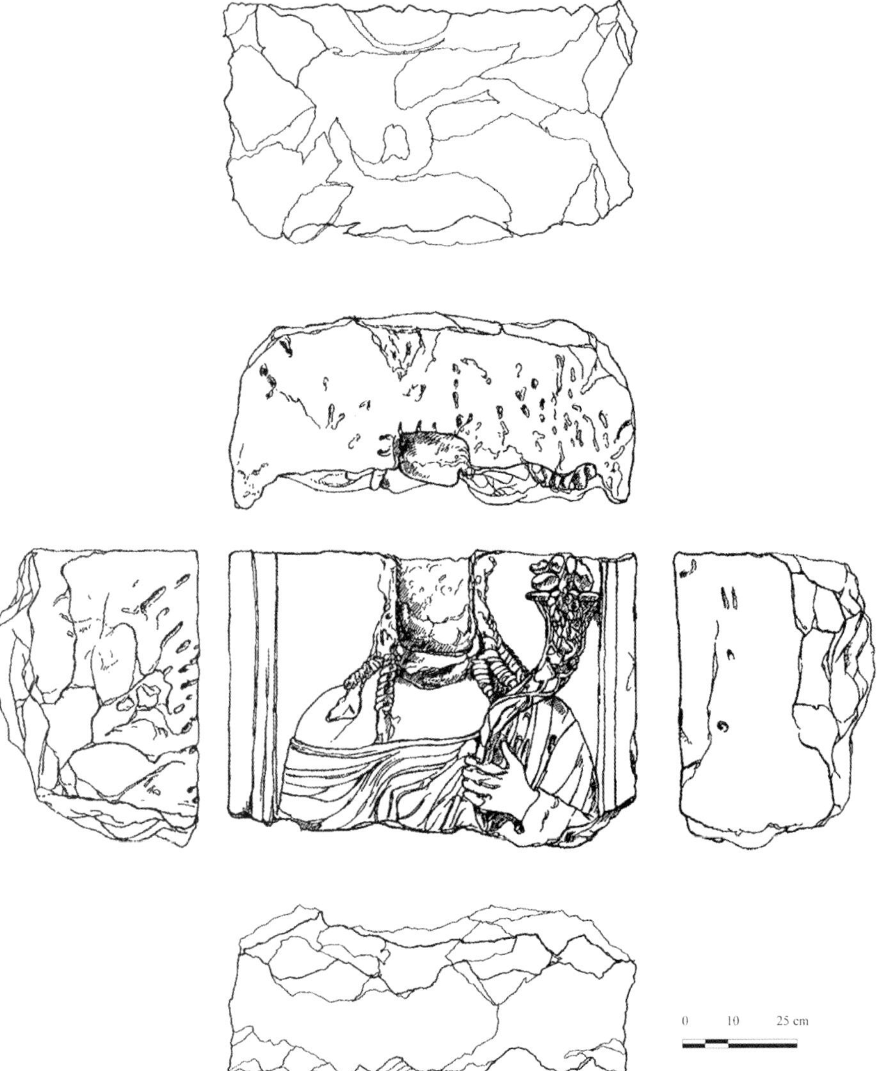

Fig. 6.7. Bust of "Tyche/Fortuna".

raised border, carved with a suggestion of a woven braid or herringbone pattern, with four open "loops" or gaps on the shoulder, between fasteners (buttons or clasps). Shallow-cut folds give an indication of the anatomy beneath (including shoulder and breast) in a "wet drapery" technique. The neckline plunges from the proper left shoulder to beneath the right breast (which is heavily damaged and mostly missing), seemingly leaving it exposed. Two corkscrew "finger curls" rest on the shoulder next to an open slot which indicates that the head was carved separately and fitted into the panel. Too little of the panel is preserved to be certain of the identification.[7]

3 (figs. 6.6-6.7). 52 cm high, 38 cm thick. Excavated in 1998 from a layer of dense gray lime associated with a supposed Late Roman/Early Byzantine re-use of the SE corner of the Lower Temenos as a lime kiln. Like the other panels, roughly worked on the back. Female figure holds a cornucopia. Full width of the panel (84 cm) is preserved from the left to the right frame. Top and bottom of the panel have been sawn or chiselled off.[8]

The figure, clad in a *chiton, vel sim.*, grasps a *cornucopia* in her proper left hand. Head missing, but a rough slot was cut where the neck should articulate, and some plaster is preserved in the slot, supporting the view that a separate head was fitted into the socket. Tyche/Fortuna or a related figure is suggested by the *cornucopia.* The carving technique, with heavy, rounded features, is similar to that of no. 2 above. The folds of the *chiton* are shallow and cut in the "wet drapery" style. A braided border, similar to that on the garment of no. 2, forms the neckline, which exposes the proper right shoulder but drapes over the breast. The proper left hand is visible. The arm is bent at the elbow, with the forearm laid across the left breast. The cornucopia, held in the left hand, is a thin, "S-curve" horn with a stylized ivy tendril wrapped round, laid across the left forearm and resting on the left shoulder. Fruits, including a bunch of grapes, emerge from the flaring mouth of the *cornucopia.* As on no. 2, corkscrew "finger curls" are arranged on each shoulder (three on the proper left, two on the right).

4 (figs. 6.8-6.9). 52 cm high, 82 cm wide, *c.*24 cm thick. Excavated in 1998 re-used in the Late Roman wall constructed between the columns of the middle row of the East Triple Colonnade, just south of where no. 2 was found. Almost the full width of the panel survives, as can be judged from the *cyma reversa* framing on both sides.

Fig. 6.8. Wreath panel.

Triumphal wreath with ribbon or fillet.[9] The foliage of the wreath (olive, perhaps) is rendered more naturalistically than, for example, the ivy tendril on the cornucopia of no. 3, and no stylistic link can be made between the ribbon/fillet of the wreath and the drapery of the figural panels.

5 (figs. 6.10-6.11). 85 cm wide, 50 cm high, 40 cm thick. Found in 1998 near the wreath (no. 4), built into a late cross-wall (fig. 6.12 shows the piece *in situ*) running SE–NW from the NW corner of the retaining wall of the monumental pool of the "Lower Market" area to the southernmost column of the middle row of the East Triple Colonnade.[10] Panel is cut down on both top and bottom and somewhat damaged. Some of the *cyma reversa* border survives on the left edge but no border is visible on the damaged right edge.

Upper torso of a male wearing a garment that covers the proper left shoulder, with the edge or neckline running diagonally to beneath the right breast. Executed in the heavy style also seen in the

7 A female figure with exposed right breast might represent Aphrodite, an Amazon, a nymph or a maenad, but any such identification remains uncertain, and the captions to the figures in Basile 2002a are misleading (see n.5).

8 Joukowsky 1999, 208-9, fig. 12; Basile 2002a, 333-36, figs. 6-7.

9 Joukowsky 1999, 209, fig. 15; Basile 2002a, 336-38, figs. 8-10.

10 Joukowsky 1999, 209; Basile 2002a, 337-38, figs. 11-12.

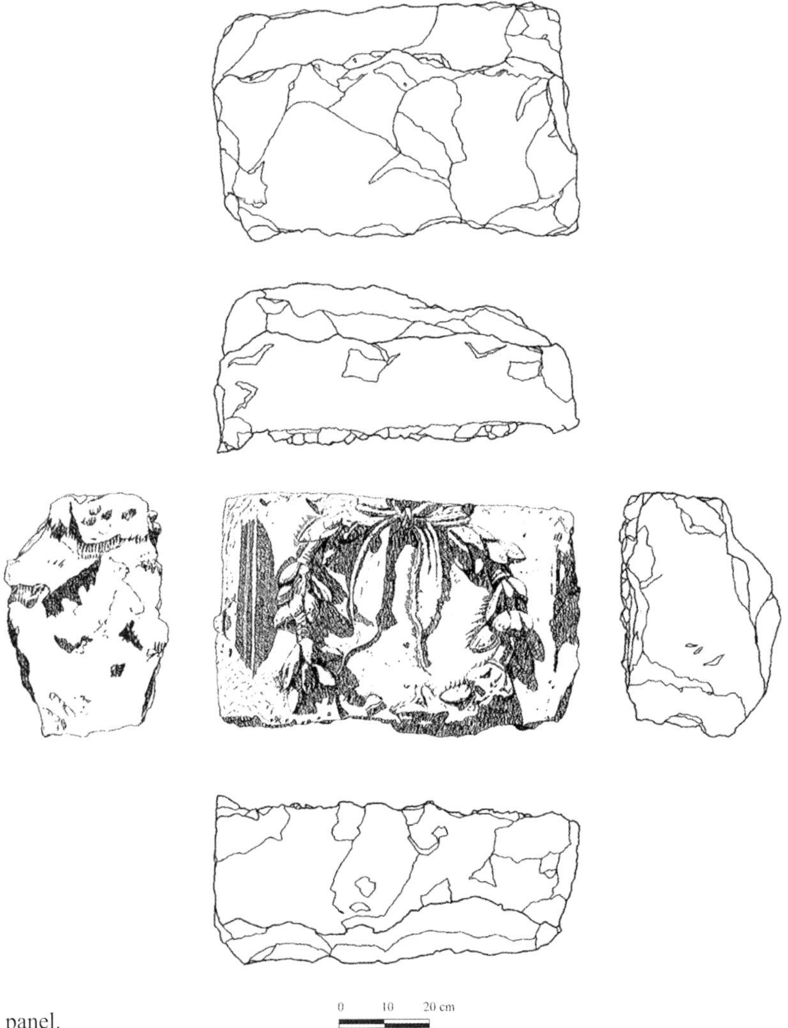

Fig. 6.9. Wreath panel.

Fig. 6.10. Male bust.

Fig. 6.12. Male bust, still *in situ*.

other figural panels. The musculature of the left shoulder is somewhat delineated under the garment. A generalized musculature is indicated on the bare right shoulder as well as on the right side of the chest. The collarbone is deeply carved. The slot where the head would have been inserted was filled with a large stone when the panel was re-used.

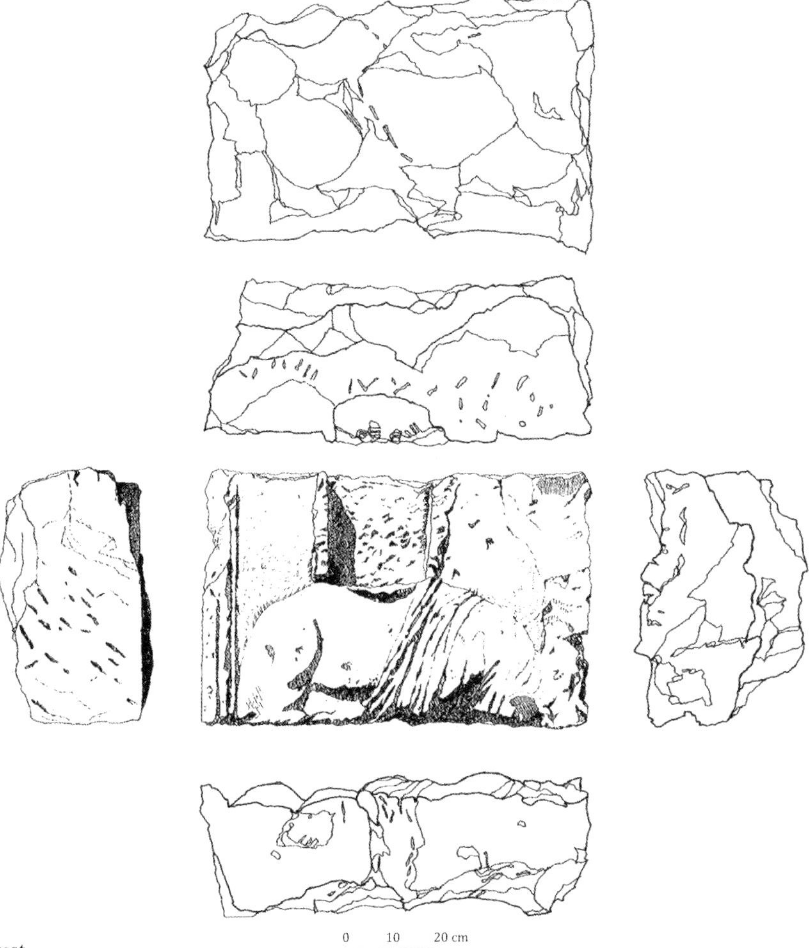

Fig. 6.11. Male bust.

6 (figs. 6.13-6.14). 53 cm wide, 40 cm high. Found in 1999 immediately adjacent to no. 5, built into the same late cross-wall.[11] Damaged and cut down.

The "twin" of the Tyche panel found the previous year, it shows the proper left shoulder, left arm, left side of the neck, and left breast of a female. Heavy folds of a *chiton* are again draped over the left shoulder and arm, while a V-shaped neckline exposes part of the neck and the left half of the slot where the head would be inserted. The left arm is bent at the elbow and folded across the breast below the left shoulder. The worn, chunky left hand holds a badly damaged *cornucopia*.

7 (figs. 6.15-6.16). 87 cm wide (almost the full width), 49 cm high (cut into a strip), 22 cm thick. Found in 1999 not on the E side of the Lower Temenos but on the W side of the Upper Temenos, built into a late "bedouin" wall.

Fig. 6.13. Partial bust of "Fortuna/Tyche".

11 Joukowsky 2000, 317; Basile 2002a, 338, fig. 13.

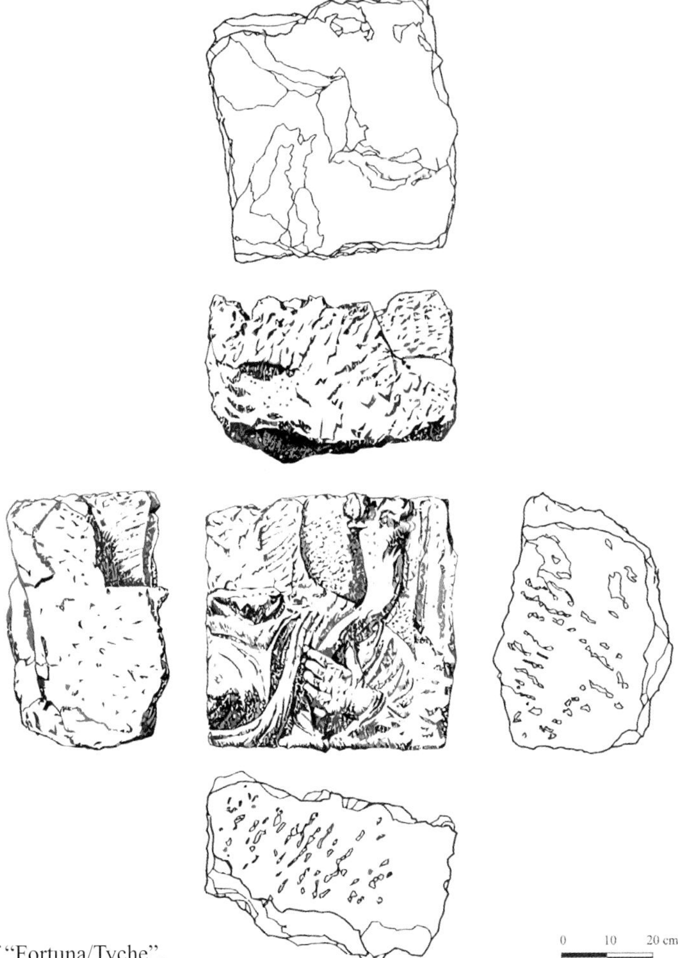

Fig. 6.14. Partial bust of "Fortuna/Tyche".

Upper part of a female with a *chiton, vel sim.* draped over the left breast.[12] The anatomy under the thick drapery is generalized, with shoulder and breast appearing as mounds under the cloth. The neckline of the *chiton* plunges from the proper left shoulder to the right breast. It is unclear whether a flat plane at the edge of the garment is meant to be a hem or a strap/baldric. It is also unclear whether the right breast is exposed.[13] Part of the square socket for an inserted head is preserved. The carving is in all repects similar to the panels described above.

Fig. 6.15. Partial female bust cut into a strip.

A number of small fragments have been recognized as probably belonging to the group of relief panels.

---

12 Joukowsky 2000, 333; Basile 2002a, 338-39.

13 Basile 2002a, 339 states that the breast was exposed, but closer examination of the piece makes this interpretation uncertain. Cf. Wenning 2004, 166, n.57.

Fig. 6.16. Partial female bust cut into a strip.

8 (figs. 6.17-6.18). 26 cm wide, 36 cm high, 42 cm thick.

Part of the left side of a panel, preserving a sculpted border and the proper right shoulder of a figure, covered in a garment with a number of pleats or folds.

9 (figs. 6.19-6.20). 41 cm wide, 17 cm high, 12.5 cm thick.

Part of a wreath of grape leaves[14] with a ribbon knotted where branches cross. It is analogous both formally and stylistically to the olive wreath (no. 4 above). Again, the leaves of the wreath are depicted in great detail and a highly naturalistic style.

10 (figs. 6.21-6.22). 90 cm wide, 45 cm high. From the Colonnaded Street, just below the courtyard of the Lower Temenos. *Cyma reversa* and fillet survive on the (viewer's) left; the frame is broken away at the right.

Well-preserved draped female bust, with heavy cloak overlying a lighter *chiton*. The *chiton* shows a braided border at the neckline and a multitude of vertical folds running from the neck to where it disappears under the heavy cloak. The anatomy beneath the thick drapery is again generalized, the shoulders resembling mounds under the heavy cloth. The proper right arm, mostly obscured under the thick cloak, appears to be bent at the elbow and drawn across the torso, covering the breasts.

Fig. 6.17. Shoulder fragment.

14 Joukowsky 2004, 165-66, fig. 12.

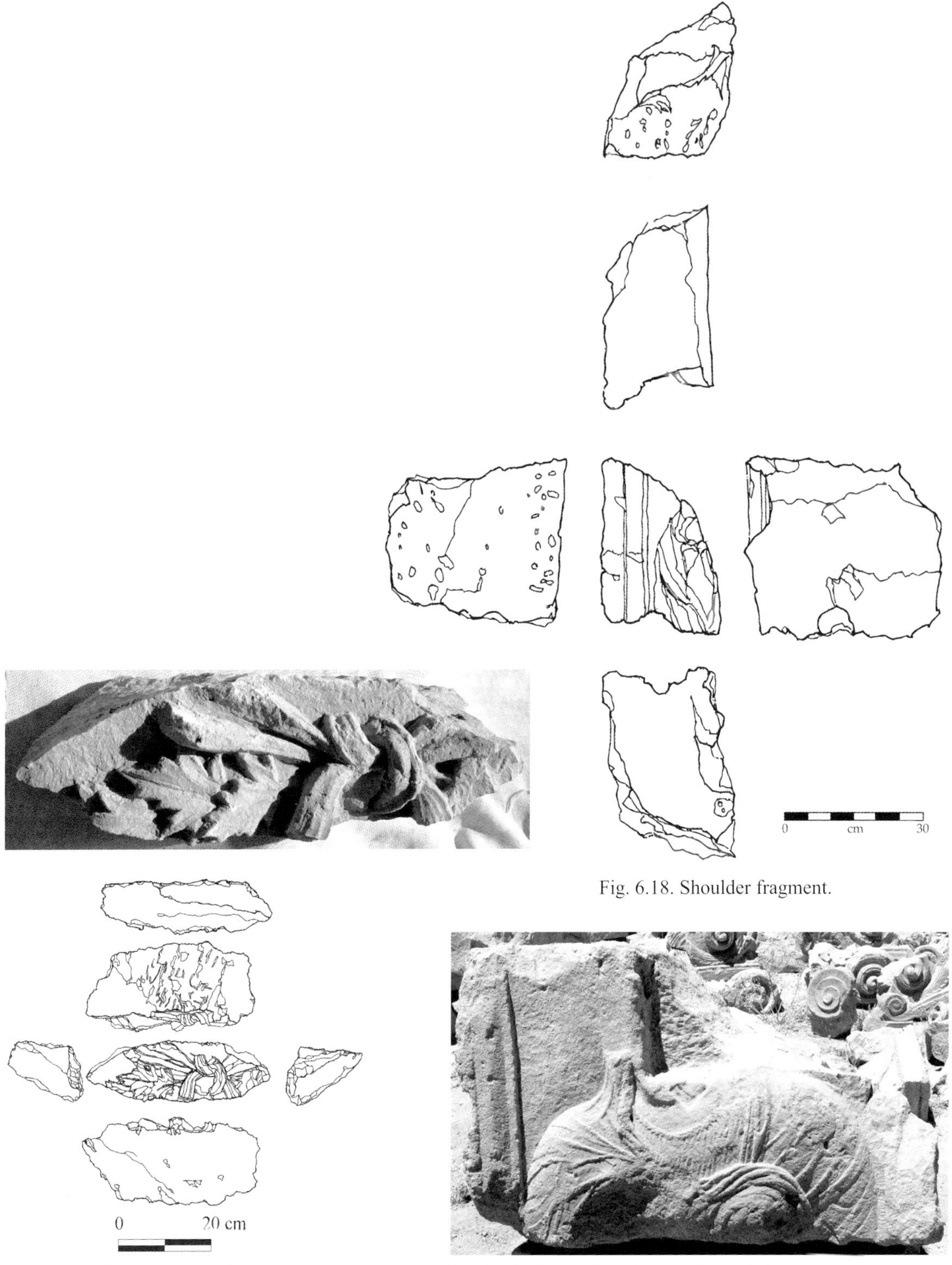

Fig. 6.18. Shoulder fragment.

Figs. 6.19-6.20. Grape wreath fragment.

Fig. 6.22. Female bust from Colonnaded Street.

Part of the square socket for the inserted head is preserved. The heavy cloak comes up the proper right side of the neck and the socket, perhaps suggesting that the head was veiled. This piece has been recognized by the author to belong to the same group of relief carvings based on its dimensions and the strong parallels in its workmanship.[15]

---

15 Roche 1985, 313-17, fig. 1; McKenzie 1988, 94, no. 65; Basile 2002a, 339, fig. 14; Joukowsky 2004, 165-66, fig. 14.

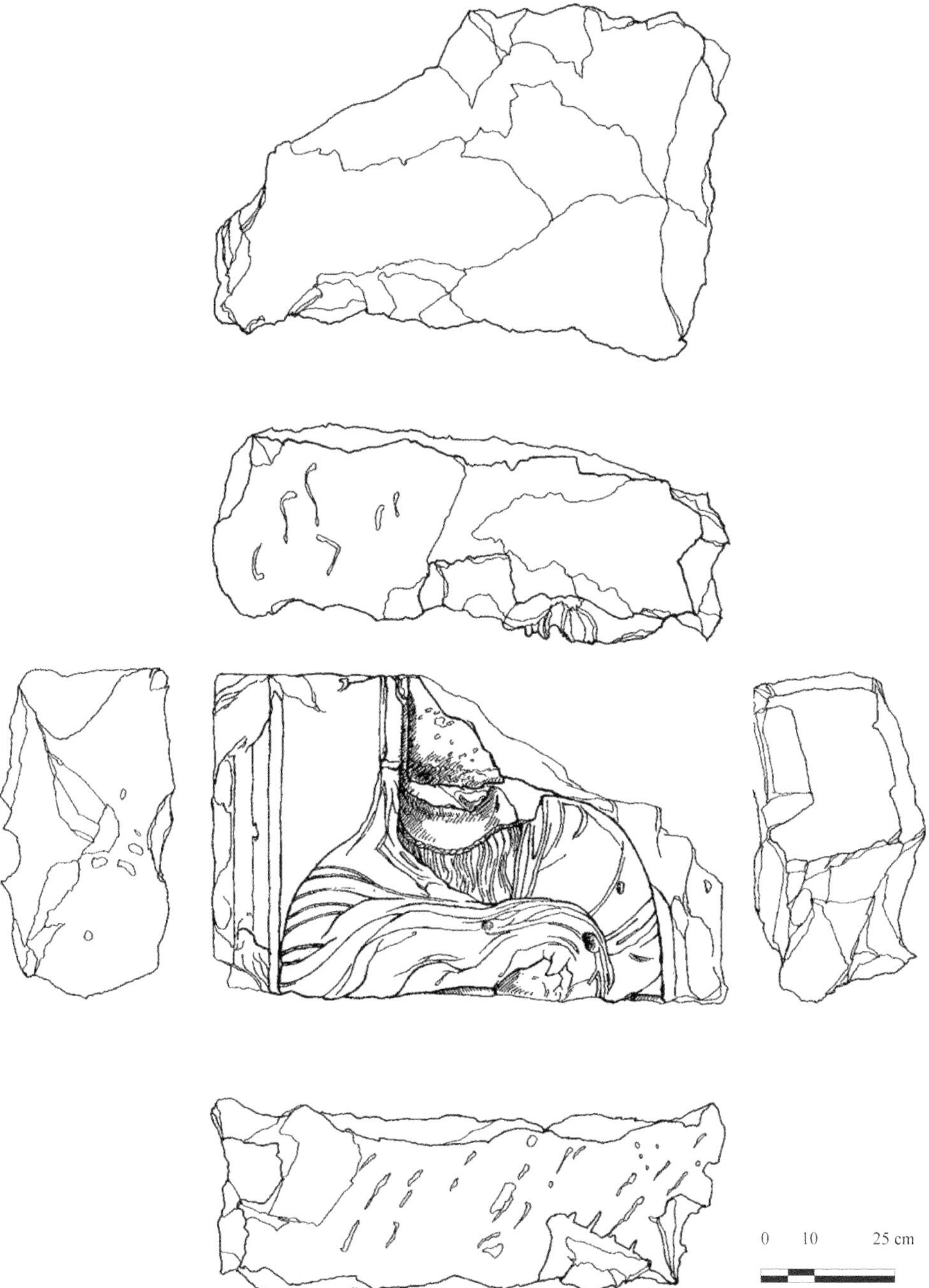

Fig. 6.21. Female bust from Colonnaded Street.

Other fragments

A number of other fragments of sculpted relief panels have been recovered from the site. In some instances they are too damaged to be assigned securely to the same relief panel group; in other instances they are made from different materials and are probably not from the same group.

A. Limestone fragment (figs. 6.23-24). 31 cm wide, 31 cm high, 38 cm thick.

Perhaps part of the group, it depicts what might be leaves or part of a wreath. What remains resembles the (olive?) wreath panel (no. 4), but the fragment is too badly damaged and weathered to be certain.

Several sandstone relief panels probably decorated some subordinate structure of the complex or a structure nearby. They include:

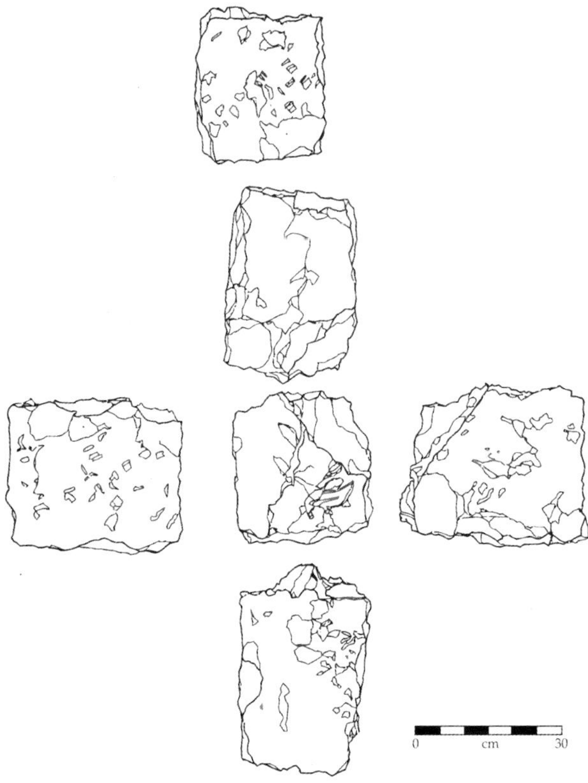

Figs. 6.23-6.24. Possible wreath fragment.

B. Sandstone relief (figs. 6.25-6.26). 68 cm wide, 29 cm high, 42 cm thick.

Found in 2003 in the Propylaeum area, it depicts a helmet in profile,[16] facing the (viewer's) right side of the block, with a curving cheek piece and volute decoration.[17] On the left of the helmet, a diagonal element running from the bottom edge of the block to the (viewer's) upper left corner might represent paired or bundled spears or javelins, although the feature is too weathered for the identification to be secure. It bears a resemblance to reliefs decorated with armor and weapons often found on Hellenistic and Roman temple friezes and victory monuments.

C. Fine-grained yellow sandstone relief (figs. 6.27-6.28). 29 cm wide, 36 cm high, 25 cm thick. A flat border is preserved on the top and side. Found in the N part of the site in 2003.

A beautifully rendered image of Athena/Minerva,[18] it preserves the (proper) right shoulder of the deity, with part of the aegis. A pair of spears or javelins appears over her right shoulder.[19] In terms of style, format, and material, the panel resembles those decorating the nearby Temenos Gate.[20]

---

16 Joukowsky 2004, 165-66, fig. 13.

17 L. M. Anderson kindly comments: "Although the top of the helmet and the bottom of the cheek flap are missing, the lack of a neck guard and shape of the brim help to place it firmly within the realm of 'Hellenistic'. The depiction of the embossed volute decoration is rather unusual. Volute decorations are common on Hellenistic helmets, but most are much tighter (resembling a snail shell) and twist toward the front of the helmet, not toward the back as in this case. The best parallels appear in sculpture (e.g, the Pergamon Altar, although cheek flaps are lacking, and the 'Altar of Domitius Ahenobarbus'); a relief of Ares, which probably belongs to the same group as the Athena relief, depicts a helmet with a loose volute, although much larger than that of this pilaster: cf. *LIMC*, Ares in Peripheria Orientalia, fig. 1."

18 Joukowsky 2004, 164-65, fig. 10.

19 L. M. Anderson comments: "The two finely carved javelins behind Athena are unusual in their number. While Roman soldiers are occasionally shown with more than one javelin or spear (cf. Bishop and Coulston 1993, figs. 3.2 and 4.2)... this relief represents the first occurrence in the iconography of Athena or Allat".

20 McKenzie 1990, 132-34, pls. 55-59.

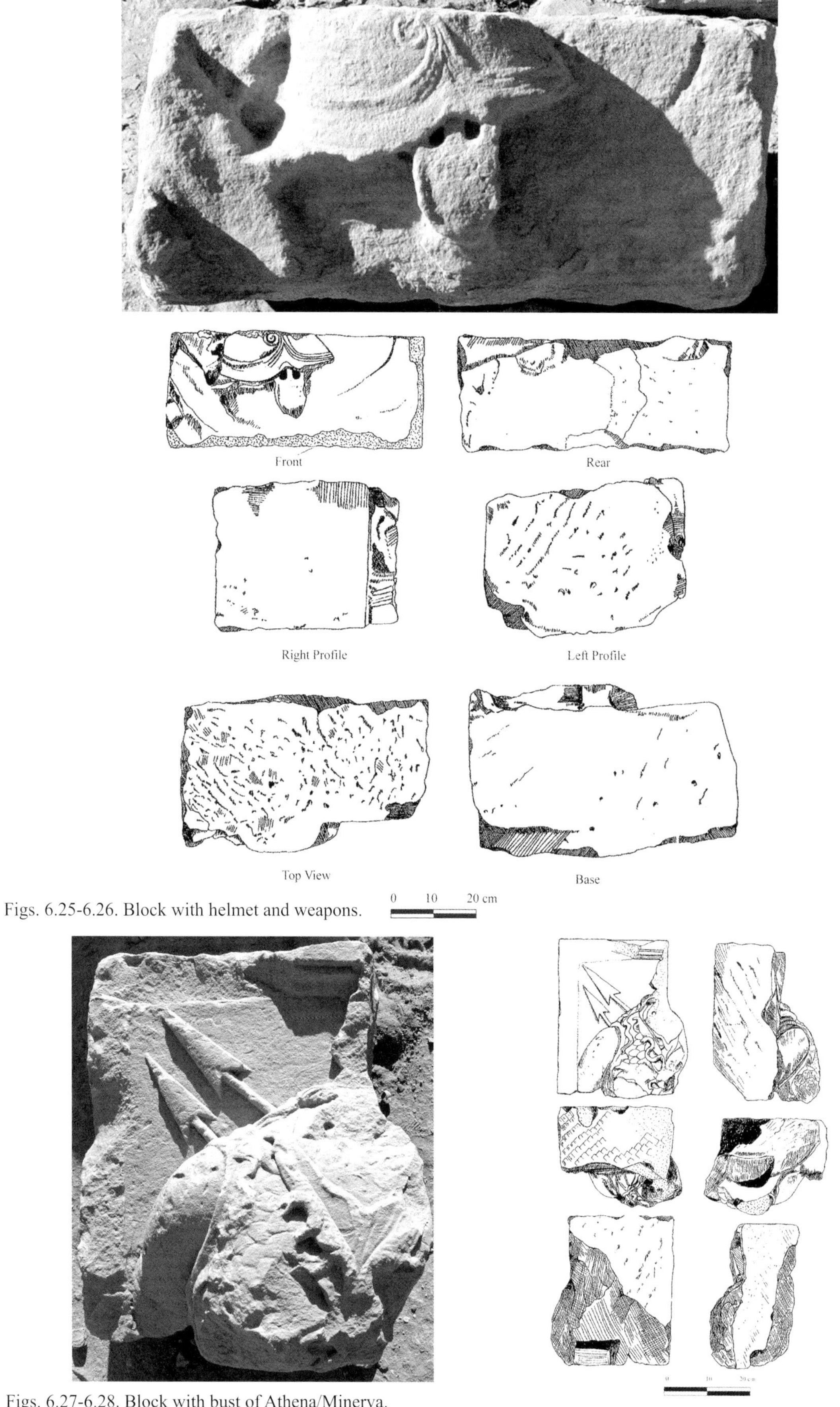

Figs. 6.25-6.26. Block with helmet and weapons.

Figs. 6.27-6.28. Block with bust of Athena/Minerva.

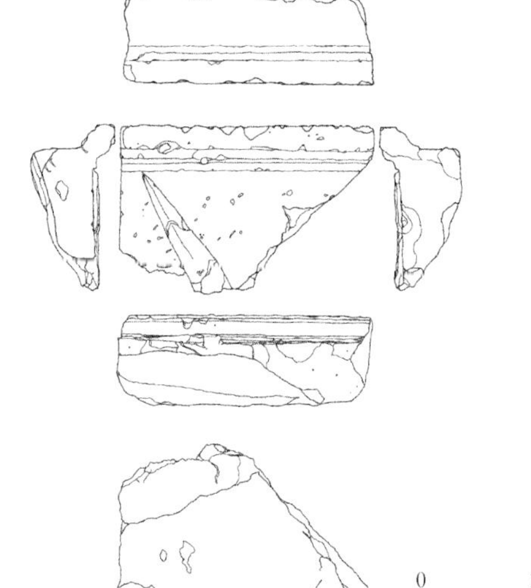

Figs. 6.29-6.30. Block with point.

D. Yellow sandstone panel (figs. 6.29-6.30). 40 cm wide, 25 cm high, 14 cm thick. Crisply carved frame of *cyma reversa* with a fillet alongside the point of the weapon and also on the other side, which suggests that the piece decorated a corner block of an *anta* wall. Found in the Propylaeum area in 2003.

A sword or spear tip, or perhaps a solar ray, runs diagonally across the face of the panel.

Discussion and interpretation

A number of scholars have written on the group of relief panels from the Great Temple, as well as on the general topic of sculpted relief panels in Nabataean art and architecture. In her 1999 dissertation on the Great Temple site, E. Schluntz took up the question of the first two relief panels discovered (nos. 1 and 2),[21] hypothesizing that they might have been part of a program that decorated the N (front) sides of the two *anta* faces of the exterior walls of the main temple. Based on her estimate of the reconstructed dimensions of the panels (*c.*90 cm), the width of the *anta* faces (1.5 m), and the reconstructed height of the temple's façade, she surmised that there might have been as many as 5 panels on each *anta* wall, arranged vertically from the top of the *anta* to the bottom. R. Wenning was critical of her ideas on their number and placement, suggesting that an original placement in the frieze course (similar to the panel metopes of the Qasr al-Bint temple) or in the exedrae or the Propylaeum of the complex is just as likely.[22] However, if these panels were meant to function as metopes, it is important to note that no triglyphs of appropriate size or design to match them have yet been recovered from the Great Temple.

Schluntz also suggested that stylistically the panels most closely resemble the group of sculptures (the "1967 Group" that figures prominently in J. McKenzie's book of 1990[23]) recovered by G. R. H. Wright in the area of the Temenos Gate of the Qasr al-Bint temple complex. Schluntz noted the same use of *cyma reversa* fillet, parallels between the male torso and the so-called "Ares" figure from the "1967 Group",[24] and similarities in the treatment of drapery between the cut-down female panel (no. 2) and the veiled female bust from the "1967 Group".[25] These similarities have a number of important implications. First, for the production of the Great Temple reliefs they suggest a date similar to that postulated by McKenzie for the "1967 Group" if we accept her conclusions — namely,

21 Schluntz 1999, 69-72.

22 Wenning 2004, 165-66, n.50.

23 Wright 1967-68, 20-29; McKenzie 1988, 85-88, figs. 10-11; ead. 1990, 134-35, pls. 60-66; Schluntz 1999, 71-72.

24 Lyttelton and Blagg 1990, fig. 6.9.

25 McKenzie 1988, fig. 11c; Schluntz 1999, 72.

the 1st c. B.C.[26] McKenzie has demonstrated archaeologically that the "1967 Group"predates A.D. 76 or 9 B.C.[27] Furthermore, she has argued that stylistically the "1967 Group" most resembles the Helios bust of the Qasr al-Bint and the relief sculptures of the Al-Khazna. Both of these are dated by several scholars to before the beginning of the 1st c. A.D.,[28] which would correspond with current dating of the main structure of the Great Temple.[29]

Work done by McKenzie on stylistic and chronological links between sculptures at Petra and Khirbet Tannur (especially relief busts from the Temenos Gate and from the "period II" altar pedestal at Tannur, dated to the 1st c. A.D. and the first quarter of the 2nd c.) further demonstrate a stylistic development in which our panels might participate: classical features in Nabataean sculptures at Petra and Khirbet Tannur are strongest in the earlier periods, and become more simplified later on.[30]

One tends to suppose that a revival of the classical style began after the Roman province came into being, operating in tandem with the more schematic styles that persist at Kh. Tannur and Dharih in the Roman era.[31] Thus, while the "1967 Group" remains closest to our group stylistically, the workmanship of some of our panels (especially in the depiction of drapery and the anatomy beneath) is less classicizing than the "1967 Group" and points to a further chronological refinement. A comparison of the veiled female bust from the "1967 Group",[32] our Tyche panel (no. 3 above) and the "bust of a female with cornucopia" from the Temenos Gate[33] is especially instructive. While our relief has more in common, perhaps, with the "1967" piece, in a certain way it stands in the middle of the sequence: the drapery is more classical than the Temenos Gate panel, but of a quality inferior to that of the "1967 Group" panel.[34] The "ringlets" or "corkscrew curls" on our panel are better executed and more fully realized than the stylized curls of the Temenos Gate panel, but are more schematic than the undulating hair of the "1967 Group" bust.[35] If McKenzie's sequence is correct, it could be suggested that, stylistically, our panels should come somewhere between the "1967 Group" (before A.D. 76 or 9 B.C.)[36] and the Temenos Gate group (after A.D. 76 or 9 B.C.).[37] Since the main architecture of the Great Temple is dated to before A.D. 100 and the relief panels are reconstructed as belonging to the main phases,[38] this would jibe with McKenzie's notion of "simplification of the earlier more classical forms as a Nabataean style develops".[39]

---

26 Schluntz 1999, 72.

27 Or, at least, some of this group; *contra* McKenzie that the "1967" sculptures form a coherent group, see Lyttelton and Blagg 1990, 98. These predate the Temenos Gate sculptures, and the Temenos Gate dates from after A.D. 76 or 9 B.C.; see Wright 1967-68, 20-29; McKenzie 1988, 85-88, figs. 10-11; McKenzie 1990, 134-35, pls. 60-66; Lyttelton and Blagg 1990, 98-99; Schluntz 1999, 71-72. For the *terminus post quem* date of the "1967 Group" as either A.D. 76 or 9 B.C., which depends upon the interpretation of the stratigraphic evidence associated with the Temenos Gate and Colonnaded Street, see Wright 1967-68, 20-29 and McKenzie 1988, 88.

28 McKenzie 1988, 86-87 and 90-92; ead. 1990, 134-35; Lyttelton and Blagg 1990, 106.

29 Pottery and stratigraphic evidence suggest that the earliest architecture of the Great Temple dates to the end of the 1st c. B.C. and 1st c. A.D.: Joukowsky 1998a, 133-40; Bestock 1999, 246-48; Joukowsky and Basile 2001, 50; and the present volume p. 24ff.

30 These show what Zayadine (1991, 56-57) would call "Graeco-Syrian" and "Parthian-Hellenistic" influences; cf. McKenzie 1988, 81 and 89.

31 Zayadine 1991, 58.

32 McKenzie 1988, fig. 11c.

33 Ibid. fig. 12d.

34 McKenzie's (1988, 88) progression from "rounded folds of various depths" to "series of flat surfaces".

35 This is characteristic of the move to "repetitive" elements in the depiction of hair in Nabataean sculpture; see McKenzie 1988, 88.

36 Ibid. 92.

37 Ibid. 91.

38 Schluntz 1999, 69-72.

39 McKenzie 1988, 88.

An attempt to identify sources of influence also points to the 1st c. B.C./1st c. A.D. and to the Hellenistic kingdoms of the Near East, the expanding Roman state, and Roman client kingdoms such as those in Syria and that of Herod the Great nearby. Hellenistic influences have already been suggested for the "1967 Group", which McKenzie placed at the beginning of a process by which classical traditions become more schematic and generalized. The "1967 Group", along with the Al-Khazna reliefs and the bust of Helios from Qasr al-Bint, the most classicizing and naturalistic, would stand at the beginning of the sequence, in the 1st c. B.C.; indeed, M. Lyttelton and T. F. C. Blagg called some pieces in the "1967 Group" "wholly Hellenistic ... without any obvious Nabataean reference".[40] Increasingly, scholars look toward Alexandria as the direct source of these influences.[41] Alexandrian influence, for instance, is seen in the "baroque" architecture (e.g., in the Al-Khazna) that some would date to the second half of the 1st c. B.C. or the first half of the 1st c. A.D. (and not to the 2nd c. A.D., when the Roman imperial baroque style reached its climax),[42] and specifically in the distinctive "floral-type" capitals on several key monuments at Petra, including the Al-Khazna and the Great Temple.[43] An important theme running through McKenzie's book is Alexandria's baroque influence on Petra's earliest monuments. While connections with other Hellenistic centers such as Pergamon can also be expected,[44] it seems that Alexandrian contact might account for the classicism not only of the "1967 Group" but perhaps also for our reliefs. As for the problem of differentiating Roman influence, Rome in the 1st c. B.C. was, in many respects (and especially in its art and architecture), a Hellenistic state, so to look for Hellenistic *and* Roman influences in Nabataean art is, in some ways, to look for the same thing. As Lyttelton and Blagg said of the period from Aretas III to Aretas IV (*c.*87 B.C. to A.D. 40), in which they saw a number of key monuments being built at Petra,

> many of the elements in the art of Petra which have been regarded as 'Roman' have probably been interpreted as such because Roman ornament was being influenced [by Hellenistic models] at approximately the same time.[45]

We need not wait for annexation to look for Roman influence — and Roman influence in the 1st c. B.C. and first half of the 1st c. A.D. would include Hellenistic elements.

Rome's client kingdoms also suggest themselves as possible sources of influence. Herod's might figure prominently, for in the same period embracing the end of the 1st c. B.C. Herod's rôle as builder and patron is paramount.[46] Lyttelton and Blagg saw a possible connection between Herod and the building programs of the later Nabataean kings, especially Aretas IV.[47] Schluntz sees Herodian influence in the Great Temple complex,[48] finding parallels between the main temple and the audience hall of Herod's "Winter Palace" at Jericho.[49] Possible Herodian links also exist with the architecture of our Lower Temenos in its resemblance to courtyards of sanctuaries (e.g., the Sanctuary of Hercules Victor at Tivoli or Fortuna at Praeneste) or fora (e.g., those of Julius Caesar and Augustus in Rome), which all predate or are contemporary with the major architectural phase on our site.[50] The Temple of Augustus at Sebaste was probably influenced both by the Kaisareia of Antioch and Alexandria and the Forum of Julius Caesar, although at Sebaste Herod did not enclose the temple structure within the portico, transforming the portico instead into a "forecourt" below

---

40 Lyttelton and Blagg 1990, 99.

41 Lyttelton 1974; Schmidt-Colinet 1980; Lyttelton and Blagg 1990; McKenzie 1990.

42 See for instance Ward-Perkins 1981, 331-34, *contra* Lyttelton and Blagg 1990, 100-4 and 106.

43 Lyttelton and Blagg 1990, 94-95; Schluntz in Joukowsky 1998a, 226-31; Schluntz 1999, 57-68.

44 Lyttelton and Blagg (1990, 96-98), for instance, see Pergamene influence in the "floral scrolls" and "weapons friezes" that appear on several Petra monuments.

45 Ibid. 105.

46 Roller 1998; Netzer 2006.

47 Lyttelton and Blagg 1990, 106.

48 Schluntz 1999, 106-13.

49 For the interpretative implications of this argument, see chapt. 8 below.

50 Basile in vol. 1, 204-6.

the temple proper.[51] The "Lower Market" of Petra, directly east of the Great Temple, has been shown by L. Bedal to be a garden and pool complex with Herodian "overtones".[52] Thus Petra in the 1st c. B.C. and A.D. stood at the intersection of a number of artistic influences, all of which trace at least some of their origins to traditions of the Hellenistic Near East of the 1st c. B.C. The classicism of our relief panels is a reflection of such influences.

The meaning and function of our panels, however, are more controversial. This is because the meaning and function of the temple itself are still open questions. The discovery of a classicizing *theatron*, replete with horseshoe-shaped *cavea* and low *pulpitum* built between the massive porch columns in what was supposed to be the *cella* of the Great Temple, a structure added sometime after the original construction,[53] threw into disarray the assumption that the Great Temple (so-called since von Bachmann's day) was a temple at all. In her dissertation, Schluntz argued that in its earliest phase (prior to the Roman province) it was in fact a royal audience hall, similar to those in Herodian palaces such as Jericho, and became a public assembly space following the addition of the *theatron*.[54] In support of this interpretation, she saw the sculptural decoration as a program designed to speak to the rôle of the Nabataean royal families.[55] In regard to the relief panels, she stated:[56]

> … the figural relief panels would be serving an appropriate propagandistic function as divine patrons of the Nabataean kings, adorning the main building's façade. Their presence would have actually been less appropriate for a temple façade, which would more likely only display imagery connected to the temple's resident divinity.

Yet this is a difficult claim to press; comparanda are not plentiful, and the architectural evidence is sometimes contradictory. First, there are no other Nabataean palaces with which we could compare the Great Temple (if it was indeed an audience-hall). A banqueting hall has recently been identified at Beidha;[57] it is decorated with relief carvings (mainly figural column capitals) that have parallels in Petra. Other Nabataean relief panels, however, can be securely associated with *sacred* architecture; often they show a mixture of symbols, iconography, and types of deity that defy the notion that temple decoration would "only display imagery connected to the temple's resident divinity". Examples would include the sculpted panels decorating the Temenos Gate. Interpreted as the gateway to the sacred *temenos* enclosure of the Qasr al-Bint temple, it is faced with square, framed sculpted panels decorated with relief busts,[58] among which a variety of deities and mythological figures has been identified. For the Qasr al-Bint structure itself, massive sculptural panels showing various deities in bust reliefs (the Helios relief is the best preserved) have been reconstructed as decorating the 'Doric-style' frieze of the temple.[59] Again, the variety of figure types contradicts the notion that the temple would only be decorated with imagery associated with the deity/deities dwelling within. One can find other examples outside Petra. The sculptural panels of the Khirbet Tannur temple decorated the façade of its inner shrine.[60] A similar situation is seen at the temple at

---

51 Roller 1998, 92; Netzer 2006, 273-74, fig. 56.

52 Bedal 2000 and 2004.

53 Vol. 1, 300-9.

54 Schluntz 1999, 82-135.

55 Ibid. 78-81.

56 Ibid.

57 Bikai *et al.* 2006, 30.

58 Some are *in situ*, some have been restored to the Temenos Gate, and some are reconstructions. A number of fragments of panels have been associated with the Temenos Gate: Parr 1957, 5-8; id. 1960, 130-32; Glueck 1965, 466-67; McKenzie 1988, 87-88; ead. 1990, 133-34; Basile 1997, 255-66; id. 1999, 223-26.

59 McKenzie 1990, 135-38.

60 Glueck's book of 1965 summarizes his work at the Khirbet Tannur temple, illustrating the sculpture from the site as well as comparanda. For the relief panel busts see ibid. 122-23, 144-46, 198-207, 222-28, 315-19, 396-99, 410-17, 465-73 and 510, with pls. 1-3, 12, 25-28, 45, 53, 55-56, 130-32, 136-37, 145-46, 153-54 and 157. For McKenzie's re-appraisal see ead. 1988, 81-107; ead. *et al.* 2002a, 451-76; and ead. *et al.* 2002b, 44-83. Also cf. Starcky 1968, 206-35; Tholbecq 1997, 1069-95; and Wenning 2004, 157-58.

nearby Khirbet edh-Dharih,[61] where relief busts of gods (including the "Castor and Pollux" relief) decorate the frieze course; the panels are linked stylistically to the reliefs of Khirbet Tannur, suggesting to some a "school" of Nabataean sculptors operating in central Jordan.[62] In both cases, the relief panels represent a number of deities and mythological types, seemingly negating the view that sculptural programs of Nabataean temples would include only images pertaining to the deity worshipped inside. In the end, the presence of a program of busts representing a number of different deities or mythological figures does not preclude a sacred function for the building, but neither does it necessarily suggest a palace, banqueting hall or audience-hall.

Conclusions

Not all questions surrounding the group of panels can be answered with certainty. Because all were removed from their original contexts (some to be re-used in secondary contexts), it is difficult to be certain about dating and function. However, associated artifacts and stylistic analysis suggest the pieces are to be dated in the first three quarters of the 1st c. A.D. or to the end of the 1st c. B.C., and that they formed part of the decorative program of the main phases of the Great Temple complex, perhaps of the temple itself. The panels show the influence of Hellenistic (probably Alexandrian, possibly Pergamene) models of the 1st c. B.C. through contacts with the Hellenistic kingdoms, the expanding Roman state, and Rome's client kingdoms in the Near East such as Herod's, and they demonstrate how art and architecture in the Nabataean kingdom were impacted by developments in neighboring states. They also demonstrate the artistic skill of the Nabataean carver, who combined native and foreign elements to produce a Nabataean style for some of the finest examples of architectural sculpture from Petra.

Acknowledgements

The team from the Maryland Institute College of Art in 2006 included Professor K. O'Meara (Department of Environmental Design), undergraduate L. Braddock, and myself. O'Meara and Braddock made a majority of the field drawings. In Baltimore the drawings were inked by O'Meara and undergraduate C. Benditsis, and electronically documented by undergraduate C. Baum. I thank all four for their invaluable contributions.

61 Villeneuve and al-Muheisen 2000, 1525-63.

62 Lyttelton and Blagg 1990, 100; Zayadine 1991, 57.

7A

The Corinthian columns of the Great Temple and the plants associated with Dionysos

Angela Murock Hussein

The Great Temple had a total of more than 140 decorated columns divided between the Lower Temenos and the temple proper. In the ancient world a large number of columns had long served to enhance the monumentality and luxury of structures, as in the cases of the Apadana of Persepolis, the Temple of Artemis at Ephesus or the Hypostyle Hall of Karnak, where veritable forests of columns overwhelmed the visitor and attested to the greatness of divine might as well as that wielded by a royal authority. Doubtless the Great Temple was intended to have a similar effect. Its most famous architectural elements are the elephant-head capitals from the Lower Temenos, a variation on the Greek Ionic capital, with elephant trunks forming the corner scrolls; they will be considered below (chapt. 7B). First, we consider the temple's columns and pilasters of the Corinthian order, itself another variation on the Ionic and thereby serving to draw together the architecture of the Lower Temenos and Temple. The same end was achieved through an iconographical program and imagery that evoked both the divinity and the secular power behind the construction.

Description

The Great Temple was originally surrounded by 22 columns and two matching pilasters (fig. 7.1). In the first stage of the building, four standard columns lined the S side, and two corner capitals, heart-shaped in section, stood at the S corners. On the E and W sides, seven standard columns ran between the heart-shaped corner column at the S end and a pilaster at the N end. Two columns between the pilasters (*antae*) at the entryway on the N side formed the original distyle *in antis* façade. An outer wall, pierced by many entrances, surrounded the structure on three sides. By Site Phase IV the outer walls were extended towards the front of the temple (fig. 7.2), terminating to form the outer *antae* of a large porch. Between these new *antae*, *c.*6.3 m from the original façade, a further 4 columns created a tetrastyle *in antis* façade.

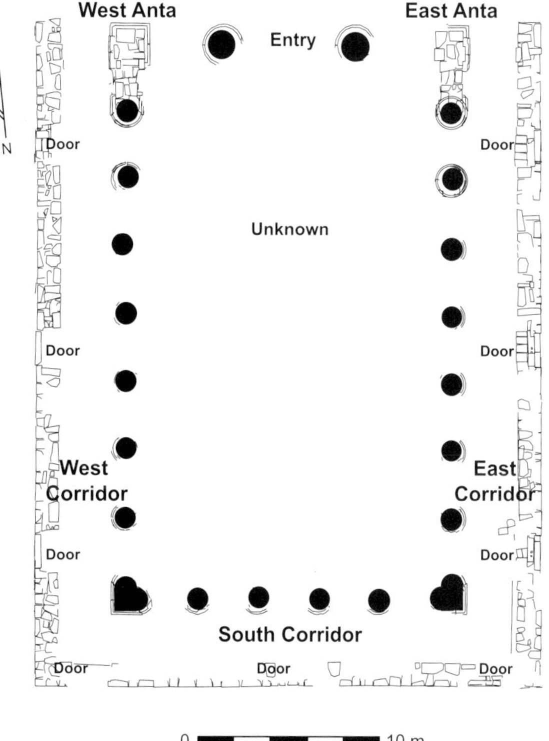

Fig. 7.1. The earlier configuration of columns of the temple (Phase II).

Each column of the temple sat on a lathe-carved Attic base of white limestone (fig. 7.3). The preserved bases of the peripteral colonnade have lower diameters of 1.32-1.42 m, upper diameters of 1.07-1.19 m, and heights of 0.051-0.6 m. The bases of the heart-shaped corner columns with two half-round bases added to square bases are *c.*2.08 m wide below and 1.83 m wide at the top. The bases of the columns of the pronaos and porch measure *c.*1.9 m in diameter below and 1.7 m at the top. The Attic bases for the pilasters of the pronaos measure *c.*2.2 x 1.5 m at the bottom (the widths are truncated since the bases flank the temple's stylobate) and 2.05 x 1.4 m at the top. The columns on the S side of the temple have an inter-axial distance of 3.27 m, while on the E and W sides the inter-axial distance is *c.*3.51 m. The inter-axial distance between each pair of

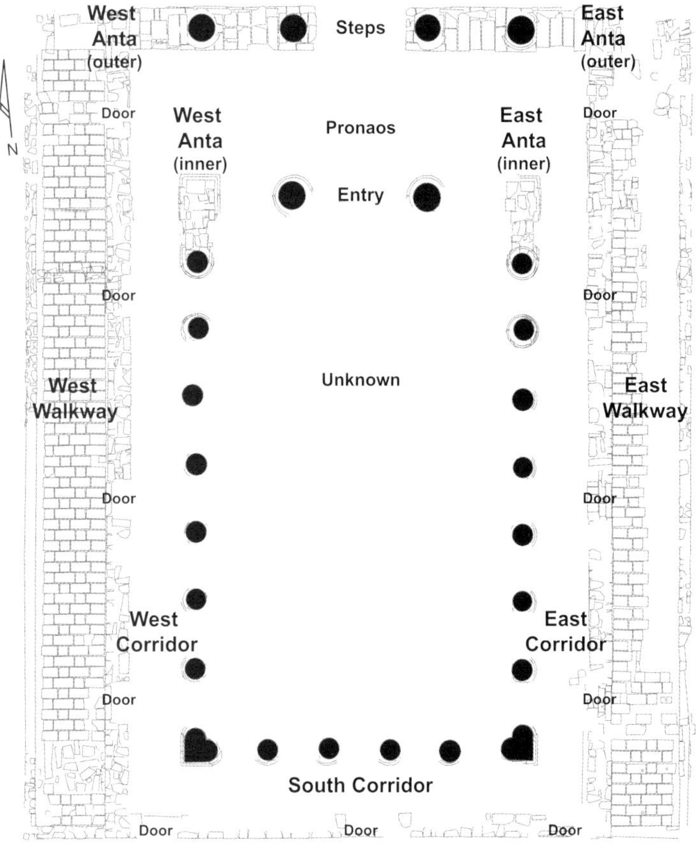

Fig. 7.2. The later configuration of columns of the temple (Phase IV).

Fig. 7.3. Attic base from the porch of the temple.

Fig. 7.4. Reconstructed columns for the heart-shaped corner capital with the lower order of the Nabataean-Corinthian capital. The drums preserve scoring to receive plaster.

Fig. 7.6. Reconstructed upper and lower orders of Nabataean-Corinthian capitals of the temple.

Fig. 7.5. Column drum with plaster coating in a cable-fluted pattern.

Fig. 7.7. A typical Nabataean-Corinthian capital of the temple.

columns on the tetrastyle façade is 5.03 m, except that the inter-axial distance between the central columns is 7.06 m.

The temple's column drums are of local sandstone (fig. 7.4). The peripteral columns have an average diameter of 1.2 m, those of the pronaos and porch *c.*1.5 m. The heart-shaped corner columns are made up of round half-drums set against square blocks and are *c.*1.5 m in combined width. The L-shaped pilasters in the pronaos measure *c.*1.5 x 2.0 m. The individual drums and blocks that make up all the shafts are rough-cut and vary greatly in height but average *c.*50 cm; gaps in between the blocks had been filled with mortar, smaller stones and pottery sherds before the surface was plastered, the columns being veneered in plaster like all of the temple's visible surfaces. The lower third of the columns, up to 3.16 m above the base, were colored either red or yellow. The upper length of the columns received white plaster moulded into cable fluting (fig. 7.5), rather than the traditional fluting associated with the Greek Ionic and Corinthian orders. The plaster coating was 7 cm or more thick. In some places plaster appears to have been re-applied several times. There may have been some degree of entasis, although it is difficult to be certain given the condition of the columns.

The Great Temple's capitals were a Nabataean variation of Greek Corinthian known as Floral or Floral Corinthian and, like the bases, were carved of white limestone. They were in two parts, assembled as two stacked drums (fig. 7.6). The lower orders were *c.*1.17 m in diameter in the case of the capitals from the peristyle and 1.50 m in diameter in the case of those from the porch. The interior capitals are reconstructed as 1.56 m high, while the porch capitals were 2 m high. The upper orders seem to have a lower diameter of *c.*1.13 m. Although many fragments are badly broken, some capitals may have had a separate abacus or an inserted boss. The capitals come in 6 different components, the lower order being manufactured in two halves, the upper order in four quarters (fig. 7.7, 7.8 and 7.13). The lower order has two rows of outcurving acanthus leaves; the bottom row has 8 leaves (fig. 7.8), the top row has 10 (fig. 7.7). With the upper order the corner volutes are sheathed above and supported below by acanthus leaves, a design with Alexandrian precedents (fig. 7.7 and 7.13).[1] Two sets of vines spiralling towards each other create the helices on each of

1 McKenzie 1990, 95.

Fig. 7.8. Half of a lower order of a Nabataean-Corinthian capital of the temple.

Fig. 7.9. Quarter drum with volute of an upper order of a Nabataean-Corinthian capital of the temple.

the four faces between the volutes; the vines terminate in poppy buds or pomegranates framed by flowers (fig. 7.13). Other vines grow outwards between the helices and volutes, terminating in flowers with pinecones at the center (fig. 7.9). Bosses of pinecones (fig. 7.10 and 7.15) framed by acanthus or grape leaves are set on each face at the center of the abacus (fig. 7.10), which is concave in plan (fig. 7.11). The astragal is a rounded ring over a disc-shaped base (fig. 7.8).

The height of the columns (including base, drums and capitals) is estimated at 15.5 m for those on the porch and 12 m in the rest of the temple. The top surfaces of the peristyle capitals are scored, indicating that they were prepared to bear an entablature. The different heights were possibly equalized by an entablature frieze above.

Most of the fragments securely identified as elephant-head capitals, with designs such as egg-and-dart or elephants (i.e., *not* Corinthian), come from the Lower Temenos. Most of those associated with Corinthian Floral capitals come from the Great Temple, much smaller percentages coming from other parts of the complex. Certain motifs, such as acanthus and helices (fig. 7.12), can belong to either elephant-head or Corinthian capitals but the majority are probably Corinthian, especially if they were found in Temple or Upper Temenos contexts. Some fragments are carved but the particular motifs are not discernible. All capital fragments that are certainly (because they have motifs unique to Corinthian capitals) or possibly Corinthian (because they have motifs common to both capital types), as well as those with indistinguishable motifs, are listed (Tables 7.1-7.2) to give the maximum possible number of Corinthian capital fragments for each area.

TABLE 7.1
CORINTHIAN CAPITAL FRAGMENTS BY AREA WHERE FOUND

Area	*Propylaeum*	*Lower Temenos*	*Upper Temenos*	*Temple*	*Total*
Column Fragments	632	1,256	1,001	2,601	**5,490**
	12%	23%	38%	47%	
Not Corinthian	353	913	56	13	**1,335**
	26%	68%	4%	1%	
Possibly Corinthian	279	343	945	2,588	**4,155**
	7%	8%	23%	62%	

TABLE 7.2
CORINTHIAN CAPITAL ELEMENTS FROM THE GREAT TEMPLE, 2006

Capital Motif	*Propylaeum*	*Lower Temenos*	*Upper Temenos*	*Temple*	*Total Fragments*
Acanthus Leaf	94	120	404	1,292	1,910
	5%	6%	21%	68%	51%
Cauliculus	5	23	29	129	186
	3%	12%	16%	69%	5%
Helix	10	20	7	21	58
	17%	35%	12%	36%	1%
Petal	13	19	83	226	341
	4%	6%	24%	66%	9%
Pinecone	6	30	32	84	152
	4%	20%	21%	55%	4%
Pomegranate/Poppy	2	8	29	103	142
	1%	6%	20%	73%	4%
Vine	24	55	121	429	629
	4%	9%	19%	68%	17%
Volute	46	67	48	186	347
	13%	19%	14%	54%	9%
TOTAL	**200**	**342**	**733**	**2,470**	**3,765**
	5.31%	**9.08%**	**19.4%**	**65.65%**	**99.4/100%**

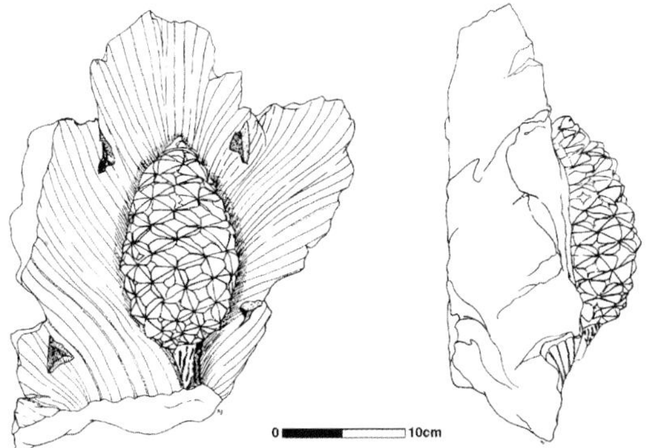

Fig. 7.10. Pinecone boss fragment (Arch. frag. PST/888).

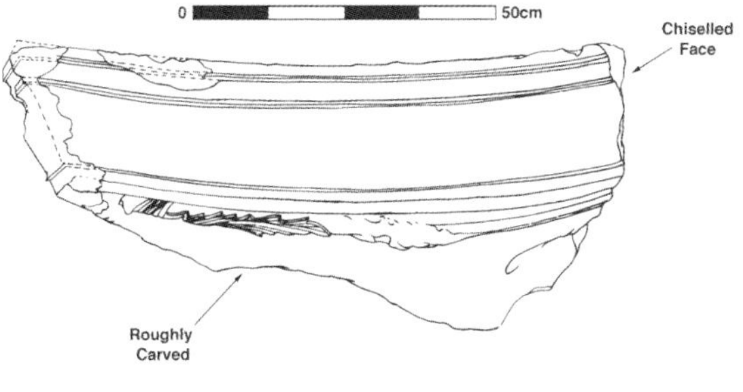

Fig. 7.11. Abacus fragment.

The majority of the fragments carved with Corinthian Floral motifs (between 54% and 73% for most motifs) come from the Temple; the one exception is for helices, which also occur on elephant-head capitals and which are fairly evenly distributed between the Temple and Lower Temenos. The next highest amount of fragments comes from the Upper Temenos surrounding the Temple — predictably, due to the placement of the Corinthian capitals on the building.

The Corinthian capitals of the Petra Great Temple were manufactured in more than one piece, a technique popularized by the Romans in the 1st c. B.C., whereas temple capitals in ancient Greece tended to be carved in one piece.[2] The one-piece technique is associated with Rome's expansion and increased influence in the Near East, seen above all in works by Herod the Great.[3] Carving capitals in sections facilitated construction, and the use of smaller pieces helping to lower transport costs. Sections could be mass-produced in a standard size, increasing the speed of work, and the simpler decoration could be done by less skilled craftsmen, increasing the efficiency of labor.

2 Netzer 2003, 160.
3 Forester 1995, 108-9.

Fig. 7.12. Volute of a capital from the upper order of the temple.

Fig. 7.13. Fragment of a capital from the upper order of the temple.

In many cases plaster still adheres to column drums and capitals from the temple, both as the original treatment and as a repair (fig. 7.12). Many major structures and temples in the region were not built of marble; instead, limestone was used because it could be quarried close to the building site. To smooth the appearance of more porous stone, give a seamless look and provide a surface for painted decoration, a plaster or stucco coating was frequently applied in the Near East to stone and mudbrick. At Petra the surfaces of most stone structures were scored with lines running at a 45° angle as a preparation for the application of plaster. It could be applied to a plain surface, moulded to create the appearance of carved stone, and was typically used to repair decoration if some element was broken in manufacture or during the life of the building, as in the case of the elaborately carved capitals where recarving would be impractical or very difficult and expensive. Paint was added to the plaster and colors such as red and yellow can still be discerned on some capitals and drums. In some cases gold leaf was applied to the carved ornament. The addition of gold to capitals adding a touch of luxury had precedents on some of the most famous Ionic buildings, such as the Temple of Artemis at Ephesos or the Erechtheion.[4]

As can be seen in Fig. 7.15 Corinthian capitals provide a more flexible field, with multiple surfaces, than did the standard Ionic.[5] A number of variations on Corinthian capitals spread throughout the Near East from the 2nd c. B.C., largely originating in the ornate architecture of Alexandria.[6] Although under Augustus the Corinthian capital developed into an order in its own right with standard decoration and proportions, becoming the norm for most Roman monuments,[7] it was evidently under Hellenistic influence that the Corinthian order made its way to non-Greek cultures in the Near East, including Petra.[8]

Floral Corinthian capitals like those from the Great Temple were first commented upon by D. Schlumberger, who identified them as "Heterodox" capitals, hybrids between Greek Corinthian

4 Dinsmoor 1975, 131 and 193.
5 Boardman 1993, 123.
6 McKenzie 2007, 86-91; ead. 1990, 96.
7 Jones 2000, 135.
8 Ronczewski 1932, 37-90; Ismail 1980, 27-29; McKenzie 1990, 70 and 94-96, diag. 14 a-f.

and the local trapezoidal capitals known as the Nabataean type.[9] More recently, J. McKenzie classified Nabataean capitals based on K. Ronczewski's system for analyzing the Corinthian capitals of Alexandria.[10] By her categories, all the Corinthian capitals from the Great Temple are Type 1 floral capitals.

Several Nabataean structures, all dated to the second half of the independent Nabataean kingdom, have columns similar to those of the Great Temple. The closest parallels are found on structures associated with Aretas IV (9 B.C.–A.D. 40). The first is the "Qasr al Bint Fir'awn" temple, dedicated to the god Dushara, which dates to Aretas IV according to the dedicatory inscription.[11] It boasts Type 1 floral capitals manufactured in 6 layers. Their acanthus lower order is very similar to, and their upper order volutes are identical to, those of the Great Temple, but pinecones are lacking, only vines and flowers being present.[12] The second is the "Temple of the Winged Lions," dedicated to either Al-Uzza or Allat and also dated to the reign of Aretas IV.[13] It possesses some floral columns very similar to those from the Great Temple.[14] Its Type A1 capitals share the same leaf sheaths on the volutes, grapevine with poppy bud motifs, pinecones on the faces, and other plants more difficult to identify. Types A2 and B also have the vines, poppy buds and pinecones, but they differ in some of the details: Type A2 has bundled ivy volutes, while the volutes of Type B are replaced by the eponymous winged lions. The Type A1 capitals are perhaps the closest parallel to those of the Great Temple. A third parallel is found at Beidha in a recently excavated building, dated to the reign of Malichos I (58-30 B.C.)[15] and interpreted as an *oecus* or wine hall, with its elephant-head Ionic capitals and Floral capitals.[16] Many different types of Floral capitals, many with Dionysiac imagery, are associated with the structure but they compare closely to the capitals of the Great Temple.[17] A fourth parallel, again at Petra, is found in the decoration on the Floral capitals on the rock-cut lower section of al-Khazna tomb (fig. 7.14); it is nearly identical to the Floral capitals on the Great Temple.[18] The tomb was perhaps carved for Aretas III (85-62 B.C.) or, more probably, for Aretas IV.[19] Thus the Great Temple capitals should be assigned to the later Nabataean kingdom, probably to the reign of Aretas IV.

Fig. 7.14. Nabataean-Corinthian capital from al-Khazna, Petra.

The vegetation is full of symbolism. In addition to acanthus leaves (traditional to the Corinthian capital), the capitals of the Great Temple were decorated with pinecones, poppy buds, pomegranates, grape vines, and a flower with 5 petals — a design unique to Nabataean monuments. The motifs on the faces of the capitals' upper sections are formed into a single plant. The vines terminate

9 Schlumberger 1933, 283-17; Negev 1974, 153-59; Lyttelton and Blagg 1990, 94-95.
10 Ronczewski 1927a and 1927b; McKenzie 1990, 95.
11 Larché and Zayadine 2003, 200.
12 Zayadine, Larché and Dentzer-Feydy 1996, 48-50, pls. 26-27. No fragment survives of what seem to be very worn attachments for fruits or buds within the flowers.
13 Hammond 1996, 14.
14 Hammond 1977, 47-51, fig. 3; id. 1996, 78-80.
15 This is based on the excavated pottery: ibid. 494.
16 Bikai, Kannelopoulos and Saunders 2008, 465ff.
17 Ibid. 481, fig. 15, in particular (f).
18 Ronczewski 1932.
19 Stewart 2003, 194.

in flowers which have pinecones, pomegranates or poppy buds at their centers; this design, which corresponds to no real plant, is an object of fantasy, borrowing elements from several plants, but the meaning is not sufficiently understood to allow us to detect a cohesive decorative program.

Fig. 7.15. Pinecone boss.

P. Bikai *et al.* have discussed Dionysiac imagery in the vines, ivy and masks on Nabataean floral capitals at Beidha.[20] Vines, ivy and masks are all symbols of the wine god in Greece, Dionysiac imagery being adapted as royal symbolism in the time of Alexander the Great and by Hellenistic rulers. Mark Anthony also made use of this association.[21] Dionysiac imagery was a sign of regal power, and that may have been a large part of its appeal for the monuments commissioned by the Nabataean royal house. Some of the other plants on the Great Temple and the Beidha capitals can also be associated with the wine god. One of the attributes of Dionysos and his followers is the *thyrsus*, a fennel stalk terminating in a pinecone, and pinecone bosses appear on the abacus as well as at the corners of the faces of the capitals of the Great Temple. The plant depicted here (fig. 7.15) is probably the Aleppo Pine (*Pinus halepensis*), which has large pinecones. Pine resin can be used to seal wine jars, preserve wine or flavor the beverage.[22] It is also possible that pine resin was used as an intoxicant in its own right; even today, ingesting or inhaling distilled pine resin (turpentine) is known to cause a dulling of the nervous system.[23] The weaker versions of the product available in antiquity may have had a less dangerous but still noticeable effect. Pine resin was also used topically for its antiseptic properties.[24]

Greek Dionysiac imagery, however, does not include the other plants (pomegranate, poppy, 5-petalled flower) present on our capitals. For those we must look to the version of the cult that was popular in the Hellenistic world. Alexander and the successor Macedonian dynasties worshipped Dionysos as he was known in Orphism, a set of beliefs with their basis in a Thracian mystery cult which worshipped Dionysos, a dying god.[25] According to Orphic versions of the myth, Dionysos was the son of Zeus and Persephone with the epithet Zagreus.[26] After he was born, Zagreus climbed onto his father's throne and held Zeus' thunderbolts, but Hera grew jealous and sent the Titans to seize the child and dismember him, despite his attempts to defend himself by changing shape.[27] The blood from his body became a pomegranate tree.[28] Dionysos was resurrected through Zeus' impregnation of Semele,[29] and he went on to raise an army and conquer India, after which he returned in triumph.[30] Dionysiac imagery could thus be used

20 Bikai, Kannelopoulos and Saunders 2008, 477-86 and 495-96.

21 Heckel and Yardley 2004, 208-10; Plut., *Ant.* 24.

22 Plin., *NH* 14.25 and 16.16; Dioscorides, *de Materia Medica* 1.86 and 5.43.

23 Dart 2003, 1313. Aleppo pine resin can be used to make turpentine, but the most common source for turpentine is the terebinth tree (*Pistacia terebinthus*). The region of Petra was known for a resinated wine made from terebinth (Dioscorides, *de Materia Medica* 1.71). However, terebinth trees lack pinecones and thus cannot be the source of inspiration for our capitals.

24 Dioscorides, *de Materia Medica* 1.86.

25 Guthrie 1993.

26 Aesch., Fr. 124, *Sisyphus*, from *Etymologicum Gudianum*; Diod. Sic. 4.4.1 and 5.75.4; Hyg., *Fab.* 155 and 167. Nonnos, *Dionys.* 6.155-69; *Orphic Hymns* 28.

27 Nonnos, *Dionys.* 6.155-69; Hyg. *Fab.* 150 and 155.

28 Clement, *Exhortations to the Greeks* 2.15.

29 Nonnos, *Dionys.* 7-8; Hyg., *Fab.* 155 and 167.

30 Diod. Sic. 4.3.1; Nonnos, *Dionys.* 14 ff.

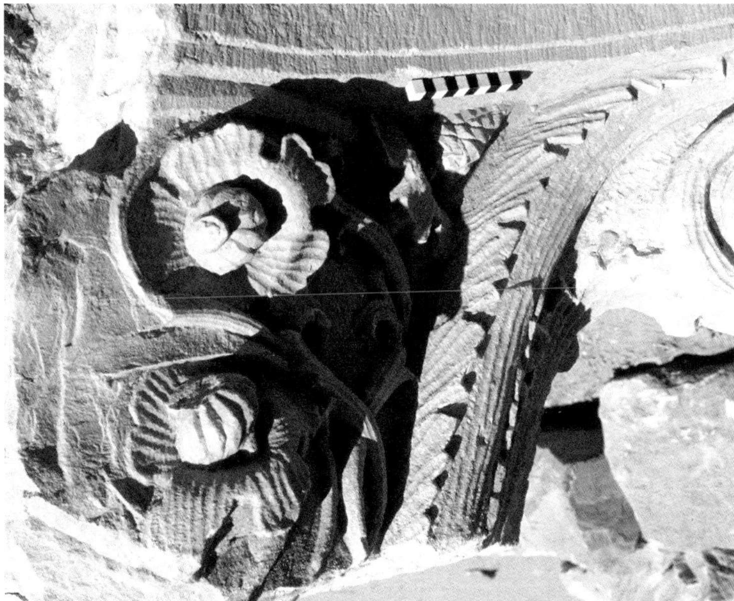

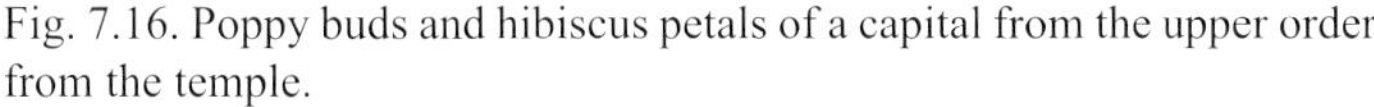
Fig. 7.16. Poppy buds and hibiscus petals of a capital from the upper order from the temple.

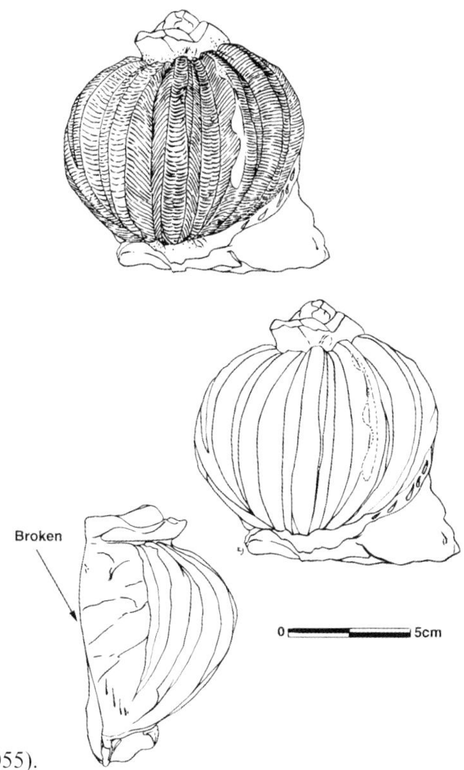

Fig. 7.17. Poppy bud (Arch. frag. PST/1055).

generally to symbolize military victory.[31] Further symbolism may also be found in the particular flowers at the center of the helices of the Great Temple's capitals, terminating in bulb-shaped objects, some of which are probably pomegranates. Persephone (Orpheus's mother) and the pomegranate were linked in Greek mythology through the myth of her abduction by Hades. She ate seeds of the pomegranate and was required to return to the underworld for half of the year.[32] The fruit of the pomegranate is a symbol of Dionysos. Pomegranates were associated with fertility because of their abundant red seeds, but they were also thought to have abortifacient properties and were recommended for birth control.[33]

Secondly, the poppy buds on the Great Temple's capitals have slits on their surfaces for the extraction of the drug (figs. 7.16-7.17). The opium poppy has long been recognized for its intoxicating and medicinal properties.[34] The poppy is the symbol of several goddesses and is often held by their statues, including Demeter, Cybele and the Titan Rhea. Cybele was the mother of Sabazios, who was identified with Thracian Zagreus and Greek Dionysos and thereby incorporated into Orphic writings; Rhea and Dionysos were worshipped together in the mystery cults of Thrace and Phrygia, which reached Greece by the 4th c. B.C.[35] According to Orphic myth, it was with Rhea that Dionysos settled until he raised his human and divine army and travelled to India.[36]

Thirdly, the 5-petalled flower on the Great Temple's capitals (figs. 7.18-7.19) has often been identified as a hibiscus. Hibiscus does not have any properties that would connect it to the other plants on the Floral capitals. Instead, I would argue that this plant is a member of the genus *Hypericum*,

---

31 In this light, the connection of the decorative program with the elephant-head capitals is obvious. Military victory would reference Dionysus' (and Alexander's) conquests of India.

32 *Homeric Hymn to Demeter* 405-33.

33 Riddle, Worth Estes and Russel 1994, 31.

34 Joukowsky 2008; Dioscorides, *de Materia Medica* 4.64.

35 Strabo 10.3.13-15; Dem., *De cor.* 259-60.

36 Nonnos, *Dionys.* 11.139 on his arrival there, 12 and 13 on the mustering of his armies and learning of the mysteries from the goddess. Cf. also Apollod., *Bibl.* 3.33.

Fig. 7.19 (above). Carved vegetal decoration on a capital from the upper order of the temple.

Fig. 7.18 (left). Quarter drum of the upper order of a Nabataean-Corinthian capital, being prepared for its journey to Providence. Note the flower with 5 petals.

commonly known as St. John's Wort,[37] a herb used since antiquity for medicinal purposes, usually as a diuretic and for hip ailments.[38] King Mithridates reportedly used the herb as an antidote against poisons.[39] Extracts derived from St. Johns' Wort are said to have antidepressant effects on users (it is marketed as such by modern herbal medicine). The flowers of St. John's Wort can look very similar to the flowers on the Great Temple's capitals; they usually have a tuft of stamens at the center that resembles the placement of the poppy buds, pomegranates and pinecones on Nabataean floral capitals.[40] Besides yellow flowers, various species of *Hypericum* are known to produce fruits with blood-red juices, and the seeds smell of pine. Perhaps because of the resemblance of the juice to wine or because of the bloody Orphic myth, one species, *Hypericum perfoliatum*, was known in antiquity as 'Dionysia'.[41]

---

37 Several of the flowers from this genus have similar chemical properties. *Hypericum perforatum* and *Hypericum perfoliatum*, species native to Europe, were specifically described by Roman medical texts. The species native to the Near East is *Hypericum calycinum* or Rose of Sharon, which most closely resembles the flowers on the Great Temple's capitals.

38 Dioscorides, *de Materia Medica* 3.154-56.

39 Jashemski 1999, 18.

40 On most parallels (al-Khazna, Temple of the Winged Lions, Qasr al-Bint) to the capitals from the Great Temple, the carved flowers have 5 petals. However, on the earlier capitals from Beidha the flowers usually have 4 petals, except for the one that most closely resembles the Great Temple. The 4-petal flowers probably represent a different species since they appear on capitals that include more prominent vine imagery. The 4-petal flowers should probably be considered from a different source to that of the capitals with vine, poppy, pomegranate, pine or 5-petal flower being discussed here. See P. M. Bikai *et al.* 2008, 481, fig. 15 f, and compare with a-d.

41 Dioscorides, *de Materia Medica* 3.156.

Thus the theme of the Great Temple's Floral capitals (and the similar capitals from al-Khazna, Beidha, Qasr al-Bint and the Temple of the Winged Lions) is plants connected to Dionysos in his Orphic guise. They can all be used for medicinal purposes and sometimes as intoxicants. Medical plants were often connected to divine powers, and the taking of drugs has precedents in the Orphic mysteries and other forms of ancient religion. Further, all of Petra's major temples, the royal wine-hall at Beida, and the resting place for a ruler display similar Floral capitals, an imagery which was doubtless connected to the royal house and the particular rulers who commissioned these structures. Yet Dionysiac imagery was not simply regal: it also signified triumph,[42] and Dionysos's association with Aretas IV would recall the defeat of the armies of Herod Antipas by the forces of Aretas.[43]

We cannot say that the similar capitals on the other temples are exact copies of those of the Great Temple; some of the plants may have been different, modified according to the particular gods associated with each context. Al-Khazna and the *oecus* at Beidha preserve the closest examples, and Dionysiac imagery would have been important in those contexts (the Beidha structure is a wine-hall, Al-Khazna is a funerary structure where Dionysiac imagery was important for the promise of new life), whereas the Dionysiac capitals on the Great Temple can perhaps be linked to the identity of the god to whom the temple was dedicated.[44] A connection between a Dionysiac mystery cult and the Great Temple should also be explored through its architectural plan and design: there are similarities between the multiple entrances in the outer wall surrounding the temple with cult buildings for mysteries in Greece, while the theatral area at the center of the temple recalls Dionysus the god of theatre.

42 An interesting connection between Judea and the Thracian mystery cult of Dionysus is brought up by Plut. (*Mor.* 4.6) in the 1st c. A.D. where he says that the Jews worship Sabazius, a guise of Dionysus similar to Zagreus (Diod. Sic. 4.4.1 equates them). This fact has been doubted by some. However, Phasaelis, the daughter of Aretas IV, was married to Herod Antipas, and a connection between the royal houses of Judea and Nabataea may have brought the cult to Judea.

43 Jos., *AntJ* 18.5.

44 A god whom the Greeks equated with Dionysos was worshipped in Arabia as far back as the 5th c. B.C. Herodotos (3.8) refers to the Arabs' worship of only two gods, Dionysus and Aphrodite, and gives their Arabian names as Orotalt and Ailiat. Nabataean images of Dionysus are known (e.g., in Wadi Farasa, where he is connected to Dushara).

7B

The elephant-head capitals of the Triple Colonnades in the Lower Temenos

Martha Sharp Joukowsky

I introduced a previous discussion[1] of the elephant-head capitals (fig. 7.20) with John Godfrey Saxe's poeticization of the Hindu tale "The blind men and the elephant",[2] which begins:

It was six men of Indostan
To learning much inclined
Who went to see the elephant
(Though all of them were blind),
That each by observation
Might satisfy his mind.

Each of the blind men proceeds to touch a different part of the animal. The first touches the elephant's side and concludes that elephants are like walls; the second feels the tusk and says that the elephant is like a spear; the third grabs the trunk and determines the elephant is a form of snake; the fourth puts his arms around one of the legs and exclaims that it is like a tree; the fifth feels the elephant's ear and decides it is a type of fan; the sixth strokes the tail and believes it is very like a rope. They all end up disputing the true nature of the elephant, each one being partly right and all of them being wrong.

Saxe's poem is a metaphorical reference to theologians in constant argument about something they cannot see. I like to apply it to archaeologists, constantly faced with evidence that is new and unusual. Although we have sight, all of us sometimes fail to see more than we have been trained to expect: in one way or another we are victims of blindness. Archaeology means many different things to different people, but the whole, as in the case of the elephant, is much more than the sum of its parts. Nabataean artists celebrated the elephant on the capitals of the Triple Colonnades of the

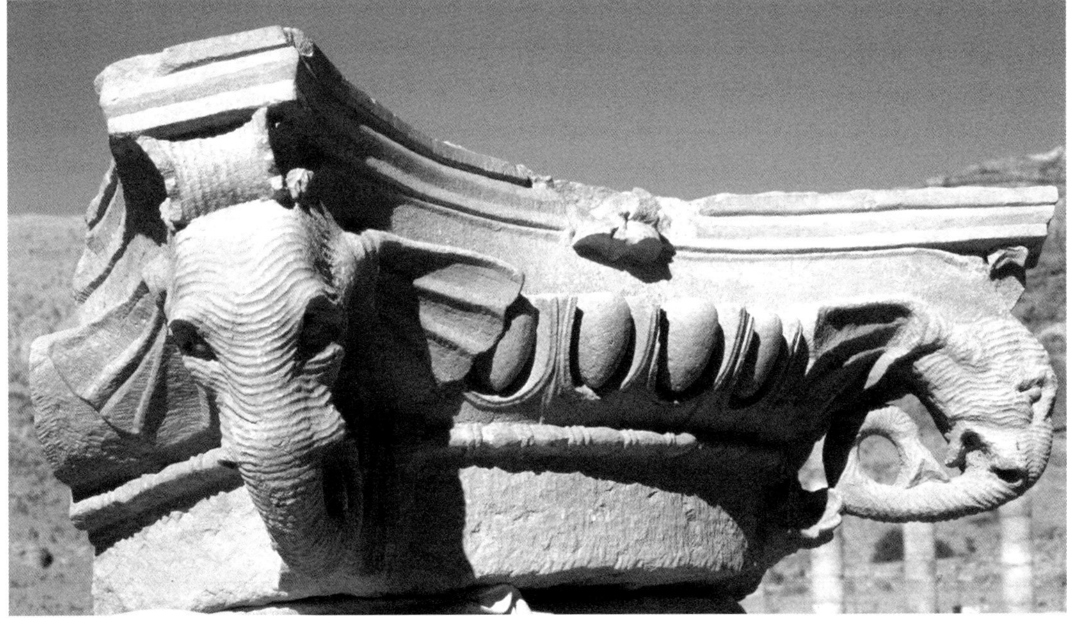

Fig. 7.20. Elephant-head capital from the Great Temple.

1 Joukowsky 1998a, 133-48.
2 Sillar and Meyler 1968, 140-41. "The Blind Men and the Elephant" is found in the *UdĀna* Hindu Scripture.

Fig. 7.21. East Triple Colonnade of the Lower Temenos, view to northeast.

the Lower Temenos and the Propylaeum, the idiosyncratic signature of elephant heads replacing traditional volutes.[3] How should we make sense of the elephant in a Nabataean cultural context? The pseudo-Ionic elephant-head capitals are dated from the last quarter of the 1st c. B.C. to the 1st c. A.D., some 50 years later than the distyle Corinthian temple capitals, when the tetrastyle is constructed and the precinct is enlarged.

Lower Temenos: the East and West Triple Colonnades and cryptoportici

The rectangular enclosure of the Lower Temenos (see fig. 1.3 on p. 20) extends from the Propylaeum Retaining Wall to the Lower Temenos Retaining Wall at the south. Elevated 8.5 m above the street and set at an average elevation of 898.70 m, the Lower Temenos measures 49.0 m N–S x 56.0 m E–W.[4] As the formal introduction to the Great Temple proper, the expanse of the Lower Temenos is integral to an understanding of what the Nabataeans sought to achieve through the monumentality of the complex.

Running the full N–S length of the plaza on its E and W sides are triple colonnades (see fig. 1.5 on p. 22; fig. 7.21 and 7.26) with a total of 120 columns (60 on each side, 20 in each row), all with elephant-head capitals, while on the N side one (possibly two[5]) E–W colonnades of 10 or 20 columns stood at the junction with the Propylaeum. For the visitor entering the precinct, elephant-head capitals

3 Elephant-head capitals publications include (in chronological order): Freyberger and Joukowsky 1997, 71-86; Joukowsky 1998a, 133-48; vol. 1, 78, 197-98, 289-90, 302; figs. iv; 5.13-5.14, 197; 5.15-5.17, 198; pl. 35; Joukowsky 2002a, 106-7; Netzer 2003, 73, Abb. 222.4-223; Joukowsky 2003, 214, figs. 234 and 236-37; Taylor 2005, 98-101, fig. 110; vol. 2, xxvii-xxviii, xxxi, xxxii, 70, 72, 81, 83, 95-96, 106, 110-11, 116, 120-21, 123, 126, 131, 161, 231, 286, 288-89, 291, 296-98, 407; figs. 1.20, 25; 2.42, 80; 2.43, 81; 3.8, 95; 3.9, 95; 3.24, 107; 3.25, 107; 3.42, 118; 6.27, 300; 18a, 366; 19a-c, 366-67; figs. 7.20a-7.20c, 368-69, and back cover; and Dimitrov 2012-13.

4 These measurements exclude the West Entry Stairway.

5 We have scant evidence of the precinct's N perimeter colonnade due to the collapse of these features.

Fig. 7.22. West Exedra of Lower Temenos, view to north, showing small columns at the entrance which carried elephant-head capitals.

were first visible running along the Propylaeum; a restored column (fig. 7.24) marks the entrance from the Propylaeum into the Lower Temenos. The E and W Triple Colonnades of the temenos rest on a stylobate constructed of alternating sandstone and white limestone ashlar slabs (average size 0.52 x 0.96 m). The columns, displaying a visible *entasis*, are made of sandstone drums (diam. 76-84 cm) spaced at regular inter-axial distances of 2.50 m. Rising to a projected height of at least 7.6 m, the shafts are clad with a bright red and yellow painted plaster topped in turn by a white plaster with cable fluting. The walkways between the colonnades are *c.*4.4 m wide; the total width of the E and W Triple Colonnades is *c.*12.5 m. Ceramic roof-tiles in the excavated fill suggest that they were roofed. The colonnades protected people from inclement weather or the sun, providing an airy meeting place for conversation and for viewing whatever entertainment was taking place in the plaza.

At the S end of the temenos, the E and W colonnades terminate at buttressed exedrae. Inside both exedrae are 5 niches (1.15 m wide, 0.55 m deep), set into the curving sandstone walls. Executed in the classical style, each exedra measures *c.*6.5 m wide (internally) and 5.5 m deep. They are fronted by two freestanding columns made of sandstone drums (diam. 0.60 m) crowned with small elephant-head capitals. The columns rest on Attic bases and project 1.2 m from the slightly incurving opening of the apse (6.8 m wide). Two freestanding columns partly survive at the front of the West Exedra (fig. 7.22). Flanking the exedrae, two engaged columns mounted on the façades are also embellished with elephant-head capitals (fig. 7.23).

Each column is crowned by an exquisitely-carved limestone capital with 4 heads of Asian elephants (*Elephas maximus*). They are covered with a light coating of white plaster. Currently there are more than 1052 elephant elements or fragments in our catalogue and database (fig. 7.25 illustrates

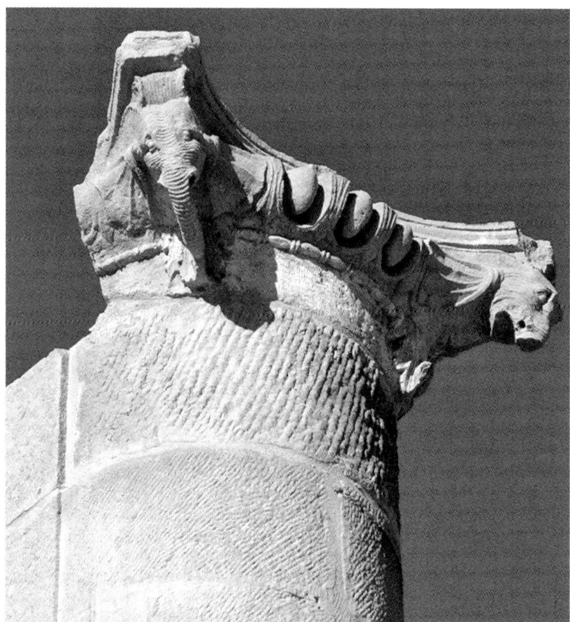

Fig. 7.23. Lower Temenos west, restored elephant-head capital on engaged column.

Fig. 7.24. Propylaeum, entry into Lower Temenos, restored elephant-head capital.

Fig. 7.25. Fragment of elephant-head capital showing the pinecone boss, egg-and-tongue, ovolos and bead-and-reel.

a capital fragment unearthed during excavation).[6] The Propylaeum and Lower Temenos yielded the bulk of the elephant heads, totalling 91% of those found in the Great Temple excavations. There must have been a minimum of 536 and a maximum of 576 elephant heads adorning columns.

The diameter of the colonnade capitals ranges from 76 to 89 cm. From top to bottom of the capitals the decoration (fig. 7.25) consists of a plain band 12 cm high; bead-and-reel 2.5 cm high, egg-and-tongue 15 cm high, and a cornice as a plain band with a tripartite moulding in a double wave, 12 cm high. The base of the astragal measures 89 cm. The corner decoration consists of an elephant head with fan-shaped ears extending to just above the bead-and-reel into the same plane as the ovolo. Unfortunately, no tusks have been found. Beneath the elephant heads is a cascading

6 Two databases with architectural fragments (a total of 751) and the catalogue (301 entries) record 1052 elephant elements. Only 4% of the capital fragments in the architectural fragment database represent elephants; heads or partial heads number 117, there are 82 ears, 27 skin fragments, and 58 eyes. More prone to breakage are the 412 fragments of elephant trunks. Combining the databases, 611 (58%) fragments were recovered from the Lower Temenos, 351 (33%) from the Propylaeum, 20 (2%) from the Temple area, and 63 (6%) from the Upper Temenos.

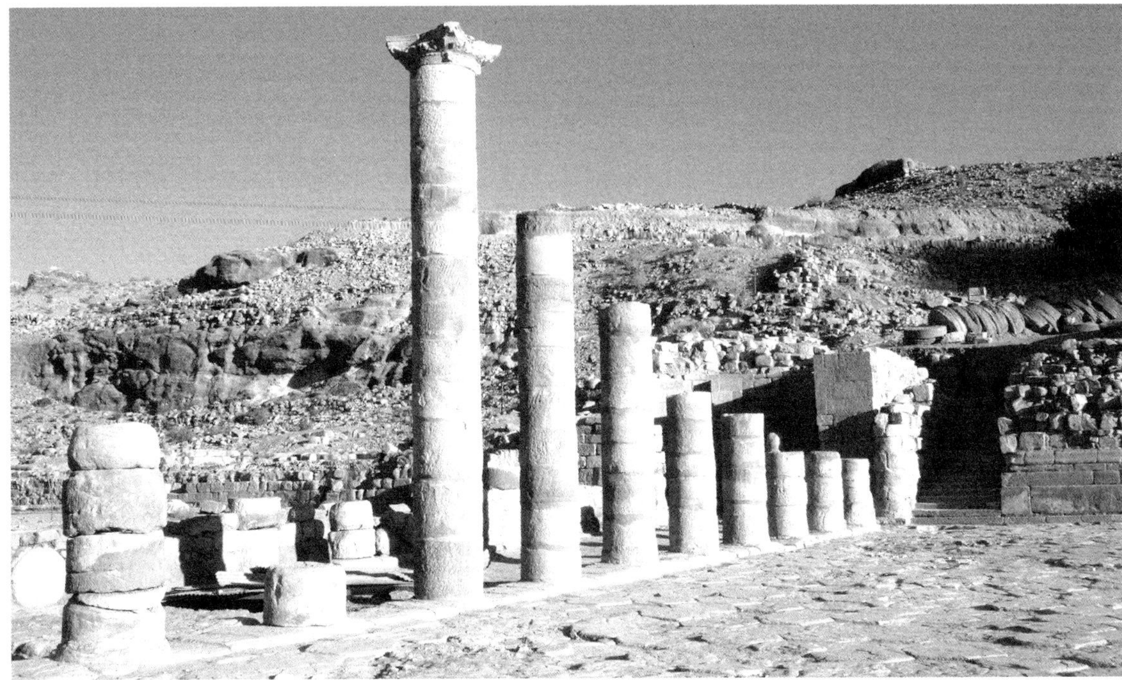

Fig. 7.26. Lower Temenos, East Triple Colonnade, view to southeast, showing restored elephant-head column with its capital.

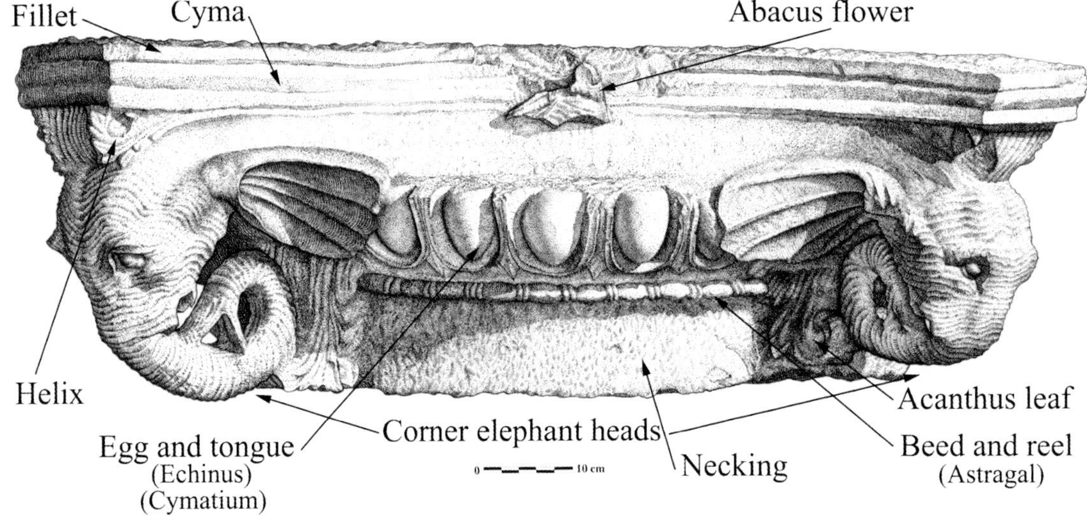

Fig. 7.27. Elephant-head capital from an engaged column in the Lower Temenos (Petra Museum).

acanthus leaf extending down; it overlies both the bead-and-reel motif and the shaft. On the sides and resting on the elephant's forehead is an incurving scroll with floral motifs. A plain band runs across the abacus. The combined height of these features is *c.*41.5 cm (see fig. 7.27). Unfortunately, they had not been discovered before E. von Merklin published his exhaustive corpus, *Antike Figuralkapitelle* (1962). We have used the term "pseudo-Ionic" when describing these capitals, but E. Netzer places them in a class he calls "Diagonale ionische Kapitelle", or "Ionic-Nabataean type C capitals".[7] Z. Dimitrov suggests they cannot be placed in the Ionic order;[8] even if the proportions and overall shape are classified as Ionic, the abacus flower is Corinthian in genre (like those

7 Netzer 2003, 160, figs. 222.4 and 223.
8 Dimitrov 2012.

of al-Khazna) and the placement of the elephant heads, instead of volutes, suggests a Corinthian design, as do the secondary decorative motifs (the abacus and *calathos*). He suggests they should be identified as a "Corinthian composite sub-type", or be placed within a group of "figural capitals with animal figures from the Imperial period".

A comparison of the Asian and African elephant shows that the ears of our elephants are fan-like and considerably smaller than those of the African elephant (*Loxodonta Africana*), which characteristically has a bent dorsal edge that is folded over. One of the distinguishing marks of the Indian elephant is that the forehead is indented, having twin domes, as do our examples.

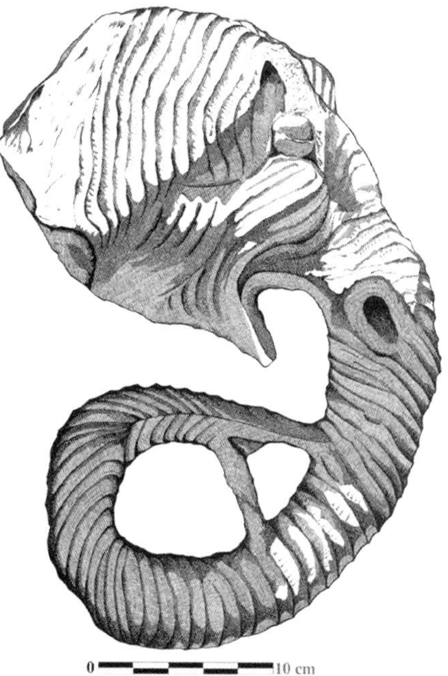

Fig. 7.28. Right profile of elephant-head capital (seq. no. 66055).

The representations on the capitals from the Great Temple are diverse, each sculptural representation being unique. Each animal reveals its own disposition (fig. 7.28): some seem intelligent, others stupid, some have 'type A' personalities, others seem lazy, some seem good-natured and pacific, others fierce and obstinate.

The adoption of the elephant by the Nabataeans seems to have been short-lived and restricted to one phase, the peak period of building from the 1st c. B.C. to 1st c. A.D. This zoomorphic apparatus does not appear to survive into the Roman period.

In addition to stray, unstratified examples found in Petra by the Temenos Gate below the Great Temple,[9] elephant-head capitals were already known at Nabataean Tell/Khirbet Brak[10] and at the Nabataean site of Khirbet Tannur, where N. Glueck misidentified the elephant as a dolphin.[11] At Beidha, a suburb of Petra, one elephant head and capital is associated with an *oecus* or banquet hall.[12] The evolution of the elephant-head capital and the context in which it was used can be traced through a series of representations and a few finds at other Nabataean sites,[13] which show that it enjoyed some popularity with Nabataean builders, but nowhere was its use so prolific as at the Great Temple.

The Indian or Asian elephant head had been represented on Hellenistic coins from the 3rd c. B.C. As India will have produced spices trafficked by the Nabataeans, the latter could have encountered the motif in Hellenistic art or in India itself, but its use replacing the scroll on the Ionic type of capital seems to have been original to the Nabataeans. Nabataean artists were well able to synthesize, modify, adapt and even invent ideas. In this instance they mingled Nabataean and Hellenistic symbols to decorate a royal building. The image of the elephant was not used because

---

9 We can only assume that many of the elephant-head capitals in the Great Temple had been carried away, like the one found inside the cistern of the Petra Church (Kanellopoulos 2001c, 174, fig. 51) and those found on the Roman street. The latter had their origins in the Propylaeum before tumbling onto the street along with some pilaster blocks; they suggest that the façade of the Propylaeum too was embellished with elephants.

10 Parr 1960a, 4-5 and 134-36; Glueck 1966, 60.

11 Glueck, 1965, 16, pl. 4.

12 Bikai *et al.* 2008, cat. no. 11, 498. This is a capital for a quarter column (Bikai *et al.* 2008, fig. 9, 475) measuring 0.36 m in diameter, possibly from an open window on an upper level, as shown ibid. fig. 10, 476.

13 See the important studies of zoomorphic capitals of the free-standing monuments at Petra by McKenzie and McKenzie and Phippen 145-65 (1987 and 1990), Blagg (1990, 131-37), Lyttelton and Blagg (1990, 91-107), Parr (1960, 134-36 and 1990), Hammond (1977, 47-51) and Zayadine (1981, 12-13 and 20-29).

its characteristics were associated with a local Nabataean god. The elephant is not recorded as a divinity or theophoric element, but, in a culture in which literacy was not universal, imagery and symbols are paramount. A passing reference to the cult of Dionysus and Alexander,[14] when coupled with recent excavations at Beidha,[15] may offer a clue (see below).

What iconographic sources served the sculptors of the elephant-head capitals when elephant-head capitals were previously unknown in Hellenistic art? Did the Nabataeans adopt the elephant as a symbol, due to its decorative value? Was it solely a visual device or did it somehow enhance the apotropaic value of the Lower Temenos and Propylaeum. Elephant images had the power to ward off or prevent evil and bring good fortune, as was celebrated in the cult of Dionysus-Alexander. Alexander was attributed many of twice-born Dionysus' characteristics, and as time went on Alexander legends were invented to explain the connection between Dionysus and Alexander.[16] The elephant can be seen both as a symbol associated with Alexander and as an allusion to the animal's own specific qualities. The relationship of the elephant to Alexander signified triumph. Qualities assigned to the elephant by the Nabataeans were that it could repel demons and provide protection against evil. Since the pseudo-Ionic capital with the elephant head remains unique to the Nabataeans, it should have been serving the wishes of some members of the Nabataean élite.[17]

The life of elephants

During a sabbatical spent in India researching the elephant and watching elephant behavior, I held extended conversations with *mahouts* in various zoos, from San Diego to New Delhi. The goal was to study plausible representations of the elephant and gather direct information about elephant personalities and character in order to understand why the Great Temple's elephants were sculpted in such diverse ways.

Asian elephants stand *c*.2.8 m high at the shoulder for a bull, shorter for a cow. They have two lumps forming parallel ridges on their angular heads and steep foreheads. They have smaller ears than their African counterparts. Their skin is smoother and their trunk has one, rather than two, "fingers" at the end. Their ivory tusks are smaller than the African elephant's (*Elephas Loxondata,* "lozenge-shaped teeth"), weighing *c*.41-50 kg; the females have small tusks if any, which protrude beyond the upper lip. Their backs are arched, compared to the flat ones of African elephants. Asian elephants (*Elephas Maximus*) are typically smaller than African. The African elephant is the Titan of the animal kingdom:[18] they can weigh 4208 kg, their tusks can weigh up to 101 kg, and they stand 2.9 m high at the shoulder.

---

14 See Coleman 2006, 156-57 (I owe this reference to M. Dickie). At Pella, Alexander grew up amidst deep roots of Dionysus worship. He identified and became syncretized with Dionysus, and was attributed many of Dionysus' attributes – wine, joy, merrymaking, vegetation, fertility of land and man, protector of theaters, and lover of peace (Strab. 15, p. 687; Eurip., *Bacc.* 13). Like Dionysus, Alexander wandered through Egypt, Syria and crossed all of Asia (Paus. 10.29; Plut., *de Flum.* 24). Dionysus built a bridge to cross the Euphrates and Tigris and travelled on to India. He conquered his enemies, killed the Amazons, and founded towns as a promoter of civilization. Alexander-Dionysus conquered his enemies, taught the Indians cultivation of the vine and various fruits, and also worship of the gods; he founded towns, gave them laws, and left behind pillars and monuments in the happy land which he had conquered and civilized, where the inhabitants worshipped him as a god (Comp. Str. 11, p. 505; Arr., *Indica* 5; Diod., *Ind.* 2.38; Philostr., *Vit. AS.* 2.9; Verg., *Aen.* 6.805).

15 Bikai, Sanders and Kanellopoulos 2008, 465-507.

16 Cf. Plin., *NH* 4.39: "[Alexander the Great] even roamed in the tracks of Father Liber [Dionysus] and of Hercules and conquered India". Alexander's character further developed in his role as promoter of civilization, lawgiver, and lover of peace (Eurip., *Bacc.* 430).

17 By the time the elephant-headed capitals were installed, the activities of the iconoclasts (people who destroy religious images) were over, so the elephant must not have been offensive to them.

18 One African forest elephant is a smaller subspecies of the gigantic elephant.

Elephants have the largest brain of any land animal and are characterized by having a remarkable intelligence, calm nature, and excellent long-term memory. Elephants exhibit empathetic social behavior: they are gregarious and quick to learn. Elephants are considerate and gentle with people; although endowed with enormous strength, it is said that an elephant will never harm a child. By nature they are placid animals that do not kill unless trained to do so, but if they are under psychological stress they can show outbursts of rage. Sometimes in captivity their natural instincts are suppressed and they become aggressive. When threatened by danger, they face their foe with courage.

Elephants relish the jungle and rain-forest environment where they can lead their lives privately with the protection of lush foliage. They are herd animals with a cohesive migratory life and stable family order. The family unit consists of 2-3 older females with their offspring that travel together, creating a life-long bond. In the dry season the family group separates from the herd, one cow staying in front, the other behind. The elders control the young. The mother guides and cares and maintains matriarchal authority over the young, as well as ensuring stability and harmony in the group. There can also be extended family groups. Generally, the bulls form bands (a lone bull can sometimes be dangerous) and a hierarchical order operates between them. The bulls join the female herds only at mating time, when the sex act is repeated several times. Mating begins before the cow comes into season, generally between December and February. Females are in heat for three weeks, pregnancy lasts 20-22 months, and the cow gives birth standing. A fellow female, an adopted aunt, is present to help her with the birthing process and care of the baby. The calf weighs about 100 kg.

Elephants have flexible knee joints: no other large animal is more agile. They have an excellent state of balance and supple physical control. Desert elephants can cover 64-80 km in a day, run 40 km per hour, and can survive without water for 3-4 days. Each day they consume 136-170 kg of food and require 68-98 liters of water. Eighteen hours are spent grazing — they can eat almost anything. If the trunk is lost, it is the elephant's death knell. The trunk provides a fine sense of direction: it can locate water sources 19 km distant. Elephants love water and are accomplished long-distance swimmers, able to cover 48 km using their trunks as a snorkel. Male elephants have temporal glands that exude from ducts on their cheeks, at which time they become restless; known as *musth*, it may in part be an indication of sexual desire. Elephants pick up different sound frequencies than humans and they distinguish between tones, tone sequences and rhythms. Purring vibrations indicate pleasure, rumbling throat sounds indicate pain, moaning squeals indicate loneliness or boredom, hissing rumbles indicate anger, and a vibrating singing sound indicates desire. Elephant communication is most intricate and complex. Studies by K. Payne[19] and others have shown that elephants make infrasonic vibrations and send each other seismic signals that travel through the ground and are below the range of human hearing. The somatosensory signals are received through their bones, feet and trunks. At night, these conversations can travel across 200 km^2, during the day 50 km^2. Their gentle melancholy eyes are weak and not designed for night vision. Their tusks are massively enlarged upper-jaw incisors that continue to grow throughout life. An elephant is old by age 60 and wanders off to die alone.

In India the *mahout* is the elephant trainer, keeper and driver; the *khotal* is the *mahout*'s assistant. At the start of the training the *mahout* is carried on the elephant's back; then he moves to the driving position on the elephant's neck. For commands, the *mahout* uses an elephant hook (*ankush*) to poke it on its sensitive trunk or behind the ears. A bond of trust and dependency develops between the *mahout* and his charge.

The elephant was revered in Hindu mythology; it was thought to be the bearer and keeper of the universe. Ganesh, the elephant-headed Hindu god, is the protector of wisdom, erudition and well-being. Ganesh is also the patron of scientists, merchants and thieves. He is considered the 'lord of the blessed host'. Represented with a human body of elephantine proportions and a large

---

19 Payne 1999.

belly, his four arms are often shown holding a whip, fork, dagger, and death's head, with only one developed tusk. Ganesh is most often accompanied by the rat. In Buddhism, Buddha, the 'enlightened one', enters the 'incarnation of the white elephant'. Before he was born, Buddha in heaven took the shape of a white elephant. His mother, Maya, mated with this white elephant and Buddha, also known as the white elephant, was born. This is one of the earliest legends about the rebirth of the white elephant (Buddha) and the virgin birth. The god Indra was shown riding through the heavens on a white elephant, Airavata, whom legend has it arose in the earliest times of the cosmos from the ocean of milk, out of which the gods churned their nectar of immortality. He is the mythological ancestor of the elephant race. The motif of the elephant has been used constantly by Hindus and Buddhists. Under the influence of Buddhism in the 3rd and 2nd c. B.C., the elephant represents the power of insight.

A brief review of the uses of elephants down to the 1st c. B.C.

A review of how elephants were used in antiquity, and particularly during the Hellenistic era, may shed light on the reasons behind its adoption by the Nabataeans at the Great Temple.

For the Egyptians the elephant became a single hieroglyph (*abu*), meaning ivory. To this was added an explanatory symbol of an elephant or a tusk. Yet the elephant played virtually no rôle in Egyptian mythology or daily life. For most of Egypt's history African elephants lived farther south in Nubia and beyond. In the New Kingdom (1550-1070 B.C.) the pharaohs gained control of Nubia and the kingdom of Kush, which supplied Egypt with gold, ivory and ebony. Egypt's port for expeditions into Kush was on Elephantine Island.

In the 8th-7th c. B.C. the Assyrians prized the elephant as game and greatly valued its ivory; as seen in the Nimrud ivories, the elephant tusk was used for small sculptures and luxury decorative objects. Ivory ('white gold') was one of the most precious materials for the ancients, and was said to have magical powers. African ivory is superior in quality to Asian ivory. Ivory statuettes are found in Minoan Crete (e.g., the snake goddess and bull jumper from Knossos). In their tombs the Egyptians used ivory for animal figures, statues, idols, furniture decoration, combs, pins and cult objects. Ivory was a luxury reserved for rulers and high officials. The Phoenicians supplied ivory to Egyptian pharaohs and were also ivory carvers, particularly of intarsia for furniture. Phidias prized ivory, using it for his chryselephantine statue of Athena. In 460 B.C. Hanno traveled down the African coast to find ivory. An ivory portrait head of Philip II, father of Alexander the Great, survives. In the 3rd c. B.C. the Ptolemies established colonies in Eritrea and Ethiopia from which they imported elephants and ivory. The Carthaginians also traded ivory. After Carthage's destruction the ivory trade was controlled by Rome which purchased most of its ivory from Axum (Ethiopia), shipping it through the port of Adulis. The Parthians also prized ivory. Forty large ivory rhytons from Nisa were each made from an elephant tusk; decorated with the deities Anahita, Mithras and Ahura Mazda as well as Greek gods (Artemis, Apollo, and Zeus), they are extraordinary for the detail of the renderings.

The naturally gentle elephant was forced into war and trained to perform tasks against its nature: the elephant became a war-machine. Carrying its driver and two or so warriors and archers, the trained elephant corps was expected to perform as the vanguard of the marching army. The elephants were trained to tear down trees for roads and campgrounds, with their tusks to destroy enemy walls, gates and towers, and in battle to trample the opposition.[20]

Elephants became a most important arm of the military about the time of the Macedonian invasion:

> The classical chronicles make it abundantly clear that in his titanic struggle against Alexander, Porus pinned his hope on the elephants in his army. In the battle-array … on that fateful day he posted the elephants along the front like bastions in a wall. He seems to have thought that these monsters

20 Chakravarti 1993, 50.

> would terrify the foreign soldiers and render the Macedonian calvary unmanageable ... Alexander, a shrewder judge of military affairs, instinctively realized the grave danger involved ...[21]

Referring to ancient Indian manuals devoted to the art of war, H. Zimmer[22] writes:

> ... so elephants belong to kings. In stately processions they are the king's symbolical mount; in warfare they are the watchtower and citadel from which he controls the strategy of battle ... Hence Hindu kings keep elephants for the welfare of their subjects ... the elephant is finally worshipped by the high officials of the realm, both civil and military ... The text [The *Hastyayurveda*] remarks, "If they did not pay worship to the elephant, the king and the kingdom, the army and the elephants would be doomed to perish, because a divinity would have been disregarded".

It was said that one good elephant was worth 50 horses in warfare.

The Persians made use of elephant power during their campaigns of conquest. The elephant corps was the pride of kings, often replacing or augmenting the functions of the cavalry, particularly when the ground was jungle, swampy, hilly or otherwise difficult for horses. Alexander the Great first saw the elephant used in battle by Darius III in 331 B.C. at Gaugamela. With Darius's murder, Alexander ascended the Persian throne and set his sights on the upper Indus where the Persians had lost control of the 20th satrapy. Setting out in 327 from Afghanistan, Alexander constructed a pontoon bridge across the Indus river; in 326, he attacked the Indian king Porus on the Hydaspes river. Although the figures are probably exaggerated, King Porus' troops numbered 50,000 infantry, 3,000 cavalry, 300 war chariots and some 200-war elephants. Alexander's troops by this time were about 30,000 men including 5000 cavalry. Although Alexander employed elephants to carry supplies, he had not previously used them in battle. A front line of war elephants shielded Porus' infantry and the cavalry. By the time Porus ordered his war elephants to attack, it was too late. Alexander unleashed his archers on the elephants, and as Arrian (*Anab.* 5. 4-17, 17.3-18) reported, a bloodbath ensued, with the elephants indiscriminately attacking and killing everything and everyone in their paths. Meanwhile Alexander's men either avoided the war elephants or shot long spears into the gigantic beasts' bodies. Porus fought with great courage but finally was wounded. Plutarch (*Alex.* 60.4-7) writes that when his elephant sensed his collapse it fell to its knees, allowing Porus to slide off its back. Using his trunk, the compassionate elephant pulled the arrows out of his body. Retracing its steps, the Greek army retreated through Persia to Babylon. With the spoils of war, Alexander now brought at least 200 war elephants into his army. Thereafter a concerted effort was made in the taming and training of elephants. Clearly Alexander was impressed by the fearsome bulk of war elephants for strengthening battle lines. The elephant was the tank of antiquity.

At the village of Mir Zakah (Afghanistan) a famous hoard of gold and silver artworks was found in a well.[23] One (fig. 7.29) is a gold medallion depicting an elephant on what is believed to be the only lifetime portrait of Alexander, issued as a commemorative for the

Fig. 7.29. Mir Zakah medallion. Obverse shows the horns of Ammon, signifying his status as a god. Elephant head and aegis indicate divine intervention for winning the battle at the Hydaspes river (drawing by N. MacDonald, *Saudi Aramco World*, Nov.-Dec. 2006; courtesy *Saudi Aramco World*).

21 Ibid. 47-48

22 Zimmer 1946, 107.

23 Four tons of coins and 770 pounds of gold and silver works of art were found. See Holt 2005, 10-19 and 2006, 4-9, for the story behind this remarkable discovery.

success of his campaign of 326. The Mir Zakah medallion depicts him with an elephant scalp on his head; on the reverse is an Indian elephant with Greek monograms. In 323, the 33-year-old Alexander died from a fever, and elephants were stationed around his grave in Babylon. From the Nile to India Alexander had established 70 Greek cities and promoted Hellenistic culture. His vision was to create a pan Macedonian-Persian union. His legacy of a hybrid culture, a mix of Greek and Oriental, blossomed, as in the hybrid architectural concepts of the Nabataean builders at Petra.

Indian and Seleucid relations became tense in 305 B.C. when Seleucus Nicator led his army against the Mauryan Empire. Instead of waging war, a pact was drawn up between Seleucus and King Chandragupta; Seleucus allowed the Hindu to keep his satrapy in exchange for 500 elephants. Then followed ambassadorial exchanges and the visit of Megasthenes to Pataliputra, the Mauryan capital on the Ganges. Overland and sea trade flourished between India and the Seleucids. Seleucid control of the Persian Gulf and trade through the ports of western India and Ceylon ensured the flow of Asian elephants to the west.

Fig. 7.30. Ptolemy's coin of Alexander depicting him as Zeus, with the ram's horn of Amon above his ear and an elephant scalp. Ptolemy copied what Alexander had already minted (drawing by N. MacDonald, *Saudi Aramco World*, Nov.-Dec. 2006; courtesy *Saudi Aramco World*).

In the period after Alexander's death, Greek kings and commanders became inordinately fond of war elephants, developing large herds of them as part of a "pre-industrial arms race".[24] In 301, at the Battle of Ipsus, Antigonos employed 70 war elephants against Seleucus. Ptolemy I Soter imported captured Asian war elephants and brought Indian *mahouts* to train Egyptians in taming and working the giant beasts. The Ptolemies opened the routes to the Red Sea, Nubia and the land of Kush. They made the Suez Canal navigable and established caravan routes to Arabia by way of Palestine and southern Syria, which included probably a stop in Petra. In the age of the Ptolemies elephants living in the wild had been forced down to the twentieth parallel south of the equator, but on the Red Sea coast of Eritrea the Ptolemies controlled the port of Adulis from which Ethiopian elephants could be transshipped to Egypt. Ptolemy's silver decadrachms of Alexander depict the latter with the ram's horn of Amon, elephant cap, and aegis of Zeus tied around his neck (fig. 7.30). These coins are copies of the Mir Zakah commemorative, struck by Ptolemy to promote his own reputation. Holt also comments:

> Ptolemy's portrait of Alexander deified proved to be so potent that rivals such as Lysimachus in Thrace and Seleucus in Syria [in 300 B.C.] soon imitated its main features: ram's horn, aegis and elephant scalp ... Only the popularity of the elephant head-dress has puzzled scholars ... Why Ptolemy dressed Alexander in this fashion, calling attention to India rather than Egypt, has remained a mystery until a recent dazzling discovery from Afghanistan yielded up a single artifact that changes all of our assumptions about Ptolemy's famous Alexander portrait.

The elephant had now become a popular subject in the Hellenistic Middle East.

Ptolemy III (246-221 B.C.) led elephant hunts and used Eritrean elephants in his successful battle against the Seleucids. Due to their training, Indian war elephants were superior to African forest elephants in war. Ptolemy IV (221-205 B.C.) realized this when he fought Antiochus III in a battle near Gaza. Polybius reports that the latter commanded 102 Indian war elephants, whereas Ptolemy IV had a majority of African elephants. Ptolemy's troops lost the battle and with it southern Palestine.

---

24 Holt 2003, 80.

The Seleucids continued the elephant trade with the Indian Hindu Maurya Empire, but cut the Ptolemies off from the Asian elephant supply, with the result that the Ptolemies had to use small African (Ethiopian and Nubian) elephants for their military exploits.

By 198 B.C. Antiochus III the Great had crushed the Ptolemaic army near Baniyas, and Petra and Jerusalem passed into Seleucid hands. Later, as Seleucid power was declining, the Hasmonaeans, successors of the Maccabees, ruled an independent Judaea from 142 to 63 B.C. Alexander Jannaeus provoked a conflict with the Nabataeans who were in control of the trade routes and cities that he coveted. Threatened, the Nabataeans joined forces with the Seleucid Demetrius III. Although they temporarily defeated the Hasmonaeans, Alexander Jannaeus regained control and then constructed fortresses along the Jordanian front. In 64 B.C. Syria was made a Roman province by Pompey. Pompey the Great's arrival in Damascus in 63 B.C. sounded the death knell for the Hasmonaeans. Pompey forced Aretas III's troops to withdraw from Jerusalem and appointed John Hyrcanus II as high priest. After a second rebellion in 55 B.C., the Romans appointed the strategist Herod Antipater as governor.

Even after the end of the Seleucid empire, war elephants continued to play an important rôle in the outcome of battles. In 46 B.C. Julius Caesar used elephants at Thapsus against Pompey. At Rome in the 1st c. A.D. the elephant was associated with the cults of Dionysus and Alexander and with the person and property of the Roman emperor. Tradition credited elephants with spontaneous worship (*proskynesis*) of the sun and the new moon. [25]

Rise of the Nabataeans and relations with Parthia

The Zenon Papyri of 259 B.C. identify the Nabataeans with the Hauran and N Transjordan, which they may have controlled as they expanded their influence to the north. Nabataean settlements on the Edomite plateau may predate their fortress in Petra, where the earliest Nabataean building dates to the mid-3rd c. B.C. Finds of this period include black-glazed wares and Phoenician, Ptolemaic and Seleucid coins. The Nabataeans borrowed art and architectural ideas from the surrounding kingdoms; Hellenistic culture was pervasive, but they also co-opted ideas from Egyptians, Assyrians, Parthians (who controlled the Silk Road to China) and the inhabitants of Arabia for their buildings and artifacts. Paradoxically, it was during the era of the Ptolemies and Seleucids that Petra and the caravan cities flourished, with increased trade and the establishment of new trading towns such as Philadelphia and Jerash. Infighting between Seleucids and Ptolemies allowed the Nabataeans to maintain control over the caravan routes between Arabia and Syria, and Greater Petra became a metropolis with a population estimated at 20,000-30,000.

In the 2nd-1st c. B.C. Parthia was a formidable enemy of the Roman Republic, interfering with Rome's desire to control the trade routes. Swift bands of Parthian horsemen and war elephants protected the trade route and their trading interests from which they derived huge profits. The Parthians invaded Palestine in 40 B.C. and put the Hasmonaean Antigonus on the throne in Jerusalem, taking John Hyrcanus II prisoner. The Nabataeans made a tactical blunder by siding with the Parthians. Rome, backing Herod the Great, defeated the Parthians and captured Jerusalem; the Nabataeans were forced to pay a heavy fine. Herod invaded Nabataean territory when the Nabataeans neglected to pay tribute to Rome. Of Nabataean descent, Herod the Great was the son of Herod Antipater; his mother Cypros was a noblewoman from Petra. Herod captured Jerusalem in 37 B.C. and Nabataea in 31 B.C., gaining control over a large part of Nabataean territory and unofficially ending its independence, although Nabataea remained nominally independent and its culture continued to flourish until its king Rabbel died in A.D. 106.

---

25 "The same motif of spontaneous worship is employed by Martial in an oblique allusion to the emperor's divinity and his power over nature": Coleman 2006, 157. Caracalla paraded with a troupe of elephants to impress the crowds that he was another Alexander: Dio 77.7.4 (I owe this reference to M. Dickie).

Figs. 7.31-32. Porphyry elephant-head capital (Vatican Museums; courtesy Musei Vaticani).

Conclusion

The Nabataeans certainly knew of elephants and how war elephants had changed the course of battles; they must also have heard how they were used in royal pageantry. There is no evidence that live elephants were kept in Petra but the army of stonecarvers must have seen live elephants, for the capitals are sculpted with a remarkable accuracy, ingenuity, quality of workmanship and painstaking attention to detail. If the sculptors were not familiar with the real animals, the capitals would have borne little relation to reality: instead, they are anatomically correct. Each animal is treated as an individual, with its own disposition. The eyes in particular can be expressive of emotion of all kinds. According to the nearly contemporary Pliny the Elder (*NH* 8.1.27), "elephants possess the virtues of honesty, consideration and justice to a higher degree than the majority of men". For the Petraeans, the elephant was a revered icon of great power, one that also reflected their pluralistic, hybrid and nomadic heritage. The symbolism of their public art likewise had to be innovative, departing from Classical forms.[26] The elephant was a reference to the force of nature. It evoked recognizable memories as well as a sense of spectacle. Its massive bulk, strength, courage and other qualities were admirable, and it reflected the pride of the nobility. The white elephant in particular was long considered priceless: the mythical Airavata was the white elephant's ancestor, and in Indian cosmic prehistory white elephants mated with clouds and were considered mediators for bringing rain and protecting against drought and famine. The capitals reveal the reverence the Nabataeans held for the animal as a sacred symbol of royal power.

A final interpretation of the Great Temple complex also depends on the arguments for a link with Dionysus. With the discovery of the Nabataean Hall at Beidha, which its excavators have identified with Dionysus, we may hypothesize a connection between the elephant-head capitals and the cult of Dionysus. The elephant portraits exalt the heroic deeds of Alexander–Dionysus, who may be the legitimizing force behind the capitals and thereby behind the identity and purpose of the Great Temple complex.

---

26 A. Oliver kindly brought to my attention these 4 elephant *protomai* from an unknown provenience now in the Vatican Museums and published by H. von Hesberg (1981-82, 43-86, figs. 1-3). In 2001 I examined one elephant-head capital of porphyry in the Vatican Museums (see figs. 7.31-32 here). I have also searched for sculptural representations in The Metropolitan Museum of Art and the Louvre, and have visited the remarkable elephant sculptures in Indian cities from Sanchi to Mumbai and Elūra, but none resembled the capitals at the Great Temple; indeed, none beyond Nabataea compared with our elephants.

Like the blind men, we may still be seeing only certain aspects of the elephant. My own archaeological version of Saxe's poem would have a different ending: the elephant would become impatient with all the touching, jabbing and fussing, and would run away, ignoring the blind archaeologists. Like the touch of the blind men, our excavations have produced evidence that is difficult to comprehend, but we may expect further eye-opening discoveries that will allow us better to understand the elephants of the Great Temple.

8

Theater-in-Temple

Rune Frederiksen

Introduction

During the excavations of 1996 Trench 47, located in the upper west part of the rectangular space within the colonnade of the Great Temple, revealed a small theater.[1] The unexpected find not only challenged the interpretation of the overall function of the Great Temple, but also proved to be a unique architectural edifice from Roman Nabataea. During the campaign of July-August 1997 the west part of a *cavea* orientated towards the north was revealed. Later the *orchestra* came to light extending 1.5 m below the narrow walkway in front of the seats. Table 8.1 lists the theater trenches excavated.

TABLE 8.1
GREAT TEMPLE EXCAVATED THEATER TRENCHES

Trench	*Year*	*Description N-S by E-W*	*Measurement (m)*	*Exavators*
Trench 40	1997	Stage west	6.00 x 9.80	Slaughter
Trench 47	1997	Theater west	9.80 x 6.00	Bedal
Trench 62	1999	Theater, stage and East Corridor north	11.00 x 12.50	Basile, Sylvester
Trench 92	2002	Pronaos/Stage	4.00 x 6.18	Fusté
Special Project 200	2005	Orchestra floor sondage	6.96 x 1.96	Libonati
Trench 123	2006	Theater seats sondage	1.30 x 2.80	Libonati

The whole complex was called a *theatron* in subsequent publications. The ancient Greek *theatron*, meaning "a place from where things can be seen," and used for many forms of seating, is attested locally as a Greek loan word in a Nabataean inscription from the Petra Church excavations on the north side of the Colonnaded Street.[2] *Theatron* may have been the word used by the Petraeans to label this fascinating structure. In the following discussion *theatron* refers to the *cavea* alone,

1 I would like to express my sincerest thanks to Martha Sharp Joukowsky for entrusting me with the general presentation and interpretation of the Great Temple Theater. My life has become richer in knowing her as well as Artemis W. Joukowsky. We shared many great moments in Petra both professionally and personally. I am also indebted to Elizabeth Gebhard, my uncrowned 'Doktormutter' of Greek and Roman theater research, who has inspired and supported me for many years in this area of research. I would like to thank Judith McKenzie for being willing to share her great knowledge of Nabataean and related architecture and building and finally Frank Sear for having read and commented on a draft, and made decisive suggestions as regards the most likely function of the building. Chrysanthos Kanellopoulos and the following excavators and surveyors of the Theater in the Great Temple, have been of great help to me in the process of understanding this building: Emma S. Libonati, Christopher A. Tuttle, Joseph J. Basile and Marshall C. Agnew. For a complete list of excavators involved in this part of the Brown University excavations at the Petra Great Temple, see Great Temple vol. 2, xxxiv-xxxviii.

2 See Jones and Bowersock in Fiema *et al.* 2001, 346-9; Joukowsky and Basile, 2001. An *in situ* inscription from Sî in the Syrian desert, identifies a structure of stepped seating in a porticoed courtyard in front of the temple of Ba'al Shamin as a 'teietra' (Semitic characters), Rossetto and Sartorio 1994, vol. 3, 214; Weber 2003, 350 with n. 2 [with refs.]), and Sear 2006, 110. It would be logical to assume that the Nabataeans borrowed 'theatron' as a loan-word from Greek, and used it in the same broad meaning as the Greeks themselves used 'theatron,' i.e., for any structure that was used for seating hundreds or more people who would watch something in front of them, cf. Frederiksen 2002, 69-76.

whereas "theater" encompasses the complete construction including the orchestra and stage. I use the word "theater" although the structure may in fact have been an odeum (more on this below).[3]

This chapter presents various components of the Great Temple Theater. The reconstruction of the monument and its relation to the pre-existing architecture of the Great Temple is discussed. Further, the architecture of the theater is analyzed in relation to Hellenistic, Nabataean and Roman theatrical architecture, and its likely function, or functions, will be considered.[4]

The main civic theater of the Romanized Nabataean capital was located further to the east beyond the Wadi Musa Siq, and at least one additional open-air performance-structure has been identified at Petra. The theater discussed here was built into the largest freestanding Nabataean structure, the Great Temple, in the center of the city. It is *sui generis* in location, design and construction. As confirmed by a deep sondage below the *cavea* of the structure (Trench 123; fig. 8.1, slightly to the north of No. 27),[5] the theater was a new installation, not based on any previous theater structure. It utilized but was also restricted by the dimensions, proportions and major architecture of the existing building. The relationship between the old and the new makes the Great Temple Theater a unique and exciting architectural phenomenon.

Theater Description

The Great Temple Theater is fully excavated and is exposed in a consolidated and partly reconstructed state. This was to stabilize it from further destruction and enable tourists and scholars to visit it. Parts of the building have been removed and others reconstructed to explore earlier phases and the construction of various elements.

The theater is designed to fit into the colonnade of the *distyle* peripteral Great Temple building measuring 30.07 m x 18.36 m (fig. 8.1). By reutilizing an already existing colonnade this structure resembles a small group of theaters and odea, for example the Roman odeum at Epidauros.[6] Except for the front, the temple is surrounded by high walls on all sides, preserved to a height of 5-6 m. The result of the 'Grand Design' rebuilding in the Great Temple Site Phase IV was its reconfiguration into an impressive *tetrastyle in antis* edifice. Between the walls and the colonnade are corridors each 3 m wide (East, South and West Corridors) surrounding the temple. The Pronaos, created by the addition of the Site Phase IV façade, was a much grander space measuring 6.5 m x 24.7 m (Fig. 1.10) in this volume.

The central feature of the theater is the stone *cavea* with its supporting ashlar substructure, consisting of three chambers and a carefully planned access-system of staircases leading to the upper parts of the *cavea* (fig. 8.1). Into the Pronaos a scene-building was installed, and between it and the *cavea* are the orchestra and the *aditus maximi*[7] (fig. 8.1 and 8.11). Access to the *theatron* from the East and West Corridors is possible from the *aditus maximi*. The *cavea* and orchestra were built together, while the various scene-constructions: the pre-stage wall, *proscaenium* and the *pulpitum*, are in part contemporary with the installation of the *theatron*, in part later additions. In the following paragraphs these architectural components will be presented and discussed.

---

3 In the words of Frank Sear (2006, 38): Many odea [...] which means that they were related very closely to theaters in terms of physical features.

4 The published reports on the Theater in the Great Temple, include *Great Temple* vol. 1, 118-28; Great Temple vol. 2, 217-77; Joukowsky 2007b, 86-87; Trench 123 on-line at *Open Context*.

5 See note 8.

6 Installed into the pre-existing gymnasium the colonnade of which was reutilized on three sides of the odeum Meinel 1980, 225-31, fig. 87.

7 The *aditus maximus*, known in Greek theater architecture as the *parodos*, is a term invented by modern theater research, and is used here because it has been generally adopted in research literature (Sear 2006, 6).

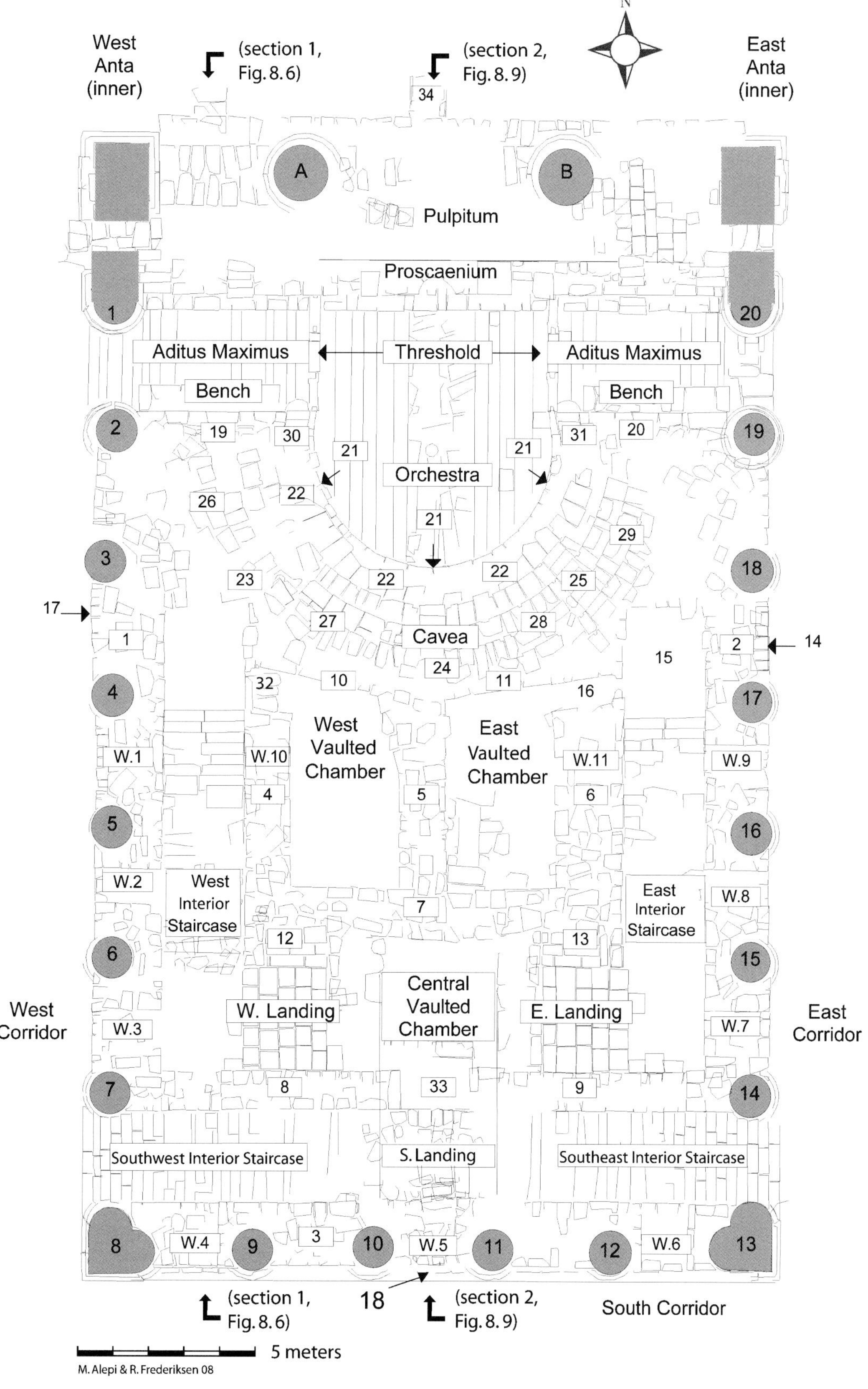

Fig. 8.1. Actual state-plan of The Great Temple with Theater (based on the Brown Univ. General Survey Plan 2002-7). Numbers represent building-features described in the text ('W' is Window).

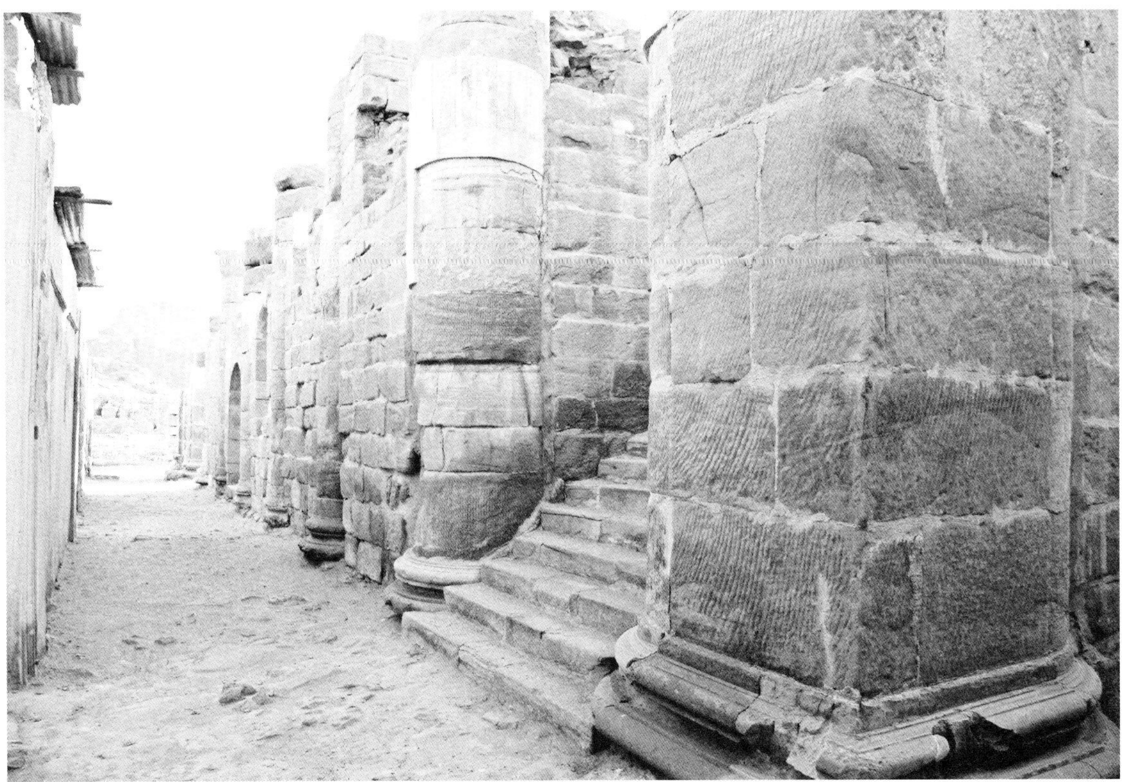

Fig. 8.2. Theater substructure placed on the foundation level of the temple columns.

Cavea and Substructure

The *cavea* and its substructure (fig. 8.1) form a rectangle inserted into the *distyle* colonnade, extending southwards from Columns 2 and 19, comprising the entire colonnade and interior, ending at the heart-shaped Columns 8 and 13. Finds of earlier structures were discovered during the excavations, but none provide decisive evidence as to the function of the Great Temple, Great Temple Site Phases I-IV, before the installation of the *cavea* in the 1st c. B.C.[8] The substructure, built of casemate ashlar walls, reused the foundation blocks and paving that had been laid inside the colonnade and in the corridors around the Great Temple (fig. 8.2). The finely turned Ionic column bases are on a higher level than the paving, and it seems an inescapable conclusion that the theater utilized the upper surfaces of the foundation socle, just under the bases of the earlier temple structure for the level of the paving which has since gone.

The outer substructure walls (fig. 8.1, Walls 1-3) are built of various sized ashlars laid in fairly even courses, preserved to a height of some 6 m towards the south.[9] Many blocks are dressed with diagonal striations to receive plaster. The exterior substructure walls utilize the footprint of the columns of the *pteron* of the temple, but leave parts of the columns and their bases visible. There is some evidence that the temple may have been damaged before the theater was built, and was repaired when the *cavea* substructure was installed (fig. 8.3).

Constructed of two outer walls (E and W, fig. 8.1 Walls 1 and 2), the substructure extends N-S from Columns 2 and 19 to Columns 7 and 14 in the south, with an E-W wall (Wall 3) to the south. These walls average 1.8 m in width and are constructed with an inner and an outer shell with rubble

8 For finds and observation relating to interior of the Great Temple and structures found under and antedating it, see *Great Temple* vol. 2, 270-75.

9 *Great Temple* vol. 2, 249, fig. 5.46. Note that the scale on the plan in *Great Temple* vol. 2 has been erroneously printed as 2 m and not 5 m.

Fig. 8.3. Stucco repair made to column base.

fill in between (fig. 8.4). Two additional E-W walls (8 and 9) 0.9 m wide extend inwards between Columns 7 and 14. Under its northernmost lowest section the *cavea* is constructed as a solid entity bonded on the south by Walls 10 and 11. The remainder of the substructure between the north and the two narrow E-W walls (Walls 8 and 9) consists of two N-S walls (4 and 6) laid parallel to the axis of the building, plus a central N-S wall (5) between them, but truncated by another E-W wall (7). The E wall (6) is considerably wider (1.92 m) than walls 5 and 4 (5:1.21 m; 4:1.27 m). These substructure walls supported vaults, landings and the *cavea* upper tiers (now collapsed).

At ground level the substructure consists of three vaulted chambers: East, West, and Central, Vaulted Chambers. Between the outer and inner substructure walls are the East and West Interior Staircases, running N-S, and two E-W staircases to the S—the SE Interior and SW Interior Staircases—all leading up to the second story of the substructure. Approximately 5 m above ground level, the second story has two paved landings (East and West Landing) providing access to two upper stairways (East and West Upper Staircases, fig. 8.1 Nos. 12 and 13), which provided access to the upper part of the *cavea*.

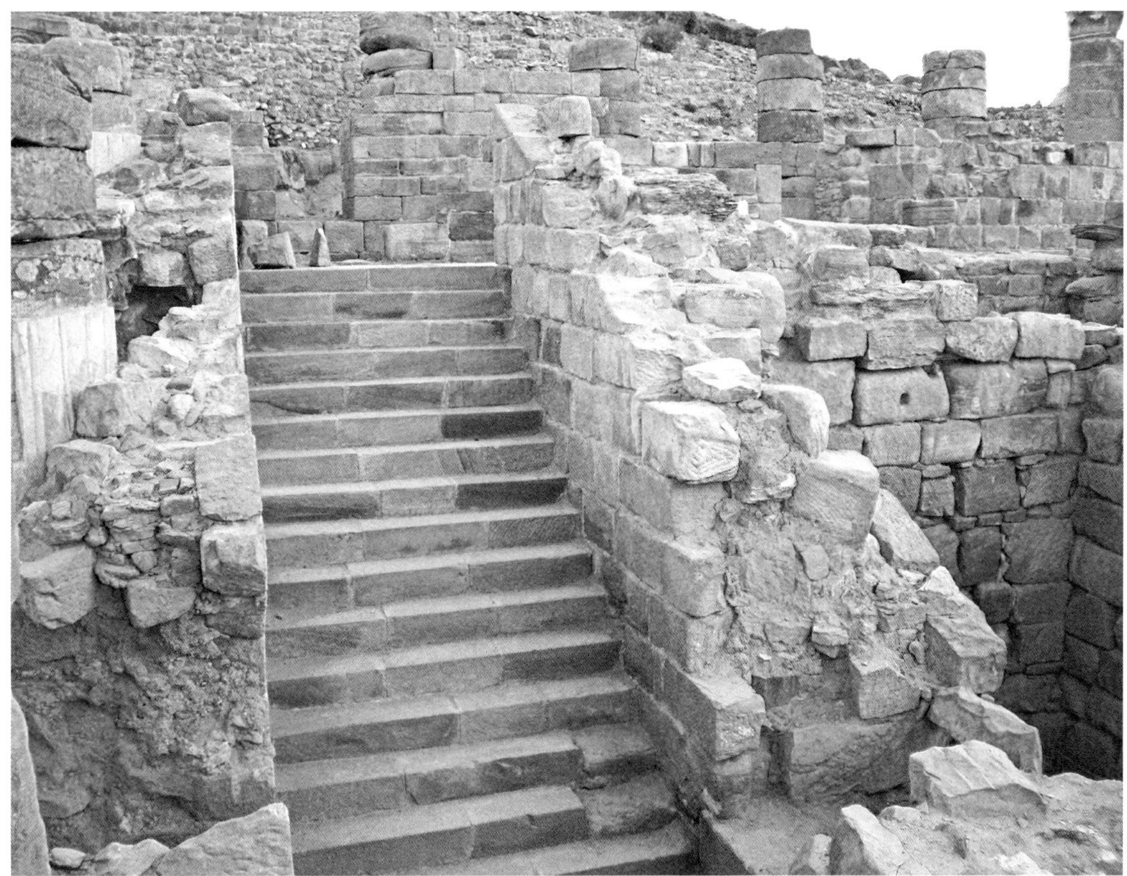

Fig. 8.4. East Interior Stairway (reconstructed) and construction of substructure walls 2 and 6, to the South.

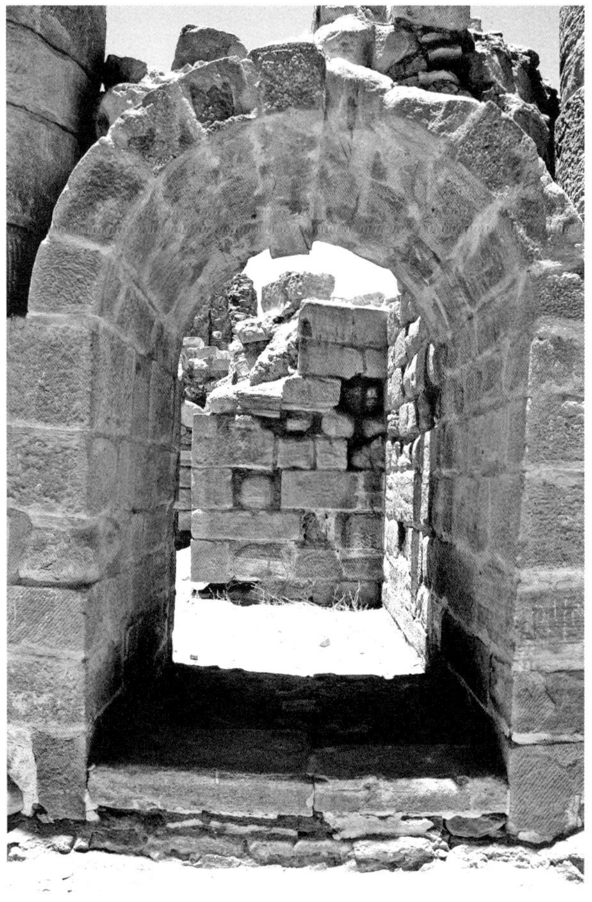

Fig. 8.5. Entrance to East Interior Staircase (see fig. 8.1, no. 14).

Fallen blocks from walls, vaults and *cavea* seats indicate that the *cavea* rose from the north in a 33-degree angle towards the south, and would have rested partially on vaults over the second story landings. The outer and inner substructure walls are pierced by vaulted windows on the W, S and E sides (W. 1-9), which provided light not only for the stairways and landings, but also for the ground-level chambers from W. 1 through W.10 and from W. 9 through W.11.

The East Interior Staircase is entered from the East Corridor via a vaulted passage through the E substructure wall (fig. 8.1, No. 14, 2.8 m in height x 1.705 m in width x 2 m in length). The passage has a threshold of two flat blocks and its semicircular[10] vault (fig. 8.5) is constructed of 10 wedge-shaped voussoirs. The height of the vault, measured from above the spring line is approximately 0.90 m, representing some 47% of the height measured below this line. This vaulted passage leads into a rectangular area (No. 15, 2.2 m wide x 3.06 m in length) leading to the stairs. On the west side is a narrow corridor (No. 16) to the East Vaulted Chamber. The East Interior staircase extends the entire

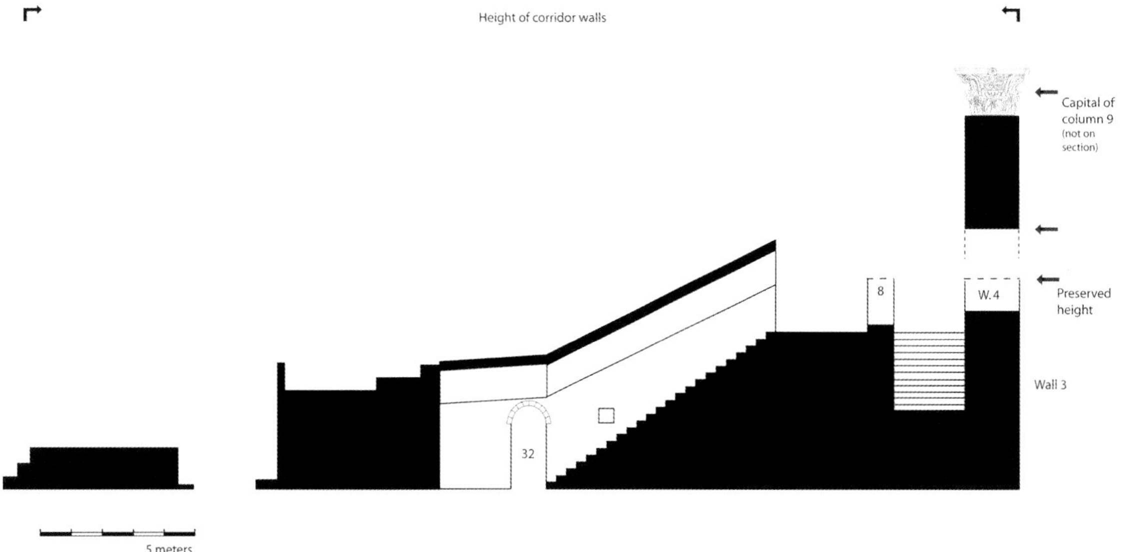

Fig. 8.6. Section 1. Reconstructed section of theater, at the center-axis of the West Interior Staircase (see fig. 8.1 for position of section). Reconstruction principle: only features of which fragments are preserved *in situ* are reconstructed. Numbers correspond to elements shown in fig. 8.1.

10 Measured at the spring line the distance of the interior height of the vault is roughly 50% of the interior width of the vault.

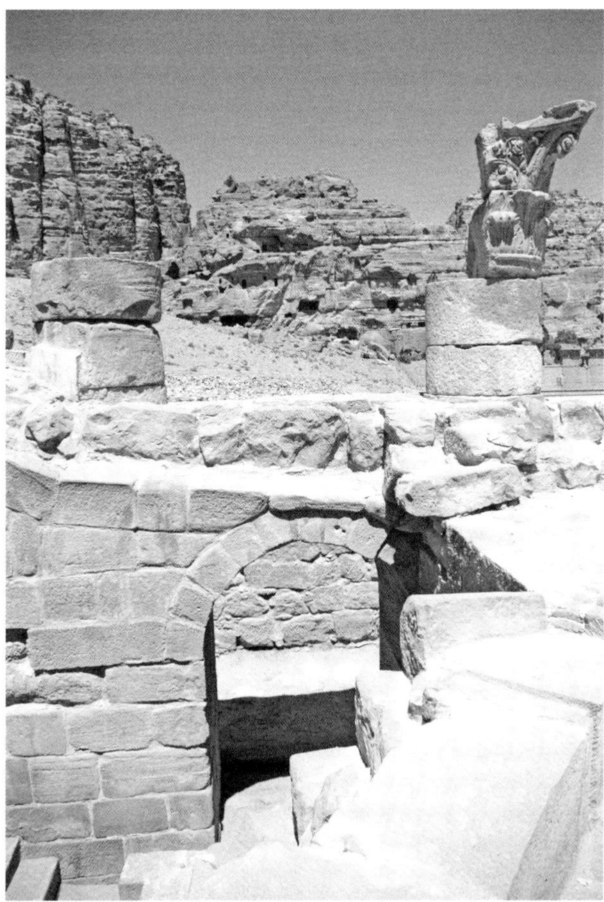

Fig. 8.7. North end of West Interior Staircase to west. Springers meet the inner voussoirs of the arch of the passage (17) leading to the West Corridor.

Fig. 8.8. East face of substructure wall No. 5 (from East Vaulted Chamber) showing masonry and spring line of the chamber vault.

2.2 m width between the walls and has 21 steps with an average height of 21 cm and depth of 33 cm. Seven meters in length, the stairway begins at the south edge of the doorway leading into the East Vaulted Chamber, and ascends to the East Landing (fig. 8.6 illustrates a section of the identical West Inner Staircase). Many steps are not *in situ* but have been reconstructed and stabilized—necessary measures for the theater's preservation. A vault, now lost, spanned the rectangular area in front of the staircase (No. 15, cf. fig. 8.7), slightly rising as it extended towards the staircase—the vault springers are still *in situ* on the west side of the E substructure wall (No. 2) and on the east side of the inner E substructure wall (No. 6). At the north these springers join the inner voussoirs of the arched passage into the East Corridor. The vault over the staircase is constructed with a 26-degree slope, which is less pronounced than the 34-degree slope of the steps themselves[11] (cf. fig. 8.6). Three windows (W. 7, W. 8 and W. 9) pierce substructure wall 2; Window 9 may have been vaulted (as is its counterpart W. 1 on the west side), and Window 8 is set 2 m higher following the upward slope of the staircase. This window may also have been vaulted, but no remains of a vault are preserved.

Irregular in plan, the East Vaulted Chamber, (3 m in width. x 5.3 m east x 5 m west in length), is entered from a narrow doorway 71 cm wide (No. 16) where dowel holes for the fitting of a door are preserved. Like the exterior walls, the walls of this chamber (essentially the walls of the inner substructure) are built of ashlars laid in even courses, but they are somewhat less carefully fitted than those of the exterior walls (fig. 8.8). In some places smaller stones are used to even out a course or to fill the interstices between blocks. The vault over the chamber has collapsed, but the preserved spring line is visible on the chamber's west side, and some of the voussoirs remain *in situ* (fig. 8.8). The vault extends from the north end of the chamber towards the south at a 23-degree angle. If the vault was of a simple semicircular type it would have been 1.5 m above the spring line

11 Distances from the upper side of the steps to the arch spring line—inner side of east wall: 10/2.18 m; 13/1.96 m; 20/1.64 m, and the outer side of inner east wall: 9/2.1 m; 12/2 m; 17/1.75 m; 20/1.6 m; 23/1.37 m.

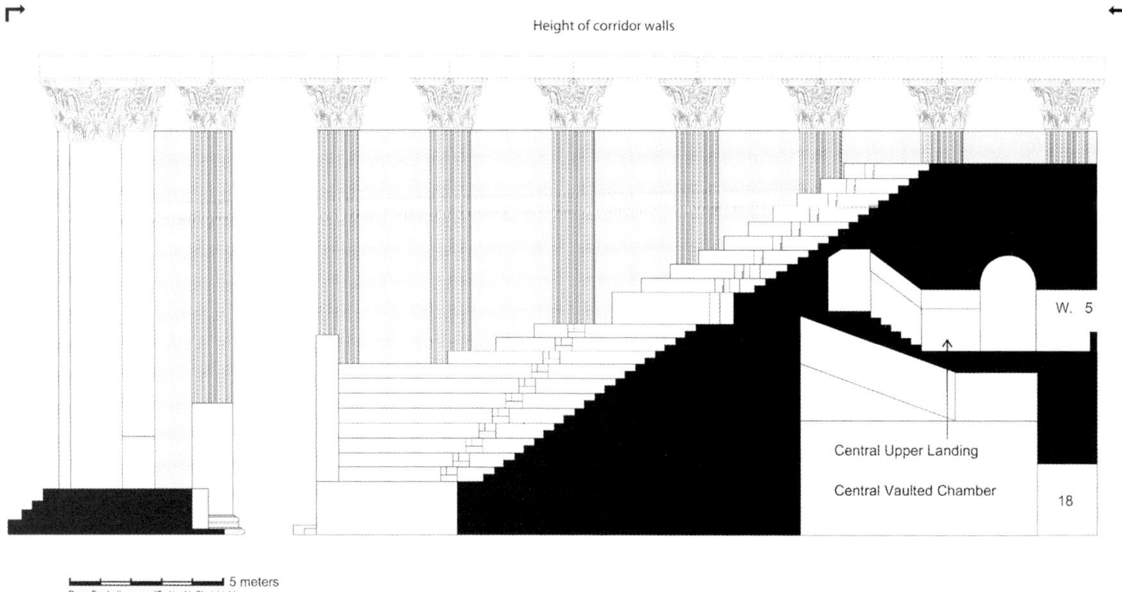

Fig. 8.9. Section 2. Reconstructed section of theater, cut through the center axis of the building (see fig. 8. 1 for position of section). Elements above the 6th row of seating in *ima cavea*, the upper termination and configuration of the central vault, and elements on the level of and above the Central Upper landing, are all hypothetic. Numbers correspond to elements shown in fig. 8.1.

Fig. 8.10. View of East Landing, over the 'Central Upper Landing' (33) towards the West Landing. East Upper Stairway (13) visible to the right and threshold to the 'Central Upper Landing' in the foreground.

(internal measurement according to the width of the room), and the total internal height (at the center of the chamber where the vault is highest) would have been 3.5 m in the north and 5.6 m in the south. On the same axis as vaulted Window 9 in the east wall of the substructure, a rectangular window (Window 11) with a straight lintel providing light for the chamber, is set in the wall between the chamber and the East Interior Staircase.

The West Interior Staircase with vault, windows, and the West Vaulted Chamber, are designed as a mirror image of the east half of the substructure. The dimensions of some features, however, are not uniform, for example the width of the passage (No. 17) leading to the West Interior Staircase is 1.75 m wide, compared to its counterpart on the east (No. 14), which is 1.70 m in width. The west interior staircase was also vaulted, and the same relationship between vault and stairway exists as on the east (figs. 8.6-7).[12] The northernmost (and lower) of the two staircase windows (W. 1) is better preserved than its east counterpart (W. 9), with similar vaulting. Both windows are constructed with 8 voussoirs of various sizes. Window 1 measures 2 m in height x 1.12 m in width, and the height of the vault above the spring line is 0.58 m —41% of the window height is below the spring line. The blocks in the W exterior substructure wall from the spring line of the vault over the West Interior Staircase partly cut into the N window voussoirs. The West Vaulted Chamber is 25 cm longer in the north than its east counterpart, but exhibits the same width. This indicates an error in the layout of the walls of the vaulted chambers (Walls 4, 5 and 6), which was compensated by building the West Vaulted Chamber further from the central axis of the building than its eastern counterpart, but not by narrowing its width.

The East and West Interior Staircases terminate in East and West Landings, two rectangular spaces measuring 2.7 m x 2.26 m. Providing light for the area in the two inter-columniations between Columns 6 and 7 and 14 and 15, is a third set of windows (W. 3 and W. 7, the south windows in the E and W substructure walls). These windows average 1.24 m in width and extend to the landings, but it is not known how high they were or if they were originally arched. The landings are furnished with rectangular pavers averaging 50 x 50 cm, laid in rows with some pavers measuring 1 m x 50 cm. A few steps are preserved of the Upper East and Upper West Stairways (Nos. 12 and 13) each 1.6 m wide, with three and four steps respectively, 20 cm in height x 29 cm in depth. Thresholds at the west edge of the East Landing and the east edge of the West Landing (fig. 8.10) mark the entrances into an area over the Central Vaulted Chamber. With the vault largely collapsed, the precise nature of this area is unknown (cf. fig. 8.1), but for convenience it is referred to as the Central Upper Landing.

Behind the East and West Vaulted Chambers is the rectangular Central Vaulted Chamber, 6.89 m x 3.21 m, with Wall 7 protruding into it. This chamber is accessed only from the South Corridor through a narrow passageway (No. 18, height 2.04 m x width 0.67 m) aligned with the central axis of the building. Consisting of 16 voussoirs, the vault is preserved to the south below the Central Upper Landing, rising from south to north at an angle of 20-degrees in an opposite direction from the East and West Interior Staircases and the East and West Chambers. The spring line is 3.17 m above ground level in the south. The vault inner height is 1.4 m or 4.57 m above ground level at this point.

Forming the rear of the substructure, inside the South Substructure Wall (3), are the SE and SW Staircases 2.4 m in width, with 25 steps averaging 19 cm in height x 29 cm in depth. Lighting the staircases are Windows 4 and 6, 1.25 m wide (the height is unknown) in the South Substructure Wall, between the easternmost and westernmost inter-columniations. Both staircases lead to the South Landing, a rectangular space 4.71 m x 2.48 m. This landing is lit by a third window (5) in the central inter-columniation on the building's axis, and it leads into the Central Upper Landing.

---

12 The distance from the top of the 4th step and the spring line is 2.62 m, the 10th step is 2.15 m and the 14th step 2.08 m.

Fig. 8.11. Orchestra with podium and ruin of theater as excavated.

Fig. 8.12. Orchestra podium.

The lower *cavea* rests on a massive soil fill with ashlar inclusions, rather than on a solid ashlar substructure.[13] The northern limits of the *cavea* are the two *analemmata* (retaining walls) Nos. 19 and 20, of ashlar construction, 60-65 cm in thickness, and a raised low wall (No. 21) or podium serving as the base for the tiers of seats. The structure of the lower *cavea* is bounded to the south by the north walls of the East and West Vaulted Chambers (Nos. 10 and 11). A walkway (No. 22) rests on the orchestra podium, 1.5 m just above the level of the orchestra. Approximately 84 cm in width, the walkway is paved with flat sandstone slabs of alternating white and dark red/purple colors to form an even surface between the first row of seats and the uppermost blocks of the orchestra

13 The excavator suggests, that this layer of fill may have been used as an anti-earthquake measure, E. S. Libonati, Trench 123 (June 24 - July 4 2006), on-line at *Open Context*.

podium. Excavation revealed that the orchestra podium is solidly constructed, with an individual foundation as wide as the walkway itself.

The orchestra podium (figs. 8.11, 8.12) is well built of rectangular ashlars, with slightly curving faces following the curve of the orchestra. The ashlars are tightly fitted, laid in straight horizontal courses, with 4 courses preserved out of an original 5. In height the two upper courses are 28 cm, while the second from the bottom is 34 cm. The surfaces of the blocks are roughly finished, many still retaining claw chiselmarks for a plaster overlay (fig. 8.12).

Fig. 8.13. Theater seats with narrow grooves on front upper edge and rough surfaces. Guidelines for uncut deep groove visible behind. Deep grooves visible on blocks on the right.

The sondage SP200 bifurcating the orchestra along its central axis to the orchestra podium, revealed that the orchestra was laid on a sterile fill of yellow sand and that the ashlars of the lowermost course of the podium were not set on an equal depth. On average they extended 20 cm below the surface of the pavers and were placed with their upper edge to equal height preparing for the even courses of masonry above. The lowest course was partially covered by the orchestra fill and pavers. Traces of plaster, some 5 mm thick, were preserved along the lower portions of the wall. In the second course, on the central axis of the theater (and the central *cavea* stairs, No. 24), a hole was cut into the center block, which was later filled in by a stone block inserted to fit it (A on fig. 8.12). Additional anomalies are found in the wall where the east and west stairs join the lower walkway (fig. 8.12 B and C; cf. fig. 8.1 Nos. 23 and 25). The ashlars of the wall's lowest course appear to have been removed and the blocks in the course above were re-cut to provide space for this repair.

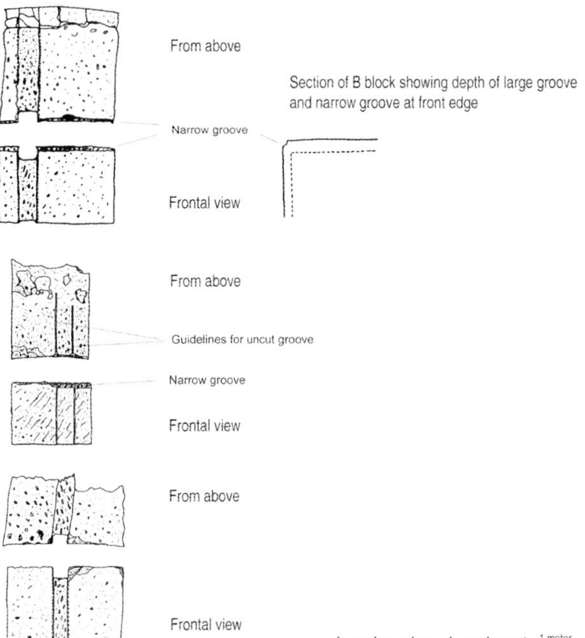

Fig. 8.14. Seats from rows B, C and D, with deep grooves, narrow grooves and guidelines for (uncut) deep grooves. See Fig. 8.28 for the location of rows.

Cavea

The *cavea* itself consists of 4 *cunei* (wedge shaped seating sections) cut by the three *scalae* (stairways), Nos. 23–25, averaging 66 cm in width, with steps on an average of 26 cm in depth x 19 cm in height (fig. 8.1). The curve of the *cavea* is greater than 180-degrees, and the orchestra podium bends inward following the same curve. However, the tangential *analemma* walls, on axis with each other, do not follow this curve. Enough seat-blocks were found *in situ* during the excavation to substantiate the existence of 5 rows of seats in the 4 *cunei* of the *ima cavea* (the reconstruction is made with 7 rows, see below).

The seats are constructed of blocks of local sandstone and limestone (figs. 8.13-14), leveled to the full height of the row. Occasionally they extend the full depth of the row, but are often supplemented with smaller stones in order to obtain the desired depth (a block from row B, fig. 8.14, may serve as an example). On average the seats are 59 cm in depth x 39 cm in height (Table 8.2). The excavators observed that the seats of the 2nd and 5th tiers were primarily of white sandstone. The seats are positioned on the massive fill of the *cavea* substructure and they do not overlap—one row begins where the other ends. The fronts and upper surfaces of the seats are not smoothly finished and chisel-marks are prominent (figs. 8.13-14).

Unusual are the deep grooves cut into some of the seat blocks on the front upper edge and throughout their complete depth (figs. 8.13, 8.14), with average dimensions of 6.6 cm in height x 9.5 cm in width (Table 8.3). Such grooves were identified on some 20 blocks; fig. 8.25 illustrates the distribution of grooved *in situ* seat blocks in the *cavea*. They appear to occur at various intervals (Table 8.4), more often at the end of a row next to the stairs.

The grooves are trapezoidal in section and are wider at the bottom than at the top (fig. 8.14). Remains of what has been interpreted as deteriorated wood and nails were found in some of the grooves. Parallel rows of incised lines, set at a distance equivalent to the width of the deep grooves, can be observed on a few seats (fig. 8.14 'C'). These seem to have been guidelines for the cutting of grooves that were left uncut. Other narrow grooves, occasionally fashioned with the use of a pointed chisel at the outer and upper edge of a few of the seat-blocks also seem to be remains of unfinished or abandoned work.

TABLE 8.2
DIMENSIONS OF ROWS OF SEATS IN THEATRE,
CF. PLAN FIG. 8.25.
Each figure is an average of 4-6 readings.

Row no.	*Height/depth (centimeters)*
B	–/59.5
C	38/59.5
D	39/58 (?)
E	39/58
F	38.5/59
G	38.5/58 (?)
Average figure	39/59

TABLE 8.3
DIMENSIONS OF GROOVES IN SEAT-BLOCKS OF THEATER,
CF. PLAN FIG. 8.25.

Groove no.	*Depth/width (centimeters)*
1	6–7/7.5–9
2	6–8/9–11
3	5–6.5/8.5–9
4	–
5	5.5–7.5/10–11
6	5–7/(vertical, 18–19)/ 9.5–11.5
7	6–8/8–9
8	–/9–10
9	6–9/9
10	8/–
11	6–10/9–11
12	3–5/9–9.5
13	6–8/10–10.5
14	–/8
15	–/5–6
16	6/9.5–11.5
17	6/11
18	6–7/–
19	7–8/11.5–13
20	5–8/10
Average	6.6/9.5

TABLE 8.4
DISTANCES BETWEEN GROOVES IN SEAT-BLOCKS OF THEATRE,
CF. PLAN FIG. 8.25.

Grove nos.	*Inner/outer (centimeters)*
1–5	122/140
2–6	157/174
3–7	184/201
8–10	146/159
10–15	108/128
9–11	103/116
11–13	86/94
13–16	96/110
12–14	96/110
14–17	137/147

The steps for the three stairways of the *cavea* (fig. 8.1 Nos. 23-25) were monolithic blocks and their proportions to the seats are approximately two-to-one. Two stairways of 5 sandstone steps each (Nos. 30 and 31), 63 cm wide and 20-25 cm in height, gave access to the podium walkway from the *aditus maximi*. The lowest steps, roughly semicircular on both sides, rest on the *aditus maximi* paving.

Orchestra and Aditus Maximi

The horseshoe-shaped orchestra is composed of two elements; an area bounded by the orchestra podium with a curve of 206-degrees and a rectangular space to the north, framed on the north by a screen-wall, the pre-stage wall. This wall predates the stage and the *proscaenium*, and is of uncertain function (see below). To the east and west are gate thresholds continuing the line of the podium (fig. 8.1). The curved portion of the orchestra has a diameter of 6.4 m, and the rectangular section measures 3.35 m x 6.2 m, giving a total area of the orchestra of approximately 37 m2.

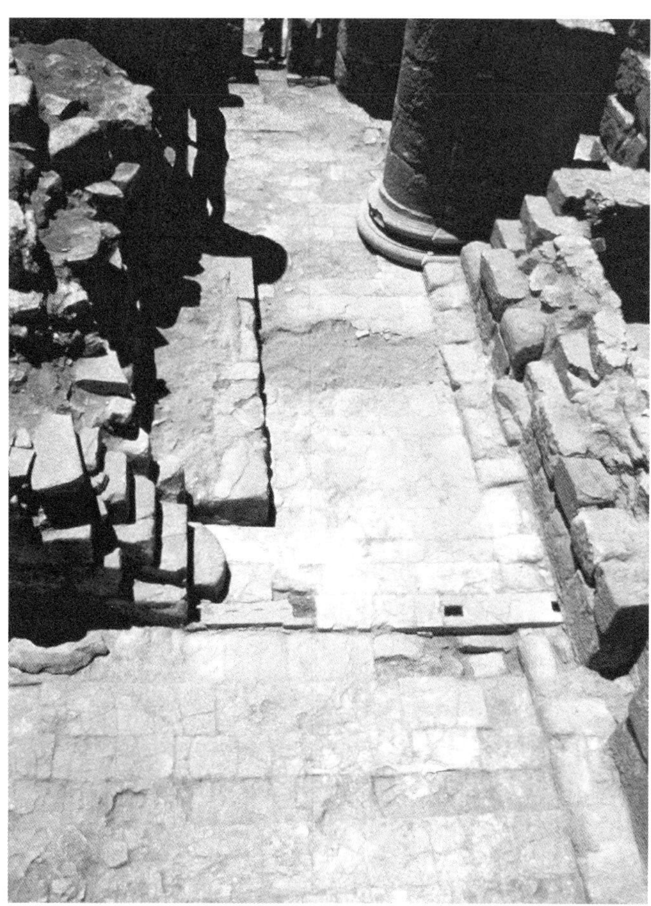

Fig. 8.15. View of west *aditus maximus*, part of orchestra, pre-stage wall, *proscaenium* and threshold for orchestra gate, to west.

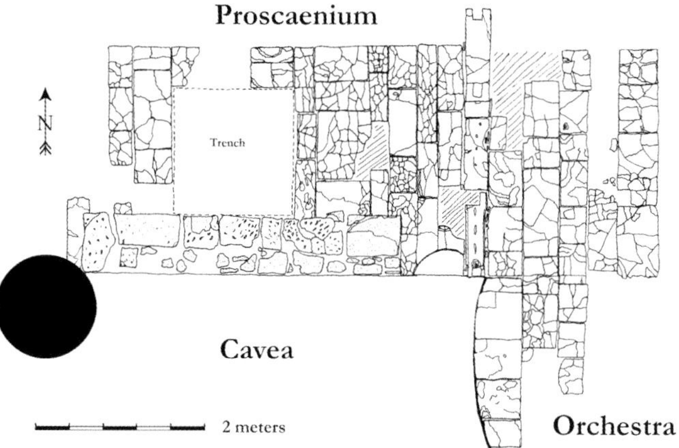

Fig. 8.16. West *aditus maximus*. Paving and bench, threshold for orchestra gate protruding under the *proscaenium* and part of the orchestra paving.

Laid against the podium, the orchestra floor is paved with rectangular sandstone pavers laid in straight rows parallel to the long axis of the building (figs. 8.15-16). The pavers are mostly of white stone, although dark red pavers were observed in the NW area of the orchestra and as a N-S line extending along the center-axis of the orchestra.[14] Differences in the color of the pavers were not obvious when this author examined them. The length of the pavers varies but their width is fixed to either 32 cm or 40 cm. No system emerges from the 16 rows of pavers, from W to E they a laid in the following manner: two wide, two narrow, two wide, two narrow, then three wide, two narrow and three wide. The pavers are laid on a sterile layer of gray-brown sand.

Under the pavers in the center of the orchestra is a small column drum with a diameter of 38 cm, and height

14 L.-A. Bedal *et al.* on Trench 47 (July 9 August 3 1997), on-line at *Open Context*.

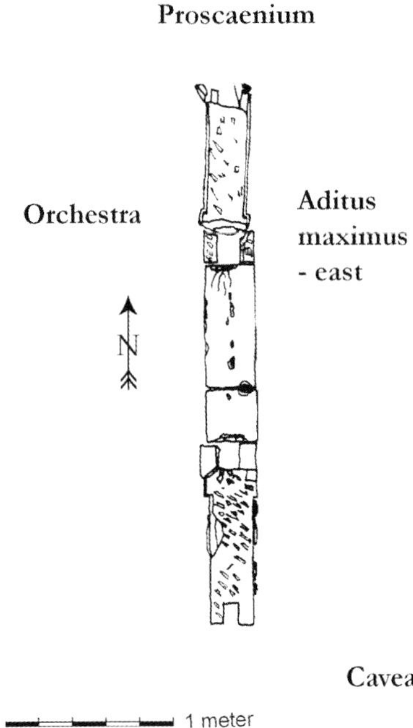

Fig. 8.17. East orchestra gate threshold.

of 22 cm.[15] Distinct, deep chisel-marks cut as a series of parallel grooves are incised over the entire surface of the stone at 45-degrees to its vertical axis. The drum stands almost upright, and its center is found to be equidistant to the center of the orchestra and the *cavea*—3.10 m from the south edge of the orchestra podium and 3.26 m from both the east and west edges of the podium.

The orchestra is delimited to the east and west by two thresholds for gates (hereafter, orchestra gates) extending from the NE and NW ends of the orchestra podium and some 60 cm into the pre-stage wall (figs. 8.15-17). The thresholds are 3.10 m in length x 30 cm in width, and each consists of three consecutive long blocks sunk deep into the fill of the orchestra, but with their upper surfaces at a higher level than the orchestra pavers. The blocks measure 1.00–1.04 m in length, the central blocks are plain with worn smooth surfaces, the other 4 have two 10 cm x 10 cm square deep slots cut at their ends, and their surfaces are left rough dressed by a flat chisel. The north and south blocks of the east threshold and the south block of the west threshold have clear profiles cut on both sides (figs. 8.15-17) clad with stucco and are thinner except at their ends where they exhibit square slots. These differences suggest that the blocks were originally made for something else and were later reused in these thresholds. The central blocks show some 7 circular shallow cavities, which perhaps means that there was an iron grill with pins that rested on the central block which then functioned as a sill.

Outside the orchestra thresholds are the *aditus maximi*, 2.7 m w. x 5.4 m in length (measuring from the center of the inter-columniation of Columns 1 and 2, and 19 and 20). Like the orchestra, the *aditus maximi* are paved but with pavers of different widths. Only the pavers in the west *aditus* are preserved well enough to discern any decorative scheme (figs. 8.18-19). Pavers of three different widths (30 cm, 46 cm and 66 cm) are interchanged with pavers of 20-22 cm.

Two benches (height 30 cm, length 3.8 m and depth 0.7 m) are placed against the *analemma*ta/*aditus maximi*-walls and installed on the pavers (fig. 8.1). Their length equals that of the *aditus maximi* adjacent to the semicircular steps of the walkway stairs (Nos. 30 and 31) and Columns 2 and 19. The benches are fashioned from rectangular and square sandstones for their entire height and at their rear is a mixed fill of smaller stones and soil (figs. 8.15-16 and 8.18). The finishing of the bench-blocks is rough with multiple chisel marks. It can be assumed they were originally covered with plaster, although no traces remain. The width of the benches restricts the effective width of the *aditus maximi* to only 2 m. In addition, the Columns (1 and 20) at the northeast and northwest corners allow only 1.4 m of passage space between the benches and the columns.

Pre-stage wall

To the north of the *cavea*, orchestra and *aditus maximi*, below the stage, is the pre-stage wall, a double-faced wall 1.4 m wide, extending 19 m under the entire width of the stage (figs. 8.15 and 8.19). The wall's south edge is located a little further south than the center of Columns 1 and 20, and it visibly protrudes beyond the stage. Only the west portion of the wall is fully known because the west third of the stage was removed by the excavators to investigate structures beneath it.

Clearly defined by its north and south faces, one course of this wall is preserved and its outer courses are built of fairly substantial blocks with a packed fill of smaller stones. The size and

15 Special Project 200; *Great Temple* vol. 2, fig. 5.80.

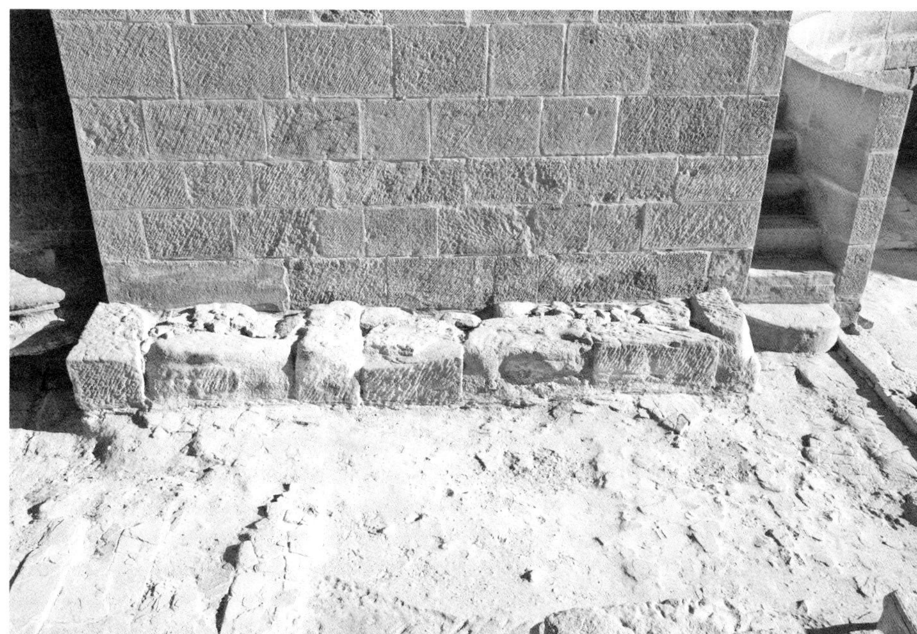

Fig. 8.18. Bench in east *adytus maximus* to south.

Fig. 8.19. Pre-stage wall (exposed section in the west).

composition of the blocks of the north side differ considerably exhibiting tool-marks from various types of chisels and hammers. The dominant feature of the construction of the south side is a system of different colored headers and stretchers of local soft limestone interchangeably laid between yellow and red blocks (fig. 8.15). The orchestra gate thresholds cut into this wall and disrupt the systematic pattern of the stones, as shown in figs. 8.15 and 8.16.

Stage

The stage itself consists of two elements, the *proscaenium* and the *pulpitum* (stage floor). These features may be contemporary, but are characterized by signs of disparate designs and execution so as to merit independent description.

Proscaenium

The *proscaenium* wall is placed above the pre-stage wall, but located a little further to the north exposing the south face of the pre-stage wall. The *proscaenium* is 87 cm wide, and extends along the entire 19 m width of the structure (figs. 8.1, 8.15, 8.21-23, 8.25). Its west side was removed to allow for a sondage of the pre-stage wall (visible in fig. 8.15). The northeast side of the *proscaenium* is overlaid by *pulpitum* pavers still *in situ*. Behind the center part, however, the *pulpitum* fill can be seen up against the north face of the *proscaenium* (fig. 8.21). The *proscaenium* is constructed

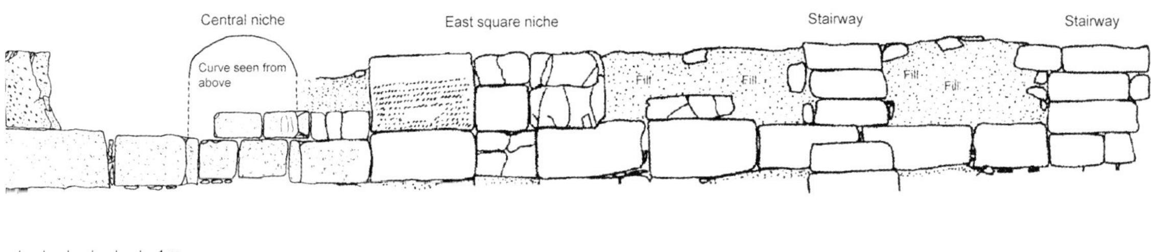

Fig. 8.20. *Proscaenium*, center and east.

with some substantial sandstone ashlars as well as with blocks of various sizes and shapes, a few measuring its entire thickness. The front (south side) of the *proscaenium* is furnished with one central semicircular niche (diameter 98 cm), of 4 curved blocks on the center axis of the theater (figs. 8.1 and 8.20). This niche is not a perfect semicircle—its west side is more curved than the east. At a distance of 1.53 m on either side of the central niche are square niches (figs. 8.1, 8.20), both 50 cm x 60 cm.

Beyond the niches of the *proscaenium*, 2.35 m to the east and west and opposite the benches of the *aditus maximi*, two stairways of 5 and 6 steps respectively lead up to the *pulpitum* (figs. 8.1, 8.20 and 8.22). The width of the steps is roughly 70 cm, wider than the stairways of the *cavea* (66 cm). At the two ends of the *pulpitum* a second set of stairways of 5 steps each—1.53 m east and west of the first pair of stairs, also provide access to the stage. Utilizing the stones of the protruding pre-stage wall as a lowest step, the steps of the 4 stairways average 26 cm in height.[16] These steps are roughly the same height as the inner stairs but they are slightly wider, measuring 80 cm. The stairways are built into the *proscaenium*, while the first two steps of the inner east stairs are added onto the pre-stage wall without cutting into it (fig. 8.22).

Pulpitum

On top of the pre-stage wall and behind the *proscaenium* is the *pulpitum*, covering a 19 m width with a depth of 5.2 m, including the width of the *proscaenium* (fig. 8.1). The north limit of the *pulpitum* is a wall, 16.35 m in width, extending beyond the footprint of the *distyle* building. It is built 45 to 50 cm from the northeast corner of the West Anta wall, and covers an additional 45-50 cm further north and 80 cm further east than the equivalent northwest point of the East Anta wall (fig. 8.1). The size of the *pulpitum* is almost 100 m2 (without deducting the space of the columns and *antae* walls).

On the short east and west sides the East and West Inner Antae walls support the *pulpitum*. Built in a more haphazard manner than the rest of the theater, the *pulpitum* floor level is approximately 1.25 m higher than the orchestra, and the *pulpitum* itself is constructed with rubble and re-used blocks. At its sides is a third set of stairs, accessing the stage directly from the East and West Corridors (fig. 8.23). On the north rear of the *pulpitum*, a ramp (fig. 8.1, No. 34) provides access to the stage from the Pronaos between the tetrastyle temple front and the (older) *distyle* façade. The ramp, approximately on axis with the central niche of the *proscaenium* and the central axis of the building, is carelessly constructed of upright flat ashlars mixed with earth and rubble. West of the ramp is yet another stairway leading up to the *pulpitum* which is also not well built. No similar stairway is found at the east rear of the *pulpitum*.

The almost 100 m2 *pulpitum* floor surrounds Columns A and B of the temple *distyle* façade (fig. 8.1). It is covered with square brightly colored pavers of various sized sandstones (ca. 40 cm

16 The norm for the stairways of the theater is 19 cm.

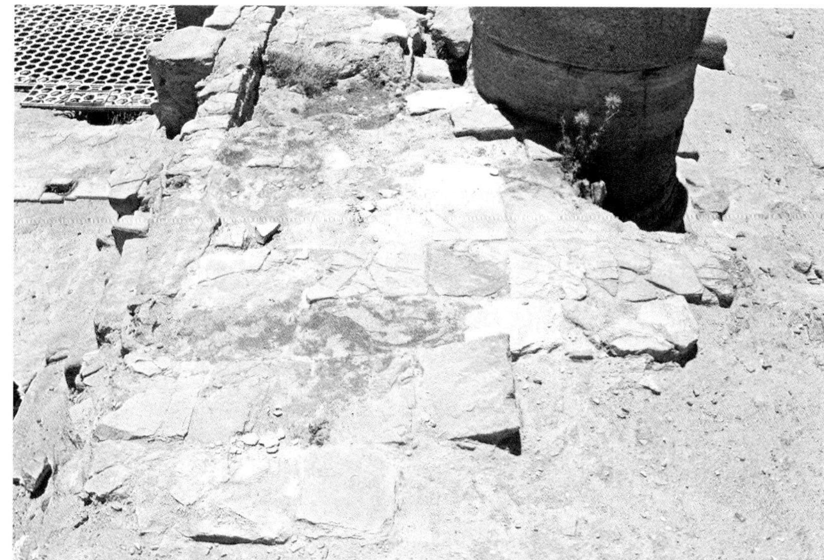

Fig. 8.21. *Pulpitum* east with pavers and the rear of *proscaenium* to the left (west).

Fig. 8.22. Extreme east stage, with pre-stage wall, *proscaenium* with two stairways and *pulpitum*, to north.

Fig. 8.23. Stairway to the *pulpitum* through opening in West Anta, to the northeast. Behind and to the right is the west *aditus maximus* and the pre-stage wall under the *proscaenium*.

x 40-60 cm) in a seemingly unsystematic mix of gray, green, red, black, white, yellow and purple. Today this paving, which would have covered the entire floor, is preserved only in the east part (figs. 8.1, 8.21 and 8.24).

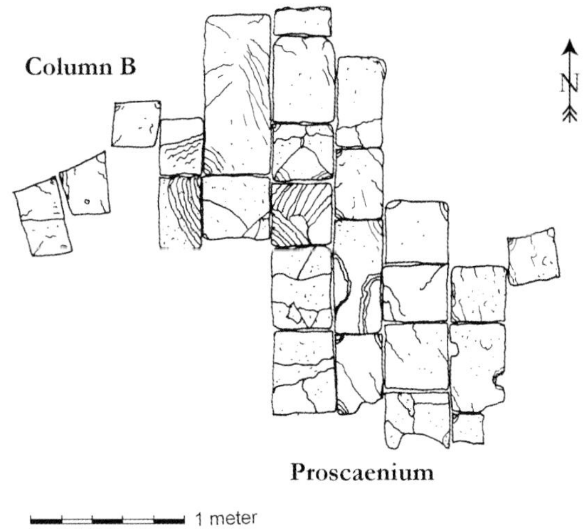

Fig. 8.24. Pavers on the *pulpitum* east.

Important finds

Numerous architectural fragments deriving from the theater edifice and found everywhere inside and around the Great Temple contribute to our knowledge of its architecture and function. Fragments have been recorded in the databases of the Great Temple excavations accessible online in *Open Context* and many can be viewed in the site *lapidaria*. Every fragment belonging to the theater held in one subterranean storage depot holding 5,000 architectural fragments has been examined twice to check previous attributions.[17] Almost every trench report refers to sizeable numbers of architectural fragments. Studies by this author confirm the basic observation made by the Brown University archaeologists that the Corinthian capital fragments from the temple are of one type (Floral Type 1), but of two different sizes.[18] Additionally the corresponding pilaster decoration of the *antae* walls is decorated in the same style. Ashlars recorded in the excavation diaries are rarely of any impressive size or exhibit special characteristics.[19] It is significant that some reports[20] state the quantitative amounts of the capital fragments in comparison to other classes of finds. Interesting are the ashlars found in the Pronaos trenches, *e.g.* Trench 23 which average 62 cm x 42 cm x 42 cm, and some are still joined with a sandy slightly pink mortar adhering to their surfaces.[21]

Fragments of marble pavers and marble wall cladding were found in Pronaos Trench 24. Dozens of painted wall plaster fragments and hundreds of molded plaster elements also were recovered from the Pronaos trenches particularly Trenches 24 and 48, the former almost certainly from the column and *antae* walls plastering—observable *in situ* on some standing columns. Plaster or stucco of at least two qualities, a thick and rough inner layer and a thin and finer outer layer, has been identified. The inner layer attached to wall blocks and columns with reeds and nails.[22] Numerous painted as well as unpainted plaster fragments are found in the East, West and South Corridor trenches (Trench 29), as are numerous fragments of terracotta roof-tiles. Mosaic *tesserae* were found in the Pronaos trenches, particularly in center-east Trench 24 with more than 1,000 recorded.

Seven fragments of 6 limestone theater-masks were found in the West Walkway. The fact that they were found together makes it likely they were associated and decorated the building. The masks, 5 female and one male, are of the tragic type, and based on their style they date to the 1st c. A.D.[23]

---

17 A few fragments were found which must derive from hitherto unidentified structures. The fragments in question may come from buildings outside the Great Temple *temene*.

18 Special Project 200; *Great Temple* vol. 2, fig. 5.80.

19 See however M. F. Slaughter on Locus 17 in Trench 40 (June 14-July 14 1997) dated August 15, 1997, on-line in *Open Context*.

20 For example the reports by L. D. Bestock of Trench 24 (June 16-August 18 1996), and by L.-A. Bedal *et al.* of Trench 47 (July 9-August 3 1997), dated August 1997, on-line at *Open Context*.

21 See Ch. 11.

22 M. F. Slaughter, Trench 40 (June 14-July 14 1997), dated August 15 1997, online at *Open Context*.

23 E. L. Schluntz, in *Great Temple* vol. 1, 232-33; Schluntz 1999. Ph.D. diss. See also the present book Ch. 22.

Around the two thresholds of the orchestra gates, a number of nails and strips of iron and other materials interpreted as deteriorated wood were recovered. It was reasoned that these were the remains of wooden doors/gates that were once in place at this spot.[24] One report mentions many large nails (one 37 cm in length),[25] which suggests a massive wooden structure of a scale larger than doors or gates fitting the dimensions of the orchestra thresholds.

An abundance of masons' marks has been observed on the ashlar blocks of the Great Temple and the Theater.[26] These are clearly Nabataean and contribute important evidence as to who built the structure.

Design and construction

The building in which the theater was installed was the Great Temple Site Phase IV the 'Grand Design' *tetrastyle* temple. The earlier *distyle* inner temple included the East and West Antae walls with the two large Columns A and B in between, and a Corinthian-Nabataean colonnade with 8-by-6 columns with southeast and southwest corner heart-shaped columns. In addition to the monumental façade of 4 columns and two *antae* walls, a wall extended from the *antae* walls around the colonnade, creating the corridor space (E, S and W) with 11 doors providing access to the East and West Walkways. Access to the temple and to the theater in this phase was from the Lower Temenos via these walkways. The overall design of the theater, its various elements and the proportional relationships between them, had to be planned in relation to the pre-existing colonnade. This was a challenge and an enhancement, and in the following discussion we will see how the architects managed to balance the theater design with the limitations imposed by the architectural features of the Great Temple.

All Roman theaters and theater-like structures effectively combine multi-storey buildings and open structures with surfaces rising gradually from ground level to one or more upper stories. In the case of our theater, the structure is already raised some 1.5 m above the ground at the north (the orchestra podium). Thereafter, the building rises at an angle corresponding to the height and depth of the seat-blocks and the *scalae* (see reconstructed section fig. 8.9). The architects would have planned the substructure to accommodate the weight of the *cavea* as well as caring for the design of the access-system to the seats.

One of the challenging circumstances in theater design is the circulation of the audience when entering and leaving their seats. The difficulty is to plan this with minimal interference to the design of the *cavea* itself—to avoid wasting valuable spectator space on too many *diazomata*,[27] *scalae*, or openings for substructure access-ways like *vomitoria*.[28] For the Romans the vaulted substructure was the basic solution to all the challenges and needs when constructing a *cavea* from level ground.[29]

The Great Temple ground plan was laid out within a fairly small rectangle requiring the structural elements of the substructure to be parallel to the long axis of the building. Normally vaulted chambers and substructure passageways expand progressively in width and height from the orchestra and outwards.[30] They expand only in height in our theater. Commonly practiced in the Empire[31] was the construction of the *ima cavea* on a massive fill, not on vaults. If vaults had been

24 Trench 40 Final Report; L-A. Bedal *et al*. Trench 47 (July 9 August 3 1997) on-line at *Open Context*.
25 Bedal *et al*. previous note.
26 *Great Temple* vol. 1, 264, 266-67; Rababeh 2005, 91-92.
27 Concentric horizontal walkways separating seating sections in a theater.
28 Entrances/exits for the audience in the seating area.
29 Sear (2006, 70-80); On sloping vaults in Roman Palestine and *Provincia Arabia* see Segal (1995, 76, n.153).
30 Sear 2006, 51.
31 And seems not, as suggested by Segal (1995, 29), to constitute a local (regional) tradition of *Provincia Arabia*; Roman theaters that reused sites of Greek style theaters, would automatically have at least a great part of the *cavea* sited on a natural slope.

installed under the *ima cavea* in our theater, they would have little practical use because of the low height of the rooms thus created.[32]

The theater was designed at the outset to include three key elements: orchestra, *cavea* and scene building. The design-process and architectural plan will now be described (figs. 8.1 and 8.25).

The point where the two retaining walls of the lower *cavea* (Nos. 10 and 11) meet in an obtuse angle at the north end of Wall 5 is exactly in the middle of the Great Temple colonnade, on the long axis of the central inter-columniations of the short sides of the *pteron*, and on axis with the centers of Columns 4 and 17 (compare figs. 8.1, 8.25). The center N-S axis divides the theater lengthwise into two symmetrical parts, and is the obvious point of reference in a design process. However the E-W axis (the line separating module 2 and 3, fig. 8.25) cannot serve the same purpose, because it does not divide the *theatron* into two symmetrical parts. The point where the two axes do meet, the 'substructure focal point' (indicated with a dot on fig. 8.25), was used as the design's center point. As seen in fig. 8.25, it is suggested that the substructure was laid out in modules, each corresponding to two inter-columniations, resulting in 4 modules. The architects probably chose to implement this modular layout at invisible parts of the substructure, wherever there was a choice of location of parts.

Not all major elements corresponded to the modules; for example, the irregular annular wall (No. 7, fig. 8.1) between the East and West and Central Vaulted Chambers is not in the 'correct' position, i.e., where modules 3 and 4 meet. The modules may reflect the superstructure seating division, but this remains theoretical because details of the *cavea* and elements of the original superstructure above the 5th row of seating are unknown (for reconstruction attempts see below).

The North Walls of the Vaulted Chambers (Nos. 10-11 on fig. 8.1) were not set on the E-W axis. Firstly, because the ground level entrances to the chambers did not provide sufficient space for the East and West Interior Staircases to extend the proscribed length to the north; thus the chamber entrance was moved to the north. Secondly, since the massive *ima cavea* is semicircular, its support—the Chambers' North Walls—had to be aligned with its shape. Instead of the walls being annular, they were constructed in straight lines with the east and west limits extended to the south to provide the requisite support for the superstructure.

As mentioned above, the E-inner substructure wall (fig. 8.1, No. 6) is wider than the central and western walls (Nos. 5 and 4), and the central wall is off center (fig. 8.25). The East and West Vaulted Chambers are of similar length and width. The E-inner substructure wall is the same width as the outer substructure wall, but it should have been narrower. This suggests the substructure was built from east to west and that there may have been a builder's mistake in the execution of the building, that is, the builder did not follow the architects' plan. If divided in two halves the building should have been perfectly symmetrical, and there is no reason in the structural design for differences in wall width. After the mistake was recognized, and when it was also realized that there would not be enough space to build the vaulted chambers to the desired size—if the rest of the inner substructure walls were to be constructed to the same erroneous width—the solution was to avoid dismantling the already constructed E-inner substructure wall, but to build the central wall thinner, and move it slightly off the central axis towards the west. The W-inner substructure wall also had to be narrower. This mistake had no visible consequences and was apparently considered of no consequence for the substructure's stability.

The entire substructure was clearly designed to support the tremendous weight of the *cavea*. A concern for this weight-factor may be seen in the irregularly shaped central substructure wall

32 There are examples of vaults under the *ima cavea* of a number of Roman theaters, but more often than not chosen since the saving of building materials by vaults would have been limited and would not have outweighed the trouble and expense involved in the construction of vaults.

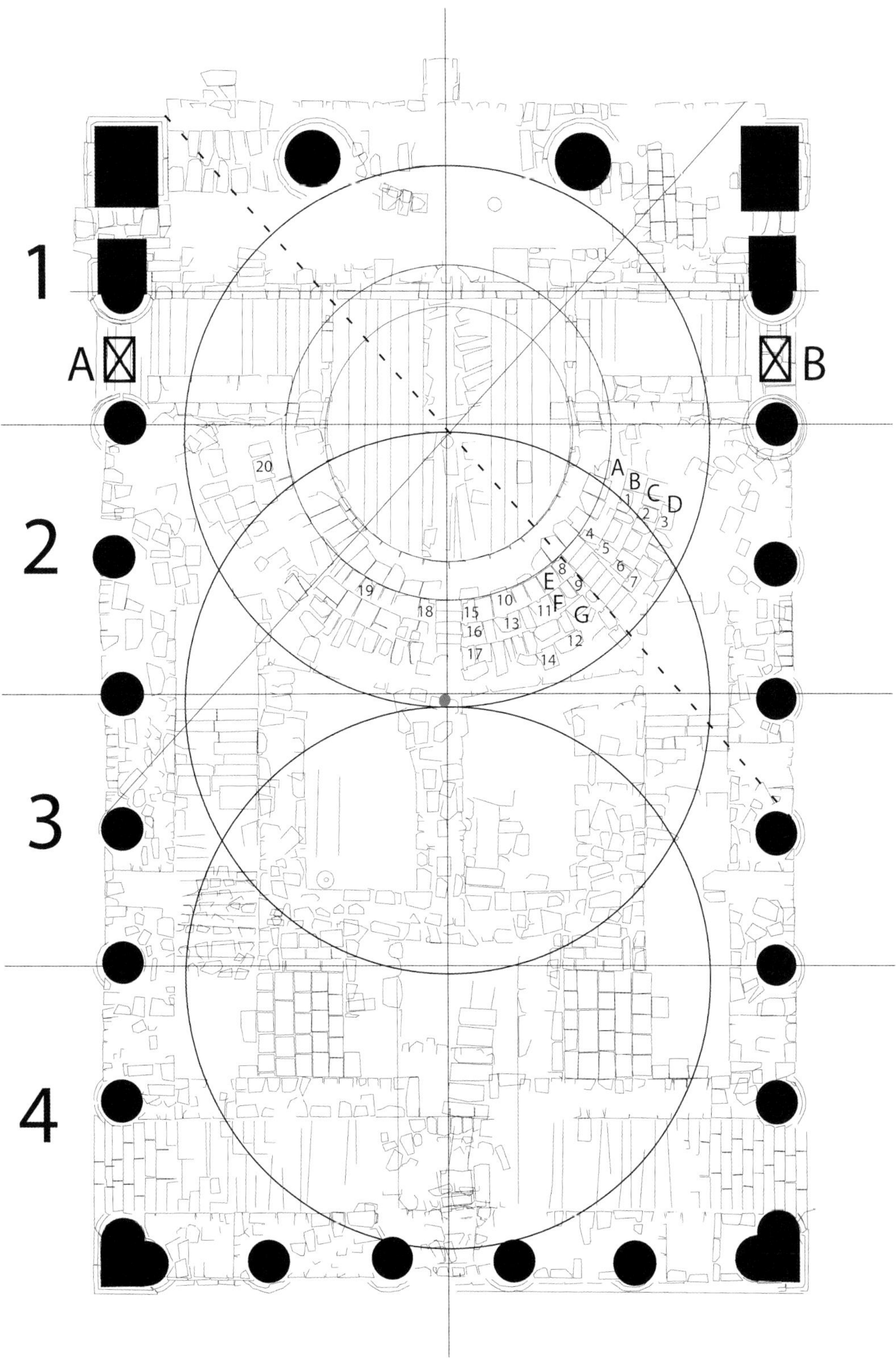

Fig. 8.25. Plan with indications of possible basic principles behind the design of the theater, 4 modules each of two inter-*columnia*. One circle indicates the continuation of the curve of the orchestra podium, another the continuation of the curve of the lower *diazoma*. The 'pivot stone' is visible just below the center of the inner circle. A-G indicate individual rows of seats in the east half of *ima cavea*, and 1-20 are locations of deep grooves in the seat blocks (See fig. 8.14 for drawings of blocks and grooves, and Table 8.3 for the dimensions of grooves).

between the East, West and South Vaulted Chambers (No. 7, fig. 8.1). This wall is wider towards the building's center axis than at its ends where it conjoins the other walls (Nos. 4 and 6) also supporting the *cavea*.

The center of the orchestra is on axis with Columns 2 and 19 (figs. 8.1 and 8.25). The distance between the orchestra center and the 'substructure focal point' equals one unit of the system explained above. The orchestra and *cavea* are designed around the orchestra center and the substructure focal point. The central *scala* is on the N-S axis—on the same axis as the center of the orchestra. The SE and SW theater steps, however, are not concentric to this center, only their inner edges are concentric to the center (indicated by lines, fig. 8.25).

It was not an option to design the Great Temple Theater according to the ideal proportions for such a building, since the proportions of the pre-existing structure governed the major layout. For example, the proportions of the rectangular colonnade into which the *cavea* was inserted resulted in an unusually deep *cavea*. As a consequence, a greater part of the audience had to sit further away from the center of the action, than would normally have been the case in a theater of this size. The size of the orchestra and the difference in height between it and the podium *diazoma* were necessary due to whatever function the theater was designed to accommodate. With a diameter of 6.4 m the orchestra is roughly one-third width of the *cavea* substructure, and this proportional relationship was likely determined by function rather than a desire for architectural harmony.

The dominant feature of the theater, the *cavea*, falls within the traditional design of the so-called, 'western Roman' type of theater[33]—the characteristic feature of which is the *analemmata/aditus maximi* walls being parallel to the stage. Because of the *aditus maximi* and the need for a certain-sized orchestra, the front of the *proscaenium* wall was located, as described above, a little to the north of the axis of Columns 1 and 20. Its exact location may have been found by completing the circle, which is the continuation of the curve of the orchestra podium (fig. 8.25), since the *proscaenium* front is close to being tangential to this circle. The (lower) *cavea* and orchestra were designed somewhat similar to a Greek theater, according to the principles of Vitruvius. Other major features of the design, however, do not seem to correspond to Vitruvian diagrams.[34] Instead, guided by proportions inherent in the colonnade, the architects used key points of the existing structure to design the *theatron* and its substructure.

The previous *distyle* building offered obvious solutions to the design but also left the architects with some problems of inserting the theater into the pre-designed space. The outer edges of the *distyle* columns and their bases were deliberately left visible for aesthetic reasons and the result is a fine interplay between the old and new structure.

The second inter-columniations (between Columns 1-2 and 19-20) were used for the *aditus maximi*. As was previously mentioned, the benches in front of the *analemmata* and Columns 1 and 20 leave only 1.4 m free access space for the *aditus maximi*. All 4 elements obstruct the broad entrances that ideally the *aditus maximi* would have provided (see A and B on fig. 8.25). The effect is not as visually striking on the ground as it appears on the plan—one can easily pass and the space feels open, perhaps because the benches are low. However, the *aditus maximi* must have constituted a dilemma for the architects. The *analemmata* had to be in line with the north edges of Columns 2 and 19 and the columns had to be partially visible as they were on the long sides. It would have appeared awkward to deviate from this principle adopted on both the long sides and the short south side.

The pre-stage wall and the *proscaenium* were set back from the south edges of Columns 1 and 20 and placed on either side of the E-W axis of the columns respectively, whereas the rear (north) side of the *pulpitum* extended beyond the footprint of the Great Temple. This was more acceptable

33 Sear 2006, 68, fig. 8.1.
34 For a recent discussion of these, see Ibid. 27-30.

to the designers, compared to the alternative solution, which would have been to position the *analemmata* slightly to the south.

The stage is low and open towards the south, with Columns 1 and 20 creating its frame. The *analemmata* originally stood some 4-5 m next to Columns 2 and 19. It would have looked unbalanced if the *analemmata* and Columns 2 and 19 were not in line, since they constitute a solid mass of some 4-5 m upwards. There may have been a southern limit to the location of the stage if we assume that the orchestra required a certain size, and the *aditus maximi* a certain width. The line of the *analemmata* was decided by the overall plan and desire for architectural harmony. It is likely the stage required a set N-S width. The position of its north edge, exceeding the footprint of the Temple behind the two Pronaos Columns A and B, was probably fixed because the *scaenae frons* would have required structural support. It is impossible to establish for certain if the south side of the stage was governed by the size requirements of the *aditus maximi* and/or the orchestra alone, or if its position simply fitted the desired depth of the stage. The benches may not have been part of the original design, but added later. If, however, they were part of the original building their installation was too insignificant an architectural element so as to influence the positioning of the *analemmata*. Original to the design or not, the installation of the benches did disrupt the aesthetics of the structure, although not significantly. The appearance of the *theatron*, and its harmony with the pre-existing structure were primary concerns, and had to be balanced with various functional necessities—the spatial reconfiguration for access-ways and seating. Optimal visibility and audibility were a priority for the architects. It has already been mentioned that the elongated design of the *cavea* left part of the spectators at some distance from the activities performed. Had the *analemmata* been located 50-70 cm further south so that the benches were in line with the north edges of Columns 2 and 19, either the entire *cavea* would have had to be moved equally in a south direction, thus expanding even further the distance between the spectators and the performance, or the space in the front part of the *cavea* would have been foreshortened—thus reducing the space for spectators in this the most valued section of seating.

A further feature for which the existing structure either dictated or provided obvious solutions, was the interrelationship between staircases, landings, and windows. Because the columns were already in place, the windows could be located only in the inter-columniations. The interior system of staircases (East and West Inner, and SE and SW) was also planned so that their landings would be lit by windows (See W.1-9, fig. 8.1).

The orchestra podium followed the arch of a semicircle beyond 180-degrees to 198-degrees. The blocks were laid in even isodomic courses sunk into a sterile layer of sand. Composed of blocks of uneven height, the lowest course was set so their upper edges stood at the same level and their lower edges extended below ground level to various depths,[35] with no visible consequences since the orchestra pavers would later cover this irregularity. There is no obvious explanation for the anomalies in the orchestra podium mentioned above (fig. 8.11 and B and C on fig. 8.12), and the disruption of the fine coursing was unimportant aesthetically because the podium wall was plastered and the ashlars therefore not visible.

No clear decorative system seems to have governed the installation of the 16 rows of flagstones covering the orchestra floor. Since they seem to be laid more to a pattern in the west than the east, it is possible that their installation sequence may have been from west to east. When it was realized that their selected dimensions would not fit in the east, this area was covered with rows of adjusted widths to fit into the fixed space of the area.

The rows of seats are not preserved well enough to establish if they curved beyond the 180-degree line. The curves of the orchestra podium, the *diazoma*, the seating blocks, the *aditus maximi-scalae* (fig. 8.1 Nos. 30-31), the central *cavea scala* (No. 24) (but not the E and W *scalae* of the *cavea*, Nos. 23

35 *Great Temple* vol. 2, 270-73, figs. 5.77-5.80.

and 25) were concentric to the center of the orchestra (fig. 8.25). The pre-stage wall is roughly tangential to the circle drawn by the orchestra diameter. The niches of the *proscaenium* all relate to the circle as a continuation of the outer curve of the *diazoma* above the orchestra podium (fig. 8.25)[36] suggesting a geometric relationship between the niches and the first row of seating. However, this may be accidental.

The column drum found under the pavers in the orchestra is likely to be a pivot-stone used for laying out the various elements of the *theatron*. Similar finds are known from other theaters, for example at Magnesia on the Meander,[37] where a stone assemblage was found exactly in the middle of the circle defining the orchestra podium and on axis with the central *scala* of the *cavea*. The stone in the Great Temple Theater is not exactly in the middle of the orchestra but some 16 cm towards the south of it, and it may have been pushed out of its original position with the sand fill in the orchestra before the flagstones were laid. No other stones were found under the pavers, and the column drum would not have been visible after the pavers had been laid, as also was the case at Magnesia. I believe the stone was used as a measuring point for the architects and masons. Its position served as a stable focal point by the builders—they would have fixed measuring strings to its exact center point, marked by color. Another interpretation is that the stone was laid to stabilize the orchestra fill, to prevent the pavers from sinking should a heavy object be placed on top of them in the middle of the orchestra. If, for example, a massive stone altar originally stood here, its installation may have been planned before the orchestra pavers were laid and the column lent the floor its requisite support.

The seat dimensions are similar to those found all over the Roman world. In Roman theaters, as opposed to Greek—the seats have no frontal vertical cavities. Exhibiting a rough finish, the seat blocks are unlikely to have been in that state during use. Grooves with chisel marks at the edges of some blocks (figs. 8.13, 8.14) may be attempts to refashion the blocks with a more pronounced curve—mistakes were made and the results remained on the blocks. This may seem extraordinary for a building, with which care was otherwise taken of its aesthetic appearance. Perhaps the seat-blocks were not meant to be visible, but designed to be covered with a fine stone veneer, wood, plaster, or cushions.

The distribution of the *scalae* and widths of the *cunei* are similar to other Roman theaters, as are the dimensions of the steps of the *scalae*—two steps equal one seat-block, a governing rule both in Greek and Roman theaters.[38]

The stage has at least two major phases of construction. The pre-stage wall was either a low wall that served as a foundation for some other structure, or originally it was built higher. Either way, it extended between Columns 1 and 20. Neither were the orchestra gate thresholds nor the *aditus maximi* benches installed at this point. Later, perhaps soon after the first phase, the *pulpitum* was positioned over the pre-stage wall set slightly to the north. This was advantageous for this new element because of the need for a greater distance to the *cavea*, or for the width of the *aditus maximi* that was narrowed by the benches installed up against the *analemmata*. With its colorful sandstone trim the south edge of the pre-stage wall was exposed and continued to be part of the adornment of the building. It also served as the lowest step for one of the 4 stairways leading from the *aditus maximi* up to the *pulpitum* floor. The installation of the *proscaenium* created a formal division between the orchestra and the *aditus maximi* and the two gates were installed.[39] The thresholds cut into the exposed south edge of the pre-stage wall and extended up to the front of the *pulpitum*. Between

---

36 The west outer corner of east square niche; the rear of the semicircular niche; and the east outer corner of west square niche.

37 Bingöl 2005, 56, 59, fig. 201. For a review of Bingöl, see Yegül 2007, 578-82.

38 See Frederiksen 2000, 142 for observations on Greek theaters; for observations of Roman theaters, cf. the bibliography: for analyses of a number of Roman theaters by this author.

39 Now only the thresholds remain.

the gates, in front of the orchestra, the *proscaenium* was decorated with niches, as was the fashion in Roman theater architecture, and outside the gates, in front of the *aditus maximi*, were stairways, two on each side.

The two massive columns in the center back of the *pulpitum* would have created a dramatic *scaenae frons* with the addition of walls between them and the *antae*. This is theoretical, but it would explain why a part of the *pulpitum* extended to the north beyond the footprint of the building.

Variegated colored stone played an important role in the Great Temple Theater design. The pattern of the pre-stage wall was probably maintained throughout the active history of the theater. The mix of white and red pavers in the orchestra must have been intentional. The *pulpitum* pavement, with colorful pavers of various colors, was apparently laid in a random although quite powerful visible mixture of color.[40] Only a fraction of the approximate 100 m2 of *pulpitum* floor remains *in situ*.

Who built this Theater-In-Temple? The Roman elements in construction and design are overwhelming. We cannot conclude, however, that the structure was built by and for Romans. The masons' marks suggest that the stonemasons were Nabataeans working in a Nabataean tradition. These masons either were under the supervision of Nabataean architects acquainted with Roman theater design, or Roman architects hired by Nabataeans.

Dating

The grand scheme of Site Phase IV, the existing structure into which the theater was installed, dates to the last quarter of the 1st c. B.C. The theater construction probably took place in the 1st c. A.D. Thereafter some damage is exhibited in the walls of the East and West Staircases and the West Anta wall. The narrowing of the doorways in the East, West and South Corridors could be contemporary with this later phase. It has been suggested that the destruction and subsequent modifications could be associated with a Roman attack on Petra, sometime around the annexation of A.D.106.[41]

Theater phase V.1

The installation of the entire *cavea* with the orchestra and its podium represents one phase. In the fill under the orchestra pavers in association with the pivot-stone, a coin of Aretas IV, dated to 4/3 B.C., was recovered,[42] thus providing a post quem not only for the installation of the pavers, but probably for the *theatron*; thus it may have been constructed sometime in the early 1st c. A.D. Less clear are the sequences of installation of various features in relation to each other, such as the paving of the orchestra and *aditus maximi*. They both seem to be contemporary with the orchestra gates because they are not disrupted by their insertion. The pre-stage wall, however, represents an older phase than the gate thresholds, since the gate blocks cut into the pre-stage wall and disturb the pattern of its layout. Perhaps there was an earlier paving associated with the theater that was renovated with the gate installations.[43] One solution to this phasing problem is the suggestion that the pre-stage wall followed the installation of the thresholds, entailing its modification.

The use of the sloping substructure barrel vaults points to a date in the second half of the 1st c. B.C.[44] while the colorful pavement of the orchestra suggests a date not prior to the Augustan

---

40 The 2nd and 5th rows of the *ima cavea* were primarily of white limestone as opposed to the grey stone of the rest. This would not have been a decorative feature, if the seat blocks were covered as it is maintained here.

41 *Great Temple*, vol. 2, 229.

42 SP200, Locus 6. Cat. No. 05-C-47, Seq. No. 200013.

43 But this is theoretical, and perhaps unlikely, since it would have been quite troublesome to exchange the entire paving with the sole gain of not having to disrupt the pattern of the pavers, which is not perfect anyway.

44 Segal 1995, 76, n.153.

period.[45] Our theater shows clear Roman elements, and can be paralleled to the large theater at Petra, which is also constructed in the late Nabataean Hellenistic period. The Great Temple Theater may be its contemporary. The pre-stage wall is contemporary with Theater Phase V.1, since the entire theater design with its *aditus maximi* relates to it. Alternating between yellow and red sandstone blocks, the pre-stage wall mirrors the decorative scheme observed in the *tetrastyle in antis* curb of the Great Temple Pronaos, and the curbing bordering the Lower Temenos Triple Colonnades. Both are dated to Site Phase IV, which supports an A.D. pre-106 date for the initial phase of the theatre as well. Another possibility is that this pre-stage wall was not originally installed with the theater but was a pre-existing wall belonging to the Great Temple Site Phase IV. This would explain the need to cut into the wall's south face and interrupt its design. Until it may persuasively be argued that this wall was a part of the temple, it will be considered as a part of the theater.

Theater phase V.2

The *proscaenium* installation should be regarded as a later addition to the original theater, since it overlies the pre-stage wall of the Theater Phase V.1. The north face of the pre-stage wall was a visible distinct architectural statement, before the *proscaenium* and *pulpitum* were installed over it, and it clearly had a functional period of its own until this happened.[46] Moreover, the *proscaenium* also slightly overlays the north ends of the orchestra gate thresholds, and would also partially have covered the north postholes of the thresholds.[47] These observations do not automatically lead to the conclusion that the function of the gates ceased with the installation of the *proscaenium*, but it seems pretty certain that the *proscaenium* was not a planned element at the time when the thresholds were put in place. The *proscaenium* installation probably does represent a change in function, alternatively and enhancement of an existing function, but certainly a change in the architecture of the theater so great that it makes sense to describe it as a distinct phase. The dating of this Theater Phase V.2 happened either later in the 1st c. A.D. or during the 2nd c. A.D.

Theater phase V.3

In this phase the space at the rear (to the north) of the *proscaenium* was filled in to create a solid foundation and the permanent paved *pulpitum* floor of colored pavers laid on top of it. The complete blocking of the access to the Central Vaulted Chamber is contemporary with the removal of the pavers in the Pronaos and the ensuing installation of the *pulpitum*. The dating of Theater Phase V.3 follows Phase V.2 later in the 1st c. A.D. or 2nd c. A.D.

Reconstruction of the Monument

The reconstruction of the theater requires an understanding of the pre-existing structure, the Great Temple, since the theater was inserted into this building. Clearly repairs were made to the temple in Site Phase IV, and this may have occurred in the first phase of the theater (V.1). The columns are an outstanding feature of the building. We are fairly certain about the height of the columns because of the general laws of proportional relationships between measured width and height. The columns of the Temple Colonnade are therefore considered to have been 14.30 m in height.[48] The architrave superstructure is largely unknown. From the earlier structure (Site Phase II-IV) the squat sandstone columns were plastered with a thick layer of painted stucco (8-10 cm) from the base one third up the shaft, topped by an un-painted (white) fluted plaster all the way up to the capitals.[49] This plastering was visible in the theater phases wherever parts of the col-

45 Sear 2006, 81.
46 This was only until the *pulpitum* was installed over it.
47 Or, alternatively, they would have been able to hold posts of a lesser thickness than envisaged in the original design.
48 The bases are 0.46 m, shafts 12.4 m, and the capitals are 1.47 m in height.
49 *Great Temple* vol. 2, 220-22.

umns and walls were exposed, and the colorful lower shafts and fluted upper shafts were thus automatically incorporated with the theater design.

Substructure: The rectangular areas in front of the East and West Interior staircases are vaulted, as are the staircases themselves. Although arch springers and sections of vaults are preserved it is not certain how the vaults were actually designed. Based on the fact that all the preserved vaults are of the simple semicircular type, I have reconstructed all the unpreserved vaults similarly (figs. 8.6 and 8.9). The vaults over the East and West Inner Staircases were sloping on a gentler angle than the stairways themselves (fig. 8.6). These vaults are not preserved, but assuming that they were semicircular, their inner height from ground level in front of the lowest step to highest inner point would be 4 m.[50] The height further up is considerably less. Over step 23 the highest inner point of the vaults would have been approximately 2.47 m (fig. 8.6).[51] The height from the steps to the spring line of the vaults decreases gradually upwards, due to the fact that the vaults would have reached too great a height in relation to the *cavea* superstructure if they were constructed with the same incline as the stairs.

The substructure construction was a paramount consideration for the architects, and it was carefully devised in accordance with the needs of the *cavea*. Seat blocks from the *cavea* seats,[52] were scattered throughout the collapsed substructure, as was mentioned previously, so we may safely conclude that the entire space above the substructure was covered with rows of seats for spectators. As suggested by Vitruvius[53] each section of the *cavea* should have its own entrance. This principle, found in many Roman theaters,[54] was most probably followed in our theater as well (figs. 8.26-27), but we lack explicit proof for the *cavea* subdivision. A *cavea* in two sections with 3 *diazomata*, suggested here, is not inspired by the size of our theater, which is small,[55] but by the fact that there are three sets of entrances: the front accesses at the orchestra podium, the East and West Interior Staircases, and South East and South West Interior Staircases. The substructure architecture suggests a simple reconstruction of the *cavea*. Illustrated in figs. 8.26 and 8.27, the space over the substructure is appointed with seats and stairways all rising at identical angles as those preserved in the lower *cavea* section. The reconstructed arrangement of seats, *scalae* and *diazomata* above the *ima cavea* is theoretical, but it is likely that the angle of the rising seats and steps is accurate, since it follows the angle of the preserved ones of the *ima cavea*. It could have been different, however, since occasionally a change of angle is found in Greek and Roman theaters, introduced at the point of the *diazomata*, simply to enhance the view of the spectators in the upper seats. As such, a change in angle is more common in larger monuments; there is no special reason to believe that the *cavea* of this modest theater included such features in its design. The lowest section, the *ima cavea*, was accessed by the *aditus maximi* with the east and west flights of steps leading up to the first *diazoma* (A). A second *diazoma* (B) is suggested which was accessed from the East and West Interior Staircases and East and West Landings feeding an (unpreserved) Upper Inner Staircase (No. 12, fig. 8.27). This *diazoma* (B) divided the *cavea* in two, and provided access to the upper part of the

---

50 The width of the stairway-space is 2.2 m. The distance from the ground level to the spring line of the vault is 2.9 m. If perfectly semi-circular, the vault would have been half that measurement or 1.1 m high, from the spring line up. Those two measurements together is 4 m.

51 Addition of height of vault (1.1 m) and the distance from upper side of step 23 to the spring line is 1.37 m.

52 The blocks are easily distinguished because of their dimensions and the grooves cut on the fronts and surfaces on a number of them (see figs. 8.13, 8.14). For their prevalence in substructure collapse see L.-A. Bedal *et al.*,Trench 47 (July 9 August 3 1997); B. A. Brown, Trench 55 (July 18 August 7 1998), dated August 1998; M. Prendergast *et al.*, Trench 57 (June 13 July 29 1998), dated August 1998, on-line in *Open Context*.

53 Vitruvius, *De Arch.* 5.3.5.

54 Sear 2006, 69.

55 According to the classification system suggested by Rossetto and Sartorio 1994, vol. 1, 80, or 'tiny' if one follows the size classification of Segal 1995, 26.

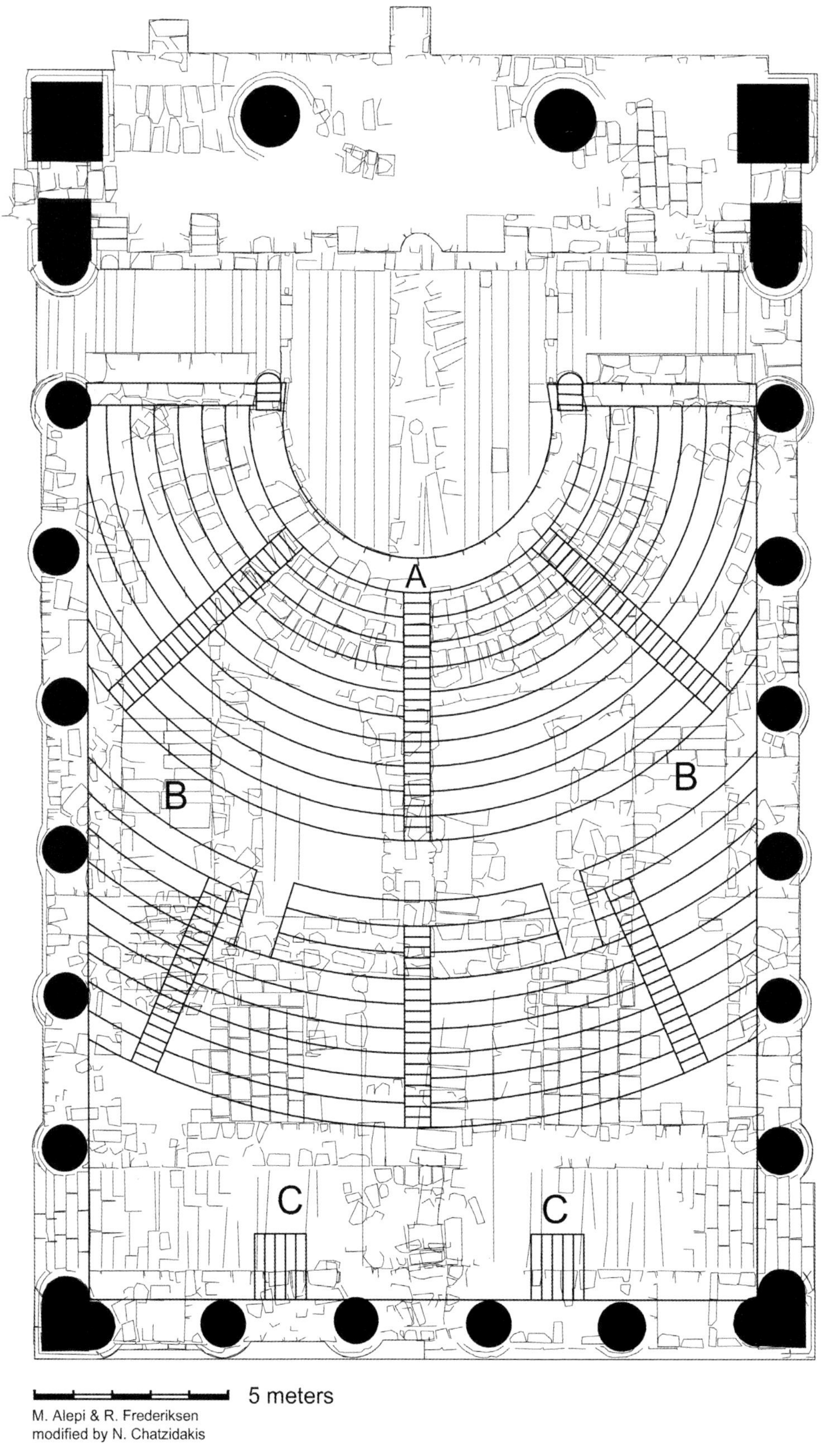

Fig. 8.26. Suggested reconstruction of the *cavea*, with *ima* and summa *cavea*, *diazomata* and *scalae*. The layout above (south of) the 6th row of the *ima cavea*, is hypothetical.

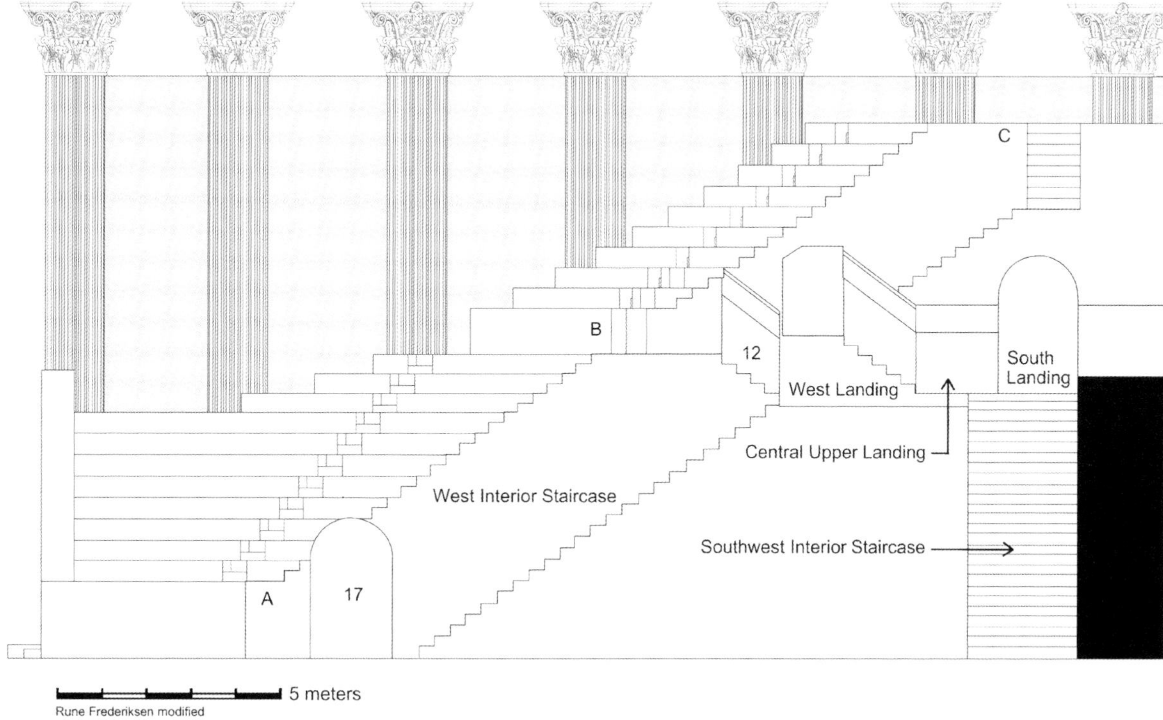

Fig. 8.27. Suggested reconstruction of the access system. Features above '12', the Central Upper Landing, the West and the South Landings, are hypothetical.

ima cavea. Additionally the SE and SW Interior Staircases would have provided an (unpreserved) access-way to the 3rd *diazoma* (C) from where the *summa cavea* could also be accessed from above. It is possible that the two rear entrances served the same access-point as the E and W Interior Staircases, via the E and W Landings. It is important to repeat that it is not clear how the upper half of the substructure and *cavea* were designed and constructed, but I believe that the two sets of staircases must have been reflected somehow in the subdivision of the *cavea*.

A Diazoma (B), between the *ima cavea* and *summa cavea*, was probably of the same width as the lowest (and preserved) *diazoma* (A), or it may have been wider to give room for the exits from the East and West Upper Staircases that must have existed in this area. These exits, or *vomitoria*, cut through the last two seats and the wall just south of *diazoma* B that served as foot-rest for the last seat-row in the reconstruction figs. 8.26-27. This is just one possible suggestion. A way to avoid the *vomitoria* to cut through seat rows would be to raise the entire *epitheatron*, but this would have reduced the number of rows towards the *diazoma* C, because the ceiling of the building set a limit to the height in this. The height is then also a likely explanation for the suggested broader *diazoma* (C) at the rear, reconstructed in this way because the installation of more seat rows – rising to the same angle as the preserved ones below – would have raised this *diazoma* to such a level that spectators would have bumped their heads into the entablature and the column capitals, or ceiling if the building had one. We assume that the theater was designed as being fully contained by the surrounding structure in all its functional aspects (figs. 8.26-27).

The third set of windows (W. 3 and 7, fig. 8.1) extending down to the East and West Landing floor levels indicates that the landing passageways were a low space restricted by the vaults and *cavea* seats above them. An alternative explanation for this placement is the corresponding windows of the East and West Corridor walls (see this volume fig. 1.16), which would have existed at this level before the theater was built.

Cavea: No seats of the NE and NW *cunei* were preserved *in situ* close enough to the *analemmata* to establish if there were seat rows set to the inner faces of these walls, or if there may have been a 4th and 5th *scala* ending the *cavea* instead of seats. Either way, the *analemmata* (collapsed) would have increased in height to the east and west respectively, half a meter or so above the height of either the seats or the stairway steps. They were probably finished on top in a (sloping) straight or a stepped line. It could be claimed, that the seats did extend to the *analemmata*, since a *cavea* of this size would not have required more than three *scalae*.[56] This is how we reconstruct this part of the *cavea* (fig. 8.26).

The orchestra podium and the *aditus maximi-scalae* followed the curve of the circle beyond 180-degrees, but the seats of the *cunei* above them would not have extended that far since they abutted the south faces of the *analemmata*, which are exactly on the 180-degree line. The space above the preserved lower rows and inside the two imagined walls, tangential to the inside of the Columns 2 and 19, continue south (fig. 8.1 and fig. 8.26), and allow for the reconstruction of 7 rows extending to slightly beyond 180-degrees. Around the center axis of the *theatron* there would have been 10 rows, and the reconstructed *diazoma* B above could have served as an 11th row. Unfortunately substructure walls 1 and 2 are not preserved to this height, so it is not possible to lift this theoretical probability into the realm of certainty.

The roughly finished seat blocks with their deep grooves (fig. 8.14), suggest that the seats were covered and were appointed with armrests. It has not been possible to identify a system for the distribution of the deep grooves, since too few are preserved *in situ* (fig. 8.25). That they existed in the entire *cavea* is confirmed by their recovery in the collapse of the center and south part of the theater.[57] The concentration of grooved seats found on either side of the East Scala (fig. 8.1, No. 25; fig. 8.25), suggests that grooves were placed at the ends of seat-rows which fits the idea that each row was a bench with armrests at either end. The problem with their interpretation as armrests is that they would have disrupted an easy access for the spectators entering the seat-rows from the *cavea* stairways.[58] Another possibility is that the trapezoidal grooves were designed to fix plates of wood or stone on the seat rows. The surfaces of the blocks are quite rough, and some covering of the upper and front surfaces of the seat-blocks is very likely.

Orchestra: The orchestra and *aditus maximi* pavements extend into the East and West Corridors and it is suggested here that the corridors were entirely paved in this manner. Situated below the original paving of the Great Temple, this paving has been entirely robbed out except for the preserved areas described above.

The orchestra podium certainly continued in its full height to the north edge of the *cavea* as it has been reconstructed (figs. 8.9, 8.26 and 8.27). The only alternative reconstruction is that the wall would have been stepped following the steps of the two north *scalae* leading from the *aditus maximi* up to the first *diazoma* above the podium wall. However such a reconstruction would have left voids between the north wall and the orchestra gates. The quantities of metal in the areas of both thresholds are likely to be remains of nails and fastenings for the screens and/or doors. The small circular cavities in the central threshold blocks may be from slide pins holding a double leaf door or a grill. Here the surface wear attests to their active use (fig. 8.17).

Aditus maximi: The benches of the *aditus maximi*, left in a roughly finished manner, are quite low (30 cm); the comfortable seat height for an average person is 35 cm. It can be reasoned that these benches may have been covered with wood, carpets and perhaps cushions.

---

56 Two additional *scalae* would have reduced the number of spectator seats considerably.

57 *Great Temple* vol. 1, 264.

58 This problem may only be theoretical since a person could step over the armrests. Alternatively the armrests could be set in two positions, horizontal and vertical. The armrest scenario is not impossible, but only leaves us with a small (potential) problem of practicality.

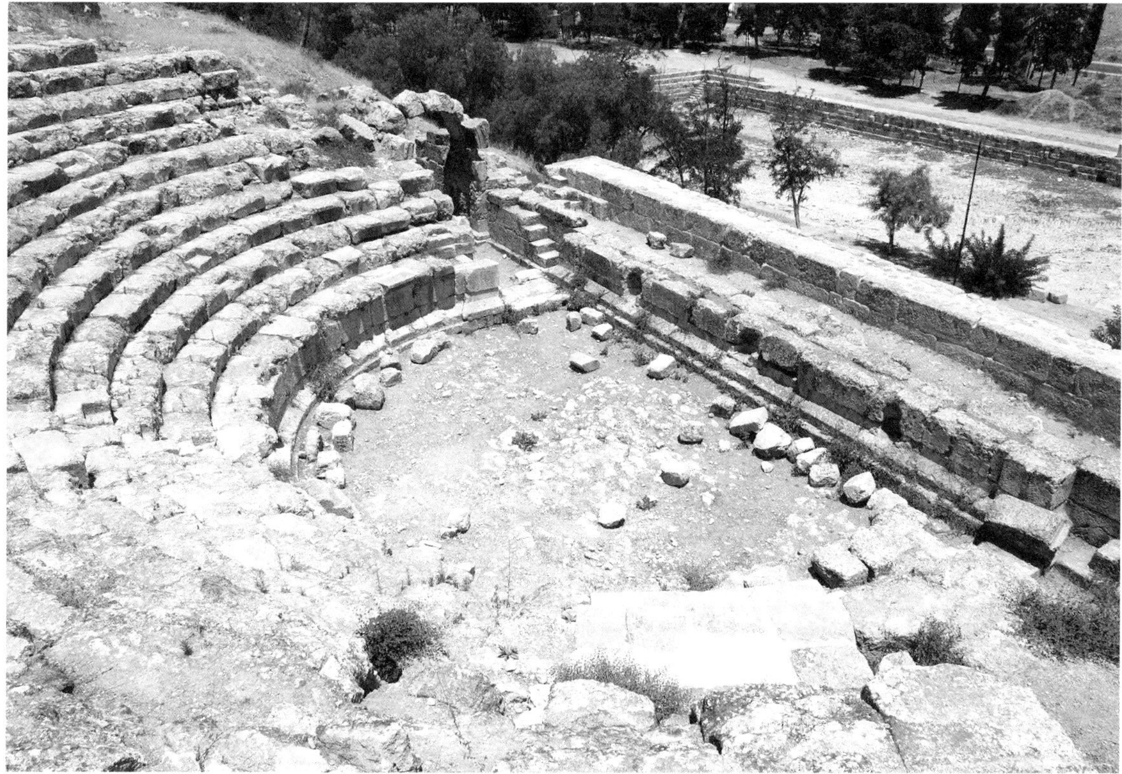

Fig. 8.28. Theater at Berketin (Gerasa) to northwest.

Pre-stage wall: This wall is part of a structure that is older than the *proscaenium* and *pulpitum* building phases. It is possible that it was considerably higher than the one course now preserved. That the south side was constructed with more attention to its appearance than the north side suggests that it was originally part of the performance architecture and was visible. The wall does not seem to have had any staircases. Its 1.4 m width is hardly spacious enough for a proper stage, but it may have served to support some sort of scenography in Theater Phase V.1.

Proscaenium and the first and second *pulpitum*: Before the space behind the *proscaenium* was filled in and the stone paved *pulpitum* was constructed, there may have been a phase with a wooden (?) *pulpitum*. In this phase the *proscaenium* was a freestanding wall with a total width of no more than 87 cm. There are numerous examples in Roman theater architecture of narrow *proscaenia* in combination with (indirectly attested) wooden pulpita (fig. 8.28).[59] We suggest the probability of such an installation in this theater. No elements were found in the remains of the stage to suggest that the space behind the *proscaenium* was used for an *aulaeum* (a stage drop curtain), as has been observed in some Roman theaters.[60]

In a later phase a permanent *pulpitum* was built by filling the area north of the *proscaenium* and by paving the area. Fragments of a base from the West Anta was reused as part of this fill, suggesting that the temple and perhaps even Theater Phases 1-2 were in a partly ruined state when the Theater Phase 2 *pulpitum* was installed. Some time had elapsed between the building of the *proscaenium*, the first *pulpitum*, and the second *pulpitum*.

The *proscaenium* and *pulpitum* (1-2) constitute a miniature Roman stage. The wall with Columns A and B embedded in it would have served as the *scaenae frons*. The inter-axial distance

59 One example is the *proscaenium* in Berketin.
60 Cf. Sear 2006, 8.

between Columns A and B is greater than the distance between *antae* walls and Columns A and B respectively.[61] The three spaces across the north edge of the *pulpitum*, between the *antae* walls and Columns A and B, correspond proportionally with the tripartite *scaenarum frontes* of other Roman theaters.[62]

However, the proportional correspondences between the design of the pre-theater building and the new theater, encourages two possible interpretations for the north side of the *pulpitum* extending beyond the *pronaos* columns. Firstly, the *pulpitum* required a certain width. With the orchestra and *aditus maximi* preventing it from expanding to the south, the only possibility for the *pulpitum* to increase was to extend beyond the footprint of the building to the north. This solution may at the same time have been purely practical so as to allow performers to move behind Columns A and B. A different interpretation of the expansion of the *pulpitum* to the north, and which I think is more likely,[63] is that the north edge of the *pulpitum* served as the structural base for a *scaenae frons* perhaps of wood or canvas.[64] If there was a *scaenae frons* it would have built up to a significant height, and probably have been placed immediately behind or between Columns A and B—between the northwest corner of the east anta wall and the northeast corner of the west anta. It also may have been partially composed of ashlars, judging from those unearthed in the Pronaos trenches from collapsed structures. This interpretation would also fit the existence of the two (more likely originally three) rear entrances leading into each of the three sections of the *scaenae frons* façade. It is possible that the inner part of the entablature extending over the *antae* walls and Columns A and B supported a roof structure, but this is of course pure theory.

In general Roman theaters are constructed with the stage structurally connected to the *cavea*. However this relationship is not confirmed from the ruins of the Great Temple Theater. If the architrave connects the columns of the *pteron*, the building was built as a single entity. The Anta Walls of the NE and NW corners of the temple were erected as a single entity with Columns 1 and 20 connected by walls, extending up to the entablature. This was also the case for the walls inserted in the other inter-columniations of the *pteron*, from Columns 2 to 19. There is no *in situ* evidence that the *aditus maximi* entrances (between Columns 1-2 and 19-20) were filled in, at some level above. These entrance areas were clearly open from the ground level at least up to a few meters. At some point, higher up, towards the architrave, vaults could have connected Columns 1 and 2, and 19 and 20. This would be a foregone conclusion given the closure of the colonnade on both sides of the entrances for the *aditus maximi*, save the vaulted entrances to the East and West Interior Staircases and the vaulted windows. It would have appeared disjointed to have 12 m high walls around a 2 m wide x 12 m high opening. A few arch springer fragments, and fragments of a smaller pilaster order, were recovered from the excavations inside and around the stage, all of which support the theory of arches and walls over the *aditus maximus* openings.

The Great Temple columns were furnished with 6-piece[65] Corinthian capitals.[66] However, it is

---

61 The *scaenae frons* with three openings is a feature characteristic of the western type theater (Sear 2006, 83). It would be incorrect to interpret the likely existence of a tripartite *scaenae frons* at the Great Temple Theater to being a deliberate result of creating a *scaenae frons* in accordance with this general type of theater, since the small scale of this theater would hardly have left other possible ways to devise a *scaenae frons*.

62 Segal 1995, 24.

63 I owe to Elizabeth Gebhard the observation that the northern edge of the *pulpitum* could be of key importance for establishing the existence of the now vanished but once substantial elements of the stage building.

64 The insubstantial construction of the *pulpitum*, in particular towards its north edge, would not have been able to support too great a weight.

65 The capitals were constructed of 6 separate blocks, the lower half with the two rows of acanthus leafs in two vertical halves, the upper volute and abacus were carved in 4 parts. Corinthian capitals in the city of Rome were constructed of two blocks in the early Empire, and from the middle of the 1st c. A.D. the capitals were monolithic (See Ch. 7A in this volume).

66 Type 1 floral capital, McKenzie 2005, 95, 190, Diagram 14.f.

unknown how the entablature was constructed. A stone entablature would seem unlikely given the relatively wide span of more than 6 m between Columns A and B (fig. 8.1). Also it is difficult to imagine how such a substantial weight could have rested securely on the 6-part composite capitals. Ashlars have indeed been found in the building collapse, and various excavation reports suggest they may derive from an entablature but a stone entablature for a building of these dimensions would have left behind numerous blocks of substantial dimensions. The upper surfaces of the capitals are dressed to receive some kind of superstructure, but it was probably wooden. In support of a proposed wood entablature are, perhaps, the huge iron nails and wood found in the orchestra area.[67] The lesser height of the inner colonnade of 12 m, compared to the 15.5 m of the porch, suggests that this entablature was 3.5 m high—the same height as the porch entablature.

The capitals of the East, West and South Corridors were clearly visible to the exterior, i.e., when seen from within the corridors. They were also visible as part of the upper interior substructure walls above the *cavea*. The inner substructure walls 1-3 (fig. 8.1) did not (structurally) extend to the top of the building. They were carrying the vaults of the substructure on top of which rested the seats. Above the level of the seats, the walls would have continued with built widths as wide as, or a little less than the columns, presumably leaving parts of the capitals exposed (fig. 8.9).

It has not been established for certain if the space over the *cavea* was roofed. A great number of roof tiles have been reported from some trenches, in particular in the South Passageway. It has been argued that these originated from the South Corridor, which is possible if the roof over this corridor was slanting upwards in a northerly direction, towards the *cavea*. In this case the entablature of the Great Temple colonnade and the corridor walls would have reached the same height.

The substantial thickness of the outer walls (fig. 8.1, Nos. 1-3, on average 1.8 m width) cannot be used as a sole argument for them having carried a roof.[68] The walls, which were certainly designed to support the vaults of the *cavea* substructure, do not seem to have extended to the same height as the top of the capitals. The columns were not carrying the substructure, but only supporting themselves. It could however be argued that the extra width of the walls, towards the interior of the building, were used for beams that could have spanned the open space over the *cavea*. The walls, although necessary for structural reasons, were clearly designed into the colonnade so that the two elements appeared together as much as an entity as possible.

Setting

Although major changes took place in the conversion of the building into a theater, there is no particular reason to believe that there was a long period of disuse between the end of the buildings original function and the new as theater. The situation cannot therefore be compared for example to the 3rd c. A.D. theater installation in the previous market building at Cyrene that was devastated by an earthquake and never repaired.[69] The installation of the *theatron* in the Great Temple, regardless of its previous function as a temple or perhaps a dining hall, appears to have been a sudden dramatic change to the functionality of the building. It is tempting to identify this change with the Roman annexation of Nabataea and Petra, although we know little in detail about this take-over and the ensuing Romanization. Most of the main structures at Petra date to the 1st c. B.C. and the 1st c. A.D.[70] If the installation of the theater was associated with the annexation after A.D.106, the Great Temple, a center of power, was transformed into a structure that symbolized its new Imperial masters. This is likely to have occurred deliberately, and it is analogous to the installation of the 'Colosseum' in Rome by the Flavians into what had been part of the private villa of Nero, the

67 Although the find spots here are somewhat remote from where beams from such an entablature are most likely to have fallen. Such finds could also, of course, have derived from a wooden roof-structure.

68 Roofing seems to have been essential for *odea*: Rossetto and Sartorio 1994, vol. 1, 138; Meinel 1980, 190 and passim; Sear 2006, 38-9.

69 Ward-Perkins and Gibson 1983, 349-53.

70 McKenzie 2005, 33-59.

last member of Julio-Claudian dynasty—from whom the Flavians wished to distance themselves. With a century long tradition of conquest the Romans at the time of Trajan—when Nabataea fell to Rome —were at the height of their power. They knew all too well the power of symbolic values, in particular in times of change.

We are not sure of the function of the Great Temple either before its metamorphosis or after. Let us revisit some basic facts and observations. It is clear that the *theatron* was not a building for the masses. Its capacity was only some 900 people.[71] A partial understanding of the Theater-in-Temple may be gained from comparing it to the Large Theater of Petra. This Theater was also placed in a location that entailed the destruction of already existing structures, but of a completely different nature—monumental tombs. The functional connection between the tomb cult (*necrolatry*) and the Great Theater has been suggested.[72] Apart from the difficulties in proposing that this huge canonic Roman theater served such a function, I conclude, alternatively, that the desire to build this civic theater was so pervasive that it was simply a practical necessity to obliterate some of the ancestors' monuments. Both theater installations would befit a Roman take-over, but it may also be argued that both theaters were constructed even a century earlier, when Nabataean kings were still in full control. If so, both theaters strengthen the image of a Nabataean culture that incorporates Roman cultural elements long before the annexation and formal incorporation of Nabataea into the Roman *Provincia Arabia* in A.D.106.

Function

I believe that we need to view theatrical structures in general, both in Greek and Roman times, as assembly places that could accommodate many different functions. In addition, buildings constructed to serve primarily one purpose, could suddenly change this function, resulting in a perhaps barely visible structural change to its architecture. These facts however, must not prevent us from trying to analyze the various theatrical ruins and come up with suggestions as to the primary scopes behind their erections. These can be deduced from the key elements of the architecture—the size of the *cavea*, the size of the orchestra and its relationship to the *cavea*, and the stage and its elements.

The Theater in the Great Temple is small, and should be interpreted in comparison with the other theater structures in Petra. I have already commented on two other Petraean theater structures, the Large Theater and a now vanished smaller one. In addition, there are stepped areas at the Temple of the Winged Lions, the Temenos seating of the Qasr al-Bint, and at the temple at Ed Deir, all of which may have been performance seating areas used in connection with ritual drama.[73] The more buildings a city purposefully builds for specific functions the more likely it is that additional buildings would also be erected primarily for specialized functions.[74] We should remember that Petra was the Nabataean capital and in the Roman period she is likely to have been equipped with the expected architectonic paraphernalia of a 2nd c. A.D. Empire metropolis.

It is possible that the Theater was used for sports activities like boxing or wrestling and such functions find potential support in the architecture. The substructure was designed so that light could enter the East and West Vaulted Chambers suggesting that they may have been used for the

71 *Ima cavea*: 400; *Summa cavea*: 500. Calculations are based on the reconstruction in fig. 8.26, and on the assumption that each spectator would require 40 cm of seating width. This measurement is believed to have been the standard space allocated to spectators in Greek and Roman theaters, Sear 2006, 6, note 102: examples from Arles, Nîmes, Pompeii and Stobi. This calculation also corresponds to space allocation in modern theaters in London (see Hansen 1996, 27). No generally accepted standards have been developed for calculating the capacity of ancient spectator spaces. Brown University excavators calculated that the theater capacity to 600 persons (Great Temple vol. 2, 267).

72 Segal 1995, 6-7.

73 For such seating facilities in general, see Nielsen 2002, passim.

74 Sear 2006, 40-1, makes the general observation that smaller towns would have one building for more purposes, and larger towns a number of specialized buildings.

performers as well as for storage. One could easily imagine how these chambers may have been reserved for contestants before a fight. The spectators ascending the East and West Interior Staircases would, perhaps, have been able to view the contestants through the windows (W.10-11, fig. 8.1).[75] The closing off, of the orchestra with gates also may support the idea of fights having taken place. However, this is speculation.[76]

The plastering of the orchestra podium wall, creating a smooth and uniform surface, may point in the direction of the orchestra having been filled up with water in connection with performances. Although the major drain or water-supply channel does extend under the orchestra, no physical connection between it and the orchestra has been identified during the excavations. It is possible that the orchestra was designed to hold water, but this author will not pursue this idea further.[77]

It has been suggested that the theater served as a *bouleuterion*.[78] This is possible, although if it so functioned, that role was secondary. The structure was clearly built as a theater, and does not resemble structures known as *bouleuteria*.[79]

The orchestra podium seems to be the key to understanding the function of the building. The difference in height between the orchestra and the first (and further) rows of seats seems to exclude the theater as a political meeting-place in a broad sense. Speakers would have been relegated to be well below their peers when addressing them. And further, since there was a stage-structure (pre-stage wall) from Theater Phase V.1, we should rather examine all the possibilities offered by dramatic performances and perhaps sports. The orchestra podium is neither high enough, nor is the orchestra large enough for gladiatorial games, a sometimes suggested explanation for such orchestra podia.[80] The separation between the 'arena' and the spectators is so insignificant in our case that such a function is unlikely.[81]

Potentially the two (main) phases of the stage constitute two different functions, both of which are most likely to have been dramatic. It might be indicative of the function, that the *aditus maximi* benches are located in front of two sets of steps respectfully leading up to the *pulpitum*. Performers such as dancers and actors would have waited on the benches following closely the course of the performance. Such waiting performers would have been largely out of sight of the audience, because of the walls (*analemmata*) behind the benches, and the orchestra gates. The gates may in fact have served to visually isolate the center of the *proscaenium* and *pulpitum* from the *aditus maximi* and perhaps even obstruct any view to the East and West *proscaenium* from anywhere in the *cavea*. This interpretation connotes that the *aditus maximi* was part of the 'backstage environment' invisible to the audience, from where there was access both into the orchestra through the gates and from the *aditus maximi* onto the *pulpitum*. If, on the other hand, the east and west thirds of the *proscaenium*

---

75 The chambers could be closed by substantial doors, but this does not help us assign a specific function to them.

76 For a brief discussion of such activities in the region, see Segal 1995, 14.

77 For the water-phenomenon to have been quite common in theaters of the area see Segal 1995, 23. For a discussion of "water dances" likely to have taken place in the "odeon" of Libyan Ptolemais, see Kraeling 1962, 92. For the Syrian festival Maïumas, which apparently contained such activities, s.v. RE 14.1, 610-11 (F. Jacoby).

78 See the summarized debate on the function of the Great Temple and the Theater in Great Temple vol. 2, 350-55. See also discussions for the building perhaps having been the Aphrodision mentioned in the Babatha Archives (Tholbecq 2007, 134-35).

79 *Bouleuteria* were sometimes shaped as theaters and could be the same size as smaller theaters, but they rarely had a stage, and the orchestra area was generally very small and never on a level 1-2 m below the first row of seating. Often *bouleuteria* had in fact a rectangular shaped koilon/*cavea*, for example, Priene (Sear 2006, 350, no. 355); Sagalassos, (Ibid., 375 no. 398); Herakleia ad Latmos, (Ibid., 337-38, no. 333).

80 Yegül (2007, 581) observes that the orchestra podium is a phenomenon that has received little, if any, interest in modern scholarship, since Bernardi Ferrero (1966, 74).

81 For a similar scepticism towards gladiatorial games and animal fights having taken place in the "Odeon" at Ptolemais in Libya with comparable architecture, see Kraeling 1962, 92.

and *pulpitum* were to be visible to the audience, these gates would not have been higher than the orchestra podium. The audience sitting in the East and West *cunei* would have been able to see the front of the *pulpitum* with its stairways and probably parts of the *aditus maximi* as well, but not the benches. Either way, this interpretation restricts the middle of the *proscaenium* between the gates as the center of activity—the focus was directed to the central part of the scene-building.

It appears that our structure was built and rebuilt for dramatic performances, but we do not know if the theater served more than one function, both in the first and the second major phase of use. For example, the orchestra gates may have been detachable permitting change of activity from one day to the other.

It has been claimed that the eastern Empire cherished only mime and pantomime,[82] but there is evidence for tragedies and comedies to have been performed in this part of the Empire as well.[83] As already argued, the architecture of our theater does not point exclusively towards a specific subcategory of dramatic activity. However, without wanting to exclude other possible dramatic functions, I would like to argue in favor of Pantomime. Pantomime, in the Imperial form, originates from the time of Augustus,[84] and often consisted of dance competitions and could involve a number of musicians. There is nothing in the architecture of the Great Temple Theater to argue against such a purpose. On the contrary, the size of the orchestra would suit a small group of musicians perfectly and would also explain the difference in elevation between the orchestra and the seating. It would have operated in the same fashion as the orchestra in a present-day ballet, opera or theater house. This suggests that the connection between the orchestra and the stage was one of audibility only, for there is no point of access between the orchestra and the stage (from the area within the orchestra gates). The dancers (or other performers) would have sat on the benches in both the *aditus maximi* in front of the two sets of steps leading up to the *pulpitum* and waited their turn to perform. The podium would have raised the audience above the direct sight of the musicians. I contend that orchestra podia were included in many Roman theaters, musicians or not, because they elevated the lowest seats to a height that ensured a clear uninterrupted line of sight to the stage. This was particularly important for small theaters where the lowest seats were closer to the stage.

The key to understand the function of this theater lies in the architecture of the building itself, however its installation into a pre-existing structure could potentially be of significance as well. Since however, it is still unclear if the pre-existing building was a temple, a royal dining hall, or perhaps an administrative building, it remains impossible to classify the building as either sacred or secular. Thus we cannot find real support for any specific function of the later theater by looking into the history of the structure.[85]

Architectonic parallels and idiosyncrasies

As mentioned earlier there were at least two other contemporary theaters at Petra. The large 1st c. A.D. Theater at the eastern entry to the city is Roman in form with a Greek style *cavea*. This theater does not exhibit any close architectonic similarities to our Theater-in-Temple.[86] The *proscaenium* wall is niched as in our theater, but this is common for Roman theaters at this time and cannot be regarded as a specific local parallel. About 450 m further west on the north bank of Wadi Musa, a smaller semicircular theater was still to be seen in the 20th century when Petra was

82 Segal 1995, 12-15, n.37.

83 Csapo and Slater 1994, 186-06.

84 For this type of pantomime see Jory (1996, 1-6). For a recent introduction to the genre in general, see Hall and Wyles, passim.

85 It is rightly observed that in antiquity sacred buildings would normally not be converted into secular buildings (McKenzie 2004, 565).

86 For this theater see Hammond 1965; Rosetto and Sartorio 1994 vol. 2, 86-89; McKenzie 2005, 35.

investigated by the Germans,[87] but this is no longer visible.[88] The German team estimated that it was older than the large theater, and because mortar was used in its construction it was dated to the Roman period. Additional theatrical structures existed at Petra associated with the Temple of the Winged Lions and the Qasr al-Bint seating in the Temenos. All these seem to have served local purposes in Nabataean Petra; they appear to be unrelated to each other and to the 'proper' theaters of Petra.

As mentioned above, our theater shows similarities in plan to the Roman theaters of the 'western type,' but it also has eastern elements like the orchestra podium, a feature more common to Roman theaters of the 'Levantine type.'[89] The use of a vaulted substructure for the theater is a general characteristic of Roman freestanding theaters;[90] whereas the paving of the orchestra with stone slabs is common for theaters of Roman Palestine and *Provincia Arabia*. The same seems to be the case for *proscaenia* with semicircular and rectangular niches without reliefs.[91] Unique elements are the *aditus maximus* benches which lack parallels in any theaters of the Roman world.

Close parallels, in terms of architectural dimensions and similarities in some elements, are to be found in the theater at the sanctuary at Berketin, just north of Gerasa, which unfortunately received only partial excavation in the 1930s.[92] This theater (fig. 8.28) is similar in size and in the layout of the orchestra and lower *cavea*. Its orchestra podium is of comparable height, the orchestra is closed off with orchestra gates which in a sense continue the podium,[93] and the podium in this way terminates at the *proscaenium*. The similar *pulpitum* is 1.6 m high, compared to 1.25 m of the Great Temple Theater, and the Berketin *proscaenium* also has three niches facing the orchestra, and stairways in the *aditus maximi* areas outside the orchestra gates. One set of stairs leads up to the *cavea* and the other to the *pulpitum*. Whereas all these features are differently executed, their basic dimensions and arrangement are similar to those of our theater. Also is found at Berketin is an almost perfect parallel to the *proscaenium* in the phase before the installation of the permanent *pulpitum* floor, where a permanent solid *pulpitum* was never installed. Inscriptions date the theater at Berketin to the late 2nd-early 3rd c. A.D., and this may be a hint to date the *proscaenium* phase of the Petra Theater to the later 2nd c. A.D.

Another theater offering some correspondences is the temple at Sahr in north Nabataea.[94] This theater faces north as well but has a high orchestra podium—2 m in height compared to 1.25 m of the Great Temple theater.[95] This is a considerable difference, but still allows us to establish that the function of both theaters demanded a considerable difference in height between the orchestra and the lowest seats.[96] Some minor details compare as well—the height of the seat-rows of the *caveas* in both are approximately 38 cm. The depth of the seats in our theater, however, is around 59 cm, almost 10 cm greater than the seats at Sahr. The *diazoma* above the orchestra podium is 84 cm in width as compared to 82 cm at Sahr.

---

87 Segal 1995, 93; von Bachmann *et al.* 1921, 32-33, figs. 1, 25.

88 Rossetto and Sartorio 1994, vol. 2, 90.

89 Sear 2006, 80.

90 Ibid. 77-80.

91 Segal 1995, 22. Strictly speaking we do not know if these niches held reliefs, but no traces of installed art works in the proper dimensions have been identified.

92 Rossetto and Sartorio 1994, vol. 2, 85 (H. P. Isler); Segal 1995, 71; Sear 2006, 312-13.

93 Thresholds like those at the Great Temple have been drawn on the old excavation plan (reproduced in Segal 1995, fig. 81), but were not obvious to me when I examined the site in July 2008.

94 Segal 1995, 38-9, fig. 2.

95 An orchestra podium of this high type is also to be observed in the theater at Wadi Sabra, 8 km south of Petra, but here as high as 2.5 m (Segal 1995, 94).

96 At Sahr the height of 2 m may have been governed solely by the fact that the entrance to the orchestra was via three vaulted passageways. They had to be high enough to allow a person to pass (Segal 1995, fig. 2).

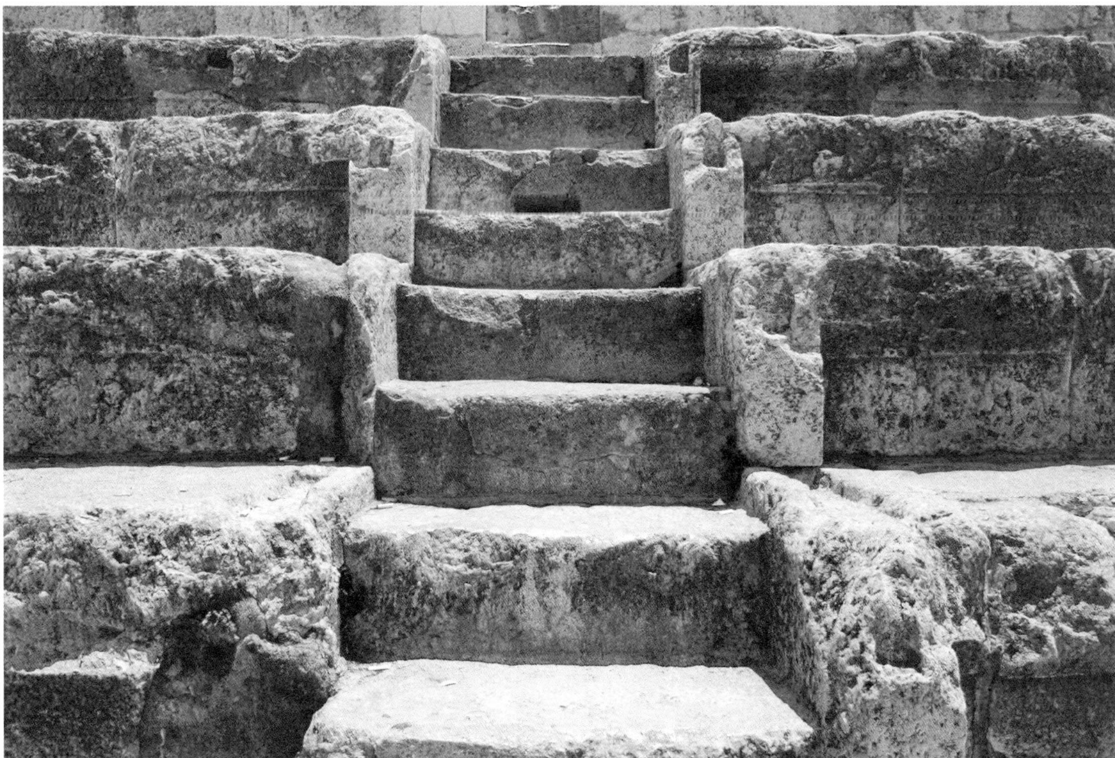

Fig. 8.29. Large theater in Amman (Philadelphia), with deep grooves in the seat blocks.

An interesting parallel to the deep grooves in the seat rows is found in the large theater in Amman (Philadelphia). Here (fig. 8.29) they are slightly narrower and less deep as the ones in Petra. If they are present then they rarely cut through the front of the seats; and if they are then only about 5 cm. At Amman they are interpreted as slots for wooden armrests,[97] which is their preferred interpretation for our theater as well.

The basic architectonic elements of our building identify it as theater, but since it is difficult to separate theaters from odea, from a strictly architectural point of view, the building may in fact have been an odeum. At least it compares well with some structures identified by scholars as odea. One example is the 2nd c. A.D. Odeum in Kanatha, Syria, which has fairly similar dimensions of the (*ima*) *cavea*, orchestra and scene building area, and has an orchestra podium. This type of odeum is called the "mixed type," by Meinel, referring to its similarity to theaters.[98] The crucial proof for identifying our theater as an odeum would be a roof spanning the whole interior of the *pteron* (figs. 8.1 and 8.26). There are indications that the building was roofed: remains of wood, huge nails, and tiles that may stem from such a roof. A complete tile-roof, however, would have constituted a very heavy load and the 6-part capitals would have served a crucial role as carrying elements, making this hypothesis seem unlikely.

In conclusion, the Theater In-Temple is not only a unique building to Petra; it is unique in Roman architecture. The installation of a theater into a pre-existing colonnade is a rare phenomenon, and no close parallels for the construction and plan of the Great Temple Theater exist. The existence of a proper theater elsewhere in Roman Petra could point in the direction of an identification of the theater as an odeum.

---

97 Sear 2006, 314.

98 For Kanatha, see Meinel 1980, 294-96, figs. 113-14.

9

The Roman-Byzantine Baths adjacent to the Great Temple

Eleanor A. Power

Introduction

The Roman-Byzantine bath complex was constructed around the time of the annexation of Petra by the Romans in A.D. 106. While many of the surrounding buildings drew upon models from the Roman architectural corpus, the bath complex is evidence of the adoption not only of a Roman form but also of a decidedly Roman social practice. Constructed at a time when Roman influence was waxing, these small baths provide evidence of the process of cultural and social fusion in the cosmopolitan city.

The bath complex was constructed against the W side of the Great Temple, alongside the West Exedra and above the West Entry Stairs (fig. 9.2). This modest yet elegant structure, measuring as exposed 47.91 m N–S by 30.84 m E–W and occupying 1477.5 m^2, took the form of a row of rooms next to a palaestra, a design often referred to as the row type or Pompeian type. Although the entirety of the complex has not been excavated (fig. 9.1), it is clear that the main entrance to the bathing suite was at the south, where there was a latrine and 'well room' for washing. From there the visitor moved north through the cold, warm and hot rooms. The furnace and associated service access were on the E side of the complex. The present chapter focuses on the architecture and phasing of the complex.

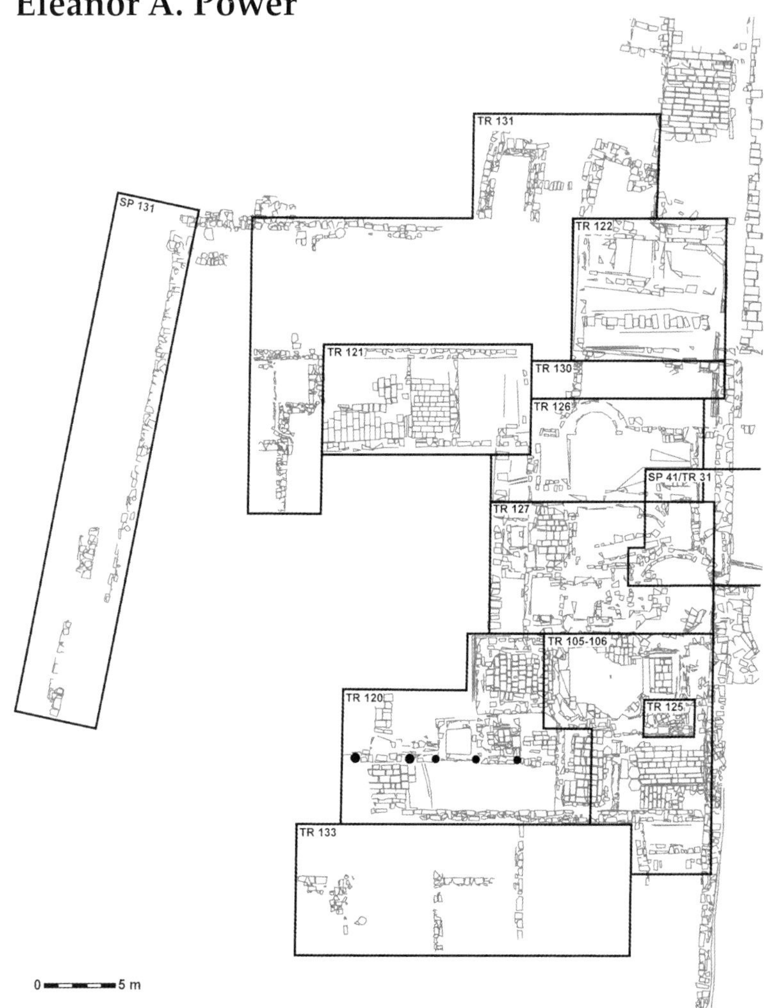

Fig. 9.1. Identification of trenches excavated in the bath complex.

Description of the main spaces

The palaestra A (fig. 9.3) is rather poorly preserved and has not been fully excavated (as exposed, it measures 20.46 m N–S x 14.30 m E–W). It seems to have been an open court enclosed by rooms on each side. Only a small part of the original floor survives towards the S side, where it consists of tight-fitting sandstone pavers. Clientele probably passed along the colonnade (B) at the south end of the palaestra, which was 3.11 m wide (it is exposed for a length of 15 m), to gain entrance to the bath complex. The S wall of the colonnade is a fine Nabataean exterior wall, pierced by a major doorway at its exposed W end and approached by a few steps leading up from the north. To the south of this wall are visible the tops of additional walls, perhaps other rooms of the baths or

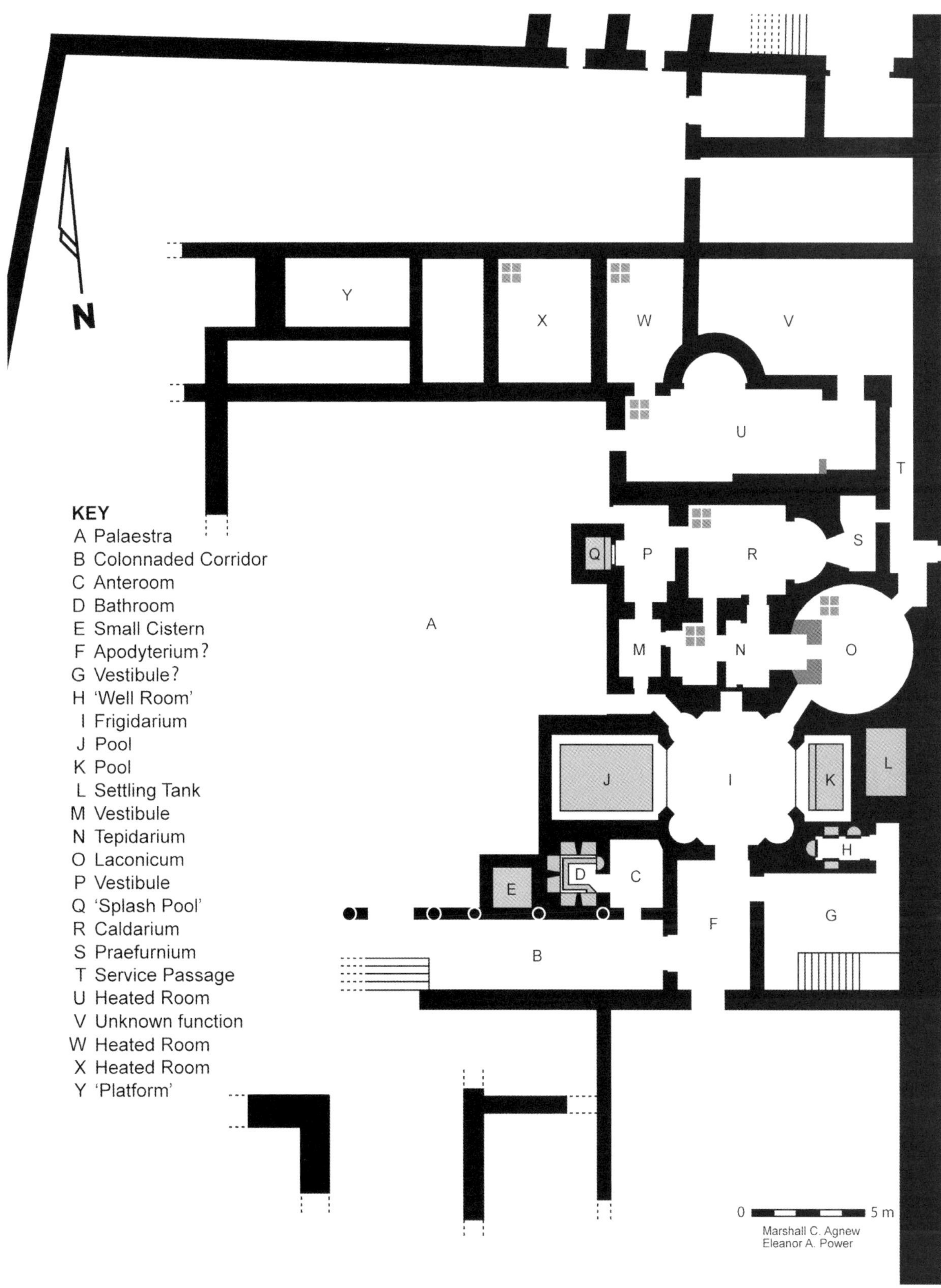
N
KEY
A Palaestra
B Colonnaded Corridor
C Anteroom
D Bathroom
E Small Cistern
F Apodyterium?
G Vestibule?
H 'Well Room'
I Frigidarium
J Pool
K Pool
L Settling Tank
M Vestibule
N Tepidarium
O Laconicum
P Vestibule
Q 'Splash Pool'
R Caldarium
S Praefurnium
T Service Passage
U Heated Room
V Unknown function
W Heated Room
X Heated Room
Y 'Platform'
0 5 m
Marshall C. Agnew
Eleanor A. Power

Fig. 9.2. Plan of the Roman-Byzantine baths.

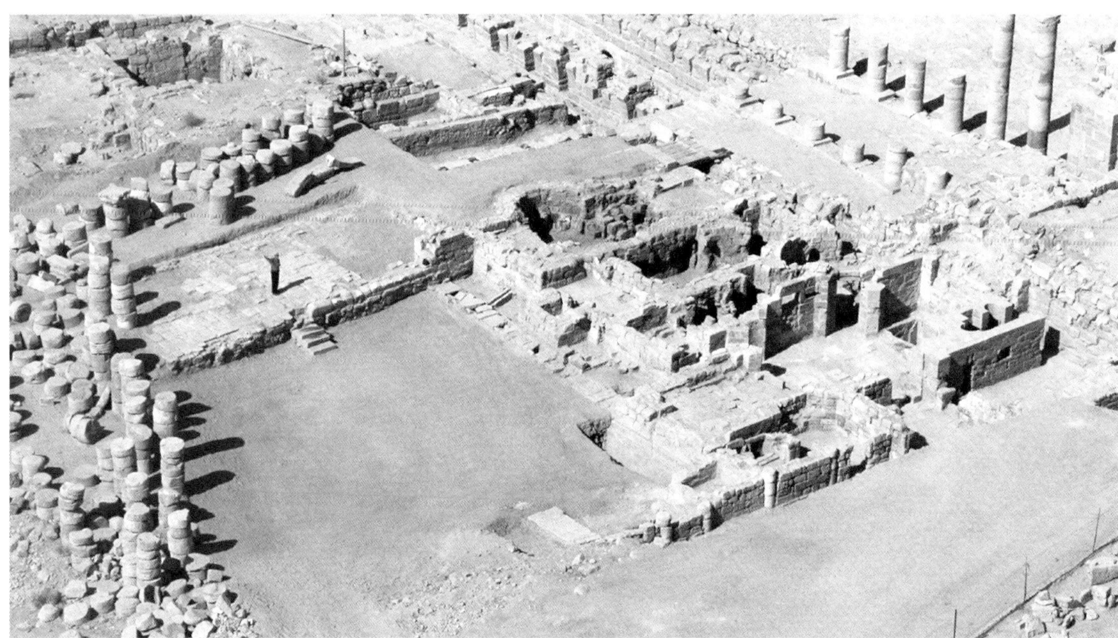

Fig. 9.3. Aerial view of the palaestra and the surrounding rooms to its east, view to the northeast (2006).

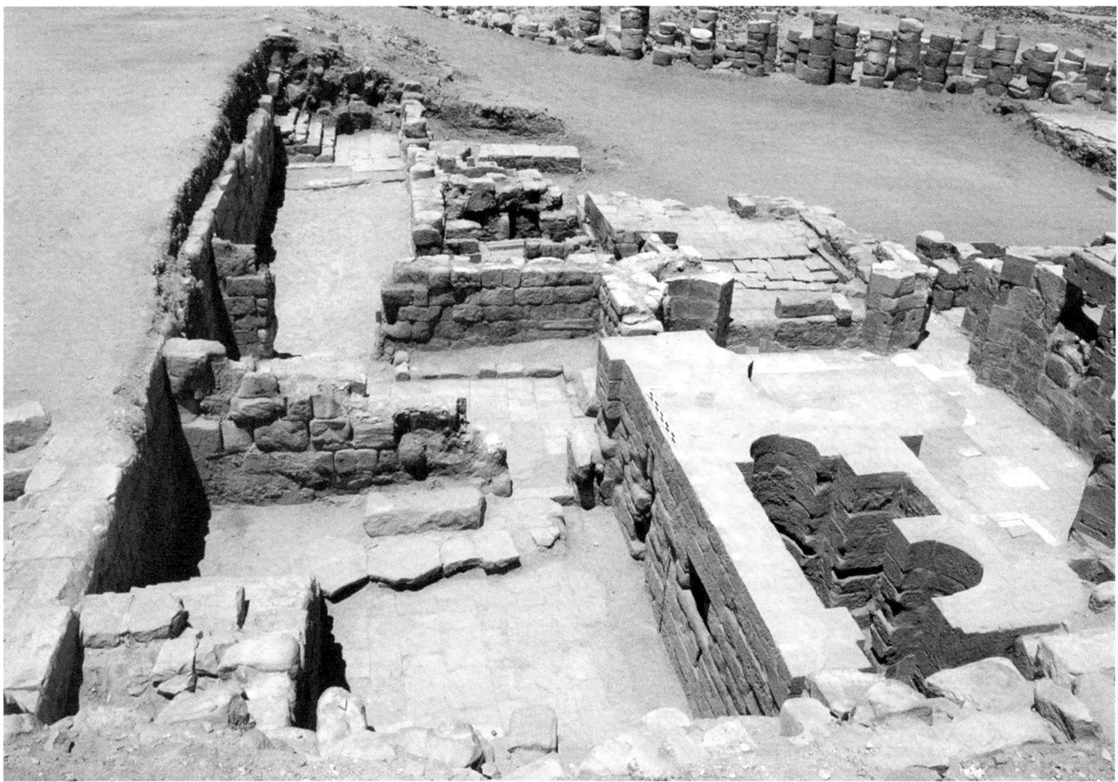

Fig. 9.4. View of the entry rooms with the Colonnaded Corridor and the apsed 'Well Room' to the right.

transitional spaces leading to the Residential Quarter. The E end of the colonnade gives access to the entry rooms of the complex (fig. 9.4); one door leads into room F, while another leads into the small room C on the left.

Room C (2.98 x 2.36 m) may be an anteroom to the latrine (D), intended to provide it with some privacy from the corridor. The latrine (2.76 x 2.78 m) is lined on three sides with niches serving as stalls; the niches are divided by low walls to support a seat and backed with fine curved plaster.

The floor (0.9 x 1.26 m), of finely laid pavers, is bordered by a raised channel on three sides. The channel starts at the NE corner of the room where there is a small semicircular limestone basin[1] at the base of a niche. Water would have flowed into the basin from a small pipe on the other side of the niche within the anteroom; from there it fell into a circular depression at the start of the channel, made the circuit of the latrine, and emptied into the SE stall. A major channel runs beneath latrine D and the small (1.75 m square internally) cistern (E) to the west.

Directly at the end of colonnade B the visitor stepped up into a rectangular room F (5.54 x 3.25 m), which was possibly an *apodyterium*, to judge by what may have been low benches made of wadi stones and rough ashlars which extend out *c.*30 cm from the walls. The room has three other doors: that in the S wall (which was later blocked) led through the Nabataean wall; that in the W wall led to room G; and that in the N wall led directly into the room I, the main hall of the *frigidarium*.

Room G to the east of room F may be another vestibule (7.15 x 6.01 m), in this case for the 'well room' (H), which is reached from its NE corner. The floor is made up of tightly-fitting flagstones laid in rows. On the S wall of this room, a stairway inserted after the original construction of the baths leads up to the West Precinct Wall and the Upper Temenos of the Great Temple. The secluded 'well room' H (1.84 x 3.12 m; its floor measures 1.06 x 2.68 m) is defined by four well-built niches still partly covered with hydraulic plaster (fig. 9.5). On the N wall are two niches, the E one semicircular with a vertical channel running down it, the W one rectangular. The W wall holds a semicircular niche; the S wall has a rectangular niche opposite that on the N wall. The collapse within the room included numerous curving limestone ashlars which probably formed half-domes over the semicircular niches. The floor of the room is suspended above a cavity that would have drawn water from all the niches into a large channel heading west. Many jugs, juglets and cups found in the sediment below the suspended floor suggest that the room was used for drawing water, whether for ablution or to quench thirst.

Fig. 9.5. Room H, "Well room" with 4 niches.

Proceeding to the north, the visitor entered the cold section of the baths. Its main hall I (fig. 9.6) is a dramatic octagon (*c.*5.7 x 5.8 m) which was probably topped by a segmented dome. At each of the four corners is an apse, the two southern ones being niches, the two northern ones being pierced by doorways. The *frigidarium* was sumptuously decorated with marble on both floor and walls. Much of the floor, made of irregular pieces of stone and marble *opus sectile* (some of them re-used), survives. A simple sandstone drain found loose above the floor of room F may have derived from here. Opening off its E and W sides are pools J (3.1 m long, 4.1 m wide, 1.45 m deep) and K (2.2.5 m long, 1.47 m wide, 1.15 m deep) marked off by low ledges. Their sides are covered by large stone slabs affixed with mortar and clamped with bronze rivets, while their floors are formed of tightly-laid pavers.

1 The basin is similar to one found in the Garden and Pool complex, next to the central platform: Bedal 2002, 229.

Fig. 9.6. *Frigidarium* to the west.

A raised platform just above and beyond the E pool contains remnants of a small tank or *castellum* (L). Both pools probably served as cold plunge baths.

All three doorways on the N side of the *frigidarium* lead into the heated section of the baths (fig. 9.7). The NW door leads into a passage that goes into the palaestra as well as to a door leading into room M (2.55 x 2.01 m), evidently a vestibule for the heated section. The central N door (blocked at a later date) leads into *tepidarium* N, while the NE door leads into the circular *laconicum* O. The *tepidarium,* a long rectangular space divided into three chambers by piers that jut into the room (1.55-3.55 m x 2.01 m), would have had a suspended floor (not extant) supported by hypocaust pillars or piers *c.*1 m above the subfloor.

The circular room (O) to the east, probably the *laconicum* or *sudatorium*, would have been domed with an oculus. It has a diameter of 5.17 m. A small arched alcove made of thin, stacked bricks between rooms N and O could have served as a potential source of embers in the room, generating dry steam. Again there was a suspended floor (some of which survives) with a hypocaust system below it, though of a different type (with stone blocks, not *pilae*) than room N and at a slightly lower elevation. On the N side of the room a low arch links it with the *praefurnium* (S) to the north, perhaps an outlet for fumes or smoke. A doorway (later blocked) in the curving NE wall leads into a narrow service corridor (T).

If we now return to the W side, room M leads to the north into a second vestibule or anteroom (P) (4.06 x 2.15 m) serving the hot rooms. On the W side of this room and separated from it by a low

Fig. 9.7. Heated rooms of the Roman-Byzantine Baths.

threshold is a small pool (Q), jutting into the area of the palaestra. It may have served as a small plunge bath for individual submersion for those coming straight from the palaestra. It is finely decorated with marble facing. Room P leads into the *caldarium* R, composed of a rectangular section (3.98 x 4.35) with an apse (N-S diameter 2.82 m, E-W radius 1.51 m) opening to the east. It could also be reached through a door (later blocked) from *tepidarium* N. The suspended floor (not extant) and walls would have been covered in marble, as large quantities of *opus sectile* fragments were found during excavation. Beneath the raised floor, passages connected to the heated room on the N and S sides, facilitating the circulation of hot air. A roughly-built channel, perhaps originating in the furnace, runs E–W across the subfloor; it may have increased the draft by directing hot air into the rooms, or it may belong to a later phase when the baths were re-used for industrial purposes. Heat also flowed into this room by way of *tubuli*, ceramic pipes built into the walls to carry the hot gases upwards. The flue tiles were of two types, tubular and squared, and both had pierced holes to allow for the flow of air.

Opening off the back of the apse is the rectangular (3.26 x 1.60 m) room S, probably the furnace (*praefurnium*). A doorway in its E wall (later blocked) would have given access to it from the service corridor (T) beyond, allowing those operating the heating system to avoid contact with the baths clientele.

A second apsed hot room (U) lies directly north of room R and the *praefurnium* (fig. 9.8). This large room (11.05 x 3.64 m) features an apse (N-S 1.34 m, E-W diameter 2.95 m) in its N face. A door in the W wall would have provided access to the palaestra. The two doors in the N wall, one in the east and one in the west, lead into the final row of rooms of the bath complex. Noticeably absent from the heated rooms are water features, apart from the small 'splash pool'. The water features may have taken the form of basins or tubs instead of permanent installations built into the architecture of the complex. The larger apse in the northern heated room possibly held a *labrum*, a

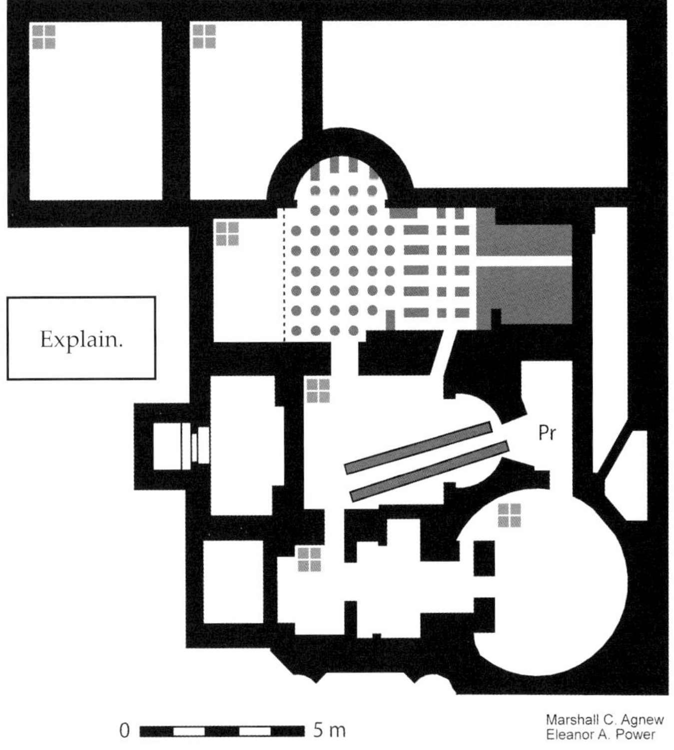

Fig. 9.8. Heating arrangements of the Roman-Byzantine Baths. Walls show subfloor connections and blockages. Rooms with hypocaust system are marked with square in top left corner. The extant hypocaust system is represented in Room U. The *praefurnium* is marked in Room S, as is the possible exhaust channel in Room R.

large basin on a stand. A water channel which emerges form the W wall of this room to carry water to the canalization system in the palaestra implies that water was present here.

Farther north are two rooms that have not been fully excavated. Room V (5.6 x 4 m), which is bounded by the West Triple Colonnade of the Lower Temenos, seems to have had direct access to the service corridor T and may have served a more utilitarian purpose. To the west of this room is what appears to be a small heated room, accessible from the N *caldaria* (Room W, 5.25 x 3.27 m). That this room is heated is deduced from its relationship to the N *caldarium* and the room to its west, which has a hypocaust system and extant dense limestone pavers (Room X, 5.30 x 4.09 m). These are the two final rooms that would have been heated; given their distance from the *praefurnium*, they may have been additional *tepidaria*. This second heated room is the first in a series of rooms (Y; 6.51 x 13.63 m as exposed) lining the N side of the palaestra. The walls enclosing these rooms were leveled off at one point, so that their lower courses are now continuous with the floors' pavers. These rooms could have marked the transition out of the formal heated rooms, perhaps providing an alternative entrance or exit from the baths onto the palaestra. Alternatively, these rooms north of the palaestra and the N *caldarium* (U) may have formed a distinct baths for one of the sexes, with the rooms to the south forming another.

The heating and water supply systems

The *praefurnium* has been identified with the deep room (S) in the east of the complex, where it could have been easily reached by the service corridor T. The *praefurnium* directed hot air into the southern *caldarium* R, in which a 'firing chamber' possibly helped funnel the air out of the furnace and into the heated rooms. Subfloor passages in the N and S walls of this *caldarium* facilitated the circulation of hot air out into the other heated rooms (fig. 9.7). The *laconicum* seems to have had a direct connection to the *praefurnium* through a low arch in their shared wall. A boiler would presumably have been located next to the *praefurnium* to keep the water for the heated pools warm, though no direct evidence was found. Substantial deposits of a very ashy, greasy black soil, indicating sustained burning, were excavated here. The fuel that created the ash would primarily have been wood, but mixed in the ash were carbonized olive pits. As the detritus from olive-oil production, the pits would have been a cheap and convenient source of fuel in a region with a limited supply or wood.[2]

The hypocaust system differed from room to room. The *laconicum* (O), for example, used stone blocks to support the suspended floor, rather than the *pilae* present in the *tepidarium* and *caldaria*.

2 Shaw 2001, 24.

Fig. 9.9. *Caldarium* (Room U), view to west showing hypocaust *in situ*.

Tubuli embedded in the walls to carry hot gases upwards are present only in the *caldaria*. The hypocaust system of the heated rooms is best preserved in *caldarium* U (fig. 9.9), where the channeled, arched and pillared hypocaust tiles are largely intact. In the E section of the room, walls built of hypocaust tiles created channels for the heated gases to circulate through, before transitioning to narrower piers of tiles and finally the more typical pillars made of thicker hypocaust tiles in the center of the room. These *pilae* are mostly composed of circular (average diameter 22 cm) tiles resting on two or three square tiles. The subfloor below this is made of the *sesquipedales*, larger terracotta tiles; the suspended floor, intact in the W part of the room and resting on brick vaults *c.*1.21 m above the subfloor, is composed of two layers of large terracotta tiles, the *bipedales*, held together with thick mortar and topped with dense limestone pavers. Notably, the bath complex takes advantage of the bedrock sloping away to the north by placing the heated rooms with their *suspensurae* on that side.

Water was brought to the bathing areas from several directions (fig. 9.10). Some water was probably brought to the settling tank (L) from the Cistern-Reservoir in the Great Temple complex by way of a ceramic channel that extends along the top of the West Precinct Wall. A lead pipe in a

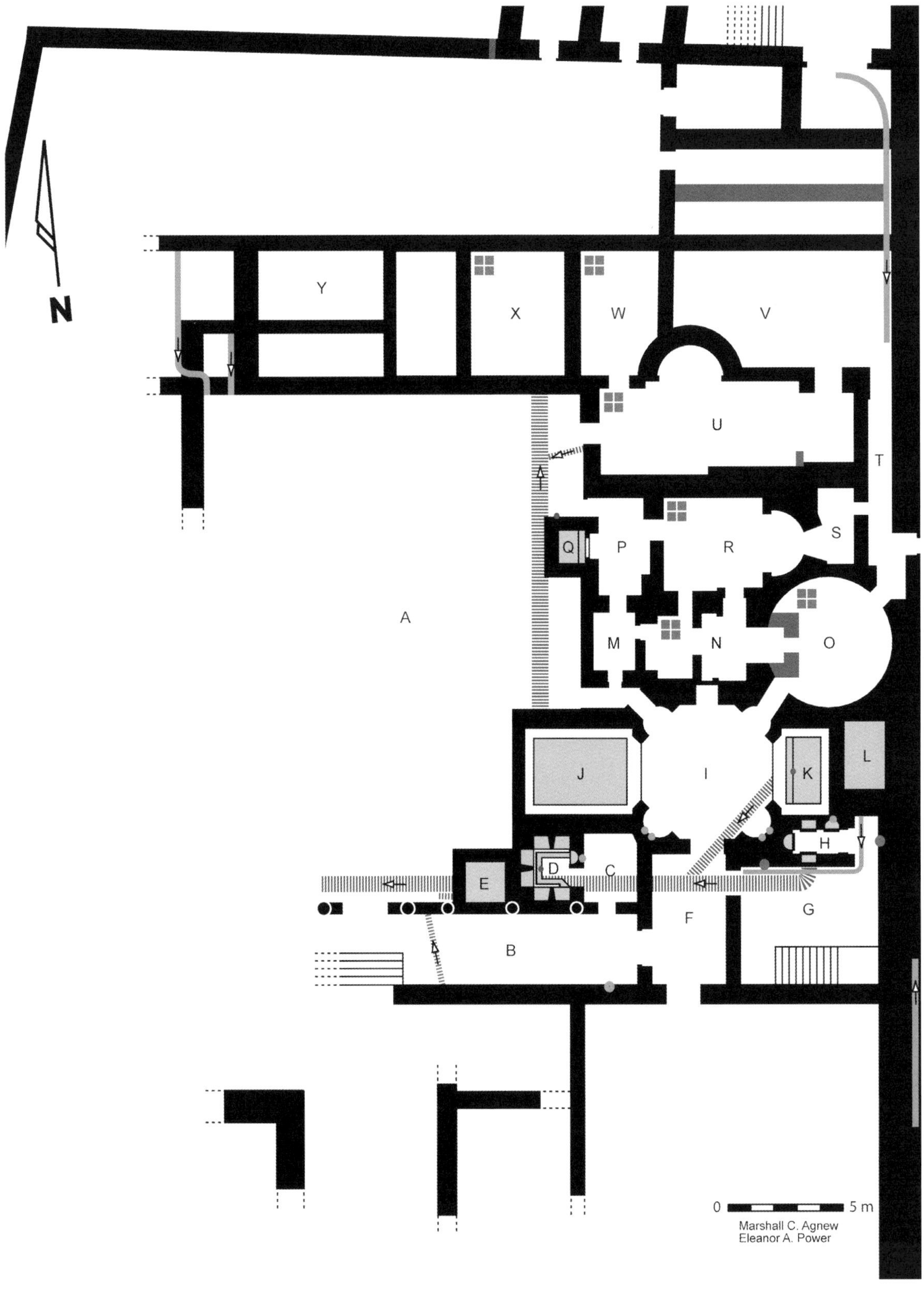

Fig. 9.10. Water systems of the Roman-Byzantine Baths. Solid gray lines denote pipes and channels bringing water into the baths, while dashed gray lines denote pipes and channels directing water out of the baths. Vertical pipes and channels are marked with circles. Arrows denote the direction of flow.

stone channel, extending across the S edge of the Lower Temenos, probably brought water from east of the Garden and Pool Complex to the hypothesized boiler next to the *praefurnium*. A third source of water was to the north: a stone channel at the upper edge of the West Entry Stairs and two channels to the northwest of the palaestra (a curving channel and a clay pipe) could also have supplied water.

The settling tank L probably provided water for the water features in the S sector of the bath complex. A short channel probably led directly west to the small pool K, while another hole and vertical channel brought water to the E semicircular niche of the 'well room' H. A lead pipe emerging from the wall just below the settling tank curves around the exterior of the 'well room' and continues to the west to emerge in the anteroom of the latrine. There, a channel is clearly carved into the back of the sink, letting water flow out into the basin and through the room. Other features in the southern rooms clearly required water, such as the ornamental pool J and the water features located in the two apses in the S part of the main hall I (indicated by carved vertical channels), but poor preservation makes it unclear which source supplied them. The small pool Q and the hypothesized basins of the heated rooms were probably served by the channels coming into the bath complex from the north.

Wastewater exited the bath complex through a second set of channels. The large E–W channel first seen in 'well room' H carried water away from most of the rooms in the S sector, including the small pool K, the latrine and cistern E, as well as water coming from further to the south across the colonnaded corridor B. The earlier, Nabataean channel in the palaestra also carried water away, in this case to the north. Water entered this channel from the N *caldarium* (U) through a small pipe in its W wall and from the small pool Q through a small plug in its N face.

Building phases

Clearly conceived of as a singular entity, almost all of the rooms of the baths were constructed contemporaneously with the full repertoire of rooms necessary for a bath complex. The architect took advantage of pre-existing features, chiefly the West Precinct Wall, which marked its E limit, and the E-W Nabataean wall at the south. Almost all of the rooms were built in Site Phase VI around the time of the Roman annexation in A.D. 106. Dating evidence comes from two lamp fragments in closed but not fully sealed contexts beneath the foundation of pool J.[3] One (fig. 9.11) is a volute lamp (of type B) decorated with rosettes; it was in use from the early 1st c. B.C. to *c.*A.D. 70.[4] The other (fig 9.12) is a local variety of a lamp with ovolo, dated to the last third of the 1st c. A.D.[5] A date of *c.*A.D. 100 is supported by the facts that the spread of bath complexes throughout the empire occurred primarily in the 2nd c. and the octagonal form of the *frigidarium* is not widely used until the 2nd or 3rd c. Yet any attempt to pinpoint the construction of the complex as specifically pre- or post-annexation must be somewhat conjectural. Still, as

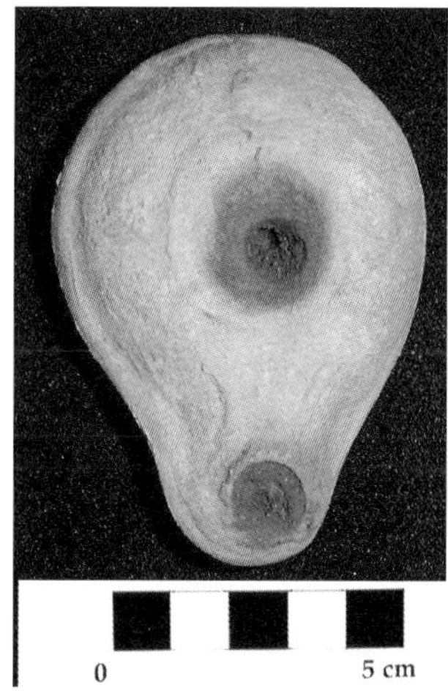

Fig. 9.11. Lamp, 06-L-4.

Fig. 9.12. Lamp, 06-L-5.

3 Vol. 2, 16.

4 Barrett 2004, 98. It is cat. no. 06-L-4 and seq. no. 127A028, from trench 127 locus 42. See further chapt. 12 below.

5 Barrett ibid. It is cat. no. 06-L-5 and seq. no. 127A036, from trench 127 locus 39. See further chapt. 12 below.

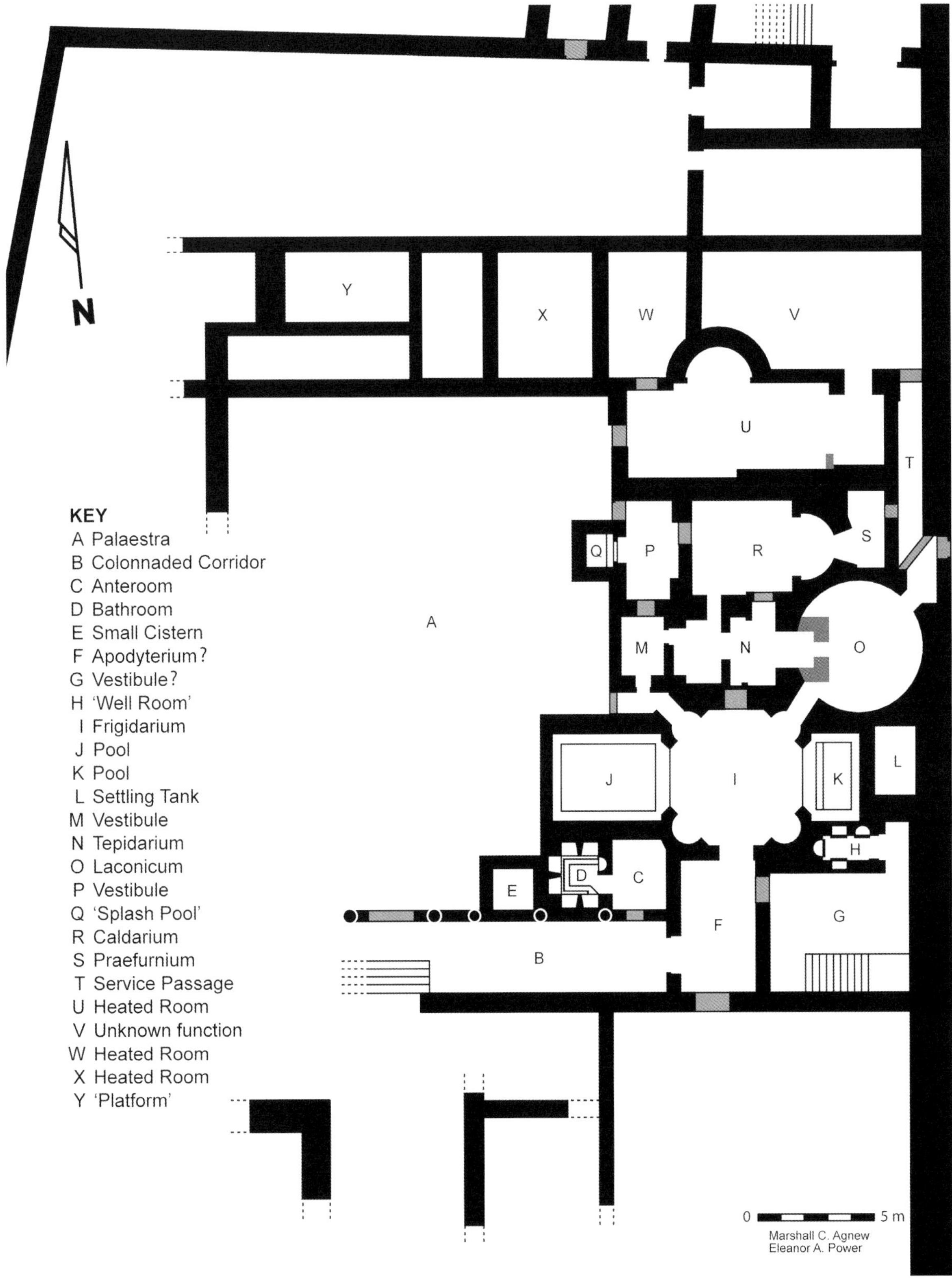

Fig. 9.13. Roman-Byzantine Baths, showing door and wall blockings. Roman-Byzantine Baths, showing door and wall blockings (marked in gray).

the rule of Rabbel II (A.D. 70-106) seems to have shown a revival of more traditionally Nabataean forms, and since a variety of other civic structures in Petra have been dated to the early 2nd c., the construction of the bath complex probably took place after the annexation, when such structures and activities would have been regularly promoted.[6]

A number of features were added to the baths at a later date, probably between the mid-2nd and mid-4th c. All are located in the S part of the complex and are associated not with its main suite of baths but with more secondary rooms. The *apodyterium* (F) was added with the construction of its W wall, the blocking of the doorway on its S wall, and the addition of a bench along its walls. To the west of this room, the latrine and its anteroom (D and C) were also constructed. To build them, walls were inserted between the columns of the corridor, and the window looking into pool J was blocked. The walls of the latrine and anteroom are of a poorer quality than those of the *apodyterium* and include some re-used ashlars, which suggests that they antedate it. Slightly later still, the small cistern E was built up against the latrine. Also at this time a stairway was added against the S wall of room G, giving an alternative point of access to the 'well room' and the bath complex. As with the walls of the latrine, the stairway was built chiefly of re-used ashlars, but it also included some column drums tipped on their sides, which could suggest that this addition was a slightly later one, perhaps after the earthquake of 363.

Also occurring during this long period of additions were modifications connected with the integrity of the heating and water systems. The central door leading out of the *frigidarium* to the heated rooms was blocked and a pier was added on the sides to provide support for the suspended floor, dividing the *tepidarium* into two sections. This may have been in response to a weakening of the floor that required repair, or to a realization that too much heat was being lost in the *tepidarium* through the direct connection to the *frigidarium*. Minor alterations can be seen in such work as the insertion of hypocaust *pilae* into the E subfloor vault connecting the two *caldaria*. Maintenance of some of the water features also appears to have been necessary. For example, 10 fragmentary marble inscriptions were re-used as revetment in the 'splash pool' Q. Two belong to a Greek inscription of the 2nd or 3rd c. in Homeric-style language; T. Gagos suggests that the first line reads: "and this building ... " and that the second contains the name of the deity Aiakos.[7]

A number of doors appear to have been blocked while rooms were still functioning as part of the baths (fig. 9.13). A fairly early blockage seems to have taken place in the service corridor T where a low wall, plastered on its S face, extends diagonally across the corridor's width. This would have isolated those working in the service passage form the clientele of the *laconicum*. Fairly early blockages of doorways are also found in rooms P, R and U. Some use rough-hewn, some use neat courses of ashlars and stones, and were carefully plastered over. It is difficult to understand the sequence of blockages; if all were in effect at the same time, they would have greatly restricted circulation through the baths.

A major destruction can be associated with the earthquake of May 19, 363, which damaged the baths to the point where it could no longer function in its original capacity. The water system that channeled water to the complex must have been compromised, as features such as the Cistern-Reservoir were destroyed and filled with sediment. As with much of Petra, the bath complex was re-used in whatever capacities it could be — both as a quarry for architectural stone and for housing continued occupation.[8]

Most of the rooms to the north of the palaestra were robbed out and leveled, while the partially destroyed N *caldarium* (U) filled up with débris and sediment. Sometime later, the apse was briefly re-used for cooking purposes: a defined and localized layer of burning, full of animal bones, was

6 Schmid 2001, 402; Fiema 2003, 49.
7 It comes from trench 127 locus 32, seq. no. 127951-52, cat. no. 06-S-13.
8 Watson 2001, 484.

found within the débris there. The S *caldarium* (R) was also partially destroyed, but it may have been at least partially cleared out. It is possible that the roughly-built channel extending across the floor of this room should best be dated to this period, perhaps serving as a furnace or kiln of sorts, in conjunction with what had been the *praefurnium* to the east. The *tepidarium* N and the *laconicum* O appear to have been cleared of collapse and re-used for some industrial purpose, perhaps associated with the proposed kiln to the north.[9] A column of re-used drums was built to support the weakened or partially collapsed dome of the *laconicum*, including a capital dated stylistically to the 4th or 5th c.[10]

The rooms further to the south generally sustained less damage than those at the north. Floors and walls are largely intact, and the rooms were all repaired and re-used in some capacity. The main hall of the *frigidarium* seems to have remained largely undamaged, though the hallway leading to it from the palaestra was probably blocked at this time. Pool J was filled in and covered with pavers, presumably after the water system that fed it had been crippled. The fill used to level the pool consisted of a number of layers of dumping, in which were found a number of Roman coins (including one thought to date to the reign of Julian)[11] and Byzantine lamps. Despite a partial collapse of the West Precinct Wall, room G was cleared out and the wall repaired. A new floor, resting on a few centimeters of sediment, was constructed in the room using hexagonal pavers taken from the Lower Temenos of the temple. At some later date, the room was filled with débris taken from the heated parts of the baths that included large quantities of ash, flue tiles, marble fragments and Byzantine pottery. The corridor B was not severely damaged, but the remaining intercolumnar spaces were filled in, other than the space between the two columns framing the stairway on the S side. Most of the pavers of the palaestra were removed. The newly exposed E–W water channel was blocked with a *stele*, dated to 253-259 by the name of the governor of Bostra, Aelius Aurelius Theon (fig. 9.14).[12] Lacking a functioning water system, the latrine and its anteroom were also blocked up and filled with dumps.

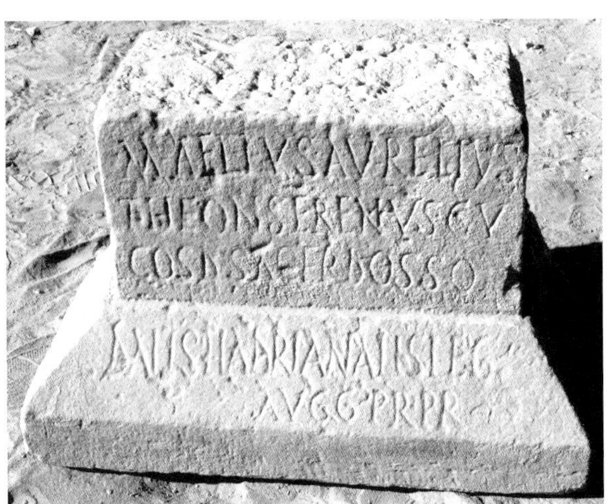

Fig. 9.14 Inscription, 06-S-18.

Overall, it appears that parts of the bath complex saw some re-use following the earthquake of the mid-4th c., after which it fell briefly into disuse before being taken over by industrial functions. The robbing of stone was probably a piecemeal affair, and the dumping of refuse may also have occurred at different times. Certainly the distinct layers of dumping suggest that the débris was brought from various locations around the Great Temple, including other parts of the bath complex itself. The pottery and glass found in the dumping layers were quite consistent, with clay and glass lamps pointing to a date after *c.*363.[13] A gradual process of abandonment ensued for some of the spaces, with wash accumulating in the main E–W channel and above the floors of some rooms (e.g., I and B).

9 Joukowsky 2006b, 35. Unfortunately the image of this inscription is not shown here, but see the discussion by T. Gagos in Ch. 16, 300-301.

10 Vol. 2, 48.

11 See chapts. 12 and 15 for more details. The coin of Julian is no. 77 from trench 120, locus 55, seq. no. 120863.

12 Trench 120, locus 46, seq. no. 120A050, cat. no. 06-S-18.

13 E.g., slipper lamps from trench 120, locus 16, date to the 4th-5th c.; a complete lamp (cat. no. 05-L-5, seq. no. 105269) from trench 105, locus 7, dates to the 3rd-4th c. Fragments of glass lamps and bowls also suggest a Byzantine date (see chapt. 14).

The final blow probably came from the earthquake of July 9, 551. Artifacts (mostly lamps) found in the final collapse layer are preliminarily dated to this general era, but it cannot be ruled out that the earthquake of 491 was responsible, not least since that earthquake was responsible for the collapse of some residences on Ez Zantur.[14] The event brought walls crashing down and dislodged marble tiles on floors and walls. A section of the ceiling of room I was found fallen on the floor, and the column erected in room O following the earlier earthquake collapsed. Other walls and ceilings collapsed on top of layers of dumping and sediment. Wash and overburden eventually covered the collapse. Long after, Bedouin would use the area for farming, clearing the surface of the last remnants of the building and constructing low walls to mark their field boundaries.

The baths in their wider context

The overall plan of the baths conforms to the single-axis row-type, also referred to as the row or Pompeian type, common in the Roman East as in the rest of the empire. Like the Stabian and Forum Baths at Pompeii and the Forum Baths at Herculaneum, it is organized into parallel, barrel-vaulted rectangular rooms with their short sides fronting the palaestra. This offered the bathing clientele an ordered progression from cool to hot rooms. Like those baths, it may have contained two separate bathing areas for the sexes, with one series of rooms (I-R) to the south and another (U-Y) to the north.

While the layout of the bath complex is typical of the row type, the many doorways giving direct access to the palaestra is not in keeping with the Campanian baths or with others in the East. This greater integration of the palaestra into the experience of the baths, however, was short-lived, as many of those doorways were blocked by the mid-2nd c. In the East, the baths that show the closest resemblance to ours are the Herodian bath buildings, also of the row type and on a comparable scale.[15] The use of locally quarried ashlars, as opposed to brick and concrete, aligns our baths more closely with others found in the East.[16] At Petra itself, the building directly to the north (termed the Baths–Palatial Complex) has been tentatively identified as a baths complex dating to the early 1st c. A.D.,[17] and would thus have been the closest reference for our baths at the time of their construction. That complex consists of two rooms and a staircase, perhaps associated with three or more additional rooms to the north, next to the Temenos Gate.[18] One of the rooms, domed with four apses at its corners and smaller apses in between, and elegantly decorated with painted plaster and marble revetment, may have been an inspiration for *frigidarium* I of our complex.[19] The other baths so far known at Petra are in the residence Ez Zantur IV, dated to the 2nd c.,[20] and on Umm al-Biyara, which, though unexcavated, shows traces of a hypocaust system and two tubs of similar construction to our pools J and K.[21]

---

14 Fiema 2002, 67.

15 Nielsen 1999, 41-41; Lee 2003, 42.

16 Dodge 1990, 114.

17 McKenzie 1990, 41. Since the structure has not been fully excavated, its function is not certain, but it is generally thought that at least the two domed rooms belong to a bath complex. The northern rooms have been variously suggested to have been a guardhouse for the Temenos Gate, a palace for the Nabataean rulers or the continuation of the baths: von Bachmann *et al.* 1921, 46-47; McKenzie 1990, 51 and 138; Schmid 2002, 49; Joukowsky 2006a, 8. If Joukowsky is right to see it as a palatial structure incorporating a small bath for the private use of the royal family and dating to the reign of Aretas IV, other than the Herodian examples it would be an unusually early adoption of this bath type in the Roman East.

18 von Bachmann *et al.* 1921.

19 McKenzie 1990, 138.

20 Kolb 2002, 261.

21 Schmid 2011. From the excavation reports of the Umm al-Biyara baths, it is posited that they were also constructed in the 1st c. The continuing excavations demonstrate that these baths have similar architectural features to the Great Temple baths. See http://www.auac.ch/iubp/season2010,iubp_2010text. And see subsequent excavation reports.

The bath complex was part of the central fabric of the city, embedded between sacred precincts, civic buildings and private residences. Pressed against the perimeter of the Great Temple complex, the decidedly indulgent social space of the baths would have contrasted markedly with the lofty purposes of the Great Temple. This bath complex shows the continued growth of Roman influence in Petra and the growing cultural presence of the empire in the new provincial capital. That this political shift was more than a bureaucratic reshuffling is demonstrated by structures such as this complex, which brought the local residents into the Roman world in a very physical, embodied way.[22] This complex, more modest than imperially commissioned baths, was one of many venues through which the multiform dialogues of Romanization were held. In an archaeological site dominated by the grand monuments of the Nabataean period, this small complex adds more detail and complexity to the later life of the city.

22 Nielsen 1990; Dodge 1990, 112; Revell 1999, 53.

10

An introduction to the catalogue of objects

Deirdre Grace Barrett

This chapter serves as a brief introduction to the organization of the catalogue of objects, which is available online at *Open Context*, <http://opencontext.org>.[1] The database provides detailed information about the special finds, along with illustrations. The entries include the following:

Cat. no. identification In addition to its sequence number and the details of its provenance, each special find is assigned a catalogue identification. The first two numbers refer to the year (99 = 1999, 02 = 2002, etc.), the letter refers to the material (most correspond to the code used in *Grosso Modo*, with the additions of L for lamp, CO or ST for stucco), and the last number is a serial number given to each special find in that material through the season.

Object A description of the type of artifact (e.g., bowl, bead, inscription, coin).

Material The material of which the piece is made.

Munsell A standardized color system to provide a description of the color of the artifact.

Condition The state of the artifact, such as complete, good, fair or poor.

Description A short description of the artifact.

Diagnostic A one- or two-word description of the most important characteristic of the piece.

Date & catalogued by The entering of the artifact into the database, normally done at the dig house shortly after it was excavated.

Comments A place for the excavator or cataloguer to give any other information that is particularly relevant.

Catalogued objects were grouped by material in 9 broad categories, plus coins. The totals (1993-2008) are as follows:

107 Bone (includes 14 ivory fragments) (86 are presented in *Open Context*, of which 9 are ivory and 32 are echinoderms);

33 Faïence (all presented in *Open Context*);

26 Glass (16 are presented in *Open Context*);

626 Lamps (includes 55 lamps from the 1994 catalogue originally classified with pottery) (280 are presented in *Open Context*);

242 Metal (bronze, copper alloy, silver, iron, etc.) (230 are presented in *Open Context*);

278 Pottery (after removing the 55 lamps classified with pottery in 1994);

6 Shell (5 are presented in *Open Context*);

451 Stone (416 are presented in *Open Context*) (stucco that was originally entered under stone is now in its own category, and that number has been deducted);

55 Stucco (44 of these are registered as stucco and 11 as plaster) (all are presented in *Open Context*)

(The Architectural Fragment database provides for objects of stone and stucco combined, which is how such pieces were originally recorded).

Coins were always classified in their own database, which can be accessed in *Open Context*:

759 Coins.

Open Context includes separate type series for coins, figurines, lamps, glass and bone.

The above totals are not the complete tally because only artifacts deemed 'museum quality'[2] were catalogued and transferred to the Department of Antiquities at the Petra Museum. The remainder were recorded and then re-buried on site for future re-examination as necessary. Material that would deteriorate if buried (e.g., bone, glass and metal) was placed in well-ventilated, dry storage in a cave above the site. Occasionally some objects were not assigned a catalogue number,

---

1 I previously presented a description of the catalogue in vol. 1, 287-315.

2 Although not of 'museum quality', initially all fragments of the elephant-head capitals and other objects the excavators thought of interest were catalogued; over time we became more selective about which objects should be catalogued. Also see Appendixes 3-5.

Fig. 10.1. Bone pin (cat. no. 95-B-7; length 10.2 cm, diam. 0.4 cm) from the Lower Temenos.

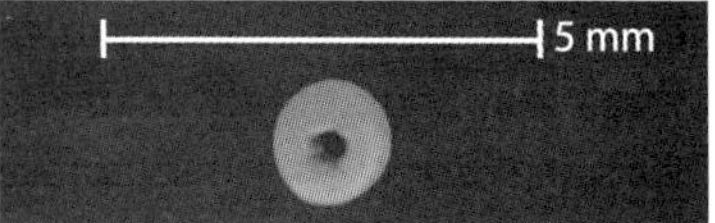

Fig. 10.2. Faïence bead (cat. no. 06-F-6; diam. 0.6 cm, ht. 0.46 cm) from the Upper Temenos.

Fig. 10.3. Glass head vase (cat. no. 06-GL-1; length 3.83 cm, w. 3.56 cm, th. 0.06 cm, wt. 7.6 gm), from the Upper Temenos.

Fig. 10.4. Indigenous Hellenistic-type/Nabataean volute lamp (cat. no. 08-L-1; length 8.7 cm, w. 5.2 cm, ht. 2.2 cm), from the Lower Temenos.

Fig.10.5a-b. Bronze handle finial, flower attachment in the form of a curved leaf, backed by a scroll; the flower with 12 petals provides the actual handle (cat. no. 97-M-3; length 6.7 cm, w. 1.64 cm, width of flower 3.81 cm), from the Lower Temenos (seq. no. 42198, trench 42, locus 24).

Fig. 10.6. Small piriform unguentarium (cat. no. 01-P-64; ht. 8 cm, th. 0.3 cm), from the Lower Temenos.

but were allocated a sequence number when they were turned over to the museum. At the culmination of each season the text of the catalogue and photographs of each object were also turned over.

In the following brief discussion of each category, objects are chosen which are of special interest. They also help to show the variety found. For greater detail on the finds in each category, see the following chapters.

1. *Bone* (fig. 10.1)

Bone, a most malleable material, was carved into various implements or decorative items. They include combs, counters, spindle whorls, needles, pins, hair ornaments, rings, beads, cosmetic palettes and spatulae, knife handles, spoons, ornamental trimmings, buckles, and small containers (see chapt. 18A-C). Animal sacrifice to the Roman and Nabataean gods and remains from meals must have provided a good supply of bones; indeed, the site has yielded an enormous number of unmodified bones (see chapt. 17A).

2. *Faïence* (fig. 10.2)

All the tiny faïence objects are pierced beads with the exception of one small decorative fragment. The manufacture of faïence is akin to glass-making in that quartz crystals are combined with other elements (e.g., sodium, calcium, magnesium, and copper oxide). After the beads were formed, they were heated and the combined elements produced a glaze reminiscent of turquoise.

3. *Glass* (fig. 10.3)

The glass is discussed in chapt. 14; M. O'Hea has also presented a type series in *Open Context*. One fragment from a head vase shown here illustrates the delicacy of the moulding practiced during the Roman period. The head appears to be that of a *putto*; it is green in color, whereas its curly hair is represented by clear glass 'bubbles'. Some Petra soil remains on the infant's right cheek.

4. *Lamps* (fig. 10.4)

Terracotta lamps were found in abundance. After the Roman annexation, the import of lamps became rare and locally-made copies of Roman lamps began to supersede earlier indigenous types. This may have been partly for economic reasons, given the presence of local clays and kilns, but it does not explain the disappearance of the indigenous Hellenistic type, which was a moulded lamp, original in design and well-made (see chapt. 12).

5. *Metal* (fig. 10.5a-b)

A large quantity of metal objects was retrieved (see chapt. 19), including fragments of military equipment (e.g., cheek pieces from helmets, arrowheads, spear points and bridle fittings); tools (e.g., axe and knife blades, nails, wire, and brackets); and miscellany (e.g., hooks, locks, handles, decorative elements of figurines, jewelry, plaques, spatulae, buttons, and spoons). Most were made from iron or bronze, like the bronze flower finial shown here.

6. *Pottery* (fig. 10.6)

This category includes the exquisitely-formed Nabataean plain and decorated (painted) pottery that defies replication even today. Many coarseware items (e.g., jugs, bowls, cups and jars) were also found. Other ceramic forms include figurines, plaques, and stamped amphorae handles. One item common to the site and to other sites within Petra is the small piriform unguentarium.[3] This small bottle would have contained fragrant oil or perfume essence, distilled from the incense and spices that were traded within the region. Its piriform-shaped base may have perched atop the central filling hole of the Nabataean lamp shown above.[4]

---

3 Few fusiform or spindle unguentaria were found; the vast majority are of a bulbous shape, dating to the second half of the 1st c. A.D. or later. See further Anderson-Stojanovic 1987, 105-22.

4 This idea was proposed by D. Johnson (1987, 70), one of the excavators at the Temple of the Winged Lions which lies directly across Wadi Musa from our site. He suggests that heat from the lit lamp would have warmed the fragrance in the unguentarium, scenting the space in which it reposed.

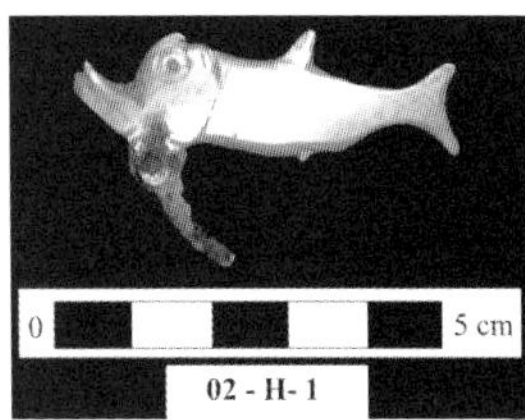

Fig. 10.7. Mother-of-pearl dolphin pendant (cat. no. 02-H-1; length 5.05 cm, w. 1.25 cm, th. 0.57 cm, wt. 6.5 gm) from the Upper Temenos.

7. Shell (fig. 10.7)

Although many shells were found on the site, most were not selected for the museum, but one exception is a shell pendant made from mother-of-pearl and carved in the shape of a dolphin (02-H-1).

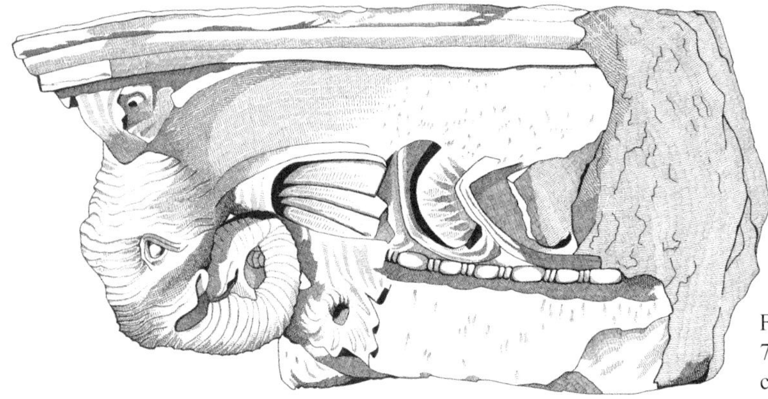

Fig. 10.8. Half of elephant capital 70101 (w. 82 cm, h. 41.2 cm, th. 37.2 cm) from the Propylaeum. Scale 1 : 3.

8. Stone (fig. 10.8)

Over 400 stone items were catalogued, many of them having been toppled by earthquakes. More than half of the stone artifacts relate to the elephant-head capitals; the remainder comprised other architectural elements, inscriptions, statuary, tools, pestles and mortars, gaming boards, loom weights and spindle whorls. Most of the head and ear fragments of the elephants were unearthed beneath the column drums. The ears and trunks were the most vulnerable features of the large heads and were the first to break, crushed beneath the larger stone elements. Their tusks have not been found: either they were of ivory or stucco and collected by scavengers, or they have not survived in a recognizable state. One small piece of ivory (95-S-5) may have served as one of the elephant's eyes.

Fig. 10.9. Decorative stucco column with stucco vine relief (length 12.8 cm, diam. 5.6 cm without cat. no.; recorded in architectural fragment database) from the Upper Temenos.

9. Stucco (fig. 10.9)

Many of the small stucco fragments were painted in vivid colors of blue, red, and yellow ochre. Some bear inscriptions, others have gold leaf. Others again derive from architectural mouldings (e.g., on friezes and column drums). One piece (cat. no. 96-S-24; see chapt. 22) found in a pile of stucco débris is identified as a nose. Coloured in a flesh tone and life-sized, perhaps it acted as a prosthesis for a statue that had lost this element. Other anatomical fragments moulded in stucco (e.g., an arm, an elbow and a torso) have also been found.

Overall, the finds reflect the diversity of Petra's industries and imports, some coming from as far away as Egypt and areas around the Red and Mediterranean Seas.

11
An overview of the ceramic assemblage from the Residential Quarter

Shari Lee Saunders

The Residential Quarter (fig. 11.1)[1] lies on an elevated bedrock platform, backed by an outcrop, just southwest of the Upper Temenos and the Temple proper. It includes caves and architectural units which incorporate columns and arched walls. A total of 32,349 pottery fragments were recovered, mostly from fills. During excavation, all fragments were collected, washed, sorted by types and counted in the field, and this information was recorded in the Grosso Modo database.[2] After counting, diagnostic sherds were bagged for future study, but at some point before they were drawn and analyzed the greater portion of the sherds were separated from the tags denoting their contexts. However, the information recorded in the database permits a general consideration of the forms and types present (a representative sample from Trench 94 Locus 75 is presented in figs. 11.2-11.3, a sample from mixed loci in the same trench in fig. 11.4), and this can add to our understanding of the Nabataean corpus. In the present chapter we discuss the range of material with reference to the *c*.350 pieces made available at *Open Context* (henceforth OC), which the reader of this chapter should consult simultaneously.

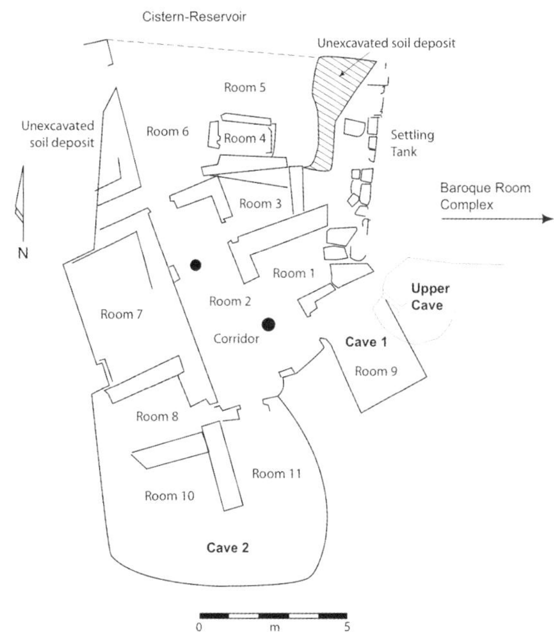

Fig. 11. 1. Plan of the Residential Quarter.

According to the database, the total assemblage from the Residential Quarter included bowls (36%), plates (26%), cooking pots (16%), jar/jugs (12%), large storage vessels (5%), jugs (3%), amphorae (0.8%), jars (0.4%), small forms (0.8%), lids (0.1%), and cups, strainers, stoppers, and a jar stand (all less than 0.1%); overall, the corpus is made up of 62% dining wares and 37% cooking wares. Particularly relevant for comparative purposes are the assemblages of painted and plain wares from Ez Zantur,[3] the Petra Church,[4] and the North Ridge Tombs 1-2.[5]

1 See the initial description in vol. 2, 197-99 and 210-11. It was excavated in 2002 by E. S. Libonati and J. I. Fusté, whose final reports can be found online in *Open Context* (*s.v.* 2002 Trench Reports).

2 See Appendix 4. This representative sample of the pottery from the whole excavation is presented online in *Open Context* takes the form of a descriptive catalogue, divided into 12 categories supported with pottery line-drawings. In the field the Residential Quarter pottery was analyzed primarily by the excavators, Libonati and Fusté, but members of the Brown team also helped in the processing and recording. Each team member's initials were entered on the Grosso Modo form.
During the 2004 and 2005 field seasons, S. L. Saunders drew, described and found comparanda for each ceramic represented. Saunders ordered the Open Context presentation, creating the classes and selecting the vessels to represent. M. S. Joukowsky and E. C. Egan drafted and inked the drawings and typed the descriptions.

3 Schmid 1996; Gerber 1997.

4 Gerber 2001a.

5 Bikai 2001.

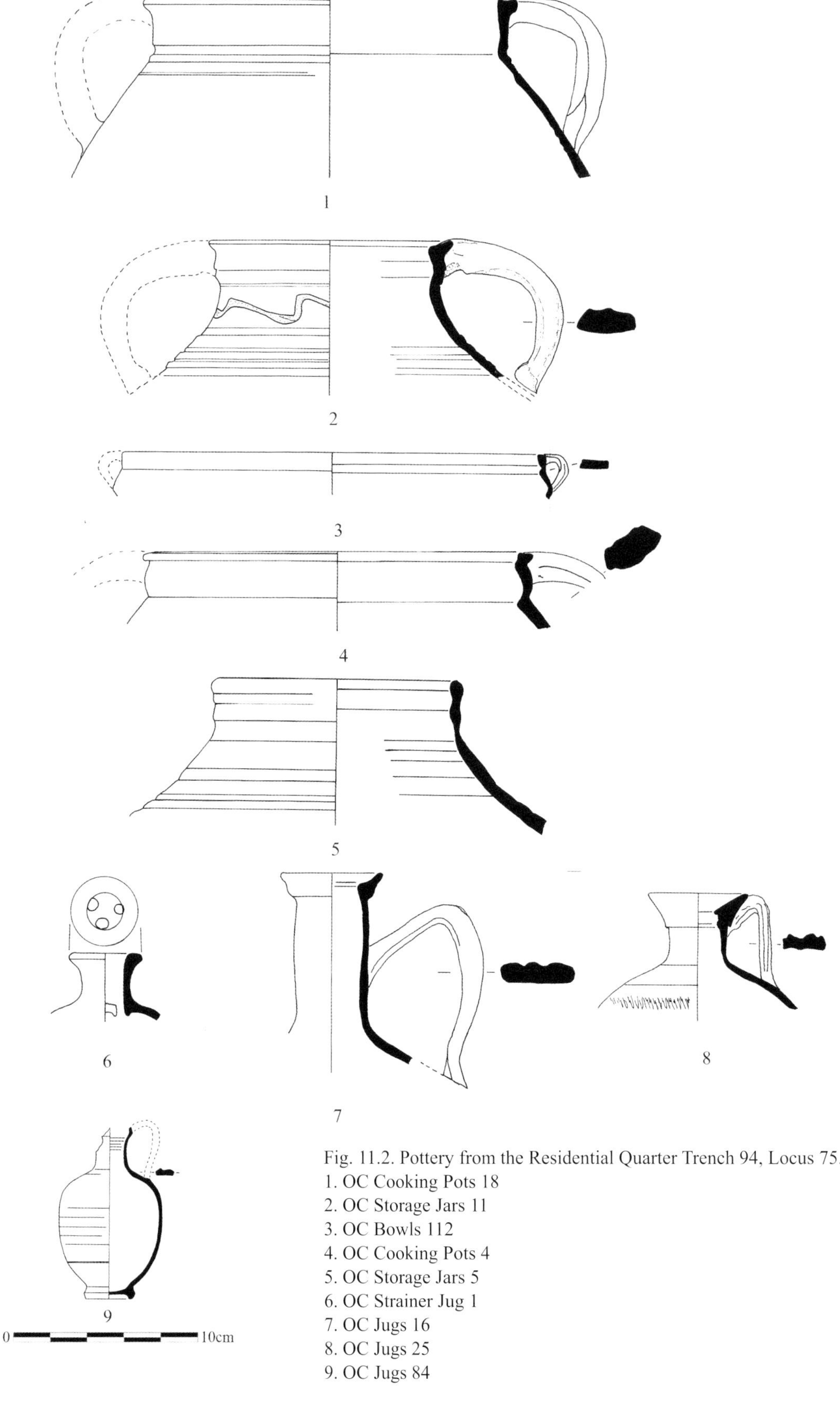

Fig. 11.2. Pottery from the Residential Quarter Trench 94, Locus 75.
1. OC Cooking Pots 18
2. OC Storage Jars 11
3. OC Bowls 112
4. OC Cooking Pots 4
5. OC Storage Jars 5
6. OC Strainer Jug 1
7. OC Jugs 16
8. OC Jugs 25
9. OC Jugs 84

1. Bowls and plates

Most may be compared with the second half of S. Schmid's typology: bowls with incurving rims (his *Gruppe 5*), bowls with deep rims slanted inwards and thick walls (*Gruppe 6*), bowls with deep rims, often beveled/moulded, and thin walls (*Gruppe 7*), small bowls (*Gruppe 8*), bowls with exterior-flanged rims (*Gruppe 9*), and bowls with everted rims (*Gruppe 10*). 'Casserole' bowls with various rim shapes and large-diameter deep bowls are also present. The rim forms run from the late 1st c. B.C. through the 2nd c. A.D.

One hemispherical bowl (OC Bowl 1) with an incurving rim belongs to Schmid's *Gruppe 2* of the late 2nd c. B.C.
The single example presented of his *Gruppe 5* (OC Bowl 2) bears a handle which places it in the mid-4th c. A.D.[6]
Of the several *Gruppe 6* bowls (OC Bowls 4-15; fig. 11.4, nos. 1-3), the most common form is OC Bowl 11; *Gruppe 6* is generally dated to the late 1st c. B.C.
Most of our bowls belong to the thin-walled *Gruppe 7*, dated to the early 1st c. A.D. Ours are divided into 6 subsets: incurving rims (nos. 18-24), thickened rims (nos. 25-30), vertical rims with strong carination (nos. 31-35), inward sloping rims with strong carination (nos. 36-45), moulded vertical rims (nos. 46-49), and moulded inverted rims (nos. 50-54). The first group includes a bowl (no. 23) that has been altered into what appears to be a candelabrum.
The bowls/cups of *Gruppe 8* (late 1st to early 2nd c. A.D.) have also been divided into small (rim diam. <10 cm) uncarinated (nos. 57-64), small carinated (nos. 65-75), and medium-sized (rim diam. >10 cm) carinated (nos. 76-77) and uncarinated (nos. 78-84).
Gruppe 9 bowls are also differentiated by their rim diameters: medium-sized (nos. 85-89; rim diam. 11-16 cm), and large-sized (nos. 78-84 and 90-93; 23-30 cm).
Gruppe 10 bowls are both shallow (no. 96) and deep (nos. 97-100); the deep examples resemble a form found at North Ridge Tomb 2,[7] but, unlike those, ours all exhibit a strong carination.
Among the casserole bowls of large diameter, some have rounded shoulders (nos. 101-4) and others have carinated shoulders (nos. 105-8). As examples of both forms carry incised decoration (wavy lines) associated with Late Roman/Early Byzantine pottery, there does not appear to be a development from rounded to carinated shoulders, or *vice versa*.
Our assemblage includes a variety of casserole bowls (nos. 109-14) with rims thickened on both interior and exterior in a T-shape.
Possibly another form used for cooking is a bowl with a moulded vertical rim, thick walls and small loop handles (nos. 116-19); comparanda for this form, which seems to derive from the *Gruppe 7* tradition, date to the 2nd c. A.D.
Our assemblage also includes bowls of large diameter with incurving rims decorated with excised grooves (nos. 120-22), S-shaped rims (nos. 123-26), and thickened rims (no. 127). As several examples in this last group have burnt exteriors, they were probably used for cooking purposes.

The bowls and plates have 5 base types: ring (93.2% of those identified), rounded (2.2%), pointed (1.6%), string-cut (1.6%), and flat (1.5%).

2. Cups and chalices

Several deep bowls with long everted or horizontal rims are present (OC cups/chalices 1-12). They may feature decorative rouletting, paint, or handles. One example (OC cups/chalices 10) is shallow and the rim is less horizontal; it bears some resemblance to a bowl of the 1st c. B.C.[8]

6 Gerber 1997, fig. 16.E.
7 Bikai 2001, fig. 8.4.
8 Gerber 2001a, fig. 1.9.

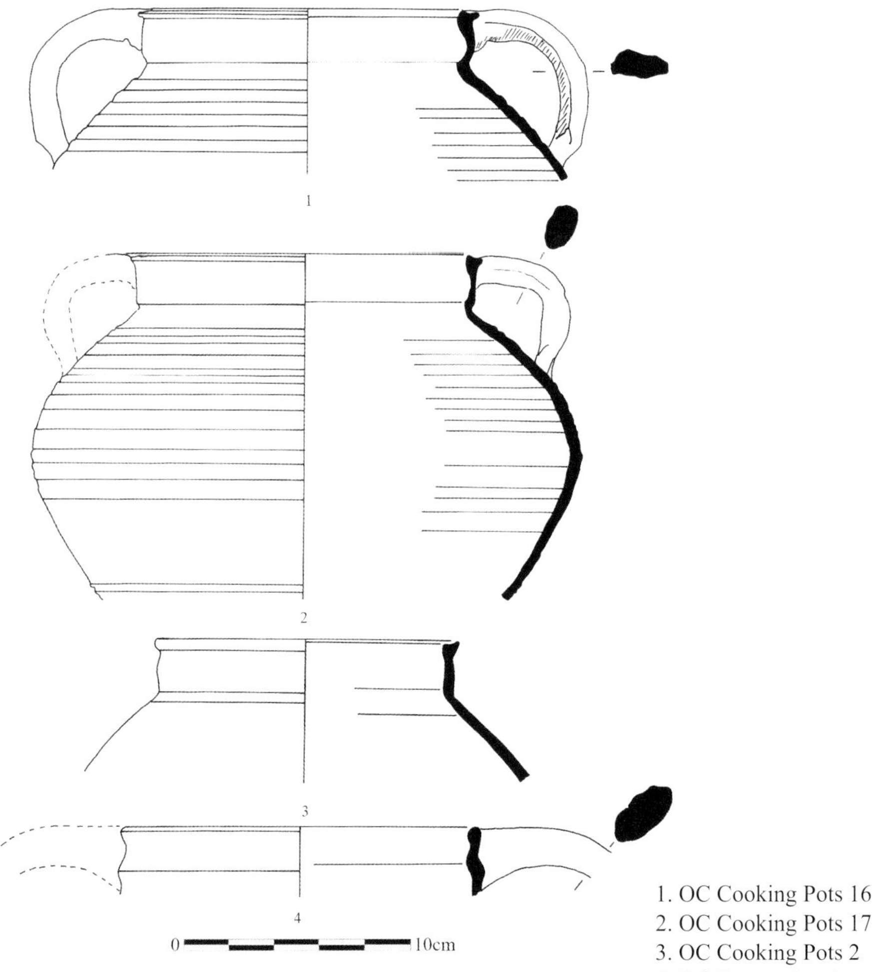

Fig. 11.3. Pottery from the Residential Quarter Trench 94, Locus 75.

1. OC Cooking Pots 16
2. OC Cooking Pots 17
3. OC Cooking Pots 2
4. OC Storage Jar 4

3. Stopper cups

Our assemblage contained several stopper cups with long, horizontal, flaring rims and ring bases. Three examples are presented (OC Stopper Cups 1-3 with additional bases nos. 4-8; fig. 11.4, no. 12), while Grosso Modo records *c*.20 other fragments of this type. Rim diameters range from 7.0 to 11.5 cm. The sides of the cups can be vertical or angled. These cups were present in the North Ridge tombs, one being set inside the mouth of a jug, which indicates its function.[9] Although our examples are not painted, a stopper cup in the Jordan Archaeological Museum bears Type 4 (Phase 3) decoration.[10]

4. Jugs

Jug and jar fragments were relatively common, comprising 15% (or 12% jars/jugs and 3% jugs) of the assemblage. The difficulty of distinguishing sherds from jugs and jars resulted in 12% being designated as 'jar/jug' in Grosso Modo; just 3% of the sherds with a recognizable function were distinguished as jugs.

Six jug forms (with 1 or 2 handles) are differentiated.

1. (OC Jugs 1-6). Long neck with rim thickened on the interior; it finds parallels in North Ridge

---

9 Bikai 2001, 66.

10 'Amr *et al.* n.d., fig. 5.

Tomb 1[11] (dated to the first half of the 1st c. A.D.) and is also present in Ez Zantur phase 2[12] (*c.*50 B.C.–A.D. 20).
2. (nos. 7-14). Flange on the rim's interior and a wide neck relative to the body; P. Bikai considers this small dipper jug a diagnostic form of North Ridge Tomb 1.[13] The moulded rim of no. 14 may represent a later development of the type.
3. Collared rim; second half of the 1st c. A.D., with comparanda in North Ridge Tomb 2[14] and the Petra Church.[15] The type comes in variations: one rim is slightly everted (no. 15); five (nos. 16-18 and 21; fig. 11.2, no. 7) have an interior flange for holding a stopper; five (nos. 22-26; fig. 11.2, no. 8) do not have a flange but have more arrowhead-shaped, everted rims. The latter has Early Roman[16] but also Late Roman comparanda.[17] This rim form also appears on a large jug (no. 27) that has fine ribbing on the upper neck and is probably later in date (2nd or 3rd c. A.D.).[18]
4. Everted rim with a sharp ridge below (nos. 28-35). Three have short necks and are related to a jug diagnostic of the finds in North Ridge Tomb 2.[19]
5. Flaring, thickened rim (nos. 36-44; fig. 11.4, no. 15). One example (no. 40) is related to a North Ridge Tomb 2 dipper jug.[20] Three other examples with moulded rims (nos. 42-44) probably represent later developments of the form.
6. Out-flaring neck, varying degrees of rim complexity (nos. 45-49).

5. Small jars

Vessels with rim diameters less than 10 cm are classified as small jars, but the similarity of some of the forms to cooking pots may have led to some misidentifications. There are four distinct forms:
1. Rim that is vertical or thickened on the interior (OC Small jars 1-4). This is perhaps the earliest, with comparanda in North Ridge Tomb 1.[21]
2. Thickened rim. Two examples (nos. 5-6) have a more globular body than the others (nos. 7-14). The rims strongly resemble cooking pots. In fact, no. 9 is very similar and only slightly smaller than a cooking pot in North Ridge Tomb 2,[22] but our example has only one handle.
3. Everted or horizontal rim (nos. 15-16). Two examples are distinguished by their twisted handles, and one has impressed chevron decoration similar to a chalice in North Ridge Tomb 2.[23]
4. Small jars or beakers with ridged bodies and string-cut bases (nos. 18-20). These distinctive vessels also appeared in other Great Temple contexts (no. 17). There are comparanda in North Ridge Tomb 2[24] and at Mampsis.[25]

6. Strainer jugs

Three general forms of strainer jugs appear:
1. Short-necked and beaded rim with a narrow diameter (OC Strainer 1 = fig. 11.2, no. 6).
2. A wider mouth with a short neck (no. 2).

11 Bikai 2001, figs. 5.14 and 5.16.
12 Schmid 2001, figs. 11.3-4.
13 Bikai 2001, figs. 6.2-3.
14 Ibid. fig. 8.8.
15 Gerber 2001a, fig. 1.17.
16 Khairy 1982, fig. 75.
17 Hendrix *et al.*, 1996, 357.
18 Gerber 2001a, fig. 1.22.
19 Bikai 2001, fig. 9.17.
20 Ibid. fig. 9.15.
21 Ibid. figs. 6.10 and 6.12.
22 Ibid. fig. 9.13.
23 Bikai 2001, fig. 7.6.
24 Ibid. fig. 9.9-10.
25 Erickson-Gini 1999, fig. 5.2.16.

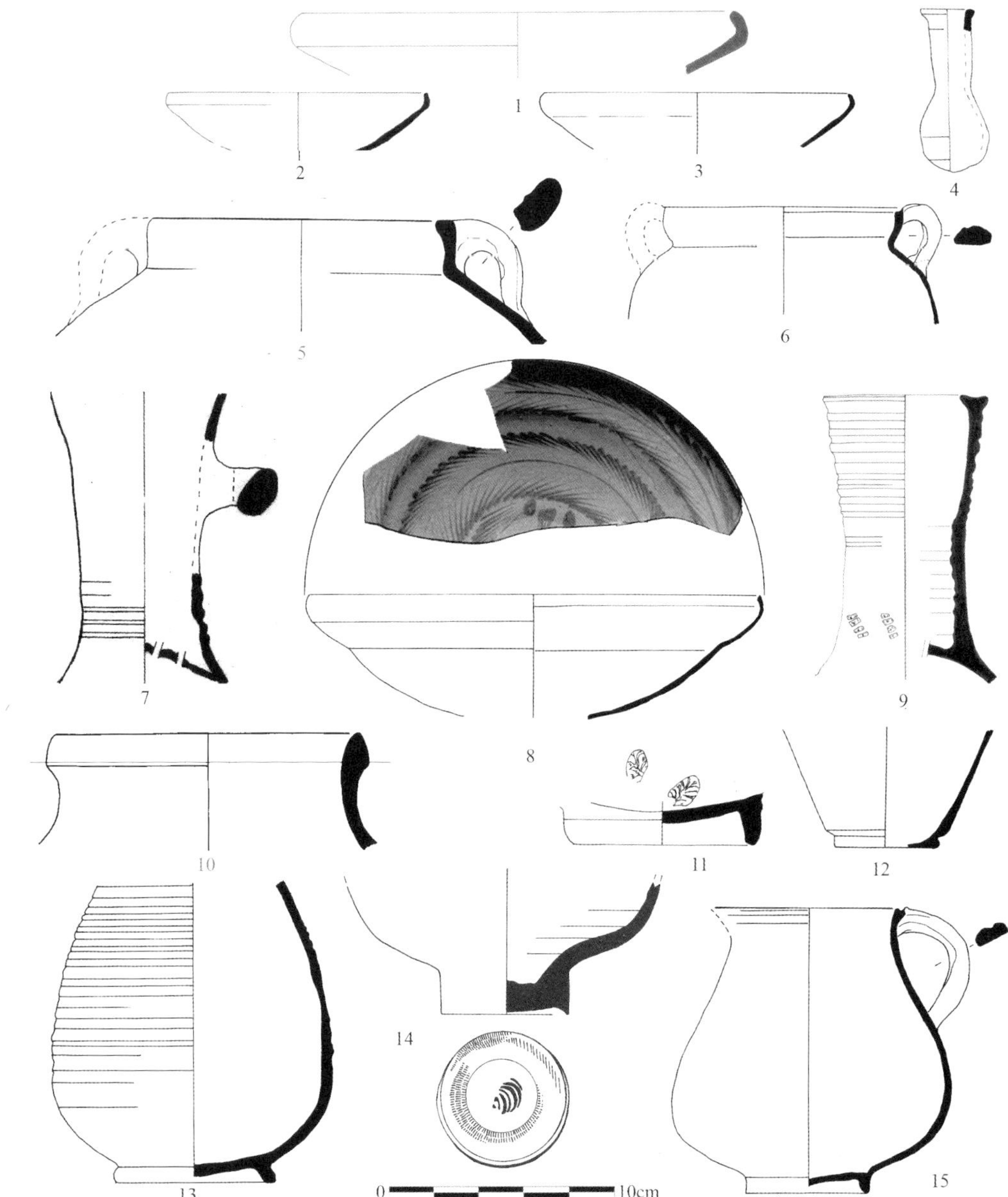

Fig. 11.4. Pottery from the Residential Quarter, Trench 94, mixed loci.
1. OC Bowls 6
2. OC Bowls 4
3. OC Bowls 18
4. (Not represented in OC)
5. OC Cooking Pots 1
6. OC Cooking Pots 3
7. OC Strainer Jugs 3
8. OC Bowls 24
9. OC Strainer Jugs 4
10. OC Storage Jars 1
11. OC Bowls 130
12. OC Stopper Cups 8
13. OC Jugs 11
14. OC Jugs 58
15. OC Jugs 36

3. A wider mouth with long necks (nos. 3-4; fig. 11.4, nos. 7 and 9), made in green ware. Two vessels of this group have holes punched into their bodies (nos. 5-6).

7. Large storage jars

A diversity of rim forms exists among our large storage jars; many are complex.

1. 'Simple' with beaded trims (OC Storage jar 1 = fig. 11.4, no. 10; 1st c. B.C.).[26]

---

26 Gerber 2001a, fig. 1.7.

2. This group shares beaded rims but they are more complex (nos. 2-6; fig. 11.3, no. 4 and fig. 11.2, no. 5). These first two groups are close in date since the complex form is diagnostic of North Ridge Tomb 1.[27]
3. Everted rim (no. 11 = fig. 11.2, no. 2). Perhaps related to vessels from other Great Temple contexts (nos. 7-10); probably mid-4th c. A.D. at Ez Zantur;[28] they may represent Nabataean amphorae as descendants of a type of the early 1st c. B.C.[29]
4. A series of ridges decorate the neck (nos. 12-13). One example has an incised wavy line on the shoulder. These attributes resemble storage jars from late contexts at Ez Zantur.
5. Thickened rim, no neck with small (no. 14) and large diameter (nos. 15-16).

8. Amphorae

Almost half of the diagnostic fragments are handles (2 lug, 2 flat, 3 round, 2 ovoid, 1 double-stranded, 1 unspecified). An off-white, cream or yellow color appears on 76% of the fragments; another 16% have self-same color slip. Brown, gray and salmon comprise the remaining colors. Two diagnostic fragments are illustrated (OC Amphoras 1-2).

9. Cooking pots

The importance of the cooking pot is evident in the relatively high numbers in the assemblage (16.3%). The earliest forms have vertical necks which date to the first half of the 1st c. A.D. A variety of forms show this early attribute. The rim of the first is thickened on the interior (OC Cooking pot 1; fig. 11.4, no. 5). The rims of nos. 2-3 (fig. 11.3, no. 3 and fig. 11.4, no. 6) are thickened on the exterior and have a shallow flange along the top edge; this form also appears in North Ridge Tomb 1.[30] Another form (fig. 11.2, no. 4) may belong to the early group because its neck is vertical, even though the curvature characteristic of later forms is evident.

Cooking pots with angled necks are generally later in date.[31] Our assemblage contains numerous examples (nos. 6-12) of rims with a pointed, usually downward-sloping collar, a form which seems to date to the second half of the 1st c. A.D.[32] A cooking pot (no. 5) from Special Project 95 in the Propylaeum East seems to be an intermediary form because the same attributes are combined with a vertical neck. Similar is a cooking pot with a thick, horizontal collar. Examples of this form (nos. 13-19; fig. 11.2, no. 1 and fig. 11.3, nos. 1-2) have larger diameters than the forms mentioned above; it may date to the 2nd-3rd c. A.D.[33] Another type (no. 21; fig. 11.3 no. 4) has an everted rim and cinched neck; its form is similar to a late storage jar (OC Storage jar 11).

10. Lids

Only 21 fragments are identified as lids in the database but 6 types can be identified:
1. Previously identified as a "flagon stopper",[34] but its 3-cm diameter (OC Lid 1) suggests use with smaller vessels, such as unguentaria, rather than flagons.
2. Tall vertical rim, out-flaring ledge, pyramidal shape (nos. 3-4). The two examples are similar in form and decoration and may have been manufactured in the same workshop. They are larger versions of a decorated stopper (no. 2) found in the 'Baroque Room'.
3. Simple bowl (no. 5) probably used as a lid for a cooking pot, as seen in modern use.
4. Shallow bowl (nos. 6-7) with perforated holes for release of steam.

---

27 Bikai 2001, fig. 6.13. See also Gerber 2001a, figs. 1.2 and 1.5 that are dated slightly earlier.
28 Gerber 1997, fig. 1.
29 Schmid 2001, fig. 11.1.5.
30 Bikai 2001, fig. 6.9.
31 Ibid. Compare the forms found in Tomb 2 (fig. 9.10 and 14) with those of slightly earlier dates in Tomb 1 (fig. 6.9).
32 Ibid. (fig. 9.10 and 14).
33 Gerber 2001a, fig. 1.20.
34 Hayes, 1997, fig. 22.

5. Incurving rim thickened on the interior (no. 8).
6. The form of the lid for large vessels (nos. 10-12) is comprised of shallow bowls with long, horizontal rims (diam. 16-24 cm).

11. Small forms

The small forms includes perfume containers, alabastroi, amphoriskoi, bottles, unguentaria and lacrymatoria; in some cases, the particular type is specified in Grosso Modo. Unguentaria and lacrymatoria account for roughly half of this category. Five representative pieces presented here can be attributed to 3 groups.
1. The earlier type has a piriform body.[35] The bodies of the North Ridge Tomb 1 and of our illustrated OC Small form no. 1 are not ribbed, but ribbed piriform unguentaria appear in other contexts of our project.[36]
2. Less bulbous bodies; the rims are beaded or everted (nos. 6-9). Both rim types are also seen in North Ridge Tomb 2.[37]
3. Out-flaring rim and ribbed neck (no. 11). No. 10, an unguentarium from Special Project 89 with a similar rim, has comparanda at the oil factory at Khirbet edh-Dharih; that piece has a flat base and is dated to the 2nd c. A.D.[38]

Three alabastroi (nos. 13-15) are identified. All are of the same type with a flat, out-flaring rim and a carinated body. All are decorated with black palmette wreaths of the Nabataean Phase 4 decorative style. Their close similarity in form and decoration point to manufacture in the same workshop.

12. Varia

Four funnels are present (OC Varia nos. 1-2). Their spouts vary in length but all are less than 2 cm in diameter, which would allow them to be used to fill unguentaria or similar small forms. A funnel of similar construction comes from North Ridge Tomb 2.[39]

The purpose of a small bowl with ribbed sides, squeezed in the top center to partly close it (no. 4), is unclear.

A decorated ceramic brazier (no. 5) perhaps used for incense, was recovered in the fill directly overlaying the floor in Rooms 10-11 (fig. 11.1). The wavy-line decoration on its exterior recalls the décor found on Late Roman/Byzantine storage jars.

The single-spouted kernos with everted rim (no. 3) lacks datable features.

Decorated wares

This category includes both painted and plastic. Nabataean painted ware comprises *c.*20% of the assemblage from the Residential Quarter. N. Zabban partially reconstructed several bowls.[40] In addition to the ubiquitous Nabataean painted bowl, the assemblage includes other painted forms, such as alabastroi (OC Small forms nos. 13-15), a casserole bowl (OC Bowl no. 114), and a candelabrum (OC Bowl no. 23). Among the various colors used, brown predominates (29% of all painted fragments); red and reddish brown paint decorates 18% of all painted pieces, while black decoration appears on almost 25%; white paint (including off-white, cream and yellow) appears on 27%; and a white band is present on 37% of the rims of bowls/plates. When compared to Schmid's

35 Bikai 2001, fig. 6.6.
36 E.g., Special Projects 85 and 84, Sequence nos. 85161, SP84036 and SP84011.
37 Bikai 2001, figs. 9.11-12.
38 Villeneuve 1990, pl. II.1.
39 P. M. Bikai, pers. comm.
40 See vol. 2, figs. 7.40-41.

typology,[41] the descriptions of motif and color of the paint noted in Grosso Modo suggest that a considerable proportion of the decorated corpus belongs to Phase 3 (96%); Late Phase 2 and Phase 4 fragments appear in negligible quantities.

Some sherds bear plastic decoration (appliqué, excision, impression, incision, moulded, perforation, ribbing, rouletting). In this category most common is ribbing (77% of the decorated fragments), followed by moulded (8%), incised (8%) and rouletted (7%) decoration. Cooking pots, cups, jars and jugs, large storage vessels and unguentaria in the assemblage are frequently decorated with ribbing. Jars and jugs are the vessel types most often decorated with incision, but some rarer forms, such as the brazier (OC Varia 5), also bear this type of decoration. Moulded and rouletted decoration appears most often on bowls and plates, yet only *c.*6% of these vessels are decorated in this manner. Vessel bases carry 72% of the examples of rouletting in the collection.

Dating of the site

Very few of the excavated contexts were undisturbed; the further loss of context information means that the mass of pottery cannot help refine the phasing of the construction, use and destruction of the Residential Quarter. According to the stratigraphic phasing by the excavators, less than 1% of the sherds belong to periods when the Residential Quarter was inhabited, and 56% belong to the period following the A.D. 363 earthquake. Some comments may be made, however, about the pottery from two contexts.

(a) Room 7

Beneath the sandstone pavement (Locus 64) in Room 7, the excavators identified three soil loci above bedrock. Locus 63, directly below the pavement, was a compact, sealed soil matrix forming the floor bedding. It contained 10 coins, three identified as Nabataean. The pottery included a bowl with an incurving rim (OC Bowl 6; fig. 11.4 no. 1) of Schmid's *Gruppe I* (second half of the 1st c. B.C.); it also included rim sherds of bowls of *Gruppen 6, 7 and 8*, in addition to the rim of a casserole bowl (OC Bowl 102) and the base of a jug (OC Jug 58).

Locus 65 below was a homogeneous dark brown soil. Pottery included a bowl fragment with Nabataean Phase 3a decoration. A mid-1st c. date is also supported by a bowl and cooking pot with comparanda in the North Ridge Tomb 1.[42] A storage jar (fig. 11.4, no. 10) is earlier (1st c. B.C.)[43] and the simple rim of the cooking pots illustrated here (fig. 11.4, nos. 5-6) also seems to belong earlier.

Locus 69 below was the original sub-floor, overlying bedrock. It contained a bowl with Nabataean Phase 2c painted decoration (OC Bowl 24; fig. 11.4, no. 8; A.D. 10-40). Of a similar date is the base of an Eastern Sigillata A plate (of the final phase) with stamped palmettes on the tondo and three rows of rouletting around the edge (OC Bowl 130; fig. 11.4, no. 11; 1st c. A.D.).[44] The pottery points to the first half of the 1st c. A.D. as the *terminus post quem* for construction of the features in Room 7.

(b) Room 3 (figs. 11.2-3)

Locus 71 is a compacted soil layer that formed the floor bedding in Room 3; it lacked pottery but produced 3 Trajanic coins.[45] Below that floor bedding was Locus 75. Here, fragments of Phase 3a and 3b painted decoration were found and recorded in Grosso Modo. Cooking pots with vertical necks point to the early 1st c. A.D. The jugs (OC Cooking pot 16 = fig. 11.2, no. 1; OC Cooking pot 4 = fig. 11.2, no. 4) have comparanda throughout the 1st c. A.D. The casserole bowl (OC Bowl 112 = fig.

41 Schmid 1996, 173-74.
42 Bikai 2001, figs. 5.3 and 6.11.
43 Gerber 2001a, fig. 1.7.
44 Hayes 1997, 57.
45 See chapt. 15 below.

11.2, no. 3), however, is similar to a bowl dated to the 2nd c. A.D., while the storage jar (OC Storage jar 11 = fig. 11.2, no. 2) bears the incised wavy-line decoration that is usually associated with Late Roman/Early Byzantine contexts. Thus the floor bedding seems to contain chronologically mixed materials. The excavators hypothesized that Nabataean tombs were once situated in the cliff above the Residential Quarter and that material from them (most of it also of a domestic nature) washed down. It would appear that there were at least two destruction events, and that débris from the first event was used to level the area for subsequent construction. The incised storage jar (fig. 11.2, no. 2) may place the latest destruction close to the A.D. 363 earthquake. Perhaps the Residential Quarter was occupied for only a brief period before its final obliteration.

12

Terracotta lamps

Deirdre Grace Barrett

Lamps and fragments thereof found by the Great Temple project from 1994 through 2008 total 626. Because of the large number, for the present chapter we present only a typology, which does include the full range of types present. The complete data for all the pieces is available online in *Open Context*.[1]

The typology comprises 24 types, classified by their attributes (shape, size, nozzle design, discus decoration, clay). All functioned as lamps except for no. 3, a lamp filler with a spout for pouring oil. Only representatives of each group are illustrated here. Where our examples are fragmentary, complete examples (e.g., from the North Ridge site at Petra or from the collections of the Semitic Museum of Harvard University) are illustrated. Photographs (taken by the author), drawings and profiles are shown at 1 : 2, unless otherwise indicated. If a lamp is incomplete, diameter measurements have been taken from a diameter chart.

The emergence of the Nabataeans in Petra during the 3rd c. B.C. coincides largely with the Late Hellenistic era (198-63 B.C.), and Petra's early ceramic repertoire shows the development of wares and forms from the Hellenistic corpus.[2] Hellenistic influence continues to be visible in the Early Roman ceramics after Pompey's conquest of the region in 63 B.C. Nabataea became part of *Provincia Arabia* in A.D. 106, but the Nabataean ceramic tradition did not disappear and their painted wares were still being produced in the 3rd c. A.D., and perhaps later.[3] Periods referred to are as defined by W. Rast (1992):

Early Hellenistic	332-198 B.C.
Late Hellenistic	198-63 (start of the Nabataean ceramic tradition).
Early Roman	63 B.C.–A.D. 135 (Nabataea annexed by Rome in A.D. 106)
Middle Roman	A.D. 135-250
Late Roman	250-360
Early Byzantine	360-491
Late Byzantine	491-640
Umayyad dynasty	661-750
Abbasid dynasty	750-1258

The numerical order of the 24 types in our classification is not a strict indication of their chronological progression since there is a considerable overlap in types within an historical period.

In 2001, seventy clay samples were taken from the Great Temple lamps and ceramics for instrumental neutron activation analysis (INAA) at the Missouri University Research Reactor (MURR). This testing was funded by an NSF grant (No. SBR-9802366), and was undertaken by H. Neff and M.D. Glascock at MURR. L.-A. Bedal (1998, 347-67) had conducted an earlier INAA analysis of Petra ceramics at MURR, and her results were compared to the plotting of the present author's INAA results. Bedal's Groups were labelled A and B, and the author's Groups were labelled 1, 2 and 3.

Despite a lack of direct evidence for provenance, Bedal (ibid) concluded from her plot results that both her Groups A and B were local to Petra. If this inference is correct, then Barrett Group 2, which subsumed both of Bedal's Groups, represents a production zone that included the Petra region.

---

1 http://www.opencontext.org. Also online at Open Context are Excel charts figs. 13.28-13.32: 13.28. Hellenistic and Miscellaneous, nos. 1GT-7GT; 13.29. Nabataean, nos. 8GT-19GT; 13.30. Roman, nos. 20GT-26GT; 13.31. Byzantine, nos. 27GT-32GT; 13.32. Islamic, no. 33GT. The Excel charts show the complete corpus, with measurements and provenience information.

2 Hendrix *et al.* 1996, 67.

3 Schmid 2000, phase 4, fig. 98.

Fig. 12.1. Delphiniform lamp (1907.64.203), in the Semitic Museum, Harvard University.

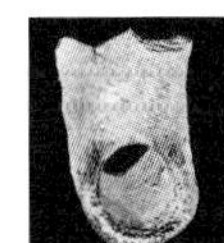

Fig.12.2. Nozzle from Hellenistic lamp (96-L-36) from Lower Temenos.

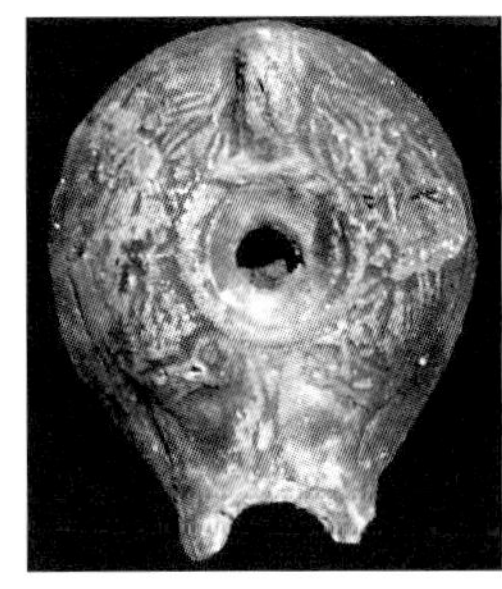

Fig. 12.3a. Syro-Palestinian lamp (02-L-5) from Residential Quarter.

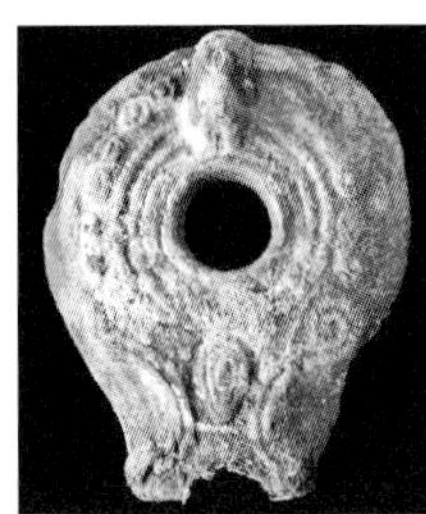

Fig. 12.3b. Syro-Palestinian lamp (02-L-11). Note schematic anthropomorphic face on nozzle, from Residential Quarter.

Fig. 12.4 Fragment of lamp filler (95-L-59) from Lower Temenos (note scale is 1 : 1).

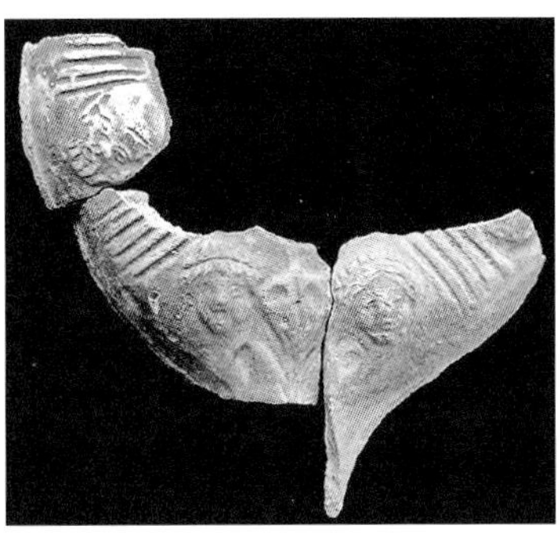

Fig. 12.5. Lamp filler from Petra's North Ridge (98-LB-122).

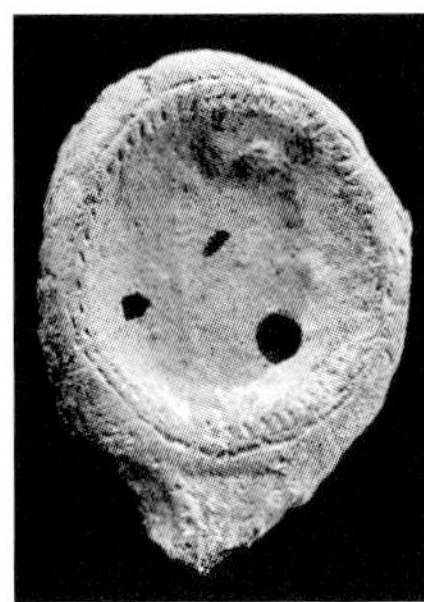

Fig. 12.6. Apprentice lamp (94-P-25) from Upper Temenos.

Fig. 12.7. Ptolemaic palmette lamp (02-L-6) from Residential Quarter.

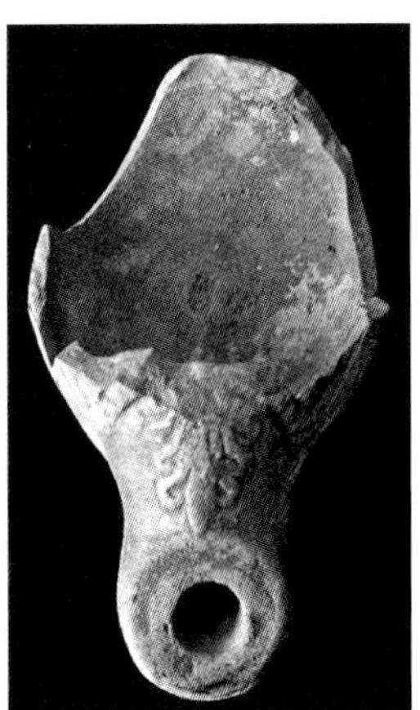

Fig. 12.8. Ptolemaic palmette lamp (02-L-7) from Residential Quarter.

Fig. 12.9. Ptolemaic palmette lamp (1931.3.173), in Semitic Museum, Harvard University.

Neff and Glascock (2001, 2) noted that the Roman lamps were less frequent in Barrett Group 2 than in Group 1, suggesting that the shift in Group 1 compositions was related partly to a difference between the ceramic resource preferences of makers of Nabataean lamps *versus* makers of Roman lamps. The origin of the clays in Group 1 was not known, thereby indicating that the 14 lamps found in this group were produced outside the Petra region, an origin that was also demonstrated in the style and fabric of the lamp. The lamps were classified as Roman because their stylistic qualities reflected those of imported Roman lamps. In the following Typology, no. 9, the Roman decorated discus lamp 94-P-37 (fig. 12.17) was identified as a member of Barrett Group 1.

Hellenistic imported lamps and local copies (mid-2nd c. B.C.–1st c. A.D.)

1. *Delphiniform and related lamps* (figs. 12.1-12.2)

The term 'delphiniform' refers to the shape of the lamp.[4] W. F. Petrie referred to them as thumb lamps from the thumb-piece at the side for holding them but noted that early examples "show that this projection was at first a dolphin".[5] Moulded lamp with a rounded, double-convex body, plain rim around the filling-hole, and flat, low disc-base. Lug-handle on one side, sometimes with volutes or an S-coil on the handle. Shoulders decorated with radiating ridges. Long nozzle with a rounded end. Mid-2nd to mid-1st c. B.C., possibly extending to the end of the 1st c. B.C. For a complete example see fig. 12.1 in the Semitic Museum at Harvard University. Our finds include elongated nozzles related to the above type. 96-L-36 (fig. 12.2) was found in the Lower Temenos.

Comparanda: Broneer Type XVIII; Lapp 1961 type 83; Rosenthal and Sivan 1978, 13, nos. 22-23; 'Amr 1984, 31, type 4; Fitch and Goldman 1994, 47-51, nos. 183-204; Barag and Hershkovitz 1994, 13, no. 2.

2. *Syro-Palestinian lamp* (fig. 12.3)

Similar to type 1 but lacking the thumb piece. Moulded lamp 02-L-5 (fig. 12.3a) has a 'pocket watch' body and vestigial knob handle at the rear of a small, depressed discus, with an olive wreath around the filling-hole as the shoulder decoration, and with half-volutes on the nozzle. A second example, 02-L-11 (fig. 12.3b), is a moulded lamp with the same rounded body and knob handle but the decoration consists of a garland of circles around the filling hole, with a schematic anthropomorphic face on the nozzle. Both were found in the Residential Quarter.

Comparanda: Howland 1958, 197-98, dated from the late 1st c. B.C. to the early 1st c. A.D.; Rosenthal and Sivan 1978, 55 no. 223, dated not earlier than the mid-1st c. A.D.; Hayes 1980, 15-16, no. 57 pl. 7, dated *c.*50 B.C.–A.D. 25.

3. *Lamp filler* (figs. 12.4-12.5)

95-L-59, a shoulder rim fragment from the Lower Temenos (fig. 12.4), is part of a lamp filler. A more complete example comes from the North Ridge excavations (98-LB-122, fig. 12.5). It takes the shape of a clock. A large central filling-hole is surrounded by a border of radials. Anthropomorphic heads in relief on the shoulder rim, separated by panels of radials. Narrow nozzle in the form of a goat's head in low relief, with ivy-leaf decoration above, strap handle on the side (Horsfield 1941 no. 50).

Comparanda: Horsfield *et al.* 1941, 123, no. 50. S. Loeschcke (pers. comm. to the Horsfields) classified this lamp filler as Nabataean, with perhaps a Ptolemaic influence, suggesting a date of the 1st c. B.C. Crelier (1995, 128, Nr. 68) dated it from the 1st c. B.C. to the 1st c. A.D.

4. *Apprentice lamp* (fig. 12.6)

These lamps are crudely and locally made, either by hand or taken from a worn mould. Often boat-shaped or mimicking the Roman discus lamp, with a shallow discus and small filling-hole. 94-P-25 (fig. 12.6), from the Upper Temenos, has an etched border around the shoulder rim and an indistinct discus relief. It may be dated from the second half of the 1st c. B.C. to the first half of the 1st c. A.D.

Comparanda: Horsfield *et al.* 1941, pl. XXI, no. 163; Hammond 1973, 34, nos. 102-3; Negev 1974, 29, pl. 17.92; Rosenthal and Sivan 1978, 98, nos. 395-98; Khairy 1990, 15, Group VI.

5. *Ptolemaic lamp with palmette* (figs. 12.7-12.9)

Violin-shaped body with geometric decoration of concentric arcs and nodules between pairs of dotted lines surrounding the small filling-hole. Palmette on nozzle, rope decoration above. Flattened base ring. 02-L-6 and 02-L-7 (figs. 12.7-12.8) were found in the Residential Quarter. For a complete example in the Semitic Museum, see fig. 12.9.

---

4 Walters 1914, 42-44.

5 Petrie 1904, 8.

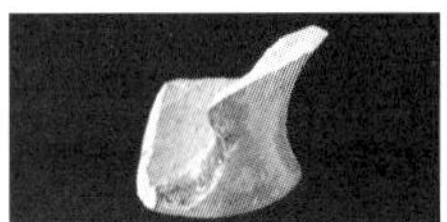

Fig. 12.10. Nozzle of Herodian lamp (04-L-6) from Propylaeum.

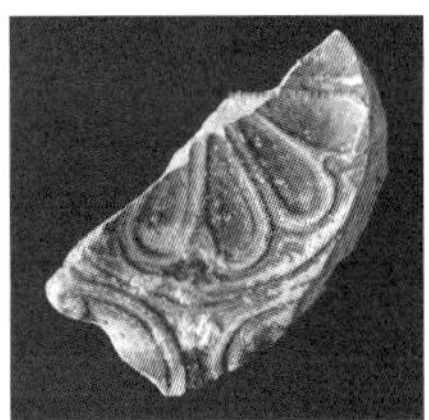

Fig. 12.12. Fragment of Roman rosette lamp (02-L-8) from Upper Temenos.

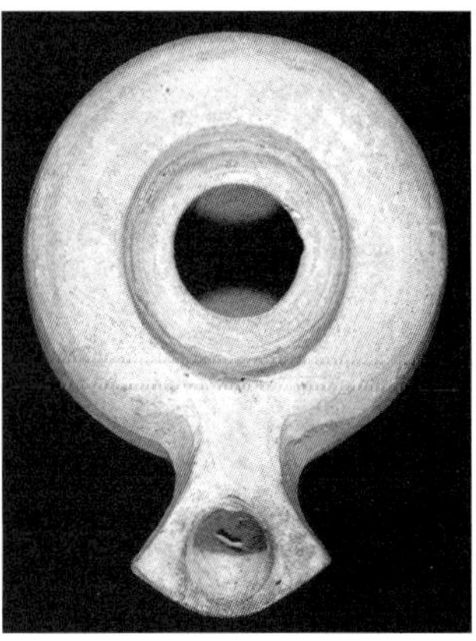

Fig. 12.11. Herodian lamp (1907.64.2) in Semitic Museum.

Fig. 12.13. Roman rosette lamp (98-LB-113), from fill of Tomb 1, North Ridge.

Fig. 12.14. Discus fragment from locally-made rosette lamp (01-L-1) from Lower Temenos.

Fig. 12.15. Discus fragment from locally-made rosette lamp (98-LB-10) from Tomb 1, North Ridge.

Fig. 12.16. Fragment from a locally-made rosette lamp (01-L-10) with moulded inscription '*slmt*' on outer wall of base, from Propylaeum West in vicinity of two standing *betyls*.

Fig. 12.17. Roman symplegma lamp (94-P-37) from Upper Temenos.

Fig. 12.18. Lamp in British Museum, Reg. No. 1971:4-26.3 (Boardman *et al.* 1988, 202).

Figs. 12.19a (left). Fragment from locally-made discus lamp, Eros as a miner (95-L-179), found in the Lower Temenos (drawn by C. Alexander).

Figs. 12.19b (right). Discus fragment found at Khirbet edh-Dharih (© French-Jordanian Mission of Khirbet edh-Dharih).

Comparanda: Petrie 1904, pl. LVIII, K30; Howland 1958, 165 Type 48E; Rosenthal and Sivan 1978, 14, no. 28; Hayes 1980, 25, no. 100, pl. 11, dated second half of 1st c. B.C. to 1st c. A.D.

6. Herodian lamp (figs. 12.10-12.11)

This type can be wheelmade or moulded, with a knife-pared, spatulate nozzle. Often plain, without decoration or handles, they were first attributed to the Herodian period by E. L. Sukenik (1934, 71). P. P. Kahane (1961, 135) suggested a comparison with Broneer type XVII. Our fragment 04-L-6 (fig. 12.10) preserves the knife-pared, spatulate nozzle without the body. For a complete (wheelmade) example, see fig. 12.11 in the Semitic Museum. Examples at Samaria-Sebaste (Crowfoot *et al.* 1957, 289-90 and 295-300, figs. 68-69) come from a context of the late 1st c. B.C.-1st c. A.D. and later. The type is most common during the 1st c. A.D. in areas inhabited by Jews (Barag *et al.* 1994, 46).

Comparanda: Sukenik 1934, 71; Harding 1946, 60, pl. XX.2; Saller and Bagatti 1949, 29-30, pl. 5.29; Sellers and Baramki 1953, 31; Kahane 1961, 133-38; Smith 1961, 53-65; Mazar *et al.* 1967, 141, pl. XXXIV.10.

Roman imported lamps and local Nabataean copies (1st c. B.C.–1st c. A.D.)

7. Roman rosette lamp (figs. 12.12-12.13)

Rosette or petal relief decoration was a popular design on the moulded discus lamp where petals of the rosette, often arranged in heart-shaped pairs, encircled a small central filling-hole, edged with a ridge. The shoulder rim was also edged with one or more ridges, and the nozzle was flanked by half-volutes (Broneer type XXI). The lamp was coated in a red or dark brown slip. 02-L-8 (fig. 12.12) is a fragment of a discus featuring two pairs of petals. For a nearly complete example see 98-LB-113 (fig. 12.13) found at the North Ridge in the fill of Tomb 1. These lamps are not locally made.

Comparanda: Negev 1974, 75, pl. 16; Rosenthal and Sivan 1978, 25, 31 nos. 69, 73-75 and 107; Bailey 1994, 79-81, nos. 138-39, 148 and 150, dated to the late 1st c. B.C. to the first half of 1st c. A.D.

8. Locally-made rosette lamp (figs. 12.14-12.16)

In addition to the rosette (or linked omegas[6]) the Nabataean version often has two ear lugs, as seen in 01-L-1 (fig. 12.14) and on 98-LB-10 from the North Ridge (fig. 12.15). An unusual example of the Nabataean rosette lamp is 01-L-10 (fig. 12.16), bearing a moulded inscription consisting of 4 Nabataean characters, translated as *slmt*, on the exterior wall of the base section. The inscription may relate to the presence of a statue of a deity. In his commentary on inscriptions accompanying betyls, J. Healey (2001, 156) writes:

> Where statues existed, the term *slm* would have been used. Thus it was used of the statue of the divine Obodat in *CIS* II, 354, and the feminine form *slmt* is used for the Tyche of Si in the bilingual mentioning her (*RES* 1092).

Our lamp was found in the vicinity of the pair of standing *betyls* in the Propylaeum West (Trench 86, Locus 17). While it is impossible to know whether the lamp was used to honor the *betyls*, it is a very rare find and its proximity to them is of interest.

Comparanda: for local rosette lamps without the inscription, see Horsfield *et al.* 1941, 195, pl. XXI, no. 162; Hammond 1973, 90; Negev 1986, 132; Khairy 1990, 12, nos. 17-18, dated to the second decade of the 1st c. A.D. until the end of the reign of Rabbel II (A.D. 106); Bailey 1988, 278, pl. 57, no. Q2289, dated to the second half of the 1st c. A.D.; Crelier 1995, 126, no. UT 60, pl. IV, dated from the second quarter to the end of the 1st c. A.D.

9. Roman decorated discus lamp (figs. 12.17-12.18)

A common type in the 1st c. A.D., widely distributed and copied across the empire. The whole upper surface forming the discus was given over to moulded reliefs of religious, mythological and daily-life themes (Bailey 1972, 22), including erotica as seen in our example. A small filling-hole was set within the motif but not necessarily in the center. The shape of the nozzle changed over time (triangular, rounded, heart-shaped) and was often bordered by volutes. Handles were sometimes added. Large discus lamps had elaborate heat shields protecting the handle. The base might be inscribed with the potter's name. The lamp was often coated with dark red or brown slip. The scene on 94-P-37 (fig. 12.17) was known on lamps found throughout the Petra region and the empire at large (cf. fig. 12.18). This lamp was found in the Upper Temenos.

Comparanda: Broneer types XXI-XXV: Horsfield *et al.* 1941, 196, pl. XIV, 424a-b; Hammond 1973, 37, nos. 149-52; Rosenthal and Sivan 1978, 19-41; Hayes 1980, pls. 21-26; Bailey 1994, 84-85; Zayadine 1982, 392, no. 169 fig. 15; Khairy 1990, 13-14, no. 20 fig. 9; Zanoni 1996, fig. 109; Barrett 1998, 277, fig. 6.39. Dated to the end of the 1st c. B.C. through 1st c. A.D.

---

6 J. Patrich (1990, 130) suggested that the petals can also be read as linked omegas, epitomizing the local "avoidance of imitation of the surrounding Hellenistic-Roman culture."

Fig. 12.20. Nabataean volute lamp type A (02-L-9) top view, Great Temple, surface find.

Fig. 12.21. Nabataean volute lamp type A (02-L-9) base view, Great Temple, surface find.

Fig. 12.22. Nabataean volute lamp type B (02-L-1), Upper Temenos.

Fig. 12.23. Nabataean volute lamp type B base (98-L-22a) inscribed 'rayt' ("I have seen"), from Upper Temenos.

Fig. 12.24. Nabataean volute lamp type B base (98-LB-28), inscribed 'rayt', from fill of Tomb 1, North Ridge.

Fig. 12.25. Round lamp with double axes on shoulder rim (01-L-14) from Great Cistern in Upper Temenos.

Fig. 12.26. Roman round lamp (94-P-15) from Lower Temenos.

10. Locally-made decorated discus lamp (figs. 12.19a-b)

Motifs on Roman discus lamps were often adapted when copied. A theme peculiar to the Petra region shows Eros engaged in an activity not represented elsewhere, as a young man with wings, wearing shackles, and carrying a pickaxe and basket. The basket was interpreted as an ingot by G. and A. C. Horsfield (1941, 123), who asked "May he [Eros] be serving his sentence in a Nabataean copper-mine such as Fenan in the 'Arabah, where convicts were sent in the Byzantine period?", suggesting that this may be "a new variant of the theme of the punished child Eros" (well-known from a marble statue in the Palazzo Pitti, Florence. The statue of Eros wears leg irons and shackles, and wipes a tear from his right eye). Our discus fragment from the lamp 95-L-179 (fig. 12.19a) is shown in a drawing, superimposed over a sketch of the complete discus. Our fragment features the torso of the shackled Eros. For a more complete image, fig. 12.19b is a photograph of a similar lamp found at Khirbet edh-Dharih (© French-Jordanian Mission of Khirbet edh-Dharih).

Comparanda: Khairy 1990, 14, no. 22, dated to A.D. 18-40; Barrett 1998, 277, fig. 6.40, dated 1st c. A.D.

Nabataean indigenous lamps dated to the 1st c. A.D.

11-12. Nabataean volute type lamps

A quintessential Nabataean lamp, found throughout the realm and beyond (e.g., at Masada).[7] I divide the type into volute types A and B. Both have half-volutes on their nozzles and a sun-ray

7 Bailey in Barag 1994, 87, no. 177.

ridged design on their shoulders, but there are subtle differences. A. Negev (1986, 134-37) named them Subtype 1a and 1b, while Khairy (1990, 9-10) named our Volute type A his Group I, and our Volute type B, his Group II.

11. Type A (figs. 12.20-12.21)

A circular, moulded lamp with rounded nozzle, flanked by half-volutes with tiny concentric circles above each volute. Shoulder rim decorated with ridged radials surmounted by four 7-petalled rosettes.[8] A groove connects the depressed plain discus with the wick-hole. Flat base with a double base-ring. Dated by Khairy (1990, 10) to A.D. 18-70 based on coins found in conjunction with the lamp. 02-L-9 (fig. 12.20–12.21) is almost complete, apart from damage to the wick-hole.

Comparanda: Hammond 1973, 33, nos. 94, 96, dated before the middle of the 1st c. A.D.; Negev 1974, 28, pl. 17.87; Rosenthal and Sivan 1978, 97, no. 394, dated 1st c. A.D.; Khairy 1990, 9-10.

12. Type B (fig. 12.22)

Our complete example (02-L-1; fig. 12.22) is a round, moulded lamp with a rounded nozzle flanked by half-volutes. The upper section of the discus is decorated with a ladder-like pattern around the filling-hole. The two volutes are connected at the back of the nozzle. On the nozzle is a symbol which might represent a chalice, torch or candlestick, consisting of a hemispherical body and a trumpet base (Khairy 1984, 10; 1990, 11). Negev (1974, 29) identified this symbol as "a double cornucopia, like the one found on the coins of Aretas IV." This symbol is restricted to Nabataean lamps and has never been recorded elsewhere. There are two rosettes composed of 4 circles, one on either side of the shoulder rim, and a rosette of 9 petals at the rear of the rim. The lamp type has been dated by Khairy (1990, 11) from the beginning of the 1st c. A.D. to the end of the reign of Malichus II (A.D. 40-70).

Comparanda: Dalman 1912, 26-27, fig. 15b (no. 871a); Murray and Ellis 1940, 26, pl. XXXVI.15; Horsfield *et al.* 1941, 122, 195, pls. XI.42-43 and XLIV.415-18; Cleveland 1960, 71-72, pl. 18A; Schmitt-Korte 1968, 514, fig. 11.42; Negev 1970, 48-51, fig. 32.2; Hammond 1973, 33-34, 36, nos. 129-32; Negev 1974, 28-29, pls. 17.87-89; Zayadine 1982, 371, no. 10; Khairy 1990, 10-11, figs. 5-7.

13. Nabataean volute type B, inscribed (figs. 12.23-12.24)

Identical to type B above except it has a variety of Nabataean characters etched on its base. The short formulae which appear most often are: "*rayt*" (translated as "I have seen"), "*slm*" ("Greetings"), and "*hny*" ("use it with pleasure").[9] With regard to "*rayt*", Khairy writes: "there is a direct and logical relation between the functional purpose of the lamp itself — as a means for helping to see in the darkness of the wilderness, tombs, dwellings, and caves — and the meaning of this word". 98-L-22a (fig. 12.23) and an example from the North Ridge site (fig. 12.24) bear the "*rayt*" inscription on their bases.

Comparanda: As for Type no. 12. Also Khairy 1984, 115-19, figs. 1-3, dated 1st c. A.D.

Imported lamps and Nabataean local copies (1st-3rd c. A.D.)

14. Double-axe decoration on the shoulder (fig. 12.25)

These lamps share the double axe symbol, which appears on either side of the shoulder rim. Found all over Syria-Palestine.[10] Neutron activation analysis gives 95-L-81, with axes on its shoulders, a possible Parthian source. Round shape with a ridge bordering a slightly depressed discus. Wide and flaring nozzle. Discus often decorated with a relief design, and there may be a potter's mark on the base. 01-L-14 (fig. 12.25), found in the Upper Temenos inside the Great Cistern, provides a *terminus post quem* for that locus.

---

8 Negev (1974, 28) wrote that the 7 petals "may have had a religious significance, as it is the case with the Jews and other people."

9 Khairy 1984, 118.

10 Rosenthal and Sivan 1978, 85.

Fig. 12.27. Local round lamp with ovolos on shoulder rim and unidentified image on discus (02-L-10), from Upper Temenos.

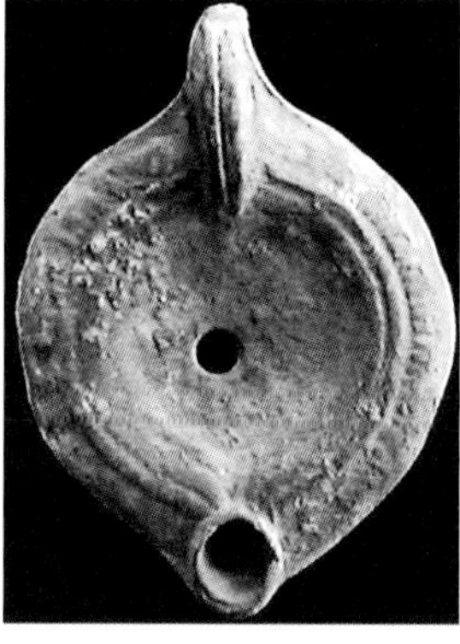

Fig. 12.28. Local round lamp with ovolos on rim of shoulder (97-L-66), from the Temple.

Fig. 12.29. Bird with grapes in beak (02-L-4) from Residential Quarter.

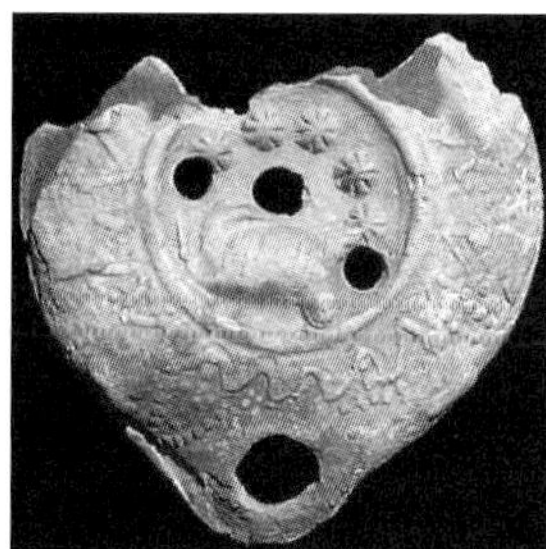

Fig. 12.30. Five stars/rosettes (02-L-3) from Residential Quarter.

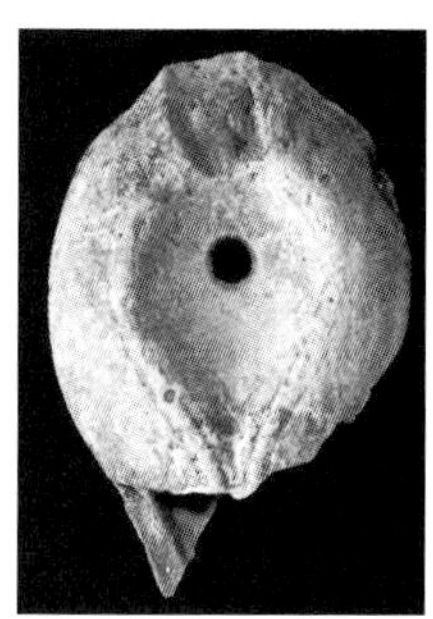

Fig. 12.31. Pear-shaped lamp (02-L-12) from Upper Temenos.

Fig. 12.34. Slipper lamp with vestigial knob handle (05-L-5) from Upper Temenos.

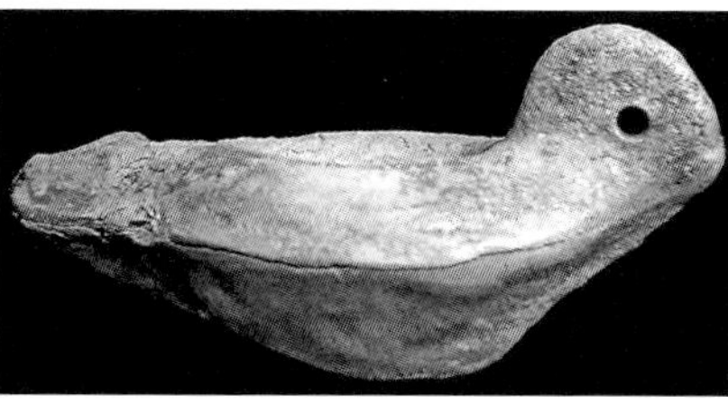

Figs. 12.32-12.33. Pear-shaped lamp (98-LB-33) from collapse of a pillar bracing the Ridge Church foundation.

Comparanda: Broneer type XXV and Loeschcke VIII; Rosenthal and Sivan 1978, 85-89; 'Amr 1987, 326, Type 6, pls. 27-28; Bailey 1988, 281 no. Q2307-9, dated last quarter of 1st to beginning of 3rd c. A.D.; Hadad 2002, 16-20, Type 7, dated late 1st through 2nd c. A.D.

15. Roman round lamp[11] (fig. 12.26)

Rounded with a broad shoulder rim, slightly depressed discus and central filling-hole. Rounded nozzle. Raised handle at the rear, sometimes perforated. Rim can be plain or impressed with vegetal or geometric shapes. Often coated with a red or reddish-brown slip. The Roman round lamp is present in abundance in the Petra area, both in imported and locally copied examples. 94-P-15 (fig. 12.26) is finely moulded, with traces of slip and a vegetal border.

Comparanda: Broneer type XXV. Loeschcke VII, dated from mid- to third quarter of the 1st c. A.D. Hayes 1980, 51, no. 231; Crelier 1995, 144, no. 135, pl. XIX.

---

11 Negev (1986, 132) included the double-axe type (our Type 14) in this group.

16. Locally-made round lamp (figs. 12.27-12.28)

A local version of no. 15 and a most popular type. Compared to the imported versions, the nozzles are less ornate and the lamps are not slipped. The size of the filling-hole varies (smaller during the 1st c. A.D., becoming much larger by the 3rd c. A.D.). 02-L-10 (fig. 12.27), dated to the second half of the 1st c. A.D., bears a close resemblance to the imported lamps. 97-L-66 (fig. 12.28) is typical of the later, locally-made and plainer, round lamps.

Comparanda: Broneer type XXV; Negev 1986, 133, no. 1156, dated from beginning of the 2nd to 3rd c. A.D.; Crelier 1995, 145, no. 138, dated from 2nd to 3rd c. A.D.; Hammond 1973, 36, 48, no. 138; Rosenthal and Sivan 1978, 98, no. 399, dated to 1st c. A.D.; Khairy 1990, 12, dated from last quarter of 1st c. B.C. to second half of 1st c. A.D.; Zanoni 1996, 317, no. 11, dated to mid-2nd c. A.D.

Early to Late Byzantine lamps (4th-7th c. A.D.)

17. Zoological motif (figs. 12.29-12.30)

Two lamps possibly imported from Egypt and dated to the 5th-6th c. A.D.

02-L-4, from the Residential Quarter, with a bird motif (fig. 12.29), preserving a partial discus featuring a stylized bird facing left with a bunch of grapes in its beak. Bunches of grapes around the shoulder rim; three small concentric circles over the nozzle. One small filling-hole. Discus coated with a reddish-brown slip on both sides.

Comparanda: Broneer type XXV. Rosenthal and Sivan 1978, 41, 42, nos. 163 and 167, are similar, both featuring birds on the discus with a decorated rim and dated to second third of the 1st through the 2nd c. A.D. This date may be too early for our example due to its proximity to the following lamp, which also features grapes on its shoulder rim and is more firmly dated to the Early Byzantine period. Rosenthal-Heginbottom (1981, 114) describes three lamps from Beit Nattif decorated with birds and bunches of grapes, a motif that survived through the Byzantine period.

02-L-3, from the Residential Quarter, with animal motif (fig. 12.30), having a highly decorated shoulder rim with bunches of grapes and a zig-zag border around the slightly depressed discus on which is an animal (a lamb?) in raised relief. In the field below are 5 rosettes or stars. Three small filling-holes are punched around the animal. In contrast to the normal conventions, the animal has its head towards the nozzle.

Comparanda: similar lamps in Rosenthal and Sivan 1978, 65 no. 267, dated to the Early Byzantine period; Bailey 1988, 266 no. Q2201 MLA, pl. 51, fig. 71, dated from the 5th through 6th c. A.D.

18. Pear-shaped lamp with tongue on nozzle (figs. 12.31-12.33)

A marriage of the popular round lamp with the Byzantine slipper lamp, it has a small filling-hole as found on lamps of the 1st c. A.D. but a slipper shape that is typical of the 4th-c. A.D. local lamps. Ovoid, depressed discus bordered by incised ridge, which extends like a tongue onto the nozzle. Handle raised and ribbed. Flattened base.

02-L-12 (fig. 12.31) has a broken nozzle and missing handle, from the Upper Temenos. 98-LB-33 (figs. 12.32-12.33) was found in the débris of a pillar bracing the foundation of the Ridge Church.[12] Vessels, including lamps, were often placed within the foundations of buildings in the Late Roman period[13] as apotropaic offerings, and this lamp may well have served such a purpose; it provides a *terminus post quem* for the foundation of the church.

Comparanda: Rosenthal and Sivan 1978, 98 no. 400, classified as Nabataean; Zayadine 1982, 371-72, fig. 5, nos. 3 and 8, dated 3rd-4th c. A.D.; Bailey 1988, 415, no. Q3305, pl. 122, a similar lamp dated 4th-5th c. A.D.

19. Slipper or candlestick lamp with knob handle (fig. 12.34)

Due to its elongated pear-shape, this type is known as a slipper lamp; because the nozzle is often decorated with a symbol resembling a branched candlestick or palm fronds, it is also known

12 Bikai and Perry 2001, 59.

13 Negev *et al.* 2005, 294.

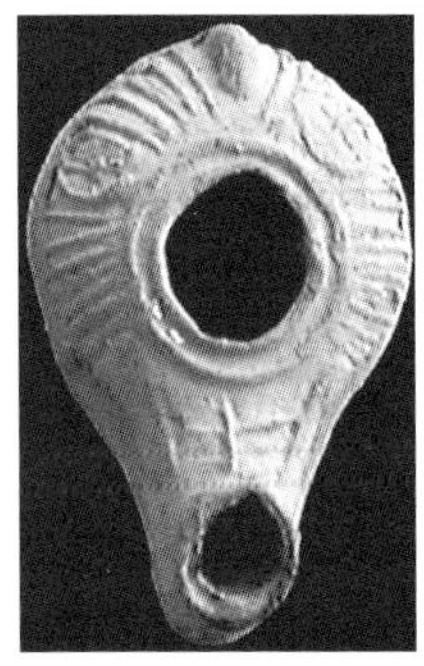

Fig. 12.35 Slipper lamp with cross and spoked wheels (98-L-34) from Lower Temenos.

Fig. 12.36. Slipper lamp with raised dots (98-L-6) from Propylaeum.

Fig. 12.37 Slipper lamp base with 'three fingers' potter's mark (04-L-9) from Lower Temenos.

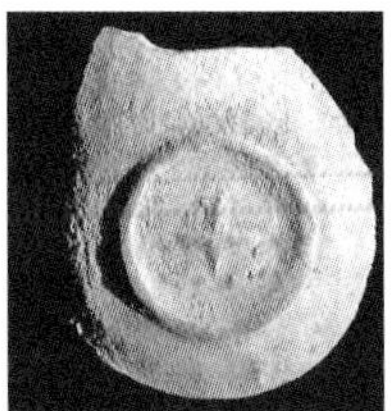

Fig. 12.38. Slipper lamp base with cross in center of base ring (04-L-8) from Lower Temenos.

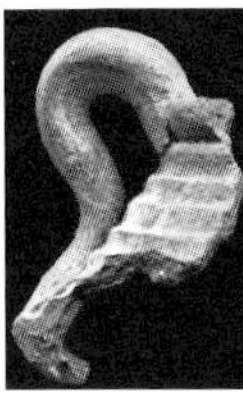

Fig. 12.39. Wheelmade boot-shaped lamp (96-L-50) from the Temple.

Fig. 12.40. Wheelmade boot-shaped lamp (99-LB-31) from a drainpipe on the North Ridge.

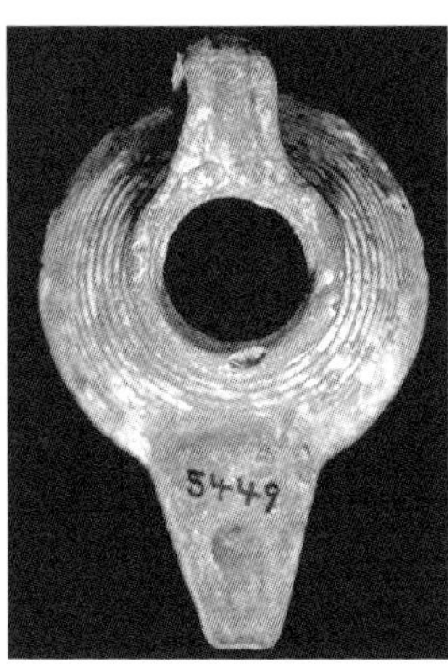

Fig. 12.41. Wheelmade boot-shaped lamp (1907.64. 185) in Semitic Museum, Harvard University.

Fig. 12.42. Umayyad ovoid-shaped lamp (00-L-3) from Upper Temenos.

as a candlestick lamp. Half volutes are also common. The rest of the body is decorated with ridges emanating from the large filling-hole, which is marked by an incised ridge. A raised ring marks the base. The Nabataean version is smaller than those found outside the kingdom and has slightly concave sides between nozzle and filling-hole. It usually has a vestigial knob handle at the rear; see our lamp 05-L-5 (fig. 12.34). 04-L-9 bears the 'three fingers' potter's mark on its base (cf. Type 22, fig. 12.37 for this detail).

Comparanda (all dates are A.D.): at Jerusalem: Aharoni 1956, 108 fig. 4.2, dated 5th-6th c.; Magness 1993, 250 Form 2, dated second half of 4th through 6th c. In Samaria: Crowfoot 1957, 376, fig. 89.5, dated from second half of 4th c. Pella: Smith 1973, 219, pl. 66 no. 369, dated 6th c. Petra: Horsfield *et al.* 1941, 137, pl. VI.5, dated 4th c.; Khairy 1990, 20, nos. 41-48; Zanoni 1996, 320-22, no. 14-29, dated 4th-5th c. Hadad 2002, 66-67 refers to the candlestick lamp at Beit Shean which is similar to that found on Nabataean sites and dates it to the 5th through 8th c.

20. Slipper lamp with crosses and/or spoked wheels (fig. 12.35)

Related to Type 19, it features the cross symbol or a cross within a wheel on the body or nozzle. The practice of depicting the cross, in any form, is thought to have begun in the mid-4th c. A.D.[14] 98-L-34 (fig. 12.35) features the 'three fingers' potter's mark on the base (cf. Type 22, fig. 12.37 for this detail).

Comparanda (all dates are A.D.): Horsfield *et al.* 1941, 159 pl. XXIX, 239, dated 3rd through 4th c. (Petra); Rosenthal and Sivan 1978, 112, dated 4th through 5th c.; Khairy 1990, 20 no. 42; Zanoni 1996, 323 nos. 30-31, found in conjunction with a coin hoard of the 4th c.

14 Tzaferis 1971, 23.

21. Slipper lamp with raised dots (fig. 12.36)

Related to Types 19 and 20, it is decorated with both radial ridges and raised dots; often spoked wheels are included. 98-L-6 includes both.

Comparanda: Khairy 1990, 19, no. 44, fig. 19 (Petra); Zanoni 1996, 332, nos. 30-31; dated 4th through 5th c. A.D.

22. Slipper lamps with potters' marks (figs. 12.37-12.38)

Related to Types 19, 20 and 21. A mark resembling an arrowhead in the form of 'three fingers' or short ridges extending upwards is usually found on the lower rear above the ridged base ring. Khairy suggested that the 'fingers' could either represent the Trinity[15] or simply be a potter's mark. 04-L-9 (fig. 12.37) shows the mark, which is peculiar to Petra. The ridged base ring of another slipper lamp, 04-L-8 (fig. 12.38) shows a 4-armed cross, another unusual potter's mark.

Comparanda for 'three fingers' lamp: Horsfield *et al.* 1941, 137, dated 4th c. A.D.; Saller 1957, 52-53, dated 4th through 6th c. A.D.; Khairy 1990, 20, nos. 41-43, dated to the Byzantine period.

Late Byzantine-Umayyad lamps (late 5th-8th c. A.D.)

23. Wheelmade boot-shaped lamp (figs. 12.39-12.41)

Also known as a cone-shaped lamp. R. A. S. Macalister (1912) gave it the soubriquet 'boot shape', a good description for the type when viewed in profile. It either has a ribbed body, tapering towards the top, or a plain body with a bulbous base which narrows as it projects upwards to end in a flat flaring rim. The ribbed version predominates in the region of Petra, like our lamp 96-L-50 found in the Temple (fig. 12.39), consisting of the nozzle and a typical handle, which were handmade and attached after the body had been removed from the wheel. A more complete version is shown in fig. 12.40, found at the North Ridge site. Figure 12.41 shows a complete example in the Semitic Museum.

Comparanda (all dates are A.D.): Aharoni 1956, 108, fig. 4.3, dated 5th through 6th c.; Rosenthal and Sivan 1978, 122 (Variant A) and Khairy 1990, 21, both dated it to the end of the Byzantine and early Islamic periods (6th-8th c.); Zanoni 1996, 329, gives a *terminus post quem* of 419 (the last earthquake to devastate ez Zantur); Hadad 2002, 72, nos. 317-18, dated late Byzantine through early Umayyad, 5th-8th c.

24. Umayyad ovoid lamp with horror vacui *decoration* (fig. 12.42)

Islamic type, body has a pointed oval shape and is a double cone in profile. Large central filling-hole surrounded by a high ridge; a second ridge extends on to the nozzle and around the wick-hole, forming a straight shallow channel. Handle can be either a cone, a small knob handle, or high and vertical, sometimes perforated. May have base-ring with a potter's mark or other symbols, or base may be completely flat and unmarked. Decoration (e.g., diagonal bands with raised dots, vegetal relief, animal motifs including chimerae, all related to the ornamental style popular under the Umayyad and Abbasid caliphs) covers the entire rim.[16] 00-L-3 (fig. 12.42), found in the Upper Temenos, exhibits the *horror vacui*.

Comparanda (all dates are A.D.): Crowfoot and Fitzgerald 1929, pl. 17.6, 36-38; Kennedy 1963, pl. XXIX types 23-24; Magness 1993, 258 Form 5, dated 8th-10th c.; Hadad 2002, 105 Type 37, dated 8th-11th c.

Distribution of lamps through the excavations

Tables 12.1-2 show the occurrence of the various types in the different areas of the excavation.

---

15 Khairy 1990, 20. The decree of the Council of Nicaea in A.D. 365, which established the Trinity of God, the Father, Son and Holy Ghost, may have persuaded a local Petraean potter to place a moulded 'thrice blessed' mark on the base of the slipper lamp, in which case the lamp would date after the A.D. 363 earthquake.

16 Cf. Rosenthal and Sivan 1978, 129-35.

TABLE 12.1
LAMP TYPES AND COUNT AT THE SITE

Type No.	*Lamp Type*	*Time Period*	*Total*	*Open Context Reference*
1	Delphiniform and related lamps	Second half of 2nd – 1st c. B.C.	8	1, 2GT
2	Syro-Palestinian	1st c. B.C. – 1st c. A.D.	1	3 GT
3	Lamp filler	1st c. B.C. – 1st c. A.D.	1	18 GT
4	Apprentice	Second half of 1st c. B.C. – 1st c. A.D.	3	8GT
5	Ptolemaic Egyptian palmette	Second half of 1st c. B.C. – 1st c. A.D.	3	4GT
6	Herodian	1st c. B.C. – mid-1st c. A.D.	3	5GT
7	Roman rosette	Last quarter of 1st c. B.C. – A.D. 106	2	20GT
8	Locally-made decorated rosette	1st c. A.D.	13	9GT
9	Roman decorated discus	End of 1st c. B.C. – 1st c. A.D.	33	21,24, 25GT
10	Locally-made decorated discus	1st c. A.D.	9	14, 15GT
11	Nabataean volute type A	Second quarter – end of 1st c. A.D.	7	10GT
12	Nabataean volute type B	Second quarter – end of 1st c. A.D.	35	11GT
13	Nabataean volute type B - inscribed	Second quarter – end of 1st c. A.D.	1	12GT
14	Double axes shoulder decoration	Last quarter of 1st – beginning of 3rd c. A.D.	5	6GT
15	Roman round	1st-3rd c. A.D.	17	22, 23GT
16	Locally-made round	1st-3rd c. A.D.	65	13, 16, 17GT
17	Zoological motif	2nd-5th c. A.D.	2	7GT
18	Pear-shaped with tongue	3rd-4th c. A.D.	1	27GT
19	Slipper with knob or tongue handle	A.D. 350-550	177	28GT
20	Slipper with crosses and/or spoked wheels	4th-5th c. A.D.	10	29GT
21	Slipper with raised dots	4th-5th c. A.D.	3	30GT
22	Slipper with potter's mark	4th-6th c. A.D.	8	31GT
23	Wheelmade boot-shaped	5th-8th c. A.D.	6	32GT
24	Ovoid-shaped with *horror vacui* decoration	8th-11th c. A.D.	3	33GT
	Unidentified fragments		210	19, 26, 34GT
	Total lamp fragments at Great Temple site		**626**	

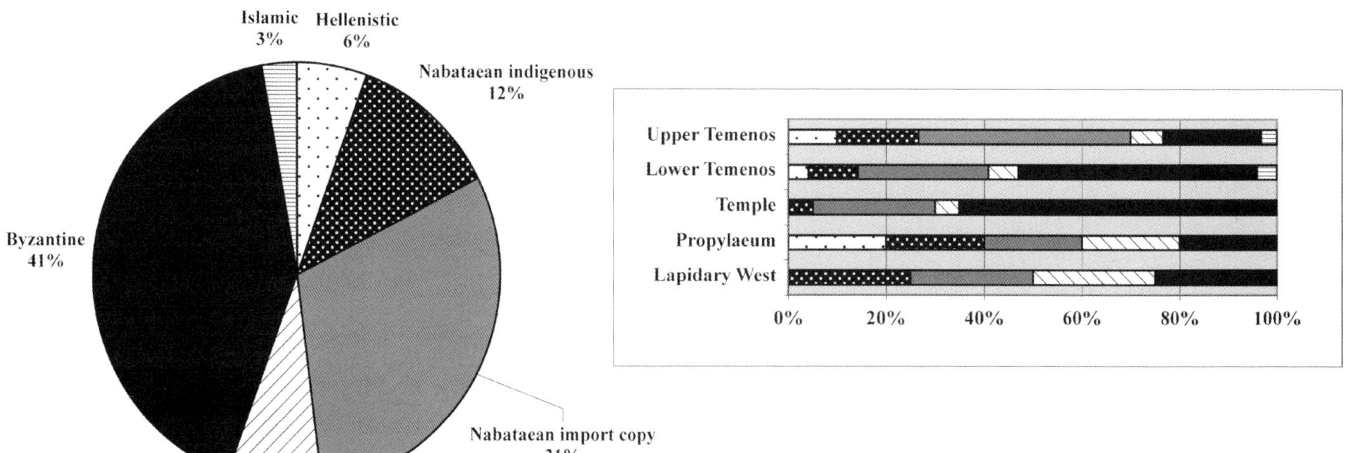

TABLE 12.2
APPROXIMATE PERCENTAGES OF LAMP TYPES AT THE SITE

Hellenistic	*Nabataean indigenous*	*Imported Roman*	*Nabataean local copies of Roman*	*Byzantine*	*Islamic*
6%	12%	7%	31%	41%	3%

Discussion

Only a small quantity of Hellenistic lamps and fragments (6%) were found, mostly from the Propylaeum. Nabataean examples (43%) comprised both Nabataean indigenous (12%) and Nabataean local copies of Roman imported pieces (31%). Imported Roman fragments comprised only 7%. Byzantine lamp fragments are the next largest group to Nabataean (41%), and Islamic the smallest (3%). One would expect to find a large number from the last period of occupation (Byzantine) particularly as the building was demolished by a series of earthquakes, a most severe one occurring in A.D. 363. Such catastrophes often cause a 'Pompeii effect', denying the occupants the opportunity to remove their possessions (Schiffer 1987, 92). Occupation probably ceased by the end of the 6th c. A.D.

Cultural change during the 1st c. A.D.

Nabataean indigenous lamps, Nabataean locally-made copies of Roman lamps, and imported Roman lamps were all in use during the 1st c. A.D. While use of the first and third of these ceased by the end of the 1st c. A.D., Nabataean locally-made copies continued in use for at least another century. Evidently the popularity of Nabataean indigenous lamps and Roman imported lamps waned as Nabataean locally-made copies of imported Roman lamps came on the scene. This cultural change is replicated elsewhere in Petra during the same period.[17] Many examples of the locally-made copies have been found at the North Ridge site, across the wadi from the Great Temple. Economic factors may have been involved: lamps made locally would not be at risk of breaking during transport by sea or by caravan, and they would be less expensive when manufactured from local clays.

Why, however, did the popular indigenous volute lamp also begin to disappear by the end of the 1st c. A.D., around the same time as the delicate Nabataean finewares? The volute lamp (figs. 12.20-12.23) was replaced by the more robust local version of the round lamp (figs. 12.27-12.28), just as the finewares were superseded by sturdier cups and bowls which lacked the earlier elegant ornamentation. This change occurred around the time of the Roman annexation, resulting in the degeneration in the style of the ceramic corpus, according to S. G. Schmid.[18] Patricia Bikai, on the other hand, suggests that the delicacy of manufacture made the earlier ceramics too impractical, and that the heavier, larger vessels were an improvement, rather than marking a degeneration of form and style.[19]

The function of lamps at our site

The lamp was a multi-functional vessel serving many purposes besides lighting households. It had both secular and sacred uses and was employed wherever extra light was required, whether in shops, theaters or the mines. Lamps also served as offerings in temples and sanctuaries and were carried in processions of different kinds; frequently they were deposited as grave goods.

Since the archaeologists have not yet established the primary nature of the Great Temple site – whether it was a sacred or a secular building (or perhaps both) – we do not know if the Nabataean and Roman lamps found there would have been used mainly for religious purposes. Pagan practices continued in many places after the conversion of Constantine; relatively few temples were closed and new temples were still being built until the end of the 4th c. A.D.[20] A kind of syncretism was also practiced at Petra, where Epiphanius of Salamis notes that many of the inhabitants still revered Dusares, the chief Nabataean god, but now included his virgin mother Chaamou in their worship.[21]

---

17 Barrett 2008, 137.
18 Schmid 2003, 81.
19 Bikai 2001, 67.
20 Cameron 1993, 57.
21 Epiphanius II.51.22.9-11 (transl. Williams, 1994).

> And they carry the image itself seven times round the innermost shrine with flutes, tambourines and hymns, hold a feast and take it back down to its place underground. And when you ask them what this mystery means, they reply that today at this hour Kore – that is, the virgin – gave birth to Aeo.
>
> This also goes on in the city of Petra, in the idolatrous temple there … They praise the virgin with hymns in the Arab language and call her Chaamou – that is Kore, or virgin … And the child who is born of her they call Dusares, that is, "only son of the Lord". And this is also done that night in the city of Elusa, as it is there in Petra, and in Alexandria.

Some churches are known at Petra to be in the proximity of the Great Temple site. Church construction on the S side of the Colonnaded Street is poorly documented, but N. Khairy has described an apse of a church found in the Al-Katute excavations on the S side of Wadi Musa[22] where similarities to the reconstruction work at the Great Temple exist in a pavement of small hexagons and in the re-use of Nabataean architecture to build the church. However, a large number of Byzantine lamps found in the area of the West Exedra in the Lower Temenos may provide direct evidence of religious practice at the Great Temple site in the 4th-5th c. A.D. Possibly the West Exedra served as a chapel during the Byzantine period since the apsidal forms would have appealed to the Christian worshipper.[23] Many luxurious decorative elements were found within its apse: they included an amethyst tessera, cut and polished slabs of marble and porphyry, and colored floor slabs or *opus sectile*.[24] A concentration of 14 glass lamp fragments, dating to the 4th-5th c. A.D., was also found within the West Exedra (see chapt. 15); some came from hanging lamps, fixtures often used in churches.[25] We recall that Z. Fiema found a large quantity of glass, including fragments from oil lamps, at the Petra Church.[26] Of the many (74) Byzantine ceramic lamp fragments found in the West Exedra, three (94-P-14, 95-L-126, 95-L-132) have decorative crosses inside wheels on their shoulders that resemble Christian symbols (fig. 12.35). Some Byzantine small slipper lamps have arrow-shaped ridging on their bases (04-L-9, fig. 12.37), and this potter's mark is sometimes compared to the 'three fingers or thrice blessed' symbol of the Trinity (Khairy 1990, 20). Another example of this type (98-L-34; fig. 12.36) was found in the East Exedra, including a complete Byzantine slipper lamp (98-L-3) with two wheel crosses on the rear shoulder and the 'three fingers' potter's mark on its base; a complete slipper lamp (98-L-4) with a herringbone design on the shoulders; and 14 lamp fragments ranging from Nabataean to Roman in date, and locally-made copies of Roman round lamps. Whether the West Exedra was used as a small Byzantine chapel from the late 4th through the beginning of the 6th c. is speculative, but it is a candidate for that kind of religious practice.

---

22 Khairy 1990, 5.

23 It was common practice to re-use a former sacred site for the new religon: Cameron 1993, 62.

24 Basile 1998, 200.

25 Cf. Whitehouse 1997, 193, no. 339.

26 Fiema 2003, 247.

13

The coroplastic artifacts: terracotta figurines, plaques, masks and vessels

Christopher A. Tuttle

The excavations recovered 93[1] fragments of clay coroplastic artifacts, of which 79 can be identified and classified with some certainty; the rest are too fragmentary for identification.[2] Their classification follows the new typology for Nabataean coroplastic objects presented in my 2009 Ph.D. dissertation, a typology based on 777 published and unpublished artifacts (the latter all found in excavations at Petra and in the Negev desert). That was a first attempt to present a classification for all types of moulded and modelled Nabataean clay objects. It had 9 major coroplastic types and 36 subtypes, some further subdivided into classes. The coroplastic corpus from the present excavations includes examples from 7 of those types, further divided into 17 subtypes, and a representative sample of them is presented here.

Chronology and contexts

An accurate chronology for Nabataean coroplastic objects is lacking.[3] The main difficulty is that each object has at least three dates associated with its particular history:[4] the first is when the type first appears; the second is when the artifact in question was created; the third concerns when the artifact entered the depositional record. For Nabataean coroplastic objects it is generally only possible to identify the date of their deposition. Rarely can we posit a date range for their manufacture since most coroplastic objects have not been published in their stratigraphic contexts with the associated artifacts. We are still in need of examples from secure stratigraphic contexts before we can begin to trace the history and evolution of the different types. Despite the fact that the contexts for most of the coroplastic pieces from our excavations were well documented, the collection has been able to contribute only minimally to the development of an overall chronology due to the site's location at the foot of a hill and its complex history of use and re-use, including recent agricultural activities. A majority of the artifacts derive from wash deposits, portions of which appear to have originated elsewhere on Ez Zantur. In a few instances pieces were recovered from deliberate fill or sedimentation deposits that yielded sufficiently consistent finds to suggest a date range. In other cases, the similarity of the decorative paint to that found on some later Nabataean fine wares might assist with dating.

Twenty-eight of the artifacts derive from contexts that suggest date-ranges for their final deposition. The catalogue at the end of this chapter includes 19 of these: no. 73 (figs. 13.32, 13.34-35) in a stratum probably of the 1st c. B.C.; no. 65, probably of the late 1st c. A.D.; nos. 7, 11 (fig. 13.11) and 32 of the 1st-3rd c. A.D.; nos. 20 and 22 perhaps of the late 1st-early 2nd c. A.D.; no. 27 (fig. 13.19) probably of the 1st-2nd c. A.D.; no. 34 of the 2nd c. A.D.; nos. 36 and 71 (fig. 13.31) of the 2nd-4th c. A.D.; no. 38 of the 1st-5th c. A.D.; and no. 44 of the 1st-4th c. A.D. Nine other objects with suggested date-ranges are not included in the catalogue: Tuttle 2009, cat. no. 262, inv. 05-P-16, perhaps of the 1st c. A.D.; Tuttle 2009, cat. no. 264, inv. 99-P-8, perhaps of the 1st-2nd c. A.D.; Tuttle 2009, cat. nos. 267-70, 292 and 294, inv. 05-P-5, 7, and 9 through 12) probably of the early 1st c. B.C.; Tuttle 2009, cat. no. 298 (inv. 04-P-9) probably of the 1st-2nd c. A.D.

---

1 An object presented in vol. 2, fig. 7.45a, as a possible figurine fragment is in fact a lamp.
2 These 13 can be seen in my dissertation and at www.opencontext.org, along with the entire typological framework. The online version also provides a comprehensive list of parallels for each artifact from the Great Temple site.
3 See the fuller discussion in Tuttle 2009, 120-23 and 234-40.
4 Burr Thompson 1963, 20.

Function and meaning

Although the Nabataeans were a literate society, virtually no texts are available to help us elucidate their own perspectives on their culture. Lacking such narratives as mythology, religious treatises, poetry or historical accounts, modern scholars have little to work with in attempting to reconstruct an allegorical framework in which to situate representational imagery in Nabataean material culture.[5] We therefore have to fall back on the objects themselves. In my dissertation I employed four methodological approaches to the data. The first involved thoroughly examining the visible manufacturing, representational, and use-related details through formal analysis. The second examined the mechanical characteristics of each object. The third classified the similarities, differences and interrelations of the object types. The fourth employed a new analytic model to try to narrow the range of plausible functions and meanings for each object type and subtype. This last took its lead from a model developed by P. Ucko[6] for analyzing prehistoric figurines from Egypt, Crete, mainland Greece, and the Near East. The model was subsequently developed by M. Voigt for studying objects from the Neolithic settlement at Hajji Firuz Tepe (Iran),[7] also touched upon for her work at Çatal Höyük (Turkey).[8] The "Ucko–Voigt model" defined 5 primary categories of function and meaning for prehistoric figurines: cultic figurines, vehicles of magic, didactic/teaching aids, human representations (living or dead), and toys. The lack of Nabataean texts creates a situation akin to studying the material cultures of preliterate societies, so a model developed for analyzing the possible functions and meaning of prehistoric material culture provides a good starting point. Yet we do possess a larger range of evidentiary sources to assist our contextualization of Nabataean artifacts than generally exists for prehistoric peoples, so the Ucko–Voigt model required expansion and elaboration before it could be applied to Nabataean objects. The new model thus provides 8 primary categories rather than the original five:

Cultic	Toys
Magic	Decorations
Didactic	Mementos
Representations	Practical.

Further, some of the main functional categories are divided into sub-categories to permit additional nuances of both function and meaning. The sub-categories are required not only because of the potential of additional evidentiary sources to provide insights, but also to encompass the possibility that distinct artifacts may have served a variety of purposes and conveyed a diversity of meanings during their functional life spans. In the catalogue below I have tried to apply this new cognitive model systematically in order to identify a range of probabilities for the function and meaning of the artifact types.[9]

Manufacturing techniques

Coroplasts created artifacts by moulding, modelling, or a combination of those. The choice of technique seems to have been determined by the nature of the artifact in question. Certain patterns may be discerned with respect to the techniques used by Nabataean coroplasts for different classes of objects.[10] Moulding is the predominant technique for anthropomorphic figurines throughout the corpus of Nabataean coroplastic objects. Human figurines made using a combination of moulding and modelling are infrequent, and modelling alone as the primary technique is rare. Nearly all

---

5 For the most thorough compilation of the data for Nabataean religion, see Healey 2001. For historical sources, see Hackl *et al.* 2003.

6 Ucko 1968.

7 Voigt 1983.

8 Voigt 2000.

9 The entire interpretative analytical model is presented in Tuttle 2009, 244-50. The suggestions of function and meaning presented here are summaries of the interpretations deemed to have the strongest probabilities. Longer discussions that include consideration of lesser probabilities are given in Tuttle 2009.

10 Tuttle 2009, 102-23.

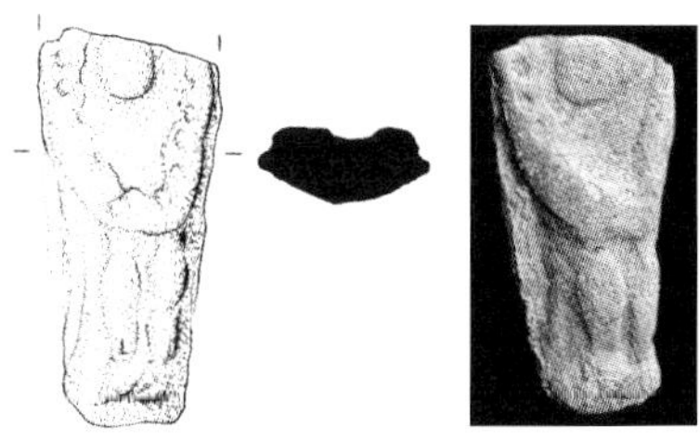

Fig. 13.1a-b. Type A.2.10, abstract figure (no. 19).

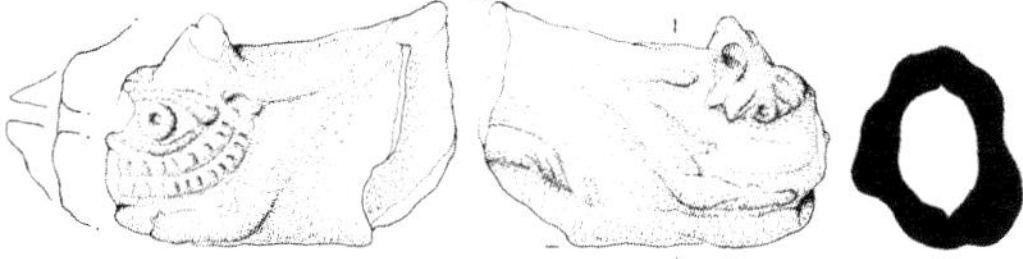

Fig. 13.3. Type F.4.1, vessel component, spout (no. 79).

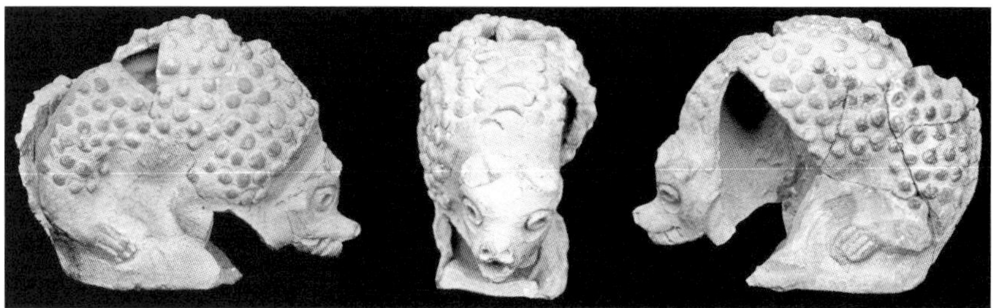

Fig. 13.2. Type C.9.2, hedgehog vessel (no. 73); see also figs. 13.32, 13.34 and 13.35.

Fig. 13.4. Type C.7.2, modelled quadruped vessel with fired paint (no. 71); see also fig. 13.31.

of the anthropomorphic figurines included here were made using moulds. Only one (no. 18; fig. 13.14) was entirely executed through modelling; another (no. 19; fig. 13.1a-b) involved modelling over a template made using an existing mould type. The techniques employed for the zoomorphic figurines and vessels is a little more varied. Throughout the Nabataean corpus only a few examples of horse or camel figurines were modelled or made with a combination of the two primary techniques, and all of the horse and camel figurines included here were manufactured using bi-valve molds. By contrast, all known figurines and some vessels depicting ibexes or other quadrupeds, including those in our catalogue, used modelling as the sole primary technique. Many of the ibex and other zoomorphic vessels, however, also used a combination of wheel-thrown bodies onto which the heads and limbs were modelled. The hedgehog vessel (fig. 13.2) used a combination of moulding and modelling. The other artifact types in our catalogue are all fashioned from moulds, as is the case throughout the Nabataean coroplastic corpus for both anthropomorphic and zoomorphic statuettes and masks/affixes. The known plaques are always made using mono-valve moulds. Moulding predominates when making vessel components: the vessel affix (no. 78; fig. 13.39) was made using a mono-valve mold, while the vessel spout (no. 79; fig. 13.3) was initially made in a bi-valve mold, but secondary modelling was employed apparently because of damage that occurred when it was removed from the mould.

Nabataean coroplasts utilized a variety of ancillary techniques to enhance their products.[11] They include appliqué, boring, excision, impression, incision, paring, and paint. We use the term "paint" to describe the application of any colour that can be distinguished as having been applied on top of the fabric of the original object. At present we only have instances of paints[12] which were applied to objects before they were fired, and thus became fired (e.g., fig. 13.4). The use by Nabataean coroplasts of (non-fired) paints, applied after an object was removed from the kiln, has not yet been demonstrated,[13] although it was a well-established practice in the Greek,[14] Hellenistic and Roman worlds. Some objects in our catalogue preserve evidence of materials that may have been non-fired paints: in two instances (no. 11 [fig. 13.11] and no. 78 [fig. 13.39]) traces of white substances adhere in grooves, but it has not been determined if these are non-fired paints or subsequent accretions during burial. No. 28 (fig. 13.20) shows patches of an orange-red substance on its belly, but it may be the flaking of a slip induced by the difference in coefficients between the clay fabric and the slip.

11 Tuttle 2009, 123-27.

12 Nos. 1, 27, 36, 40-41, 48-51, 61, 71 and 78.

13 Tuttle 2009, 125-27.

14 Higgins 1963, 11.

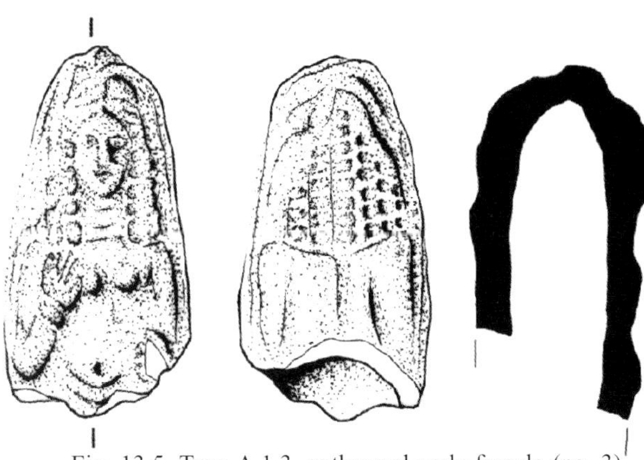

Fig. 13.5. Type A.1.3, enthroned nude female (no. 3) (1 : 1).

Fig. 13.6. Type A.1.1, standing draped female (no. 1) (1 : 1).

Fig. 13.7. Type A.1.3, enthroned nude female (no. 4) (1 : 1).

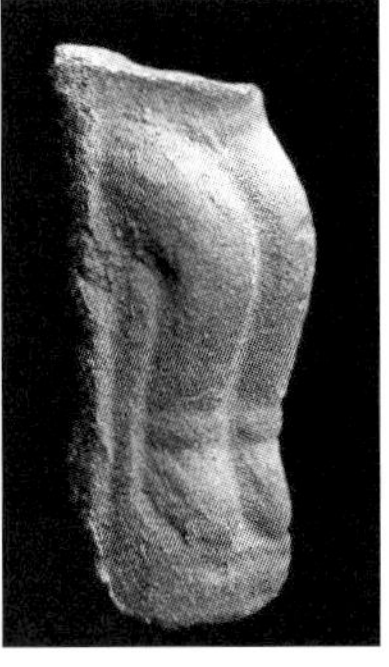

Fig. 13.8. Type A.1.3, enthroned nude female (no. 5) (1 : 1).

Fig. 13.9. Type A.1.4, enthroned draped female (no. 6) (1 : 1).

Fig. 13.10. Type A.2.1b, camel rider (no. 10).

Type series

A. Anthropomorphic

1. Female (nos. 1-9), divided into 4 subtypes: (i) standing draped females; (ii) enthroned nude females, (iii) enthroned draped females, and (iv) enthroned females, details uncertain. The enthroned nude are the most frequent, followed closely by the enthroned draped and the details uncertain. The standing draped figurine is without any direct parallel.

Female figurines are the second commonest type in Nabataean contexts, only slightly surpassed by horse figurines.[15] Due to their relative uniformity, small sizes and ease of portability, the majority of the female figurines may well have served as personal cult items. They could have played devotional rôles in the home or workspace, or even while a person was moving around; possibly their owners believed that protection was afforded by being in close proximity to the image of a deity. They could also have served as dedicatory, petitionary, propitiatory or apotropaic votives.

(i) The fragmentary standing draped female (fig. 13.5) is dressed and cradling in her left arm an item which could be a feather, palm frond or wheat stalk. The slight *contrapposto* stance and apparent attempt to render the mantle as windblown may suggest that the figure is to be thought of as

15 Tuttle 2009, 145.

in motion, but it may instead be standing on a pedestal. It belongs to our category of "Representations", whether as an emblematic personage (e.g., a maenad) or an icon of a deity. It bears some resemblance to a possible maenad from Oboda.[16] This may be supported by imagery in and around Petra drawn from Dionysiac cult activity.[17] Alternatively, the item being cradled and the possible presence of a pedestal may point to an icon which served a cultic function for its owner. If the item is a stalk of grain, a Nabataean version of a syncretization of Syrian Atargatis with the city Tyche may be intended. Atargatis-Tyche sometimes holds a *cornucopia* or stalks of grain to symbolize "wealth and well-being".[18] Or it may represent a syncretization of the Nabataean al-Lat and/or al-'Uzza with Tyche, or simply Tyche herself.[19] Possibilities are that it was personal and devotional, that it served in a dedicatory or petitionary capacity as a votive, or that it was an iconic decoration in a house, shop or shrine.

(ii) The enthroned nude females (figs. 13.6-13.7) are fairly standardized, with a nude figure, right hand raised and left resting in her lap (perhaps clasping an object). She is seated on a throne, her feet on a footstool. The figures wear bracelets, anklets and footware (sandals or slippers) (figs. 13.6-13.8). Their divinity is suggested by the nudity,[20] the right hand raised in a probable blessing[21] and the use of a throne.[22] Previous scholars plausibly suggested that the enthroned nude demales depict the Nabataean goddess al-Lat/al-'Uzza.[23] The nudity may be a standard component of this deity's identification or possibly refer to an aspect such as fertility.[24] The relative frequency of this subtype is likely to permit the eventual development of a Nabataean coroplastic type series.

(iii) Enthroned draped females and (iv) Enthroned females, type uncertain, are probably also images of goddesses. In the case of the former (fig. 13.9), the type may be intended to be a replica of a known statue of a deity, perhaps a seated Isis similar to the two rupestral images in the Sadd al-Mreriyyeh in Wadi Siyyagh[25] and in Wadi Wigheit/Waqit/Abu Olleiqa on the route to Jebel Haroun.[26] Functionally, this type may have served in funerary cult activity, for in two of the rare instances where figurines have been found in tombs or burials they were of this type. Thus the type may have served a communal cultic[27] or an apotropaic/dedicatory rôle for the deceased.[28]

2. Male (nos. 10-16), divided into 3 subtypes: (i) camel riders, (ii) bearded males with diadem, and (iii) nude youths standing. The "nude youths standing" type is the third most common subject in the Nabataean corpus (following the horses and enthroned nude female). In general, male figurines exist in a greater range of forms than females.[29]

(i) The camel rider figurine (fig. 13.10) can be readily identified by comparison with previously known examples.[30] All of the figurines or statuettes from the Nabataean milieu that depict human riders on camels and horses may be classified as emblematic representations of people, although the specific activity is not certainly identifiable. They may have been suitable as martial, sporting

---

16 Rosenthal-Heginbottom 1997, pl. 3, 30a.
17 Bikai *et al.* 2008; Patrich 2005; Healey 2001.
18 Lindner and Zangenberg 1993; Bilde 1990 and Hörig 1979.
19 Images of Tyche are known at Petra: Basile 1997 and 1999; Meshorer 1975.
20 Frankfort *et al.* 1940; Gorgerat 2006; *contra* Pritchard 1943, 85; cf. Bahrani 1996 and Bonfante 1989.
21 Parr 1990; El-Khouri 2002; Gorgerat 2006.
22 Thrones, or *mwtb'*, have been identified as playing some rôle in Nabataean religious iconography: see Will 1986, Zayadine 1990 and Healey 2001. For the wider context of enthroned goddesses, see Jung 1982.
23 Parlasca 1990 and 1993; El-Khouri 2002.
24 El-Khouri 2002 and 2007.
25 Merklein and Wenning 1998 and 2001; Janif 2004.
26 Parr 1962; Linder 1989 and 2003.
27 Farajat and Al-Nawafleh 2005, fig. 24E, which is a Type A.1.4 enthroned draped female figurine found in a tomb beneath the al-Khazneh façade in Petra.
28 Tuttle 2009, no. 025, from Tomb 2 on Petra's North Ridge.
29 Tuttle 2009, pp. 262.
30 Parlasca 1990, 1991 and 1998; id. *et al.* 1997; El-Khouri 2002; Bignasca 1996; Parr 1990.

Fig. 13.11. Type A.2.2a, bearded male, with diadem (no. 11) (1 : 1).

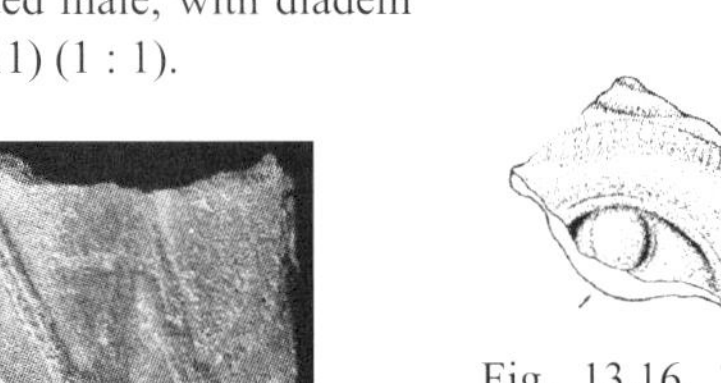

Fig. 13.15. Type B.1.1, statuette feet (no. 22).

Fig. 13.12. Type A.2.5a, nude youth, standing (no. 12)

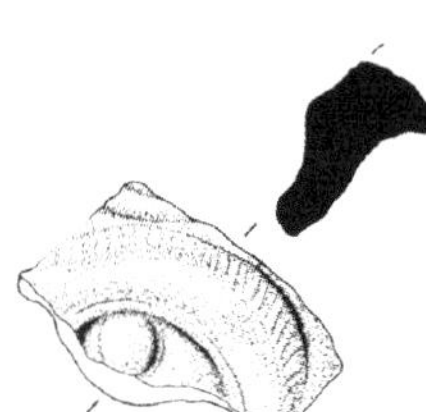

Fig. 13.16. Type B.2.4, mask/architectural affix (no. 23).

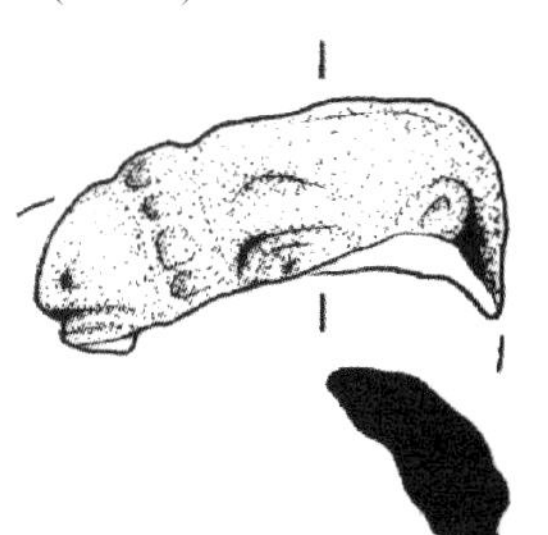

Fig. 13.18. Type C.2.1a, camel head (no. 25) (1 : 1).

Fig. 13.13. Reverse of Type A.2.5a, nude youth, standing, with a vent hole that may be intended to represent the anus (no. 14) (1 : 1).

Fig. 13.19. Type C.2.2a, camel with tack and weapons, without stand (no. 27) (1 : 1).

Fig. 13.14. Possible Type A.3.2, musician, individual (no. 18).

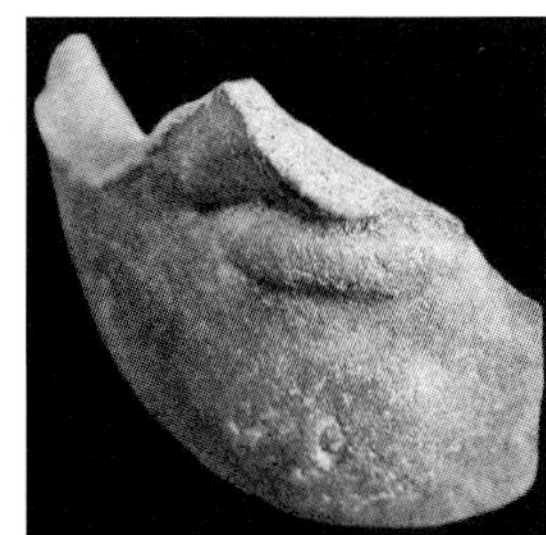

Fig. 13.17. Type B.2.4, mask/architectural affix (no. 24) (1 : 1).

or trade-related mementos. It is also possible that they served as toys since a camel-rider statuette was a rare grave good found in a child's burial in a tomb on the Me'eisra ridge at Petra.[31]

(ii) The bearded male with diadem (fig. 13.11) is currently unique. Possibly it is a portrait or emblematic representation of a notable; the diadem across the forehead and apparent presence of a lip ring could suggest a divinized king.[32] More plausibly it is an iconic representation of a deity such as Dushara.

(iii) The nude youth standing is present in several examples (e.g., figs. 13.12-13.13). Nudity, the position of the arms, and the presence of a *lunula* pendant necklace are ubiquitous characteristics, probably in an iconic representation of a deity. Like the enthroned nude females, the naked boys always have their right hand raised (in a gesture of blessing(?), the left possibly clasps an object against the abdomen, and they wear bracelets. The inverted lunate necklace distinguishes the fragments of this type from the female examples. It has been interpreted as a signifier of childhood[33] or a symbol of lunar worship,[34] but we do not know enough about Nabataean religion to be sure. Based on the consistency of the iconography and frequency of the type, we suggest that a deity is represented, but the objects could have served personal cult, devotional and/or apotropaic purposes; they may also have served as votives.

3. Musicians, in 2 subtypes: (i) musicians, group, and (ii) musicians, individual. The musician figurines can be considered emblematic representations of people; they may also have served as decorations or as mementos from performances.

---

31 Horsfield and Horsfield 1938, 113.

32 See Healey 2001, 147-51 and 173-74, for discussions on the deification of Nabataean kings.

33 Parlasca 1993; El-Khouri 2002.

34 Parr 1990.

(i) Musicians, group (cat. no. 17) is recognisable from the parallels.[35] It is the rightmost figure in a group, but we do not know if it belonged to a duo or trio (both are known) or which instrument is held.

(ii) Musician, individual (fig. 13.14), but there is some uncertainty because of the break along the left side of the figure, which could instead mean that it was the leftmost figure in a group. At present this is the only published example that may be of the musician, individual, subtype.[36]

4. Anthropomorphic pieces of uncertain identity. All three are without parallels in the known corpus.

(i) The clothed figure (95-P-13, cat. no. 19) might be a hermaphrodite, as it seems to have breasts yet also wears the *lunula* pendant that is otherwise known only in the male nude youths, standing. If a deity, it may be an iconic representation or some sort of cultic object.

(ii) Cat. no. 20 could be a goddess, such as Aphrodite, or it might represent an iconic figure or cult object, or even an emblematic representation of a person as an aesthetic decoration.

(iii) The unique abstract figure (cat. no. 21, figs. 13.1a-b) was created by modifying an object taken from a mould of the enthroned nude females subtype. The subject matter is unidentified.

B. Anthropomorphic: other artifact types

One fragment belongs in the "statuettes, feet" and two in the "masks/architectural affixes" categories. They can readily be considered decorative, possibly iconic or apotropaic.

(i) Cat. no. 22 (fig. 13.15) could be part of an image of a deity that served a communal or personal cultic purpose, even a copy of a particular statue, or it may be of a notable personage.

(ii) Cat. nos. 23-24 (figs. 13.16-13.17) may have been suspended by a cord or attached directly to a surface to serve a decorative function. The subjects are probably iconic, emblematic or portrait representations.

C. Zoomorphic figurines and vessels

This type includes 50 objects (cat. nos. 24-73), more than half of all the coroplastic artifacts recovered from our excavations, which is in line with the general pattern with Nabataean coroplastic objects, of which 43% are zoomorphic figurines or vessels.[37] They are divided into 5 subtypes. All can be placed in our "representations, environmental" category since all the animals depicted were known in the Nabataean environs. All could have served simply as decorations or as toys, though it is possible that some could have been used as dedicatory or petitionary votives or in sympathetic magic.

(i) Camels: heads, or camels with tack and weapons without stands

Despite the fragmentary state of the three pieces (cat. nos. 25-27; (figs. 13.18-13.19), they can be identified by comparison with known parallels. Nearly all of the moulded Nabataean camels that are well enough preserved display weaponry mounted on the animal's tack.[38] It usually consists of a sword, shield and quiver. The tip of a sword scabbard can be seen on no. 27 (fig. 13.19). They never show any evidence of having had a separate rider figure (nor are such figures known). No pieces show the animals as beasts of burden, perhaps surprisingly at a supposed caravan city. Perhaps they served as mementos of warfare, sport or trade. Those with weapons may represent animals used in a Nabataean dromedary corps.[39] It is also possible that some served in sports such as organized camel racing (still popular in the region today); the variations in the types of

35 Khairy 1990; Parlasca 1991; El-Khouri 2002.

36 An unequivocal example of a single musician was recovered from a tomb in front of al-Khazna during recent excavations conducted by the Department of Antiquities. The figurine depicts a male double-flute player seated on a stool. This artifact is now on display in the Petra Museum but remains unpublished.

37 Tuttle 2009, 229-30.

38 Tuttle 2009, 278-83; French 1988.

39 Bowsher 1989; Graf 1994.

Fig. 13.20. Type C.3.1a, horse with tack, without stand (no. 28) (1 : 1).

Fig. 13.21. Type C.3.1a, horse with tack, without stand (no. 30).

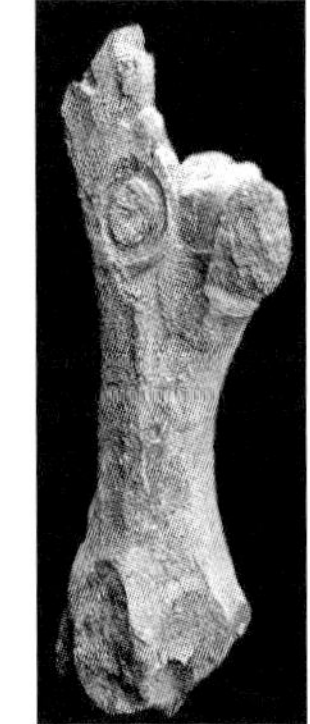
Fig. 13.22. Type C.4.1, ibex figurine (no. 33).

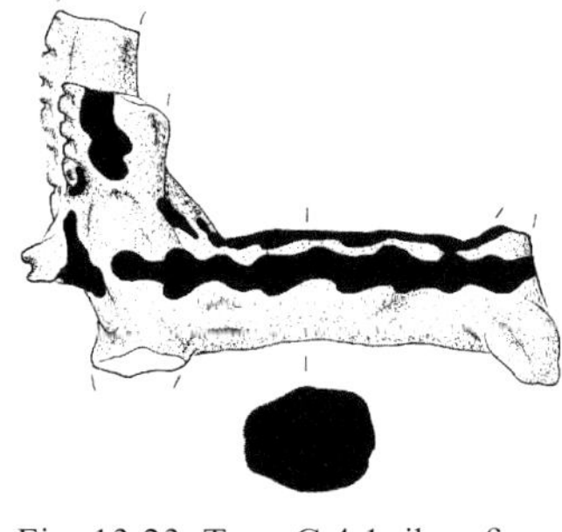
Fig. 13.23. Type C.4.1, ibex figurine (no. 36).

Fig. 13.24. Type C.4.2, ibex vessel (no. 41).

Fig. 13.25. Type C.4.2, ibex vessel (no. 42).

Fig. 13.26. Type C.4.3, ibex, type uncertain (no. 46).

Fig. 13.27. Type C.4.3, ibex type uncertain (no. 48).

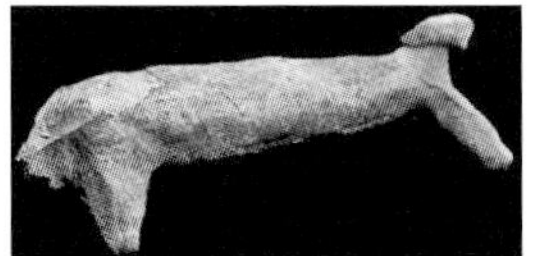
Fig. 13.28. Type C.7.1, modelled quadruped figurine (no. 61).

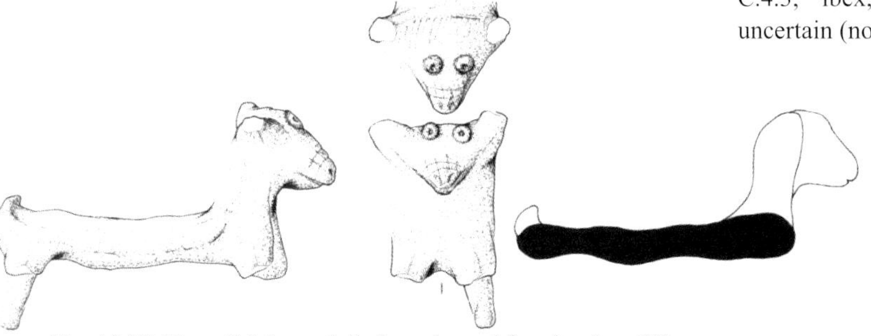
Fig. 13.29. Type C.7.1, modelled quadruped figurine (no. 68).

Fig. 13.30. Type C.7.1, modelled quadruped figurine (no. 69) (1 : 1).

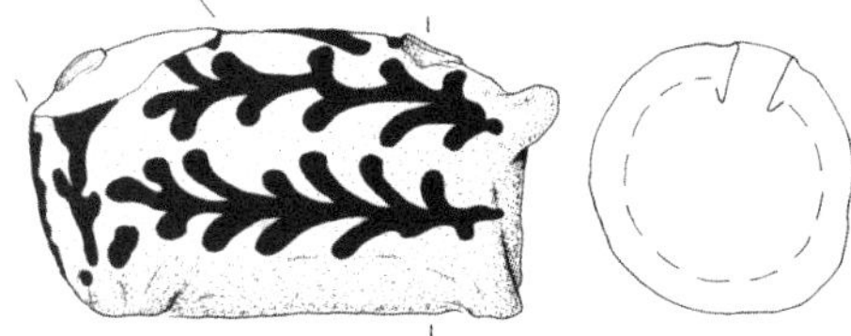
Fig. 13.31. Type C.7.2, modelled quadruped vessel (no. 71); see also fig. 13.4.

martial equipment may then allude to different types of events in which riders demonstrated their mounted prowess with the particular weapons. Thirdly, it is possible that they depict animals used by caravan protection forces.

(ii) Horses: horses with tack without stand

Four examples of horse figurines are present (nos. 28-31). Unlike camels, no horse figurines with weaponry have been recorded in the Nabataean coroplastic corpus. Usually horses are depicted only with riding tack, which can be quite elaborate and fairly accurate (e.g., figs. 13.20-13.21). Decorative elements, such as *phalerae* and a variety of pendants that hang from the harnessing (nos. 28 and 30), are frequently present. In many cases the horses have large, inverted *lunulae* hanging from the strap across their chests.[40] No evidence for figurines of separate riders exists. Some may be

40 Tuttle 2009; Bishop 1988, 152-54.

shown as on military parade,[41] but no weapons are present. Most probably the images are drawn from a Nabataean sporting milieu. Horse and camel racing are likely to have been organized, public sports which did not require large permanent infrastructures such as hippodromes, generally absent in Nabataean territory.[42] The horse figurines could represent participants in such races, especially the favorites, with close attention paid to the details of the harness and pendants.[43] Such details may also refer to different kinds of awards or honors earned by victors.

Yet we cannot rule out that both the camel and horse figurines may have served as toys. The subject matter would have been of interest to children who observed adults engaged in these types of activities. We note the presence of both horse and camel rider statuettes in a burial of a mother and child in a tomb at Petra.[44] It is also possible that both camel and horse figurines could have had magical or votive uses, the images being dedicated to win influence on behalf of an animal and its rider or aiding in a curse of a rival in a competition.

(iii) Ibex: figurines, vessels, or type uncertain

The excavations produced 6 figurines (cat. nos. 32-37; figs. 13.22-13.23), 6 zoomorphic vessels (nos. 38-43; figs. 13.24-13.25), and 12 fragments of type uncertain, which could belong to either ibex figurines or vessels (nos. 44-55; e.g. figs. 13.26-13.27). The ibex figurines may have been decorative objects or toys. Possibly they were employed for purposes related to hunting, as dedicatory or petitionary votives, or served as mementos of hunting outings. Another possibility is that characteristics seen as innate to the male ibex (e.g., strength, agility, endurance, virility) were evoked in sympathetic or apotropaic magic.

The ibex vessels can be assigned to the "practical" functional category. They have been interpreted as possible aquamaniles (ritual vessels for washing hands), lamp fillers, or feeders for infants,[45] but there are difficult questions regarding their practicality in functioning as aquamaniles or lamp-fillers.[46] Intact pieces in the existing corpus had a volume capacity of between *c.*50 and *c.*150 ml of fluid, but unequivocal aquamaniles nearly always have much larger capacities;[47] and if they were lamp-fillers, why would the effort be made to fill an ibex vessel with only enough for one or two refills, rather than just refilling the lamp directly? Infant feeders may thus be a more likely interpretation. But another possibility is that they served as an applicator of medicine, for which the possible symbolic values of the ibex might be pertinent: the intent could have been to convey attributes of the ibex to a child or sick person.

(iv) Unidentifiable quadrupeds: modelled quadruped figurines; modelled quadruped vessels; moulded quadrupeds, type uncertain; and quadruped legs/feet

In these cases we cannot identify the animals depicted (figs. 13.4 and 13.28-13.31), although some may be ibexes. One can safely assume that these were known to the Nabataeans (thereby they would fall into our category of "representations, environmental", as well as into the "practical" category). Possibly they depict hunted animals and could have served as hunting mementos. They could also have been decorations or toys, and used as teaching instruments or as vehicles of sympathetic magic.

(v) Hedgehog vessel

The single, nearly intact hedgehog vessel (cat. no. 73, figs. 13.2 and 13.32-13.36) depicts a member of the *Paraechinus aethiopicus pectoralis* species of desert hedgehog that is indigenous to Petra

41 Tuttle 2009, 285; Hyland 1990, 190-91.
42 Tuttle 2009, 263-64.
43 El-Khouri 2002, figs. 66-68, who provides sketches of the predominant pendant designs.
44 Horsfield and Horsfield 1938 and 1941.
45 Aquamaniles: Baramki 1934 and 1935, Franken 1991, Erickson-Gini 1999 and 2004, and Erickson-Gini and Israel 2003; Lamp-fillers: Bignasca 1993 and 1996, Barrett 1998; Infant feeders: Barrett 1998.
46 Tuttle 2009, 295-302.
47 Cf. Bloch 1982; Müller 2006.

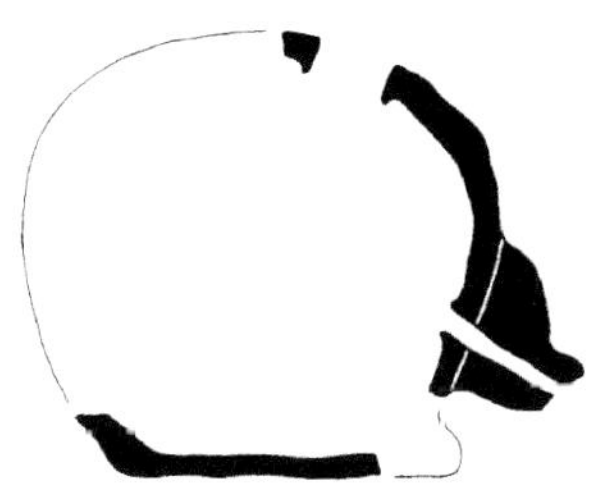

Fig. 13.32. Section of Type C.9.2, hedgehog vessel (no. 73).

Fig. 13.33. *Paraechinus aethiopicus pectoralis.*

Fig. 13.34. Type C.9.2, hedgehog vessel (no. 73) (1 : 1).

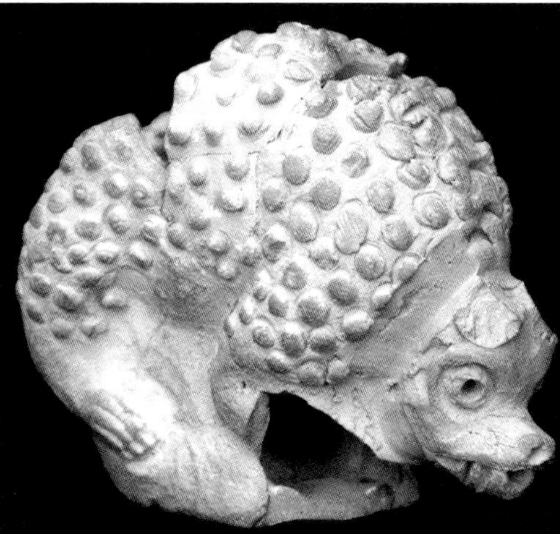

Fig. 13.35. Hedgehog vessel (no. 73) (1 : 1).

Fig. 13.36. *Paraechinus aethiopicus pectoralis* in a similar pose to fig. 13.35.

Fig. 13.39. Type F.1.1b, moulded appliqué for vessel, figural, male (no. 78).

Fig. 13.37. Type D.2.2, zoomorphic mask/affix (no. 74) (1 : 1).

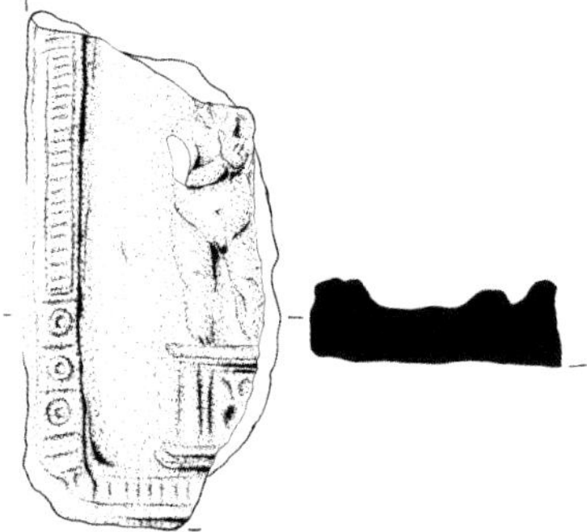

Fig. 13.38. Type E.1.1, anthorpomorphic plaque, nude youth (no. 75).

Fig. 13.40. Type G.3, moulded type, uncertain (no. 80).

and most of the Nabataean realm.[48] As the only known example of this vessel type, it helps elucidate another fragment found at Petra in the 1930s.[49] Coroplastic hedgehog figurines and vessels are known in the Near East from at least the Bronze Age; they may have been chosen because of the creature's natural abilities to confront both scorpions and snakes.[50] This vessel surely served practical purposes.[51] Due to its mechanical characteristics, it can only hold liquid when its rump is cupped in the palm of the hand and the snout held at an upward angle. The vessel's use was thus

48 Ruben and Disi 2006; Bodenheimer 1960.

49 Horsfield and Horsfield 1941, no. 260.

50 Leonard 2000.

51 Tuttle 2009, 299-302.

probably situational. Like the ibex vessels, it was very possibly used as to feed infants or to apply medicine. In either case, the intent may have been to transfer the protective, and possibly curative, qualities of the hedgehog against snakes or scorpions. At the same time it may have served a sympathetic magic or apotropaic rôle for the Nabataeans.

D. Zoomorphic: other artifact type

A single object in the catalogue is assigned to this type (No. 74, fig. 13.37). A fragment of a horse head (cat. no. 74; fig. 13.37) is probably part of an architectural affix, perhaps for decoration. It has no known parallels.

E. Plaques

One object (cat. no. 75; fig. 13.38) belongs to the subtype "anthropomorphic plaques of nude youths", one (no. 76) to the "enthroned nude females", and one (no. 77) to the "plaques, steles, surmounted by masks". Although none preserved direct evidence for suspension, plaques were often meant to be suspended, which could perhaps emphasize iconic or apotropaic cult and decorative functional aspects. The plaque in the "stele surmounted by a mask" category is probably best assigned to iconic or replica representations, along with a devotional function. It is probably a dual iconic/aniconic representation of a Nabataean god, possibly Dushara, since it recalls an aniconic *betyl* stele, with a figural bust in a carved circle directly above, carved on the rupestral shrine above Wadi Farasa (East),[52] which one scholar[53] has interpreted as a dual depiction of the god. The *stele* plaques could be replicas of that shrine, or at least be intended to convey the same kind of imagery.

F. Vessels

One artifact (cat. no. 78; fig. 13.39) is identified as a Moulded appliqué for vessel, figural, male, while the other (no. 79; fig. 13.3) is a vessel component (spout). Both are unique in the existing Nabataean corpus. Both are likely to be aesthetic decorations, with the spout also serving a practical purpose for the complete object.

G. Unknown/uncertain artifact type

The fragmentary state of no. 80 (fig. 13.40)[54] precludes its certain identification. It appears to be part of a male torso clad in a garment gathered on the left shoulder. If so, it could be classified as an iconic representation of a deity or perhaps an emblem or portrait of a particular personage. Its relatively poor execution would appear to argue against it having been a decorative object.

Conclusions

The diversity of coroplastic items produced by the Nabataeans is seen in the number of different types, the combinations of manufacturing techniques employed, variations in the quality of execution, and the range of possible functions and meanings of the objects. Coroplastic arts were amongst the crafts mastered to varying degrees by Nabataean artisans. The reason for their attention to this craft must lie in the fact that there was a demand for the items by the populace. Much work remains to be done in expanding the corpus and implementing standardized methodologies to correlate all the data quantitatively and qualitatively, with the hope that these small-scale representational objects may yet elucidate aspects of Nabataean worldviews and reveal some of the mechanisms through which individuals defined and interacted with those views.

---

52 Taylor 2002, 123.

53 Zayadine 1975, 336-37; *contra* Hammond 1968.

54 Previously published in vol. 2, fig. 7.45c.

Catalogue

This catalogue contains all of the identifiable coroplastic objects recovered from the Great Temple excavations. Each entry provides the empirical and provenience data, citations to any previous publications, and short descriptions of the artifact, with dimensions in cm.

The artifacts are arranged according to the new typology of Nabataean coroplastic objects created for the author's dissertation (Tuttle 2009). Also to be found in that study are thorough descriptions of each object based on formal analysis and examinations of the fabric and manufacturing techniques, as well as a list of published parallels.

A. Anthropomorphic figurines

No. 1. 99-P-1 (fig. 13.6). Type A.1.1 Standing Draped Females. From Temple, Tr. 64, Locus 16, East Corridor, fluvial deposit. Deposit date: Site Phase IX. L 8.33 cm; w 4.1 cm; th 0.73 cm. Fabric: red 2.5 YR 6/6, red slip, red paint. Monovalve mould, incision, paint. See El-Khouri 2002 no. 73; Tuttle 2009 no. 001.
A standing female is shown wearing a *peplos*, *chiton*, and *himation*/mantle. Also depicted are a necklace and a belt/sash. A possible palm branch, feather or stalk of grain is cradled by the missing left arm. The figure depicted cannot be identified with certainty.

No. 2. 02-P-29. Type A.1.3 Enthroned Nude Females. From Upper Temenos, Tr. 94, Locus 53, Residential Quarter, Room 7, fluvial deposit. Deposit date: Site Phase IX. L 4.7, w 2.8, th 0.45 cm. Fabric: pink 5YR 7/4, red slip. Bivalve mould, incision. See Tuttle 2009 no. 002.
Only the face is extant on the front; the hair, back, arms, and upper buttocks are preserved on the reverse. The figure is shown smiling, and the pupils of the eyes are rendered. The hair is shown in plaits and is parted in the middle on the forehead. No details of the throne are evident, but it can be inferred from parallels.

No. 3. 02-P-25 (fig. 13.5). Type A.1.3 Enthroned Nude Females. From Upper Temenos, Tr. 94, Locus 41, Residential Quarter, Cave 2, Rooms 10-11, fluvial deposit. Deposit date: Site Phases XI-XIII. L 4.4, w 2.25, th 0.4 cm. Fabric: red 10R 5/8, red slip. Bivalve mould, incision, paring. See Tuttle 2009 no. 003.
The upper portions of both the front and back are preserved. The nose and upper lip are skewed to the left from damage done during the finishing process. The hair on the forehead is depicted as tresses sweeping to each side from a central part. The rest of the hair is shown as hanging plaits of curls, which appear to emerge from beneath the tresses beside the face. The clavicle is indicated, as are the breasts. The belly swells slightly, and its pendency is emphasized by the placement of the navel and two moulded, curved grooves. The right forearm is raised and the hand is shown palm outward. A bracelet is shown around the right wrist. The throne is not extant, but it can be inferred from parallels.

No. 4. 00-P-6 (fig. 13.7). Type A.1.3 Enthroned Nude Females. From Upper Temenos, Tr. 77, Locus 20, East Perimeter Wall, fluvial deposit. Deposit date: Site Phases XI-XIII. L 4.56, w 2.7, th 0.47 cm. Fabric: red 2.5YR 6/8, red slip(?). Bivalve mould, incision, paring. See Joukowsky 2007 fig. 7.44a-b; Tuttle 2009 no. 004.
The head and parts of the torso and right arm are extant. The facial features are well-preserved. The hair tresses on the forehead sweep from a central part to either side. The hanging hair is arranged in plaits of curls, which appear to emerge from beneath the tresses on the front. Two curved parallel relief bands across the neck suggest a necklace, which may be segmented into beads by faint vertical lines. The breasts are moulded in relief. The right forearm is raised with the palm of the hand facing outward. A bracelet is shown on the wrist.

No. 5. 00-P-18 (fig. 13.8). Type A.1.3 Enthroned Nude Females. From Upper Temenos, Tr. 77, Locus 22, South Canalization, sedimentation(?). Deposit date: Site Phase XI. L 3.92, w 1.82, th 0.4 cm. Fabric: red 2.5YR 6/6, red slip. Bivalve mould, paring. See Tuttle 2009 no. 014.
The body is extant from below the waist. This is one of the few examples of a figurine made of halves from two different mould types. The front is from the A.1.3 type, in which the legs are shown held together. The figure wears anklets on both legs. The feet appear to be wearing sandals, resting on a footstool. The rear is from the A.2.5a (Nude Youths, Standing) type. It depicts naked buttocks and the segments of the lower legs. The disparity between the two mould types is remedied by the liberal use of extra clay for the joins.

No. 6. 01-P-11 (fig. 13.9). Type A.1.4 Enthroned Draped Females. From Upper Temenos, Tr. 83, Locus 5, South Passageway, overburden/fluvial deposit. Deposit date: Site Phases XI-XIV. L 5.4, w 2.32 cm. Fabric: pink 5YR 8/4, red slip. Bivalve mould, incision, paring. See Tuttle 2009 no. 016.
This nearly intact figurine is missing only its head and feet. It is poorly executed and the halves are slightly misaligned. Moulded breasts are evident, indicating that it is a female. Several faint features, such as a possible drapery fold between the breast, a waistband, and a hem suggest that the figure is clothed. There is also

an anklet shown on the right leg. The arms are bent and the forearms rest on the abdomen. The throne is not evident, but both the posture of the figure and comparison to parallels indicate that this is an enthroned type.

No. 7. 99-P-7. Type A.1.6 Enthroned Females, Details Uncertain. From Temple, Tr. 65, Locus 21, East Corridor, collapse/sediment. Origin date 1st-3rd c. A.D.(?); deposit date: Site Phase XI. L 3.65, w 1.45 cm. Fabric: red 2.5YR 6/8, red slip(?). Bivalve mould, boring. See El-Khouri 2002 no. 17; Tuttle 2009 no. 021.
The lower portion with the legs, feet, and a footstool is present. As the fragment is very eroded, not enough details are preserved to determine if it is nude or draped. A circular vent hole (0.15 cm) is bored through the base from the exterior. It can be tentatively dated based on associated lamps in the deposit (Barrett 2005 and 2008).

No. 8. 02-P-21. Type A.1.6 Enthroned Females, Details Uncertain. From Upper Temenos, Tr. 90, Locus 8, East Plaza, fluvial deposit. Deposit date: Site Phases VIII-XIII. L 2.04, w 2.05, th 0.51 cm. Fabric: weak red 2.5YR 5/4, red slip. Bivalve mould, incision, boring. See Tuttle 2009 no. 023.
The feet, part of the anklets, and footstool are preserved. The toes are articulated in the mould but are now only faintly visible due to wear. The V-shaped relief on top of each foot probably indicates sandal straps. The front of the footstool is decorated with a horizontal rectangular pattern. One half of a vent hole (0.1 cm) is extant on the base; it is bored through the join seam.

No. 9. 04-P-2. Type A.1.6 Enthroned Females, Details Uncertain. From unknown trench. L 2.00, w 3.4, th 0.76 cm. Fabric: light reddish brown 2.5YR 7/3, self slip(?). Bivalve mould, incision(?), boring. See Tuttle 2009 no. 026.
The bottom front edge of a footstool from an enthroned female figurine is present. The front surface of the footstool has a slightly recessed rectangular panel enclosed by a rectilinear frame. The base has a concave depression through which a tiny pinhole vent (0.01 cm) is bored from the exterior.

No. 10. 95-P-4 (fig. 13.10). Type A.2.1b Camel Riders. From Lower Temenos, Tr. 20, Locus 1, East Colonnade, topsoil. Deposit date: Site Phases XI-XIII. L 5.1, w 4.8, th 0.4 cm. Fabric: light red 10R 6/8, reddish/pink slip. Bivalve mould, excision. See El-Khouri 2002 no. 275; Tuttle 2009 no. 029.
Parts of a draped human hip, right hand, and camel saddle are preserved. The hand is angled in toward the abdomen, and appears to have a cuff/bracelet on the wrist. The hand clasps the end of a goad in its fingers, part of which can be seen extending to the right below the hand. The moulded ellipse is the seat of the camel saddle. The vertical grooves above the seat are the drapes of the figure's garment. The vertical grooves below the seat, which do not align with the upper grooves, are part of the saddle bag.

No. 11. 00-P-10 (fig. 13.11). Type A.2.2a Bearded Males, with Diadem. From Upper Temenos, Tr. 76, Locus 9, Between Temple and West Precinct Wall, débris(?)/fluvial(?) deposit. Origin date: 1st-3rd c. A.D.(?). Deposit date: Site Phase IX. L 3.02, w 1.9, th 0.18 cm. Fabric: light red 10R 6/8, self slip. Bivalve mould, incision, paring. See Joukowsky 2007, fig. 7.45d; Tuttle 2009 no. 030.
The entire head is extant. The nose is slightly flattened in the moulding process. In the lower lip appears to be a ring, which is rendered frontally by a small moulded disk/circle of clay. The parallel vertical lines across the forehead seem to be depicting a diadem. The beard and moustache are incised, but there is no detailing of the hair behind the diadem. The fragment can be tentatively dated by association with two complete lamps in the deposit (Barrett 2005 and 2008).

No. 12. 02-P-2 (fig. 13.12). Type A.2.5a Nude Youths, Standing. From Upper Temenos, Tr. 89, Locus 3, Shrine/Baroque Room/West Cistern, fluvial deposit. Deposit date: Site Phases XI-XIII. L 4.9, w 3.3, th 0.5 cm. Fabric: light red 10R 7/6, self slip(?). Bivalve mould. See Tuttle 2009 no. 031.
The front of the head, torso, and two hands are preserved. The features are moulded, and the hair is shown arranged in plaits extending back from the forehead. The ears emerge from beneath the hair. The figure wears a necklace, which consists of 8 moulded beads and an inverted lunate pendant. Two small breasts are shown in relief to each side of the pendant. The belly swells slightly, and its pendency is enhanced by the placement of the navel and the use of two curved relief lines to suggest fat. The right forearm is raised, with the palm of the hand facing outward. The left arm is foreshortened; its hand is shown clasping an unidentifiable object against the abdomen. Bracelets are shown on both wrists. Despite the presence of breasts, the male gender is confirmed by preserved genitalia on parallels.

No. 13. 00-P-7. Type A.2.5a Nude Youths, Standing. From Upper Temenos, Tr. 77, Locus 20, south/east corner, fluvial deposit. Deposit date: Site Phases XI-XIII. L 3.8, w 2.54, th 0.55 cm. Fabric: red 2.5YR 6/8, self or red slip(?). Bivalve mould, incision, paring. See Joukowsky 2007, fig. 7.45b; Tuttle 2009 no. 032.
The front of the head, torso and two hands are preserved. This figure has the same features as no. 12 above. The only exceptions are that the hair plaits are not depicted on the crown of the head, and the necklace has 11 beads.

No. 14. 02-P-16 (fig. 13.13). Type A.2.5a Nude Youths, Standing. From Upper Temenos, Tr. 94, Locus 43, Residential Quarter, Room 2, fluvial deposit. Deposit date: Site Phase IX. L 4.4, w 2.46, th 0.46 cm. Fabric: red 2.5YR 6/8, self slip. Bivalve mould, paring (?). See Tuttle 2009 no. 033.

Parts of both the front and back of the upper body are extant. The fragment is very eroded, but the same details as on nos. 12-13 can still be discerned. Hair plaits can be seen extending across the crown to the back of the head. Only 5 beads can be seen in the necklace. The two halves of the figurine are poorly aligned, with the reverse side offset toward the right, which may be the result of slippage along the joins.

No. 15. 99-P-5. Type A.2.5a Nude Youths, Standing. From Temple, Tr. 62, Locus 39, East Corridor, deposit unknown. L 4.1, w 2.08, th 0.6 cm. Fabric: red 2.5YR 6/6, red slip. Bivalve mould, impression, excision(?), paring, boring. See El-Khouri 2002 no. 87; Tuttle 2009 no. 035.

The backside of the figure, from the waist to the ankles, is preserved. The buttocks, thighs, calves, and ankles are schematically demarcated by 3 straight impressed lines. These features are moulded, but the impressions were used for enhancement. The vent hole is bored from the exterior; its placement at the base of the buttocks may be intended to depict the anus.

No. 16. 98-P-4. Type A.2.5a Nude Youths, Standing. From unknown context. L 3.1, w 2.36, th 0.8 cm. Fabric: red 10R 5/6, red slip. Bivalve mould. See Tuttle 2009 no. 039.

The right arm and part of the torso are extant. Three beads of a necklace are visible along the neck break. A bracelet is shown around the wrist of the upraised right forearm.

No. 17. 05-P-6. Type A.3.1 Musician Group. From Upper Temenos, Tr. SP108, Locus 8, Sondage north of Upper Temenos support wall, fluvial deposit. Deposit date: Site Phase IX. L 2.53, w 2.54, th 0.65 cm. Fabric: red 2.5YR 6/8, red slip. Bivalve mould. See Tuttle 2009 no. 042.

The head of the right figure from a musician group is preserved. The break from the group is evident on the left. A row of hair curls curve across the forehead. The head is covered by a veil, part of which can be discerned hanging down on the right along the face. The back side of the head is smooth.

No. 18. 02-P-14 (fig. 13.14). Type A.3.2 Musician, individual(?). From Upper Temenos, Tr. 89, Locus 5, Baroque Room, fluvial deposit. Deposit date: Site Phases XI-XIII. L 6.05, w 3.19, th 1.16 cm. Fabric: pale red 2.5YR 7/4, red slip. Modeled, appliqué. See Tuttle 2009 no. 046.

Part of the body, right arm, and a membranophone (tambourine or frame drum) are preserved. No details of the body are indicated. The arm and instrument are modelled separately and appliquéd. The arm bends at the elbow, the forearm extending across the torso to the instrument. A small extrusion of clay behind the instrument is attached to both it and the body; this may be the left hand, or merely a support for the instrument. The break along the right of the fragment suggests that it is attached to a larger piece; this could be the leftmost figure from a musician group, rather than an individual.

Parallels are known from both the Iron Age and Hellenistic periods. The ware and slip of this fragment are comparable to other Nabataean coroplastic artifacts.

No. 19. 95-P-13 (fig. 13.1a-b). Type A.5.2 Clothed Figures. From Temple, Tr. 19, Locus 9, East Staircase(?), deposit unknown. L 2.9, w 3.3, th 0.5 cm. Fabric: reddish yellow 5YR 7/6. Bivalve mould, incision. See Barrett 1998, 304; El-Khouri 2002 no. 100; Tuttle 2009 no. 048.

Part of the torso with breasts, a necklace, and two arms are extant. The thick necklace consists of 4 rectilinear beads with an inverted lunate pendant. Two round breasts are shown in relief, and the left side of the lunate rests on the breast. The arms are visible from the shoulder to wrists, lying down along the sides of the torso. Incised lines along the arms appear to render garment drapery.

The breasts suggest the figure is female, but the lunate pendant is heretofore known only from the standing nude youths type. This necklace has not previously been associated with this particular posture (arms down), or the possible clothing, presented on this figurine.

No. 20. 95-P-3. Type A.5.9 Possible Figures. From Lower Temenos, Tr. 20, Locus 4, East Colonnade, intentional fill(?). Origin date: late 1st-early 2nd c. A.D. Deposit date: Site Phases XI-XII. L 5.5, w 3.0, th 0.6 cm. Fabric: reddish yellow 5YR 7/6, reddish-brown slip. Bivalve mould, incision. See Barrett 1998, 302; Tuttle 2009 no. 068.

The imagery of this fragment is uncertain. It exhibits a group of 7 folds/strands in moulded relief along the left when viewed in a vertical position. In this orientation, the folds/strands gather slightly closer together at the top and then separate and widen as they disappear into the bottom break. There is evidence that the folds/strands are enhanced by incision before firing. In the vertical orientation, a faint, roughly-incised circle in the upper center is evident. There is also possibly a small, raised, vertical lump visible below and to the right of the incised circle.

This piece was originally identified as part of a human figure with drapery (Barrett 1998), but this interpretation is difficult to substantiate as close study does not reconcile the preserved contours and folds/strands of the fragment with body parts usually shown draped. Another possibility is that it represents part of the head and neck of a female whose face is turned right from the center axis of her body. In this case the circle and lump would be the left eye and nose, and the folds/strands a portion of her long hair preserved along the left. The faintness of the facial features suggests it was produced in a worn mould, thus requiring the use of incision to delineate the eye and hair strands. In this reading, the pose and emphasis of the hair detail are iconographic elements that might suggest that this is a female head, possibly from an Aphrodite figure.

The artifact was found in what appears to be an intentional fill. It can be tentatively dated by association with Nabataean and Roman import lamps (Barrett 2005 and 2008).

No. 21. 02-P-22. Type A.5.10 Abstract Figures. From Propylaeum, Tr. 97, Locus 6, Room 1, fill/sediment deposit. Deposit date: Site Phases IX-XIII. L 5.62, w 2.85 cm. Fabric: pink 5YR 8/4, red slip. Monovalve mould, modeling, impression, paring, appliqué. See Tuttle 2009 no. 070.

A seated anthropomorphic figurine whose legs and poorly rendered feet are modeled over moulded elements. The upper part of the figure has two bands of clay that extend along the sides to meet in the "lap", which may represent arms with clasped hands. These "arms" are modeled by pressing the original moulded torso details outward and adding new clay. Some 10 impressed circle decorations are visible on the surface of these modeled elements; these circles continue across the "hands". A flattened disk (*c.*1.0 cm diam.) was appliquéd to the "chest".

This seems to be an instance where an existing mould (probably the enthroned nude female type) is used to create a template to model a different image. Only the front monovalve mould was used; the concavity on the reverse from the mould was then filled with lumps of clay and roughly smoothed.

B. Anthropomorphic, Other Artifact Types

No. 22. 94-P-2 (fig. 13.15). Type B.1.1 Statuettes, Feet. From Lapidary West, Tr. 7, Locus 9, fill/sediment deposit. Origin date: 1st-early 2nd c. A.D. Deposit date: Site Phases X-XI(?). L 4.2, w 4.6, th 0.35 cm. Fabric: pale yellow 2.5Y 7/4. Bivalve mould, incision, paring. See Tuttle 2009 no. 071.

These feet with sandals derive from a hollow statuette. The sandal straps are formed by moulded double strands, which are detailed to appear coiled by the use of small incisions. The right side of the right foot shows a moulded, vertical side-strap; its join to the corresponding V-strap is marked by a faint circular feature, perhaps a button or ring. A small rectangular vent hole is preserved on the base. The fragment can be tentatively dated to the 1st to early 2nd c. A.D. based on associated lamps in the deposit (Barrett 2005 and 2008).

No. 23. 02-P-28 (fig. 13.16). Type B.2.4 Masks/Architectural Affixes. From Lower Temenos, Tr. SP92, Locus 1, sondage, overburden. Deposit date: Site Phase XIV. L 2.73, w 4.7, th 0.64 cm. Fabric: reddish brown 5YR 6/4, red/brown slip(?). Molded (monovalve?). See Tuttle 2009 no. 073.

The upper part of the left eye, brow ridge, eyebrow, and a hair tress are present. The iris is offset from center toward the right (nose) and is partially covered by the upper eyelid. This positioning suggests that the figure's gaze is turned upward. Above the brow, along the right edge of the top break, two curved, moulded relief-lines define a single tress of hair, swept toward the side from the center, lying along the forehead.

No. 24. 05-P-14 (fig. 13.17). Type B.2.4 Masks/Architectural Affixes. From Upper Temenos, Tr. 105, Locus 28, overburden/fluvial deposit(?). Deposit date: Site Phases XI-XIV(?). L 2.3, w 4.37, th 0.40 cm. Fabric: light red 10R 7/8, red slip(?). Monovalve mould. See Joukowsky 2007, fig. 7.54; Tuttle 2009 no. 074.

The chin, lower lip, and right side of the upper lip are preserved. The chin is well-formed, with subtle contours to differentiate it from the jaw line. A small circular incision is centered on the chin, the purpose or meaning of which is unknown.

C. Zoomorphic Figurines and Vessels

No. 25. 95-P-12 (fig. 13.18). Type C.2.1a Camels, Heads. From Upper Temenos, Tr. SP30, Locus 12, NE Platform/Podium, sedimentation deposit. Deposit date: Site Phase VII. L 3.4, w 1.7, th 0.75 cm. Fabric: light reddish brown 2.4YR 7/4, brown slip. Bivalve mould. See Barrett 1998, 303; El-Khouri 2002 no. 267; Tuttle 2009 no. 091.

Part of the left side of the head is extant, with muzzle, eye, ear and halter. The characteristic cleft of a camel's muzzle is suggested by faint moulded lines on top of the snout. Between the nose and the mouth is a slightly curved excised line. The eye has a small impression toward the front half to indicate the pupil. Behind the eye is part of an ovoid ear that realistically angles toward the back of the head. The halter spans the bridge of the snout; it is depicted as a twisted rope by diagonal lines.

The fragment was previously identified as possibly deriving from an anthropomorphic figurine (Barrett 1998), but later correctly identified by El-Khouri (2002).

No. 26. 05-P-3. Type C.2.1a Camels, Heads. From Lower Temenos, Tr. 102, Locus 1, West Entry Stairs, collapse/sediment deposit. Deposit date: Site Phase XIV. L 3.19, w 3.04, th 0.52 cm. Fabric: light red 10R 6/8, self slip(?). Bivalve mould, excision(?), incision(?). See Tuttle 2009 no. 092.

The right side of the neck and head is preserved. The surface is extremely eroded. The excised divot of the moulded ear is faintly visible, as is a slight circular relief , which is probably the eye. A shallow groove indicates the mouth. A shallow depression at the tip of the muzzle may be a nostril, but it could have resulted from flaking. The muzzle harness is depicted by a vertical band in relief with faint, moulded diagonal hatch-marks to give it the appearance of twisted rope. Two parallel incised lines spanning the neck horizontally may be an attempt to render a collar or part of the harness.

No. 27. 01-P-15 (fig. 13.19). Type C.2.2a Camels with Tack and Weapons, without Stand. From Upper Temenos, Tr. 84, Locus 9, East Perimeter Wall, Room A, mixed fill/fluvial deposit. Origin date: 1st-2nd c. A.D.(?). Deposit date: Site Phases VI-IX. L 3.06, w 2.65, th 0.5 cm. Fabric: pink 5YR 7/4, self slip, red paint. Bivalve mould, paint. See Tuttle 2009 no. 095.
The forelegs of a camel are preserved. The feet are indicated by moulded inverted crescent impressions. The right side has the tapering portion of a dagger/sword scabbard. The length of the scabbard is decorated with 4 parallel moulded lines. A single line of red paint can be seen on the left (inner) side of the leg extending onto the foot; it appears to be intentional.
The piece cannot be dated with certainty due to the mixed nature of the deposit. A coin from this locus is of either Aretas IV (A.D. 18-40) or Rabbel II (A.D. 65-101).

No. 28. 01-P-07 (fig. 13.20). Type C.3.1a Horses with Tack, without Stand. From Upper Temenos, Tr. 84, Locus 8, East Perimeter Wall, Room A, fluvial deposit. Deposit date: Site Phases X-XIII. L 4.0, w 4.0, th 0.49 cm. Fabric: light red 2.5YR 7/6, red slip. Bivalve mould, incision, paring, paint(?). See Tuttle 2009 no. 111.
Present are the right rear haunch with parts of the saddle, harness, tail and hindleg. The schematic hoof is indicated by a moulded inverted crescent. The tail extends down the exterior edge of the leg. Both a saddle pad and a saddle are shown. For the harness, the girth and the crupper are both shown as consisting of two strands each. The position of the crupper is schematic, appearing to cross the top of the tail rather than lie beneath it. Two pendants hang from the crupper; decorated with incised inverted chevrons, they appear to represent feathers. Patches of an orange-red substance adhering to the belly and girth may suggest the use of non-fired paint.

No. 29. 04-P-11. Type C.3.1a Horses with Tack, without Stand. From Lower Temenos, Tr. 98, Locus 3, West Cryptoporticus West, fluvial/sedimentation deposit. Deposit date: Site Phases IX-XIII. L 6.35, w 3.3, th 0.84 cm. Fabric: pink 5YR 7/4, self slip. Bivalve mould, incision, boring. See Tuttle 2009 no. 112.
Part of the left side with the saddle and harness is extant. A V-shaped saddle is positioned between the withers and loin on a square saddle pad. The saddle appears anchored to the girth by diagonal straps; the straps and girth are all depicted as double strands. Two circular moulded reliefs cap where the straps join the saddle proper; these may represent junction rings, *phalerae*, or schematic, foreshortened saddle horns. The crupper (viewer right), also double-stranded, extends from the ring junction or horn to the break. A single pendant hangs from the crupper, on which no decoration is presently visible. Part of a double-strand shoulder-strap angles from the forward ring junction/horn to the break. Half of a rectilinear vent-hole through the join seam in the belly is present, made by 3 consecutive punctures with a wedge-shaped tool rather than a single stroke.

No. 30. 00-P-3 (fig. 13.21). Type C.3.1a Horses with Tack, without Stand. From Upper Temenos, Tr. 77, Locus 10, South East Perimeter, fluvial deposit. Deposit date: Site Phases XI-XIII. L 6.14, w 5.0, th 0.62 cm. Fabric: light red 2.5YR 7/6, red slip. Bivalve mould, incision. See Joukowsky 2007, fig. 7.46b; Tuttle 2009 no. 113.
Part of the left side with the hind leg, saddle and harness is extant. The schematic hoof is indicated by a moulded inverted crescent impression. The area of the saddle pad is defined by two parallel moulded relief lines arranged in a square to depict its edge, yet this is visually confusing since the technique is identical to how the harness straps are rendered. The saddle is V-shaped. It is not clear if the diagonals of the V-shape represent the saddle-frame or straps anchoring it to the girth. Faint moulded lines give these diagonals the appearance of being braided, which may support the strap interpretation. Two circular moulded reliefs cap where the "straps" join the saddle proper; these may represent junction rings or schematic saddle horns. The crupper (viewer right) extends from the edge of the saddle pad (rather than the ring junction/horn) to the break. Two pendants hang from the crupper, each decorated with inverted nested chevron lines which may depict feathers. In front of the saddle (viewer left), a breast strap extends from the saddle junction ring/horn to the neck break; at its midpoint there is a moulded junction ring from which a plain relief band hangs; the absence of decoration on this element suggests it is a plain pendant strap. The girth, crupper and breast straps are all moulded double strands delineated by incision. Parts of the reins can be seen as two parallel lines lying on the neck. The proportionality and positioning of the tack is poor, with the saddle/pad extending on to the neck, rather than being centered between the withers and loin.

No. 31. 06-P-64. Type C.3.1a Horses with Tack, without Stand. From Upper Temenos, Tr. 84, Locus 38, East Perimeter Wall, Room B, fluvial deposit. Deposit date: Site Phases X-XIII. L 8.2, w 4.0, th 0.7 cm. Fabric: light red 2.5YR 7/6, red slip. Bivalve mould, incision, boring. See Tuttle 2009 no. 114.

Present is part of the left side with the saddle and harness. The trapezoidal saddle pad is decorated by a hatched border, with the rear edge angled up on to the croup. The V-shaped saddle appears centered between the withers and loin. The outer edge of the saddle frame is rendered by a simple moulded relief line; the relief line of the inner edge is decorated with hatching. Surmounting the front and back top edges of the saddle are low relief knobs which are delineated from the saddle "V" by horizontal relief bands; these may represent saddle horns. The saddle is anchored by a girth. The crupper (viewer right) extends from beneath the rear horn to the break; two faint moulded reliefs suggest that two pendants hang from the crupper. A shoulder or breast strap extends from beneath the front horn to the break. All of the harness straps are depicted as moulded double strands enhanced by incision. The proportion and position of the saddle and harness is very good. A small rectilinear vent hole is bored through the join seam on the belly.

No. 32. 95-P-8. Type C.4.1 Ibex Figurines. From Lower Temenos, Tr. 20, Locus 21, East Triple Colonnade, ash/trash dump. Origin date: 1st-early 2nd c. A.D.(?). Deposit date: Site Phase X. L 4.2, w 2.7 cm. Fabric: light red 10R 6/8. Modeled, boring, paring. See Barrett 1998, 303; El-Khouri 2002 no. 293; Tuttle 2009 no. 159.
The head and neck are preserved. Breaks in this crudely modeled figurine indicate where the forelegs, body and horns are originally joined. The body is cylindrical, the forelegs are elliptical. The face is rendered with two eyes and a muzzle. The eyes were made by boring a tapered tool into the head. The right side of the muzzle is broken away, and there are no traces of any attempt to indicate nostrils or the mouth.

No. 33. 99-P-4 (fig. 13.22). Type C.4.1 Ibex Figurines. From Upper Temenos, Tr. 68, Locus 1, East Perimeter Wall, overburden. Deposit date: Site Phases IX-XIII. L 6.85, w 1.6 cm. Fabric: red 2.5YR 5/6, self slip. Modeled, appliqué, excision, incision, paring. See El-Khouri 2002 no. 292; Tuttle 2009 no. 160.
The neck and the right half of the head with part of a horn are extant. The muzzle is formed from a separate piece of clay and appliquéd. A shallow mouth is rendered on the lower part of the muzzle; there is no break on the underside to suggest that there is a "beard". The eyes, positioned on the exterior surface of the horn bases, are indicated by circles with shallow punctures for the pupils. On the head the size of the breaks indicates that the horns would have been quite large. Three wedge-shaped, excised notches are preserved on the base of the right horn. The forelegs are elliptical and the body is cylindrical, but their respective lengths cannot be estimated.

No. 34. 04-P-7. Type C.4.1 Ibex Figurines. From Lower Temenos, Tr. 97, Locus 15, West Cryptoporticus East, sediment deposit. Origin date: 2nd c. A.D. Deposit date: Site Phases VI-VIII. L 4.0, w 3.2 cm. Fabric: red 10R 5/6, self slip. Modeled, appliqué, excision, paring. See Tuttle 2009 no. 161.
The right eye and part of the muzzle are extant. The neck tapers down to the join with the body. The muzzle is elliptical, and set to angle upward toward the front. The preserved eye is made from an irregular ovoid disk of clay with excised pupil that is appliquéd to the base of the right horn. A small divot at the base of the left horn indicates where the other eye was attached. Two irregular elliptical breaks on the crown show where the horns are set; these are not positioned along the front-to-back axis but on slight diagonals, so they would have angled in toward each other at their apexes. It can be dated by stratigraphy and associated finds to the 2nd c. A.D.

No. 35. 01-P-12. Type C.4.1 Ibex Figurines. From Upper Temenos, Tr. 83, Locus 9, South Passageway, fluvial deposit. Deposit date: Site Phases XI-XIII. L 3.8 cm, w 2.8 cm. Fabric: pinkish gray 5YR 7/2, red slip. Modeled, appliqué, incision, paring, boring. See Tuttle 2009 no. 162.
Part of the neck/head with muzzle and horn stumps is preserved. The head/neck is crudely modeled. The horns and muzzle are appliquéd onto the neck/head. The muzzle is a cone of clay with a possible incised line used to render a mouth on the underside. The left eye is indicated by a shallow bore-hole on the upper side of the muzzle. The underside of the fragment has a concave depression that suggests the head and body are made separately.

No. 36. 02-P-6 (fig. 13.23). Type C.4.1 Ibex Figurines. From Upper Temenos, Tr. 94, Locus 41, Residential Quarter, Cave 2/Rooms 10-11, fluvial deposit. Origin date: 2nd-4th c. A.D. Deposit date: Site Phases XI-XIII. L 8.8, w 3.6 cm. Fabric: light red 2.5YR 7/6, red slip, black paint. Modeled, excision, appliqué, paint. See Tuttle 2009 no. 163.
The body, neck/head, parts of both horns, one leg and the tail are preserved. The body and legs are cylindrical. The neck and head are truncated into one element. The body and neck/head are modeled as one piece; the muzzle and eyes are appliquéd and faint contour lines and fingerprints suggest that the legs, tail and horns are appliquéd as well. The mouth is shown at the tip of the muzzle. The eyes are formed with clay disks and the pupils are rendered by circular excisions. The characteristic ibex horn notches are evident on the horns. The body and horns are decorated with wavy lines of black, fired paint. The origin date range is suggested by comparison of the black paint to that used on the Phases 3b-4 pottery (Schmid 2000).

No. 37. 02-P-3. Type C.4.1 Ibex Figurines. From Upper Temenos, Tr. 94, Locus 43, Residential Quarter, Room 2, fluvial deposit. Origin date: 2nd-4th c. A.D. Deposit date: Site Phase IX. L 5.6, w 3.4 cm. Fabric: light red 2.5YR

5/6, red slip. Modeled, excision, appliqué, paring, boring. See Tuttle 2009 no. 164.
The extant parts of the head, muzzle, and horns are modeled as one piece. The muzzle is conical and well-proportioned to the head and has an excised, slightly curved mouth. Beneath the mouth hangs a small beard (1.15 x 0.7 cm), which is shaped from the muzzle clay rather than appliquéd. The eyes are formed with appliquéd disks, of which the right disk is extant, but the left is evident only by a faint impression on the surface of the face. The pupils are made by boring holes through the disks, not by excision. The horns are rectilinear and nearly flat on each side; one characteristic notch is preserved on the right horn. The head is hollow (1.8 cm int. diam.); it is likely the head was modeled separately and then attached to the (missing) body.

No. 38. 95-P-6. Type C.4.2 Ibex Vessels. From Upper Temenos, Tr. 16 (I), Locus 9, West Exedra, rubble/fill deposit. Origin date: 1st-5th c. A.D.(?). Deposit date: Site Phase XI. L 4.5, w 2.5 cm. Fabric: light red 10R 6/6, red slip. Modeled, wheel, excision, appliqué, paring, boring. See Barrett 1998, 303; El-Khouri 2002, 301; Tuttle 2009 no. 165.
The head and parts of the neck and one horn are preserved. The horns are roughly cylindrical, and only a fragment of one notch is visible on the left horn. The neck is hollow. The conical muzzle/spout is modeled separately and appliquéd. The mouth aperture (0.4 cm int. diam.) is bored at an angle from the exterior into the hollow neck. The eyes are indicated by two bore-holes in the muzzle/spout. A sherd from the wheel-thrown body is still attached inside the neck. The outflow aperture (0.5 cm diam.) that allowed liquid to flow from the body through the neck to the muzzle/spout is preserved; the aperture was bored from the exterior into the body before the head was attached. The inclusive date range given here is based on its association with lamps and coins (Barrett 1998).

No. 39. 00-P-4. Type C.4.2 Ibex Vessels. From Lower Temenos, Tr. 71, Locus 28, West Cryptoporticus, burnt fill deposit. Deposit date: Site Phase X. L 3.5, w 2.24 cm. Fabric: red 2.5YR 6/8, deposition discoloration. Modeled, excision, boring. See Tuttle 2009 no. 166.
Parts of the head, neck and horns are preserved. The horns are cylindrical; no characteristic notches are extant. The eyes are excised circles. The muzzle/spout is broken away but it had a maximum interior diameter of 0.9 cm. The neck is hollow (0.7 cm int. diam.) and is modeled to be roughly cylindrical; at the top a small outflow aperture (0.35 cm diam.) is bored at a downward angle from the exterior. The head is modeled separately and overlaid onto the neck — the layers of clay are evident in the basal break. The head/spout is slightly misaligned to the neck aperture, suggesting the neck aperture is bored prior to the emplacement of the head. The nature of the body cannot be determined.

No. 40. 02-P-9. Type C.4.2 Ibex Vessels. From Upper Temenos, Tr. 74, Locus 43, Residential Quarter, Room 2, fluvial deposit. Origin date: 2nd-4th c. A.D.(?). Deposit date: Site Phase IX. L 6.3, w 3.7 cm. Fabric: red 10R 5/8, red slip, black paint. Modeled, excision, boring, appliqué, paint. See Tuttle 2009 no. 168.
Parts of the neck, head, and one horn are preserved. The neck is modeled in a hollow hourglass shape and the spout hole (0.5 cm diam.) is bored from the exterior. The muzzle/spout, eye(s), and horns are then appliquéd onto the neck. A protuberance on the back of the head indicates the shape of the neck/mouth prior to placing the head features. The muzzle is conical and the spout is a bore-hole (0.7 cm diam.). The two separately-made holes are aligned during the appliqué process. The right eye is a disk appliquéd below the horn base; it has an excised pupil. The preserved right horn is elliptical and part of one notch is preserved. A sherd of the wheel-thrown body is preserved inside the break; the curvature of the body is evidenced by the arc in the basal break visible at the front of the artifact. The origin date range is suggested by comparison of the black paint to that used on the pottery of Phases 3b-4 (Schmid 2000).

No. 41. 02-P-24 (fig. 13.24). Type C.4.2 Ibex Vessels. From Upper Temenos, Tr. 94, Locus 54, Residential Quarter, Cave 2, fluvial deposit. Origin date: 2nd-4th c. A.D.(?). Deposit date: Site Phase IX. L 4.22, w 3.17 cm. Fabric: red 10R 5/8, red slip, black paint. Modeled, wheel, excision, boring, appliqué, paint. See Tuttle 2009 no. 169.
Parts of the neck, head and horns are preserved. The neck is a wheel-thrown, hollow cylinder (2.2 cm int. diam.). There is a small aperture (0.5 cm diam.) bored from the exterior through the neck wall. The muzzle/spout, eyes and horns are modeled and then appliquéd to the neck. The muzzle/spout (1.0 cm diam.) is bored from the exterior and then positioned over the pre-existing neck aperture. A break on the underside of the muzzle indicates that a beard broke away. The eyes are appliquéd elliptical disks; the pupils are rendered by excisions. The horns are flattened ellipses, with two excised notches extant on the left horn. Wavy lines are painted on the head with a fired black paint. The origin date range is suggested by comparison of the black paint to that used on the Phases 3b-4 pottery (Schmid 2000).

No. 42. 02-P-30 (fig. 13.25). Type C.4.2 Ibex Vessels. From Upper Temenos, Tr. 94, Locus 54, Residential Quarter, Cave 2, fluvial deposit. Deposit date: Site Phase IX. L 4.77, w 3.84 cm. Fabric: light red 10R6/6, self slip. Modeled, wheel, excision, boring, appliqué, paring. See Tuttle 2009 no. 170.

Parts of the neck, head, horns, and body are preserved. The neck is a modeled hollow cylinder (int. diam. 1.5 cm), the outline of which is visible in profile; there is an outflow aperture from the neck to the muzzle/spout. The head details are modeled separately and appliquéd to the neck. The muzzle/spout is conical with a circular aperture (0.7 cm diam.) bored from the exterior. A flattened triangular beard is appliquéd to the underside of the muzzle. The eyes are rendered by two appliquéd clay disks, with excised pupils. The horns are elliptical and several of the characteristic ibex horn notches are evident. The right eye disk slightly overlays the lowest notch, indicating that the eyes were attached after the horns. A curved, wheel-thrown body sherd is preserved inside the neck break; an elliptical outflow aperture (0.4 x 0.2 cm) is bored from the outside through the sherd.

No. 43. 06-P-6. Type C.4.2 Ibex Vessels. From Upper Temenos, Tr. 127, Locus 31, Baths *caldaria*, Destruction/sedimentation deposit. Deposit date: Site Phases XI-XII. L 5.17, w 3.9 cm. Fabric: light red 10R 6/8, red slip. Modeled, wheel, excision, boring, appliqué. See Tuttle 2009 no. 171.
Parts of the neck, head, horns and body are preserved. The neck and body are wheel-thrown. The outflow aperture in the neck is bored from the exterior. The head details are modeled separately and appliquéd to the neck. The muzzle/spout is conical with a circular aperture (0.7 cm diam.). The eyes are elliptical in shape. Five characteristic ibex horn notches are evident on each horn. A sherd from the wheel-thrown body is preserved inside the neck break.

No. 44. 98-P-1. Type C.4.3 Ibex, Type Uncertain. From Lower Temenos, Tr. 52, Locus 2, East Exedra, gray mortar/lime deposit. Origin date: 1st-4th c. A.D.(?). Deposit date: Site Phase X. L 3.9, w 2.7 cm. Fabric: red 2.5YR 6/6. Modeled, excision/impression(?). See Tuttle 2009 no. 172.
The crown of the head and parts of two horns are preserved. The extant portions of the fragment are modeled as one piece. The horns are cylindrical with characteristic notches preserved on both. The underside of the head has a slight hollow (*c.*1.5 cm diam.); this could indicate that the head was modeled separately before its attachment to the body.
The fragment could derive from either a figurine or a zoomorphic vessel. The origin date range is suggested by association with lamps from the locus (Barrett 2005 and 2008).

No. 45. 98-P-2. Type C.4.3 Ibex, Type Uncertain. From Lower Temenos, Tr. 52, Locus unknown, East Exedra. L 2.6, w 2.6 cm. Fabric: red 2.5YR 5/5, self slip(?). Modeled, excision. See Tuttle 2009 no. 173.
The crown of the head and parts of the two horns are preserved. The extant portions of the fragment are modeled as one piece. The horns are elliptical with characteristic notches evident on both. The interior of the head has an ovoid hollow cavity (2.1 x 0.8 cm); this suggests that the head was modeled separately before its attachment to the body. The fragment could derive from either a figurine or a zoomorphic vessel.

No. 46. 02-P-27 (fig. 13.26). Type C.4.3 Ibex, Type Uncertain. From Upper Temenos, Tr. 94, Locus 41, Residential Quarter, Cave 2/rooms 10-11; fluvial deposit. Deposit date: Site Phases XI-XIII. L 8.2, w 5.4 cm. Fabric: very pale brown 10YR 8/3. Modeled, excision, incision, boring, appliqué. See Tuttle 2009 no. 174.
A slice of the head with parts of the two eyes and ears as well as one horn. The eyes are formed by two concentric disks of clay appliquéd to the face; the pupils are excised holes in the center of the upper disks. The ears are appliquéd after the horns were modeled; the ears are pierced by holes made by boring. The horn is modeled as a piece with the head; the 5 characteristic notches were then appliquéd along the raised frontal ridge of the horn. The fragment could derive from either a figurine or a zoomorphic vessel. Bore holes in the ears suggests that it could have been suspended.

No. 47. 97-P-12. Type C.4.3 Ibex, Type Uncertain. From Temple, Tr. 48, Locus 1, Northeast Pronaos, sedimentation deposit. Deposit date: Site Phases IX-XIII. L 3.85, w 1.0 cm. Fabric: light red 2.5YR 6/6, self slip. Modeled, incision, boring, appliqué. See Barrett 1998, 304; Tuttle 2009 no. 175.
This ibex horn with an eye is from the left side of the original object. It is modeled with 6 incised, shallow lines to indicate the notches characteristic of the ibex figurines/vessels. The eye is made from a small, appliquéd disk with a bored pupil. The fragment could derive from either a figurine or a zoomorphic vessel.

No. 48. 00-P-9 (fig. 13.27). Type C.4.3 Ibex, Type Uncertain. From Upper Temenos, Tr. 77, Locus 20, East Perimeter Wall, fluvial deposit. Origin date: 2nd-4th c. A.D.(?). Deposit date: Site Phases XI-XIII. L 4.7, w 1.2 cm. Fabric: light red 10R 6/6, red slip, black paint. Modeled, excision, paring, paint. See Joukowsky 2007, fig. 7.46c; Tuttle 2009 no. 176.
This modeled ibex horn fragment has a slight curve back to the right at the tip when viewed frontally. Fourteen characteristic ibex horn notches are extant. Black paint is visible on both sides of the artifact. The fragment could derive from either a figurine or a zoomorphic vessel. The origin date range is suggested by comparison of the black paint to that used on the Phases 3b-4 pottery (Schmid 2000).

No. 49. 02-P-10. Type C.4.3 Ibex, Type Uncertain. From Upper Temenos, Tr. 94, Locus 41, Residential Quarter, Cave 2/rooms 10-11, fluvial deposit. Origin date: 2nd-4th c. A.D.(?). Deposit date: Site Phases XI-XIII. L 6.0, w

1.8 cm. Fabric: light red 2.5YR 6/8, self slip, black paint. Modeled, excision, paring, paint. See Tuttle 2009 no. 177.
This ibex horn has 12 characteristic notches preserved. The horn has a smaller circumference at the base. The basal break is elliptical, but the section is "hourglass" in shape due to paring along the length of the sides. Black paint is visible only on the right side of the object. The fragment could derive from either a figurine or a zoomorphic vessel. The origin date range is suggested by comparison of the black paint to that used on the Phases 3b-4 pottery (Schmid 2000).

No. 50. 02-P-11. Type C.4.3 Ibex, Type Uncertain. From Upper Temenos, Tr. 94, Locus 41, Residential Quarter, Cave 2/rooms 10-11, fluvial deposit. Origin date: 2nd-4th c. A.D.(?). Deposit date: Site Phases XI-XIII. L 4.8, w 1.6 cm. Fabric: red 2.5YR 5/6, self slip, black paint. Modeled, excision, paring, paint. See Tuttle 2009 no. 178.
This ibex horn has 14 characteristic notches extant. Faint excised lines extend the length of the fragment to either side of the raised notches; they probably originate from the paring away of excess displaced clay resulting from excising the notches. Black paint can be discerned only on the left side. The angle of the basal break and the fragment's stance suggest this horn derives from the left side of the head, which would make the paint visible only on the object's exterior. The fragment could derive from either a figurine or a zoomorphic vessel. The origin date range is suggested by comparison of the black paint to that used on the Phases 3b-4 pottery (Schmid 2000).

No. 51. 02-P-12. Type C.4.3 Ibex, Type Uncertain. From Upper Temenos, Tr. 94, Locus 41, Residential Quarter, Cave 2/rooms 10-11, fluvial deposit. Origin date: 2nd-4th c. A.D.(?). Deposit date: Site Phases XI-XIII. L 5.76, w 1.7 cm. Fabric: light reddish brown 5YR 6/4, red slip, black paint. Modeled, excision, paring, paint. See Tuttle 2009 no. 179.
This ibex horn has 14 characteristic notches extant. Black paint is found on both sides of the fragment, but it is more extensive on the left. The angle of the basal break and the stance both suggest this would have been the left horn of the original artifact. The fragment could derive from either a figurine or a zoomorphic vessel. The origin date range is suggested by comparison of the black paint to that used on the Phases 3b-4 pottery (Schmid 2000).

No. 52. 02-P-31. Type C.4.3 Ibex, Type Uncertain. From Upper Temenos, Tr. 94, Locus 54, Residential Quarter, Cave 2, fluvial deposit. Deposit date: Site Phase IX. L 4.5, w 1.8 cm. Fabric: red 10R 5/6, red slip. Modeled, excision. See Tuttle 2009 no. 180.
The curve of the apex of this ibex horn is shaped and tapered by hand. It has 23 characteristic notches preserved. It is not possible to determine from which side of the head the fragment originates. It could belong to either a figurine or a zoomorphic vessel.

No. 53. 01-P-8. Type C.4.3 Ibex, Type Uncertain. From Upper Temenos, Tr. 84, Locus 8, East Perimeter Wall, Room A, fluvial deposit. Deposit date: Site Phases X-XIII. L 4.1, w 1.3 cm. Fabric: light red 2.5YR 6/6. Modeled, excision. See Tuttle 2009 no. 181.
This ibex horn is formed from a rolled cylinder of clay and shaped manually. A central air pocket is visible in the modern break. Nine characteristic notches are extant on the front of the horn. The fragment could derive from either a figurine or a zoomorphic vessel.

No. 54. 06-P-8. Type C.4.3 Ibex, Type Uncertain. From Lower Temenos, Tr. 126, Locus 1, Baths, N hypocaust chamber, sedimentation deposit. Deposit date: Site Phases XI-XIV. L 4.75, w 1.6 cm. Fabric: light red 10R 6/6, red slip. Modeled, excision, incision, paring. See Tuttle 2009 no. 182.
The curvature of this ibex horn is shaped by paring. Seven characteristic notches are extant. It is not possible to determine from which side of the head the fragment originates. It could derive from either a figurine or a zoomorphic vessel.

No. 55. 06-P-1. Type C.4.3 Ibex, Type Uncertain. From Lower Temenos, Tr. 120, Locus 7, Baths, colonnaded corridor, collapse deposit. Deposit date: Site Phase XI. L 3.7, w 2.5 cm. Fabric: light reddish brown 2.5YR 7/4, self slip. Modeled, incision. See Tuttle 2009 no. 184.
This ibex horn is roughly cylindrical. The 9 characteristic horn notches are rendered by incision rather than excision. The angle of the basal break indicates this is the left horn of the original artifact. The fragment could derive from either a figurine or a zoomorphic vessel.

No. 56. 94-P-1. Type C.7.1 Modeled Quadruped Figurines. From Upper Temenos, Tr. 2, Locus 23, West Forecourt/podium, destruction debris/fluvial deposit(?). Deposit date: Site Phase XIV. L 4.4, w 2.7 cm. Fabric: pink 5YR 7/3. Modeled, excision. See Tuttle 2009 no. 185.
Parts of the head, torso and forelegs are extant. The body is slightly flattened and elliptical in shape, whereas the neck and forelegs are cylindrical. Two ovoid breaks at the top of the head indicate missing parts, which are probably horns rather than ears. The right eye is preserved as a raised oval with a slight tail angled to the

lower right; the eye is sculpted rather than appliquéd; the pupil is formed by excision. The snout is broken away.

No. 57. 00-P-15. Type C.7.1 Modeled Quadruped Figurines. From Propylaeum, Tr. 69, Locus 1, South Gallery, overburden/fluvial deposit. Deposit date: Site Phases XI-XIII. L 4.5, w 2.7 cm. Fabric: light reddish brown 2.5YR 6/4, self slip. Modeled, excision, appliqué, boring. See Joukowsky 2007, fig. 7.46a; Tuttle 2009 no. 186.
Parts of the head, neck, and torso are extant. The damaged face/muzzle is worked into a separate lump of clay appliquéd to the head. The eyes are rendered by two small, round bore-holes. A slightly, curved wedge-shaped excision creates the mouth. There are no traces of nostrils. Two elliptical breaks indicate that appendages once surmounted the crown, the sizes of which suggest that these would have been horns rather than ears. The breaks for the missing body and forelegs indicate the former was ovoid and the latter cylindrical/conical.

No. 58. 95-P-2. Type C.7.1 Modeled Quadruped Figurines. From Lower Temenos, Tr. 14, Locus 14, East Triple Colonnade, Burnt lime fill/dump. Deposit date: Site Phase X. L 6.2, w 1.8 cm. Fabric: light reddish yellow 5YR 7/6. Modeled. See Barrett 1998, 301; El-Khouri 2002 no. 320; Tuttle 2009 no. 187.
As the front portion and hind legs are broken off, the original size of the piece cannot be estimated. The tail, curved toward the left, was formed by pinching a clay extrusion upward; the direction of motion is evident from impressions beneath the tail. Similar tails are found on other figurines.

No. 59. 98-P-5. Type C.7.1 Modeled Quadruped Figurines. From Upper Temenos, Tr. 53, Locus 2, East Cistern, fluvial deposit. Deposit date: Site Phases IX-XIII. L 6.0, w 3.3 cm. Fabric: light red 2.5YR 6/6, red slip. Modeled, paring(?). See El-Khouri 2002 no. 319; Tuttle 2009 no. 188.
The body, parts of the neck, three legs and tail are preserved. The body is roughly cylindrical, although thicker at the front and tapering toward the rear. The legs also appear cylindrical and are modeled as a piece with the body. The tail was formed from a pinched extrusion of clay from the body. The neck is angled forward from the body. A long gouge along the top of the back cannot be explained.

No. 60. 98-P-6. Type C.7.1 Modeled Quadruped Figurines. From Lower Temenos, Tr. 52, Locus Unknown, East Exedra, deposit unknown. L 3.3, w 1.9 cm. Fabric: light red 2.5YR 6/6, red slip. Modeled. See El-Khouri 2002 no. 322; Tuttle 2009 no. 189.
A hindquarter of the body is preserved with parts of the legs and a tail. The body is cylindrical but the legs seem to have been conical. The tail has a slight curve toward the left. It was formed by pinching an extrusion of clay from the body.

No. 61. 02-P-7 (fig. 13.28). Type C.7.1 Modeled Quadruped Figurines. From Upper Temenos, Tr. 94, Locus 41, Residential Quarter, Cave 2/rooms 10-11, fluvial deposit. Origin date: 2nd-4th c. A.D.(?). Deposit date: Site Phases XI-XIII. L 7.6, w 2.4 cm. Fabric: red 2.5YR 5/8, brown slip(?), black paint. Modeled, excision, appliqué, paring. See Tuttle 2009 no. 190.
Completely preserved are the body, left legs, and tail, parts of the muzzle and right hind leg. The body is cylindrical; the legs range between cylindrical and conical in shape. Impressions around the join of the left foreleg to the body suggest that the legs were modeled separately before attaching. The tail was formed by pinching a long extrusion from the body and then doubling it back upon itself. The muzzle is appliquéd to the front of the body between the forelegs, and is twisted *c.* 20° off the central axis toward the left. The mouth is rendered by a slightly-curved excision. Faint traces of black paint can be seen on the body. The overall proportions seem poor, although the apparent disparity between length and height may have been offset if this figure had horns. By contrast, the axial quality is good, indicating that the figure could have stood on its own even with a large head. The origin date is suggested by comparison of the black paint to that used on the Phases 3b-4 pottery (Schmid 2000).

No. 62. 02-P-6. Type C.7.1 Modeled Quadruped Figurines. From Propylaeum, Tr. 82, Locus 1, East Room 3, overburden/fluvial deposit(?). Deposit date: Site Phases IX-XIII. L 7.5, w 1.9 cm. Fabric: light red 2.5YR 7/6, self slip(?). Modeled. See Tuttle 2009 no. 191.
The body, 4 legs, tail and part of the neck are extant. The body is cylindrical. The legs and tail were formed by pinching extrusions of clay from the body. These appendages remain complete. At the neck break an internal nub of clay is surrounded by an outer layer, which suggests a two-stage modeling process: the body is formed with a rudimentary neck, the head was then modeled separately, and the join was secured by smoothing and working an extra clay layer into the body. The tail is nearly the same length as the legs, which suggests odd proportions for the complete figurine. However, the axial quality of the extant fragment is very good, suggesting that the complete form could have stood on its own.

No. 63. 02-P-1. Type C.7.1 Modeled Quadruped Figurines. From Upper Temenos, Tr. 89, Locus 5 Baroque Room, fluvial deposit. Deposit date: Site Phases IX-XIII(?). L 8.9, w 2.3 cm. Fabric: light red 2.5YR 6/6, self slip. Modeled, boring, incision. See Tuttle 2009 no. 192.

The body and part of the left hind leg are preserved. Elliptical breaks indicate where the head, legs, and tail have broken away. The position of the neck break indicates that the neck/head would have angled forward from the body. Beneath the tail break on the rump are unusual marks, a small circular bore-hole above a diagonal wedge-shaped incision; these appear to render the anus and vagina, indicating that a female quadruped is represented.

No. 64. 02-P-26. Type C.7.1 Modeled Quadruped Figurines. From Upper Temenos, Tr. 94, Locus 54, Residential Quarter, Cave 2, fluvial deposit. Deposit date: Site Phase IX. L 6.24, w 2.76 cm. Fabric: reddish yellow 5YR 6/6. Modeled. See Tuttle 2009 no. 193.
Body fragment of a quadruped. To judge by the Great Temple Catalogue description, it is a body with 4 leg stumps. This object could not be located in the museum storage, but it had been photographed for the catalogue.

No. 65. 97-P-1. Type C.7.1 Modeled Quadruped Figurines. From Upper Temenos, Tr. 44, Locus 7, East Plaza, fluvial deposit. Origin date: late 1st c. A.D.(?). Deposit date: Site Phases XI-XIII. L 3.6, w 2.95 cm. Fabric: light reddish brown 5YR 6/4. Modeled. See Barrett 1998, 304; Tuttle 2009 no. 194.
The base of the neck where it joins the body and forelegs remain. The right foreleg seems complete and is conical; the body is a flattened ellipse. The neck appears to angle upward slightly to the left.
Four Roman lamp fragments of the late 1st c. A.D. were found in the same locus (Barrett 1998). Although found in a fluvial deposit, the consistent date of the lamps may provide an approximate date for this fragment.

No. 66. 04-P-1. Type C.7.1 Modeled Quadruped Figurines. From Propylaeum, Tr. 100, Locus 1, Cryptoporticus room 3, collapse/débris/fill deposit. Deposit date: Site Phases IX-XIII. L 3.3, w 2.2 cm. Fabric: light red 2.5YR 6/6, self slip. Modeled, appliqué. See Tuttle 2009 no. 195.
Parts of the body and neck, as well as the right foreleg are extant. The body is elliptical but neck and foreleg are cylindrical. The leg(s) and neck are modeled separately and appliquéd to the body; a piece of the secondary clay layer is evident on the neck break.

No. 67. 02-P-13. Type C.7.1 Modeled Quadruped Figurines. From Upper Temenos, Tr. 89, Locus 3(?),Shrine/Baroque Room/West Cistern, fluvial deposit. Deposit date: Site Phases IX-XIII(?). L 7.8, w 3.0 cm. Fabric: light red 10R 6/6. Modeled, excision, appliqué(?). See Tuttle 2009 no. 196.
The whole body is extant, along with parts of the head/neck and left foreleg. The body is cylindrical and tapers in thickness from front to back. A possible break at the rear may indicate that there is also a tail. It seems that there is no distinction between the head and neck. The protrusion rising on the right side on the front appears to be the base of a horn. Two diagonal excisions on the front beneath the "horn bases" may be schematic "eyes". No muzzle is extant, although surface irregularities on the front suggest an appliqué may have broken away.

No. 68. 02-P-23 (fig. 13.29). Type C.7.1 Modeled Quadruped Figurines. From Upper Temenos, Tr. 94, Locus 54 Residential Quarter, Cave 2, fluvial deposit. Deposit date: Site Phase IX. L 8.7, w 3.6 cm. Fabric: light red 2.5YR 6/6, red slip. Modeled, excision, incision, boring, appliqué. See Tuttle 2009 no. 197.
Head, body, tail and left hind leg are preserved. The body is a flattened slab, the legs tapering cylinders. The tail curves in toward the body, and was formed by pinching the clay upward from the body. Faint incised lines on the tail may be an attempt to render fur. The head is seated on a neck that rises in a piece from the body. The face is triangular, with the muzzle tapering to a rounded point. Two incised parallel lines curve across the muzzle bridge; the area between is subdivided by short vertical incised lines, perhaps suggesting whiskers. The tip of the muzzle has two excisions and a curved, incised line to indicate nostrils and mouth. The eyes are formed of appliquéd clay disks and the pupils are bored. Ovoid breaks at the side edges on the crown indicate where ears or horns are broken away. Eleven short, parallel incised lines, aligned front to back, are visible on the crown between these breaks and may be another attempt to depict fur.
The figurine was probably intended to depict a gazelle or ibex. The use of incised lines to render details of the animal's fur is very rare in the known corpus of figurines. Cf. also no. 69.

No. 69. 02-P-8 (fig. 13.30). Type C.7.1 Modeled Quadruped Figurines. From Upper Temenos, Tr. 94, Locus 3 Residential Quarter, overburden/fluvial deposit. Deposit date: Site Phase IX. L 2.8, w 3.5 cm. Fabric: light red 2.5YR 6/8, red slip. Modeled, excision, incision, boring, appliqué. See Tuttle 2009 no. 198.
Only the head and part of the neck are preserved. The muzzle is bifurcated by a deep excision, the top of which is now broken away. This excision extends a little along the left side to represent the mouth. No nostrils are shown. A single fine incised line curves across the muzzle bridge. A single, short incised line on the right extends diagonally from the arc-line to the broken muzzle, but no similar lines are extant on the left. The eyes are formed of appliquéd clay disks and the pupils are bored. Ovoid breaks at the side edges on the crown indicate where ears or horns are broken away. Eight short, mostly-parallel incised lines, aligned front to back, are visible on the crown between these breaks; they may be an attempt to depict fur (cf. no. 68, muzzle and crown details).

The piece is likely intended to depict a gazelle or ibex. The use of incised lines to render details of the animal's fur is rare in the known corpus of figurines. Cf. also no. 68.

No. 70. 01-P-9. Type C.7.1 Modeled Quadruped Figurines. From Upper Temenos, Tr. 83, Locus 29 South Corridor, fill/sedimentation deposit(?). Deposit date: Site Phases XI-XIII. L 8.8, w 3.6 cm. Fabric: red 2.5YR 5/8, red or self slip. Modeled, boring, appliqué. See Tuttle 2009 no. 199.

The body, parts of 3 legs, tail and an upright rectilinear projection from the top of the rump are extant. The piece has an inner cylindrical core that is at least partly hollow (when found, it was full of sand that readily poured out through the bore-hole). The body features are modeled (appliquéd) in a secondary layer of clay over this core. The legs are roughly cylindrical; the axial stance indicates the figure could easily have stood on its own. The tail was formed by pinching an extrusion from the body. A small bore-hole (purpose unknown) above the tail pierces through into the inner core. There is no other hole to suggest that a spout was present in the missing head/neck. The rectilinear upright is enigmatic but may be part of a support for a separable piece (rider, cargo?). The size of a large elliptical break on the top in front may suggest either a robust neck or that a second upright projection has broken away along with the neck/head.

No. 71. 02-P-4 (figs. 13.4 and 13.31). Type C.7.2 Modeled Quadruped Vessels. From Upper Temenos, Tr. 94, Locus 41 Residential Quarter, Cave 2/rooms 10-11, fluvial deposit. Origin date: 2nd-4th c. A.D.(?). Deposit date: Site Phases XI-XIII. L 7.85, w 4.15 cm. Fabric: light red 2.5YR 7/6, red slip, black paint. Modeled, boring, paring, appliqué, paint. See Tuttle 2009 no. 201.

The preserved body of this zoomorphic vessel is ovoid in shape and hollow. What may be a faint join seam along the base suggests that it was inverted when it was modeled, the base being added last to seal the hollow interior. The "belly" is flattened. The legs are appliquéd, and the size of the breaks suggests they are not much larger than what survives; the flattened "belly" may have functioned as the base, the legs being iconic or decorative. The tail is appliquéd; the break at its tip suggests that it extends to the right, possibly curled back on itself. Two holes are evident, both bored from the exterior: the rear one (0.8 cm diam.) is probably the "filling" hole, while the front one (1.0 cm diam.) is the outflow aperture to the missing spout. A large break around the front hole indicates where the head/spout is attached. Nested chevron patterns in black paint decorate the piece: horizontal bands along the sides, and vertical bands on the front. Those along the left are nested from front-to-back, while those on the right are back-to-front. The left vertical band on the front is isolated, while the two on the right are extensions of the horizontal side bands — the combined directionality of the decoration may suggest that it was painted while being turned in a clockwise motion, starting on the left. Although this nested chevron pattern is not explicitly paralleled on any of the heads presented here, the paint itself suggests that this could be a body from an ibex zoomorphic vessel. The origin date is suggested by comparison of the black paint to that used on the Phases 3b-4 pottery (Schmid 2000).

No. 72. 04-P-10. Type C.7.6a Moulded Quadrupeds, Type Uncertain, Legs/Feet. From Lower Temenos, Tr. 98, Locus 4, West Cryptoporticus West, sediment deposit. Origin date: 2nd-4th c. A.D.(?). Deposit date: Site Phase IX. L 4.9, w 2.9 cm. Fabric: light red 2.5YR 6/6, self slip(?). Bivalve mould. See Tuttle 2009 no. 204.

The right rear leg and traces of the tail are preserved. The orientation is shown in the drawing and photograph. The raised contour renders the hind leg. A faint series of moulded diagonal hatch-lines extend down along the outer edge of the leg to depict the tail. A fragment of the curve where the leg joins the underbelly can be seen at far right. The fragment could derive from either a horse or camel figurine.

No. 73. 08-P-1 (figs. 13.2, 13.32, 13.34 and 13.35). Type C.9.2 Hedgehog Vessels. From Upper Temenos, Tr. SP110, Locus 46, Early terrace of wadi stones, the piece was found between stones. Origin date: 1st c. B.C.(?). Deposit date: Site Phase I. L 7.9, w 4.0 cm. Fabric: light red 2.5YR 6/6. Bivalve mould, modeling, incision, paring, boring, impression, appliqué. See Joukowsky 2006, fig. 16; ead. 2007, fig. 4.94; Tuttle 2009 no. 229.

The vessel is nearly complete, missing only the forepaws and rump. The body is covered with raised relief bumps to simulate the hedgehog's bristly fur. The body is formed in a bivalve mould; the joining is finely executed, the only evidence of the seam being the circular impressions used to mimic the raised-relief fur texturing. The head was modeled separately and appliquéd to the body. The details of the head are finely executed. The eyes are circles with the pupils bored into the central relief disk created by the incisions; the nostrils are indicated by two bore-holes above the spout. The division of the mouth is made by a deep horizontal incision to each side of the spout; the whiskers are rendered on each side by two vertical incisions below the mouth. The ears are broken away. The hind legs are proportional and realistically depicted, including incisions to indicate long toes/claws on each paw. The spout is a hole (0.24 cm diam.) bored from the outside through the muzzle. The filling hole (1.1 cm diam.) is set just before the crest of the hunched back; it was bored from the outside through the seam after joining. The base is flat and smooth, and the vessel still stands evenly.

The hedgehog may also have been used as a subject for figurines (cf. Horsfield and Horsfield 1941 no. 260). This artifact can be tentatively dated by the context to the 1st c. B.C.

D. Zoomorphic, Other Artifact Types

No. 74. 00-P-5 (fig. 13.37). Type D.2.2 Masks/Affixes, Equids. From Upper Temenos, Tr. 77, Locus 28, S East Perimeter, deposit unknown. L 4.5, w 3.0 cm. Fabric: red 2.5YR 6/8, red slip. Monovalve mould, Modeling, incision, excision, appliqué. See Tuttle 2009 no. 230.
A section from a moulded horse preserving the right side of the head with the eye and parts of the ears. The eye is ovoid and tapers toward both sides; the pupil is an excised hole. Above the eye is a curving brow ridge in relief, bounded by upper and lower incisions. The right ear is 'teardrop' in shape, its interior rendered by a shallow excision. The ears were modeled separately and then appliquéd to the head. Faint moulded contours along the back of the neck may render tresses of the mane. The absence of a join seam and the unfinished left ear suggest that the object is to be viewed from only one side. The limited mechanical characteristics suggests it is perhaps an architectural affix.

E. Plaques

No. 75. 97-P-7 (fig. 13.38). Type E.1.1 Anthropomorphic Plaques, Nude Youths. From Temple, Tr. 47, Locus 13, Theatre West, fluvial/sediment deposit. Deposit date: Site Phases IX-XIII. L 8.4, w 4.33 cm. Fabric: light red 2.5YR 6/6, red slip. Monovalve mould, incision, paring. See Barrett 1998, 300; El-Khouri 2002 no. 103; Joukowsky 1998b, fig. 16; Tuttle 2009 no. 231.
Part of the body of a nude male child standing on a pedestal within a frame is preserved. Predominantly frontal in representation, an attempt is made to show the body *contrapposto*, with the left leg slightly forward and angled outward. The body is generally well-proportioned, with well-moulded details. The right arm is raised, the hand held to the extant part of the lower face; the forefinger is extended and the rest of the digits are distinct. Contours at the wrist suggests a bracelet. The belly swells slightly; a curved, moulded line separating it from the genitalia also gives it a hint of pendency, and the position of the navel toward the lower edge of the belly enhances this aspect. The testes and penis are both evident in the genitalia, which are delineated from the top of the thighs by two grooves. The thighs are fleshy and are proportional to the belly. The knees are moulded, the shins tapering beneath them. The toes of the right foot are articulated but all the same size. The figure stands on a moulded pedestal but the design on the front of the pedestal is indecipherable. The plaque is enclosed within a frame with an ornate design consisting of straight and circular incisions; this frame may be part of an aedicule. The posture of the raised hand with forefinger extended toward the mouth may suggest that this is an image of the child god, Harpocrates.

No. 76. 02-P-15. Type E.1.2 Anthropomorphic Plaques, Enthroned Nude Females. From Upper Temenos, Tr. 94, Locus 41, Residential Quarter, Cave 2/rooms 10-11, fluvial/sediment deposit. Deposit date: Site Phases XI-XIII. L 4.6, w 4.74 cm. Fabric: very pale brown 10YR 8/4, red slip. Monovalve mould, modeling, incision, paring. See Tuttle 2009 no. 233.
The legs, feet and footstool of an enthroned nude female image are present. The knees are shown together; the thighs angle back to each side to match the width of the throne. Anklets with central openings are shown on each leg. A V-shaped moulded relief on the top of each foot indicates sandal straps. The feet rest on a footstool, which has two incised horizontal lines of a rectilinear pattern evident on the front. The figure is flanked by two vertical grooves; they are from the original edge of the mould. The plaque was created by using only half of a bivalve mould of the "Enthroned Nude Females" type. The outer edges of the plaque are created by additional clay modeled to the original edges.

No. 77. 00-P-8. Type E.2.1 Plaques, Steles, Surmounted by Masks. From Upper Temenos, Tr. 77, Locus 9, East Perimeter Wall, fluvial deposit. Deposit date: Site Phases XI-XIII. L 2.35, w 2.48 cm. Fabric: pale red 2.5YR 7/4, red slip. Monovalve mould, incision, paring. See Joukowsky 2007, fig. 7.45e; Tuttle 2009 no. 236.
A nearly circular medallion with a head. The details are very faint but a fleshy face surmounted by a headdress can be discerned. The face is well moulded; even in its present state the different contours are evident. The headdress, which appears to have two successive peaks, sits on the crown of the head; the band across the forehead is decorated with faint vertical, moulded hatch-lines. A moulded extrusion extends at a 60° angle from beneath the headdress down to the right; there is also a fragment of the same at the left. These could be tresses of hair or a part of the headdress. The front edge of the medallion is encircled by a relief ridge defined by an incised line made after the moulding. The shape of the medallion is finished by paring. The reverse surface is finely smoothed, with finger traces evident.
The subject cannot be identified with certainty. This piece is only part of the original object; it probably surmounted a *stele* (or herm), which may have been plain or have displayed a different image. Similar artifacts have been described as 'theatrical masks" depicting helmeted youths. The headdress on our example appears more like a 'crown' or 'diadem'.

F. Vessels

No. 78. 02-P-32 (fig. 13.39). Type F.1.1b Moulded Appliqués for Vessels, Figural, Males. From Upper Temenos, Tr. 94, Locus 41, Residential Quarter, Cave 2/rooms 10-11, fluvial deposit. Deposit date: Site Phases XI-XIII. L 3.35, w 4.6 cm. Fabric: reddish yellow 5YR 7/6, red slip, red paint(?). Moulded (monovalve?), incision(?), paint(?). See Tuttle 2009 no. 238.

Part of a male torso, shown clad in a mantle or possibly togate, is preserved. Details of the garment are rendered on the left and across the lower edge of the fragment by moulded raised reliefs that are enhanced by incision. The contoured surfaces rise from the center of the figure toward the right; this slight swell seems to render the different planes of the sternum and the bare, right pectoral muscle (the left pectoral is covered by the garment). A small curved piece of the broken top edge, aligned with the proposed sternum, suggests the slope of the neck. The small fragment extending out to the left may be part of the surface of an arm. Traces of a white substance appear in some of the garment folds, which may indicate the use of ancillary, non-fired paint. A single line (droplet?) of red fired paint is visible extending from the top break onto the right "pectoral". The fragment is slightly curved across the horizontal axis. The absence of a join seam suggests that it was made in a monovalve mould. The curvature of the fragment, along with the presence of the red paint, may suggest that this is an appliqué from the surface of a painted vessel; the droplet could merely be an error.

No. 79. 05-P-15 (fig. 13.3). Type F.4.1 Vessel Components, Spouts. From Upper Temenos, Tr. SP110, Locus 29, Southwest Cistern/Reservoir, dump/fill deposit. Deposit date: Site Phase IX. L 6.23, w 3.74 cm. Fabric: red 2.5YR 6/8, red slip. Bivalve mould, Modeling, incision, boring. See Tuttle 2009 no. 253.

The head, forelegs, and right hind leg of a recumbent animal are extant. The head rests on the outstretched forelegs. The left side is better formed. A curved moulded line separates the face and the top of the head. The eye is an ovoid relief that tapers to each end with an incised pupil. The moulded ear is raised and bifurcated by a vertical incised line. Below the eye, the stylized mouth is disproportional, rendered as two curved relief rows divided into teeth. The contours of the foreleg are visible, but the details of the paw are broken away. The features of the right side are damaged, perhaps during the removal from the mould and/or in the joining process. There is no dividing line between face and head. The ovoid eye is misshapen and shows evidence of a hasty attempt to redefine it by incision; the pupil is incised. The ear did not survive the mould and is crudely remodeled and incised with a bifurcating line. Only one faint moulded relief line suggests the mouth. The foreleg lacks details, and a clear finger impression damaged its form during the joining process. The paw of the hind leg has three toes indicated by incisions. The fragment is hollow. The join seams are poorly aligned, resulting in an uneven surface for the base. A spout hole (0.54 cm diam.) is bored from the outside through the mouth into the hollow neck. The stylized animal cannot be identified with certainty, but a similar piece has been interpreted as a rabbit. It is possibly a spout from a rhyton.

G. Unknown/Uncertain Artifact Type

No. 80. 00-P-11 (fig. 13.40). Type G.3 Molded, Valve. Type Uncertain. From Propylaeum, Tr. 69, Locus 6, South Gallery, fluvial/sediment deposit(?). Deposit date: Site Phase IX. L 4.93, w 3.19 cm. Fabric: light red 10R 7/6, self slip(?), reduction discoloration. Molded, incision, paring. See Joukowsky 2007, fig. 7.45c; Tuttle 2009 no. 293.

The object cannot be identified with certainty. It may be part of a torso clad in a *chiton* or mantle. The garment is bound by a girdle. The graduated lines above the girdle may be an attempt to render the slope of the garment up to where it crossed the left shoulder; the right shoulder would thus have been bare. The incisions below the girdle could then be the skirt. Although the fragment suggests a slight hourglass shape, the breaks are problematic; it is difficult to reconcile them with a human pose.

14

The glass (1998-2006)

Margaret O'Hea

Introduction

The glass excavated from 1998 to 2006 provides material for better understanding how Nabataean culture and trade interacted with its region and beyond during the first two centuries A.D. Previous publications of early glass at Petra have been cursory,[1] with the exception of the exemplary study of the Swiss-Liechtenstein excavations of a mansion on Ez Zantur,[2] the ridge overlooking our site. Yet even with data for Ez Zantur, the total amount of published early glass suggests the lack of any local glass industry,[3] and our assemblage seems to support this hypothesis. Our Early Roman corpus includes an unusually high percentage of imported, high-quality glass that includes decolourized intaglio vessels, facet-cut and painted beakers. Stratigraphic evidence at the Great Temple confirms their Flavian-Trajanic date range. Along with case flagons from the W Mediterranean, their presence at Petra contributes to the study of Nabataean globalized markets and trade patterns into and beyond Nabataea. The early glass falls into two groups: pieces that follow the generic traditions of glass workshops throughout the Levant, and those which were imported from the W Mediterranean, from Roman Egypt, or from specialised workshops in Phoenicia or Judaea, the second group comprising nearly three-quarters of a minimum number estimate (MNE) of 61 Early Roman vessels and revealing a profoundly different assemblage from that recognized in most Levantine cities, particularly after the Julio-Claudian period (see further below).

Three-quarters of the Julio-Claudian and Flavian assemblage is drinking ware, beakers, drinking bowls or wine flagons. None was found complete or was fully reconstructable, not even from rooms providing evidence of early 2nd-c. architectural collapse, which suggests that the rooms' contents had already been partially cleared before the roofs collapsed. Such drinking wares could have been used in ritual feasts in Nabataean temples (note the presence of dining rooms surrounding the courtyard of the later temple at Khirbet et-Tannur).[4]

The glass associated with the destruction of the adjacent baths (figs. 9.1.2) by the earthquake of A.D. 363 adds to the picture of persistent Egyptian stylistic influences on contemporary glass-workshops already provided by the mansion on Ez Zantur, confirming a distinctive southern Levantine *koine* of glass forms and decoration; it also confirms an early dating for the appearance of circular blown windowpanes. A clear differentiation in the use of glass appears between the Roman and the so-called Byzantine period. Most of those from the latter period (MNE 335) are either light fittings or flasks for perfumed oil found in the baths (see fig. 14.11 below). Nearly a third are flasks or jars, and nearly half are hanging lamps (more if beakers and goblets are counted as lighting equipment). Absent are any forms that are typologically purely 6th c. or Islamic (e.g., Late Byzantine and Umayyad slab-footed blown bowl bases). Since Umayyad glass is usually plentiful on urban sites in the region, it reinforces the notion that this part of the city was not occupied in that period.

The glassware will be discussed in chronological groups following Roman Mediterranean rather than Nabataean historical periodization. Within the catalogue, the illustrated type (identified by Type Series or TS number) is described, with variations of decoration or fabric. The MNE is based on either rims or bases, depending on which gives the larger minimum estimate, as well as any body fragments that by their fabric or form do not belong to identified rims or bases. Fabric colors were identified by looking through sections of sherds wetted with ethanol (this reduces the distortion of surface hydration). All dimensions are in

1 E.g., Murray and Ellis 1940.
2 Keller 2006.
3 Ibid. 183.
4 McKenzie *et al.* 2002, fig. 4.

centimeters: h = height, rdiam = rim diameter, bdiam = base diameter, w = width, and th = thickness. All simple blown rims are fire-rounded unless otherwise stated. Only the earliest datable contexts are treated as useful chronological indicators.

Late Hellenistic glass

Sagged drinking bowls are the earliest mass-produced glass vessels of antiquity. Syrian, Judaean or Decapolis sites with Late Hellenistic occupation from *c*.150 B.C. onwards typically yield these bowls in the hundreds.[5] They testify to a thriving and widespread glass industry in the Levant. An MNE of just 4 comes from our assemblage. Conical bowls probably begin early in the series but continue into the early 1st c. B.C., overlapping with hemispherical bowls (TS 97) and parabolic bowls (TS 166). All are simply decorated, with lathe-cut internal grooves, and all function as drinking cups. Core-formed vessels are wholly absent even though they had a ritual and funerary use. Such bowls are ordinarily much rarer than sagged drinking bowls in Late Hellenistic domestic contexts, although one was found at Ez Zantur.[6] That so few Late Hellenistic glass vessels were retrieved could simply reflect a scarcity of contemporary houses in the immediate area. Yet no identifiable Hellenistic glass came from the Petra Church beneath which Late Hellenistic occupation was clearly identified.[7] The scarcity of Hellenistic glass does not support the idea of local glass production, nor indeed of much importing of glassware from Judaea or the Decapolis region.

Commonplace on Late Hellenistic sites throughout the Levant are hemispherical glass counters (TS 73), made as simple drops onto a flat surface. They are used as gaming pieces, being depicted as such in tombs,[8] but they were also used as appliqué decoration on Third-Style wall paintings.[9] A total of 4 are present in our assemblage, including those from earlier seasons.[10]

Clearly an Egyptian import is the small fragmentary inlay TS 92 (fig. 14.2). It belongs to a tradition of Late Ptolemaic rectangular inlays for tables, couches, and boxes. Excavated examples in Egypt and N Africa provide only a broad range of *c*.100 B.C.–A.D. 100,[11] and our site provides only a broadly 1st c. A.D. context. Such inlays have not yet been published for other Levantine sites. The floral architectural roundel found in 1997[12] may also be Egyptian, despite the fact that later adaptations of floral motifs were made in Italy.[13] Rectangular inlays have either simple Egyptian motifs or small half-theatrical masks[14] specifically associated with Antony and Cleopatra.[15] No published parallel has been found for a yellow line spanning both green and blue, but the row of triangles may indicate a hair strand, as part of an unusual form of mask.

Fig. 14.1 TS 104. Sagged conical bowl rim (MNE 2). rdiam 15. Polished rim on conical body; single extant groove below rim interior. Strongly olive greenish. Iridescent flaking. Another example of the type is decolorized.

TS 97. Sagged deep bowl rim (MNE 1). rdiam 10. Polished rim on deep hemispherical body. No extant grooves; wheel-polished interior. Decolorized. Black on iridescence.

TS 166. Sagged parabolic bowl rim (MNE 1). rdiam 11. Slightly flaring rim, deep bowl. Pair of close-set grooves below rim interior, another pair extant on upper body. Indeterminate fabric.

TS 73. Counter (MNE 1). (fig. 14.1, 1) h 0.5, bdiam 1.2 . Solid dome, complete. Indeterminate fabric. Black on iridescence.

TS 92. Mosaic cane inlay (MNE 1) (fig. 14.1, 2). Extant h 1, w 1, th 0.5. Flat thick edge fragment of rectilinear inlay. Dark cobalt blue and opaque mid-green, with fine yellow line through both green and blue, and fine corkscrew line of cobalt blue in green. Iridescence. Sagged.

---

5 O'Hea 2005, 45.
6 Keller 2006, 37-39, pl. 10 type 1.1.
7 Fiema 2001, 11.
8 O'Hea 2002, 260.
9 Bacchelli *et al.* 2000, 86-87.
10 Karz 1998, 333.
11 Stern and Schlick-Nolte 1994, 376.
12 Karz 1998, 333.
13 de Bellis 1998, 50, 69, no. 5.
14 Grose 1989, 354.
15 Stern and Schlick-Nolte 1994, 376-77.

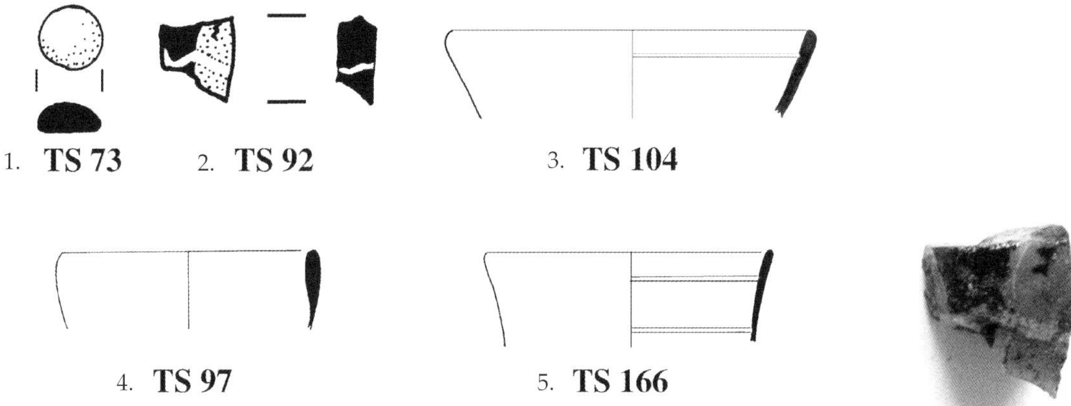

Fig. 14.1. Late Hellenistic and Early Roman glass (TS 73 and TS 92 are at 1 : 2, TS 104, TS 97 and TS 166 are at 1 : 3).

Fig. 14.2. Fragment of Late Hellenistic mosaic cane inlay plaque (2 : 1).

Julio-Claudian glass

Three ribbed sagged bowls with slightly kicked bases belong to a ubiquitous Roman series beginning in the mid-1st c. B.C. and lasting into the Flavian period. They seem to have been produced for local use throughout the empire. They were also standard drinking ware for the Roman army, whether manufactured in forts or imported.[16] Our examples might be purely Julio-Claudian,[17] along with three more from Ez Zantur[18] and an upcast in the Petra Church.[19] As with the Hellenistic glass, their low numbers make it difficult to be certain whether they were made locally or imported. As elsewhere in the Levant, they are unmistakeably a sign of the adoption of Roman fashions in tableware in the 1st c. A.D. by local glass workshops.

Fig. 14.3. Opaque grey-blue glass chunk (TS 169) (1 : 1).

The presence of one small chunk of raw, opaquely-colored glass (fig. 14.3) might be taken to imply that glass working of some kind (jewelry, inlays or vessel production) occurred at Petra. Raw glass was transported from Late Hellenistic and Roman glass-making sites, such as the Belus river in Phoenicia, to workshops across the provinces primarily in the form of chunks. The retrieval of the chunk from within a wall of the first half of the 2nd c. A.D. suggests a Julio-Claudian date at the latest; in fact, its distinctive opaque pale blue color is specific to this period, especially in Italy,[20] although it also occurs in Egyptian inlays. How and why it reached Petra remains a mystery. The fabric is not found on any published glass from Petra, and this makes it difficult to take it as evidence of vessel production within the city. One possibility is that it arrived as a tithe or temple offering in a shipload of Egyptian raw glass destined for India, since E. M. Stern noted a similarly colored bowl from Arikamedu.[21]

Thick-walled piriform unguentaria appeared in the second half of the 1st c. A.D. across the empire, especially in tombs, where they were deposited as ritually impure items after being used to anoint the dead. Longer-necked versions in naturally tinted hues probably became the 'bread and butter' of Early Roman glass workshops in the Levant, since they were used in large numbers

---

16 Price 2005, 100; Lightfoot 1993, 34-37.
17 Grose 1989, 247.
18 Keller 2006, 37.
19 O'Hea 2001, 371, no. 32.
20 Scatozza Höricht 1986, 36-37, pl. 26, nos. 47-50.
21 Stern 1991, 143.

for funerary and ritual purposes. However, they are largely absent from Nabataean tombs, including those at Oboda and Mampsis. A. Negev mentions only one secondary burial recorded with glass.[22] This might explain why they were so few in the sanctuary at Petra or at Khirbet et-Tannur. If these were not locally produced, they would probably have been imported from Judaea or the Roman province of Syria, along with the ribbed bowls. Contexts of the 1st c. A.D. have yielded at least three glass unguentaria, of which at least two thick-walled piriform-bodies (TS 84) are typologically Julio-Claudian. Our rims of Type 72 might belong to these, while the other could be as late as the early 2nd c.

The mould-blown fragments of TS 60 are closely related to late Julio-Claudian and early Flavian "Sidonian" mould-blown beakers, bowls and jugs[23] through the presence of a tongued border with possible running scroll above or below. These were high-quality tablewares, exported or produced in limited numbers across the E Mediterranean and as far west as Italy. Jugs and beakers signed by Ennion (a Semitic name) cluster in Phoenicia and Judaea,[24] although most datable examples are from the western provinces and Italy.[25] That these last are also the earliest datable mould-blown vessels has cast doubt on D. B. Harden's hypothesis that Ennion moved his workshop from Sidon to Italy.[26] While TS 60 might not be an Ennion-signed vessel,[27] it probably belongs to a contemporary Phoenician series of piriform jugs with tongues below a running scroll;[28] as such, it is certainly an import from beyond Nabataea.

Two other mould-blown fragments are perhaps from a small flask or jug, with a small relief circle on an indented panel. Neither is well enough preserved for one to be certain of their original form, but the motif does appear on an Ennion jug now in New York[29] and on small Jerusalem flasks.

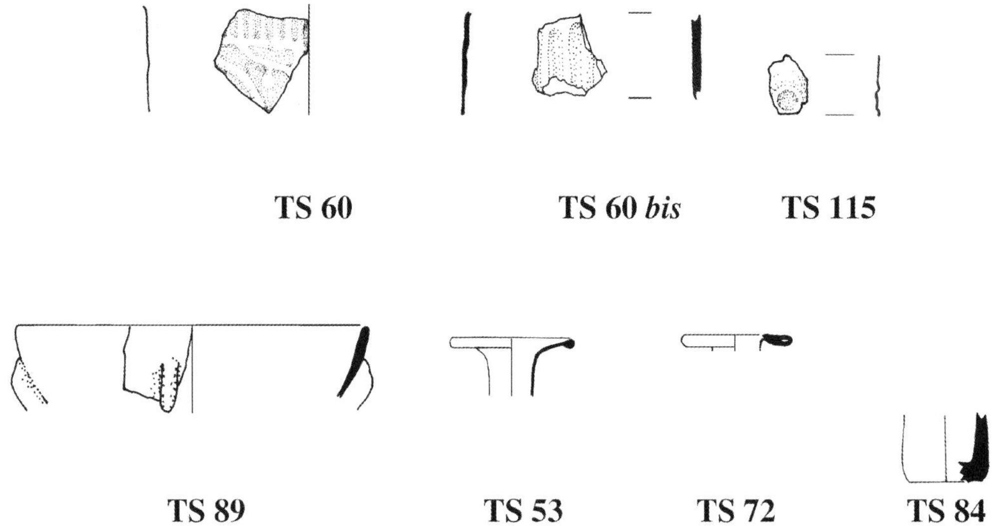

Fig. 14.4. Late Hellenistic and Early Roman glass (TS 60, TS 60 bis and TS 115 are at 1 : 2, TS 89, TS 53, TS 72 and TS 84 are at 1 : 3).

22 Negev 1971, 119 and 122.
23 Harden 1935, 165 and 168, pl. xxviii c-d.
24 Barag 1996, 89-90.
25 Price 1991, 64 and 71.
26 Harden 1935, 165.
27 Although one was retrieved at Petra in 1942: Barag 1996, 89.
28 Stern 1995, 15-153, nos. 55-58.
29 Vessberg 1952, 142.

Fig. 14.4 TS 89. Ribbed sagged bowl rim (MNE 3). rdiam 14. Rim polished round on top, sloping straight in. Narrow, widely spaced ribs below rim. Medium-thick walled, bluish. Iridescence. One example is decolorized; the other is strongly pinkish/aubergine, indicative of a failed attempt at decolorizing using manganese in the batch.

TS 53. Ledge unguentarium rim (MNE 2). rdiam 5. Wide simple ledge rim, cylindrical neck. Medium walled, blue-greenish. 4 fragments. Black on iridescence. One of these is certainly 1st c. A.D. by context; the other could be Roman or Byzantine.

TS 72. Ledge unguentarium rim (MNE 11). rdiam 4. Flat ledge rim, folded flat on top, on narrow neck. Thin walled. Blue-greenish. At least 2 of these are Early Roman by context, but the rim itself is a long-lived type and was used on 4th-c. flasks. One piece is strongly dark amber.

TS 84. Piriform unguentarium base (MNE 2). bdiam 3. Splayed, round heel; flat base with large pontil ring. Thick-walled, indeterminate fabric. Abraded; black on iridescence. One example is blue-greenish.

TS 60. Mould-blown glask or beaker fragment (MNE 1). bdiam 8. 2 non-joining body fragments: relief-borders above and below narrow incuse tongues; relief line sloping down to right, with pendant dot below, to right of circular border of modillion or scroll. Medium-thick walled, strongly lime greenish. Black on iridescence. Neither fragment is from a well-dated context.

TS 115. Mould-blown fragment (MNE 2). Thin-walled, with relief small circle. Blue-greenish or bluish.

Fig. 14.3 TS 169. Small chunk (MNE 1), 5.3 x 3.5 x 1.4 cm. 27 g. Opaque grey-blue glass; all surfaces flaked. Iridescence.

Flavian to A.D. 106

The number of glass vessels jumps from MNE 9 in the Julio-Claudian period to at least 52 for the later 1st c., probably because of the greater preservation of material in architectural collapse of the 2nd c. A.D. Whereas the provenance of most of the earlier glass is difficult to identify since they were generic forms produced widely, the Flavian glass can be more clearly sourced. Nearly three-quarters were probably imports from Roman Egypt and the Mediterranean, while one other vessel was imported either from Phoenicia, Judaea or Italy. These are the decolorized tablewares, crate flagons and mould-blown flask of fig. 14.5. A high percentage of imported glass is also found in the private house at Ez Zantur in the assemblage of *c.*A.D. 108,[30] but this is emphatically not the pattern seen elsewhere in Levantine cities of this period and thus requires some comment here. As I have argued more fully elsewhere,[31] our Flavian glass assemblage most closely resembles that from Nabataean Aila[32] and the Egyptian Red Sea ports of Myos Hormos[33] and Berenike.[34] But why is the glass from a public building in the Nabataean royal capital closer to known assemblages from ports on the edges of the empire than, say, to contemporary glass from Jerusalem or cities such as Gerasa, Samaria-Sebaste[35] or Berytus[36]? It is not simply because more 1st c. A.D. material survives here than elsewhere. At the simplest level, the answer seems

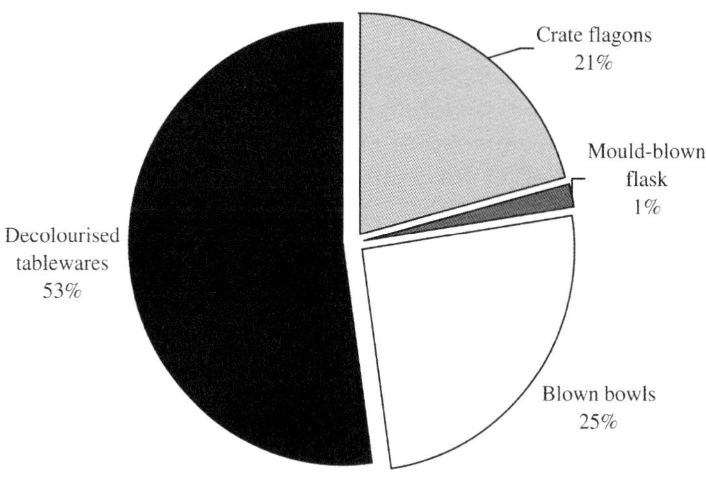

Fig. 14.5. Relative percentages of decolorized vessels, crate flagons, mould-blown flask and blown bowls (MNE 67) of the late 1st to mid-2nd c. A.D.

30 Keller 2006, 42-50.
31 O'Hea, 2010b forthcoming.
32 Jones 2000, 147.
33 Meyer 1992, pls. 5-13; Peacock *et al.* 2000.
34 Nicholson 2001, 152.
35 Crowfoot 1957, fig. 93.
36 Jennings 1998, 115.

to be that most Early Roman glass excavated on Nabataean sites, including Petra, came from Egypt rather than from the Levant. This suggests both that Petra did not produce its own glass in the way that other major centers such as Jerusalem did, and that Petra did not import most of its glassware from its immediate neighbors to the north at precisely the time when their glass workshops were producing more than ever before — this was, after all, the region which probably invented the greatest technique for mass-production, glassblowing, in the 1st c. B.C. Instead, Petra seems to have imported most of its Flavian glass via and from Roman Egypt.

Imported Levantine glass

Only one vessel can be said with certainty to have been imported from elsewhere in the Levant, probably Judaea. A single date flask (see figs. 14.11-14.12) was found in the fill of a Byzantine burial. Datable examples are no earlier than Claudian and no later than the later 2nd c. A.D.[37] These vessels could have been cast from moulds made from real fruit.[38] A Sidonian production center has been suggested, since Phoenicia was renowned for date palms,[39] but the distribution horizon excludes the Lebanon while including Galilee and Samaria. Jericho was as famous for its dates as its balsam; both were grown on estates owned by Julio-Claudian imperial women in precisely this period, which might explain why so many such vessels appear in Italy. The excavators of the Herodian and later palaces have attributed some unusual installations to the extraction of date juice.[40]

At least three blown bowls of naturally colored fabrics (fig. 14.9), with and without trailed handles, are indistinguishable from common bowls of Romanized forms made in the same fabrics in local workshops across the Levant. They could therefore be either Levantine products imported overland from the north or made in Nabataea, following Levantine workshop fashions and using the same sources for raw glass. More were found at Ez Zantur in Petra[41] and at Aila;[42] they also appear in Judaea[43] and in the Decapolis (Philadelphia,[44] Pella[45] and Gerasa[46]).

Imported non-Levantine glass

The examples fall into two groups. The smallest and very homogeneous assemblage consists of at least 13 square-sectioned, mould-blown crate-flagons of Isings Form 50a-b, commonly (if less precisely) also called "square jugs". Although only two have 1st-c. A.D. contexts in Petra, evidence from the western provinces shows quite clearly a production that began in the mid-1st c. A.D. but expanded in the Flavian period.[47] Both fabric and form suggest that they are indeed western, if not actually Italian, imports (sites include Herculaneum[48] and, still in their crates, Pompeii). They appear in two natural colored fabrics, blue-greenish and bluish, but there is no technical reason to suppose different sources for them. They seem to come in two sizes, one with a large rim (nearly 5 cm diam.), one half that size. As noted by D. Barag,[49] Early Roman crate-flagons were uncommon in Phoenicia-Palestine, and plain examples in naturally-colored fabrics tended rather to be cylindrical versions. That said, at least four appear, along with Julio-Claudian opaquely-colored wares and Flavian vessels, in tombs at Castra near Haifa.[50] Recent excavations in S Judaea and just north

37 Stern and Schlick-Nolte 1994, 93.
38 Stern 1995, 92.
39 Ibid. 93.
40 Netzer *et al.* 2004, 134-35.
41 Keller 2006, 210, type VII.19b.
42 Jones 2000, 148.
43 Barag 1962, figs. 4-5.
44 Dussart 1998, 59, BI.1322b.
45 McNicoll *et al.* 1982, 84 and 87 pls. 132.9 and 133.3; da Costa *et al.* 2002, 520, fig. 13.
46 Meyer 1988, 185, figs. 5g-h.
47 de Alarcão 1975, 47.
48 Scatozza Höricht 1986, pl. XXX.
49 Barag 1987, 111.
50 Goren-Rosen 1998, 20-21.

of Jerusalem have yielded comparable flagons. Although not fully quantified, they do not seem to appear in the numbers that would justify the claim that some mould-blown square flagons were "local".[51] 'En Gedi may have produced two, although only their rims are preserved,[52] and Jerusalem itself does not yet have any published examples. Only one has been published for a Decapolis city (Gerasa);[53] Pella, with several glass-rich Flavian tombs, has yielded none. By comparison, at least 26 have been recorded at Ez Zantur from Flavian and later contexts,[54] giving Petra a total of at least 39. Some also appear at Nabataean Humayma.[55] The only other published Levantine site with such a concentration is Dura Europos, where the MNE of 44 comprises *c.*18% of the recognisably Flavian-Trajanic glass imported into the fort, coinciding perhaps with an expansion of the garrison there. The valued item would have been the wine, not the glass. The Mediterranean–Egypt–Red Sea trade route (of which Aila to Petra was by this time a branch-line) connected to central India, which imported wine, principally Italian, according to the contemporary *Periplus of the Erythraean Sea*.[56] Yet it is odd that no crate-flagon has been identified at Myos Hormos or in India itself.[57] India could, of course, have imported its wine entirely in ceramic amphorae, but, when considered alongside the presence of crate-flagons in quantity at Dura Europos, it raises the possibility that these western imports were not necessarily mass items of Red Sea trade. Perhaps the diplomatic presence of Romans with military responsibilities at the royal court in Petra during the Augustan period persisted into the Flavian and could have been the avenue by which these vessels arrived in such concentrations in Petra.

The second (much larger: MNE 31) group covers a range of forms but shares a deliberately colorized fabric decorated by intaglio or relief cutting or painting (fig. 14.5). These vessels may have been among the most expensively produced glassware of the 1st c. A.D., but they should still have been cheaper than bowls or cups made of rock crystal, agate, silver or gold. We may consider painted or cut glass rare and special (ancient writers talked of them as both) but they surely could not have rated high in the royal world described by Strabo (16.4.26) a century earlier, where royal symposia involved up to 11 different gold cups per guest. The best-preserved colorized and cut bowls in the Levant came from the caves used by Bar-Kokhba rebels, including modest landowners such as Babatha, a widow from within what had been Nabataea and not at the highest level of Judaean or Nabataean society.

Petra, Egypt and Begram

The overland and sea route from Egypt to Petra via Aila predated Roman control of Egypt. Although under the Julio-Claudians Nabataea lost its monopoly of the trade into the Roman world of Arabian and Indian spices, herbs and luxury goods, it did not cease to be part of that route. Indeed, the glass from Aila shows that it was still one offshoot of the Egypt–Arabia–India route. This should not be surprising. The *Periplus* makes it clear that for Flavian traders leaving the Egyptian coast, the first Red Sea port of call after Myos Hormos remained the Nabataean port of Leuke Kome on the Arabian coast,

> through which there is a way inland up to Petra, to Malichas, king of the Nabataeans. This harbor also serves in a way the function of a port of trade for the craft, none large, that come to it loaded with freight from Arabia. For that reason as a safeguard there is dispatched for duty in it a customs officer to deal with the fourth [tax] on incoming merchandise as well as a centurion with a detachment of soldiers.[58]

---

51 Katsnelson 2009,166, fig. 6.1 and 6.4.
52 Jackson-Tal 2005, 138, 75* and fig. 1.12-13.
53 Dussart 1998, 159, BXL.231.
54 Keller 2006, 199, Type IV.3.
55 J. Jones pers. comm.
56 Casson 1989, chapt. 49.
57 Stern 1991.
58 Casson 1989, chapt. 19; 61 and 63.

Arabian spices could still have entered Nabataea directly, even if the extent of onward trade to her Judaean and northern neighbours cannot be determined. On the basis of inscriptions and field surveys, G. Young has recently argued that the Arabian caravan route for spices did not collapse in the 1st c. A.D., nor did the level of Nabataea's wealth drop.[59] The fact that Leuke Kome imposed a 25% duty (the same imperial tax rate applied in Alexandria and 2nd-c. Palmyra[60]) implies that it was still an active gateway for imports. But the glass shows that Nabataea herself still remained a consumer of traded items from Egypt, whether via the overland Negev route from Rhinocolura or via the Gulf of Aqaba.

Paradoxically, the strongest argument in favor of Roman Egypt as a source for the Petra glass comes from the enigmatic collection found at Begram (Kushan, now Afghanistan). There imported Roman glass included high-relief and intaglio-cut and painted vessels, at *c.*180 vessels the most richly decorated assemblage ever found on one site.[61] With them, J. Hackin's team found a massive cache of Indian ivories, plaster toreutic tondi for casting metal reliefs, bronze vessels, weights and statuettes, rock crystal, and Chinese lacquer bowls in two adjacent storerooms[62] that may have been a trader's warehouse, a customs house or royal treasury. Where identifiable, provenances for objects from within the Roman empire lead only to Egypt (the millefiori glass bowls) and Alexandria (the "Pharos" beaker and the plaster tondi). Nearly every published discussion of the Begram glass has pointed to Alexandria as a source of the faceted, cut, and painted glass vessels, while acknowledging that there is no direct proof of this. While there are occasional references to Egyptian glass in Roman sources, Alexandria was not always specified;[63] the *Periplus* mentions only Diospolis in Middle Egypt as a source for exported (colored) glass.[64] If we consider the categories of Flavian-Trajanic glass found at Begram and at our site, the first are the decolorized, cut bowls. They often have a slight lime greenish hue when viewed though a section, and all hydrate to a distinctive, chalky surface that is not found on later decolorized and lathe-cut beakers and bowls. They belong to what D. Grose has called the "international style" of glass tableware from the Flavian period into the early 2nd c.,[65] and were common in the West,[66] as well as in Egypt, Nubia[67] and N Africa. What has not been fully appreciated is that they are rare within late 1st- to 2nd-c. contexts in most Levantine cities. An MNE of just 3 has been published for Gerasa,[68] and a possible unpublished bowl base from Pella's main tell, but none from its glass-rich Flavian tombs, yet they dominate at Nabataean Aila,[69] and were prized possessions in the Cave of the Treasure by the Dead Sea.[70]

Our excavations give an MNE of 4 large footed bowls (TS 87 and 90) with ledge rims ground away to leave ridges on top and an overhanging edge.[71] These are probably the commonest form of decolorized cut bowl, although elsewhere they appear in a wider range of sizes and decoration.[72] Another large but straight-sided, faceted bowl (TS 91) is similar in form and dimensions to a

59 Young 2001, 21 and 106-12.
60 Casson 1989, 14 and 144.
61 Whitehouse 2003, 437.
62 Hackin 1954.
63 Whitehouse 1999, 74-75.
64 Casson 1989, chapt. 6, 53.
65 Grose 1991, 16.
66 Italy: Grose 1991, 12-14; Tarpini: id. 2003, 95-98; German *limes*: Hoffmann 2000, 172; Britain and Spain: Price 1987, 72-80.
67 Cool 1996, 203, fig. 3.1.
68 Meyer 1988, 187-88, fig. 5P-S.
69 Jones 2005, 135.
70 Yadin 1962, 234. There are also fragments from the Cave of Horrors: Barag 1962, 210, no. 6.
71 Isings 42a, variant Limburg.
72 Price 1987, 74-76.

shallow footless bowl with Dionysiac intaglio cutting from Begram[73] and is related to a large bowl with arcading under faceted rim from Lejjun.[74] At least two have firm Flavian contexts at Petra, and two more come from early- to mid-2nd c. destruction débris. Other fragments are reported but not quantified from the first 4 seasons of the Great Temple excavations,[75] and there is a bowl rim and base from the Petra Church.[76] Two small bowls with everted rims but no overhanging edges (TS 65) have only ridges extant on the upper body; whether they were footed is unclear, since published examples elsewhere are both rarer than the ledge-rimmed bowls and lacking full profile.[77]

Related and contemporary are decolorized and faceted beakers, squat, conical and ovoid. Convincingly identified by A. Oliver as a purely Flavian to mid-2nd c. group,[78] these too are found across the empire, especially in the western provinces, but are unusual elsewhere in the Roman Levant, with the notable exceptions of Aila, Petra and Dura Europos. A third of those identified at our site (MNE 8) are squat-footed beakers with flaring rims TS 42. At least three have surviving facet decoration. At least two more have been excavated elsewhere at Petra.[79] The majority are ovoid beakers (called jars by Oliver,[80] barrel-shaped beakers by D. Whitehouse[81]) and one-handled versions of the same (called pitchers by Oliver, pear-shaped jugs by Whitehouse), which are probably simply tankards. All external surfaces were ground down, leaving square-cut narrow ridges below the rim and often just above the footed base, with additional intaglio decoration. This puts them all into Oliver's Group II.[82] At least two were in contexts at Petra dating before *c.*A.D. 105. At least 9 are clearly identifiable (TS 52 and 129); another 5 bases without extant feet might be closely related, but they have sharper heels on a sagging body (TS 170). Petra's 9 ovoid beakers are unlike any other published examples, including three cobalt colored and faceted "pitchers" from Begram.[83] Not only is the profile broader, with a less constricted mouth, but Petra's beakers have vegetal scrolls, quatrefoil flowers, and a single frieze of a leopard striding through vegetation, all in intaglio and with finely-incised internal details, such as lightly-ground spots on the leopard's rear leg and tufted hair on its tail. The plant motifs on other fragments could be background details for a figured scene, as on the shallow bowl with Dionysiac subject from Begram.

Flavian-Trajanic decolorized glass with intaglio figural decoration is distinct and rare: 5 bowls/beakers from Britain, one with a Nilotic scene; a skyphos from Siphnos; 2 or 3 plates, 1 bowl, 1 tall beaker from Begram;[84] and the Nilometer beaker now in the British Museum, which uses circular floral buds for the background,[85] as do the ovoid beakers from our site. On typological grounds the British Museum piece has been dated to the early 3rd c., although the technical similarities to Flavian-Trajanic cut glass have been recognized.[86] Its base and rim are both quite close to rim TS 52 and base TS 134 at our site; the latter in turn parallels a faceted beaker from Cyprus.[87] Both Petra forms appear only in later deposits: there is scant evidence for 3rd-c. use at the site. In Egypt, Karanis has yielded at least 7 fragments of shallow bowls and at least 2 deep bowls with vegetal motifs or possible figured scenes,[88] mostly from houses dated to the 2nd c. A.D. at the earliest. Denderah

---

73 Inv. MG 91214.
74 Jones 2006, fig. 18.1.3.
75 Karz 1998 (database).
76 O'Hea 2001, 370-71, no. 15.
77 As at Nicopolis ad Istrum: Shepherd 1988, 310, fig. 11.1.5.
78 Oliver 1984, 44.
79 Murray and Ellis 1940, 15; Keller 2006, 194, type II.10a.
80 Oliver 1984, 42.
81 Whitehouse 2001, 441; Hamelin's Group D.
82 Oliver 1984, 36.
83 Ibid. 42.
84 Massabo 1998, 25-37.
85 Harden *et al.* 1987, 200.
86 Ibid. 182, no. 109.
87 Bourriau *et al.* 1978, 104.
88 Harden 1936, pl. XIII, nos. 182-85 and 187-90; 119, pl. XIV, nos. 311-12.

and Medinet Madi also yielded faceted or cut decolorized glass dated to the Antonine-Severan periods.[89] A mythological bowl at Berenike is decorated in the same style but lacks good stratigraphic dating[90] while one from Myos Hormos was tentatively dated 2nd or 3rd c.[91] If the British Museum's Nilometer beaker is contemporary with our cut glass, it would support the idea of a Egyptian production center in the late 1st to mid-2nd c.

Another tiny fragment (TS 132) from our site belongs to the class of relief-cut vessels which is also represented in small numbers at Begram, but not enough survives to determine its form. Beakers, bowls and flasks with raised ovals and other motifs overlapped with the repertoire of forms and fabrics used for faceted and intaglio glass; again, more are found in western provinces than in the east.[92]

Yet significant differences also exist between the Begram glassware and ours. Begram yielded many fish-flasks (not one has been recorded at Petra) and its enigmatic trailed flasks and beakers have no close parallels anywhere.[93] Our site has yielded several examples of a sharp-heeled, almost piriform body (TS 170) which, while Flavian by context, has no direct published parallels, although the bodies show a broad similarity to handled beakers at Begram and elsewhere at Petra. As none preserves a full profile, it is unclear if the entire wall of the body lacked decoration — only surviving are grooves on their bases. Also unusual is TS 111, a small group (MNE 4) of trumpet-footed vessels which had simple cut-away linear decoration on the bodies, even sharing the same "projecting knob" that Oliver observed on the underside of the more common cut and facetted beaker bases,[94] but that larger group did not have high trumpet feet on small bodies (roughly the size of an eggcup). Nor did Levantine artisans make footed beakers with such high bases in this period. A typological parallel of sorts is found only in decolorized glass of the late 2nd-early 3rd c. in the western provinces, but it lacks cut decoration.[95] A preference for cobalt-blue glass alongside decolorized wares is strongly evident at Begram but not Petra, although a single fragment of Early Roman cobalt bluish translucent glass (TS 82; fig. 14.6) might once have had a line of white bobs painted around it (flaky hydration makes this difficult to verify); if it were painted, it would parallel a cobalt beaker from Begram and beakers from the 2nd c. A.D. cemetery at Nubian Sedeinga.[96]

Fig. 14.6. Cobalt blue glass (TS 82) (1 : 1).

A unique decolorised fragment from earlier excavations at Petra has two deliberate cuts through the vessel wall, containing remnants of "decomposed blue glass".[97] Its closest parallel is another unique fragment of a faceted decolorized beaker from Begram that had round lapis lazuli and turquoise gems inserted into cut-out holes penetrating the vessel wall.[98]

The third and most striking overlap between Begram's and our glass are the decolorized, cut beakers with painted decoration. At least two beakers are probably represented by the 10 fragments. Eight body fragments show a mythological figure on one beaker (figs. 14.7-14.8). All come from domestic occupation in the Tabun Cave Room, which ended with a destruction in the mid-2nd c. A.D. Another body fragment (fig. 14.10) comes from Room A in the Upper Temenos, which probably collapsed early in the same century; a tenth fragment, which probably belongs to the same beaker, came from topsoil in the same area. Since both beakers are of exactly the same form

89 Silvano 2005, 119-20.
90 Nicholson 2001, 152.
91 Meyer 1992, 24, 15??, no. 88.
92 von Saldern 1991, 112-17.
93 Whitehouse 2001, 442 and 445.
94 Oliver 1984, 36.
95 Foy *et al.* 2005, 124, fig. 1.4-7, pl. 26.
96 Cool 1996, 206.
97 Murray and Ellis 1940, 26, no. 25, pl. 15.
98 Hamelin 1953, 128; Dussubieux and Gratuze 2003, 456.

and decorative program, they should be contemporary, and a Flavian-Trajanic dating for the production is likely based upon our contexts. As with Begram's Group 10,[99] our figured beakers were probably tall conical forms using decolorized fabric whose surfaces were ground away to leave flat-topped ridges like the Group II faceted beakers, the faceting simply being replaced with a painted scene. As Oliver suggested, the glass is likely to have been made (if not decorated) in the same workshops which produced the faceted and figurally-cut beakers.[100] The Begram beakers and a pair from Lübsow (Poland)[101] share the form, fabric and double borders of reddish-brown and yellow lines with our fragments, but the dotted florets that appear above and below the borders on the Begram beakers have not survived here, nor has any rim or base. Mythological scenes at Begram include Homeric battles, Orpheus, Ganymede and Europa, and one which has been identified as showing Isiac (Isis-like) rituals of women weaving garlands. At Begram different painting styles are apparent, with a single or double register of figures, but all the mythological styles use fine black lines for internal details, as on our piece TS 51. One clear difference is that none of our fragments has traces of blue or green paint, whereas both the gladiatorial and mythological beakers at Begram and at Myos Hormos[102] have both, particularly for vegetal motifs. At Petra, only black, brown, pink and yellow were used on the surviving fragments. Nevertheless, stylistic similarities are close enough to suggest contemporaneity at the least, and the source for both the Petra and Begram painted beakers could be the same, namely Egypt.

Although a Flavian-Trajanic dating for the faceted glass now seems universally accepted, the painted and high relief beakers from Begram remain under debate. F. Coarelli's attribution to them of a late-antique Hellenizing style is not well argued,[103] although a 3rd c. A.D. date for the painted glass has been followed on different grounds by K. Painter,[104] M. Menninger[105] and B. Rütti.[106] Meticulous typological comparisons of the painted beakers at Begram with Oliver's Group II tall faceted beakers[107] are confirmed by excavated examples from mid-1st to mid-2nd c. graves in Germany[108] and now also by our contexts at Petra.

The identification of the figure on our beaker (fig. 14.7) is not certain. As the "Isiac" beaker at Begram has both genders in the same pinkish-brown skin, the relatively dark skin tone cannot establish whether our figure is male or female. While the hair is Dionysiac, the head-dress must be a variant of the *atef* crown (white with ostrich plumes) often worn by Osiris, sometimes by Isis (fig. 14.8). The tight-fitting, transparent yellow over-garment and general outline of the body are not overtly female; comparable are the breasts and musculature outlined on a male Dionysiac figure on a painted beaker from Britain, now in the British Museum.[109] There are no Isiac corkscrew curls in the hair, nor an Isis knot and mantle on the body. Serapis wears the same headdress as our figure on a wall-painting in the Temple of Isis at Pompeii,[110] but the Petra male cannot be Serapis since he is always bearded. However, since Isis, Osiris and Serapis all overlap in their different head-dresses in the Roman period, it indicates nothing other than that this is likely to be a male figure from Isiac myth. It certainly cannot be Osiris as the object of cult worship, since he is always shown

99 Hackin 1954, 104.
100 Oliver 1984, 38.
101 Ibid. 38. fig. 10.
102 Peacock *et al.* 2000.
103 Coarelli 1962.
104 Painter 1987, 260.
105 Menninger 1996, 71.
106 Rütti 1999, 131-33.
107 Koster and Whitehouse 1989, 31.
108 Whitehouse 2003, 441.
109 Inv. P&EE 1995, 3-1 1.
110 Tran Tam Tinh 1990, 768, no. 77.

Fig. 14.7. Painted fragments of beaker (1 : 1) (TS 51 from SP 84, Locus 7).

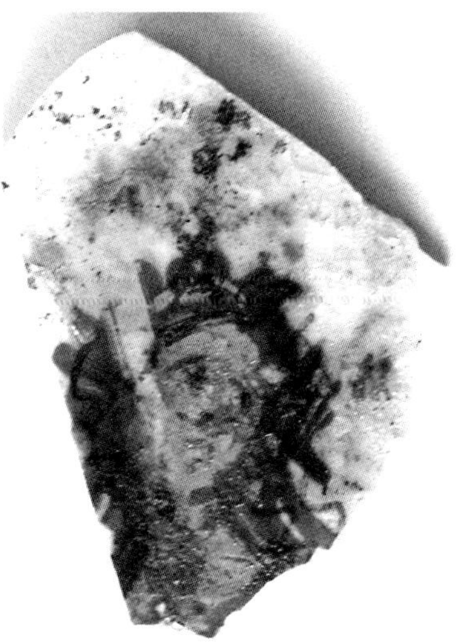

Fig. 14.8. Detail of head on painted beaker (TS 51) (2 : 1).

mummiform,[111] but Osiris as part of a mythological narrative is a different issue; and, like his son Harpocrates, he was syncretized by the Romans with Dionysus. The yellow semi-transparent robe on the Petra figure has literary parallels, as in Tibullus' "Tribute to Messala" (1.7.45-48), in which Osiris has "… saffron tunics flowing down to soft young feet … and little baskets with their ritual secrets". The hand-on-hip pose also, very broadly, recalls the "dancing Indian" stance seen in terracotta figurines of Harpocrates where he was syncretised with Dionysus as an Indian youth. What the black wedge-shape between the figure's thighs was meant to represent is unclear, but it is unlikely simply to be a shadow, given its lack of gradation and the absence of shadowing anywhere else on the surviving fragments. Although clearly not the same thing, it recalls the treatment of the front of the charioteer's gown worn by Dionysus in triumph on the handle of a Roman silver bowl from the Near East and now in the Metropolitan Museum.[112] The brown cone adorned with a ribbon on an adjacent section of the beaker seems more like a torch than *cornucopia*, although it could be an oddly-shaped *thymiaterion* (there is no cross-hatching to suggest a woven basket). If it was a very stubby torch, it could also relate to the *lychnapsia* ritual.[113] In a loose sense, then, an Isiac myth is likely to be depicted here, and Osiris-as-Dionysus is, for the moment, the best candidate.

Three possible hypotheses emerge from the above. The least contentious is that the source for Petra's Flavian-Trajanic imported glass is likely to be the source for Begram's glass of the same period, even though the full assemblages were not identical. The decolorized cut bowls and faceted beakers found at Petra could have come from any region within the empire with the exception of the Levant, since they are most scarce where local glass workshops appear to have been most prolific. Second, the eastern distribution of these non-Levantine products points at least to Egypt as the conduit for their arrival into Petra, and at most to Egypt as the source for their production. Given that decolorized cut glass occurs at Aila and Humayma, the likeliest route into Petra would have been via the Red Sea ports, rather than overland via Rhinocolura, Mampsis and Zoara, though Aila was itself connected to the Mediterranean Sea by overland routes through the Negev.[114] Third, if both these hypotheses are correct, the likeliest route for the Begram glass was also via the Red Sea route, rather than through Syria and across to India, thence into the Kushan.

---

111 Leclant and Clerc 1994, 107-16.
112 Alexander 1955, 64-67.
113 Witt 1971, 92, nn. 38-39.
114 Parker 1997, 21.

Blown bowls

Fig. 14.9 TS 71. Crimped trail-handled rim (MNE 1). rdiam 14. Upright rim, folded to exterior; carinated to deep bowl, sloping in; crimped handle added to rim. Thin walled, bluish. Iridescent flaking.

TS 130. Volute handled rim (MNE 1). rdiam 9.5. Down-turned rim, folded flat on top, shallow bowl. Volute trail added to rim. Very thin walled, greenish. Black on iridescence.

TS 70. Ledge-rim (MNE 2). rdiam 21. Large simple ledge rim, carinated to deep bowl. Very thin walled. Faintly blue-greenish. Iridescent flaking. Although from Byzantine contexts, one or both could be Flavian. No handles extant; these examples could be from either trail-handled or handleless bowls.

TS 85. Flanged bowl (MNE 1). bdiam 16. Upright wall, folded to form horizontal flange. Thin walled. Faintly greenish. Iridescence.

TS 62. Low folded foot (MNE 17). bdiam 5.5. Thin-walled bowl, with low folded ring-base, center slightly kicked. Small pontil mark. Greenish. Iridescence. At least two came from Early Roman contexts. Just under half were decolorized, with blue-greenish and lime/greenish also present; bases range from 4 to 6 cm.

Decolorized and cut ledge-rimmed bowls

TS 90. Rim (MNE 2). rdiam 24. Down-turned edge, carinated to wide ledge rim, sharply carinated to deep bowl. Medium walled. Edge polished; wide shallow groove cut along ledge rim, leaving ridges at both carinations. Truly decolorized. Iridescence. Type repeat is smaller.

TS 87. Rim (MNE 2). rdiam 15-16. Bevelled edge, on wide ledge rim, chipped on top at carination to convex bowl. Medium walled. Narrow groove at top of bevel; wide cut grooves along ledge. Decolorized, very faintly greenish. Calcified.

TS 91. Rim (MNE 1). rdiam 24-25. Simple rounded but polished rim, on uniformly medium-thick wall sloping shallowly into bowl (missing). External decoration, ground-away rim leaving flat-topped ridge above and row of squat ovals below; below, row of close-set "rice" facets, remainder missing. Decolorized, very faintly greenish. Iridescent flaking.

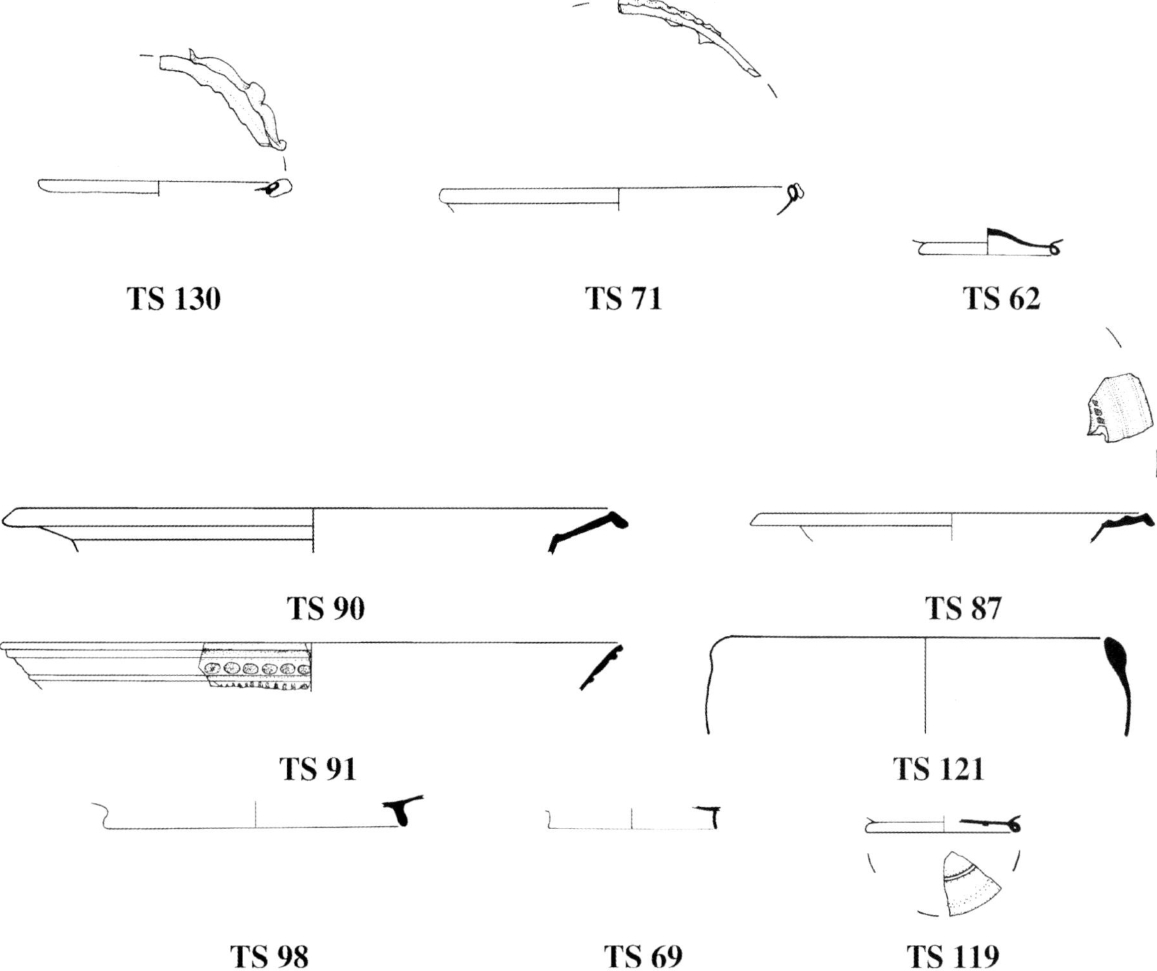

Fig. 14.9. Late Hellenistic and Early Roman glass (1 : 3).

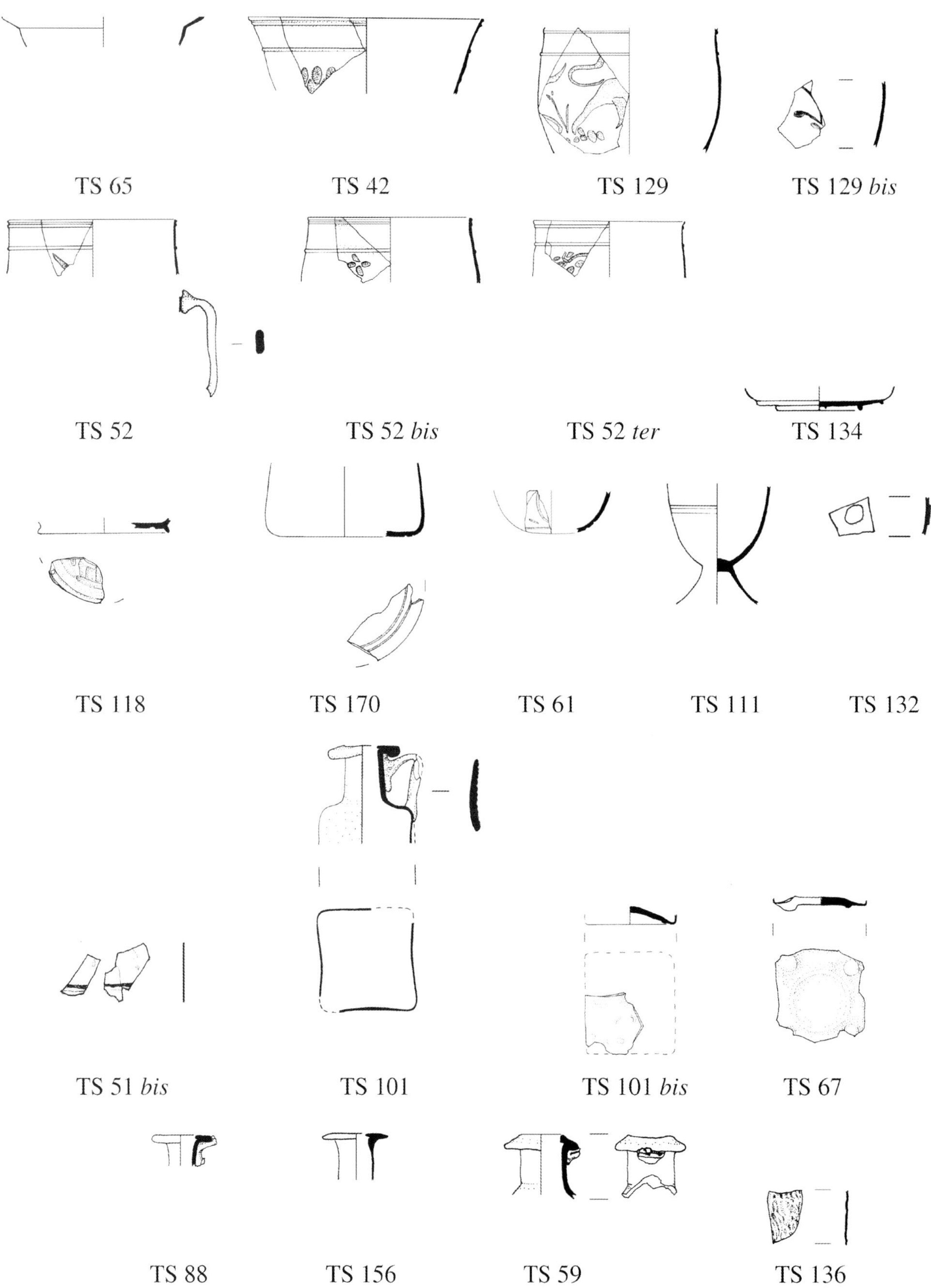

Fig. 14.10. Flavian-Trajanic decolorized glass, high-relief cut ware and mould-blown vessels (1 : 3).

TS 121. Bevelled rim (MNE 1). rdiam 17. Slightly incurved rim, thickened and bevelled to exterior; deep convex body. Medium walled. Decolorized, faintly greenish. Calcified. An almost identical deep bowl/beaker rim from a house at Humayma was found with extant intaglio circle or arch.[115]

TS 98. Footed base (MNE 4). bdiam 12. Shallow large bowl, center missing; low, slightly splayed slab foot. Internally wheel-polished. Decolorized, faintly greenish. Iridescence. Diameters range from 8 to 17 cm.

TS 69. Small footed base (MNE 4). bdiam 5-6. Flat base, sagging slightly to center (missing). Uniformly medium-thick walled. Upright slab foot, very slightly splayed at end. Almost colorized, faintly greenish. Calcified. All the duplicate examples are of the same diameter.

TS 119. Ring-foot (MNE 1). bdiam 6. Rounded heel, folded to small ring-foot; flat base, ridged circle on base exterior. Thin-walled body. Almost decolorized, faintly greenish. Calcified.

Decolorized faceted and cut beakers

Fig. 14.10 TS 65. Everted rim (MNE 2). rdiam 10. Rounded edge on everted rim carinated sharply to deep convex bowl. Thick walled. Ridged borders at mid-body. Almost decolorized, faintly lime greenish. Iridescent flaking. Another example of the type has a cut-away ridge immediately below the rim carination.

TS 42. Conical beaker rim (MNE 8). rdiam 13. Flaring rim, ground flat on top; deep body, base missing. Ridge below rim exterior, another on upper body, above narrow almond-shaped facets. Medium-thin walled. Decolorized. Calcified surface. Only 2 other examples of the same type have extant facets.

TS 129. Ovoid body (MNE 2). bdiam 10. Rim and base missing; deep hemispherical bowl. Widely-spaced pair of ridges above single main frieze or panel. Cut decoration, with internal finely scratched or incised details within cuts. At left, horn or tail curving up to right, with fine internal incised strokes; to right, tail with tufted end curving up behind outstretched rear right leg of leopard striding to right. Fine circles incised up leg, fine diagonal strokes on underbelly. 3 long tufts of grass springing from arc of overlapping large dots; more vegetation below? Medium walled. Decolorized, very faintly greenish. Calcified. Another example has extant tendril.

TS 52. Ovoid handled beaker (MNE 10). rdiam 9, bdiam 9. Upright rim, ground flat on top; slightly ovoid body. Widely-spaced pair of ridges below rim and above field with single extant diagonal lanciform groove. Non-joining narrow strap handle, probably attached below rim to mid-body. Medium-thin walled. Almost decolorized, faintly lime greenish. Many fragments, some joining. Calcified. A slightly smaller example of the type has more complete decoration (fig. 14.10) of gouged 4-petalled flowers, another has floral motif or scroll.

TS 170. Piriform base (MNE 5). bdiam 9. Double close-set groove around flat base just below heel exterior. Thin walled. Almost decolorized, faintly lime greenish. Many fragments, some joined. Calcified. 3 more examples have no extant grooves.

TS 134. Base (MNE 1). bdiam 6. Rounded heel with small ridge; flat base with large ridged circle on center exterior. Small solid half-pontil mark. Medium-thin walled. Almost decolorized, faintly greenish. Calcified and flaking.

TS 118. Footed base (MNE 1). bdiam 7. Flat base, with deep slanting cuts on exterior; circling close-set cuts at center of base; added short slab foot. Almost decolorized, faintly greenish. Iridescent flaking.

TS 61. Lower body (MNE 1). bdiam >6. 2 convex body fragments; extant oval and circle thickly cut with single vertical dash between them. Thick walled, faintly lime greenish. Calcified.

TS 111. High base (MNE 4). bdiam 5. Upper body missing; deep ovoid body, 3 lightly incised grooves mid-body. Added hollow trumpet foot, edge missing. Medium-thick walled. Almost decolorized, faintly greenish. Iridescent flaking. 2 fragments, joining. One example has extant ridge on lower body.

TS 132. Cut body fragment (MNE 1). bdiam 8-9. Convex fragment, exterior surface cut away and flat relief oval extant. Thick walled. Strongly blue-greenish. Abraded.

Painted cut and decolorized beakers

Figs. 14.7-14.8 TS 51. Body fragments (MNE 2). bdiam 7. Rim and base missing. Tapering tall body. Medium-thin walled. 8 fragments, some joining. Almost decolorized, faintly lime greenish. Iridescent flaking.

3 fragments, dark red-brown vertical linear border or edge with yellow inner line; to left/right, brownish-black tendril or perhaps animal paw. 3 joining fragments, yellow blobs, multi-lobed brown tendrils, and yellow vegetal tendrils with heart-shaped leaves and thick yellow buds, on either side of tapering brown cone filled with mound of yellow, through which rises a brown spiral; fine black hanging ribbon tied below rim. Pale pink arc extant above cone is probably either a torch or *thmiaterion* free-floating in background.

2 joining fragments: of head and figure and musculature outlined in brown with pinkish-brown skin. Face and hair detailed in fine black lines. Head turned back to left, long curly red hair with yellow highlights. On

115 Jones, pers. comm.

head, large yellow diadem, with central solar disc or stone, from which 2 outer yellow horn/plumes and 2 higher, inner brown plumes rise. Two yellow staffs or rays emanate from behind both shoulders. Translucent yellow wash over extant torso indicating sleeveless long tunic. Underlying brown modelling of torso makes it unclear if a girdle is slung from left hip to crotch, from which hangs a thick black triangular-shaped object, perhaps a tassel or central kilt. Right arm missing; left arm is bent with open hand placed at left hip. Indeterminate yellow dash sloping down to right in field behind body; brown-bordered solid object sloping up to right behind lower left leg.

Another example of the same type is of the same diameter and fabric, with extant brown and yellow borders.

Fig. 14.6 TS 82. Body fragment (MNE 1). Medium walled, dark cobalt body fragment. Iridescent flaking. It is possible that there was once white over-painted decoration (perhaps vegetal) with linear black outline, but the fragment is too heavily hydrated for this to be certain.

Crate flagons

Fig. 14.10 TS 101. Large flagon (MNE 9). rdiam 4. Ledge rim folded on top; short narrow neck, flat shoulder on square-sectioned body, base missing. Strap handle attached neck to upper body. Fragmented. Medium walled. Blue-greenish; mottled blue-greenish/amber handle. Iridescence.

TS 67. Base (MNE 2). bdiam 5. Square-sectioned mould-blown base. Thickened at center; 4 rounded knob-legs and relief circle in center of exterior of the base; smaller and very faint circle within. Thin-walled, strongly blue-greenish. Iridescence. Another example has a more domed base, with indistinct raised knob-pattern.

TS 88. Small rim (MNE 2). rdiam 2.5. Ledge rim folded on top; narrow neck. Strap handle attached rim to neck. Thick walled. All strongly blue-greenish. Black on iridescence.

TS 59. Small rim (MNE 3). rdiam 3. Bevelled rim, folded on top; short wide neck, pinched above sloping shoulder. Thick walled. Three-stranded, narrow strap handle attached the rim and upper neck. Strongly bluish. Iridescence.

TS 136. Fig. 14.12 Date flask (MNE 1). Nearly flat in section, two-part mould-blown 'wrinkled' fragment with protruding smooth mould-seam. Strongly amber-yellow. Iridescence.

Fig. 14.12. Date flask (TS 136) (1 : 1).

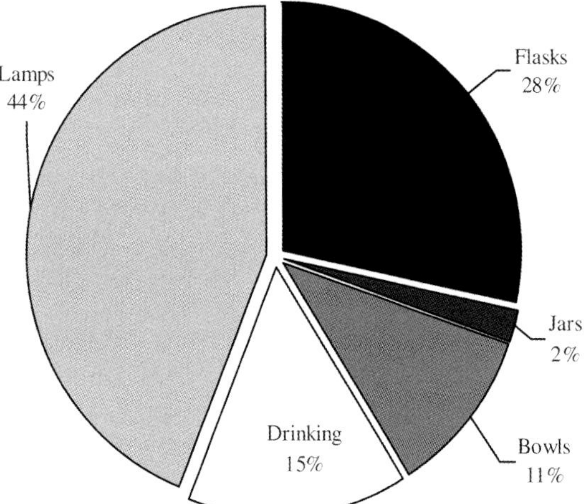

Fig. 14.11. Relative percentages of basic functional groups of Early Byzantine glass vessels (MNE 335) from the Great Temple site.

Byzantine glass

Most of the glass vessels (MNE 335) come from the use, collapse and rebuilding of the bath complex to the west of the Great Temple. Less than 3% of them were mould-blown. The majority are oil flasks, lamps, and windows (fig. 14.11), which fits the pattern for other Near Eastern bathhouses, including Hammat Gader.[116] A small amount is related to dining and drinking, not unknown in Roman *thermae*. Given their very different architectural contexts, it is surprising that the range of forms is similar to that found at the 4th-c. church at Nabataean Aila.[117]

Regional preferences

Byzantine glass workshops have now been identified at many sites across the Levant; Samaria-Sebaste,[118] Bet She'arim,[119] Jalame[120] and Bet Shean[121] are but a few. They shared a repertoire of forms, a range of fabric colors, and used similar technical and decorative traditions. Subtle regional differences can, however, be seen in the relative popularity of different forms in both

116 Cohen 1997, 396.
117 Jones 2005, 135-37.
118 Crowfoot 1957, 404-5.
119 Vitto 1996, 134 and 139.
120 Weinberg 1988.
121 Mazar and Bar-Nathan 1998, 27-29.

domestic and ecclesiastical assemblages. In the southern Levant, the same forms and range of fabrics appear in roughly the same proportions at Petra, Mezad Tamar,[122] Rehovot,[123] Aila[124] and Deir 'Ain 'Abata, as studied by the author. Most of these forms and fabrics re-appear in N Palestine and Syria, but some were less common than other lamp types, even though it is clear that they were produced in the region.

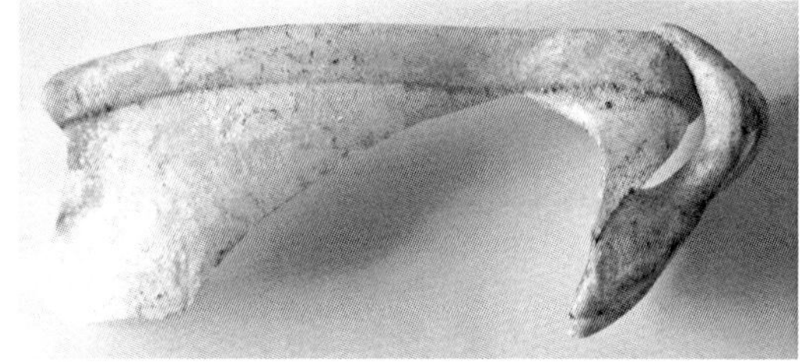

Fig. 14.13. Melted beaker-lamp (TS 34) from Lower Temenos, Trench 126. (1 : 1).

For example, three-handled beaker lamps with folded rims are found across the empire. They hung from hooked chains and had floating wicks, clipped with small lead clasps. Our excavations give an MNE of 23, at least 12 of which had added wick-tubes on their bases. Many show signs of high temperatures, caused by a fire (fig. 14.13). The sub-category with tubes seems to have appeared first and in the greatest numbers in 5th-c. contexts in the southern Levant rather than in Egypt (e.g., MNE 242 at the Monastery of St Lot at Deir 'Ain 'Abata, and MNE 53 from the Petra Church; they were also used at Jebel Harun[125] and Rehovot in the 5th c.,[126] but are absent from Karanis, Ashmunein and Naqlun). In more northern cities, they are either completely absent (none comes from three churches at Pella) or present in relatively smaller numbers from well-dated Late Byzantine phases, as at Gerasa.[127] The Petra examples include some that pre-date 363, which would make them amongst the earliest with a firm dating. They spread more widely throughout the Levant in the Islamic period.

Our site has yielded many more tall beaker lamps (MNE 37) with sharp, 'cracked-off' rims, light lathe-cut horizontal incisions, and contrasting dark cobalt bluish or mid-bluish trails and/or prunts (applied blobs). All have cupped rims on either a conical body in lime greenish fabric (TS 10 and 16) or a swelling body (TS 1 and 57) which then tapers to small flat base or thick solid toe (the latter are mostly in a strongly olive-greenish fabric, but amber and bluish examples also occur; the olive and amber colors may have been artificially selected from glass made from specific types of sand, so as to resemble bronze). The use of contrasting-coloured prunts[128] places them in a wider category of 4th-6th c. bowls and beakers found in N Italy, Greece, the Balkan provinces, the Black Sea region and Egypt. They seem concentrated, however, in the Black Sea region and especially Egypt.[129] Only in *Palaestina Salutaris Tertia* were they as common as in Egypt, as listed by D. M. Bailey,[130] even though conical forms were made at Jalame[131] in the Galilee in the later 4th and early 5th c. They first appear at our site in collapse from the earthquake of 363, and they were the most common lamps in use in the house on Ez Zantur in the same period.[132] Many were also retrieved from the 4th-c. church at Aila.[133] Caution must be exercised, however, when making regional comparisons. Their relative scarcity further north, such as at Gerasa,[134] might be exacerbated by an absence of comparable 4th- or 5th-c. destruction deposits, since most glass lamps from Decapolis cities come from churches with Umayyad earthquake destructions. At Pella, a warehouse which was demolished in

---

122 Erdmann 1977.
123 Patrich 1988.
124 Jones 2005.
125 Lindblom 2005, 164.
126 Patrich 1988, 134-36, pl. XII.
127 Meyer 1988, 205, fig. 10.
128 A small blob of glassed fused to another piece of glass either to provide decoration or to help provide a firm grip in the absence of a handle.
129 Harden 1936, 161-62, pl. XVI nos. 436-66; Bailey 1998, 151, pl. 93.
130 Bailey 1998, 151.
131 Weinberg 1988, 87-93.
132 Keller 2006, 56-57.
133 Jones 2005, 136.
134 Meyer 1988, 198, fig. 8 w.

the 4th or early 5th c. yielded a small number of prunted beakers (MNE 5)[135] all yielding a small number of prunted beakers (MNE 5). It may well be that their absence from the Petra Church and the monastic church at Deir 'Ain 'Abata reflects their construction dates after the 4th c. Yet some lathe-cut hemispherical bowl lamps with cupped and sharp rims, which were exactly contemporary with beaker lamps with 'cracked off rims', are to be found in later ecclesiastical assemblages, such as the Petra Church. This may be because relatively complex decoration made them worthy items to be donated. Most, however, were decorated simply with either lightly lathe-cut bands or deep lathe-turned linear grooves; bowls with deep grooves are typically thicker-walled but share the same forms, and the earliest at Petra (TS 100) also appeared before 363. Their simple lathe-turned decoration and ubiquity on Early Byzantine sites throughout the Levant suggest they were produced in local workshops everywhere, including at Jalame.[136] Certainly, hemispherical bowl lamps were by far the most common form (MNE 82) at our bath complex. They occur mostly in naturally colored fabrics that typically weather to a black surface on iridescence, although the relative thinness of the wall can make these bowls seem decolorized. At least some engraved examples were clearly used for drinking. Within the MNE of 82 bowls, at least 9 were lightly abraded with figured and/or vegetal decoration. The best preserved is TS 75 (fig. 14.14), which must predate 363. It may show a naked fisherman hauling a net or pulling at the edge of a boat; the same subject appears on a contemporary bowl in Rome.[137] TS 150 was inscribed, with both an E and I preserved: perhaps ΠΙΕ ΖΕΣΕΣ, 'Drink that you may live'. Other examples with this light abraded technique include a figured bowl from the Petra Church[138] and one with inscription (perhaps also ΠΙΕ ΖΕΣΕΣ) from a pre-church context at Deir 'Ain 'Abata (TS 107). The product of a perhaps Anatolian workshop that used double-lines for abraded inscriptions was found at Ez Zantur.[139]

Fig. 14.14. Figural engraved hemispherical glass bowl TS 75 (1 : 1).

In sum, the range and relative proportions of southern Levantine forms is closer to those of contemporary Egyptian sites, although Egypt has additional forms and fabrics (oval bowls at Karanis,[140] Byzantine millefiori bowls at Ain et-Turba, Bagawat and Douch[141]) not found in *Palaestina Salutaris Tertia*. There is thus no reason to suppose that Petra or other southern sites simply imported Egyptian glass; rather, local Arabian production in late antiquity was more closely influenced by Egyptian glass-working traditions than by northern workshops.

Glass types in use in A.D. 363

All the types which appear in the collapse of A.D. 363 appear in greater numbers in the next earthquake collapse, which may be assigned to the early 6th c. For the architectural glass, lamps and windows, it seems that the initial construction and the post-363 refurbishment occurred close enough in time (perhaps all within the 4th-early 5th c.) that no typological differences can be identified. Of the bowl types, only the unusual scalloped rim bowl (TS 133) and tubular-folded bowls (TS 116) lack examples from pre-363 contexts. The latter were produced in great numbers at late 4th c.-/early 5th-c. Jalame[142] and are found across the Levant. The former has a general parallel from

135 da Costa *et al.* 2002, 518.
136 Ibid. 96-97.
137 Hayes 1928, 24, fig. 1.
138 O'Hea 2001, 370, no. 9.
139 Keller 2006, 212, pl. 12. There may also have been a specifically Syro-Phoenician workshop with a different style and technique: de Tommaso 1998, 422. A later, different workshop could have produced the deep chi-rho bowl from Gerasa with its internal engraving: Bowsher 1986, 263, fig. 25.
140 Harden 1936, 48.
141 Hill and Nenna 2003, 88; Nenna 2003, 93-94.
142 Weinberg 1988, 53.

4th-6th c. Karanis[143] and from Ez Zantur, where Keller argues convincingly for a mid- to late 4th c. date on the basis of ceramic parallels and finds across the empire.[144] In addition to the listed bases there are splayed folded feet on a flat bowl center (MNE 4), ranging from 8 to 16 cm in diameter, in olive, greenish and faintly blue-greenish fabrics, all dating to the 4th c. at the earliest. Stacked coil bases, on the other hand, appear throughout the 4th to 6th c. across the empire. Three of the 4 examples here pre-date the earthquake of 363, placing them early in the series. They also appear at the Petra Church.[145] Wheel-incised beakers (not lamps) are also found commonly in both northern and southern Levant in contexts of the 4th-5th c. All our types (MNE totalling 21) must have been made in the first half of the 4th c. Also typical of 4th-5th c. beakers and the occasional flask is the solid pad base (TS 124, 54–55: the last two types find examples in the collapse of 363). Fragments of at least 10 indented beakers of the same period were also present (too fragmented to illustrate); some have simple domed bases.

Goblets became increasingly popular throughout the Byzantine and Umayyad Levant. Although many must have functioned as drinking vessels (as mosaics show), their repeated appearance in churches suggests that some functioned as oil-lamps for niches and benches. Only 6 are attested at our site; none has handles so they were not used as hanging lamps. At least one dates from the first half of the 4th c. Although solid-stems only became dominant among Late Byzantine and Umayyad goblets, the added solid disc-feet do occur in the 4th c. at Sardis.[146] Everted or folded rims (MNE 18) could belong to goblets, hollow-stemmed lamps, or beakers (TS 81, 128, 96 and 21). Bowl lamps (TS 27, 24), beaker lamps and stemmed lamps are all present in the collapse of 363. Of the bowl lamps, only bases have survived, but more complete profiles from Gerasa show that they are three-handled shallow bowls.[147] All but one of the hollow-stemmed lamps (MNE 5) at our site came from the collapse of 363, placing them at the start of a long-lived series present in 5th-and 6th-c. churches across Syria, *Palaestina Secunda et Tertia.* The unguent or oil vessels are overwhelmingly small, funnel-mouthed flasks, although tall-mouthed flasks also appear. Rare here (MNE 6) are jars that may have contained perfumed salves or oil, since they are common in contemporary graves; two-thirds of them are the typically collared types of the 4th and early 5th c.

Flasks TS 32 and 17 are broadly 3rd-4th c. by their context. The other flask bases all appear in the collapse of 363, implying an early to mid-4th c. dating at the latest, as do piriform flask bases and fragments. Notable (smashed) concentrations (MNE 23) of flasks with bases TS 9 and 16 came from the débris of 363 in the Upper Temenos Trench 105 Loci 6-16, especially Locus 7; another 5 were found in Lower Temenos Trench 127 Locus 19. Indented flasks are common in the Byzantine period but rarely take the exaggerated form of our TS 7; they occur in the mid-4th c. collapse. Possibly this variant had a deliberately cruciform cross-section, where other Christian flasks used mould-blown Christian symbolism. The complete profile is unknown; to my knowledge, the only published parallel is a less well-preserved and aptly described "very strange shape" from Karanis.[148] Three head flasks (TS 8) from the baths may be added to a pair found in the prior seasons.[149] It is unclear if they were double-headed or single head flasks of young boys, but they were probably perfumed oil flasks (they are more common in graves than in domestic contexts). This distinctive long-haired type is known from a Karanis Period-C house[150] and at Cairo,[151] as well as from an unpublished Justinianic tomb at Pella. At least one of the Petra flasks confirms a

143 Harden 1936, 97, Form 259, pl. 25q.
144 Keller 2006, 209, Type VII.16, pl. 10k.
145 O'Hea 2001, 371, no. 25.
146 von Saldern 1980, 56-57, no. 323.
147 Baur 1938, 528 and 530, fig. 23.
148 Harden 1936, 251, no. 766.
149 Karz 1998, 334.
150 Harden 1936, 214, no. 629.
151 Edgar 1905, 38-39, no. 32.573, pl. VI.

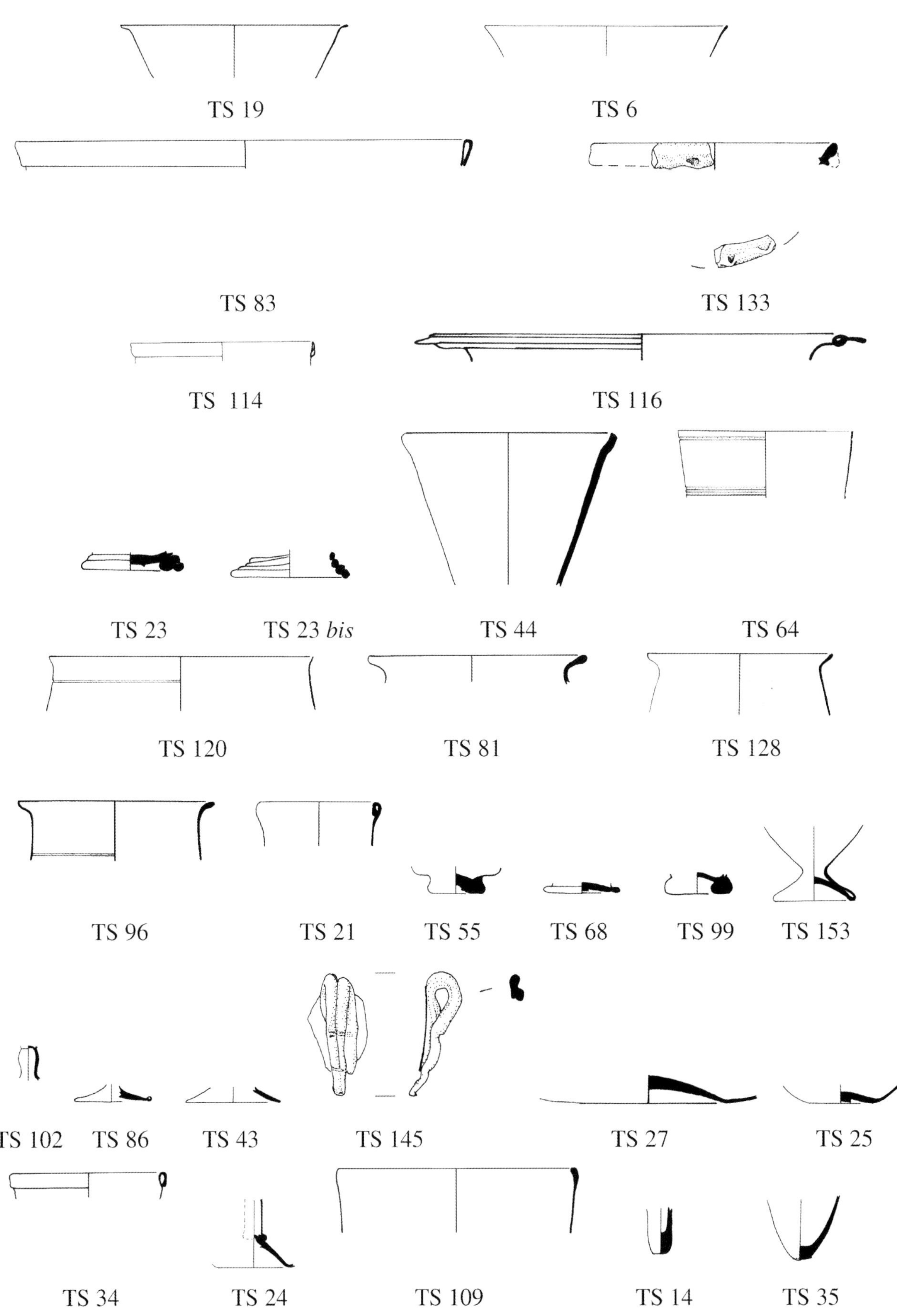

Fig. 14.15. Early Byzantine glass bowls, beakers, handled and hollow-stemmed lamps (1 : 3).

broadly 4th-c. dating. An indistinctly patterned mould-blown fragment and three polygonal (perhaps square-sectioned) fragments are present in Byzantine contexts at the Great Temple.

Bowls

Fig. 14.15 TS 19. Small ledge-rim (MNE 10). rdiam 12. Narrow ledge rim, carinated to deep bowl. Thin walled. Bluish. Iridescence. Most other examples are faintly lime or greenish, with one blue-greenish.

TS 6. Flaring rim (MNE 21). rdiam 13. Simple flaring rim, on straight shallow bowl. Thin walled, bluish. White enamel-like surface. Fabrics are almost evenly divided between greenish, blue-greenish and bluish. This bowl form was also found in the Petra Church.[152]

TS 83. Folded rim (MNE 1). rdiam 25. Rim folded out on steep convex bowl. Thin walled. Greenish. Black on iridescence.

TS 133. Tooled rim (MNE 1). rdiam 13. Bevelled thick dropped edge, pinched to form scallops; deep convex bowl. Thick walled. Strongly olive greenish, mottled lime. Black on iridescence.

TS 114. Tubular folded bowl (MNE 1). rdiam 10. Upright thin wall, folded against itself. Indeterminate fabric.

TS 116. Tubular flanged rim (MNE 2). rdiam 26. Ledge rim, folded on top as tubular ridge; carinated to deep bowl. Thin walled. Indeterminate fabric. Black on iridescence. Another example is a body fragment from smaller (10-16 cm diam.) bowls.

TS 85. Tubular flanged bowl (MNE 1). bdiam 16. Rim missing; upright wall, folded to form tubular flange, carinated into bowl (missing). Thin walled. Faintly greenish. Iridescence. This rim occurs on both 1st-c. and Early Byzantine bowls and pyxides,[153] but since the fragment does not come from a secure Early Roman deposit it is classified as Byzantine.

TS 23 Coiled base (MNE 5). bdiam 4. 4 stacked coils making footed base, rest missing. Greenish. Iridescent flaking. Base diam. range 4-6 cm; other examples have 3-4 coils.

Goblet or beaker rims

TS 44. Conical beaker rim (MNE 16). rdiam 11. Cupped cut rim on deep, slightly convex wall. Medium-thick walled. Single extant, lightly incised band on cupped exterior of rim. Indeterminate fabric. Black on iridescence. Other examples of the type include faintly lime greenish or decolorized fabrics.

TS 64. Wheel-incised beaker rim (MNE 4). rdiam 9. Straight wall, sloping steeply inwards. Cut rim, narrow deep groove below rim, another close-set pair down the body. Very thin walled. Faintly lime greenish. Other examples are lime greenish and decolorized.

TS 120. Everted beaker rim (MNE 1). rdiam 15. Everted cut rim, ground to point; swelling body (mostly missing). Narrow single groove below carination. Very thin walled. Decolorized, faintly greenish. Calcified.

TS 81. Everted rim (MNE 2). rdiam 11. Everted thickened rim, carinated to swelling body. Medium-thick walled. Strongly lime greenish. Iridescent flaking. Another example is decolorized with pinkish tint.

TS 128. Everted rim (MNE 1). rdiam 10. Everted simple rim, carinated to swelling body. Medium walled. Strongly lime greenish. Iridescence. Rims such as TS 128 can belong to beakers, goblets or hollow-stemmed lamps.

TS 96. Flaring rim (MNE 6). rdiam 10. Flaring rim, upright body. Non-joining rounded heel to thin base. Thin walled, many fragments. Blue-greenish. Black on iridescence. Other examples are faintly greenish.

TS 21. Folded rim (MNE 9). rdiam 6. Slightly everted rim, folded in, on nearly upright wall. Medium-thin walled. Probably bluish, 3 fragments, non-joining. Iridescence. Externally folded rims are usually lamps or goblets.

Beaker bases

TS 55. Pad base (MNE 9). bdiam 3.5. Flat heel curving in to solid pad base, slightly domed. Small incuse pontil mark. Thin walled. Strongly bluish. Black on iridescence. Occurs almost equally in bluish, greenish and blue-greenish fabrics.

TS 68. Footed base (MNE 1). bdiam 4. Heel slightly pinched on flat thickened base. Pared, solid pontil mark. Thin walled body. Bluish. Abraded.

TS 99. Small ring-foot (MNE 1). bdiam 3.5. Rounded heel, base kicked with reamer. No pontil mark. Added thick solid trail as ring-foot. Decolorized. Black on iridescence.

Goblet bases

TS 153. Hollow stemmed goblet (MNE 2). bdiam 4.5. Narrow bowl tapering to short hollow stem, on folded

---

152 O'Hea 2001, 371, no. 20.

153 Hayes 1975, 174, no. 295, fig. 9.

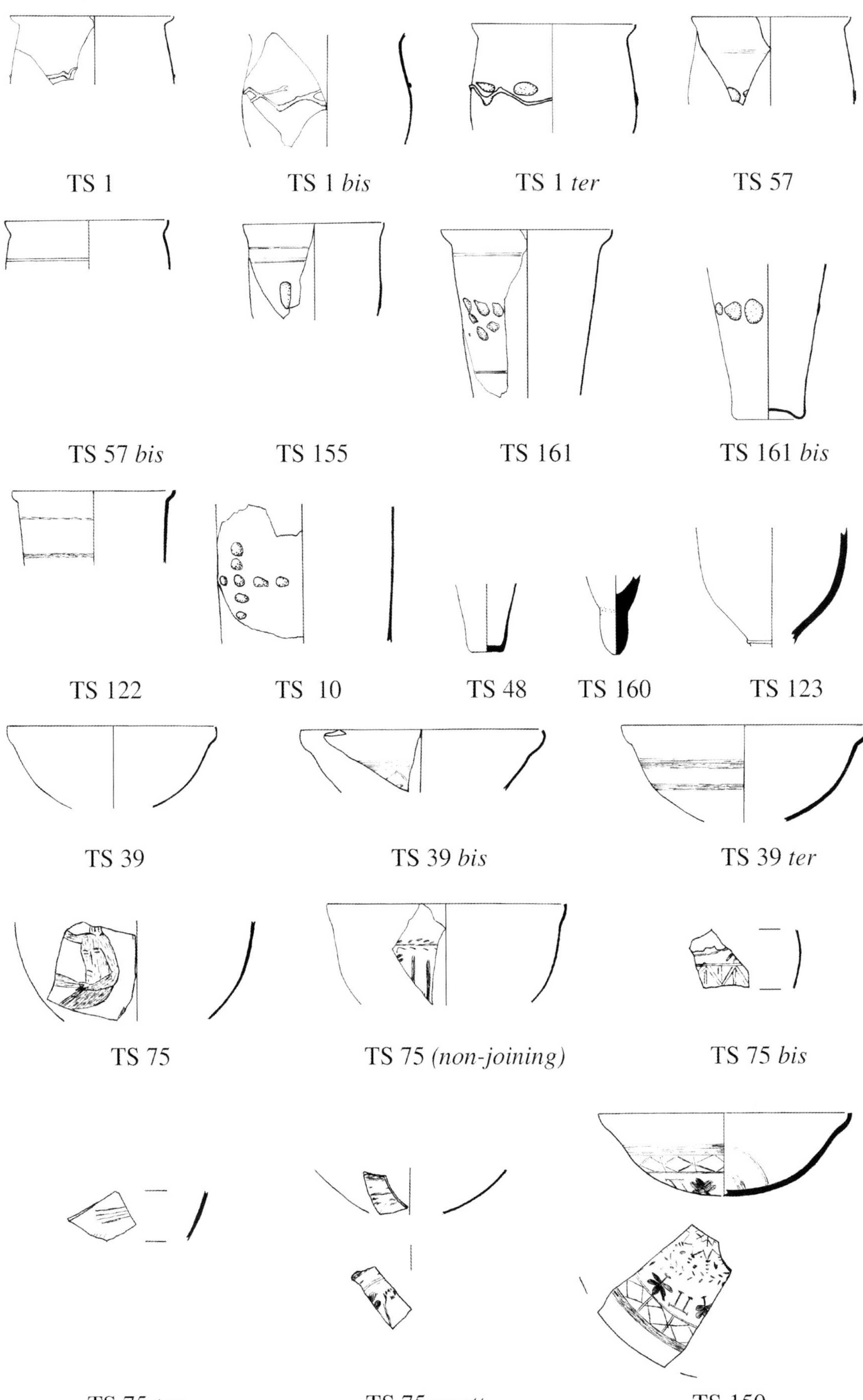

Fig. 14.16. Early Byzantine glass conical, ovoid beaker lamps and wheel-incised bowl lamps (1 : 3).

foot, pushed up at base. Medium walled. Strongly olive greenish. Iridescent flaking.

TS 102. Hollow stem (MNE 4). Hollow, bulbous stem, flaring to missing folded foot. Medium walled. Strongly blue-greenish. Iridescence.

TS 86. Hollow stemmed goblet foot (MNE 2). bdiam 4. Folded low foot only. Strongly bluish. Iridescent flaking.

TS 43. Solid stemmed goblet foot (MNE 1). bdiam 5. Solid disc foot only; some tool marks. Strongly olive greenish. Black on iridescence.

Beaker and bowl handled lamps

TS 145. Handled bowl lamp (MNE 1). bdiam 20. Convex bowl fragments; 2 extant vertical double-stranded handles, trailed up and looped down body. Tooled horizontally across handle at body. All faintly blue-greenish. Iridescent flaking.

TS 27. Large simple base (MNE 6). bdiam 8. Very shallow heel, on slightly domed large base. No pontil mark extant. Strongly blue-greenish. Iridescence. Half of the examples are blue-greenish, with lime greenish and bluish instances.

TS 25. Simple base (MNE 36). bdiam 4. Shallow body on rounded heel; thickened flat base, with thick pontil blob in solid relief. Medium walled. Blue-greenish. Iridescence. Two-thirds of the examples are blue-greenish, the remainder lime greenish or bluish. Some have pared, solid pontil marks.

TS 34. Handled beaker folded rim (MNE 23). rdiam 8.5 (fig. 14.12). Upright rim, folded out; thin wall sloping steeply in. Single extant handle attached to rim exterior (mostly missing). Indeterminate fabric. Black on iridescence. Most other examples are blue-greenish; at least 8 are without extant handles.

TS 24. Wick-tubed beaker lamp base (MNE 15). h 3.7, rdiam 1.5. Rim rolled in, flattened on top; tapering tube, squashed onto beaker base (missing). Indeterminate fabric, either blue-greenish or greenish. Black on iridescence.

Hollow-stemmed lamps

TS 109. Deep hollow-stemmed lamp rim (MNE 4). rdiam 12. Thickened, slightly incurved simple rim on upright thin wall. Faintly lime greenish. Iridescence. One other example is bluish.

TS 14. Hollow-stemmed lamp (MNE 5). Pared base, thick-walled cylindrical stem. Strongly blue-greenish. Iridescence. Other examples of the type include bluish.

TS 35. Hollow-stemmed lamp (MNE 5). Pres. h 3.7 max., w 4.4. Convex conical hollow stem, pared at base. Medium-thick walled. Faintly greenish. Iridescence.

Beaker lamps

Fig. 14.16 TS 1. Trailed ovoid (MNE 10). rdiam 8. Cupped cut rim, carinated to ovoid thin-walled body. Strongly olive greenish. Single extant zigzag cobalt blue trail around upper body. Iridescent flaking. Other examples are olive, one is strongly amber; at least 3 have lightly incised narrow bands below the rim. Other examples have single zigzag with prunts and interlacing zigzags, as at Ez Zantur and Karanis.[154] The earliest stratigraphic dating is broadly 4th c.

TS 57. Prunted ovoid (MNE 22). rdiam 8. Cupped cut rim, carinated to ovoid thin-walled body. Strongly olive greenish. Single lightly wheel-incised narrow band below carination; single extant row of mid-bluish prunts. Iridescence. At least 5 other examples have dark cobalt-bluish prunts. Fabrics include lime greenish, amber, bluish and decolorized fabrics. Rims range from 7 to 13 cm.

TS 155. Prunted narrow tapering beaker (MNE 1). rdiam 7. Cupped cut rim, carinated to ovoid thin-walled body. Bluish. Single extant row of large, vertically oval prunts, all mid-bluish. Iridescent flaking.

TS 161. Conical beaker (MNE 1). rdiam 8. Cupped cut rim; tall conical body, base missing. Lime greenish. Narrow, lightly wheel-incised bands below carination and mid-body; triangle of 6 cobalt prunts. Black on iridescence. Another example has simple domed base, no pontil mark.

TS 122. Conical beaker (MNE 2). rdiam 8. Cupped cut rim; tall conical and thick-walled body. Strongly lime greenish. Narrow, lightly-incised band below carination, wide band lower down body. Iridescent flaking. Although no prunts survive, the fabric suggests that it belongs to the series of lamps, rather than beakers such as TS 64.

TS 10. Large conical body (MNE 1). bdiam 7. Rim and base missing; conical body. Cross of close-set cobalt-bluish oval prunts; top and right bar are complete, suggesting horizontal row of 5 intersected by at least 5 in a column. Medium walled. Strongly lime greenish. 2 fragments, joining. Direct parallel at Karanis.[155]

---

154 Keller 2006, pl. 21q VII. 67; Harden 1936, 161, nos. 444-45.

155 Harden 1936, 161, no. 443.

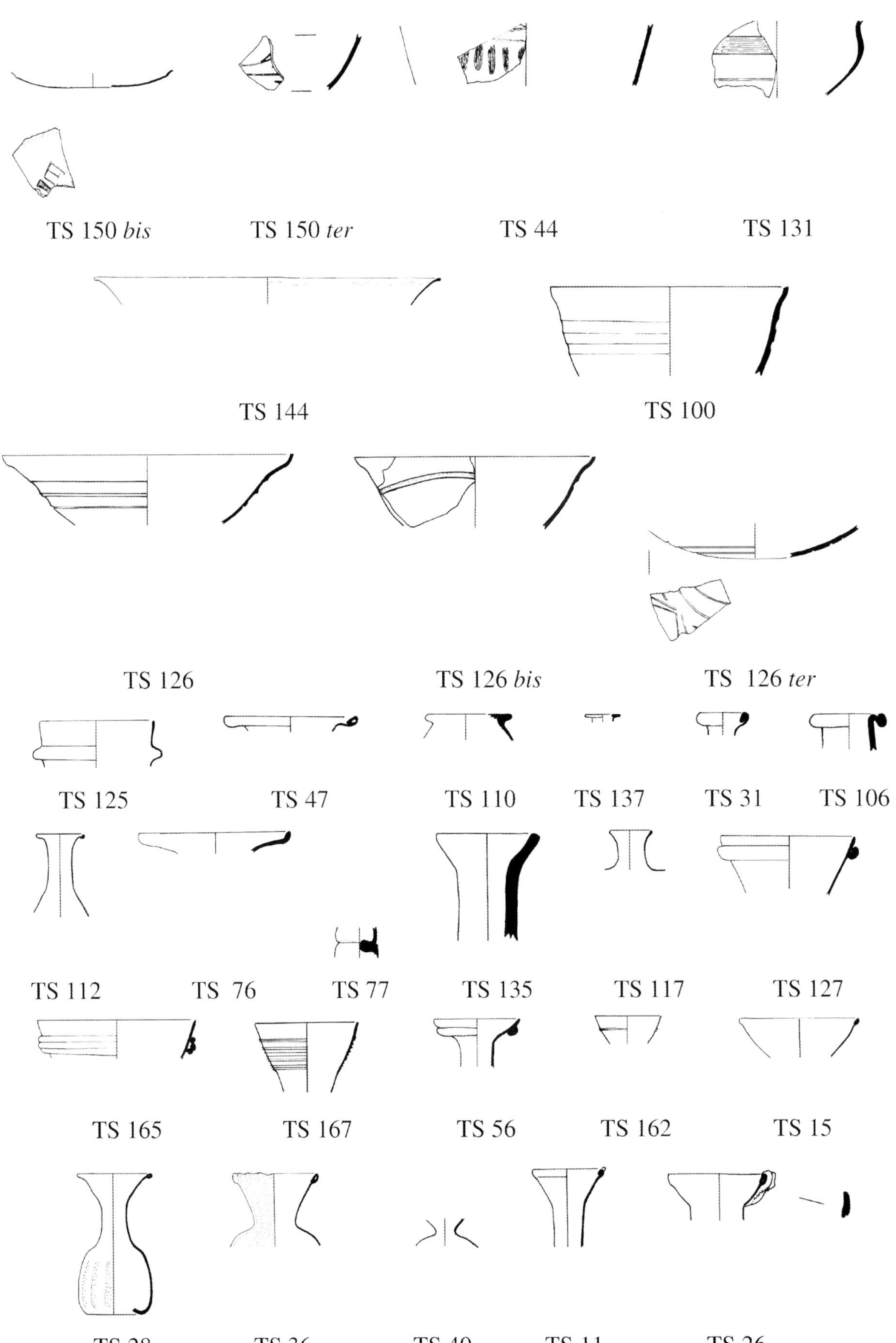

Fig. 14.17. Early Byzantine wheel-incised bowl lamps, jars, funnel-mouthed flasks and flagons (1 : 3).

TS 48. Conical base (MNE 10). bdiam 1.5. Flat base, not pared, hollow base flaring concavely to missing upper body. Medium walled. Strongly olive greenish. Black on iridescence.

TS 160. Solid conical base (MNE 2). Solid short tapering stem on thick conical base. Strongly lime greenish. Parallel at Karanis.[156]

TS 123. Body (MNE 3). bdiam 8. Convex body, tapering to pointed base. Very thick walled. Greenish. Iridescence. Other examples are lime greenish, one with cobalt prunt. Compare example at Ashmunein.[157]

Incised hemispherical bowls

TS 39. Rim (MNE 45). rdiam 15. Upright ground cupped rim, carinated to steep bowl sloping in. Uniformly thick walled. Wide band of light wheel-incisions around upper body. Faintly greenish. Iridescence. Half of the other examples are greenish, with small numbers bluish or blue-greenish and one decolorized. The earliest can be attributed to the mid-4th c. at the latest; almost all the remainder probably belonged to the mid-4th c. refurbishment of the baths and were collapsed into the rooms in *c*.512 by another earthquake. Rims vary from *c*.10 to 15 cm.

Thirty-six hemispherical bowl bases have light, wheel-incised bands around the exterior and a deep pair of concentric grooves around the center interior. At least three predate the collapse of 363. Where known, all but one have greenish fabrics.

TS 75. Figured bowl (MNE 8). (figs. 14.14 and 14.16). Hemispherical bowl body, thin walled, thickening slightly to rounded base. External decoration only. Body fully lightly and vertically abraded and outlined with slightly heavier cutting: naked male figure faces left, with right arm raised in front and left arm bent at his side, holds edge of shallow basin or net. Both legs are together, slightly forward of body. Head mostly missing, possibly bearded. Single nipple dot and forked vertical line down the center of torso to indicate musculature; fingers indicated by straight, deeper abraded lines. Non-joining fragments: horizontal laurel wreath above 2 tips of lines slanting up to right, to left of 2 vertical lines; below, upright dashes (grass?) and tapering diagonal line. Faintly bluish. Black on iridescence.

The decolorized and lime greenish examples of this form show curled tendril and petals between broad, lightly incised borders; vertical borders and 2 widely-spaced lines; lightly incised band above leaf or tendril tip above thick guilloche/wavy line around base; ribbon above arch; and 4 parallel lines with ovoid tips. Similar motifs may appear at Mezad Tamar.[158]

TS 150. Hemispherical bowl (MNE 2). rdiam 13. Cupped ground rim, carinated in to hemispherical bowl. Thick walled. Wide shallow groove below rim; abraded hollow lozenges in divided band, above alternating Greek letters (π extant) with serifs, and 5-lobed leaves. Below, wreath above large star with dashed finials; smaller central rosette with pointed petals within. 2 lightly incised concentric circles on interior of base. Strongly blue-greenish. Black on iridescence. Non-joining fragment from Locus 40, ε adjacent to arm of a cross. Greenish example of this type has 2 sets of hatched triangles on exterior.

Fig. 14.17 TS 131. Shallow bowl (MNE 5). bdiam 10-11. Rim missing; probably everted or cupped, carinated to rounded shoulder, sloping shallowly to missing base. Thick walled. Wide, lightly incised band around upper shoulder, fine lines around lower body. Blue-greenish or bluish. Black on iridescence. The earliest dating is late 4th c.

TS 144. Shallow bowl (MNE 1). rdiam 18. Everted rim, shallow bowl; lightly wheel-incised rim interior; pair of lightly incised bands on upper bowl exterior. Thin walled. Probably blue-greenish. Iridescence.

Deeply incised hemispherical bowls

TS 100. Rim (MNE 13). rdiam 12. Slightly cupped ground rim on deep bowl. Thick walled. 2 very wide, deep grooves below carination. Greenish. Iridescent flaking. Rims range 12-15 cm. Another example from the Petra Church.[159]

TS 126. Shallow bowl rim (MNE 8). rdiam 16. Cupped ground rim, carinated to shallow hemispherical bowl. 2 wide, deep grooves below carination. Thick walled. Strongly greenish. Abraded. One example has part of a scroll or medallion.

Jars

TS 125. Collared jar rim (MNE 1). rdiam 6. Upright simple rim, folded out to collar. Medium-thin walled. Aubergine color. Black on iridescence.

---

156 Ibid. no. 466, pl. XVI.
157 Bailey 1998, 151-52, Y 39.
158 Erdmann 1977, 143, nos. 903-4.
159 O'Hea 2001, 370, no. 13.

TS 47. Ledge jar rim (MNE 4). rdiam 7. Wide ledge rim, folded flat on top, curving in to wide neck. Medium-thin walled. Faintly blue-greenish. Iridescence.

TS 110. Ledge jar rim (MNE 1). rdiam 4. Flat rim, folded on top, neck swelling to body. Medium-thick walled. Blue-greenish. Iridescent flaking.

Flask rims

TS 137. Folded rim (MNE 2). rdiam 1.5. Tiny ledge rim, folded in on top. Narrow thin neck. Indeterminate fabric. Black on iridescence.

TS 31. Folded rim (MNE 3). rdiam 2.5. Everted rim, folded in; pinched at top of narrow neck. Thin walled. Greenish. Black on iridescence.

TS 106. Folded rim (MNE 2). rdiam 4. Flat rim, folded down against self to form dropped edge; narrow neck. Thick walled. Greenish. Black on iridescence. Another example is amber, with trail on rim.

TS 112. Funnel-mouthed flask (MNE 3). rdiam 2.5. Rim rolled in on shallow small funnel-mouth, narrow neck with tapering shoulder, rest missing. Thin walled. Blue-greenish. Iridescence. One other example has 2 trails wound around the lower neck.

TS 76. Possible sprinkler flask rim (MNE 1). rdiam 8.5. Upturned rounded edge on shallow mouth, curving in to narrow neck. Thick walled. Decolorized. Black on iridescence. Alternatively this could be a lid (inverted).

TS 77. Sprinkler flask (MNE 2). bdiam 2.5. Upright neck, curved in to flat base, swirled and pierced from top; added body with sloping shoulders. All greenish. Black on iridescence. Not later than A.D. 363.

Funnel-mouthed flasks

TS 135. Rim (MNE 3). rdiam 5. Simple rim on tall neck. Thick walled. Blue-greenish. Iridescence.

TS 117. Flaring rim (MNE 1). rdiam 2.2. Simple flaring rim; short narrow neck, sunken wide shoulder. Medium walled. Decolorized, faintly greenish.

TS 127. Large trailed rim (MNE 2). rdiam 7. Simple funnel mouth; large single trail immediately below rim. Thick walled. All greenish. Iridescent flaking. One other example is bluish.

TS 165. Trailed rim (MNE 1). rdiam 8. Simple funnel mouth; thick trail closely wound below rim. All bluish. Black on iridescence.

TS 167. Trailed rim (MNE 1). rdiam 5.5. Simple funnel-mouth; fine trails below rim. Thin walled. Black on iridescence.

TS 56. Trailed rim (MNE 4). rdiam 4.5. Simple rim on narrow neck. Single large solid trail immediately below rim. Decolorized, faintly greenish. Thick walled. 2 fragments joining. Iridescent flaking.

TS 162. Trailed rim (MNE 1). rdiam 2.5. Simple, slightly cupped rim; fine trail wound around middle. Thin walled. Blue-greenish. Black on iridescence.

TS 15. Large rolled rim (MNE 2). rdiam 6. Rim rolled in, very wide and shallow convex mouth. Medium walled. Bluish. Iridescence.

TS 28. Optically blown flask (MNE 1). rdiam 5, h 7.4. Rim folded in; shallow mouth on narrow neck; sloping shoulder on cylindrical narrow body with rounded heel and domed base, center missing. Thin walled. Vertically ribbed body. Blue-greenish. Black on iridescence. Not later than A.D. 363.

TS 36. Ribbed flask (MNE 2). rdiam 4, h >5.5. Rim folded in on deep mouth, carinated to rounded shoulder. Non-joining short pomiform body; rounded heel, base missing. Medium-thin walled. Widely-spaced narrow ridges run vertically from rim to lower body. Blue-greenish mottled to greenish. Iridescence.

TS 40. Neck (MNE 1). Int. diam. 1. Rim missing, flaring mouth curving concavely to pinch above wide rounded shoulder. Medium walled. Strongly olive yellowish. Iridescence.

Handled funnel-mouthed flasks

TS 11. Rim (MNE 14). rdiam 3.5. Rim folded in; funnel mouth on narrow neck, slightly splayed towards missing body. Medium-thin walled. Blue-greenish. Traces of handle at rim exterior. Iridescence. At least 7 come from the one area (Trench 105, Loci 7-9) and 3 from Trench 120, Loci 14-16, suggesting concentrations of these vessels in the Baths. The earliest date is before A.D. 363.

Flagon

TS 26. Funnel mouth (MNE 10). rdiam 4. Shallow mouth, rim folded in, on narrow neck. Medium-thin walled. Single strap handle attached to rim exterior, folded against self, then outwards. Faintly blue-greenish to greenish.

Tall-mouthed flasks

Fig. 14.18 TS 29. Rim (MNE 7). rdiam 5, bdiam 6, h 6. Upright rim, folded in; upright mouth; neck missing. Rounded shoulder on cylindrical body. Rounded heel. Thin, domed base, center missing. Thin walled. Bluish. Iridescence.

TS 22. Rim (MNE 15). rdiam 3. Simple upright rim. Medium walled. Faintly blue-greenish. Iridescent flaking. Other examples in blue-greenish, greenish and bluish fabrics; at least 4 predate A.D. 363.

TS 94. Trailed rim (MNE 3). rdiam 3. Simple upright rim, with fine trails from rim top down neck. Medium-thin walled. All lime greenish. Iridescence. Other examples are greenish and bluish, both with mid-blue trails. Comparative examples are 5th-6th c.

TS 164. Rim (MNE 2). rdiam 5. Rim rolled in; steeply tapering mouth. Thin walled. Lightly swirl-ribbed. Blue-greenish. Iridescent flaking.

Indented flasks

TS 17. Indented polygonal flask (MNE 2). Internal diam. *c*.3, max. diam. 4. Flat, thickened base; pared solid pontil mark. 4 deep right-angled indentations from heel to shoulder, forming cruciform-sectioned body, with each wall paddled flat. Non-joining indented upper body fragments with cylindrical neck or mouth slightly sunken into shallow shoulder. Medium-thin walled. Blue-greenish. Iridescent flaking. These seem to be a pair from adjacent areas in the Upper Temenos.

Trefoil-mouthed flasks

TS 149. Rim (MNE 1). rdiam 3.5. Rim folded in, on shallow funnel mouth carinated to narrow neck. Handle folded against rim exterior. Medium walled. Blue-greenish.

TS 163. Rim (MNE 1). rdiam 5. Everted rim, rolled in; large tall mouth. No extant handle. Thin walled. Bluish.

Miscellaneous forms

TS 33. Handled fragment (MNE 1). Int. diam. 1. Loop handle attached to lower neck. Medium-thin walled. Indeterminate fabric.

TS 37. Body (MNE 1). bdiam 7. Rim missing; wide neck, rounded shoulder on pomiform body, base missing. Thin walled. Bluish, almost blue-greenish. Many fragments.

TS 113. Trailed neck (MNE 1). Neck diam. 1.2. Narrow long neck swelling to sloping shoulder on piriform body. 2 fine trails at base of neck. Medium-thick walled. Decolorized, faintly greenish. 2 fragments, joining.

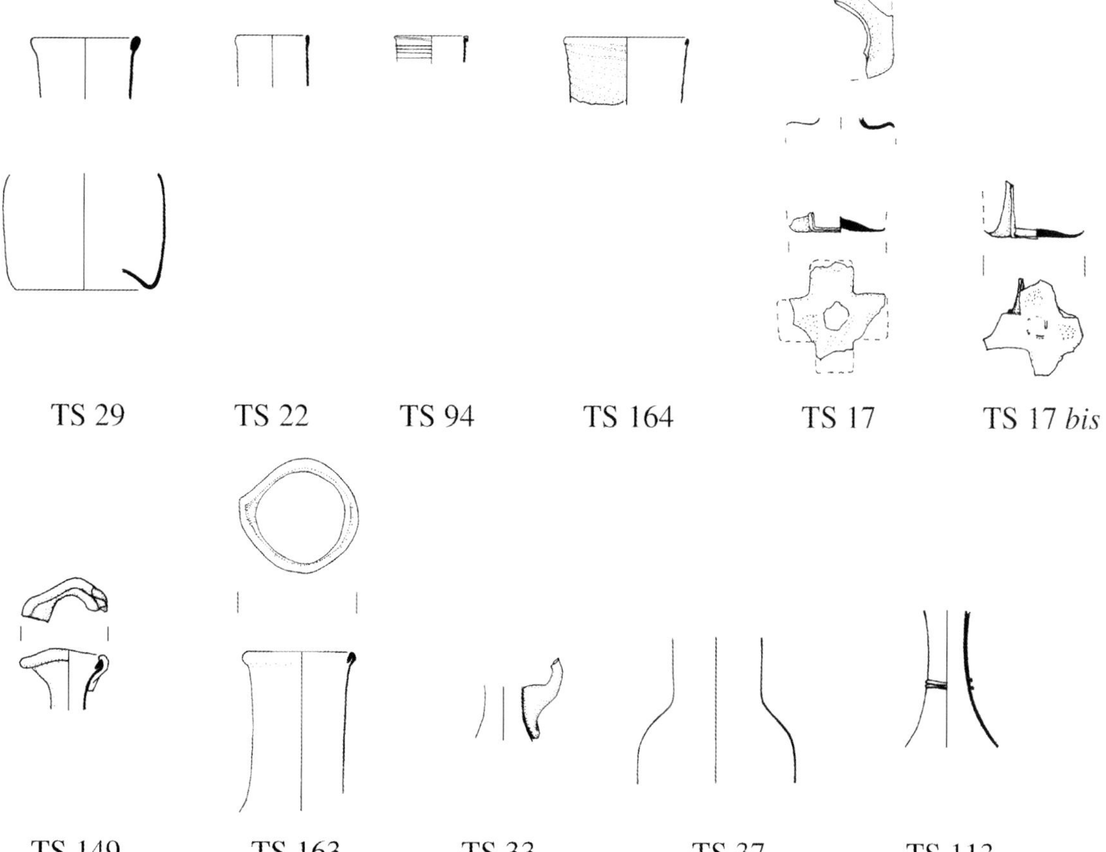

Fig. 14.18. Early Byzantine glass flask rims and flask or beaker bases (1 : 3).

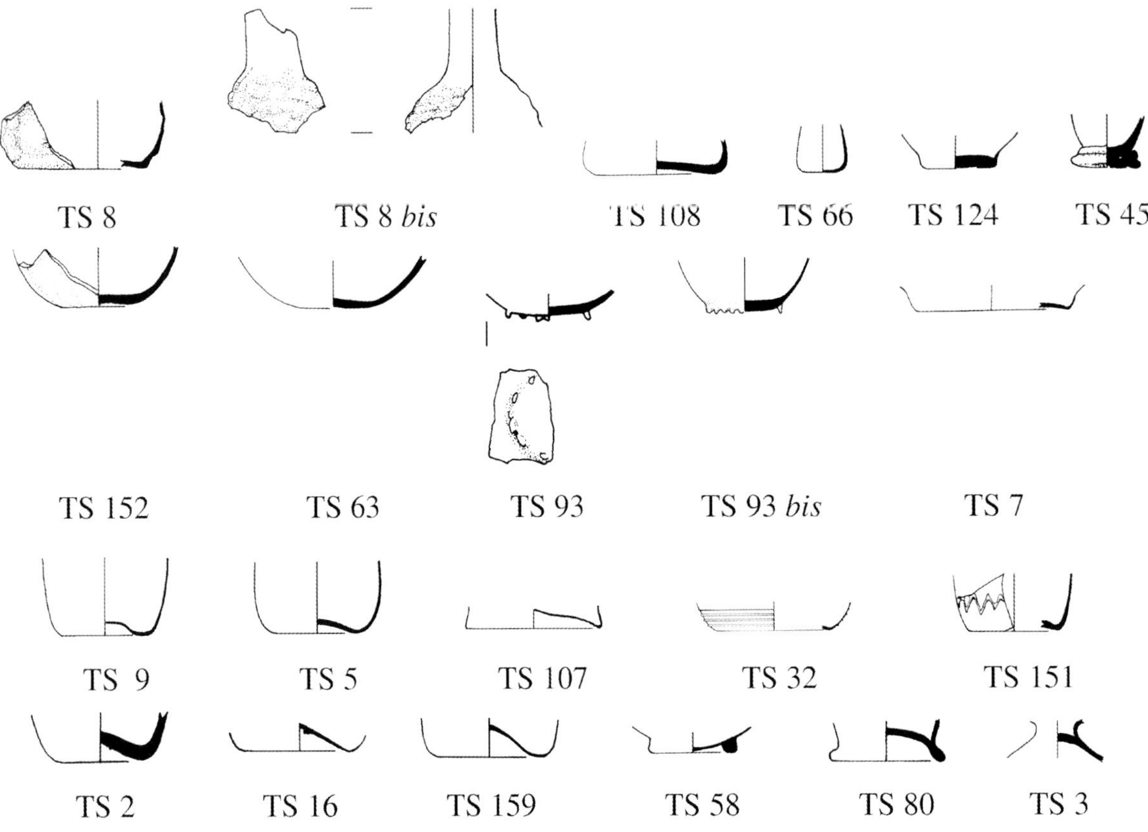

Fig. 14.19. Early Byzantine glass flask rims and flask or beaker bases (1 : 3).

Mould-blown flasks

Fig. 14.19 TS 8. Head flask (MNE 3). bdiam <5. Base fragment of head flask, knobbly hair to base; extant right cheek, dimpled to chin, mostly missing. Head offset slightly to flat and thickened base. Medium walled. Lime greenish. Iridescent flaking. Other examples of the type are lime greenish and amber.

Bases

TS 108. Piriform base (MNE 4). bdiam 5. Upright cylindrical body, sharply carinated to very flat base, no pontil mark. Medium-thick walled. Blue-greenish. Iridescent flaking. Other examples are faintly lime greenish.

TS 66. Small tubular flask base (MNE 2). bdiam 2. Narrow, piriform body, rounded heel very slightly domed. Center missing. Medium-thin walled. Lime greenish. Iridescent flaking.

TS 124. Pad base (MNE 4). bdiam 3.5. Tapering body; thick pad base with incised dot in center exterior. Thin walled. Lime greenish. Iridescent flaking.

TS 45. Coil base (MNE 3). bdiam 2.5. Flat coil-wound base on narrow conical body. Medium walled. Body now faintly pinkish, coil fabric indeterminate. Black on iridescence.

TS 152. Optically-blown pomiform body (MNE 1). bdiam 4. Flattened base, very slightly domed, no pontil mark. Light vertical ribbing from heel. Thick walled. Strongly dark greenish.

TS 63. Flask flat base (MNE 11). bdiam 4. Rounded body on simple flat base, very slightly domed in center, no pontil mark. Thick walled. Strongly bluish. Iridescent flaking. Range for base diam. is 4-6 cm, some with pared, solid pontil mark.

TS 93. Multi-footed base (MNE 3). bdiam 3. Rounded base on mostly missing flask, with at least 6 tiny pulled-out feet. No extant pontil mark. Medium walled. Lime greenish. Iridescent flaking.

TS 7. Low base (MNE 4). bdiam 8. Body carinated in to narrower rounded heel; slightly thickened simple base, center missing. Thin walled, 3 fragments, 2 joining. Decolorized, faintly bluish or blue-greenish. Iridescent flaking.

TS 9. Domed base (MNE 23). bdiam 4. Tall cylindrical body; rounded heel, thin domed base, no pontil mark. Medium-thin walled. Bluish. Iridescence. Most other examples are bluish; range of base diam. is 4-6 cm.

TS 5. Domed base (MNE 17). bdiam 4. Rounded heel on low domed base, uniformly medium walled. Faintly bluish or blue-greenish. Black on iridescence.

TS 107. Domed base (MNE 1). bdiam 5. Splayed heel on thin domed base, no pontil mark. Very thin walled, perhaps mould-blown. Indeterminate fabric. Black on iridescence.

TS 32. Trailed domed base (MNE 1). bdiam 4-5. Shallow heel, sloping in to slightly domed base, center missing. Medium-thin walled. Widely spaced fine trails wound around body to just above heel. Indeterminate fabric. Iridescent flaking.

TS 151. Trailed domed base (MNE 1). bdiam 4. Body tapering slightly to rounded base, center domed and thickened. Medium walled. Blue-greenish. Fine mid-bluish zigzag above heel.

TS 2. Kicked base (MNE 5). bdiam 4. Piriform body, rounded heel; base kicked with reamer over large pontil scar. Thick walled, strongly blue-greenish. Mottled white enamel-like surface.

TS 16. Kicked base (MNE 16). bdiam 4. Rounded heel; thickened and kicked base. Light pontil scar. Greenish. Iridescent flaking.

TS 159. Kicked base (MNE 15). bdiam 4. Upright wall, small base highly kicked. No pontil mark. Very thin walled. Yellowish olive. Some of these could be conical lamp bases.

Footed bases

These footed flask bases cannot be closely dated by typological comparisons. None from our site dates from the first half of the 4th c. The added ring base is unusual for Byzantine-era flasks in the Levant, where it has no secure dating by context. At Ashmunein, similar but not exact parallels exist in 4th- and 5th-c. contexts.[160]

TS 58. Ring base (MNE 1). bdiam 3.5. Rounded base; solid ring added. No pontil mark. Thin walled. Very faintly greenish. Iridescence.

TS 80. Folded foot (MNE 6). bdiam 4. Tapering body, folded to low foot, base pushed up as dome. No pontil mark. Medium walled. Decolorized, very faintly yellowish. Iridescence. Other examples are bluish, blue-greenish, greenish and amber.

TS 3. Folded foot (MNE 7). bdiam >3. Narrow, tapering base on splayed folded foot, base pushed in with reamer; edge missing. Large pontil scar. Greenish. Iridescent flaking.

Miscellaneous

Rod fragment TS 95 has no firm stratigraphic dating. Stirrers are found in Byzantine-era houses throughout the Levant; similar rods were made at Jalame.[161]

Fig. 14.20 TS 95. Spiral-twisted rod fragment (MNE 1). Pres. h 1.8, diam. 0.6. Straight rod, round section, finely twisted. Faintly greenish. Black on iridescence.

Window panes

The earliest form was a rectilinear, pan-moulded form, beginning in the 1st c. A.D. (TS 4). At least 40.3 gm came from 1st- or early 2nd-c. phases of the temple precinct, since they were found in fill for mid-2nd c. walls. Since none was *in situ*, their original location is unclear. This must be emphasised since there is no evidence for panes in any pagan temple architecture, whether Egyptian, Roman, Greek or Nabataean. Window panes seem to have remained restricted chiefly to baths in private houses and bathhouses in public architecture in the Levant; they were present in pre-363 phases of the Nabataean house on Ez Zantur,[162] but as to whether they were found only in its western bath rooms[163] we await the final publication. The bulk (at least 67.9 gm) of the rectilinear panes at our excavation came from the pre-363 phase of the Baths.

Circular panes, made like shallow blown bowls in natural hues, appeared only in the 4th c. At the Great Temple they appear in the collapse of 363 (at least 144.2 gm), making them among the earliest datable examples of the type. As elsewhere, circular panes normally had folded rims (TS 13), but they were so unevenly rolled or folded that the simple rims of TS 78 probably belong to the same generic group. Of the total amount (1607.5 gm) which came from the Baths, circular panes

160 Bailey 1998, 153-54, Y70-71.

161 Weinberg 1988, 232-33, no. 33c.

162 Keller 2006, 117.

163 Kolb 2002, 261.

Fig. 14.20. Early Byzantine glass stirrer rod TS 95 (1 : 2) and windowpanes TS 4, TS 13 and TS 78 (1 : 3).

form 55% by weight. Plaster on both types of panes suggests that they were directly fixed into the windows, rather than set into timber or metal mullions.

TS 4. Rectilinear panes 759.3 gm (MNE 59). pres. w 6.7, pres. length 6.6, max. th 0.4. Rounded edge extant; neither surface matte. Decolorized. Black on iridescence.

TS 13. Circular panes with folded rim 736.7 gm (MNE 28). pres. diam. 21. Flat thin walled rim folded on top; non-joining, very thick center with relief pontil ring. Greenish. Iridescent flaking.

TS 78. Circular pane with simple rim 151.8 gm (MNE 9). pres. rdiam 26-27. Thin, fire-rounded rim on flat circular pane, thickening *c.*0.6 cm to center. Greenish. Iridescence.

Fig. 14.21. Early Byzantine raw glass chunks TS 41 (1 : 1).

Glass chunks (fig. 14.21)

All come from one context associated with the collapse of the Baths (UT Trench 110, Loci 27-29). Since no glass wasters, trails, kilns or crucibles were identified in our excavations, there is no suggestion that glass working — either for window panes or for mosaics — occurred within the bath complex itself, but they must have been associated with a workshop somewhere in the city. The 4th-c. workshop at Samaria-Sebaste[164] and its later counterpart at Bet Shean both produced windowpanes in the town center.[165] Mosaicists used much larger glass bun-shaped ingots for cutting glass tesserae at Gerasa,[166] the Petra Church[167] and Pella,[168] so they cannot be associated with that kind of minor repair work. The reason for their presence remains unknown.

Acknowledgements

I thank Martha Sharp Joukowsky for granting me permission to publish this material and for her unstinting kindness in providing contextual data to aid my analysis. I would also like to thank Christopher A. Tuttle for his invaluable help both in Petra and at the American Center of Oriental Research, Amman, and the staff at ACOR for providing facilities for post-excavation processing of the glass. Any errors remain my own.

---

164 Crowfoot 1957, 421.
165 Mazar and Bar-Nathan 1998, 29.
166 Baur 1938, 517-18.
167 O'Hea 2001, 370.
168 O'Hea 1994, 258, fig. 8.

15

Coins from the Great Temple excavations: an overview

Christian F. Cloke

Introduction

The coin catalogue for the excavation includes 760 items[1] excavated between 1994 and 2006 (no coins were found in 1993). Some were already described by D. G. Barrett, in vol. 1, 317-24. The full database,[2] created with the FileMaker program and accessible at *Open Context* (http://www.opencontext.org), can be searched and sorted by any of the recorded criteria (date, culture, and so on).

At the conclusion of each season the coins and their associated records were first turned over to the Department of Antiquities at the Petra Museum until permission was granted by the Directorate to take the coins to the American Center for Oriental Research (ACOR) in Amman for cleaning. From 1994 to 1998, the coins were freed from dirt and encrusted salts in the ACOR laboratory and then stabilized and preserved by Pierre Bikai and M. S. Joukowsky. Since 1998, N. Zabban at ACOR undertook both the coin cleaning and stabilization. The coins were then returned to the Petra Museum.[3] In 2004, A. W. Joukowsky, assisted by Barrett, photographed all coins. Images of coins found from 2005 onwards were created using a flatbed scanner. C. Augé (Université of Paris I) completed the readings of all the coins, details of which are recorded in the catalogue. In 2007 the present author traveled to Petra to read the coins recovered in 2005-6 and review the full collection.

Many of the coins were too worn or corroded to allow for a clear reading: the Petra soil is very acidic and Nabataean base metal issues (which make up a large proportion of the finds) are prone to deterioration. Yet the many identifiable coins have aided in developing the site's phasing and chronology.

In broad terms the finds include:

Jewish (from the mid-1st c. B.C. to the time of the First Jewish Revolt)	3
probable Hellenistic (including 4 coins of Arados or Sidon)	7
certainly or probably Nabataean	138
Roman (including Greek provincial issues), 1st through 3rd c.	51
Roman, 4th c. or later (including many struck after the mid-4th c. earthquake)	296

- The few coins probably minted at Arados suggest that Petra participated in regional monetary commerce during the 3rd-2nd c. B.C., even before the Nabataeans began minting their own coins.
- Nabataean coinage of the following centuries (punctuated by the occasional foreign arrivals[4]) abounds, including the earliest and latest known issues as well as most of those in between.
- Roman coins paint a picture of Petra as firmly entrenched within the economic sphere of the E Mediterranean. Some issues minted at Rome (e.g., by Trajan and Constantine I) made their way to the site, but locally and regionally minted issues are far more common. Following the annexation of Nabataea in A.D. 106, some of the first new coins to arrive were silver drachms of Trajan (02-C-68A and 68C) probably minted in nearby Bostra. Also dating from around this time is a small bronze issue (02-C-22) bearing the monogram of the newly-designated Petra Metropolis. Bronze coins of Septimius Severus and Julia Domna minted at Petra suggest that at least some of the city's coin supply was produced locally well after the annexation.

---

1 A small handful were found not to be coins but simply pieces of metal.

2 Following excavation and numbering in the field, the coins were entered into the catalogue by D. G. Barrett.

3 Except for 3 coins accessioned by the National Jordan Museum in Amman, two of which (01-C-16 and 01-C-23) are included below and identified with the assigned "JMA" numbers.

4 Such as a small bronze of the emperor Galba (97-C-33) excavated in 1997: see vol. 1, 318.

- Most of the Roman coins belong to the 3rd-4th c. The range of mint-marks reflects the distances over which coins traveled to Petra; by far the most common mints represented are Alexandria and Antioch, but Constantinople, Cyzicus, Heraclea, Nicomedia, Thessalonica, and possibly Siscia (in Pannonia)[5] appear too, as well as the occasional product of the Rome mint. Trench 57, below the central arch of the Great Temple proper, yielded 159 coins, mostly small bronzes of the 4th-5th c. The legible pieces derived mainly from the mints of Antioch and Cyzicus. Overall, the fairly limited range of mints argues strongly that the coins supplied to and used in this part of the province of *Arabia* were largely produced in the East.

What follows is a selection of coins excavated since the first report published in 1998. The selection includes coins whose identification was the most secure, but it remains generally representative of the range of types present.

Diameter (diam.) and thickness (th.) are given in cm, weight (wt.) in gm. *AR* = silver, *AE* = base metal.

SELECT CATALOGUE

Phoenician

Fig. 15.1. 02-C-62. Phoenician from Sidon or Arados.

02-C-62. 3rd-2nd c. B.C. (fig. 15.1).
Area UT, Tr. 94, Loc. 63. Very worn.
Obv.: head of Tyche with mural crown, right. Rev.: ship's prow, left.
Diam. 1.90, th. 0.38, wt. 6.4. Die axis uncertain. AE. Mintmark uncertain.
Refs: *BMC Phoen.* (Arados) 15, nos. 97-102, pl. III, 10-11[6] (226-187 B.C. or later); 16, no. 103, pl. III, 12 (187-185 B.C.); *BMC Phoen.* (Sidon) 157, no. 98, pl. XXI, 12 (2nd c. B.C.).

Fig. 15.2. 05-C-11. Phoenician from Sidon or Arados.

05-C-11. 3rd-2nd c. B.C. (fig. 15.2).
Area LT, SP 104, Loc. 3. Very worn.
Obv.: head of Tyche with mural crown, right. Rev.: ship's prow, left.
Diam. 1.28, th. 2.1, wt. 2.2. Die axis 2 o'clock. AE. Mintmark uncertain.
Refs.: *BMC Phoen.* (Arados) 15, nos. 97-102, pl. III, 10-11 (226-187 B.C. or later); 16, no. 103, pl. III, 12 (187-185 B.C.); *BMC Phoen.* (Sidon) 157, no. 98, pl. XXI, 12 (2nd c. B.C.).

Fig. 15.3. 05-C-60. Phoenician from Sidon or Arados.

05-C-60. 3rd-2nd c. B.C. (fig. 15.3).
Area T, SP 107, Loc. 2. Very worn.
Obv.: head of Tyche with mural crown, right. Rev.: ship's prow, left.
Diam. 1.43, th. 0.15, wt. 1.0. Die axis 5 o'clock. AE. Mintmark uncertain.
Refs.: as for 05-C-11.

Fig. 15.4. 95-C-42. Phoenician.

95-C-42. 3rd to 2nd c. B.C. (fig. 15.4).
Area LT, Tr. 16, Loc. 23. Worn.
Obv.: head of Tyche with mural crown, clearly veiled, right. Rev.: ship's prow, left; legend effaced at top.
Diam. 1.50, th. 0.15, wt. 3.36. Die axis 11 o'clock. AE. Mintmark unclear, so it is uncertain whether this is a coin of Sidon, Arado s, or perhaps Carne.
Refs.: as for 05-C-11.

5 This is a tentative identification; the piece (98-C-01) may instead have been a product of Antioch.

6 Numbers of images within plates will be given only when they do not correspond exactly with the respective catalogue number.

Nabataean

Fig. 15.5. 05-C-69. Aretas III.

05-C-69. Aretas III, 87-60 B.C.[7] (fig. 15.5).
Area P, SP 150, Loc. 5. Worn and corroded, but legible.
Obv.: helmeted head, right. Rev.: winged Nike, standing left, holding uncertain object in left hand and a wreath in right. In field left, crescent and letter Λ.
Diam. 1.13, th. 0.24, wt. 3.0. Die axis 12 o'clock. AE.
Refs.: Meshorer 1975, 85, no. 1, pl. I; Schmitt-Korte 1990, 106, no. 1, pl. X.

Fig. 15.6. 05-C-22. Syllaeus/Aretas IV.

05-C-22. Syllaeus, 9-6 B.C.[8] (fig. 15.6).
Area LT, Tr. 102, Loc. 1. Small scratches on the rev.
Obv.: laureate head, right; linear border. In field,ש ח (although the ש is off the flan to the left). Rev.: 2 cornucopiae crossed; linear border. On right, ח (off the flan), on left, Meshorer's monogram 3 (שלי; Syllaeus).
Diam. 1.32, th. 0.23, wt. 2.5. Die axis 1 o'clock. AE.
Ref.: Meshorer 1975, 93, no. 44, pl. III.[9]

Fig. 15.7. 05-C-26. Syllaeus/Aretas IV.

05-C-26. Syllaeus, 9-6 B.C. (fig. 15.7).
Area LT, Tr. SP 105, Loc. 3.
Obv.: Laureate head, right; linear border. In field,ש ח (but the ח is off the flan to the left). Rev.: 2 cornucopiae crossed; beaded border. On right, ח (off the flan); on left, Meshorer's monogram 3 (שלי; Syllaeus).
Diam. 1.07, th. 0.16, wt. 1.8. Die axis 12 o'clock. AE.
Ref.: Meshorer 1975, 93, no. 44, pl. III.

Fig. 15.8. 02-C-28. Aretas IV for Phasael.

02-C-28. Aretas IV for Phasael, 5 B.C.[10] (fig. 15.8).
Area UT, Tr. 90, Loc. 8. Very clear and legible.
Obv.: laureate head, right. Rev.: 2 parallel cornucopiae, right, with a palm branch below. פצאל (Phasael) on left.
Diam. 1.26, th. 0.12, wt. 1.4. Die axis not recorded. AE.
Ref.: Meshorer 1975, 97, no. 61, pl. IV.

Fig. 15.9. 05-C-09. Aretas IV for Phasael.

05-C-09. Aretas IV for Phasael, 5 B.C. (fig. 15.9).
Area LT, SP 105, Loc. 7. Some light wear, but virtually as struck.
Obv.: laureate head, right; beaded border. Possibly an "o" visible in the field right, but difficult to discern.
Rev.: 2 parallel cornucopiae, right, with a palm branch below; beaded border. In field right below, פצ; above at left, ח.
Diam. 1.29, th. 0.15, wt. 1.8. Die axis 12 o'clock. AE.
Refs.: Meshorer 1975, 97, no. 61a, pl. IV; cf. Schmitt-Korte 1990, 115, no. 47, pl. XIII.

---

7 For a discussion of the earliest Nabataean coins and the king who issued them, see Schmitt-Korte 1990, 125-26, who posits that the first Nabataean coins were minted by Aretas III during the time he held Damascus (84-71 B.C.). Huth (2010, 213, 221, Table 2) agrees that the first wholly Nabataean coins were struck under Aretas III (from 87 to 60 B.C.), rather than Aretas II. Meshorer (1975, 85), probably incorrectly, attributed these issues to Aretas II, and dated them to 110-96 B.C. On pre-Aretas III Nabataean issues, see Hoover and Barkay 2010, 197-99.

8 On the dating of coins of Syllaeus, perhaps issued jointly with Aretas IV, see Huth 2010, 219-20.

9 See also a discussion of these types by Schmitt-Korte (1990, 111-13 and 127-29).

10 For a discussion of Phasael's identity, and the date of these issues, see Huth 2010, 221-22, who argues that she was Aretas' daughter, born in 5 B.C.

Fig. 15.10. 06-C-86, Aretas IV.

06-C-86. Aretas IV, 4/3 B.C. (fig. 15.10).
Area UT, Tr. 127A, Loc. 39. Very worn, with a porous surface.
Obv.: laureate head, right. Rev.: crossed cornucopiae. ה between the cornucopiae (with pomegranates?), another ה, field right, and a third ה, field left.
Diam. 1.35, th. 0.25, wt. 1.92. Die axis 1 o'clock. AE.
Refs.: Schmitt-Korte 1990, 114, no. 40, pl. XII; cf. Meshorer 1975, 99, no. 69/69a, pl. V, with some slight variation.

Fig. 15.11. 02-C-56. Aretas IV/Shaqilat.

02-C-56. Aretas IV/Shaqilat, A.D. 16.[11] (fig. 15.11).
Area UT, Tr. 94, Loc. 63.
Obv.: king standing as soldier, left, right hand raised with spear. in field, Meshorer's monogram 4, a ligature of רח (for Aretas). Rev.: queen standing left, right hand raised. Inscription unclear but should read (in 3 lines) ת/יל/שק (Shuqa/ila/t).
Diam. 1.16, th. 0.15, wt. 1.5. Die axis 12 o'clock. AE.
Refs.: Meshorer 1975, 103, no. 97, pl. VI; Schmitt-Korte 1990, 119, no. 66, pl. IV.

Fig. 15.12. 00-C-03. Aretas IV/Shaqilat.

00-C-03. Aretas IV/Shaqilat, A.D. 16 (fig. 15.12).
Area UT, Tr. 77, Loc. 3.
Obv.: king standing as a soldier, left, right hand raised with spear, cuirassed; palm branch at left; dotted border. Letter at right is off the flan. Rev.: queen standing left, right hand raised, wearing a long garment; wreath at left. (In 3 lines) ת/יל/שק (Shuqa/ila/t).
Diam. 1.40, th. 0.15, wt. 1.1. Die axis 12 o'clock. AE.
Refs.: Meshorer 1975, 103, no. 97, pl. VI; Schmitt-Korte 1990, 119, no. 66, pl. XIV.

98-C-11. Aretas IV/Shaqilat, A.D. 20-39/40.[12]
Area UT, Tr. 53, Loc. 12.
Obv.: jugate busts of the king and queen, right. Above the busts, שלם (whole), ש in field right, ח in field left. Rev.: 2 cornucopiae crossed. (In 3 lines) לת / שקי / חרתת (Aretas/Shuqai/lat).
Diam. 1.54, th. 0.20, wt. 3.2. AE.
Refs.: Meshorer 1975, 105, no. 112, pl. VII.

Fig. 15.13. 04-C-03. Aretas IV/Shaqilat.

04-C-03. Aretas IV/Shaqilat, A.D. 20-39/40 (fig. 15.13).
Area P, SP 87, Loc. 10. Corroded, but images are distinct.
Obv.: jugate busts of the king and queen, right. Above the busts, perhaps 3 letters off flan, reading שלם (whole), ש to the right, left field off flan (should be a ח). Rev.: 2 cornucopiae crossed. (in 3 lines) לת/שקי/ חרתת (Aretas/Shuqai/lat).
Diam. 1.65, th. 0.19, wt. 3.4. Die axis 12 o'clock. AE.
Ref.: Meshorer 1975, 105, no. 112, pl. VII.

01-C-08. Aretas IV/Shaqilat, A.D. 20-39/40.
Area UT, Tr. 83, Loc. 18.

---

11 Meshorer (1975, 103) dates this issue to A.D. 18/19, but Schmitt-Korte (1990, 119 and 129-30) argues for an earlier date coinciding with the marriage of Aretas IV and Shaqilat in A.D. 16, the 25th year of the former's reign as king.

12 Whether the date of this issue should be lowered to begin in A.D. 20 is taken up by Schmitt-Korte (1990, 122 and 129-30). Yet in the absence of the mark of "X" on the reverse of this example (something Schmitt-Korte takes as a sign of the fourth year in Shaqilat's marriage to Aretas, which occurred in A.D. 16), it is not certain whether this version ought to be lowered in date.

Obv.: jugate busts of the king and queen, right. above the busts, שלם (whole), ש in field right, ח in field left. Rev.: 2 cornucopiae crossed. (in 3 lines) חרתת/שקי/לת (Aretas/Shuqai/lat), although the first line is largely illegible.
Diam. 1.70, th. 0.30, wt. 4.3. Die axis 12 o'clock. AE.
Ref.: Meshorer 1975, 105, no. 112, pl. VII.

Fig. 15.14. 05-C-34. Aretas IV/Shaqilat.

05-C-34. Aretas IV/Shaqilat, A.D. 20-39/40 (fig. 15.14).
Area UT, Tr. SP 108, Loc. 5.
Obv.: jugate busts of the king and queen, right, with V-shaped ornaments on their heads. ש in field right, ח in field left. Rev.: 2 cornucopiae crossed. (In 3 lines) חרתת/שקי/לת (Aretas/Shuqai/lat).
Diam. 1.67, th. 0.21, wt. 3.7. Die axis 12 o'clock. AE.
Ref.: Meshorer 1975, 105, no. 114, pl. VII.

Fig. 15.15. 06-C-71. Rabbel II/Gamilat.

06-C-71. Rabbel II/Gamilat, A.D. 101/102 (fig. 15.15).
Area LT, Tr. 127, Loc. 40. A weak strike in places, double-struck in others.
Obv.: design is almost entirely off the flan except for part of a linear border and some of the king's hair. Rev.: single cornucopia, at left, nicely executed. A second lies parallel, somewhat more faintly, to its right. This presumably was an error of engraving or striking (it seems very probable that this coin was overstruck or restruck). To the right of the clear cornucopia and on top of the second one are 2 lines of a Nabataean inscription, the second of which includes the name "Gamilat". The complete inscription presumably read (in 2 lines) רבאל/גמלת (Rabbel/Gamilat).
Diam. 1.70, th. 0.21, wt. 2.03. Die axis unclear. AE.
Ref.: Meshorer 1975, 110-11, nos. 162-63, pl. VIII; compare with Schmitt-Korte 1990, 124, no. 86, pl. XV.

Fig. 15.16. 01-C-09. Rabbel II/Gamilat.

01-C-09. Rabbel II/Gamilat, A.D. 101/102 (fig. 15.16).
Area UT, Tr. 83, Loc. 18.
Obv.: jugate busts of the king and queen, right. Rev.: 2 cornucopiae crossed. Between cornucopiae (in 2 lines) רבאל/גמלת (Rabbel/Gamilat).
Diam. 1.60, th. 0.25, wt. 3.4. Die axis 12 o'clock. AE.
Ref.: Meshorer 1975, 110-11, no. 163, pl. VIII; compare with Schmitt-Korte 1990, 124, no. 86, pl. XV.

Fig. 15.17. 00-C-14. Rabbel II /Gamilat.

00-C-14. Rabbel I/Gamilat, A.D. 101/102 (fig. 15.17).
Area LT, Tr. 71, Loc. 14.
Obv.: jugate busts of the king and queen, right. The king's shoulders are visible, wearing a mantle. The queen wears a pleated garment. Rev.: 2 cornucopiae crossed. Between cornucopiae (in 2 lines) רבאל/גמלת (Rabbel/Gamilat).
Diam. 1.40, th. 0.20, wt. 1.9. Die axis 12 o'clock. AE.
Ref.: Meshorer 1975, 111, no. 163a, pl. VIII.

Roman

Fig. 15.18. 02-C-68B. Trajan.

02-C-68B.[13] Trajan, A.D. 101-102 (fig. 15.18).
Area UT, Tr. 94, Loc. 71.
Obv.: laureate bust of Trajan, right. IMP CAES NERVA TRAIAN AVG GERM PM. Rev.: Victory,

13 The first three coins in this group were found corroded together in 2002, and thus have similar numbering.

draped, advancing left, holding a wreath in extended right hand, and a palm upright in left. PM TRP COS IIII PP.
Diam. 1.68, th. 0.13, wt. 2.7. Die axis 8 o'clock. AR (*denarius*). No mintmark (minted at Rome).
Refs.: *BMCRE* III 46, no. 123; *RIC* II 248, no. 60.

Fig. 15.19. 02-C-68A. Trajan.

02-C-68A. Trajan, A.D. 113-114 (fig. 15.19).
Area UT, Tr. 94, Loc. 71.
Obv.: laureate bust of Trajan, right. Largely off the flan, the complete legend should read, ΑΥΤΟΚΡ ΚΑΙΣ ΝΕΡ ΤΡΑΙΑΝ ΣΕΒ ΓΕΡΜ ΔΑΚ. Rev.: Arabia, personified as a full-length female figure, standing left; she holds a scepter with her left arm and in her right hand extends a branch of frankincense above a camel. ΔΗΜΑΡΧ ΕΧ ΙΗ (18) ΗΥΠΑΤ [ϛ] (6).[14]
Diam. 1.83, th. 0.13, wt. 2.9. Die axis 6 o'clock. AR (drachm). No mintmark (probably minted at Bostra).
Refs.: Sydenham 1933, no. 189, 65, fig. 54; *BMC Galatia, Cappadocia, and Syria* 54, nos. 62-64, pl. IX, 15; Metcalf 1975, 107, no. 17, pl. XIII; Spijkerman 1978, 32-35, nos. 6-14, pl. I-IV, 6-20; cf. *BMCRE* III 96-97, nos. 474-76, pl. XVII, 8, and *RIC* II 261, no. 245, the same type with a Latin legend (dated A.D. 112-114).

Fig. 15.20. 02-C-68C. Trajan.

02-C-68C. Trajan, A.D. 113-114 (fig. 15.20).
Area UT, Tr. 94, Loc. 71. Reverse poorly struck.
Obv.: laureate bust of Trajan, right. Largely off the flan, the complete legend should read ΑΥΤΟΚΡ ΚΑΙΣ ΝΕΡ ΤΡΑΙΑΝ ΣΕΒ ΓΕΡΜ ΔΑ[Κ]. Rev.: Arabia, personified as a full-length female figure, standing left. She holds a scepter with her left arm and in her right hand extends a branch of frankincense above a camel. ΔΗΜΑΡΧ ΕΧ ΙΗ (18) ΗΥΠΑΤ [ϛ] (6).
Diam. 1.75, th. 0.19, wt. 3.1. Die axis 7 o'clock. AR (drachm). No mintmark (probably minted at Bostra).
Refs.: Sydenham 1933, 65, no. 189, fig. 54; *BMC Galatia, Cappadocia, and Syria* 54, nos. 62-64, pl. IX, 15; Metcalf 1975, 107, no. 17, pl. XIII; Spijkerman 1978, 32-35, nos. 6-14, pls. I-IV, 6-20; cf. *BMCRE* III 96-97, nos. 474-76, pl. XVII, 8, and *RIC* II 261, no. 245, the same type with a Latin legend (dated A.D. 112-114).

Fig. 15.21. 98-C-32. Trajan.

98-C-32. Trajan, A.D. 106-117 (tribunician and consular dates on the reverse are illegible) (fig. 15.21).
Area LT, Tr. 52, Loc. 25.
Obv.: laureate bust of Trajan, right. ΑΥΤΟΚΡ ΚΑΙΣ ΝΕΡ ΤΡΑΙΑΝ ΣΕΒ---. Rev.: Arabia, personified as a full-length female figure, standing left; holds a scepter with her left arm and in her right hand extends a branch of frankincense above a camel. ΔΗΜΑΡΧ Ε[Χ] --- ΗΥΠΑΤ.
Diam. 1.84, th. 0.15, wt. 2.8. Die axis 7 o'clock. AR. No mintmark (probably minted at Bostra).
Refs.: Sydenham 1933, 63-65, nos. 183-85 or 189, fig. 54; *BMC Galatia, Cappadocia, and Syria* 54, nos. 62-64, pl. IX, 15; Metcalf 1975, 106-7, nos. 14-17, pl. XIII;

14 ΔΗΜΑΡΧ 18 ΗΥΠΑΤ 6 = TRIB POT 18 (A.D. 113-114), COS 6 (A.D. 112-117). ΗΥΠΑΤΟΣ 6, Trajan's 6th consulship, should be designated "ΗΥΠΑΤ ϛ," but the lower-case sigma is either off the flan or not included in the legend.

Spij-kerman 1978, 32-35, nos. 6-14, pl. I-IV, nos. 6-20; cf. *BMCRE* III 73, nos. 297-300, pl. XIV, 19; 96-97, nos. 474-76, pl. XVII, 8; *RIC* II 250, no. 94; 253, no. 142; and p. 261, no. 245, similar types with a Latin legend (dated A.D. 112-114).

Fig. 15.22. 98-C-15. Trajan.

98-C-15. Trajan, A.D. 114-117 (fig. 15.22).
Area UT, Tr. 53, Loc. 26.
Obv.: head of Hercules, with lion's skin, right. [IMP] CAES TRAIAN [AVG GE]RM. Rev.: boar walking right. If there was an SC in exergue, it has been worn off.
Diam. 1.44, th. 0.20, wt. 2.7. Die axis 6 o'clock. Copper (quadrans). No mintmark (minted at Rome).
Refs.: *BMCRE* III 226, nos. 1062-67, pl. XLIII, 10-12; *RIC* II 294, no. 702.

Fig. 15.23. 02-C-22. Quasi-autonomous Petra Metropolis.

02-C-22. Quasi-autonomous coin of Petra Metropolis (struck following the annexation of Arabia, A.D. 106-117)[15] (fig. 15.23).
Area P, Tr. 87, Loc. 7. Rather worn.
Obv.: veiled bust of Tyche, right. Rev.: 2 cornucopiae crossed; between them, a monogram ΠΜ (only the Π is visible), standing for Petra Metropolis.
Diam. 1.06, th. 0.15, wt. 0.7. Die axis 6 o'clock. AE. Mintmark: ΠΜ (Petra Metropolis).
Refs.: Spijkerman 1978, 220-21, nos. 1a-1b, pl. XLVIII; *SNGANS* VI, no. 1359, pl. XLVII.

Fig. 15.24. 00-C-4. Faustina Senior.

00-C-04. Faustina Senior (posthumous), A.D. 141-144 (fig. 15.24).
Area UT, Tr. 77, Loc. 2. Very worn.
Obv.: veiled bust of Faustina I, right, draped hair coiled on top of head; dotted border. ΘΕΑ [ΦΑVCΤΕΙΝΑ or ΦΑVCΤ]. Rev.: 3 ears of barley fastened together, inside a wreath; letters worn off (should read NT B/O).
Diam. 1.30, th. 0.15, wt. 1.3. Die axis 6 o'clock. AE (half quadrans). No mintmark (minted at Bostra).
Refs.: Spijkerman 1978, 70-71, no. 15; Kindler 1983, 108, no. 11a, pl. I; *SNGANS* VI, nos. 1183-85, pl. XL.

Fig. 15.25. 02-C-16. Septimius Severus.

02-C-16. Septimius Severus, A.D. 193-211 (fig. 15.25).
Area P, Tr. 87, Loc. 6. Very worn, especially on the reverse.
Obv.: bust of Septimius Severus, right. All that is legible are the letters "CΕΠΤ" above the bust. Rev.: Tyche seated, left, holding trophy with her right hand and a *stele* with her left. Legend only partially preserved but a variation on [ΑΔΡΙΑΝΗ ΠΕΤΡΑ] ΜΗΤΡΟ[ΠΟΛΙC].
Diam. 2.31, th. 0.22, wt. 7.2. Die axis 12 o'clock. AE. No mintmark (minted at Petra).
Refs.: Spijkerman 1978, 226-29, nos. 28-32, pl. L; *BMC Arabia, Mesopotamia, and Persia* 36, no. 15; cf. *SNGANS* VI, no. 1369, pl. XLVII.

00-C-01. (JMA 1996) Julia Domna, A.D. 193-217 (fig. 15.26).
Area P, SP 70, Loc. 8. Very worn and weakly struck.
Obv.: bust of Julia Domna, right, draped; dotted

15 These issues may also have been struck during the reign of Hadrian.

Fig. 15.26. 00-C-01. Julia Domna.

Fig. 15.27. 02-C-37. Valerian II as Caesar.

Fig. 15.28. 98-C-01. Probus.

Fig. 15.29. 98-C-30. Probus.

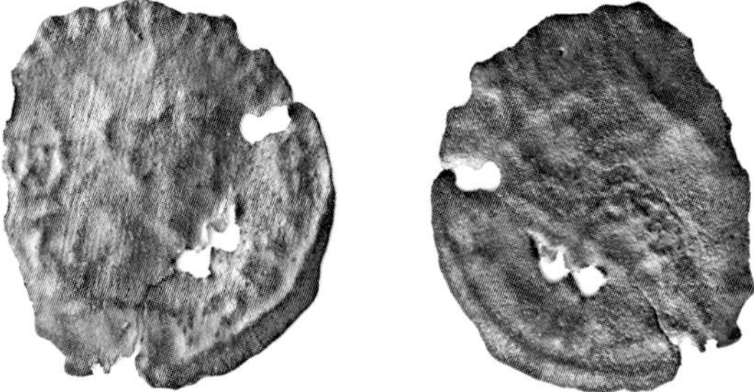

Fig. 15.30. 02-C-26. Imitation of a coin of Probus.

border. There was a countermark but it is virtually illegible. Greek inscription but illegible. Rev.: Tyche seated, left, within a distyle temple with triangular pediment with no visible decoration, holding a trophy against her left shoulder and a small *stele* in her right hand. ΑΔΡΙΑ ΠΕΤ[ΡΑ ΜΗΤ].
Diam. 2.8, th. 0.35, wt. 10.2. Die axis 11 o'clock. AE. No mintmark (minted at Petra).
Refs.: similar, but not identical, to Spijkerman 1978, 230-31, nos. 38-40, pl. LI.

02-C-37. Valerian II, as Caesar, A.D. 254-255 (fig. 15.27).
Area T, Tr. 92, Loc. 4.
Obv.: radiate bust of the young Valerian II, right. VALERIANVS NOBIL CAES. Rev.: prince standing left, holding a spear and shield, crowning a trophy. PRINCI[PI IVVENTVTIS].
Diam. 2.28, th. 0.10, wt. 2.4. Die axis 12 o'clock. AR (*antoninianus*). No mintmark (minted at Antioch).
Refs.: *RIC* V.1, 122, no. 49, pl. IV, 69.

98-C-01. Probus, A.D. 276-282 (fig. 15.28).
Area LT, Tr. 52, Loc. 2.
Obv.: bust of Probus, right, radiate and draped. IMP C [M A]VR PROBVS P F AVG. Rev.: emperor, standing right and holding a scepter, receiving a globe from Jupiter, standing left and holding a scepter. CLEMENTIA TEMP; A(?) in field between them; in exergue, XXI.
Diam. 2.04, th. 0.11, wt. 3.2. AE, still clearly silvered (*antoninianus*). Mintmark uncertain (either Siscia or Antioch, the latter perhaps more likely).
Refs.: *RIC* V.2, 86, no. 643 (Siscia, undated) or 119-20, no. 920 or 922 (Antioch, undated).

98-C-30. Probus, A.D. 276-282 (fig. 15.29).
Area LT, Tr. 52, Loc. 25. Reverse is quite corroded and had also been badly struck.
Obv.: extremely good image of Probus, right, radiate, draped. IMP C M AVR PROBVS PF AVG. Rev.: unclear, but it probably shows the emperor, standing right and holding a scepter, receiving a globe from Jupiter, standing left and holding a scepter. Several letters legible ---ENT---TEMP (CLEMENTIA TEMP).
Diam. 2.05, th. 0.11, wt. 2.3. AE (*antoninianus*). No mintmark can be clearly read.
Refs.: see 98-C-01 for several possibilities.

02-C-26. Imitation of a coin of Probus, A.D. 276-282 (fig. 15.30).
Area P, Tr. 88, Loc. 1. Badly corroded.
Obv.: radiate bust of Probus, right. (left side of inscription is off the flan) ---PROBVS PF AVG. Rev.: illegible.
Diam. 1.77, th. 0.04, wt. 0.5. Die axis uncertain. AE (imitation of an *antoninianus*).

04-C-41. Carinus, A.D. 283-285 (fig. 15.31).
Area LT, Tr. 98, Loc. 3. Porous.
Obv.: bust of Carinus, right, radiate, cuirassed, and draped. IMP M AVR CARINVS PF AVG. Rev.: emperor, standing right and holding a scepter,

Fig. 15.31. 04-C-41. Carinus.

Fig. 15.32. 01-C-16. Diocletian.

Fig. 15.33. 01-C-23. Constantine I.

Fig. 15.34. 02-C-40. Licinius I (or Constantine I).

receiving Victory from Jupiter (or Carus), standing left and holding a scepter. CLEMENTIA TEMP; letter in field (Δ?); in exergue, XXI.
Diam. 2.04, th. 0.13, wt. 3.0. Die axis 1 o'clock. AE, silvered (*antoninianus*). Mintmark: Cyzicus (Δ?) or Antioch.
Refs.: *RIC* V.2, 178, no. 324, pl. VII, 16 (attributed to Cyzicus); Waagé 1952, 110, no. 1291 (attributed to Antioch).

01-C-16. (JMA 1221) Diocletian, pre-reform, A.D. 293-295 (fig. 15.32).
Area P, Tr. 80, Loc. 2. Practically as struck.
Obv.: radiate bust of Diocletian, right, draped; dotted border. IMP CC VAL DIOCLETIANVS AVG. Rev.: Emperor, standing right and holding a scepter, receiving victory from Jupiter, standing left and holding a scepter; dotted border. CONCORDIA MI-LITVM (in 2 parts); B in middle lower field, between the figures; in exergue, XXI.
Diam. 2.2, th. 0.2, wt. 9.6. Die axis 2 o'clock. AE, silvered (*antoninianus*). Mintmark probably Cyzicus (B).
Refs.: *RIC* V.2, 253, no. 306 (attributed to Cyzicus); see also 256, no. 322 (attributed to Antioch); cf. Waagé 1952, 111, no. 1302 (post-reform, from Antioch), and 111, no. 1304 (pre-reform, from Heraclea).

01-C-23. (JMA 1222) Constantine I, *c.*A.D. 313-317 (fig. 15.33).
Area UT, Tr. 84, Loc. 10.
Obv.: bust of Constantine, right, laureate and draped; dotted border. IMP CONSTANTINVS PF AVG. Rev.: Sol standing right, hand raised, holding a globe; *chlamys* across left shoulder. SOLI INV-I-CTO COMITI; in exergue, R P.
Diam. 1.8, th. 0.18, wt. 2.6. Die axis 12 o'clock. AE (follis). Mintmark R P (Rome P).
Refs.: *RIC* VII, 303, no. 56; see 296, no. 5 (and 296-303 for other possibilities, since the fields around the figures may once have contained other symbols; see also Waagé 1952, 199, no. 1407.

02-C-40. Licinius I (or Constantine I), A.D. 317-320 (fig. 15.34).
Area P, Tr. 81, Loc. 1. The obverse is badly corroded, particularly on the left side.
Obv.: bust of the emperor, left, laureate, draped in consular robes; his hand is visible (this type should show him holding a scepter in his left hand and/or *mappa* in his right); the shape of the features suggest it may be Licinius, rather than Constantine. (Only the lower right side of the inscription is legible) ---NIVS (perhaps -INVS?) AVG. Rev.: Jupiter standing, left, holding victory on a globe in his right hand, leaning on a scepter with his right; palm branch at lower left, angled toward the left. IOVI CONS-ERVATORI AVGG; at right, Greek letter (B? or E?);[16] in exergue, SMN.

16 If the Greek letter to the right of Jupiter is an E, this is more likely a coin of Licinius I, as *RIC* VII 603-4 does not record this particular mintmark for the corresponding issue of Constantine I.

Diam. 1.82, th. 0.12, wt. 2.9. AE (follis). Mintmark Nicomedia.
Refs.: *RIC* VII 603-4, no. 24 (Licinius) or no. 23 (Constantine), see pl. XX, 23 (for the Constantine example).

Fig. 15.35. 04-C-26. Constantine I.

04-C-26. Constantine I, A.D. 325-326 (fig. 15.35).
Area LT, Tr. 97, Loc. 10.
Obv.: bust of Constantine, right, laureate. CONSTANTINVS AVG. Rev.: camp gate with 2 turrets, no doors; above, a single star with 8 rays. PROVIDEN-TIAE AVGG; in exergue, SMALB.
Diam. 1.77, th. 0.17, w 3.1. Die axis 5 o'clock. AE, silvered (follis). Mintmark Alexandria B.
Ref.: *RIC* VII 709, no. 34; see also *LRBC* I, 31, no. 1402.

Fig. 15.36. 04-C-33. Helena.

04-C-33. Helena, A.D. 324-329 (fig. 15.36).
Area P, Tr. 100, Loc. 14. Quite worn, porous from corrosion.
Obv.: bust of Helena, right, draped, hair gathered on top of head and covered with an elaborate headdress. [FL] HELENA AVG[VSTA]. Rev.: standing female, probably a personification of Securitas (or perhaps Pax). Inscription illegible.
Diam. 2.01, th. 0.09, wt. 2.7. Die axis 11 o'clock. AE, silvered (follis). Mintmark illegible.
This type was ubiquitous during the second half of the 320s and was issued by virtually all Imperial mints (see *RIC* VII and *LRBC* I for numerous examples).

Fig. 15.37. 04-C-29. Constantine II as Caesar.

04-C-29. Constantine II, as Caesar, A.D. 330-333 or 335 (fig. 15.37).
Area LT, Tr. 97, Loc. 13. Heavily corroded on the obverse.
Obv.: bust of Constantine II, right, laureate and cuirassed, wearing an aegis. CONSTANTINVS IVN NOB C. Rev.: 2 soldiers standing, facing one another, each holding a spear in his outer hand, inner hand resting on a shield set on the ground; between them, 2 standards. GLOR-IA EXERC-ITVS; in exergue, SMANE.
Diam. 1.73, th. 0.10, wt. 1.6. Die axis 12 o'clock. AE, silvered (follis). Mintmark Antioch E.
Refs.: *RIC* VII 693, no. 87; *LRBC* I 30, no. 1357.

Fig. 15.38. 06-C-32. Constantine II.

06-C-32. Constantine II, A.D. 333-335 (fig. 15.38).
Area LT, Tr. 126, Loc. 1. Significant corrosion on both sides.
Obv.: bust of Constantine II, right, laureate and cuirassed. [CONSTANTIN]VS IVN NOB C. Rev.: 2 soldiers standing, facing one another, each holding a spear in his outer hand, inner hand resting on a shield set on the ground; between them, 2 standards. [GLORIA EXERC-]ITVS; in exergue, SMAL[A], left edge of final A is just visible.
Diam. 1.73, th. 0.12, wt. 1.71. Die axis 12 o'clock. AE (follis). Mintmark Alexandria A.
Refs.: *RIC* VII 711, no. 59; *LRBC* I 32, no. 1329.

Fig. 15.39. 06-C-90. Constantius II.

06-C-90. Constantius II, 9 Sept. 337 to late 347 (fig. 15.39).
Area LT, Tr. 121, Loc. 3. Weakly struck around the edges and on the reverse.
Obv.: head of Constantius II, right, wearing a pearl diadem with rosette decoration at forehead.

CONSTAN-TIVS AVG. Rev.: 2 helmeted soldiers standing, facing one another, each holding a spear in his outer hand, inner hand resting on a shield set on the ground; between them, a single standard. GLOR-IA EXERC-ITVS; in exergue, SMANΓ.
Diam. 1.50, th. 0.15, wt. 1.71. Die axis 6 o'clock. AE 4. Mintmark Antioch Γ.
Refs.: *RIC* VIII 515, nos. 54 and 56; *LRBC* I 31, nos. 1388 and 1391.

Fig. 15.40. 06-C-20. Jovian.

06-C-20. Jovian, 27 June 363 to 16 Feb., 364 (fig. 15.40).
Area LT, Tr. 127, Loc. 21.
Obv.: bust of Jovian, right, with pearl diadem, draped. DN IOVIAN-VS PF AVG. Rev.: VOT V MVLT X in 4 lines inside a wreath. SMNA (or, less likely, SMKA) in exergue.
Diam. 1.50, th. 0.13, wt. 1.26. Die axis 12 o'clock. AE 4. Mintmark difficult to read, either Nicomedia or Cyzicus.
Refs.: *RIC* VIII 485, no. 129 (Nicomedia) or 501, no. 132 (Cyzicus); *LRBC* II 97, no. 2513 (Cyzicus) (this type is not listed for Nicomedia by *LRBC* II).

Fig. 15.41. 98-C-112. Theodosius I.

98-C-112. Theodosius I, 9 August 378 to 25 August 383 (fig. 15.41).
Area T, Tr. 57, Loc. 11.
Obv.: bust of Theodosius, right, draped and cuirassed, with a pearl diadem. DN THEODO-SIVS PF AVG. Rev.: in wreath, VOT X/MVLT/XX; SMKΓ at bottom.
Diam. 1.39, th. 0.08, wt. 0.90. Die axis 1 o'clock. AE 4. Mintmark Cyzicus Γ.
Refs.: *RIC* IX 244, no. 21c(3); *LRBC* II 98, no. 2557.

Fig. 15.42. 98-C-52. Arcadius.

98-C-52. Arcadius, 25 August 383 to 28 August 388 (fig. 15.42).
Area T, Tr. 57, Loc. 11.
Obv.: bust of Arcadius, right, draped and cuirassed, with a pearl diadem. DN ARCADIVS PF AVG. Rev.: wreath with inscription VOT/X/MVLT/XX (in 4 lines); in exergue, ANΔ.
Diam. 1.29, th. 0.11, wt. 1.20. Die axis 12 o'clock. AE 4. Mintmark Antioch Δ.
Refs.: *RIC* IX 292, no. 65c(3); *LRBC* II 101, no. 2743.

Fig. 15.43. 01-C-14. Valentinian II.

01-C-14. Valentinian II (A.D. 383-392) (fig. 15.43).
Area P, Tr. 82, Loc. 1. Weakly struck in places.
Obv.: bust of Valentinian, right, cuirassed, draped, and with a pearl diadem; dotted border. DN VALENTI-NIANVS PF AVG (much of the right side is unclear or off the flan). Rev.: victory dragging a captive toward the left; in field left, a cross. SALVS [REI-PVBLICAE]; in exergue, mintmark off the flan.
Diam. 1.20, th. 0.15, wt. 0.90. Die axis 5 o'clock. AE 4.
Refs.: see *RIC* IX 133, no. 64a (Rome), 246, no. 26a (Cyzicus), 262, no. 45a (Nicomedia), 292, no. 67a (Antioch), and 303, no. 20a (Alexandria); see also *LRBC* II 62, nos. 796 and 799 (Rome), 94, nos. 2403, 2406, 2411, 2415 and 2418 (Nicomedia), 98, no. 2568 (Cyzicus), 102, nos. 2763 and 2768 (Antioch), and 105, nos. 2898, 2901 and 2904 (Alexandria), for possible examples.

Fig. 15.44. 98-C-161. Theodosius I.

98-C-161. Theodosius I, 28 August 388 to 17 January 395 (fig. 15.44).
Area T, Tr. 57, Loc. 13.
Obv.: bust of Theodosius, right, draped and cuirassed, with a pearl diadem. DN THEODO-SIVS PF AVG. Rev.: victory and captive. SALVS REI-PVBLICAE; in exergue, SMKΓ.
Diam. 1.28, th. 0.12, wt. 0.80. Die axis 6 o'clock. AE 4. Mintmark Cyzicus.
Refs.: *RIC* IX 246, no. 26b(3), or 247, no. 30b; *LRBC* II 98, no. 2577.

Fig. 15.45. 06-C-15. Arcadius.

06-C-15. Arcadius, A.D. 401-403 (fig. 15.45).
Area LT, Tr. 122, Loc. 5. Obverse is very weakly struck, and a chunk is missing from the coin's edge.
Obv.: helmeted bust of Arcadius, facing, diademed, cuirassed, spear in right hand, held over right shoulder and behind head (the point emerges above left shoulder); on his left arm is a decorated shield with a cross. Legend is partial due to the chunk missing from 7 to 10 o'clock, but what remains (on the right side of the coin) reads -VS PF AVG. Rev.: Constantinopolis enthroned facing, head left, holding a long scepter and victory on a globe; beneath right foot, a prow. CONCORDI[-A AVGG] (only the first part remains); in exergue, SMNA.
Diam. 1.70, th. 0.15, wt. 1.92. Die axis 12 o'clock. AE 3. Mintmark Nicomedia.
Refs.: *RIC* X 248, no. 91; *LRBC* II 95, no. 2442.

Fig. 15.46. 00-C-07. Theodosius II.

00-C-07. Theodosius II, A.D. 408-423 (fig. 15.46).
Area LT, Tr. 71, Loc. 18. Very worn, although well preserved.
Obv.: Bust of Theodosius II, right, draped, with pearl diadem; at his left is a 6-pointed star. DN [THEODO-] SIVS PF AVG. Rev.: 2 emperors, standing facing, each holding a spear and resting his hand on a shield. GLORIA ROMA-NORVM; in exergue, TESA.
Diam. 1.60, th. 0.02, wt. 2.10. Die axis 6 o'clock. AE 4. Mintmark Thessalonica A.
Refs.: *RIC* X 271, no. 396; *LRBC* II 82, no. 1877.

Conclusions

The excavated coins as a whole typically had not traveled far to reach Petra. Nabataean coins, minted locally or nearby, seem to have been in regular use. Among the Roman issues (almost all of them post-dating the annexation of *Provincia Arabia*) there are numerous local issues, while many others were struck by mints throughout the Roman East. The largest group of identifiable coins belongs to the waning years of regular use of our site, in the Late Empire, when Petra's inhabitants and visitors to the city relied chiefly on the mints of Alexandria and Antioch for most of their new currency.

Almost all are small coins of base metal in an array of denominations. This is typical of site finds and suggests that we are dealing primarily with the currency of daily exchange, lost, or in several cases secreted, in places of congregation or public business.

The chronological range of the finds reveals an interest in coined money as early as the 3rd-2nd c. B.C., before the city itself had been substantially monumentalized. The earliest pieces, minted during the Hellenistic period, probably found their way to the site in the hands of traders who were conducting business with the Ptolemaic and Seleucid kingdoms and the cities on the Phoenician coast. The latest coins, of the 5th c. A.D., suggest continued activity at our site even after the mid-4th c. earthquake that we believe inflicted serious damage on the precinct.

16

Inscriptions

Traianos Gagos†

Fragments of a Greek inscription on marble

In 2006, 8-10 fragments[1] of marble inscriptions in Greek were found in the *caldarium* of the Roman-Byzantine Baths. Some have drill-holes preserved, and traces of bronze dowels used to mount such panels are still found in the walls of the building. Most of the fragments are very small and provide no valuable information, but the three presented here (one of them found in 2005) appear to belong to the same inscription since the formation of the letters is very similar and all seem to preserve the uppermost part of the inscription and margin. I transcribe them separately and then attempt to join them:

06-S-13 (fig. 16.1)

L.22.87, w. 16.36, th. 2.37 cm. The largest surviving fragment of a marble panel. The upper part of the left side is preserved intact and the same is probably true for the top where the marble is cut very evenly. In terms of palaeography, the writing of the letter A is notable because the crossbar is formed with two strokes angled in relation to each other. This form of A has a long history and was still in use in the 2nd c. Overall, the form of the letters (and especially the A) present similarities with three other inscriptions from Petra that date from the early period of the annexation (*I. Jord.* IV, 37.1-3)

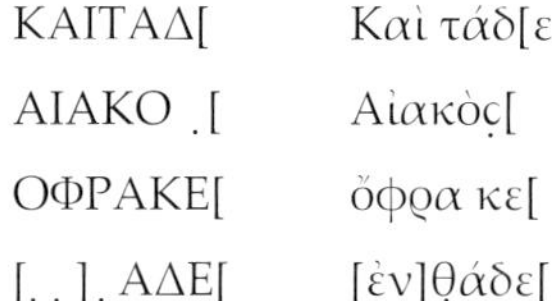

ΚΑΙΤΑΔ[	Καὶ τάδ[ε
ΑΙΑΚΟ .[	Αἰακὸς̣[
ΟΦΡΑΚΕ[	ὄφρα κε[
[. .]. ΑΔΕ[	[ἐν]θ̣άδε[

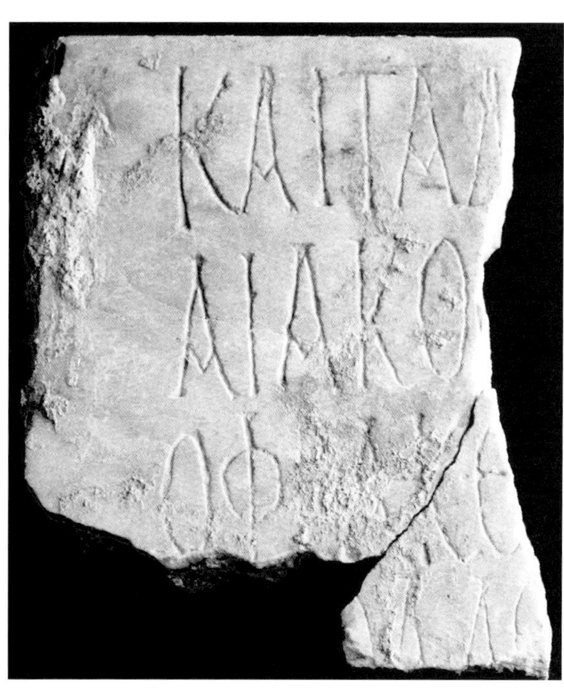

Fig. 16.1. 06-S-13.

1. καὶ τάδ[ε or καὶ τὰ δ[.

2. Not much is left of the last letter before the break, but it could match well the curve of a lunate *sigma* (written in the same style as the curved *epsilon* in l. 4.

More likely the letters represent the name Αἰακός̣[, but αἱ ἄκος̣[(= cure, remedy) is another possibility; it is unlikely that a form of ἄκοϲμοϲ,or ἀκοϲμία was involved.

3. To be read certainly as ὄφρα κε(ν), (final or temporal conjuction). This is the element that makes us think that the inscription was written in the Homeric style and perhaps metrically.

4. [ἐν]θ̣άδε or [ἔν]θα δέ.

06-S-9 (fig. 16.2)

L. 9.57, w. 9.49, th. 2.55 cm. The cut of the marble at the top appears to be regular, which this suggests that what survives was probably the first line of the inscription.

---

1 Cat. nos. 06-S-6, 06-S-7, 06-S-8, 06-S-9 (2 fragments together), 06-S-10, 06-S-11, 06-S-12, and 06-S-13 (2 fragments together), all from Tr. 127, Locus 32.

Fig. 16.2. 06-S-9.

]ẸPNHT[κυβ]ẹρνητ[

]ị[

The writing at the top is undoubtedly a form of the Greek word κυβερνήτηc = "skipper" or, in a metaphorical sense, "guide, governor" (see LSJ *s.v.*).

05-S-7

L. 15.96, w.13.66, th. 3.87 cm. This fragment was found in 2005 in an adjacent locus to those found in 2006. The top left is evenly cut, suggesting the uppermost part of the inscription.

]AΘPAK ̣[   ]αθρα κ ̣[

] ̣ C̣HΠINΥ̣[   ] ̣ c̣η πινυ̣[τ

] ̣[   ] ̣[

1. μέλ]αθρα (= "house") or β]άθρα, which has multiple meanings ranging from "base, pedestal" to "foundations" of a building or city to "bench, seat" (see *LSJ s.v.*).
2. A form of πινυτόc (= "prudent") or πινυτόφρων (= "of wise or understanding mind") (see *LSJ s.v.*)

Putting the fragments together

A large portion of this inscription is missing, but it looks as if these fragments belong to the top and left side, perhaps in the sequence 06-S-13 + 05-S-7 + 06-S-9. Although the last two fragments may be very close to each other (e.g., the *kappa* and the stroke that follows it an — *upsilon*? It may represent the first two missing letters of κυβ]ερνητ[), there is no conclusive evidence that they connect directly. Yet even this disjointed text is rather intriguing.

καὶ τάδ[ε ?   ]αθρα κ ̣[? κυβ]ερνητ[
Αἰακὸc̣[?   ] ̣ c̣η πινυ̣[τ   ?   ]ị
ὄφρα κε[
4 [ἐν]θ̣άδε [

"And these [...] the base/seat/house [...] governor [...] |
Aeacus [...] prudent [...] so that/until [...] here [...]"

The demonstrative pronoun of the first line clearly looks forward to the partial word that could mean "house" or "base/pedestal/foundation/bench/seat", with perhaps an adjective missing in-between. These first words must have described the object or building to which this inscription was attached. The reference to a κυβερνήτηc should not be read literally (= "skipper"), but metaphorically (= "guide/governor") and may somehow be connected with Aiacus in the next line.

The inscription was probably written in Homeric style and was metrical. It was attached to either a building (the Great Temple?) or perhaps the base of a statue or a seat (in the *theatron* of the Temple?). Whatever it was attached to, the object or structure appears to have had a strong connection with the notions of judgement, piety and justice. The use of marble (unusual in this part of the world) underscores the importance of the inscription and the object to which it was attached.

Overall, the phrasing and the constituting elements of the inscription are very much in accord with late-antique epigrams for governors, which normally emphasized the justice meted out by the honorand and the buildings *vel sim.* he caused to be constructed.[2] If this inscription dates later than suggested by the style of the

---

2 An inscription in Homerizing verse (echoing the beginning of the *Odyssey*), but of a much later date, which honors Horion, who renovated the city walls and saved the province of *Palestina Salutaris* from barbarian-speaking enemies (βαρβαρόφωνοι), was found a few years ago in Petra; see the unauthorized edition in R. Merkelbach and J. Stauber, *Steinepigramme aus den griechischen Osten* Bd. 4 (Munich 2002) 445 (#22/71/01). The inscription is mentioned in brief by G. W. Bowersock, "The Nabataeans in historical

letters, it is possible that the mention of Aiakos might be an allusion to Q. Aiacius Modestus Crescentianus, a governor of the Severan age.[3]

06-S-18. Honorific Latin inscription on sandstone[4] (fig. 16.3)

This large Latin inscription on sandstone was unearthed in the columned corridor in secondary use as an architectural element to block the water passage (Tr. 120, Locus 48). It is a complete footed *stele* with well-dressed surfaces.[5] L. 63, w. 31.5, th. 18 cm.

Diplomatic text

M AELIUS AURELIUS
THEON SERENUS CV
COS D SACERDOS SO
DALIS HADRIANALIS LEG´
AUGG´ PR´ PR´

Edited text

M(arcus) Aelius Aurelius
Theon Serenus c(larissimus) v(ir),
co(n)s(ul) d(esignatus), sacerdos, sodalis Hadrianalis, leg(atus)
Aug(ustorum) pr(o) pr(aetore).

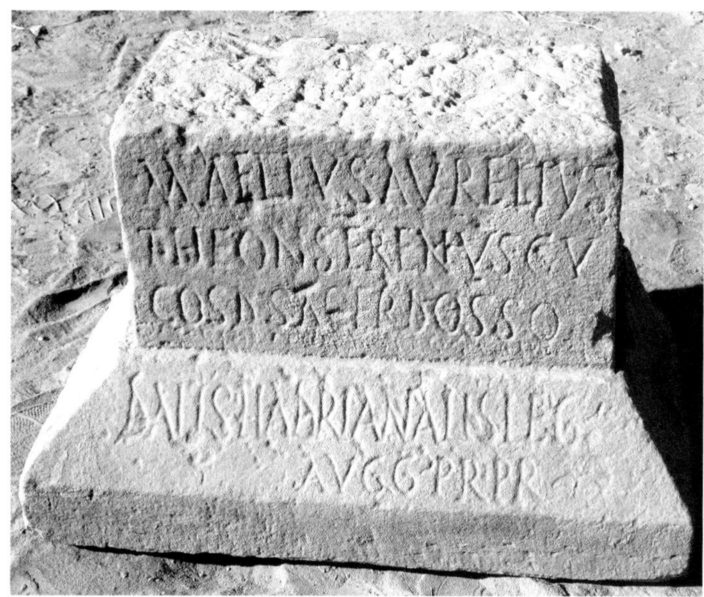

Fig. 16.3. 06-S-18.

"Marcus Aelius Aurelius Theon Serenus of senatorial rank, designated consul, priest, member of the fraternity of the cult of Hadrian, imperial legate as governor".

1-4. This man must be the same as (M.) Aelius Aurelius Theon mentioned in three inscriptions from Bostra, *IGLSyr.* XIII 9078-80, as well as in *PPUAES* IIIA 2, App. v, 10a, and *CIL* XI 376; see *PIR*² A 0150. He was governor of Arabia between A.D. 253 and 259; see *IGLSyr.* XIII 9078 note (153) and M. Sartre, *Trois études sur l'Arabie romain et byzantine* (Brussels 1982) chapt. 2, entry 38.
The *cognomen* Marcus and his honorary office of *sodalis Hadrianalis* are found only in the *CIL* inscription, but none records him with the name Serenus as here. Earlier inscriptions show that he was *sodalis Hadrianalis* before he was *legatus*, which would be typical. The puzzle is the word *sacerdos* juxtaposed to *sodalis Hadrianalis*, which could be an interpretation (a gloss?) of the latter or simply an error (this may be the case also with the name Serenus).

5. The two emperors referred to here are undoubtedly Valerian and Gallienus, who co-reigned until the capture of the former in about June of A.D. 260.

Discussion

As I argued in my article in *JRA* 22 (2009) 388-89, the recent excavations at the Great and Small Temples have increased significantly the existing data-set of inscriptions, especially those dating from immediately after the annexation. While these inscriptions may be disappointing in illuminating the function of the various structures in which they were found (all of them are in secondary use), they do underscore Petra's leading rôle vis-à-vis Bostra, the presumed capital in the north, and underline Petra's importance within the province of *Arabia*. Earlier interpretations of the

---

context," in G. Markoe (ed.), *Petra rediscovered. The lost city of the Nabataeans* (Cincinnati, OH 2003) 25. The *locus classicus* for such inscriptions is the long essay by L. Robert, "Epigrammes du Bas-Empire," *Hellenica* IV (Paris 1948).

3 Eight dedications by the governor Q. Aiacius Modestus are found in the Qasr al-Bint (*I.Jord.* IV nos. 1-8).

4 I wish to thank David Potter for advice and suggestions on this inscription.

5 It was described briefly in vol. 2, 208-9 with fig. 4.106.

existing evidence before the recent excavations considered Bostra to be the metropolitan capital of the province of *Arabia*. However, the recording of Petra as a "native mother of colonies" in two inscriptions from the Small Temple and in the carbonized papyri from Petra some three centuries later underscore Petra's primacy within *Arabia*. If the argument for Bostra is still valid, then *Arabia* had two metropolitan centers (capitals). The Roman prefect spent part of his time in each one and used the *via nova Traiana* as the main highway to meet and control the nomadic population.

17A

Food production and procurement in residential areas at the Great Temple

Sarah Whitcher Kansa

Introduction: background and aims

The first faunal analysis undertaken at the Great Temple site, this study explores the diversity of the fauna in order to define how animals contributed to the diet and economy. At the site faunal remains were found in contexts spanning the Nabataean through Byzantine periods. Significant historical events falling within this timespan are the annexation by Rome in A.D. 106, with a cultural shift from Nabataean to Roman, and a major destruction in A.D. 363. We may expect to find changes in the animal economy over this long span, and the results should be compared to those from contemporary sites in the region. Particular attention will be given here to remains from Nabataean contexts in order to increase our knowledge of Nabataean diet and economic practices, which are not yet well understood.

This analysis also aims to explore ways in which the faunal assemblage can advance understanding of the occupants' daily activities. How did they acquire their daily bread? Do the goods they consumed reflect contacts beyond the Petra region? Did their daily activities include a ritual component? Can we identify élite and 'common' foods within the assemblage? The Great Temple faunal assemblage offers an opportunity to move beyond defining the meat contribution to the diet to explore dietary preferences, environmental impacts, economic pressures and choices, and decisions related to religion, identity and status.

Faunal remains from later contexts at Petra have been studied by J. Studer[1] and by N. Desse-Berset and Studer[2] at the generally Late Roman excavations at Ez Zantur, which is close by the Great Temple. Within the region as a whole there is a general dearth of information about dietary and economic practices related to animals. The comparative literature for Transjordan in this period is sparse because faunal studies have not been a priority of most excavations. Only two studies provide overviews of animal exploitation from classical sites in this region. In his review of meat consumption across the Roman world, A. King touched on the Near East, but a lack of published analyses precluded an in-depth discussion.[3] J. Lev-Tov took on the challenge with a thorough discussion of the use of animals in Palestine in the classical period, noting that, although more than 1000 sites are known from the Hellenistic through Byzantine periods and many of those have been excavated, only a dozen or so have seen faunal analyses.[4] While acknowledging that it is difficult to speak in terms of a "Hellenistic" or "Roman diet" in Palestine, he highlighted the importance of fish in the Roman diet. Another potentially useful source is S. Weingarten on food in Roman Palestine,[5] but, while comprehensive in its review of literary sources, it provides only a brief discussion of the faunal remains of meat consumption, and is limited to fish and pig remains.

Overview of the faunal assemblage from the Great Temple excavations

The Great Temple excavations recovered a total of 27,658 faunal specimens. The assemblage discussed here consists of 8,694 specimens (Table 17A.1) from 7 seasons (1995-96, 2000-4)[6] selected primarily from residential areas. The other two-thirds of the total has not yet been analyzed and is

1 Studer 1996, 2002a and 2002b.
2 Desse-Berset and Studer 1996.
3 King 1999.
4 Lev-Tov 2003.
5 Weingarten 2007.
6 The vast majority of the specimens were recovered during the 1995 and 2000-2002 seasons. Only a handful of specimens from 1996, 2003, and 2004 have been analyzed to date.

TABLE 17A.1
LIST OF ALL SPECIMENS FROM THE GREAT TEMPLE EXCAVATIONS (ALL PERIODS COMBINED)

Taxon	*NISP*	%
Domestic		
Sheep (*Ovis aries*)	179	8.3
Goat (*Capra hircus*)	175	8.1
Sheep/goat	735	34.1
Pig (*Sus scrofa*)	270	12.5
Chicken (*Gallus gallus*)	292	13.5
Cattle (*Bos taurus*)	28	1.3
Camel (*Camelus* sp.)	92	4.3
Donkey (*Equus asinus*)	28	1.3
Horse (*Equus caballus*)	3	0.1
Indeterminate equid (*Equus* sp.)	24	1.1
Dog (*Canis familiaris*)	32	1.5
Cat (*Felis catus*)	2	0.1
TOTAL domestic specimens	1860	86.2
Wild		
Gazelle (*Gazella gazella*)	33	1.5
Goat - wild (*Capra aegagrus*)	6	0.3
Sheep - wild (*Ovis orientalis*)	15	0.7
Sheep - wild? (cf. *Ovis orientalis*)	11	0.5
Deer (*Cervus elaphus* or *Dama dama*)	5	0.2
Pig - wild (*Sus scrofa*)	1	<0.1
Hare (*Lepus* spp.)	11	0.5
Fox (*Vulpes* sp.)	2	0.1
Ostrich (*Struthio camelus*)	1	<0.1
Other bird*	109	5.1
Rodent	1	<0.1
Frog	1	<0.1
Fish**	101	4.7
TOTAL wild specimens	297	13.8
TOTAL domestic and wild specimens	2157	
Other***		
Egg shell	4	
Large mammal	197	
Medium-sized mammal	993	
Small mammal	25	
Total other specimens	1219	
Unidentified fragments****	5318	
TOTAL specimens in assemblage	8694	

* "Other bird" includes specimens of pheasant, partridge, peafowl, dove and quail, described in the "Other birds" section of this chapter.

** The 101 recovered fish bones were analyzed by R. Ceron-Carrasco and are described in chapt. 17B.

*** "Other" denotes specimens not identified to genus or element.

**** This is the only table where the count of unidentified fragments will be shown. All subsequent tables do not take unidentified fragments into consideration.

TABLE 17A.2
OVERVIEW OF TOTAL FAUNAL REMAINS BY AREA

Area	*NISP**	*% of assemblage*
Upper Temenos	5314	62%
Lower Temenos	2174	25%
Temple	625	7%

* The total number of specimens identified to genus and element in the database is 8694; however, 108 specimens could not be assigned to an area.

TABLE 17A.3
OVERVIEW OF TOTAL FAUNAL REMAINS BY SITE PHASE

Phase	*No. of specimens*
Pre-site phase I	15
II*	77
IV	248
VI	502
VI and VII	32
VII	461
VIII	463
IX	1374
IX and X	94
IX, X, XI, XII and XIII	2364
X	704
X, XI, XII and XIII	177
XI	356
XI, XII and XIII	1452
XII	112
XII and XIII	16
XIII	7
XIV	48
TOTAL	8502**

* Phase II contains remains of a burnt offering, representing the only faunal material identified from this phase. It dates to the Nabataean period but because of its special nature has not been included with the rest of the bones for this analysis. These remains are discussed in detail on pp. 331-332.

** The total number of specimens identified to genus and element in the database is 8694; however, 192 specimens could not be assigned to a phase.

stored on site. Of the analyzed sample, *c*.25% (2,157 specimens) could be identified to both element and taxon and most of the results presented here draw upon those 2,157 specimens, but in some cases data from specimens not identified to taxon are employed (e.g., for consideration of burning or fragmentation).

The assemblage is dominated by remains of sheep and goat, present in roughly equal numbers in all areas. Next most common is chicken, followed by pig and fish. Cattle, camel and equid remains are present in very low numbers. Except for fish, wild animals (which include wild sheep and goat, gazelle, deer, fox, and birds) number very few.

Faunal remains were recovered from all areas of the site (Table 17A.2), with the majority of those analyzed (62%) coming from the Upper Temenos. The assemblage spans the Nabataean through the Byzantine periods, but the majority of analyzed specimens come from the Byzantine period (later 4th-5th c., following the earthquake) (Tables 17A.3-4).

TABLE 17A.4
RELATIVE ABUNDANCE OF TAXA PER CULTURAL PERIOD
(percentage of total specimens per cultural period)*

	Nabataean	*Roman annexation*	*Roman*	*Byzantine*
	NISP=58	NISP=191	NISP=200	NISP=1607
Sheep/goat	41.3	29.3	46.5	34.8
Sheep	6.9	2.1	7.0	8.3
Goat	22.4	8.9	5.5	7.6
Pig	1.7	13.1	11.0	13.0
Chicken	3.4	35.5	9.5	13.5
Other bird	-	3.2	5.0	4.6
Cattle	-	-	1.5	1.5
Camel	10.3	0.5	3.5	4.5
Equid	5.2	0.5	2.0	2.4
Dog	-	0.5	1.0	1.2
Cat	0.1	-	-	-
Gazelle	3.4	2.6	1.5	1.3
Fish	5.2	1.0	2.0	5.7
Other	0.1	2.8	4.0	1.6

* This Table does not include elements identified only to an animal size category. It also counts multiple fragments from the same individual as "1". This accounts for the discrepancy in totals, where the entire assemblage contains 2,157 identified specimens while this Table is based on 2,056 specimens.

Methods employed in the analysis

Collection and organization

Each trench supervisor presorted finds in the field by material. Bones were separated and kept in plastic bags. The supervisor labeled each bucket, and, except for the bone, its contents were washed, sorted, read, counted and recorded, and entered into the computer. Study artifacts were then transferred to numbered plastic bags[7] which were placed in plastic crates. After processing, all the bone was stored in crates on site or in a cave above the site.

The faunal sample reported on here comprised 9 boxes of remains excavated primarily from residential areas and shipped to San Francisco for analysis. Their analysis by the author took place at the Alexandria Archive Institute in San Francisco from 2004 through 2008. All identified

7 A master bag list was filled out weekly in triplicate for the trench supervisor, field director and project files. Bag numbers include the initials of the site (P/ST = Petra Southern = Great Temple) followed by the trench number and the bag number. Thus, P/ST101 stands for the Great Temple, Trench 1, Bag no. 1. The year excavated appears on the top of the form. The bag's contents are described on the master list.

fragments were assigned a unique bone catalogue number (GT-0001 to GT-3831). All unidentified fragments from each context were counted and jointly assigned a single bone catalogue number. Recording was done directly into an Excel spreadsheet with fields for the various quantitative and qualitative data: context information, bone number, taxon, element, side, fragmentation, skeletal area, sex, age, cut marks, gnaw marks, pathologies, burning, other comments, and measurements. As of December 2009, the faunal sample reported on here is stored at the Joukowsky Institute for Archaeology and the Ancient World at Brown University in Providence. Each of the 9 boxes is labeled with the project name and the range of bone catalogue numbers within. The full catalogue of the animal bones that forms the basis for this analysis is published online in Open Context.[8]

Comparative materials used

Reference manuals were used in lieu of a modern reference collection. Identification was aided primarily by illustrations and distinctions provided by Schmid 1972. Distinctions between sheep and goat were facilitated by Boessneck *et al.* 1964, Boessneck 1969, and Prummel and Frisch 1986. A description of the specific elements used for distinguishing sheep from goat is provided in Table 17A.5. Questionable identifications were checked against modern specimens at the Museum of Vertebrate Zoology of the University of California at Berkeley. A complete chicken skeleton from the author's reference collection facilitated analysis of avian specimens. All measurements follow the methods and abbreviations provided in von den Driesch 1976.

TABLE 17A.5
ELEMENTS USED TO DISTINGUISH SHEEP AND GOAT

Element	*Age fusion occurs*	*Taxon*	*Morphological criteria*
Humerus, distal	<10 months	Sheep	Lateral epicondyle is broad; from medial aspect, medial epicondyle ends in a right angle
		Goat	Lateral epicondyle is narrow; from medial aspect, medial epicondyle ends in a point
Radius, proximal	<10 months	Sheep	Short ulnar scar; pronounced sulcus of lateral margin
		Goat	Long ulnar scar; small sulcus of lateral margin
Metacarpal, distal	1.5–2.25 years	Sheep	Relative size of trochlear condyles indicates goat; bone short and broad; proximal aspect is wide
		Goat	Relative size of trochlear condyles indicate sheep; bone is long and thin
Metatarsal, distal	1.5–2.25 years	Sheep	Bone is long and narrow; depth of proximal aspect is greater than width
		Goat	Bone is short and broad; depth and width of proximal aspect are equal
Calcaneus	2.5–3 years	Sheep	Two facets on processus anterior are not attached
		Goat	Two facets on processus anterior are attached

Note: The above elements were the most reliable in this study for making the sheep/goat distinction. The criteria for distinction have been demonstrated in a separate study undertaken by members of our team to return a correct identification to almost 100% reliability (Buckley *et al.* 2010). Detailed descriptions of the distinction criteria given in this Table can be found in Boessneck *et al.* 1964, Boessneck 1969, and Prummel and Frisch 1986.

Identification

Of the 8,694 fragments sent to San Francisco, 2,157 specimens (25%) were deemed "identifiable", meaning that both the skeletal element and the taxon could be determined. "Taxon" refers to the animal group, which is often achieved to the species level but sometimes only to the level of genus or broader. 1,215 fragments were identified to element but only to a broad taxonomic category such as "large mammal", "medium-sized ungulate", or "fox / bird", depending on the

8 Kansa 2010; see http://opencontext.org/tables/0dfc42274ae780c7f55ea45c05941557

distinguishing features preserved on each specimen.[9] Finally, 5,318 specimens were "unidentified", meaning that the specific element could not be determined. This report presents analytical results on the 2,157 "identifiable" fragments.

Quantification

Unless otherwise indicated, all results are based on NISP (number of identified specimens) counts, according to which each specimen is counted as representing one individual. However, in cases where specimens clearly articulated or paired, they were counted together as one individual in order to avoid intentional over-quantification. Similarly, each of the three partial dog skeletons is counted as one specimen (and given an NISP of "1" in the database), in order to avoid inflating the presence of dog bones. This method was undertaken on a context-specific level (i.e., no attempt was made to pair or articulate bones from different loci).

Mortality patterns

The age at which an animal was killed provides information about the environment, the importance of that animal for meat or other products, and decision-making on the part of the herder, butcher or consumer. To determine the age at which the animals in the assemblage were being killed, two common methods were used: bone fusion stages and mandibular tooth eruption and wear.

As mammals mature, their bones undergo a consistent pattern of ossification. This occurs at different stages depending on the species and the element. Bone fusion is a useful method for determining the broad kill-off pattern of a species up to maturity, when fusion for all elements is complete. While this method provides limited information,[10] it is particularly useful for smaller assemblages in which tooth data are not available; it is also informative when used in conjunction with mortality patterns detected through an examination of eruption and wear stages on teeth.

Tooth eruption and wear patterns offer a more complete picture of animal exploitation because they provide information on very young individuals and on older individuals. The method is based on the fact that both the deciduous and the permanent teeth of mammals erupt according to a more or less specific pattern. Once fully erupted, permanent teeth wear down slowly over the entire duration of an animal's life, creating patterns on the biting surface which vary by age.

This study employs two approaches to determine mortality patterns among sheep/goat through tooth eruption and wear analysis: Payne (1973) and Zeder (1991, 92–3) who expanded on Payne's method. Sheep and goat fusion stages are based on the work of Silver (1969). Due to the small number of specimens of other taxa in the assemblage, this study uses bone fusion data alone to investigate the age of death of cattle, pigs, camels and equids.[11]

Fragmentation and butchery

Fragmentation can reveal information about both natural taphonomic processes and human activities that affect bone. Natural processes affecting bone fragmentation include gnawing by rodents, crushing by carnivore teeth, and breakage due to dryness or trampling. Human actions

9 For example, 197 specimens were identified as "large mammal", which means they could have come from equids, cattle, camels or large deer (the four large mammal taxa identified in the assemblage) or from another large mammal not identified in the assemblage.

10 The use of bone fusion stages to determine cull patterns has a number of analytical drawbacks. One is that the latest-fusing long bones fuse at or soon after the point of maximum growth (adulthood), rendering inaccessible the mortality profile for the portion of the population that survived beyond that particular age. Another drawback is that the age groups for various species are broad and overlapping, with the result that any kill-off profile using bone fusion must be taken as a rough and incomplete reflection of the actual mortality pattern. Finally, the nature of the fusion categories themselves is vague; if an element is unfused, we can only say that that individual died younger than a certain age.

11 Where age estimation is given, the estimate follows Silver 1969; otherwise, the distinction is only between "juvenile" (i.e., unfused) and "adult" (i.e., fused).

include butchery, crushing for marrow extraction, breakage for particular functions (e.g., making soups), cooking, and various methods of discard. Fragmentation is difficult to document and almost always subjective. As there is no standard way of noting fragmentation, this study describes the fragment size as a percentage of the original bone remaining (e.g., "50% of complete bone").

Cut marks on archaeological bones can be seen as evidence for particular butchery practices. Cut marks made by humans[12] are identified here by their location on the bone, their frequency, the direction of the mark, and how the direction reflects dismemberment techniques. They are distinguished from the parallel lines of rodent gnawing and the opposing punctures or more random chewing striations made by carnivore teeth both in appearance and in their location on the bone. Cut marks can be used to understand the way in which a carcass was processed into consumable parts. While butchery practices will differ by animal, a general rule of thumb is that cut marks on the shaft of meat-bearing bones are usually indicative of meat removal or filleting; cuts around the foot area (metapodials, carpals/tarsals and phalanges, where little meat is found) are indicative of hide removal; and cuts on the articular ends of bones result from disarticulation of the carcass. Here, cut marks were noted when they were visible to the naked eye during laboratory analysis.

Analytical results by taxon

First I present results for each major taxon identified in the assemblage. For each, I give its relative abundance in the assemblage, age, sex, body parts present, and skeletal disorders. Then I provide results on human and natural modifications, such as butchery, gnawing and burning. I discuss differences by phase and area, and, where applicable, comparisons with contemporary sites.

Sheep and goat

Remains of sheep and goats dominate the assemblage in all periods (Table 17A.4). Because of the diversity of behavioral and economic factors in the keeping of sheep and goats, it is important to distinguish between the two whenever possible. Fortunately, the well-preserved and abundant material from Petra allows for a distinction between sheep and goat to be made on certain elements (see Table 17A.5).

TABLE 17A.6
RATIO OF SHEEP TO GOATS BY SITE PHASE

	Nabataean	*Roman annexation*	*Roman*	*Byzantine*
Sheep	4	4	14	122
Goat	13	17	11	133
Ratio (S : G)	1 : 3.3	1 : 4.3	1.3 : 1	1 : 1.1

Note: Multiple samples observed to have come from one individual have been counted as "1" for the purpose of generating this ratio. The calculation considers all elements listed in Table 17A.5 where sheep and goats could be distinguished.

Though based on small sample sizes, the data for the sheep to goat ratio show four times more goats than sheep in the Nabataean period and at the Roman annexation than in subsequent periods, when it shifts to *c.*1 : 1. The keeping of goat-dominated herds by highly mobile people is not surprising given the greater suitability of goats to harsh conditions. Goats can generally thrive for longer periods without water and in hot, dry climates than can sheep. Their dominance in Nabataean phases at our site indicates the presence, if not of mobile herders *per se*, then of a population that was still following the economic and dietary traditions of mobile herders to the extent that this pattern survived in the zooarchaeological record.

---

12 Cut marks made by humans often result from mistakes due to carelessness, expedience or inexperience in butchery. It is presumed that if an individual is experienced at butchering he or she will know just what areas of the carcass to slice so as not to encounter bone.

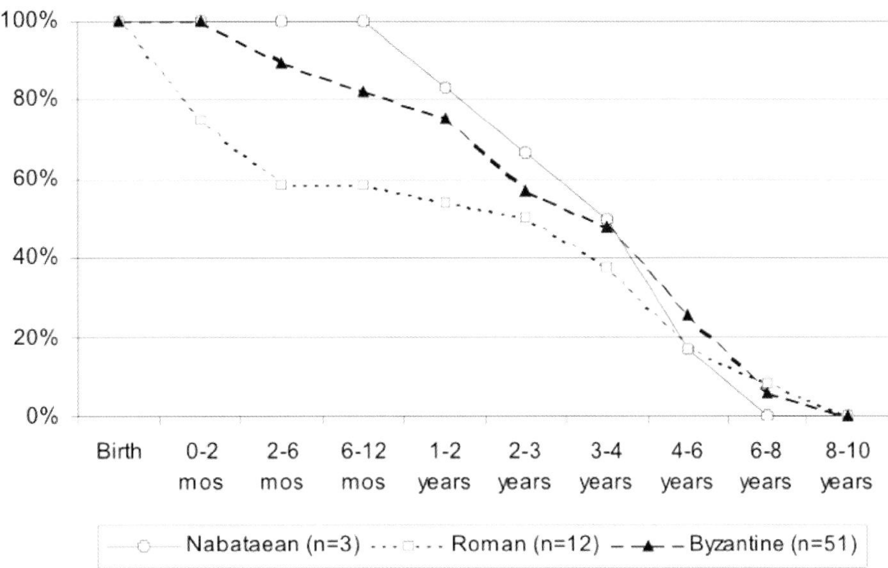

Fig. 17A.1. Sheep/goat mortality by phase (based on mandibular tooth eruption and wear).

In the Roman and Byzantine periods the zooarchaeological record indicates that sheep increased in value. Sheep were an important resource in Roman times: they were primarily used for wool, but also for milk and cheese.[13] Their meat was also eaten, including meat from sacrificed lambs. Age data (see below) show that sheep at our site were kept to older ages than goats, presumably for their wool, which offers a fiber of a more diverse quality and function than goat hair. In Roman Italy goats were kept in smaller numbers than sheep because of a tendency for epidemics to spread among the herd, their voracious appetities, and their destructive feeding practices;[14] but in the Roman and Byzantine periods at Petra we find either a slight preference for goats or an equal ratio of sheep to goat, which probably reflects a local environment more suited to goats.

Mortality data for sheep and goats suggest some possible explanations for the shift in the sheep to goat ratio. Sheep and goat tooth data, combined from all periods (though the majority comes from the Byzantine phase), suggest that meat was not the primary objective. Figure 17A.1 shows that the greatest kill-off occurs between 3-4 and 4-6 years of age, which are both beyond the prime age of slaughter (about 2 years of age) if meat was the sole aim. Fusion data (Table 17A.7), which

TABLE 17A.7

FUSION DATA FOR SHEEP AND GOAT, ALL PERIODS COMBINED*

		Sheep		*Goat*		
Element	*Age fusion occurs*	*# fused*	*# unfused*	*# fused*	*# unfused*	*Total*
Radius, proximal and Humerus, distal	10 months	24	0	30	4	58
Metapodials, distal	1.5-2.25 years	23	5	12	12	52
Calcaneus, proximal	2.5-3 years	9	5	2	6	22

* While data from all phases are combined, the vast majority comes from Byzantine contexts.

are more abundant than tooth data and by which sheep and goat can sometimes be distinguished, are useful here for detecting what might be skewing the combined tooth mortality curve toward older ages. Fusion data for sheep and goat separately show clearly that goats were being killed at a much younger age than sheep (fig. 17A.2). This pattern begins as early as 10 months of age, where

13 MacKinnon 2004, 112.

14 Ibid. 119.

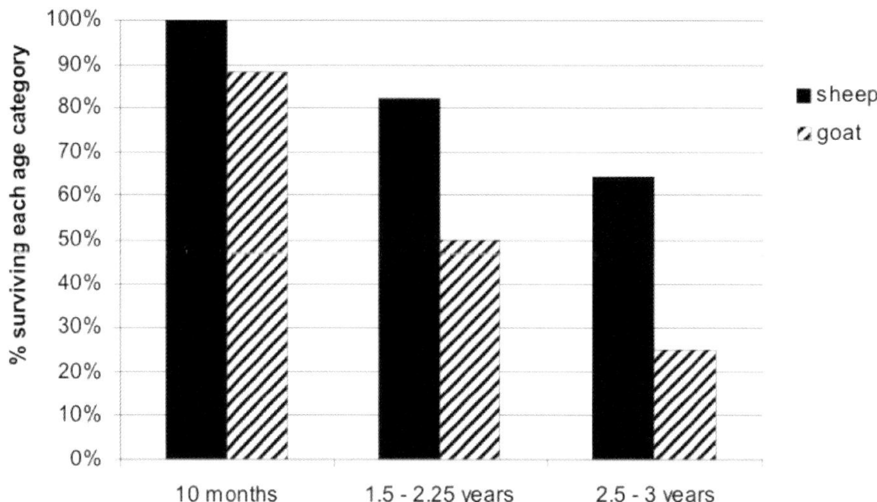

Fig. 17A.2. Differential sheep and goat kill-off at the site, all periods combined (based on fusion data for 132 specimens listed in Table 17A.7).

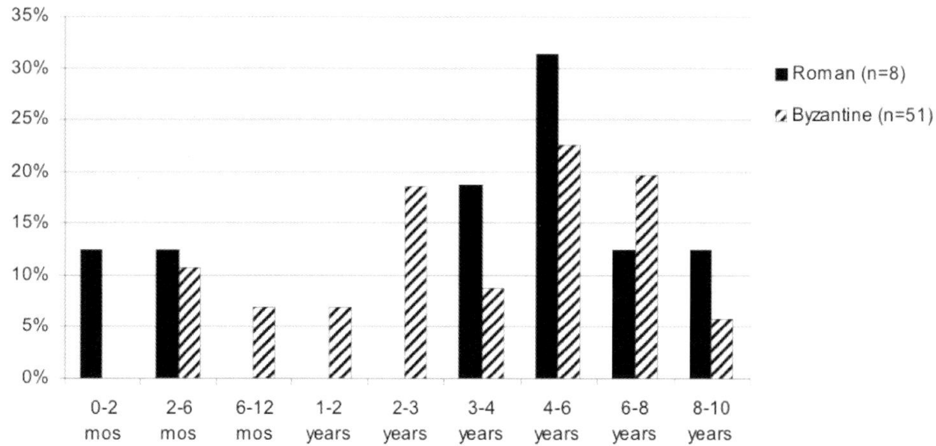

Fig. 17A.3. Sheep/goat fusion by period, showing the proportion of specimens killed in each age category (based on mandibular tooth eruption and wear).

we see only goats selected for culling. By the prime age of 2 years, only 20% of sheep are killed, while 50% of goats are killed; by 3 years of age, only 30% of sheep are killed, while 75% of goats are killed. These data offer strong evidence for the keeping of sheep for their wool and milk, while goats were primarily killed at younger ages for their meat (it is likely that goats provided milk and hair too, but perhaps on a less intensive scale than sheep).

At nearby Ez Zantur, Studer found that the combined age curve for sheep and goats pointed to a focus on milk and wool and the culling of young males, but since only 11 specimens could be distinguished she called for more exploration of these preliminary results. The sheep and goat data from our site, which show a similar pattern, are based on a larger sample size of distinguished and aged elements. Culling young goats is supported by Roman literary sources: there are no recipes for mature goats and only one for mature sheep, but numerous recipes for lamb and kid, which were also expensive to purchase.[15]

Though data from the Roman period are few, tooth data also point to different procurement strategies in the Roman and Byzantine periods. This is supported by both fusion data and the

15 Ibid. 206.

data for tooth eruption and wear (figs. 17A.1 and 17.3). In the Roman period we find a bimodal cull pattern reflecting both very young (under 1 year) and older animals (peaking at 4-6 years). This pattern may indicate consumption of a non-local supply in the Roman period, when surplus young males and some older, non-productive individuals were being brought in. Indeed, all 6 specimens of pelvis from the Roman period were from males. The Byzantine period, by contrast, shows a much broader cull of animals of all ages, with most (*c*.80%) surviving to 2 years and most being killed by 3 or 4 years of age. Though this pattern is complicated by the maintenance of sheep to older ages for their wool, the trend points to consumption of local herds during the Byzantine period. The sex ratio supports this interpretation: the ratio in Byzantine times of nearly 2 : 1 in favor of adult females supports the view that herds were raised locally, the archaeological record more closely reflecting the true herd demographics with a broader range of ages and more females.

TABLE 17A.8
BODY PARTS PRESENT FOR EACH OF THE MAJOR TAXA

	Head	*Upper forelimb*	*Upper hindlimb*	*Feet*	*Ratio of non-meat to meat-bearing*[16]	*Total NISP per taxon*
Sheep/goat	26%	21%	14%	39%	2 : 1	1095
Pig	36%	17%	16%	31%	2 : 1	269
Chicken	1%	46%	47%	6%	1 : 13	125
Cattle	38%	7%	0%	55%	13 : 1	29
Camel	21%	11%	8%	60%	4 : 1	91
Donkey	46%	9%	2%	43%	8 : 1	56
Dog	22%	22%	22%	33%	1 : 1	27
Gazelle	18%	30%	3%	48%	2 : 1	33

Note: This does not include vertebrae and ribs, as distinctions could not be made reliably with each animal size category (for example, vertebrae and ribs for cattle, camel and equid were lumped into the "large mammal" category). Categories: head = cranium, mandible, teeth; upper forelimb = scapula, humerus, radius, ulna; upper hindlimb = pelvis, femur, tibia, fibula; feet = carpals/tarsals, metapodials, phalanges. Non-meat bearing = head and feet; meat-bearing = upper forelimb and upper hindlimb.

All parts of the carcass (meat-bearing and non-meat-bearing) are present in our assemblage. Non-meaty parts occur twice as often as meaty parts (Table 17A.8), which suggests that butchery of sheep and goats took place on site — that is, whole animals were led on the hoof into town before butchery, rather than meaty parts being brought to markets. This pattern occurs in all periods except for that of the Roman annexation, when we see an over-representation of meat-bearing parts. Taken together with the sex data, this may indicate that the annexation involved the influx of new people who required market provisioning of meat (whole animals, but also, apparently, meat cuts).

Left and right side elements are present in roughly even numbers. There is no indication of a preference for forelimb or hind limb parts. An occurrence of *c*.10% cut marks noted on sheep/goat elements (see Table 17A.12 below) is consistent with preparation for consumption (for food and for products such as hides and sinews).

On the sheep/goat bones and teeth, 24 instances of pathologies were noted. This occurrence is low and suggests a generally healthy population. Predominant was periodontal disease, with 4 cases of swollen root tips, 12 of dental calculus, and 1 of malocclusion. Swollen root tips are related to periodontal infection, possibly resulting from chronic, low-grade infection;[17] among domestic herd animals low-grade infection might be caused in part by poor pasture or by crowded living conditions. Dental calculus (tartar build-up) is normally found on the teeth of mature bovids,[18]

16 Redding argues (1984) that, if whole animals were entering the archaeological record, non-meat-bearing bones would outnumber meat-bearing bones by a ratio of 2 : 1.

17 Baker and Brothwell 1980, 151.

18 Miles and Grigson 1990, 560.

both wild and domestic; it may be related to diet and pasture, such as an intake of sand during grazing,[19] which may have occurred to our sheep and goats grazing in a desert environment. A small number of additional pathological conditions were observed on sheep and goats.[20]

Chicken

Domestic fowl (*Gallus gallus*) is the second most common food taxon present. Among the nearly 300 chicken bones (13.5% of the assemblage), there are only 2 head bones, 4 vertebrae, 1 rib and 1 toe bone, which means that meat-bearing bones make up the vast majority (over 90%) of this taxon's assemblage (Table 17A.8). Dog activity and the methods of archaeological recovery may account for some of the absence of small bones such as toes and vertebrae, but the near-absence of those parts together with the high presence of other small, meat-bearing bones suggests that the non-meaty bones were simply never present. This is further supported by the counts of specific elements. The tibiotarsus and the tarsometatarsus are robust bones of roughly equal size, but the tibiotarsus is three times more common in our assemblage than the tarsometatarsus. The tibiotarsus is a meat-bearing bone (the 'drumstick'), while the tarsometatarsus farther down on the leg bears no meat. Given their similar size and robustness, human behaviour probably accounts for their differential presence here — i.e., chickens were butchered elsewhere and only their meaty parts made it into the Great Temple assemblage.

Spurs were noted on the shafts of 6 out of 11 tarsometatarsi, representing males who survived beyond 1 year of age (roughly the time when spurs begin to appear). Since sex determination can only be made on mature animals, however, this does not necessarily indicate a 1 : 1 sex ratio. We can assume that hens were often kept to older ages for egg production while males were culled for meat, probably well before reaching 1 year of age. Thus the spur-less tarso-metatarsi perhaps come from females or from young individuals of either sex, though more probably from young males killed for their meat. Chickens eaten at the site were predominantly adults since *c.*95% of the elements were fused.

The only pathology observed was a coracoid (wing bone) with a healed break near the distal part of shaft, resulting in a bulge in the bone and a false articulation surface. The break probably occurred to the juvenile chicken and it had time to heal before the chicken was killed for food.

The assemblage produced only a small number (4) of eggshells. This stands in contrast to the assemblage from the Late Roman levels at Ez Zantur, which produced high quantities of eggshell but very few chicken bones.[21]

A high occurrence of domestic fowl has been documented at other Roman and Hellenistic period sites in this region. L. Horwitz suggests that, with the ease of raising poultry and its tastiness, poultry may have provided the majority of the meat in the diet, while sheep, goats and cattle were raised mainly for their secondary products.[22] Our assemblage shows a sharp rise in birds from the Nabataean period (when they are almost non-existent) to the Roman annexation, when they dominate the assemblage at nearly 40%.

---

19 As demonstrated by Baker and Britt 1984.

20 They include: 2 metatarsals with erosion on the proximal articular surface, possibly resulting from bone thinning (osteoporosis) from calcium loss in lactating females (Horwitz and Smith 1990);
1 femur with thin cortical bone at the caput, also perhaps due to osteoporosis;
1 sheep/goat metatarsal and 1 goat metacarpal, both with swelling and woven bone at the distal metaphysis;
1 goat first phalanx with a healed, twisted fracture;
1 goat ulna with porosity on both sides of olecranon (a photograph was taken);
1 goat radius with a healed fracture; and
1 sheep first phalanx with exostosis.

21 Studer 1996.

22 Horwitz 1998.

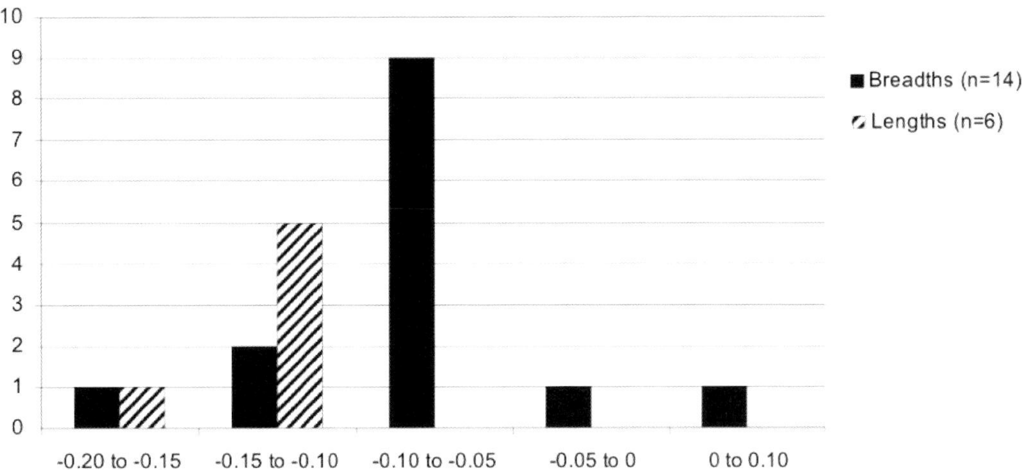

Fig. 17A.4. Pig size at the Great Temple.

Pig

Pigs comprise 12.5% (270 elements) of the overall Great Temple assemblage. As the bones come predominantly from young individuals, withers height calculations are impossible. We were able, however, to determine the overall size of the population compared against a 'standard' wild female boar from Turkey.[23] Based on a very small available sample of fused elements, the Petra pigs appear to have been stocky (see the comparison of lengths and breadths in fig. 17A.4).

Pigs provide no secondary products (such as fibers or milk) to make it worth keeping them alive beyond the age of maximum growth, and so we assume that they were raised for food. Indeed, 25 specimens (*c.*10%) have cut marks resulting from butchery for food preparation. Furthermore, there is a preponderance of young individuals: fusion data show that just over half of the individuals represented by the assemblage survived beyond their first year of life, while only 20% survived the second and a mere 3% survived beyond 3 years (Table 17A.9). Tooth eruption and wear data show an even stronger kill-off of pigs by 12 months of age: of 11 specimens, 10 were killed before they reached their first birthday, and only one is from an animal that may have lived to 2 years of age. If pigs were being produced for consumption at Petra, we would expect to see both young and older animals, the latter representing older sows no longer breeding. The observed pattern of a preponderance of young pigs up to 1 year of age supports a consumption pattern where pigs were being raised elsewhere (perhaps nearby) and brought for sale in the markets. On-site butchery is supported by skeletal element representation where all body parts are present. Non-meat-bearing elements outnumber meat-bearing elements by a ratio of 2 : 1 and this is the expected pattern when whole animals are entering the archaeological record.[24] It suggests that pig butchery, consumption and discard all occurred within the area of our site.

TABLE 17A.9
PIG FUSION DATA, ALL PERIODS COMBINED

Age category	*no. fused*	*no. unfused*	*% Surviving age category*
1 year	20	17	54%
2-2.5 years	10	41	20%
3-3.5 years	1	32	3%

23 As reported in Hongo and Meadow 2000.
24 Redding 1994.

C. Grigson has proposed an environmentally-dependent distribution of pigs in the Levant, according to which pigs are present in assemblages at sites in areas which received over 350 mm of annual rainfall, and generally absent from sites which received less than that.[25] Petra lies in an arid region that today receives a maximum of 200 mm of rainfall annually, making it a poor candidate for pig-keeping. Yet their presence in significant numbers in our assemblage suggests that they may have been raised nearby. Water-management practices and the manipulation of natural springs by the town's residents may have created pig friendly local conditions. Desse-Berset and Studer[26] describe how different Petra's landscape was during the Nabataean period because of artificial water-management systems:

> The outskirts of the town were woodlands, the water flowed more regularly, and the landscape was maintained as terraces and did not therefore present the same wadi-like aspect [as today]. The climatic conditions did not change radically, but deforestation and the abandoning of the upkeep of the terraces led to desertification (Becker 1991). Nowadays, Wadi Musa and Wadi Araba, near the site, have a very low rate of water flow. During the Nabataean period, the situation was quite different as the region had a highly developed irrigation system, including dams.

It is possible, then, that pigs were raised nearby, with the prime-age animals being supplied to the markets in Petra while the less desirable, older animals were consumed at the production site or elsewhere. In the Roman-Nabataean Negev (at 'Ein Haseva and Mesad Dafit, but not Mo'a), D. Hakker-Orion[27] found that pigs were raised in addition to sheep and goats, in spite of the less-than-ideal environmental conditions for keeping pigs.

Beyond questions of environmental suitability, the exploitation of pigs may relate to dietary preferences, cultural taboos and political factors.[28] Indeed, pigs are all but absent in the Nabataean phase of our site (only 1 of the 270 specimens in the assemblage). An absence of pigs fits well with nomadic traditions that appear to have characterized the early Nabataean population. By contrast, pigs are ubiquitous throughout the Roman world and are often the most abundant taxon in faunal assemblages.[29] At our site the relative proportion of pig jumps from just under 2% in the Nabataean period to 10-15% at the moment of the Roman annexation and beyond. Pigs were the meat of choice in the Roman diet: "Apicius lists more recipes involving pork, ham, and sausages than any other meat".[30] All parts of the pigs were used and pigs were intentionally raised for food. Perhaps because of the water management systems established by the Nabataeans, the Roman and later populations at the site found ways of acquiring this food which was so desirable a component in the contemporary diet.

Camel

Camel bones make up an average of 4.3% of the overall assemblage from our site. With Petra located at the crossroads of major caravan routes, camels and other beasts of burden were important to the inhabitants for the long-distance transport of goods that formed the backbone of the economy. This is illustrated by terracotta camels and equids, suggested to have been made as "offerings for safe returns from expeditions".[31] Hakker-Orion reported a very high number of camel bones at Negev sites of the Nabataean-Roman period, stating that camels, in addition to transporting goods to the coast, also contributed the majority of meat to the local diet.[32] Camels also provide rich milk. One might assume that camels were too valuable to kill for food, but our assemblage contains all the body parts and rates of fragmentation consistent with food preparation. Of 98 camel bones, 10 show evidence of butchery, and they come from all phases; this rate of

25 Grigson 1995, 254.
26 Desse-Berset and Studer 1996, 386.
27 Hakker-Orion 1994.
28 Hesse 1990; Zeder 1996.
29 MacKinnon 2004, 243.
30 Ibid. 206.
31 Bignasca 1993, 66.
32 Hakker-Orion 1994.

butchery marks is consistent with patterns observed on other known food mammals (sheep, goats and pigs) at the site (Fig. 17A.5 and Table 17A.12).

Camel bones with cut marks are predominantly toe bones showing evidence of skinning and/or disarticulation. One specimen of a cranium has cuts in the foramen magnum, indicating removal of the head. A number of specimens are split in half; camel bones in general show a high degree of fragmentation. The ratio of non-meat-bearing to meat-bearing bones is 4 : 1, indicating that there were twice as many non-meaty bones entering the archaeological record than would be expected if whole animals were present at the site. While it seems camels were eaten, an abundance of non-meaty limb bones may reflect their use for other purposes (e.g., the import of hides for tanning).[33]

The majority of the bones come from adult animals, suggesting that they were eaten only after they had served other purposes. Analysis of fragmentation patterns at nearby Ez Zantur led to the same conclusion that camels were eaten but that they were not specifically bred for meat.[34] It is likely that camel meat, bones and hides from mature individuals arrived at Petra by way of the caravans, to be used as food or in some industry.

There is some evidence, however, that camels occasionally were intentionally killed for food at younger ages. About 20% (7 out of 36 specimens) of the elements for which age could be determined came from juveniles less than 5 years of age. These may represent surplus young males killed for special events requiring large amounts of food, as has been suggested by Studer. Indeed, with a body mass of 300-690 kg, camels would have provided an abundance of meat that, in the absence of refrigeration or curing, would lend itself to large-scale distribution or feasting. Burning on camel bones is higher than on all other taxa, and it occurs in all phases (see Table 17A.15). Of all camel elements, 15% are partly burned, whereas other taxa show generally less than 5% burning. The high occurrence of burning on camel bones, and specifically on foot bones, supports a different type of preparation (e.g., roasting) than other food animals and provides further support for camels being consumed as part of large-scale events.

Donkey and horse

Equid remains make up 2.5% of our assemblage. Half (28 bones) were identified as donkey (*Equus asinus*) bones, 3 bones were identified as horse (*Equus caballus*), and 25 were indeterminate. Equid remains are more abundant during the Nabataean period than subsequently (Table 17A.4). Equids were not normally eaten in the Roman period,[35] but, based on cut marks on donkey bones, Studer suggested that donkey meat was consumed at Ez Zantur during the Late Roman period.[36] She also questioned whether horsemeat may not have been eaten because horses held higher status. In our assemblage, out of 57 equid specimens only 1 shows butchery marks: saw marks on a donkey scapula indicate dismemberment at the shoulder.

While the dearth of butchery marks suggests that equids were not eaten at our site, fragmentation on equid bones is high (fig. 17A.5), paralleling that of the known food mammals. This unusual combination of low butchery marks and high fragmentation suggests that equid carcasses were being processed for some purpose other than meat or skin (which would have left filleting or skinning marks on the bones). Body part representation suggests one explanation: Table 17A.8 shows that the equid remains from our site are almost all head and foot bones (the non-meaty parts of the carcass), which raises the question of equid bones being used for tool, tallow or hide production, rather than for meat consumption.

---

33 It is also possible that camel foot bones are readily identifiable whereas their limb bones, if fragmented, may be present but grouped within the broader "large mammal" category, leading to an over-representation of non-meaty bones.

34 Studer 1996.

35 MacKinnon 2004, 96.

36 Studer 1996.

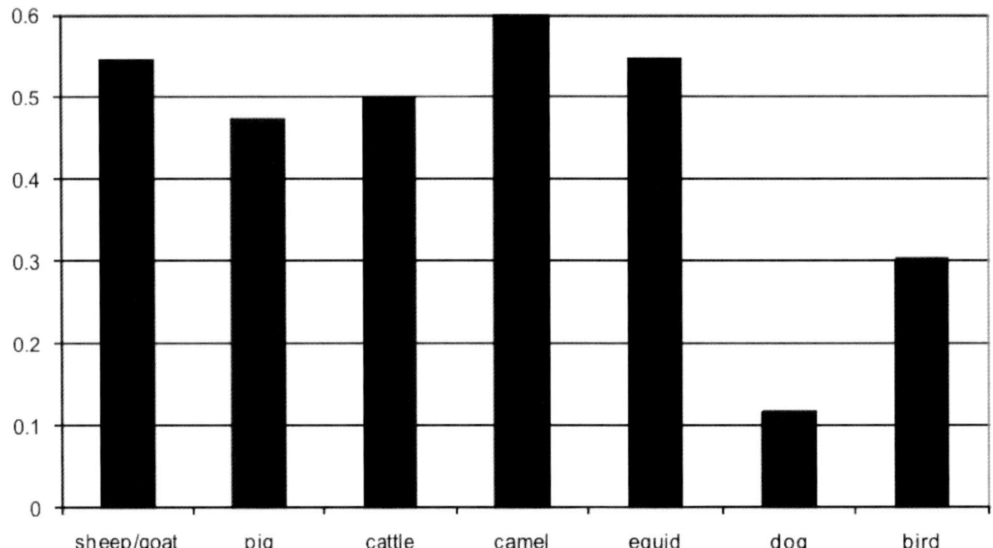

Fig. 17A.5. Percentage of specimens per taxon fragmented to one quarter or less of the original bone (data from Table 17A.14).

Overall, the small population of equids appears to have been healthy. Two pathologies were noted: one donkey metacarpal appears to have had a healed fracture, with a large area of exostosis near the distal part of the shaft; and one tooth from an unidentified equid has swollen roots.

Cattle

Cattle bones make up a small proportion (1.3%) of our assemblage, with only 27 identified specimens, all from Roman and Byzantine contexts. No cattle remains were found in Nabataean and Late Nabataean to Roman annexation contexts. The majority of the cattle elements come from the foot, with a ratio of 13 : 1 non-meat-bearing to meaty body parts. This extreme disproportion in body parts offers strong evidence that whole animals were not present at the site and that the elements present were brought in from elsewhere.

The few specimens to provide age data are mainly phalanges (toe bones) from individuals older than 18 months. One unfused metapodial came from a juvenile less than two and a half years old, while two mandible fragments contain permanent teeth in intermediate stages of wear.

Pathological conditions include one tooth showing malocclusion and an exostosis on a 3rd phalanx, resulting from an infection. When pathologies such as osteoarthritis occur on the foot bones of cattle, they might be related to the cattle having been used for draught[37] or some other repeated or excessive task.

Cut marks, noted on 3 out of 29 specimens (*c.*10%), are consistent with disarticulation and skinning. As with equids, the vast majority of the specimens come from the head or foot, with the exception of two bones from the upper forelimb (a radius and a scapula). The paucity of evidence for cattle meat and milk may be due both to Petra's location in an arid region unsuitable for cattle-keeping and to dietary preferences. According to texts that mention meat in the Roman diet, beef was tough and inexpensive, and cattle milk was not commonly consumed fresh.[38]

The near-absence of meat-bearing elements suggests that beef, if it was consumed at all, arrived at Petra not attached to the bone, but the very low representation of cattle overall suggests that beef was not in fact common in the diet. The head and foot bones may simply represent the remains of butchery that occurred nearby, the meaty parts having been despatched elsewhere or remaining in

---

37 Baker and Brothwell 1980, 117.

38 MacKinnon 2004, 205.

an unexcavated part of our site. The lower limb bones and the metapodials, in particular, are ideal materials for making tools, but no blanks or by-products of tool production have been found so it may be that the bones arrived at our site attached to skins to be used in tanning on a small scale.

Dog

Dog bones make up 1.5% of our assemblage. They represent all parts of the carcass. Of the 32 specimens (including 3 partial skeletons, each counted as "1" in this analysis), 72% (23 of 32 specimens) are half or more complete. None displays cut marks (see Tables 17A.12-13 below), indicating that these bones were not processed like the bones of the food animals. Based on 3 left fused proximal femora, 1 unfused right proximal femur and 1 puppy skeleton, the specimens represent a minimum number of 5 dogs. Dog remains come mainly from the Roman and Byzantine periods, with only one partial skeleton found in an annexation context and no remains from the Nabataean period. Although the overall sample is small, it raises the question of whether dogs only made an appearance in Petra after the Nabataean period.

A partial skeleton including fragments of a cranium, mandible and vertebrae from a puppy was found in a Late Nabataean/Roman annexation context (Site Phase VI) in the Upper Temenos. Another partial skeleton including fragments of a cranium, mandible, vertebrae and upper limb bones came from a juvenile dog in a Roman context (Site Phase VIII) in the Lower Temenos. Another partial skeleton of a an older, diseased individual[39] (cat. no. GT-0095) was found in Byzantine levels of the Upper Temenos; it included the cranium and mandible, half the vertebrae and ribs, both scapulae but no forelimbs, a pelvis, both femora and tibiae, but no fibulae or feet.

Roman texts suggest that neither dogs nor cats were consumed,[40] and our dog remains support this conclusion, being few in number and showing none of the characteristic damage associated with food preparation that is seen on the bones of the main food animals. The partially complete skeletons may indicate that dogs were intentionally buried, but the other scattered remains indicate that often they were simply discarded alongside other general household débris.

Cat

Two bones in our assemblage were identified as belonging to domestic cats, a femur[41] and a humerus[42] both coming from adult animals. Studer[43] identified a bone of a probable domestic cat at the Byzantine monastery at Jabal Harûn. Based on the absence of cat in the assemblage from nearby Ez Zantur, she suggested that cats appeared at Petra only during the Byzantine period. Of the 2 cat bones identified in our assemblage, one comes from a Byzantine context while the other could not be assigned. Given the large size of our Byzantine assemblage, this single specimen suggests that cats were perhaps not as common as dogs around the residential areas; cats are also relatively independent of humans and might be less likely to end up in the archaeological record.

Wild taxa

Our assemblage contained a variety of wild animals (Table 17A.1: wild sheep, wild goat, ibex, deer, hare, ostrich, fox and wild pig) represented by only a handful of specimens; the exception is gazelle, which yielded 33 specimens. The gazelle specimens come from all parts of the carcass and both sides of the body in roughly equal proportions, although the forelimb (10 specimens) is much

---

39 The dog is determined to be of advanced age based on high wear on the teeth (all worn down to the dentine). Thinning of the ischium and 3 deformed arches in the lumbar region also point to an older age. The dog's left femur shows signs of an infection or possibly a tumor. The bone is thin on the articular ends and the cortical bone is exposed on the distal lateral condyle. The same femur has a lesion on the shaft, characterized by swelling, striations and woven bone, as well as a large hole penetrating the shaft.

40 MacKinnon 2004, 207.

41 Measurements (mm): Bp: 19.7; DC: 9.3; SD: 7.7.

42 Measurements (mm): Bd: 13.7; Bt: 9.4; SD: 4.5.

43 Studer 2002a, 171.

better represented than the hind limb (1). That single element comes from the less-meaty distal part of the tibia, whereas the forelimb elements chiefly represent the meaty upper forelimb (scapula and humerus), suggesting that the forelimb was the preferred cut for gazelle meat.

At Rome, large game such as gazelles, deer, wild sheep and goats formed part of wealthier diets,[44] and rabbit and hare meat was one of the most expensive to purchase. At our site, remains of rabbits and hares are present only in Roman and Byzantine contexts. This could be a result of the small sample size of the preceding periods, but it may also reflect Roman influence on the diet, with more wild animals being consumed after the annexation. The bones come from the shoulder and limbs (no feet or head bones are present in our sample).

The Byzantine levels bring the highest proportion and diversity of wild taxa, including the entire sample (15) of wild sheep specimens. One wild pig bone and one ostrich bone were identified in Byzantine contexts. Studer identified one ostrich specimen in the Nabataean period at nearby Ez Zantur and observed that ostrich was very uncommon by the Byzantine period.[45]

Other birds

While chickens dominate the bird assemblage, there is a small number of specimens from other birds. Other than 4 specimens from dove-like birds (Family: *Columbidae*), all identified non-chicken specimens come from *Phasianidae,* the same family as chicken. Species present include partridge (27 specimens), pheasant (6), peafowl (1) and quail (1). These wild birds inhabiting scrub or brush environments were probably acquired through occasional hunting outside the town. None comes from a Nabataean context. All but quail are present in Roman contexts, and examples of each are present in Byzantine contexts. The single specimen of a peacock,[46] from the Roman annexation period, is the first documented at Petra and may be an élite or ritual item.

Fish

The fish remains were analyzed by R. Cerón-Carrasco and are reported in chapter 17B. It is worth mentioning here that fish, of which 91% of the assemblage belongs to the Byzantine phase, made a much smaller contribution to the overall diet than was observed by Studer for the Late Roman period at Ez Zantur and at the Byzantine monastery of Jabal Harûn. Further, mackerel and tuna dominate our Byzantine assemblage, with groupers a distant second. By contrast, parrotfish dominated the Jabal Harûn Byzantine assemblage, while parrotfish and groupers made up the majority of the Late Roman fish at Ez Zantur. Red Sea and Mediterranean fish dominate all three assemblages but dietary preferences or supply-chain variations evidently caused particular taxa to be favoured in each location.

Taphonomic (human and natural) impacts on the assemblage

Animal damage

A total of 46 bones (*c.*1% of the assemblage) show evidence for gnawing or digestion. Gnawing is present in all the excavated areas at roughly the same rate. In most cases, the bones had been gnawed by medium-sized animals, leaving punctures and depressions on fresh bone. This can be attributed to dogs since their bones are present in the assemblage and they prefer gnawing on fresh bones for meat and marrow. Most of the gnawing damage is on chicken limb bones and sheep/goat

---

44 MacKinnon 2004, 208.

45 Studer 1996.

46 This specimen is a tarsometatarsus with a greatest length of 132.6 mm. A pronounced spur indicates that it comes from a peacock. The measurements fit with the size of males of *Pavo cristatus*. A light cut-mark on the proximal end is consistent with removal of the lower leg, suggesting that this bird was eaten. Photographs are available in Open Context at: http://opencontext.org/subjects/88C44010-19FA-4E23-3E2E-E53ED07CEB6E

foot bones (see Tables 17A.10-11). Two partially digested bones also attest to a limited amount of scavenging by dogs.[47] The fact that dogs are present as non-food animals in the faunal assemblage but their presence is not strongly attested through damage to the assemblage may suggest that some effort was made to keep them out of the main habitation areas.

Rodent gnawing was observed on only a small number of bones (15 specimens, less than 0.5% of the assemblage). This suggests that food refuse was quickly covered up or disposed of in some other way that led to little rodent damage on our site. The exception to this is chicken, which account for more than half the rodent-gnawed bones.

TABLE 17A.10
OCCURRENCE OF GNAWING BY TAXON

Taxon	*no. of gnawed specimens**	*Total NISP*	*% gnawed*
Sheep/goat	16 (5)	1,089	1.5%
Pig	4 (1)	270	1.5%
Camel	3	92	3.3%
Dog	1	32	3.1%
Chicken	15 (8)	292	5.1%
Other bird	2	109	1.8%
Sheep - wild?	1	11	9.1%
Large mammal	1	179	0.6%
Medium-sized mammal	2 (1)	640	0.3%
Small-medium mammal	1	53	1.9%

*The number in parentheses shows how many of the observed specimens were gnawed by rodents

TABLE 17A.11
OCCURRENCE OF GNAWING BY PART

Element	*no. of gnawed specimens**
Cranium	1 (1)
Coracoid	2 (2)
Scapula	4 (1)
Humerus	3
Radius	1
Ulna	1
Rib	1
Pelvis	1
Femur	12 (5)
Tibia	2 (1)
Tibiotarsus	3 (1)
Calcaneus	1
Astragalus	3 (1)
Metacarpal	2
Phalanx 1	8 (3)
Phalanx 2	1

Butchery and fragmentation

A much greater impact came from human activity associated with preparing a carcass for consumption. Evidence for butchery ranges from crushing and fragmentation of long bones for accessing the marrow, to deep chops on bones resulting from disarticulation, down to the much finer slices on bones that result from skinning and removal of muscles from bones. Fragmentation occurs on 84% of the bones in the assemblage. The remainder are either from taxa that were not eaten or from parts that were discarded in butchery or cooked whole (e.g., foot bones, which account for 75% of the sample of complete bones). Figure 17A.5 shows the percentage of specimens from each of the predominant taxa that are fragmented to a quarter or less of the original element. It reveals the high fragmentation on equid and camel bones mentioned above.

Fragmentation alone cannot be taken as evidence for consumption, but in the absence of evidence for animal damage fragmentation normally points to human activities aimed at food or other primary products in instances where carcasses (e.g., of dogs) were not simply discarded whole. Further evidence for food production is found in cut marks, which indicate skinning, disarticulation or defleshing, and occur on *c.*10% of the specimens for every species that made up a normal part of the diet (see Table 17A.12-13). Equids show a much lower occurrence of cut marks,

47 The partially digested bones are small, rounded bones that could easily be swallowed by dogs but are dense enough to survive partial digestion. Identified in our assemblage are one phalanx 2 and one astragalus, both from a sheep or goat. These bones are from the extremities (non-meaty parts) of the body and may have been cast aside in the butchery process.

suggesting that they were not processed in the same way as the main food animals. Chickens also display few cut marks, but since chickens are small their meat would have been cooked on the bone, rather than filleted like the meat of larger animals; and since their small bones do not produce marrow, there would be little point in breaking them. This is reflected in the low proportion of highly fragmented chicken bones, as compared to other food taxa (Table 17A.14; fig. 17A.5).

TABLE 17A.12
CUT MARKS BY TAXON FOR PRIMARY TAXA

	no. of cut specimens	*Total NISP*	*% cut by taxon*
Sheep/goat	114	1,102	10.3%
Pig	25	270	9.3%
Chicken	16	401	4.0%
Cattle	3	29	10.3%
Camel	9	90	10.0%
Donkey	1	28	3.6%
Gazelle	1	32	3.1%
Hare	1	11	9.1%
Dog	0	32	0%

TABLE 17A.13
CUT MARKS BY AREA

Area	*no. of specimens with cut marks*	*Total NISP*	*% cut marks by area*
Upper Temenos	253	2,353	11%
Lower Temenos	79	981	8%
Temple	19	233	8%
Propylaeum	19	251	8%
TOTAL	370	3818	10%

TABLE 17A.14
FRAGMENTATION BY TAXON

Taxon	*< 25%*	*0.25*	*0.5*	*0.75*	*Complete*	*Total NISP*
Sheep/goat	261	248	135	79	209	932
Pig	55	39	24	23	58	199
Cattle	6	4	3	2	5	20
Camel	33	12	5	12	13	75
Equid	13	4	2	5	7	31
Dog	0	3	5	9	9	26
Bird	20	35	34	53	40	182

Burning

Overall, 10% of the assemblage (n=213) is charred, an indication of contact with elevated heat. Although there is no direct evidence (such as 'spit marks') for cooking over an open fire, there are some notable differences by taxon and body part. All major taxa have burning on elements from all parts of the skeleton, with the exception of camels whose feet are the only part showing burning (see Tables 17A.15-16). Possibly other camel body parts were burned but were not identified, for some of the unidentified "large mammal" specimens have burning on the cranium, limbs and back bones, and these are likely to be camel to judge by the proportion of camel in the assemblage; alternatively, the burning only on the feet may result from their having been cooked differently (e.g., roasted for large events).

The wild taxa show more evidence of burning than do the domestic animals (Table 17A.15). If the meat of wild animals was preserved by smoking before making the trip to market in Petra, near-fire smoking may have left burn marks on the non-meaty parts of the bones (specifically the lower limbs).

TABLE 17A.15
OCCURRENCE OF BURNING BY TAXON*

	no. of burned specimens	*Total NISP*	*% burned by taxon*
Domestic taxa			
Sheep/goat	79	1089	7.3%
Pig	10	270	3.6%
Cattle	2	28	7.1%
Camel	14	92	15.2%
Dog	1	32	3.1%
Chicken	5	292	1.7%
Donkey	1	28	3.6%
Wild taxa			
Gazelle	4	33	12.1%
Goat - wild	1	5	20.0%
Sheep - wild	1	15	6.7%
Sheep - wild?	3	11	27.3%
Deer	3	9	30.0%
Other taxa			
Bird, indeterminate	1	109	1.0%
Equid, indeterminate	1	27	3.7%
Large mammal	21	179	11.7%
Medium-sized mammal	53	777	6.3%
Medium to large-sized mammal	6	125	4.4%
Small to medium-sized mammal	2	53	3.8%

* Only taxa on which burning was observed are listed.

TABLE 17A.16
OCCURRENCE OF BURNING BY SKELETAL AREA

Skeletal Area	*% specimens burned*
Head	5.7%
Back	4.8%
Upper forelimb	7.3%
Upper hindlimb	5.1%
Feet	10.3%

Observations on the spatial contexts

Specimens from the Upper (62%) and the Lower Temenos (25%) make up the majority of our faunal assemblage (Table 17A.2). The samples from the Temple and the Propylaeum, at 7% and 6% of the total assemblage, respectively, though small, also provide some interesting results.

A Nabataean burnt offering

The Propylaeum has a very high occurrence of burning (Table 17A.17), nearly three times more than all other areas. The high occurrence of burning here is due to extreme burning in one special context (SP 88, Locus 3) in Site Phase II of the Propylaeum sequence, the first phase of major Nabataean construction at the complex in the 1st c. B.C. Nearly 80% of the bones in this context are burned (they were described as "burned deposits (offerings?) ... made up against the north face of the Portico Wall").[48] This context produced 36 identified and 42 unidentified fragments. Of the identified bones, 27 were burnt, most to the point of becoming black (charred). A quarter of the burned bones

48 Vol. 2, 70.

TABLE 17A.17
BURNING ON BONES BY AREA

Area	*no. of burned specimens*	*Total NISP*	*% burned by area*
Upper Temenos	107	1,344	8%
Lower Temenos	69	601	11%
Temple	6	159	4%
Propylaeum	31	113	27%

are calcined (white), indicating prolonged and/or repeated exposure to heat. All of the bones in this context are highly fragmented; in addition to the 42 unidentified fragments, 91% of the identified specimens are small fragments representing one-fourth or less of the original element. This high degree of fragmentation is unusual and further reinforces the special nature of this context and repeated activities in this one spot which led to extended periods of burning and high breakage.

While our assemblage overall contains *c.*50% sheep/goat, this deposit contains 90% sheep/goat (including fragments identified as "medium-sized mammal" and "medium-sized ungulate"). Two sheep/goat specimens were identified as coming from male animals. This context also contained fragments from 1 possible wild sheep, 1 pig, and 1 deer. Elements from the left and right side of the carcass are represented in more or less equal numbers. Notably, bones of the cranium and the feet (bones distal to the metapodials) are missing. In other words, this deposit is predominantly meat-bearing elements from sheep and goats.

The nearest comparison from a known Nabataean ritual context is found at the temple at Khirbet et-Tannur,[49] where the small animal assemblage of 255 fragments (57 identified to taxon and element) was dominated by sheep/goat. The assemblage was judged to be of a ritual nature based on the following criteria: a narrow range of species (sheep/goat, cattle and birds), a high occurrence of burning (over 90%), specific body parts (limb and skull fragments, whereas bones of the back and feet are absent), and a narrow range of ages (juvenile sheep, goats and cattle). There was a positive correlation between burning and fragmentation, which is not surprising as burning makes bones friable. The same is true in our context, which shares some of the indicators of ritual; a narrow range of species (sheep/goat), specific body parts (limbs and back bones), and a high occurrence of burning and fragmentation.[50] We suggest that it is an "offering" context, and it would be the only one of its kind in our overall assemblage.

The Temple area

The small sample recovered from the Temple area displays significant changes over time. From the Nabataean period the 22 specimens, which represent limbs and feet but no heads, include 6 sheep/goat, 4 camel and 2 fish (4 specimens come from the right side of the body, none from the left). The Roman period produced a typical range of 64 specimens, except that there was a strong under-representation of birds (4%, whereas other areas yielded *c.*15% birds) and no fish (other areas have 2% fish in this period). Of the 26 sheep/goat specimens, there is a preference for left-sided elements (11, as opposed to 4 right-sided). The Byzantine period yielded 83 specimens identified to taxon and element. As in the case of the Roman period, the assemblage contains no fish, which is notable when fish make up 4% of the Byzantine assemblage overall. As in the Roman period, the Byzantine assemblage contains fewer birds (7%, as opposed to 15% overall). Right-sided sheep/goat elements are twice as common as left.

---

49 MacKenzie *et al.* 2002; Kansa 2013.

50 A high occurrence of burning (100%) characterized the sample of bones studied by L. Horwitz from the Persian period at Mt. Gerizim, an assemblage also dominated by remains of sheep and goats (Magen 2008, 161); research currently underway at Haifa University on the extensive assemblages (*c.*300,000 specimens) from the Persian and Hellenistic periods promises to inform our understanding of both the taphonomic and cultural aspects of animal sacrifice.

Thus, birds are consistently under-represented in the Temple area, and fish are absent. This is not surprising for phases with few bones, but it is surprising in the Byzantine, a larger assemblage that should have produced at least a few specimens of fish. There is some indication of a bias for right-sided elements of sheep/goat in the Nabataean and Byzantine periods, and the opposite pattern in the Roman. The exclusion of certain taxa and a preference for certain sides of the body are two criteria for ritual uses of animals.[51] These patterns persist over time in the Temple area; though based on small sample sizes, they deserve further exploration.

Observations through time

The large size of the assemblage as a whole permits comparison of the cultural phases (Table 17A.4). We may expect to see changes in economic practices. For example, is there evidence for continuity of earlier Nabataean dietary traditions after the Roman annexation, or do we find a shift to Roman traditions?

The relative abundance of taxa over the different cultural phases reveals some temporal changes in animal exploitation. While the sample from the Nabataean period is small, it produces some strong patterns, in particular a dominance of goats and camels, reflecting a tradition of mobility. Supported by a near-absence of pigs, chickens and cattle, it suggests a herding economy without well-established agricultural practices. During the Nabataean period we find very little evidence for exploitation of pigs (1.7%) or birds (3.4%), which stands in contrast to subsequent periods. The Nabataean contexts have a much higher proportion of camel (10.3%) and equid (5.2%). At the Roman annexation and beyond, the abundance of camel and equid drops to less than half the Nabataean numbers. Fish amount to 5% of the Nabataean and Byzantine assemblages, but feature much less prominently in the Roman. This stands in contrast to Lev-Tov's observation that an increase in the number and types of fish, rather than an increase in pork or poultry, characterizes the Roman diet in Palestine.[52] At our site we find a heavy influence of nomadic traditions on the diet of the Nabataean inhabitants, although it remains to be determined if this pattern is specific to the Late Nabataean occupation at Petra or if mobility characterizes other Nabataean assemblages as well.

Following the Roman annexation one would expect to see changes in the diet. Elsewhere the Roman military diet had a strong impact on local dietary traditions:[53] there was a general increase in the amount of beef in the diet, at the expense of sheep (generally the least beef occurs at rural sites, the most on military sites). Emulation of the legionary diet often appears to have changed the local diet over time. Yet in the eastern provinces the 'Roman diet' appears to have had little effect: assemblages from the East continue the tradition of focussing on sheep and goats, with low numbers of cattle and pigs,[54] a pattern that suits the arid conditions in much of the region.

With the Roman annexation of Petra, sheep became a focus. They were kept to older ages than goats, indicating a focus on wool-production not observed in the Nabataean assemblage.[55] While Nabataean herds were dominated by goats, in Roman and Byzantine periods sheep became dominant, outnumbering goats by a ratio of 2 : 1. A dietary shift occurred around the point of the annexation, when pigs and birds increased to 13.1% and 38.7%, respectively. Both remain dominant in the Roman and Byzantine periods. R. Redding interpreted a similar increase of pigs and domestic fowl at Roman Tel Anafa in the Galilee as marking a distinction from the Hellenistic diet

51 Horwitz 1987.

52 Lev-Tov 2003.

53 King 1999, 182-183.

54 Ibid. 187.

55 A strong preference for goats in Site Phase IV continues into Phase VI around the time of the Roman annexation, probably reflecting a mixing of Nabataean and Roman material.

at that site.[56] At our site, the shift to a high relative proportion of chickens and pigs around the time of the annexation supports one of two things: new people arriving with different dietary practices and more luxury food items, or a general increase in wealth and prosperity. The two are not mutually exclusive, however, and the most likely scenario may be a combination of the two: following the annexation, a new, more prosperous population arrived with different dietary practices involving more diverse and luxury food items such as pork and chicken. This population may have been largely military. Studer states that chicken and other game birds can be seen as "luxury" foods because they probably cost more than the ubiquitous sheep and goats.[57] The pattern of increased fowl and pork consumption established at the time of the annexation persists in our assemblage into the Byzantine era, showing that the new dietary components became incorporated into the local dietary tradition.

Summary and conclusions

The spectrum and relative percentages of taxa in the faunal assemblage from our site — a predominance of sheep and goats, with cattle, pigs and some other domestic and wild taxa occurring in smaller numbers — fits the general pattern observed in Near Eastern faunal assemblages since Neolithic times. Changes in the relative proportions of taxa over time reflect a combination of environmental, economic, political and social factors. At our site sheep, goats and fowl contributed the bulk of the meat to the diet in all periods. Cattle bones, present in very small numbers, represent non-meaty parts, which suggests that beef was not a common item on the menu, unless it arrived at the site off the bone without leaving an archaeological trace. Even when we remember that one cow provides up to 10 times more meat than one sheep or goat, the extremely small number of specimens attests an insignificant contribution of beef to the diet. The low occurrence of cattle is probably related to Petra's location in an arid zone, which would have posed great challenges for keeping cattle, which require frequent watering and high-quality pasture.[58] Pigs and chickens contributed almost nothing to the Nabataean diet, but were present in much greater numbers from the time of Rome's annexation, pointing to the arrival of new inhabitants with different dietary practices. The high meat value of pigs, amounting to over 10% of the assemblage in non-Nabataean periods, suggests that pork featured frequently in meals, but the focus on a narrow age range suggests that production occurred elsewhere and that pork was supplied to the site through a market. The near-absence of chicken heads and feet in an assemblage of 300 chicken bones indicates that chicken parts were also probably purchased in the market, while butchery took place elsewhere, perhaps in an unexcavated area of the site. Camels are frequent in arid zones along caravan routes, and our site is no exception; while particularly common in the Nabataean period, camels are present in all periods. They appear to have served primarily as beasts of burden and secondarily as sources of meat.

The animal economy also involved the exploitation of secondary products. A distinct difference in kill-off patterns for sheep and goats indicates that sheep and goats were kept for different products: goats were killed by prime age for meat, while sheep were kept to older ages, presumably for wool production. Camels were highly valued as beasts of burden and for their products such as milk and wool, but their meat was also valued with the consumption of adult but also of young camels. A different pattern of burning on camel bones suggests that they were prepared in a different way, possibly roasted. The pattern of cut marks on chicken bones also points to differential treatment: chickens were probably cooked "bone-in" and not subjected to the same processing with knives as the other, larger food animals.

---

56 Redding 1984.

57 Studer 2002b, 280.

58 Cattle occur in higher numbers on sites farther north with higher annual rainfall; not surprisingly, these less arid sites also have few to no cattle remains.

Temporal differences are more difficult to assess due to the high number of specimens deriving from contexts attributed to multiple phases. However, the Nabataean phases show a preference for goats, while the Byzantine phases show sheep and goats in roughly equal numbers. This may indicate a preference for mutton in later periods, yet the sheep to goat ratio suggests that the change has to do with wool exploitation. It may be that the Nabataeans, accustomed to a herding lifestyle, kept goats primarily for meat, milk and hair, whereas in the Byzantine era wool became a more important focus of the economy. Fish were present in all periods, providing evidence for long-distance contacts since they derive from the Red Sea and Mediterranean Sea. Certain other food items, such as gazelle forelimbs, may also have reached the site by way of long-distance trade networks.

Our assemblage reflects a mix of market economy, local agricultural activities and industry. The chicken parts point to market supply of poultry. The dearth of cattle points to little agricultural work that would require ploughing. The presence of all body parts of sheep and goats in all periods, and all parts of pigs in the Roman through Byzantine periods, indicates that whole animals were brought to the site before butchery. Kill-off patterns for pigs (Roman and Byzantine periods) and for sheep and goats (Roman) suggest non-local production; in the Byzantine period there was a shift towards local production of sheep and goats. This emphasis on local production and decreased market activity may hint at a lowering in standards of living in the Byzantine period. A similar scenario was noted at Bet She'an (*Scythopolis*) in the Early Islamic period, where a shift in kill-off for sheep and goats, together with an increase in cattle and equids, pointed to intensified agricultural practices following a major earthquake.[59] A preponderance of head and foot bones, specifically of cattle but also of equids and camels, suggests that the inhabitants of Petra were undertaking some other kind of industry, such as tanning.

There is little evidence for class distinctions within our assemblage. MacKinnon described some possible distinctions:[60] Roman assemblages in general appear to support the notion that greater wealth is correlated with more meat in the diet, although tougher cuts and older cattle have been associated with slave deposits, while young pigs, in particular, as well as other young and wild animals have derived from élite areas. Our site has evidence both for a focus on young pigs and on the exploitation of wild taxa, including hare, one of the most expensive meats in the Roman market. These may indicate a generally wealthy population, but no specific areas or deposits can be attributed to different classes.

Although marked changes have been attributed to Roman influence on dietary practices in other regions,[61] these changes do not seem to be so marked in the Near East, possibly because of the arid environment which would not have allowed for cattle- and pig-keeping on a large scale, because of well-established dietary practices, or because Roman influence impacted the diet in different ways, such as changes in the use of flavorings and spices or in the use of non-mammalian taxa such as fish.[62] At Petra we find no increase in cattle at the time of the annexation but we do find other changes then that might be particular to the Roman presence, such as changes in the faunal spectrum and in the relative proportions of taxa. While not the beef-heavy diet attested in other parts of the Roman world,[63] the focus on pigs and chickens from the time of the annexation suggests a marked demographic change. Intensive pig production in central Italy has been interpreted as a response to increasing population density,[64] pigs being fast-producing and easy to keep in a household where they would eat kitchen scraps. Chickens also fit this model of a low-maintenance and tasty food source that fits easily into urban life. Perhaps the increase in pig and

59 Manor and Horwitz. 1997.
60 MacKinnon 2004, 225.
61 King 1999, 182-183.
62 Lev-Tov 2003.
63 King 1999, 182-183.
64 MacKinnon 2007, 489.

chicken exploitation was a response to the influx of a new population that could not be supported by the small-scale local production of the Nabataean period.

Our assemblage has provided some rare insight into Nabataean cult practices related to animal offerings. The data from the apparent offering in the Propylaeum, alongside the evidence from Khirbet et-Tannur, suggest that Nabataean cult sometimes involved animals. These probable cultic offerings are different from the daily food refuse in that they focus on a specific species and specific body parts and contain a high occurrence of burning and fragmentation. Not only in the presence of bones but also in their absence can we find evidence for possible cultural or cultic preferences; thus the absence of fish remains across our site (with the exception of two bones from the Nabataean period) is remarkable. The area of the temple has produced an assemblage that is not necessarily a "normal" refuse deposit: some other factors are impacting the faunal spectrum, and they merit further consideration.

Acknowledgements

I would like to thank Martha Sharp Joukowsky for providing me with the opportunity to analyze this assemblage and for her patience with my work, which spanned the births of my two daughters. I am grateful to Judith McKenzie and Priscilla Lange for providing helpful advice and tracking down relevant publications. Sincere thanks go to Michael MacKinnon and Justin Lev-Tov for their pertinent comments on the penultimate draft. Above all, as always, my thanks go to Eric Kansa for being my sounding board.

17B

Fish remains

Ruby Cerón-Carrasco

The primary aim of the analysis was to establish taxonomic identification and provenance of the fish remains recovered during excavations and to provide information about the contribution of fish to the diet of the inhabitants of Petra. Since the site is *c.*100 km from the sea, the assemblage was examined to determine the provenance of the fish and evaluate their importance. The implications of the movement of such an easily perishable product in terms both of supply and demand and of long-distance exchange networks will also be discussed.

Methods

The fish remains were hand-collected and dry-sieved. Taxonomic identification was made by reference to modern fish bone skeletons. All the remains were examined and identified to the highest taxonomic level (i.e., to species or family). In cases where identification was not possible due to lack of reference material, specimens were classed as "Indeterminate". Where extreme fragmentation of the skeletal element had occurred, specimens were recorded as "Unidentifiable". The nomenclature used for the skeleton follows Wheeler and Jones 1989, while taxomic nomenclature follows Beauchot and Pras 1993, Dor 1984, Goren and Dor 1994, Shpigel 1997, and Whitehead *et al.* 1986.

The recording of preservation of the bone was based on two characteristics: texture on a scale of 1 to 5 (fresh to extremely crumbly) and erosion on the same scale (none to extreme). The sum of both was used as an indication of bone condition; fresh bone would score 2, while extremely poorly preserved bone would score 10.[1] Quantification was done by number of identified species per fragment count (NISP).

Results

A total of 101 fish remains were recovered (14% of the total archaeozoological assemblage). The average preservation of the bone was quite good; bones were 40-70% whole, and 80% of those recovered being identifiable to species or family. Thirteen taxa, all belonging to marine fishes, were identified, 7 to species and 6 to family level; no freshwater fish remains were present in this assemblage. The results of the identification are given in the species representation by NISP (Table 17B.1); element representation is shown in Table 17B.2. The majority of fish remains (91% of the assemblage) were recovered from deposits dating to the Byzantine period (Table 17B.1).

Taxonomical analysis

The remains belong to species from the Mediterranean and Red Sea. They represent the following family groups (in descending order of abundance in the assemblage): *Scombridae, Serranidae, Scaridae, Sparidae, Sciaenidae,* and *Muglidae.*

The family *Scombridae* (mackerels, tunas and bonitos) includes many of the most important and familiar food fishes. Scombrids are generally predators of the open ocean and are found worldwide in tropical and temperate waters. They are capable of considerable speed, due to a highly streamlined body and retractable fins. Some members of the family, in particular the tunas, are notable for being endothermic (warm-blooded), a feature that also helps them to maintain high speed and activity. Species length varies from the 20 cm length of the mackerel to the 458 cm recorded for the immense northern blue fin tuna.

---

1 After Nicholson 1991.

TABLE 17B.1
FISH SPECIES BY NISP (per fragment count)

Family	*Genus*	*Species*	*Nabataean*	*Late Nabataean – Roman takeover*	*Roman*	*Byzantine*	*Total*	%
muglidae						2	2	1.98
Scaridae						18	18	17.82
Sciaenidae			1		1	1	3	2.97
	Sciaena	*Cf. umbra*				2	2	1.98
Serranidae			1	1	2	14	18	17.82
	Epinephelus	*Cf. fasciatus*				3	3	2.97
Scombridae								
	Euthinnus	*alletteratus*				22	22	21.78
	Thunnus	*Cf. alalunga*				2	2	1.98
Sparidae					1	4	5	4.95
	Diplodus	*Cf. noct*				1	1	0.99
	Diplodus	*Cf. vulgaris*				1	1	0.99
Indeterminate			2	2		20	24	23.76
TOTAL			4	3	4	90		101
Percentage			3.96%	2.97%	3.96%	89.11%		100.00%

Two species of this family were present, though only in Byzantine deposits: *Euthynuus alleteratus* (33.6%) and *Thunnus alalunga* (1.9%). The Little Tuna (*Euthynuus alletteratus*[2]) exists worldwide in tropical to temperate waters, including the Mediterranean Sea where it is found close inshore. It is a schooling species, and, in addition to hook and line, specialized traps (*madragues*) are commonly used to catch it. *Madrague* means "enclosure for catching tuna" and derives from the Arabic, *al mazraba*. Nets were staked down and fishermen would drive the tuna towards them.[3] The Little Tuna has a robust, torpedo-shaped body built for powerful swimming. Its flesh is darker and stronger-tasting than that of the other large tunas, which makes it suitable for salting and/or smoking. It may attain a maximum length of 122 cm. The albacore (*Thunnus alalunga*[4]) also occurs in the temperate waters of the Mediterranean Sea. These highly migratory fish move with seasonal currents. Albacore travel in large schools of mixed species that include skipjack, yellow fin and blue fin tunas. The schools are usually formed around floating objects such as sargassum weeds. The maximum recorded size is 140 cm.

Serranidae (groupers) are one of the largest families among bony fishes. Twelve species are known in the Gulf of Aqaba (Red Sea). In our assemblage only one species could be identified: *Epinephelus fasciatus* (1.9%). It was present in Nabataean, Roman and Byzantine deposits and accounts for 17.8% of the assemblage. *Epinephelus fasciatus*[5] (Black tip Grouper) is one of the most abundant groupers in the Gulf of Aqaba. As an adult it can reach up to 40 cm. Commonly found in outer reef slopes at depths below 15 m, it also swims in protected bays in shallow waters up to 4 m in depth. It is a common angling fish and can be caught by line.

Scaridae (parrot fish) derive their name from their brilliant colors and distinctive beak-like dental plates formed by the premaxilla, dentary and fused teeth. They are typical coral-reef fish, abundant in the Red Sea, Indian and Pacific Oceans. The maximum size does not vary greatly within the family, most species ranging between 30 and 45 cm in length. Parrot fish are active diurnally and commonly seen in schools in the reefs. At twilight, the schools break up and each fish finds a nighttime shelter. It secretes a thick coating of mucus in which it lies enshrouded in the reef throughout

---

2 Rafinesque 1810.
3 Toussaint-Samat 1994.
4 Bonnaterre 1788.
5 Forsskal 1775.

the night. Bedouins take advantage of this habit and catch the fish with their bare hands. One species in particular, the Bicolor Parrot Fish (*Cetoscarus bicolor*), is recorded as being caught in this manner.[6] Species of this family may also be caught using lines. The group is present only in the Byzantine deposits (13.8%).

Sparidae (breams and porgies) are found in shallow temperate waters. The family occurs in both the Mediterranean and Red Sea. The group made up 4.9% of the assemblage. They were found mainly in Byzantine deposits, with just 0.9% in Roman contexts. Two species were identified. *Diplodus vulgaris*,[7] which attains a length of 45 cm, spawns in the Mediterranean from October to November and is found in rocky and sandy substrata. It is an important fish food. *Diplodus noct*,[8] the Red Sea sea bream, is also an important fish food. Endemic to the Red Sea, it is found above sandy substratas, coral reefs and shallow coastal waters. It may attain up to 25 cm in length and can be caught on line. It is present in Roman and Byzantine deposits. *Scianidae* (croackers or drummers) are found mainly in warm seas along sandy shores. Most of the species produce a peculiar sound, hence the name "croackers". It is present in both the Mediterranean and Red Sea. One particular Mediterranean species, *Sciaena* cf. *umbra*, is present in Byzantine deposits (1.9%), while the group is present in both Roman and Byzantine contexts (4.9% of the assemblage). *Sciaena umbra*[9] may reach up to 50 cm in length. In the Mediterranean Sea the species spawns from April to July and is found in shallow coastal waters in rocky and sandy substrata. It is an important fish food. The otoliths are reportedly used today for medicinal purposes in areas of Turkey to treat urinary track infections.[10]

Muglidae (mullets or grey mullets) are found in temperate waters of the Mediterranean Sea. They are an important fish-food in our region, particularly during the Roman period.[11] The group is present only in the Byzantine deposits (1.9% of the assemblage).

General discussion

Species from both the Mediterranean and Red Sea were recovered in all the main periods, which implies that consumption of fish was not unusual at Petra. The acquisition of fish involved interactions with more than one source of supply, with fish from both the Mediterranean and Red Sea reaching the city through wider procurement systems that connected the north Jordan valley to the Mediterranean coast and the Gulf of Aqaba. This involved transporting fish over great distances. The presence of Red Sea fish suggests the existence of transport routes extending along the Rift Valley.

It is not clear from the remains if they were transported as processed fish (dried, salted or smoked). The skeletal evidence shows that most of the smaller species were brought whole, since elements from the head and vertebral column were recovered (Table 17B.2). Here it is worth noting that tuna salting in the Mediterranean region can be traced back to the Greek period when salted tuna marinated in oil was already common.[12] In the Levant there is evidence for the inland transport of Mediterranean and Red Sea fish as far back as the Chalcolithic period.[13]

The presence of marine fish at inland sites reflects both supply and demand and an exchange network. Fish may have been in real demand at Petra to fulfil social or religious purposes. In coastal communities where fish were easily collected in quantity in certain seasons (e.g., at times of

6 Shpigel 1997.
7 Geoffroy Saint-Hilaire 1817.
8 Valenciennes 1830.
9 Linné 1758.
10 Frimodt 1995.
11 Radcliffe 1926.
12 Kurlansky 2002; Toussaint-Samat 1994.
13 Cerón-Carrasco 2005.

TABLE 17B.2
FISH BONE ELEMENTS REPRESENTED BY NISP

Element	*Family*								
	Scombridae	*Serranidae*	*Scaridae*	*Scianidae*	*Sparidae*	*Muglidae*	Unknown	**Total Count**	Percentage
cleithrum		1						**1**	0.99%
dentary		2	4					**6**	5.94%
maxilla		2	1	2			1	**6**	5.94%
premaxilla		1						**1**	0.99%
quadrate					1			**1**	0.99%
vomer								**0**	0.00%
posttemporal		1	1					**2**	1.98%
hyomandibular							1	**1**	0.99%
pharyngeal		1			1			**2**	1.98%
ceratohyal			1				1	**2**	1.98%
lachrimal				1				**1**	0.99%
fin rays	1						6	**7**	6.93%
branchiostegals							6	**6**	5.94%
atlas vertebra							1	**1**	0.99%
precaudal veterbrae	8	4	1		2			**15**	14.85%
caudal vertebra	15	9	10		3	2	2	**41**	40.59%
Unidentified fragment								**8**	7.92%
TOTAL	24	21	18	3	7	2	26	101	
Percentage	23.76%	20.79%	17.82%	2.97%	6.93%	1.98%	25.74%		

spawning), a temporary local surplus could have been converted into a valuable exchange product. The scale of the activity is suggested by the presence in the Byzantine phase of more than one species of both Red Sea and Mediterranean origin. While very few remains were recovered from Nabataean and Roman deposits, the available remains show traces of similar instances of fish procurement not unlike those of the Byzantine period. We may note that at nearby Ez Zantur the excavation of Byzantine domestic deposits yielded large amounts of fish remains, as well as 12 taxa from Nabataean deposits and 8 taxa from Late Roman deposits. Species from the Red Sea were mainly present, although some, such as the Eastern Little Tuna, may have originated in the Mediterranean.[14]

Conclusion

The marine species from the Red Sea and the Mediterranean are indicative of the long-term exchange of marine species to this inland site. The presence of fish remains in a variety of deposits over long periods implies the inhabitants' use of regular sources from coastal areas. Unlike other marine products brought from the coast such as shell beads, which could last for years, fish, whether fresh, dried or salted, are a consumable. The fish bone assemblage provides evidence for frequent and continuing interactions with coastal communities, perhaps as part of a wider framework for the acquisition of other products of the sea and shore.

14 Desse-Berset and Studer 1996; Studer 2002.

TABLE 17B.3
CATALOGUE OF FISH REMAINS, PETRA GREAT TEMPLE

Bone #	*Period*	*Element/side*	*Count*	*Taxa*	*Texture*	*Erosion*	*Condition*	*Element %*	*Comment*
GT3367-GT3371	Byzantine	precaudal vertebra	2	Tuna	3	3	6	65	
		dentary/right	1	*Scaridae*	3	4	7	60	proximal
		precaudal vertebra	1	*Serranidae*	3	4	7	60	
GT357	Byzantine	caudal vertebra	1	Tuna	3	4	7	65	
GT3418-GT3419	Byzantine	caudal vertebra	1	Tuna	3	3	6	65	
		caudal vertebra	1	Unidentifiable	4	4	8		
GT2080	Byzantine	caudal vertebra	2	Tuna	3	3	6	65	
		fragments	2	Unidentifiable	3	4	7	10	
GT0937	Byzantine	precaudal vertebra	4	Tuna	3	3	6	65	
		caudal vertebra	10	Tuna	3	3	6	65	
		fin ray	1	Tuna?	3	3	6	65	
GT0938	Byzantine	precaudal vertebra	2	*Serranidae*	3	3	6	65	
GT3514- GT3515	Byzantine	precaudal vertebra	2	Tuna	3	4	7	60	
GT229- GT234	Byzantine	dentary/right	1	*Serranidae*	4	4	8	60	proximal
		maxilla/right	1	*Serranidae*	4	4	8	50	proximal
		vomer	1	*Scaridae*	3	4	7	65	proximal
		premaxilla/right	1	*Serranidae*	4	4	8	40	proximal
GT1298	Byzantine	dentary/left	1	*Scaridae*	3	4	7	70	proximal
GT1207-GT1208	Roman	posttemporal	1	*Scaridae*	3	4	7	70	proximal
		maxilla/left	1	*Scaridae*	3	4	7	60	proximal
GT3023	Byzantine	dorsal fin	1	Indeterminate	3	4	7	60	
GT149-GT150	Byzantine	maxilla/left	1	*Sciaena cf umbra*	3	3	6	70	proximal
		fin ray	1	Indeterminate	3	4	7	60	
GT75-GT81	Byzantine	dentary/left	1	*Epinephalus cf fasciatus*	3	4	7	60	proximal
		pharyngeal	1	*Serranidae*	3	4	7	75	
		caudal vertebra	1	*Epinephalus cf fasciatus*	3	3	6	75	
		branchiostegal	2	Indeterminate	3	4	7	40	
		fin ray	1	Indeterminate	3	4	7	40	
		posttemporal	1	*Serranidae*	3	4	7	60	medial
GT885	Byzantine	maxilla/right	1	Indeterminate	3	4	7	60	medial
GT720	Byzantine	maxilla/right	1	*Sciaena cf umbra*	3	3	6	70	proximal
GT2828-GT2831	Byzantine	dentary/right	1	*Scaridae*	3	4	7	70	proximal
		dentary/left	1	*Scaridae*	3	4	7	70	proximal
		caudal vertebra	1	*Scaridae*	3	4	7	65	
		ceratohyal	1	*Scaridae*	3	4	7	60	
GT407	Byzantine	caudal vertebra	5	*Scaridae*	3	4	7	65	
GT2802	Byzantine	precaudal vertebra	5	*Scaridae*	3	4	7	65	

Bone #	*Period*	*Element/side*	*Count*	*Taxa*	*Texture*	*Erosion*	*Condition*	*Element %*	*Comment*
GT2126	Byzantine	caudal vertebra	4	*Scaridae*	3	4	7	65	
GT15- GT18	Byzantine	caudal vertebra	1	cf Albacore	3	3	6	60	
		precaudal vertebra	1	*Pagrus sp*	3	4	7	60	
		atlas vertebra	1	Unidentified					
GT260	Byzantine	precaudal vertebra	1	*Diplodus cf noct*	3	4	7	60	
GT200	Byzantine	caudal vertebra	1	*Diplodus cf vulgaris*	3	4	7	60	
GT3535	Byzantine	ceratohyal	1	Indeterminate	4	4	8	50	medial
GT3475-GT3476	Byzantine	skull fragment	1	Indeterminate	4	4	8	40	
		fin ray	1	Indeterminate	3	4	7	65	
GT1773	Unknown	precaudal vertebra	1	*Serranidae*?	4	4	8	60	
GT1317	Byzantine	caudal vertebra	1	*Serranidae*	3	4	7	60	
GT205	Byzantine	caudal vertebra	1	*Muglidae*	4	4	8	50	
GT0671-GT0673	Roman	quadrate/right	1	*Sparidae?*	3	4	7	60	proximal
		hyomandibular	1	Indeterminate	4	4	8	50	medial
		branchiostegal	1	Indeterminate	4	4	8	40	
GT3679- GT3680	Roman	caudal vertebra	2	*Serranidae*	3	4	7	60	
GT3263	NAB/ROM	skull fragment	1	Indeterminate	4	4	8	30	
GT302	Byzantine	caudal vertebra	1	*Serranidae*	3	3	6	60	
GT2412	Byzantine	caudal vertebra	1	*Serranidae*	4	4	8	50	
GT2562- GT2563	Byzantine	caudal vertebra	1	*Diplodus cf Sargus*	3	4	7	65	
		pharyngeal	1	*Sparidae*	3	4	7	60	
GT2290	Byzantine	cleithra/left	1	*Serranidae*?	4	4	8	60	medial
GT2482	Byzantine	fin ray	1	Indeterminate	4	4	8	30	
		branchiostegal	3	Indeterminate	4	4	8	30	
GT0589	Roman	fin ray	1	Indeterminate	3	4	7	50	
GT2206	Roman	caudal vertebra	1	*Sparidae*	4	4	8	60	
GT182	Byzantine	caudal vertebra	1	*Serranidae*	4	4	8	60	
GT821	Byzantine	maxilla/left	1	*Sciaenidae*	4	4	8	50	proximal
GT3742	Nabataean	lachrimal	1	*Sciaenidae?*	4	4	8	50	medial
GT2606	Roman	caudal vertebra	1	*Serranidae*	3	4	7	60	
GT1156	Nabataean	caudal vertebra	1	*Serranidae*	3	4	7	65	
		caudal vertebra	1	Indeterminate	4	4	8	60	

17C

Human skeletal remains (2000-2003)

Megan A. Perry

Human skeletal remains were recovered during the 2000, 2001 and 2003 seasons from various contexts along the East Perimeter Wall of the Temple and from the East Propylaeum. All of the remains come from contexts following the A.D. 363 earthquake destruction, with the exception of a jar burial recovered from Tr. 84, Locus 31.[1]

Burials along the East Perimeter Wall

The remains of 4 infants and 1 adult were recovered from deposits along the East Perimeter Wall of the Temple complex. Two of these individuals were recovered as separate but incomplete skeletons, two as disarticulated remains, while the fifth was represented by only 3 arm bones.

Tabun *Cave Room, Tr. 77, Locus 1*

Excavations in 2000 in a natural cavity in the bedrock at the S end of the East Perimeter Wall (the *Tabun* Cave Room) revealed disarticulated skeletal remains in the uppermost strata. They derived from two individuals, a child *c.*7 years (± 24 months) and a male adult.[2] Fusion of the epiphyses indicates that this is an adult individual, but a more exact age could not be estimated.

The skeletal remains were recovered from sloping layers within the cave, probably fluvial deposits. The bones were very water-worn and in poor condition. It is not clear if these individuals had been buried in the cave and been displaced or damaged by water entering the area, or if they had been washed down from above the cave. The initial excavation report indicated that the arms of one individual were in correct anatomical position, providing support for the first scenario over the second.

Room B, Tr. 84, Locus 10

In 2001, the bottom half of a jar containing an infant burial was found in a terminal corridor (Room B) within the casemate of the East Perimeter Wall.[3] The jar lay on top of the bedding (Locus 35) for the original 1st c. B.C./1st c. A.D. pavers, which had been robbed in the mid-2nd c. The burial thus falls anywhere between the mid-2nd c. and the earthquake of A.D. 363 that caused the room to be filled with architectural débris, covering the jar. The jar contained the incomplete skeletal remains of an infant who died around the time of birth (i.e., gestational age of 9 months). The growth of the deciduous dentition suggests that the child died anywhere between birth and 2 months of age,[4] but estimations of body length from long bone and scapula measurements imply that the child died 9-9.5 months after conception,[5] i.e., right around the time of birth.[6] The newborn had active *cribra orbitalia* in the upper portion of its eye orbits, a condition that often results from iron-deficiency anemia but can be caused by other conditions such as vitamin C deficiency.[7] This

1 Perry and Joukowsky 2006, 171.
2 Vol. 2, 176 (incorrectly identified them as a male child and an adult). The age of the child was determined by its stage of dental development following standards developed by Moorrees *et al.* 1963 and by Ubelaker 1989. The sex of the adult individual was estimated through morphological observations of cranial fragments following Buikstra and Ubelaker 1994.
3 Perry and Joukowsky 2006.
4 Moorrees *et al.* 1963a.
5 Fazekas and Kósa 1978.
6 It was mistakenly estimated as 9 months old after birth, not 9 months after gestation, in Joukowsky and Perry 2006, 173.
7 Aufderheide and Rodríguez-Martín 1998; Wapler *et al.* 2004.

evidence for a poor diet more directly reflects that of the mother, since the child was *in utero* during most if not all of its existence before it died.

Room A,Tr. 84 Locus 14

In the same season, the almost complete burial of another newborn was recovered from Locus 14, a thick layer of fluvial and windblown deposits that covered Rooms A and B in the casemate of the East Perimeter Wall. The date of these deposits ranges anywhere from the 4th-5th c. A.D. up through the Late Islamic period. The infant bones, which were discovered near the skull of a dog, originally had been collected as faunal remains and were missing many elements (e.g., the vertebrae, parts of the skull, and portions of the pelvis). The age of this individual was achieved primarily from long bone and ilium measurements. The long bone measurements indicate that this infant died *c.*11-12 weeks after birth.[8] He or she suffered from a systematic infection that caused porosity and periostitis on many of the bones (e.g., femur, tibia, humerus, radius, ulna and clavicle), but its cause cannot be determined.

Room A, Tr. 84, Locus 9

In the same season, the scant remains of another infant were discovered in fill (Locus 9) that collected naturally within Room A directly on top of the supposed collapse caused by the A.D. 363 earthquake. The bones recovered include the right femur and left radius and ulna probably from a single individual. Their proximity to the jar burial of Locus 10 made it tempting to suggest that these unassociated arm bones came from that individual, but a left ulna and radius already present inside the jar show these bones come from completely different individuals. The long bones provide an estimate of 11-12 weeks old from birth.[9] The bones presented no pathologies or other anomalies.

The East Propylaeum

Tr. 96, Locus 1

In 2003, two adult bones, possibly from the same individual, were recovered from the uppermost layer within the E section of the Propylaeum. They consist of a second metacarpal from the hand and talus from the foot. Sex and a more precise age could not be estimated, nor were any pathologies or other anomalies observed.

Summary

The remains of 4 infants were recovered from post-occupational deposits along the East Perimeter Wall of the Great Temple. One was discovered buried in a large jar of an unknown date, but its stratigraphic context suggested that the infant was buried between the 2nd and 4th c. A.D. Another relatively complete infant skeleton, found at a higher stratum in the same vicinity, dates to after the earthquake of A.D. 363. A third infant was found within the Tabun Cave deposits at the S end of the wall. Lastly, three bones of another infant were found on top of same earthquake's débris. These data suggest that the East Perimeter Wall may have served as an informal location for the interment of infants from the Roman through the Islamic eras, although adult bones were also found at the S end of the same perimeter wall. The two adult bones found in the East Propylaeum probably washed down from a burial placed in the upper sector of the Temple, perhaps indeed close to those along the East Perimeter Wall.

These data should provide further evidence for use of southern parts of the city center for burials after the earthquake and subsequent seismic events levelled the buildings in this area. We may also note that Byzantine-era burials were recovered near Qasr al-Bint, to the west of the Great Temple,[10] and that more burials may exist in the débris between these two monuments.

---

8 Scheuer *et al.* 1980.
9 Ibid.
10 Zayadine 2003, 96.

18A

The worked bone objects

Martha Sharp Joukowsky and Etan Ayalon

This section presents the bone objects deserving of attention, with the exceptions of the handle in the form of a leg and the hippopotamus tusk presented in the following sections.

The use of bone was well established in antiquity, and it appears to have been very popular for personal adornment and tools, alongside other common raw materials. We know less about worked bone than we do about pottery, stone or glass because bone is a more perishable material and does not survive as well. Bone was carved into a wide range of artifacts including rings, hairpins and hair ornaments, needles and combs, gaming pieces, *styli*, spindle whorls, and spoons, as well as various working tools. It was also employed for parts of other objects such as knife or mirror handles, decorative inlays for furniture, and small items like boxes.

In the catalogue containing 59 objects as many as 22 pieces (36%) derive from Site Phase IX around the time of and following the A.D. 363 earthquake, while 9 derive from Site Phase XI (after the earthquake of 551), both being part of what we term the Byzantine period. The Upper Temenos deposits produced 24 (41%), the Lower Temenos 18 (31%), the Temple sector 12 (20%), and the Propylaeum 5 (8%). One object was registered without a context. All of our objects are made of animal bone, primarily large domesticates such as cattle, camels and donkeys. Usually leg bones and shoulder blades were favored; a few objects were identified as ivory, but none was examined by an osteologist. This chapter does not consider the technological aspects of bone and ivory production.

Functional categories and discussion

The uses to which many objects were put in antiquity are often difficult to identify. Some objects could be used in various ways, and many modern works reach different assessments of the same kind of object. Decorated inlay, rings and handles are usually identifiable, but a wide array of other objects is often difficult to differentiate (e.g., buttons from spindle whorls, spools from rings, pins from needles or piercers). Many bone objects are unique, for a bone tool cannot be precisely duplicated.[1] Many kinds of objects remain in use over a long period (e.g., the pin throughout the Roman and Byzantine periods).

The bone implements were arranged in 9 broad groups. There are 9 rings and ring fragments, 3 discoid objects, 8 pins and 3 pin heads/crowns, 4 possible spoons, 3 likely containers, 7 decorative pieces including 2 probable comb-like pieces for inlay, 2 hinge heads, and 4 buttons. One-of-a-kind pieces include a container tag, a furniture mount, and hand-held tools like the awl, a *stylus,* a handle and an engraver. There is also a bead, a point, a spool, a rod, a gaming piece, and miscellaneous pieces such as industrial waste, an unidentified object, a lid, the head of a tool, and an eye socket.

Rings

Six ring or ring fragments have been recovered. They are all simple hoops and only partially preserved. Only two (no. 40 of Site Phase X and no. 47 of Site Phase XI) are decorated: the first is decorated with a series of engraved circles enclosing dots, while the second is incised with X's and dots. Some may have been suitable for simple finger rings, or, in the case of no. 50, possibly as an earring. Conceivably some undecorated rings were used to provide a footing for small containers, while others may have served as buttons, as K. M. Elderkin suggested.[2] Rings are commonplace in

1 Ayalon 2005, 5.
2 Elderkin 1928, fig. 1.

European bone assemblages and could also have served as part of a chain or decoration, even part of the closing apparatus for a sack or bag. Ring production was widespread in Petra.[3] Items nos. 17 and 20 might be rough waste remains and not finished rings.

Disks

Disks include items that could have served as buttons or spindle whorls. Often they were catalogued in the field as spindle whorls as all but one is discoid in shape and features a central hole. No. 11 (fig. 18.4) without a conical hole may have been an unfinished button or industrial waste. No. 46 may probably be classed as a button because of its shape. At Corinth, G. R. Davidson used size and appearance to classify spindle whorls[4] while distinguishing spindle whorls from buttons, and we have followed her lead but have still grouped them all as "disks" because we are unable to identify their functions securely. It is possible that well-balanced objects of the same thickness throughout, with few signs of use wear in the central hole, were spindle whorls, as spinning necessitated balance while the weight is well fixed on the rod. On the other hand, a button does not have to be balanced and its hole should show much wear caused by the string tying it. Davidson suggested that similar items possibly served as bottle stoppers;[5] indeed, nos. 46 and 48 could have been *pyxis* lids.

Pins[6]

This large group includes objects that are characterized by being long and pointed. Most are made from the compact leg bones of large animals. Superior to wooden objects, they are hard and relatively strong. They could serve as pins, needles, piercers, cosmetic applicators, or *styli*. Bone pins are attested well before Nabataean times, and they were not completely replaced by metal pins and needles.

Included in this category are a needle (no. 39, fig. 18.16), a possible engraver (no. 38) and a piercing tool (no. 52). Only 4 pins are complete with their decorated finials: no. 14 (fig. 18.6 middle), no. 53, no. 43 (figs. 18.6 left and 18.16), and no. 28 (fig. 18.12). The shape of the finial and the presence of any embellishments such as carved lines have been noted in the catalogue. Four pieces were found in the Upper Temenos, the Lower Temenos and the Temple area. None was recovered from the Propylaeum.

The best representative of pins or pointed tools is no. 43 (figs. 18.6 left, 18.16) dated to Site Phase X, with a series of grooves on the elongated oval head. Most pins feature a finial. Terminal crowns could also be the decoration for surgical tools or other objects, but we have grouped them with pins. A few carry a carved finial (ovoid, round, globular, flame-like, or pyramidal). With such a diversity of finials, we assume they were used for decorating female dress or hair. Hairstyles depicted in the Late Roman period are often held together or adorned with hairpins.

One pin (no. 53) has a bronze attachment. This pin was held in place by wrapping the bronze thread around the shaft near the end. No. 12, a pin head/crown from Site Phase VIII, may have been the finial for any number of different tools. The well-preserved needle no. 39 (fig. 18.16) may be of ivory. No. 52 may have been used for piercing holes in cloth, similar to an awl in function. It and pin no. 15 (fig. 18.7) are examples of the *ad hoc* use of slightly modified animal bones as tools.

---

3 Cf. Schneider-Naef 2005. Compare finds at Caesarea: Ayalon 2005, 150-51, with further parallels; Dray 2005.

4 Davidson 1952, 172.

5 Ibid. 296.

6 At the beginning of our project we classified sea urchin spines (echinoderms) as bone pin fragments because we found a few that had been modified. When we realized what they were, we eliminated them from the field catalogue. In 2008 in the Bath Complex we found a dump of *c.*5500 sea urchin spines.

Items previously considered spatulas

Three objects, no. 35 (fig. 18.14), no. 21 and no. 55, were originally categorized as spatulas because the working end is flat, but the first finds its closest parallel in a so-called "container tag" found in the Lyon collection, no. 21 is identified as a rod, and no. 55 has been classified as a spoon like similar objects from Ez Zantur and Alexandria. We appear to have no spatulas.

Other objects like no. 38, may be *stylus* or engraver. At Corinth, Davidson suggested that the *stylus* class was probably employed for mixing unguents.[7]

Spoons

Two spoons with oval bowls, no. 44 (fig. 18.19) and no. 59 (fig. 18.22) are generally referred to as *ligulae*, which had various functions.[8] No. 55 is also a fragmented spoon.

Spools

The three small spools catalogued here (nos. 8, 24, 1) look like the modern bobbin, but they may have served a different function. They are too small in diameter (1.48, 1.22, 1.34 cm, respectively) to be classed as rings, and they do not appear to be lids or buttons. Possibly they served as furniture mounts, hinge heads or as added decoration for hand-held tools. They are characterized by a central hole and raised rings around the body.

Containers

Three fragmentary bone containers were perhaps used for precious unguents, kohl or perfumes, but we have found no close parallels. One (no. 22) with a ring base. No. 54 is a neck fragment perhaps of a box or a *pyxis*. No. 3 is enigmatic and was found in a Nabataean context. No. 22 is from Site Phase IX and no. 54 is from Site Phase XIII. Two came from the Upper Temenos and one from the Temple.

Decorative elements and those without a clear category

Two fragmentary items were found in the Upper Temenos and one in the Propylaeum, neither in contexts earlier than the Roman annexation. No. 18 (fig. 18.9) and no. 31 are thought to be decorative piece inlays.[9] Both belong to Site Phase IX in the Propylaeum. No. 9 with its pyramidal-shaped teeth may have served a different purpose.

Six additional items are classified as decorative motifs. No. 45 possibly served as a gaming piece. No. 32 was cut into a specific shape to decorate a small object such as a powder box or piece of furniture. No. 34 (fig. 18.13) is an elegant piece of carved bone presumably used as an inset for furniture. We suggest no. 7 (fig. 18.2) may have served as a decorative element for the lid of a box. No. 16 is carved on both sides with engraved designs of intricate encircled dots. No. 42 (fig. 18.17) is an unusual insert, an elliptical eye socket that probably embellished a piece of sculpture. A bone handle, no. 37, is also included in this final grouping; bone produces a natural socket for the tang of a knife, dagger, or mirror to be inserted.

It is clear that raw bone materials were readily available at the site. Techniques for bone working (drilling, cutting, polishing) had been developed long before the Nabataean era. There is no firm evidence to suggest that any of these pieces were imported as finished luxury items, but at Ez Zantur (Schneider-Naef 2005) the amount of bone roughs and waste found proved that a workshop for the production of bone items operated within Petra itself. Nos. 11, 17, 20-21, 23-24 and 32-33 may belong to this category. We therefore assume that some of our collection was locally made while others were imported.

---

7 Ibid. 182.

8 Ibid. 189.

9 Joukowsky first identified them as string instrument bridges, a suggestion also made by Alice Choyke and László Bartosiewicz (pers. comm.).

CATALOGUE

A sample of objects excavated from 1993 to 2006 is presented here, arranged according to Phase (from Pre-Site Phase I to Phase XIII, followed by unassigned finds). Dimensions are given in cm. Additional photographs but at varying scales can be found in *Open Context*.

For comparanda we have turned chiefly to the following sources: the Petra excavations at Ez Zantur (Schneider-Naef 2005) and the Petra Church (Fiema *et al.* 2001), and Hesban (Ray 2009). Further afield are the excavations at Alexandria (Rodziewicz 2007) and Caesarea Maritima (Ayalon 2005; Dray 2005). Other Israeli sites considered include Ashkelon (Wapnish 1991, 2008), Tel Beth Shean (Ayalon 2006), Samaria-Sebaste (Kenyon 1957), Ein Gedi (Chernov 2007), and Ramat Hanadiv (Kol-Yaakov 2000). Comparanda further afield are in France (Sautot 1978; Béal 1983), Augusta Raurica (Deschler-Erb 1998) in Switzerland, Hungary (Bíró 1994; Bíró *et al.* 2012), and Corinth (Davidson 1952).

The use of certain objects, such as the pin or needle, is fairly clear, but the variety of worked bone testifies to a wide range of activities, from personal adornment or gaming to spinning and weaving or furniture inlay. No attempt is made here to justify our suggested identifications, and alternatives are sometimes offered. In some cases we have changed an identification from that given in the online database; the latter is then retained in parenthesis following the new identification. Joukowsky's identification in 2009 of the items catalogued here was based on photographs and the catalogue. In the field, each supervisor plotted and recorded bone artifacts in the notebook and also maintained a log with the sequential listing of the artifacts by trench for the online catalogue. The bone items were originally recorded and identified by D. G. Barrett and Joukowsky.

Pre-Site Phase I

1. 05-B-10
Furniture mount or spool ring. Diam. 1.34, inner diam. 0.65, th. 0.57, wt. 1.1 gm. The perforation cavity is partially squared-off.
Temple, SP107, Locus 9.
Cf. pieces from Alexandria (Rodziewicz 2007, pl. 42, no. 249) identified as a hinge or (pl. 43, no. 259) as a furniture mount; Corinth (Davidson 1952, pl. 64, no. 868: furniture joint); Hesban (Ray 2009, fig. 13.2.31, Object 299). It could also be a stopper through which an applicator or handle was inserted.

Site Phase I

2. 05-B-1
Button ("spindle whorl"). Diam. 2.55, wt. 0.9 gm. Half of the object is present, resembling a wheel.
Lower Temenos, SP104, Locus 20.
A button from Caesarea (Ayalon 2005, fig. 6, no. 58) is comparable; one from Alexandria (Rodziewicz 2007, pl. 59, no. 477) also resembles our button, there identified as appliqué; Hesban (Ray 2009, fig. 12.2.31, no. 299).

Site Phase IV

3. 00-B-10 (fig. 18.1)
Container. Ht. 3.42, diam. 2.80, th. 0.35, int. diam. 1.55. The interior has been carved away as if to hold a liquid or precious object.
Upper Temenos, Tr. 77, Locus 93.
Cf. a furniture mount from Caesarea dated to the Early Arab period (Ayalon 2005, fig. 45, no. 422), and a box dated to the Roman period (ibid. fig. 12, no. 129).

4. 96-B-1
Button ("spindle whorl"). Diam. 3.05, th. 0.68, central hole 0.45.
Upper Temenos, Tr. 18, Locus 3.
Cf. a "game counter" or "button" from Alexandria (Rodziewicz 2007, pl. 63, no. 518; pl. 58, no. 466).

5. 95-B-6
Ring fragment ("unidentified fragment"), a plain loop of bone. Diam. 3.2, th. 0.6.
A plain simple loop of bone. Too large to serve as a finger ring unless to be worn on a thumb, probably from waste of ring production.
Lower Temenos, Tr. 16, Locus 23.
Cf. a Roman "lathe carved ring" at Caesarea (Ayalon 2005, fig. 51, no. 496).

6. 95-B-8
Ring fragment, ring waste-production ("unidentified fragment"). Diam. 3.2. Roughly one-third of a ring, sharp lower and upper edges, top and sides smoothly finished; rough underneath probably due to breakage. Unevenly carved with a rather large central hole.
Lower Temenos, Tr. 16, Locus 23.

Fig. 18.1: cat. no. 3.

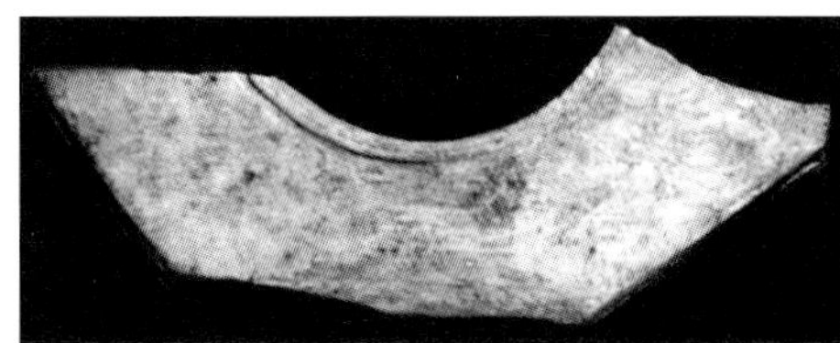
Fig. 18.2: cat. no. 7.

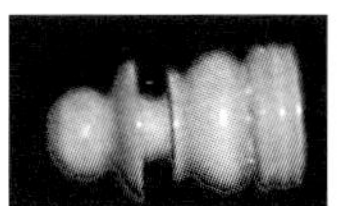
Fig. 18.3: cat. no. 10.

Fig. 18.4: cat. no. 11.

Site Phase V

7. 97-B-3 (fig. 18.2)
Decorative fragment ("unknown"). L. 5.94, w. 1.28, th. 0.51. A flat triangular, possibly hexagonal fragment with a curved cut-out, etched with a ridge on one side.
Upper Temenos, Tr. 41, Locus 21.
From Caesarea comes a similarly decorative piece (Ayalon 2005, fig. 54, no. 517), identified as "disk production waste", dated to the Roman period. It is suggested (ibid. 116) that it may also be "a lid, inlay or blank for a circular object". It could be made to receive an additional round inlay (possibly of a different material), inserted in its hole, or it could be the lid of a hexagonal container, with a central hole to hold an applicator or a handle.

Site Phase VI

8. 02-B-8
Hinge head. H. 1.03, w. 1.66.
Upper Temenos, Tr. 89, Locus 28.
For a close parallel at Caesarea, cf. a hinge of the 3rd-4th c. A.D. (Ayalon 2005, fig. 15, no. 154); Hungary (Bíró *et al.* 2012, 113, no. 331).

9. 02-B-7
Decorative piece inlay ("comb?"). L. 8.43, h. 1.07, th. 0.57. Width of the tooth at widest part 1.47. Four pyramidal-shaped, evenly spaced teeth along the shaft.
Upper Temenos, Tr. 94, Locus 63.
This unusual object is probably a decorative piece/inlay, like a cornice. For the general shape (but not identical) cf. Alexandria (Rodziewicz 2007, pl. 29, nos. 112-13), classified as a flat "triangular tympanum", decoration for a box lid; En-Gedi (Chernov 2007, 526, fig. 69, mentioning a similar object from Nessana, which is identified as "binding strips for papyri"). An object from Szöny, Hungary (Bíró 1994, pl. 67, no. 578) is classified as a double-sided furniture inlay with holes.

10. 01-B-16 (fig. 18.3)
Hinge crown ("pin crown or finial"). H. 1.47, th. 0.84, wt. 0.8 gm. Intricately-carved hinge crown, finished with decorative knobs. Perforated from top to bottom with a side hole that could be accidental or served to accommodate the insertion of a metal pin.
Upper Temenos, Tr. 84, Locus 18.
Cf. Corinth (Davidson 1952, 190, pl. 84, no. 1394). This terminal shape at Corinth is attached to an ivory spoon; no interior perforation is noted. Cf. Szöny (Bíró 1994, pl. 70, no. 596), which is a little different, and (ibid. pl. 62, nos. 539-540) "spindle heads"; longer, socketed handle heads from Dijon (Sautot 1978, pl. 18, nos. 6-9).

Site Phase VII

11. 01-B-15 (fig. 18.4)
Industrial waste ("counter"). Diam. 1.87, th. 0.36, wt. 2.2 gm. Small round counter that originally may have been stained red (traces of stain on one surface).
Upper Temenos, Tr. 84, Locus 15.
Industrial waste (output of drilling a hole in a flat piece of bone) or unfinished object (disk, lid, button, etc.).

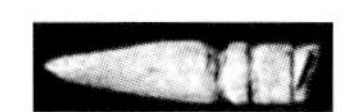

Fig. 18.5: cat. no. 13.

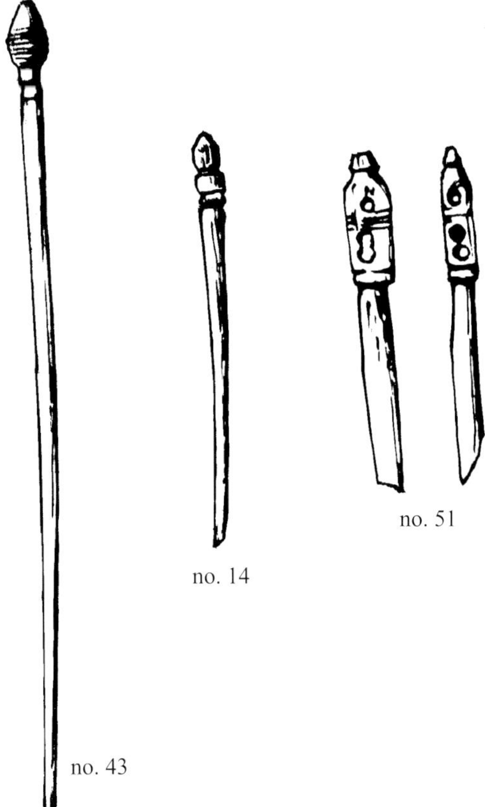

Fig. 18.6. Pins no. 43 (left), cat. no. 14 (middle), cat. no. 51 (right).

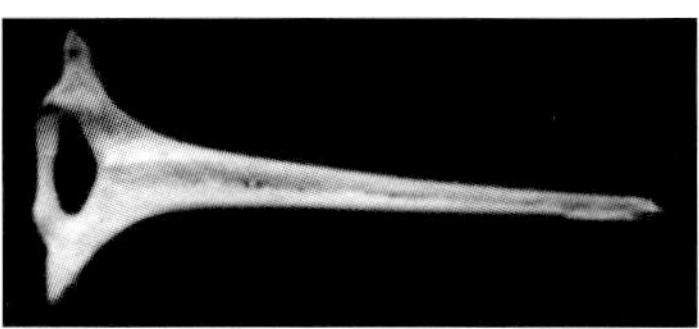

Fig. 18.7: cat. no. 15.

Site Phase VIII

12. 06-B-3
Pin head. L. 4.77, th. 0.41, wt. 1.1 gm. Crown is intact but point is missing. The shaft narrows near the point.
Upper Temenos, Tr. 125, Locus 18.
Cf. Corinth (Davidson 1952, 186, pl. 83, no. 1362). Caesarea (Ayalon 2005, fig. 21, no. 206) is similar to ours, but our pin head has a pronounced projecting collar.

13. 95-B-2 (fig. 18.5)
Pin crown ("peg"). L. 2.6, w. 0.6. Fragment tapered to a point with two grooves carved at the neck and a fragmented third groove.
Lower Temenos, Tr. 20, Locus 22.
Caesarea (Ayalon 2005, fig. 22, no. 236) bears a close resemblance, although it is grooved and identified there as a "pin with a grooved drop-shaped head". Also at Caesarea 7 pins of this type are found from the Hellenistic to the Byzantine period. One pin (Late Byzantine period) was gilded. A flame-like finial from Alexandria is comparable (Rodziewicz, 2007, no. 313). A similar object appears at Ashkelon (Wapnish 2008, fig. 34.17). Previously published in vol. 1, fig. 6.120.

14. 95-B-11 (fig. 18.6, middle)
Pin. L. 5.3, w. 0.35. Triple grooves below the crown, quadrilateral head, polished to a high sheen.
Temple, Tr. 23, Locus 7.
This pin is similar to no. 27 (02-B-4) in shape, with a decorative ovoid knob at the end offset by decorative grooves. Cf. Szöny, Hungary (Bíró 1994, pl. 29, nos. 318-19; Bíró *et al.* 2012, 89, nos. 125 and 128) and Augusta Raurica (Deschler-Erb 1998, pl. 35, no. 3398).

15. 97-B-4 (fig. 18.7)
Pin. L. 4.3, w. 1.82. The top has an ovoid opening and "wings". *Ad hoc* use of a slightly modified animal bone as a tool.
Temple, Tr. 34, Locus 14, 1997.
Cf. Ez Zantur (Schneider-Naef 2005, fig. 52, no. 8). Previously published in vol. 1, fig. 6.119.

16. 95-B-9
Incised decorative fragment ("unidentified ornamental fragment"). L. 3.3, th. 0.8. Carved design of irregularly placed dots and grooves on the front surface, random slashes on the back. Tapered from the middle to the thin end with decorations made by a drill.
Temple, Tr. 23, Locus 7.
The object could be part of a doll, handle or even castanet handle. Cf. Caesarea (Ayalon 2005, fig. 57, no. 546); Beth Shean (Ayalon 2006, 670, fig. 23.1, no. 7); Alexandria (Rodziewicz 2007, pl. 34, no. 146). Previously published in vol. 1, fig. 6.119.

Site Phase IX

17. 01-B-13 (fig. 18.8)
Ring or its production waste ("unknown"). Diam. 3.44, th. 0.35, wt. 1.9 gm. Broken with ridging and flare at the bottom. Too large for a finger ring, it may have been used as a vessel support.
Propylaeum, Tr. 80, Locus 16.
Two rings from Caesarea bear comparison. The first (Ayalon 2005, fig. 51, no. 495) is a "lathe-carved ring" (Roman-Byzantine). The second (ibid. fig. 25, no. 264) (2nd-4th c.) may be closer in shape to our piece. Cf. also Ez Zantur (Schneider-Naef 2005, fig. 11, no. 53, 4th c.).

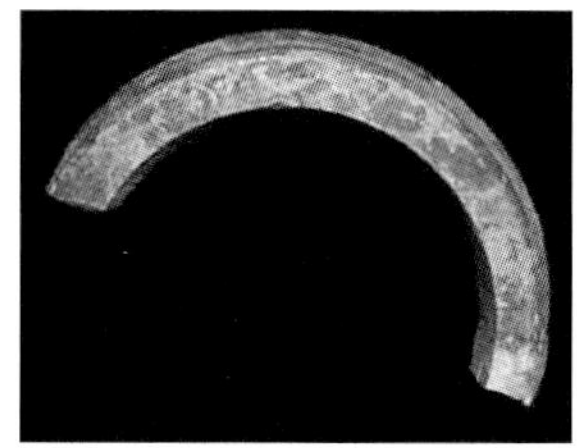
Fig. 18.8: cat. no. 17.

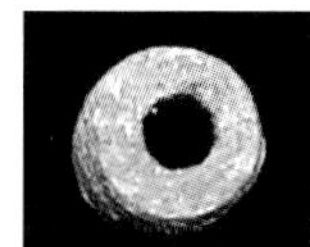
Fig. 18.10: cat. no. 24.

Fig. 18.9: cat. no. 18.

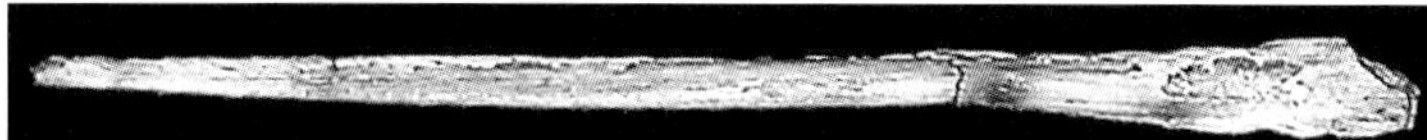
Fig. 18.11: cat. no. 23.

18. 03-B-1 (fig. 18.9)
Decorative inlay ("unidentified object"). L. 3.5, w. 0.04, th. 0.04. This object has 11 slots cut on the diagonal, perhaps to insert some sort of decorative inlay.
Propylaeum, Tr. 96, Locus 1.
Cf. Alexandria (Rodziewicz 2007, pl. 29, nos. 112-13), classified as a flat "triangular tympanum", decoration for a box lid. Cf. above for the possibility that it was a string instrument bridge (but contrast the different shape in Caesarea [Ayalon 2005, fig. 58, nos. 273-74]).

19. 04-B-09
Point ("pin/spatula"). L. 5.59, th. 0.74, wt. 0.7 gm. *Ad hoc* use of a slightly modified animal bone as a tool, with a sharpened tip, showing use wear.
Lower Temenos, Tr. 97, Locus 9.
Perhaps comparable to Caesarea (Ayalon 2005, fig. 4, no. 44).

20. 01-B-14
Ring or ring production waste. Diam. 1.74, th. 0.29, w. 0.2 gm. A plain, simple loop, half missing.
Upper Temenos, SP84, Locus 27.
Many of these were found at Ez Zantur where ring production took place (Schneider-Naef 2005, fig. 11, no. 53, 4th c.). Similar is Caesarea (Ayalon 2005, fig. 51, no. 497), a lathe-carved ring, dated Late Byzantine.

21. 01-B-9
Rod ("spatula or pin"). L. 5.53, th. 0.66, wt. 2.5 gm. Broken, top missing.
Lower Temenos, Tr. 79, Locus 3.

22. 99-B-3
Container/small receptacle ("cosmetic spoon"), but it is not typical of the *ligula* or *cochlear*. Diam. of ring base 1.96, h. 0.67, th. 0.25. Bowl-shaped fragment with partial ring base and fragmented handle. Possibly intended to hold a small amount of a precious substance.
Temple, Tr. 65, Locus 21.

23. 99-B-2 (fig. 18.11)
Pin/needle/rod blank ("needle"). L. 9.36, th. 0.37. It lacks a perforated eye and may originally have been longer.
Temple, Tr. 65, Locus 21.
Our unfinished piece may find parallels in a "rod blank" at Caesarea (Ayalon 2005, fig. 49, nos. 461-62), at Alexandria (Rodziewicz 2007, pl. 72, no. 591), and in Hungary (Bíró *et al.* 2012, 30, fig. 15), "half finished pin".

24. 01-B-20 (fig. 18.10)
Bead? Drilling waste? Diam. 1.22, inner diam. of central perforation 0.5, h. 0.86. Possible bead or waste consisting of a cylinder with a central perforation.
Propylaeum, Tr. 80, Locus 35.
At Ez Zantur there are 74 such beads (Schneider-Naef 2005, fig. 13, nos. 72 and 74). Cf. also from Hungary (Bíró *et al.* 2012, 57, fig. 27), "waste of circle-and-dot cutting".

25. 02-B-3
Discoid object ("spindle whorl"). Diam. 5.95, h. 0.71, wt. 9.9 gm. Half of a discoid object with a raised base ring and a depressed discus with a perforation in the center. Perhaps too large to be a button, it may have served as a collar for a perfume bottle.
Upper Temenos, Tr. 94, Locus 54.

26. 02-B-6
Discoid object or button ("spindle whorl"). Diam. 2.79, diam. of perforation 0.35, h. 1.06. Polished, two concentric grooves decorate the convex surface.
Upper Temenos, Tr. 94, Locus 45.
Cf. Ez Zantur (Schneider-Naef 2005, fig. 4, no. 19).

27. 02-B-4
Pin. L. 4.58, th. 0.43, wt. 0.9 gm. Circular shaft is broken, missing the pointed tip. Knobbed crown has two ridges around the neck ending in a plain band.
Upper Temenos, Tr. 94, Locus 41.
Cf. Caesarea (Ayalon 2005, fig. 21, no. 206). Although this pin has a pronounced neck collar, the finials are similar. Cf. Samaria-Sebaste (Kenyon 1957, fig. 114, no. 26), Roman; Mati (Sautot 1978, pl. II, no. 9); Augusta Raurica (Deschler-Erb 1998, fig. 5, no. 53); Szöny in Hungary (Bíró 1994, pl. 29, no. 317) (the last two have only one ridge).

28. 02-B-5 (fig. 18.12)
Pin. L. 9.10, th. 0.31, wt. 1.3 gm. Complete with knobbed crown having 2 grooves around the neck, ending in a plain band.
Upper Temenos, Tr. 94, Locus 54.
Cf. parallels for no. 27 above.

29. 00-B-7
Unknown ("unidentified object"). L. 8.85, th. 0.99. Piece with carved double lines that could represent a figure or be production waste (i.e., of disks). 'Soapy' feel.
Propylaeum, Tr. 69, Locus 8.

30. 04-B-13
Disk button ("spindle whorl"). Diam. 2.88, diam. of perforation 0.75, th. 0.56, wt. 2.3 gm.
Upper Temenos, SP94, Locus 8.
Cf. Caesarea "buttons, plano-convex, undecorated", or "whorls" (Ayalon 2005, fig. 6, nos. 58-59).

31. 04-B-11
Decorative piece/inlay. L. 4.31, h. 0.52, th. 0.54, wt. 2.1 gm. Object has 18 slots ('teeth') cut; one is squared off, perhaps to inlay some decorative element.
Propylaeum, Tr. 100, Locus 24.
This unusual object is probably a type of cornice. For the general shape (but not identical) cf. Alexandria (Rodziewicz 2007, pl. 29, nos. 112-13) classified as a flat "triangular tympanum", decoration for a box lid; En-Gedi (Chernov 2007, 526, fig. 69), referring to a similar object from Nessana, which is identified as "binding strips for papyri". See also Szöny in Hungary (Bíró 1994, pl. 67, no. 578), classified as a double-sided furniture inlay with holes. Cf. no. 18 for the possibility that it is a string instrument bridge.

32. 05-B-6
Inlay/decoration/waster? ("unknown"). L. 3.26, th. 0.68. Arched shape with ridging on the exterior and interior. Triangular piece with 2 straight sides and 1 concave side, beveled on 2 sides. Presumably it served as inlay for furniture or a box.
Lower Temenos, Tr. 98B, Locus 3.
Cf. Ez Zantur (Schneider-Naef 2005, fig. 24, no. 150; fig. 25, nos. 158-63; fig. 26, nos. 164-68), dated to the 2nd-1st c. B.C. to 1st c. A.D.; Petra Church (Fiema *et al.* 2001, 423, no. 101), identified as an "inlay"; Alexandria, "wasters" (Rodziewicz 2007, pls. 76-77, nos. 627-40).

33. 05-B-5
Ring production waste ("unknown"). H. 3.75, w. 3.54, th. 0.75, wt. 9 gm.
Rimmed edge. One section has horizontal incised ribbing with 4 ribs present. Highly polished exterior. 3 fragments.
Lower Temenos, Tr. 98B, Locus 2.
Cf. similar wasters of ring production from Ez Zantur (Schneider-Naef 2005, fig. 19, nos. 129-30, 2nd-1st c. B.C.; figs. 20-22, up to 2nd c. A.D.) and Caesarea (Ayalon 2005; Dray 2005).

Fig. 18.13: cat. no. 34.

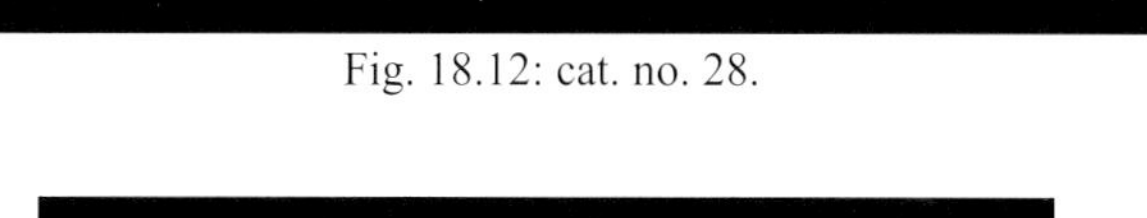

Fig. 18.12: cat. no. 28.

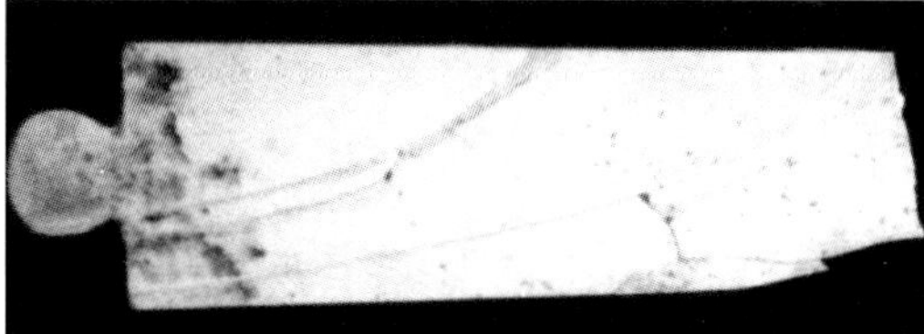

Fig. 18.14: cat. no. 35.

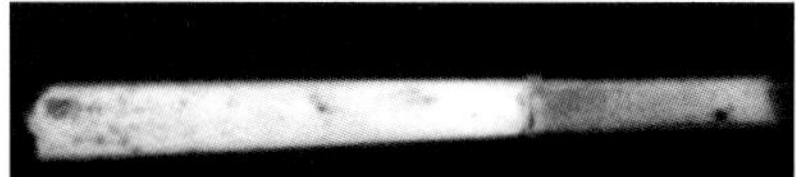

Fig. 18.15: cat. no. 36.

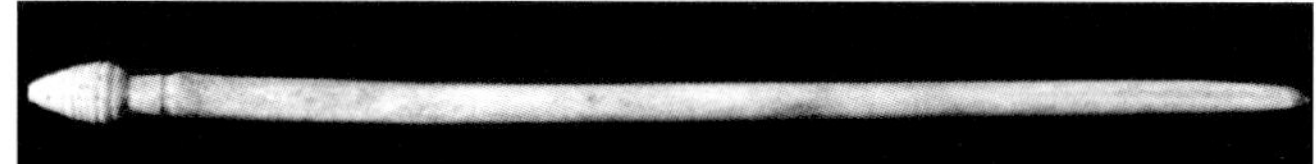

Fig. 18.16: cat. no. 43.

34. 96-B-2 (fig. 18.13)
Decorative insert, possibly unfinished ("decorative motif"). L. 4.19, th. 0.45. Beveled on all sides, originally with a pair of volutes taking the form of a "c" turned toward the center core element, a triangular-shaped flower? Perhaps an accessory for a piece of furniture, or an insert for furniture or a decorative box. Previously published in vol. 1, fig. 6.109 (*fleur-de-lys* design).
Temple, Tr. 29, Locus 14.

35. 96-B-4 (fig. 18.14)
Container tag? ("cosmetic spatula"). L. 6.48, th. 0.14. Circular protrusion at one end, flat.
Temple, Tr. 22, Locus 16.
Similar objects are widespread in Europe and usually defined as tags for containers sometimes bearing inscriptions. Cf. Lyon (Béal 1983, pl. 61, no. 1329); Augusta Raurica (Deschler-Erb 1998, fig. 28, no. 1968). In Hungary it was called a "ruler for writing tablet" (Bíró *et al*. 2012, 109, nos. 278 and 280). Previously published in vol. 1, fig 6.110.

36. 96-B-5 (fig. 18.15)
Stylus? ("needle"). L. 6.10, th. 0.29. Found in two fragments. The shaft is somewhat flattened; the end shows traces of burning.
Temple, Tr. 22, Locus 16.
Although the shape finds no parallel, traces of burning or stained tips for the application of cosmetics are known at Caesarea (Ayalon 2005, fig. 10, nos. 119 and 122).

37. 96-B-7
Handle. L. 6.08, w. 1.93, th. 1.19. Rounded socketed end of a handle, upper shaft is fragmentary. Perhaps used for a mirror or knife.
Temple, Tr. 22, Locus 16.
An ivory handle at Caesarea (Ayalon 2005, fig. 55, no. 521) is similar in shape; Alexandria (Rodziewicz 2007, pl. 35, nos. 158-59), the same shape (no. 158 is ivory); Lyon (Béal 1983, pl. 63, no. 1331).

38. 94-B-01
Engraver/*stylus* ("echinoderm"). L. 6.2, th. 0.5, diam. 0.6. The surface is polished and the stem well-finished, but the shaft is broken.
Temple, Tr. 10, Locus 14.
Cf. Caesarea (Ayalon 2005, fig. 4, no. 40).
Previously published in vol. 1, fig. 6.112.

39. 96-B-3 (fig. 18.17)
Pin or needle. L. 10.45, th. 0.35, eye diam. 0.16. Possibly ivory, in excellent condition. Found in the same location as no. 35 above.
Temple, Tr. 22, Locus 16.
Cf. Corinth (Davidson 1952, pl. 78, no. 1259); Caesarea (Ayalon 2005, fig. 9, no. 100); Hesban (Ray 2009, fig.

11, no. 10) is similar. An ivory needle (Baramki 1935, pl. 5.8) from the Beit Nattif cistern and two needles from Samaria-Sebaste (Kenyon 1957, fig. 114, nos. 41-42), are dated to the Roman period. In Hungary an example was defined as "sewing or knitting needle" (Bíró *et al.* 2012, 108, no. 264). Previously published in vol. 1, fig. 6.111.

Site Phase X

40. 05-B-3
Ring. Diam. 2.43, th. 0.66, wt. 2.6 gm. Broken; a second fragment was found separately. This hoop has a series of engraved circles with a central dot. For the same motif, see no. 16.
Upper Temenos, Tr. 105, Locus 9.
Cf. Corinth (Davidson 1952, pl. 107, nos. 1996-97).

41. 95-B-3
Decoration ("unidentified object"). L. 4.9, w. 1.9. A carved piece with an unidentifiable image that resembles a bow or could be part of a doll. It may have served as a handle for an unguent container or cosmetic box.
Lower Temenos, Tr. 20, Locus 21.
Cf. Caesarea (Ayalon 2005, fig. 39, no. 363), identified as a "carved piece", probably an inlay.

42. 95-B-5 (fig. 18.18)
Eye socket inlay/decoration. L. 3.2, w. 1.9, th. 1.4. An elliptical eye socket from a statue or perhaps an elephant head. This piece may be ivory. A faint pin hole may have held a colored pupil in place.
Lower Temenos, Tr. 20, Locus 21.
Cf. Dijon (Sautot 1978, pl. XLIV, no. 1), where the eye decorates part of a finger ring.

Site Phase XI

43. 95-B-7 (figs. 18.6 left, 18.16)
Pin. L. 10.3, diam. 0.4. Shank tapers to a point and is polished; series of grooves beneath a long ovoid head, shaped like a pinecone. Apparently lathe-made. Elaborately decorated with a series of grooves on the neck below a long ovoid head.
Lower Temenos, Tr. 16, Locus 13.
Cf. Corinth (Davidson 1952, pl. 118, no. 2312) but of ivory and dated to the 1st-2nd c. A.D. Corinth (ibid. no. 2278, pl. 119), dated to the 4th c. A.D., better resembles ours; Cagnet (1916-20, vol. 2, fig. 600) illustrating a number of pins with elegant finials; Caesarea (Ayalon 2005, fig. 22, no. 236); Alexandria (Rodziewicz 2007, pl. 47, no. 310).

44. 95-B-1 (fig. 18.19)
Spoon. L. 6.4, w. 2.1, th. 0.2. Only the almond-shaped oval bowl is present with the stub of a handle extending from the back. It may have served for cosmetics.
Lower Temenos, Tr. 20, Locus 4.
Cf. Ez Zantur (Schneider-Naef 2005, fig. 2, nos. 8-10) dated to the 1st and 4th c. A.D.; Caesarea (Ayalon 2005, fig. 17, no. 161), dated 6th c. Cf. a similar spoon shape at Alexandria (Rodziewicz 2007, pl. 57, no. 461) and Corinth (Davidson 1952, pls. 84, 189, no. 1393). Also cf. Cagnet (1916-20, vol. 2, 437).

45. 00-B-12
Gaming piece? ("unknown"). Diam. (of base) 1.05, h. 1.33, wt. 1.1 gm. Small, roughly-finished pyramidal object with a round base.
Upper Temenos, Tr. 77, Locus 9.
Cf. Caesarea (Ayalon 2005, 75, fig. 28, no. 290) "conical circular gaming piece?", dated 3rd-4th c.; Alexandria (Rodziewicz 2007, pl. 63, no. 527), identified as a "game counter".

46. 06-B-4
Button ("spindle whorl?"). Diam. 2.96, diam. of perforation 0.73, th. 0.55, wt. 7.0 gm. Discoid with a central hole. Or it may be the lid of a cosmetic box.
Lower Temenos, Tr. 127, Locus 39.
Cf. Caesarea (Ayalon 2005, fig. 6, no. 59, "whorl/button"; fig. 7, no. 80, "button"); Corinth (Davidson 1952, pl. 99, no. 1707), "counter;" Horvat 'Eleq on Mt. Carmel (Kol-Yaakov 2000, 491, no. 80, pl. VII, no. 16).

47. 05-B-9
Ring. L. 1.61, th. 0.25, w. 0.3 gm. Broken (2 frags.). Incised design of X's with dots on the band.
Upper Temenos, Tr. 106, Locus 3.

48. 00-B-2
Button/lid ("spindle whorl"). Diam. 3.45, w. of squared perforation 0.52, th. 0.51, wt. 7.0 gm. Has a finished and an unfinished side. Square perforation in the center. Faint ridge around the edge on both sides. Notch in the side, broken. Perhaps the lid of a cosmetic box.
Upper Temenos, Tr. 77, Locus 9.

Fig. 18.17: cat. no. 39.

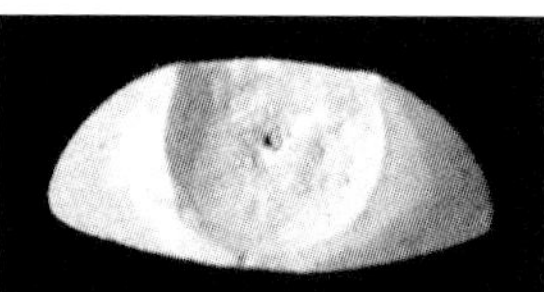

Fig. 18.18: cat. no. 42.

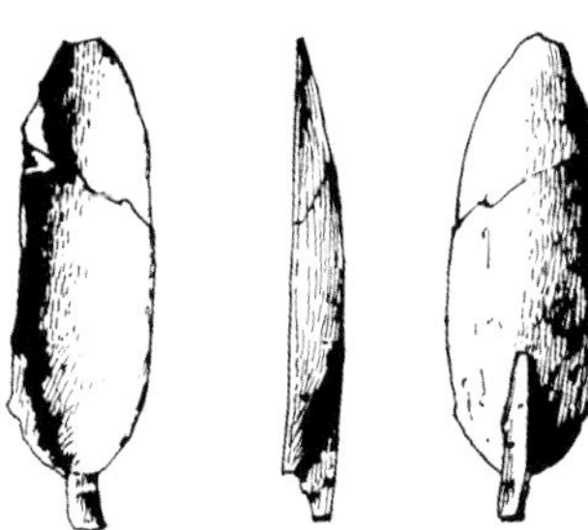

Fig. 18.19: cat. no. 44.

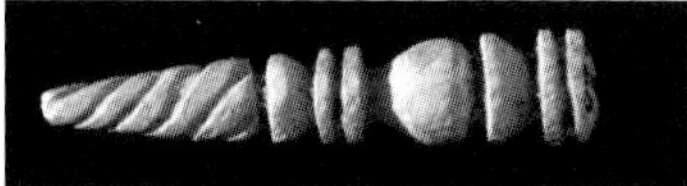

Fig. 18.20: cat. no. 49.

49. 00-B-8 (fig. 18.20)
Head of a tool like a *stylus* or engraver. Two fragments, each weathered differently. L. 3.77, one diam. 0.70, other diam. 2.8, wt. 1.3 gm. Perforated in the center, diam. of perforation 1.5. Heavily decorated head crown, terminating in a stylized flame atop 6 rings of different sizes.
Upper Temenos, Tr. 77, Locus 93.

50. 95-B-4
Ring or decorative piece ("eye line insert?"). Diam. 2.4. Half circle, polished ivory(?), from a statue or elephant head, or possibly part of an earring.
Lower Temenos, Tr. 16, Locus 13.

51. 95-B-12 (fig. 18. 6, right)
Head crown of a pin. L. 4.4, w. 0.6. Rectangular, highly polished, intricately carved and perforated, tapers to a small knob on the top. Rounded finial pierced in two places, with a flattened head and an offset shoulder. One eye is circular, the other has two eyes drilled very close together, roughly in the shape of a figure-8.
Lower Temenos, Tr. 5, Locus 22.
Cf. Caesarea (Ayalon 2005, 63, fig. 23, no. 242), a pin "with a head like perforated tower", dated Late Roman-Byzantine. Cf. Ez Zantur (Schneider-Naef 2005, fig 10, no. 44). Previously published in vol. 1, fig 6.115.

Site Phase XIII

52. 05-B-8
Awl, pin or piercer? L. 6.72, w. 1.89, th. 0.79, wt. 3.3 gm. Classed separately from the other pins because of its point. Its shape suggests that it served as a piercing tool for soft materials. Probably created from a horse fibula in an *ad hoc* use of a slightly modified animal bone as a tool.
Upper Temenos, SP110, Locus 27.
Cf. Caesarea (Ayalon 2005, 19 and fig. 4, no. 44) for references.

53. 05-B-7
Decorated pin of bone and bronze. L. 10.18, w. 1.28 (i.e., diam. of the head plus the bronze attachment), th. 0.26 (i.e., median width of the stem), wt. 2.4 gm. A small strip of bronze extends from the center of the pin's flattened head to the neck to secure the pin in place.
Upper Temenos, SP110, Locus 27.
The rounded finial resembles a pin found at Corinth (Davidson 1952, pl. 82, no. 1324; also see pl. 83, nos. 1343 and 1345), but the Corinthian shaft no. 1324 is decorated while ours is circular in section. At Corinth this type of head is also found attached to an ear spoon (ibid. 81). Pins with metal strings are known in Hungary (Bíró 1994, 23-25).

54. 05-B-4
Container/ partial neck of a box/*pyxis* or small vessel fragment. H. 3.97, th. 0.36, wt. 7.2 gm. The upper rim is ridged with 3 grooves on its upper surface; there are 2 finely incised grooves near the exterior of the rim.
Upper Temenos, SP110, Locus 26.
Cf. Ez Zantur (Schneider-Naef 2005, fig. 13, no. 79; 1st-2nd c.); Caesarea (Ayalon 2005, fig. 12, no. 128); Alexandria (Rodziewicz 2007, pl. 44, nos. 264-66); Corinth (Davidson 1952, pl. 69, no. 965; Roman).

55. 98-B-1
Spoon. L. 7.93 (width of paddle), w. 0.99, th. of stem 0.37. Fragmented, one end snapped off, the other has a broken paddle. Possibly Nabataean since it is associated with a Nabataean assemblage.
Upper Temenos, Tr. 53, no locus designated.

Cf. Ez Zantur (Schneider-Naef 2005, fig. 2, nos. 8-10) dated to the 1st and 4th c.; Caesarea (Ayalon 2005, fig. 17, no. 161), 6th c. A.D. Also cf. a similar spoon shape in Alexandria (Rodziewicz 2007, pl. 57, no. 461); Corinth (Davidson 1952, 189, pl. 84, no. 1393); Cagnet (1916-20, vol. 2, 437).

56. 99-B-1
Ring. Diam. 1.95, inner diam. 1.36, th. 0.35. Fragmentary. Decorated with incised lines on the external circumference. Etched line on the face.
Lower Temenos, Tr 61, Locus 2.
Cf. a "lathe-carved ring" at Caesarea (Ayalon 2005, fig. 51, nos. 495 and 497).

Without a site phase

57. 00-B-4
Lid, gaming piece or furniture joint. Diam. 2.24, th. 0.32, wt. 0.9 gm. Fragmentary, poor condition.
Upper Temenos, Tr. 75, Locus 1.
Cf. Caesarea (Ayalon 2005, fig. 12, no. 136), a box lid.

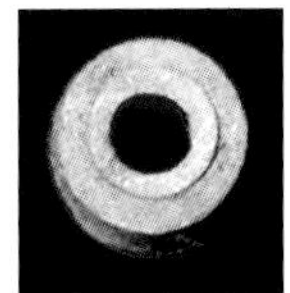

Fig. 18.21: cat. no. 58.

58. 00-B-5 (fig. 18.21)
Spool or furniture joint ("spindle whorl"). Diam. 1.48, th. 0.71, wt. 1.4 gm. Inner diam. of the central hole 0.58. One side is flat and unfinished; on the finished side there is a raised ring around the central hole.
Lower Temenos, Tr. 71, Locus 28.
Cf. Corinth (Davidson 1952, pl. 64, no. 867). Cf. perhaps "drilling waste" at Caesarea (Ayalon 2005, fig. 50, no. 484); "hinge base" in Hungary (Bíró *et al*. 2012, 115, no. 346).

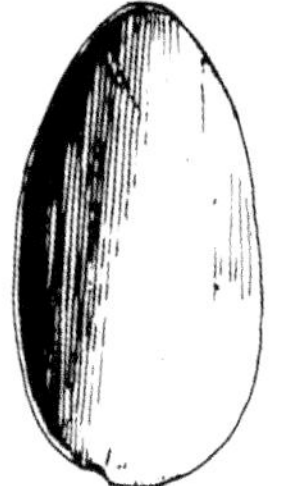

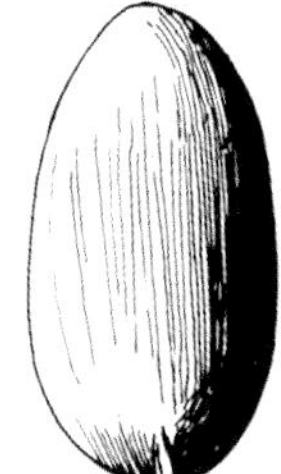

Fig. 18.22: cat. no. 59.

59. 95-B-10 (fig. 18.22)
Large spoon (*ligula*). L. 6.5, w. 3.4. Oval bowl only, handle missing.
Temple, SP23, no locus designated.
Cf. Corinth (Davidson 1952, pl. 84, no. 1393); also Cagnet (1916-20, vol. 2, 437). Cf. a 6th-c. example at Caesarea (Ayalon 2005, 48, fig. 17, no. 161); Alexandria (Rodziewicz 2007, pl. 57, no. 461).

Concluding remarks

A bone workshop was recently discovered at Ez Zantur just up the hill from the Great Temple. Its output seems to have been dependent on a few popular items, such as the pin, while adapting some traditional forms.

The fact that these tools were found in separate Great Temple locations suggests that no specific area served a cultic function at the time they were left there. We speculate that these small objects of personal use came to rest accidently where they were found. Therefore no specific activities can be inferred from the worked bone repertoire to evaluate the locational use of the Great Temple complex.

This modest collection is not unlike other worked bone assemblages from the region. There are certainly shared traditions and stylistic details between Petra and Caesarea Maritima; indeed, the existence of so many correspondences between their finds is remarkable. It would also appear that finished bone implements were brought in from commercial centers such as Ashkelon and Alexandria with a tradition of manufacturing by skilled artisans and a history of marketing. Yet worked bone was also part of a general cultural *koine* throughout the Mediterranean world during the Roman and Byzantine periods.

18B

A bone handle in the form of a leg from the Residential Quarter

Martha Sharp Joukowsky, Sarah Whitcher Kansa, François Poplin, David Bartus and Donna Strahan

The archaeological context

Southwest of the temple enclosure in the Upper Temenos is a Residential Quarter which includes two caves subdivided into 11 rooms. These cave households are based on a Nabataean style of urban planning characterized by compact, concentrated structures laid out in an organic plan. The Residential Quarter is only part of a larger domestic zone that has still to be fully defined by excavation. The larger west cave (Cave 2) measures 6.50 m N-S x 6.65 m E-W, and the height from floor to ceiling is 3.85 m.

A bone handle in the form of a leg was recovered in the débris in Rooms 10 and 11 (Tr. 94, Locus 41) excavated in 2002. Located in the rear of Cave 2, Room 10 measures 4.94 m N-S x 4.16 m E-W, while Room 11 measures 6.17 m N-S x 2.96 m E-W. Locus 41 refers to the artifact-rich sediment of a very dark brown fill covering an area of *c.*6.5 x 5.4 m, 1.9 m deep (7.5 YR 2.5/2).[1] The layer was unusually full of cultural materials, including large amounts of pottery, bone, glass, metal, shell, stucco, stone cornices, and a vine carved in relief. The pottery included 9 nearly complete pieces (ranging from beer strainers to Nabataean painted jugs and plain wares), 5 lamps (ranging from the 1st c. B.C. to the 5th c. A.D.), and 9 fragmentary figurines of votives, gazelles and a horse. There were also 2 Roman provincial coins of the 2nd-3rd c. A.D. Of the 5 jewelry objects, one was a faience bead and one a mother-of-pearl dolphin. Thirteen metal items were catalogued, including knife blades, axe-heads, an arrowhead, and a cross. Stone artifacts included an alabaster foot, a loom weight, a limestone gazelle head, and a button. There was also a single bone pin. The animal bone assemblage from this context consisted of 200 fragments, 33 of which could be identified to both an element and a taxon. Compared with the overall assemblage, this context had a disproportionate number of camel foot bones and a high proportion of large mammal vertebrae. A complete metacarpus of a young donkey is another unusual find. Also found in the bone assemblage was a long fragment of a large mammal long bone that has been roughly worked into a point. The bone handle (figs. 18.23-18.27) was discovered subsequently amongst the bone fragments given to S. W. Kansa for analysis.[2]

The destruction stratum in Rooms 10-11, which is mixed with earlier remains, formed part of the massive destruction in Site Phase IX associated with the earthquake of A.D. 363. This stratum is well distinguished from Site Phase VIII below and from Site Phase X above.

Description (by D. Strahan[3])

The leg (9.8 cm in length) was carved from a single piece of bone with a slight bend at the knee. When examined under magnification, the typical bone structure of small vein holes is especially evident along the bottom (back) edge of the upper thigh. The toes, now missing, were pinned to the foot by a copper-alloy pin (fig. 18.25). Whether this is a repair or the original method of fabrication

1 *ADAJ* 53 (2009) 226, figs. 14-15.

2 The piece was subsequently catalogued as 08-B-1 and deposited with the Jordanian Department of Antiquities at the Petra Museum in 2008. Additional photographs are published in Open Context (Strahan 2009).

3 Conservator, Sherman Fairchild Center for Objects Conservation, The Metropolitan Museum of Art. The other four authors are most grateful to Donna Strahan for the kindnesses she has shown to the project over many years, especially in identifying bone, ivory and antler materials.

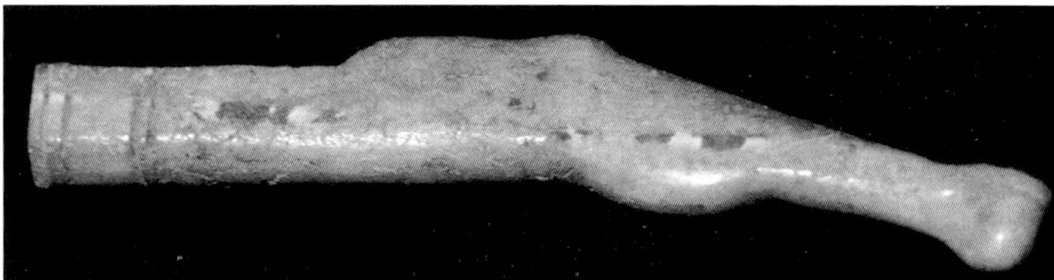

Fig. 18.23. Bone handle, left side.

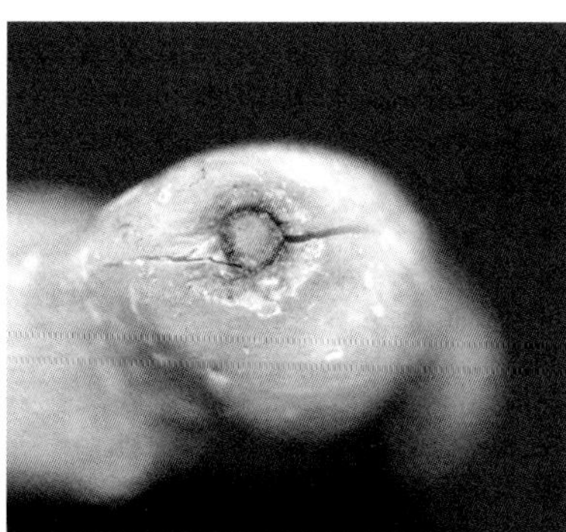

Fig. 18.25. Pin of the foot for attaching the toes.

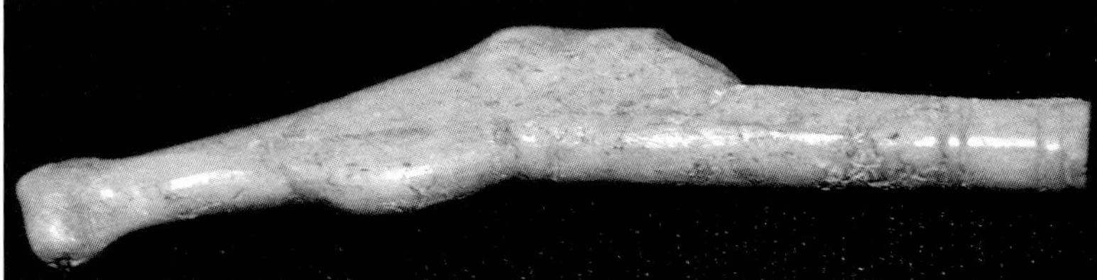

Fig. 18.24. Bone handle, right side.

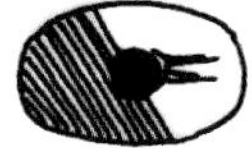

Fig. 18.26. Drilled hole in the top of the leg.

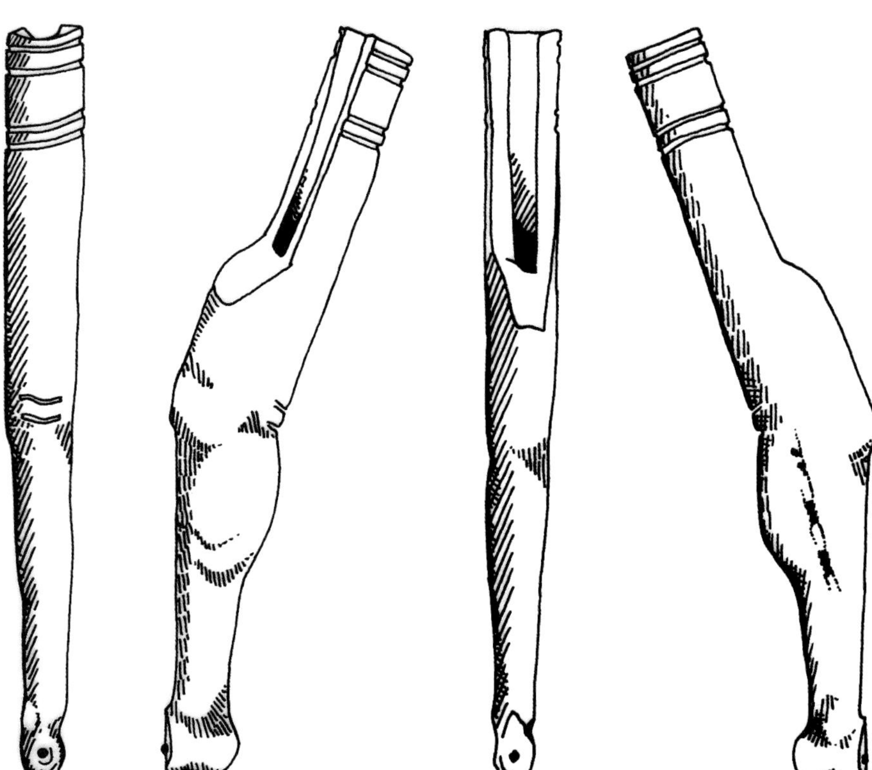

Fig. 18.27. Drawing of the bone handle: top, right side, rear and left side (E. C. Egan).

is unclear. The remains of the pin extend from the front and back of the foot; it is severely corroded and has cracked the bone across the bottom of the foot.

The leg appears to be the handle portion of an object. The slight curve of the leg helps it fit comfortably in a small hand. The toes would have extended upward below the hand of the person holding the handle, making a "stop" behind his or her little finger. The top of the thigh is finished and has 4 decorative lines running around its circumference.

A 3.5 cm-deep channel is drilled into the top of the leg (figs. 18.26-18.27). It was probably drilled to hold the tang of an object such as a blade or comb. A large loss runs across the top of the thigh down the length of the hole. If the leg was held as a handle and a strong downward force applied, it may have caused pressure from a possible 'blade' to crack the bone, causing the loss across the top of the hole. As the hole does not have any visible traces of corrosion from metals such as iron, copper or silver, it is unclear what was held by the handle. The lack of metal corrosion does not rule out the likelihood that the handle held a metal blade. Indeed, when the handle broke, a blade would have been removed and recycled for use with another handle, leaving the channel empty. A radiograph[4] shows that the drilled hole stops just below where the object broke, supporting the interpretation that the break relates to pressure from an inserted blade. In addition, there are traces of some material (now missing) that ran the length of the leg on both sides; they are visible to the naked eye as an alternating pattern of dark and light (fig. 18.23) and in the radiograph as a slightly less dense (i.e., eroded) region of bone on either side of the piece.

Discussion and comparanda

Our object was carved from a thick fragment of a long bone of a large mammal (e.g., camel, equid or cattle). Fresh bone was easy to procure and cheaper than ivory; it can be easily cut and carved with intricate designs.

Bone handles have been found in many parts of the Roman world.[5] Our piece is more elaborately carved than most. It is most likely to have been a handle, but its form is unique.[6] The handle could belong to a knife, razor or toilet knife, but it is not a typical "Klappmessergriff" (Roman pocket-knife), which represent the majority of the figural decorated knives. Other objects similarly executed in the form of human body parts include Roman bone pocket-knife handles with human legs from Ephesos, Rome, Cologne and Berlin.[7] A Roman ivory handle in the form of a human leg is in the collections of the Vatican Museums,[8] and bronze pieces have been found at Trier[9] and Cologne.[10] Excavations at Ostia[11] produced a bone knife-handle in the shape of a human finger,[12] and bone or ivory knife-handles in the shape of a human arm,[13] a human leg[14] and two examples of a sandaled human foot. These human-leg handles fit rather well with a series of foot- or leg-handles for folding knives, frequently in cleft-foot examples. The blade of the knife when folded

---

4 We are grateful to the VCA Albany Animal Hospital (Albany, CA) for providing a radiograph of the piece: see http://opencontext.org/media/260BCE41-95B1–4F42-2511–A787A163CD89.

5 Weitzman 1972.

6 We appreciate the assistance of various members of the International Council for Archaeozoology's Worked Bone Research Group (ICAZ WBRG), who viewed the object online and provided comments about its rarity and its probable function.

7 Ephesos: Mercklin 1940, Anm. 31, pl. XXXVI.6; Rome: Mercklin 1940, Anm. 31-32; Cologne: Banerjee-Schneider 1996, 338, Kat. 2, pls. 14a-b; Berlin: Mercklin 1940, Anm. 32, pl. XXXVII.1.

8 Mercklin 1940, Anm. 31.

9 *Arbeitsgebiet des Landesmuseums Trier* 1937, 196, pl. 2.

10 Franken 1996, 126, no. 163, pls. 245-46.

11 See the Ostia Virtual Museum, Hall of Bone Objects: http://www.ostia-antica.org/vmuseum/small_4.htm

12 Ostia Virtual Museum: http://www.ostia-antica.org/vmuseum/small_4.htm, Object set E27336A, 1.

13 Ibid. Object set E27326, 2.2.

14 Ibid. Object set E27344, 1.6.

(closed) lay in a groove carved between the toes, on the back (plantar, or sole) side of the foot.[15] The socket insert in the Petra handle is uncommon; it is found more frequently in large knives.[16] From the quality of the handle's execution, its uncommon form, and the care taken to drill a socket and carefully attach the toe, we may infer that this was an item of value.

Our piece also shows a link with doll-making. Bone dolls' limbs were often long and thin like this piece. Their appearance reflects the available raw materials, the long bones of such animals as cattle and deer, which provided ample length but just enough thickness to form willowy limbs. Dolls' legs, however, are generally simpler in shape, straighter, and have a transverse hole at the top for articulation and movement of the limb.

---

15 Ibid. Object set E27344, 1.5 and E27326, 3.3.

16 Ward 1911.

18C

A worked hippopotamus tusk

Martha Sharp Joukowsky with Donna Strahan

Ivory is a term used to describe any mammalian teeth or tusks large enough to be carved. Derived from the hard white dentine in the tusks and teeth of animals, ivory from the elephant and hippopotamus has been used since Chalcolithic times for a broad range of precious objects. Both the Greeks and the Romans used ivories for high-value goods. In the 1st c. B.C. ivory was traded along the Silk Roads. After elephant ivory, hippopotamus ivory is prized for carving, being denser and finer in grain.

The second-named author examined a group of 4 worked bones (figs. 18.28-18.29),[1] concluding that they are all hippopotamus tusk,[2] and not elephant, bone or antler. They come from the mammal's curved lower canine tooth.[3] Discovering also that they all fit together, she restored them to form a single fragment, which may have been a part of a small object such as a cosmetic box. The finished side or top of the tusk measures 6.8 cm in length, 0.05 cm in thickness, and 1 cm in width. Its upper surface is striated horizontally, while its lower surface exhibits a raised projecting ridge as if it were carved to serve as a cover.

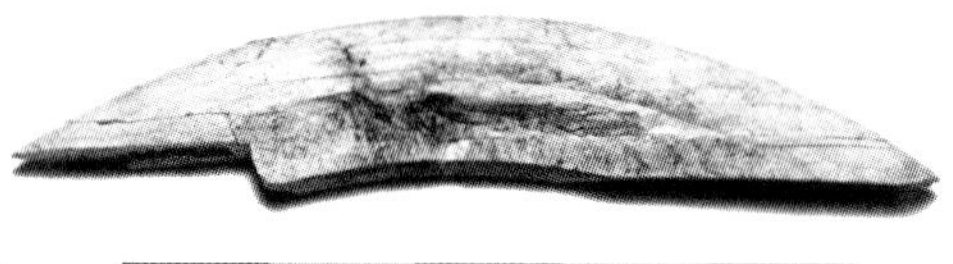

Figs. 18.28-29. Hippopotamus tusk, top (left) and bottom (right).

The tusk came from trench 131 in the Roman-Byzantine Baths, excavated in 2008.[4] Work was focused west of the upper platform of the West Entry Stairs, an area lying to the south of the spiral staircase of the Baths–Palatial Complex excavated in the 1960s by the Jordanian Department of Antiquities. In a staircase room on the NE side (dimensions 4 m N-S x 3.75 m E-W, excavated to a depth of 1.57-1.61 m below the 'platform' elevation of the Baths) the tusk was found in Locus 6, a loose, silty and dark brown soil (7.5YR 2.5/3; *c.*0.04 m in depth) with a substantial amount of ash in the matrix. It is part of regular dumping in the area, with little clear stratigraphy.[5] Locus 6 is placed in Site Phase VIII (late 2nd c. A.D.) when this period of disuse and dumping is thought to have occurred. This ashy, artifact-rich lens also yielded 3 complete lamps — a Darom or moulded Judaean lamp (08-L-4)[6] and 2 Nabataean volute lamps (08-L-3, 08-L-2) — all found next to one

---

1 The 4 separate fragments as found were published in *ADAJ* 53 (2009) 224, fig. 11. It is now catalogued as 09-B-1 and has been deposited with the Jordanian Department of Antiquities at the Petra Museum. At the Great Temple, ivory may also have been used to form the white of the eye for a statue (see chapt. 17, no. 42, fig. 17.19).

2 Today the *Hippopotamus amphebius* is concentrated in Sub-Saharan Africa. Whereas the incisors are peg-shaped, the largest teeth, the curved lower canines, are triangular in cross-section and can be 60 cm long with a thick enamel coating.

3 Compare half of a left lower hippopotamus canine (44 cm length) found at Alexandria (Rodziewicz 2007, pl. 84; also ibid. pl. 25, nos. 103-4, for a carved floral relief engraved on a hippopotamus ivory).

4 See *ADAJ* 53 (2009) 220-24. Also Ch. 9 in this volume.

5 Each day of excavation of this dump received its own locus number. In an effort to establish the floor level, a 1 x 1 m sondage was sunk in the SW corner of the room. When no floor was found at the expected level (calculated from the threshold in the W doorway to the room), the baulk at the W threshold was pushed back, and the staircase was unearthed in Locus 7.

6 Identified by D. G. Barrett and dated *c.*A.D. 70-135 (cf. Israel and Avida 1988, 50, no. 88; 61, nos. 134-36). Other such lamps have been recovered at Masada in the rooms in the casemate wall occupied by the Zealots, dating from the last decade or so before the siege and fall.

another, as well as a complete cup and a bronze pendant. Most surprising were the more than 5000 sea urchin spines (echinoderms) and 1682 shells (primarily oyster), along with substantial amounts of pottery (9016 fragments).

Popular in the classical world is the pyxis, a small, squat, flat-bottomed cylindrical box with a separate lid.[7] Used by women to keep jewelry or cosmetics, this small trinket box might be made of ivory, glass, pottery or wood, or of other more precious materials. It may well be that the hippopotamus fragment enhanced the lid of such a small box.

7 At Alexandria, a typical cylindrical pyxis (h. 4 cm, w. 3.3 cm) is represented by Rodziewicz 2007, pl. 44, no. 264.

19

"Mettle Enough in Thee" Metal Artifacts from the Petra Great Temple

Angela Murock Hussein

"Though care killed a cat, thou hast mettle enough in thee to kill care."
Claudio, *Much Ado About Nothing*, Act 5, Scene 1.
William Shakespeare.

Introduction

"Mettle"/metal, or lack thereof, is a particular problem in artifact studies on most archaeological sites. Although common in many ancient societies, metal artifacts, particularly those made of iron, are a somewhat rare find in many archaeological contexts, since metal is easily corroded in wet or acidic soil. Therefore our picture of metal use in the ancient world is biased by artifact survival rates. Fortunately, Petra is located in a desert environment and therefore many metal pieces are relatively well preserved for us to study. These artifacts offer us clues about ancient technology, building techniques, and human activities across the landscape. More importantly for this study, enough metal objects were recovered to allow for a robust examination.

During the excavation seasons of 2000–2003 a large sample of over 300 metal pieces were recovered from each of the 4 areas of the Petra Great Temple complex. In addition, 242 metal artifacts were entered in the catalog, with photographs[1] and measurements[2] taken for study. The array of object types in these samples is extremely diverse, from structural elements, technological tools, and decorative items.

This work is divided into two sections. The first will examine the different kinds of metal objects that were found at Petra Great Temple providing evidence of the diverse and varied uses for metals. Objects are divided by material, i.e. iron, bronze, lead, silver and gold, and subdivided according to function. The second section will analyze the different contexts in which the finished metal artifacts were found to extract information about areas of activity. Three notable concentrations of metal artifacts and their significance will be examined in detail.

I. Metal artifacts

The majority of the metal artifacts from Petra Great Temple were integral construction elements to the structure itself. For example the largest group of iron artifacts are nails, thousands of which would have been utilized in the wooden components of the Temple. Other iron structural components include door locks, hooks, and latches. Bronze was employed for some of these same uses, but was probably intended for more decorative contexts like leaf finials[3]. Artifacts of other metals, such as silver and lead, were also recovered.

A. Structural elements

Structural elements include different sizes of nail, Large, Medium, Thin and Tacks. Nail shaped objects such as chisels, will be discussed below under tools. Also discussed in the structural elements category are artifacts such as braces and iron and bronze sheathing.

---

1 Not all the existing illustrations of the metal artifacts are included here. Additional photographs are filed in the Great Temple archives.

2 All measurements are in centimeters, with abbreviations for L.= length, Th.= thickness, Diam.= diameter, Ht.= height.

3 See below for description of bronze artifacts

1. Nails

Around 484 objects could be securely identified as nails and nail fragments. The total number was most likely higher, but several pieces could not be securely identified as nails to the exclusion of all other object types. Nails were used for construction in all areas of the temple complex.

In Petra large iron nails were used on the walls of stone buildings. Large nails were driven between stone blocks keying the stone surface for the initial heavy coats of plaster. The nail heads would then be covered by thinner plaster topcoats.[4]

Typically, the Petra Great Temple is of Greek inspiration in form, where a stone building supported a roof of wood covered by tiles. On Greek stone monuments, colonnades were surmounted by a stone entablature that held the primary timber frame—large beams evenly spaced to provide the skeleton of the roof. Over the primary timbers, smaller, lighter secondary timbers would have provided a base for the roofing tiles, which were sometimes packed onto the wood with clay and straw.[5] In Petra, tiles were probably bonded to the timbers and to each other with stucco or plaster. Terracotta roof tile fragments have been found around much of the temple area. Decomposition of the wood and other organics have left the tiles and nails as the only evidence for the roofing of the Petra Great Temple including the Temple corridors that remains.[6] Doors were also constructed using nails to fit boards together, to affix iron locks, braces and handles, and to reinforce wooden doors with iron studs.

Unfortunately the most extensive iron nail typologies have been published for Romano-Britain.[7] The British samples do not match our examples closely in time or place and so the typologies cannot be applied directly. There are also some problematic methods of recording, for example, some of these typologies register nail weights, a practice that is not extremely helpful due to the large amount of corrosion that has altered artifact mass. Nevertheless, nail typologies can be useful models when looking at nail distribution and which specific nails are used for what purposes. The nails in the Petra Great Temple sample closely match examples published from the Petra Church.[8]

In the sample, 5 types of nail shaped objects are recognized as appearing frequently, one of these types is likely a chisel rather than a nail. There are also two types of nail that appear infrequently in the sample but whose purpose can be ascertained by means of parallels with modern carpentry. The exact original sizes cannot be known, these are handmade objects with substantial corrosion. Therefore, there is some overlap in the measurement ranges for those objects cannot be identified as nails with absolute security. Therefore the evidence used for the statistics below is based on nail fragments for which two or more dimensions are identifiable.

Nail typology

Large Nails: These nails have large mushroom heads and thick tapering shafts. Measurement Range: Head: One dimension at least 2.7, other at least 2.2, up to 4.2. Shaft Th.: At least 1.2, but usually, 1.3-1.6 up to 2.1. L. between 13 and 7.3.

Medium Nails: Smaller heads, thick shafts, only slightly smaller than the large nails. Measurement Range: Head: 2.7-1.4. Shaft Th. 1.4-0.9, L. 6.8-9.3.

Thin Nails: These have long thin shafts and the mushroom heads like the larger sizes. Measurement Range: Head: 0.8-1.8. Shaft Th. 0.5-1.0, L. 4.5-8.4.

---

4 Hammond 1965, 68-69, pl. 45,1-3; Hammond 1996, 61-62; Hammond 2000, 146; Rababeh 2005, 46, and Ch. 3 in this volume.

5 Hodge 1960, 62-67.

6 *Great Temple* vol. 1, 213-14; *Great Temple* vol. 2, 250, and the colonnades of the Lower Temenos (Ibid. 95).

7 Angus *et al.* 1962; Manning 1985, 134-37; Simpson 2000, 112-16.

8 Fiema *et al.* 2001, 174-75.

Tack: Relatively wide round heads, very short shafts. Measurement Range: Head: 2.1 and 1.0. Shaft Th. 0.6-1.1, L. 3.3-6.5 with one at 1.0.

Chisels: Very large nail shaped objects, probably not used as nails.[9] Measurement Range: Head: 4.0-4.2. Shaft Th. 1.8-2.9, L. 15.5-21.9.

Single variations: In addition to the main nail types used, there are other nail types evident in the sample.

Dome Headed Nail: This has a rounded head different from the other nails.[10] Probably intended for some decorative purpose with the head meant to protrude. Measurements: Head diam. 2.5, Shaft Th. 1.1, L. 7.6.

Wide Headed Nail: One nail has a very wide flat round head and a long thin shaft. This type of nail is used today for affixing soft materials such as plaster plaques without too much pressure to damage the surface or crack it. Measurements: Head, 2.9 x 2.8, shaft Th. 0.8, L. 9.3.

Fig. 19.1. Medium Nail (top) and Large Nail Head (bottom) from the Temple (Seq. No. 85225).

Comment: *Large* and *Medium* nails are the most common in the sample.[11] These two types are closely related; the best way to differentiate them is by head measurements (fig. 19.1). However, the present differences may be due to the extensive corrosion or variation between craftsmen. If variations do not reflect different intended purposes then these were likely used for similar jobs. Large nails tend to come from the temple area and the rooms of the Propylaeum, roofed parts of the complex and so the nails may have fallen from the rafters. However, not many nails in this sample come from the colonnades of the Lower Temenos, the other roofed portion of the temple complex. This dissimilarity could be due to a different roofing technique in the Lower Temenos. It is certain that the large and medium nails were used for wooden doors. Large nails are still embedded in door locks from the rear entrance to the Temple,[12] and an iron brace element from the Propylaeum.[13]

Thin nails tend to be utilized for finer jobs involving smaller wooden boards as opposed to the larger beams affixed with Large and Medium nails (fig. 19.2). There are lower numbers of nails of this type in this sample which may be due to reduced survival rates than the more robust larger sizes. In two clear cases, thin nails were found on heavily corroded objects of bronze[14] possibly for decorative usages such as grille work.

Fig. 19.2. Thin Nails from the Propylaeum (Seq. No. 95875) with corroded copper on the surfaces. 85225).

Tacks, with their wide heads and short shafts, were used for hanging and affixing thin materials to wood. This could include decoration or molded tiles. For example, 9 tacks come from the Baroque room, which has elaborate stucco decoration.[15]

A comparison between the nail distribution from the studied sample and the reported numbers from the Grosso Modo artifact database reveal that the sample yields similar results to the overall distribution pattern.

---

9 Discussed further under tools.

10 Fiema *et al.* 2001, 413, no. 201.

11 *Great Temple* vol. I, 306, Cat. No. 96-M-3.

12 Seq. No. 85017.

13 Seq. No. 80225.

14 Seq. Nos. 95875 and 95863.

15 Seq. Nos. 89809, 89826, 89277, 89240, 89251.

Table 19.1
TOTAL NAILS FROM THE PETRA GREAT TEMPLE
(GROSSO MODO AND CATALOG)

Lower Temenos	*Upper Temenos*	*Temple*	*Propylaeum*	*Total*
68	143	191	86	488
14%	29%	39%	18%	100%

Table 19.2
STUDIED SAMPLE OF GREAT TEMPLE NAILS

	Lower Temenos	*Upper Temenos*	*Temple*	*Propylaeum*	*Total*
Large	2	6	41	14	**63**
Medium	3	5	15	5	**28**
Thin	0	14	0	5	**19**
Tack	1	9	1	2	**13**
Total	6	34	57	26	**123**
	5%	28%	46%	21%	

Even assuming that there are limitations to these data, for example that the sample may be skewed towards nails of the larger sizes because these were more likely to be preserved, we can see some patterns. These facts may be an indication of the different types of construction in the various areas.

The temple had the majority of nail finds and these were structural nails- mostly Large and Medium in size. This suggests usage was affixing beams, either for roofing or doors. Propylaeum nails are also mostly structural (Large and Medium) as well but with somewhat sizable proportions of other types, meaning that this section probably had both structural and decorative elements.

The fewest total nails originated in the Lower Temenos, with almost equal proportions Large and Medium nails. The Upper Temenos has the most diverse deposits, no doubt due to its proximity to the Residential Quarter and other surrounding structures with varied functions. Most of the nails from the Upper Temenos are Thin nails or tacks and specifically all of the tacks originate in the Baroque room in the Upper Temenos.

The rarity of nails of any kind in the Lower Temenos could be explained as this area having no doors. Another factor to explain this distribution could be the tile roofs of the Lower Temenos were smaller and had less area to span between vertical supports (columns) and so may have had a less complex roofing structure than the temple.

Technology

The finds from the Great Temple context are extremely uniform for an archaeological site. This may imply that the majority of the nails come from a single building phase.

Many of the nails are well preserved enough that one can see evidence of the blows used to shape them. They are all square in section, but heads can be round, oval or roughly square. Thin nails are much more delicately shaped than the larger sizes or tacks.

A great number of nails have clay or plaster on the shafts, particularly the larger sizes. Most of the roof tile fragments have the same material adhering to them, indicating that these nails were used in construction for the roof. As mentioned above, clay and plaster packing was used to adhere tiles each other and to the roof timbers. This substance would also have been applied to the nails when they were used in the keying system for wall plastering.

Several thin nails are bent in a precise and intentional manner. These bends form the nails into squared J or L-shapes. These may have been intended for use as hooks, driven into walls and then bent to provide places for hanging items such as garlands. There are also some Large nails bent at various angles (fig. 19.3). Bent nails are also found in the Petra Church and were interpreted as having been used on thinner sections of wood.[16]

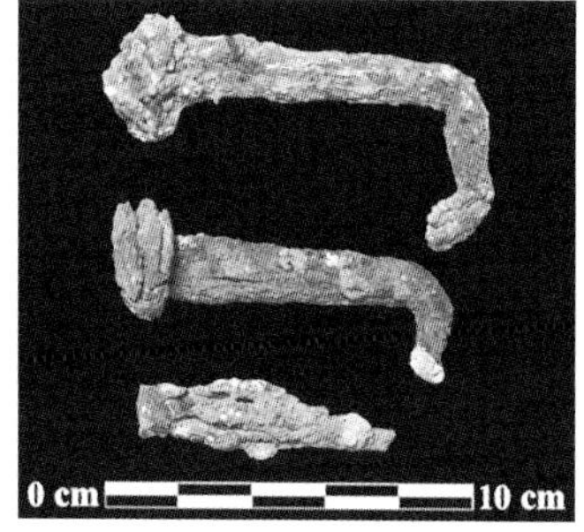

Fig. 19.3. Bent Large Nails from the Temple (Seq. No. 85042).

Aside from nails, several architectural components associated with wooden doors are found among the iron samples taken from the Petra Great Temple. These include door locks, iron sheathing and a brace. There are also hooks and what may be attachments and door lock catches.

No hinges have been found and the doors evidently moved on pivots, the shafts for which can still be seen in the jambs of several doorways. Cuttings for drop locks are evident in several threshold stones. Doorways also have rectangular slots about halfway up the sides of the vertical doorposts, to catch the crossbars used to lock the doors.

2. Door locks

Iron door locks. Seq. No. 85017. Condition: Corroded. Temple, Trench 85, Locus 1.
Lock A: L. 32.8, W. 5.2, Max. Th. 2.8 (fig. 19.4).
Lock B: L. 29.6, W. 4.3, Max. Th. 2.2.

Fig. 19.4. Door Lock from the South Corridor of the Temple (Seq. No. 85017).

Comment: These items consist of two slabs of iron with two large nails driven through each, to affix them to wood.[17] The only doorway in this area that was not blocked was in the North wall of the South Corridor. However the locks could have possibly fallen from one of the doors in the South wall when other doorways were blocked in antiquity.

The heads of one nail on each of the locks protrude slightly, either to receive ties or a bar or where the knobs were once attached. A substantial amount of a white substance remains on the backs of these locks, indicating that the doors were plastered or painted.

3. Brace:

Seq. No. 80225. Iron Brace. Condition: Corroded. Propylaeum, Trench 80, Locus 7. L. 15.4, W. 10.7, Th. 4.7.

Fig. 19.5. Iron Brace from the Propylaeum (Seq. No. 80225).

Comment: An iron brace bent into a squared C-shape (fig. 19.5).[18] Metal strips such as this were used to bind boards together for boxes, carts and structural elements. One nail was driven into the brace at either end, and evidence of a third nail was at the center. The brace comes from the Propylaeum West where there were several doorways and rooms. On the inner side of the brace are traces of the grain of the wood to which it was once affixed.

16 Fiema *et al.* 2001, 175.
17 Ibid. 2001, 412, no. 137.
18 Manning 1985, 142.

4. Sheathing:

Seq. No. 79376. Iron sheet metal shaped to fit around an edge. Condition: Corroded. Lower Temenos, Trench 79, Locus 21. Maximum preserved W. 3.9, Th. 0.2.

Comment: Some iron sheathing was recovered from the central area of the West Cryptoporticus. One fragment of thin sheet curves slightly to fit around the edge of a wooden board or door and has a nail driven through it. From the same locus a large iron nail driven through a fragment of bronze sheeting was found. This may have served for affixing a dedication, such as armor or arms, for display on the temple walls, or for decorative bronze elements on doors.[19]

B. Non-structural elements

Besides the metal objects that made up parts of buildings, there are several additional metal artifacts in the sample. These include tools, ornaments and writing implements.

1. Iron tools

There are additional iron tools recovered that were for day-to-day use. Some examples are cataloged below where their function can be identified based on extant components. These include chisels and awls as well as some other recognizable tool fragments. Many additional broken pieces of iron objects survive, the functions of which are unknown.

Chisel A: Seq. No. 85079. Iron chisel. Condition: Corroded. Temple, Trench 85, Locus 1. Preserved L. 14.9, Head Diam. 4.1, Shaft Th. 2.0.

Chisel B: *Seq.* No. 85257. Iron chisel. Condition: Corroded. Area: Temple, Trench 85, Locus: 19. Preserved L.15.5, Head Diam. 4.2, Shaft Th. 2.9.

Comment: Two iron chisels have a form similar to nails, however their size suggests that they were likely mortise chisels.[20] Additionally, they flatten towards the end of the shaft. All come from the South Corridor of the Temple, near the South Perimeter Wall where there was extensive evidence of sandstone quarrying and the cutting back of the escarpment.[21] Chisel B is sharply bent and may have been discarded because it was broken. A third shaft fragment was also collected, which is thick enough to be a chisel,[22] but lacks the head.

Awls

Awl A: Seq. No. 83028. Iron shafts, tapering to a point at both ends, probably used as awls. Condition: Fair. Upper Temenos, Trench 83, Locus 5. L. 10.1, max. Th. 1.2.

Awl B: Seq. No. 85017. Iron shafts, tapering to a point at both ends, probably used as awls. Condition: Fair. Temple, Trench 85, Locus 1. L. 7.4, max. Th. 1.0.

Comment: These are metal shafts with points on both ends.[23] Tools like this were used for punching holes, especially for wood and leatherwork. Awl A is square in section and bent towards one end. Awl B is rounded in section and covered with plaster at one end.

Socket: Seq. No. 84011. An iron tube, broken on both ends. Condition: Fair. Upper Temenos, Trench 84, Locus 7. L. 11.1, Diam. 2.2, Sheet Th. 0.4. Description: Sheet of iron bent in a circle to form shafts to attach tools or weapons to handles.[24]

Needle eye: Seq. No. 79018. Iron needle eye: Condition: Corroded. Lower Temenos, Trench 79, Locus 1. Preserved L. 6.2, Shaft Th. 1.2. Description: The eye end of a large iron packing needle. Large needles can be used for binding large bundles of coarse cloth as well as for leather work.[25]

Chain link or buckle: Seq. No. 89735. Iron chain link: Condition: Corroded. Upper Temenos, Trench 89, Locus 41. L. 6.0, w. 3.6, Th. 1.2. Description: Large iron chain link or buckle, broken at one corner.[26]

---

19 Fiema *et al.* 2001, 410, no. 69.

20 Manning 1985, 23.

21 *Great Temple* vol. 2, 144-45 and 182-85.

22 Seq. No. 85257.

23 Manning 1985, 39-41.

24 Manning 1985, 160-71.

25 Ibid. 36.

26 Ibid. 139.

2. Bronze objects from the sample

Bronze artifacts were less commonly found than iron ones, and were often decorative objects or smaller more precise tools. Four bronze artifacts were examined from the study sample. A further 9 bronze objects were cataloged from the seasons between 1994 and 2003.

Drills: Seq. No. 89858

Drill set. Condition: Fair. Upper Temenos, Trench 89, Locus 41.

Tubular drill: L. 9.9, Diam. 0.8–0.9.

Bronze drill: L. 6.4, Th. 0.4.

Iron drill: L. 10.6, Th. 0.8-0.5.

Comment: Among the most interesting pieces was a group of three tools that may represent a drill kit for lapidary work or bead making.[27]. One is a tapered bronze object, another, a thin bronze tube, the third, an iron point. Bronze was well suited to drilling because of its fine, thin point for precision work. The tube is a tubular drill bit for making round bead cores or circular markings. The iron shaft is another drill bit or a shaft on which to attach the bronze bits to the lathe.

Stylus: Seq. No. 84158. Bronze stylus end. Condition: Very good. Upper Temenos, Trench 84, Locus 18. Preserved L. 5.5, W. 2.1, Th. 0.3. Description: This object is a small flat bar, becoming thinner towards one broken end.[28] This piece may be a stylus or writing implement for wax tablets. The flat end would be used to wipe away the writing to prepare the wax surface for the next use.

Plaque: Seq. No. 96151. Fragment of bronze sheet. Condition: Very good. Propylaeum, Trench 96, Locus 10. L. 16.7, w. 14.0, Th. 0.5. Description: The corner of a bronze plaque with two edges preserved, the other side was torn (fig. 19.6). The remains of one iron nail driven through the bronze near one edge, possibly used to affix this plaque to wood or stone. No evidence of writing or decoration. This object was found in the Propylaeum, which was the area where the temple complex fronts the Roman Street. Any written dedications or decrees would have been well placed in this area.

Coil: Seq. No. 95908. Fragment of a bronze coil, broken on one end. Condition: Fair. Propylaeum, Trench 95, Locus 11. L. 2.3, W. 1.6, Th. 0.4. Description: A small bronze coil from the Propylaeum implies a decorative affix to some vessel or object.

Fig. 19.6. Corner of a Bronze Plaque (Seq. No. 96151). Iron nail fragment can still be seen near the upper edge.

C. Cataloged bronze objects

There are several bronze items that are worth mention from the catalog. These, items are primarily decorative, which is the reason they were selected for special notice.

1. Handles

Handle A: Seq. No. 42199, Cat. No. 97-M-2. Condition: Very good. Lower Temenos, Trench 42, Locus 24. L. 5.5, W. 4.0.

Handle B: Seq. No. 42198, Cat. No. 97-M-3. Condition: Very good. Lower Temenos, Trench 42, Locus 24. L. 6.7, W. 1.64.

Comment: Two cast bronze handles. Attachment is in the form of a serrated leaf, with a protruding scroll under a flower with 12 petals.[29]

2. Pins

Pin A: Seq. No. SP110172, Cat. No. 05-M-12. Long bronze pin. Condition: Fair. Upper Temenos, Trench SP110, Locus 10. L. 10.

---

27 Lucas and Harris 1962, 42-44; Boardman 2001, 379-81.

28 Jacobi 1897, pl. 70.

29 *Great Temple* vol. 1, 309-10; *Great Temple* vol. 2, 397.

Pin B: Seq. No. SP107104, Cat. No. 05-M-20. Long bronze pin. Condition: Fair. Temple, Trench SP107, Locus 9. L.15.9, Th. 0.45.

Pin C: Seq. No. SP110318, Cat. No. 05-M-18. Long bronze pin. Condition: Fair. Upper Temenos, Trench SP110, Locus 27. L. 8.88, W. 0.35, Th. 0.2.

Pin D: Seq. No. 97903, Cat. No. 04-M-75. Long bronze pin. Condition: Fair. Lower Temenos, Trench 97, Locus 2. L. 7.52, Th. 0.15.

Pin E: Seq. No. 97458, Cat. No. 04-M-69. Long bronze pin. Condition: Fair. Lower Temenos, Trench 97, Locus 10. Preserved L. 5.66, Th. 0.43.

Pin F: Seq. No. 94199, Cat. No. 02-M-26. Long bronze pin. Condition: Good. Upper Temenos, Trench 94, Locus 71. L. 14.1, Th. 0.54.

Comment: Six extremely long nail-shaped objects come from the Temple, Upper Temenos and Lower Temenos. These bronze pieces are too long to have been used as nails in wood, the metal was soft and would have bent too easily. Instead, these may have functioned as decorative pins for hair or clothing. The shapes of the heads vary; Pin A is conical, that of Pin C is round.

3. *Buttons*

Button A: Seq. No. 55A060, Cat. No. 99-M-2. Bronze button or stamp. Condition: Good. Temple, Trench 55A. L. 1.81, Diam. 1.74.

Button B: Seq. No. 89956, Cat. No. 02-M-13. Condition: Fair. Upper Temenos, Trench 94, Locus 54. Diam. 1.57, Ht. 0.9.

Comment: Possible bronze buttons. Both have shanks on the back with thread holes. A is more decorative, with a long molded shank. It could possibly have been a decorative stamp seal, but no incisions remain on the face. Button B is a small rounded button.

4. *Bronze plaque fragments*

Plaque A: Seq. No. 53286, Cat. No. 98-M-2. Bronze inscription plaque fragment. Condition: Good. Upper Temenos, Trench 53, Locus 24. L. 13.55, W. 6.27, Th. 0.48.

Plaque B: Seq. No. 52258, Cat. No. 98-M-3. Bronze inscription plaque fragment. Condition: Good, Upper Temenos, Trench 53, Locus 24. L. 5.21, W. 3.17, Th. 0.64.

Comment: Two bronze plaque fragments (compare Seq. No. 96151). Plaque A bears the remains of an inscription in Nabataean, "MLKT" and possibly "H."[30] Plaque B is a trapezoid shaped fragment preserving one edge of the plaque with a raised loop for hanging. It is too corroded to read. The two pieces do not join and are of different thickness, so are unlikely to be from the same inscription.

5. *Spatula*

Bronze spatula. Seq. No. 53190, Cat. No. 98-M-5. Condition: Fair. Upper Temenos, Trench 53. L. 85.6, Th. 0.39. Description: A twisted rod of metal with ends terminating in wide flat shapes. Possibly a double-ended spatula.

6. *Bronze nails*

Nail A: Seq. No. 95891, Cat. No. 03-M-2. Bronze nail. Condition: Good. Propylaeum, Trench 95, Locus 10. L. 6.6, Th. 0.6, Diam. 2.0.

Nail B: Seq. No. 100A129, Cat. No. 04-M-123. Bronze Nail. Condition: Good. Propylaeum, Trench 100, Locus 24. L. 7.9, W. 1.83, Th. 0.75.

Comment: These two bronze nails were found in the Propylaeum. They both have shafts square in section. A has a domed head, B a flat one. These were likely used for decorative studs.

7. *Spoons*

Spoon A: Seq. No. 89853, Cat. No. 02-M-11. Bronze spoon. Condition: Fair. Upper Temenos, Trench 94, Locus 41. L. 11.65, Bowl L. 1.21, Bowl W. 0.83.

---

30 Joukowsky 2003, 220, fig. 239; *Great Temple* vol. 2, 377, fig. 7.6).

Spoon B: Seq. No. 89940, Cat. No. 02-M-16. Bronze spoon. Condition: Poor. Upper Temenos, Trench 94, Locus 54. L. 2.91, Diam. 1.37.

Comment: Two small spoons were discovered in the Upper Temenos. Spoon A has a long handle and small bowl. Spoon B is shallow and broken. These items may have served as cosmetic spoons.

8. Jewelry

Bead: Seq. No. 12, Cat. No. 95-M-7. Half of a metal bead. Condition: Fair. Temple, Trench 19, Locus 8. L. 0.67, w. 0.37, Th. 0.37. Description: Half of a metal bead, broken lengthwise, black in color.

Bracelet A: Seq. No. 97506, Cat. No. 04-M-82. Half of a bronze bracelet. Condition: Poor. Lower Temenos, Trench 97, Locus 10. Th. 0.36, Diam. 5.49. Bracelet A is ca. half of a bracelet, broken at both ends.

Bracelet B: Seq. No. 70184, Cat. No. 00-M-3. Bronze bracelet fragment. Condition: Fair. Propylaeum, Trench 70, Locus 1. L. 5.5, Th. 0.48. Bracelet B, around one-third extant, the non-broken end terminates in a knob.

Earring(?) A: Seq. No. 33024, Cat. No. 96-M-2. Droplet of metal. Condition: Fair. Propylaeum, Trench 33, Locus 1. L. 0.023, Th. 0.0042. This is a piece of wire that terminates in a teardrop shape. The broken end may have formed the hook.

Earring B: Seq. No. 105399, Cat. No. 05-M-15. Loop of metal. Condition: Poor. Lower Temenos, Trench 105, Locus 13. L. 2.16, W. 1.63, Th. 0.22. A loop of metal with one pointed end.

Bronze Pendant. Cat. No. 94-M-3.Condition: Corroded. Temple, Trench 9, Locus 45. L. 2.25, W. 1.4. Description: Bell-shaped bronze pendant, broken off at the wider end.

Bronze rings:

Ring A: Seq. No. 17506, Cat. No. 96-M-1. Condition: Fair. Lower Temenos, Trench 17, Locus 26. Diam. 3.17, Th. 0.53.

Ring B: Seq. No. 31176, Cat. No. 96-M-13. Signet Ring. Condition: Corroded. Lower Temenos, Trench 31, Locus 51. Diam. 2.23, Th. 0.25.

Ring C: Seq. No. 23191, Cat. No. 95-M-4. Knotted Ring: Condition: Corroded. Temple, Trench 23, Locus 7. Diam. 1.9.

Ring D: Seq. No. 52533, Cat. No. 98-M-8. Large Ring: Condition: Fair. Lower Temenos, Trench 52, Locus 2. Diam. 2.24.

Ring E: Seq. No. 82005, Cat. No. 01-M-1. Ring bezel. Condition: Poor. Propylaeum, Trench 82. L. 2.3, W. 1.02, Th. 0.23.

Ring F: Seq. No. 79111, Cat. No. 01-M-2. Condition: Poor. Lower Temenos, Trench 79, Locus 3. Diam. 1.91, Th. 0.45.

Ring G: Seq. No. 89797, Cat. No. 02-M-2. Ring bezel. Condition: Poor. Upper Temenos, Trench 94, Locus 43. W. 2.82, Th. 0.42, Ht. 1.67.

Ring H: Seq. No. 89928, Cat. No. 02-M-10. Large Ring. Condition: Poor. Upper Temenos, Trench 94, Locus 54. Diam. 2.47.

Ring I: Seq. No. SP150036, Cat. No. 05-M-19. Twisted Ring. Condition: Fair. Propylaeum, Trench SP150, Locus 5. Diam. 3.19, Th. 0.67.

Ring J: Seq. No. 97769, Cat. No. 04-M-74. Condition: Good. Lower Temenos, Trench 97, Locus 13. Diam. 1.98, Th. 0.49.

Ring K: Seq. No. 105334, Cat. No. 05-M-16. Signet Ring. Condition: Poor. Upper Temenos, Trench 105, Locus 7. Diam. 1.65, Th. 0.25.

Ring L: Seq. No. 105252, Cat. No. 05-M-17. Condition: Poor. Upper Temenos, Trench 105, Locus 7. Diam. 1.72, Th. 0.16.

Comment: Several bronze rings were found in many areas of the Petra Great Temple. Many are jewelry, most are signet rings and ring bezels. The function of some rings is less apparent—they could have been used for curtains, chains or decorative trappings.

9. Sculpture

Sculptural Fragment: Seq. No. SP108180, Cat. No. 05-M-9. Upper Temenos, Trench SP108, Locus 19. Condition: Fair. L. 6.56, W. 2.67. Description: One piece created of two mended fragments, may be hair for a human figure.

Figurine: Seq. No. 84112, Cat. No. 01-M-4. Upper Temenos, Trench 84, Locus 14. Condition: Fair. L. 3.07, Th. 0.38. Description: Small figurine of an ibex.

D. Lead Objects

From the Sample

Water pipe: Seq. No. 89102. Flattened lead water pipe. Condition: Good. Upper Temenos, Trench 89, Locus 11. L. 13.4, flattened W. 6.9. Estimated circumference on torn end, 15.9, estimated circumference on large end, 18.3, Th. metal sheet, L. .2. Description: Lead water pipe, crushed flat and broken at one end. The flaring end is intact. It came from the Upper Temenos where pipes were found for the Roman-Byzantine baths.[31]

Hangers

Hangar A: Seq. No. 95859. Condition: Good. Propylaeum, Trench 95, Locus 11. L. 6.1, Th. 0.4, paddle w. 0.8. Broken on one end, the other end terminating in a flattened paddle.[32] A white patina has formed on the surface.

Hangar B: Seq. No. 76056. Condition: Good. Upper Temenos, Trench 76, Locus 6. L. 6.7, Th. 0.6. Broken at both ends.

Cataloged Item

Amulet: Seq. No. 15279, Cat. No. 95-M-6. Lead pendant. Condition: Corroded. Temple, Trench 15, Locus 105. L. 1.5, w. 1.3, Th. 0.15. Oval shaped lead pendant with worn incised decoration on one side in the form of a cross or a human.

E. Silver Object

From the sample

Ring: Seq. No. 95267. Condition: Very good. Propylaeum, Trench 95, Locus 4. Diam. 2.0-1.8, Th. 0.2. Description: Thin silver wire wrapped into a circle.

Silver cataloged objects

Silver decoration: Seq. No. 98B037, Cat. No. 05-M-14. Molded piece of silver. Condition: Good. Lower Temenos, Trench 98B, Locus 1. W.1.49, Th. 0.06. Description: Roughly pear shaped piece of silver with molded design. Starting near the tapering end are two rows of vertical hatching over a band of heart shaped leaves.

Pendant: Seq. No. 22084, Cat. No. 96-M-12. Silver pendant. Condition: Fair. Temple, Trench 22, Locus 8. L. 1.82, Th. 0.13. Description: Silver piriform pendant.

Bracelet: Seq. No. 126356, Cat. No. 06-M-5. Condition: Good. Lower Temenos, Trench 126, Locus 12. L. 5.1, W. 2.97, Th. 0.28. Description: Silver bracelet of twisted wire with the ends formed into coils.

F. A Gold Object

Gold clasp: Seq. No. 95332, Cat. No. 03-M-1. Condition: Very good. Propylaeum, Trench 95, Locus 4. L. 1.6, W. 0.5, Th. >0.01. Description: Gold clasp, the center is a flower with four petals each marked with a diamond shape. The flower is flanked by diamond shapes and flattened spheres. Spheres are marked possibly to receive perforations. The clasp is made of sheet metal formed in a mold.

II: Context studies: three examples of metal artifact concentrations

In addition to the review of individual artifacts, the evidence from the Petra Great Temple showed certain distribution patterns that are worthy of further study.

A. Evidence of arms and armor

In the northwest of the Temple complex, in the Lower Temenos and Propylaeum are found a concentration of ballista balls.[33] Along with these artifacts were items such as arrowheads, spear points, helmet cheek pieces, a scabbard and horse trappings including decorative pendants, iron rings and a buckle. The items are overwhelmingly military in nature. These artifacts may be evidence of military storage or debris from an attack.[34]

---

31 *Great Temple* vol. 2, 191.

32 Hammond 1996, 126-27; Rababeh 2005, 47.

33 See Ch. 21.

34 *Great Temple* vol. 2, 79-80 and 116.

1. Arrowheads

A total of 106 iron arrowheads were found in the Petra Great Temple (fig. 19.7). All are from the northwest Propylaeum and Lower Temenos.[35]

Lower Temenos: Trench SP104 (West Cryptoporticus east, sondage). Locus 1-*4*; Locus 7-*4*; Trench 97 (West Cryptoporticus east). Locus 10-*2*, Locus 13-*34*, Locus 15-*35*, Locus 22-*1*; Trench 5 (East part of the West Exedra). Locus 46-*1*.

Propylaeum: Trench SP87 (Propylaeum West) Locus 7-*2*, Locus 8-*3*, Locus 9-*5*, Locus 10-*3*; Locus 11-*11*, and Locus 15-*1*.

Measurement Range of the Arrowheads: L. 2.16-5.36, W. 0.42-1.69.

Fig. 19.7. Arrowheads from the Lower Temenos, West Cryptoporticus.

Almost all of the arrowheads are tanged with a trilobate profile, which was a design of central Asiatic origin. The type was common throughout the Roman Empire before the 2nd c. A.D. and continued to be used on the Roman Eastern frontier thereafter.[36] The side lobes are drawn back to form barbs. A close parallel for these pieces comes from the Cave of Letters in Israel from the 2nd c. A.D.[37] A few are more leaf shaped, lacking barbs, but still tanged with a trilobate profile. One arrowhead (Lower Temenos Trench 5) has an elongated tanged shape. These latter shapes are comparable to finds from the Petra Church.

2. Spears

Spear A: Seq. No. 102463, Cat. No. 05-M-8. Bronze spear point. Condition: Poor. Lower Temenos, Trench 102, Locus 1. L. 7.30, W. 3.59, Th. 0.29. A broad leaf-shaped spear point preserving the upper section.

Spear B: Seq. No. SP87067, Cat. No. 04-M-22. Bronze spear point. Condition: Fair. Propylaeum, Trench SP87, Locus 7. L. 11.6, W. 9.7. Description: Most of the point and shaft are preserved.

3. Horse Trappings

Harness fragment: Seq. No. 126811, Cat. No. 06-M-6. Horse harness. Condition: Fair. Lower Temenos, Trench 126, Locus 27. L. 9.5, Th. 1.06. Description: Two iron rings, one larger than the other, joined by a bolt.

Horse trapping A: Seq. No. 97A324, Cat. No. 04-M-127. Perforated Bronze Disc. Condition: Fair. Lower Temenos, Trench 97, Locus 13. Diam. 1.42, Th. 0.14.

Horse trapping B: Seq. No. 97A332, Cat. No. 04-M-128. Half of a crescent pendant. Condition: Poor. Lower Temenos, Trench 97, Locus 13. L. 3.17, W. 1.02, Th. 0.12.

Horse trapping C: Seq. No. 97A333, Cat. No. 04-M-129. Leaf shaped pendant. Condition: Fair. Lower Temenos, Trench 97, Locus 13. L. 2.33, Th. 0.08.

Horse trapping D: Seq. No. 97A330, Cat. No. 04-M-130. Crescent pendant. Condition: Fair. Lower Temenos, Trench 97, Locus 13. L. 4.16, W. 3.23, Th. 0.15.

Horse trapping E: Seq. No. 97A327, Cat. No. 04-M-131 (fig. 19.8). Crescent pendant. Condition: Fair. Lower Temenos, Trench 97, Locus 13. L. 4.18, W. 3.75, Th. 0.1.

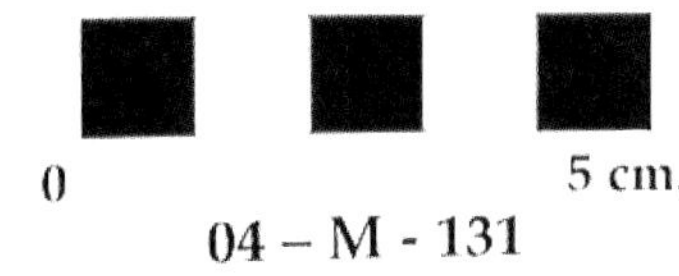

Fig. 19.8. Crescent-shaped Bronze Pendant for Horse Trappings (04-M-131).

35 Ibid. 116, fig. 3.44.
36 Coulston 1985, 264-65; Coulston 2001.
37 Yadin 1963, 91, nos. 38-40.

Horse trapping F: Seq. No. 97A328, Cat. No. 04-M-132. Crescent pendant. Condition: Fair. Lower Temenos, Trench 97, Locus 13. L. 3.99, W. 3.29, Th. 0.8.

Horse trapping G: Seq. No. 97A329, Cat. No. 04-M-133. Crescent pendant. Condition: Fair. Lower Temenos, Trench 97, Locus 13. L. 4.27, W. 3.75, Th. 0.1.

Horse trapping H: Seq. No. 97A331, Cat. No. 04-M-134. Leaf pendant fragment. Condition: Poor. Lower Temenos, Trench 97, Locus 13. L. 1.6, W. 1.54, Th. 0.9.

Comment: From a single locus in the Lower Temenos comes a hoard of bronze pendants, a bronze ring and a scabbard.[38] The pendants have loops at the top for attachment. Two of these sheet metal pendants are leaf shaped, one is a disc. The crescent pendants were discs with curved snips on the bottom to create crescent shapes with a round tab in the middle.

4. Helmet cheek pieces

Iron helmet cheek piece or ax blade. Seq. No. 97584, Cat. No. 04-M-67. Condition: Poor. Lower Temenos, Trench 97, Locus 15. L. 14.09, w. 7.57, Th. 0.47. Description: Sheet of iron shaped roughly into a bent trapezoid.

Bronze helmet cheek piece: Seq. No. SP87090, Cat. No. 04-M-32 (fig. 19.9).

Condition: Very good. Propylaeum, Trench SP87, Locus 9. L. 15.3, W. 10.9, Th. 0.26. Description: Slightly convex bronze sheet, formed into a wide sickle shape.[39] This probably belongs to a cavalry helmet.[40]

Fig. 19.9. Cheek piece for a bronze cavalry helmet (04-M-32).

5. Iron rings

Ring A: Seq. No. 97A347, Cat. No. 04-M-140. Condition: Fair. Lower Temenos, Trench 97, Locus 23. Diam. 2.71, Th. 0.66.

Ring B: Seq. No. 97A336, Cat. No. 04-M-126. Condition: Poor. Lower Temenos, Trench 97, Locus 13. Diam. 2.4.

Ring C: Seq. No. 97A335, Cat. No. 04-M-125. Condition: Poor. Lower Temenos, Trench 97, Locus 13. Diam. 2.13.

Ring D: Seq. No. 97773, Cat. No. 04-M-76. Condition: Poor. Lower Temenos, Trench 97, Locus 13. Diam. 2.18.

Ring E: Seq. No. 97780, Cat. No. 04-M-71. Trench 97, Locus 10. Diam. 2.21.

Ring F: Seq. No. SP87099, Cat. No. 04-M-27. Condition: Fair. Propylaeum, Trench SP87, Locus 10. Diam. 2.64, Th. 0.77.

Ring G: Seq. No. SP87313, Cat. No. 04-M-29. Ring fragment. Condition: Fair. Propylaeum, Trench SP87, Locus 11. L. 2.44, Th. 0.59.

Ring H: Seq. No. SP87319, Cat. No. 04-M-20. Ring fragment. Condition: Poor. Propylaeum, Trench SP87, Locus 11, L. 2.75, Th. 1.25.

Comment: These 8 iron rings and ring fragments come from the northwest side of the temple complex. These could be used as fasteners, horse trappings or for arms and armor. The use is usually indeterminate, but their concentration in this area with the associated military finds suggests they were used with weaponry.

6. Buckles

Bronze buckle: Seq. No. 31121, Cat. No. 96-M-16. Fastener. Condition: Good. Lower Temenos, Trench 31, Locus 21. L. 4.24, Th. 0.53. Description: A rectangular bronze sheet for application attached to a figure-8 shaped fastener.

38 Cat. No. 04-M-136.

39 *Great Temple* vol. 2, 116, fig. 3.45.

40 Warry 1995, 168.

Iron Buckle: Seq. No. 97777, Cat. No. 04-M-79. Condition: Fair. Lower Temenos, Trench 97, Locus 10. L. 6.15, W. 3.78, Th. 0.34, Width of interior opening: 1.13. Description: Oval buckle.

7. Boss

Iron boss: Seq. No. 97A293, Cat. No. 04-M-124. Iron, knob shape. Condition: Poor. Lower Temenos, Trench 97, Locus 10. Diam. 3.43, Ht. 3.27. Description: A round boss of iron, possibly from a shield.

8. Scabbard:

Scabbard Seq. No. 97A326, Cat. No. 04-M-136. Tip of a bronze scabbard (fig. 19.10). Condition: Poor. Lower Temenos, Trench 97, Locus 13. Preserved l.: 8.81, Th. 0.55. Description: Fragmentary bronze scabbard with a round terminal at the point.

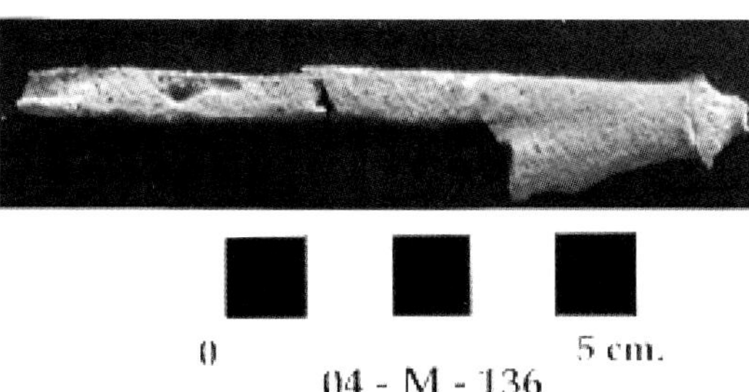

Fig. 19.10. Point of a bronze scabbard (04-M-136).

B. Evidence of blades

In the Residential Quarter near the Upper Temenos, several iron blades as well as a bronze blade, were found in a single locus. Four cataloged knife blade fragments[41] were recovered from a locus in the Residential Quarter, along with two small ax blades. This locus in the Residential Quarter was below higher ground, and it was theorized was a deposit of soil that washed down from above. It was an extremely rich and varied deposit. These objects may testify to metallurgical activity on the high ground above the Residential Quarter, involving the maintenance or manufacturing of tool blades.

1. Iron knife blades

Blade A: Seq. No. 89793, Cat. No. 02-M-7. Condition: Poor. Upper Temenos, Trench 94, Locus 41. L. 8.63, W. 2.28.

Blade B: Seq. No. 89798, Cat. No. 02-M-8. Knife blade. Condition: Poor. Upper Temenos, Trench 94, Locus 41. L. 15.56, Th. 0.57.

Blade C: Seq. No. 89810, Cat. No. 02-M-17. Knife blade. Condition: Poor. Upper Temenos, Trench 94, Locus 41. L. 5.33, W. 1.25.

Blade D: Seq. No. 89792, Cat. No. 02-M-18. Knife blade. Condition: Poor. Upper Temenos, Trench 94, Locus 41. L. 6.78, W. 1.40.

Comment: Commonly the blades of these knives are curved. For blades A, C and D, only the ends are preserved. Blade B is complete.

2. Bronze knife blades

Knife blade: Seq. No. 89878, Cat. No. 02-M-9. Condition: Poor. Upper Temenos, Trench 94, Locus 41. L. 4.55, W. 1.33. Description: Bronze knife blade with curved edge.

3. Iron ax blades

Ax blade A: Seq. No. 89832, Cat. No. 02-M-22. Ax blade. Condition: Poor. Upper Temenos, Trench 94, Locus 41. L. 9.24, W. 4.37, Th. 0.51.

Ax blade B: Ax blade. Condition: Fair. Upper Temenos, Trench 94, Locus 41. L. 6.56, W. 7.18,Th. 0.23. Description: Corroded ax blade with curved edge.

---

41 As well as an additional object that was not cataloged, Seq. No. 89805.

C. Evidence of metallurgy

In addition to the metal artifacts themselves, there is extensive evidence for metallurgy, specifically the creation of copper alloy, in the precinct of the Petra Great Temple. The finds are highly concentrated in the east side of the Upper Temenos. Slag and metal waste was recovered from many of the trenches excavated in this area. From the southwestern part of the Upper Temenos, the Baroque Room complex, comes a rich array of finished copper alloy objects as well as a large piece of copper ore. The finds on the western side of the Upper Temenos may indicate that a processing site was located here, while the east side of the Upper Temenos may have served as a dump for the byproducts of this industry.

There were local sources of copper to the south of Petra.[42] The collected ore was ground into small pieces and mixed with charcoal. It was then heated in a furnace to extract the metal. Metal would separate from the ore and be on the bottom of the crucible while the vitrified slag and waste that remained on top would be chipped off. The metal could then be reheated in crucibles made of pottery to remove the air. Molten copper could be combined with tin to create bronze. Refined copper or bronze alloy was then poured into molds for casting.[43] Several different artifacts were found representing almost all the steps in the smelting and casting process.

Upper Temenos East

Copper slag (Seq. Nos. SP84048, SP84128, SP85159, 77341, 77322, SP84024, 84041, SP84114, SP84082, SP84101, 84180). Porous materials, partially vitrified from the smelting process, with charcoal embedded in them.

Crucible fragment (Seq. No. 84070). One piece of a spout of clay, vitrified with copper residue on some surfaces.

Amorphous fragments of copper or bronze. (Seq. Nos. 84070, 84172, SP84220, 84058, 84079, 91036, 84025, SP84077, 91021).

Amorphous piece of a white powdery substance. (Seq. No. 90026). Possibly corroded tin.

Small bronze corner or lip. (Seq. No. 84147). Possibly from a vessel or molded sheet.

Small greenish stone. (Seq. No. 77322). Possibly ore.

Upper Temenos West

Bronze pins (Seq. Nos. 89735, 89775, 89923, 83313). 0.006-0.002 thick, tapering to points.

Amorphous pieces of copper or bronze (Seq. No. 89923).

Drill set (Seq. No. 89858, See above).

Bronze hook (Seq. No. 89009). W. 0.005, Th. 0.003, Bent L. 0.04.

Bronze vial? (Seq. No. 89873). Diam. 0.017 x 0.015, Ht. 0.015. Remains of the end of a bronze tube, with white substance in it. Possibly a container for some substance.

Copper ore (Seq. No. 89748). An amorphous piece of copper bearing stone.

Chemical analyses

Three samples of copper alloy excavated from different contexts at the Petra Great Temple were sent for scientific analysis. The tests were performed by Laboratory Testing Inc. and Thielsch Engineering, Inc. of Cranston, RI. The tests consisted of chemical analyses; the procedures were MAS-ICP, Rev. 5, analysis of metals and their /lloys by ICP. Small pieces of the test items were sectioned for microscopic examination.

Sample 1: *Metal* plate for inscription, Seq. No. 96151. Primary elements: 70.64% Copper, 23.69% Lead; 5.25% Tin, Trace elements .098% Antimony, .071% Arsenic, .058% Calcium, .040% Iron, .036% Nickel, .020% Silicon, and .010% Magnesium.

Comment: This plaque consists primarily of copper, but the secondary ingredient is lead, while tin is third. Microscopic examination revealed that the lead and tin were evenly distributed, which

42 Hodges 1974, 56.
43 Ibid. 71-75 and 143-44.

proves that they were intentionally alloyed with the copper, rather than naturally occurring elements. Lead was often added to bronze to make it more pliable for sculpting, reducing the porosity of the metal and the casting temperature.[44] For statues or decorative plaques, it was not important to harden the metal, as opposed to copper alloys that were used to make tools.

Sample 2: Amorphous metal lump, Seq. No. 87392. Primary elements: 87.64% Copper, 11.35% Tin, Trace elements .81% Lead, .065% Iron, .038% Arsenic, and .036% Antimony.

Comment: The second object sampled was an amorphous lump of copper alloy with exterior corrosion but which was still extremely dense, indicating that a metal core remained intact. This alloy was found to be tin-bronze. It is likely that this object was an ingot fragment. Metals in antiquity (gold, silver, lead and copper) were extracted from the ore and the molten metal was put into molds to form ingots. These ingots were traded in bulk. Pieces were broken off as needed and weighted for metal working or the production of coinage.

Sample 3: Nail, Seq. No. 95875. Primary elements: 99.83% Copper, Trace elements .052% Iron, .021% Tin. This sampled object is a Thin Nail (see the Nail Typology above).

Comment: This object was covered with copper oxide corrosion, making it extremely difficult to see if it was made of bronze or if the corrosion was merely the object that was once affixed by the nail. The results were surprising, since the nail is almost pure copper. Nails were usually composed of copper alloyed with tin to harden it. However, the context of this nail might indicate that it was used to affix to molded plaster which would not require a great deal of strength or hardness. It would have been more important that the metal not expand when corroded, as iron does, causing the plaster to flake and crack.

The nail was also cut into a section to examine its structure. Microscopic examination indicates that this nail was cast into shape and then cold pounded to form the head and to flatten the sides of the spike.

Overall, the elements in the tested pieces are extremely pure. There are only small levels of trace elements, considered to be naturally occurring, in any of the samples and all elements which occur in high percentages would seem to have been added intentionally. The metal extraction techniques were evidently highly refined.

Conclusions

The metal artifacts from the Petra Great Temple provide extremely valuable insight about metals in their entire cycle of use, from their manufacture, to consumption, to deposition.

From nails and other iron artifacts, we gain clues about the structure of the buildings. Because of the dry climate and relatively good preservation of the iron artifacts, we have valuable clues about the wooden and metal elements, parts of structures not commonly archaeologically visible on ancient buildings.

This study also provides a glimpse into the array of ancient metal use. Iron, due to its strength, was most often used for utilitarian purposes, building and tools. In addition, we have ample evidence for bronze mostly used for decorative purposes, both on personal and structural ornaments. However, it could also be formed into tools and weapons. Infrequently evidence was found of precious metals, the Petra Great Temple produced only one decorative artifact in gold and some silver jewelry, likely because of the value of the metal. Lead was usually utilized for functional purposes but could also serve as decoration.

There were three examples metal artifact concentrations which seem to indicate Great Temple areas of metal working activities. In the northeast sector of the Temple complex was strong evidence

44 Nicholson and Shaw 2000, 154-55.

for military activity, either storage of military equipment or perhaps of military operations. Near the Residential Quarter, there was evidence for some form of work on tools such as blades. Finally, the smelting and casting of copper alloy took place in the area around the southwest corner of the Temple, while waste products from this process were disposed of around the eastern side of the Temple.

20

A store of ballista balls

Martha Sharp Joukowsky

The geographical setting of Petra would have made the city an awkward place to attack for a hostile force. Because of its erratic rift valley topography, any assailant would have found it impossible to ensure the sealing of the city by a cordon of troops. The most important building within central Petra, the Qasr al-Bint, would have been out of effective range for any enemy artillery.[1] If the Romans did attack the city at the time of the annexation, they may have set up their siege engines on the N slope overlooking the Wadi Musa, *c.*40-50 m across the wadi from the Great Temple, since that was the most vulnerable building in central Petra. The evidence for the use of ballista balls at Petra comes primarily from the Propylaeum West, where 421 rounded stone projectiles intended for use by anti-personnel stone-projectors[2] were discovered.

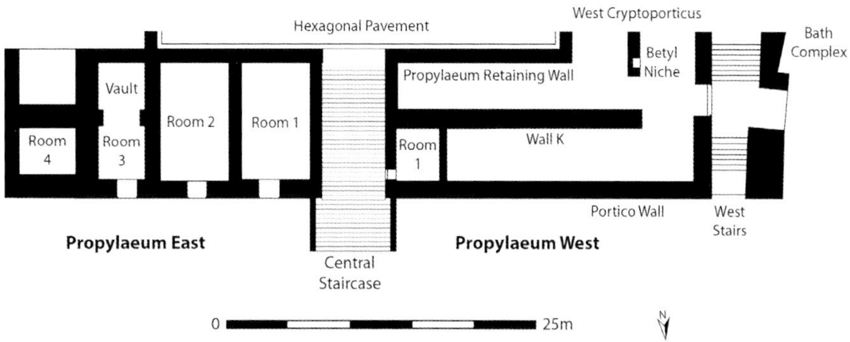

Fig. 20.1. Plan of Propylaeum.

Context of the finds

The Propylaeum (55 x 12.5 m) is the first component to be encountered at the N end of the Great Temple complex, behind the Portico Wall and directly adjacent to the Roman Street[3] (figs. 20.1-20.2).[4] The Portico Wall,[5] now in a state of ruin, dates to the mid-1st c. B.C. (Site Phase II); 6 ashlar courses remain bordering the Roman street (figs. 20.1, 20.3-4). Additions to the Propylaeum were constructed to the south behind the Portico Wall in Site Phase IV (1st c. B.C. to 1st c. A.D.). This was when a parallel wall, the Propylaeum Retaining Wall,[6] its N face supporting columns with elephant-head capitals, was built atop a cryptoporticus;[7] at the same time the Portico Wall was reconfigured and modified.[8] Noted on the plan (fig. 20.1) are two parallel galleries running E-W, separated by Wall K.[9] The North Gallery is 3 m wide and 25 m long (fig. 20.3 shows its W end, where it turns

1 Marsden (1969, 91) estimated that ancient artillery had an effective range of between 400 to 500 yards (366 to 457 m). Josephus (*War* 5.6.3 [270]) records that one-talent shot fired by *ballistae* at the siege of Jerusalem travelled two *stades* (370 m) or more.

2 Although the first catapults had been developed for Dionysius I, tyrant of Syracuse, around 399 B.C., the type of torsion engine that would have used these forms of projectiles was probably introduced by the corps of engineers working for Philip II of Macedon. Artillery barrages formed a standard element of the Roman siege repertoire. See Diod. Sic. 41.1-6 and 42.1; Marsden 1969, 48-58.

3 Just beyond the Portico Wall is the Roman Street, and parallel to it is an immensely steep, deep embankment created by the Wadi Musa gorge.

4 For a general description of the Propylaeum, see vol. 2, 52-85.

5 The Portico Wall with Wall K and the parallel Lower Temenos Retaining Wall behind it are still visible today.

6 This 17-course ashlar wall today measures 6.7 m in height.

7 The stubs of 10 vaults across the width of the wall remain today.

8 It is difficult to restore the original height of the Portico Wall; possibly it was built as high as the Propylaeum Retaining Wall.

9 In the excavations of the Colonnaded Street, Wall K was so named by P. J. Parr (1970, 351 fig. 1, 353).

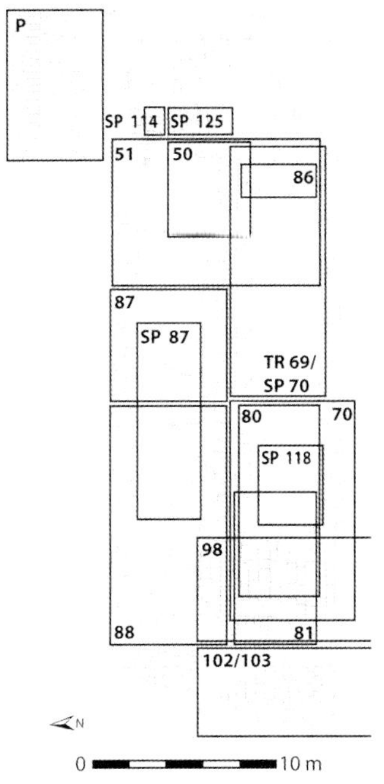

Fig. 20.2. Trenches excavated in the Propylaeum.

south; fig. 20.4 defines the N and S galleries, with Wall K dividing the galleries). The South Gallery in this Nabataean phase was vaulted and entered from the W end (from the West Entry Staircase, also of Phase IV). In the middle of the North Gallery a two-course stone bench (14.52 m long, 0.71 wide), running along the N face of Wall K, was set on top of a ceramic tile pavement. The plaster on Wall K (in which a Nabataean graffito was inscribed[10]) extended behind the top course of the bench, indicating that it was applied before the bench was constructed. The earliest stage of the North Gallery included a beaten earth floor laid over unshaped rocks set into fill.

Excavations of the North Gallery earlier than 2004

Beginning in 1997, excavation in the North Gallery removed 2 m of accumulated overburden and many fallen architectural fragments. The considerable evidence for earthquake damage included the collapse of columns of the Lower Temenos/Propylaeum Retaining Wall into the cryptoporticus of the South Gallery.[11] Ballista balls were first encountered in 2002[12] in Trench 87.[13] The first 1.8 m of fill was excavated in successive 50-cm passes across the trench that were interrupted by earthquake collapse of wall and arch ashlars and column drums. Next, homogeneous fill was removed and a ceramic tile floor exposed both in the NW corridor and in Room 1 to the west of the Central Staircase. The tile floor extended 15.25 m E–W across most of the trench; it was 2.92 m wide at its widest point. One coin (02-C-16) dating to A.D. 193-211 was found in the fill of Room 1 (Locus 6). Thirty-nine ballista balls were found in the fill of Tr. 87, Locus 7 (the locus measured 19.5 m E–W x 4.39 m N–S). Also in this deposit were 11 coins from the Nabataean period onwards, the majority being 4th or 5th c. A.D. (02-C-4, 02-C-5, 02-C-7, 02-C13).

He dated Wall K to later than the beginning of the reign of Aretas IV, or to some point in the 1st c. A.D. Our phasing places its construction to approximately the same time, sometime in the mid-1st c. A.D. It is assumed that in antiquity it stood nearly as high as the Lower Temenos Retaining Wall, to support their shared vaulted cryptoporticus over the South Gallery.

10 Vol. 2, fig. 7.30, p. 378.

11 Vol. 2, fig. 2.40, p. 78.

12 Three ballista balls were recovered in Tr. 87 Room 1, and 42 more in the North Gallery. Farther west in Trench 81 (fig. 20.2, final report Joukowsky 2002b, 11-12) 9 ballista balls were found, while 3 were found nearby in Trench 88 at the West Entry Stairs (final report, Joukowsky 2002c, 10).

13 Trench 87 (not to be confused with Special Project 87) was 19.41 m long and 5.3-4.39 m wide. The phases encountered in this trench are as follows. Stage 1 represents the construction of the Portico Wall (Site Phase II) and Wall K (Site Phase IV); the original lower courses of these two walls predate the construction of the temple complex, as suggested by P. J. Parr. Stage 2 (Site Phase IV) saw the construction of the Lower Temenos Retaining Wall with its cryptoporticus and columns. The Portico Wall and Wall K were breached and a west doorway accessing the West Entry Stairs to the cryptoporticus system was constructed. A window in Wall K in Room 1 was probably constructed and plastered. Stage 3 (Site Phases IV-V) saw the division of the cryptoporticus. The W wall of Room 1 was constructed abutting Wall K, separating it from the main passageway to the west. (Possibly some form of access to Room 1 existed to the east, but it remains undiscovered.) Stage 4 saw the paving of the area (Site Phase VI, dated to *c.*A.D. 106). The floors in Room 1 and in the Northwest Corridor were laid. It is possible that the plastering of the W face of the W wall of Room 1 and the N face of Wall K in the Northwest Corridor also occurred now. In Stage 5 the E wall of Room 1 was constructed with a doorway leading to the Great Temple Central Stairs (Site Phase VII). It was laid over the ceramic floor tiles, and a bench against the N face of Wall K was built atop the tiles. Room 1's Wall K window and Room 1 doorway were blocked and the room abandoned. Finally, the vaults of the South Gallery cryptoporticus collapsed, fill accumulated, and the columns fell (Site Phase IX, associated with the earthquake of 363).

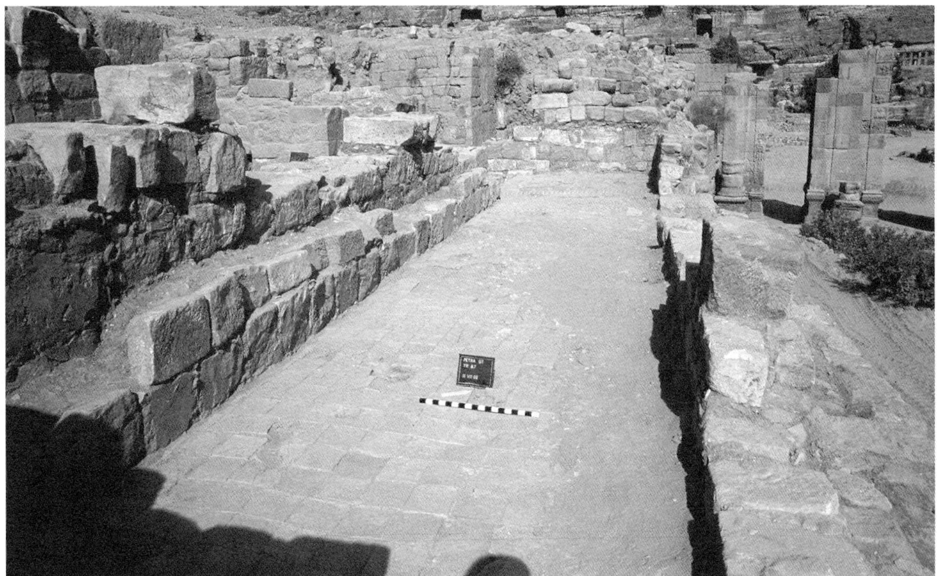

Fig. 20.3. Propylaeum West, North Gallery, view to west.

Fig. 20.4. Propylaeum West, North and South Galleries, view to east.

2004-2005 excavations

It was still unclear whether the ballista balls had been used underneath to level the pavement or had been set on top of the pavement; their relationship to the bench was also unclear. Therefore in 2004 S. K. Reid supervised the excavation of Special Project 87[14] to the west of Room 1 between the Portico Wall on the N side[15] and the bench abutting the N side of Wall K on the S side. To assess the

14 Previous excavation in Trenches 50, 51, 87 and SP53 removed a depth of *c*.3.7 m of earthquake collapse full of architectural fragments before SP87 was opened.

15 The majority of ballista balls were found inside the Portico Wall in the North Gallery, not along the bottom of the wall. If a battle did take place, the Romans concentrated their efforts on the top half of the wall

Fig. 20.5. Ballista balls recovered in the North Gallery and then set against the Portico Wall.

stratigraphic relationship between the ballista balls and the tile pavement, the E central area of our special project (7.66 x 1.96) was excavated below the tile floor (Locus 9) in the center of the North Gallery (figs. 20.2 and 20.6-20.7). Locus 2 formed the top layer of ballista balls in the W central area of the trench; they were mixed with a sandy and silt-like soil (7.5YR 5/4) and randomly distributed cobble-sized rocks. Here a total of 40 densely-packed ballista balls and trilobate iron arrowheads were found. Locus 10 was an upper layer of ballista balls in the E part of the trench. It too had a sandy, silt-like soil (7.5YR 5/4). Here a coin (04-C-03) dating to A.D. 39/40 was recovered.[16] Associated artifacts in SP87 included many trilobite iron arrowheads[17] and several finds of a probable or possible military nature, including a bronze scabbard tip, the left cheek plate of an helmet,[18] a tear-drop-shaped bronze scale possibly from a suit of armor, fragments of 3 iron rings, a bronze hook, a bronze shafted spearhead, and a bronze loop of uncertain purpose. The sparse pottery included a few Nabataean plate fragments, one decorated with red-painted fine radiating lines, another with red painted palmettes.[19] Locus 12 yielded the partial spatulated nozzle of a Herodian lamp (04-L-08), dating between *c.*50 B.C. and A.D. 70.

To summarize the loci of Special Project 87: the deliberate fill beneath the floor tiles included limestone and sandstone ballista balls (Loci 2-3, 6-12, 15, 18), roughly contained by a series of N–S lines composed of unshaped, flat limestone and sandstone rocks (Loci 13, 16-17, 19). This ballista ball and rock fill was then covered with a gray mortar (Locus 5), after which the floor of ceramic tiles was laid on top. The excavator, S. K. Reid, wrote in the trench report as follows:[20]

(see vol. 2, figs. 2.2, 2.23 and 2.26) where the ashlars have been breached. It is unclear if there is a correlation between the breaks in the wall and the concentrations of ballista balls in the North Gallery.

16 Meshorer, 1975, no. 112, 105. The locus 10 deposit was initially placed in a later phase, but this coin and Locus 10 are now dated to Site Phase VI, or *c.*106-113/114 (earthquake).

17 Vol. 2, figs. 3.44 and 119. These can be paralleled at Gamla (Syron 2002, fig. 9.5); Josephus (*BJ* 3.211) refers to Nabataean bowmen.

18 Cat. no. 04-M-32; see vol. 2, fig. 3.45.

19 These painted wares can be dated to S. G. Schmid's Phase 3b (2003, fig. 63), *c.*A.D. 70/80-100; there were also plain, white-slipped ribbed wares in these loci.

20 See *Open Context*, 2004 Trench Reports, SP 87.

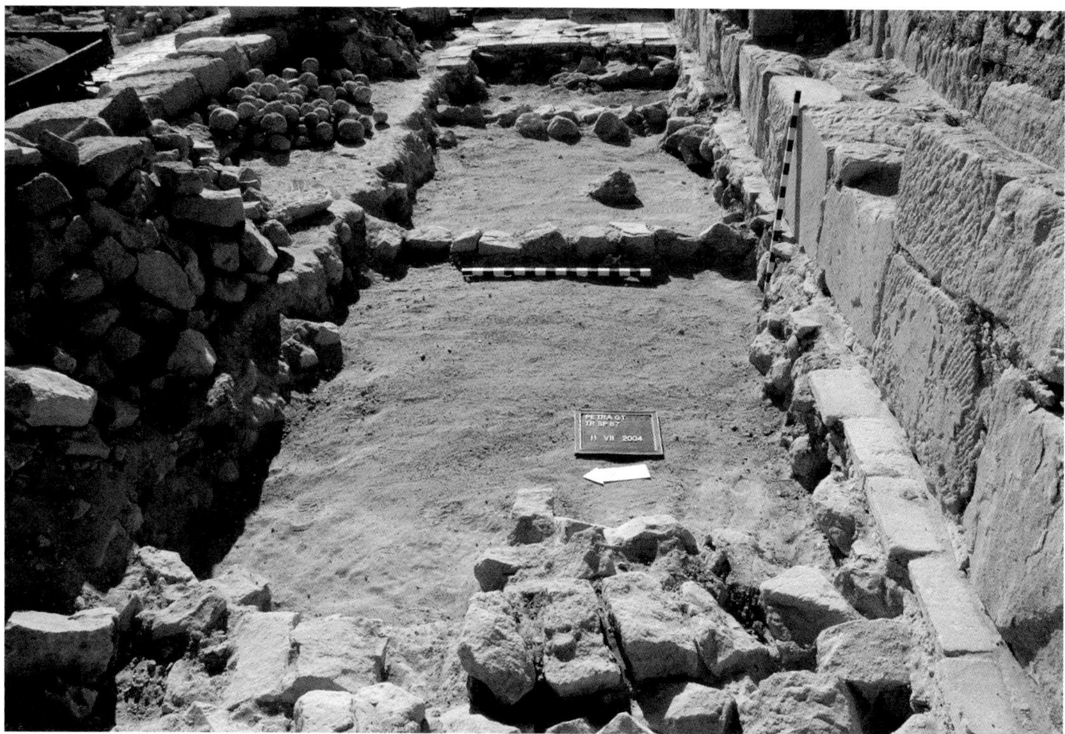

Fig 20.6. SP87 during excavation, view to north.

Fig. 20.7. SP87 during excavation, view to east.

The 56 ballista balls discovered at or above floor level in Trench 87 are dwarfed by the over 350 ballista balls *below* floor level in Trench SP87. The even distribution of the ballista balls suggests intentional use as fill as opposed to chance deposition through warfare or other event unrelated to construction. The density of the ballista ball loci in the subfloor is also an unlikely pattern in which to find the results of an attack. Had the Propylaeum been attacked from across the wadi (from the north), one would expect to find ballista balls scattered over a wide area within the radius of the

Fig. 20.8. SP87, North Gallery, mapping of ballista balls, showing the relationship between them and the tiled pavement, view to north.

> range of the siege engines and in the general cardinal direction of the intended target, with occasional outliers. That each of over 350 ballista balls from Trench SP87 landed in essentially the same place, piling up on each other in such a manner, is difficult to believe. Again, the density of ballista balls seems far more indicative of intentional placement, rather than a representation of the randomness of artillery fire from a distance.
>
> Although the author (Sara Karz Reid herself) believes the ballista balls were deliberately employed as subfloor fill, it is more difficult to evaluate whether or not they had been used as weaponry prior to that use. It is possible, for example, that these ballista balls had been launched at the Great Temple by Cornelius Palma or another attacker, then collected and re-used in the subfloor at a later time. It is also possible that they were collected from a much wider area, perhaps encompassing several structures that had been under attack, before being placed in the subfloor. Or the ballista balls may never have been used but rather simply stored at the Great Temple (or some other structure) for an anticipated use; after the danger had passed, they were relegated to the subfloor fill. These are only some of the many possible scenarios that could have preceded their use as fill.

A total of 361 densely packed ballista balls (85% of the entire collection) were excavated from beneath the pavers in SP87. Prior to its removal, each layer of balls was mapped in a multi-step process (fig. 20.8). After cleaning, the layer was photographed to give a top plan on which to map each ball within a layer. A unique sequence number was assigned to each ballista ball, which was then recorded on the form for architectural fragments and on the ballista ball itself.[21]

Next, still within 2004, Reid and M. S. Zimmerman excavated SP125 (see fig. 20.2), a sondage beneath the surviving Propylaeum Central Staircase. It found a continuation of the tile floor and an earlier set of stairs belonging to Site Phase VII.

---

21 The ballista balls were not assigned Special Finds numbers but were given Sequence Numbers. Special information, including date of recovery, trench and locus, material (limestone, sandstone, chert, granite), diameter, and Site Phase, can be found in the Architectural Fragment database. When the balls were removed, their position in the trench was recorded and each was marked with its Sequence Number, but their weighing had to be postponed.

A final effort to clarify the story of the ballista balls was made in 2005 by T. M. Khanachet (SP114). He excavated the west pavement of the Central Staircase adjacent to Room 1 to determine whether the ballista balls lay on top of the floor and so were later than the pavement, or whether they were beneath the staircase treads and would be earlier. He confirmed that the balls predated the installation of the Central Staircase (cf. vol. 2, 70-72):

> Special Project 114 confirms that at the entry to Room 1, the ballista assemblage is not under the stairs, so the ballista balls used as rubble fill and leveling of the flooring of the Propylaeum West do not continue under the pavers of the landing for the earlier steps. If the terracotta tiling under the pavers of the landing is understood to be the same as that found in the two west rooms of the Propylaeum, then the ballista balls predate both staircases of the Propylaeum. If that is the case, then two possibilities emerge: if the current date, Site Phase VI, A.D. 106-113/4, for the ballista balls is correct, then both the early and later stairs must be dated to the Roman period; alternatively, the ballista balls could be earlier and the earlier stairways could be dated from the Nabataean period. A careful re-analysis of the remains will have to be made to shed more light on the dating of this area of the Propylaeum.

The ballista balls: material, shape and weight

Fig. 20.9. Weighing a ballista ball.

Our database contains 421 ballista balls, of which 417 (99%) came from the Propylaeum, 4 from the Lower Temenos, and 2 from the Upper Temenos. As many as 416 (98%) are associated with Site Phase VI, which begins with the Roman annexation, while 7 are assigned to Site Phases IX-XIII, following the devastating earthquake of 363. The majority are sandstone (222 = 52%) or limestone (199 = 47%); two are recorded as granite, and one is chert (limestone). We assumed that all would be spheroid in shape, but 15 were recorded as different: 4 have one flat side, 3 are lumpy and not really spherical, 1 has a chunk missing, and 1 has a depression on one side; 1 was noted as being more ovoid than spherical, 2 were noted as oblong or lemon-shaped, and other single examples were recorded as pear-, fig- and peanut-shaped.

The ballista balls were weighed with a digital scale (fig. 20.9). Of the original total of 421 from all areas, 24 are not considered in the following discussions of weight and diameter because they were incomplete spheres. The weights may shed light on what size range was preferred and on the system of measurement being used.[22]

In our database many of the entries have the weights listed, ranging from 0.965 to 8.345 kg.[23] Most of the balls have diameters between 12 and 16 cm, but some are as large as 18 cm (fig. 20.10).[24]

---

22 S. K. Reid (2004, 4) made the following observation: "A further analysis of the weights of the ballista balls might be able to provide a clue as to who was responsible for their production. While it is only a simple matter of using long division to transform ballista ball weights in kilograms to historical units of measurement, such as the Roman *libra* or any of the varieties of Greek *minae*, the process of determining which (if any) of these standards were applied is more complex. However, it is important to recognize that the mere identification of the unit used in no way guarantees the identification of the producer. For example, if the ballista balls are, in fact, identified as having been produced in specific increments of the Roman *libra*, this cannot be taken on its own to indicate that Romans (or the Roman military) was responsible".

23 The heaviest ballista ball is Seq. No. SP87162 weighing 8.345 kg, followed by Seq. No. SP87248 at 7.870 kg, and Seq. No. SP87404 at 7.800 kg. The lightest balls are Seq. No. SP87023 at 0.965 kg, and Seq. No. SP87038 and Seq. No. SP87201, each at 1.140 kg.

24 Vol. 2, 30-31.

The surviving 101 balls[25] (24% of the original collection; see Table 1) indicate that an average sandstone ball weighs 2.872 kg and is 13.9 cm in diameter, while an average limestone ball weighs 3.154 kg and is 13.7 cm in diameter. Per unit of weight measurement, an average sandstone ball weighs 90% less than a limestone ballista ball. The graphs of the diameters and weights of this sample (taken in 2008) of 101 ballista balls are found below. The figures on the following page show the distribution of the balls according to kilograms, *mina* and the Roman *libra*.

TABLE OF BALLISTA BALLS

Sample size= 101 (out of 421 recovered)

Statistical analysis based upon 2008 recovered sample size of 101:

Average weight = 2.21 kg	Average diameter = 13.81 cm
Median weight = 2 kg	Median diameter = 13 cm
Weight range = 0.865 to 6.225 kg	Diameter range = 10 to 21 cm

Correlation between weight and diameter= r^2= 0.84

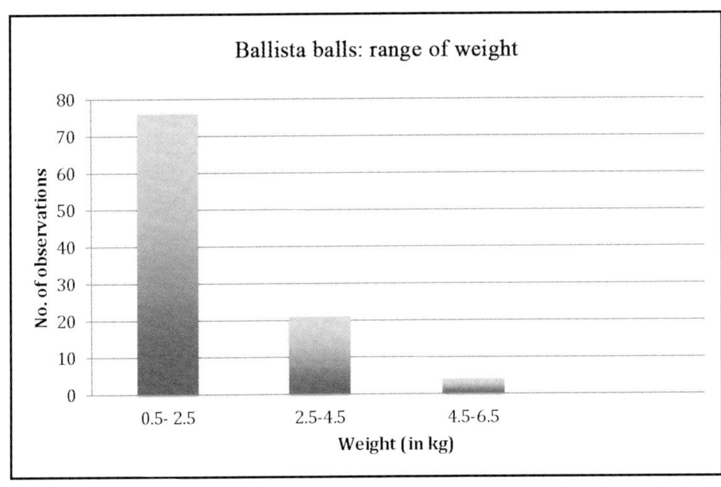

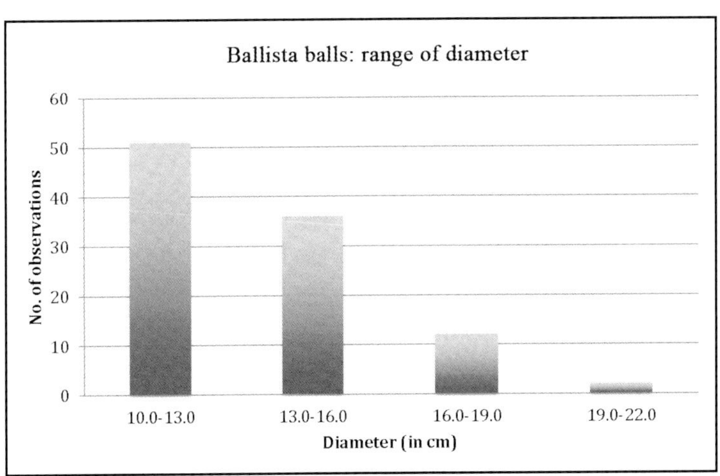

25 The original field records of 2004 for weights and diameters of the ballista balls (which included sequence numbers and descriptions) were loaned to a student in 2004-5 for analysis but were stolen in the burglary of his automobile, leaving us with only the annotated database. At the close of the 2002 season the ballista balls were left in a heap against the Portico Wall (see fig. 20.5). When in 2004 we realized that some were missing, we moved the whole pile to the fenced-in Sculpture Garden, where large architectural fragments were also stored. Returning in 2006, we saw that more balls had been stolen from the Sculpture Garden. The remaining 101 balls were then transferred to the West Cryptoporticus behind a locked gate, where in 2008 S. M. Köprülü re-measured and weighed them. As many of the inked sequence numbers were no longer visible, they were assigned new numbers. They remain today in the secure West Cryptoporticus storage.

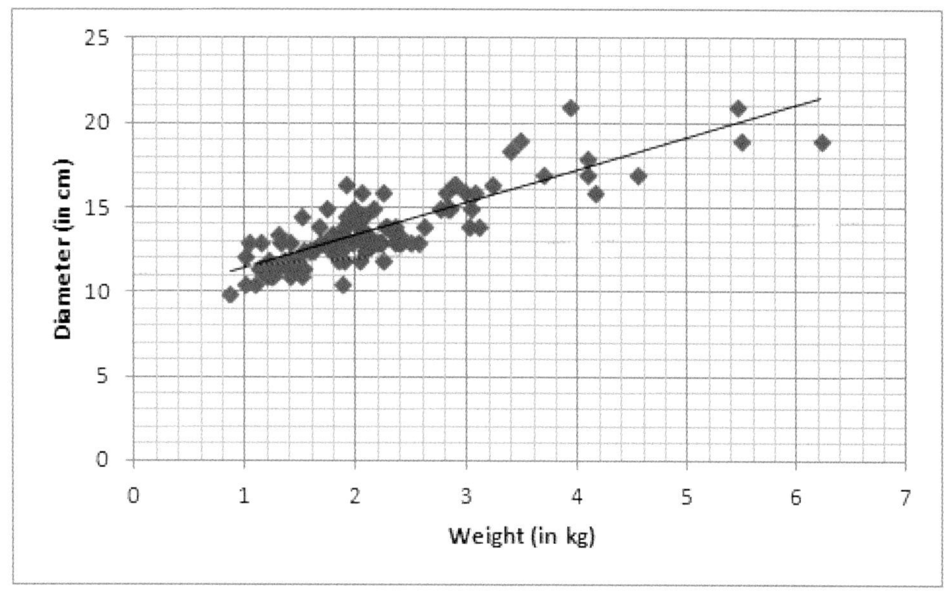
Diameter (in cm)
Weight (in kg)
0 5 10 15 20 25
0 1 2 3 4 5 6 7

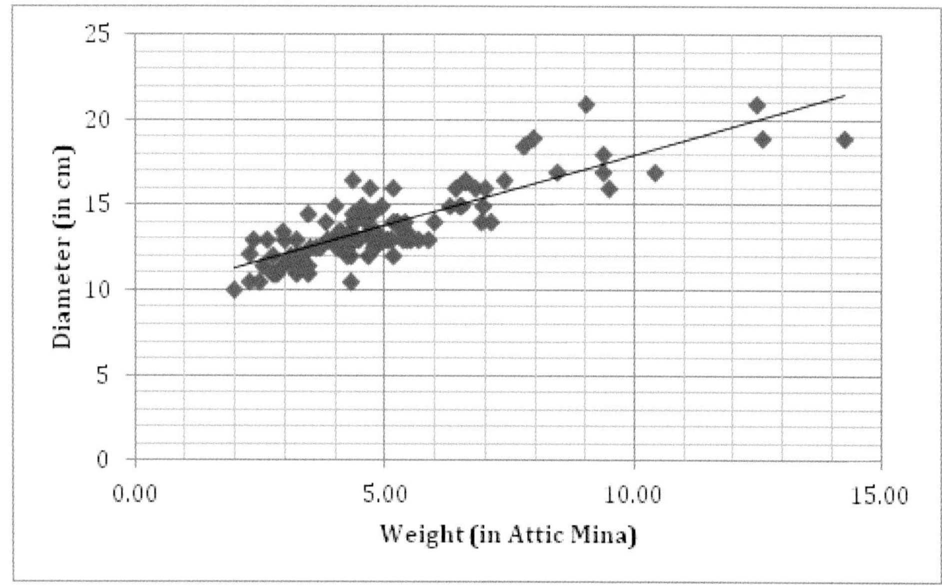
Diameter (in cm)
Weight (in Attic Mina)
0 5 10 15 20 25
0.00 5.00 10.00 15.00

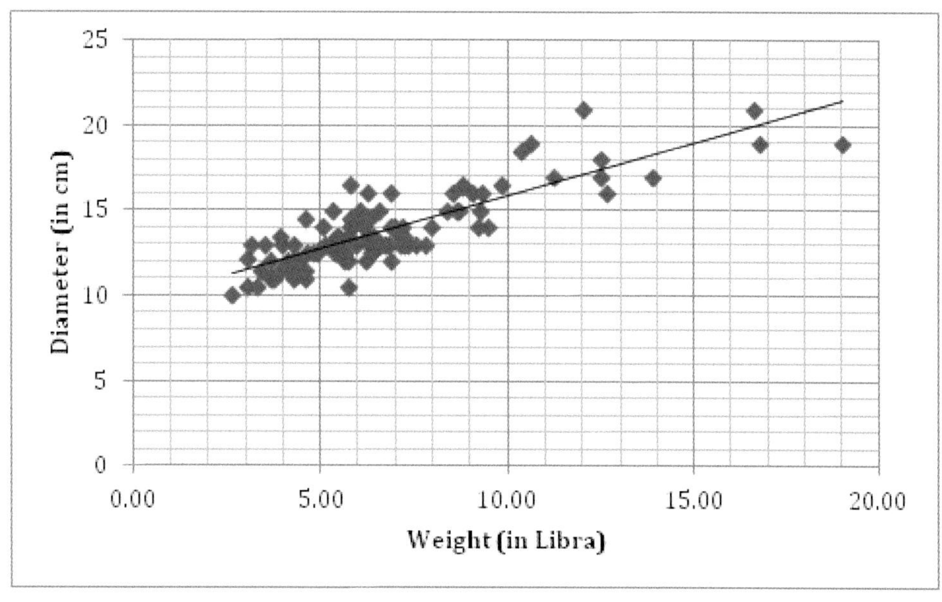
Diameter (in cm)
Weight (in Libra)
0 5 10 15 20 25
0.00 5.00 10.00 15.00 20.00

TABLE 1

No.	Weight (kg)	Diameter (cm)	No.	Weight (kg)	Diameter (cm)
1	3.93	21	51	5.445	21
2	1.765	12.5	52	2.05	16
3	1.9	16.5	53	2.025	14
4	1.445	12	54	1.575	12.5
5	2.825	15	55	1.285	11.5
6	1.88	13.5	56	2.175	13
7	1.405	12	57	1.2	12
8	4.08	17	58	1.115	11.5
9	3.105	14	59	1.31	13
10	1.505	11	60	1.845	12
11	4.54	17	61	1.4	11
12	2.97	16	62	1.29	13.5
13	4.145	16	63	2.885	16.5
14	4.09	18	64	2.25	16
15	2.105	13.5	65	1.79	13.5
16	2.285	14	66	1.615	12.5
17	2.089	12.5	67	1.68	13
18	1.78	13	68	1.89	14
19	0.995	10.5	69	1.145	13
20	5.49	19	70	1.665	14
21	2.155	13	71	2.48	13
22	2.16	15	72	2.25	12
23	1.03	13	73	1.505	14.5
24	3.06	16	74	1.98	15
25	2.055	13.5	75	1.225	11
26	3.475	19	76	1.85	12.5
27	3.675	17	77	1.885	12
28	3.385	18.5	78	2.375	13
29	2.085	12.5	79	3.225	16.5
30	1.195	11	80	2.04	12
31	2.06	14.5	81	2.345	13.5
32	1.9	14.5	82	2.255	14
33	1.52	12.5	83	1.725	13
34	1.09	10.5	84	2.355	14
35	1.78	13.5	85	1.98	14.5
26	2.38	13.5	86	1.955	13
37	2.605	14	87	2.2	13
38	1.35	12	88	2.8	16
39	6.225	19	89	1.24	11
40	2.23	13	90	2.88	16.4
41	1.915	14	91	2.345	13
42	2.745	15	92	1.375	11.5
43	2.045	13.5	93	3.015	14
44	1.475	11.5	94	1.88	10.5
45	1.515	11.5	95	0.865	10
46	2.405	13	96	2.555	13
47	2.845	15	97	1.765	13
48	1.788	13	98	1.4	13
49	3.035	15	99	2.06	13
50	1.74	15	100	1.005	12.2
			101	1.85	12.5

Fig. 20.10. Sample of different sizes and shapes of ballista balls.

Ancient ballista balls: some comparanda

The two chief descriptions of *ballistae* are found in Philo of Byzantium chapts. 51-55 (3rd c. B.C.) and Vitruvius' Book 10.10-11 (1st c. B.C.). To capture a town through a siege, Philo said that one must use catapults[26] and other war engines, try to starve the inhabitants, bribe people to assist, use poison recipes, and pass secret messages. Vitruvius had direct experience of *ballistae*, having served in the Roman army. Both authors included specifications and formulae to calculate the dimensions of different caliber engines and tables of the standard ammunition weights that were in use.

Collections of ballista balls are known from several sites, including Carthage, where 5,600 were found, very irregular in size and with a flattened side,[27] and Pergamon, of a more regular size.[28] Both groups exhibit different calibers of ammunition, but most were larger caliber and crafted according to the Attic Greek units of measure:[29] 1½ talent (*c.*39.3 kg), 1 talent (26.2 kg), 40 *minae*[30] (17.5 kg), 30 *minae* (13.1 kg), and 20 *minae* (8.75 kg). At Carthage (but not at Pergamon) there was also a 15-*minae* (6.55 kg) caliber.[31] Artillery projectiles from the city of Rhodes evidently had their weights carved and painted on their surfaces;[32] the calibers most used were 25 *minae* (10.9 kg) and 30 *minae* (13.1 kg), but some examples are marked with weights as small as 5 *minae* (2.19 kg).

The large groups of ballista balls of smaller calibers found at Masada and Gamla can be associated with the Roman sieges during the Jewish War.[33] Following the siege at Gamla, ballista balls were evidently left where they ended up. Of the more than 1,310 balls found,[34] a large number was concentrated in a large breach in the walls where a barrage took place; many had been collected at night so that they could be thrown back at the Romans.[35] Another cache of balls was found stacked in a pile *c.*300 m outside the walls, apparently at a launch site. The most common weights

26 Cf. Soedel and Foley 1979, 124-25 on catapults.

27 Rathgen 1909-11, 236-44; von Röder 1909-11, 311 ff.

28 von Szalay and Boehringer 1937, 50-51.

29 Marsden 1969, 81-82.

30 The *mina* is a Near Eastern unit of weight equivalent to 60(50) sheckels. The value of the mina is calculated at 1.25 pounds or 0.571 kg per mina.

31 Marsden 1969, 81-82.

32 Laurenzi 1938, 31-36; 1964, 141-51.

33 A. Holley 1994, 353-59; Syon 2002.

34 A. Holley, "The stone projectiles from Gamla and the use of artillery in the siege of Gamla," in D. Syon, *Gamla* III: *finds and studies* (IAA Reports, forthcoming).

35 Syon 2002, 141. "I suggest that the defenders gathered the ballista stones together after they had been fired into the city so they could throw them by hand at the Romans as they assaulted the walls" (Andrew Holley, pers. com.).

at Masada were 2 *minae* (0.88 kg), 4 *minae* (1.74 kg), and 6 *minae* (2.62 kg).[36] Masada shows that smaller balls were preferred in this region by the Roman military, possibly because they were more easily transported in the baggage train.[37] For Gamla A. Holley commented:

> It seems more likely to me that the size of ballista stones is an indication of the role they were intended to fulfil (i.e., small anti-personnel shot, as opposed to larger shot intended to damage walls and fortifications) rather than due to the convenience of transportation. For example, at the siege of Masada the majority of the ballista balls recorded were small in size (Holley 1994, 355). Forty-two out of a total of 50 complete stones weighed less than 3 kg (1994, 364), implying that small caliber engines were probably used by the Romans to subdue the defenders on the walls whilst the battering ram in the siege tower was deployed (1994, 363). At Gamla, 607 out of the total of 808 stones that were analysed as possible ballista balls weighed 5 kg or less.[38] However, much larger stones were apparently used at the sieges of Yodfat (Jotapata) and Jerusalem, where Josephus refers to one-talent shot (26.2 kg) being fired by Roman artillery (*Jewish War* III. 167; V. 269-270). This one-talent shot is equivalent to the 80-*libra* caliber mentioned by Vitruvius (Book XI, 3).

The historical context at Petra

The Nabataean kingdom was annexed by the Roman governor of Syria, A. Cornelius Palma in A.D. 106. Some evidence, including reports in Ammianus Marcellinus (14.8.3) as Cassius Dio (68.14),[39] suggests the province was brought under Roman rule partly by subjugation, but it has never been clear if Cornelius Palma or another man led a military expedition against Petra. That Palma oversaw a peaceful takeover seems to be indicated by the coins issued 5 years after the fact.[40] The Babatha papyri state that the last Nabataean king, Rabbel II, had a son, meaning that the royal line was not coming to an end, yet the period when a king was dying offered a prime opportunity for Rome to plan a strategic takeover.[41] Perhaps a planned Roman operation was awaiting the death of Rabbel II to be put into effect. The fact that the governor of neighboring Syria was involved is of interest. Note also that two cohorts[42] (*I Hispanorum* and *I Thebaeorum*) were moved from Egypt to Judea the year before 106, possibly so as to be available for direct intervention when circumstances so allowed,[43] while cohorts from the *III Cyrenaica*, known to have been involved in construction work in 107 in S Arabia near Petra, may have arrived the year before. Thus Roman forces were present to the west and south of the city,[44] and a local Safaitic graffito possibly refers to military engagement when it says 'the year the Nabataeans revolted against the people of Rome'.[45]

In short, based upon the historical sources it is likely that skirmishes occurred between the Romans and Nabataeans, but we still lack historical proof of a major siege of Petra. The large

---

36 Holley (1994, 353-59) suggests that the Roman *ballistae* at Masada may have been built by artillerymen using the Attic *mina* rather than Roman *libra* as the weight system, even if they appear to have used even numbered weights as suggested by Vitruvius.

37 G. Davies notes: "Josephus attests balls of c. 25kg used during the siege of Jerusalem…again, this merely shows that the surviving projectiles at Masada/Gamla demonstrate the use of anti-personnel weapons at these siege sites…the Romans would have had access to heavier caliber weapons when they needed them." Holley comments: "It would obviously make more sense to manufacture ballista stones at the site of a siege rather than transport them to the site in the baggage train (although it is likely that a baggage train would have included at least some artillery shot). For example, at Gamla most of the ballista balls were made from local basalt".

38 Holley (supra n.34).

39 Bowersock (1983, 79-82) provides a summary of this evidence and the sources.

40 Coins minted in A.D. 111 are inscribed with *Arabia adquisita*, not *Arabia capta*, perhaps reflecting a relatively peaceful takeover. Note that Trajan never held the title of *Arabicus*.

41 G. Davies pers. comm.; Yadin 1962, 239-40; id. 1963, 230.

42 Such auxiliary cohorts had 6 different possible configurations; they could have been equitatae (a combination of 120 cavalry military and 480 infantry forces in each formation).

43 Speidel 1977, 709-10 and 719.

44 *P. Mich.* vol. 8 (1951) no. 466.

45 The reference is taken from Bowersock (1983, 79-80, n.13). It reads: *snt mrdt nbt 'l 'l rm*. Bowersock refers to a graffito published by Winnett and Harding (1978, 406-7, no. 2815).

collection of ballista balls now adds a further archaeological dimension to the question of whether Petra was attacked at the time of annexation or whether the takeover was peaceful. Based on the archaeology, we cannot say for certain that some ballista balls crashed through the walls and floor-tiles to become embedded, but there is the possibility that the Propylaeum was bombarded in some kind of skirmish — stone-throwing siege engines could have been set up on the N side of the Wadi Musa, at a distance of just 40-50 m. Indeed, it is tempting to associate the ballista balls with some collapses on site attributed to Site Phase VI (*c.*106), including that of the South Gallery here, the cryptoportici in both Propylaeum East and West, and the SW Cryptoporticus in the Lower Temenos. Following damage, and during the same site phase but evidently before the earthquake attributed to 113/114, the tiled floor of Propylaeum West was laid, making good use of the mass of ballista balls as fill beneath.

Effectively, there seem to be two main choices for explaining the large number of ballista balls found:

1. The ballista balls are Nabataean, were stockpiled against an anticipated attack from across Wadi Musa, but were never used (at least not these particular ones).
2. The ballista balls are Roman and represent the stored ammunition of the Roman garrison in the immediate wake of the occupation of Petra. The balls had been employed in action, and did cause damage to the Propylaeum, prompting the repairs undertaken in the subsequent years. At that point they were gathered up by the repairers and used as fill beneath floors.

At Masada, one encounters a similar conundrum: the projectiles may have been launched at, or they may have been intended to be launched from, the fortress.[46]

In short, the discovery of ballista balls beneath the floor of the Propylaeum does not preclude their prior use in an attack, although it does make the identification of such an attack (both its instigator and date) difficult, if not impossible, without datable finds in sealed contexts or historical texts referring to an attack. Besides the Nabataean coin, the lamp and a few pottery fragments, there is no secure dating evidence in the main layer beneath the tiled floor. At the least, the large quantity of ballista balls present seems to show that a siege was anticipated, whether or not one actually took place. At a certain moment, then, the Nabataeans believed they were going to be attacked. Balls launched at the Great Temple would result in a scatter; balls systematically gathered up, as here, would rather suggest that they had been stacked awaiting use. On balance then, it seems more likely that a ballista armory had been prepared by the Nabataeans in anticipation of an attack.

A cautious interpretation of the archaeological evidence will be that there is no proof of military action involving *ballistae*. Yet it seems certain that resistance to Rome was in the minds of many Nabataeans shortly before the annexation, even if no violent struggle occurred, resistance at that time proving futile. It is in this historical context, which is not at odds with the phasing of the site, that the sizeable armory of ballista balls found re-used in the repair/rebuilding of the Propylaeum West perhaps makes the most sense.

Acknowledgements

This chapter owes much to the input of several members of the Brown University team, particularly Angela Murock Hussein. I wish to express my appreciation particularly to the excavators K. M. Haile, M. G. Parker, and J. M. Rogér; A. Henry should also be credited for excavation efforts. S. K. Reid supervised the excavations of SP87, ably assisted by C. F. Cloke. Thanks are due to Artemis W. Joukowsky, T. M. Khanachet, S. M. Köprülü and M. S. Zimmerman who aided in weighing the ballista balls. We are indebted to S. Farajat, S. Al-Nawafleh, and the Jordanian Department of Antiquities for going to great lengths on three separate occasions to provide a digital scale for weighing the ballista balls. Manas Gautam is to be credited for the graphs. Lastly, it is a particular pleasure to acknowledge Gwyn Davies and Andrew Holley, specialists of the Roman army in the East, who generously shared their ideas and, in the case of the former, contributed an Appendix.

---

46 Holley 1994, 360-62.

APPENDIX

Gwyn Davies

I would suggest that what we have here is the re-use of redundant ballista shot as a handy make-up for the laying of a new floor in some 2nd-c. peacetime context. The nature of the remains and their distribution argue against them being *direct* evidence for any military action. That said, we have to explain the occurrence of such shot and their re-use for this purpose. It would only make sense to re-use these projectiles if they had been available in close proximity to the new floor. This suggests a stockpile of ballista balls located in one of the rooms/corridors of the Great Temple Propylaeum.

There would seem to be three explanations:

1. That they represent a Nabataean arsenal perhaps stockpiled when it became clear that the Romans were about to liquidate the client kingdom. Their location, then, would make sense only if the Great Temple was to be used as a *reduit* or citadel for last-ditch resistance *and* if the Nabataeans had access to anti-personnel stone-projectors. If the Great Temple was envisioned as playing some such rôle, the question must be asked: How was the complex to be defended? The *ballistae* could have been emplaced in the (open?) corridor behind the Portico wall to maintain indirect fire against positions on the opposite side of the wadi (the Portico Wall was too narrow to mount any engines on it directly). In that case, since the ground slopes up quite quickly on the N side of the wadi, the effectiveness of any such close-fire support when fired 'blind' would have been limited.[47]

2. That this is a stock of projectiles that *had* been discharged in the course of an actual military operation and that had subsequently been gathered up in clearance operations *ex post facto,* to be piled neatly in the Propylaeum. In that case, it need not necessarily represent a stockpile for active defense in the future, but could simply indicate Roman military discipline where 'tidying up' after a battle was regarded as a suitable exercise for otherwise under-employed garrison troops: the rationale could have been that these missiles *might* be useful in the future (whether to be transported elsewhere or to be employed directly in place).

3. That they represent the stored ammunition of the Roman garrison in the immediate wake of the takeover of the city, and that the Great Temple was pressed into service as a temporary strongpoint where a garrison may have been billeted. In this case, we need not necessarily believe that *ballistae* were emplaced to provide direct fire-support for a Roman military presence (again we are left with the question as to how and where the artillery would have been mounted), but that there were artillery pieces stored in the Temple as part of the garrison's *impedimenta.* When the troops were withdrawn, the engines would have gone with them, but it may have been considered unproductive at that time to move the bulky shot. This might also explain the fairly limited range of other *militaria* recovered from the site as lost or discarded pieces of equipment belonging to a supposed early garrison force.

---

47 It is not intrinsically implausible that the Nabataean capital may have had a limited stock of the requisite artillery pieces or engines as products of Roman 'technical assistance' provided to loyal clients, but whether the Nabataeans maintained the appropriate cadre of trained personnel is perhaps more questionable.

21

Nefesh, betyls and miscellaneous sculpture

Martha Sharp Joukowsky

Following the Corinthian Nabataean capitals of the temple itself, the elephant-head capitals of the Lower Temenos, and the pilaster blocks, all presented in prior chapters, some additional aspects of ornament and sculpture remain to be treated. Here we record the aniconic *nefesh* and *betyls* and other sculpture, a total of 33 objects found chiefly in contexts of collapse at the Great Temple yet whose purpose would have been to embellish the site in its heyday. Following the *nefesh* and *betyls*, we present deities, a male head, a heroic warrior torso, a male youth, a table support, and lion heads. Then come sculptural components (eye sockets, a nose, arm, and a drapery fragment); based on some lifesized and over lifesized body elements, we will argue that a monumental sculpture stood in the temple. Last come a crude carving of a divinity in a shrine, the relief of a possible torch or animal, and theater masks.

Many of these pieces represent a Nabataean translation of classical art. Some may be Roman imports, like the male bust/warrior (no. 10). The deity in a shrine (no. 28) and the theater masks (nos. 30-33) show the individualistic character of Nabataean art forms. Note particularly the variety of forms present and the variety of sculptural adaptations made by Nabataean artists, some of them locally inspired, some imported, and some adapted to local needs, so as to convey the city's prestige and status to its patrons and visitors.

The entries give catalog number, sequence number, Site Phase (the deposit in which the artifact was found, not its period of manufacture), specific excavation context, description (with measurements in cm) and prior publication if any. The photographs are not all to the same scale; the reader should compare the dimensions given in the descriptions. If an object carries only a sequence number and not a catalogue number, it indicates that when excavated the piece was immediately turned over to the Department of Antiquities/Petra Museum. Images of pieces not illustrated here can be found online in the catalog in *Open Context*.

Nefesh and *betyls*

A *nefesh*[1] is a sacred Nabataean commemorative monument, carved to consecrate a person or a family and to be the receptacle of the soul. The Nabataeans often represented the dead with a

---

1 Cf. Gawlikowski 1972, 5-6: "Among the Aramaic funerary terms there is one which seems of primary importance: this is the *nefesh*, of which the premier meaning in all the Semitic languages is "[breath/inspiration-of-genius], soul, person", and which designates the monuments stood up or carved in relation with the tomb. The paramount importance of the monument around tombs in the funerary architecture of Syria was thus associated by scholars with the concept conveyed by the term which expresses the belief that the soul of the deceased is [incorporated/integrated] in the monument of its burial. However, to look at it more closely, the use of the word *nefesh* proves relatively late … As the meaning of the monument around tombs is present also in the south-Arabic *nfs*, and as it is attested at Tema … earlier than in Syria, it seems likely that the custom to identify the soul of the dead with the monument came to Arabia and Syria around the 2nd c. B.C., as a consequence of Nabataean migration. It is indeed in Nabataean that the term is most widespread". Cf. also Healey 2001, 170-71: " …*npš'*, referring normally to the pyramidal stele engraved on rock-faces, may have more religious significance [than other terms for "tomb" and "burial"]. It appears to mean "funerary monument", the equivalent of Greek mnēmeion (Cantineau 1932, II, 121; J. Hoftijzer and K. Jongeling. 1995, 748). In *CIS* II, 196, 102 (the Madaba inscription) we have the phrase *mqbrt' wtry npš' dy ['l]' mnh*, ("the tomb and the two funeral monuments above it"), making a clear distinction between the tomb and the associated memorial monuments. The *napšā* does not necessarily have a burial immediately associated with it. A series of *napšātā* at the entrance to the Sīq at Petra is of this kind. They are essentially commemorative". According to J. Patrich (1990, 122-23), "the primitive view of the *napšā* appears to have been that it embodied the individual in his or her post-mortal state, but this ideology was rooted in a nomadic past and was gradually lost by the urbanized Nabataeans, so that the term came to be used for "funerary monument" (also see Gawlikowski 1982, 302). This is very

pyramidal or conical form, as in Petra's Obelisk Tomb. Often no burial is associated with the *stele*, as is the case with no. 1.

Fig. 21.1. *Nefesh*, Lower Temenos, West Entry Stairway, platform 2005.

1. *Nefesh* (fig. 21.1). Seq. no. 102926, Site Phase IV. Lower Temenos West Entry Stairway, Tr. 102, Locus 13 (2005). White limestone/sandstone stele with incised obelisk carved above a squared cut *betyl* block, which is removable. Stele width 78.5, height 57, carved obelisk height 19, width 13.5 cm. Two *betyls* are associated with this *nefesh*, one being carved in the *stele* itself, the other being freestanding, having been recovered beside it (fig. 21.3). The small *betyl* insert measures 13.5 cm wide x 13 cm high. When the small *betyl* block was removed from the *stele*, it was found that the slab had been completely carved through, and the *betyl* had been affixed into the square window of the *stele* with white mortar. For safekeeping, the *nefesh* stele was turned over to the Petra Museum, but a reproduction was created and placed at the original findspot. Previously published at vol. 2, fig. 7.35, 382-84; Joukowsky 2006, fig. 10, 359, n.9.

C. A. Tuttle reports that a fragmentary but similar *nefesh* was recovered from the Temple of the Winged Lions, East Lapidaria, in 2009. That *nefesh* looks similar to ours, having a clearly incised obelisk of similar proportions. Below the carved obelisk, it too may have held a *betyl* since the fractured lower edge of the *stele* may have been carved out to incorporate a lower *betyl*.

The Nabataeans represented their gods as *betyls*. A *betyl* is a standing stone shaped as a conical, rectangular or pyramidal libation stone that signifies the god's home and/or presence. It is usually freestanding and can be undecorated or carry schematic facial features.

Fig. 21.2. *Betyl* accompanying the *nefesh* in fig. 21.1.

2. *Betyl* (figs. 21.2-3 (left)), accompanying the *nefesh* no. 1. Object now lost. Seq. no. 102928, Site Phase IV. From Lower Temenos West Entry Stairway, Tr. 102 (2005). H. 40, w. 30, th. 20 cm. Betyl sits on a carved base. No features on its front surface, rear surface is roughed out. Previously published in vol. 2, fig. 7.35, 382-84; *ADAJ* 50 (2006) fig. 10, 359.

Beneath Trench 102, 2005, débris collapse and fill off to the west, between the two uppermost flights of the West Entry Stairs, is a landing or platform (4.97 x 4.35 m). Behind this platform to the west is a narrow corridor (unexcavated) leading to the West Baths-Palatial Complex. The *nefesh*, accompanied by the *betyl*, were found on the platform just below the corridor doorway in front of an ash-discolored deposit and next to many collapsed ashlars attributed to Site Phase XIII. As the area has also been subject to erosion over the millennia, the deposits were not sealed.

The West Entry Steps were an important point of access from the Roman Colonnaded Street to the Upper and Lower Temenos of the Great Temple in Site Phase IV, and they remained in use for some 500 years. This roughly-carved freestanding bas-relief placed on the West Entry Stairway raises several questions regarding its rationale and placement. Why does the *nefesh* in Fig. 21.1 contain both the *betyl* and an obelisk with a freestanding

---

clear in the inscriptions on the *napšātā* found at the entrance to the Sīq at Petra (Starcky 1965). The specific meaning of the word *napšā* became gradually devalued so that the word often meant simply 'stele' or the like."

Fig. 21.3. *Betyl* and *nefesh* of figs. 21.1-2 *in situ*.

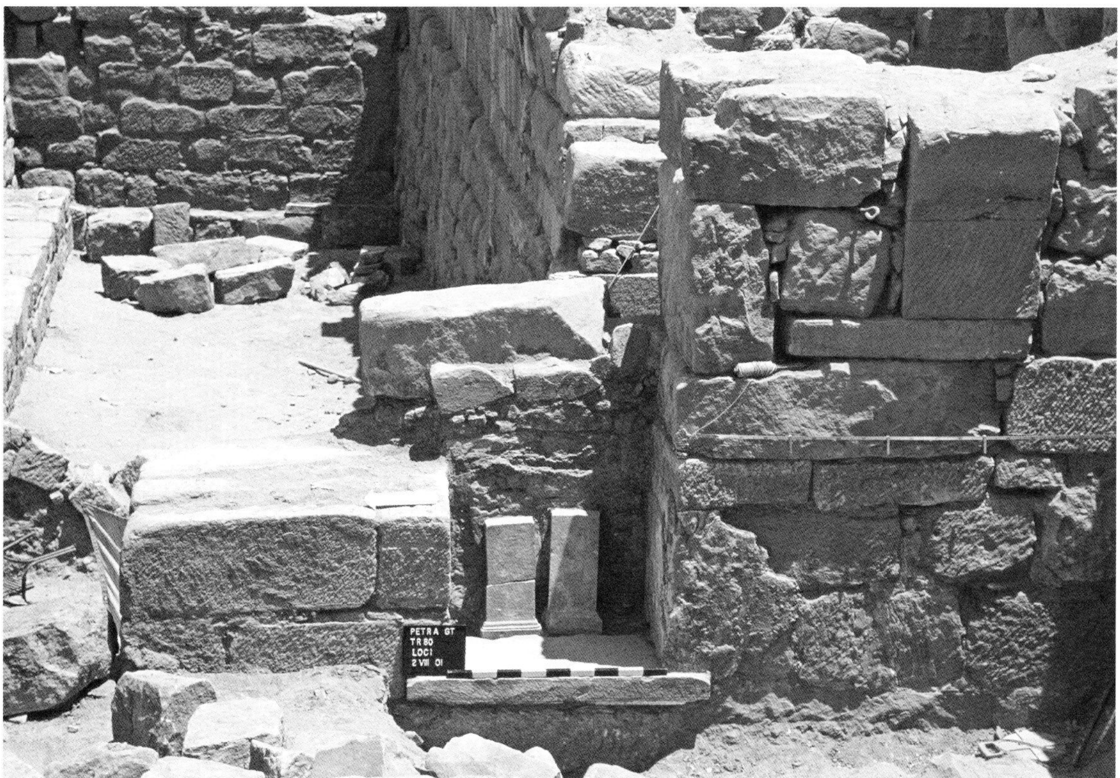

Fig. 21.4. Twin *betyls* (01-S-38, 01-S-39) from the Propylaeum, as excavated in 2001 (north *betyl* to left).

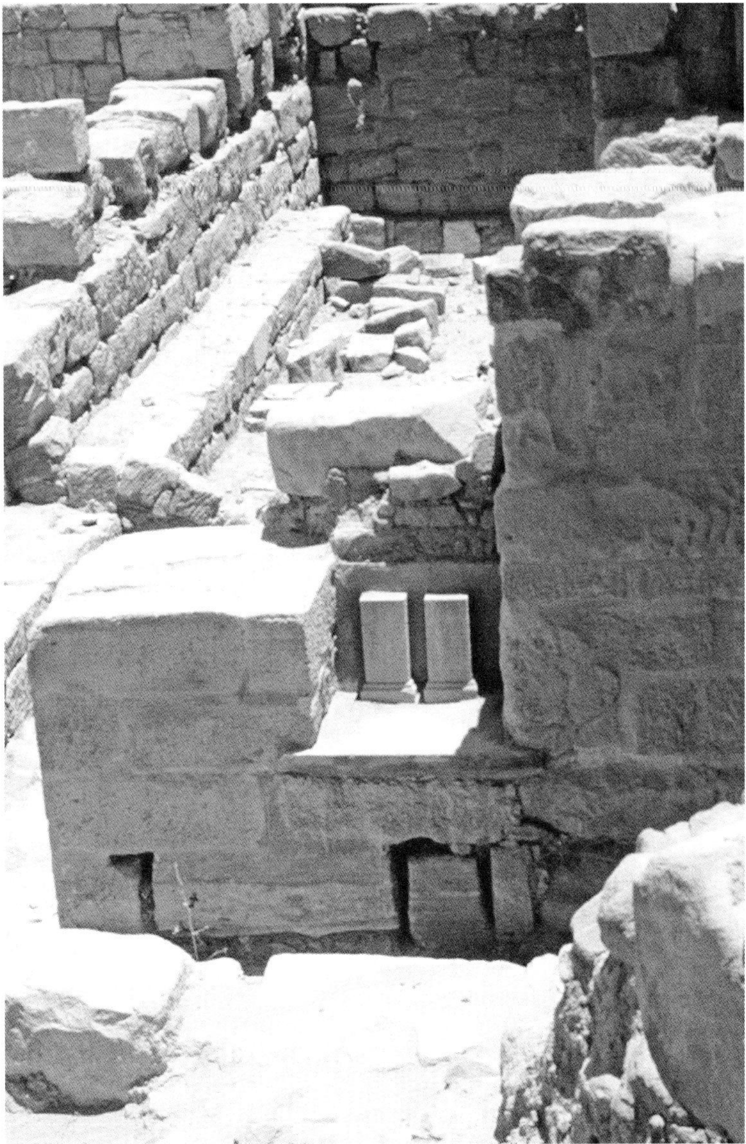

Fig. 21.5. Restored (facsimile) *betyls* of fig. 21.4.

rectilinear *betyl* placed next to it? According to R. Wenning,[2] the *nefesh* is commonly found along the "paths of the city". The monument should indicate that some dedicatory ritual was performed here as a tribute to the god and perhaps to a person of influence.

3. *Betyl* from Propylaeum West (left northern of pair) (figs. 21.4-5). 01-S-38. Seq. No. 80432A, 80432B. Site Phase V. From Propylaeum Tr. 80, Loci 35 and 40 (2001). Limestone. Th 9.80 (at upper edge), w 21, h 50.9 cm. Flat base (wider than no. 4), with a rounded bottom. Chisel mark on its left side possibly indicates where a cut remained from chiseling the block. Fragmented diagonally, since repaired. Previously published in vol. 2, 63, figs. 2.19, 2.20; p. 64, 66. *ADAJ* 46 (2002) 317-18, figs. 4-5, p. 318.

4. *Betyl* from Propylaeum West (southern of pair) (right fig. 21.4). 01-S-39. Seq. no. 80433. Site Phase V. Propylaeum Tr. 80, Loci 35 and 41 (2001). Limestone. W 21, h. 50, th. (at upper edge) 9.9 cm. Intact, but back left edge has a small chip. Set with no. 3 in a niche, fine rounded pedestal base decorated in the classical style. Previously published in vol. 2, 63, figs. 2.19, 2.20-21, 64, 67, 83, 93, 126, 146, 185, 291, fig. 6.20; 297, 354, 383-84. *ADAJ* 46 (2002) p. 317-18, figs. 4-5, p. 318. Joukowsky 2002, fig. 5, p. 317-19.

A sacred niche cut out of the W face of the central stylobate foundation wall holds a rectangular sandstone block which probably served as an altar for two limestone betyls (double gods) found *in situ*, plastered to the wall (fig. 21.3). The niche, at *c.*1 m above floor level, lies diagonally across from the W entrance into the Propylaeum West from the street. The *betyls* would have been visible as one entered the Great Temple by way of the West Entry Stairway and entry into the Propylaeum. The *betyls* are in remarkably good condition. Unlike the *betyls* found throughout the Siq, most of which are carved out of the sandstone bedrock and are badly weathered, these twin freestanding *betyls* are carved in a high-grade limestone, their edges remaining well-articulated and their faces flush. Both exhibit a fine dressing at a 45° angle on their N and S faces. Their W faces and tops are smooth to the touch. They slope 3-4° in opposite directions (the left *betyl* slopes to the south, the right one to the north). The finely carved Attic pedestals are very classical in their design. Their bottoms differ, the right pedestal having a fine rounded bottom while the left pedestal has a simple flat base. Perhaps they were originally positioned elsewhere to fit another location, since in their present locations there is no apparent reason for them to have differently carved bottoms. Figure 21.5 shows the restored betyls as they appear on the altar today; possibly further roughed-out *betyl* blocks form part of the wall supporting the altar.

2 Wenning 2001, 87.

Fig. 21.6. Portable *betyl*, 00-S-93 from Great Temple (2000).

While their general shape and size coincides with the majority of the *betyls* in and around Petra, other aspects are quite rare. The commonest shape for betyls is a rectangle, usually with a smooth surface and a width of half or less than half its length,[3] but these Attic bases or pedestals are special. G. Dalman found only 7 *betyls* with elaborate bases ("postaments"), and "… stelae with a rounded top are quite rare."[4]

The altar which serves as a shelf for the niche exhibits fine diagonal dressing on its W edge. It seems to have two circular niches on its E edge. The *betyls* do not rest on this ledge but sit just to the east, plastered into the wall niche. To insert the altar stone into the wall two incisions (one into the N addition to the central stylobate foundation wall, the other into the foundation wall itself) were carved.

Possibly these aniconic representations represent Dushara and his consort Atargatis or al 'Uzza. J. Patrich points out that the representation of a deity varies and that a particular shape does not always coincide with the same deity; thus, "it is not surprising that we cannot find any clear one-to-one relationship between the stele and the god".[5] The Nabataeans may have intended them to have an apotropaic function, perhaps not least following the collapse of one of the cryptoporticus arches in the E corridor of the West Cryptoporticus.

5. *Betyl* (fig. 21.6). 00-S-93. Seq. no. 73138, Site Phase XI. From Great Temple, Tr. 73, Locus 22 (2000). Limestone. H. 34, w. 21 cm. Plain *betyl* with pyramidal-shaped top and a flat, irregular base. The surfaces are roughly worked. This portable *betyl* was found in the Temple's East Walkway in the second doorway leading into the East Corridor. No niches are associated with these walls. Previously published in vol. 2, fig. 5.57 (drawing), 255; Joukowsky 2001, no. 1, 5-6. For a comparandum, see Dalman 1908, no. 324, semicircular in shape and not quite as triangular as our piece. The context of our object, the collapse of the East Walkway, is not helpful for determining its original placement.

6. Incised Al-'Uzza or Allat votive (fig. 21.7). 04-S-03. Seq. no. 97567, Site Phase IX. From Lower Temenos, West Cryptoporticus, Tr. 97, Locus 16 (2004). Sandstone 2.5Y 8/6 yellow. L. 5.96, w. 4.51, th. 2.57 cm, wt. 53.7 gm. Small oval stone, flattened on one side. A face with two eyes, probably the image of Al-'Uzza, is carved into the sandstone surface. A cross with two bars is incised between two eyes. The forehead and left side of the face are incised with a shallow groove. There is a clear association between the incised cross and the eye *betyl*. The cross with two bars can be found at the Qattar ed Deir, Petra,[6] but the combination of the cross with the eye betyl finds no ready parallel.

Fig. 21.7. Incised Al-'Uzza representation, 04-S-3 from Lower Temenos (2004).

3 Patrich 1990a, 76.
4 Ibid. 87.
5 Ibid. 104.
6 Wenning 2001, fig. 2, p. 82.

Sculptural representations

7. Sculpted head of a deity (fig. 21.8). 05-S-8. Seq. no. SP110195, Site Phase XIII. From Upper Temenos, SP110, Locus 16 (2005). Sandstone. L. 14.83, th. 6.07, w. 13.98 cm. Previously published in vol. 2, fig. 4.95, 201; *ADAJ* 50 (2006) fig. 15, 363. Sculptured high relief of a male head, perhaps Dushara, Hercules, Daedalus, Asklepios, Serapis, or perhaps Laocoön (there is no specific attribute to aid the identification). Carved in Hellenistic style with tousled curling hair, thin moustache, and beard with a double row of curls; eyes wide and staring, gazing heavenward in the Alexandrian manner. The irises of the eyes are not drilled. The open gaping mouth reflects suffering. Marked furrow in the high forehead, which is modeled with a rising peak. Nose worn away or broken off (an old break). Head slightly turned to the left, but broken at the neck whether accidentally or intentionally. Back of head is flattened, indicating that the figure was set as a relief against a wall niche or flat surface. Present condition rough, with the surface is exfoliating. A similar head from Amman[7] is dated to the Antonine period. Our piece possibly parallels an Asklepios head from Jerash.[8]

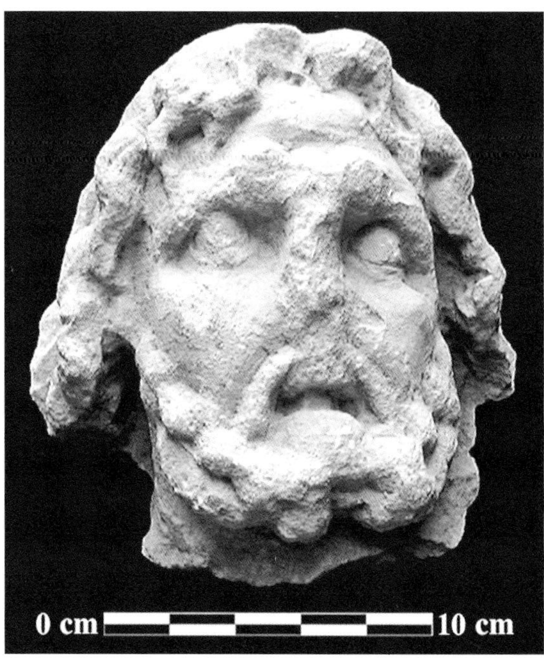

Fig. 21.8. Head of a male deity (05-S-8) from the Upper Temenos (2005).

8. Lower half of lifesize male head (fig. 21.9). Deposited with the Department of Antiquities. Seq. no. 93095, Site Phase IX. From Propylaeum East, Tr. 93, Locus 1 (2002). Limestone, L. 18, w. 18, th. 27 cm. Fleshy cheeks, evocative open mouth. Hair tendril just beside the proper right ear. Head looks to the proper right. Face separated from the neck by a chisel line extending below the chin and along the jaw bone. Mouth and nose damaged, encrustation on the face. No evidence of drilled pupils. Perforation pierced in ear lobe of proper right ear. Right check has a vertical scar. Proper left cheek has longitudinal encrustation. Previously published in vol. 2, fig. 2.32, 73; *ADAJ* 47 (2003) fig. 13, 397. The curl before the ear, the open mouth, the soft modeling of the chin, and the upward proper right tilt of the face recall the bust of Helios from Petra;[9] and there is also a resemblance to a head of Ares also from Petra.[10]

Fig. 21.9. Male head from the Propylaeum (2002).

9. Head of a deity, deliberately(?) defaced, badly weathered (figs. 21.10-11). Deposited with the Department of Antiquities. Seq. no. SP131041, Site Phase IX. From Upper Temenos, West Perimeter Wall, SP131, Locus 1

7 Hannestad, 2001. 518, pl. 6a.
8 Stemmer 1976, pls. 1-2, in Amman National Museum, no. J 2212.
9 McKenzie 1999, pl. 68c.
10 Ibid. pl. 61a.

Figs. 21.10. Head of a female deity, proper left side, from the Upper Temenos West Perimeter Wall (2008).

Figs. 21.11. Head of a female deity, front, from the Upper Temenos West Perimeter Wall (2008).

(2008). Previously published in *ADAJ* 53 (2009) 217, fig. 6. Crystalline marble. Head measures 14 cm to the eye, thickness 23 cm, width 24 cm; eye 3 cm in width and 2 cm in height. The proper left almond-shaped eye is proportionally smaller in relation to the face. Proper left side (fig. 21.10) is skillfully modeled with a full cheek and open eye. Nose is battered, as is the proper right side of face (fig. 21.11). Hairstyle is similar to that of a Greek goddess. The hair hangs in wavy tendrils encircling the cheek; drill-hole present where hair and neck meet. Hair of figure's proper left side flows to rear. Hair tresses not deeply carved. On the battered right face the hair is more crudely sculpted. The hair on the left and the ridges in the back may have held a diadem, crown, wreath or *stephane*, or the figure may have been veiled. Faint indication on the proper left of a jeweled band with some 9 small round decorative studs(?) (interrupted by the fracture); behind this, the faint outlines of a headband hold 5 clumps of hair. The proper left cheek has taken a harsh blow and there is a gauge next to the left eye; the eye itself and the forehead has received a severe hit.

Figs. 21.12-15. Male bust/warrior, front, proper left side, proper right side, and rear, from the Upper Temenos West Perimeter Wall (2008).

10. Warrior, life-sized torso (double-sided) on a base (figs. 21.12-15). Deposited with the Jordanian Department of Antiquities. Seq. no. SP131040, Site Phase IX. From Upper Temenos West Perimeter Wall, SP131, Locus 1 (2008). Previously published in *ADAJ* 53 (2009) p. 217-18, figs. 7-8. Brilliant white crystalline marble. Headless torso carved from a single block. Ht. from the shoulders to the base 45.5 cm. The base (h.10, length 35, w. 21 cm; fragmented on the proper right side) is not well articulated. Chest breadth 37 cm; arm-to-arm width 53 cm; thickness 22.5 cm. The front (fig. 21.12) is broken at the neck but has hair extending over the shoulders. The clavicle is emphasized, as is the scapula. Hollow in the neck 2 cm high. Base of the neck itself 14 cm wide. The figure's proper right breast is bare and effeminate with emphasized pectoral muscles. Nipple is battered. The front is sculpted with a single V-shaped baldric (proper right baldric h. 65-70 cm, left baldric h. 65 cm). Adjacent to the proper left baldric are two raised areas demarcated by two diagonal shallow grooves following the line of the baldric. Over the figure's proper left shoulder is a partial cuirass embellished with a curly breastplate fringe, suggesting he wears both a breastplate and a back plate. Two raised areas show a sculpted fringed cuirass and a sheath, perhaps representing leather. Proper right chest also sheathed with a baldric (10 cm wide at its top). Left arm (fig. 21.13) h. 27 cm, w. 10 cm, with complete armband h. 10 cm. Right arm (fig. 21.14) is partly battered but was once protected with an armband (the complete armband can be seen from the rear). Deeply chiseled groove between arm and chest. At the back on the nape of the neck (fig. 21.15) the hair tresses are damaged (by erosion?). The proper right rear (fig. 21.15) shows a double baldric with the fleecy fringe from the front continuing over the shoulder.

It is rare to see such long hair tresses on a warrior. The tresses of flowing hair, which are not deeply cut, extend over the shoulders to 14 cm. The locks are emphasized by deep grooves; individual locks are grouped or bunched in clumps. On the proper right, only 13 locks of hair are bunched together; on the left shoulder, 17 locks of hair are grouped. Including the shoulder locks, the hair is grouped in several wavy bunches. Were it not for the hair, this monumental statue might have served as a battle trophy.

Several drill-holes in the rear probably served for attachments. At the rear from right to left, the cuirass fringe also has a deep drill-hole. On the baldric strap at the shoulder another puncture may have held a decoration of some kind. The baldric is also notched. Two perforations drilled into the rear baldric suggest that appliqués, such as weapons or discs (*phalerae*), may have been attached.

Although the sculpture is to be viewed from both sides, the rear is not as well sculpted as the front, and portions of the back of he figure appear to be rough and unfinished. Overall, the carving is coarse.

An inscription, scratched like a graffito and irregularly incised on the front of the base, may be a later addition:

L – Φ - I E I

After the Roman annexation, the Nabataean army (*c*.4500-6000 men) was absorbed by the Roman military as 6 Petraean cohorts. Possibly this warrior (or god or demigod) was erected to promote the new military order, or it may commemorate a Roman victory perhaps as a votive. The piece was mounted at a high level so it could be seen from a distance. The presence and iconography of this warrior bust suggests that the portico of the West Perimeter Wall served in some official capacity, perhaps for ceremonies. We may compare the sculpture (from Petra) with the edge of the cuirass shown with the Medusa head.[11]

---

11 McKenzie 2003, 167, fig. 171.

11. Three fragments of idealized nude male youth (figs. 21.16-17). 01-S-5. Seq. no. 80267, Site Phase IX. From Propylaeum, Tr. 80, Locus 16 (2001). Pale yellow limestone 2.5Y 8/2. L. 15.84, w. 5.26, th. (body) 3.38 cm. A young, physically fit male, his weight probably on his (missing) proper left leg, *contrapposto*. A well-modeled proper right leg, a small fragment of his left forearm, and a muscular torso, twisted to the proper right, are preserved. The rear is flat and unfinished, suggesting that this small piece was set in relief against a flat surface. Previously published in vol. 2, figs. 7.27a-b (drawing), p. 376; *ADAJ* 46 (2002) fig. 18, p. 329.

A terracotta sculpture at Corinth[12] resembles our youth but shows a greater elongation of the thigh. G. Davidson suggested that drapery may have been attached,[13] but no signs of any attachment appear on our piece.[14]

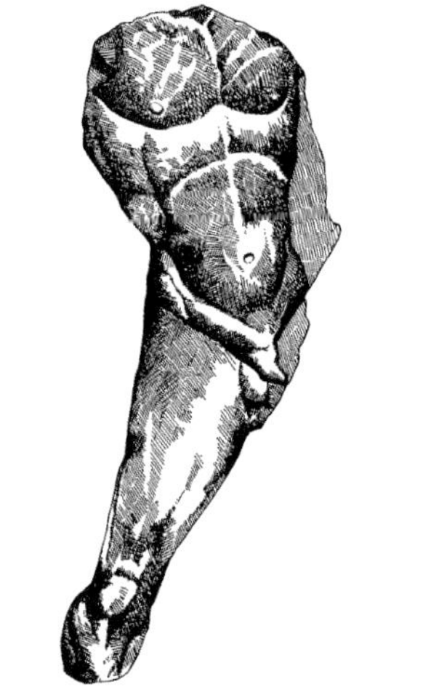

Fig. 21.16. Male youth (01-S-5) from Propylaeum (2001).

12 Davidson 1952, no. 190, pl. 13.
13 Ibid. 38.
14 *AJA* 10 (1906) 160, no. 4.

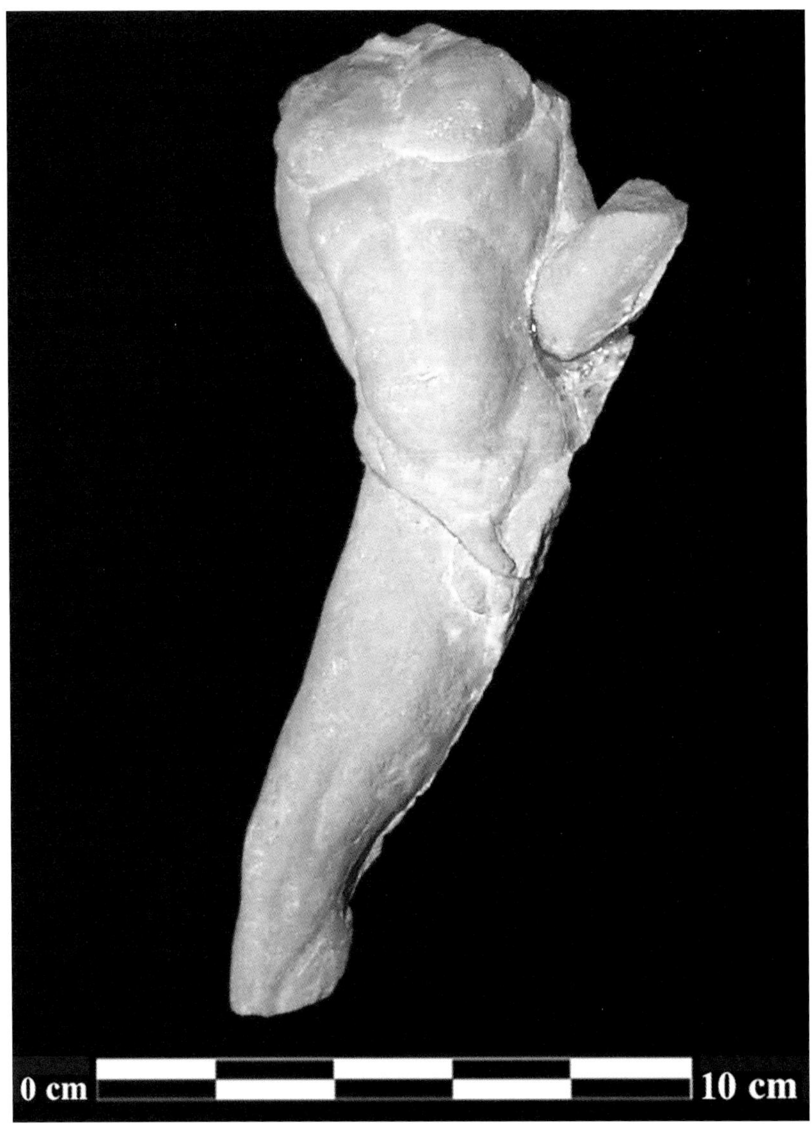

Fig. 21.17. Youthful male athlete (01-S-5) from Propylaeum (2001).

12. Fragment of table support (fig. 21.18a-b). 01-S-4. Seq. no. 83042, Site Phase XI. From Upper Temenos, Tr. 83, Locus 5 (2001). Pinkish white marble, 5YR 8/2. H. 15.10, w. 9.89 cm. Base fragment, once attached to an architectural component. Folds of a toga or cloak and part of the left foot and ankle survive. Only one toenail, finely articulated, is visible. Some anklet ornament surrounding the left calf may be indicative of a soft leather shoe or *calceus*. Two drilled holes exist for the attachment, one at the rear, whic is flattened and unpolished, and another at the front to the right. The left front has part of a human foot with one toe; above the ankle a cuff is ornamented with a panther or lion(?) and two fastenings on either side. To the right of the foot is perhaps the remains of a tree trunk.

Table supports from Aphrodisias show similar characteristics.[15] Boots decorated with panther heads are seen on the Mars Ultor sculpture (*c.*A.D. 90) in the Musei Capitolini.[16] For similar shoes, see the E frieze of the Altar at Pergamum (2nd c. B.C.) with Artemis' dog is biting the giant, where Artemis wears a similar leather shoe.[17] The Gemma Augustea in its lower register depicting Roman soldiers setting up a trophy with barbarians looking on has one soldier at right wearing such footwear.[18] Compare also the sarcophagus of Endymion (*c.*150-160) where Aura wears similar shoes.[19]

Fig. 21.18a. see caption for fig. 21.18b.

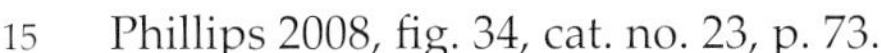

15 Phillips 2008, fig. 34, cat. no. 23, p. 73.
16 Siebler 2007, 55.
17 Boardman 1993, fig. 155 D, p. 164.
18 Ibid. pl. XVIII, nos. 271, p. 274.
19 Ibid. p. 342-43, fig. 351.

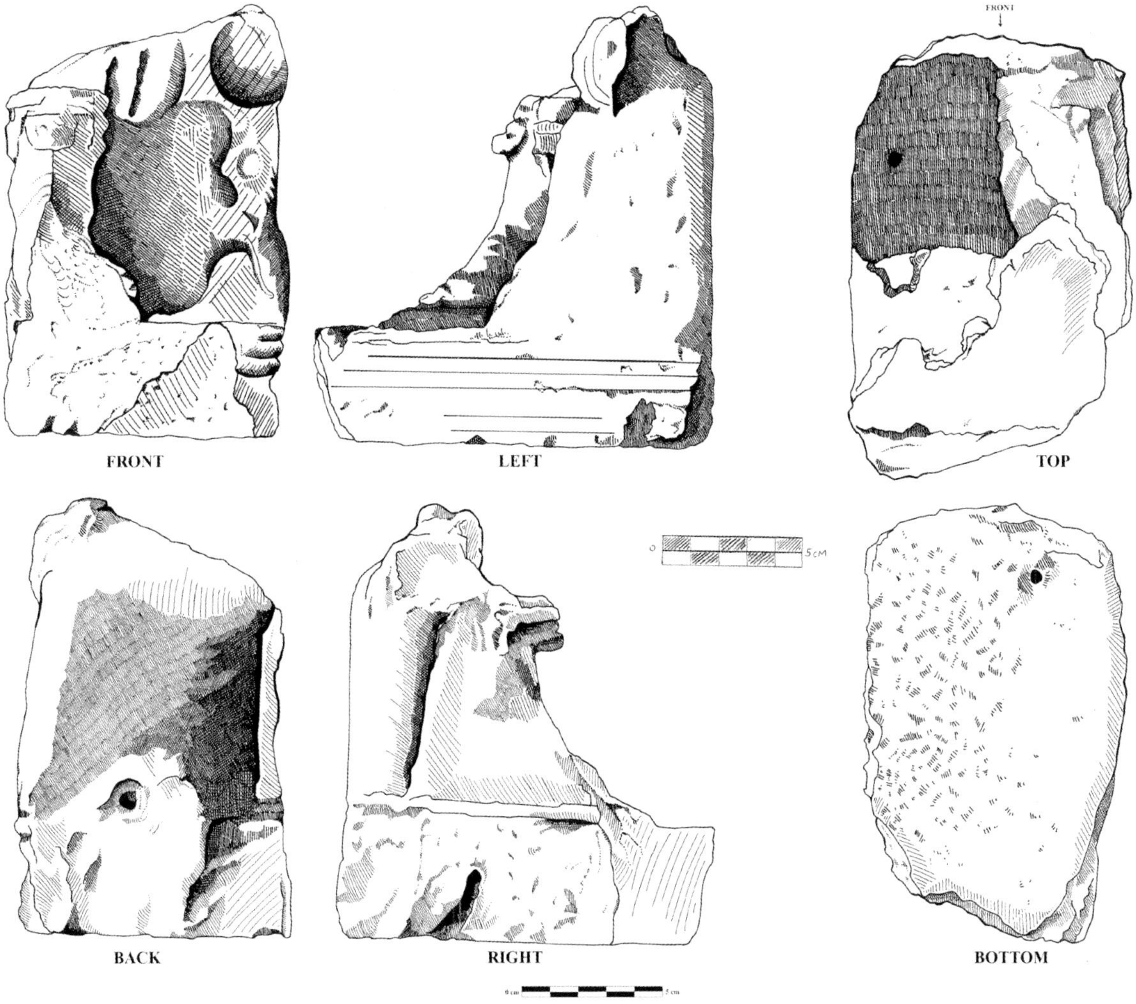

FRONT LEFT TOP

BACK RIGHT BOTTOM

Fig. 21.18b. Marble table support (01-S-4) from Upper Temenos (2001).

13. Fragment of lion head (fig. 21.19). 97-S-33. Seq. no. SP53007, Site Phase XI. From Propylaeum, SP53, Locus 1 (1997). Very pale brown limestone, 10YR 7/3. L. 12.38, th. 4.87, w. 6.61 cm. Both eyes, the upper part of the broad nose, the proper left cheek, and the proper left side of the mane with thick tresses or tufts of hair remain. Vestiges of red/brown paint on the underside of the left cheek. Previously published in Joukowsky 1998, fig. 4, 297; vol. 1, figs. 6.67-68 and fig. 6.69, p. 291; vol. 2, fig. 5.58, p. 234.

Fig. 21.19. Small lion's head (97-S-33) from Propylaeum (1997).

The lion, like the elephant, held an abstract and actual meaning for the Nabataeans, as attested by the Temple of the Winged Lions and Great Temple. Lions were frequently sculpted by the Nabataeans as "stand-ins for the paramount goddess of their pantheon". A lion in high relief, perhaps from a cornice, at Qasr Rabbah[20] resembles ours. Cf. also the lion head found in the al-Khazna courtyard.[21]

14. Fragment of a relief of a lion (fig. 21.20). 02-S-44. Seq. no. 87183, Site Phase IX. From Propylaeum, Tr. 87, Locus 7 (2002). Limestone. L. 42, w. 30, th. 18.5 cm. Mane carved in low relief. Based on the eyes, this seems to be a sleeping lion, although the beginnings of the mouth indicate that it was open. On the proper right there is a large 'C'-shaped ear. A solar symbol, the lion became a hallmark of Hellenistic influence.[22]

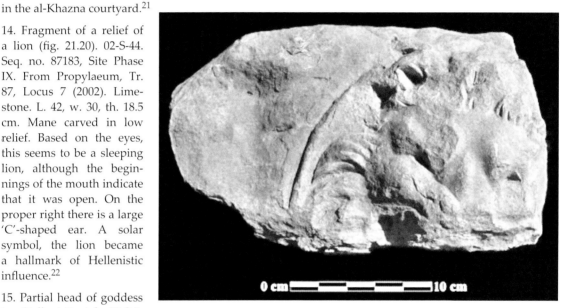

Fig. 21.20. Lion in relief (02-S-44) Propylaeum (2002).

15. Partial head of goddess in a Hellenistic style. 02-S-3. Seq. no. 93095a, Site Phase IX. From Propylaeum East, Tr. 93 Locus 1 (2002), a major destruction deposit. Pink limestone, 2.5YR 8/3. H. 15.52 from the chin up to the mid-face (the rest is missing), w. 18.70, th. 30, depth (from the front of the face to back of the slab) 52 cm. Present are the tapering chin and slightly opened small mouth; wavy hair and curl on the figure's right side. The rest of the face is missing, the rear of head is roughened, and the head is quite worn.

The following 5 fragments derive from sculptures found in the Propylaeum (nos. 16 and 20), and the Upper Temenos (nos. 17-19). The subject matter is diverse and the catalogued pieces illustrate the range.

16. Eye socket (fig. 21.21). 04-S-01. Seq. no. SP87114, Site Phase VII. From Propylaeum West, SP87, Locus 11 (2001). Found under tile floor within the subfloor fill of ballista balls. Limestone. L. 3.27, h. 1.81 cm, wt. 15.5 gm. Similar inserts, sometimes of white marble, are well known. The bronze portrait head of Augustus from Meroe carries such an insert.[23]

17. Eye socket. 01-S-3. Seq. no. 83120, Site Phase IX. From Upper Temenos Tr. 83, Locus 9 (2001). Found in the early excavation of the South Passageway and the Shrine Room in a layer of collapse. Very pale brown marble

20 Glueck 1956, pl. 164a, p. 367.
21 Farajat and al-Nawafleh 2005, fig. 20.
22 Glueck 1965, 287.
23 Siebler 2007, 45.

(10YR 8/2). W. 1.66, h. 2.92 cm, wt. 19.1 gm, diam. at widest part of cavity 1.97 cm. Possibly an amulet?

18. Plaster nose (fig. 21.22). 96-S-24. Seq. no. 29053, Site Phase IV. From Great Temple, Tr. 29, Locus 6 (1996). L. 4.54, w. 2.97 cm. Possibly an ancient repair for a lost limestone feature. Published in vol.1, fig. 6.73.

19. Arm fragment. 06-S-16. Seq. no. 121003, Site Phase VII. From Upper Temenos, Tr. 121, Locus 3 (2006). Marble. L. 13.19, th. 7.87 cm. Section of a limb (possibly the lower left arm in the round) of a human or deity. Some damage on one side perhaps where the arm was placed against a wall or attached to a body.

20. Toga fragment from the shoulder of a figure (fig. 21.23). 06-S-14. Seq. no. 120728, Site Phase XI. From Upper Temenos, Tr. 120, Locus 39 (2006). Marble. L. 15.47, w. 13.98, th. 4.49 cm. Drapery carving skillfully carved in the round with deep folds. Fracture at either end. E. Friedland[24] illustrates toga folds dated to the mid 2nd c. A.D. Cf. the marble *togatus* found in the area of the East Baths at Jerash, now in the Amman Museum, Inv. J. 262.[25] Cf. also the *peplos* of a winged Nike in high relief from the basilica at Ascalon.[26]

Fig. 21.21. Eye socket from statuary (01-S-3) from Propylaeum (2001).

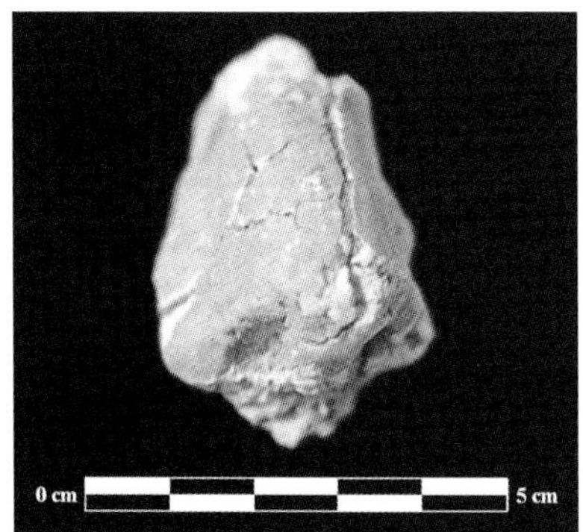

Fig. 21.22. Plaster nose (96-S-24) from Great Temple (1996).

Fragments of statuary from the Great Temple

From isotope analysis[27] we know that the majority of the marble at the Great Temple came from the region of Marmara, probably from the island of Prokonnesos,[28] but because all of the following pieces are in a white medium to large crystalline stone they may have originated from another source, such as Luna (Italy). Ten fragments (nos. 22-28) were recovered from the Great Temple itself. No. 21, an elbow fragment (Site Phase I) probably belongs to a separate marble sculpture, but no. 22 (Site Phase VIII) and nos. 23-27 (Site Phase IX, the 4th-c. earthquake), can be assumed to belong to larger-than-life-size sculpture, which may well have adorned the temple, since all were found scattered within the building itself.

Fig. 21.23. Drapery fragment (06-S-14) from Upper Temenos (2006).

From Tr. 23 (NW central Temple pronaos) came several fragments: the hand, no. 22 (95-S-45) (fig. 21.25), and the 4 fragments collectively catalogued as no. 27 (95-S-46). Three other statuary fragments are from the temple Tr. 65 (East Corridor center and south): the arm or breast no. 24 (99-S-23) from Locus 16; a limb or knee fragment no. 26 (99-S-29) from Locus 21, and from Locus 17 came another knee, no. 26 (99-S-24). A second hand fragment, no. 23 (00-S-1; fig. 21.24), came from the upper levels of the South Corridor (Trench 77, Locus 27). The similarities between the fragments, including their greater than life size, suggest they derive from the same massive sculpture. All were found in or near the Great Temple's central Pronaos, a commanding position for a major sculpture to be set overlooking the Lower Temenos.

24 Friedland 2001, fig. 14 in particular, Cat. 4, pp. 471-74.
25 Weber 1990, fig. 2.
26 Fischer *et al.* 1995, fig.14a.
27 Reid 2005, 140-41.
28 Proconnesian marble was also used prolifically at Umm Qeis (Gadara).

21. Elbow fragment (biceps and forceps) from a nude upraised arm. 99-S-21. Seq. no. 55A152, Site Phase I. From the Great Temple's E Vaulted Chamber. Tr. 55A, Locus 20 (1999), from the leveling terrace for the subterranean drainage system extending under the floor. Marble. L. 6.81, arm th. 3.04, th. at elbow join 3.88 cm. Damaged on the inner section.

Upraised arms are common in imperial portraits but this fragment appears more appropriately to be from a female figure. Cf. the battle sarcophagus of the Greeks against the Gauls from Via Amendola (*c*.A.D. 170), where a Greek brandishing an axe has her arm in a similar position.[29] From the sculptor's workshop at Antioch (second half of the 1st c. A.D.) T. Najbjerg illustrates a cache of 28 arms and hands with two fragments (top row, 3rd and 4th from the left) similar to ours.[30]

22. Fragment of over-lifesize left hand (fig. 21.24). 00-S-1. Seq. no. 77225, Site Phase IX. From the S part of the Great Temple Tr. 77 SP72, Locus 27 (2000). Marble. L. 11.12, w. 13.52, th. 7.3 cm. The fingers, thumb and wrist are missing. Since the size is comparable, it may be the mate for no. 23, 95-S-45 (fig. 21.25). Previously published in Joukowsky 2001, fig. 17, 341.

The proper left hand of the Weary Hercules from the Baths of Caracalla (early 3rd c.) could serve as a comparandum.[31]

Fig. 21.24. Fragment of marble left hand (00-S-1) from Great Temple (1995). (Trench 77, locus 27)

23. Fragment of c. 1.5 times lifesize wrist and part of hand (fig. 21.25). No. 95-S-45. Seq. no. 23224, Site Phase VIII. From the Great Temple, Tr. 23, Locus 7 (1995), the NW part of the central Pronaos between the W pronaos column and the interior W anta in a deposit containing Late Nabataean pottery. Crystalline marble. L. 11.5, w. 14.5 cm. Square opening in center of wrist for a pinhole attachment to the arm. Plaster survives inside the opening. Once attached to a large sculpture which was broken and repaired in antiquity since thin plaster is visible in the repaired break. Previously published in vol. 1, fig. 6.81 (drawing), fig. 6.82, 296 (photo).

The hand may have been raised in blessing, as is commonly seen on sculptures of the gods. Cf. Titus as a magistrate gesturing with his right hand.[32]

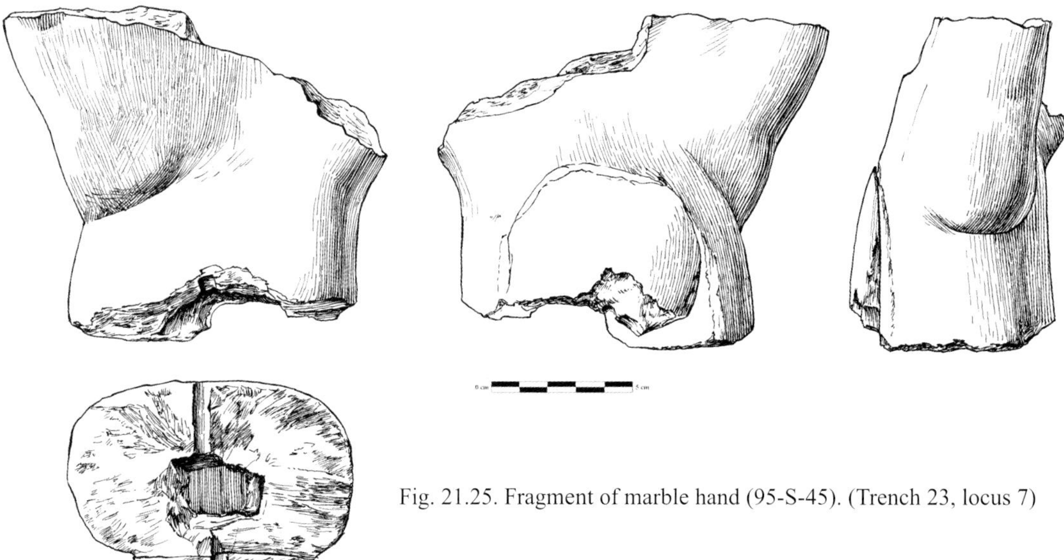
Fig. 21.25. Fragment of marble hand (95-S-45). (Trench 23, locus 7)

29 Ibid. fig. 228, p. 258.
30 Najbjerg 2001, pl. 92.
31 Kleiner 1992, fig. 305, p. 339.
32 Ibid. fig. 143.

24. Fragment of statue, possibly from an arm or breast. 99-S-23. Seq. no. 65278, Site Phase IX. From Great Temple, East Corridor, Tr. 65, Locus 16 (1999). Very fine marble. L. 9.67 cm, w. 9.18 cm, th. 4.47 cm. Carved hollow for a pin in a roughened area at the rear. Length of pin allowance 3.33, width of pin allowance 1.45 cm.

25. Possible limb of a statue. 99-S-29. Seq. no. 65369, Site Phase IX. From Great Temple, Tr. 65, Locus 21 (1999). Marble. L. 16.51, w. 13.30, th. 4.43 cm. Aperture for a nail on the right side (nail opening diam. 0.37 cm, nail drill-hole length 3.91 cm. Polished on the modeled side. The base(?) is smoothed and finished.

26. Part of a knee? 99-S-24. Seq. no. 65331, Site Phase IX. From Great Temple Tr. 65, Locus 17. Marble. H. 12.75 (obtaining by placing the piece in a kneeling position), w. 21, th. 8.39 cm. Drill hole at the top.

27. Four marble fragments and metal. 95-S-46. Seq. no. 23008, Site Phase VIII. From Great Temple, Tr. 23, Locus 7. Largest fragment length 8, w. 5.3, th. 3.9 cm. Broken, rust stains. Each fragment has attachment grooves. The collection includes two rusted iron pegs, which do not fit the fragments found in association. The lower fragment has an iron pin (left) adhering to its side.

Figs. 21.26-27. Divinity in a shrine (99-S-25) from Great Temple (1999).

Miscellaneous

28. Divinity in a shrine (figs. 21.26-27). 99-S-25. Seq. no. 65346, Site Phase IX. From Great Temple, Tr. 65, Locus 19. Very pale brown limestone, 10YR 8/3. L. 9.41, w. 8.90, th. 4.82 cm. Partial block with low-relief bust of an androgynous figure. The hair is long and the facial features (e.g., small nose) appear more feminine. *Chiton* draped over the left shoulder. Arms are held stiffly to the sides. An *aedicula* with a decorated pediment, topped by capitals, fluted columns and stylobate surround the figure. Scratched cross-hatching on the stylobate may be a weather-worn inscription. Figure is crudely carved. Previously published in *ADAJ* 44 (2000) fig. 10, p. 328; vol. 2, fig. 5.37 (drawing), fig. 5.38, p. 244.

29. Relief (no catalogue no. (not illustrated)). Seq. no. 95837, Site Phase VII. From Propylaeum, Tr. 95, Locus 19 (2003). L. 24 , w. 10, th. 17.5 cm.

Possibly a comet, a torch or Zeus's lightening bolt(?), or it might represent a hero's killing of a lion or perhaps a fox, being carried in a shoulder sack. The animal is characterized by its wavy tresses or flowing mane. Reliefs of this kind are often associated with maenads or satyrs who have animal skins hanging from their shoulders.[33]

33 Cf. Bieber 1961, figs. 450-51.

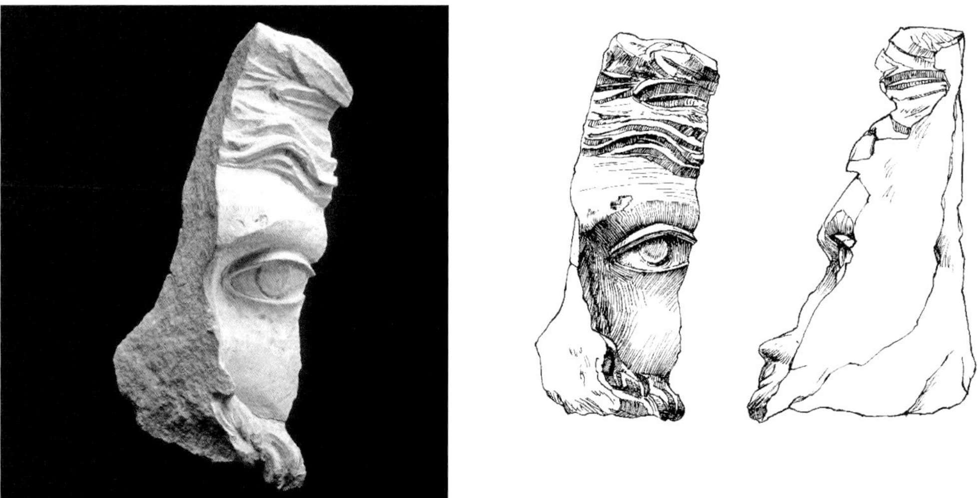

Figs. 21.28-29. Male theater mask (94-S-02) from Great Temple (1994).

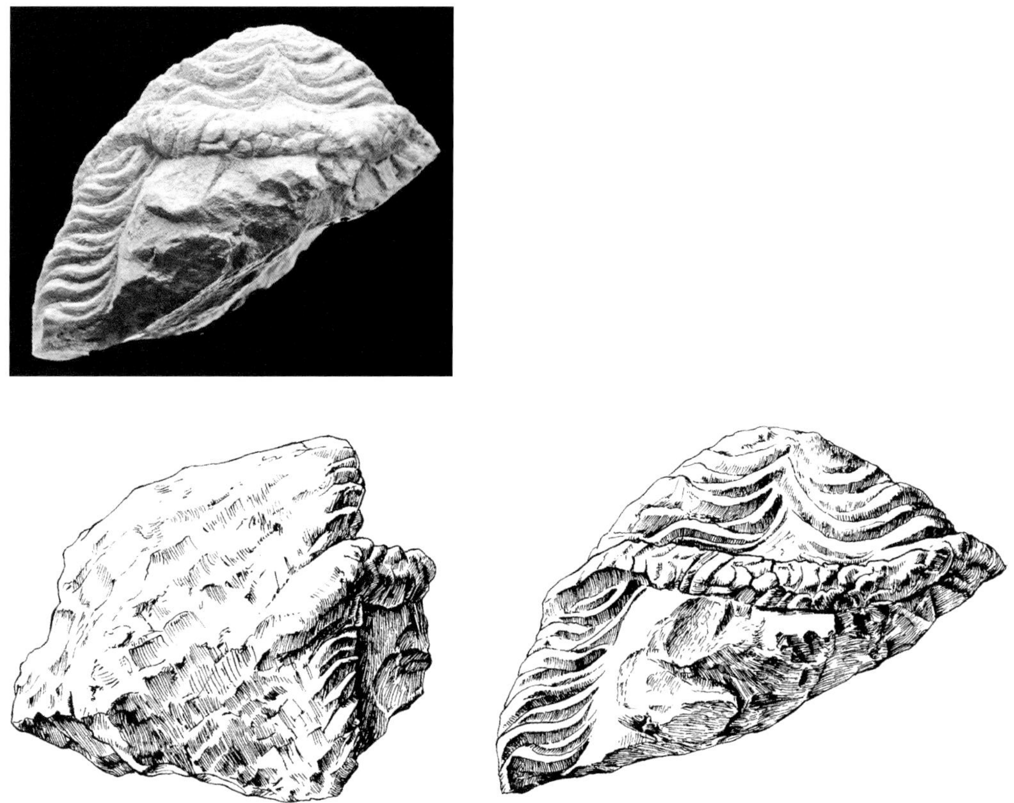

Figs. 21.30-31. Garlanded forehead of a theater mask (94-S-05) from Great Temple (1994).

Theater masks

The Great Temple included sculptural images associated with the theater, perhaps alluding to the theater-in-temple as a ceremonial site (see chapt. 8 above). The theater, built in the 1st c. A.D. (Site Phase V), is a local hybrid of the Greco-Roman theater. The prototype was probably to be found in Alexandria with its *Ptolemaia*, sacred gatherings in honor of the gods.

Seven Graeco-Roman theater masks were discovered near the small doorway in the temple's W corridor wall.[34] Two have joining fragments: 94-S-8 and 94-S-9 belong together, as do 94-S-1 and 94-S-3, so a total of 4 masks is presented here. Two appear to be tragic masks (Melpomene with a weeping face) but without their mouths. The facial expressions of nos. 30 and 31 are unknown, but because they were found in the same context we suggest they formed part of the same program that embellished the theater. All but one represent females and are under-lifesize, but the male mask, perhaps Dionysos himself, is over-lifesize and may have been exhibited in a central position on the exterior façade of the theater. The masks are shown frontally, the male with a moustache, while the hair of one of the females is in tight ringlets in the Nabataean style. All are sculpted from a local pale yellow limestone (5Y 8/4). The joining fragments were all discovered in SP2 (1994) in loci dated to Site Phase IX, a collapse associated with the earthquake of A.D. 363. We posit that the masks were sculpted for the theater's decorative program of Site Phase V. While they are based on Graeco-Roman deities and reflect a borrowing from classical theaters, we may detect Nabataean influences. As E. L. Schluntz has written,[35] "these startling heads appeared to have adorned a frieze, possibly one that was situated across the lintel or on the doorjambs within [a] doorway. The fragments were not carved in the round, but rather appear to have been broken off from a relief".

30. Male theater mask (figs. 21.28-29). 94-S-2. Seq. no. SP2017, Site Phase IX. From the Great Temple, SP2, Locus 6. Frieze fragment, larger than life-size limestone head facing right. L. 27, w. 8.5, th. 7.3 cm (measured at the eyebrow). Crisp carving of a laurel leaf diadem. Nearly complete proper left eye with a raised pupil and the beginning of a beard. There is a pit in the eyebrow and a small crack in the beard line. Previously published in *ADAJ* 39 (1995) fig. 21, p. 258; vol. 1, fig. 5.53, p. 232; vol. 2, fig. 5.62, p. 258.

31. Garlanded forehead of a female theater mask(?) (figs. 21.30-31). 94-S-5. Seq. no. 8003, Site Phase IX. From the Great Temple, Tr. 8, Locus 6. Frieze fragment, head in yellow limestone. L. 19.5, w. 9, th. 14.5 cm. Garland around the forehead; elaborate arrangement of hair parted in the middle on top and flowing into waves onto the proper right side of the face. Previously published in vol. 1, fig. 5.54, 233. As this fragment was associated with nos. 30 and 32-33, found in Tr. 8 Locus 6, we assume it is part of a theater mask, but conceivably it belongs to an unrelated sculpture.

32. Tragic theater mask (two joining fragments) (figs. 21.32-35). 94-S-1 (proper right) and 94-S-3 (proper left). Seq. nos. SP2029 and SP2018, Site Phase IX. From the Great Temple, SP2, Locus 6. Frieze fragments, head in yellow limestone. Proper right: length 12, w. 8.5, th. 5 cm. Open mouth (lower lip) and half of open eye with raised pupil, cheek, chin, and the beginning of a wisp of hair. Proper left: length 11, w. 4, th. 8 cm. Lower chin (open mouth) and part of proper left cheek. Previously published in *ADAJ* 39 (1995) fig. 20, p. 258; vol. 1, fig. 5.57, p. 233.

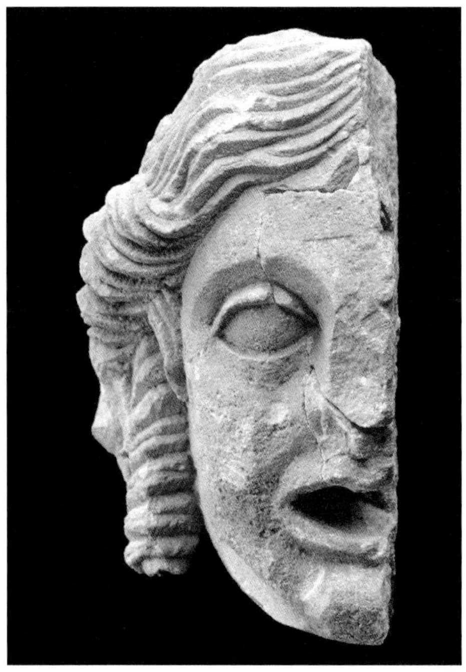

Fig. 21.32. Fragment of female tragic theater mask, proper right side, from Great Temple (1994).

34 One piece is too fragmentary to catalogue here. A further fragment of a mask found on the Roman Street is stored in the Site Museum: Schluntz 1998, 232.

35 Ibid.

33. Tragic theater mask (two joining fragments) (figs. 21.36-39). 94-S-8, Seq. no. SP2029 (proper right). 94-S-9, Seq. no. SP2028 (proper left). Site Phase IX. Both from the Great Temple, SP2, Locus 1. Frieze fragments, head in yellow limestone. Proper right: length 20.1, w. 14.2, th. 10.8 cm. Lower chin (open mouth) and part of a cheek, partial eyebrow and eye (no raised pupil). Nose fragmented in 4 pieces (labeled B and C for reconstruction of the nose). Proper left: length 19.6, w. 14.2, th. 10.3 cm. Lower chin (open mouth) and part of the left cheek, eyebrow and eye (no raised pupil). Hair with Nabataean-style tight corkscrew ringlets and a well-defined side curl set before the ear; hair modeled on top of the head. Only the corner of the mouth remains. Previously published in *ADAJ* 39 (1995) fig. 19, p. 258; vol. 1, fig. 5.55, 233; vol. 1, fig. 5.56, p. 233; vol. 2, fig. 5.64, p. 258.

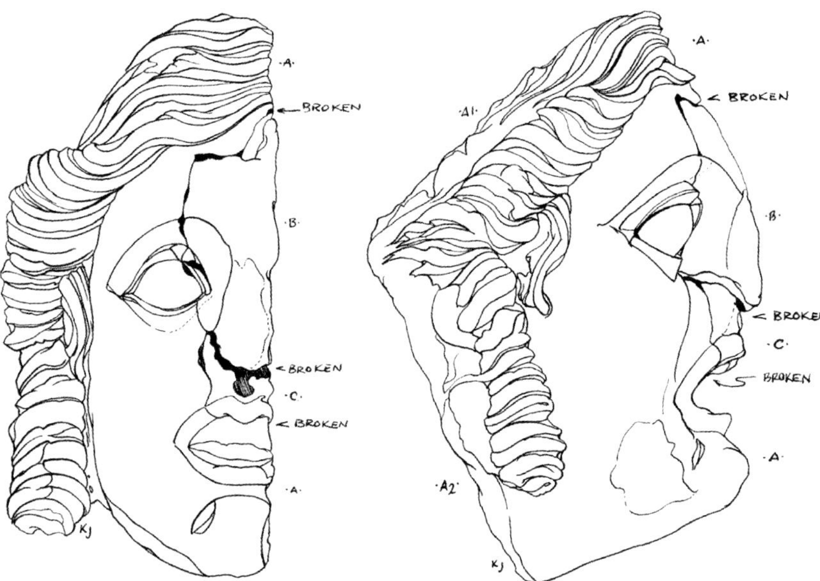

Fig. 21.33. Fragment of tragic theater mask with Nabataean-style tight ringlets (94-S-08), proper right side, from Great Temple (1994).

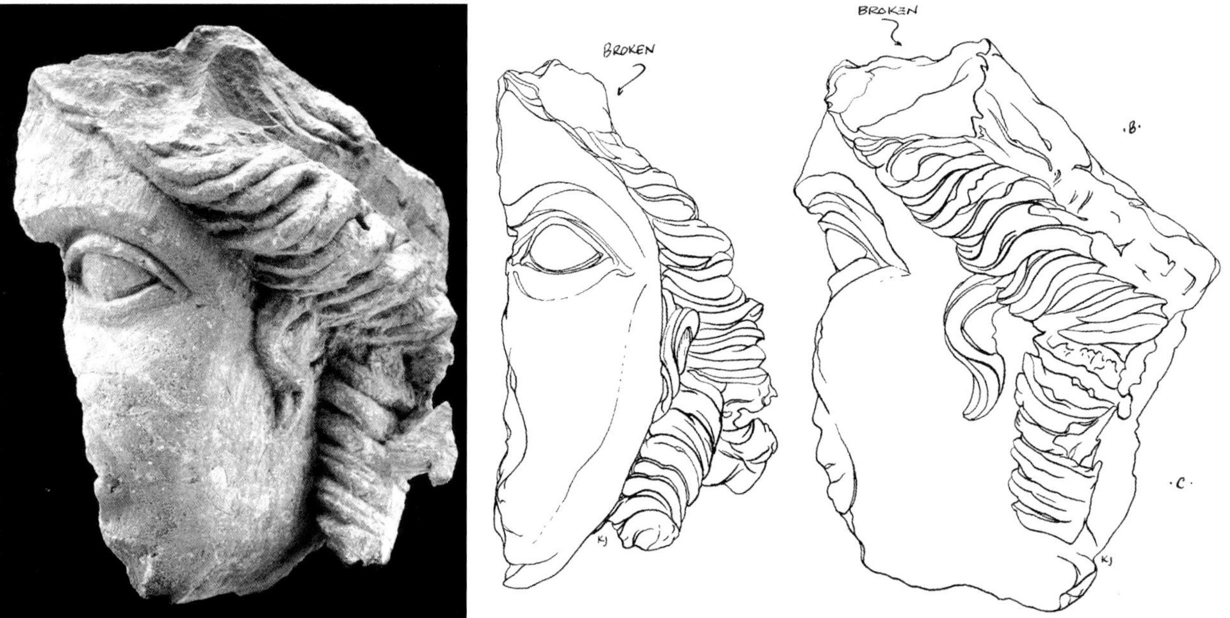

Fig. 21.34-35. Fragment of tragic theater mask with Nabataean-style tight ringlets (94-S-09), proper left side, from Great Temple (1994).

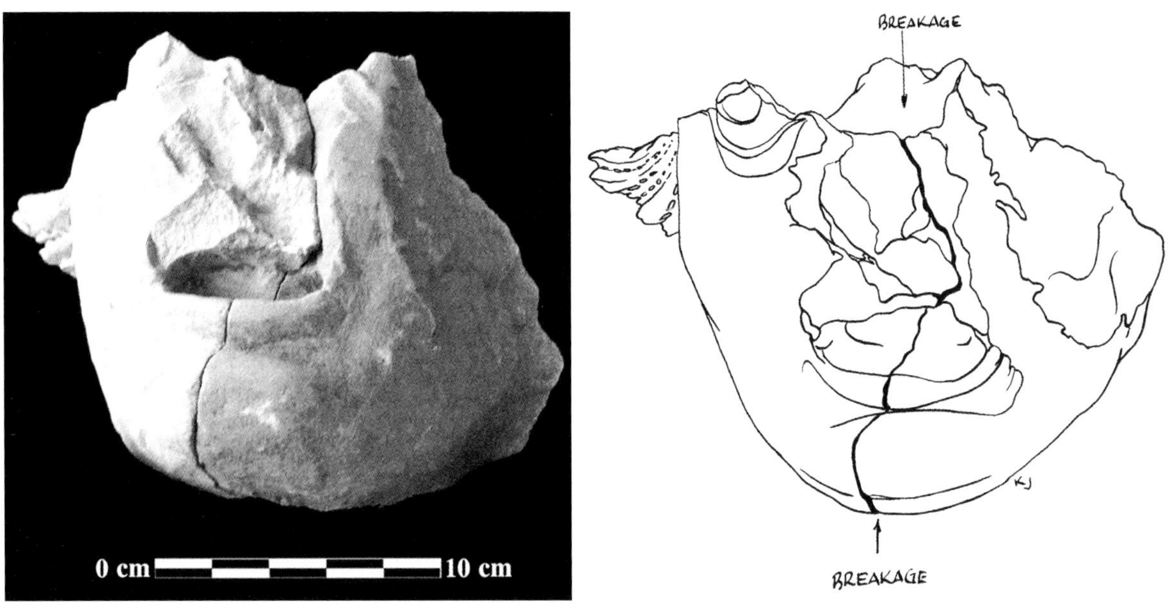

Fig. 21.36

Fig. 21.37

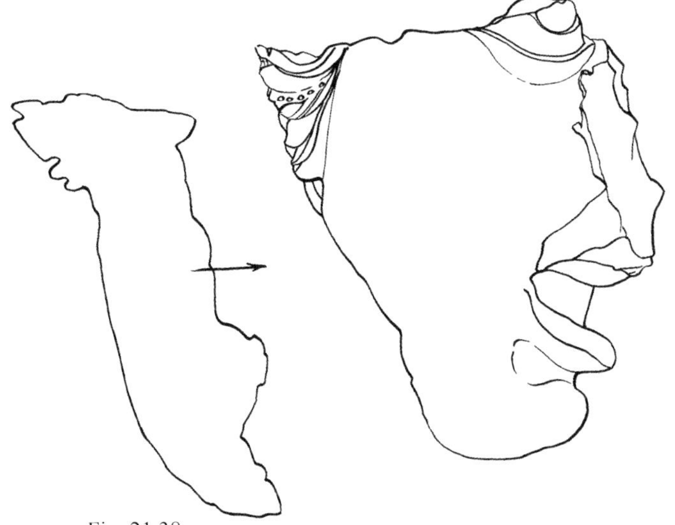

Fig. 21.38

Fig. 21.36-39. Fragments of tragic theater masks 94-S-01 (proper right and profile drawing) and 94-S-03 as well as frontal views Fig. 21.36-37, from Great Temple (1994).

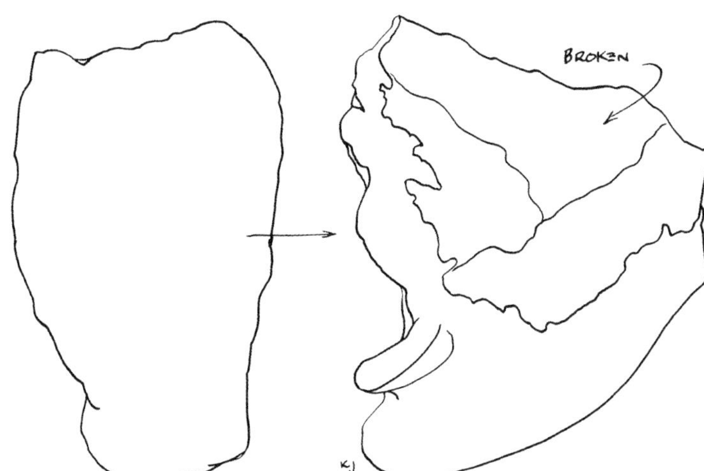

Fig. 21.39

Conclusions

The subjects, iconographies, techniques and styles draw on a wide range of traditions — Nabataean, Hellenistic and Roman. Some, like the *nefesh* and *betyls*, are related stylistically to native Nabataean antecedents, being visible symbols of the Nabataeans, but a new Roman order also makes itself felt on the site.[36] As H. Dodge has written,[37]

> Roman influence was exerted upon the architecture of the Eastern provinces on several levels, dependent upon the local materials available. On one level these were localized, short-lived direct imports ...On another level the Roman impetus was only one of many influences, which were blended and adapted to local practices and the use of local materials.

Acknowledgements

I am indebted to D. G. Barrett for her work in producing the finds catalogue over many seasons. I am grateful to R. Wenning and T. M. Weber for reading this chapter in an earlier draft and offering many valuable corrections and suggestions.

36 Dodge 1990, 108.
37 Ibid. 118.

22
Summary and Conclusions
Martha Sharp Joukowsky

Introduction

Great Temple Volume I examined the Great Temple's first five years of excavation results, and *Great Temple Volume II* focused on the archaeological contexts of the remains, the stratigraphy, and conservation measures used to preserve and protect important features. This volume, *Great Temple Volume III,* takes the evidence a step further to address the results of the Great Temple precinct's architectural design and bring the site's artifact record into sharper focus.

The Brown University excavations of the Petra Great Temple in 16 seasons of fieldwork have uncovered a wealth of information. In this volume we have found architecture that is revolutionary and informative, a myriad of artifacts originally used in the precinct, plus a précis of Great Temple subsistence patterns. From 1993 until 2009 the Brown University archaeological team has opened some192 trenches, site phased the deposits, and has recorded close to a million artifacts.

Here is presented the description and analyses of the architecture and specific artifact classes, both in terms of the overarching culture of the Great Temple itself, but also in the broader context of Nabataean architecture and art. Because we are still discovering the Nabataeans, these remains provide essential clues toward a broader understanding of the Great Temple, Petra, and the choices the Nabataeans made in building their capital city. The well-developed style and the exceptional quality of the Great Temple architecture and its artifact record when viewed against the background of existing Nabataean scholarship, both within Petra itself and in its caravan cities, also is providing enticing new information for determining the aesthetic sense of the Nabataeans through periods in which the Great Temple is constructed and used.

The temple is the product of the Nabataeans who created an independent 'Nabataean style' and craftsmanship that served the demands of its dynamic trading society with its own desert nomadic folk tradition. And it is for that reason Nabataean art and architecture were the products of eclectic decisions that exhibit spontaneity in the establishment of Petra as the creative and monumental capital of its vast desert kingdom.

Borrowing Hellenistic architectural paradigms and concepts this Nabataean artistic tradition invariably changes with the historical events that affected those who commissioned the Great Temple; first in the Late Hellenistic period (*ca.* first century-63 B.C.) until Roman influence becomes pervasive (63 B.C.-A.D. 360), through to the Byzantine period (A.D. 360-640) when the center of power is transferred to 'New Rome' or Constantinople. For this reason it is important to study the Nabataeans through the lens of the Great Temple, not only for the historic and political contexts of Nabataean times, but also to discover the emergence of their own individualistic Nabataean artistic traditions. In their choices of architecture, sculpture, and pottery and in the various industries covered in these pages, we find artistic concepts influenced by Hellenistic, Roman and Byzantine symbolic iconography, but are dictated in part by Nabataean ideas of power and royal succession. As seen at Petra, the truth is that architecture played a paramount role in the political world of the Nabataean monarchy. This study of Petra centers on the Great Temple that offers the focal point for a greater understanding in its reflection of the complex processes involved with Nabataean cultural development.

Part I – Great Temple Architecture

Temple Architecture—Introduction

Whatever scatters of earlier structures there may have been on the Great Temple site, the Nabataean city planners razed them all, and at some point they must have realized that the location of the building site had enormous limitations i.e., whatever was to be built had to be constructed on very uneven ground. There was a large spur of sandstone bedrock in the south, which would compete with any structure placed there, and an appreciable breakdown of the west sandstone bedrock, which dramatically dropped away. As for the south spur of sandstone, they instructed stonemasons to create a strong and substantial bedrock platform by cutting away the south sandstone spur to a depth of 12 m. in preparation for the temple.

Some of the discrepancies in elevation would be offset by the creation of a tri-tiered precinct, including Propylaeum, Lower Temenos and Upper Temenos. The processional way was approximately 7 m below the Great Temple Propylaeum, and from the Propylaeum the precinct rose another 7 m to the Lower Temenos, and Approximately 7 meters above the Lower Temenos is the Upper Temenos, the leveled bedrock shelf, and the site of the earliest Great Temple.

Once the plan was established, in Site Phase II, the Great Temple with an impressive distyle *in antis* façade was erected on the hill well above the central city. From the archaeological record, it appears that in Site Phase III, dated from the mid-to-late first century B.C to A.D. first century, there were some structural problems with the temple construction that had to be rectified, and at that time a major decision must have been undertaken to correct the problems and redesign the temple with a grand tetrastyle *in antis* addition with a significant raised Upper Temenos and a porch (entry, Pronaos) to the temple itself.

In any event, the local dynast, probably King Arteas IV (9/8 B.C. - A.D. 40) and his collaborators in the ruling class must have recognized the requisite need to enlarge the precinct for it is during Great Temple Site Phase IV that architectural innovations were introduced and the precinct was rebuilt with an ambitious ground plan which was far more imposing and replete with areas of interest. Attention was showered on the whole precinct. Nabataean wealth and power had to be evident. Thus the architects were to build a larger and more elaborate precinct that was planned to be unique to the Nabataean world. Such a lavish display of unusual architecture would in reality connote Nabataean Petra's success and its ruler's high-ranking and worldly economic status.

Despite the differences in elevation the architects consciously designed the Great Temple precinct in Site Phase IV in a royal setting with additional Propylaeum walls behind the Portico Wall on the north flanking the great processional way[1], which was the principal artery to the central city. Now the Propylaeum and its Portico Wall itself was to be embellished with a great display of relief sculpture that served to convey perceptions of divinity and power. On the west the Propylaeum Portico Wall is reconfigured to allow the building of the West Entry Stairway to serve as the grand entry to the precinct where access would flow from the processional way either to the Propylaeum west entry for a visit to the twin *betyls* or continue up the stairs for entry into Lower Temenos.[2]

However, before construction could begin many factors had to be considered in the planning and building, in particular of the great Lower Temenos, which was to be an intended venue for parades and celebrations. It was to be designed with columned triple walkways decorated with elephant headed capitals. And these covered walkways would lead into east and west exedras located on both sides of the vast hexagonally paved limestone plaza.

---

1 In Roman times this became the Colonnaded Street (the cardo).

2 The Central Stairway seen today as the main access to the precinct was constructed in Site Phase VII in the mid-second century A.D. This renovation plan may have been put in motion with the paving of the Roman Colonnaded Street.

Nevertheless before these plans could be set in motion, the architects had to solve the problems of additional and even more severe elevation discrepancies particular to the Lower Temenos. The ground of the monumental Lower Temenos with its planned colonnaded walkways and exedras had to be somehow compensated, because these planned features were to be located where the natural bedrock had broken down. They invented ingenious solutions to solve the elevation disparities— where there was an approximate 2-4m m bedrock drop off they would import enormous amounts of fill and level the area, and when the drop off was 5m or greater, they would construct subterranean galleries, vaulted cryptoporticoes, which they purposefully designed to be covered over, so that they would not be visible.

In studying the Lower Temenos, we can only speculate analysis of the preserved remains and the technical problems faced by Nabataean architects to conceive such a utilitarian, visually stimulating and yet massive space. Enormous amounts of fill had to be imported to level the area. Thus the original ground level of the monumental Lower Temenos plaza with its hexagonal pavement, exedras, and triple colonnades[3] initially had to be leveled, before the buildings themselves could be constructed.

The situation was similarly complicated on the Upper Temenos west because here too the natural bedrock dramatically dropped off. In order for the features on the west, including the Great Temple's West Corridor, the West Walkway and the West Perimeter Wall to be stabilized, a five to eight course East-West Support wall[4], 5 m in height, was built directly on the bedrock and supported an artificial platform that was created to reinforce the area. In sum, preserved portions of the Lower Temenos like the exedras and Upper Temenos walls, colonnades, and even the west temple itself were buttressed by subterranean architectural reinforcements and fill.

Also in Great Temple Site Phase IV, dated most likely to the A.D. first century, surrounding the temple and built into or on the Upper Temenos sizeable bedrock shelf are notable features, such as the temple's Central Arch Room, the Nabataean-excavated Great Cistern in the East Plaza, and to temple south, the Baroque Room Complex, and the Residential Quarter. These features were all constructed on or into the same bedrock as the temple itself as well as into caves (Residential Quarter) that rose just above the temple's South Passageway or near the casemate East Perimeter Wall (as was the case for the Tabun Room). At completion the temple stood some 34 meters above the processional way and roughly 7 m above the Lower Temenos. Now built on the solid bedrock in the site's Upper Temenos stood the Great Temple displaying its reconstruction. Towering above the precinct with its raised forecourt and tetrastyle *in antis* façade, the temple had become a Nabataean statement—an imposing building of majestic proportions.

This arrangement reflected Nabataean choices for spatial relationships and monumentality. Once inside the Great Temple Portico the dynast of the time could roam its brightly frescoed corridors, walkways, multiple staircases and or visit the central theater-odeon (of later Site Phase V). These structures provide a unique opportunity to study how they were built and integrated into the overall very complicated precinct plan. Fortunately we can correlate this architectural information with Great Temple site phases to pin down when we posit each feature was constructed and remained in use.

Now we turn to the discussions presented here in Volume III.

---

3 The architects knew there was a problem with the Lower Temenos design. At a 5 m below the Lower Temenos Triple Colonnade walkways are vast cryptoporticoes built onto artificial fill. The architects ingeniously compensated for the bedrock drop off by building the cryptoporticos to provide a structural base for the Triple Colonnades, which they built directly above the cryptoporticos shortly after the cryptoporticoes support structures were erected.

4 *Vol. 2,* Figs. 4.21, 4.23, p.150, 157, 192, 194, 259.

Survey

From the 1993 inception of the excavations the Brown University team has site surveyed using a total station. Assisted by GIS (Geographic Information System) with thousands of measurements, a systematic survey of the Great Temple precinct covering 17 years of excavations has been instituted. Now these measurements are fully integrated into an AutoCAD system of mapping and reconstruction. We have excavated 12,601.57 m^2 of area (multiplied by 7 m in average depth, or approximately 88,211 m cubed). Moreover these excavations have contributed new data to the Petraean central city mapping project undertaken by the American Center of Oriental Research (ACOR) in Amman and the Hashemite University of Jordan in Zerqa.[5] Our survey work has helped to define the Nabataean capital, particularly the central city, and the extraordinary features of the Great Temple precinct.

Water Systems

The semiarid climate of Petra generates unpredictable precipitation and heavy, sometimes-torrential rainfall, from October to March, however, the risk of drought is ever present today as it was in antiquity. The manipulation of water sources from 'Ain Musa and 'Ain Brak suggest a consistent concern of the Great Temple planners. Run-off rainwater is captured in surface drains of the Lower Temenos, and above ground and subterranean drainage systems litter the site, running below all its built areas. The need for a secure supply of water is dramatically demonstrated by the Great Temple subterranean canalization systems. The builders of the Great Temple devised various subterranean water channels which they put in place even before they constructed the precinct, including canalization dispersal conduits, stone-lined channels, sluices, stopcocks, reservoirs, settling tanks, closed pipe conduits and lead water pipes.

Besides these features there is the presence of the sizeable Upper Temenos Great Cistern constructed in Site Phase IV, with an overall interior breadth of approximately 327.64 cubic meters —with an astonishing capacity of 86,562.488 gallons or 327,640 liters of water. This is the largest cistern yet documented in the Petra central city, and it appears it also provides sufficient supplies for the Roman-Byzantine Baths, and may have served the Garden-Pool complex located to the east of the Great Temple. During the excavations it was difficult to obtain a clear picture of the complete system, because it was buried beneath the temple architecture. However, we have arrived at an expert reconstruction of the ingenious Great Temple's vast hydraulic network.

Temple Architecture

The large-scale Great Temple architecture of all the areas was constructed with quarried building materials that were available by the local natural geology, including those in nearby quarries and perhaps the sandstone bedrock that was chiseled away at the rear of the temple itself. Highly skilled stonemasons[6] quarried, chiseled, and dressed rectangular ashlar sandstone blocks that they set in leveled horizontal courses. Ashlar masonry had a long tradition in Egypt and by the third millennium its use for architecture had spread to the Levant. Once set in place, Great Temple sandstone ashlars were diagonally chiseled to hold a stucco facing. Once in place the ashlar blocks were bound together with a strong mortar. This type of construction was used not only for the temple, but also for the wide variety of buildings, walls and staircases in the precinct. The quality of construction exhibits great care both in the design layout and construction.

---

5 *Vol. 2*, Figs. 1.1, 4; 1.2, 5.

6 There must have been a thriving industry for the stonemasons not only in the quarries but for the mass production of ashlars. The industry for the manufacture of roof and pavement tiles must also have been significant.

As the Nabataeans became a wealthy political force and expanded their control of the trade routes, architects were commissioned to find ideas for architectural forms that served the needs of their monarch. They decided to adopt formal artistic Hellenistic traditional and prestigious building forms, wanting to create meaningful architectural spaces for themselves and their capital city. We have found they retained Hellenistic ideas and at the same time developed fresh ideas to serve their own needs.

Stucco Revetments[7]

The 27,000 molded and often polychrome stucco fragments from the Great Temple give us new insights into the temple's sumptuous decoration. The excellent colored and cable-fluted plastering of the columns and walls with colorful cassettes points to the Petraean adoption of the Pompeian 'Second Style' decorative scheme. Little of the stucco *in situ* now survives but elements of this decorative program with molded cassettes and stucco cornices cover the long corridor walls of the temple and provide a narrative linking the iconography of the frescoes with the temple architecture. Designed to represent false columns, *trompe d'oeil* designs, polychrome diamonds, and marbleizing motifs it serves as an interior embellishment for the temple architecture. This study provides an interesting and clear perception of the Nabataean idea of interior space and the use of impressive wall decoration.

In the elaborately decorated Baroque Room is the spectacular ceiling that collapsed in Site Phase VI of the A.D. second century. Here we find an idiosyncratic plaster relief painted in reds and blues with some sections gilded. We can envision raised plaster reliefs fashioning the large ceiling decoration with its extraordinary central pomegranate medallion in high relief encircled by raised relief acanthus leaves and molded dentils.[8] The Nabataean predilection for a "grand style" also finds three-dimensional raised plaster leaves decorating columns or grape clusters and brightly painted Ionic columns and swirling vine and leaf patterns.

Sculpted Relief Panels

Traveling over the desert trade routes is a precarious business, but the potential for amassing riches is possible for those who succeed. Elevated on the Propylaeum and Great Temple walls, sculpted stone relief panels adorning the façade of the Propylaeum charts the direction of the processional way to the monumental Temenos Gate leading to the entrance to the Qasr al-Bint's vast Temenos and to the majestic Qasr temple itself. The worship of divine figures—Fortuna and Tyche, who were regarded as the providers of fertility and commercial success, decorate both the Propylaeum and the temple itself, symbolizing the prosperity of Nabataean traders. Although there seems to be little connection between the figures themselves, they symbolize the choices that were made and defined a more intimate involvement with a wide range of cultic needs.

These figurative panels are Nabataean adaptations reflecting the Petraean indigenous tastes for styles they recognize. These remarkable pilasters are not peripheral or atypical works, and they are significant not only as a Nabataean improvised art form, but serve as an integral part of the Great Temple's rich tapestry of styles. The busts are placed frontally towards the spectator and some of the females are represented with corkscrew curls. They reflect an artistic formal language and truly represent the Petraean canon for the Nabataean period—surely they are part of the official world they serve.

---

7 Many of these fragments are recorded on the Grosso Modo forms. If they deserved particular attention they were classed with other architectural fragments and entered into the Architectural Fragment database.

8 *Vol. 2*, 46, 157,185-186, 187, 188-189, 190, 192, 194, 244, 288, 296, 361.

Nabataean Corinthian and Elephant-headed Capitals[9]

The sculpted temple capitals find their geneses in the Hellenistic world. A Nabataean variant of the rich Corinthian capitals decorating the temple indicates these types of columns represent a visual metaphor for the status of the building. Their visual imagery and aesthetic can be directly related to the Great Temple patrons who commissioned the building. Some elite person or group took the decision not to use the traditional Corinthian capital to adorn the structure, but to commission sculptors to create deeply carved capitals delicately adorned with hibiscus petals, pinecones, pomegranates or poppies, acanthus leaves and vines—in a distinct Nabataean style symbolic of the earliest *distyle* temple, their city, and possibly their reverence for the god Dionysus.

What role did the elephant headed capitals play in the Lower Temenos? Elephant-headed capitals bordering the Lower Temenos plaza indicate that the elephant enjoyed an exotic status and the sculptural program of the Lower Temenos provides abundant evidence for the Asian elephant holding an intrinsic power for the Nabataeans. Surely these capitals are a sculptural anomaly that is difficult to explain for they are neither part of the Hellenistic tradition, nor can they be explained by a native tradition. Did the elephants guard the Lower Temenos and the temple? Obviously Hellenistic architecture and sculptural ideas had an impact on Nabataean sculptural designs, however experimenting with new ideas as seen in these capitals must have served as catalysts for the political trade-directed world of the Nabataean monarchy.

The sculptors who executed these works used their chisels with an extraordinary degree of delicacy for the heads and the facial expressions are minutely detailed. Furthermore it is suggested that the Great Temple elephant heads are carved in sufficient physiological detail to suggest that the Nabataean sculptors have firsthand experience with elephants and the master sculptor who directed the atelier bases these 500+ sculptures on actual observation at least.

Theater-In-Temple

Unique to the Great Temple as well as to ancient architectural models is the Theater-in-Temple dated to Site Phase V or to the A.D. first century. This anomalous building has modified our understanding of the architecture and function of the building. Its dramatic arrangement would seem to confirm the Great Temple served as a locus for performance—and was a celebratory emblem of the political, religious and cultural assertion of these functions.

With a detailed architectural plan a new picture has emerged, one that includes a clear view of the pioneering architectonics the theater-in-temple represents both in layout and function. There is nothing quite like the Great Temple *theatron* in Nabataean architecture, it seems to exhibit fresh architectural ideas that harken back to an early Hellenistic paradigm archetypes. Inside the Temple-in-Theater is found a considerable part of the original architectural program of the building. This unusual architecture offers valuable new research evidence, which throws light on the relationship between the Nabataean architectural dynamic and the eclectic ideas of its patrons.

Roman-Byzantine Baths

While the architecture of the Great Temple itself has drawn much interest, it is only since 2005 that attention has turned to a systematic study of the lavish Roman-Byzantine Baths.[10] The research conducted on the architecture and other artifacts recovered from this 24-room complex

---

9 Components of these sculpted capitals can be found in the Architectural Fragments database < http://www.open context.org >. They have all been recorded by material, measured, and classed by motif.

10 The Great Temple Roman-Byzantine Baths are built to the west of the Lower Temenos lie adjacent to the underground palatial earlier baths What is the interplay between the Great Temple baths and the earlier first century B.C. Nabataean palatial baths? This question has yet to be answered.

demonstrate that this small bath system is constructed on a row type Pompeian architectural plan. Here the architecture, including the platform, apodyterium, praefurnium, "splash pool," vestibule, tepidarium, laconicum and settling tank, multiple caldaria, frigidarium, and an elegant toilet, are described along with the known hydraulic and heating systems. There is also a consideration of the extent to which the facilities are modified in the post-earthquake environments of A.D. 363 when multiple changes take place and to the point when a further unfortunate earthquake strikes in A.D. 551 after which the baths are no longer in use.

Part II. Great Temple Material Culture

Great Temple Catalogue[11]

The Petra Great Temple Catalogue of hundreds of objects demonstrates the broad range of artifacts in various materials, sizes and shapes that have been deposited with the Department of Antiquities in Petra. These objects are briefly presented by material—stone, bone, faience, shell, metal and pottery, and are discussed within the larger context of the site as a whole. An analysis of the objects that were chosen for use by the Great Temple patrons is significant for our understanding of the range of Great Temple activities taking place.

Residential Quarter Ceramics

A significant result of the 2002 excavations is the discovery of the Residential Quarter extending 15.48 m north-south x 9.22 m east west covering an area of 142.72 m^2. It lies a few meters to the south of the Upper Temenos just beyond the West Precinct Wall. Isolated from the Great Temple it is most likely that these private residence(s) of Site Phases IV and V of the Nabataean period represent a high-density complex with apartments for several families, consisting of two caves and 11 rooms. Its strata serve as a time capsule in constant use from the first century B.C. to the A.D. 363 earthquakes. Here we have taken the opportunity to trace the development of both Nabataean fine wares and plain wares, numbering some 32,349 fragments unearthed in these household contexts. This ceramic analysis demonstrates the rich collection of both painted and plain wares at the Great Temple.

Lamps[12]

The presence of 626 lamps, and the frequency or absence of specific lamp types provides another avenue to place this artifact into context with Great Temple activities taking place at the site. Lamps appear in all periods, but only small quantities occur in the Hellenistic and Islamic periods. Nabataean fragments (both Nabataean indigenous fragments and Nabataean local copies of Roman imported fragments) account for a major portion of the assemblage. The percentage of imported Roman fragments is small, whereas there is a substantial quantity of Byzantine lamp fragments.

In addition to the locally made common lamps and locally made copies of Roman lamps are some unusual imports such as those from Syro-Palestine and further a field from Rome, and perhaps Parthia, clearly reflecting Petra's position as an entrepôt on the trade route.

---

11 The Catalogue can be found on-line at *Open Context,* < http://www.open context.org >.

12 Created by Deirdre G. Barrett, the lamp database can be found on-line at *Open Context,* < http://www.open context.org >.

Figurines[13]

Eighty terracotta figurines have been found at the Great Temple ranging in date from the Nabataean period A.D. late in the first century to the A.D. fifth century with the majority recovered from later site phases where they are dispersed among building and debris contexts. Several types of figural images are presented portraying anthropomorphic subjects as well as masks, zoomorphic figures, plaques and vessels. Representations of Isis and Harpocrates attest to the presence of Egyptian connections. There is evidence provided by the presence of many animal figurines that reflects the basic world—the cult life—the early Petraeans as a food producing economy based on animal husbandry.

Glass[14]

Here is defined the typological and technical evolution of glass styles and shapes at the Great Temple set against the stratigraphy and site phases. Although blown glass is developed in the A.D. first century, the existence of a local glass production cannot proven but trade contacts are detected with other regions of the Near East. Present are decolorized intaglio vessels, and facet-cut and painted beakers confirming a Flavian-Trajanic date (A.D. 69-116). The Byzantine glass, from the A.D. 363 earthquake destruction of the Roman-Byzantine Baths, suggests a persistent Egyptian stylistic influence on contemporary glass-workshops. Of special note for glass experts is the early dating for the appearance of circular blown windowpanes found in the bath complex. These factors and the Great Temple glass repertoire substantiate a distinctive southern Levantine *koine* of glass forms and decoration.

Numismatics[15]

One of the features of the Great Temple excavations is the registry of 759 coins, however not all of the collection is identifiable. Of the group, 46 coins are presented chronologically, which have not been published before.[16] They show a broad range of both time periods and stylistic diversity. Of particular interest are four early Phoenician coins from Sidon and Aradus, dated from the third to second centuries B.C. The full range of stereotypical Nabataean coins follows with the various kings on the obverse, and on the reverse the crossed cornucopia and often a palm branch (or less often, the queen standing with her hand raised). These are followed by a broad range of Roman coinage, but of particular interest are the extraordinarily well preserved silver coins of Trajan, No. 98-C-32A and 98-C-32C, dating to A.D. 112-114. Roman coins signify that Petra is firmly entranched within the economic sphere of the eastern Mediterranean. The latest issue is of the Byzantine ruler Theodosius II (A.D. 408-423). This numismatic evidence abundantly reflects cross-cultural currents of exchange far beyond the borders of Nabataea.

Epigraphic Evidence

Epigraphic evidence from the Great Temple is scanty. The Great Temple Nabataean inscriptions have been published, including the bronze plaque[17], the faint Nabataean inscription on a plaster

---

13 The Figurine Catalog, authored by Christopher A. Tuttle, is found on-line at *Open Context,* < http://www.open context.org >.

14 The glass typology and distribution patterns created by Margaret O'Hea can be found at *Open Context,* < http://www.open context.org >. This is a continued study from the report published in *Great Temple I,* 325–343. Total glass fragments numbered (1993-2006) 4672, which were recorded on the Grosso Modo forms. A large selection of this material has been studied.

15 The complete coin catalogue prepared by C. F. Cloke and M. S. Joukowsky can be found on-line at *Open Context,* < http://www.open context.org >.

16 In *vol. 1* p.317-324 where several Nabataean, Roman and Byzantine issues are presented.

17 Joukowsky 2003, fig. 2.39, p. 220.

molding[18], and the Nabataean grafitti carved into the mortar of the West Propylaeum wall.[19] There are a few ostraca fragments[20], and stamped jar handles[21], but of note are the three Roman Imperial inscriptions[22], including the Trajanic inscription recovered from the West Chamber of the Great Temple[23]. Masons' marks on temple components are discussed as well—both here in Chapter 2, and in previous publications[24].

A series of new later inscriptions are examined in detail, which are found associated with the Roman-Byzantine Bath Complex. Of interest is that the dating of the baths cannot be based on these inscriptions, because they were reused in secondary contexts. However they do provide an indication as to when the bath renovations took place in the Byzantine period.

Faunal Analysis[25]

What can faunal analysis tell us about the food choices of the Great Temple occupants? As is expected sheep and goat remains are found throughout all site phases and in all areas of the precinct. Chicken is the second most common food in the assemblage with pig also represented. Camels, donkeys and horses, cattle, dogs and wild taxa also appear in significant numbers. The Great Temple assemblage is dominated by goats and camels, which support Nabataean nomadic style practices. With the Roman annexation, chicken, game birds and pigs indicate an abrupt shift from earlier consumable choice patterns. This contribution also discusses the ages and variety of animals and with the analysis of bone cut marks, butchering techniques were also analyzed.

The examination of the Great Temple fish remains contributes to our understanding of the archaeological process involved with the importation of fish. Food fish include tuna, groupers, and parrotfish which were consumed in all sectors of the site. Determining the source from which the fish are recovered indicates that the occupants of the Great Temple favored fish both from the Red Sea and the Mediterranean. As these sources are located at a 100 km distance from Petra, these fish imports indicate a regularized pattern beginning (from the Great Temple remains) in the Nabataean period.

Worked Bone[26]

The function of a worked bone tool kit signals the presence of trade as well as the local manipulation of bone. Sixty objects were examined and noteable finds include decorated pins, spatulae, styli, bottons, spoons and combs. The study of worked bone provides information not only about the small collection itself, but about Nabataean women, for it is assumed that women

---

18 Ibid. 7.29a, p. 378.

19 Ibid. fig. 7.30.

20 Ibid. fig. 7.31a.

21 Ibid. fig. 7.31d.

22 *Great Temple vol. 1,* Figs, 6.83-684, p. 297)

23 Ibid. Ch. 8, p. 369–375).

24 See vol.1, p.114, 264 266; vol. 2, p.166, 241, 259, 358, and 359.

25 Various faunal analyses charts prepared by S. W. Kansa can be found at *Open Context*, < http://www.open context.org >. A large selection of the 27,658 (1993-2006) bones is studied.

26 Worked bones are part of the Great Temple Catalogue. There is no separate database for these objects.
Commonly encountered during the excavations are shells. In the field collection of all available evidence, shells are collected and recorded. A representative sample will be analyzed for origin, taxonomy and diversity throughtout the site phases. Shells are recognized as objects for food and ornamentation. The exquisite mother-of-pearl dolphin pendant (02-I I-1, Fig. 10.7) recovered from the Residental Quarter in 2002 is placed within the Great Temple archaeological contexts belonging to Site Phase IX. Shells are recorded as part of the Grosso Modo input where 1676 entries were entered. They are not distinguished by taxa. Separately bagged in the field, only a portion of the complete repertoire has been examined by D. S. Reese who has planned to publish a separate report on his findings.

are primarily responsible for textile and clothing production. It was theorized that they are the principal consumers utilizing this worked bone kit for household purposes.

A tantalizing find is the hippopotamus tusk fragment, which originally may have been part of a small box or pyxis designed to keep trinkets or make-up. This is of particular interest, because the shores of the Nile serve as a primary source for the hippo. Comparable tusks from other sites are documented, and interpretation is given. The overland and sea route from Egypt up to Petra via Aila pre-dated the Roman control of Egypt. Although Nabataea lost its trade monopoly under the Julio-Claudians (CE 14-70), this does not suggest that the city is no longer part of that route in the Byzantine period. It is assumed that in antiquity this hippopotamus tusk traveled north from Egypt to Petra via intermediate sites, and was prized for its special exotic qualities.

Metalwork[27]

Metal craft specialization is found at the Great Temple. In the southwest of the temple precinct the evidence suggests that smelting and casting of copper may have taken place. Here are found objects including slag, fragments of a crucible and a possible pot bellows used for draft.

Clearly different metals are used for different purposes. By examining the metal artifacts, we find traded objects alongside local items. Structural architectural components such as nails and door locks are commonly recovered implements in the assemblage. Non-structural iron objects including chisels, awls, sockets and needles also were utilized. Less common are bronze objects but handles, buttons, plaques, horse trappings and helmet cheek pieces also appeared in the repertoire. Although we know that local sources of copper are located to the south of Petra, we assume that most of the metal implements found at the site are imported. Metal tools may have reached Petra by various routes—but overland from the Mediterranean coast to the east is probably the preferred scenario. The *Via Traiana* provides an additional overland route for the import of metals from either the north or south.

Ballistae[28]

The ballista (Gk. *ballista*, "ballo," to throw) is an artillery weapon developed by the Greeks for launching projectiles. The excavations at the Great Temple recovered an armory of 421 ballista balls at the front the temple precinct in the north gallery of the Propylaeum West. These missiles are of particular interest and attest to the Great Temple's preparation for an attack, or they may offer evidence of the result of an attack, which is posited to take place just before or during the Roman annexation of Nabataea in A.D. 106.This weaponry was weighed to provide information on the system of measurements for calibration used by either the Nabataean or Roman military, and an assessment of the stone used and the average size range of the ballistae are also presented.

Nefesh, betyls and Miscellaneous Sculpture[29]

In attempting to present a general discussion and photographic catalogue for a few, very varied extant sculptural pieces, attention is drawn to the aniconic display of the *nefesh* and *betyls* as well as the iconic sculptures, including human forms and animals. The surviving *nefesh* is without doubt a public memorial set where passers-by could view the stele. As for the *betyls*, the various styles of this idiosyncratic body of sculpture deserve study, not only in relation to the Great Temple

27 Metals are collected in the field, bagged separately, and recorded on the Grosso Modo form. If they are of museum quality they are cataloged and can be found in the Great Temple catalogue registered by D. G. Barrett. A total of 4799 metal pieces are found from 1993 to 2006, most of which was not cataloged.

28 All ballistae are recorded in the Architectural Fragments database at *Open Context* < http://www.opencontext.org >.

29 Most of these fragments have been recorded in the Great Temple Catalog, however, many of them were turned over to the Jordanian Department of Antiquities as soon as they were recovered, and are not registered in the site catalog.

sequence of site phases, but for their own individuality. As has been mentioned in Chapter 21, betyls represent the physical presence of the Nabataean god. (These were beliefs that extended back to the third millennium B.C.) The physical presence of the god provided the people with the guarantee of deific beneficience and prosperity.

The Nabataean period was a producive time for art, not only for the Nabataean Corinthian temple capitals embellished with a profusion of fruits and vines, but the prolific carving of elephant headed capitals and the pilasters in relief. And the theater-odeum masks illustrate this particular eclecticism as well. Unknown sculptors created these hybrid variants of typical masks, and their adaptations differ significantly from typical Hellenistic or Roman models. Assuming they represent symbols of drama and culture, they are distinctly Nabataean in taste and are well suited to theatrical symbolism. Details that may be relevant to a better understanding of the possible sources for these sculptures are presented so that their stylistic analysis and broader significance carefully can be determined by sculpture experts.

As for the sculptures presented here, there is a sense of mystery associated with the aniconic, incised Al-'Uzza *betyl* (Fig. 21.7), and in contrast we sense a theatrical pathos conveyed in the figurative expression of the classicized head of a deity (Figure 21.8). Or perhaps we can fathom more from the lack of drama exemplified in the iconography of the heroic warrior in Figure 21.10? Found associated with the West Perimeter Wall and it was probably erected to be seen in honor of the Roman (and perhaps Nabataean?) military, or to celebrate a triumph. In any event this heroic warrior representation is a wholly new portrayal of the heroic for Petra. We assume that both his dress and equipment is closely linked to an evolving political role in the Roman Empire and this scupture was commissioned as a message of Imperial propaganda.

In Appendixes 1 and 2 we review the

1. List of Trenches and Special Projects Excavated by Area; 2. The excavation Trenches in the Propylaeum, 1993-2008, 3. Excavation Trenches in the Lower Temenos, 1993-2008, 4. Excavation Trenches in the Upper Temenos, 1993-2008, 5. Excavation Trenches in the Temple, 1993-2008; and

Appendix 2 lists the Dimensions and Elevations of features in the Great Temple Precinct.

In Appendixes 3-5 Database Methodology

Database methodology with an eye to developing a practical method to capture bulk finds has been central to our excavations. In Toto we have registered 405,297, artifacts, plus thousands from the 2008 and 2009 seasons, using a model known as "Grosso Modo,"[30] which can be accessed on-line at Open Context <opencontext.org >. Drawing on stylistic changes as seen in approximately 317,977 pottery fragments (1993-2006), plus 19,255 architectural fragments, spotlights a reconsideration of the distribution patterns that continued through the few centuries of the Great Temple's existence. The presence of these bulk artifacts provides importance in establishing the activity trends taking place at the site. Using the data from this system, an extensive overview is offered of the ceramic repertoire in Appendix 4 and the architectural fragments in Appendix 5, using databases as indicators of socioeconomic change.

Appendix 4 reiterates that pottery is the single most abundant artifact class of objects at the Great Temple where 318,000 ceramic fragments are analyzed and recorded along with several complete objects. Petra's kilns are producing massive quantities of ceramics, and become a production center of pottery for the local market and for export to the corners of the Nabataean empire and further a field to cities along the eastern Mediterranean littoral. Examples of fine, high-quality Nabataean local pottery have particular importance for a definitive ceramic sequence for the site. Thin walled (1-2 mm) Nabataean ceramics of the highest quality are produced during the reign of King Aretas IV

30 The Grosso Modo database can be searched on line at *Open Context*, <http://www.open context.org >.

(9 B.C.-A.D. 40), and continue to be manufactured even after the Roman annexation in A.D.106 until the fifth century. The unusual craftsmanship of the popular thin-walled painted bowls of the Nabataean period also are very popular at the Great Temple and at sites further a field. Painted Nabataean conical bowls, paint-decorated on the interior are the most consistent horizon markers of the Nabataeans, painted with monochrome red and later brown or dark brown to black patterns. Traditional motifs include floral designs, fine lines, eyes and dots. They reach their apogee under Aretas IV.

In Appendix 5 we take a look at the Architectural Fragments database, reminding ourselves that building materials were determined by the basic Petrean geology. The Nabataean builders used designs and methods that had been well-established by Hellenistic times. They adapted and changed to their own needs. It is assumed that architects and sculptors worked together on the Great Temple overall building program.

We have presented the Great Temple's birth and architectural and artistic development at the time when Petra's world revolved around being a dominant international entrepôt of economic wealth and political power. The Nabataeans controlled the trade routes and Nabataea became an individual and different ruling power building her capital in Petra with borrowed Hellenistic, Roman and Byzantine cultural traditions. As far as we know Petra becomes the largest and most celebrated city in the Nabataean kingdom. Blending their tribal nomadic past with the cultures that surrounded them, the eclectic and individualistic Nabataeans create their own mixed artistic tradition, and that is referred to here as 'Nabataean architecture and art.'

Political circumstances intervened when the Romans subsumed the Nabataeans in A.D.106. This is the time at which Petra and Nabataea no longer enjoyed economic supremacy and the Romans took control the desert trade routes, provoking a Nabataean and Petraean economic crisis. In the beginning of Roman control, to some extent Nabataean art production (particularly in ceramic production and sculpture) retained its identity. But slowly over time a striking passivity sets in as Nabataean artisans are influenced by Roman rule, resulting in the loss of Nabataean artistic individuality. With time Nabataean identity vanishes. Thereafter in the A.D. fourth century when the Byzantine Empire assumes the leading political rule, the Great Temple reflects this period's art and culture by assimilating its ideas. By this time Nabataean art had all but disappeared completely and by the A.D. late fifth early sixth centuries it did not reappear thereafter throughout the entire history of the Near East.

This volume covers an interdisciplinary approach to the Great Temple and the special problems involved in conducting an extensive archaeological excavation. In examining the multi-period Great Temple, with its extensive architecture and artifact recovery, a methodological survey combining the study of architecture and cultural materials has been presented. All of these research areas are of special value for the reconstruction of the site and the people who brought life to the valley and its city. And when integrated with other results, we know more about the food patterns, the large-scale architectural and artistic foundations of the Nabataeans, the technology and the products of bone, ceramic, glass, metal, and sculpting industries favored by the Petraeans.

At the Great Temple we find the reality of life, not only the lives of royalty and the elite, but the city planners, architects, sculptors, painters, potters, mosaic artists,[31] smiths, butchers and soldiers, in short the ethos of the people[32] who lived, worked and worshipped in Petra. We find a land that is barely adequate for sheep and goats with some pasturage. Today as in antiquity we find herdsmen

---

31 Scattered in all areas of the Great Temple only 593 large white limestone chunks set in plaster of *tesserae* have come to light, indicating that the mosaics industry is not of particular importance to the Great Temple builders. There are a few examples of glass or faience *tesserae* and small black *tesserae* as well. They have been recorded in the Grosso Modo database.

32 There are so many professions that come to mind, including engineers, wine makers, teachers, merchants, shopkeepers and grocers, fruit and vegetable pickers, dyers, camel, donkey and horse drivers, healers, scribes, money changers, and probably physicians and lawyers.

and farmers, living in a comparatively infertile pastoral and agricultural community. There are scattered family clans that have formed tribes, and they acknowledge one central authority—2000 years ago it was the Nabataean kingdom—today it is the Hashemite kingdom of Jordan.

The results of the Great Temple excavations clearly have demonstrated an active and prosperous vibrant city from the Nabataean period through to the Roman and Byzantine periods. As the Great Temple has become a major Nabataean-Roman-Byzantine type-site for Petra, we have assessed the cultural affinities of the Petraeans and the choices they made in building, working and living at the Great Temple. Beyond doubt, the Great Temple represents one of the most important sites where not only Nabataean traditions survive, but it also provides an outstanding reference and reflection of Petra's contacts and developments within the fabric of the Nabataean, Roman and Byzantine Near East.

Avenues for Further Research—Unfinished Business

It should be noted that the name, "Great Temple" is conjectural. It was named, "Grosse Tempel" by von Bachmann some 100 years ago. In the beginning I elected to identify the precinct "The Southern Temple" and in 1997 I changed the name back to von Bachmann's identification, to the "Grosse Tempel", or the Great Temple, the identity with which most Petra scholars clearly identified the precinct. I also accepted von Bachmann's identification of the building as a temple. I have argued for the Great Temple serving both as a religious structure and administrative structure although we all know that it also shares in a residential purpose as well. Critics argue that it may have served as a palace with a great dining hall. I think most of the critics would agree that the precinct may have functioned both as an administrative and residential center, but they assert that there is little evidence for any cultic connection.

There are several temples in the Petra central city—the Qasr al Bint, and the Temple of the Winged Lions, and we assume indigenous architects built them. Prestigious temples like the Qasr al Bint and the Great Temple are designed with large courtyards—spaces where great royal processions can take place. Perhaps the Qasr al Bint being the largest edifice served the royals and the Great Temple may have been created to serve some sort of specific rites or a specific cult. Although there are *nefesh*, *betyls*, and numerous horned altars at the Great Temple, there are no inscriptions to help us understand to whom it was dedicated.

The Great Debate[33]

What is clear is that the Great Temple has been identified, however, all scholars do not universally accept that it represents Nabataean sacred space. Debate will continue as to the identification of this structure as a temple or administrative edifice. I argue that it served in both capacities as an administrative and religious center, but nothing from our excavations has been left unsaid, so let the debate continue!

West Entry Stairway—Research

As for the early Great Temple architecture, further examination should be directed to better define the grand West Entry Stairway and its approach into the Great Temple precinct. Joining the processional way (Colonnaded Street) to the Great Temple compound, all traffic in Site Phase IV would have had to be channeled to move up the West Entry Stairway in order to gain formal entrance either to the Lower Temenos plaza and or the Upper Temenos complex or the temple. Working with the extant archaeological evidence, perhaps this information, which is not yet clear, can be given thoughtful consideration.

---

33 Cf. *vol.1* p.125, 128; *vol. 2*, p. 399.

The Great Temple and the Garden-Pool Complex—Future Research

As for future study, I propose an in depth project conjoining the Great Temple and the Garden-Pool Complex. The Great Temple was clearly part of a larger architectural plan which included the Garden-Pool complex or *paradeisos* located to its east and excavated over the past few years by Leigh-Ann Bedal. Combined these precincts dominated the south side of the Wadi Musa and the central city, and were aligned as part of Petra's urban fabric. The two precincts were adjacent and we know were closely interrelated. Each was part of a separate modern day excavation, however, in antiquity—in Nabataean times—they were part of a single, interconnected, high prestige and sophisticated building program. The one precinct, Great Temple and Garden Pool complex were similarly constructed roughly facing north south on a longitudinal axis. Together they were part of a larger setting, and their unusual configuration suggests they were intended to "work" together.

Now it is hoped they will be studied in combination and thought to be sharing a single context. This overall design is unlike any other existing remains in Petra and the concept of a Greek *paradeisos,* (literally, an enclosed park), is dependent on a surviving Persian tradition. The trade-driven merchant Nabataean society carried home eastern ideas (including elephant-headed capitals), and the monarch elected to incorporate an eastern-inspired architectural presence in the Garden-Pool complex as well. We do not know, but perhaps the Petraean use of these eastern art forms in cultic settings may have been a purposeful construct to comfort journeying merchants from the east? Serious examination must be given to these structures for their vernacular Nabataean legacy and the role(s) both Levantine and more eastern ideas had on native Nabataean builders and architects.

APPENDICES

DIMENSIONS AND ELEVATIONS: GREAT TEMPLE PRECINCT

APPENDIX 1. Table 1.

PETRA GREAT TEMPLE TRENCHES BY AREA 1993–2008

Propylaeum	*Lower Temenos*	*Upper Temenos*	*Temple*
Trench 50 (SP53). 1997	Trench 5, Part I. 1994	Trench 1. 1993	Trench 9 (SP7, 52). 1994
Trench 51. 1998	Trench 5, Part II. 1995	Trench 2, Part I. 1993	Trenches 8, 10, 11. 1994
Trench 69. 2000	Trench 6, Part I. 1994	Trench 2, Part II.1994	Trench 12 (SP14). 1994
Trench 70. 2000	Trench 6, Part II. (SP45, 46). 1997	Trench 3. 1993	Trench 15, Part I (SP8). 1994
Trench 80. 2001	Trench 13.1994	Trench 4. 1993	Trench 15, Part II. 1995
Trench 81. 2002	Trenches 14, 20 (SP22, 24, 29). 1995	Trench 7. 1994	Trench 19. 1995
Trench 82. 2001	Trench 16, Part I. 1995	Trench 18. 1996	Trench 22, Part I. 1995
Trench 86. 2001	Trench 16, Part II. 1996	Trench 18A. 1997	Trench 22, Part II. 1996
Trench 87. 2002	Trench 17, Part I (SP25). 1995	Trench 32. 1996	Trench 23. 1995
Trench 88. 2002	Trench 17, Part II. 1996	Trench 38.1996	Trench 24. 1996
Trench 93. 2002	Trench 21 (SP31, 32, 33). 1995	Trench 41.1997	Trenches 26, 27 Part I. 1996
Trench 95. 2003	Trench 25.1996	Trench 44.1997	Trench 35, Part I. 1996
Trench 96. 2003	Trench 28.1996	Trench 46.1997	Trench 27, Part II. 1997
Trench 99. 2004	Trench 30.1996	Trench 49.1997	Trench 29. 1996
Trench 100. 2004	Trench 31, (SP41). 1996	Trench 53.1998	Trench 34, Part I (SP42, 43). 1996
Special Project P. 2005	Trench 33. 1996	Trench 54.1999	Trench 34 Part II. 1997
Special Project 70. 2000	Trench 36. 1996	Trench 67.1999	Trench 35 Part II. 1997
Special Project 87. 2004	Trench 37. 1996	Trench 68 (SP61). 1999	Trench 40. 1997
Special Project 88. 2002	Trench 39. 1996	Trench 72. 2000	Trench 45. 1997
Special Project 95. 2003	Trench 42, (SP48, 49). 1997	Trench 75. 2000	Trench 47. 1997
Special Project 114. 2005	Trench 43. 1997	Trench 76. 2000	Trench 48. 1997
Special Project 118. 2005	Trench 52. 1998	Trench 77, Part I. 2000	Trench 55. 1998
Special Project 125. 2004	Trench 60. 1999	Trench 77, Part II. 2000	Trench 55A. 1999
Special Project 150. 2005	Trench 61. 1999	Trench 83 (SP83). 2001	Trench 56. 1998
	Trench 66. 1999	Trench 84 (SP91). 2001	Trench 57. 1998
	Trench 71. 2000	Trench 89. 2002	Trench 58. 1998
	Trench 79. 2001	Trench 90. 2002	Trench 59. 1998
	Trench 97. 2004	Trench 91. 2002	Trench 62. 1999

APPENDIX 1. Table 1. (continued)
PETRA GREAT TEMPLE TRENCHES BY AREA 1993–2008

Propylaeum	*Lower Temenos*	*Upper Temenos*	*Temple*
	Trench 98. 2004	Trench 94. 2002	Trench 63. 1999
	Trench 98B. 2002	Trench 101. 2008	Trench 64. 1999
	Trenches 102-103. 2005	Trench 105-106. 2005	Trench 65, Part I. 1999
	Trench 104. 2005	Trench 120. 1998	Trench 65, Part II. 1999
	Trench 121. 1998	Trench 125. 1998	Trench 73. 2000
	Trench 122. 1998	Special Project 4, Part I. 1993	Trench 85. 2001
	Trench 126. 1998	Special Project 4, Part II. 1994	Trench 92. 2005
	Trench 127. 1998	Special Project 4, Part III. 1995	Trench 123. 1998
	Special Project 20. 1995	Special Project 21. 1993	Special Project A. 1993
	Special Project 26. 1995	Special Project 30. 1995	Special Project 1. 1994
	Special Project 27. 2008	Special Project 35. 2008	Special Project 2. 1994
	Special Project 28. 2008	Special Project 44. 1997	Special Project 3. 1994
	Special Project 36. 1995	Special Project 60. 1999	Special Project 9. 1994
	Special Project 37. 1995	Special Project 84. 2001	Special Project 10. 1994
	Special Project 38, Part I. 1995	Special Project 85. 2001	Special Project 11. 1994
	Special Project 38, Part II. 1996	Special Project 89. 2004	Special Project 12. 1994
	Special Project 39, Part I. 1995	Special Project 94. 2004	Special Project 13. 1994
	Special Project 39, Part II. 1996	Special Project 96. 2004	Special Project 15. 1994
	Special Project 47. 1997	Special Project 108. 2005	Special Project 16. 1994
	Special Project 51. 1997	Special Project 110. 2005	Special Project 23. 1995
	Special Project 54. 1997	Special Project 111. 2005	Special Project 34. 2008
	Special Project 56. 1998	Special Project 120. 2004	Special Project 40. 1996
	Special Project 57. 1998	Special Project 121. 2004	Special Project 50. 2008
	Special Project 73. 2000	Special Project 123. 2004	Special Project 71. 2000
	Special Project 92. 2002	Special Project 21 (Baths). 1995	Special Project 72 (Tr. 77, Part I). 2000
	Special Project 104. 2005	Special Project 131. 2008	Special Project 93. 2002
	Special Project 105. 2005	Trench 133. 2008	Special Project 107. 2005
	Special Project 124. 2004		Special Project 109. 2005
	Trench 130. 2008		Special Project 200. 2005
	Trench 131. 2008		

APPENDIX 1. Table 2.
PETRA GREAT TEMPLE TRENCHES EXCAVATED IN THE PROPYLAEUM

Trench	*Year*	*Description*	*Measurement (m) N-S x E-W*	*Excavators*
Sidewalk and Roman Street				
Special Project 88	2002	Sidewalk and Roman Street north of the Propylaeum Central Staircase	6.10 x 34.30	M. S. Joukowsky
Propylaeum Central Staircase				
Special Project P	1994	Cleaning of the Propylaeum Central Staircase	20 x 6.00	M. S. Joukowsky
Special Project 125	2004	Propylaeum Steps	6.35 x 1.20	Zimmerman, Reid
Special Project 114	2005	Propylaeum Steps	0.86 x 0.36	Khanachet
Propylaeum East				
Trench 82	2001	Upper levels of the Propylaeum East, Room 3	6.00 x 12.00	Basile
Trench 93	2002	Upper levels Propylaeum East	15.45 x 13.00	M. S. Joukowsky
Trench 95	2003	Propylaeum East, Rooms 1 and 2	10.50 x 23.50	M. S. Joukowsky, Saunders
Trench 96	2003	Propylaeum East Room 3	6.50 x 4.00	M. S. Joukowsky, Saunders
Special Project 95	2003	Sub-floor deposits in Propylaeum East, Room 1	2.00 x 2.40	M. S. Joukowsky, Saunders
Trench 99	2004	Northeastern corner of the Propylaeum	5.5 x 8.00	Basile
Trench 100	2004	Propylaeum East, Room 3	17.34 x 3.80 to 4.30	M. S. Joukowsky
Special Project 150	2005	Propylaeum East, Room 2	2.30 x 2.30	Tuttle

APPENDIX 1. Table 2. (continued)
PETRA GREAT TEMPLE TRENCHES EXCAVATED IN THE PROPYLAEUM

Trench	*Year*	*Description*	*Measurement (m) N-S x E-W*	*Excavators*
Propylaeum West				
Trench 50 (SP53)	1997	Upper levels of the north gallery west of the Propylaeum Central Staircase	4.55 x 4.75	Haile, Parker, M. S. Joukowsky
Trench 51	1998	Upper levels of the north and south galleries west of the Propylaeum Central Staircase	3.76 x 7.00	Haile, Roger
Trench 69	2000	Propylaeum West, south gallery, cryptoporticus	5.9 x 4.50	Larsen, Brown
Trench 70	2000	Intersection of the Propylaeum West south gallery and the Lower Temenos west cryptoporticus	8.30 x 11.8	Larsen
Special Project 70	2000	East sector of the Propylaeum West, south gallery	4.17 x 12.25	Larsen
Trench 80	2001	Continuation of Trench 70 in the Propylaeum West, south gallery to the west of SP70	7.00 x 12.00	Sneag, Egan, Brown
Trench 86	2001	Test trench of the lower levels of the Propylaeum West, south gallery	4.20 x 2.00	Brown
Trench 81	2002	Propylaeum West, south gallery	11.70 x 6.70	M. S. Joukowsky
Trench 87	2002	Propylaeum West, north gallery, east and Propylaeum West Room 1	4.39/5.30 x 19.41	Henry, M. S. Joukowsky
Trench 88	2002	Propylaeum West Stairs	10.10 x 3.80/2.80	M. S. Joukowsky
Special Project 87	2004	Propylaeum West	1.96 x 7.66	Reid
Special Project 118	2005	Propylaeum West, south gallery	2.35 x 3.00	Tuttle

APPENDIX 1. Table 3.
PETRA GREAT TEMPLE TRENCHES EXCAVATED IN THE LOWER TEMENOS

Trench	*Year*	*Description*	*Measurement (m)* *N-S x E-W*	*Excavators*
East Triple Colonnade and East Cryptoporticus				
Trenches 14 and 20 (SP22, 24, 29 combined)	1995	Central Area between the inner and middle stylobates of the East Triple Colonnade	TR. 14= 8.20 x 11.00 TR 20= 9.00 x 4.30 (SP22=4.00 x 2.00; SP24 =7.00 x 2.20; SP29 2.00 x 2.00	Sisson, Bell
Trench 17, Part I (SP25)	1995	East Triple Colonnade and sondage north of Trenches 14 and 20	10.00 x 14.00 1.60 x 2.50	Payne
Special Project 27	1995	Column #3 to the south of SP24	No measurements taken	M. S. Joukowsky
Special Project 28	1995	The second column in the East Triple Colonnade	No measurements taken	M. S. Joukowsky
Special Project 38, Part I	1995	Sondage in the East Colonnade east	No measurements taken	M. S. Joukowsky
Trench 17, Part II	1996	Continuation of the 1995 excavations in Trench 17	10.00 x 14.00	Payne
Trench 25	1996	East Perimeter Wall of the Lower Temenos and adjacent area of the East Triple Colonnade	26.67 x 2.37	Slaughter, Butler, Goldstein
Trench 28	1996	East Triple Colonnade south of Trench 25	13.00 x 2.80	Bestock, Gimon
Trench 30	1996	East Triple Colonnade west of Trench 25	19.00 x 4.00	M. S. Joukowsky
Trench 33	1996	East Triple Colonnade north and west of Trenches 25 and 30	4.70 x 6.00	Warnock
Trench 36	1996	East Triple Colonnade west of Trench 28	11.00 x 4.00	Bestock, Gimon
Special Project 38, Part II	1996	Continuation of SP38	3.00 x 3.00	Goldstein, Butler
Special Project 39, Part II	1996	Brief investigation of the southern part of the East Triple Colonnade, just north of the East Exedra	19.00 x 4.10 x 1.90	M. S. Joukowsky
Special Project 45	1997	Recovery of the southernmost column in the central row of the East Triple Colonnade, north of the East Exedra	No measurements taken	Payne
Special Project 46	1997	Recovery of the second column from the south in the central row of the East Triple Colonnade, north of the East Exedra	No measurements taken	Payne

APPENDIX 1. Table 3. (continued)
PETRA GREAT TEMPLE TRENCHES EXCAVATED IN THE LOWER TEMENOS

Trench	*Year*	*Description*	*Measurement (m) N-S x E-W*	*Excavators*
East Triple Colonnade and East Cryptoporticus continued				
Special Project 51	1997	East Triple Colonnade (space for reerection of columns)	No measurements taken	Haile, Parker
Special Project 54	1997	Excavation by British team of an *in situ* decorated pilaster block, reused in the inter-columnar wall between the columns of the East Triple Colonnade.	1.00 x 0.60	British Excavation team, Schluntz
Special Project 56	1998	Sondage in the East triple Colonnade to remove an island of earth created during the excavation of SP54	1.80 x 2.60	Ginsberg
Special Project 57	1998	Sondage in the East Triple Colonnade to remove a "tongue" of earth adjacent to Trench 14	2.00 x 1.60	Ginsberg
Trench 61	1999	East Triple Colonnade, center	6.00 x 13.70	Karz
Special Project 73	2000	Inter-columnar wall in the center row of the East Triple Colonnade	26.00 x 3.50	Karz
East Exedra				
Trench 37	1996	East Exedra	19.00 x 15.00	M. S. Joukowsky
Trench 52	1998	East Exedra	15.30 x 18.00	Basile, Sylvester, and Karz
West Triple Colonnade and West Cryptoporticus				
Special Project 37	1995	Cleaning of a Bedouin wall north of the West Exedra	No measurements taken	M. S. Joukowsky
Special Project 39, Part I	1995	Search for the Lower Temenos west perimeter wall	No measurements taken	M. S. Joukowsky
Trench 31 (SP41)	1996	West Triple Colonnade and West Bath, southwest of the West Exedra	7.50 x 9.72, 1.65 x 1.65	Butler, Goldstein
Special Project 47	1997	Recovery of a portion of the west stylobate of the West Triple Colonnade	No measurements taken	Haile, M. S. Joukowsky
Trench 71	2000	West Triple Colonnade and Cryptoporticus, north of the West Exedra	22.50 x 19.80	M. S. Joukowsky
Trench 79	2001	Central area of the West Cryptoporticus	13.50 x 12.50	M. S. Joukowsky
Trench 97	2004	West Cryptoporticus East	25.77 x 6.10	Tuttle

APPENDIX 1. Table 3. (continued)
PETRA GREAT TEMPLE TRENCHES EXCAVATED IN THE LOWER TEMENOS

Trench	*Year*	*Description*	*Measurement (m) N-S x E-W*	*Excavators*
West Triple Colonnade and West Cryptoporticus continued				
Trench 98	2004	West Cryptoporticus West	32.00 x 4.20	Khanachet, Power
Trench 98B	2005	West Cryptoporticus West	17.21 x 4.04	Khanachet
Special Project 104	2005	West Cryptoporticus East, sondage	4.00 x 4.30	Tuttle
Special Project 105	2005	West Cryptoporticus East, below pavement	1.50 x 4.20	Tuttle
West Exedra				
Trench 5, Part I	1994	East part of the West Exedra	7.00 x 10.00	Beckman, Retzleff, Schluntz
Trench 5, Part II	1995	East part of the West Exedra	9.00 x 4.00 and 2.00 m probe	Basile, Rucker
Trench 16, Part I	1995	West part of the West Exedra	7.00 x 10.00	Basile, Rucker
Trench 21 (SP31, SP32, SP33)	1995	East part of the West Exedra	4.00 x 7.00	Basile, Rucker, Khalidi
Special Project 26	1995	East part of the West Exedra	2.00 x 2.00	Khalidi
Trench 16, Part III	1996	Search for the foundations of the Byzantine canal and of the northwest wall of the West Exedra, found in 1995	1.20 x 1.95	Brown, Takian
Hexagonal Pavement and Subterranean Canalization System				
Trench 6, Part I	1994	South center of the Hexagonal Pavement, north of the Central Staircase	9.00 x 4.00	Payne
Trench 13	1994	Center of the Hexagonal Pavement	10.00 x 10.00	M. S. Joukowsky
Special Project 36	1995	Cleaning of a sink hole associated with the main subterranean canalization artery	No measurements taken	M. S. Joukowsky
Special Project 20	1995	Subterranean canalization system collapse in Trench 13	1.50 x 2.50	Payne, Barrett
Trench 39	1996	Southwest section of the Hexagonal Pavement	4.00 x 4.00	Brown
Trench 6, Part II	1997	South center of the Hexagonal Pavement, north of the Central Staircase	8.00 x 3.00	Basile, Najjar, Sylvester

APPENDIX 1. Table 3. (continued)
PETRA GREAT TEMPLE TRENCHES EXCAVATED IN THE LOWER TEMENOS

Trench	*Year*	*Description*	*Measurement (m) N-S x E-W*	*Excavators*
Hexagonal Pavement and Subterranean Canalization System continued				
Trench 42 (SP48, SP49)	1997	West center of the Hexagonal Pavement and the adjacent part of the West Triple Colonnade	18.00 x 14.00	Haile, Parker, Brown
Trench 43	1997	Hexagonal Pavement between Trenches 6 and 13	4.00 x 9.70; 1.45 x 2.30	Basile, Najjar, Sylvester
Trench 60	1999	East center of the Hexagonal Pavement	25.30 x 11.30	Karz
Trench 66	1999	Hexagonal Pavement west	13.50 x 9.00	M. S. Joukowsky, Karz
Special Project 92	2002	Sondage directly south of the Propylaeum Central Staircase	2.00 x 3.00	Brown
Special Project 124	2004	Central Staircase	5.90 x 4.56	Libonati, Egan
Trench 104	2005	Hexagonal Pavement northwest sondage	8.00 x 10.00	Khanachet
West Entry Stairway				
Trench 102-103	2005	West Entry Stairway	30.75 x 4.55	M. S. Joukowsky
Trench 122	2006	West Entry Stairway south	7.90 x 9.00	M. S. Joukowsky, Khakpour
Roman-Byzantine Bath Complex				
Trench 121	2006	Bath Complex northwest	9.00 x 16.00	Khakpour
Trench 126	2006	Bath Complex northeast	4.55 x 13.00	Tuttle
Trench 127	2006	Bath Complex central	0.11 x 14.00	M. S. Joukowsky
Trench 130	2008	Bath Complex northwest	5.00 x 11.50	Power
Trench 131	2008	Bath complex north and west	13.00 x 17.00	Power
Trench 133	2008	South of the Colonnaded Corridor	11.00 x 28.50	M. S. Joukowsky
Special Project 133	2008	West Perimeter Wall	40.00 x 7.20	M. S. Joukowsky

APPENDIX 1. Table 4.

PETRA GREAT TEMPLE TRENCHES EXCAVATED IN THE UPPER TEMENOS

Trench	*Year*	*Description*	*Measurement (m)* *N-S x E-W*	*Excavators*
Temple Forecourt and Subterranean Canalization Systems				
Trench 1	1993	Temple Forecourt center, stair bedding and podium	9.00 x 9.00	Schluntz
Trench 2, Part I	1993	Temple Forecourt, podium and west stylobate	6.00 x 10.00	Smolenski, Thorpe
Trench 3	1993	Temple stylobate and West Forecourt	4.50 x 5.00	M. S. Joukowsky
Trench 4	1993	Temple Forecourt and stylobate, Upper Temenos east	4.00 x 10.00	Shubailat
Special Project 4, Part I	1993	Subterranean canalization system	1.00 x 1.50	Schluntz
Trench 2, Part II	1994	Temple Forecourt and west podium	6.00 x 10.00	Schluntz
Special Project 4, Part II	1994	Subterranean canalization system beneath the Central Staircase	4.00 x 2.00	Payne
Special Project 4, Part III	1995	Subterranean canalization system beneath the Central Staircase	9.75 x 2.80	Payne, Slaughter, Barrett
Special Project 30	1995	Temple northeast podium at the intersection of the East Staircase and the small hexagonal pavementof the Forecourt	4.60 x 7.20 x 8.20	Tholbecq
Special Project 35	1995	Extension of SP4 to the east	No measurements taken	Slaughter
Trench 18	1996	West Staircase and Lower Retaining Wall	17.50 (S) x 16.00 (N) 14.50 (E) x 10.00 (W)	Basile
Trench 32	1996	Western half of the temple Forecourt	17.65 (N) x 3.60 (E) 15.36 (S) x 16.45 (W)	Brown
Trench 18A	1997	Lower Temenos Retaining Wall between the West and Central Staircases	7.35 (N) x 7.50 (S) 14.50 (E-W)	Basile, Najjar, Sylvester
Trench 46	1997	Lower Temenos Retaining Wall between the Central and East Staircase	7.00 (N) x 8.00 (S) 14.50 (E-W)	Basile, Najjar, Sylvester
Trench 49	1997	East Staircase	6.00 x 17.70 (E) 14.50 (W)	Basile, Najjar, Sylvester
Special Project 60	1999	Temple Forecourt sondage north of the West Walkway	2.00 x 1.50	M. S. Joukowsky

APPENDIX 1. Table 4. (continued)
PETRA GREAT TEMPLE TRENCHES EXCAVATED IN THE UPPER TEMENOS

Trench	*Year*	*Description*	*Measurement (m) N-S x E-W*	*Excavators*
East 'Cistern'				
Trench 38	1996	East arch of the East 'Cistern,' south of the East Exedra	7.50 x 4.00	M. S. Joukowsky
Trench 41	1997	Upper strata of the East 'Cistern,' south of the East Exedra	4.50 x 9.50	Bestock, Mattison, Sistovaris
Trench 53	1998	Lower strata of the East 'Cistern,' south of the East Exedra	3.15 x 11.05	Bestock, Sullivan, Schwartz
East Perimeter Wall and Reservoir				
Trench 67	1999	East Perimeter Wall, Reservoir and associate canalization of the Upper Temenos	9.90 x 3.50	A. W. Joukowsky, M. S. Joukowsky
East Perimeter Wall				
Trench 68 (SP61)	1999	East Perimeter Wall south of Trench 67	15.90 x 5.20	A. W. Joukowsky, M. S. Joukowsky, Qublan
Trench 84 (SP91)	2001	East Perimeter Wall interior, Rooms A and B	10.53 x 6.46	Fusté
Trench 91	2002	East Perimeter Wall	2.74 x 0.80	Fusté
East Plaza				
Trench 44	1997	East Plaza, south of the East 'Cistern'	10.10 x 8.85 (W) 9.75 (E)	Bestock, Mattison, Sistovaris
Trench 54	1999	East Plaza northwest of the East 'Cistern'	10.20 x 5.05	Karz
Trench 72	2000	Continued excavation of the bedrock shelf south of Trench 54	6.00 x 6.40	M. S. Joukowsky
Trench 75	2000	Removal of the balk between Trenches 54 and 67	9.00 x 0.96	J. Farley, P. Farley, McCracken
Trench 77 Parts I and II	2000	Southeast areas of the East Perimeter Wall, the South Perimeter Wall and the south canalization systems	18.40 x 5.20	McCracken, A. W. Joukowsky
East Plaza Great Cistern				
Special Project 84	2001	Tabun Cave Room and early investigation of the Great Cistern	4.58 x 3.20	Cloke
Special Project 85	2001	East Plaza Great Cistern, Part I	2.50 x 1.50	Cloke
Trench 90	2002	East Plaza Great Cistern, Part II, and the East Artery, platform, and associated canalization	36.00 x 13.00	Cloke

APPENDIX 1. Table 4. (continued)
PETRA GREAT TEMPLE TRENCHES EXCAVATED IN THE UPPER TEMENOS

Trench	*Year*	*Description*	*Measurement (m) N-S x E-W*	*Excavators*
South Passageway				
Trench 83 (SP83)	2001	South Passageway and preliminary excavation of the Anteroom and the Shrine Room	6.45 x 31.20	Libonati, Egan
Trench 89	2002	Shrine Room and Baroque Room	6.65 x 9.28	Libonati, Fusté
Special Project 89	2004	Baroque Room North Door	0.30 x 1.30	Egan
Trench 101	2004	Settling Tank	5.25 x 4.82	Libonati, Khanachet
Special Project 121	2004	Sondage in the South Passageway	1.50 x 1.50	Zimmerman
Special Project 123	2004	Sondage in the Shrine Room	0.86 x 0.60	Libonati, Egan
Residential Quarter				
Trench 94	2002	Residential Quarter	16.00 x 10.00	Libonati, Fusté
Special Project 96	2004	Southwest Bedrock Plateau	No measurements taken	Egan, Libonati
Special Project 94	2004	Corridor between Settling Tank and Residential Quarter	4.90 x 1.66	Khanachet
Special Project 111	2005	Removal of Residential Quarter steps	4.90 x 1.66	Khanachet
West Upper Temenos				
Special Project 21	1995	Belaying examination of the West Palatial Complex Baths	No measurements taken	Clapp
Special Project 44	1997	South of the West Exedra (West Palatial Complex Baths Dump)	No measurements taken	Brown
Trench 76	2000	Area west of the West Walkway	3.00 x 11.00	P. Farley, J. Farley
Special Project 108	2005	West Bedrock Plaza and Temple East-West Support Wall	12.40 x 9.20	Libonati
Special Project 110	2005	West Precinct Wall and Cistern- Reservoir	62.00 x 2.50	M. S. Joukowsky
Roman-Byzantine Bath Complex				
Trench 105-106	2005	Bath Complex southeast	18.00 x 12.00	Power, Agnew
Trench 120	2006	Bath Complex southwest	13.50 x 17.00	Power, Khakpour, Agnew
Trench 125	2006	'Well' Room	1.93 x 2.52	Libonati
Lapidary				
Trench 7	1994	Lapidary West	2.00 x 3.00	Retzleff

APPENDIX 1. Table 4. (continued)
GREAT TEMPLE TRENCHES EXCAVATED IN THE TEMPLE

Trench	*Year*	*Description*	*Measurement (m) N-S x E-W*	*Excavators*
Porch/Pronaos				
Special Project A	1993	No excavation undertaken. Measurements of the collapsed debris on top of the temple porch columns	2.00 x 28.00	Payne
Trench 12 (SP14)	1994	Northwest Pronaos and Interior West Anta	10.00 x 10.00	Parr, M. S. Joukowsky
Special Project 10	1994	East Pronaos column	No measurements taken	M. S. Joukowsky
Trench 23 (SP23)	1995	Northwest central Pronaos	10.00 x 6.50, 3.00 x 3.60	Schluntz, Harris
Special Project 34	1995	East Anta	No measurements taken	Qublan
Trench 24	1996	Northeast central Pronaos	9.80 x 9.95	Bestock
Trench 48	1997	Northeast Pronaos	2.00 x 10.00	Slaughter
Special Project 107	2005	Pronaos East Sondage	6.40 x 3.55	Libonati
Temple East				
Special Project 9	1994	Search for the third and fourth columns from the south in the temple East Colonnade	No measurements taken	M. S. Joukowsky
Special Project 11	1994	Search for the sixth column from the south in temple East Colonnade	No measurements taken	M. S. Joukowsky
Special Project 12	1994	Search for the fifth column from the south in the temple East Colonnade	No measurements taken	M. S. Joukowsky
Trench 15, Part I (SP8)	1994	East Interior Staircase and landing	6.00 x 5.00	Austin
Trench 15, Part II	1995	East Interior Staircase and landing	7.35 x 2.23	Harris, Khalidi
Trench 19	1995	East Staircase, north of the East Walkway between the temple Forecourt and Porch	5.20 x 3.40	Tholbecq, Habboo
Trench 34, Part I (SP42 and 43)	1996	Further excavation of Locus 6 of Trench 34 in the East Corridor south	14.00 x 5.00	A. W. Joukowsky
Trench 34, Part II	1997	Continued clarification of the southeast wall of the temple	5.00 x 4.00	Brown, M. S. Joukowsky
Special Project 50	1997	Moving four column drums from East Porch column to central East Porch column	No measurements taken	M. S. Joukowsky
Trench 55	1998	Upper levels of the East Vaulted Chamber	7.50 x 4.80	Brown

APPENDIX 1. Table 5.
GREAT TEMPLE TRENCHES EXCAVATED IN THE TEMPLE

Trench	Year	Description	Measurement (m) N-S x E-W	Excavators
Temple East continued				
Trench 58	1998	East Corridor including the third, fourth and fifth columns from the south in the East Colonnade	11.00 x 3.00	Schwartz, Haile
Trench 55A	1999	East Vaulted Chamber	7.50 x 4.80	Brown
Trench 64	1999	Extension of the East Walkway at the point where it abuts the temple Pronaos in the east	6.80 x 3.80	M. S. Joukowsky, Sylvester, Karz
Trench 65, Part I	1999	East Corridor center and south	14.00 x 3.50	Brown
Trench 65, Part II	1999	East Corridor center and south	21.00 x 3.15	M. S. Joukowsky
Special Project 71	2000	Sondage along the East Walkway cutting into Trench 72 in the east and Trench 73 in the west	1.30 x 1.50	Brin
Trench 73	2000	Area between the East Corridor Wall and the East Colonnade	21.00 x 3.60	Stern
Temple West				
Trench 9 (SP7, SP52)	1994	West Interior Staircase and landing	7.50 x 10.00	Bedal
Special Project 1	1994	West Walkway and drain sondage	Absorbed into Tr. 8, 10, and 11	M. S. Joukowsky
Special Project 2	1994	West Walkway sondage	Absorbed into Tr. 8, 10, and 11	M. S. Joukowsky
Special Project 3	1994	Brief exploration of the West Walkway Wall	Absorbed into Tr. 8, 10, and 11	M. S. Joukowsky
Trenches 8, 10, and 11	1994	West Walkway	18.50 x 7.00	Slaughter, A. W. Joukowsky
Special Project 13	1994	Removal of fallen column drums in the temple west in taken preparation for the excavation of Trench 12	No measurements taken	M. S. Joukowsky
Special Project 16	1994	Search for the northernmost column of the West Colonnade	No measurements taken	M. S. Joukowsky
Trench 22, Part I	1995	West Vaulted Chamber and West Interior Staircase	7.50 x 10.00	Bedal
Trench 22, Part II	1996	West Vaulted Chamber and West Interior Staircase	7.50 x 10.00	Bedal
Trench 29	1996	West Corridor north	8.25 x 3.36	Slaughter
Trench 45	1997	West Corridor, west of the Theater	7.50 x 3.00	Payne, M. S. Joukowsky
Trench 56	1998	West Corridor center	8.50 x 3.00	A.W. Joukowsky, M. S. Joukowsky

APPENDIX 1. Table 5. (continued)
GREAT TEMPLE TRENCHES EXCAVATED IN THE TEMPLE

Trench	*Year*	*Description*	*Measurement (m) N-S x E-W*	*Excavators*
Temple West continued				
Trench 59	1998	West Corridor and western part of the South Corridor	11.18 x 3.40	A.W. Joukowsky, M. S. Joukowsky
Trench 63	1999	West Walkway	22.70 x 3.74	A.W. Joukowsky
Special Project 109	2005	West Walkway	2.00 x 3.06	Khanachet
Temple South				
Special Project 15	1994	Investigation of a localized plaster deposit in grid square D5	No measurements taken	Jacobsen
Trench 26	1996	Central Arch and Rear East Staircase	5.50 x 4.50	Payne
Trench 27	1996	Central Arch and Rear East Staircase	4.75 x 3.50	Payne
Trench 35, Part I	1996	Central Arch and Rear East Staircase	3.75 x 3.50	Payne
Special Project 40	1996	Southeast double-engaged column	5.00 x 2.60	M. S. Joukowsky
Trench 27, Part II	1997	Central Arch and Rear East Staircase	4.75 x 3.50	Payne
Trench 35, Part II	1997	Bottom of East Rear Staircase	2.47 x 4.38	Brown, Parker
Trench 57	1998	Central Arch	6.96 x 3.32	Libonati, Prendergast, Sullivan
Trench 77, Part III (SP72)	2000	Upper levels of the temple South Corridor	4.50 x 21.80	M. S. Joukowsky
Trench 85	2001	South Corridor	2.73 x 17.27	Egan, Libonati
Special Project 93	2002	Sondage into the foundation platform and subterranean features in the southwest of the South Corridor	2.00 x 2.50	Cloke
Special Project 120	2004	Central Arch Water Systems	2.26 x 3.60	Libonati, Egan
Theater and Stage				
Trench 40	1997	Stage west	6.00 x 9.80	Slaughter
Trench 47	1997	Theater west	9.80 x 6.00	Bedal
Trench 62	1999	Theater, stage and East Corridor north	11.00 x 12.50	Basile, Sylvester
Trench 92	2002	Pronaos/Stage Platform west sondage	4.00 x 6.18	Fusté
Special Project 200	2005	Orchestra Floor Sondage	6.96 x 1.96	Libonati
Trench 123	2006	Theater seats sondage	1.30 x 2.80	Libonati

APPENDIX 2

DIMENSIONS AND ELEVATIONS: GREAT TEMPLE PRECINCT

Elevations and dimensions of major Temple precinct components in meters
Note: All measurements are external (ext.) or internal (int.) and include wall thicknesses unless otherwise noted. When a depth is irregular e.g., steps, it is averaged.

Great Temple site datum control points

El-Katute — Elevation 930.81 m, UTM 734783.05 m E, 3357608.15 m N.

CP 513 — Elevation 916.03 m, UTM 735050.56 m E, 3357722.02 m N.

CP 103 — Elevation 914.99 m, UTM 734836.86 m E, 3357673.11 m N.

Summary of Great Temple Precinct Features — Dimensions in meters

Great Temple precinct: From the Portico wall in the Propylaeum to the preserved south Precinct Wall: 135.00 m N-S x 56.00 m E-W.

Total Temple Area: 7560 m2 (3/4 hectare).

Added precinct excavated features

Sidewalk and Curbing: 5.25 m N-S x 56.68 m E-W—Total area 297.57 m2.

Roman-Byzantine Baths: 47.91 m N-S x 30.84 m E-W; Total area 1477.54 m2.

West Entry Stairs: 37.2 m N-S x 4.6 m E-W; Total area 171.12 m2.

Cistern-Reservoir: 7 m N-S x 5.4 m E-W; Total area 37.8 m2.

Baroque Room complex: 6.12 m N-S x 18.29 m E-W; Total area 111.87 m2.

Residential Quarter: 15.48 m N-S x 9.22 m E-W; Total area 142.73 m2.

East Perimeter Wall: 36.69 m N-S x 4.00 m E-W; Total area 146.94 m2.

West Perimeter Wall: 40 m N-S x 7.50 m E-W; Total area 300 m2 (excavated).

Additional Precinct Features and Measurements Total: 2685.57 m2.

Total Great Temple Features Excavated (excluding the Small Temple): 10,245.57 m2.

Small Temple Precinct: 76 m N-S x 31 m E-W; Total area 2356 m2.

Small Temple (internal) 14.62 x 14.62: Total area 213.744 m2; Small Temple and Portico: Total area 338 m2.

Brown University Excavations 1993-2008 Total Excavated Area, 12,601.57 m2

Propylaeum (also Roman Street Excavations)

Propylaeum measurements: (ext.) 12.41 m N-S x 56.68 m E-W; (int.) 9.81 m N-S x 53.98 m E-W.

Great Temple sidewalk and curbing: 5.25 m N-S x 56.68 m E-W = 297.57 m2.

Propylaeum and Roman Street elevations

Colonnaded Street: Crown directly north of the Propylaeum, 890.33 m; South gutter directly North of the Propylaeum: 890.15 m.

Propylaeum: Curbing—890.66 m; Lowest Step—890.75 m; Upper Step—897.25 m.

Propylaeum dimensions

Propylaeum: (ext.) 12.41 m N-S x 56.68 m E-W; (int.) 9.81 m N-S x 53.98 m EW.

Propylaeum East: From Room 4 east wall to Propylaeum Steps: N-S 22.41 m.

Room 1: (internal) 10.2 m N-S x 6.4 m E-W x 4.8 m depth.

Room 2: 1 m N-S x 6.7 m E-W x 5 m depth.

Room 3: (corridor) 19 m N-S x 4.2 m E-W x 4.8 m depth.

Room 4: (internal) 3.74 m N-S x 5.4 m E-W x 4 m depth.

East Propylaeum Wall Dimensions

Room 1: (North) 1.13 m; (South) 1.1 m; (East) 1.03 m; (West) 1.09 m.

Room 2: (North) 1.24 m; (South) 1.1 m; (East) 1.26 m; (West) 1.03 m.

Room 3: (North) 1.37 m; (South) 1.1 m; (East) 1.53 m; (West) 1.26 m.

Room 4: (North) 1.7 m; (South) 1.1 m; (East) 1.2 m; (West) 1.53 m.

Propylaeum Stairs

(Partially restored) 17 m N-S x 7.4 m E-W.

Earlier Propylaeum Stairs (excavated): 6.35 m N-S x 1.2 m E-W.

Propylaeum West

From West Stairs to the Propylaeum Steps: 25.05 m E-W.

Wall K bench, south: 0.76 m N-S x 17.19 m E-W x 0.5 m depth.

West Entry into the West Propylaeum: 2.29 m N-S x 1.47 m E-W x 0.07 m depth.

West Entry into South Gallery on W of Wall K: 2.38 m N-S x 1.2 m E-W x 0.14 m depth.

North Gallery: (ext.) 6.46 m N-S x 21.52 m E-W x 1.3 m depth; (int.) 3.45 m N-S x 19.6 m E-W.

Room 1: (ext.) 6.52 m N-S x 4.75 m E-W x 2.6 m depth; (int.) 3.93 m N-S x 3.39 m E-W.

Bench along north face of Wall K: 0.77 m N-S x 14.59 m E-W x 0.43 m depth.

Ceramic Pavement: 3.4 m N-S x 19.55 m E-W x 0.1 m depth.

South Gallery: (ext.) 6.78 m N-S x 20.56 m E-W; (int.) 4.36 m N-S x 18.13 m E-W; voussoir inter-axial distance: 0.53 m.

West Entry Stairs: 37.2 m N-S x 4.8 m E-W.

West Entry Doorway: 2.42 m N-S x 1.5 m E-W x 2.18 m depth.

West Entry Threshold: 2.18 m N-S x 0.3 m E-W x 0.12 m depth.

Betyl Wall: 3.91 m N-S x 1.50 m E-W x 2.72 m depth.

Betyl Wall Bench: 3.63 m N-S x 0.72 m E-W x 0.77 m depth.

Limestone Pavement in *betyl* entry: 6.5 m N-S x 3.94 m E-W.

West Propylaeum wall dimensions (thickness and height)

Portico Wall: 1.3 m N-S x 25.05 m E-W x 2.44 m depth.

Wall K: 1.2 m N-S x19.74 m E-W x 1.42 m depth.

Propylaeum Retaining Wall: 1.45 m N-S x 35.12 m E-W x 6.7 m depth.

West Wall: 11.62 m N-S x 1.47 m E-W x 3 m depth.

West Room 1 West Wall: (N) 1.34 m; (S) 1.1 m; (E) 0.9 m; (W) 0.9 m.

Lower Temenos

Lower Temenos measurements

From the Propylaeum Retaining Wall to the Lower Temenos Retaining Wall: 49 m N-S x 56 m E-W.

Lower Temenos Elevations of Major Features

Hexagonal Pavement: 898.67±0.12 m.

Trench 13 lowest elevation below Hexagonal Pavement—898.24 m.

Easternmost Colonnade: 898.63±0.16 m (pavers and stylobate slope downward slightly).

Sondage SP 25 elevation: 891.97 m.

West Exedra (maximum height): 903.52 m.

Porch column stylobate elevation: 899.35 m.

Byzantine platform: 900.25 m.

West Stairway lowest step-curb: 899.14 m; restored upper step: 903.94 m.

East Exedra: Maximum height: 905.16 m; Porch Column stylobate: 899.15 m.

East Stairway: Lowest step curb: 899.14 m; Excavated upper step: 902.58 m.

Lower Temenos dimensions of major features

From the Propylaeum Retaining Wall to the Lower Temenos Retaining Wall: 49 m N-S x 56 m E-W.

East Exedra to the West Exedra: 32.7 m E-W.

East and West Exedra columns. 0.60 m diameter.

Triple Colonnade columns: 0.76-0.84 m diameter. Inter-axial distance between Triple Colonnade columns: 1.8 m.

Hexagonal Pavement: 49 m N-S x 31 m E-W.

East Lower Temenos

East Triple Colonnade: From the East Exedra to the Propylaeum Retaining Wall: 54 m N-S x 11.8 m E-W.

East Exedra: 5.4 m N-S x 6.8 m E-W x 4.8 m depth.

West Lower Temenos

West Triple Colonnade: (external) from the West Exedra to the Propylaeum Retaining Wall 50.19 m N-S x 11.96 m E-W width.

West Exedra: 5.30 m N-S x 6.5 m E-W x 4.8 m depth.

West Cryptoporticus: (ext.) 38.89 m N-S x 12.08 m E-W x 5.18 m depth; (int.) 38.89 m N-S x 9.50 m E-W.

West Cryptoporticus East: from Cryptoporticus Retaining Wall 36.89 m N-S x 4.3 m E-W x 4.39 m depth.

West Cryptoporticus West: 39.03 m N-S x 4.30 m E-W x 5.18 m depth.

West Cryptoporticus Bench W: 39.16 m N-S x 0.74 m E-W x 0.66 m depth.

West Cryptoporticus Bench S: 0.68 m N-S x 3.63 m E-W x 0.53 m depth.

West Entry Stairs: 37.15 m N-S x 4.6 m E-W: Total area 171.12 m2

Lower Temenos wall dimensions (thickness and height)

East Exedra: (S) 4.68 m height; (E) 3.21 m height; (W) 3.22 m height.

West Exedra: (S) 4.33 m height; (E) 3.31 m height; (W) 3.17 m height.

Retaining Wall: 1.01 m N-S x 28 m E-W x 2.76 m height.

Byzantine Platform: 8.13 m N-S x 5.45 m E-W x 1.4 m height.

Cryptoporticus East (E): 1.18 m thickness x 4.60 m height.

Cryptoporticus West (W): 1.46 m thickness x 3.40 m height.

Cryptoporticus Center vault wall: 1.88 m thickness x 5.33 m height.

Upper Temenos

Upper Temenos measurements

Temple Central Stairs from LT to UT T. Forecourt: 5.9 m N-S x 4.56 m E-W.

East and West Staircases (30 treads) from LT to UT T. Forecourt: 9m N-S x 2.70 m E-W x 0.35 m deep.

South Passageway: (ext.) 5.8 m N-S x 27.2 m E-W x 5.44 m depth; (int.) 2.9 m NS x 24.7 m E-W.

South Perimeter Wall: 1.1 m N-S x 55.46 m E-W x 7.11 m depth.

Baroque Room Complex: From the Anteroom to the Settling Tank: 5.77 m N-S x 17.26 m E-W.

Residential Quarter: From the Settling Tank in the east to west (excavated extent): 15.48 m N-S x 9.22 m E-W.

East Upper Temenos

East Perimeter Wall: 36.69 m N-S x 1.33 m E-W x 6.4 m depth; Southeast corner ca. 6.4 to 12 m depth.

East Plaza: 45.37 m N-S x 9.53 m-to-14 m E-W.

West Upper Temenos

West Plaza: 49.33 m N-S x 10.2 m E-W.

Cistern-Reservoir: 7 m N-S x 5.4 m E-W; Total area 37.8 m2, 74 m3.

Roman-Byzantine Baths: 47.91 m N-S x 30.84 m E-W.

Upper Temenos features — elevations in meters

Temple Forecourt: 904.02 m.

East Archway East 'Cistern' Arch Upper Elevation: 905.23 m.

Lowest excavated elevation (west quarry): 898.76 m.

Lowest plaster floor: 900.62 m.

Temple Forecourt, capstone upper elevation—903.85 m.

Floor elevation—901.6 m.

Upper Temenos South dimensions

South Passageway: (ext.) 5.8 m N-S x 27.2 m E-W x 5.44 m depth; (int.) 2.9 m NS x 24.7 m E-W.

Baroque Room Complex: From the Anteroom to the Settling Tank: 5.77 m N-S x 17.26 m E-W.

Anteroom: (ext.) 3.9 m N-S x 4.9 m E-W x 2.19 m depth, (int.) 2.7 m N-S x 5.54 m E-W.

Shrine Room: (ext.) 6.78 m N-S x 4.67 m E-W x 3.1 m depth; (int.) 3.79 m N-S x 5.7 m E-W.

Shrine Room niche: 0.74 m height x 0.53 m width x 0.33 m depth.

Baroque Room: (ext.) 5.85 m N-S x 5.27 m E-W; (int.) 4.55 m N-S x 3.54 m E-W.

Baroque Room East Door: 1.05 m N-S x 0.51 m E-W x 1.6 m depth.

Baroque Room North Door: 0.44 m N-S x 1.02 m E-W x 0.7 m depth.

Baroque Room Corridor: 1.32 m N-S x 9.77 m E-W x 2.49 m depth.

Settling Tank: (ext.) 5.39 m N-S x 4.82 m E-W x 1.46 m depth; (int.) 3.86 m N-S x 3 m E-W.

Residential Quarter

From the Settling Tank in the east to west (excavated extent) N-S 15.48 m x 9.22 m E-W.

Steps between the Settling Tank and Residential Quarter Room 3: (ext.) N-S 2.91 m x 1.18 m E-W; (int.) 2.91 m N-S x 0.77m E-W x 1.01 m depth.

Cave 1: 4.6 m N-S x 3.46 m E-W x 2.4 m depth.

Room 9: 4.6 m N-S x 3.46 m E-W x 2.4 m depth.

Cave 2 (with rooms 10, 11): 6.5 m N-S x 6.65 m E-W x 3.54 m depth.

Room 7: (ext.) 5.94 m N-S x 3.42 m E-W x 2.24 m depth; (int.) 4.82 m N-S x 2.59 m E-W.

Room 8: (ext.) 3.18 m N-S x 3.95 m E-W x 3.4 m depth; (int.) 1.94 m N-S x 3.37 m E-W.

Room 10: (ext.) 4.94 m N-S x 4.16 m E-W x 3.8 m depth; (int.) 4.14 m N-S x 3.68 m E-W.

Room 2 Corridor: (ext.) 7.79 m N-S x 3.47 m E-W-by x 3.57 m depth; (int.) 6.85 m N-S x 2.08 m E-W.

Room 11: (ext.) 6.17 m N-S x 2.96 m E-W x 3.54 m depth; (int.) 5.71 m N-S x 2.4 m E-W.

Other rooms:

Room 1: (ext.) 2.91 m N-S x 3.59 m E-W x 2.17 m depth; (int.) 1.95 m N-S x 2.53 m E-W.

Room 3: (ext.) 2.94 m N-S x 3.05 m E-W x 2.39 m depth; (int.) 1.92 m N-S x 2.57 m E-W.

Room 4: (ext.) 1.82 m N-S x 2.15 m E-W x 0.86 m depth; (int.) 1.20 m N-S x 1.80 m E-W.

Room 5: (ext.) 1.96 m N-S x 7.12 m E-W x 1.57 m depth; (int.) 1.40 m N-S x 6.10 m E-W.

Room 6: (ext.) 6.10 m N-S x 3.37 m E-W x 1.19 m depth; (int.) 4.27 m N-S x 2.49 m E-W.

Upper Cave: 3.24 m N-S x 5.14 m E-W x 2.32 m depth.

East Upper Temenos and East Perimeter Wall

East Perimeter Wall: 36.69 m N-S x 1.33 m E-W x approximately 11 m depth.

East Plaza: 45.37 m N-S x 9.53 m-to-14 m E-W.

East Reservoir to the S. escarpment: 45.37 m N-S.

Reservoir: 8.3 m N-S x 2.8 m E-W x 1.3 m depth.

From the East 'Cistern' behind the East Exedra to the south escarpment: 58.81 m N-S.

Great Cistern: 8.5 m N-S x 7.8 m E-W x 5.17-to-5.88 m depth, 37.64 m cubed = 86,562 gallons of water or 327,640 liters. Shaft depth1.64 m, shaft diam. 1.41 m.

Room A: (ext.) 8.69 m N-S x 3.15 m E-W x 4.35 m depth; (int.) 7.75 m N-S x 1.53 m E-W.

Room B: (ext.) 4.77 m N-S x 2.45 m E-W x 1.83 m depth.

Tabun Room: 6.19 m N-S x 2.34 m E-W x 1.2 m depth.

Stairway between Room A and Tabun Room: 3.17 m N-S x 0.77 m E-W x 1.80 m depth.

West Upper Temenos

West Plaza: 49.33 m N-S x 10.2 m E-W.

Cistern Reservoir: 7.00 m N-S x 5.4 m E-W.

Upper Temenos Wall Dimensions (thickness and height)

South Precinct Wall: 1.50 m thickness x 3.00 m height.

East Perimeter Wall: 1.34 m thickness x 6.40 m height.

East Perimeter Wall: 36.69 m N-S x 1.33 m E-W x approximately 11 m depth.

East Perimeter Wall Arch: (ext.) 5.50 m N-S x 4.88 m E-W x 7.83 m depth—(int.) 4.05 m N-S x 3.32 m E-W.

West Perimeter Wall: (excavated), 40 m N-S x 7.50 m E-W x 4.55 m depth.

South Perimeter Wall: 1.10 m N-S x 55.46 m E-W x 7.11 m depth.

Small arch/vault: 6.70 m N-S x 2.50 m depth.

(The Roman-Byzantine Bath Complex Dimensions are given in Chapter 9.)

Great Temple(s)

Temple dimensions

Distyle Temple: 30.07 m N-S x 18.36 m E-W.

Tetrastyle Temple: 42.5 m N-S x 27.1-to-35.5 m E-W.
(Tetrastyle Temple: the largest freestanding structure in Petra)

Porch stylobate: 2.2 m N-S x 28 m E-W.

From the East Walkway to the West Walkway: 35.5 m.

Porch inter-axial distance between the East Anta and East Porch Column: 4.4 m.

Porch and Pronaos Columns: 1.5 m diameter.

East Porch columns inter-axial distance: 5.03 m.

Central Porch columns inter-axial distance: 7.06 m.

West Porch columns inter-axial distance: 5.03 m.

Heart-shaped south columns: c. 1.2 m (center).

East, West and South Corridor columns ca. 1.1- 1.2 m. diam. Side columns inter-axial distance east and west: 3.51 m. Rear columns inter-axial distance: 3.27 m.

Preserved height of West Anta: 2.60 m.

Pronaos

Width from the stylobate south edge to the front of the East Anta and West Anta: 6.5 m N-S x 24.7 m E-W.

Temple south

South Corridor: (ext.) 5.8 m N-S x 27.1 m E-W x 6.9 m depth; (int.) 3.1 m N-S x 24.7 m E-W.

Rear E-W Stairs East: 2.4 m N-S x 8.5 m E-W x 5.12 m depth.

Rear E-W Stairs West: 2.4 m N-S x 8.6 m E-W x 5.12 m depth.

South doorways (average) 2.06 m width x 6.90 m height x 1.18 m depth.

Temple east

East Corridor: (ext.) 33.9 m N-S x 6.12 m E-W x 5.89 m depth; (int.) 31.35 m NS x 3.12 E-W.

East Walkway: 41.55 m N-S x 3.67 m E-W x 0.2 m depth.

East Chamber: (ext.) 7.16 m N-S x 4.37 m E-W x 5.1 m depth; (int.) 5.3 m N-S x 3 m E-W.

Central N-S Stairs East: 6.60 m N-S x 2.27 m E-W x 4.8 m depth.

East Corridor Doorways: (average) 2.05 m width x 4.37 m height x 1.29 m depth.

Temple West

West Corridor: length from the front of the West Anta to the rear: 12 m N-S x 3 m E-W x 2.21 m depth.

West Walkway: from the front of the West Anta 33.30 m N-S x 3.67 to 3.7 m E-W x 0.81 m depth.

West Corridor doorways: (average) 2.05 m width x 2.21 m height x 1.35 m depth.

West Chamber: (ext.) 6.88 m N-S x 4.66 m E-W x 4.78 m depth; (int.) 5.52 m N-S x 3.03 m E-W.

Central N-S Stairs West: 6.82 m N-S x 2.23 m E-W x 4.76 m depth.

Temple center

Central Arch: (ext.) 9.81 m N-S x 5.77 m E-W x 5.58 m depth (int.) 6.89 m N-S x 3.21 m E-W.

East steps (rear of theatron): 2.5 m N-S x 0.9 m E-W x 1.54 m depth.

West steps (rear of theater): 2.5 m N-S x 0.9 m E-W x 1.54 m depth.

Theater

Orchestra floor diameter: 6.43 m.

Proposed diameter of outermost seats according to reconstruction 33.2 m x 2.96 m depth.

Estimated seating capacity (0.5 m per person) 565; (0.45 m per person) = 620 capacity.
As per R. Fredericksen's calculations (Ch. 8) = 900 persons.

Great Temple(s) elevations

Stylobate: 905.63 ± 0.05 m.

Pronaos: 905.345 ± 0.04 m.

Restored porch columns average: 907.96±0.10 m.

West Anta (inner) elevation: 909.15 m.

East Anta (inner) elevation: 907.75 m.

West Walkway elevation: 905.54±0.01 m.

West Corridor elevation: 905.47 ± 0.06 m.

West Corridor maximum elevation: 909.02 m.

East Corridor elevation: 905.53 m.

East Corridor maximum elevation: 910.07 m.

Theater elevations

Orchestra: 905.53±0.02 m.

Lowest diazoma: 907.11±0.02 m.

Lowest seating: 907.50±0.01 m.

Uppermost excavated seating: 908.59 m.

Projected last seat (approximate): 914.667 m.

Lowest step: 905.97 m.

Restored uppermost step: 910.49 m.

Upper (rear) platform: 910.49 m.

East Stairway (N-S)

Floor at the bottom of the stairs: 905.61 m.

Lowest step: 905.98 m.

Restored uppermost step: 910.52 m.

Upper Platform: 910.53 m.

West Stairway (N-S)

Floor at the bottom of the stairs: 905.63 m.

Lowest step: 905.97 m.

Restored uppermost step: 910.49 m.

Upper platform: 910.49 m.

Central Arch

Top of keystone: 910.51 m.

Heart-shaped east rear column restored elevation: 912.49 m

Temple wall dimensions (thicknesses and heights)

West Interior Anta wall: 5.97 m N-S x 1.57 m E-W x 3.86 m height.
East Interior Anta wall: 6 m N-S x E-W 1.57 m x 2.3 m height.
South Corridor wall: 1.18 m thickness x 5.36 m height.
East Corridor wall: 1.29 m thickness x 5.51 m height.
East Walkway wall: 0.66 m thickness x 0.6 m height.
East Chamber wall: 1.92 m thickness x 2.8 m height.
East and West shared wall: 1.21 m thickness x 3.2 m height.
West Corridor wall: 1.35 m thickness x 3.9 m height.
West Walkway wall: 0.67 m thickness x 1.32 m height.
West Chamber wall: 1.27 m thickness x 3.2 m height.
Central Arch: arch 0.4 m thickness x 5.9 m height.
East Steps (rear of *Theater*): 1.7 m thickness x 1.4 m height.
West Steps (rear of *Theater*): 1.7 m thickness x 0.8 m height.

If the Great Temple is 19 m in height as we posit, the temple would stand some 34 m above the Colonnaded Street.

APPENDIX 3

DATABASE METHODOLOGY AND RESULTS

Martha Sharp Joukowsky

Artifacts and artifact databases

Material remains form part of the Great Temple's cultural story. From 1993 onwards, as Great Temple archaeologists began their discoveries, their encounters with a vast array of artifacts created a great deal of interest.[1] In this appendix we have captured this information in our databases, which along with the stratigraphy transformed the way the artifact record was seen and understood.[2] Here we explore Nabataean choices regarding cultural material—what they made, imported and used. This chapter focuses on the main aspects of our database management and the results of our general recording database in Filemaker 6.[3] It was dubbed 'Grosso Modo,' and it incorporated the full range of material culture found at the site. The same computer program was used in recording the architectural fragment database. The recovery of these data reflects a Great Temple community who were deeply engaged in a world of artifacts.

The application of computerization at the Petra Great Temple excavations has offered us a powerful tool helping us disentangle the remains. Now we can assess the extent to which computer use during the multi-year course of our excavations has awarded us with insights about the artifact record. We have placed our artifact assemblages in serial order and within the context of the stratigraphy have constructed a relative chronology for the site. Underlying the concept of the Great Temple artifact record is the fact that the artifacts of the Nabataean period at the Great Temple have a recognizable style and are characteristic of the local Petraeans who produced and/or used them. The fashion choices over time and these changes reflect the Petra local chronology with artifact sequences that now can be understood. This chapter provides an overview of artifact tabulation by material.

Specialist Artifact Studies

Specialist studies pose several questions about each artifact data set. They direct their inquiries to the range of artifacts they analyze; they want to know where each artifact is discovered and its stratigraphic context. Then the question arises about when and where the artifact was originally produced, and finally, what parallel correspondences can be drawn from like artifacts and their contexts. Each specialist, therefore, is concerned with space, time, and how the artifact arrived at the Great Temple and its site archaeological context. Of course, the larger implications of such studies are a better understanding of the Great Temple's human story and its symbolic heritage.

The 626 lamps are a considerable number in the pottery corpus and are significant as artifacts that can be dated. A discussion of Great Temple lamps by Deirdre Grace Barrett appears above in

---

1 These appendices—Appendix 3, general Artifact recording and results, Appendix 4 Pottery, and Appendix 5 Architectural Fragments are the result of many people patiently laboring in the hot sun during the excavation day, and encoding the data on computers during the evening hours and far into the night. It was the Great Temple team over the years who were patient, as they were forced to adapt to never-ending days of wrestling with nearly half a million artifacts—their careful excavation, their cleaning and recording process—annotation of their specific characteristics, their measurements, and their preservation, and their identification and safe storage. The Great Temple team kept up each other's spirits and never complained. They were generous—helping one another with washing, brushing, annotation, and recording. All of them need to be thanked for helping us complete this work, which is a testament to their assistance and perseverance.

2 It is important to note that this discussion is based on 14 years of excavation findings, 1993-2008. The 2008 artifacts from the Roman-Byzantine Baths have not been included here.

3 The Great Temple database program was designed by Donna D'Agostino.

Chapter 12. The Coroplastic art of terra cotta figurines found in Great Temple contexts is indicative of Nabataean socio-religious ideas. In Chapter 13 Christopher A. Tuttle discusses these miniature sculptures in all their variety.

Bone accounts for 27,658 fragments or nearly seven percent of the total materials. All the faunal remains are saved, 7658 fragments, and zooarchaeologist, Sarah Whitcher Kansa, focuses on part of this collection in Chapter 17A. Kansa's study will answer many questions we have about Nabataean subsistence and diet. (Her extensive faunal data sets are presented in *Open Context*.) During the process of analysis, Kansa also found an interesting bone handle, which is presented here in Chapter 18B, and thereafter the taxonomic identification of the Great Temple fish remains is presented by Ruby Cerón-Carrasco in Chapter 17B.

Stucco/plaster fragments are numerous as well. Numbering 26,901 pieces, they represent over 6% of the materials. It appears that every built surface, including walls, columns and capitals, of the Great Temple are plastered. We saved all the plaster fragments with identifiable secondary characteristics, i.e., painted or sculpted surfaces, Here in Chapter 5, Emily Catherine Egan focuses on the stucco/plaster decoration as an integral part of the decorative vocabulary of the Nabataeans.

Glass fragments number 4672, and although it represents only 1% of the database. With the glass typology corpus, Margaret O'Hea explores many interesting questions, including the origin(s) of the pieces. Her contribution is not only in Chapter 14, but also in the extensive glass database she developed, which can be accessed on-line at *Open Context*.

Excepting the 760 coins (which are recorded in a separate database, see Chapter 15 by Christian F. Cloke), metal artifacts number 4799 or 1% of the total Great Temple collection. Although recognizable pieces are catalogued, the remaining artifacts needed to be properly analyzed, like the flower finials (fig. 10.7) the arrowheads,[4] and other objects, like the probable bronze ibex, Cat. No. 01-M-4, are documented in the catalogue. Angela Murock Hussein analyzes other bits and pieces here in Chapter 19. She has explored a selection of the metal corpus, with overall numbers of 917 objects. She presents the outcome of her examination along with a chemical analysis of a selection of the metal artifacts.

Over the 1993-2006 years we collected 508 vegetable matter samples, and P. Warnock[5] has been sent many questionable samples, but the results generally confirm they are weeds. Botanical remains like the olive pits we have found are recorded in the field. A questionable burned deposit that I thought to be incense underwent chemical analysis by Brown University geologists, who concluded that it was mixed collapse debris. Only 67 wood fragments have been recognized. A section of the large juniper beam found in East Corridor collapse was sent to Cornell University's Malcolm and Carolyn Wiener Laboratory for Aegean and Near Eastern Dendrochronology. It was determined to be "stressed juniper." The remaining wood remnants remain in on-site storage and are available for analysis. No Great Temple wood has been analyzed for radiocarbon dates—perhaps such studies will be performed in the future. However stucco from the Lower Temenos Colonnade has produced some results.[6]

Shell collected over the span of our campaigns numbers 1676 specimen or 0.40% of the total material. All the shell is saved, and David S. Reese, has analyzed a sample of this collection, and will present these results in a separate publication. One sculpted shell with a bronze attachment,

---

4 *Vol. 2,* and fig. 3.44); It is also found in Joukowsky 2003, 405, fig. 22.

5 *Great Temple* Vol. 1, 167 ff.)

6 Samples of plaster provided radiocarbon dates from the Great Temple were reported in 2009 by Khaled al-Bashaireh from the Department of Archaeology, Yarmouk University, Jordan. Plaster Sample 41 covered a column of the East Colonnade (we assume this indicates a Temple column, not the East Colonnade of the Lower Temenos), and was dated between A.D. 126 and A.D. 128, which fits in well for the possible re-plastering of the column in the first quarter of the A.D. second century in Site Phase VI, dated to the Roman takeover.

the stunning dolphin pendant, is published above in Figure 10.7. "Eggshell" is not commonly found. Delicate shell fragments are recorded and saved, but generally disintegrate. The majority of these are due to the modern Great Temple nesting snake population.

Stone fragments number 20,833 or 5% of the total materials. When their function is known, from a small section of *opus sectile* pavement, or a smoothed pebble perhaps used either for pulverizing materials or as a pottery burnishing tool, this was indicated on the Grosso Modo form. "Chips of the old block" that were small and unidentifiable were recorded and discarded. Any with telltale signs of use or carving was saved and stored for future analysis or reconstruction. Often we found chipped stone elements, part of the Neolithic tool kit in a deposit. These too were retained for study; we reasoned that they were probably part of the original soil fill brought in by the Nabataean architects to build up the platform of the Great Temple Lower Temenos.

Six faience fragments are recorded in Grosso Modo,[7] but there are 33 pieces in the site catalogue. (Only those pieces of museum quality are registered in the Great Temple Catalogue.) In general faience must have been imported from a Hellenistic site like Alexandria, Egypt, for few faience artifacts is found in Petra.

Once again we now turn to review the Great Temple site phases

Great Temple Site Phases

Based on a complicated site deposition and dateable evidence from lamps, coins, and pottery stylistics, the general sequence of some 15 Site Phases, Pre-site I, I–XIV, is now evident for the Great Temple construction, collapse and abandonment. Although these sequences (progressing from earliest to latest) indicate stages of construction, destruction, and abandonment, building periods are sometimes separated from artifact periods moving the latter to *later* phases, depending upon the context in which the materials are found. Therefore even if we know that a particular Nabataean artifact was made in the A.D. first or second century, in Site Phase IV, it is placed in Site Phase IX where it is found mixed and tumbled together with other elements of the 363 CE collapse.

Once the stratigraphy had been analyzed and the 15 site phases established, the artifact repertoire was distributed between the registered six databases and each database was set against the phasing. But here we have to add a word of caution: One of the significant results of any of our database analyses is the mixture found in the stratigraphic and resulting artifact record. The results presented here correspond with the stratigraphy and the deposition record. There are few clear transitions between the Site Phases. Obviously we have a sequence with few stratigraphic breaks and mixtures of material culture.

Taking place in the first century B.C., Nabataean *Site Pre-Phase I and Phase I* are assigned to the preparation of the site for building, odd walls and cup marks are found in the bedrock from earlier inhabitants, the bedrock is stripped away in a massive quarrying operation particularly on the east and south for the placement of the building and its immediate surround. An early canalization system also is constructed under the planned temple forecourt. Tentatively the evidence suggests that originally the Great Temple is to occupy the highest position on the south side of Central Petra.

Site Phase II is dated to the mid-first century B.C., and is characterized by the building of the distyle *in antis* temple in the earliest major Nabataean construction phase. It is to be embellished with columns supporting pseudo-Corinthian capitals. A Propylaeum East-West Portico Wall is also constructed separating the independence of the nascent precinct, fronting the then major thoroughfare in Central Petra. In the beginning this distyle temple stands as an isolated structure, constructed sometime in the last quarter of the first century B.C. by Nabataean architects and perhaps foreign craftsmen who combine their native traditions with the classical spirit. The beginning

7 See Joukowsky 1988, 239.

of the Great Temple is postulated to be constructed during the reigns of either Nabataean King Malichus I (62–30 B.C.), or King Obodas II (30–9 B.C.). A temple Central Stairway is also constructed from the then Lower Temenos area to access the fill creating the upper terrace and the temple's Forecourt.

In *Site Phase III* dated to the mid-to-late first century B.C. There is minor damage to the distyle temple building. It is difficult assess what may have happened, but most likely it experienced structural problems.

Site Phase IV of the first century B.C. to A.D. first century is known as "The Grand Design" when the precinct dramatically expands. In the Propylaeum two additional east west walls are added behind the earliest Portico Wall. It also may be at this time that the sculpted pilaster blocks were mounted on the Propylaeum façade. The West Entry Stairs leading from then major thoroughfare[8] to the temple precinct are constructed. Commemorative *nefesh* and *betyls* are placed along its stair platforms.

In the Lower Temenos this phase also includes the construction of East and West Cryptoporticoes under the East and West Triple Colonnades These Triple Colonnades flank the massive Lower Temenos courtyard on the east and west and are ornamented with elephant-headed capitals. Also built at this time are twin, semicircular East and West Exedrae to the east and west of the Lower Temenos, as well as the massive east-west Lower Temenos Retaining Wall delimiting the Lower Temenos to its south and the terraced raised Upper Temenos to its north. Additionally there is the embellishment of the sizeable Lower Temenos plaza with a limestone hexagonal pavement.

In the Upper Temenos, the walls and arches of the East 'Cistern', the precinct's casemate East Perimeter Wall, and the East Plaza are also constructed. Excavated into the bedrock of the East Plaza, the subterranean Great Cistern is chiseled out of the bedrock as well. The west flank of the temple has to be supported by subterranean walls where the bedrock has fallen away. It is also during this time that the Residential Quarter and the Baroque Room are woven into the fabric of the Upper Temenos and the newly renovated temple. The then freestanding Great Temple columns are erected along with the East and West Corridors and exterior East and West Walkways, and a raised temple Forecourt is put in place. Other monumental structural changes take place as well, for this is when a great porch (Pronaos), is added onto to the distyle temple adorned with four elaborately sculpted pseudo-Corinthian capitals. This transforms the structure into a majestic Great Temple tetrastyle with its tetrastyle *in antis* façade.[9]

In the A.D. first century, in *Site Phase V*, again finds major redesign in the precinct. In the Propylaeum double *betyls* are added to an interior altar. There is a major remodeling when the construction of the earlier distyle temple interior is reconfigured with a Theater-like[10] arrangement, and there is the construction of inter-columnar walls (walls between the previously free-standing corridor columns), to provide additional support for the theater east and west stairways). This renovation we place sometime near the end of the reign of King Aretas IV, ca. A.D. 40/44, or to the rule of King Malichus II (A.D. 40/44–70), and possibly to the reign of the last Nabataean king, King Rabbel II (A.D. 70–106). It is therefore suggested that these modifications take place sometime in the A.D. first or early second centuries.

Dated to the A.D. mid-second century, around the time of the Roman annexation of Petra, Nabataean-Roman *Site Phase VI* follows a minor collapse when a Central Propylaeum Stairway is built to provide a more formal entry from the major thoroughfare to the Lower Temenos, the Lower Temenos East Cryptoporticus now has east west cross-walls built to stabilize its north-south walls and is intentionally covered over with fill.

---

8 In site phase VII this thoroughfare becomes an impressive Colonnaded Street.

9 On the basis of the floral decoration, especially seen on the limestone capitals and elements of the entablature, the Petra Great Temple's iconography appears to be similar to that of the Great Temple's neighbor, the monumental Al-Khazna.

10 As Chapter 8 suggests, this may have been an Odeon.

PETRA GREAT TEMPLE SITE PHASING SUMMARY

Site Phases	*Dates*	*Major Construction-Destruction*
Pre-Site Phase I	ca. Pre 1st c. B.C.	Odd walls and cup marks in bedrock
Site Phase I	ca. Early 1st c. B.C.	Bedrock Preparation
Site Phase II	Mid-1st c. B.C.	Distyle *in Antis* temple Portico Wall, Lowest Steps of Central Steps
Site Phase III	Mid -to-Late 1st c. B.C. A.D. 1st c.	Minor Damage
Site Phase IV	ca. 1st c, B.C. – A.D. 1st c.	Grand Design (Expansion) Tetrastyle *in Antis* Temple; Full Propylaeum; West Entry Stairway(*Nefesh*); Lower Temenos Triple Colonnades; Exedrae; Upper Temenos Great Cistern, East Perimeter Wall; Residential Quarter, Baroque Room
Site Phase V	ca. A.D. 1st c.	Nabataean Redesign and Repair: Theater Added to Great Temple *Betyls* in Propylaeum
Site Phase VI	ca. A.D. 106	Roman Takeover; Damage to West Propylaeum; Repairs to Lower Temenos; Baroque Room Collapse; Temple Doorways and Corridors Narrowed; Bath Complex Constructed
Site Phase VII	A.D. Mid 2nd c.	Propylaeum Repair, Wall K Razed in East, Rebuilt in West; West Room 1 Constructed; Roman Street Paved; East Propylaeum Rooms 1-3 Constructed; East Exedra Repair; Lower Temenos East-West Crosswalls in East Colonnade; Benches; Temple Doorways narrowed and Walled-In; Theater Stage Constructed
Site Phase VIII	A.D. Late-2nd c.	Damage, Abandonment, Collapse, Dumping
Site Phase IX	A.D. 363 Earthquake	Collapse of Propylaeum and Lower Temenos West Triple Colonnade; West Cryptoporticus Collapse; Upper Temenos Added Features; Temple West Columns Fall; Robbing of Staircases, Pavements and Walls
Site Phase X	A.D. 4th–5th c. Byzantine Reuse	Abandonment, Fluvial Deposit Accumulates; Lower Temenos Reconstruction of Colonnades with Reused Ashlars; Domestic Secondary Reuses in all Temple Areas
Site Phase XI	Post A.D.512 Earthquake	Further Collapse; East Triple Colonnade Collapse; West Entry Stairs Collapse; Temple East Porch Columns Collapse; Baths Out of Use
Site Phase XII	Late Byzantine A.D.512-640	Abandonment and Robbing
Site Phase XIII	Islamic Period	Series of Major Collapses
Site Phase XIV	Modern Period	Farming of the Lower Temenos by Bedouin; Dumping, Construction of Bedouin Walls; Brown University Excavations, 1993

Site Phase VII, also dated to the later A.D. mid-second century, the Roman Colonnaded Street (the earlier thoroughfare) is paved and adorned with a colonnade.[11] In the Propylaeum Wall K (the Wall behind the Propylaeum Portico Wall) is razed in the east and rebuilt in the west, and a room (Room 1) is constructed. In the East Propylaeum the Portico Wall is reconfigured so that Rooms 1-3 can be erected, with bars inserted in their thresholds.[12]

The Lower Temenos finds the East Exedra under repair, and east west cross walls are built to support the East Triple Colonnade.

In the Great Temple makeshift benches are built and doorways between the walkways and the temple corridors are narrowed and the Theater Stage is constructed.

Site Phase VIII is dated to the ca. A.D. late second century. This is a time of collapse and perceptible damage to the site, dumping, and temporary abandonment.

In *Site Phase IX* the major devastating earthquake of A.D. 363 brings about the collapse of the Propylaeum and the Lower Temenos West Triple Colonnade falls below into the West Cryptoporticus, which in turn collapses.

In *Site Phase X* there is abandonment of the Great Temple and this is represented by the accumulation of a deep fluvial deposit. This is Site Phase X of ca. A.D. 4th–5th centuries, is a period of Byzantine reuse. In the Lower Temenos there is a reconstruction of the Triple Colonnade walls with reused ashlars.[13] Signs of domestic reuse are present in all the precinct areas.

Site Phase XI marks a period after the A.D. 551 earthquake, and tremors bring about further collapse of what precinct architecture is left standing There is industrial reuse of both Exedras in the Lower Temenos, and domestic secondary uses are found in the temple areas, including the Theater stage, Vaulted Chambers, Great Cistern, Central Arch, and in the East Corridor. The West and South Walkway doors are blocked, an east-west wall is constructed across the Walkway South, the Walkway west exterior wall is re-erected, the collapse of the Lower Temenos East Colonnade occurs, and at the same time the Great Temple east Porch columns collapse.

Site Phase XII (A.D. 551-640) is a time of further collapse, abandonment, and robbing. Another fluvial deposit then accumulates and there is the major robbing of the upper stair treads of all the temple stairways.

In *Site Phase XIII* there are a series of major collapses, and Phase XIV encompasses roughly the modern era when the Lower Temenos is used for Bedouin farming and a dump is dug between the fallen east porch columns.

Site Phase XIII is roughly dated to the Islamic Period and is a time of a series of major collapses.

Site Phase XIV is dated to the modern period when the Lower Temenos is utilized for wheat farming, odd Bedouin walls are found on the site, and the Brown University excavations begin.

Overall results

The aim of Appendix 3 is to summarize the recovered artifacts by material, based on the 1993-2008 data. This appendix presents a large-scale review of the Great Temple artifact record, by overall materials, for evidence of characteristics that mark site phases as distinct. Conclusions are based on the actual finds—the result of the various choices that the Great Temple potters, architects, and people made, and the decisions we made in categorizing the various data sets and the classification of various elements. With these facts, finally, we can theorize how the artifact record relates to the

11 This is now known as the Colonnaded Street, but the colonnade ends well before the east perimeter of the Great Temple precinct.

12 However their function is unknown.

13 We recovered the sculpted wreath pilaster reused as a wall block in the East Triple Colonnade wall.

stratigraphy and the Great Temple site phases. In this chapter we complement the abovementioned specialist artifact/ecofact analyses with the overall database results and an overarching discussion about the frequency of artifact occurrence in relation both to the stratigraphy and the Great Temple site phases. Great Temple consumers left phenomenal remnants behind for us to quantify and analyze. Let us be grateful for the complex culture of the Nabataeans!

As outlined in Great Temple Volume I,[14] our procedures using Sequence Numbers for the charting and control of every field process remained constant throughout the years of our excavations. All of the Great Temple databases are available online at *Open Context*. Some of these findings have been defined and presented in previous Great Temple publications, but here, for the first time we present and discuss the overall results.

This appendix presents the overall results of our largest and most complicated artifact database, Grosso Modo, to which we now turn.[15]

The Grosso Modo Database

While each artifact in the Architectural Fragments database and the Catalogue is recorded individually and given a unique FileMaker Pro page, in Grosso Modo each page is given to an entire container. Every artifact type in each locus is given a distinct container number for each day (e.g. pottery in Locus 5 would have one container, while the pottery in Locus 6 would have another, and Locus 5 pottery on the next day would have yet another container). Each bucket is allocated an artifact material serial number by locus: P-1 (Pottery container 1), G-3 (Glass container 3), etc., and there is a separate database record or "page" for each of those containers.

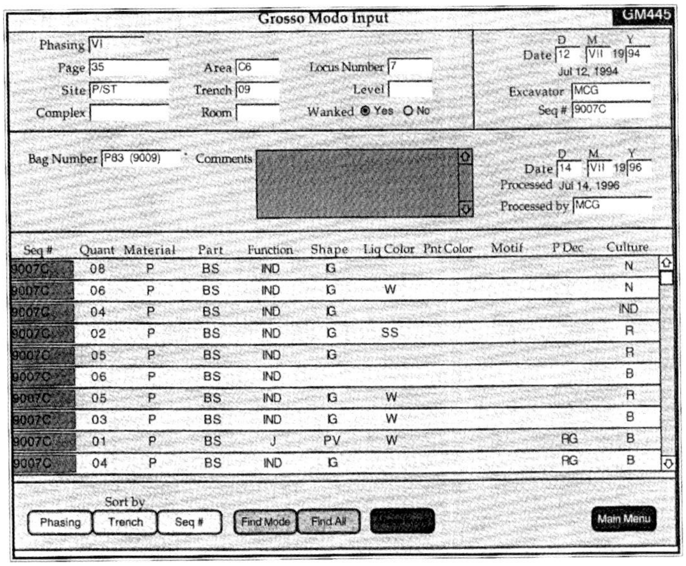

Grosso Modo Input GM445

Phasing VI
Page 35 Area C6 Locus Number 7
Site P/ST Trench 09 Level
Complex Room Wanked ● Yes ○ No

Date (D M Y) 12 VII 19 94
Jul 12, 1994
Excavator MCG
Seq # 9007C

Bag Number P83 (9009) Comments

Date (D M Y) 14 VII 19 96
Processed Jul 14, 1996
Processed by MCG

Seq #	Quant	Material	Part	Function	Shape	Liq Color	Pnt Color	Motif	P Dec	Culture
9007C	08	P	BS	IND	G					N
9007C	06	P	BS	IND	G	W				N
9007C	04	P	BS	IND	G					IND
9007C	02	P	BS	IND	G	SS				R
9007C	05	P	BS	IND	G					R
9007C	06	P	BS	IND						B
9007C	05	P	BS	IND	G	W				R
9007C	03	P	BS	IND	G	W				B
9007C	01	P	BS	J	PV	W			RG	B
9007C	04	P	BS	IND	G				RG	B

Sort by
Phasing Trench Seq # Find Mode Find All Main Menu

App. 3. Fig. 1. Address of the Grosso Modo Form.

In addition to the date excavated that is present in every database, the Grosso Modo database also indicates the date(s) that the container was processed in the field and keypunched into the computer. This would frequently occur back at the dig house in the days following the original excavation.[16]

The main part of each Grosso Modo page comprises a chart showing the particular information about each individual artifact by material within the bucket. Each material is assigned a different sequence number. Each artifact is given a row, and the various columns pertain to various features

14 2008, 239.

15 Several artifact databases were employed during the Great Temple excavations. These are described and illustrated in vol. 1. The Great Temple excavation team analyzed and encoded each artifact's various factors on specific forms during the excavations, and, thereafter each team member keypunched the results into the computers prepared databases, using FileMaker Pro. Whatever revisions had to be incorporated were undertaken annually by database designer and coordinator, Donna D'Agostino, during the postseason intervals.

16 This was particularly true for pottery that had to be washed and dried before it could be sorted for processing.

of the artifact. If a number of artifacts are identical, they are listed together in the same row. The key codes we used will be generally described at the end of this appendix.

Initially we shall look at the overall results of the Great Temple corpus. Several tables here present summary accounts and quantitative distributions, and the statistics reveal the presence or absence of materials. The Grosso Modo data allows us an extensive look at the vast corpus of Great Temple material—a phenomenal 405,297 objects from the 1993 to 2008 excavations are represented by Great Temple area in Appendix 3, Table 1.

Bulk finds, fragments of bone, charcoal, eggshell, faience, glass, metal, pottery, stone, shell, stucco/plaster, vegetable matter, and wood are the materials recorded. Here the totals of combined materials are given for each of the four areas excavated. What conclusions might we offer about Appendix 3, Table 1?

The Upper Temenos deposits significantly outweigh the remaining three areas of the Great Temple site, representing nearly 50% of the results, and that is due to the fact that these were recovered accumulated remains left by people who actually occupied the site and abruptly left, most probably for some unpleasant reason.

Propylaeum numbers are the lowest of the three areas; it is obvious that fewer materials are found there, and that may be because it is a point of entry and a pass through to other areas engaged in activity. As is reported by Sarah W. Kansa in Chapter 17A, a burnt bone deposit mixed with cache of early (Schmid Phase 3b[17] broken Nabataean painted pottery we posit is associated with a Great Temple early altar. The ceramics, bones, and a considerable ash deposit are found between the interstices between the early altar and the later Site Phase VII reconstructed Propylaeum Wall.

APPENDIX 3. Table 1.
GREAT TEMPLE: TOTAL ARTIFACT MATERIAL BY AREA

Area	*TOTAL*	*Percentage of Great Temple Site*
PROPYLAEUM	27,432	6.80%
LOWER TEMENOS	107,627	26.50%
UPPER TEMENOS	199,713	49.30%
TEMPLE	70,448	17.40%
OTHER (No Area)	77	–
TOTAL	**405,297**	**100%**

APPENDIX 3. Table 2.
GREAT TEMPLE: SPECIFIC RAW MATERIALS EXCAVATED AND RECORDED IN GROSSO MODO
1993-2008

*Material**	*TOTAL*	*Percentage*
Bone	27,658	6.80%
Charcoal	65	–
Eggshell	135	–
Faience	6	–
Glass	4672	1.20%
Pottery	317,977	78.50%
Stone	20,833	5.10%
Shell	1676	0.40%
Stucco/Plaster	26,901	6.60%
Vegetable	508	0.10%
Wood	67	–
TOTAL	**405,297**	**98.7%**

**Note: Metal artifacts were studied separately, and are not included here.*

The Lower Temenos represents 27% of the materials collected, and the Temple area accounts for only 17% of the overall artifact corpus.

Clearly the Nabataean culture is enjoyed throughout the Great Temple site, but it is often difficult to discern what specific activities are taking place in various areas of the precinct.

17 Phase 3b is dated to A.D. 70 to the beginning of the 2nd c.

In Appendix 3 Table 2, the percentage figures in the right column are set against the total representation of each area. The total figures at the bottom of each section are set against the total of 405,297 artifacts.

Pottery far outweighs other materials excavated representing 317,977 fragments or 78.5% of the corpus. The second highest percentage is bone at nearly 7% with 27,658 pieces or 7%, and 26,901 stucco/plaster artifacts or 6.6 % of the materials corpus. Glass has a negligible showing representing 4672 fragments or 1% of the recorded corpus. This is understandable because it is uncommonly found in Nabataean contexts until the Roman period. The figure for stone at 20,833 or 5% of the corpus is reasonable, because with the unsettled tectonics of the area—some of these fragments are probably the result of splinters that were bashed off the surfaces of collapsing architectural fragments. Shell numbers 1676 fragments, only 0.40%, and it is of interest to know if they are fresh water or salt water species. (This study is yet to be published.) 508 specimens or 0.10 % represents vegetable matter, and many of these are olive pits. Although we set out to capture numbers for charcoal deposits only 65 pieces were recovered, and although they were saved most were reasoned to be too small-sized for radiocarbon analysis.

To summarize, pottery remains dominate the Great Temple Grosso Modo collection—317,977 pottery fragments represent close to 80% of the materials found at the Great Temple, and bone and stucco/plaster each represent nearly 7% of the collection.

Undoubtedly in antiquity the Great Temple was an active, living site. Goats or perhaps sheep were prepared for a meal, pottery was used to serve the meal to people who were surrounded by a glorious stucco decorated environment with walls that were interlaced with a few wood beams, and glass was sparingly employed.

Raw Materials by area

Clearly the Nabataean culture is enjoyed throughout the Great Temple site, but it is difficult to discern what specific activities are taking place in various areas of the precinct, except for the Upper Temenos where there appear to be basic household activities taking place.

Ceramics far out weigh other artifact deposits, accounting for 66% of the Propylaeum materials, 78% of those in the Lower Temenos, 83% of the Upper Temenos and 70% of the Temple. Bone materials find their highest numbers in the Temple accounting for 8.5% of that collection, with 7% of the finds in both the Propylaeum and the Lower Temenos, with the Upper Temenos representing 6% of the collection for that area.

Glass finds its lowest numbers in the Temple (0.40%) and its highest representation in the Upper Temenos (1.5%). And metal represents its highest representation in the Temple (2.40%) with the Propylaeum numbers just behind at 2%. This may be partially due to the number of attachments associated with sculpted pieces located in the Temple, and the door lock and room threshold attachments recovered from the Propylaeum.

Shell has a poor representation with the highest numbers found in the Upper Temenos (1%) and the other three areas hovering around 0.30%. The Propylaeum finds a high number for stone at 12%, with the Temple at 8% and the Lower Temenos and Upper Temenos representing approximately 4% of their assemblages. The counts for stucco/plaster percentages of the assemblages correlate well with the stone results, for the Propylaeum again finds the highest percentage of that material at 11%, the Temple at 10% the Lower Temenos at 7% and the Upper Temenos at 4%. Clearly the areas with significant architectural embellishments such as capitals and sculpture reflect the highest numbers.

APPENDIX 3. Table 3.

GREAT TEMPLE: TOTAL SPECIFIC RAW MATERIALS BY AREA*

PROPYLAEUM

*Material**	*TOTAL*	*Percentage of Area*
Bone	1817	6.60%
Glass	186	0.70%
Metal	542	2%
Pottery	18,087	65.90%
Shell	75	0.30%
Stone	3351	12.20%
Stucco/Plaster	3089	11.30%
Vegetable	285	1%
TOTAL	**27,432**	**6.80% of Great Temple site**

LOWER TEMENOS

*Material**	*TOTAL*	*Percentage of Area*
Bone	7435	7%
Eggshell	117	0.10%
Glass	1223	1.10%
Metal	1570	1.50%
Pottery	84,452	78%
Shell	338	30%
Stone	4412	4%
Stucco/Plaster	8002	7.40%
Vegetable	78	0.07%
TOTAL	**107,627**	**26.50% of Great Temple site**

**The percentage figures in the right column are set against the total representation of each area. The total figures at the bottom of each section are set against the total of 405,297 artifacts.*

UPPER TEMENOS

*Material**	*TOTAL*	*Percentage of Area*
Bone	12,408	6.20%
Charcoal	64	–
Faience	5	–
Glass	2952	1.50%
Metal	998	0.50%
Pottery	166,403	83.30%
Shell	1045	1%
Stone	7159	3.60%
Stucco/Plaster	8611	4.30%
Vegetable	55	–
TOTAL	**199,713**	**49.30% of Great Temple site**

TEMPLE

*Material**	*TOTAL*	*Percentage of Area*
Bone	5990	8.50%
Charcoal	1	–
Eggshell	18	–
Faience	1	–
Glass	304	0.40%
Metal	1688	2.40%
Pottery	48,979	69.50%
Shell	218	0.30%
Stone	5907	8.40%
Stucco/Plaster	7198	10.20%
Vegetable	144	0.10%
Wood	53	0.10%
TOTAL	**70,448**	**17.40% of Great Temple site**
OTHER	**77**	
TOTAL	**405,297**	

Materials by Site Phase

In Appendix 3, Table 4 is an accounting of selected materials[18] by site phase. In most phases pottery and bone are among the most numerous finds, which indicates the phases with the highest count of materials are Site Phase IX[19] with 63,209 objects, representing 15.6 percent of the total, and Site Phase VIII, which has 23,336 or 5.80 percent. Results are found for Site Phases X and XI, with more than 20,000 materials each. Thereafter follows Site Phase VI with 18,315, Site Phase VII with 16,295 or 4 percent, Site Phase XIV with 14,764 or 3.6 percent, and Site Phase XIII with 11,563, 2.90 percent. The artifact evidence is admittedly uneven, however, we can assume that these numbers reflect a thriving Nabataean community. The phases with the lowest occurrences are the early phases: Site Phases Pre-I, I, II, and III, and later Site Phase XII. Of course Site Phases Pre-I-III, and I are periods of site preparation and construction. Site Phase V is a time of redesign when the Theater is being inserted into the center of the temple. And Site Phase XII reflects the abandonment of the site in Late Byzantine times when little activity other than the robbing of architectural elements was taking place. Site Phase XIV is problematic because of the tricky problem of erosion and debris falling down from the precipitous hillside above the Great Temple, the reuse of the Lower Temenos for Bedouin farmers' fields, and the discovery of an Israeli shell casing in the Great Temple Forecourt. As would be expected, in most phases pottery and bone are among the most numerous finds. The phases with the highest count of materials are Site Phase IX with 63,209 objects, representing 15.6% of the total, and Site Phase VIII, which has 23,336 or 5.80%. Results are found for Site Phases X and XI, with more than 20,000 materials each. Thereafter follows Site Phase VI with 18,315, Site Phase VII with 16,295 or 4%, Site Phase XIV with 14,764 or 3.6%, and Site Phase XIII with 11,563, 2.90%. We can assume that these numbers reflect a thriving Nabataean community. The phases with the lowest occurrences are the early phases: Site Phases Pre-I, I, II, and III, and later Site Phase XII. Of course Site Phases Pre-I-III, and I are periods of site preparation and construction. Site Phase V is a time of redesign when the Theater was being inserted into the center of the temple, and Site Phase XII reflects the abandonment of the site in Late Byzantine times when little activity other than the robbing of architectural elements was taking place. Site Phase XIV is problematic because of the tricky problem of erosion and debris falling down from the precipitous hillside above the Great Temple, the reuse of the Lower Temenos as Bedouin farmers' fields, and the discovery of an Israeli shell casing in the Great Temple Forecourt.

Significant trench deposits of materials

The nine trenches outlined in Appendix 3, Table 5 are significant for the role each plays in defining the indigenous character of the Great Temple site. This is because the Upper Temenos trenches were Nabataean living or working spaces particularly in the west Residential Quarter caves, and the temple east *Tabun* Room and the isolated Room A inside the casemate East Perimeter Wall. Although the archaeological evidence is admittedly uneven, it is the result of how these areas are used and abandoned, however, some patterns of activity can be revealed. These deposits increase our understanding of how people actually lived, worked, and used the Great Temple precinct. Also significant to this understanding, is the Upper Temenos East 'Cistern' dump and the Temple South Passageway, because they reflect the final depositions of large numbers of artifacts. Finally beyond the temple area, the Roman-Byzantine Baths are discussed for their unique composition of finds. These deposits are presented in the order of their size of artifact frequency, beginning with the highest frequencies set into their archaeological contexts. Now we turn to the defining material deposits of each of these excavations. Together these areas represent 128,355 materials or nearly 32% of the total Grosso Modo results for the Great Temple excavations.

---

18 Only those artifacts designated as belonging to one specific phase by the excavation team.

19 Site Phase IX is dated to the A.D. 363 devastating earthquake that wrought havoc at the Great Temple and to Petra.

APPENDIX 3. Table 4.
GREAT TEMPLE: SELECTED SITE PHASES BY MATERIAL

Great Temple Site Phase	*Material*	*TOTAL*	*Percentage of Phase and 405,297*
PRE-I	Bone	567	36.70%
	Glass	8	0.50%
	Metal	14	0.90%
	Pottery	922	59.80%
	Shell	3	0.19%
	Stucco/Plaster	24	1.50%
	Vegetable	3	0.19%-
	TOTAL	**1541**	**0.38% of 405,297**
I	Bone	1104	20.90%
	Glass	2	–
	Metal	207	3.90%
	Pottery	3305	62.50%
	Stone	474	9%
	Shell	10	0.20%
	Stucco/Plaster	187	3.50%
	Vegetable	2	–
	TOTAL	**5291**	**1.30% of 405,297**
II	Bone	118	7.80%
	Metal	9	0.60%
	Pottery	941	62.30%
	Stucco/Plaster	442	29.30%
	TOTAL	**1510**	**0.40% of 405,297**
III	Bone	38	30.90%
	Glass	1	0.80%
	Metal	1	0.80%
	Pottery	55	44.70%
	Stucco/Plaster	28	22.80%
	TOTAL	**123**	**–**
IV	Bone	795	8.00%
	Glass	29	0.30%
	Metal	55	0.60%
	Pottery	7278	73.30%
	Stone	95	1.00%
	Shell	25	0.30
	Stucco/Plaster	1635	16.50%
	Vegetable	19	0.20%
	TOTAL	**9931**	**2.50% of 405,297**
V	Bone	832	16.00%
	Glass	50	1.00%
	Metal	191	3.70%
	Pottery	554	68.50%
	Stone	248	4.80%
	Shell	28	0.50%
	Stucco/Plaster	273	5.30%
	Vegetable	9	.17%
	TOTAL	**5185**	**1.30% of 405,297**
VI	Bone	1564	8.50%
	Glass	169	0.90%
	Metal	363	2.00%
	Pottery	11,131	60.80%
	Stone	473	2.60%
	Shell	236	1.30%
	Stucco/Plaster	4373	23.90%
	Vegetable	6	—
	TOTAL	**18,315**	**4.50% of 405,297**
VII	Bone	1044	6.40%
	Charcoal	1	–
	Glass	91	0.60%
	Metal	612	3.80%
	Pottery	13,073	80.20%
	Stone	355	2.20%
	Shell	28	0.20%
	Stucco/Plaster	1089	6.70%
	Vegetable	2	–
	TOTAL	**16,295**	**4.00% of 405,297**
VIII	Bone	1558	6.70%
	Glass	1252	5.40%
	Metal	302	1.30%
	Pottery	16,467	70.60%
	Stone	2607	11.20%
	Shell	65	0.30%
	Stucco/Plaster	927	4.00%
	Vegetable	158	0.70%
	TOTAL	**23,336**	**5.80% of 405,297**

APPENDIX 3. Table 4. (continued)
GREAT TEMPLE: SELECTED SITE PHASES BY MATERIAL

Great Temple Site Phase	*Material*	*TOTAL*	*Percentage of Phase and 405,297*
IX	Bone	2901	4.60%
	Faience	3	–
	Glass	614	1.00%
	Metal	567	0.90%
	Pottery	53,223	84.20%
	Stone	3195	5.10%
	Shell	136	0.20%
	Stucco/Plaster	2499	4.00%
	Vegetable	27	–
	Wood	44	0.10%
	TOTAL	**63,209**	**15.60% of 405,297**
X	Bone	1992	9.40%
	Eggshell	18	0.10%
	Glass	419	2.00%
	Metal	140	0.70%
	Pottery	16,758	79.20%
	Stone	804	3.80%
	Shell	269	1.30%
	Stucco/Plaster	726	3.40%
	Vegetable	22	0.10%
	TOTAL	**21,148**	**5.20% of 405,297**
XI	Bone	1751	7.60%
	Eggshell	117	0.50%
	Glass	190	0.80%
	Metal	53	0.20%
	Pottery	19,532	85.00%
	Stone	378	1.60%
	Shell	76	0.30%
	Stucco/Plaster	871	3.80%
	TOTAL	**22,968**	**5.70% of 405,297**
XII	Bone	13	5.90%
	Glass	6	2.70%
	Metal	10	4.50%
	Pottery	186	84.50%
	Shell	5	2.30%
	TOTAL	**220**	**0.10% of 405,297**
XIII	Bone	1303	11.30%
	Glass	102	0.90%
	Metal	93	0.80%
	Pottery	9685	83.80%
	Stone	111	1.00%
	Shell	32	0.30%
	Stucco/Plaster	136	1.20%
	Vegetable	101	0.90%
	TOTAL	**11,563**	**2.90% of 405,297**
XIV	Bone	866	5.95%
	Glass	186	1.30%
	Metal	52	0.40%
	Pottery	11,333	76.80%
	Stone	614	4.20%
	Shell	62	0.40%
	Stucco/Plaster	1651	11.20%
	TOTAL	**14,764**	**3.60% of 405,297**
	TOTAL	**215,399**	**53% of 405,297**

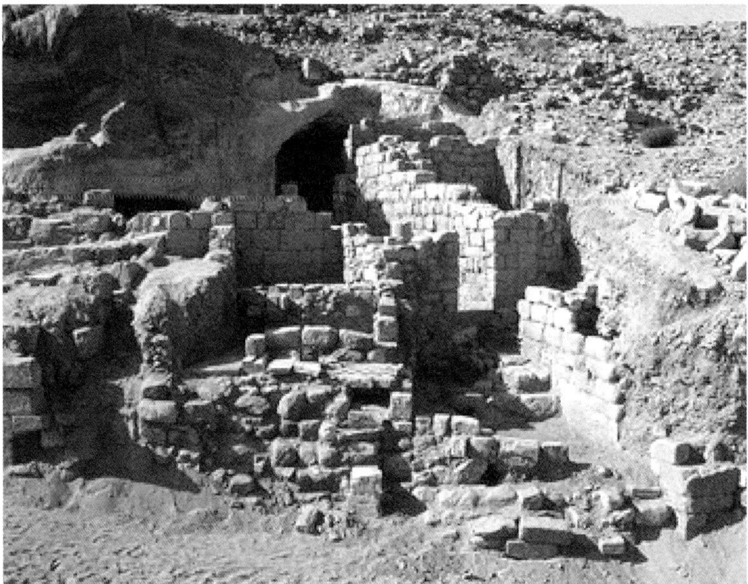
App.3. Fig. 2. Upper Temenos Residential Quarter.

1. *Upper Temenos Trench 94, the Residential Quarter.* Housed in a series of two caves, 11 masonry rooms are discovered, nestled deep within the Great Temple's southwest escarpment. Cave 1, the smaller east cave, measures 3 m in N-S length x 4 m in E-W width. Cave 2 is the larger west cave measuring 6.25 m in length x 5.4 m in width and a standing height of 3.85 m from floor to ceiling. Situated above Caves 1 and 2 is the "Small Upper Cave," 2.9 m in N-S length x 2.5 m in E-W width with a height of 3.05 m. This is the largest domestic complex at the Great Temple providing archaeological evidence for Nabataean life ways. The Residential Quarter deposits are robust with 33,668 objects. Of these, 32,349 are pottery fragments, representing 96% of the total materials objects collected in its excavation. This area also has a noteworthy collection of bone (864 pieces) but modest amounts of plaster (40 fragments), an indicator perhaps that not all of its surfaces are stucco/plastered. Ninety metal pieces are found in Trench 94, and 161 shells, and this is the location of the decorative shell dolphin pendant,[20] shown above in Chapter 10.

Trench 94's phenomenal collection represents 33,668 total materials, 8.3% of the materials recovered from the Great Temple site. More about this trench's extraordinary pottery collection is discussed above in Chapter 12.

2. *Temple, Trench 73.* In the temple is Trench 73 with 14,691 materials or 3.6% of the collected materials. This trench measures 21 m N-S x 3.60 m E-W, and is located on the east flank of the temple between the East Corridor Wall and the East Walkway Wall. The excavators also cleared the debris-ridden doorways between the East Corridor Wall and the East Walkway. The depth of deposit measured from 2.50 m in the north to 9.00 m depth in the south. Not only is a considerable amount of pottery found here (1147 fragments), but there are sizeable amounts of bone (777) and sculpted and painted plaster (392 pieces) that most likely slid off the walls.

3. *Upper Temenos, Special Project 110* (SP110). SP110 is excavated to recover the West Precinct Wall and the Cistern-Reservoir. This trench measures 11.5 m N-S x 9.2 m E-W. The area is largely comprised of fill to a 3.25 m depth containing 12,905 objects. Besides vast numbers of pottery fragments (11,243), there are considerable amounts of bone (1,160 items), and a small amount of metal (42 fragments). Its finds represent 3.20% of the total materials recovered from the Great Temple excavations.

4. *East 'Cistern' south of the East Exedra, Trench 53.* This vaulted room, 3.15 m N-S x 11.05 m E-W, also has a narrow seven-step staircase accessing it from the East Stairs leading up from the Lower Temenos to the Upper Temenos. The room originally was in use as a cistern with a bedrock floor, and after it ceased to function as a cistern it served as a dump. 11,960 artifacts register from this deposit number. There are 4035 plaster fragments in the Grosso Modo collection, which slipped

20 Joukowsky 2003, 405, fig. 22.

APPENDIX 3. Table 5.
GREAT TEMPLE: SIGNIFICANT TRENCH DEPOSITS OF MATERIALS

Area	*Trench/Special Project*	*Total Materials*	*Percentage-Total Materials*
UPPER TEMENOS	Trench 94 Residential Quarter	33,668	8.30%
	Trench 53 East 'Cistern' south of East Exedra	11,960	3%
	Trench 84 East Perimeter Wall, Rooms A and B	11,856	2.90%
	Trench 83 South Passageway	11,560	2.90%
	Special Project 110 West Precinct Wall and Cistern-Reservoir	12,905	3.20%
	Special Project 84 "Tabun Cave" Room	10,866	2.70%
	Trench 77 East Plaza	10,775	2.70%
	Trench 105-106 Roman-Byzantine Bath Complex	10,074	2.50%
TEMPLE	Trench 73 Great Temple, East side	14,691	3.60%
TOTAL		**128,355**	**PERCENTAGE of Total Materials 31.6%**

off the walls and are found in the fill. Stone artifacts total 507 objects, part of a marble storage or dump deposit of large unworked chunks. Pottery numbers are high as well—5883 fragments are found along with Nabataean inscribed bronze fragments,[21] a startling face painted on stucco,[22] and a painted inscription on plaster.[23] Its finds represent 3% of the total Great Temple materials recovered.

5. *Upper Temenos Trench 84 East Perimeter Wall Rooms A and B.* Excavated in 2001, Room A (Trench 84 and its continued excavation in Trench 91 in 2002), is located in the Upper Temenos within the casemate East Perimeter Wall. A total of 11,856 objects, or nearly 3% of the total, are recovered from the interior rooms of the East Perimeter Wall—a casemate construction consisting of two interior rooms labeled A and B. Leading into Room A from the East Plaza is a door on the west spanned with an extraordinarily engineered 7-ashlar, flat arch lintel.[24] The cache of pottery unearthed in

21 *Vol. 2,* fig. 7.6.
22 Ibid. fig. 7.9.
23 Ibid. fig. 7.29a-b.
24 *Vol. 2,* fig. 56; also see Rababeh 2005, figs. 6.3 and 6.4.

App. 3. Fig. 3. Upper Temenos, East 'Cistern'.

Room A is noted as a group, and there are also sizeable quantities of other objects—614 bones, 958 stones, and 795 stucco/plaster fragments.

Room A consists of a single room with internal measurements of 7.75 m N-S x 1.53 m E-W x 4.35 m depth. Its interior is embellished with two very high, finely crafted arched niches on the east and north walls. On the south side of the room, rock-cut stairs lead up to the Tabun Room above the Great Cistern and the two rooms serve as part of the same installation. The stratigraphy spans from Site Phases V and VI through to Site Phase IX.

Dating to Site Phase V, a hearth is built into the north niche, a water basin in the east niche, and a *tabun* (oven) into the southwest corner. Associated with the hearth is a deposit of numerous cooking pots found directly on top of the bedrock floor suggesting that cooking activity in this room is probably public. The excavator theorizes that with Room A's access to the *Tabun* Room above, Room A is used for holding Nabataean ritual feasts, while the *Tabun* Room is used for their preparation and cooking.

6. *Upper Temenos Trench 83* embraces the South Passageway behind the Great Temple and is located between the South Corridor Wall and the South Perimeter Wall and its bedrock escarpment. The trench measures 6.45 m N-S length in the E and 12.21 m length in the W, and is 31.20 m E-W. The average depth of deposit is 5.3m. The artifact collection numbers 11,560 objects, or nearly 3% of the total Great Temple materials. There are 1371 pieces of bone, and 8540 pottery fragments, the majority of which are collapsed roof tiles that cascaded down from the temple South Corridor into the South Passageway.

7. *Upper Temenos Special Project 84 (SP84)* is also known as the "Tabun Cave"[25] Room.[26] Located above the Great Cistern, this is an open cave where 10,866 or 2.70% of materials are collected. Measuring 6 m N-S x 5.6 m E-W, this room has a plaster-coated rock-cut basin serving as its main focus in its earliest stage of use. After the basin no longer serviced the occupants, an oven was built. During the room's later use a large amount of pottery was used for leveling the floor. We are unsure

25 The room derives its name from the oven (tabun in Arabic), as the Tabun Room or the *Tabun* Cave Room.

26 The *Tabun* Room also is connected to Trench 84 Room A of the East Perimeter Wall via interconnecting rock-cut steps.

App. 3. Fig.4. Upper Temenos, Tabun Room. .

of the origin of these wares but assume they are part of the room's accumulated dump. Thereafter the room is abandoned and more fill accumulates, completely obscuring the cave, the wall, and the Great Cistern lying below. The *Tabun* room is filled with 9668 ceramic fragments. Bone (or 982 bone fragments) is common as well, and 70 glass fragments are recovered, one of which dramatically depicts a human figure.[27]

8. In *Trench 77 of the Upper Temenos East Plaza,* 10,775 artifacts are collected representing 2.7% of the total materials collected. Measuring 18.4 m N-S x 5.2 m E-W is a large swath extending from the East Walkway Wall to the East Perimeter Wall, and from the north of the East Perimeter Wall to the South Perimeter Wall. It is little wonder that it contained such a wealth of material; the upper levels held erosional wash from the Ez Zantur excavations on the hill just south of the Great Temple.

9. Trench 105-106—Roman-Byzantine Bath Complex is located in the Upper Temenos to the west of the West Precinct Wall. We have to remember that the Bath Complex was constructed some time after Site Phase VI, after the Roman annexation of Petra, and most of the material evidence must belong to later phases. It is not obvious how the baths functioned within the fabric of the Great Temple complex, but it must have played an important role within the temple setting.

The baths excavation team collects 10,074 artifacts, which represent 2.5% of the 405,297 total. Measuring 18 m N-S x 12 m E-W, this trench produces an interesting repertoire, distinguished by its function as a small bath complex. This corpus amounts to 8063 of pottery, 239 of stone, 115 of metal, and 1181 glass fragments—the highest occurrence of glass, a modest 0.3% at the Petra Great Temple. This is not unexpected for in these Late Roman and Byzantine periods glass was a celebrated commodity. There are also 73 plaster fragments, 51 shells, and 348 bone finds. This deposit is considered to be very important, for not only is the architecture exceptional, but also the amounts of marble opus sectile, used for the flooring. The Special Finds include dateable inscriptions,[28] such as beads and lamps.[29]

Appendix 3, Table 6 presents a listing of total material by trench. There is fairly even distribution of materials by trench with nine exceptions, which are highlighted. The majority of these deposits are from the Upper Temenos, as would be expected.

---

27 *Vol. 2,* fig.7.48.
28 Ibid. fig. 4.106.
29 Ibid. fig. 4.104.

APPENDIX 3. Table 6.
GREAT TEMPLE TOTAL MATERIAL BY TRENCH*

Trench	*Bone*	*Glass*	*Metal*	*Pottery*	*Shell*	*Stone*	*Stucco*	*Veg*	*Msc.*	***TOTAL***	%
1	151	–	–	5632	–	278	75	–	–	6136	**1.50**
2	21	–	26	914	4	122	484	–	–	1571	**0.40**
3	1	–	12	275	–	10	71	–	–	369	**0.10**
4	–	–	–	32	–	23	21	–	–	76	–
5	231	–	22	6868	23	354	480	–	–	7978	**2**
6	30	–	–	512	–	22	1	–	–	565	**0.10**
7	423	–	–	4851	3	2	222	–	–	5501	**1.40**
8	–	–	1	16	24	1	1	–	43	–	
9	5	–	–	1053	6	153	175	–	18	1410	**0.30**
10	9	–	7	172	1	–	26	–	–	250	**0.10**
11	1	–	2	85	1	–	9	2	–	100	–
12	–	–	–	87	–	–	97	–	–	184	–
13	–	–	–	154	–	–	–	–	–	154	–
14	4	–	–	93	1	–	–	–	–	98	–
15	–	–	–	633	37	32	–	–	702	0.20	
16	608	–	46	10,604	74	474	220	117	–	12,143	**3%**
17	388	–	14	2856	3	25	290	–	–	3576	**0.90**
18	320	–	8	3294	11	7	30	–	–	3670	**0.90**
18A	43	–	13	1560	11	32	8	–	–	1667	**0.40**
19	–	–	1	733	–	–	–	–	–	734	**0.20**
20	404	–	3	5686	30	167	207	–	–	6497	**1.60**
21	1	–	–	949	2	7	–	–	–	959	**0.20**
22	297	–	160	3344	1	380	263	–	–	4445	**1.10**
23	178	–	23	1194	2	366	46	–	–	1809	**0.40**
24	69	–	29	718	–	1044	264	–	–	2124	**0.50**
25	–	–	–	301	1	–	–	–	–	302	**0.10**
26	29	–	12	632	–	28	48	–	–	749	**0.20**
27	8	–	2	172	–	19	10	–	–	211	**0.10**
28	28	–	–	501	2	–	2	–	–	533	**0.10**
29	240	–	70	537	–	535	580	–	–	1962	**0.50**
30	8	–	–	105	–	9	20	–	–	142	–

APPENDIX 3. Table 6. (continued)
GREAT TEMPLE TOTAL MATERIAL BY TRENCH*

Trench	*Bone*	*Glass*	*Metal*	*Pottery*	*Shell*	*Stone*	*Stucco*	*Veg*	*Msc.*	***TOTAL***	*%*
31	64	–	8	2211	2	33	431	–	–	2749	**0.70**
32	28	–	6	1492	1	1	4	–	–	1532	**0.40**
33	–	–	–	120	–	7	–	–	–	127	**–**
34	167	–	168	230	–	462	164	44	–	1235	**0.30**
35	64	–	46	422	3	135	186	1	–	857	**0.20**
36	46	–	3	402	3	6	–	–	–	460	**0.10**
37	58	–	1	2275	4	89	23	–	–	2450	**0.60**
38	–	–	–	170	–	96	–	–	–	266	**0.10**
39	5	–	1	120	–	1	55	–	–	182	**–**
40	203	–	117	2181	1	42	407	–	–	2951	**0.70**
41	824	–	30	4029	22	673	268	–	–	5846	**1.40**
42	243	–	19	2151	4	75	590	–	–	3082	**0.80**
43	–	–	10	615	1	19	1	–	–	646	**0.20**
44	439	–	7	3681	214	648	101	–	–	5090	**1.30**
45	393	–	93	581	2	58	398	–	–	1525	**0.40**
46	73	–	8	1133	4	125	16	–	–	1359	**0.30**
47	222	–	112	491	3	13	159	–	–	1000	**0.20**
48	125	–	6	431	2	11	64	–	–	639	**0.20**
49	391	–	35	2512	29	427	36	–	–	3430	**0.80**
50	17	–	6	195	–	380	6	–	–	604	**0.10**
51	151	15	50	1051	3	258	240	–	–	1768	**0.40**
52	1161	120	218	6960	59	612	825	–	–	9955	**2.50**
53	950	103	237	5883	245	507	4035	–	–	11,960	**3**
54	54	2	1	521	12	7	7	–	–	604	**0.10**
55	10	5	12	189	6	11	48	7	–	288	**0.10**
55A	123	41	43	2204	7	60	25	–	1	2504	**0.60**
56	163	3	59	345	1	22	596	6	1	1196	**0.30**
57	378	21	69	3315	43	616	169	2	–	4613	**1.10**
58	–	–	4	27	1	–	307	–	–	339	**0.10**
59	28	10	145	218	43	21	238	–	–	703	**0.20**
60	5	8	–	185	4	23	38	–	–	263	**0.10**

APPENDIX 3. Table 6. (continued)
GREAT TEMPLE TOTAL MATERIAL BY TRENCH*

Trench	*Bone*	*Glass*	*Metal*	*Pottery*	*Shell*	*Stone*	*Stucco*	*Veg*	*Msc.*	*TOTAL*	*%*
61	40	36	5	728	2	31	41	–	–	883	**0.20**
62	365	21	78	3238	15	40	517	–	–	4278	**1.10**
63	131	25	25	543	12	42	38	–	–	816	**0.30**
64	91	8	7	901	2	24	116	–	–	1149	**0.30**
65	695	64	150	4085	3	356	427	17	–	5797	**1.40**
66	2	–	–	154	–	–	83	–	–	239	**0.10**
67	96	10	1	1803	3	55	13	–	–	1981	**0.50**
68	68	23	13	2874	1	7	6	–			
69	257	15	63	3413	2	1680	280	8	–	5718	**1.40**
70	13	4	11	245	–	12	76	–	–	361	**0.10**
71	210	82	6	3120	11	117	1060	–	–	4606	**1.10**
72	14	5	–	90	–	16	–	–	–	125	**–**
73	777	54	7	13147	12	302	392	–	–	14,691	**3.60**
75	96	3	–	905	7	50	14	–	–	1075	**0.30**
76	421	48	52	7098	35	480	493	–	–	8627	**2.10**
77	375	116	21	9719	30	467	46	–	1	10,775	**2.70**
79	371	123	50	2958	7	145	204	20	–	3878	**1**
80	132	5	66	2309	5	362	897	1	–	3777	**0.90**
81	37	2	16	330	–	76	78	–	–	539	**0.10**
82	7	8	1	781	9	296	106	–	–	1208	**0.30**
83	1371	91	19	8540	27	1197	293	9	13	11,560	**2.90**
84	614	73	54	10,558	13	333	210	–	1	11,856	**2.90**
85	89	7	192	3046	2	958	795	57	–	5146	**1.30**
86	122	1	21	293	1	1	17	–	–	456	**0.10**
87	117	27	51	1733	10	36	487	1	–	2462	**0.60**
88	12	–	1	131	1	8	59	–	–	212	**0.10**
89	365	37	61	3888	21	16	874	–	–	5262	**1.30**
90	354	21	2	3551	8	569	260	5	–	4770	**1.20**
91	78	7	2	1445	4	–	10	–	–	1546	**0.40**
92	25	19	5	294	1	–	1	–	–	345	**0.10**
93	14	2	7	156	4	1	35	–	–	219	**0.10**

APPENDIX 3. Table 6. (continued)
GREAT TEMPLE TOTAL MATERIAL BY TRENCH*

Trench	*Bone*	*Glass*	*Metal*	*Pottery*	*Shell*	*Stone*	*Stucco*	*Veg*	*Msc.*	*TOTAL*	*%*
94	864	143	90	32,349	161	18	40	–	3	33,668	**8.30**
95	8	10	37	258	6	–	58	16	–	393	**0.10**
96	3	3	3	573	2	3	27	–	–	614	**0.20**
97	596	65	702	4269	21	91	724	21	–	6489	
98	625	113	80	3538	31	1015	340	7	–	5749	**1.40**
98B	180	13	7	1538	6	926	278	–	–	2948	**0.70**
99	237	65	44	2905	11	24	274	–	–	3560	**0.90**
100	316	6	13	400	9	55	65	251	–	1115	**0.30**
101	58	5	–	569	2	2	1	–	–	637	**0.20**
102-103	25	17	7	650	4	24	218	–	–	945	**0.20**
104	6	2	1	172	5	–	4	–	–	190	**–**
105-106	348	1181	115	8063	51	239	73	4	–	10,074	**2.50-**
120	663	552	38	3586	31	2 6	2	20	–	4954	**1.20**
12071	–	–	–	–	7	–	–	–		7	**–**
121	–	1	–	63-	–	–	–	–	–	64	**–**
122	19	58	2	1093	5	4	70	–	–	1251	**0.30**
123	57	3	8	347	11	4	26	1		457	**0.10**
125	73	265	12	2101	1	12	17	–	–	2481	**0.60**
126	390	168	70	3832	6	3	656	16	–	5141	**1.30**
127	159	403	23	3583	9	1	47	3	–	4228	**1**
SP	–	–	–	8	–	–	–	–	–	8	
SP	7	–	–	54	–	1	–	–	–	63	**–**
SP	2	–	–	38	–	–	–	–	–	40	**–**
SP	–	–	–	–	–	–	16	–	–	16	**–**
SP1	–	–	–	17	1	7	–	–	–	25	**–**
SP2	–	–	–	71	–	–	62	–	–	135	**–**
SP3	–	–	–	6	–	–	–	–	–	6	
SP4	21	–	4	2385	–	12	103	–	–	2525	**0.60**
SP9	–	–	–	6	–	–	27	–	–	33	**–**
SP10	–	–	3	–	–	–	6	–	–	9	**–**
SP15	–	–	–	–	–	–	31	–	–	31	**–**

APPENDIX 3. Table 6. (continued)
GREAT TEMPLE TOTAL MATERIAL BY TRENCH*

Trench	*Bone*	*Glass*	*Metal*	*Pottery*	*Shell*	*Stone*	*Stucco*	*Veg*	*Msc.*	*TOTAL*	*%*
SP20	38	–	–	516	1	–	–	–		555	**0.10**
SP22	–	–	–	64		–	–	–	–	64	–
SP23	–	–	–	463	–	–	290	–	–	753	**0.20**
SP24	23	–	1	728	–	5	9	–	–	766	**0.20**
SP25	147	–	13	1079	–	11	707	–	–	1957	**0.50**
SP26	90	–	–	299	1	2	–	–	–	392	**0.10**
SP29	–	–	–	101	–	8	–	–	–	109	–
SP30	88		–	2790	–	28	134	–	–	3040	**0.80**
SP31	–	–	–	71	1	22	–	–	–	94	–
SP38	1	–	1	236	–	2	–	–	–	240	**0.10**
SP39	2	–	–	141	–	–	–	–	–	143	–
SP40	–	–	–	16	–	–	–	–	–	16	–
SP41	21	–	–	715	–	22	20	–	–	778	**0.20**
SP42	3	–	–	134	–	1	5	–	–	143	–
SP43	57	–	–	22	1	–	–	–	–	80	–
SP44	–	–	–	–	–	1				1	–
SP45	–	–	–	22	1	–	–	–	–	22	–
SP45a	–	–	–	484	–	9	–	–	–	493	**0.10**
SP47	–	–	–	110	–	–	2	–	–	112	–
SP48	–	–	–	63	–	2	4	–	–	69	–
SP53	4	–	2	104	2	108	60	–	–	280	**0.10**
SP56	4	–	–	191	–	4	1	–	–	200	–
SP57	–	–	–	5	–	–	–	–	–	5	–
SP70	95	7	9	667	2	23	173	–	–	976	**0.20**
SP71	1	–	–	255	–	43	3	–	–	302	**0.10**
SP72	32	16	13	794	3	7	86	–	–	951	**0.20**
SP73	2	6	42	–	–	–	8	–	–	58	–
SP83	4	1	–	2	–	–	–	–	–	7	–
SP84	982	70	18	9668	11	96	17	4	–	10,866	**2.70**
SP85	434	15	13	5894	8	341	265	60	–	7030	**1.70**
SP87	66	–	118	249	1	4	7	5	–	450	**0.10**

APPENDIX 3. Table 6. (continued)
GREAT TEMPLE TOTAL MATERIAL BY TRENCH*

Trench	*Bone*	*Glass*	*Metal*	*Pottery*	*Shell*	*Stone*	*Stucco*	*Veg*	*Msc.*	*TOTAL*	*%*
SP88	60	2	1	659	–	–	–	–	–	722	**0.20**
SP89	66	?	1	8	–	1	42	12	–	132	–
SP91	–	–	–	21	–	–	–	–	–	21	–
SP92	5	2	1	180	5	–	5	–	–	198	–
SP93	122	–	–	338	2	–	–	–	–	462	**0.10**
SP94	142	7	14	1379	1	1	–	–	–	1544	**0.40**
SP95	1	–	1	55	–	–	–	–	–	57	–
SP96	35	11	2	758	1	18	67	1	–	893	**0.20**
SP104	684	5	240	2543	3	1	51	10	–	3537	**0.90**
SP105	66	1	18	591	1	1	3	1	–	682	**0.20**
SP107	811	1	16	1031	4	–	41	3	–	1907	**0.50**
SP108	249	27	29	3168	15	37	51	1	–	3577	**0.90**
SP109	12	–	3	67	–	69	6	–	–	157	–
P110	1160	139	42	11,243	53	211	57	–	–	12,905	**3.20**
SP111	52	–	–	99	1	–	26	3	–	181	–
SP114	10	–	–	22	–	–	1	–	–	33	–
SP118	6	–	7	83	–	1	–	–		97	–
SP120	–	–	8	–	–	–	–	–	–	8	–
SP123	3	–	1	7	–	–	19	–	–	30	–
SP124	8	–	2	80	1	–	184	–	–	275	**0.10**
SP125	20	14	7	407	4	18	3	3	–	476	**0.10**
SP150	110	–	7	947	3	3	140	–	–	1210	**0.30**
SP200	18	–	–	57	–	1	21	–	–	96	–
SPA4	–	–	–	1	1	–	3	–	–	5	–
SPC5	–	–	–	47	1	–	–	–	–	47	–
SPD1	–	–	–	–	–	3	20	–	–	23	–
SPGB	26	7	–	2673	3	34	96	–	–	2839	**0.70**
SPP	–	–	–	83	–	2	–	–	–	85	–
SPW	–	1	–	27	–	–	–	–	–	28	–
XXX	–	–	–	25	–	4	1	–	–	30	–

* The 7 highlighted trenches account for 27%of all the materials collected. Trench 94 of the Upper Temenos has the most significant repertoire representing more than 8% of the total artifacts registered in the Grosso Modo database.

Concluding Remarks

In the beginning of our excavations we addressed the range of artifacts we were recovering as we excavated. We constructed a basic classification system to better understand and chart their recovery. What we have attempted to do is to use discrete attributes of the Great Temple materials recovered and to have a look at the presence and frequency of materials within temple areas and within different site phases and different trenches. And it is clear that we have been able to infer some of the functional and social aspects of the Great Temple areas through calculated frequency distributions and the overall results of the associative factors that have been presented.

Using the Petra Great Temple Databases

The Petra Great Temple Excavation has a number of databases with which the material culture of the site is organized and understood. The information in each database is gleaned from the forms filled out by the trench supervisors in the field, and is usually entered into the site computers during the field season. The **Grosso Modo** database (originally in FileMakerPro) houses all the recorded information on the vast majority of material culture of the Petra Great Temple; pottery, glass, stucco, bone, shell, metal, and worked stone. The **Architectural Fragments** (also originally in FileMakerPro) database is for the recording of each architectural element recovered in the trenches, including ashlars, floor pavers, arch elements, column drums, and capital fragments. The **Catalogue** (originally in FileMakerPro) is reserved for the Special Finds, those artifacts that are particularly informative, and worthy of a more detailed description. Such artifacts regularly include complete vessels, coins, beads, and other particularly interesting artifacts. In the earlier years of the excavation, all elephant capital fragments were included in this database, as were many lamp fragments, and while such finds are no longer entered into the Catalogue, but reported on in separate databases, these earlier records are left as they were originally recorded.

The Grosso Modo Database[30]

While each artifact in the Architectural Fragments database and the Catalogue is recorded individually and given a unique FileMaker Pro page, in Grosso Modo each page is given to an entire bucket. Every artifact type in each locus is given a bucket for each day (e.g. pottery in Locus 5 would have one bucket, while the pottery in Locus 6 would have another, and Locus 5 pottery on the next day would have yet another bucket). Each bucket is given an artifact number: **P-1, G-3, M-7, SH-15,** etc., and there is a database page for each of those buckets.

In addition to the date excavated that is present in every database, the Grosso Modo database also shows the date that it was processed, as this would frequently happen back at the dig house in the days following the original excavation.

The main part of each Grosso Modo page is made up of the chart showing the particular information about each individual artifact within the bucket. Each artifact is given a row, and the various columns pertain to various features of the artifact. If a number of artifacts are identical, they are listed together in the same row. The columns of the chart will now be generally described, and the key to the codes used in these fields is presented.

Quantity: This column records the number of artifacts that are described together. This is usually one, but if a number of artifacts are "identical," they will be listed together, and the quantity will reflect that.

Material: This column describes the type of artifact being recorded. The codes are as follows: Vegetal Matter: **Veg**; Bone: **B**; Faience: **F**; Glass/Glass Slag: **G**; Stone: **S**; Metal: **M**; Pottery: **P**; Shell: **SH**; Stucco/Plaster: **ST**.

---

30 While these codes were published in *vol. 1,* p. 237 ff., they have been revised over the years, and the final categories are reported here.

Part: This column records the part of the full vessel or object is represented in each individual artifact, such as base, rim, body sherd, or architectural fragment. The codes are as follows:

Architectural Fragment: **AF**; Base: **B**; Bead: **BD**; Body Sherd: **BS**; Handle/Base: **CHB**; Handle/Neck: **CHN**; Handle/Neck/Rim: **CHNR**; Handle/Rim: **CHR**; Rim/Base: **CRB**; Rim/Neck: **CRN**; Spout/Base: **CSB**; Other composite: **CD**; Construction Material: **CM**; Discus (lamps): **D**; Handle: **H**; Lid: **L**; Neck: **N**; Rim: **R**; Spout: **S**; Indeterminate: **IND**; Other: **O**; Unknown: **UN**.

Function: This column records the reasoned function for which the artifact was used, such as bowl, unguentarium, or wall decoration. The codes are as follows:

Amphora: **A**; Amphoriskos: **AS**; Bowl: **B**; Canalization Tile: **CT**; Cooking Pot: **CP**; Decorative: D; Figurine: **F**; Floor Tile: **FT**; Glass Slag: **GS**; Hypocaust Tile: **HT**; Jar: **JR**; Jar/Jug: **JJ**; Jug: **JG**; Kiln Waster: **KW**; Lachrymatory: **LY**; Lamp: **L**; Lid: **LD**; Large Store Vessel: **LS**; Loom Weight: **LW**; Mosaic: **M**; Nail: **N**; Pipe: **PP**; Pithos: **P**; Plate: **PLT**; Roof Tile: **RT**; Small Form: **SF**; Spindle Whorl: **SW**; Stopper: **SR**; Tessera(ae): **T**; Unguentarium: **U**; Wall Tile: **WT**; Indeterminate: **IND**; Other: **O**; Unknown: **UN**.

For Stucco/Plaster

Architectural Decoration (for moldings): **AD**; Column Decoration: **CD**; Wall Decoration (for wall plaster):**WD**.

Shape: This column describes the shape of the artifact, and is particularly important for pottery. The codes are applicable to rims, bases and handles and are as follows:

Acanthus Leaf: **AL**; Button: **B**; Disc: **D**; Double-Stranded: **DS**; Everted: **E**; Flaring: **FG**; Flat: **F**; Floral: **FL**; Fluted: **FD**; Horizontal: **H**; Incurving: **IG**; Inverted: **ID**; Lug: **LG**; Ogee/pedestal: **OP**; Ovoid: **OV**; Pendant: **PT**; Plain Vertical: **PV**; Pointed: **PD**; Raised Banded: **RB**; Ring: **RG**; Rounded: **RD;** Squared-Off: **SO**; String-cut: **SC**; T-Shaped: **TS**; Trefoil: **T**; Triangle: **TE**; Tubular: **TR**; Twisted: **TW**; Umbilical: **U**.

For Stucco/Plaster

Identification: Abacus: **AB**; Boss: **BO**; Dentil: **DL**; Egg & Dart: **ED**; Egg and tongue: **ET**; Egg: **EG**; Dart: **DT**; Tongue: **T**; Flat: **F**; Floral: **FL**; Leaf: **LF**; Ribbed/cable fluted (for column plaster): **RI**; Other String Course: **OS**; Vine: **VI**; Volute: **VO**.

Liquid Color: This column describes the color of the artifact. The codes are as follows: Black: **BK**; Blue: **BE**; Brown: **BN**; Brownish-Black: **BB**; Cream: **C**; Glazed: **GL**; Gray: **GY**; Green: **GN**; Multi-colored: **M**; Off-White: **OW**; Pompeian Red: **PR**; Purple: **P**; Purplish-Black: **PB**; Red: **R**; Red-Brown: **RB**; Salmon: **S**; Self-Same: **SS**; Tan: **TN**; Terra Sigillata Black: **TSB**; Terra Sigillata Red: **TSR**; Turquoise: **T**; White: **W**; Yellow: **Y**.

Paint Color: This column describes the paint color on the artifact, if any is present. The codes are the same as those for liquid colors.

Motif: This column describes the motif of any notable decoration of the artifact, which pertains primarily to paint designs on pottery. This factor is annotated on the sheet and includes circles, crosshatching, dots, drips, floral elements, birds, leaves, splash, wavy lines and zigzags.

Plastic Decoration: This column records the artifact's plastic decoration, again mostly used in pottery pieces, such as appliqué or molding. The codes are as follows:

Appliqué: A; Excision: **E**; Impression: **IM**; Incision: **IN**; Molded: **MD**; Perforation: **P**; Ribbing: **RG**; Rouletting: **R**.

Culture: This column describes the culture to which the artifact can be attributed. It is frequently not entered, as it is preferred to leave the task to the excavation's experts, who will study special artifacts in more detail. The codes are as follows: Byzantine: **B**; Byzantine/Islamic: **B/I**; Classical: **CL**; Contemporary: **CY** or **M**; Crusader: **CR**; Edomite: **E**; Hellenistic: **H**; Islamic: **I**; Nabataean: **N**; Roman: **R**; Roman/Byzantine: **R/B**; Roman/Nabataean: **R/N**; Indeterminate: **IND**; Other: **O**; Unknown: **UN**.

APPENDIX 4

GREAT TEMPLE POTTERY

Martha Sharp Joukowsky

Introduction

Nabataean pottery is unique. It is what archaeologists refer to as a "horizon-marker" or an "index fossil," because it is different from any other wares produced at this time. Origins of Nabataean pottery are obscure, but it makes its earliest appearance at Petra during the reign of Aretas II, or between 100 and 92 B.C., and appears to continue in favor at the Great Temple until the earthquake of A.D. 551. Not only has it been found in prodigious numbers at Petra[1] and other known Nabataean sites in Jordan like Khirbet et Tannur,[2] and the settlement of Khirbet edh Dharih,[3] Nabataean remains further north include Gerasa (Jerash)[4], Umm el-Jimal,[5] and other sites found along the trade routes from Damascus to Bostra.[6] South of Petra is the site of Humayma,[7] which is a well-researched site along the trade route. Nabataean painted wares are also found in large quantities in Saudi Arabia,[8] the Sinai[9] and the Negev[10] at sites like Oboda ('Avdat),[11] Sobota (Shivta);[12] Mampsis,[13] Nessana,[14] and Elusa. Further afield into the Sinai, Nabataean pottery has also been found in Oman, Qana on the South Arabian coast and

App. 4. Fig. 1.
Nabataean Painted Bowl. Cat. No 01-P-35, Trench 84, Locus 22, Rdiam. 22, Ht. 4.5, of 2.5YR5/8 red ware, painted interior 2.5YR4/6 red. Wheel burnishing on exterior below inverted rim, with very pale brown 10YR8/2 paint on rim. Motifs include parallel lines in all directions, palm leaves, circles and rounded triangles, painted base.

---

1 Particularly at Ez Zantur (Bignasca 1993, Bignasca *et al.*1996; Schmid 1995a, 1996b, 2003); the sounding on the Petra Colonnaded Street (Parr 1970, 348-381); and the North Ridge Tombs 1 and 2, Bikai and Perry 2001, 59-78; and further afield at Beidha, (Bikai, Kanellopoulos and Saunders) 2008, 465-507.

2 The Jordanian Department of Antiquities and N. Glueck undertook excavations in 1937. For a reinterpretation and re-publication of the site and its architecture, see McKenzie 2001, 96-112; McKenzie, Reyes, and Gibson 2002, 44-83; 2003,165-191; and also see online document: http://www.ocla.ox.ac.uk/pdf/khirbet_tannur.pdf.

3 al-Muheisen and Villeneuve, 2001, 139-141; 2000, 1525-1563; 1999, 43-46; 1994, 735-757; 1993, 486-489; 1992, 356-359; 1988, 458-479; Villeneuve 1990, 367-384; Villeneuve and al-Muheisen 2003, 83-100.

4 Vincent 1940, 120-129.

5 Parker 1998, 149-152.

6 Near Madaba in central Jordan is the settlement of Khirbat al-Mudayna where Nabataean-Early Roman remains of a housing complex and a reservoir have been excavated. See Daviau, Mulder-Hymans and Foley 2000, 271-282.

7 Nabataean *Hawara* or *Auara*, see Oleson and Eadie 1986, 49-76; Oleson 2010, 51.

8 L. Nehmé, Th. Arnoux, J-C. Bessac, et. al. 2006.

9 Bestock 1999, 241-248 has written specifically on the Great Temple East 'Cistern' collection.

10 Erickson-Gini and Israel 2003, 9-14.

11 Negev 1974; Negev 1970, 48-51; 1974b; 1986; Negev and Gibson 2001a, 371-375.

12 Negev and Gibson 2001d, 474-475.

13 Negev 1988a; 1988b; Negev and Gibson 2001d, 310-312, Negev and Siwan 1977.

14 Negev and Gibson 2001b, 367-368.

from Yemen to the Persian Gulf. Nabataean pottery also has been located in Mediterranean and Aegean port sites.

Ceramic Specialist Studies

Numerous pottery studies of Petraean Nabataean wares have been undertaken by Khariah 'Amr[15], Avi-Yonah and Negev[16]; Bikai, Kanellopoulos and Saunders[17], Bikai and Perry[18], Hammond [19], Iliffe[20], Khairy[21], Parr[22], Schmid[23], and Gerber[24]. Figurines have also undergone study by Parlasca[25], El-Khouri[26], and Tuttle[27].

Nabataean pottery kilns have been found just outside central Petra at the Zurrabah kilns, excavated by 'Amr[28], who published the neutron activation (INAA) results[29] as has Barrett[30]; and Bedal[31] has published the Great Temple INAA results. Bestock[32] has written specifically on the Great Temple East 'Cistern' collection.

A single pottery fragment consists of an indefinite number of attributes that constantly recurs. Primary factors in the construction of the Great Temple pottery typology were defined by multiple characteristics of fabric, shape and surface finish, decoration, and function. For rims and bases it was presumed function, preserved profile, stance and decoration that differentiated one from another. Classes were based on function, a most important level of abstraction, and function provided consistent parameters for organizing an extensive collection, such as the Great Temple's. An additional and most important level of abstraction was the attributes of shape and decorative features. These were primary factors in the construction of the Great Temple typology—in large, the corpus was represented only by fragments of complete pots. For rims and bases it was their profile, stance and function that differentiated one from another. Initial assessments were made during the 1993 excavation fragments were labeled and drawn, with copies stored in each field supervisor's field notebook. When a new shape or decorative motif appeared with a significant frequency, additions to the typology were made.[33] Pottery classes—bowls, jugs, storage jars and

15 'Amr, 1986, 319-328, 1987.
16 Avi-Yonah and Negev, 1974, 944-947.
17 Bikai, Kanellopoulos and Saunders, 2005a, 339-344.
18 Bikai and Perry, 2001, 59-78.
19 Hammond 1973b, 27-49.
20 Iliffe, 1934, 132-135.
21 Khairy, 1975.
22 Parr, 1970, 348-381.
23 Schmid, 1995a, 637-647; 1995b; 1996b, 151-218, 1997a, 413-420.
24 Gerber, 1995, 1997, online; 2001a, 359-366.
25 Parlasca, 1986a, 200-213; 1986b, 192-199; 1990, 87-92; 1993, 60-63.
26 El-Khouri, 2002.
27 Tuttle, 2009.
28 'Amr 1991, 313-323.
29 'Amr, 1986, 319-328 and 1987.
30 Barrett 2008.
31 Bedal, Great Temple Vol. I, 345–367; this includes the Great Temple INAA results.
32 Bestock, 1999, 241-248.
33 In 2009-2010, Saunders re-appraised the typology, drew and described the components and re-ordered it. The majority of the pottery drawings were drafted by Emily C. Egan and in lesser numbers by this author, who digitized them and mounted the figures, and edited the descriptions for *Open Context*. The purpose of publishing the pottery online was to make available as early as possible the Great Temple ceramic repertoire. Shari L. Sanders initiated a comprehensive Great Temple ceramic study in 2001. She measured and drew, described, and ordered the approximate 350 fragments presented in *Open Context* in 56 figs. Recognizing the need for database analysis, statistical data can now be presented along with a site phase discussion. When completed the illustrations and their descriptions were arranged for online viewing by the *Open Context* staff. A few ceramic parallels have been cited in the *Open Context*

cooking pots—were then created to define those types that could be classified together on the basis of assumed function.[34] In the beginning the Great Temple corpus was represented only by fragments of complete vessels, but with the additional recovery of many complete forms from four special pottery collections, the type series was enlarged and the shape corpus supplemented with a greater range of forms.[35]

Great Temple wares and types—selection of data

Excavated by Fawzi Zayadine[36] in the nineteen eighties is a pottery workshop at Zurrabah which was thought to be the primary pottery production center for Petra. This excavation was followed by further excavation undertaken by Khairieh 'Amr[37] who discovered two additional pottery kilns.[38] Subsequently 'Amr and James Mason undertook studies of Nabataean pottery manufacturing techniques and experiments for the replication of fine ware bowls published in 1990.[39] 'Amr went further to perform compositional analysis, instrumental neutron activation analysis (INAA), which she subsequently published.[40]

App. 4. Fig. 2.
Nabataean goblet with stamped leaf impressions, Cat. No. 01-P-28. Seq. No. 84187. Trench 84, Locus 22. Ht. 10 cm, rdiam. 10.7 cm, dated from A.D. 30 to 100. Impressed designs of palm leaves, dotted triangles, and horizontal linear incisions on the base and just below the flaring rim with a rounded lip; with a flat base with incised concentric circles.

Also in the 1980s, additional composition analysis to determine the cluster analysis of 32 elements of 149 Great Temple pottery samples[41] was undertaken by L-A. Bedal[42]at the facilities of the Missouri University Research Reactor (MURR).[43] S. G. Schmid had chronologically ordered these fragments into seven phases,[44] and the cluster signatures of Nabataean wares[45] determined that their trace elements fell into two main ware groups both of which were produced in the Petra area. More importantly however, there

descriptions, but no attempt has been made here to list possible occurrences of forms at other sites.

34 Not all the shapes produced by Nabataean potters are included here. Nevertheless the pottery types from the Great Temple provide a framework for discussions regarding the definition of Great Temple pottery in particular and Nabataean pottery in general.

35 Early special collections included Lower Temenos Trench 20 (*Great Temple* Vol. I fig. 6.13), Trench 25 (Ibid. fig. 6.15), and Trench 42 (Ibid. figs. 6.15-6.16).

36 Zayadine 1981, 350-351, 1982, 380-383; 1986, 185-189.

37 'Amr 1991, 313-323.

38 Ibid. 1999,175-194.

39 Mason and 'Amr 1990, 287-307.

40 'Amr 1986, 319-328; 1987. Also see 'Amr, Akasheh and Na'es online.

41 The majority of these samples were taken from Trench 7, the Lapidary West, located 44 m W of the Temple. A few lamps of Nabataean, Roman (*Great Temple* Vol. 1, Fig. 7.5), and Byzantine dates, were also tested. The Roman lamps were discovered to be imports from coastal Palestine.

42 *Great Temple* Vol.1, Ch. 7, 345-367.

43 This is a method whereby samples are ground down to 200 mg and placed into small vials to be irradiated in a nuclear reactor This provides a means of identifying minute trace elements in parts per million so that ware "fingerprints" can be compared to the trace elements found in known proveniences. In these tests 32 elements were tracked.

44 This report is on file at Brown University.

45 Originally identified by K. 'Amr 1987, 198; 'Amr, NABPF sub-groups XVa and XVb. Also see 'Amr's Group V, Table 4.15, distinguishing subdivisions, ESA a-c.

was a change in clay sources in the Petra valley sometime in the early A.D. 1st century (between 9 B.C. and A.D. 40), and this change was reflected in a complete shift to a new geological clay stratum in ceramic production; not only at the Great Temple and Petra, but also at the site of 'Avdat/Oboda[46] in the Negev that imported pottery from Petra.[47] The results of the INAA analyses indicated that there were the two local ware groups used at the Great Temple; earlier P/ST A (23 fragments)[48], and then the shift to a newer later source P/ST B (109 fragments),[49] which continued to be used until the A.D. 4th c. There was also a group of Outliers P/ST C (17 fragments)[50] having compositional origins in coastal and hill regions of Palestine, in Syria and Cyprus, and other as yet unknown sources. Although the tests failed to identify the fingerprints of the majority of P/ST C samples, should they be obtained, the results will indicate the extent of the Petra Great Temple's sphere of regional interaction.[51] What is characteristic of Petra fabrics is their brilliant ware color, which is due to the iron in the clay as well as their even firing temperatures and complete oxidation in the kiln.

In the Field at the Great Temple

In the Great Temple pottery database, the intention was to capture a broad cross section of material within the time framework of the field operations. We knew we would not find enough time to compare rim shapes according to a specific type series. We did, however, classify basic shapes and function. All diagnostics[52] were double bagged and tagged, and saved for future study and can be found in the Great Temple on-site storage areas.[53] As the excavation progressed restored vessels of museum quality were catalogued, drawn and described, and disposed with the Jordanian Department of Antiquities at the Petra Museum.

---

46 Negev 1974; Slane, Elam, Glascock and Neff 1994, 51-64.

47 Gunneweg *et al.* 1991, 342, identified as NAB-I and NAB-II.

48 Illustrated in *Great Temple* Vol. I, fig. 7.12, 1-18.

49 Ibid. figs. 7.13-7.15.

50 Ibid. Outliers are illustrated in fig. 7.12, 20-27.

51 Additional analyses at the MURR facilities were undertaken on the Petra lamp database by D. G. Barrett (2005, 303-312) in 2001 with 35% of the collection of Roman lamps from the Great Temple. The results were disappointing, but confirmed that the Roman lamps originated from outside Petra. It is hoped they will find matches for their clay origins when the data bank is enlarged.

52 All rims, bases, necks, handles, spouts, and decorated wares. Our chief pottery restorer, N. Zabban, who worked with the Residential Quarter wares, noted that he had found fragments that joined from the same bowl from two and sometimes three different loci. So in collecting what we think is a "pure sample" is in fact mixed.

53 *Great Temple* Vol. II, 281-341. In 2014 the pottery was rebagged. A copy of my correspondence with the authorities details the history of the Great Temple pottery storage. Dr. Monther Jamhawi, Director General of the Department of Antiquities, Cc: Mr. Aktham Oweidi, Head of Excavation and Survey Dr. Emad Hijazeen, Commissioner, Petra Archaeological Park, Eng. Tahani Salhi, Director of CRMI would like to thank you for your consideration of the Petra Great Temple restoration and fieldwork for the maintenance of the structure, which I excavated between 1993-2009. I heartedly approve of the document for the re-bagging and storage of the pottery collected during the course of the excavations and stored in the Lower Temenos excavated areas, and I authorize the authors of this document to undertake this project, which was submitted to me by Dr. Barbara Porter, Director of ACOR, and co-written by Elena Ronza and Glenn Corbett, TWLCRM co-directors. This document clearly outlines the discussions I held some time ago with Chris Tuttle, before he started to work on the Temple of the Winged Lions. During the course of the excavations, on multiple occasions, I had requested a safe dry place to store the pottery, but no place was assigned, and I was told to re-bury it. I stored the pottery in plastic bags, some 317,977 fragments with tytek labels marked with their trench and locus numbers, the date month and year of excavation along with their sequence numbers, their container numbers and the supervisor's initials. The data for this collection have been recorded in our databases and can be found on-line under *Open Context, Petra Great Temple*. Over the course of the excavation that the bags disintegrated, and we re-bagged the collection, but I'm afraid that many of these contexts have been lost due to the in-ground storage conditions, which is, of course a great pity. cc. Dr. Barbara Porter, ACOR Director, Elena Ronza and Glenn Corbett (TWLCRM co-directors).

The purpose of the Great Temple ceramic typology was to quantify the occurrence of pottery types recovered from successive Great Temple site phases. The pottery could then be studied in relation to the stratigraphy and analyzed as changes took place over time. The Great Temple typology provides a framework for discussions regarding a broad definition for Great Temple pottery and Nabataean pottery in general.

When a series of new shapes, fabrics or decorative motifs appeared with a significant frequency, additions to the typology were made. Pottery classes—bowls, jugs, jars, storage jars and cooking pots—were then created and added to as our excavations continued to define those functional classes that could be classified together on the basis of assumed function.[54] In Grosso Modo, the intention was to capture a broad cross section of material within the time framework of the field operations. We did classify their basic shapes and function. As mentioned previously, all diagnostics are saved for future study and can be found in the Great Temple on-site storage areas.

Function

Function is separated by ware-fabric types and finishing techniques—argillaceous fine wares, such as cups, bowls and plates; gritty cooking wares; gritty and argillaceous storage wares such as jars, jugs and pithoi; and small forms—*unguentaria* (oil and perfume containers), *amphoriskoi*, bottles, and lamps. Pottery classes—bowls, jars, jugs, storage jars and pithoi as well as cooking pots—were then created to define those types that could be classified together on the basis of assumed function.

Here we look at the basic shapes, which can be found as classes in Appendix 4, Figures 15-19. But we begin with the basic groups of rims, bases, handles, and thereafter follows a discussion of slip surface color. The vessel assemblage is then described by plastic decoration traits such as incision, excision, rouletting, ribbing, shaving, and impression. The bodies of many jars and jugs can be globular or ovoid, and their body surfaces often are characterized by ribbing. Paint and painted motifs associated with fine wares are then briefly described. With all of these characteristics, there are changes over time, and these modifications are what we hoped to capture in the recording of various features.

Phasing Rationale: Petra Great Temple

Based on the preponderance of pottery fragments recovered from the Petra Great Temple, (not *in situ*) the question arises whether to phase the fragments according to the phase in which they are found or to identify them with the phase in which they were originally manufactured. While the relative date of manufacture for more distinctive fragments like Nabataean painted ceramics, lamps, and coins is easily determined, too many examples are extremely fragmentary (e.g, parts of fragmented artifacts, like other pottery fragments, broken floor tiles, making it difficult to assign them to a specific period of manufacture. Therefore we elected to phase all artifacts including those not in closed contexts, i.e., *in situ,* within the contexts in which they were excavated. This method more accurately reflects their deposition in the archaeological record. If the pottery were phased where we presume they originally belonged it is difficult to interpret their archaeological context

54 Not all the shapes produced by Nabataean potters are included here. Nevertheless the pottery types from the Great Temple provide a framework for discussions regarding the definition of Great Temple pottery in particular and Nabataean pottery in general. We knew we would not find enough time to physically compare specific rim shapes, according to a distinct type series, but annotated their overall shapes. Our chief pottery restorer, Naif Zabban, who worked with the Residential Quarter wares, noted that he had found fragments of the same bowl from two and sometimes three different loci. So what we consider a "pure sample" is in fact mixed. Not all the shapes produced by Nabataean potters are included here. Nevertheless the pottery types from the Great Temple provide a framework for discussions regarding the definition of Great Temple pottery in particular and Nabataean pottery in general.

as they were recovered during excavation. Therefore, by phasing the fragments within the locus, in which they are found, the archaeological, contextual history of each piece is more fully preserved. A note of when they were made is often entered into the "notes" field attached to each fragment and locus record.

Total pottery by area

Although there are significant size disparities between Great Temple areas, we elected to compare the results between them.

The Propylaeum produced 18,087 fragments (6% of the corpus), the Lower Temenos 83,912 (26%), the Upper Temenos 166,403 (52%), and the Temple 48,979 (15%).[55] A Grosso Modo report showing the total pottery by Great Temple Trench or Special Project can be found at the end of Appendix 4 in Tables 12 and 13.

APPENDIX 4. Table 1.
GREAT TEMPLE: POTTERY BY AREA

Area	*TOTAL*	*Percentage*
PROPYLAEUM	18,087	5.68%
LOWER TEMENOS	83,912	26.38%
UPPER TEMENOS	166,403	52.33%
TEMPLE	48,979	15.40%
TOTAL	**317,977**	**100%/99.7%**

Because pottery is the most common class of material, representing 317,977 fragments and 78% of the total artifacts analyzed, we summarize its representation, moving from the general to the particular. The pottery is characterized by a preponderance of material found in the living quarters of the Upper Temenos. When reporting on each trench, 30% of the pottery corpus is recovered from the Upper Temenos Residential Quarter of Trench 94, representing 10% of the total pottery found at the Great Temple with 32,349 fragments. Other exceptions, showing significant yields, are Trench 73 in the Temple with 13,147 or 4% of the site results, the Upper Temenos Special Project 110 with 11,243 fragments or 4% of the total ceramics recovered, Lower Temenos Trench 16 also with 10,604 potsherds (hereafter, sherds) or 3%, Upper Temenos Trench 84 with 10,558 fragments or 3%, and Trench 77 and SP84 (also Upper Temenos trenches), each accounting for 3% of the corpus, respectively. Added together these specific ceramic deposits by trench represent 27% of the pottery recovered from the Great Temple site throughout the excavations.

Special Collections

Listed in Appendix 4, Table 2 are seven special collections of pottery from the Great Temple.[56] Together these deposits represent 97,288 fragments or 30% of the total Great Temple pottery recovery. Six of the deposits originate in the Upper Temenos. Only Trench 73 of the Temple East Walkway with 13,147 fragments represents 4% and each of the remaining deposits represents 4%-to-3% of the total sherds recovered. Heading the list is the massive amounts of ceramics from the Residential Quarter, Trench 94 are presented here in Chapter 12.

The excavation and collection of fine wares found in Room A, Trench 84, of the East Perimeter Wall, we briefly summarize below, and have selected many pieces from this extraordinary collection to illustrate this appendix.

Upper Temenos Room A, Trench 84

In Site Phase VI, lying under a sealed deposit, in a now defunct tabun this cache appears to be a storage depot with a wealth of various Nabataean vessel types. Stacked and purposefully packed

55 Appendix 4, Table 12 gives the occurrence of selected pottery for the Propylaeum and the Lower Temenos trenches by site phase, and Appendix 4 Table 13 gives the occurrence of selected pottery for the Upper Temenos and Temple by trench and by Site Phase.

56 The ceramics from the East 'Cistern,' Trench 53, have been published by Bestock, 1999.

APPENDIX 4. Table 2.
GREAT TEMPLE: TRENCHES WITH SIGNIFICANT NUMBERS OF POTTERY

Area	*Trench* *Special Project*	*Fragments*	*Percentage set against* *317,977 total pottery*
Upper Temenos	Trench 94, 2002 Residential Quarter	32,349	10%
Temple	Trench 73, 2000 East Walkway	13,147	4%
Upper Temenos	Special Project 110, 2005 West Precinct Wall and Cistern-Reservoir	11,243	4%
Lower Temenos	Trench 16, 1996 West Exedra, West	10,604	3%
Upper Temenos	Trench 84, 2000 East Perimeter Wall	10,558	3%
Upper Temenos	Trench 77, 2000 East and South Perimeter Wall	9719	3%
Upper Temenos	Special Project 84, 2001 East Fluvial Deposit	9668	3%
TOTAL		**97,288**	**30%**

The combined figures of Great Temple area trenches with significant numbers of pottery show the Upper Temenos with 23% or 73,537 fragments, the Temple with 13,147 fragments or 4%, and the Lower Temenos with 10,604, or 3%. There are no trenches in the Propylaeum with significant numbers of pottery recovered.

together are 12 Nabataean ring based cups alongside three fine ware goblets; each of very thin ware and flat-based red slipped, with impressed designs of palm fronds and dotted lines around the exterior.[57] Additionally there are juglets, a small globular jar with twisted handles, ribbed globular jars and a tall spindle bottle shaped jar, a bulbous *unguentarium*, perhaps intended for holding a precious oil, and a few cooking pots, ribbed and slipped in pale yellow. A most extraordinary piece is a light red-slipped pilgrim flask with rouletting on its body, shown below in Appendix 4, Figure 9.[58]

Rouletted decoration is commonly found to embellish ring bases of plates, and rouletted patterns are often found around the rim as well. Furthermore, there are several ring based inverted rim bowls with pale yellow paint[59] on the exterior rim and several Nabataean painted bowls. These are decorated in red,

App. 4. Fig. 3.
Interior of a plain ware Nabataean bowl, Cat. No. 01-P-33, UT, Trench 84, Locus 22; ring base, inverted rim with rounded lip, Rdiam. 6.6, Ht. 4.7, of 7.5YR6/6 reddish-yellow ware, exterior-interior self-same slip with wheel burnishing on the exterior beneath the rim; 10YR8/2 very pale brown paint on rim exterior.

57 Ibid. Fig.7.38).
58 Ibid. Figs. 4.58,7.39.
59 Munsell color, 2.5YR8/2.We have identified this as a so-called "slurry paint", see note 69.

APPENDIX 4. Table 3.
GREAT TEMPLE: PERCENTAGES OF RIM SHAPES BY SITE PHASE

SITE PHASE	*Everted*	*Flaring*	*Incurving*	*Inverted*	*Pendant*	*Plain Vertical*	*Trefoil*	*Percentage*
Pre-I	2%	30%	7%	6%	6%	47%	–	98%
I	4%	21%	35%	7%	4%	28%	–	99%
II	17%	3%	19%	31%	2%	28%	–	100%
III	–	54%	15%	–	–	31%	–	100%
IV	15%	13%	23%	16%	–	33%	–	100%
V	14%	11%	11%	37%	8%	19%	–	99.1%
VI	14%	16%	8%	34%	10%	17%	0.10%	99.2%
VII	26%	11%	8%	17%	5%	32%	0.20%	99.3%
VIII	12%	11%	44%	6%	2%	24%	0.30%	99%
IX	15%	5%	23%	8%	18%	30%	–	99.2%
X	12%	7%	35%	12%	3%	30%	0.20%	99.2%
XI	21%	12%	12%	7%	5%	41%	0.30%	98.3%
XII	18%	13%	4%	–	9%	55%	–	99%
XIII	26%	7%	9%	26%	3%	27%	0.90%	98.9%
XIV	16%	13%	17%	19%	3%	32%	0.70%	100%

red brown, or very pale brown paints depicting parallel lines, floral and geometric designs of palm leaves, circles, and rounded triangle designs. This is an excellent array of dateable pieces, including the painted bowls dating to the Nabataean 3b period, from A.D. 70 to 100.[60] The room itself has 51 catalogued objects, 34 belonging to this cache dating to Great Temple Site Phase VI. [61] which has been dated to the period of Roman annexation, A,D. 106. The collection comprises a collection of 10,558 pieces representing 3% of the of the overall total Great Temple pottery collection.

Great Temple shape types

As mentioned earlier, 317,977 pottery fragments are recorded in Grosso Modo, accounting for 78% of the 405,297 artifacts recorded in the database. Since all of the Great Temple databases appear online in *Open Context*, accessing the on-line database can search specifics there.[62] In the following section we provide overarching summary comments about the various strengths of the data. Beginning with basic rim shapes, we now turn to their descriptions and database results.

---

60 The Catalog database in *Open Context* and Grosso Modo counts of the locus-by-locus fragments indicates the impressive array of these ceramics.

61 Food preparation and consumption in conjunction with a temple precinct may indicate that women were assigned a role within the temple setting.

62 The codes we use to record various features are found at the end of this Appendix.

Rims

Rim shapes vary considerably. Six rim shapes are differentiated in the Great Temple typology shown in Appendix 4, Figure 4. Their shape classifies rims as open or closed forms. The rim is the widest part of the vessel for open forms and includes rims that are plain (Appendix 4, Figures 4. 1-2), everted (Appendix 4, Figures 4. 9-10), and flaring shapes (Appendix 4, Figures 4. 7-8). Plain rims are simple vertical shapes that rise directly from the body of the vessel. Flaring rims are simple out-curving forms ending in a tapered lip. Pendant rims Appendix 4, Figures 4. 11-12) often are exaggerated in their pronounced angular thickening and their downward slope, and are commonly associated with cooking pots.

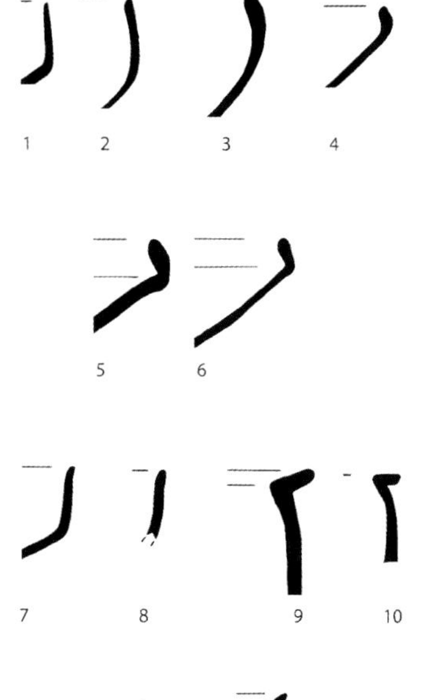

App. 4. Fig. 4. Principal Great Temple Rim shapes.
1-2=Plain;
3-4=Incurving;
5-6=Inverted;
7-8= Flaring;
9-10=Everted;
11-12= Pendant.

Closed forms are turned inwards by the potter—the potter actually folds the clay to the vessel interior, closing the rim towards the center of the vessel. Closed forms include inverted (Appendix 4, Figures 4. 5-6), and incurving shapes (Appendix 4, Figures 4. 3-4), anti-splash devices) Incurving rims are turned inwards and may be plain or rounded in shape. Inverted rims have a more restricted[63] diameter than open forms, having the lip turned to the interior of the vessel, (an anti-splash device), and they are easily identified by a sharply defined exterior corner point.

Rim Percentages by Site Phase

Appendix 4, Table 3 shows a comprehensive percentage distribution of diagnostic rim shapes over the selected corpus of the site phases.[64] Rims account for 23,047 fragments, or 7% of the Great Temple pottery corpus, and their highest count is in Site Phase IX when they represent 27% of the total rims. Also charted are rim and neck combinations (588 fragments) necks alone accounted for 789 sherds, and rim and base fragments numbered 171. Added together with overall rims, rim elements total 23,806 fragments. Again in Site Phase IX most of these combinations are recovered.

Six commonly found rim shapes in Site Phase Pre-I indicate that plain vertical shapes are most popular at 47%. In Site Phase I, the incurving shape, dominates the collection, representing 35% of the total rims, but plain vertical forms are still favored at 28%, and flaring shapes represent 21%. Plain vertical forms return to find favor in Site Phase II, at 28%, but more popular are inverted shapes representing 31%. Flaring forms reach their apogee in Site Phase III at 54%, and the plain vertical rim shape is 31% of the sample. In Site Phase IV the plain vertical shape attains a high of 33% and the incurving shape is still popular at 23%, inverted at 16%, everted at 15%, and flaring at 13%, showing that there is a broad diversity of forms during this time. Plain vertical shapes lose popularity in Site Phase V when inverted shapes, at 37% are dominant, and plain vertical rim shapes decline to represent only 19%. In Site Phase VI, the inverted rim shape represents 34% of the sample, and the plain vertical rim at 17%, has much the same distribution as in the preceding

---

63 See Shepard, 1968, 228-231, fig.21.

64 It will be found that the majority of the pottery evidence comes from the turmoil created in Site Phase IX or dating to the earthquake of A.D. 363. Unfortunately these finds are problematic, and cannot placed in closed contexts. More trustworthy results can be found in Site Phases IV-VII.

phase. The trefoil rim makes its appearance at the Great Temple in this phase and appears with a modest representation throughout most of the succeeding site phases. In Site Phase VII, the plain vertical shape returns as the dominant form at 32%, and the inverted form has lost some popularity, now representing only 17%—a 50% loss from Site Phase VI.

Incurving forms dominate the rim shapes at 44% in Site Phase VIII, but the plain vertical shape is still popular at 24%. That trend continues in Site Phase IX with 30% plain vertical and 23% incurving rims still representing the most popular shapes. In Site Phase X they again switch positions with incurving at 35% and the plain vertical at 30%. Another shift in popularity occurs in Site Phase XI with plain vertical shape at 41%, well beyond other shapes, and everted rim shapes represent 21%. All other forms during Site Phase XI are far fewer in representation. In Site Phase XII, the plain vertical rim swells in numbers to 55% and everted forms rise to 18%, and in Site Phase XIII, the plain vertical rim holds its lead at 27% and everted and inverted shapes are just behind, each representing 26%. We assume these changes in fashion would also be reflected in similar proportions at other sites in Petra.

Bases

Bases are integral to our typology. Illustrated in Appendix 4, Figure 5 is several base shapes including the flat, pointed, conical, round, ring (and ogee or pedestal base), string cut, disc, and umbilical shaped bases. The shape, size, and construction of the base can be directly related to the vessel class and the size of the object. Base statistical analysis aids in an approximation of the number of vessels in a given locus and site phase. At the Great Temple a total 11,977 bases are recorded, representing 3.8% of the total fragments analyzed. From unmixed site phases, bases number 11,977, and reach their peak in Site Phase IX with 4010 or 33% base fragments for that phase.[65]

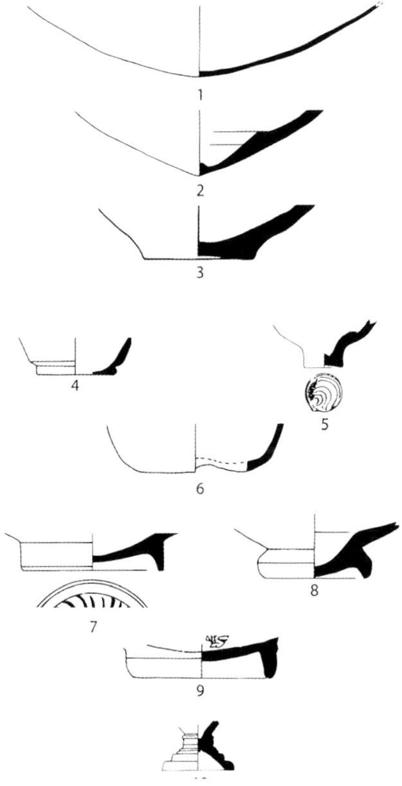

App. 4. Fig. 5.
Principal Great Temple Base shapes.
1=Round; 2=Pointed; 3=Flat;
4=Disc; 5=String-cut; 6=Umbilical;
7-9=Ring; and 10=Ogee or Pedestal.

The flat base (Appendix 4, Figure 5.3) is formed from a single slab of clay with the rest of the vessel. It is cut off the wheel with a string and given its flat bottom surface by scraping when the vessel is sufficiently dry and hardened. Flat bases represent 55% of the bases. Like the flat base, string cut bases (Appendix 4, Figure 5.5) are formed by cutting the vessel from a lump or cone of clay with a string. The string-cut base is flat with smoothed over spiral-like marks on the bottom. The height of the base varies according to the point at which the vessel is cut away from the parent clay. It generally measures 2-3 cm in diameter and belongs to a small class of vessels often with unfinished interiors like the *unguentarium* (Appendix 4, Figure 19.2, or the lid, Appendix 4, Figure 19.9), and accounts for 2% of the major bases analyzed.

The conical base (Appendix 4, Figure 5.2) is most closely associated with the Nabataean painted bowl, represents 0.6% whereas the hemispherical round base (Appendix 4, Figure 5.1) has a gradual more rounded

65 Relatively rare to recover is the rim still attached to its base, which gives the complete profile of the original vessel.

curvature and is associated with wide-bodied vessels, like cooking pots. Round bases account for 25% of the total bases processed.

Ring bases (Appendix 4, Figures 5. 7-9) represent 17% of the bases in the Great Temple repertoire. Ring base subtypes are distinguished by the size and their base profiles. Ring bases may be high or low, vary in shape (upright, triangular, tapered, flattened or not), and vary in diameter size (2-15 cm), or thickness (rounded), as well as in stance. They may be vertical or flaring in shape.

As the vessel rotates on the wheel, the potter manipulates the clay outwards to the exterior of the vessel. A separate bottom ring also may have been added as the vessel is rotated upside down on the turning wheel—the object is to center the ring. Scraping and wet smoothing the wet surface with a self-same slip or frequently white painting finishes the base.[66]

The medium ring base diameter (Bdiam.), varies from 4 to 8 cm, and is attached to open forms like small cups and bowls (Appendix 4, Figures 5.7-9), whereas the small ring base belongs to the jug class. The ring is often smoothed with a wet cloth or scraped with a tool and may be flattened and can be incised with rouletting (a favorite decorative technique used by Nabataean potters). On angular ring bases (Appendix 4, Figure 5.8), turning marks are visible indicating they belong to closed vessels. Ring bases also may support plain ware large bowls. Often these are low ring bases 2 to 6 mm in height and 6 to 12 cm in Bdiam. where as large ring bases belong to deep bowls, and range from 5 to 15 mm in height and from 6 to 14 cm in Bdiam. Technically ogee or pedestal bases (Appendix 4, Figure 5.10) are high ring bases, generally with a flaring shape.

The umbilical-shaped base (Appendix 4, Figure 5.6) finds a knob at its center lending the base its appearance.[67] The diameter of the ring varies from 4 to 8 cm. It has a rounded ridge for its support and can also be classified as a depressed very low ring base. The umbilical base has a minimal showing of 0.3% in the typology for only 180 fragments were classified in selected unmixed phases. The disc base appears infrequently in the Great Temple repertoire and represents only 0.1%. It is characterized by its torus-like profile, and is associated with closed forms.

Base Percentages by Site Phase

Appendix 4, Table 4 tabulates the percentages of base shapes by site phase. Ten base types are charted, and the flat, ring and round base are the most popular, with the ring base dominating the bases from Site Phase Pre-I to Site Phase III. In Site Phase IV, the flat base is the most represented shape, constituting 45%, and the ring base represents 23%. In Site Phase V, the round base represents 50% of the assemblage and continues similarly in Site Phase VI. These figures are due to the high numbers of cooking wares found relating to this phase. As we mentioned earlier, most cooking pots have round bases, which sometimes are difficult to detect because they are so similar to ribbed body sherds. In Site Phase VII, the round base dramatically drops from 42% to 8% and the flat base reaches its highest occurrence in all site phases, representing 76%. Then in Site Phase VIII a dramatic change takes place when again the round base dominates the

App. 4. Fig. 6. Cooking Pot. Cat. No. 01-P-41, Seq. No. 84187, UT, Trench 84 Locus 22 with painted round base, plain vertical rim, Rdiam. 14, Ht. 20.5, two plain vertical loop handles extend from rim to shoulder, of 2.5YR4/8 red ware, Worn away pale yellow exterior slip 2.5Y8/3, Exterior ribbing, burned, blackened exterior.

66 The term, "slurry" means a light aqueous solution of the parent clay and the same color as the fabric.

67 See jug, Appendix 4, Figure 16.6.

APPENDIX 4. Table 4.
GREAT TEMPLE: PERCENTAGES OF BASE SHAPES BY SITE PHASE

SITE PHASE	*Button*	*Disc*	*Flat*	*Pedestal*	*Pointed*	*Ring*	*Round*	*String-cut*	*Umbilical*	*Lug*	%
Pre-I	1%	–	21%	–	–	71%	6%	–	–	–	99
I	0.70%	–	33%	0.70%	4%	44%	9%	6%	0.70%	1%	99
II	–	–	28%	–	–	53%	11%	6%	–	2%	100
III	–	–	–	–	50%	50%	–	–	–	–	100
IV	–	0.08%	45%	0.10%	1%	23%	28%	1%	0.30%	–	98
V	0.80%	0.60%	27%	0.10%	–	18%	50%	2%	0.06%	–	99
VI	0.08%	0.05%	31%	0.10%	1%	13%	50%	4%	0.05%	0.02%	99.3
VII	0.30%	0.02%	76%	0.10%	–	13%	8%	2%	0.02%	0.10%	99.5
VIII	0.80%	0.10%	66%	0.10%	1%	9%	17%	4%	1%	–	99
IX	1%	0.10%	69%	0.08%	0.10%	25%	0.30%	2%	0.20%	0.05%	98
X	0.40%	0.40%	49%	0.05%	2%	10%	34%	3%	0.50%	0.10%	99
XI	0.50%	0.05%	21%	0.10%	0.10%	13%	62%	3%	0.20%	0.09%	100
XII	8%	–	20%	–	–	52%	20%	–	–	–	100
XIII	0.60%	0.50%	58%	0.10%	2%	21%	15%	1%	0.30%	0.05%	99
XIV	0.30%	0.10%	56%	0.10%	2%	13%	25%	2%	0.20%	0.10%	98

class at 66%. This site phase is also a high point for fine wares associated with both the flat and ring bases. The flat base climbs to 69% in Site Phase IX[68] with the ring base at 25%, and the round base appears to be eclipsed by these two shapes. Once again the flat base returns to favor in Site Phase X, representing 49% of the class. The round base is at 34%, and the ring base accounts for only 10%. In Site Phase XI the round base represents 62%, flat 21%, and ring 13%. Cooking pots at this time are at their apogee, representing 18% of the finds, and the round base percentage also is indicative of this factor. The ring base achieves its high point in Site Phase XII with 52%, and the flat and round bases each represent 20%. In Site Phase XIII the flat base dominates the group with a 58% showing, with the ring base at 21% and the round base at 15%. In Site Phase XIV, the flat base continues to outweigh the other base shapes with a 56% representation.

Handles

Handles are generally recovered complete and are most commonly found with jugs generally having a single handle, and jars with two. They are important for the statistical understanding of how many vessels are present. Often found in excavation, unattached to the parent pot, handles are classified by form, size, ware type and function. As the last element to be added to a vessel, they appear on jugs, jars, juglets, large bowls and cooking pots. Large elongated handles are associated with storage jars, as well as those triangular in section. Double strand handles and vertical loop handles accompany jugs (Appendix 4, Figures 16. 5,10). Ridged and combed handles are wide with

68 See note 67.

APPENDIX 4. Table 5.
DISTRIBUTION OF HANDLES AND HANDLE ATTACHMENTS BY SITE PHASE

PHASE	*Handles*	*%*	*Handle-Rim*	*%*	*Handle-Neck-Rim*	*%*	*Handle-Neck*	*%*
PRE-I	16	0.3%	10	0.3%	–	-	–	–
I	56	1%	11	0.3%	1	0.2%	1	0.4%
II	15	0.3%	6	0.2%	–	–	–	–
III	2	0.4%	1	0.3%	–	–	–	–
IV	223	5%	82	3%	4	0.8%	3	1%
V	73	2%	55	2%	7	1%	1	0.4%
VI	232	5%	170	6%	3	0.6%	11	5%
VII	226	5%	171	6%	29	6%	4	2%
VIII	378	9%	314	11%	34	7%	10	5%
IX	1241	28%	917	32%	199	42%	41	19%
X	547	12%	357	13%	60	13%	31	14%
XI	515	11%	340	12%	21	4%	19	8%
XII	9	0.2%	1	0.3%	–	–	–	–
XIII	380	9%	164	6%	22	5%	7	3%
XIV	491	11%	217	8%	90	9%	93	42%
TOTAL	**4404**	**100%**	**2816**	**100%**	**470**	**100%**	**221**	**100%**

vertical ridges or grooves along their exteriors, whereas small ridged, slightly twisted and grooved loop handles are cooking pot components (Appendix 4, Figures 18, 5, 6). Small loop handles are found with juglets (Appendix 4, Figure 16.7), and twisted small handles also can be linked to small forms like the small cup shown in Appendix 4, Figure 15.6. In Toto, singular handles number 4404 classified and represent 1.38% of the total number of fragments in the corpus.

Remaining elements of the Great Temple pottery corpus include combined forms like ceramics with one or more features, including rims-attached to handles, rims with necks, and rims attached to both handles and their bases. Handles found attached to rims number 2816 fragments plus handle and neck fragments number 221 fragments, so total

App. 4. Fig. 7. Nabataean ovoid jug. Cat. No.01-P-45, UT, Trench 84, Locus 22. Ring base, plain sloping rim with thinned out lip. Rdiam. 5.2, Ht. 16.5, of 2.5YR 6/8 light red ware, interior ribbing. Flattened vertical loop handle with vertical incision, exterior self-same slip. Maximum Body diameter 7.0.

handles number 7441 pieces or 2.3% of the pottery corpus. In Site Phase IX, 32% of the handle-rim combinations fragments are the most popular. There are also 470 handle-neck-rim fragments, and Site Phase IX finds their highest occurrence. Handles attached to necks are at their most popular in Site Phase XIV.

Other forms, such as stoppers, lids, necks, spouts, lamp fragments, beads, and varia are also charted, but their numbers are insignificant.

Body sherds and construction materials

93,001 fragments are body sherds representing 29% of the pottery processed. Body sherds are those fragments with no distinguishing functional characteristics, but they may carry liquid decoration such as slip or paint and/or plastic decoration such as rouletting or ribbing, both of which are discussed below. Significant numbers also are captured for ceramic architectural construction materials servicing the building industry, including floor tiles (1969, 0.6% of the corpus), canalization pipes (2740, 0.9% of the corpus), roof tiles (38,762, 12% of the corpus), and hypocaust tiles from the bath complex (1322, 0.4% of the corpus). Taken together construction materials represent 14% of the 317,977 materials analyzed. There is a measured gain in both body sherds and construction materials between Site Phases VI and IX, followed by a decline in Site Phase X. Both body sherds and architectural fragments enjoy their greatest popularity in Site Phase IX,

APPENDIX 4. Table 6.
GREAT TEMPLE: DISTRIBUTION OF BODY POTSHERDS AND CERAMIC ARCHITECTURAL FRAGMENTS BY SITE PHASE

SITE PHASE	*Body Sherds*	*Percentage Fragments*	*Ceramic Architectural Fragments*	*Percentage*
Pre-I	698	0.7%	–	–
I	2466	3%	28	0.1%
II	680	0.7%	–	–
III	37	0.03%	–	–
IV	5033	5%	345	0.2%
V	2570	3%	33	2%
VI	7784	8%	110	0.6%
VII	7138	8%	2730	17%
VIII	7972	9%	3210	20%
IX	31,757	34%	4780	29%
X	10,340	11%	1453	9%
XI	10,565	11%	2311	14%
XII	135	0.1%	–	–
XIII	19	0.02%	303	2%
XIV	5807	6%	953	6%
TOTAL	**93,001**	**100%**	**16,256**	**100%**

and the lowest distribution of both classes is found in Site Phase III, when architectural construction materials are all but absent from the record.

Now that we have looked at individual diagnostics such as rims, bases, and handles, we will turn our attention specifically to Nabataean ceramic surface treatments.

Surface treatments— slip

The surface treatments of all vessels are also analyzed with regard to their liquid decoration (slip and paint). Slip colors and paints are also an indicator of change. Appendix 4, Table 7 charts the total numbers and percentages of slipped fragments by site phase— the number of slipped or painted fragments and their respective percentages are set against the number of slipped or painted pieces recovered from the phase.[69] The highest percentage of slipped wares can be found in Site Phase IX with 33% of the wares slip finished. In Site Phases VIII and X, 10% of the fragments are so decorated. These numbers are diminished in Site Phases VI and XI, each with an 8% representation and Site Phase XIII with 7%. Together these deposits represent 76% of the total slipped wares. Other site phases do not carry high percentages for slipped wares.

Appendix 4, Table 8 tabulates predominant slip colors by site phase. Nine colors, black, brown, gray, white (and off-white and cream) red, red brown, salmon, self-same (the same color as the body fabric), and tan are also recorded. Overall trends for slip colors set against site phases indicate that in Site Phase II, 67% of the fragments for the phase exhibit a self-same slip, in Site Phase III brown slip colors represent 37% of the slipped wares, in Site Phase IV white slips appear on 41% of the fragments, and red slip is at its high point in Site Phases VI and VII representing 12% and 24% of the slipped sherd corpus. Black has its strongest showing in Site Phase VIII at 21%, and by Site Phase IX self-same slips return to popularity representing 47%. In Site Phase XI white slip represents 46%, but in Site Phase XII there appears to be a return to the use of self-same slips representing 54% of the total for that

69 Counted in the slip color numbers but not presented in the chart are Black Slip Pottery (BSP) and Eastern Sigillata Wares (ESA) frequencies, which will be discussed below. Yellow and green slips (and in one case, a blue slip) are part of the corpus but are not included in Appendix 4 Table 7.

App. 4. Fig. 8. Flaring rimmed cup. Cat. No.02-P-5, UT, Trench 94, Locus 29. Flaring rim, Rdiam. 8.01, Ht. 6.71. Small, very deep cup of fine thin fabric, 2.5YR6/8 light red ware with a self-same slip. Faint, spiral lines around body. Broken horizontally halfway down the body. See Hammond, 1973, 46, No. 91. (PEQ 105, 27-49).

APPENDIX 4. Table 7.
GREAT TEMPLE: TOTAL SLIPPED WARES BY SITE PHASE

SITE PHASE	*Fragments*	*Percentage*
Pre-I	908	0.7%
I	3232	2.5%
II	738	0.6%
III	55	0.04%
IV	4644	3.6%
V	3372	2.6%
VI	10,569	8.3%
VII	9051	7.1%
VIII	12,966	10.2%
IX	42,219	33%
X	13,007	10%
XI	10,401	8%
XII	177	0.1%
XIII	8698	7%
XIV	6631	5%
TOTAL	126,698	98.7%

APPENDIX 4. Table 8.
GREAT TEMPLE: PREDOMINANT SLIP COLORS BY SITE PHASE

SITE PHASE	*Black*	*Brown*	*Gray*	*White*	*Red*	*Red Brown*	*Salmon*	*Self-Same*	*Tan*	*TOTAL %*
Pre-I	91 10%	129 14%	136 15%	40 4%	16 2%	5 0.5%	–	432 47%	57 6%	**906** **0.7%**
I	252 8%	196 6%	251 7%	552 17%	177 5%	110 3%	41 1%	1427 44%	215 6%	**3221** **2.5%**
II	33 4%	17 2%	62 8%	44 6%	13 1%	60 8%	1 –	494 67%	14 2%	738 **0.6%**
III	8 14%	20 36%	6 10%	– –	– –	– –	– –	13 23%	7 12%	54 **0.04%**
IV	460 10%	435 9%	412 9%	1,902 41%	206 4%	29 0.6%	196 4%	780 16%	130 2%	4550 **3.6%**
V	174 5%	243 7%	259 7%	901 26%	300 9%	100 3%	307 9%	793 23%	270 8%	3347 **2.7%**
VI	844 8%	255 2%	817 8%	3516 33%	1325 12%	101 0.9%	71 0.6%	3116 29%	493 5%	10,538 **8.3%**
VII	437 5%	221 2%	331 3%	2683 29%	2209 24%	13 0.14%	448 5%	2208 24%	446 5%	8996 **7%**
VIII	2779 21%	970 7%	1450 11%	1732 13%	762 6%	5 –	916 7%	2966 23%	1208 9%	12,788 **10%**
IX	732 2%	582 1%	3740 9%	12,084 28%	1117 2%	174 0.4%	832 2%	20,000 47%	2572 6%	41,833 **33%**
X	1266 10%	1209 9%	1531 12%	3750 29%	405 3%	16 0.12%	1078 8%	2290 17%	1156 9%	12,701 **10%**
XI	752 7%	301 2%	975 9%	4804 46%	482 4%	2 0.01%	– –	2332 22%	321 3%	10,604 **8.4%**
XII	20 11%	5 2%	7 4%	35 20%	– --	1 –	85 0.9%	96 54%	11 6%	175 **0.1%**
XIII	234 2%	107 1%	820 9%	4257 49%	30 0.3%	– –	721 12%	2972 34%	109 1%	8614 **7%**
XIV	473 7%	296 4%	504 8%	2365 36%	567 8%	2 0.03%	721 12%	830 12%	654 10%	6412 **5%**
TOTAL	**8555** 7%	**4986** 4%	**11,301** 9%	**38,665** 31%	**7609** 6%	**618** 0.5%	**5331** 4%	**40,749** 32%	**7663** 6%	**125,477** 98.5/99.5%

phase. Finally in Site Phases XIII-XIV yellowish-white slips dominate the assemblage representing 49% and 36% respectively of the slipped pottery corpus.

Self-same slips are the most popular accounting for 40,749 or 32% of the 125,477 fragments. In the overall assemblage self-same slips account for 67% in Site Phase II, 54% in Site Phase VI and 47% in Site Phases Pre-I and IX.

In Site Phase III brown slips account for 36%. In Site Phase VI the yellowish-white slip is most popular at 41%, in Site Phase V the self-same slip represents 25% in Site Phase VI yellowish-white slip accounts for 33%, and in Site Phase VII it accounts for 29%, and black slips have their strongest showing in Site Phase VIII with 21%. Self-same slips return to popularity in Site Phase IX representing 47% of the fragments so decorated. White slips return to popularity in Site Phase X with a 29% representation, and in Site Phase XI white represents 46%. Self-same slips represent 54% in Site Phase XII, and white slip predominates in Site Phase XIV at 49%.

Plastic decoration

Pottery finishing techniques include a myriad of surface treatments, and one or more is usually applied to the exterior of the vessel while the vessel clay is in a semi-hardened state before firing. At the Great Temple such decoration includes excision, incision, ribbing, rouletting, shaving, appliqué, impression, and perforations. The decoration can act to seal the surface pores. Ribbing, which is particularly popular on Great Temple cooking pots, jars and jugs, is a series of regular horizontal ridges fashioned on the surface of the pot and is purposefully created by the potter while the pot is being built on the wheel. Rouletting, seen on the body of the pilgrim bottle/flask in Appendix 4 Figure 9 is the engraving of the clay. Often rouletting is applied by a hand-held wheel-engraved with designs that is rolled or stamped on the area to be decorated. Nabataean potters particularly enjoyed rouletting ring bases, and rouletting is generally found to accompany plain fine wares.

App. 4. Fig. 9. Nabataean Pilgrim Bottle/Flask. UT, Trench 84. Cat. No.01-P-42, Seq. No. 84147. Everted rim, Rdiam. 2.5, Max body diam.16.3, Ht. 38 of 5YR7/6 reddish yellow ware, exterior light red slip 2.5YR6/8. Interior slip 2.5YR4/2 dusky red, rouletting around both sides. Two incised vertical loop handles extend from mid-neck to shoulder.

Appendix 4, Table 9 charts nine commonly used plastic decoration techniques. The evidence is uneven. Totals are set against the percentages of total fragments in each site phase, indicating that 31,847 pottery fragments exhibit plastic decoration, with Site Phase IX having the highest occurrence of 11,155 fragments or 35% exhibiting plastic decoration. Overall ribbing appears on 81% of the fragments, incision is found on nearly 9%, and rouletting occurs on 5.3% of the sample. Clearly excision, appliqué, and perforation are not commonly employed potter techniques. Patterns reveal that because ribbing is most often associated with storage and food preparation, these activities appear to be common at the Great Temple site.

APPENDIX 4. Table 9.
GREAT TEMPLE: OCCURRENCE OF PLASTIC DECORATION BY SITE PHASE

SITE PHASE	*Incision*	*Excision*	*Impression*	*Appliqué*	*Molded*	*Perforation*	*Rouletting*	*Ribbing*	*Modeled*	*TOTAL %*
Pre-I	31	12	–	–	–	–	–	31	–	**74**
	41%	16%	–	–	–	–	–	41%	–	0.2%
I	85	4	14	1	3	1	6	274	1	**389**
	21%	1%	4%	0.2%	0.7%	0.2%	2%	70%	0.2%	1.2%
II	15	–	2	–	–	–	12	91	–	**120**
	13%	–	2%	–	–	–	10%	75%	–	0.37%
III	6	2	–	–	–	–	–	5	–	**13**
	46%	15%	–	–	–	–	–	38%	–	0.04%
IV	126	4	27	–	4	–	11	717	–	**889**
	14%	0.4%	3%	–	-0.4%	–	1%	80%	–	2.8%
V	51	3	29	1	–	–	30	434	6	**554**
	9%	0.5%	5%	0.01%	–	–	5%	78%	1%	1.7%
VI	214	2	50	–	2	2	114	2894	2	**3280**
	6%	0.06%	1%	–	0.06%	0.06%	3%	88%	0.06%	10%
VII	128	12	26	59	6	2	90	1811	–	**2134**
	6%	0.5%	1%	2%	0.3%	0.09%	4%	55%	–	6.7%
VIII	128	8	3	5	37	6	52	2097	–	**2336**
	5%	0.3%	0.1%	0.2%	0.3%	0.2%	2%	89%	–	7%
IX	1,018	12	81	1	279	27	1014	8299	424	**11,155**
	9%	0.1%	0.7%	0.008%	3%	0.2%	9%	75%	4%	35%
X	254	3	22	12	8	3	75	2999	–	**3376**
	7%	0.08%	0.7%	0.4%	0.2%	0.08%	2%	88%	–	10.6%
XI	266	5	19	24	4	124	188	2616	–	**3246**
	8%	0.2%	0.6%	0.7%	0.1%	4%	6%	83%	–	10%
XII	3	–	–	–	1	–	–	26	–	**30**
	10%	–	–	–	3%	–	–	87%	–	0.09%
XIII	324	23	29	18	3	26	49	1463	–	**1935**
	16%	1%	1%	0.9%	0.1%	1%	3%	76%	–	6%
XIV	143	3	20	22	2	5	62	2052	7	**2316**
	6%	0.1%	0.8%	0.9%	0.08%	0.2%	3%	89%	0.3%	7%
TOTAL	**2792**	**93**	**322**	**143**	**349**	**196**	**1703**	**25,809**	**440**	**31,847**
	8.7%	**0.29%**	**1%**	**0.4%**	**1%**	**0.6%**	**5.3%**	**81%**	**1.3%**	**99.59%**

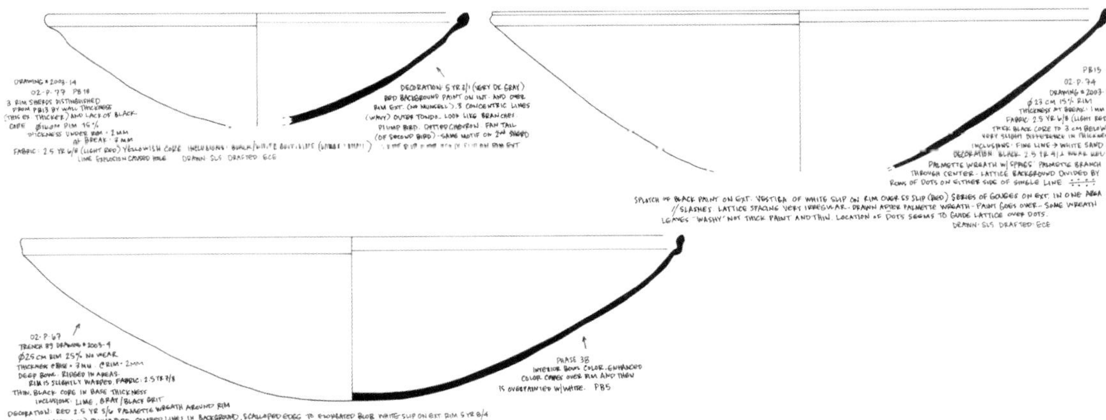

App. 4. Fig. 10. Study drawings of Great Temple Nabataean Bowls (Emily Catherine Egan).

Nabataean fine wares

Strabo (16.4.26) is worthwhile quoting:

> The Nabataeans are a sensible people, and are so much inclined to acquire possessions that they publicly fine anyone who has diminished his possessions and also confer honours on anyone who has increased them. Since they have but few slaves, they are served by their kinsfolk for the most part, or by one another, or by themselves; so that the custom also extends even to their kings. They prepare common meals together in groups of thirteen persons; and they have two girl-singers for each banquet. The king holds drinking bouts in magnificent style, but no one drinks more than eleven cupfuls, each time using a different golden cup. The king is so democratic that, in addition to serving himself, he sometimes even serves the rest himself in his turn. He often renders an account of his kingship in the popular assembly; and sometimes his mode of life is examined.

Unfortunately at the Great Temple we did not unearth golden cups, but could the quantities of painted Nabataean bowl fragments found throughout Petra be indicative that each time the bowl was emptied, it was ceremoniously broken? If breaking their bowls was routine, with 13 in the group, dining together, discussing the affairs of the day, and drinking at one time, dinner must have been a raucous occasion, and it is little wonder that we find such an abundance of Nabataean painted fragments scattered over the site.

The Nabataean bowl has a distinctive look and feel, having an exceptional clay fabric with painting on the interior. Appendix 4, Figure 10 illustrates a preliminary study of Great Temple Nabataean bowls. The Nabataean bowl exhibits technical proficiency in its manufacture with its extremely high quality fabric and surface finish. The bowl's shape is open and conical to hemispherical in profile, with a conical base, a flaring body, and an incurving rim, sometimes folded to the interior. Purposefully designed to be held in the hand, it is often accompanied by the small ring-based small cup, (illustrated in Appendix 4, Figure 15.5), but the decorated bowl is the most characteristic and easily identifiable element of the Nabataean fine ware repertoire. The Nabataean painted bowl is a well-levigated ware, meaning that there are few inclusions in the clay, which has been well purified in water during the levigation process. The ware is fine, very thin, wheel-thrown, and crisp—a so-called "ringing" ware. Characteristically, its ware-fabric colors are salmon to red,[70] which in part are created from its even firing temperatures and the high ferris content in the clay.

The surface treatment varies. On the exterior, most often wheel marks can be seen, and as the vessel turned, horizontally shaved with a sharp thin edged tool. Much of it is covered with a self-same slip having a finer composition than the ware itself. The bowl is painted on the interior before it is fired, and some bowls have traces of a white slip or paint on the exterior and on the exterior rim. Generally it is well fired without a discolored gray or black core. Appendix 4, Figure 11 illustrates a reassembled painted Nabataean bowl from the Great Temple Residential Quarter.

Nabataean Painted Fine Wares

S. G. Schmid[71] has created the widely used Nabataean fine ware pottery typology charting a shape and decoration sequences from his analysis of the Ez Zantur[72] ceramics. Hereafter when reference is made to "Schmid (Phase)," it is for cross dating the Petra Great Temple pottery, and we paraphrase his conclusions in the following descriptions of painted decoration.[73] Our stratigraphic and chronological sequences confirm Schmid's painted ceramic typological sequence, [74] and the dominating features are that red painted decoration is earlier than black or dark brown painted decoration, and this transition takes place somewhere around the beginning of the A.D. second century.

App. 4. Fig. 11. Complete profile of a Nabataean Bowl, Cat. No.03-P-64, UT, Trench 94. Rdiam. 17, of 10R5/8 red ware; painted with dark gray 10YR4/1 with palm fronds wreaths with dotted chevrons; white slip on the exterior rim. Dated Phase 3c.

---

70 Munsell light red 2.5YR6/8 - 2.5YR7/6.

71 Schmid 1996a, 1996b, 2000a.

72 The Ez Zantur site is located on the slope above the Great Temple. Since 1988 the site has been excavated by a Swiss team from the University of Basel.

73 Particular Great Temple motifs can be accessed using *Open Context*.

74 Early bowls are haphazardly red painted on the interior with wavy lines and teardrop strokes around the rim. In Phase 2a, from 50 B.C. to 30/20 B.C., painted palmette branches radiate from the base to the rim. In Phase 2b, from 30/20 B.C. to the turn of the century, the stylized palmettes are placed horizontally around the upper interior near the vessel rim. And in Phase 2c, from the turn of the century to A.D. 20, palmette designs become finer in painted technique, and below the rim are palmette sprigs intermixed with peacock eyes. Bowls are more often inverted in form. In Schmid's Phase 3, the bowls have extremely thin walls and vertical rims. Schmid then subdivides the phases into 3a, A.D. 20 to 79, Phase 3b, A.D. 70 to the beginning of the 2nd c. A.D.; Phase 3c, 100 A.D.; and Phase 3d, A.D.100 and later. In Phase 3a delicate designs of ivy and other leaves with lines of dots cover the vessel interior, and with time, the painting becomes darker in color. The decoration is precisely drawn with attention to detail. In Phase 3b, bowl shapes become shallower and the rims are reduced in size. Covering the background is a grid, and darker colors emerge to decorate palmettes, pomegranates, and geometric shapes, like stylized triangles. Phase 3c decoration is the same as Phase 3b, but the execution of the designs is cruder, and the background grid has disappeared. Phase 3d exhibits careless painting, the wares are coarser, and figural representations of birds can appear. The open bowl is decorated on the interior with red, dark brown or black designs of feathers, dots, branches, pomegranates and other fruits.

A later Nabataean bowl group, dated to A.D.100, is of comparatively inferior quality. Although the forms remain basically the same, the clay is not as well processed (levigated), and it is coarser and sandy to the touch. Firing techniques have fallen off as well, and the cores often are discolored. This group exhibits less precision in the painting; it is sloppy in production and shows considerably less detail. These are features that stand in stark contrast to the characteristics of the earlier Schmid Phase 2 Nabataean bowl.

APPENDIX 4. Table 10.

GREAT TEMPLE: PREDOMINANT PAINT COLORS BY SITE PHASE

SITE PHASE	*Black*	*Brown*	*Gray*	*White*	*Red*	*Brown*	*Red Tan*	*Other*	*TOTAL*
Pre-I	16	27	1	4	51	1	1	–	**101**
	16%	26%	0.9%	4%	50%	0.9%	0.9%	–	
I	81	67	14	106	214	13	4	24	**523**
	15%	3%	2%	20%	41%	2%	0.7%	4%	
II	2	–	–	–	2	1	–	–	**5**
	40%	–	–	–	40%	20%	–	–	
III	2	–	–	–	2	1	–	–	**5**
		40%	–	–	–	40%	20%	–	–
IV	78	44	5	51	100	2	3	–	**283**
	27%	15%	1%	18%	35%	0.7%	1%	–	
V	52	77	11	46	92	13	8	1	**300**
	17%	25%	3%	15%	30%	4%	2%	0.03%	
VI	105	120	3	143	75	55	3	–	**504**
	20%	23%	0.5%	28%	15%	11%	0.5%	–	
VII	65	146	5	1596	42	86	2	5	**1947**
	3%	7%	0.2%	81%	2%	4%	0.1%	0.2%	
VIII	432	138	85	603	52	47	11	38	**1406**
	30%	10%	6%	43%	3%	3%	0.7%	2%	
IX	1535	2369	47	1527	456	739	3	26	**6702**
	23%	35%	0.7%	22%	6%	11%	0.04%	0.3%	
X	200	220	44	321	127	5	2	63	**982**
	20%	22%	44%	33%	13%	0.5%	0.2%	6%	
XI	111	113	–	17	107	26	–	–	**374**
	29%	30%	–	4%	29%	7%	–	–	
XII	2	–	–	1	1	3	–	–	**7**
	28%	–	–	14%	14%	42%	–	–	
XIII	40	64	37	156	45	27	–	–	**369**
	11%	17%	10%	42%	12%	7%	–	–	
XIV	125	44	6	171	99	–	6	12	**463**
	27%	10%	1%	37%	21%	–	1%	2%	
TOTAL	2846	3429	258	4742	1465	1019	43	169	**13,971**
%20%	24.5%	1.8%	34%	10%	7%	0.3%	1.2%	**98.8%**	

Numbers of painted fragments and their respective percentages are set against the number of painted pieces in the phase.[1]

1 Counted in the slip color numbers but not presented in the chart are Black Slip Pottery (BSP) and Eastern Sigillata Wares (ESA) frequencies, are discussed below. Yellow and green slips (and in one case, a blue slip) are part of the corpus but are not included in the chart.

In Great Temple Site Phase IV, there are 283 painted fragments of which 100 are red painted, representing 35%, 78 black painted fragments number 27% of the phase collection, and brown painted fragments number 44 or 15%.

From the comments written on the Great Temple encoding forms, I calculated that Nabataean painted bowl fragments number 2036 fragments. Bowls with red painting represent 32%, salmon pink 2%, and red brown 6%, which together make up 40% of the painted Nabataean bowls. Black painted fragments number 635 or 31%, brown black 2%, purple-black 2%, and brown 24%. Together the dark colors represent 59% of the collection, indicating that black painted wares enjoyed greater popularity, and that the Great Temple it appears that the Great Temple painted fine wares collection as a whole is chronologically later, and can be dated to Schmid's later painting phases 3b and 3c, between A.D. 70 to 80 and A.D. 100 and later. During the recording process, paint and painted motifs are written on the form and the designs are described—(unfortunately we did not code specific designs, so these calculations are based on the annotations written on the encoding document). What was written in includes, "stylized triangles, circles, crosshatching, dots, drips, floral and fruit elements, such as—palmettes, pomegranates, leaf fronds, branches, or birds, and splashes, lines, wavy lines and zigzags." [75]

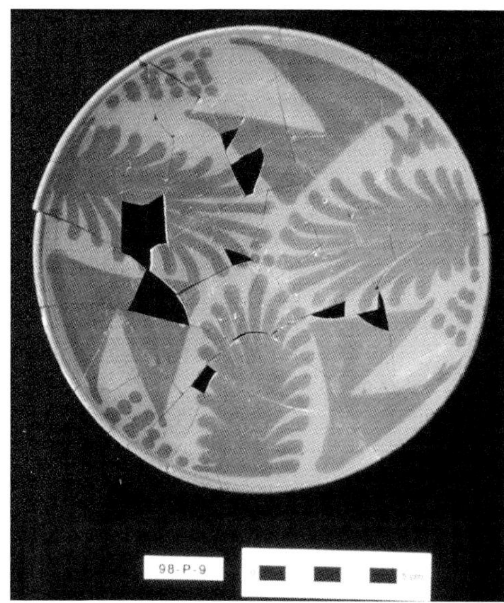

App. 4. Fig. 12. Reassembled Painted bowl. Cat. No. 98-P-9, Seq. No. 53036, UT, Trench 53, Locus 2, Phase IX, inverted rim, Rdiam.17, of 2.5 YR5/6 red ware, with dots, a zigzag, and triangular division of geometric and vegetal forms.

In Site Phase V, 300 fragments are painted with designs, 92 or 30% are red painted designs, 52 or 17% are black painted and 77 fragments or 25% are brown painted designs. It is in Site Phase VI we find only 15% are red painted, (75 fragments); black painted designs represent 20% (105 fragments), and brown-painted fragments count for 120 fragments or 23 % of the phase painted pieces. This clearly shows by this time the transition from Nabataean red painted pieces to darker paints has taken place.

App. 4. Fig. 13. Painted Nabataean round bowl base. Cat. No. 03-P-73. UT, Trench 94. Of 2.5YR 6/8 light red ware, red decoration, 2.5YR 4/8, with feathered bands on either side of single line, branch of myrtle leaves surrounded by dots. Multiple lines of dots with a single solid line down the center and lattices.

Appendix 4, Figure 12 illustrates a later painted Nabataean bowl from Trench 53, designed with a triangular division of geometric and vegetal forms. The actual numbers demonstrate that decorative painting was not particularly favored as an instrument of decoration, for only 4.3% of the Great Temple collection is painted fine ware.

Appendix 4 Table 10 is a record of overall painted wares found at the Great Temple, and does not include the numbers of Nabataean painted bowl figures mentioned above. Paint percentages are divided by the site phase of total painted fragment

75 Unfortunately time precluded that these designs be reported here.

count of 13,971 painted fragments. The overall Great Temple collection of painted wares indicates that Site Phase IX with its earthquake collection has the largest representation of painted wares with 6702 painted fragments or 48% of the collection, followed by Site Phase VII with 1947 painted pieces, or 14%, and Site Phase VIII with 1406 fragments or 13% of the collection. Thirty-four percent of the overall collection, representing 4742 fragments is white painted, [76] 24.5% is brown painted (3429 fragments), and 2846 fragments are dark gray or black painted, like the bowl shown above in Appendix 4, Figure 11, representing 20% of the total painted wares. Lesser paint colors include red 10% and red-brown at 7%.

A Note about Eastern Terra Sigillata Wares (ESA) and BSP

The ESA (Eastern Sigillata A ware) and BSP[77] wares found during our excavations are important to mention. These wares are distinctive and easily recognized as fine wares with a clean fabric. ESA wares are covered with a bright semi glossy reddish yellow, or reddish orange, slip. They are first manufactured anywhere between 144 and 128 B.C. and continue through to the 3rd c. A.D.[78] BSP wares[79] have essentially the same fabric as ESA wares, but they are covered with a deep black to deep brown slip. A predecessor of ESA ware, BSP ceramics are manufactured only in the 2nd c. B.C.

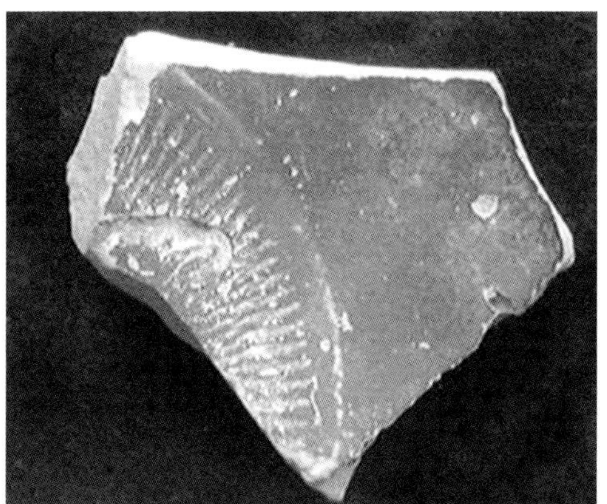

App. 4. Fig. 14. BSP base, Cat. No. 04-P-12,Trench 97, Locus 10. Eastern Terra Sigillata A, bowl fragment, 2.5YR6/8 red, glaze, 7.5YR4/2 dark gray. Ref: Hayes 1997:15 fig. 3, No. 1. Mirroring metal ware, this black gloss bowl fragment represents the final phase of Eastern Sigillata A in A.D. first century. Palmettes impressed over rouletted border on surface of bowl (see Ibid. 57). Exterior base and foot are not impressed, but glossed; simple foot profile: projecting molding at base, NB. Negev 1986:Vol. XVIII, QEDEM 22 INAA indications are that all the Eastern Sigillata wares at Oboda originated in Cyprus.

In the overall Grosso Modo results, 279 ESA wares appear throughout the deposits of the Great Temple. Representing 0.08% of the ceramics studied, their highest occurrence is found in the Upper Temenos, but they are also scattered throughout the other three areas as well. BSP wares number 57 fragments (only 0.017% of the corpus). Both wares are used for plates and bowls with ring bases; however, ESA forms are more varied. Several flat and ring bases, necks, and handles are charted, and rims include flaring and plain vertical jug rims, as well as the expected everted bowls and plates, for which ESA wares are well known.

In the Selected Site Phases, ESA first appears in Site Phase I with one fragment, 10 fragments are found in Site Phase IV, one in Site Phase VI, five in Site Phase VII, 12 in Site Phase VIII, four in Site Phase IX, 2 in Site Phase X, 11 in Site Phase XI, 4 in Site Phase XIII, and seven in Site Phase XIV. Clearly they do not occur in large quantities at the Great Temple. One fragment of BSP ware appears in Site Phase IX, so it is obviously a stray holdover in this late context. Some of these 57 fragments from selected site phases are diagnostic, but the majority of the collection is body sherds. The scarcity of this ware reflects the tendency of the Petraeans of the Great Temple enjoying their own potting culture, and not importing ESA or BSP wares in large quantities. The specifics of these wares and their possible assigned functions can be found in *Open Context.*

---

76 Designs are always painted in red, red-brown, gray or black colors. However, many Nabataean plain and painted ware bowl rims bear an exterior slurry white painting. This is an aqueous mixture of clay and water that is lighter than a slip, and is likely to deteriorate or flake off.

77 See Appendix 5, Architectural Fragments.

78 Hayes 1985, 12-13.

79 Slane 1997, 269-71.

APPENDIX 4. Table 11.
GREAT TEMPLE: DISTRIBUTION OF MAJOR POTTERY CLASSES BY SITE PHASE

SITE PHASE	*Fine Wares*	*Cooking*	*Storage*	*Small Forms*	*TOTAL*
Pre-I	13%	4%	53%	0.90%	**71%**
I	17%	7%	21%	3% 4	**7%**
II	30%	1%	13%	9%	**54%**
III	20%	–	78%	–	**98%**
IV	10%	8%	15%	4%	**37%**
V	14%	9%	18%	1%	**42%**
VI	11%	11%	9%	7%	**38%**
VII	8%	5%	13%	1%	**27%**
VIII	12%	6%	23%	3%	**44%**
IX	20%	7%	15%	3%	**45%**
X	14%	11%	21%	7%	**53%**
XI	6%	18%	10%	3%	**37%**
XII	15%	2%	44%	4%	**65%**
XIII	11%	9%	33%	12%	**65%**
XIV	9%	12%	18%	5%	**44%**
Average for all site phases	14%	7.3%	25.6%	4%	**51% for all site phases**

Distribution of Major Pottery Classes by Site Phases

An average of 51% of the Great Temple ceramics from all site phases could be distinguished on the basis of their function—fine wares, cooking, and storage wares are examined to observe whether a shift occurs in the overall collection without being selective as to vessel function or class. Appendix 4, Table 11 provides a combined typological overview of the collection as a whole. It expresses these counts as percentages set against each site phase. (It should be noted that serving wares were not examined separately)

In Site Phases I-III storage wares appear to be important as well as fine wares. In Site Phase IV storage wares represent 15% of the phase, fine wares 10%, and cooking wares 8%. Small forms represent only 4% of that phase. Storage wares represent 18% of the pottery classes in site Phase V with fine wares at 14%, and 9% cooking wares. Both cooking wares and fine wares account for 11% of the classes in Site Phase VI. Site Phase VII finds 13% Storage wares, 8% fine ware, and 5% cooking wares. In Site Phase VIII, storage wares rise to 23%, fine wares represent 12% and cooking wares gain a percentage to 6% over the previous phase. Site Phase IX is a period of disruption, and storage vessels represent 15% of that phase, and fine wares reach a high 20%. Site Phase X finds storage wares at a high of 21% and fine wares at 14%, fine wares having lost six percentage points from the previous phase. Cooking activities appear to gain in Site Phase XI; storage jar components at 10% lose 11% points over the previous phase. In Site Phase XII storage jars are at a high of 44%, and fine wares represent 15%. In Site Phase XIII storage components continue to be popular, representing 33% of the pottery, but there is a marked increase of small forms to 12%. Site

Phase XIV has storage wares representing 18%, cooking wares 12%, and fine wares 9%. Small forms continue to find moderate favor at 5%.

When thinking about Strabo's statement that "they [the Nabataeans] prepare common meals together in groups of thirteen," we can imagine the Nabataeans formally dining in a *triclinium* and celebrating the life and memories of a kinsman, or sitting on woven mats around a lovely fire, convivially serving themselves from cooking pots and decorated fine ware bowls, much as the Bedouin do today.

Because the excavators found site phases either telescoped or the result of erosion, the site phase range of a particular trench deposit was often mixed. After the excavation was completed, as a team we deduced the range of the materials and assigned a deposit within a given range, and some were assigned to multiple site phases, for example, often a span was given for site phasing between two or more phases, e.g. Phases VII-X". For the analysis presented here, we selected only site phases to compare that were not mixed and were therefore distinct.[80]

As we mentioned earlier, differences can be found between phases, but there are always overlaps in the record, which confirms the fact that there are few clear stratigraphic indicators within the Great Temple continuum. Based on this factor we close this account with Appendix 4, Tables 12 and 13, charting the numbers of *selected pottery* recovered from trenches Propylaeum, Lower Temenos, Upper Temenos and Temple by site phase.

During excavation when the stratigraphy and the finds indicated that more than one phase was present, the excavators may have assigned the deposit and its pottery to two or more phases; in their minds the deposits spanned more than a single phase perhaps the deposition was disturbed. Tables 12 and 13 give the pottery fragment results for single trench or special project loci by site phase. Appendix 4, Tables 12 and 13 show the distribution of 166,874 pottery fragments that are considered "pure", and the excavation team assigned them to a single discrete phase. Appendix 4, Table 12 outlines the selected deposits and pottery counts by Site Phase for the Propylaeum and Lower Temenos, and Appendix 4, Table 13 covers the selected results for the Upper Temenos and Temple trenches. Together these selected deposits in total have produced 166,874 pieces of pottery, the Propylaeum total represents 6476 pieces, or 3.8% of the total selected deposits, the Lower Temenos 48,536 fragments or 29% of the collection. As would be expected, the Upper Temenos represents nearly 50%, or 83,019 fragments, whereas the Temple accounts for only 28,843 fragments or 17% from the selected deposits. In comparison with Appendix 4 Table 1, Great Temple overall pottery by area, the percentages are more or less similar for the Upper Temenos and the Temple.

In Appendix 4 Table 12 shows the Propylaeum and Lower Temenos distribution of pottery overall by selected site deposits by site phases and indicates that there are higher pottery fragment counts for later site phases, VIII—XIV, and the Lower Temenos. Site Phase VII in the Propylaeum has 1041 fragments, whereas the Lower Temenos for the same phase has 3479 fragments. The Propylaeum phases thereafter have insignificant numbers of pottery, whereas the Lower Temenos has 9694 sherds in Site Phase IX, 7534 in Site Phase X, and 8934 in Site Phase XI. Thereafter the numbers drop off until Site Phase XIV where 10,041 fragments are ascribed to that site phase.

The Upper Temenos and Temple appear to have earlier and more prolific secure deposits, and in the main, the few closed contexts we have are related to trenches in the Upper Temenos. Early Upper Temenos produce some pottery, but in Site Phase IV, 4125 sherds are collected from 21 trenches and Special Projects. The numbers diminish in Site Phase V to 1231 fragments, but in Site Phase VI, 8675 fragments are recovered. Site Phase VII shows less pottery with 3567 pieces, but numbers swell in Site Phase VIII with 7113 sherds, and the largest number for any single phase occurs in Site Phase IX with 33,592 fragments or 20% of all the selected deposits from 10 trenches. The high counts come from Trenches 105-106 of the bath complex and Trench 94 of the Residential Quarter. In Site Phase X seven trenches produce 4535 fragments, Trench 120 in the

80 However we did combine Site Phase O and pre-Phase I.

APPENDIX 4. Table 12.
GREAT TEMPLE: SELECTED POTTERY BY SITE PHASE AND TRENCH
GREAT TEMPLE PROPYLAEUM AND LOWER TEMENOS

Propylaeum	*Trench*	*Total*	*Lower Temenos*	*Trench*	*TOTAL*
SITE PHASE					
Pre-I				–	–
I	Tr. 86	**12**		SP104	**1062**
	SP125	**38**			
	SP150	**947**			
II	Tr. 95	**29**		SP104	**93**
	SP88	**522**			
	SP95	**55**			
III	–	–		–	–
IV	Tr. 86	**167**		Trench 5	**37**
	Trench 95	**6**		Trench 122	**6**
	Trench 99	**6**		Trench 127	**197**
	SP87	**1**		Trench 16	**49**
				Trench 17	**23**
				Trench 21	**427**
				Trench 25	**27**
				Trench 28	**127**
				Trench 36	**103**
				Trench 42	**565**
				Trench 71	**4**
				Trench 79	**33**
				Trench 97	**71**
				Trench 98B	**52**
				SP105	**227**
				SP20	**118**
				SP48	**41**
V	SP87	**2**		SP105	**372**
				SP104	**951**
VI	Trench 51	**44**		Trench 104	**85**
	SP114	**22**		Trench 127	**63**
	SP118	**83**		SP104	**435**
	SP125	**9**		SP20	**206**
	SP87	**246**			

APPENDIX 4. Table 12. (continued)

GREAT TEMPLE: SELECTED POTTERY BY SITE PHASE AND TRENCH

GREAT TEMPLE PROPYLAEUM AND LOWER TEMENOS

Propylaeum	*Trench*	*Total*	*Lower Temenos*	*Trench*	*TOTAL*
SITE PHASE					
VII	Trench 51	**37**		Trench 17	**2189**
	Trench 82	**191**		Trench 61	**1**
	Trench 86	**114**		Trench 97	**479**
	Trench 87	**1**		SP25	**413**
	Trench 99	**1635**			
	SP125	**32**			
VIII	Trench 100	**8**		Trench 5	**329**
	Trench 69	**459**		Trench 122	**652**
	Trench 80	**118**		Trench 126	**39**
	Trench 82	**90**		Trench 127	**20**
	SP125	**366**		Trench 20	**1446**
	Trench 31	**239**			
				Trench 37	**269**
				Trench 52	**485**
IX	–	–		Trench 5	**3742**
				Trench 105-106	**11**
				Trench 122	**435**
				Trench 126	**1167**
				Trench 97	**2030**
				Trench 98	**871**
				Trench 98B	**1397**
				SP94	**41**
X	–	–		Trench 5	**1313**
				Trench 104	**87**
				Trench 14	**93**
				Trench 16	**567**
				Trench 17	**46**
				Trench 20	**2065**
				Trench 31	**18**
				Trench 36	**68**
				Trench 42	**206**
				Trench 52	**174**
				Trench 61	**419**
				Trench 71	**1513**

APPENDIX 4. Table 12. (continued)
GREAT TEMPLE: SELECTED POTTERY BY SITE PHASE AND TRENCH
GREAT TEMPLE PROPYLAEUM AND LOWER TEMENOS

Propylaeum	*Trench*	*Total*	*Lower Temenos*	*Trench*	*TOTAL*
SITE PHASE					
X				Trench 98	**347**
				Trench 98B	**89**
				SP24	**344**
				SP26	**49**
				SP56	**94**
				SP73	**42**
XI	Trench 99	**97**		Trench 16	**7669**
				Trench 21	**468**
				Trench 31	**165**
				SP26	**94**
				Trench 7	**538**
XII	–	–		SP104	**2**
XIII	Trench 100	**392**		Trench 127	**122**
				SP41	**252**
				SP48	**22**
XIV	–	–		Trench 5	**11**
				Trench 6	**153**
				Trench 20	**190**
				Trench 25	**274**
				Trench 28	**374**
				Trench 30	**105**
				Trench 31	**753**
				Trench 33	**120**
				Trench 36	**231**
				Trench 42	**551**
				Trench 52	**5299**
				Trench 71	**1172**
				Trench 97	**4**
				SP22	**64**
				SP24	**217**
				SP41	**463**
				SP92	**60**

APPENDIX 4. Table 13.
GREAT TEMPLE: SELECTED POTTERY BY SITE PHASE AND TRENCH:
GREAT TEMPLE UPPER TEMENOS AND TEMPLE

Upper Temenos Site Phase	*Trench*	*Total*	*Temple Site Phase*	*Trench*	*TOTAL*
Pre I	SP96	121	**PRE-I**	123	113
	SP108	216		SP107	472
I	1	41	I	8	2
	SP121	54		123	156
	SP108	216		55A	21
	SP110	41		57	175
	SP30	39		85	2
	SP96	276		SP107	396
II	1	32	**II**	123	5
	SP123	7		SP107	43
	SP4	53		SP9	2
III	-	-	**III**	SP107	55
IV	1	22	**IV**	19	166
	2	1		24	18
	18	1530		45	79
	18A	42		64	259
	32	352		SP3	6
	44	46		SP93	338
	46	85			
	49	233			
	53	92			
	54	33			
	67	201			
	75	33			
	77	92			
	91	14			
	94	39			
	SP111	99			
	SP124	73			
	SP30	14			
	SP4	1028			
	SP94	79			
	SP96	17			
V	41	1190	**V**	123	73
	46	41		15	8

APPENDIX 4. Table 13. (continued)
GREAT TEMPLE: SELECTED POTTERY BY SITE PHASE AND TRENCH:
GREAT TEMPLE UPPER TEMENOS AND TEMPLE

Upper Temenos Site Phase	*Trench*	*Total*	*Temple Site Phase*	*Trench*	*TOTAL*
V			**V**	34	14
				55A	22
				58	19
				SP107	65
				SP200	30
VI	105-106	1	**VI**	73	1263
	120	323			
	53	3717			
	83	70			
	84	4078			
	89	378			
	SP108	58			
	SP30	42			
	SP89	8			
VII	1	35	**VII**	23	26
	2	22		24	310
	120	121		26	19
	44	292		40	1478
	77	53		73	2000
	84	189		92	294
	90	61		SP200	17
	SP21	10		SP23	260
	SP30	858			
	SP84	1926			
VIII	105-106	5067	**VIII**	15	88
	125	1706		23	1158
	54	210		24	53
	84	3		34	61
	89	127		35	94
				40	611
				47	313
				55A	1648
				57	92
				62	526
				65	21

APPENDIX 4. Table 13. (continued)
GREAT TEMPLE: SELECTED POTTERY BY SITE PHASE AND TRENCH:
GREAT TEMPLE UPPER TEMENOS AND TEMPLE

Upper Temenos Site Phase	*Trench*	*Total*	*Temple Site Phase*	*Trench*	*TOTAL*
VIII				SP109	41
				SP23	128
IX	101	569	**IX**	9	55
	105-106	2119		34	140
	76	6297		58	6
	77	1023		62	36
	94	20,460		65	3916
	SP108	1173		73	4667
	SP110	1113		85	1114
	SP30	496			
	SP4	22			
	SP94	320			
X	2	3	**X**	9	184
	120	1670		15	240
	125	15		57	2067
	41	1117		62	2093
	44	1556		85	79
	54	174		SP109	26
XI	120	1101	**XI**	70	347
	125	346			
	77	1217			
	83	5323			
	SP108	901			
	SP30	1266			
XII	SP108	184	**XII**	–	-
XIII	32	629	**XIII**	9	24
	SP110	6579		40	20
	SP83	2		73	412
	SP94	766		SP43	22
	SP96	344		SPC5	47
	SPA4	1			
	SPWW	27			
	XXX	24			
XIV	4	6	**XIV**	–	–
	120	337			

APPENDIX 4. Table 13. (continued)
GREAT TEMPLE: SELECTED POTTERY BY SITE PHASE AND TRENCH:
GREAT TEMPLE UPPER TEMENOS AND TEMPLE

Upper Temenos Site Phase	*Trench*	*Total*	*Temple Site Phase*	*Trench*	*TOTAL*
XIV	125	34			
	18	62			
	76	119			
	SP124	7			

Roman-Byzantine Bath Complex with 1670 pieces, Trench 41in the upper strata of the East 'Cistern' (south of the East Exedra) with 1117, and Trench 44, south of the West Exedra (West and Palatial complex) with 1556 fragments. Upper Temenos Site Phase XI shows a measurable increase of 10,154 fragments from six trenches, including Trench 120, again from the Byzantine bath Complex with some 1101 fragments, Trench 125 from the so-called 'Well Room of the Bath Complex, Trench 83 from the South Passageway and the preliminary excavation of the 'Shrine Room' in the temple South Passageway where 5323 fragments are recovered.

As for the Great Temple results of pottery from selected deposits by site phase are as follows: Early site phases Pre-I to Site Phase III produce fewer numbers: Site Phase Pre-I there are only 922 sherds; Site Phase I has 3478 pieces, Site Phase II, 941 sherds, and Site Phase III has only 55 sherds from selected deposits. Higher numbers occur in Site Phase IV with 7278 fragments, or 4.3% of the selected trenches, Site Phase V has 2787, representing 1.6%, Site Phase VI has 11,878 or 7%, and site phase VII has 13,063 or 7.8% of the selected trenches. In Site Phase VIII there are 16,467 fragments or 10% of this corpus, but Site Phase IX has 53,220 selected fragments representing 31% of the selected deposits. Ten Upper Temenos trenches and special projects are noted, but specific loci in Trench 94 of the Residential Quarter alone produce 20,460 fragments of the 33,592 collected for Site Phase IX. Site Phase IX numbers 53,220 pieces or 31% of the selected corpus. Site Phase XI has 19,532 sherds or 11%, Site Phase X with 16,758 pieces represents 10% of the selected deposits, and Site Phase VIII produces 16,467 fragments or 9.9% of the total selected corpus. In Site Phase XI, the numbers increase to 19,532 sherds. However in Site Phase XII the numbers dramatically decrease for only 186 fragments are so phased, but the numbers again dramatically increase for Site Phase XIII with 9685 fragments and in Site Phase XIV are assigned 10,041 sherds.

Area Trenches—Propylaeum and Lower Temenos

A test trench at the eastern end of the Propylaeum West, Trench 86, produced only 12 pottery fragments, however among them was recovered the earliest evidence of a Nabataean painted bowl found at the Great Temple. Dating from 50 to 25 B.C. (Schmid's Phase 2a, or to the last quarter of the A.D. first century[81], it confirmed the early date of this wall, Wall K's construction. An East Propylaeum trench with a high count of ceramics is Trench 99 located in are the northeast corner of the Propylaeum in Site Phase VI with 1635 fragments and Site Phase XIII with 392, also recovered from the Propylaeum East Room 3. As can be noted in Appendix 4, Table 12, there are few other large deposits from the Propylaeum.

In Site Phase X, Lower Temenos Trench 20 has a high number of 2065 fragments. This is located in a central area in the East Triple Colonnade between the stylobates supporting the elephant-headed capitals. In Site Phase XI. Trench 16 located in the west part of the West Exedra recovers

81 Great Temple, Vol. II, Fig. 2.46

7669 fragments, and in Site Phase XIV Trench 52 from the excavation of the East Exedra are found 5299 fragments. More prolific are the later site phases of the Lower Temenos with Site Phase IX producing 9694 fragments from seven field projects.

Area Trenches—Upper Temenos and Temple

In Site Phase IV Upper Temenos trenches with notable deposits include Trench 18, the excavation of the Lower Temenos retaining Wall and West Staircase leading from the Lower Temenos up to the temple area with 1530 sherds, and Special Project 4, the Subterranean Canalization system extending from the Upper to Lower *Temenoi* with 1028 pieces. As would be expected, Upper Temenos trenches produced significantly higher counts, particularly after site Phase V. In Site Phase VI, Trench 53, lower strata of the East 'Cistern' produces 3717 pieces, and Trench 84 has 4078. High pottery counts for Site Phase VII includes Special Project 84 with 1926 examples. (Clearly the Nabataeans continued to celebrate their own cultural identity by producing their painted wares, although by this site phase the Romans had been in control for some time.) This trench includes the Tabun Cave Room in the East Perimeter Wall and the early investigation of the Great Cistern, mentioned earlier in Appendix 4. In Site Phase VIII, The southeast sector of the Bath Complex, Trenches 105-106 produce 5067 fragments and the 'Well Room' of the Bath Complex, Trench 125, produces 1706 fragments. Again from later Bath Complex deposits in Site Phase IX Trench 105-106 finds 2119 sherds. In an area excavated to the west of the West Walkway Trench 76 has 6297 pieces of pottery. As we remarked earlier, the Trench 94 Residential Area has a high count of 20,460 sherds assigned to this phase. Site Phase X has three large deposits in Trenches 120, again the Bath Complex; Trench 41, the upper strata of the East 'Cistern', and in Trench 44 in the East Plaza, south of the East 'Cistern'. Site Phase XII has an insignificant showing, but Site Phase XIII has one large deposit of 6579 pieces in Special Project 110 near the West Precinct Wall and the Cistern-Reservoir.

In the Temple area, there are no high pottery counts before Site Phase VI, where in an area between the East Corridor Wall and the East Colonnade in Trench 73, 1263 sherds are collected, and in Site Phase VII a later deposit of 2000 pieces are also processed from this same trench. The only notable deposit in Site Phase VIII comes from the East Vaulted Chamber of the Theater, Trench 55A where 1648 pieces are recovered. Temple Site Phase IX has 4667 fragments from an even later stage of Trench 73 in the Great Temple East Colonnade. In the Temple Site Phase X are two notable deposits found in the temple Central Arch in Trench 57 with 2067 sherds and the Theater Stage and its connection with the temple East Corridor north, Trench 62, with 2093 sherds. Site Phase XII has no pottery registered from the Temple area, and Site Phase XIII has few significant deposits, and there is no pottery recovered from the Temple Area in Site Phase XIV.

This pottery account provides some useful information. Clearly throughout the Great Temple site phases pottery served the needs of the community around or living in the Great Temple. These deposits represent continuity and support our understanding of the daily ebb and flow of the community. There is continuity before and after the Romans emerge to take over the site, although reflected in the collection are Roman-influenced wares. The point is that Nabataean wares continue to be produced which also reflects continuity, although Rome emerges as a force, and at that time there is a restructuring of the site to include the baths, which play a major role at the site. The pottery of Site Phase VIII before the devastating earthquake of A.D. 363 in Site Phase IX also appears to show continuity in the ceramic record.

Conclusion

Pottery provides a single most important yardstick for measuring technological and stylistic developments. Also it is in common use within the economic reach of all segments of society. For that very reason pottery is an index of Nabataean taste, providing a means by which to judge the aesthetic and practical sense of its manufacturers and of the people who actually used and enjoyed it. The Great Temple collection also provides an understanding of Petra's internal structure and its foreign contacts. Several constants can now be stated regarding the Great Temple and Nabataean pottery traditions.

Site Phase Pre-I or pre-1st c. B.C. belongs to an already established Nabataean culture.

Site Phase VI is intriguing and problematic to define, because we are unable to correlate any changes in the ceramic record with the Roman takeover. With the exception of lamps, there appear to be no discernable changes in the ceramic record associated with Roman control.

Remnants of the typical Nabataean decorated bowls and plates still survive in a major fashion in Site Phase IX, and in a minor way in Site Phase XIV. The relative dates accorded to the phased deposits substantiate the longevity of the Nabataean ceramic culture. This offers solid evidence for the continuation of a Nabataean potting tradition beginning in the pre-1st c. B.C. and continuing at least to the 5th c. A.D.

At the Great Temple no evidence suggests a wide-scale importation of pottery from beyond the Nabataean realm. The scarcity of imports, including ESA and BSP wares, reflects the fact that the Great Temple people favored their own material culture and ceramic traditions.

The Great Temple has yielded an exceptional number of Nabataean wares, which exceeds that recorded at any other Nabataean site. Its large corpus, which previously had been dealt with as either plain wares or fine (painted) wares, it brings together the establishment of a separate shape typology for Nabataean wares, and confirms the significance of Nabataean pottery as a primary source of information for reconstructing the history of the Petra Great Temple and the site as a whole.

These ceramics represent reflect local choices and represent a Nabataean cultural idiom.

Except for the Nabataean bowl, the stylistic profile reflects the Hellenistic origin for the bulk of the repertoire, probably inspired from Alexandria.[82] Wherever its origins, certain forms are assimilated and adapted by the Nabataeans.

The Nabataean potting tradition has a stylistic diversity, which might reflect the cultural diversity of the Nabataeans.

Large-scale local pottery production took place exclusively in Petra workshops, primarily for local consumption.

The Nabataean painted bowl first appears in Site Phase Pre-I at the Great Temple, and continues through the Great Temple site phases until the site is abandoned.

The dominating features are that red painted decoration is in favor earlier than black and dark brown painted decoration, and this change takes place at the Great Temple by Site Phase V, or by the late A.D. 1st century

Painted bowls display a choice of particular motifs that is the same as those from Ez Zantur, and the North Ridge tombs,[83] which implies that there was a uniform Petraean potting tradition. These sites have the same stylistic profile, and it can be assumed they are closely related and enjoyed the same potting culture.

The Great Temple collection of pottery addresses the questions of continuity in the artifact record. In particular, Nabataean painted pottery demands us to ask, what from the Nabataean culture survived to influence later periods? Based on Great Temple record, it is not difficult to determine continuity, because ultimately Nabataean pottery was no longer produced, and little survived into later periods.

We identify Nabataean pottery as a group identity with a recognizable interplay between materials and design features. Typical examples can be found in the drawings presented in Appendix 4 Figures 15 with common bowl shapes, Figure 16 Jugs, Figure 17 Storage jars, Figure 18, Cooking Pots, and Figure 19,with Varia and small miscellaneous forms.

---

82 The archaeological evidence from Alexandria, however, is inconclusive.
83 Bikai and Perry, 2001.

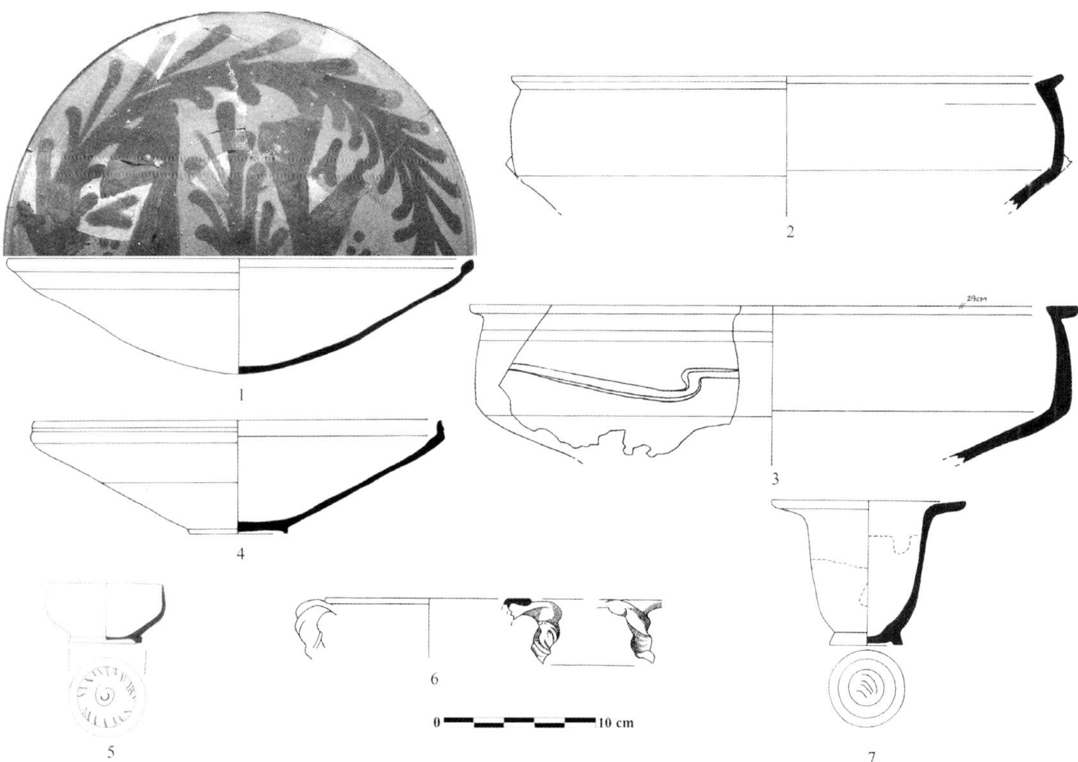

App. 4. Fig. 15. Bowls.
All vessels are provenienced from the Upper Temenos Trench 94 Residential Quarter contexts unless noted; only the locus is indicated. Measurements are in cm and mm, please check the descriptions for accurate dimensions.

App. 4. Fig. 15.1. Bowl. Cat. No. 03-P-64. Rdiam.17, Th. 1–2 mm. Yellowish brown 10YR 5/8 ware with lime, straw and grit inclusions; self-same slip on interior with Phase 3c Nabataean decoration in black 10R 4/1. White 7YR 8/4 slip on rim exterior. Cf., North Ridge Tomb 2 (Bikai 2001, fig. 7, 10; Ez Zantur, (Schmid 1996, Phase 4, no. 704, 209).

App. 4. Fig. 15.2. Bowl. Rdiam. 20, Th. 4 mm. Fine light red 2.5YR 7/8 ware. Very pale brown 10YR 8/2 slip on rim edge and upper body. Surfaces are rough. Slip is worn. Cf., Oboda (Negev 1986, 729) but smaller diameter and angle not as oblique; Ez Zantur (Brogli 1996, no. 813, Type CIIa, No. 86, 263). The Great Temple rim is a variation of this general shape.

App. 4. Fig. 15.3. Casserole bowl. Rdiam. 29, Th. 4-5 mm. Coarse light red 2.5YR 6/8 ware. Pink 7.5YR 8/4 slip on rim edge and extending over carination in irregular blotches. Excised horizontal groove on exterior below rim. Wavy line excised on upper body. Large (1 mm) lime inclusions, lime spalls and rough surface. Counterpoint is irregular resulting from lime spalls. Cf., Oboda (Negev 1986, 948), but much smaller diameter; Ez Zantur, (Brogli 1996, no. 813, Type CIIa, No. 86, 263). The Great Temple rim is a variation of this general shape.

App. 4. Fig. 15.4. Bowl. Rdiam. 15, Bdiam. 2.5, Th. 2 mm. Coarse light red 2.5YR 7/6 ware with black core. Self-same slip unevenly applied on interior. Pinkish white 7.5YR 8/2 slip on exterior rim. Cf., Ez Zantur (Schmid 1996, Gruppe 7, no. 656, 187).

App. 4. Fig. 15.5. Bowl. Rdiam. 6.8, Bdiam. 4.4, Ht. 3.4, Th. 2-3 mm. Fine light red 2.5YR 7/8 ware. Self-same light red 10R 6/8 slip on exterior and interior. Rouletting on ring base. Location: Locus 53. Seq. No. 94072. Cf., Ez Zantur, (Schmid 1996, Gruppe 8, no. 661, 189).

App. 4. Fig. 15.6. Small jar. Rdiam. 7.5, Th. 2 mm. Fine light red 2.5YR 6/8 ware. Self-same slip on exterior. Horizontal rim. Twisted handle.

App. 4. Fig. 15.7. Stopper cup. Rdiam. 7, Bdiam. 2.7, Ht. 5.1, Th. 1.5-3 mm. Light red 2.5YR 6/6 ware. Exterior fabric color: reddish yellow 5YR 7/6. Interior fabric color: 5YR 7/4. Red 10R 5/6 slip applied sloppily to upper body, exterior and interior. String-cut markings on base suggest cup made from clay hump, cut off and then the ring base created by excising clay from stump. Cf., North Ridge Tomb 2 (Bikai 2001, fig. 8, 13), 2nd half 1st c. A.D. Base similar to North Ridge Tomb 1 (Bikai 2001, fig. 5, 17).

App. 4. Fig. 16. Jugs
(Jugs Fig. 4)
All vessels are provenienced from the Upper Temenos Trench 94 Residential Quarter contexts unless noted; only the locus is indicated. Measurements are in cm and mm, please check the descriptions for accurate dimensions.

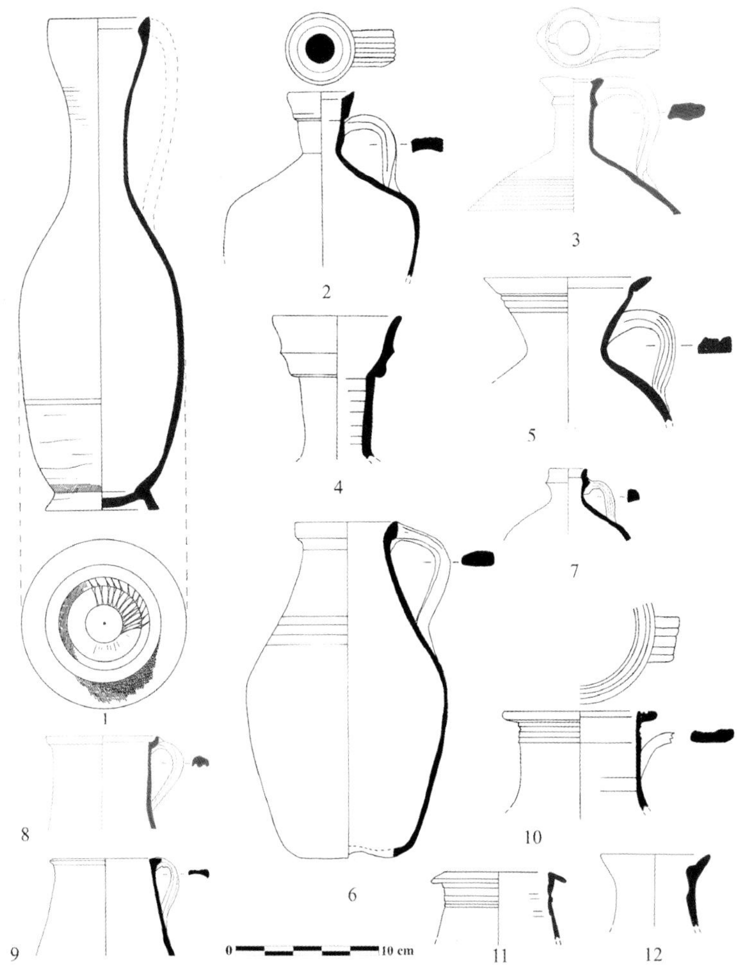

App. 4. Fig. 16.1. Jug. Pottery container P-25 (no dimensions). Reddish yellow 5YR 6/8 ware with very dark grayish brown 10YR 3/2 core. Red 10R 5/8 slip on exterior. Location: UT, Great Cistern Special Project 85, Locus 23, bottom of cistern. Seq. No. 85172.

App. 4. Fig. 16.2. Jug. Rdiam. 2.7, Th. 1.5 mm. Fine light red 2.5YR 6/8 ware. Self-same red 2.5YR 5/6 slip on exterior. Combed loop handle.

App. 4. Fig. 16.3. Jug with trefoil spout. Rdiam. 3.8, Th. 3 mm. Coarse light red 2.5YR 7/8 ware. Very pale brown 10YR 8/3 slipped exterior and interior upper neck. Location: Locus 41. Room 10. Seq. No. 89875.

App. 4. Fig. 16.4. Jug. Rdiam. 5, Th. 3 mm. Light red 2.5YR 7/8 ware. Interior color is light reddish brown 2.5YR 7/4. Pink 7.5YR 8/3 slip on exterior.

App. 4. 16.5. Jug. Rdiam. 6.5, Th. 2.5 mm. Light red 2.5YR 6/6 ware. Interior fabric color: reddish yellow 5YR 7/6. Self-same red 10R6/6 slip on exterior and interior neck. Neck decorated with 3 ridges. Flat loop handle with two ridges on top and combed sides.

App. 4. Fig. 16.6. Jug. Cat. No. 02-P-45. Rdiam. 6.6, Ht. 20.5, Th. 3 mm. Light gray 10YR 7/2 ware. Exterior may have been white slipped; color is light gray 10YR 7/2. Blackened handle. Location: Locus 41. Room 10. Seq. No. 89827.

App. 4. Fig. 16.7. Jug. Rdiam. 2.3, Th. 3 mm. Dark gray 7.5YR 4/1 ware. Exterior color light red 2.5YR 6/6. Handle has combed incisions on side. Location: Locus 53. Seq. No. 94050.

App. 4. Fig. 16.8. Dipper jug. Rdiam. 7, Th. 3.5 mm. Fine light red 2.5YR 7/8 ware. Handle ridged. Location: Locus 53. Seq. No. 94050. Cf., Ez Zantur, variation of Töpfe Typ AIIb, (Brogli 1996, nos. 28. 29, 240).

App. 4. Fig. 16.9. Jug. Rdiam. 7, Th. 2-3 mm. Fine light red 2.5YR 7/8 ware. Self-same light red 2.5YR 6/8 slip on interior. White slip exterior. Location: Locus 60. Room 10. Seq. No. 94009.

App. 4. Fig. 16.10. Jug/jar. Rdiam. 6, Th. 1.5-2.5 mm. Fine light red 2.5YR 6/8 ware.

App. 4. Fig. 16.11. Jug. External Rdiam. 5.3, Internal Rdiam. 4, Th. 1.5 mm. Fine light red 2.5YR 6/8 ware.

App. 4. Fig. 16.12. Jug. Rdiam. 4.2, Th. 2-3 mm. Coarse red 2.5YR 6/6 ware. Break at body. (Two examples of this form in the same context.) Location: UT, Great Cistern, Special Project 85, Locus 23. Seq. No. SP85172. Cf., North Ridge Tomb 1 (Bikai 2001, fig. 5, 19), 1st half of 1st c. A.D.; Phase 2c/3a.

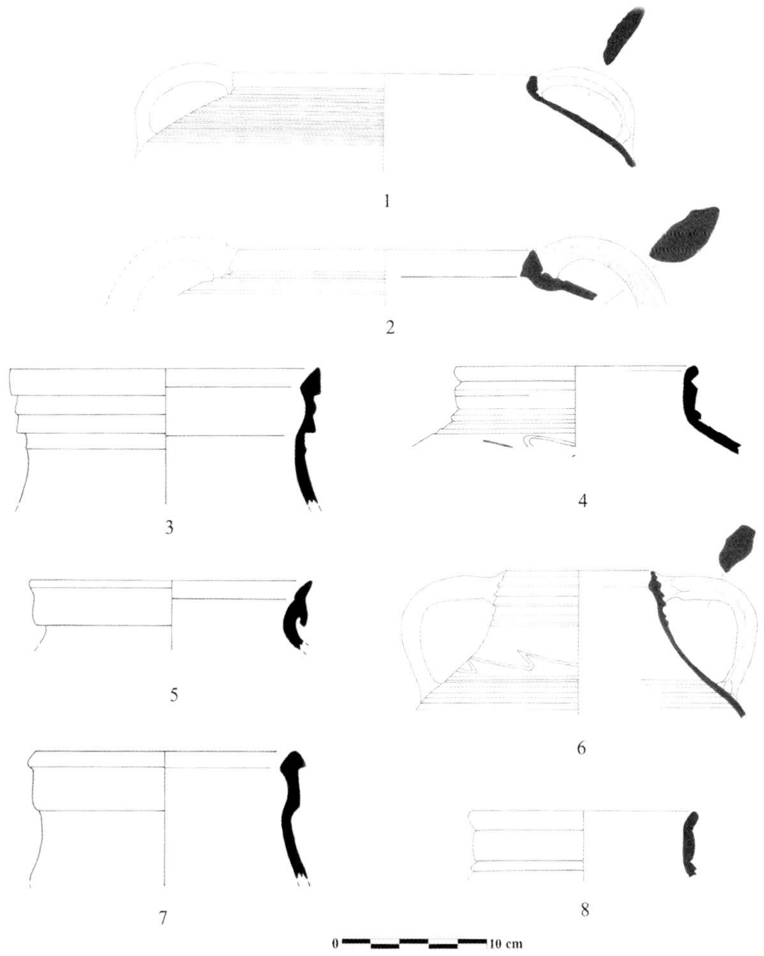

App. 4. Fig. 17. Storage Jars
Storage jars App. 8 Fig. 5.

All vessels are provenienced from the Upper Temenos Trench 94 Residential Quarter contexts unless noted; only the locus is indicated. Measurements are in cm and mm, please check the descriptions for accurate dimensions.

App. 4 Fig. 17.1. Cooking jar. Rdiam. 29, Th. 6 mm. Light red 2.5YR 6/8 ware. Very pale brown 10YR 8/2 slip on exterior. Light reddish brown 2.5YR 6/4 slip on interior. Location: Locus 43. Seq. no. 94070. There are three similar handles in the Residential Quarter assemblage.

App. 4 Fig. 17.2. Storage jar. Rdiam. 18, Th. 4.5 mm. Coarse reddish yellow 5YR 7/8 fabric with black core. Very pale brown 10YR 8/2 slip on exterior. Location: Locus 60. Seq. no. 94009.

App. 4 Fig. 17.3. Storage jar. Rdiam. 12, Th. 3 mm. Red 2.5YR 6/8 ware with dark gray core. Pinkish white 5YR 8/2 slip on exterior. Location: UT, Great Cistern, Special Project 85, Locus 23. Seq. no. SP85172.

App. 4 Fig. 17.4. Storage jar. Rdiam. 15, Th. 5 mm. Coarse light red 2.5YR 6/8 ware with gray core along interior. Very pale brown 10YR 8/2 slip on exterior. Incised wave pattern on shoulder. Location: Locus 43. Seq no. 94070. Cf., Mampsis (Erickson-Gini 1999, fig. 9, 1, 12), early Roman, but without incised decoration.

App. 4 Fig. 17.5. Storage jar. Rdiam. 10, Th. 5 mm. Yellowish red 5YR 5/6 ware with black core. Yellow 10YR 7/6 slip on exterior. Location: UT, Trench 86, Locus 68. Seq. No. 86063. Cf., Ez Zantur (Gerber 2001a, fig. 1), A.D. middle of 4th c.

App. 4 Fig. 17.6. Storage jar. Rdiam. 9, Th. 3 mm. Light red 2.5YR 7/8 ware. Pink 5YR 8/3 slip on exterior body and handle. Incised wavy line on shoulder. Location: Locus 43. Seq. no. 94110.

App. 4 Fig. 17.7. Storage jar. Rdiam. 10, Th. 4-5 mm. Red 2.5YR 6/8 ware. Thick very pale brown 10YR 8/2 slip on exterior and rim interior. Location: UT, Great Cistern, Special Project 85, Locus 23. Seq. No. SP85172.

App. 4 Fig. 17.8. Storage jar. Rdiam. 14, Th. 7 mm. Light red 2.5YR 6/6 ware. Pinkish white 7.5YR 8/2 slip on exterior while red 10R 5/6 slip on interior. No evidence of handle attachment to rim. Location: Locus 43. Seq. No. 94070. Cf., Petra Church (Gerber 2001a, fig. 1, 2), 1st c. B.C.; Mampsis (Erickson-Gini 1999, fig. 9, 1,12), early Roman. Ez Zantur, (Brogli 1996, no. 763, 253).

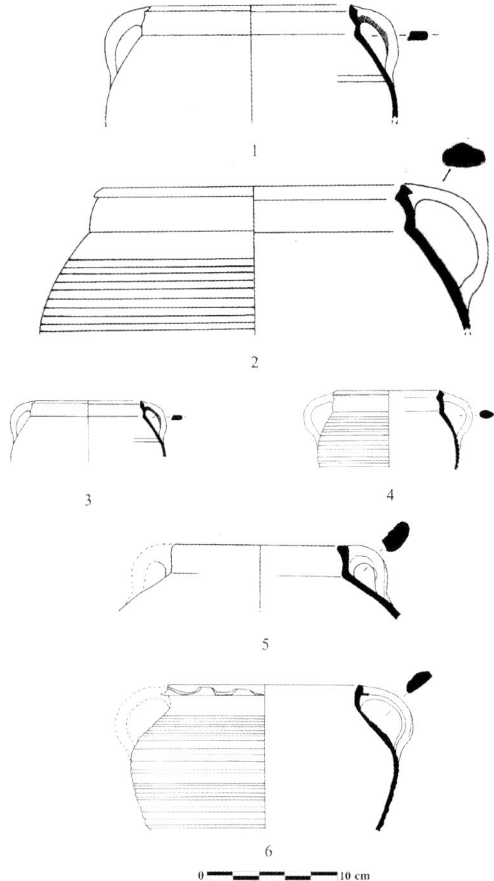

App. 4. Fig. 18. Cooking Pots
All vessels are provenienced from the Upper Temenos Trench 94 Residential Quarter contexts unless noted; only the locus is indicated. Measurements are in cm and mm, please check the descriptions for accurate dimensions.

App. 4. Fig. 18.1. Cooking pot. Rdiam 9, Th. 2 mm. Light red 2.5YR6/8 ware with quantity of fine lime inclusions, some 1 mm. Gritty surface. Inward sloping, short convex neck. Loop handle. Pink 7.5YR8/4 slip on exterior body and interior rim. Cf., Ez Zantur (Stucky *et al.,* 1994, fig. 16, F, 15, T; (Brogli 1996, no. 732, 243). The Great Temple rim is a variation of this shape.

App. 4. Fig. 18.2. Cooking pot. Rdiam. 16, Th. 3-4 mm. Light red 2.5YR 7/8 ware with shell, straw, black sand inclusions. Very pale brown 10YR 7/8 slip on exterior. Ribbed body. Location: UT, Great Cistern, Special Project 85, Locus 23. Seq. No. SP85172. Cf.,Ez Zantur (Brogli, 1996, no. 741, 245).

App. 4. Fig. 18.3. Cooking pot. Rdiam 9, Th. 2 mm. Light red 2.5YR6/8 ware with quantity of fine lime inclusions, some 1 mm. Gritty surface. Inward sloping, short convex neck. Loop handle. Pink 7.5YR8/4 slip on exterior body and interior rim. Cf., Ez Zantur, (Stucky *et al.,* 1994, fig. 16, F, 15, T).

App. 4. Fig. 18.4. Cooking pot. Rdiam 13, Th. 3.5-6 mm. Light red 2.5YR 7/8 ware with large lime and black grit inclusions. Very pale brown 10YR 8/3 slip on exterior and over rim top. Some burning on exterior. Location: Locus 43. Cf., Oboda (Negev 1986, 1007), dated to Middle Nabataean, 30 B.C.–A.D. 50; Ez Zantur (Stucky *et al.,* 1994, Fig. 15, Q), 2nd half 1st c. B.C.; see also Brogli 1996, nos. 738, 741, 245, but the Great Temple example has handles; North Ridge Tomb 2 (Bikai 2001, Fig. 9, 14), 2nd half of 1st c. A.D.; Khirbet edh-Dharih (Villeneuve 1990, pl. VI 5-6), A.D. early 2nd c.

App. 4. Fig. 18.5. Cooking pot. Rdiam. 13, Th. 4-5 mm. Coarse reddish yellow 5YR 7/6 ware with grog and numerous black pebbles. Pink 7.5YR 7/3 slipped exterior and light red 2.5YR 7/6 slipped interior. Handle is burnt. Location: Locus 65. Seq. No. 94131. Cf., Ez Zantur, (Brogli 1996, no. 749, 248 or no. 750, 249).

App. 4. Fig. 18.6. Cooking pot. Rdiam. 14, Th. 3.5 mm. Light red 2.5YR 7/8 ware. Exterior ledge of rim has been pushed up in places along the rim to create a wavy pattern. Pale yellow 2.5Y 8/3 slip on exterior. Burnt exterior. Location: Locus 60. Seq. No. 94009.

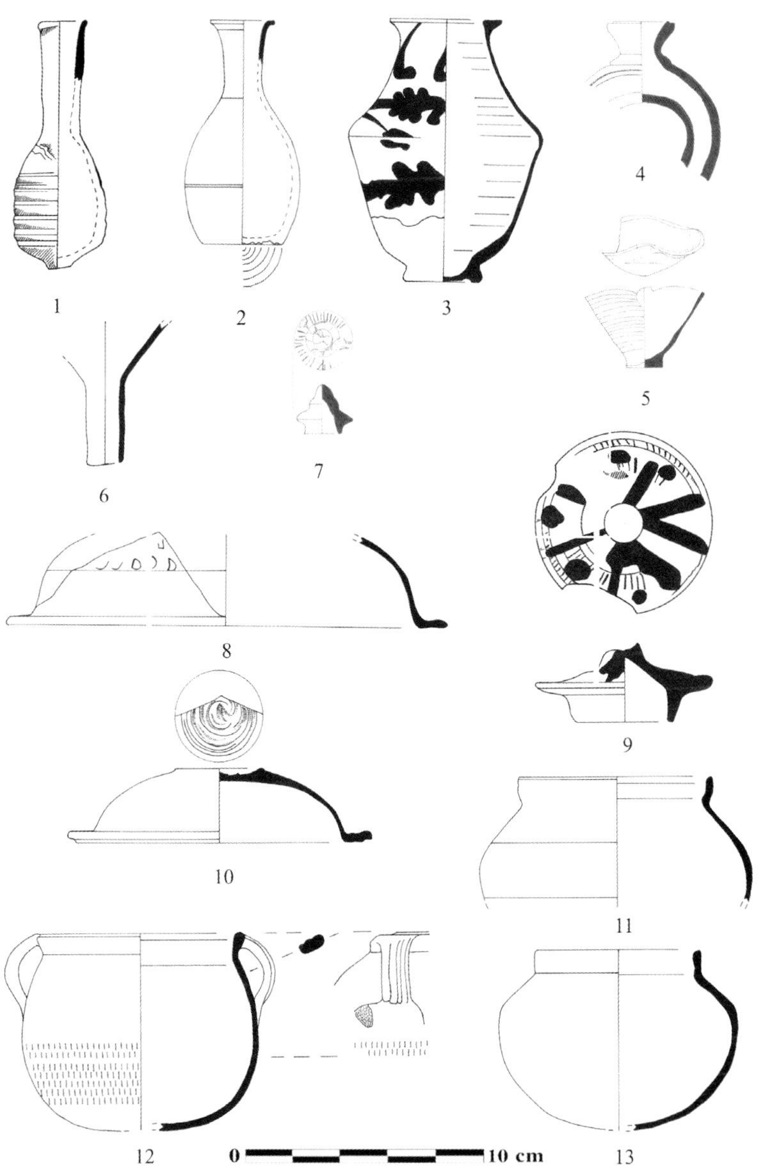
1
2
3
4
5
6
7
8
9
10
11
12
13
0
10 cm

App. 4. Fig. 19. Cooking Pots Small miscellaneous forms, App. 8. Fig. 19.

All vessels are provenienced from the Upper Temenos Trench 94 Residential Quarter contexts unless noted; only the locus is indicated. Measurements are in cm and mm, please check the descriptions for accurate dimensions.

App. 4. Fig. 19.1. *Unguentarium*. Cat. No. 01-P-65. Rdiam 2.0, Th. 3 mm, Ht. 8.7. Dark gray 10YR4/1 ware with red 10R4/8 core. Location: UT, Great Cistern, Special Project 85, Locus 19. Seq. no. SP85125. Cf., North Ridge Tomb 2 (Bikai 2001, fig. 9, 7), dated to the 2nd half of the 1st c. A.D.

App. 4. Fig. 19.2. *Unguentarium*. Rdiam. 2.4, Bdiam. 2.8. Red 2.5YR 5/8 ware. Two fine incised lines around widest point. Burnished. Base incised with spiral. Location: Locus 54. Seq. No. 89917.

App. 4. Fig. 19.3. *Alabastron*. Rdiam. 4, Bdiam. 2.8, Th. 1-3 mm, Ht. 9.1. Medium coarse, reddish yellow 5YR 6/6 ware with thick gray 5YR 5/1 core. Flat rim. Concave base with excised groove to create ring. Red 2.5YR 5/6 slip on exterior to mid-body and over rim to interior of neck. Two palmette wreaths with line of tadpoles between and vertical commas on neck in dark reddish gray 2.5YR 4/. Rim and base potsherds do not join. Similar painting is found at Ez Zantur, phase 4, cf. (Brogli 1996, no. 706, 209).

App. 4. Fig. 19.4. Small pilgrim flask. Rdiam. 4, Th. 5 mm. Pale yellow 2.5Y 8/3 fabric. Excised ridge on thick everted rim. Location: Locus 41. Room 10. Seq. No. 89875.

App. 4. Fig 19.5. Basket bowl. Bdiam. 2.2. Fabric black throughout. Ribbed exterior. String-cut base. Blackened slip on interior. Location: Locus 41. Room 10. Seq. No. 89875.

App. 4. Fig. 19.6. Funnel neck. Rdiam. 1.1, Th. 2 mm. Light red 2.5YR 6/8 ware. Plain vertical rim. Scant remains of white slip. Thick encrustation on interior and exterior. This is the shortest spout in the assemblage. Cf., North Ridge Tomb 2 (Bikai personal communication) their example also has areas of white slip.

App. 4. Fig. 19.7. Stopper. Cat. No. 02-P-18. Rdiam. 2.1. Light red 2.5YR 7/8 fabric. Reddish brown 2.5YR 5/3 radiating lines from top of lid to widest point in a star pattern. Rouletting on lower tier. Location: UT, Baroque Room, Trench 89, Locus 5.

App. 4. Fig. 19.8. Lid. Rdiam. 16, Th. 2 mm. Fine, light red 2.5YR 6/8 fabric. Self-same slip on exterior in light red 10R 6/8. Shallow rouletting above carination. Cf., Ez Zantur, Schmid 1996, a variation of no. 630, 181.

App. 4. Fig. 19.9. Lid. Flange Rdiam. 3.5, Bdiam. 6. Light red 2.5YR 7/8 fabric with pale gray core. Self-same slip 2.5YR 6/8 on exterior with dark reddish gray 10R 4/1 decoration composed of radiating lines and black dots. Rouletting on rim edge and along mid point. Slip is cursorily applied to underside. Similar painting is found at Ez Zantur in phase 4 (Brogli 1996, no. 706, 209).

App. 4. Fig 19.10. Lid. Rdiam. 11, Bdiam. 3.3, Ht. 2.6, Th. 1.5-2.5 mm. Light red 2.5YR7/8 fabric with thick reddish gray 2.5YR6/core. Pink 7.5YR 8/4 slipped rim top and light red 10R 6/8 interior. Groove excised from exterior edge of rim. Concave top. Cf., Ez Zantur, (Schmid 1996, Gruppe 3 rims, esp. no. 624, 181).

App. 4. Fig 19.11. Small globular jar. Rdiam.7, Th. 1.5 mm. Light red 2.5YR 6/6 ware. Plain vertical rim. Pink 7.5YR 8/4 slip on exterior and over rim top. Lines in slip suggest slip applied with brush on wheel. Band of black on exterior, perhaps from firing. White slip was applied over the vessel top so band is part of clay.

App. 4. Fig 19.12. Small globular jar. Rdiam. 7.5, Ht. 6.8, Th. 2 mm. Light red 2.5YR 6/8 ware. Simple rouletting on exterior lower body. Vertical lines 2 mm long x approximately 2 mm apart. Loop handle ridged; slip attached and thumb pressed. Rim warped at handle. The rouletting is reminiscent of that found on an Ez Zantur bowl, (Schmid 1996, no. 664, 189).

App. 4. Fig 19.13. Small globular jar. Rdiam. 6, Ht. 6.2, Th. 1.5 mm. Light red 2.5YR 6/8 ware. Rounded base. Light red 2.5YR 6/8 slip on exterior and over interior rim. Burning on widest area on interior and exterior. Clay is very friable. Cf., Ez Zantur, (Brogli 1996, no. 803, 262).

Now we turn a summary or Précis of Great Temple Pottery by site phase

Shape, function, and decoration précis of Great Temple Pottery by Site Phase

The following is a summary of function, classes, shapes, and decoration by site phase.[84]

Site Phase Pre-I

Site Pre Phase I can only be dated to the pre-1st c. B.C. It has no coherent architectural plan, but is composed of odd walls and a small collection of pottery.

In Pre Phase I, plain vertical rims dominate the collection representing 47%. Flaring shapes are second with a 30% showing, and incurving, inverted and pendant forms are present at a significantly lower percentage. Ring bases represent 71%, and flat bases 21% with the button and round bases present in lower percentages. The results of Site Phase Pre I distribution into functional classes indicate that 13% are bowls and plates, 4% are cooking pots, jars and jugs represent 26%, large storage jars account for 27%, and small forms have a negligible showing. 67% in this phase has recognizable vessel types.

As for bowls and plates, plain vertical shapes (33%) outnumber flaring (3%), and inverted (4%) shapes. No cooking pots are recorded in this phase. In the jars and jugs class, flaring rimmed jars and jugs (29%) are found, and outnumber plain vertical (11%) rim types. The bases in this phase find that the ring base (71%) outnumbers both the flat (21%) base and round (6%) base, but the button base is also present.

In this site phase 98% of the fragments are slipped. Self-same slips represent 47%, 15% are gray, 14% are brown, and 10% are black, representing 86% of the decorated fragments. Fine ware painted fragments represent 2% of the corpus. Red leads with a 50% showing followed by brown 26% and black 16%. There are no bowls with white painted rims. The most common motifs are drips, splashes, and squiggles. In Pre-I Site Phase only 9% of the pieces exhibit plastic decoration. Incision is found on 3% of the potsherds, including body fragments, bases, bowls, cooking pots, and jars and jugs. Ribbing is also found on 3% of the surfaces, and 1% exhibit excisions, and this single example is on a jar or jug.

Site Phase I

This phase is dated to the early 1st c. B.C. It is a time of site preparation with the razing of earlier structures on the site, importation of fill to create a level platform for the Lower Temenos and the installation of the Great Temple canalization systems.

For Site Phase I, the rim class finds incurving shapes dominating the assemblage with a 35% showing. Plain vertical shapes drop to 28% and flaring shapes also are in decline to 28%. Inverted shapes make a percentage point gain. The ring base maintains its popularity representing 45% of the bases, followed by the flat base representing 34%. Site Phase I has 49% of its collection divided into functional classes. Fine ware bowls and plates account for 17%, cooking pots 6%, jar and jug 13% and large storage vessels 8%. Small forms like lamps represent 2% of the assemblage. Construction materials—roof tiles, canalization pipes, and floor pavers represent 1%.

Most common fine ware bowls and plate rim shapes are the plain vertical (29%) form, which outnumbers the inverted (10%) shape. There is also a small representation of flaring (6%) and everted (3%) shapes. From the beginning of our cooking pot samples the flaring shape is predominant. As for jars and jugs, the flaring (45%) shape predominates this phase and overpowers plain vertical (13%) types by 12%. And in this phase ring (45%) bases far outnumber flat (28%) and round (9%) bases, however, string cut (6%) bases are present.

84 For Site Phases IV-IX painted wares and motifs and plastic decoration have already been discussed and will not be repeated here.

The total fragment count for this phase is 3305, and of these 3232 is slipped representing 97% of the phase. Self-same slips represent 44%, white 17%, black 8%, brown 6%, and gray 7%. A yellow slip also appears in this phase at 0.2%. Only 1% of the phase fine wares are painted with red (41%) painting leading white (20%), black (15%) and brown (2%). Commonly found are white painted bands around fine ware bowl rims, which begin in this phase; 155 such fragments are present, representing 16% of the white banded bowls found at the Great Temple. Other common motifs are simple red painted dots around the rim, or short strokes around the interior rim and bunch of stylized leaves. In this Site Phase, 11% of the collection exhibits plastic finishing including incision, molding, notching, rouletting, ribbing, impressions, and appliqué. Most common is ribbing 70%, with incision 21%, and 3% of the vessels have impressions. A wide range of pottery exhibits these primary and secondary manufacturing traits, but jars and jugs bear 21% of these distinctive characteristics, particularly ribbing and incision.

Site Phase II

Site Phase II is dated to the mid first century B.C. It is associated with the construction of the distyle in antis temple.

Site Phase II ceramics has 54% of its pottery as recognizable shapes, with 30% representing fine ware bowls and plates. Cooking pots account for only 1% for this phase, whereas jars and jugs represent 11%, and large storage vessels 2%. No construction materials are present.

The inverted rim shapes now dominate the rim corpus and plain vertical shapes hold on to their Site Phase I, 28% standing. Incurving shapes drop to 19%—a 9% decline, and flaring shapes fall off considerably from the Site Phase I corpus, a 17% decline. As for bases, the ring base ascends to its peak of 53% and the flat base represents 28%, and the round base is beginning to climb in representation to 11% of the corpus.

For bowls and plates, inverted (39%) forms and plain vertical (32%) shapes dominate the assemblage. The everted (9%) cooking pot shape dominates in this phase, and for jars and jugs the everted (10%) shape also is the leading shape, but flaring (4%) rims are also present. Flat (28%) bases continue, in use most probably for large vessels, but ring (52%) bases predominate the assemblage, most probably in use for plates and small jars.

Some 738 fragments in this phase are slipped, or 78% of the pottery. Self-same slips represent 67%, 8% are red brown, 6% are white, 8% are gray, 4% are black, and red slip stands at 1%. Only 1% of this collection bears painted decoration on the interior of their fine wares. There is an even distribution between red and black, both representing 40%. Red brown paint also has strength at 20%. Of the motifs there are lines of blobs or dots, swirls and a few finely red painted leaf designs. Also in Site Phase II plastic decoration occurs on 12% of the fragments, of which 9% are ribbed. Incisions and rouletting occur on 1%, respectively, of the vessel surfaces.

Site Phase III

Dating to ca. 35-30 B.C. it is little wonder that Site Phase III has a paucity of material culture. As yet there is a yet unexplained upheaval and minor damage is found throughout the site, particularly in the temple area.

In Site Phase III rim counts, flaring shapes account for 54%, and now dominate the corpus. Plain vertical forms increase their numbers to 31%, and most surprising are the total lack of inverted shapes and the slight decline of incurving forms. As for bases, pointed and ring bases share the honors, each accounting for 50% of the base group.

This phase is represented by few diagnostics. Fine ware bowls and plates account for 20%, 56% are jars and jugs, and 22% are large storage vessels. Recognizable shapes represent 97% of this small collection, but no cooking pots are found. Although the bowl and plate fine ware sample is poor, plain vertical (54%) rims appear to dominate this class. In the jar and jug class, flaring (54%) rims predominate this phase. The ring (50%) base is most popular during this phase and shares its use with the pointed base used for large forms such as jars.

The majority of fragments of this phase are slipped. Self-same slip accounts for 16%, brown, which is the most popular of the phase at 36%, black, gray 10%, and tan 12%. No white, red, red brown or salmon slips appear to be present. Painted decoration on the fine ware bowl interiors is similar to Site Phase II with an even distribution of red and black paints, each representing 40%, and 20% is red brown. No white painting is present. Designs represented include red painted drips, wavy lines and horizontal palm fronds. Site Phase III has 23% of its wares exhibiting incision, ribbing and excision on its fine ware bowls and storage vessels.

Site Phase IV

Dating from ca. the last quarter of the first century B.C. to the mid-1st c. A.D., Site Phase IV is a period of expansion for the Grand Design of the tetrastyle in antis temple. Constructed are the full Propylaeum, the West Entry Stairway with its nefesh, the Lower Temenos Triple Colonnades with their exedrae and cryptoporticoes. Also constructed are the Upper Temenos Great Cistern, the East Perimeter Wall, the Residential Quarter, and the Baroque Room Complex. Site Phase IV is both a time of construction and a time of intensive use.

Site Phase IV has 44% of its corpus identified as diagnostic shapes—of these 9% are bowls and plates, 8% are cooking pots, 11% are jars and jugs, and 3% represent large storage vessels. As for Site Phase IV's rim shapes, plain vertical forms show a modest gain to 33% and dominate the corpus. Incurving shapes show a modest increase, and there is a fairly even distribution of everted, inverted, and flaring shapes. Plain vertical (25%) fine ware bowl shapes predominate, but inverted (11%) and everted (8%) forms are also found. Plain vertical (5%) cooking pots far outweigh everted and flared forms. Plain vertical jars and jugs continue in popularity, but everted and incurving shapes are also present. Site Phase IV bases find the flat base dominating the assemblage at 45%.

The round base trails it at 28% and the ring base at 23%. During this phase ring bases appear to begin their decline.

Sixty-three percent or 4644 fragments are slipped. Liquid decoration indicates that white slip is dominant at 41%. Self-same slip is 16%, brown and gray are each at 9%, and black stands for 10% of the slipped fragments. Eighty fragments are coated with a yellow slip representing 1% of the slipped wares.

Site Phase V

A continuation of Site Phase IV, Site Phase V, dated to the late 1st c. A.D., is characterized by the Nabataean redesign of the Great Temple with the Theater inserted into its center.

In Site Phase V, 41% of the pottery is diagnostic in function. Fine ware bowls and plates represent 14%, cooking pots 9%, jars and jugs 5%; small forms have a negligible presence, and large storage vessels 13%. Construction materials also exhibit a minimal showing.

Site Phase V rims show the inverted shape to represent 37%, and everted, flaring, incurving and plain vertical shapes maintain a strong presence with the plain vertical rim accounting for 19% of the assemblage. In Site Phase V bases, the round base now ascends to the top place among base types with a 50% showing. The round base is generally associated with cooking pots, for the base sits easily into the fire pit. Ring bases amount to 13% and flat bases are at 11%.

The bowls and plates of this phase are characterized by the inverted (49%) rim shape, which is the most popular, with a small representation of plain vertical (14%) and incurving (9%) shapes. Of this phase's 139 cooking pots, the majority are divided between inverted and flaring rim shapes.

Everted jars and jugs remain the most popular shape with flaring and plain vertical shapes also present.

There are 3372 slipped fragments in Site Phase V, representing 94% of the slipped sherds. White slip at 26% dominates the phase, with self-same slip at 23%, gray and brown each representing 7%, and black is at 5%. Sixteen fragments are coated with a yellow slip or 0.4% of the total.

Site Phase VI

This phase is attributed to before and after the Roman annexation of Petra in A.D. 106. There is damage to the Great Temple site due, perhaps to the Roman takeover and/or because of the A.D. 113/114 CE earthquake. In the Lower Temenos repairs are made to the Hexagonal Pavement and to the East Exedra walls, and the subterranean canalization system is retrofitted due to soil accumulation—which contains some 1st c. A.D. ceramics. In the Upper Temenos is the probable collapse of the Baroque Room and damage occurs in both the Anteroom and Shrine Room, and shortly thereafter there is the abandonment of the Shrine Room and modification of the Anteroom's east wall. This phase may also be the terminal use of the Residential Quarter. In the temple proper, the E., W. and S. corridor doorways are blocked or narrowed restricting access to the sanctuary's interior. Further collapse is indicated by damage to the east and west walls of the E. Interior Staircase, the major walls of the temple structure, however, remained standing. Clearly damage is evidenced in various areas. The building of the Bath Complex also takes place during this period.

Site Phase VI is a large collection of 11,131 fragments, 43% of which can be divided into functional classes. Fine ware bowls and plates are 10%, cooking pots 11%, jars and jugs are 7%, small forms also represent 7%, and large storage vessels represent 1%.

Inverted fine ware bowls and plates account for 38% of the shapes and continue to dominate the assemblage, however, incurving (11%), and to a lesser extent plain vertical forms are also present. As for the Site Phase VI rim corpus, the inverted shape maintains its popularity representing 34%—a slight percentage decrease over the previous phase. The trefoil rim makes its appearance at the Great Temple during this phase. Although incurving forms drop off from Phase V to an 8% representation, other shapes—everted, flaring and plain vertical types maintain a presence. Pendant rims also maintain a modest showing at 10%. As for bases, the round base maintains its dominance maintaining a 50% showing. The ring base remains at 13% and the flat base also is 13%. In this phase, the everted cooking pot continues to dominate by a large percentage. Flaring jar and jug rims maintain their popularity with everted shapes finding slightly less favor. Incurving and inverted shapes are also represented. Round bases represent 77% of this phase with the ring base accounting for 23% of the bases present.

Ninety-four percent of this Site Phase VI assemblage is slipped with the white slip maintaining its dominant position at 33%. Self-same slips are 29%, red at 12%, black and gray each at 8% and tan at 5%.

Site Phase VII

This phase is dated to the mid-2nd c. A.D. when repairs and rebuilding are taking place.

Fifty-five percent of the Site Phase VII fragments are classed into functional shapes. Eight percent are fine ware bowls and plates, 5% cooking pots, 10% are jars and jugs with 3% representing large storage vessels and pithoi. Small forms are represented, as are construction materials. The Site Phase VI rims find plain vertical shapes returning to popularity, showing 32% dominance in the collection. Inverted and flaring forms maintain their percentages, however, flaring forms decrease and inverted shapes decrease from 34% in the Site Phase VI repertoire to a 17% presence in Site Phase VII. In this phase 39% of the bowl and plate rims are plain vertical shapes. Inverted rims account for 32% with lesser percentages for everted, incurving and flaring shapes. Everted cooking pot shapes are accompanied by plain, vertical, flaring and incurving shapes. This phase finds 35% of the jars and jugs with everted rims, and plain vertical shapes represent 23%, followed by flaring, inverted, and a few incurving rims. In this phase 70% of the bases are flat with ring bases representing 12% of the base shapes, and only 6% of the collection favoring the round base.

In Site Phase VII, 9051 fragments are slipped or 69% of the total corpus. White slip leads with a 29% showing followed by self-same and red slip, each with 24%. Black, salmon and tan colors each are at 5% presence. Forty-two fragments bear a yellow slip, representing 0.4% of the phase, and 6 pieces are decorated with a green slip.[85]

Site Phase VIII

Dating from the late 2nd c. A.D. to the A.D. 363 earthquake, this phase has a conspicuous profile of damage, partial abandonment, collapse, and dumping. Even with these disruptive events, life at the Great Temple appears to continue.

In Site Phase VIII, 69% of the collected pottery is classed into functional classes. Fine ware bowls represent 12%, cooking pots 6%, jars and jugs 18%, and large storage vessels 5%. Small forms increase their presence from the previous phase and now account for 3% of the assemblage. Construction materials represent 25% of this phase's collection.

Site Phase VIII rims find a marked decrease in everted shapes of 14% above the Site Phase VII rims. The everted rim now represents 12% of the rim group. Incurving shapes appear to be dominant with a 36% increase over Site Phase VII to represent 44% of the shapes. Flaring shapes maintain their 11% strength, inverted shapes markedly decrease to a low of 6%, and plain vertical shapes, although popular, decrease from 32% to 24% in this phase. As far as bases are concerned, flat bases continue to be dominant at 66%, ring bases have declined to 9%, and round bases reappear with a strong 17% showing.

The fine ware plain vertical bowl and plate rims continue in popularity (33%) with flaring (22%), incurving (20%), followed by everted (12%) and inverted (10%) shapes. Phase VIII cooking pots are dominated by incurving shapes, 61%, and well below those in numbers are everted, plain vertical, inverted, and finally flaring shapes. A change takes place in the jar and jug class with incurving rims representing 51% followed by plain vertical forms representing 21%. Flaring forms account for 14% and everted rims are 10%.

There are three glazed fragments appearing in this phase, and 164 fragments or 1% are yellow slipped, and 39 fragments are green slipped. The 12,996 slipped sherds represent 78% of the phase. Self-same slips represent 23%, black 21%, and white 13%. Gray is 11% followed by tan at 9%, brown and salmon each at 7%, and red at 6%.

Site Phase IX

The earthquake of A.D. 363 CE leaves clear footprints of collapse throughout the site, however, there are obvious indications that there are areas still in use.

Rims in Site Phase IX find the plain vertical rim back in great favor with a 30% showing as the dominant form for the phase. Everted forms slightly increase in numbers, whereas flaring forms decrease, as do incurving rims. Pendant forms make a sizeable increase from 2% in Site Phase VIII to 18% in Site Phase IX. Flat bases maintain their popularity at 69%, and again ring bases represent 25%, but the numbers for all other shapes decrease.

Popular in Site Phase IX are fine ware bowls and plates accounting for 19% of this phase. Cooking pots are 7%, jars and jugs 11%, large storage vessels 4%, and construction materials decline from

---

85 Stucky, Schmid, *et al.* 1994, 281-286.

the previous phase and represent 17%. Small forms account for 3%. Sixty-three percent of this pottery can be placed in functional classes.

The fine ware bowl and plate shape patterns established in the previous phase seem to continue, for plain vertical bowl rims account for 30%, followed by incurving rims 29%, and inverted rims represent 13%. In the cooking pot class, pendant or down turned rims are favored with a 49% representation, however, 38% represent everted shaped rims. Plain vertical shapes account for 7% and flaring and inverted forms each represent 2%. As for jars and jugs, this phase has a high occurrence of rims with pendant, flaring and everted forms, each representing some 27%, 24% and 23% respectively. Plain vertical shapes account for 16%.

Self-same slips regain the lead with a 47% rate, followed by white 28%, gray 9%, and tan 6%, and red and black each representing 2%. Sherds numbering 281 are yellow slipped accounting for 0.6% and 66 are green slipped or 0.1%. The 42,219 slipped pieces in this phase represent 79% of the large phase corpus of 53,223 elements.

Site Phase X

Dated from the 4th to 6th c. A.D., this approximate 200 year phase indicates that this is a period of abandonment characterized by the accumulation of a sizeable fluvial deposit in the East Plaza. There is some reconstruction by the creation of shoddy intercolumnar walls in the Lower Temenos East Colonnade, and there is secondary domestic reuse in all the temple areas. Site Phase X dramatically ends with the A.D. 551 earthquake.

With 63% recognizable forms from Site Phase X, 14% fine ware bowls and plates are found—2343 such fragments. Cooking pots represent 11%, 15% are jars and jugs with 5% of the repertoire classed as large storage vessels and pithoi. Small forms, including lids, lamps, unguentaria and amphoriskoi, account for 4%. Construction materials slightly decrease in the corpus representing 13% (they represented 17% in Site Phase IX).

Incurving rims appear to be most popular in Site Phase X, representing 35% of the shapes. There is a modest decrease in everted forms, a significant decrease in pendant forms, and flaring and inverted shapes find modest increases. Plain vertical shapes maintain their 30% presence. Inverted fine ware bowl and plate forms account for 29% of the bowl rims, but plain vertical shapes represent 27%, and incurving shapes are 26%. Everted rims are now at 13% and flaring forms represent 3%. There are few cooking pots represented in this phase, and there appears to be a fashion change in this phase, for 55% are incurving shapes, 25% are plain vertical forms, and 11% are everted. Forty-nine percent of the jars and jugs vessels are incurving in shape and only 23% are plain vertical rims. Everted forms represent 12% and flaring 10% with only 4% being inverted in shape. In Site Phase X, 48% of the bases are flat and 35% are round—these two shapes seem to dominate this assemblage. Ring bases represent 9% and string cut bases 2%. Umbilical bases are also present.

In Site Phase X, white is the dominant slip color, 29%, with self-same 17%, gray 12%, black 10%, followed by brown and tan each at 9%, and salmon at 8%. Yellow slip is found on 284 fragments representing 2% of the total; green is also present. One piece is found slipped in blue. Slipped in this phase are 77% of the sherds representing the 13,007 fragments that are processed in the field. Painted fine wares in Site Phase X appear on 5% of the pottery. Black paint continues to be popular at 20% and surpassing it is dark brown at 22%, which is 44% of the dark paints so representative of earlier phases as well. Red represents 13% and white maintains its use on 33% of the painted fragments, but banded bowls are not as prolific in this phase. In Site Phase X fewer designs are present. Feather designs and floral motifs are prominent, and dots are a favored motif. Fragments with plastic decoration in Site Phase X number 3376; 20% of the site phase pottery. Jars and jugs number 3505 showing that 17% are characterized by ribbing. Ribbed cooking pot fragments are 880, or 46% of the cooking pot fragments registered for this site phase. Fine ware bowls decorated with rouletting number 16 (1%) out of the 193 (13% of the bowls for this phase) that carry plastic decoration. Jars and jugs and large storage vessels number 3505, and only 17% display plastic decoration—the majority is ribbed (17%), and many, 80, carry incisions. Plastic decoration on 1476 body sherds accounts for 90% of the total pottery in this phase and 1340 or 90% of these, exhibit ribbing, and the remaining fragments are incised, rouletted or impressed.

Site Phase XI

The earthquake of A.D. 551 brings about all but the complete collapse of the temple and its surround. There is scant evidence that domestic tasks continue, albeit in the rubble.

Site Phase XI rims finds plain vertical shapes dominant and jumping to 41%—an 11% rise in popularity from Site Phase X. Incurving forms significantly decrease by 23% to a 12% representation. Everted, flaring and pendant shapes have modest boosts, as do trefoil shapes. Inverted shapes, however, appear to be non-existent, for none appear in this phase. As far as bases are concerned, round bases outstrip others at 62%, and the flat base, so popular from Site Phase VII to Site Phase X, shrinks to 11%.

In Site Phase XI there is a decrease of fine ware bowls and plates to 5%, whereas cooking pots increase over the previous phase to 18%—a 7% increase over Site Phase X. Jars and jugs decrease in popularity representing 6%, as do storage jars and pithoi to a 3% representation. Construction materials witness a sharp rise to 28% of the pottery examined, and small forms are at a 3% level.

As for fine ware bowls and plates, plain vertical rims outnumber the remaining shapes, representing 51% of the total bowl assemblage. Incurving plate rims number 18%, and everted shapes are 10%. This phase represents a dramatic change in the cooking pot class of vessels, for plain vertical rims represent 72% of that class. Inverted in form are 14% and everted types represent 8%, and flaring 4%. In this phase there is a relatively even distribution between the four leading jar and jug shapes. Everted shapes are 26%, flaring and plain vertical shapes each represent 23%, and the incurving shape accounts for 17%. In Site Phase XI, round bases account for 53%, flat bases represent 18%, and ring and squared-off bases each account for 12%. String cut bases and umbilical shaped bases are also part of the group.

Fifty-three percent of the fragments in this phase are slipped 10,401 of the 19,532 fragments. White slips are favored at 46%; self-same slips represent 22%, gray numbers 9%, black 7%, salmon 6%, red 4%, and tan 3%. Yellow and green slips are both present representing 0.6 and 0.02 percent respectively. One glazed potsherd is present. Six percent of the fine ware collection is painted. Black painted decoration is found on 29%, dark brown on 30%, together totaling 59% of the painted decoration. Red is making a comeback representing 29%, and red brown is at 7%. White, which enjoyed such an accelerated rate in earlier phases, is now present at only 4%, which is its lowest level since Site Phase I. This phase is similar to its predecessor as far as fine ware bowl designs are concerned in that floral designs predominate along with lines and crosshatching. There are 3133 fragments exhibiting plastic surface treatments in Site Phase XI, or 16% of the total fragments collected for the phase. Fine ware bowls with plastic surface treatment number 102, or 15% of the class registered. Of these 53% are incised, 22% are rouletted and 21% are ribbed. Fine ware plates are fewer in number representing 23 fragments—two bear incisions. Eighteen are rouletted and three are ribbed. Cooking pots, numbering 1199, exhibit surface treatment. Some 1206 or 28% of the cooking pot fragments in this phase are ribbed. Some 316 storage jars and jugs, or 16% of the jars and jug class, have plastic surface decoration, and 261 or 82% of these also are ribbed. Small forms bear incisions, ribbing, rouletting and perforation, and many small shapes are molded.

Site Phase XII

This phase represents a paucity of remains—the site is all but abandoned. Ascribing a relative date to it places it sometime in the later 6th c.

Site Phase XII signals three rim shapes vying for popularity. Everted forms are at 26%, a significant rise from Site Phase XI, the inverted shape reappears at 26%; again a significant jump, and plain vertical shapes share the lead at 27%. However, from Site Phase XI, the plain vertical shape has experienced a downward trend to 28%. The ring base becomes dominant in Site Phase XII, and round and flat bases have tumbled to 28%, respectively.

Site Phase XII is characterized by 15% fine ware bowls and plates, 2% cooking pots, 21% jars and jugs, 23% large storage vessels and pithoi, and there is an absence of construction materials. Small forms represent 4% of the collection. As for fine ware bowls and plates, this phase is poorly represented and will not be described in detail. As mentioned previously, Site Phase XII lacked a significant number of types, so cooking pots, jars and jugs, and bases will not be discussed.

The paucity of fragments in this phase, 177 sherds, makes it difficult to compare and contrast with either preceding or succeeding phases, however, 95% of the collection is slipped. Self-same slip continues in popularity to 54%, and the white slipped fragments represent 20% with black slips accounting for 11%, tan slips 6%, gray 4%, and brown 2%. Only 0.1% of this phase 's fine ware collection bears paint. Red brown colors represent 42%, black is 28%, and red and white paints each account for 14% of the colors. Designs that are registered include dots, drip designs, as well as floral motifs. Unfortunately, Site Phase XII does not have a large sample, but the results indicate are that 30% of the pottery is ribbed—body potsherds, cooking pots, and jars and jugs. Incisions also appear on a few of the jars. Unfortunately more conclusive evidence is not available.

Site Phase XIII

This phase broadly represents the late Byzantine and Islamic periods—the end of 6th and 7th c. but the site appears to have been sporadically in use by squatters who settle on it, despite the series of major collapses.

Three rim shapes vie for popularity during this time. Leading forms that share the highest percentages are everted shapes, 26%, inverted shapes 26%, and plain vertical forms at 27%.

In Site Phase XIII, 72% of the pottery fragments have a recognizable function. Fine ware bowls and plates represent 11%, cooking pots 8%, jars and jugs 30% which is a considerable increase over those in Site Phase XII. Large storage containers are 3%. Small forms account for 12% and despite the lack of construction materials in the previous phase, they now amount to 8% of the collection.

This phase finds 59% of the bowl and plate rims inverted, which demonstrates a departure from site Phase XI, however, plain vertical rims represent 32%, everted 11% and flaring rims 10% of the bowl rims. There are a few cooking pots in this phase, and 79% of this class of vessel and 9% are plain vertical, 6% are flaring and 5% are inverted shapes. (Perhaps our squatters are dining elsewhere?) Four jar and jug rims are represented in this phase with everted shapes leading the class with 35%, followed by flaring 32%, and plain vertical 27% with a few inverted shapes. In this phase, flat bases account for the majority of forms or 59%. Ring bases are 18% and round bases are 15%. String cut and umbilical bases continue to be represented as well.

Eighty nine percent of the 9685 fragments are slipped, or 8698 pieces. White represents 49%, self-same 34%, gray 9%, black 2%, and brown and tans each cover 1% of the pieces. Yellow slip is found at 0.8% with 77 sherds so-colored. Green slip is also present. Only 3% of the fine ware pottery is painted. White is the leading color with a 42% showing. Dark brown represents 17% and black 11%. In this phase the favored designs are dots, net and lines, and there is some crosshatching, dashes and rays. Site Phase XIII accounts for 1917 pottery fragments with plastic surface treatment, or 19% of the total so decorated. Of the 950, 828, or 87% of the fragments exhibit ribbing; 86 fragments, or 9% of the total, bear incision. Surface treated bowl fragments number 57 in total, of which 34, exhibit ribbing. Plates so decorated number 56, of which 46 are ribbed, three are excised, and one has a scalloped piecrust rim. Of the 378 cooking pots, 45% of these vessels for this phase, 47 bear incisions and 331 fragments or 87% with plastic decoration display ribbing. Forty percent of this vessel class is ribbed. Besides cooking pots, other body sherds bearing plastic decoration number 241 and 56% of these are ribbed, and 155 or 36% bear incisions. Small forms carry impressions, incisions and excisions, ribbing, rouletting, and two are perforated.

Site Phase XIV

This phase is broadly defined as the "modern period." In its early time, parts of the site are in domestic use, whereas other areas, like the Lower Temenos, serve for industrial purposes such as the manufacture for lime with a kiln located in the East Exedra.

In Site Phase XIV, fine ware bowls and plates have an 8% occurrence, cooking pots 11%, jars and jugs 14%, and large storage vessels and pithoi 3%. In this phase, construction materials account for 20% of the assemblage, and small forms represent 5%.

For rims, plain vertical forms represent the majority at 32%. Other top rim shapes are inverted forms at 19%, incurving types 17%, everted forms 16%, and flaring forms at 13%. As for bases, the flat base dominates this period as it did in the previous period at 56%. The round base represents 25%, and the ring base is 13%. All three of these forms represent 94% of Site Phase XIV corpus.

As for bowls and plates, this terminal site phase sees the inverted bowl well entrenched in the record, representing 36% of the sample. Present are lesser forms in numbers—plain vertical shapes account for 22%, incurving 21%, everted 11%, and the least represented at 7% is the flaring form. Like Phase XIII, there are few cooking pots in this phase. The plain vertical rimmed cooking pot represents 37% with everted shapes 23%, followed by incurving forms (21%). Flaring rimmed cooking pots represent 11% and inverted shapes 5%. The jars and jugs in this phase are dominated by plain vertical rims 52% followed by lesser representations of everted rims (19%), inverted (15%) and 12% are incurving shapes.

White slip is favored and has a 36% showing, followed by self-same at 12%, salmon at 11%, tan at 11%, and brown 4%. Red and gray slip each account for 8% and black is 7%. Yellow slips represent 2% and green 0.5% of the phase. Of the 11,333 fragments, 58% are slipped correlating to 6631 pieces. Painted decoration is present on over 3% of the fragments. Black accounts for 27% of the phase collection, red accounts for 21% and white still maintains its popularity at 37%. This phase does not appear to have a break in tradition from Site Phases XII and XIII for the designs are the same, except more cursory designs like zigzags appear. Fragments carrying distinctive surface finishes number 2316, or 20% of the total number of fragments for this phase. Body sherds number 1227 and 92% of these are ribbed wares, 3% bear incisions and 2% exhibit rouletting. Fragments with other features, such as perforation, excision, impressions, and appliqué are also present in fewer numbers. Of the 39 bowls and 33 plates, some show incision and ribbing. Of the 488 surface manipulated cooking pots, 92% are ribbed, representing 34% of the total cooking pots for this phase. Surface finished jars and jugs number 492 with a surface finish, indicating that 24% of the phase total jars and jugs are treated. Incisions on jars and jugs account for 72 fragments, or 14% of those vessels so finished, but most popular is ribbing, amounting to 82% of the decorated jar and jug fragments. A few jars and jugs have perforations and seven bear finger impressions. Twenty-four small forms are finished with ribbing, incisions and rouletting.

Now we turn to the codes we used to record the Great Temple pottery.

Grosso Modo — Pottery Codes

The particular location of each artifact is shown in each database: the **Area**, **Trench**, and **Locus** of each artifact is noted. The Great Temple is divided into four Areas: the Propylaeum (P), the Lower Temenos (LT), the Upper Temenos (UT), and the Temple (T). The Trench or Special Project number is listed with the locus being excavated.

The **Date** on which the artifacts are excavated, and the **Excavator** is recorded on each form. The **Sequence Number** is a distinct serial number given to every form, plan, locus, container, or artifact, enabling the excavator to reconstruct the sequence of activity and discovery in the trench. It also provides a control over the coding sheets themselves. The Sequence Number is a three digit number, preceded by the Trench's number—Trench 97 would thus begin 97000, 97001, 97002, 97003, etc.

The **Site Phase** of each artifact is entered in after the season, when each trench has been fully excavated, and the excavator writes proposed history of the trench. This entails the appointment of each locus into a number of trench stages that comprise the particular history of the trench. These Stages are then fit into the 15 Petra Great Temple Site Phases (Pre-Site Phase I through Site Phase XIV).

Every pottery collection from each locus is given a container for each day (e.g. pottery in Locus 5 would have one container, while the pottery in Locus 6 would have another, and Locus 5 pottery on the next day would have yet another container). Each container is given an artifact number: P-1, P-2, P-3 etc., and a Sequence Number. For pottery processing each page or series of pages is given to an entire container.

Quantity: This field records the number of artifacts that are described together. This is usually one, but if a number of artifacts are identical, they will be listed together, and the quantity will reflect that.

Material: This column describes the type of artifact being recorded. Since all the pottery is recorded together, a "P" would be entered.

Part: This column records the part of the full vessel or object is represented for each individual artifact, such as base, rim, body potsherd, or architectural fragment. The codes are as follows:

Arch. Fragment: AF, Base: B, Bead: BD, Body Sherd: BS, Handle/Base: CHB, Handle/Neck: CHN, Handle/Neck/Rim: CHNR, Handle/Rim: CHR, Rim/Base: CRB, Rim/Neck: CRN, Spout/Base: CSB, Other composite: CD, Construction Material: CM, Discus: D, Handle: H, Lid: L, Neck: N, Rim: R, Spout: S, Indeterminate: IND, Other: O, and Unknown: UN.

Function: This column records the function for which the artifact was used, such as bowl, unguentarium, or wall decoration. The codes are: Amphora: A, Amphoriskos: AS, Bowl: B, Canalization Tile: CT, Cooking Pot: CP, Decorative: D, Figurine: F, Floor Tile: FT, Hypocaust Tile: HT, Jar: JR, Jar/Jug: JJ, Jug: JG, Kiln Waster: KW, Lachrymatory: LY, Lamp: L, Lid: LD, Large Storage Vessel: LS, Loom Weight: LW, Pipe: PP, Pithos: P, Plate: PLT, Roof Tile: RT, Small Form: SF, Spindle Whorl: SW, Stopper: SR,

Unguentarium: U, Indeterminate: IND, Other: O, and Unknown: UN.

Shape: This column describes the shape of the artifact, and is particularly important for the pottery. The codes are: Button: B, Disc: D, Double-Stranded: DS, Everted: E, Flaring: FG, Flat: F, Incurving: IG, Inverted: ID, Lug: LG, Ogee/pedestal: OP, Ovoid: OV, Pendant: PT, Plain Vertical: PV, Pointed: PD,

Raised Banded: RB, Ring: RG, Round: RD, Squared-Off: SO, String-cut: SC, T-Shaped: TS, Trefoil: T,

Triangular: TE, Tubular: TR, Twisted: TW, Umbilical: U

Liquid Color: This column describes the color of the pottery. The code are: Black :BK, Blue: BE, Brown: BN, Brownish-Black: BB, Cream: C, Glazed: GL, Gray: GY, Green: GN, Multi-colored: M, Off-White: OW, Pompeian Red: PR, Purple: P, Purplish-Black: PB, Red: R, Red Brown: RB, Salmon: S, Self-Same: SS, Tan: TN, Terra Sigillata Black: TSB, Terra Sigillata Red: TSR, Turquoise: T, White: W, and Yellow: Y.

Paint Color: This column describes the paint color on the artifact, if any is present. The code is the same as that of liquid color.

Motif: This column describes the motif of any notable decoration of the artifact, which pertains primarily to paint designs on pottery.

Plastic Decoration: This column records the plastic decoration on the artifact, again mostly used in pottery pieces, such as appliqué or molding. The codes are: Appliqué: A, Excision: E, Impression: IM,

Incision: IN. Molding: MD, Perforation: P, Ribbing: RG, and Rouletting: R.

APPENDIX 5

GREAT TEMPLE ARCHITECTURAL FRAGMENTS

Martha Sharp Joukowsky

The Nabataeans were a nomadic people with no tradition of monumental architecture. They learned to build as they settled themselves in Petra. They were free to explore architectural ideas and they created unusual structures like the Great Temple complex in a paradisiacal setting with a surround of gardens and pools, and with a Lower Temenos that accommodated a crowd for displays of ceremonial processions and pomp, with an upper terrace that formed a raised entrance to the temple itself, not to mention a Propylaeum entry and staircases of massive scale. We must remember that the Great Temple was visible from the north side of the wadi, but coming down the Roman Street it was hidden behind a once glorious façade of the Propylaeum decorated with refined sculpture. We might think that visibility would be a concern in its placement; because it's distinctive Nabataean style architecture was at the heart of what the Nabataeans wanted to project—prestige. The Great Temple occupied the highest position on the south flank of Central Petra. From its early beginnings as an isolated temple the Nabataeans incorporate it into a larger complex of a Propylaeum leading to a large, grand courtyard of the Lower Temenos and a garden-Pool or paradeisos complex to its east. When reaching the top of the Propylaeum Central Stairway can we imagine the view of the forceful, dominating temple environment. The complex made these buildings distinct from other buildings in Petra and announced the complex had its own cultural identity, and was special.

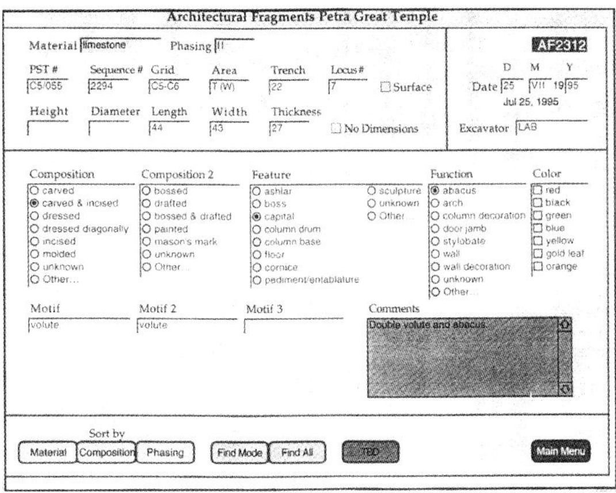

App. 5. Fig. 1. Architectural Fragment Recording Form.

The Architectural Fragment record allows us to accumulate data with which to begin addressing scholarly inquiries. Work to date has focused on the ordering of this epic collection. Simple patterns of cataloging and inventory have evolved that have identified the basic nature and attributes of the architectural data units. Now we have to question this data and inter-relate it with other features of the site to amplify both it's meaning and relate that meaning to the site as a whole.

The fragments discussed in this section reflect those components of the Great Temple displaying the typical characteristics of the Nabataean builder's architectural vocabulary.[1] The Architectural Fragment database defines the basics of the diagnostic architectural language of the Great Temple. Not only are there massive amounts of ashlars, there are the deeply drilled and carved Nabataean Type floral Corinthian capitals, the astonishing elephant headed capitals, column drums, cornices, and marvelous pinecone bosses and volutes. Beyond this, mundane ground stone tools are also classified in the Architectural Fragment database. Our goal here is to convey a complete picture in response to the challenges of a dynamic architectural collection, the demands of scholarship, and the opportunities created by new technologies. We also wish to preserve these rare materials.

1 Figures discussed herein do not include architectural components from the Small Temple.

App. 5. Fig. 2. Great Temple jumble of architectural fragments before excavation, 1993.

A presentation of related publications appearing over the past few years can be found in the notes.[2] Now we launch into the results of the database.[3]

Organization

This section progresses from a general overview of architectural fragments characteristics, to a more particular look at selected phases of the database results set against the site phases. First, the architectural fragment database is presented, by the

APPENDIX 5. Table 1.
GREAT TEMPLE: ARCHITECTURAL FRAGMENTS PROCESSED BY YEAR

Year	*Total Fragments*	*Percentage*
1993	697	4%
1994	1,409	7%
1995	1,235	6%
1996	905	5%
1997	836	4%
1998	1,193	6%
1999	987	5%
2000	896	4%
2001	851	4%
2002	1,021	5%
2003	976	5%
2004	3,266	17%
2005	2,610	14%
2006	2,373	12%
TOTAL	19,255	98%

2 An excellent outline of the architectural decorative elements has been published by Erika L. Schluntz (1998), in *Great Temple* vol. 1, Ch. 5, and in her dissertation (1999). Emily Catherine Egan (2001a, 2001b, 2002) has published the temple stucco decoration and its hypothetical reconstruction, and continues in this volume with her conclusions here in Ch. 5. The stuccos have been analyzed by Corbeil and Helwig (1999) at the Institut Canadien de Conservation. J. J. Basile (1997, 1999, 2001, 2002a, 2003) has published the Tyche head, and many of the relief carved pilaster blocks, and he contributes Ch. 6 to this volume. The elephant-headed capitals are already published by this writer (Joukowsky 1998a) and here in Ch. 7B, and the architectural components of the Great Temple are discussed in detail by S. Rababeh both here in Ch. 3 and in his *How Petra Was Built* (2005).

3 Field procedures are discussed in Appendix 5.

masons' raw materials—sandstone, limestone, and marble along with other media, such as ceramics and basalt. We turn then to the functional classes of capitals, column bases and drums, cornices, pediments and entablatures, and give their frequency of occurrence.[4]

Architectural fragments from the Great Temple

The sizeable number of 19,255 architectural fragments defined here as Nabataean originated in Great Temple contexts.[5] Appendix 5 Table 1 charts architectural fragments by field campaign, and reflects their proportionate amounts. From 2004 to 2006 approximately 43% of the fragments are registered, indicating that these campaigns are dealing with significant numbers of architectural components.

Appendix 5, Table 2 shows the most prominent occurrences of architectural fragments by area and trench, and it conveys high fragment counts.[6] All of these well-represented elements reflect the results of structural collapse when successive earthquakes and tremors batter the site. Until they were recovered by excavation, the evidence

APPENDIX 5. Table 2.
PROMINENT OCCURRENCES OF ARCHITECTURAL FRAGMENTS BY AREA AND TRENCH

Propylaeum			
Trench/ Special Project	*Architectural Fragments*	*Total*	*% Total 19,255*
87	361		
95	850		
SP87	365		
100	984		
		2,560	29%
Lower Temenos			
97	914		
98B	319		
126	463		
98	661		
127	797		
102-103	913		
		4,067	46%
Upper Temenos			
105-106	936		
2	309		
		1,245	14%
Temple			
47	357		
62	489		
		846	10%
Total		8,718	45%

4 The reader can search the *Open Context* database to find listings by trench and locus for architectural fragment type as a particular object's specific dimensions, for each fragment is entered into the database as an individual record.

5 From Site Phase II, the Temple was decorated with 8 columns on its E and W sides and 6 columns in the rear. The columns lying behind the East and West Antae walls are two-part engaged columns, and the columns in the rear are 4-to-5-part, heart-shaped columns. Excluding these engaged and heart-shaped columns, there are originally 6 freestanding columns flanking the Temple sides and 4 in the rear. The 6 rear columns are better preserved, where in antiquity, the soil, collapse, and inter-columnar walls provided them with support. The Temple south inter-columnar walls also are in a better state of preservation, for they too are surrounded by massive amounts of fill. We found many of these columns with their bases and shafts *in situ*. During the Site Phase IX A.D. 363 earthquake, the west column drums were knocked away from their shafts and tumbled to the E, into the temple. Judging from the remains of the upper drums of the W columns (which toppled into the central temple); they range from 1.08 to 1.10 m in diameter and from 0.32 to 0.65 m in height. These measurements correspond with those of the drums of the temple east, which were found slumped out of position further to the east.

6 The reader further interested in specific trench counts should refer to *Open Context*.

strongly suggests that architectural components, rest where they fell some 2000 years ago. What is recovered reflects the character of the architecture placed there, making it clear that architectural fragments do not travel far from their point of origin.

In the Lower Temenos the high numbers, 46% of the architectural fragment corpus, reflect the collapse of the West Triple Colonnade into the West Cryptoporticus. These cryptoportici excavations yielded copious amounts of column drums and elephant headed capitals. During excavation, Trench 102-103 of the West Entry Stairway (913 fragments) and the collections from Trench 97 of the West Cryptoporticus East (914 fragments) are overwhelmed with wall ashlar and column collapse. The Propylaeum represents 29% of the corpus with dramatic collapses found in Trench 95 Propylaeum East Rooms 1 and 2 with 850 fragments, and Trench 100 of the Propylaeum East Room 3 with 984 fragments. In the Upper Temenos, where 14% of the corpus was recovered, Trench 105-106 of the Roman-Byzantine Bath excavations produce a high number of fragments (936), and many of these are marble *opus sectile* floor and wall tiles. The Temple excavations found only 10% of the corpus, and the majority of these 489 fragments were found in the area of the Theater Stage and the East Corridor, indicating the pattern of collapse to the east. Additionally, Trench 2 reflects elements from the Great Temple collapse onto the temple Forecourt. Here the architectural fragments are comprised of column drums and capital fragments, along with finely decorated capital elements and ashlars. In general, material, function, part, form attributes, and dimensions clearly indicate the architectural vocabulary of each Great Temple area.

Materials

Of the total fragments classified, it will be noted that 49%, or 9462 fragments, are of sandstone; 38%, or 7289 fragments, are of limestone, marble represents 8% or 1642 fragments, and 4%, or 717 fragments, are of stucco or plaster. Eighty-one sandstone ashlars display incised mason's marks, all of which are recorded.[7] Table 11.11 charts architectural fragments by materials and site phase. As mentioned previously, small stucco fragments without visible detail were classified in the 1996-2006 Grosso Modo and numbered 26,901, or almost 7% of that database. With the two databases combined, they represent 27,618 stucco-plaster fragments. Stucco embellishments are an integral element of the Great Temple architecture.

Forty-one objects are of basalt, which are not architectural fragments at all, but are tools such as grindstones, mortars, and rotating grain mills that served for domestic purposes. These are briefly described at the end of this section.

Architectural fragments were recovered from every part of the site. Architectural fragments by area show that 19%, or 3690, were registered from the Propylaeum, and 6229 fragments, or 32%, were found in the Lower Temenos. Twenty-one percent, or 4098, were recovered from the Upper Temenos, and 26%, or 4961 fragments, were located in the confines of the Great Temple itself. A combined fragment area count shows that 51% are from the Propylaeum and the Lower Temenos, which is indicative of the corresponding architecture of the two areas with their stately colonnades and elephant-headed capitals. The distribution of architectural fragments across the Great Temple site is uneven, but informative.

Ashlar blocks

In Nabataean masonry for the walls of the Great Temple and the Propylaeum, the ashlars are especially prepared, squared off and shaped to fit together with precision. Most of the Great Temple ashlars and columns are dressed with diagonal chisel marks to provide a footing for decorative plaster. Hammering the claw or toothed chisel on the face of the ashlar block creates the desired

---

7 These are not presented in detail in this study. Several masons' marks are illustrated in *Great Temple* Vol. I, fig. 6.27, and *Great Temple* Vol. II, fig. 2.7-8.

APPENDIX 5. Table 3.

GREAT TEMPLE: SELECTED ARCHITECTURAL MATERIALS BY SITE PHASE

SITE PHASE	*Alabaster*	*Basalt*	*Ceramic*	*Granite*	*Limestone*	*Marble*	*Mortar*	*Sandstone*	*Stucco*	*Other*	*Total*
Pre-I	–	–	–	2	9	–	–	–	–	–	**11** **0.1%**
I	–	–	–	–	4	–	–	6	2	–	**12** **0.1%**
II	–	–	–	–	17	–	–	30	4	–	**51** **0.5%**
III	–	–	–	–	1	–	–	6	–	–	**7** **0.07%**
IV	–	–	–	–	107	1	–	41	57	–	**206** **2.2%**
V	–	1	–	–	36	–	1	68	10	–	**116** **1.2%**
VI	–	–	–	–	247	18	2	342	27	2	**638** **6.8%**
VII	1	–	1	–	79	4	–	63	9	–	**157** **1.6%**
VIII	–	–	1	–	132	110	–	95 1	3	–	**351** **3.76%**
IX	–	9	15	36	789	799	3	1,566	97	1	**3,315** **35.6%**
X	–	–	–	–	428	72	–	202	15	1	**718** **7.7%**
XI	–	–	–	–	87	68	–	264	6	–	**425** **4.5%**
XII	–	–	–	–	6	–	–	9	–	–	**15** **0.1%**
XIII	–	2	2	–	816	12	–	1,665	28	2	**2,527** **27%**
XIV	–	1	1	–	455	38	1	260	6	–	**762** **8%**
Total	**1**	**13**	**20** **0.2%**	**38** **0.4%**	**3,213** **35%**	**1,122** **12%**	**7**	**4,617** **50%**	**274** **3%**	**6**	**9,311**

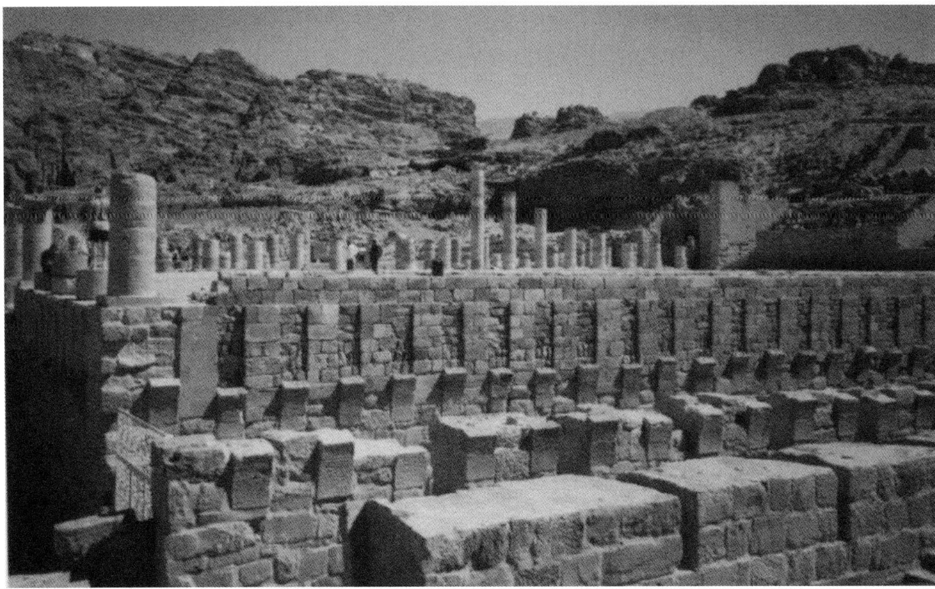

App. 5. Fig. 3. Restored West Cryptoporticus sandstone wall with ashlars and voussoirs.

effect, and it is essential that the incisions are angled between 15 and 45 degrees.[8] Of the total collection of 19,255 architectural fragments, 7315, or 38%, are ashlar blocks, and of these, 1,664, or 23%, of the ashlars are arch-voussoir fragments, while 282 doorjambs account for 4% of the ashlars. As surface dressing is charted along with other factors in the database, some 184 ashlars are found with a marginal draft and 8 with a marginal draft and bossed. This indicates that the marginal draft is not a popular form of stone dressing at the Great Temple, but it is employed on some ashlars.

From the Great Temple rear collapse, 18 ashlars are carved with channels 0.06 to 0.08 m in depth cut into either side. These channeled ashlars serve for the theater seating (and the grooved channels, we suggest, are for armrests), for they are similar to the blocks that remain *in situ* in the Theater *cavea*.[9] These ashlar fragments are found where they fall alongside other architectural elements. Had we not found them *in situ*, in the temple back rooms in association with other architectural fragments, we might have overlooked their original purpose.

Architectural moldings

Cornice fragments number 1376, and of these, 704, or 51%, are manufactured from limestone; 342 are of sandstone, and 298 are fashioned from stucco. Egg and dart fragments number 117, but the majority, or 132 fragments, are identified with an egg and tongue motif. The pattern of alternating short and long beads, otherwise known as bead and reel design (usually placed on the astragal below the egg and dart motif), decorates only 53 fragments, and these are found fashioned both from sandstone and limestone. As far as pediment and

App. 5. Fig. 4. Limestone detail with egg and tongue motif.

8 *Great Temple* vol. II, fig. 6.17. In Appendix 5 Table 2, we chart the instances of dressing and carving of selected architectural fragments by site phase, and Site Phase IX shows the most common incidence of dressing and carving. Site Phase XIII, with 26%, indicates the continued popularity of diagonal chiseled dressing at the Great Temple, ascribed to the collapsed elements recovered from these phases.

9 R. Frederiksen discusses these seat blocks in Ch. 8.

entablature fragments are concerned, only 79 pieces are registered. They are found in all media—sandstone, limestone and stucco. Unfortunately, they do not offer us a clear design idea of the temple's overall façade.

App. 5. Fig. 5. Column collapse of the Great Temple East Porch columns.

Column drums

Column drum fragments or complete drums number 1464, or 6%, of the total collection. Almost all of the drums are sandstone (1301, or 89%), and 154 (11%) are of limestone. In the Lower Temenos, 353 drums are found; their diameters average 0.78 m, and they average 0.46 m in height. Similar to these, 460 drums are found in the Propylaeum or 31% of the collection. The Temple claims 238 drums or 16% of those recovered.

App. 5. Fig. 6. Column collapse of the West Propylaeum.

The Great Temple Porch and Pronaos drums average 0.40 to 0.42 m in height, and the heights of these drums decrease the higher the drum is positioned on the column. The fall of the east Porch Columns was measured, and because the easternmost column shaft had the greatest number of drums (29 drums had fallen, which remain *in situ),* it is estimated that the original height of the column shaft (without the capital or the base) originally was about 12.4 m. These drums measure between 1.50 and 1.53 m in diameter. We know that the Pronaos columns were embellished with red stucco, for traces remain on the lower column shaft. We are less sure about the stucco color of the Great Temple Porch Columns, but we assume their lower shafts were brightly colored with red and/or yellow stucco plaster with white cable fluting extending above to the collar below the capital.

Rising to a projected height of at least 7.60 m and coated with a protective bright red and yellow painted plaster topped by white plaster cable fluting, the columns of the Lower Temenos Triple Colonnades provided a spectacular and imposing border for the Lower Temenos central plaza. The columns display a visible *entasis* and are constructed of stacked sandstone drums measuring 0.76 to 0.84 m in diameter spaced at regular north-south inter-axial intervals of 2.50 m. The columns of the West Colonnade became dislodged and tumbled directly onto the Hexagonal Pavement below, leaving well-defined impressions where the individual drums impacted the surface. This Site Phase IX disturbance also resulted in the accumulation of soil in the West Cryptoporticus, which became riddled with architectural debris, including fragments of elephant-headed capitals.

Column bases

App. 5. Fig. 7. Great Temple Attic column base.

Column bases of the Great Temple are well-articulated Attic bases that are sculpted in either limestone or in white, fine-grained sandstone. The *in situ* Porch Column bases are one of the components we have used as a guide for determining the height of the Porch and Pronaos columns. The east Porch base measures 0.63 m in height; however, the center east Porch base is slightly smaller, measuring 0.60 m in height. These bases were manufactured in two parts, as two vertical halves. A rectangular, flat sandstone slab is used as a leveled foundation block to support the Attic style bases. They are characterized by a torus (or large convex molding) at the bottom, with a concave molding above the torus, known as the cavetto, with another torus atop, above which is a finished top molding.[10] Plaster and straw mixed with plaster serve as bonding agents for the joins between the drums. Based on our excavations, we found that the Great Temple side and rear columns were still *in situ*, held in place by their support surround of inter-columnar walls.

Column base elements number only 102, which is not surprising considering that the columns of the Lower Temenos colonnades are baseless, i.e., the columns rest directly on the stylobates of the colonnade, and some remain on site *in situ*. Although battered, the twin columns in the entry to the West and East Exedrae still rest on their original bases as well.

Capitals and decorated pieces

App. 5. Fig. 8. Restored Great Temple capital.

The temple capitals are the earliest sculptural decoration at the Great Temple, dating to the mid-late 1st c. B.C. when the *distyle* edifice was constructed. Capitals represent 28%, or 5445 fragments, of the Great Temple collection. Of these, 5145, or 94%, are fashioned from limestone; 110, or 2%, are stucco fragments; and 185, or 3%, are sandstone. Eighteen percent, or 958, are from the Upper Temenos, and 1,253, or 23%, were unearthed in the Lower Temenos. The largest number, or 2601 (31%), is recovered from the Great Temple itself.

As mentioned above, it is not clear if in the collection we find capital elements of either the Porch or Pronaos columns; however, in style we assume that their capitals were similar in composition to the capitals decorating the sides of the building and to those in the temple rear.

The decorative program of the capitals flanking the Great Temple has been defined. These capitals are comprised of a two-part lower order of bushy acanthus leaves, which measure approximately 1.43 m in width and 0.58 m in height. The upper order is comprised of a four-part capital that measures as much as 0.89 m in height or as little as 0.78 m in height. Together, these elements measure 1.47 m in height. These capitals range around 0.69 m in width and are 0.56 m in thickness. The decoration is comprised of

10 Profiles of these column bases can be viewed in *Great Temple* Vol. II, fig. 5.12.

an intricate, deeply carved array of vines and plant stalks with hibiscus petals that frame different fruits—pinecones, pomegranates and poppies, springing forth from the petal centers. These capitals resemble those of the lower order of the al-Khazna, and one can reason that they were manufactured by the same sculpture school, at the same time or because of their deeper carving, just before the al-Khazna capitals.[11]

The Great Temple capitals, therefore, are part of a given sequence of Hellenistic motifs used by the Nabataeans, who employed master stone carvers and sculptors with technical virtuosity to embellish metropolitan Petra in the 1st c. B.C. One finds little justification for regarding the capitals of the Petra Great Temple as being unique, but as McKenzie has illustrated,[12] there are clear distinctions between the capitals of the Nabataean Floral Type I Corinthian order and the traditional Corinthian order. Although Nabataean capitals are too delicate for the height at which they would have been seen, we assume that this vibrant decorative element is what the Nabataeans intended to commission from the artists they employed and what they desired for public consumption.

App. 5. Fig. 9. Poppies and pinecones emerging from hibiscus flowers sculpted on the upper order of a Great Temple capital.

Visual movement and energy characterizes these sculptures. A preference is shown for the poppy that is most often represented dynamically bursting forth from a hibiscus flower or the pinecone emerging from a network of vines or acanthus leaves. Although the juxtaposition of the various vegetal elements is contrived, each component is carved realistically, with pure lines. The plants and fruits burst out from the background, and the pattern shows skill in the combination of motifs that are hardly mimicry of nature. The physical strength of the sculptural pattern lies in the innovative ornamental patterns themselves, clearly demonstrating the Nabataean decorative fascination with three-dimensional high relief, created by chiseling, gouging and channeling the leaf stems, flowers and fruits. In the comparison of these capitals one sees that the patterns are repeated, but they do not occur in a predictable order, i.e., sometimes where a poppy is expected in the design, a pinecone is represented instead. This unpredictability makes each of these upper order capitals unique and a technical tour de force. The individuality and skill in the execution of each capital is, in short, astonishing.

App. 5. Fig. 10. Fragment of an upper order capital with rich foliage.

Thirty-five percent of the capital fragments, or 1923 fragments, are identified with some acanthus leaf decoration. In the Great Temple, 1238 acanthus fragments, or 64%, were recovered, and 377, or 20%, were from the Upper Temenos. Only 207 acanthus fragments were recovered from the Lower Temenos, accounting for 4% of the assemblage, and the Propylaeum has only 100 representing 5%. Thus, the Temple and the Upper Temenos combined represent 84% of the collection. The

11 McKenzie 1990.

12 Ibid.190f.

larger implications of this are obvious; the temple is essentially the place of their original position as well as where they are found.

Fluted cauliculi represent 161, or 3%, of the temple capital fragments. These include 323 volutes and an additional 97 corner volutes, together representing 420 pieces, or 8%, of the capital fragments. More minor in representation are hibiscus petals, numbering 124, or 2% of embellishments, but an additional 145 floral fragments may include hibiscus petals as well. Only 55 fragments are classified as spirals on the face of the capital (helices) and 367 flat elements forming the top of a capital (abacus fragments). Other decorated fragments are vines representing 471, or 9% of the capital fragments. Many of these are crossed vines. Poppy or pomegranate fragments number 124, representing 2% of the decorative motifs.[13] Pinecones account for 202, or 4%, of the capital fragments. Additionally, there are 121 boss fragments—that projection of the abacus that at the Great Temple, like the al-Khazna, is decorated with a center pinecone.

The design of architectural decoration suggests that the vast majority of the elements cataloged in the database are originally part of the *distyle* architecture, which continues through the prime periods of the Great Temple's life, from Site Phase II to the collapse of the temple colonnade in Site Phase IX.

Elephant-headed capitals

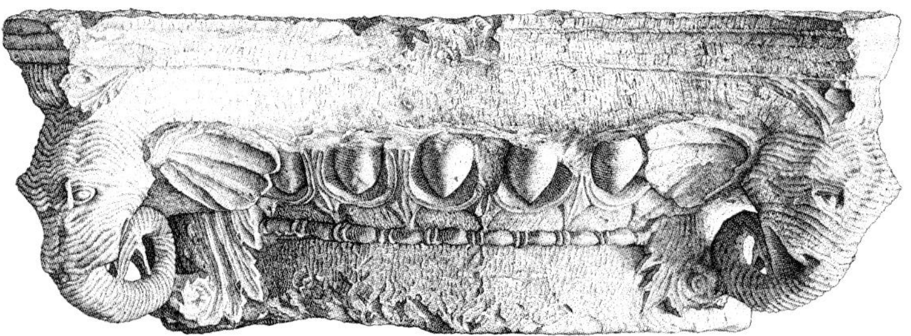

App. 5. Fig. 11. Elephant-headed capital from the Lower Temenos Triple Colonnade, drawn by John Phillip Hagen.

The Asian elephant headed capitals are dated from the last quarter of the 1st c. B.C. to the A.D. 1st c., an approximate 50 years later than the *distyle* temple capitals when the *tetrastyle* temple and the precinct are enlarged. A total of 751 elephant-headed fragments are registered in the architectural fragment database, plus 301 pieces in the catalog, totaling 1052 elephant parts from the two databases. Thus, only 4% of the capital fragments in the architectural fragment database are decorated with either elephant heads or elephant parts. The majority, 698 of the elephants, was manufactured from limestone, and one is registered as being fashioned from sandstone. Many of these fragments are covered with a thin film of white plaster, so they would all appear white to the viewer. More prone to breakage, 412 fragments are pieces of elephant-trunks, which account for 59% of the elephant remains. [14] In the architectural fragment database, heads or partial heads number 117, or 16%, 82 separate pieces are recognized as ears, 27 as skin fragments, and 58 separate eye fragments. Combining the catalog and the architectural fragment database, 611 (58%) fragments are recovered from the Lower Temenos, and 351 fragments from the Propylaeum or 33%, 20 (2%) fragments from the temple area and 63 (6%) fragments from the Upper Temenos, so it is reasonable to assume that the Propylaeum and Lower Temenos colonnades, accounting for 91% of the total are the areas these zoomorphic capitals decorated.[15] Several capitals are found on the Roman Street during the excavations there. We posit that these originated in the Propylaeum and tumbled onto the street along with some of the pilaster blocks.[16]

---

13 For comments on this motif, see Joukowsky 2008a.

14 Unfortunately no tusks have been found.

15 Seven fragments were surface stray finds.

16 In Ch. 7B, the elephant motif and the elephant headed capitals of the Great Temple are given a full discussion.

App. 5. Fig. 12. Limestone male Theater mask, Cat. No. 94-S-2, L. 27, W. 8.5; Temple, SP2; Photograph, David L. Brill.

Masks: Seven mask fragments were found in 1994 in the West Walkway of the Great Temple. [17] They are all carved out of limestone, and three are modeled out of a yellow limestone. Two (94-S-1 and 94-S-3) are the two halves of the same mask of a female head. Illustrated in our discussion on architectural sculpture,[18] these masks must have fallen from the Great Temple Theater façade.

App. 5. Fig. 13. Honorific pilaster block of limestone carved with a wreath and a (fillet) ribbon, tied around the top. LT, Trench 52, Locus 1, Seq. No. 54210. L. 82, W. 52, Th. 24. Panel was found upside down, reused as an inter-columnar wall block.

Tyche: A sandstone Tyche head is one of the few puzzling pieces, which may derive from the Great Temple or from some other nearby structure. The head may have been dumped on the site during one of the earthquakes that occurred at Petra, and it probably suffered damage to the face at that time.[19]

Pilasters: Many unusual and important pilaster blocks are registered in the database, which are described in detail in Chapter 6 by J. J. Basile.

App. 5. Fig. 14. Baroque Room stucco ceiling collapse.

Plaster/Stucco and painted plaster/stucco

Stucco/plaster represents 3% of the architectural fragment database with 274 fragments recorded; however there are 1360 fragments registered in the Grosso Modo database, totaling 1634 fragments.[20]

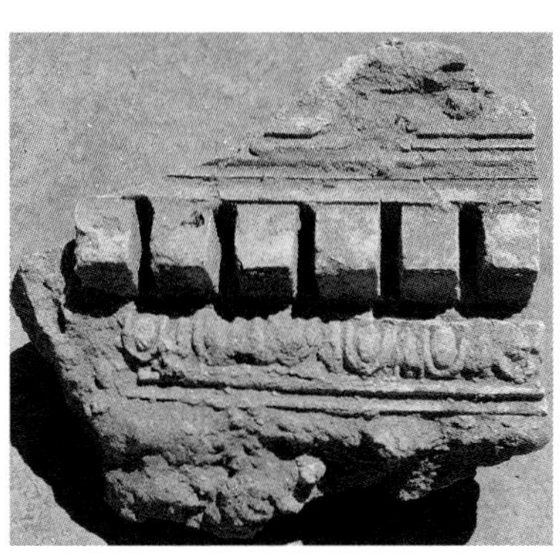

App. 5. Fig. 15. Stucco/plaster ceiling embellishment, showing dentilations.

Fragments of either capitals or wall decoration are found painted. Of these, 115 or 36% are painted red; 70 or 22% are black; 51 or 16% are green; a surprising 225, or 71%, are blue; 32% are yellow. And of the remainder, 26 fragments are recovered with gold leaf, and three fragments are painted orange. Seventeen have white painting, one has purple paint, and another has brown. One particularly lovely and colorful cassette is from the South Corridor wall,[21] there is the green-painted ionic style column from the Baroque Room,[22] the remarkable face fragment,[23] as well as other pieces with lively designs.[24]

---

17 These are presented as a group here in Ch. 21.

18 *Great Temple* vol. 2, figs. 5.62-5.64.

19 Basile 1997; *Great Temple* Vol. 1, figs. 6.79a-b, 6.80.

20 Stucco revetments and the use of stucco at the Great Temple are discussed further in Chapter 5.

21 *Great Temple* Vol. II, fig. 5.42.

22 Ibid. fig. 4.79.

23 Ibid. fig. 7.9.

24 Ibid. figs. 7.10 and 7.11.

The phase-by-phase collection

The total fragments for the phase-by-phase study number 9311, or 48% of the architectural fragment corpus.[25] Phase II has the lowest number of fragments with only seven, or 0.07% of the total, and Site Phase IX is the highest with 3315 fragments registered or 36% of the total. Site Phase XIII follows with 2527 fragments or 27% of 9311.

Materials. In Table 11.15, 10 materials are set against site phases. The most meaningful occurrences are sandstone at 50%, limestone at 35% and marble at 12%. Sandstone appears popular in all site phases—4617 sandstone architectural fragments are recorded. Sandstone use peaks in Site Phase IX representing 17% of the 9311 materials studied, and 47% of the materials are of sandstone for that phase. It appears frequently in Site Phase XIII when it accounts for 18% of all the materials and 66% of the materials for the phase.

Limestone architectural fragments number 3213 or 35% of the materials studied. Like sandstone, it is a constant throughout the site phases. In Site Phase IX it accounts for 25% of all the materials processed and 24% of the architectural fragments for that phase. It maintains popularity in Site Phase X where it represents 5% of the total architectural fragments, but it represents 60% of the assemblage for the phase. It is also most popular in Site Phase XIII where it is 9% of the assemblage and 32% of the phase materials. In Site Phase XIV it declines in overall percentage of materials to 5%, however, it maintains its presence as 60% of the assemblage for that phase.

Marble represents 12% of the architectural fragment assemblage with 1122 artifacts. Its popularity is sporadic until Site Phase VIII when it represents 31% of the materials for that phase. It achieves its height usage in Site Phase IX, when it totals 71% of the marble class and 9% of the total architectural fragments. From the evidence, we can deduce that marble was used in the temple only on rare occasions; a notable exception to this is in the large-scale embellishment of the Roman-Byzantine Baths where it appointed floors, lower walls and coping.

Although marble is in large-scale use at the Small Temple,[26] which is contemporary with, and lies on a terrace below the Roman-Byzantine Baths (A.D.106-post A.D. 551), much of it found there indicates that the slabs were reused for repairs after the A.D. 363 earthquake. [27]

Appendix 5,Table 4 shows the occurrence of selected architectural fragments by phase. We limited this study to process those architectural fragments belonging to specific phases. Later phases reflecting more collapses are dramatic, particularly Site Phase IX. As would be expected, the early phases were a time of building, and show no instances of collapse, with considerably fewer architectural fragments in the archaeological record.

We selected 26 features to follow, and for an overall idea of the frequency of occurrence we elected to chart seven architectural components by phase, from the selected sample. In Appendix 5,

---

25 Based on site deposition, the general sequence of some 15 phases (Site Phases Pre-I through XIV), we now have confirmed architectural evidence for the Great Temple construction, collapse and abandonment. As we have said previously, although these sequences (progressing from earliest to latest) indicate stages of construction, it is important to remember that building periods are sometimes separated from artifact periods moving the latter to *later* phases depending upon the context in which the materials are found. Therefore, even if an a poppy or pomegranate we ascribe to the temple capitals was put in place in Site Phase II, it is ascribed to Site Phase IX where it was found mixed in with other elements originating with the A.D. 363 collapse. A word of caution—we have difficulty in establishing absolute dates, and just as we reuse excavated elements for our Great Temple architectural reconstruction program today, the Great Temple builders also reused and retrofitted buildings with stones they salvaged and recycled.

26 Reid 2005.

27 Marble sources from the Small Temple are published by Reid (2005, 113-47), who carried out extensive isotopic analysis to determine their sources, the majority of which are found in western Anatolia, the Balkan Peninsula and the Cyclades. Of the cornice fragments analyzed, the highest probability is that 81% originated in the Marmara region of Turkey.

APPENDIX 5. Table 4.

OCCURRENCE OF SELECTED ARCHITECTURAL COMPONENTS BY SITE PHASE

SITE PHASE	*Ashlar*	*Boss*	*Capital*	*Column Base*	*Column Drum*	*Cornice*	*Pediment*	*TOTAL*
Pre-I	–	–	–	–	–	–	–	**0**
I	4	–	4	–	–	4	–	**12**
II	17	–	3	10	4	–	–	**34**
III	6	–	–	–	1	–	–	**7**
IV	46	–	79	2	4	17	4	**152**
V	56	–	8	–	3	5	–	**72**
VI	89	1	42	2	5	13	–	**152**
VII	27	3	53	8	12	14	–	**117**
VIII	88	1	74	1	23	26	2	**215**
IX	1,364	12	599	4	173	124	1	**2,277**
X	101	4	276	6	38	104	2	**531**
XI	195	1	56	2	27	44	2	**327**
XII	6	–	5	–	2	1	–	**14**
XIII	1,262	3	579	13	448	132	10	**2,447**
XIV	156	7	343	8	71	78	7	**670**
TOTAL	3,417	32	2,121	56	811	562	28	**7,027**
% Archit. Frags.	48%	0.4%	30%	0.7%	12%	8%	0.3%	**99.4%**
% Selected Archit. Fragments	36%	0.30%	23%	0.70%	12%	8%	0.30%	**75%**

Table 4, 7027 architectural fragments are studied representing 75% of the 9311. The percentages beside the total are taken against the total number of 7027, and the percentages at the bottom of the chart reflect the rate of occurrence against the selected count of 9311.

As would be expected, ashlar blocks from arch and wall collapse dominate the group representing 49% of the fragments. Appendix 5 Table 5 shows the occurrence of surface dressing by site phase; 90% of the blocks are dressed. Bosses are separate sculpted entities in the Great Temple, manufactured from a separate block of limestone inserted between two upper orders of the Nabataean floral capital. The temple capitals were carved for the *distyle* structure, and the remains of what we have found belong to that building.[28] Bosses for each capital number four, so there would be 64 bosses for the temple structure alone. Here only 32 are registered, but in our databases, overall, 121 complete or fragmented bosses have been recovered.

Flooring and *opus sectile* fragments

The occurrences of flooring with marble *opus sectile* fragments account for 1420 artifacts. Floor fragments can either be ceramic tiles or limestone slabs; they number 981. Beginning in Site Phase Pre-I ceramic floor fragments number 0.3% of the 1420. In Site Phase I none appear, in Site Phase II they account for 13%, and they disappear from the record in Site Phase III. In Site Phase IV they represent 0.7%, Site Phase V, 4%, and in Site Phase VI, 5%. Their numbers decline in Site Phase VII to 2%, and are 4% in Site Phase VIII/ In Site Phase IX they reach their peak usage representing 54% of the two classes. In Site Phase X they decline to 16%, and take a further drop in Site Phase XI to 7%. In Site Phases XII and XIII they represent 4% in both phases, and finally in Site Phase XIV they are at 3%.

Opus sectile pieces number 439. None are found before Site Phase VIII when 17% are represented. Eighty percent appear in Site Phase IX, they are absent in Site Phase X, and seem to be in nominal use from Site Phase XI to XIV.

App. 5. Fig 16. Limestone pinecone boss. Seq. No.85046, Temple, Trench 85, Locus 1, pinecone boss, Ht. 16, L. 19. Pinecone set into an acanthus leaf.

Other stone objects

Additional objects captured by our database are ground stone tools, consisting of pestles, mortar/querns, grindstone presses, and rotating grain mills. None of these objects is found in Site Phases Pre-I to IV. In Site Phase V one press is recovered, and in phase VI, one grindstone is recovered. In Site Phase IX there are four mortars/querns, three grindstones, one press, and three rotating grain mills. No more household stone objects are reported until Site Phase XIV when only one mortar is registered.

Conclusion

Since we started our site survey in 1992, the possibility of unearthing and interpreting the precinct from the Propylaeum to the Great Temple itself remained one of the great journeys of exploration. Until now, the P/GT has surrendered its architectural mysteries, piece by piece. These have become classic Nabataean icons and have provided us with a fertile array of subjects to study. The Great Temple capitals—pseudo-Corinthian and elephant-headed capitals, pilaster blocks that embellished the overall architectural design announced the Great Temple as special, and allowed it

28 No capitals, as far as we know, have survived from the *tetrastyle* façade.

to dominate the setting in which it operated. The Great Temple operated in a city state environment and must have owed its existence to royal patronage—it represents a royal tool of propaganda.

In closing, our computer databases have provided us with a coherent body of data that does have an accountable and significant impact on our understanding of this rich artifact repertoire.

The application of computerization at the Petra Great Temple excavations has offered us a powerful tool helping us disentangle the remains. Now we can assess the extent to which computer use during the multi-year course of our excavations has awarded us with insights about the artifact record. We have placed our artifact assemblages in serial order and within the context of the stratigraphy have constructed a relative chronology for the site. Underlying the concept of the Great Temple artifact record is the fact that the artifacts of the Nabataean period at the Great Temple have a recognizable style and are characteristic of the local Petraeans who produced and/or used them. The fashion choices over time and these changes reflect the Petra local chronology with artifact sequences that now can be understood. This chapter provides an overview of artifact tabulation by material. Thereafter by pottery will be examined separately in Appendix 4 and architectural fragments in Appendix 5. We turn now to a brief review of the Great Temple site phases.

Great Temple Site Phases

Based on site deposition and dateable evidence from lamps, coins, and pottery stylistics, the general sequence of some 15 Site Phases, Pre-site I, I–XIV, is now evident for the Great Temple construction, collapse and abandonment. Although these sequences (progressing from earliest to latest) indicate stages of construction, destruction, and abandonment, building periods are sometimes separated from artifact periods moving the latter to *later* phases, depending upon the context in which the materials are found. Therefore even if we know that a particular Nabataean artifact was made in the A.D. first or second century, in Site Phase IV, it is placed in Site Phase IX where it is found mixed and tumbled together with other elements of the 363 CE collapse.

Great Temple Vol. III: Bibliography

Adam, J.-P. 1994. *Roman building: materials and techniques*. (A. Mathews, transl. 1984 French edn. London).

Adams, R.B. (ed.) 2008. *Jordan: An archaeological reader*. Equinox, (London, Oakville, CT).

Aeschylus (Aesch.) Fragment,124. *Etymologicum Gudianum* 227.40, Cramer, *Anecdota Graeca Oxoniensia* ii, 443. 11.

Aharoni, Y. 1956. "Excavations at Ramath Rahel," *IEJ* 6, 102-11,137-57.

Akurgal, E. 1969. *Ancient civilisation and ruins of Turkey*. (J. Whybrow and M. Emre, transls. Istanbul).

Alexander, C. 1955. "A Roman silver relief: the Indian triumph of Dionysos," *MMAJ* 14.3, 64-67.

American Numismatic Society. 1981. *Sylloge nummorum Graecorum. ANSMN. Part 6: Palestine-South Arabia*. (New York).

Ammianus, Marcellinus. 1963. *Res gestae libri*. J. C. Rolfe (trans.) *LCL*.

'Amr, K. 1999. "The discovery of two additional pottery kilns at az-Zurrāba/Wādi Mūsā," *ADAJ* 43, 175-94.

'Amr, K. 1991. "The Petra National Trust site projects: preliminary report on the 1991 season at Zurrabah," *ADAJ* 35, 313-23.

'Amr, K. 1987. *The pottery from Petra: a neutron activation analysis study*. *BAR-IS* 324.

'Amr, K. 1986. "Instrumental neutron activation analysis of pottery and clay from the Zurrabah kiln complex," *ADAJ* 30, 319-28.

'Amr, K., T. Akasheh, and M. Na'es. n.d. *Recovery and reproduction technology of Nabataean painted fine ware*. www.cultech.org/Amr

Anderson-Stojanovic', V. R. 1987. "The Chronology and Function of Ceramic Unguentaria," *AJA* 91, 105-22.

Angus, N. S., G. T. Brown, and H. Cleere. 1962. "The iron nails from the Roman legionary fortress at Inchtuthil, Perthshire," *Journal of the Iron and Steel Institute* 200, 956-68.

Apollod. (Apollodorus). *Bibliotheca* (*Bibl.*, The Library). 1921. J. G. Frazer (trans.) Cambridge, MA.

Arnold, D. 1991. *Building in Egypt: pharaonic stone masonry*. (Oxford).

Arrian. (Arr.) *Anab.* (*Anabasis*). 1989. G. P. Goold, (ed.) *LCL*.

Athenaeus (Ath.) 1854. *The Deipnosophists*. C. D. Yonge (trans.). On-line, www.attalus.org/old/athenaeus.html

Aufderheide, A. C. and C. Rodríguez-Martín. 1998. *The Cambridge encyclopedia of human paleopathology*. (Cambridge).

Avi-Yonah, M. and A. Negev. 1960. "A city of the Negeb: excavations in Nabataean, Roman and Byzantine Eboda," *ILN* 237, 944-47.

Bacchelli, B., R. Pesqualucci and V. Mashrodonato. 2000."Interior decoration and furniture of the Roman imperial period," in *Annales du 14e congrès de l'AIHV,* Venezia-Milano 1998. *AIHV* (Lochem) 86-88.

Bachmann, W. von, C. Watzinger, and T. Wiegand. 1921. *Petra, wissenschaftliche veröffentlichungen des Deutsch-Türkischen denkmalschutz-kommandos*. (Berlin).

Bahrani, Z. 1996. "The Hellenization of Ishtar: nudity, fetishism, and the production of cultural differentiation in ancient art," *Oxford Art Journal* 19, 3-16.

Bailey, D. M. 1998. *Excavations at el-Ashmunein V. Pottery: lamps and glass of the Late Roman and Early Arab Periods. BMQ.*

Bailey, D. M. 1994. "Chapter 2: catalogue and discussion," in D. Barag and M. Hershkovitz (edd.) *Masada IV*, The Yigael Yadin excavations 1963-1965. *IES* vol. 4, 11-106, (Jerusalem).

Bailey, D. M. 1988. *A catalogue of the lamps in the British Museum. Roman provincial lamps*, vol. 3. (London).

Baker, J. and D. Brothwell. 1980. *Animal diseases in archaeology*. (London).

Banerjee, A. and B. Schneider. 1996. "Römisches elfenbein–zerstörungsfreie materialprüfung mit optischen und spektralphotometrischen methoden," *KölnJb* 29, 331-42.

Barag, D. 1962. "Glass Vessels from the Cave of Horror," *IEJ* 12, 208-14.

Barag, D. 1987."Recent important epigraphic discoveries related to the history of glassmaking in the Roman period," *Annales du 10e congrès de l'AIHV.* Madrid-Segovie 1985. *AIHV*, (Amsterdam) 109-16.

Barag, D. 1991. "The contribution of Masada to the history of Early Roman glass," in M. Newby and K. Painter (edd.) *Roman glass: two centuries of art and invention. Ant.J* 137-40.

Barag, D. 1962. "Glass vessels from the Cave of Horror," *IEJ* 12, 208-14.

Barag, D., and M. Hershkovitz. 1994. "Lamps from Masada," in D. Barag and M. Hershkovitz (edd.) *Masada IV:* The Yigael Yadin excavations 1963-1965. (Jerusalem).

Baramki, D. C. 1935. "Two Roman cisterns at Beit Natif," *QDAP* 5, 3-10.

Baramki, D. C. 1934. "An early Christian basilica at 'Ein Hanniya," *QDAP* 3, 113-17.

Barbet, A. 1995. "Les characteristiques de la peinture murale à Petra," *SHAJ* 5, 383-90.

Bar-Kochva, B. 1976. *The Seleucid army.* (Cambridge).

Barrett, D. G. 2008. *The ceramic oil lamp as an indicator of cultural change within Nabataean society in Petra and its environs circa CE 106*. Gorgias diss. Near Eastern Studies 32. (Piscataway, NJ).

Barrett, D. G. 2005. *The ceramic oil lamp as an indicator of cultural change within Nabataean society in Petra and its environs, circa CE 106*. Ph.D. diss., Brown Univ.

Barrett, D. G. 1998a. "The lamps," in M. S. Joukowsky, (ed.) *Great Temple:* vol. 1, 275-86.

Barrett, D. G. 1998b. "Other small finds," in M. S. Joukowsky, (ed.) *Great Temple*, vol. 1, 287-24.

Bartoseiwicz, L., W. Van Neer and A. Lentacker. 1997. "Draught cattle: their osteological identification and history." *Annales Sciences Zoologiques* 281. (Belgium).

Basile, J. J. 2003. "The relief sculpture program from the Great Temple at Petra, Jordan," *AIA, 104th Annual Meeting Abstracts*, 61.

Basile, J. J. 2002a. "Recently discovered relief sculptures from the Great Temple at Petra, Jordan," *ADAJ* 46, 331-46.

Basile, J. J. 2002b. "Two visual languages at Petra: the aniconic and representational sculpture of the Great Temple," *NEA* 65. 4, 255-58.

Basile, J. J. 1999. "Preliminary report of the notes on the head of the goddess Tyche from Petra, Jordan," *ADAJ* 42, 223-26.

Basile, J. J. 1998. "Architectural sculpture and reconstruction: the Lower Temenos," in M. S. Joukowsky (ed.) *Great Temple* vol. 1, 189-08.

Basile, J. J. 1997. "A head of the goddess Tyche from Petra, Jordan," *ADAJ* 41, 255-66.

Baur, P. C. V. 1938. "Glassware" in C. Kraeling, (ed.) *Gerasa, city of the Decapolis.* (New Haven) 505-46.

Beauchot, M. L. and A. Pras. 1993. *Guía de los peces de mar de España y Europa*. (Barcelona).

Becker, C. 1991. "The analysis of mammal bones from Basta, a pre-pottery Neolithic site in Jordan: problems and potential," *Paléorient* 17.1, 59-75.

Bedal, L.-A. 2003. *The Petra pool-complex. A Hellenistic paradeisos in the Nabataean capital: results from the Petra "Lower Market" survey and excavations, 1998*. Gorgias diss. vol. 4. (Piscataway, NJ.).

Bedal, L.-A. 2002. "Desert oasis: water consumption and display in the Nabataean capital," *NEA* 65. 4, 225-34.

Bedal, L.-A. 2001. "A pool complex in Petra's city center," *BASOR* 324, 23-41.

Bedal, L.-A. 2000. *The Petra pool-complex: a Hellenistic paradeisos in the Nabataean Capital.* Ph.D. diss., Univ. of Pennsylvania (Philadelphia PA).

Bedal, L-A. 1998. "Neutron activation analysis of pottery," *Great Temple,* vol. 1, 345-67.

Begley, V. and R. DePuma (edd.) 1991. *Rome and India*. (Madison, WI).

Bernardi Ferrero, D. 1966-1974. *Teatri classici in Asia Minore*, vols. 1-4. (Rome).

Bestock, L. D. 1999. "Nabataean pottery from the 'cistern:' some finds from the Brown Univ. excavations at the Petra Great Temple," *ADAJ* 42, 241-48.

Bignasca, A. 1996. "Terrakotten aus spätrömischen befunden. Petra," in Bignasca, A. *et al.* (edd.) *Ez Zantur I. Ergebnisse der Schweizerisch-Liechtensteinischen ausgrabungen 1988-1992*. Terra Archaeologica, Band II. (Mainz) 283-94.

Bignasca, A. 1993. "Die terrakotten. Petra und die weihrauchstrasse: ausstelung," in R. A. G. Stucky (ed.) *Antikenmuseum Basel und Sammlung Ludwig*. (Zurich) 65-67.

Bignasca, A. *et al.* (edd.) *Ez Zantur I. ergebnisse der Schweizerisch-Liechtensteinischen Ausgrabungen 1988-1992*. Terra Archaeologica (Mainz).

Bikai, P. M. 2005b. "The high place at Beidha," *ACORN* 17. 2, 1-3.

Bikai, P. M, 2002. "North Ridge project," *ACORN* 14, 1-4.

Bikai, P. M., C. Kanellopoulos, and S. L. Saunders. 2008. "Beidha in Jordan: a Dionysian hall in a Nabataean landscape," *AJA* 112.8, 465-07.

Bikai, P. M., C. Kanellopoulos, and S. L. Saunders. 2006. *Beidha documentation project, "'out of the desert'."* Khalid Shoman Foundation, Darat al-Funun, Amman, Jordan.

Bikai, P. M, C. Kanellopoulos and S. L. Saunders. 2005a. "Bayda documentation project," *ADAJ* 49, 339-44.

Bikai, P. M., and M. A. Perry. 2001. "Petra North Ridge tombs 1 and 2: preliminary report," *BASOR* 324, 59-78.

Bilde, Per. 1990. "Atargatis/Dea Syria: Hellenization of her cult in the Hellenistic-Roman Period," in P. Bilde, T. Engberg-Pedersen, L. Hannestad, and J. Zahle (edd.) *Religion and religious practice in the Seleucid kingdom*. Studies in Hellenistic Civilization, 1. Aarhus Univ. (Aarhus) 151-87.

Bingöl, O. 2005. "Theatron," in *Magnesia on the Meander*. (Istanbul).

Bishop, M. C. 1988. "Cavalry equipment of the Roman army in the first century A.D," in J. N.C. Coulston, (ed.) *Military equipment and the identity of Roman soldiers. BAR-IS* 394, (Oxford) 67-194.

Bishop, M.C. and J.N.C. Coulston.1993. Roman military equipment from the Punic Wars to the fall of Rome. (London).

Blagg, T. F. C. 1990. "Column capitals with elephant-headed volutes at Petra," *Levant* 22, 131-37.

Bloch, P. 1982. *Aquamaniles: objets sacrés et profanes du Moyen Age*. (Milan).

Boardman, J., (ed.) 1993. *The Oxford history of classical art*. (Oxford).

Boardman, J., J. Griffen, and O. Murray (edd.) 1986. *The Oxford history of the classical world.* (Oxford).

Boardman, J. 2001. *Greek gems and finger rings: Early Bronze age to Late Classical*. (2nd edn. London).

Bodel, J. and S. K. Reid. 2002. "A dedicatory inscription to the emperor Trajan from the Small Temple at Petra, Jordan," *NEA* 65, 4, 249-50.

Bodenheimer, F. S. 1960. *Animal and man in bible lands*. Collection de travaux de l'Académie Internationale d'Histoire des Sciences 10, (Leiden).

Boessneck J. 1969. "Osteological differences between sheep (*Ovis aries Linné*) and goat (*Capra hircus Linné*)," in D. Brothwell and E. Higgs, (edd.) *Science in archaeology*. (Santa Barbara) 331-58.

Boessneck, J., H-H. Müller, and M.Teichert, 1964. "Osteologische unterschiedungsmerkmale zwischen schaf (*ovis aries linne´*) und ziege (*capra hircus linne´*)," *Kühn-Archiv* 78, 1-129.

Bonfante, L. 1989. "Nudity as a costume in classical art," *AJA* 93, 543-70.

Bourriau, J. D. *et al.* 1978. *Glass at the Fitzwilliam Museum*. (Cambridge).

Bowersock, G. W. 2003. "The Nabataeans in historical context," in G. Markoe (ed.) *Petra rediscovered. The lost city of the Nabataeans*. (New York) 25.

Bowersock, G. W. 1982. Review of A. Spijkerman, *The coins of the Decapolis, JRS* 72, 197-98.

Bowersock, G. W. 1983. *Roman Arabia*. (Cambridge, MA).

Bowsher, J. M. C. 1989. "The Nabataean army," in D. H. French and C. S. Lightfoot (edd.) *The eastern frontier of the Roman empire*. *BAR-IS* 553 (Oxford) 19-30.

Bowsher, J. 1986. "Two glass vessels from area a," in F. Zayadine, (ed.) *Jerash archaeological project 1981-1983.* (Amman) 262-64.

Boyd, T. 1978. "The arch and the vault in Greek architecture,"*AJA* 82, 83-00.

British Museum department of coins and medals, 1965. *Catalogue of the Greek coins of Arabia, Mesopotamia, and Persia (Nabataea, Arabia Provincia, S. Arabia, Mesopotamia, Babylonia, Assyria, Persia, Alexandrine empire of the east, Persis, Elymais, Characene). BMCRE* (Bologna).

British Museum department of coins and medals, and W. W. Wroth. 1964. *Catalogue of the Greek coins of Galatia, Cappadocia, and Syria*. (Bologna).

British Museum department of coins and medals, and H. Mattingly. 1936. *Coins of the Roman Empire in the British Museum* vol. 3. "Nerva to Hadrian." (London).

British Museum department of coins and medals, and G. F. Hill. 1910. *Catalogue of the Greek coins of Phoenicia*. (London).

Broneer, O. 1977."Terracotta lamps," in *Isthmia. Excavations by the University of Chicago under the auspices of the American School of Classical Studies at Athens,* vol. 3. (Princeton NJ).

Broneer, O. 1930. "Terracotta lamps," in *Corinth.* vol. 4, part 2. (Cambridge, MA).

Brünnow, R. E., A. von Domaszewski and J. Euting. 1904-1909. *Die provincia Arabia*. (3 vols.). (Strasburg). *Die Provincia Arabia, auf Grund zweier in den Jahren 1897 und 1898: unternommenen Reisen und der Berichte früherer Reisender beschrieben*. Strassburg.

Bruun, P. M. 1966. "Constantine and Licinius. A.D. 313-337," in C. H. V. Sutherland and R. A. G. Carson (edd.) *The Roman imperial coinage*, vol. 7. *BMCRE.*

Buckley, M., S. W. Kansa, S. Howard and S. Campbell. 2010. "Distinguishing archaeological sheep from goat bones using a single collagen biomarker," *JAS* 37. 1, 13-20.

Buikstra, J. E. and D. H. Ubelaker. 1994. *Standards for data collection from human skeletal remains.* (Fayetteville, AR).

Burr Thompson, D. 1963. "The terracotta figurines of the Hellenistic period," in *Troy, excavations conducted by the University of Cincinnati, 19321938.* Suppl.vol. 3, (Princeton, NJ).

Butcher, K. 2003. *Roman Syria and the Near East*. British Museum (London).

Cagnat, R. and V. Chapot. 1916–1920. *Manuel d'archéologie Romaine*. vol. 2. (Paris).

Cameron, A. 1993. *The later Roman empire*. (Cambridge, MA).

Cantineau, J, 1932. *Le Nabatéen*. (Paris).

Caron, B. 1997. "Roman figure-engraved glass in The Metropolitan Museum of Art," *MMAJ* 32, 19-50.

Carrington, R. 1958. *Elephants*. (London).

Cassius Dio (Cass. Dio.) 1914. *Roman History*, vol. 8. E. Carey (trans.). LCL.

Casson, L., (ed.) 1989. *The Periplus Maris Erythraei.* (L. Casson, trans. with commentary, Princeton, NJ).

Casson, L. 1980. "Three notes on the text, *Periplus Maris Erythraei*." L. Casson (trans. and ed.) *CQ* 30, 495-97.

Cerón-Carrasco, R. 2004. forthcoming. *The fish remains from Tell esh Shuna, Jordan*.

Clairmont, C. 1977. *Excavations at Dura-Europos conducted by Yale University*, final report IV.5, (New Haven).

Claridge, A. 1998. *Rome*. (Oxford).

Clement of Alexandria. (Clem. Al.) 1919. *Exhortations to the Greeks.* G. W. Butterworth (trans.) LCL 92. Cambridge, MA.

Cleveland, R. L. 1960. "The excavation of the Conway High Place (Petra) and soundings at Khirbet Ader," *AASOR* 34-35, 55-97.

Cloke, C. 2003. *Water in the desert: the water systems of the Petra Great Temple.* Brown Univ. (Providence RI).

Coarelli, F. 1962. "The painted cups of Begram and the ambrosian Iliad," *EW* 13, 317-27.

Cohen, E. 1997. "Roman, Byzantine and Umayyad glass," in Y. Hirschfeld and G. Solar (edd.) *Hammat Gader excavations 1979-1982. IES* 396-31.

Coleman, K. M. 2006. Mart. (Martial *Spect.*) *Martial. Liber spectaculorum*. (Oxford).

Comer, D. C. 1997. *Enhancing the utility of SIR-C radar imagery in the analysis and monitoring of archaeological sites by georeferencing with larger scale imagery: a test project at Petra, Jordan*. Submitted September 25, 1997. National Park Service, Denver, RPG, Applied Archeology Center. (On file, National Park Service).

Cool, H. E. C. 1996. "Sedeinga and the glass vessels of the kingdom of Meroë," in *Annales du 13e congrès de l'AIHV,* Pays-Bas 1995. *AIHV* (Lochem) 201-12.

Corbeil, M - C. and K. Helwig. 1999. *Analysis of fresco fragments from the Petra Great Temple.* Analytical research laboratory report 3779, March 19, 1999. Institut Canadien De Conservation. (Toronto).

Coulton, J. 1977. *Ancient Greek architects at work*. (Oxford).

Coulton, J. 1976. *The Architectural development of the Greek stoa*. (Oxford).

Coulton, J. 1974. "Lifting in early Greek architecture," *JHS* 94, 1-19.

Coulston, J. C. N. 1985. "Roman archery equipment," in M. C. Bishop, (ed.) *The production and distribution of Roman military equipment*. Proceedings of the Second Roman Military Equipment Seminar. (Oxford), 220-366.

Coulston, J. C. N. 2001."Arrow-heads," in Z. T. Fiema, C. Kannelopoulos, T. Waliszewski, and R. Schick, (edd.) *The Petra Church*. (Amman) 395-96.

Crelier, M-C. 1995. *Die frühen lampen von ez Zantur, Petra*. Lizentiatsarbeit, Basel Univ. (Basel).

Creswell, K. 1989. *A short account of early Muslim architecture*. (J. Allan rev., Cairo).

Crowfoot, G. M. 1957. "Glass," in J. W. Crowfoot, G. M. Crowfoot, and K. Kenyon (edd.) *The objects from Samaria. PEFA*, (London), 403-22.

Crowfoot, J. W. and G. M. Fitzgerald.1929."Excavations in theTyropoeon valley," *PEFA, Ann.* V. (London).

Crowfoot, J. W., G. M. Crowfoot and K. M. Kenyon. 1957. "The objects from Samaria," in J. W. Crowfoot, G. M. Crowfoot, and K. Kenyon (edd.) *Samaria-Sebaste: reports of the work of the joint expedition in 1931-1933 and of the British expedition in 1935*, vol. 3. *PEFA*, (London).

Csapo, E. and W.J. Slater. 1944. *The context of ancient drama* (Michigan).

Curtius, L. 1930. "Poenitentia," in *Festschrift für James Loeb*, (München), 53-62.

da Costa, K. *et al.* 2002. "New light on late antique Pella: Sydney Univ. excavations in area XXXV, 1997," *ADAJ* 46, 503-33.

Dalman, G. 1912a. *Neue Petra-Forschungen. Palätinische forschungen zur archäologie und topographie*, Band II. (Leipzig).

Dalman, G. 1912b. *Neue Petra forschungen und der heilige felsen von Jerusalem*. (Leipzig).

Dalman, G. 1908. *Petra und seine felsheiligtümer*. (Leipzig).

Daremberg, C. 1881–1929. *Dictionnaire des antiquités Grecques et Romaines, d'après les textes et les monuments ... ouvrage rédigé par une société d'écrivains spéciaux, d'archéologues et de professeurs sous la direction de mm. Ch. Daremberg et Edm. Saglio, DarSag.*

Dart, R. (ed.) 2003. *Medical toxicology*. (3rd edn. Philadelphia).

Davidson, G. R. 1952. "The minor objects," in *Corinth* vol. 12.

de Alarcão, J. 1975. "Bouteilles carrées à fond décoré du Portugal Romain," *JGS* 17, 47-53

de Bellis, M. 1998. "Cento frammenti di antichi vetri adriesi custoditi nel Rijks Museum van Oudheden di Leida (Olanda)." (Adria).

De Franciscis, A. 1978. *The buried cities, Pompeii and Herculaneum*. (London).

Demosthenes. (Dem.) *de Corona (De cor.)* [*on the Crown*]. 2001. H.Yunis (trans.) Cambridge.

Dentzer, J.-M., P.-M. Blanc, and T. Fournet. 2002. "Le development urbain de Bosra de l'époque Nabatéenne à l'époque Byzantine: bilan des recherches Françaises 1981–2002," *Syria* 79, 75-54.

Desse-Berset, H., and J. Studer. 1996. "Fish remains from Ez Zantur (Petra, Jordan)," in A. Bignasca *et al.*, (edd.) *Petra, Ez Zantur 1: Ergebnisse der Schweizerische-Liechtensteinischen Ausgrabungen 1988-1992*. (Mainz) 318-27.

Deth, Koethe and Hussong. 1937. "Fundchronik für die Zeit vom 1. Juli bis 31. Dezember 1936, arbeitsgebiet des Landesmuseums Trier," *Germania* 21,196.

de Tommaso, G. 1998. "Vetri incisi di fabbriche orientali?" *ArchCl* 50, 419-33.

De Vries, B. 1982. *Umm el-Jimal: a tour guide*. (Amman).

De Vries, B. and A. Lain. 2006. "The legionary bath (area C.10)," in S. T. Parker (ed.) *The Roman frontier in central Jordan. DOP.*

Dinsmoor, W. B. 1975. *The architecture of ancient Greece.* (London and New York).

Diod. Sic. (Diodorus Siculus). 1933-1967. Oldfather, C. H. *et al.*, (trans.) *LCL.* (London).

Diod. Sic. (Diodorus Siculus) *Universal History. (Bibliotheca Historica)* Books XVIII-XIX. 1947. R. M. Geer (trans.) *LCL.*

Dioscorides. 2000. *De materia medica.* T. A. Osbaldeston (trans.) R. P.Wood (notes). Johannesburg.

Dodge, B. A. 1955. "Elephants in the bible lands," *ASOR* 18.1,17-20.

Dodge, H. 1990. "The architectural impact of Rome in the east," in M. Henig (ed.) *Architecture and architectural sculpture in the Roman Empire.* Oxford Univ. Com. for Arch., Monog. 29 (Oxford), 108-20.

Dor, M. 1984. *Checklist of the fishes of the Red Sea.* The Israel Academy of Science and Humanities (Jerusalem).

Driesch, A. von den. 1976. *A guide to the measurement of animal bones from archaeological sites.* (Cambridge, MA).

Dussart, O. 1997. "Les verres," in C. Clamer, O. Dussart, and J. Magness, (edd.) *Fouilles archéologiques de 'Ain ez-Zâra/Callirrhoé villégiature hérodienne. FIFAO,* (Beirut) 96-02.

Dussart, O. 1998. "Le verre en Jordanie et en Syrie du sud," *FIFAO* (Beirut).

Dussubieux, L. and B. Gratuze. 2003. "Analyse quantitative de fragments de verre provenant de Begram," *Topoi* 11, Fasc.1, 451-72.

Eadie, J. W. and J. P. Oleson. 1986. "The water-supply systems of Nabataean and Roman Humayma," *BASOR* 262, 49-76.

Edgar, C. C. 1905. *Catalogue général des antiquities Égyptiennes du musée du Caire XXII, Graeco-Egyptian Glass. FIFAO* (Leipzig).

Egan, E. C. 2002a. "Stucco decoration from the south corridor of the Petra Great Temple: discussion and interpretation," *ADAJ* 46, 347-61.

Egan, E. C. 2002b. *Putting the pieces together: an analysis and interpretation of the stucco finds recovered from the south corridor of the Petra Great Temple in Petra, Jordan during the 2001 excavation season.* Unpub. thesis, Brown Univ. (Providence RI.)

Elderkin, K. 1928. "Buttons and their use on Greek garments," *AJA* 32, 333-45.

El-Khouri, L. S. 2007. "Fertility as an element in Late Nabataean beliefs: the archaeological evidence considered," *Levant* 39, 81-90.

El-Khouri, L. S. 2002. *The Nabataean terracotta figurines. BAR-IS* 1034. (Oxford).

Epiphanius. 1994. *The Panarion of Epiphanius of Salamis.* F. Williams (trans.) vol. II. Brill, Leiden.

Erdmann, E. 1977. "Die glasfunde von Mezad Tamar (Kasr Gehainije) in Israel," Saalburg Jahrbuch 34, 98-46.

Erickson-Gini, T. 2004. *Crisis and renewal – settlement in the Central Negev in the third and fourth centuries C.E., with emphasis on the finds from recent excavations in Mampsis, Oboda, and Mezad 'En Hazeva.* Ph.D. diss., Hebrew Univ. (Jerusalem).

Erickson-Gini, T. 1999. *Mampsis: a Nabataean-Roman settlement in the Central Negev highlands, in the light of the ceramic and architectural evidence found in archaeological excavations during 1993–1994.* Unpub. M.A. thesis, Tel Aviv Univ. (Tel Aviv).

Erickson-Gini, T. and Y. Israel. 2003. "Recent advances in the research of the Nabatean and Roman Negev," in R. Rosenthal-Heginbottom (ed.) *The Nabateans in the Negev*. Rebuen and Edith Hecht Museum, Univ. of Haifa, 9-14.

Eschebach, H. 1977. "Die entwicklung der schola labri in den Vesuvstädten, dargestellt am labrum des mannercaldariums der stabianer thermen in Pompeji," *CronPomp* III, 156-76.

Fagan, G. G. 1999. *Bathing in public in the Roman world*. (Ann Arbor, MI).

Farajat, S. and S. Al-Nawafleh. 2005. "Report on the Al-Khazna courtyard excavation at Petra, 2003 season," *ADAJ* 49, 373-93.

Fazekas, I. G. and F. Kósa.1978. *Forensic fetal osteology*. (Budapest).

Ferdowsi, A. 2006. *Shahnameh, the Persian book of kings*. D. Davis (trans., New York).

Fiema, Z. T. 2008. *Petra—the mountain of Aaron: the Finnish archaeological project in Jordan*. (Helsinki, Finland).

Fiema, Z. T. 2003a. "Roman Petra (A.D. 106-363): a neglected subject," *ZDPV* 119, 38-58.

Fiema, Z. T. 2003b. "The Byzantine church at Petra," in G. Markoe (ed.) *Petra rediscovered: lost city of the Nabataeans,* (New York), 239-49.

Fiema, Z. T. 2002. "From the annexation to Aaron: Petra in Roman and Byzantine times,"in J. Frösén and Z. T. Fiema (edd.) *Petra: a city forgotten and rediscovered.* Amos Anderson Art Museum, exh. cat. (Helsinki, Finland).

Fiema, Z. T. 2001. "Reconstructing the history of the Petra Church: data and phasing," in P. M. Bikai (ed.) *The Petra church*. Amman, 7-137.

Fiema, Z. T., C. Kanellopoulos, T. Waliszewski and R. Schick. 2001. In P. M. Bikai (ed.) *The Petra church*. Amman.

Fiema, Z. T., C. Kannelopoulos, T. Waliszewski, and R. Schick, 2001. "Nails," in P. M. Bikai, (ed.) *The Petra church*. Amman, fig. 54,175.

Fischer, M., *et al.* 1995. "The basilica of Ascalon: marble, imperial art and architecture in Roman Palestine," in J. H. Humphrey (ed.) *The Roman and Byzantine Near East: some recent archaeological research,* JRA, Suppl. 14, 121-50.

Fitch, C. R. and N. W. Goldman.1994. *Cosa: the lamps.* Memoirs of the American Academy in Rome. vol. 39. (Ann Arbor, MI).

Foerster, G. 1995. "Art and Architecture," in J. Aviram, G. Foerster and E. Netzer, (edd.) *Masada V: The Yigael Yadin excavations 1963-1965 final reports,* vol. 5. (Jerusalem).

Foy, D., M. - P. Jezéguet and S. Fontaine. 2005. "La circulation du verre en Méditerranée au début du IIIe siècle: le témoignage de L'Epave Ouest Embiez 1 dans le sud de la France (fouilles 2001-2003)," in *Annales du 16e congrés de l'AIHV*, London 2003. *AIHV*, Nottingham, 122-26.

Franken, H. J. 1991. "A history of pottery making," in P. Bienkowski (ed.) *The art of Jordan.* (Gloucestershire) 62-85.

Franken, N. 1996. "Die antiken bronzen im Römisch-Germanischen Museum Köln," *KölnJb* 29, 7-205.

Frankfort, H., S. Lloyd, and T. Jacobsen. 1940. *The Gimilsin temple and the palace of the rulers at Tell Asmar*. *OIP* 42, (Chicago).

Fraser, P. M. 1972. *Ptolemaic Alexandria*. (Oxford).

Frederiksen, R. 2000. "Typology of the Greek theatre building in Late Classical and Hellenistic Times," Proceedings of the Danish Institute at Athens 3, 135-75.

Frederiksen, R. 2002."The Greek theatre, a typical building in the urban centre of the polis," in T. H. Nielsen (ed.) *Even more studies in the ancient Greek polis,* Acts from the Copenhagen Polis Centre 6. (Stuttgart) 65-24.

French, E. 1988. "Nabataean warrior saddles," *PEQ* 120, 64-67.

Freyberger, K. S. and M. S. Joukowsky. 1997."Blattranken, greifen und elefanten: sakrale architektur in Petra und ihr bauschmuck neuausgegrabene peripteral-tempel, Petra," in N. T. Weber and R. Wenning (edd.) *Antike felsstadt Zwischen Arabischer tradition und Griechischer.* (Mainz) 71-86.

Friedland, E. A. 2001. "The Roman marble sculptures from the east baths at Jarash," *ADAJ* 45, 461-77.

Friedland, E. A. 1997. *Roman sculpture from the Levant: the group from the sanctuary of Pan at Caesarea Philippi (Panias).* Ph.D. diss. Univ. of Michigan.

Frimodt, C. 1995. *Multilingual illustrated guide to the world's commercial warmwater fish.* Fishing News, (Oxford).

Frösén, J. and Z. T. Fiema (edd.) 2002. *Petra: a city forgotten and rediscovered.* Amos Anderson Art Museum, exh. cat., (Helsinki, Finland).

Gager, J. G. (ed.)1992. *Curse tablets and binding spells from the ancient world.* (Oxford.)

Galling, K. 1923. "Die beleuchtungsgeräte im Israelitisch-jüdischen kulturgebiet," *ZDPV* 46,1-50.

Garnsey, P. K. Hopkins and C. R. Whittaker (edd.) 1983. *Trade in the ancient economy.* (Berkeley, CA).

Gates, C. 2003. *Ancient cities: the archaeology of urban life in the ancient Near East and Egypt, Greece, and Rome.* (London and New York).

Gawlikowski, M. 1982. "The sacred space in ancient Arab religions," *SHAJ* 1, 301-03.

Gawlikowski, M. 1972. "La notion de tombeau en Syrie Romaine," *Berytus* 21, 5-16.

Gerber, Y. 1997. "Coarse ware pottery from room 6" in *Ez Zantur IV. Swiss-Liechtenstein excavations at ez-Zantur in Petra 1997- The eighth season.* < www.ez-zantur.ch/seasons/1997/IX.html. >

Gerber, Y. 2001a. "Selected ceramic deposits," in Z. T. Fiema, *et al.*, (edd.) *The Petra church.* (Amman).

Glueck, N. 1965. *Deities and dolphins: the story of the Nabataeans.* (New York).

Glueck, N. 1956. "A Nabataean painting," *BASOR* 141, 13-23.

Glueck, N. 1939."Excavations in Eastern Palestine III,"*AASOR* 18-19, (New Haven).

Goren, M. and M. Dor.1994. *An updated checklist of the fishes of the Red Sea. I.* (Jerusalem).

Goren-Rosen, Y. 1998. *Ancient glass from the Holy Land.* (Brisbane, CA.).

Gorgerat, L. 2006. "The anthropomorphic terracottas of the Nabataeans," in C. C. Mattusch, A. A. Donohue, and A. Brauer (edd.) *Common ground: archaeology, art, science, and humanities,* Proceedings of the XVIth Int. Congress of Classical Archaeology, Boston, August 23-26, 2003. (Oxford75-78).

Gowers, W. and H. H. Scullard. 1950. "Hannibal's elephants again," *NC* 6.10.

Graf, D. F. 1996. "The Roman East from the Chinese perspective," in Palmyra and the Silk Road. *AAS* 42,199-16.

Graf, D. F. 1994. "The Nabatean army and the cohortes ulpiae Petraeorum," in E. Dabrowa, (ed.) *the Roman and Byzantine army in the east.* Instytut Historii, Univ. of Kraków, (Kraków) 265-11.

Grigson, C. 1995. "Plough and pasture in the early economy of the Southern Levant," in T. E. Levy (ed.) *The archaeology of society in the Holy Land.* (New York) 245-68.

Grigson, C. 2006. "Farming? feasting? herding? large mammals from the Chalcolithic of Gilat," in T. E. Levy, (ed.) *Archaeology, anthropology and cult: the sanctuary at Gilat, Israel.* (London) 215-19.

Gröning, K. and M. Saller. 1999. *Elephants: a cultural and natural history*. Cologne.

Grose, D. 1991. "Early imperial Roman cast glass: the translucent coloured and colourless fine wares," in M. Newby and K. Painter (edd.) *Roman glass: two centuries of art and invention. Ant.J* 1-18.

Grose, D. 1989. "Early ancient glass: core-formed, rod-formed, and cast," in *Vessels and objects from the Late Bronze Age to the Early Roman Empire, 1600 B.C. to A.D. 50.* (New York).

Gunneweg, J., I. Perlman and J. Yellin. 1983. *The provenience, typology and chronology of Eastern Terra Sigillata*. Qedem 17.

Guthrie, W.K.C. 1993. *Orpheus and Greek religion: a study of the Orphic movement.* (Princeton, NJ).

Hackett, Sir John (ed.)1989. *Warfare in the ancient world*. (New York).

Hackin, J. 1954. *Nouvelles recherches archéologiques à Begram (ancienne Kâpicî) (1939–1940),* vols. 1-2, in Mémoires de la délégation archéologique Française en Afghanistan XI. (Paris).

Hackl, U., H. Jenni, and C. Schneider. 2003. "Quellen zur geschichte der Nabatäer. textsammlung mit übersetzung und kommentar," in *Novum Testamentum et Orbis Antiquus* 51, Univ. Freiburg Schweiz (Göttingen).

Hadad, S. 2002.*The oil lamps from the Hebrew University excavations at Bet Shean*. *Qedem* 4.

Haile, K. M., and M. G. Parker. 1997. "Trench 50 and Special Project 53 final report: Propylaeum, upper levels of the north gallery west of the central Propylaeum staircase. 1997 Great Temple Trench Reports," online in *Open Context* < http://www.open context.org >.

Haile, K. M., and J. M. Rogér. 1998. "Final report. Trench 51, Propylaeum upper levels of the north and south galleries west of the central Propylaeum staircase. 1998 Great Temple Trench Reports,"online in *Open Context* < http://www.open context.org >.

Hakker-Orion, D.1993. "Faunal remains from sites along the frankincense and myrrh route," in H. Buitenhuis and A. T. Clason (edd.) *Archaeozoology of the Near East*, (Leiden) 77-87.

Hall, E. and R. Wyles. 2008. *New directions in ancient pantomime.* (Oxford).

Hamelin, P. 1953. "Matériaux pour servir à l'étude des verreries de Bégram," *CahByrsa* 3, 121-28.

Hammond, P. C. 2000. "Nabataean metallurgy: foundry and fraud," in L. E. Stager, J. A. Greene and M. D. Coogan (edd.) *The archaeology of Jordan and beyond: essays in honor of James A. Sauer*. (Winona Lake, IN) 145-56.

Hammond, P. C. 1996. *The temple of the winged lions Petra, Jordan 1973-1990.* (Fountain Hills, AZ).

Hammond, P. C.1995. "Nabataean architectural technology," *SHAJ* 5, 215-21.

Hammond, P. C. 1987."Three workshops at Petra (Jordan)," *PEQ* 129-41.

Hammond P. C. 1977. "The capitals from the'Temple of the Winged Lions,' Petra," *BASOR* 226, 47-51.

Hammond, P. C.1973a."The Nabataeans—their history, culture and archaeology,"*SIMA* 37.

Hammond, P.C. 1973b."Pottery from Petra,"*PEQ* 105, 27-49.

Hammond, P. C. 1968."The medallion and block relief at Petra," *BASOR* 192, 16-21.

Hammond, P.C. 1965. *The excavations of the main theater at Petra 1961-1962, final report*. (London).

Hannestad, N. 2001. "The marble group of Daidalos, Hellenism in late antique 'Amman," *SHAJ* 7, 513-19.

Hansen, M. H. 1996. "Reflections on the number of citizens accommodated in the assembly place on the Pnyx," in B. Forsén and G. Stanton (edd.) *The Pnyx in the history of Athens*. (Helsinki) 23-33.

Harden, D. B. 1959."The Highdown Hill glass goblet with Greek inscription," *Sussex Archaeological Collections* 97, 3-20.

Harden, D. B. 1936. *Roman Glass from Karanis*. Michigan Univ. Press, (Ann Arbor, MI).

Harden, D. B. 1935."Romano-Syrian glasses with mould-blown inscriptions," *JRS* 25, 163-86.

Harden D. B. *et al.* 1987. *Glass of the Caesars*. (Milan).

Hayes, J. W. 1997. *Handbook of Mediterranean Roman pottery*. Trustees of the British Museum (London).

Hayes, J. W. 1980. *Ancient lamps in the Royal Ontario Museum: Greek and Roman clay lamps, a catalogue* vol. 1. Royal Ontario Museum, (Toronto).

Hayes, J. 1985. "Sigillate orientali. Atlante delle forme ceramiche II: Ceramica fine Romana nel bacino Mediterraneo," in *Enciclopedia delle'arte antica classica e orientale* (Rome) 1-96.

Hayes, J. 1975. *Roman and Pre-Roman glass in the Royal Ontario Museum*. Royal Ontario Museum, (Toronto).

Hayes, W. C.1928. "An engraved glass bowl in the Museo Cristiano of the Vatican Library,"*AJA* 32.1, 23-32.

Healey, J. F. 2001. *The religion of the Nabataeans: a conspectus. Religions in the Graeco-Roman World.* 136. (Leiden, Boston).

Heckel, W. and J. Yardley. 2004. *Alexander the great: historical texts in translation*. (Malden, MA).

Hellmann, M.-Ch. 2002. *L'architecture Grecque I, les principes de la construction*. (Paris).

Hendrix, R. E., P. R. Drey, J. B. Storfjell. 1996. *Ancient pottery of Transjordan, an introduction utilizing published whole forms, Late Neolithic through Late Islamic*. The Institute of Arch., Siegfried H. Horn Archaeological Museum, (Berriens Springs, MI).

Henig, M. (ed.) 1983. *A handbook of Roman art: a comprehensive survey of all the arts of the Roman world.* (Ithaca, NY).

Henry, A. G. 2002. "Final report, Trench 87, 2002 Great Temple trench reports;: Propylaeum, northwest gallery and Propylaeum Room 1," online in *Open Context* < http://www.open context.org >.

Herod. (Herodotus). 1998. *The histories*. R. Waterfield (trans., Oxford).

Hesberg, H. von. 1981-1982. "Elemente der frühkaiserlichen aedikulaarchitektur," in *Jahreshefte des österreichischen archäologischen instituts in Wien*.53, (Vienna) 44ff.

Hesse, B. 1990. "Pig lovers and pig haters: patterns of Palestinian pork production," *Journal of Ethnobiology* 10, 195-26.

Higgins, R. A. 1963. *Greek terracotta figures*. Trustees of the British Museum, (London).

Hill, M., and Nenna, M. - D. 2003. "Glass from Ain et-Turba and Bagawat necropolis in the Kharga Oasis, Egypt," in *Annales du 15e congrès de l'AIHV*, New York-Corning 2001. *AIHV* (Nottingham) 88-92.

Hill, P. V., J. P. C. Kent, and R. A. G. Carson. 1960. *Late Roman bronze coinage, A. D. 324-498*. 2 vols. (London).

Hirschfeld, Y. 1997. "The Roman baths at Hammat Gader," *IES* 15-45.

Hodge, A. T. 2000. *Purity of water: handbook of ancient water technology*.(Boston) 95-99.

Hodge, A. T. 1960. *The woodwork of Greek roofs*. (Cambridge).

Hodges, H. 1974. *Technology in the ancient world*. (New York).

Hoepfner, H. von. 1983. "Das hierothesion des königs Mithradates I, kallinokos von Kommagene nach der ausgrabungen von 1963 bis 1967," in F. K. Dörner (ed.) *Arsamaeia am Nymphaios II.* (Tübungen).

Hoffmann, B. 2000. "Gläs von ausseren limes; ein uberblick,"in *Annales du 14e congrèsde l'AIHV,* Venezia-Milano 1998. *AIHV* (Lochem) 172-74.

Hoftijzer J.and K. Jongeling. 1995, *Dictionary of North-West Semitic inscriptions (HdO)* I/XXI, vols.1-2. (Leiden).

Holley, A. E. 1994. "The ballista balls from Masada," in D. Barag and M. Hershkovitz (edd.) *Masada IV, The Yigael Yadin excavations 1963-1965 final reports, IES.*

Holt, F. L. 2006. "Ptolemy's Alexandrian postscript," *Saudi Aramco World*, vol. 57, No. 6.

Holt, F. L. 2005. "Stealing Zeus's thunder," *Saudi Aramco World*, vol. 56, No. 3.

Holt, F. L. 2003. *Alexander the Great and the mystery of the elephant medallions.* (Berkeley).

Holt, F. L. 1999. *Thundering Zeus: the making of Hellenistic Bactria.* (Berkeley).

Holy Bible 1980. KJV (King James Version). B. Thompson (design, New York, Oxford).

Homeric Hymn to Demeter. 2000. G. Nagy (trans.). www.uh.edu/~cidue/texts/demeter.html.

Hongo, H. and R. H. Meadow. 2000. "Faunal remains from prepottery Neolithic levels at Çayönü, southeastern Turkey: a preliminary report focusing on pigs (*Sus* sp.)," in M. Mashkour, A. M. Choyke, H. Buitenhuis, and F. Poplin (edd.) *Archaeozoology of the Near East IV A. Proceedings of the fifth international symposium on the archaeozoology of southwestern Asia and adjacent areas.* (Groningen)121-40.

Hongo, H. and R. H. Meadow. 1998. "Pig exploitation at Neolithic Çayönü Tepesi (southeastern Anatolia)," in S. Nelson (ed.) *Ancestors for the pigs: pigs in prehistory. MASCAP* 77-98.

Hörig, M. 1979. *Dea Syria: Studien zur religiösen tradition der fruchtbarkeitsgöttin in vorderasien.* Kevelaer. (Neukichen-Vluyn).

Horsfield, G., and A. C. Horsfield. 1941a."Sela-Petra, the rock of Edom and Nabatene," *QDAP* 7, 1-60.

Horsfield, G. and A. C. Horsfield. 1941b. "Sela-Petra (IV), the rock of Edom and Nabatene: the finds," *QDAP* 9, Nos. 2-4, 105-04.

Horsfield, G. and A. C. Horsfield. 1939. "Sela-Petra, III, the rock of Edom and Nabatene: the excavations," *QDAP* 8, No. 3, 87-15.

Horwitz, L. K. 1987. "Animal offerings from two Middle Bronze age tombs," *IEJ* 37, 251-55.

Horwitz, L. K. 1998. "Animal bones from Horbat Rimmon: Hellenistic to Byzantine Periods," *'Atiqot* 35, 65-76.

Horwitz, L. K. and P. Smith. 1990. "A radiographic study of the extent of variation in cortical bone thickness: Soay sheep," *JAS* 17, 655-64.

Horwitz, L. K., E.Tchernov and S. Dar. 1990. "Subsistence and environment on Mount Carmel in the Roman-Byzantine and Mediaeval periods: the evidence from Kh. Sumaqa," *IEJ* 40, 4, 287-04.

Hourani, G. 1951. *Arab seafaring.* (Princeton, NJ).

Howland, R. H. 1951. *The Athenian agora IV: Greek lamps and their survivals.* (Princeton).

Huntingford, G. (ed.) 1980. *The periplus of the Erythraean Sea.* Hakluyt Society. (London).

Hyginus. (Hyg.) 1934. *Fabulae (Fab.)* H. J. Rose (transl.) *LCL.*

Hyland, A. 1990. *Equus, the horse in the Roman world.* (New Haven, CT).

Iliffe, J. H. 1938. "Sigillata wares in the Near East: a list of potters' stamps," *QDAP* 5, 4-53.

Iliffe, J. H. 1934. "Nabataean pottery from the Negev: its distribution in Palestine," *QDAP* 3, 132-35.

Ismail, Z. 1980. "Les chapiteaux de Pétra," *Le Monde de la Bible* 14, 27-29.

Israel, Y. and U. Avida. 1988. *Oil lamps from eretz Israel: the Louis and Carmen Warschaw collection at the Israel Museum*. (Jerusalem).

Jacobi, H. 1913. *Führer durch das Römerkastell saalburg bei Homburg vor der Höhe: mit einem Anhang: Die sammlungen der Saalburg*. Homburg v. d. H. "Taunusbote" Druckerei.

Jacobson, D. 2002. "Herod's Roman temple," *BAR* March-April, 60-61.

Janif, M. M. 2004. "L'écrit et le figuré dans le domaine religieux des Nabatéens. Le sanctuaire rupestre du Sadd al-Mreriyyeh à Pétra," *Syria* 81,119-30.

Jashemski, W. F. 1999. *A Pompeian herbal: ancient and modern medicinal plants*. (Austin, TX).

Jennings, S. 1998."The Roman and early Byzantine glass from the souks excavations: an interim statement," *Berytus* 43, 111-46.

Johnson, D. 1987. *Nabataean Trade:Intensification and Culture Change*. Univ. of Utah, Ph.D diss. (Salt Lake City, UT).

Jones, J. 2006. "The glass in the Roman frontier in central Jordan," in final report by S. T. Parker *et al. The Limes Arabicus project, 1980-1989*, (Washington, DC), 393-12.

Jones, J. 2005."Glass vessel finds from a possibly early fourth-century church at Aila (Aqaba), Jordan," in *Annales du 16e congrés de l'AIHV*, London 2003. *AIHV* (Nottingham) 135-39.

Jones, J. 2000. "Roman export glass at Aila (Aqaba)," in *Annales du 14e congrès de* l'AIHV, Venezia-Milano 1998. *AIHV* (Lochem)147-50.

Jones, M. W. 2000. *The principles of Roman architecture*. (New Haven, CT).

Jory, E. J. 1996. "The drama of the dance in Roman theater and society," in W. J. Slater, (ed.) E. Togo Salmon Papers I. (Ann Arbor, MI)1-27.

Josephus. (Joseph.) *Jewish antiquities (AJ)*. Books 18-19 (Bks. XVIII-XIX). L. H. Feldman (trans.) *LCL* 410.

Joukowsky, M.S. 2015."An Architectural Marvel: The Petra Great Temple," in Z. Weiss (ed.), *Ehud Netzer Volume*. Eretz-Israel: Archaeological, Historical and Geographical Studies vol. 31, Israel Exploration Society (Jerusalem) 69-78.

Joukowsky, M. S. 2013. "Der 'Grosse Tempel' in Petra," in S. G. Schmid (ed.), *Petra, Wunder in der Wüste. Auf den Spuren von J.L. Burckhardt alias 'Scheich Ibrahim', 1812-2012*. Begleitbuch zur Ausstellung, Antikenmuseums Basel und Sammlung Ludwig in Zusammenarbeit mit dem Ministry of Tourism and Antiquities/ Department of Antiquities of Jordan und dem Jordan Museum, Amman, Antikenmuseum Basel und Sammlung Ludwig, 23 Oktober 212 bis 17. März 2013, exh. cat. (Basel). *1812-2012*. exh. cat. (Basel),157-161.

Joukowsky, M. S. 2009. "Extraordinary revelations from the 2008 Brown University Petra Excavations," *ADAJ* 53, 211-28.

Joukowsky, M. S. 2008a. "Common name: poppy; habitat: Nabataean sculpture; the Petra Great Temple," in S. Thompson and P. der Manuelian (edd.) *Egypt and beyond: essays presented to Leonard H. Lesko*. Brown Univ. Dept. of Egyptology and Ancient Western Asian Studies. (Providence RI), 197-08

Joukowsky, M. S. 2008b. "Into the land of research: 2007 Brown University Petra Great Temple documentation," *ADAJ* 52, 279-93.

Joukowsky, M. S. 2007a. *Great Temple,* vol. 2: *archaeological contexts of the remains and excavations*. Brown Univ. (Providence, RI).

Joukowsky, M. S. 2007b. "Exciting developments: the Brown University 2006 Petra Great Temple excavations," *ADAJ* 51, 81-02.

Joukowsky, M. S. 2006a. "Challenges in the field: The Brown University 2005 Petra Great Temple excavations," *ADAJ* 50, 351-72.

Joukowsky, M. S. 2006b. "Roman Byzantine central bath complex: Trench 127. 2006 Great Temple trench reports," online in *Open Context*, < http://www.open context.org >.

Joukowsky, M. S. 2004. "Brown University 2003 excavations at the Petra Great Temple: the eleventh field campaign," *ADAJ* 48, 155-70.

Joukowsky, M. S. 2003a. "The Great Temple," in G. Markoe (ed.) *Petra Rediscovered, Lost City of the Nabataeans*. (New York) 214-22.

Joukowsky, M. S. 2003b. "More treasures and Nabataean traditions at the Petra Great Temple: the Brown University tenth campaign," *ADAJ* 47 389-06.

Joukowsky, M. S. 2002a. "The Brown University 2001 Petra Great Temple excavations offer more surprises," *ADAJ* 46, 315-30.

Joukowsky, M. S. 2002b. "Final report. Propylaeum, Propylaeum West Cryptoporticus, Trench 81, 2002 Great Temple trench reports," online in *Open Context*, < http://www.open context.org >.

Joukowsky, M. S. 2002c. "Final report. Propylaeum, Propylaeum West Entry Stairs, Trench 88, 2002 Great Temple trench reports," online in *Open Context*, < http://www.open context.org >.

Joukowsky, M. S. 2001. "Petra: Great Temple excavations," *ACORN*, vol. 13, 1.5-6.

Joukowsky, M. S. 2000. "Brown University 1999 excavations at the Petra Great Temple," *ADAJ* 44, 313-34.

Joukowsky, M. S. 1999a. "Brown University 1998 excavations at the Petra Great Temple," *ADAJ* 43, 195-22.

Joukowsky, M. S. 1999b. "The Lower Temenos hexagonal pavement, Trench 66, 1999 Great Temple trench Reports," online in *Open Context*, < http://www.open context.org >

Joukowsky, M. S. (ed.) 1998a. *Great Temple* vol. 1. (Providence, RI).

Joukowsky, M. S. 1998b. "Brown University 1997 excavations at the Petra Great Temple," *ADAJ* 42, 293-18.

Joukowsky, M. S. 1998c. "Re-discovering elephants at Petra!" in L. H. Lesko, (ed.) *Ancient Egyptian and Mediterranean studies in memory of William A. Ward.* Dept. of Egyptology, Brown Univ. 133-48.

Joukowsky, M. S. 1997. "The 1996 Brown University archaeological excavations at the 'Great' Southern Temple, Petra." *ADAJ* 41, 195-19.

Joukowsky, M. S. 1996a. "Elefanten in Petra, der neuausgegrabene peripteral-tempel," *Antike Welt*.

Joukowsky, M. S. 1996b. "1995 archaeological excavation of the Southern Temple at Petra, Jordan," *ADAJ* 40, 177-07.

Joukowsky, M. S. 1994. "1993 archaeological excavations and survey of the Southern Temple in Petra, Jordan," *ADAJ* 38, 293-33.

Joukowsky, M. S. and J. J. Basile. 2001."More pieces in the Petra Great Temple puzzle," *BASOR* 324, 23-41.

Joukowsky, M. S. and E. L. Schluntz. 1995. "1994 archaeological excavations and survey of the Southern Temple at Petra, Jordan," *ADAJ* 39, 241-66.

Jung, H. 1982. *Thronende und sitzende götter: zum griechischen götterbild und menschenideal in geometrischer und früharschaischer zeit*. Habelts diss. Reihe Klassische Archäologie, Heft 17, (Bonn).

Kahane, P. P. 1961. "Rock-Cut tombs at Huqoq: notes on the finds," *'Atiqot* 3,126-47.

Kanellopoulos, C. 2004. "The temples of Petra: an architectural analysis," *AA* 1, 221-39.

Kanellopoulos, C. 2002. "The layout of the pool and garden complex in Petra: a metrological analysis," *ADAJ* 47, 149-57.

Kanellopoulos, C. 2001a. "The architecture of shops and colonnaded street in Petra," *BASOR* 324, 9-22.

Kanellopoulos, C. 2001b. "The monumental entrance to the upper market and the Trajanic inscription at Petra, the architectural context," *ADAJ* 46, 295-08.

Kanellopoulos, C. 2001c. "Architecture of the complex," in Fiema *et al.*, P. M. Bikai (ed.) *The Petra church* (Amman) 151-91.

Kansa, S. W. 2004. "Food and religion in the Petra region: a zooarchaeological study of two Nabataean temples." Unpublished Paper, *ASOR* Ann. Meeting, San Antonio, TX.

Kansa, S. W. 2010. "Petra Great Temple animal bones" in projects: Petra Great Temple Excavations. Led by: Martha Sharp Joukowsky. Table generated by: Open Context Editors. Open Context. < http://opencontext.org/tables/0dfc42274ae780c7f55ea45c05941557 > California Digial Library Archival Identifier, < ark:/28722/k2mw28d4j >

Karz, S. 1998. "The Roman and Byzantine glass of the Great Temple," in *Great Temple* vol. I, 325-43.

Katsnelson, N. 2009. "Early Roman glass from Judea–locally produced glass? A preliminary report," *AIHV*, 163-69.

Keller, D. 2006. "Die gläser aus Petra" in *Petra ez-Zantur III. Ergebnisse der Schweizerisch-Liechtensteinischen ausgrabungen*, Teil 1. (Mainz).

Kennedy, C. A. 1963. "The development of the lamp in Palestine, *Berytus* 14, 67-15.

Kent, J. P. C. 1981. "The family of Constantine I. A.D. 337-364," in C. H. V. Sutherland and R. A. G. Carson (edd.) *The Roman imperial coinage,*vol. 8. (London).

Kent, J. P. C. 1994. "The divided empire and the fall of the western parts. AD 395-491," in R. A. G. Carson, J. P. C. Kent and A. M. Burnett (edd.) *The Roman imperial coinage* vol.10. (London).

Khairy, N. I. 1990. *The 1981 Petra excavations,* vol. 1. Abhandlungen des Deutschen Palästinavereins, Band 13 (Wiesbaden).

Khairy, N. I. 1984. "Preliminary Report of the 1981 Petra Excavations," *ADAJ* 28, 315-20.

Khairy, N. I. 1984. "Neither 'TLT' nor 'ALT' but 'RAYT,'" *PEQ* 116, 115-19.

Khairy, N. I. 1982. "Fine Nabataean ware with impressed and rouletted decorations," *SHAJ* 1, 275-83.

Khairy, N. I. 1975. *A typological study of the unpainted pottery from the Petra excavations*. D. Phil. diss. Univ. College (London).

Khanachet, T. M. 2005. "Final report, propylaeum, sondage of Propylaeum west pavers, Special Project 114, 2005 Great Temple Trench Reports," online in *Open Context*, < http://www.open context.org >.

Kindler, A. 1983. *The coinage of Bostra*. (Warminster).

King, A. 1999. "Diet in the Roman world: a regional inter-site comparison of the mammal bones." *JRA* 12,168-02.

Kirkbride, D. 1958. "A short account of the excavation at Petra in 1955-1956," *ADAJ* 4-5, 117-22.

Kleiner, D. E. E. 1992. *Roman sculpture*. (New Haven, CT).

Knauf, E. A. 1990."Dushara and Shai'al-Qaum,"ARAM 2. 195-83.

Kolb, B. 2003. "Petra—from tent to mansion: living on the terraces of Ez-Zantur," in G. Markoe (ed.) *Petra rediscovered: Lost city of the Nabataeans*, (New York) 230-37.

Kolb, B. 2002."Excavating a Nabataean mansion," *NEA* 65, 4, 260-64.

Kolb, B. *et al.* 2000. "Swiss-Liechtenstein excavations at Ez-Zantur/Petra: the tenth campaign," *ADAJ* 44, 355-72.

Kolb, B. *et al.* 1998. "Swiss-Liechtenstein excavations at Ez-Zantur in Petra 1997," *ADAJ* 42, 259-78.

Kolb, B. *et al.* 1993. "Preliminary report of the Swiss-Liechtenstein excavations at Ez-Zantur in Petra 1992: the fourth campaign," *ADAJ* 37, 417-26.

Koster, A., and D. Whitehouse.1989."Early Roman cage cups," *JGS* 31, 25-33.

Krencker, D. 1929. *Die trierer kaiserthermen*. Dr. Benno Filser G. m. b. H. Augsburg.

Kurlansky, M. 2002. *Salt: a world history*. (London).

LaBianca, O. S. and A. von den Driesch (edd.) 1995. *Faunal remains: taphonomical and zooarchaeological studies of the animal remains from Tell Hesban and vicinity*. Hesban 13. Andrews Univ. Press, (Berrien Springs, MI).

Lapp, P. W. 1961. "Palestinian ceramic chronology 200 BC-70 AD," *ASOR* (New Haven).

Larché F. and F. Zayadine. 2003. "The Qasr al-Bint of Petra," in G. Markoe (ed.) *Petra rediscovered: lost city of the Nabataeans* (New York), 199-13.

Lawrence, A. 1996. *Greek architecture*. (R A. Tomlinson, Rev.). Yale Univ. Press, (New Haven, CT).

Laurenzi, L. 1938. "Projettile dell'artigliueria antica scoperti a Rodi," in *Memorie vols. 1-3.* Pubblicate a Cura dell'Istituto Storico-Archeologico FERT (2). Rodi, (Rhodes, Greece).

Laurenzi, L. 1964. "Perchè annibalici non assediò Roma," in *Studi Annibalici.* Atti del Convegno Svoltosi a Cortona-Tuoro sul Trasimeno-Perugia, Ottobre 1961 (Cortona).

Lawrence, A.W. 1983. *Greek architecture*. Rev. by R. A.Tomlinson. (5th edn. New Haven, CT and London).

Leclant, J., and G. Clerc. 1994. "Osiris,"in *LIMC, VIII.1-2*. (Zurich) 107-16.

Lee, R. Y. T. 2003. *Romanization in Palestine: A study of urban development from Herod the Great to AD 70.* (Oxford).

Leonard Jr., A. 2000. "Why a hedgehog?" in L. E. Stager, J. A. Greene, and M. D. Coogan (edd.) *The archaeology of Jordan and beyond: essays in honor of James A. Sauer*. (Winona Lake, IN) 310-16.

Lev-Tov, J. 2003. "'Upon what meat doth this our Caesar feed…?' A dietary perspective on Hellenistic and Roman influence in Palestine," in S. Alkier and J. Zangenberg, edd.) *Zeichen aus text und stein. studien auf dem weg zu einer archaeologie des Neuen Testaments*. (Tübingen) 420-46.

Libonati, E. S. and J. I. Fusté. 2002. "Upper Temenos, Residential Quarter, southwest ridge caves and associated architecture, Trench 94, 2002, June 19, 2002-August 9, 2002, final report," online in *Open Context,* Great Temple 2002, Trench Reports.

Lightfoot, C. 1993. "Some examples of ancient cast and ribbed bowls in Turkey," *JGS* 35, 22-38.

Lindblom, J. 2005. "Chronological and economic aspects of glass lamps from the Finnish excavations at Jabal Harun near Petra,"Annales du 16e congrés de l'AIHV, London 2003, *AIHV* (Nottingham) 162-66.

Lindner, M. 1989. "Ein nabatäisches klammheiligtum bei Petra. Petra und das königreich der Nabatäer" in M. Lindner (ed.) *Lebensraum, geschichte und kulture eines Arabischen volkes der antike.* (5th edn. Delp) 286-92.

Lindner, M. 2003. "Über Petra hinaus; archäologische erkundungen im südlichen Jordanien." (Rahden-Westf).

Lindner, M. and J. Zangenberg. 1993. "The re-discovered baityl of the goddess Atargatis in the iyyag Gorge of Petra (Jordan) and its significance for religious life in Nabataea, *ZDPV* 109, 141-51.

Ling, R.1991. *Roman painting.* (Cambridge).

Ling, R.1999. *Stuccowork and painting in Roman Italy.* (Brookfield).

Littman, E.A. 1914, *Nabataean inscriptions from the Southern Hauran, Princeton Expedition.* XI-XII, Div. IV (Leiden).

Loeschcke, S. 1919. *Lampen aus Vindonissa: ein beitrag zur geschichte von Vindonissa und des antiken Beleuchtungswesen.* (Zürich).

Lucr. (Lucretius Carus Titus). 1982. *De rerum natura.* W. H. D. Rouse (trans.), *LCL.*

Lucas, A. E. and J. R. Harris, 1962. *Ancient Egyptian materials and industries.* (London).

Lyttelton, M. B. 1974. *Baroque architecture in classical antiquity.* (London).

Lyttelton, M. and T. Blagg. 1990. "Sculpture in Nabataean Petra and the question of Roman influence," in M. Henig (ed.) *Architecture and architectural sculpture in the Roman Empire.* Oxford Univ. Comm. for Arch., Monog. 29, 91-07.

Macalister, R.A.S. 1912. *The excavations of Gezer.* vols. 1-3, *PEF.*

MacGregor, A. 1985. *Bone, antler, ivory and horn.* (New Jersey).

MacKinnon, M. 2004. *Production and consumption of animals in Roman Italy: integrating the zooarchaeological and textual evidence.* JRA Suppl. 54.

MacKinnon, M. 2007. "Osteological research in classical archaeology," *AJA* 111, 473-04.

Magen, Y. 2008. *Mount Gerizim excavations,* vol. 2*: a temple city* in Judea and Samaria. Publications (JSP 8). Israel Antiquities Authority (Jerusalem).

Magness, J. 1993. *Jerusalem ceramic chronology: circa 200-800 CE,* vol. 9. JSOT/ASOR Monog. (Sheffield).

Magness, J. 1996. "Masada 1995: discoveries at camp F," *BA* 59. 3,181.

Manning, W. H. 1985. *Catalogue of the Romano-British iron tools, fittings and weapons in the British Museum.* Trustees of the British Museum (London).

Manor, M., R. R. and L. K. Horwitz. 1997. "Diachronic changes in urban diet: the historical periods at Bet She'an, Israel," *Archaeozoologia* VIII 1, 2, 15-16, 89-04.

Markoe, G. (ed.) 2003. *Petra rediscovered: lost city of the Nabataeans.* (New York).

Marsden, E. W. 1969. *Greek and Roman artillery: historical development.* (Oxford).

Mart. (Martial) *Epigrams.* 1978-1979. Walter C. A. Ker (trans.) *LCL.*

Mart. (Martial) *Spect. (Spectacula) Liber Spectaculorum.* (2006 edn.) K. M. Coleman, (trans. Oxford).

Martín, R. 1965. *Manuel d'architecture grecque 1: matériaux et techniques.* (Paris).

Massabo, B. 1998. "Grande piatto in vetro blu figurato ad incisione e ad intaglio da una tomba della necropoli di Albigaunum (Albenga)," *JGS* 40, 25-44.

Massabo, B. 2000. "La più antica produzione di vetri figurati ad incisione e ad intaglio de età romana." Annales du 14e congrès de l'AIHV, Venezia-Milano 1998. *AIHV* (Lochem) 68-75.

Mattingly, H. and E. A. Sydenham. 1926."Vespasian to Hadrian," in *Roman imperial coinage,* vol. 2. (London).

Mazar, B. and I. Dunayevsky, I. 1967. "En-Gedi, fourth and fifth seasons of excavations, preliminary report," *IEJ* 17, 133-43.

Mazor, G. and R. Bar-Nathan. 1998. "The Bet She'an excavation project: 1992-1994," in R. Pommerantz, R. Kudish, and N. Bahat-Silberstein (edd.) *Excavations and surveys in Israel,* vol.17. I. Israel Antiquities Authority (Jerusalem) 7-38.

McCredie, J. *et al.* 1992. *Samothrace. The rotunda of Arsinoe.* (Princeton, NJ).

McKenzie, J. S. *Khirbet et-Tannur Nabataean temple project, Jordan.* Online document: < http://www.ocla.ox.ac.uk/pdf/khirbet_tannur.pdf > (Accessed 7 October 2009).

McKenzie, J. S. 2007. *The architecture of Alexandria and Egypt 300 BCE-AD 700.* (New Haven and London).

McKenzie, J. S. 2005. *The architecture of Petra.* Oxford Univ. Press, repr., (Oxford).

McKenzie, J. S. 2004. "Temples, tombs, and other recent discoveries from the rose red city," *JRA* 17, 559-68.

McKenzie, J. S. 2003. "Carvings in the desert: The sculpture of Petra and Khirbet et-Tannur," in G. Markoe (ed.) *Petra rediscovered: lost city of the Nabataeans.* New York, 165-91.

McKenzie, J. S. 2002. "Reconstruction of the Nabataean temple complex at Khirbet et-Tannur," *PEQ* 134, 44-83.

McKenzie, J. S. 1990. *The architecture of Petra.* (Oxford).

McKenzie, J. S. 1988. "The development of Nabataean sculpture at Petra and Khirbet Tannur," *PEQ* 120 July-December, 81-07.

McKenzie, J. S. 1983. "An alternate method for measuring inaccessible mouldings by a surveying method as applied at Petra," *Levant* 17, 157-70.

McKenzie, J. S., A. T. Reyes and S. Gibson. 2002. "Khirbat at-Tānnur in the ASOR Nelson Glueck archive and the reconstruction of the temple," *ADAJ* 46, 451-76.

McKenzie, J. S. and A. Phippen. 1987. "The chronology of the principal monuments at Petra," *Levant,* XIX, 145-65.

McNicoll, A. W., R. H. Smith and J. B. Hennessy.1982. *Pella in Jordan 1. An interim report on the joint Univ. of Sydney and the College of Wooster excavations at Pella 1979-1981.* Australian National Gallery (Canberra).

McNicoll, A. W., R. H. Smith and J. B. Hennessy 1973. *Pella of the Decapolis,* vol. 1. College of Wooster, (Cincinnati).

Meinel, R. 1980. *Das odeion. untersuchungen an überdachten antiken theatergebäuden.* (Frankfurt am Main).

Menninger, M. 1996. *Untersuchungen zu den gläsern und gipsabgüssen aus dem fund vom Begram (Afghanistan).* (Würzberg).

Mercklin, E. von. 1962. *Antike figuralkapitellen.* (Berlin).

Mercklin, E. von, 1940, "Romische klappmessergriffe," in *Festchrifte Victoru Hoffileru.* (Zagreb) 339-52.

Merkelbach R. and J. Stauber. 2002. *Steinepigramme as den griechiscehn Osten.* Band 4 (München/Leipzig) 445.

Merklein, H. and R. Wenning. 1998. "Ein verehrungsplatz der Isis in Petra, neu untersucht," *ZDPV* 114, 162-78.

Merklein, H. and R. Wenning. 2001. "The veneration place of Isis at Wadi as-Siyyagh, Petra: new research," *SHAJ* 7, 421-32.

Meshorer, Y. 1975. *Nabataean coins. Qedem* 3.

Metcalf, W. E. 1975. "The Tell Kalak hoard and Trajan's Arabian mint," *NNM* 20, 39-08.

Meyer, C. 1988. *Glass from the north theater, Byzantine church and soundings at Jerash, Jordan, 1982–1983*. AASOR Suppl. 25, 175-19.

Meyer, C. 1992. *Glass from Quseir el-Qadim and the Indian Ocean trade*. Studies in Ancient Oriental Civilization 53. *OIP* (Chicago).

Miles, A. E. W. and C. Grigson. 1990. *Colyer's variations and diseases of the teeth of animals.* (rev. edn., Cambridge).

Moorrees, C. F. A., E. A. Fanning and E. E. Hunt (1963) "Formation and resorption of three deciduous teeth in children," *American Journal of Physical Anthropology* 21, 205-13.

al-Muheisen, Z. and F. Villeneuve. 2000. "Nouvelles recherches à Khirbet edh-Dharih (Jordanie du Sud) 1996-1999," *CRAI* 1525-63.

Müller, U. 2006. "Zwischen gebrauch und bedeutung: studien zur funktion von sachkultur am beispiel mittelalterlich handwaschgeschirrs (5-6 bis 15-16. Jahrhundert," *ZfA,* Beiheft 20, Habelt, (Bonn).

Murray, M. A. and J. C. Ellis. 1940. *A street in Petra*. British School of Arch. in Egypt (London).

Najbjerg, T. 2001. "Sculpture from Antioch," in M. J. Padgett (ed.) *Roman sculpture in the Art Museum. Princeton Univ.* (Princeton NJ).

Negev, A. 1986. *Nabatean archaeology today.* (New York and London).

Negev, A. 1988a. *The architecture of Mampsis, final report, vol. 1: the middle and late Nabataean periods. Qedem* 26.

Negev, A. 1988b. *The architecture of Mampsis. final report. vol. 2: the late Roman and Byzantine periods. Qedem* 27.

Negev, A. 1974. "Nabataean capitals in the towns of the Negev." *IEJ* 24,153-59.

Negev, A. 1974. *The Nabataean potter's workshop at Oboda*. Suppl. 1. (Bonn).

Negev, A. 1970. "Die töpferwerkstatt in Oboda (Avadat), Die Nabatäer," in *Ein vergessenes volk am toten meer 312 v.-106 n. Chr.,* (München) 48–51.

Negev, A. 1986. *The Late Hellenistic and Early Roman pottery of Nabataean Oboda. final report*. Qedem 22.

Negev, A., and S. Gibson, (edd.) 2005. *Archaeological encyclopedia of the Holy Land*. (New York).

Negev, A. 1971. "The Nabataean necropolis of Mampsis (Kurnub)," *IEJ* 21, 110-29.

Nehmé, L. 2003. "The Petra survey project," in G. Markoe (ed.) *Petra Rediscovered. Lost City of the Nabataeans,* Harry N. Abrams in Association with the Cincinnati Art Museum (New York) 145-63.

Nenna, M. - D. 2003. "Verreries de luxe de l'antiquité tardive découvertes à Douch, Oasis de Kharga, Égypte," Annales du 15e congrès de l'AIHV. New York-Corning 2001, 93-97.

Netzer, E. 2003. *Nabatäische architektur*. (Mainz).

Netzer, E. 2001. *The palaces of the Hasmoneans and Herod the Great. IES.*

Netzer, E. 1977. "The winter palaces of the Judean kings at Jericho at the end of the Second Temple period," *BASOR* 228, 1-13.

Netzer, E., R. Laureys-Chachy and Y. Meshorer. 2004. "Stratigraphy and architecture, the coins," in *Hasmonean and Herodian palaces at Jericho. Final reports of the 1973-1987 excavations.* vol. 2. *IES* (Jerusalem).

Netzer, E. and Z. Weiss. 1995. "New evidence for Late-Roman and Byzantine Sepphoris," in J. H. Humphrey (ed.) *The Roman and Byzantine Near East: some recent archaeological research*. JRA Suppl. 14, 164-76.

Nicholson, P. 2001. "Roman glass from Berenike (Egypt): some new work," Annales du14e congrès de l'AIHV, Venezia-Milano 1998. *AIHV* 151-55.

Nicholson, P. and I. Shaw. 2000. *Ancient Egyptian materials and technology*. (Cambridge) 154-55.

Nicholson, R. A. 1991. *An investigation into variability within archaeologically recovered assemblages of faunal remains: The influence of pre-depositional taphonomic processes*. D. Phil. diss., Univ. of York.

Niehr, H. 1998. *Religionen in Israels umwelt*. (Wurzburg).

Nielsen, I. 2002. *Cultic theatres and ritual drama: a study in regional development and religious interchange between east and west in antiquity*. Aarhus.

Nielsen, I. 1990. *Thermae et balnea: the architecture and cultural history of Roman public baths.* 2 vols. (Aarhus).

Nielsen, I. 1999. "Early provincial baths and their relations to early Italic baths," in J. Delaine and D. E. Johnston (edd.) *Roman baths and bathing*: Proceedings of First Int. Conference on Roman Baths Held at Bath, England, 30 March-4 April 1992. *JRA*.

Nonnos. *Dionysiaca*. W. H. D. Rouse (trans.) Vol. I, Books 1-15. *LCL* 344.

O'Hea, M. (forthcoming) "Looking Alexandrian, becoming Roman? aspects of Early Roman glass from the Petra Great Temple, Jordan," Annales du 18e congrés de l'AIHV, Thessaloniki 2009. AIHV, (Thessaloniki).

O'Hea, M. 2005. "Late Hellenistic glass from some military and civilian sites in the Levant: Jebel Khalid, Pella and Jerusalem," *Annales du 16e congrés de l'AIHV*, London 2003, *AIHV* 44-48.

O'Hea, M. 2002. "The glass and personal adornment. Jebel Khalid on the Euphrates. report on excavations 1986-1996, vol. 1," in G. W. Clarke, *et al.* (edd.) *Mediterranean Archaeology Suppl. 5. MeditArch*, 245-72.

O'Hea, M. 2001. "Glass from the 1992–1993 excavations," in P. M. Bikai (ed.) *The Petra church* (Amman) 370-76.

O'Hea, M. 1994. "The glass industry of Pella and the Decapolis," *ARAM* 4, 1-2. (Oxford) 253-64.

Oleson, J. P. 2004. "'Romanization' at Hawara (Al-Humayma)? The character of 'Roman' culture at a desert fortress," *SHAJ* 8, 353-60.

Oleson, J. P. 1995. "The origins and design of Nabataean water-supply systems," *SHAJ* 5, 707-19.

Oliver, A. 1984. "Early Roman faceted glass," *JGS* 26, 35-58.

Orlandos, A. 1966. *Les matériaux de construction et la technique architectural des anciens Grecs 1.* (Paris).

Orlandos, A. 1968. *Les Matériaux de construction et la technique architectural des anciens Grecs 2.* (Paris).

Orpheus. 2007. *The Hymns of Orpheus: With the Life and Theology of Orpheus.* T. Taylor (trans.) www.forgottenbooks.org.

Ortloff, C. 2005. "The water supply and distribution system of the Nabataean city of Petra (Jordan), 200 BC-AD 300," *CAJ* 15.1, 93-109.

Ostia Virtual Museum, "Hall of bone objects." < http://www.ostia-antica.org/vmuseum/small_4.htm > (Accessed December 8, 2009).

Ostrogorsky, G. 1969. *History of the Byzantine state.* (4th edn. New Brunswick, NJ).

Painter, K. 1987. "Groups J and K: introduction," in D. B. Harden *et al.* (edd.) *Glass of the Caesars.* (Milan) 259-68.

Papyrus Michigan (8) 1951, no. 466. http://wwwapp.cc.columbia.edu/ldpd/app/apis/search?mode=search&institution=michigan&pubnum_coll=P.Mich.&pubnum_vol=8&pubnum_page=466&sort=date&resPerPage=25&action=search&p=1 (Retrieved on May 13, 2009).

Parker, S. T. 1997. "Preliminary report on the 1994 season of the Roman Aqaba project," *BASOR* 305,19-44.

Parlasca, I. 1998. "Neues zu den Nabatäischen kamelterrakotten," in U. Hübner, E. A. Knauf, and R. Wenning (edd.) *Nach Petra und in königreich der Nabatäer. notizen von reisegefährten für Manfred Lindner zum 80.* Bonner Biblische Beiträge, Band 113, Philo, Bodenheim, (Geburtstag) 60-63.

Parlasca, I. 1993. "Probleme Nabatäischer koroplastik: aspekte der auswärtigen kulturbeziehungen Petras," in A. Invernizzi and J. - F. Salles (edd.) *Arabia antiqua. Hellenistic centres around Arabia. IsMeo* LXX 2. 55-79.

Parlasca, I. 1991. "Terrakottenfunde aus Petra," in M. Lindner and John P. Zeitler (edd.) *Petra, königen der weihrauchstrasse.* (Fürth) 111-27.

Parlasca, I. 1990. "Terrakotten aus Petra, ein neues kapital nabatäischer archäologie," in F. Zayadine (ed.) *Petra and the caravan cities* (Amman) 87-92.

Parlasca, I. 1986a. "Die Nabatäischen kamelterrakotten—Ihre antiquarischen und religionsgeschichtlichen aspekte," in M. Lindner (ed.) *Petra. Neue Ausgrabungen und Entdeckungen.* (Munich) 200-13.

Parlasca, I. 1986b. "Priester und gott, bemerkungen zu terrakottafunden aus Petra," in M. Lindner, (ed.) *Petra. Neue Ausgrabungen und Entdeckungen.* (Munich) 192-99.

Parlasca, I., S. Schmid, F. Zayadine, K. 'Amr, and R. Rosenthal-Heginbottom. 1997. "Terrakotten, trinkschalen und goldschmuck," in T. Weber and R. Wenning (edd.) *Petra antike felsstadt zwischen Arabischer tradition und Griechischer norm.* (Mainz) 126-44.

Parr, P. J. 2003. "The origins and emergence of the Nabataeans," in G. Markoe (ed.) *Petra rediscovered: lost city of the Nabataeans.* Harry N. Abrams in Association with the Cincinnati Art Museum (New York) 27-35.

Parr, P. J. 1990. "A commentary on the terracotta figurines from the British excavations at Petra, 1958–64," in F. Zayadine (ed.) *Petra and the caravan cities.* Amman, 77-86.

Parr, P. J. 1970. "A sequence of pottery from Petra," in J. A. Sanders (ed.) *Near Eastern archaeology in the twentieth century: essays in honour of Nelson Glueck* (New York) 348-81.

Parr, P. J. 1967-1968. "Recent discoveries in the sanctuary of the Qasr Bint Far'un at Petra: account of the recent excavations," *ADAJ* 12-13. 5-19.

Parr, P. J. 1962. "A Nabataean sanctuary near Petra: a preliminary notice," *ADAJ* 6-7, 21-23.

Parr, P. J. 1960a. "Nabataean sculpture from Khirbet Brak," *ADAJ* 4-5, 134-36.

Parr, P. J. 1960b. "Excavations at Petra, 1958-59," *PEQ* 92, 124-35.

Parr, P. J. 1957. "Recent discoveries at Petra," *PEQ* 89, 5-16.

Patrich, J. 2005. "Was Dionysos the wine god venerated by the Nabataeans?" *ARAM* 17, 95-13.

Patrich, J. 1990a. "The formation of Nabataean art: prohibition of a graven image among the Nabataeans, the evidence and its significance," *ARAM* 2, 185-96.

Patrich, J. 1990b. *The formation of Nabataean art: prohibition of a graven image among the Nabataeans.* Magnes Press. Hebrew Univ., Jerusalem.

Patrich, J. 1988. "The glass vessels," in Y. Tsafrir (ed.) *Excavations at Rehovot-in-the Negev, vol. 1, the northern church. Qedem* 25, 134-41.

Payne, E. E. 1998. "Evidence for the Nabataean subterranean canalization system," in *Great Temple,* vol. 1. 171-78.

Payne, K. 1999. *Silent Thunder: in the presence of elelphants* (New York and London).

Payne, S. 1973. "Kill-off patterns in sheep and goats: the mandibles from Asvan Kale," *AnatSt* 23, 281-03.

Peacock, D. *et al.* 2000. "Myos Hormos–Quseir al-Qadim: a Roman and Islamic port site. interim report 2000: the glass," < http://www.arch.soton.ac.uk/Projects/ > (Southampton).

Pearce, J. W. E. 1951."Valentinian I to Theodosius I," in H. Mattingly, C. H. V. Sutherland and R. A. G. Carson (edd.) *The Roman imperial coinage*, vol. 9. (London).

Pedersen, P. 1989. *The Parthenon and the origins of the Corinthian capital.* Odense Univ. Classical Studies, vol. 13. Univ. Press of Southern Denmark (Odense).

Peripl. M. Rubr. (Periplus Maris Rubri/Periplus Maris Erythraei). 1989. (Princeton).

Perlzweig, J. 1961. *The Athenian agora, results of excavations conducted by the American School of Classical Studies at Athens*, vol. 7. (Princeton).

Perry, M. A. and M. S. Joukowsky 2006. "An infant jar burial from the Petra Great Temple," *ADAJ* 50, 169-77.

Petrie, W. M. F. 1904. *Roman Ehnasya (Herakleopolis Magna)*: [Plates and text supplementary to Ehnasya]. *EEF* (London).

Pflüger, F. 1995. "Archaeo-geology in Petra, Jordan," *ADAJ* 39, 281-97.

Phillips, L. K. 2008. "Figural table supports: aspects of the archaeology of dining in the Roman world," in C. Ratté and R. R. R. Smith (edd.) *Aphrodisias Papers 4: New Research on the City and its Monuments.* JRA Suppl.70.

Plin. (E) Pliny (the Elder) *HN* (*Naturalis historia)*. 1968-1984. H. Rackham (trans.) *LCL.*

Philo of Alexandria (Philo of Byzantium). 1970. *Belopoiika* (Mechanik Buch IV und V). H. Diels and E. A. Schramm (edd.) Leipzig 51-55.

Plommer, H. 1956. *Ancient and classical architecture.* (London).

Plut. (Plutarch). 1986. *Alex.* (*Alexander)*. B. Perrin (trans.) *LCL.*

Plut. (Plutarch). 1909-14. *Plutarch's Lives: Antony.* C. W. Eliot (ed.) New York.

Plut. (Plutarch). 1878. *Mor. (Moralia) (Plutarch's Morals, Symposiacs).* W. W. Goodwin (trans., ed.) vol. 3. (Boston).

Plut. (Plutarch). 1988. *Antonius (Ant.) [Life of Antony].* C.B.R. Pelling (ed.) Cambridge.

Pollitt, J. J. 1986. *Art in the Hellenistic age.* (Cambridge).

Polb. (Polybius). *Histories, book V.* 1923. W. R. Patron (trans.). *LCL.*

Power, E. A. 2008. "Trench 131, final trench report. 2008, Great Temple 2008 trench reports," online in *Open Context* < opencontext.org >

Price, J. 1987. "Late Hellenistic and early imperial cast vessel glass in Spain," Annales du 10e congrès de l'AIHV, Madrid-Segovie 23-28 Septembre 1985. *AIHV*, (Amsterdam) 61-80.

Price, J. 1991. "Decorated mould-blown glass tablewares in the first century AD," in M. Newby and K. Painter (edd.) *Roman glass: two centuries of art and invention. Ant.J* (London) 56-75.

Price, J. 2005. "Glass from the fort at Hod Hill in Dorset and other mid first-century hilltop sites with Roman military occupation in Southern England," in *Annales du 16e congrès de l'AIHV*, London 2003. *AIHV* (Nottingham) 100-04.

Pritchard, J. B. 1969. *The ancient Near East in pictures relating to the Old Testament.* (2nd edn. Princeton).

Pritchard, J. B. 1943. *Palestinian figurines in relation to certain goddesses known through literature.* American Oriental Series 24, American Oriental Society (New Haven, CT).

Prummel W. and H. J. Frisch. 1986. "A guide for the distinction of species, sex and body side in bones of sheep and goat," *JAS* 13, 6. 567-77.

Pulleybank, E. G. 1999. "The Roman Empire as known to Han China," *JAOS* 119, 71-79.

Rababeh, S. M. 2005. *How Petra was built: an analysis of the construction techniques of the Nabataean freestanding buildings and rock-cut monuments in Petra, Jordan. BAR-IS* 1460, (Oxford).

Rababeh, S. 2010a; Mashaleh, M.; Malaabeh, A.; "Factors Determining the Choice of the Construction Techniques in Petra, Jordan," in *International Journal of Architectural Heritage and Conservation,* Vol. 5, Issue 1, Pp: 60-83.

Rababeh, S. 2010b. "Nabataean Architectural Identity and its Impact on Contemporary Architecture in Jordan," *Dirasat, Engineering Sciences,* Vol. 37, No.1, Pp: 27-53.

Rababeh, S. 2011. "The Temples of Zeus and Artemis and Their Relation to the Urban Context of Gerasa," ARAM 23:177-189, doi 102143/ARAM.23.0.2959656.

Rababeh, S.; Al Qablan, H.; El-Mashaleh, M. 2013. "Utilization of tie-beams for strengthening stone masonry arches in Nabataean construction," in *Journal of Architectural Conservation* 19(2):118-130. DOI:http://dx.doi.org/10.1080/13556207.2013.819656.

Rababeh, S.; Al Rabady, R.; Abu-Khafajah, S. 2014a. "Colonnaded Streets within the Roman Cityscape: A 'Spatial' Perspective," in Journal of Architecture and Urbanisim: 293-305. Permanent link and DOI is: http://dx.doi.org/10.3846/20297955.2014.992168, Permanent link.

Rababeh, S.; Al Qablan, H. ;Abu-Khafajah, S.; El-Mashaleh, M. 2014b. "Structural Utilisation of Wooden Beams as Anti-Seismic and Stabilising Techniques in Stone Masonry in Qasr el-Bint, Petra, Jordan," in *Construction and Building Materials* 54(c): 60-69. DOI:10.1016/j.conbuildmat.2013.12.018

Rababeh, S. 2015. "Technical Utilization of Lifting Devices For Construction Purposes in Ancient Gerasa, Jordan," in *International Journal of Architectural Heritage: Conservation, Analysis, and Restoration,* 9:8, 1023-1036, DOI: 10.1080/15583058.2014.910283.

Radcliffe, W. 1926. *Fishing from the earliest of times.* (London).

Rast, W. E. 1992. *Through the ages in Palestinian archaeology: an introductory handbook.* (Philadelphia, PA).

Rathgen, B. 1909–1911. "Die Punischen geschosse des arsenals von Karthago und die geschosse von lambaesis," in *Zeitschrift für Historische Waffenkunde.* (Dresden).

Redding, R. 1984. *Theoretical determinants of a herder's decisions: modeling variation in the sheep/goat ratio. BAR* S202, Oxford, 223-41.

Redding, R. 1994. "The vertebrate fauna," in S. C. Herbert (ed.) *Tel Anafa, part 1: final report on ten years of excavation at a Hellenistic and Roman settlement in northern Israel.* Kelsey Museum of the Univ. of Michigan. (Ann Arbor, MI) 279-22.

Reid, S. K. 2006. *The Small Temple: a Roman imperial cult building in Petra, Jordan.* Gorgias diss. Near Eastern Studies: GD 20, NES 7 (Piscataway, NJ).

Reid, S. K. 2002. "Excavations at the Petra Small Temple 2000-2001," *ADAJ* 46, 363-79.

Reid, S. K. 2004. "Final report, propylaeum; subfloor ballista balls in the Propylaeum west, Special Project 87; 2004 Great Temple trench reports," online in *Open Context* < http://www.open context.org >.

Renou, L. 1958. *Civilization of ancient India.* (Calcutta).

Revell, L. 1999. "Constructing romanitas: Roman public architecture and the archaeology of practice," in P. Baker, *et al.* (edd.) *TRAC 98: Proceedings of the Eighth Annual Theoretical Roman Arch. Conference.* (Oxford) 52-58.

Riddle, J. M., J. Worth Estes, and J. C, Russel. 1994. "Ever since Eve: birth control in the ancient world," *Archaeology* 47, 29-31, 34-35.

Robert, L. 1948. "Epigrammes du Bas-Empires," *Hellenica* IV, Paris.

Roche, M.- J. 1985. "À propos d'un bas relief inédit de Pétra," *Syria* 62, 313-17.

Röder, E. von. 1909-1911. *Die kaliber der antiken geschütze. ZfA* (Dresden).

Roller, D. W. 1998. *The building program of Herod the Great.* (Berkeley, CA).

Ronczewski, K. 1927a. *Les chapiteaux corinthiens et varies du Musee Gréco-Romain d'Alexandrie. BSRAA* Suppl. 22, 3-36.

Ronczewski, K. 1927b. *Description des chapiteaux corinthien et variés du Musee d'Alexandrie.* Acta Universitatis Latviensis XVI, 3-32.

Ronczewski, K. 1932. "Kapitelle des El Hasne in Petra," *AA.* 37-90.

Rosenthal-Heginbottom, R. 1997. "Small finds from the excavations (1958–61)," in *The architecture of Oboda, final report. Qedem* 36,193-14.

Rosenthal-Heginbottom, R. 1981. *Römische bildlampen aus östlichen werkstätten.* (Wiesbaden).

Rosenthal, R., and R. Sivan. 1978. *Ancient lamps in the Schloessinger collection. Qedem* 8 (Jerusalem).

Rosetto P. C. and G. P. Sartorio. 1994. *Teatri Greci e Romani; alle origini del linguaggio rappresentato,* 3 vols. (Rome).

Rowland, B. 1956. *The art and architecture of India.* (2nd edn. Harmondsworth).

Ruben, I. and A. Disi. 2006. *Field guide to the plants and animals of Petra.* Petra National Trust (Amman).

Rütti, B. 1999. "Der pharos becher von Begram—ein spätantikes figurendiatret," in R. Lierke *et al.* (edd.) *Antikes glastöpferei. ein vergessenes kapitel der glas geschichte.* (Mainz) 129-34.

Saldern, A. von. 1980. *Ancient and Byzantine glass from Sardis.* (Cambridge, MA).

Saldern, A. von. 1991. "Roman glass with decoration cut in high-relief," in M. Newby and K. Painter (edd.) *Roman glass: two centuries of art and invention.* (London) 111-21.

Saller, S. J., and B. Bagatti.1949. *The town of Nebo (Khirbet el-Mekhayyat).* (Jerusalem).

Sartre, M. 1982. *Trois etudes sur l'arabie romain et byzantine* (Brussels).

Scatozza Höricht, L. 1986. *I vetri romani de Ercolano.* (Rome).

Schiffer, M. B. 1987. *Formation processes of the archaeological record.* (Albuquerque NM).

Schlumberger, D. 1933. "Les formes anciennes du chapiteau corinthien en Syrie, en Palastine et en Arabie," *Syria* 14, 283-17.

Schluntz, E. L. 1999. *From royal to public assembly space: the transformation of the "Great Temple"complex at Petra, Jordan*. Ph.D. diss. Brown Univ. (Providence RI).

Schluntz, E. L. 1998a. "The Upper Temenos and the Great Temple," *Great Temple* vol. 1, 209-24.

Schluntz, E. L. 1998b. "The architectural sculpture of the Great Temple," *Great Temple* vol. 1, 225-36.

Schluntz, E. L. 1997. "The architectural sculpture of the Southern Temple at Petra, Jordan," *AJA* 101, 339.

Schmid, E. 1972. *Atlas of animal bones*. (London).

Schmid, S. G. 2003. "Nabataean Pottery" in G. Markoe (ed.) *Petra rediscovered: lost city of the Nabataeans*. (New York) 75-81.

Schmid, S. G. 2002. "From Aretas to the Annexation: Petra and the Nabataeans," in J. Frösén and Z. T. Fiema (edd.) *Petra: a city forgotten and rediscovered*. Amos Anderson Art Museum, exh. cat. (Helsinki, Finland).

Schmid, S. G. 2001a. "The Nabataeans: travellers between lifestyles," in B. MacDonald, R. Adams and P. Bienkowski (edd.) *The archaeology of Jordan*. (Sheffield).

Schmid, S. G. 2001b. "The impact of pottery production on the sedentarization of the Nabataeans," in J. R. Brandt and I. Karlsson (eds.) *From huts to houses: transformations of ancient societies*. Proceedings of an Int. Seminar organized by the Norwegian and Swedish Institutes in Rome, 21-24 September 1997. (Stockholm) 427-36.

Schmid, S. G. 2001c. "The 'Hellenization' of the Nabataeans: a new approach," *SHAJ* 7, 407-19.

Schmid, S. G. 2000a. "Die feinkeramik der Nabatäer: typologie, chronologie und kulturhistorische hintergründe," in *Petra – Ez Zantur II: ergebnisse der Schweizerisch-Liechtensteinischen ausgrabungen*. (Mainz) 1-199.

Schmid, S. G. 2000b. *Petra ez Zantur II: ergebnisse der Schweizerisch-Liechtensteinischen ausgrabungen teil I.* terra archaeologica IV: Schweizerisch-Liechtensteinschen stiftung für archäologische forschungen in Ausland (FSLA). (Mainz).

Schmid, S. G. 1997a. "Nabataean fine ware pottery and the destructions of Petra in the late first and early second century A.D. *SHAJ* 6, 413-20.

Schmid, S. G. 1996a. "Die feinkeramik der Nabatäer im spiegel ihrer kulturhistorischen kontakte, Hellenistische und kaiserzeitliche keramik des östlichen Mittelmeergebietes," Kolloquium Frankfurt 24-25, April 1995, 127-45.

Schmid, S. G. 1996b. "Die feinkeramik," in R. A. Stucky, (ed.) *Petra: ez Zantur I: ergebnisse der Schweizerisch-Liehtensteinischen ausgrabungen 1988-1992,* vol. 1. (Mainz) 151-18.

Schmid, S. G. 1995a. "Nabataean fine ware from Petra," 5th Int. Conf. on the History and Archaeology of Jordan, April 1992, Irbid (Jordan), *SHAJ* 5, 637-47.

Schmid, S. G. 1995b. *Die feinkeramik der Nabatäer: typologie, chronologie und kulturhistorische hintergründe*. Ph.D. diss., Univ. of Basel, (Basel).

Schmid, S. G. and B. Kolb (edd.) 2000. *Petra. Ez Zantur II, ergebnisse der Schweizerisch-Liechtensteinischen ausgrabungen*. (Mainz).

Schmidt-Colinet, A. 1980. *Nabatäische felsarchitektur, bemerkungen zum gegenwärtigen forschungsstand*. *BJb*180, 189-30.

Schmitt-Korte, K. 1968. "Beitrag zur Nabatäischen keramik," *AA* 83. 469-19.

Schmitt-Korte, K. 1990. "Nabataean coinage – part II, new coin types and variants," *NomChron* 150, 105-33.

Scullard, H. H. 1974. *The elephant in the Greek and Roman world.* (London).

Sear, F. 2006. *Roman theatres: an architectural study.* (Oxford).

Sear, F. 1982. *Roman architecture.* (London).

Segal, A. 1995. *Theatres in Roman Palestine and Provincia Arabia.* (Leiden).

Sellers, O. R., and D. C. Baramki. 1953. "A Roman Byzantine burial cave in northern Palestine," *BASOR* 15-16, 7-55.

Seneca. Sen. (Y). 1985. *De Ira (On Anger).* J. Basore (ed.) *LCL.*

Shaw, J. 2001. "A LM IA ceramic kiln in south-central Crete: function and pottery Production," Hesperia Suppl. 30, 5-13; 15-24.

Shepard, A. O. 1971."Ceramic analysis: The interrelations of methods: the relations of analysts and archaeologists," in R. H. Brill (ed.) *Science and archaeology.* (Cambridge, MA) 55-63.

Shepard, A. O. 1968. *Ceramics for the archaeologist.* Carnegie Inst. of Washington, no 609 (Washington, D.C.).

Shepherd, J. D. 1999. "The glass," in A. Poulter, R. K. Falkner and J. D. Shepherd (edd.) *Nicopolis ad Istrum: a Roman to Early Byzantine city* [the pottery and glass]. (London) 297-78.

Sherratt, A. G. 1981. "Plough and pastoralism: aspects of the secondary products revolution," in I. Hodder, G. Isaac and N. Hammond (edd.) *Patterns of the past: studies in honour of David Clarke,* (Cambridge), 261-05.

Sheuer, J. L., J. H. Musgrave, and S. P. Evans. 1980. "The estimation of late fetal and perinatal age from limb bone length by linear and logarithmic regression," *Annals of Human Biology* 7, 257-65.

Shpigel, M. 1997. "Fishes of the Red Sea," *Red Sea Magazine, Ra'Anana.*

Sidebotham, S. and R. Zitterkoph. 1995. "Route through the eastern desert of Egypt," *Expedition* 37, 2.

Siebler, M. 2007. *Roman art,* N. Wolf (ed.) Los Angeles.

Sillar, F. C. and R. M. Meyler 1966. *Elephants ancient and modern.* (New York) 140-41.

Silvano, F. 2005. "Glass finds from Medinet Madi, Egypt," London 2003. *AIHV* 119-21.

Silver, I. A. 1969. "The ageing of domestic animals," in D. Brothwell and E. Higgs, (edd.) *Science in archaeology.* (London) 283-02.

Simpson, G. 2000. *Roman weapons, tools, bronze equipment and brooches from the Neuss-Novaesium excavation 1955-1972.* (Oxford).

Slane, K. W. 1997. *Tel Anafa II,* vol.1: *The Hellenistic and Roman pottery: the fine wares.* JRA Suppl. 10, Part 2.

Smith, R. H. 1961. "The Herodian lamp of Palestine: types and dates," *Berytus* 14, 53-65.

Soedel, W and V. Foley: "Ancient Catapults," *Scientific American,* Vol. 240, No. 3 (March 1979), 124-25.

Speidel, M. 1977. "The Roman army in Arabia," *Aufstieg und Niedergang der Römischen Welt* (II.8) (Berlin).

Spijkerman, A. 1978. *The coins of the Decapolis and Provincia Arabia.* (Jerusalem).

Starcky, J. 1968. "Le temple nabatéen de Khirbet Tannur: à propos d'un livre recent," *RBibl* 75, 206-35.

Starcky, J. 1965. "Nouvelles stelles funeraires à Pétra," *ADAJ* 10, 43-49.

Stemmer, K. 1976. "Ein Asklepios—Koph in Amman," *ADAJ* 21, 33-41.

Stern, E. M. 1991. "Early exports beyond the empire," in M. Newby and K. Painter (edd.) *Roman glass: two centuries of art and invention. Ant.J*, 141-54.

Stern, E. M. 1995. *Roman mold-blown glass: the first through sixth centuries.* (Rome).

Stern, E. M., and B. Schlick-Nolte. 1994. *Early glass of the ancient world 1600 B.C. A.D. 50.* (Ostfildern).

Stewart, A. 2003. "The Khazneh," in G. Markoe (ed.) *Petra rediscovered: lost city of the Nabataeans.* 193-98.

Strabo. 1967 edn. *The geography of Strabo.* vol. 7. H. L. Jones (ed. and trans.) *LCL.*

Strong, D. E. 1958. "Some early examples of the composite capital," *JRS* 50, 119-28.

Strong, D. 1961. *Roman imperial sculpture.* (Harmondsworth).

Strong, D. 1976. *Roman crafts.* D. Brown (ed. London).

Stucky, R. A., Y. Gerber, B. Kolb and S. G. Schmid. 1994. "Swiss-Liechtenstein excavations at Ez-Zantur in Petra 1993, the fifth campaign," *ADAJ* 38, 281-86.

Studer, J. 1996. "La faune romaine tardive d'ez Zantur, a Petra," in A. Bignasca *et al.* (edd.) *Petra ez Zantur I: ergebnisse des Schweizerisch-Liechtensteinischen ausgrabungen 1988-1992* (Mainz) 359-75.

Studer, J. 2002a. "City and monastery: animals raised and consumed in the Petra area," in J. Frösén and Z. Fiema (edd.) *Petra: a city forgotten and rediscovered.* Amos Anderson Art Museum, exh. cat. (Helsinki, Finland) 167-72.

Studer, J. 2002b. "Dietary differences at ez Zantur Petra, Jordan (1ST century BC-AD 5th century)," in H. Buitenhuis, A. M. Choyke, M. Mashkour and A. H. Al-Shiyab, (edd.) *Archaeozoology of the Near East V: Proceedings of the 5th Int. Symp. on the archaeozoology of southwestern Asia and adjacent areas.* (The Netherlands).

Suet. (Suetonius). *De vita Caesarum VII-VIII.* 1930. G. W. Mooney (trans., London).

Sukenik, E. L. 1934. "A Jewish tomb-cave on the slope of Mt. Scopus," *Qobes* 3, 62-73, Jerusalem.

Sydenham, E. A. 1933. *The coinage of Caesarea in Cappadocia.* (London).

Syon, D. 2002. "Gamla, city of refuge," in A. M. Berlin and J. A. Overman, (edd.) *The Jewish revolt: archaeology, history and ideology.* (London, New York).

Szalay, A. von, and E. Boehringer. 1937. *Altertümer von Pergamon X.* Online: < Die hellenistischen arsenale, Garten der Könige. > (Berlin, New York).

Tarpini, R. 2003. "La forma isings 42a var. limburg 1971," *AIHV* (Corning NY) 95-98.

Taylor, G. 1967. *The Roman temples of Lebanon.* (Beirut).

Taylor, J. 2002. *Petra and the lost kingdom of the Nabataeans.* (Cambridge, MA).

Taylor, R. 2003. *Roman builders: a study in architectural process.* (Cambridge, GB).

al-Tel, S. 1969. "The new archaeological studies in Jordan," *ADAJ* 14, 29-37 [Arabic].

Tholbecq, L. 1997. "Les sanctuaires des Nabatéens, état de la question à la lumière de recherches archéologiques récentes," *Topoi* 7, 1069-95.

Tholbecq, L. 2007. "Nabataean monumental architecture," in K. D. Politis and S. Moorhead (edd.) Proceedings of the Int. Conference: *The World of the Herods and the Nabataeans.* London, British Museum 1-19 April 2001. (Stuttgart) 103-43, 133-5.

Tib. (Tibullus). *The Poems of Tibullus.* 1972 edn. P. Dunlop (trans. *LCL*).

Tomlinson, R. 1961. "Emplekton masonry and Greek structura," *JHS* 81, 133-40.

Toussaint-Samat, M. 1994. *A history of food*. (London).

Toynbee, J. 1973. *Animals in Roman life and art*. (Ithaca, NY).

Tracy, S. V. 1998a. "The dedicatory inscription to Trajan at the 'metropolis' of Petra," in J. H. Humphrey (ed.) *The Roman and Byzantine Near East, some recent archaeological research.* JRA Suppl. 31. 2, 51-58.

Tracy, S. V.1998b. "An imperial inscription, Petra," *Great Temple,* vol. 1, 339-75.

Tran Tam Tinh. 1990. "Isis," in *LIMC*, vol.1-2, 761-96.

Tuttle, C. A. 2009. *The Nabataean coroplastic arts: a synthetic approach for studying terracotta figurines, plaques, vessels and other clay objects*. Ph.D. diss. Brown Univ. (Providence RI).

Tzaferis, V. 1969. "Tombs in western Galilee," *'Atiqot* 5, 72-79.

Tzaferis, V. 1971. *Christian symbols of the fourth century and the church fathers*. (Jerusalem).

Ubelaker, D. H. 1989. *Human skeletal remains,* (2nd edn. Washington DC).

Ucko, P. J. 1968. *Anthropomorphic figurines of predynastic Egypt and Neolithic Crete with comparative material from the prehistoric Near East and mainland Greece.* Royal Anthropological Institute of Great Britain and Ireland, Occasional Papers 24, (London).

Vessberg, O. 1952. *Roman glass in Cyprus*. *OpArch* VII. Lund.

Villeneuve, F. 1990. "The pottery from the oil-factory at Khirbet edh-Dharih (2nd century A.D.)," *ARAM* 2, 367-84.

Vitto, F. 1996. "Byzantine mosaics at Bet She'arim: new evidence for the history of the site," *'Atiqot* (HS) 28, 126-41.

Vitr. (Vitruvius) *De arch.* (*De architectura/The ten books on architecture*) 1995, (repr. 1999). D. Rowland (ed. and trans., Cambridge).

Voigt, M. 1983. *Hajji Firuz Tepe, Iran: the Neolithic settlement*. Univ. Museum, Univ. of Pennsylvania (Philadelphia, PA).

Voigt, M. 2000. "Çatal Höyük in context: ritual at Early Neolithic sites in central and eastern Turkey," in I. Kuijt (ed.) *Life in Neolithic farming communities: social organization, identity and differentiation*. (New York) 163-90.

Waage, D. B. 1952. *Antioch on-the-Orontes IV. Part Two. Greek, Roman, Byzantine and Crusaders' coins.* (Princeton NJ).

Walbank, F. W. 1981. *The Hellenistic world*. (Sussex).

Wapler, U., E. Crubézy, and M. Schultz. 2004. "Is cribra orbitalia synonymous with anemia? analysis and interpretation of cranial pathology in Sudan," *American Journal of Physical Anthropology* 123, 333-39.

Wapnish, P. 1981. "Camel caravans and camel pastoralists at Tell Jemmeh," Near Eastern Society of Columbia Univ. 13, 101-21.

Ward, J. 1911. *The Roman era in Britain*. (London).

Ward-Perkins, J. B. 1981. *Roman imperial architecture*. (New Haven, CT).

Ward-Perkins, J. B. and S. Gibson. 1983. "The market–theatre at Cyrene," *Libya antiqua* 13-14, 331-75.

Warry, J. G. 1980. *Warfare in the classical world: an illustrated encyclopaedia of weapons, warrior, and warfare in the ancient civilisations of Greece and Rome*. (New York).

Watson, P. 2001. "The Byzantine period," in B. MacDonald, R. Adams and P. Bienkowski (edd.) *The archaeology of Jordan*. (Sheffield) 461-02.

Webb, P. H. 1927. *The Roman imperial coinage*, vol. 5. part I. H. Mattingly and E. A. Sydenham (edd., London).

Webb, P. H. 1933. *The Roman imperial coinage*. vol. 5. part II. H. Mattingly and E. A. Sydenham (edd. London).

Weber, T. 1990. "A survey of Roman sculpture in the Decapolis, preliminary report," *ADAJ* 34, 351-54.

Weber, T. M. 2003. "Sahr al-Ledja. La statuaire d'un sanctuaire tribal de Syrie du Sud et ses relations romano-mésopotamiennes," *TOPOI* suppl. 4, 349-77

Weinberg, G. D. 1988. *Excavations at Jalame*. (Columbia, MO).

Weingarten, S. 2007. "Food in Roman Palestine: ancient sources and modern research," *Food & History* 5, 2, 41-66.

Weitzman, K. (1972) *Catalogue of the Byzantine and early medieval antiquities in the Dumbarton Oaks Collection,* vol. 3*: ivories and steatites*. (Washington, DC).

Wenning, R. 2004. "Nabatäische büstenreliefs aus Petra—zwei neufunde (mit einem beitrag von Ulrich Hübner)," *ZDPV* 120/2, 157-81, Pl. 24-26.

Wenning, R. 2003. "Hellenistische Denkmäler aus Petra," in G. Zimmer (ed.), *Neue forschungen zur hellenistischen plastik: Kolloquium zum 70. Geburtstag von Georg Daltrop*. (Eichstätt-Ingolstadt).

Wenning, R. 2003. "The rock-cut architecture of Petra," in G. Markoe (ed.) *Petra rediscovered: lost city of the Nabataeans*. Harry N. Abrams in Association with the Cincinnati Art Museum (New York) 133-42.

Wenning, R. 2001. "The betyls of Petra," *BASOR* 324, 79-95.

Wenning, R. 1990. "Das Nabatäer—reich: Seine archäologischen und histoischen Hinterlassenscchaften," in H. - P. Kuhnen *Palästina in griechisch-römischer Zeit, Handbuch der Archäologie II*. (Munich) 367-15.

Wenning, R. 1987. *Die Nabatäer—denkmäler und geschichte. Eine bestandesauf-nahme des archäologischen befundes*. Novum Testamentum et Orbis Antiquus. 3 (Gottingen), 296-98.

Wheeler, A. and A. K. G. Jones.1989. *Fishes*. (Cambridge, GB).

Whitehead, P. J., P, M. - L. Bauchot, J. - C. Hureau, J. Nielsen and E. Tortonese. 1986. *Fishes of the north-eastern Atlantic and the Mediterranean*, vol. 2, *UNESCO*.

Whitehouse, D. 1999. "Glass in the epigrams of Martial," *JGS* 41, 73-81.

Whitehouse, D. 2003. "Begram: the glass," *Topoi* 11.1, 437-49.

Whitehouse, D. 1997. *Roman glass in the Corning Museum of glass*, vol. 1. (Corning, New York).

Will, E. 1986. "Du motâb de Dusarès au trône d'Astarté," *Syria* 63, 343-51.

Wilson, L. M. 1938. *The clothing of the ancient Romans*. (Baltimore).

Winnett, F. V., and G. L. Harding. 1978. *Inscriptions from fifty Safaitic coins*. (Toronto).

Witt, R. 1971. *Isis in the Graeco-Roman world*. (London).

Wright, G. R. H. 1961. "Structure of the Qasr Bint Farun, a preliminary review," *PEQ* 93, 8-37.

Wright, G. R. H. 1967-1968. "Recent discoveries in the sanctuary of the Qasr Bint Far'un at Petra: some aspects concerning the architecture and sculpture," *ADAJ* 12-13, 20-29.

Wright, G. R. H. 1958. "Petra—the arched gate," *PEQ* 124-35.

Yadin, Y. 1988. *Masada: Herod's fortress and the Zealot's last stand*. (Jerusalem).

Yadin, Y. 1963a. *The finds from the Bar Kokhba period in the cave of the letters. IES* (Jerusalem).

Yadin, Y. 1963b. *The Nabataean kingdom, Provincia Arabia, Petra and En-Geddi in the documents from Nahal Hever*. Ex Oriente Lux 17 (Leiden).

Yadin, Y. 1962. "Expedition D: the cave of the letters," *IEJ* 12, 227-57.

Yegül, F. 1992. *Baths and bathing in classical antiquity*. (Cambridge, MA).

Yegül, F. 2007. "When a theatron is not a theater: 'a place for viewing,' Magnesia on the Meander," *JRA* 20, 578-82.

Young, G. K. 2001. *Rome's eastern trade: international commerce and imperial policy, 31 BC - AD 305*. (New York).

Zanoni, I. 1996. "Tonlampen," in Bignasca, A. *et al.* (edd.) *Petra ez Zantur 1:ergebnisse der Schweizerisch-Liechtensteinischen ausgrabungen 1988-1992*, vol. 1. (Mainz).

Zayadine, F. 1991. "Sculpture in ancient Jordan," in P. Bienkowski (ed.) *The art of Jordan*. National Museums and Galleries on Merseyside, 31–61.

Zayadine, F. 1990. "The god(dess) Aktab-Kutbay and his (her) iconography," in F. Zayadine (ed.) *Petra and the Caravan Cities*. (Amman) 37-52.

Zayadine, F. 1987. "Decorative stucco at Petra and other Hellenistic sites," *SHAJ* 3, 131-43.

Zayadine, F. 1982. "Recent excavations at Petra (1979-81)," *ADAJ* 26, 365-93.

Zayadine, F. 1981. "Recent excavations and restorations of the [Jordanian] Department of Antiquities (1979-1980)," *ADAJ* 12-13, 20-29.

Zayadine, F. 1975. "Un ouvrage sur les Nabatéens," *RA* 70, 333-38.

Zayadine, F. 1974. "Excavations at Petra," *ADAJ* 19, 135-50.

Zayadine, F. *et al.* 2003a. *Le Qasr al-Bint de Pétra l'architecture, le décor, la chronolgie et les dieux*. (Paris).

Zayadine, F. 2003b. "Évaluation chronologique," in F. Zayadine, F. Larché, and J. Dentzer-Feydy (edd.) *Qasr al-Bint de Pétra: l'architecture, le décor, la chronologie, et les dieux*, (Paris) 81-97.

Zayadine, F., F. Larché, and J. Dentzer-Feydy, 2003. *Le Qasr Al-Bint de Pétra: l'architecture, le décor, la chronologie et les dieux*. (Paris).

Zeder, M. A. 1991. *Feeding cities: specialized animal economy in the ancient Near East*. (Washington, DC).

Zeder, M. A. 1996. "The role of pigs in near eastern subsistence from the vantage point of the Southern Levant," in J. D. Seger (ed.) *Retrieving the past: essays on archaeological research and methodology in honor of Gus Van Beek,* Cobb Inst. of Arch. (Starkville MS), 297-12.

Zenon Papri. 1926. *Greek papyri in the library of Cornell University*. W. L. Westermann and C. J. Kraemer, Jr. (edd. New York).

Zimmer, H. 1976. *Spiel um den elefanten*. (Cologne, Düsseldorf, Munich).

Zimmerman, M. S., and S. K. Reid. 2004. "Final report. Propylaeum sondage in the Propylaeum Steps, special project 125; 2004 Great Temple trench reports," online in *Open Context*, < http:// www.open context.org >.

Zimmerman, P. 2000. "Mapping Petra," *Expedition*, 42.2, 37-41.

Petra Great Temple: Site Bibliography

PETRA GREAT TEMPLE: Major Publications

1988. Joukowsky, M.S. (Ed.) *Petra Great Temple: Brown University Excavations, 1993-1997*. Vol. I. Brown University, Petra Exploration Fund.

2007. Joukowsky, M.S. 2007. *Archaeological Contexts of the Remains and Excavations, History of Excavations and Methodology at the Petra Great Temple*. Vol. II. Brown University, Petra Exploration Fund.

2016. Joukowsky, M.S. (Ed.) *Petra Great Temple. History of Excavations:* Part I. Architecture, Part II. Great Temple Material Culture. Vol. III. Brown University, Petra Exploration Fund.

1993

1) Joukowsky, M. S. 1993. "The Southern Temple at Petra," *ACORN* 5, 2,11.

2) Khuri, R.1993a. "Results of first year dig," *Jordan Times*. September 8, (Amman), 37.

3) Khuri, R.1993b. "Results of first year dig," *Al Ra'i Daily Newspaper*, September 8 (Amman). [Arabic].

4) Zeitler, J. P. 1993. "Excavations and surveys in Petra 1989-90," in Chronique Archéologique," *Syria* 70, 205-273.

1994

5) Joukowsky, M. S. 1994a. "1993 archaeological excavations and survey of the Southern Temple at Petra, Jordan," *ADAJ* 38, 293-332.

6) Joukowsky, M. S. 1994b. "Archaeological survey of the Southern Temple at Petra, Jordan," *L'Orient Express* 2, 43-44.

7) Joukowsky, M. S. 1994c. "Petra Southern Temple," in G. L. Peterman (ed.), "Archaeology of Jordan, 1993 Season." *AJA* 98, 543-544.

8) Joukowsky, M. S. 1994d. "Petra: the Brown University excavations," *BUFB* 6. 3, 15-18.

9) Rodan, S. 1994. "Bedouin secrets," *The Jerusalem Post Magazine,* 29 July, (Jerusalem).

1995

10) Joukowsky, M. S. 1995a. "Le "Temple Sud" à Pétra," *Le monde de la bible, Archéologie et Histore,* 94, 43.

11) Joukowsky, M. S. 1995b. "Petra, the Southern Temple," in P. M. Bikai and D. Koorings (edd.), "Archaeology of Jordan, 1994 Season." *AJA*, 99, 518-520.

12) Joukowsky, M. S. 1995c. "Archaeological survey of the Southern Temple at Petra," *Syria* 72, 1-2, 133-142.

13) Joukowsky, M. S. 1995d. "Petra Southern Temple," *ACORN* 7. 2, 7-8.

14) Joukowsky, M. S. and E. L. Schluntz. 1995. "The Southern Temple at Petra: 1994 excavations," *ADAJ* 39, 241-266.

15) Mamalaki, D. 1995. "From the field," *Haffenreffer Museum Newsletter*, Brown Univ. Dept. of Anthropology (Providence).

16) Myers, J. W. and E. Myers. 1995. *Low altitude aerial photography*. JRA Suppl. 14, 284-285, figs. 5, 6, 7.

17) Negev, A. 1995. "The Petra Southern Temple," *Qadmoniot* 28. 2, 110 [Hebrew].

1996

18) Barrett, D. G. 1996. *How can the ceramic analysis of lamps reveal the impact of empire on the Southern Temple at Petra?* MA Thesis, Brown Univ., Dept. of Anthropology, (Providence).

19) Blackburn, J. 1996. "Ancient city in the sands," *Views. Rhode Island School of Design Alumni Magazine* (Providence), 8. 3, 20-21.

20) Joukowsky, M. S. 1996a. "Petra, the Southern Temple," in P. M. Bikai and V. Egan (edd.), "Archaeology in Jordan, 1995 season." *AJA* 100. 3,525-26.

21) Joukowsky, M. S.1996b. "The Petra Southern Temple: or what I do on my 'summer vacations,'" *BUFB*, 8.3, 30-35.

22) Joukowsky, M. S. 1996c. "The Petra Southern Temple: the fourth season, 1996," *98th Annual Meeting Abstracts*, *AJA* 20, 6-7.

23) Joukowsky, M. S.1996d. "Petra, the 'great' Southern Temple," *ACORN* 8.1, 6-7.

24) Joukowsky, M. S. 1996e."1995 archaeological excavations of the Southern Temple at Petra, Jordan," *ADAJ* 40, 177-206.

25) Joukowsky, M. S. 1996f. *Excavation and consolidation of archaeological structures: an example from the Great Temple at Petra, Jordan"* [Unpublished] in F. E. S. Kaplan (ed.), *Guardians of Monuments and Museums*, New York Univ., Graduate School of Arts and Science, Museum Studies Program.

26) Khouri, R. 1996a. "Excavations unravel mysteries of Petra's Great Southern Temple," *Jordan Times*, April 23, (Amman), 6-7.

27) Khouri, R. 1996b. "Fourth season of excavation clarifies important architectural aspects of Petra's Southern Temple," *Jordan Times,* December 14 (Amman), 7.

28) Schluntz, E. L. 1996. "The architectural sculpture of the Southern Temple at Petra, Jordan," *Abstracts, 98th Annual Meeting. AJA* 20,7.

29) Zimmerman, P. C. 1996. "MiniCad 6—Another View," *CSA Newsletter: A Quarterly Newsletter for Architectural Historians and Archaeologists* 9.3, 9-11.

1997

30) Basile, J. J. 1997. "A head of the goddess Tyche from Petra, Jordan," *ADAJ* 41, 255-266.

31) Freyberger, K. S. and M. S. Joukowsky.1997. "Blattranken, greifen und elefanten: sakrale architektur in Petra und ihr bauschmuck neuausgegrabene peripteral-tempel," in N. T. Weber and R. Wenning (edd.), *Petra: antike felsstadt zwischen Arabischer tradition und Griechischer.* (Mainz), 71-86.

32) Joukowsky, M. S. 1997a. "The water canalization system of the Petra Southern Temple," *SHAJ* 6, 303-311.

33) Joukowsky, M. S. 1997b. "The Southern Temple at Petra," in E. M. Meyers (ed.), *The Oxford encyclopedia of archaeology in the Near East.* vol. 4. (New York), 306-307.

34) Joukowsky, M. S. 1997c. "The Petra Southern Temple: the fourth season, 1996," *AJA* 101, 339.

35) Joukowsky, M. S. 1997d. "Brown University Petra Great Temple excavations," *BUFB* 10.1, 29-32.

36) Joukowsky, M. S. 1997e."Brown University excavations at the 'Great' Temple of Petra, Jordan," *ASOR Annual Meeting Abstracts*, 47, 2, A-35.

37) Joukowsky, M. S. 1997f. "Petra: Great Temple," *ACORN* 9.1, 7.

38) Joukowsky, M. S. 1997g. "The Great Temple at Petra," in P. M. Bikai, V. Egan, (edd.) "Archaeology in Jordan, 1996 season," *AJA* 101. 3, 520-521.

39) Joukowsky, M. S. 1997h."1997 Brown University excavations at the "Great" Southern Temple of Petra," *Abstracts AIA 99th Annual Meeting, AJA* 21, 100.

40) Joukowsky, M. S. 1997i."1996 Brown University archaeological excavations of the 'Great' Southern Temple at Petra, Jordan," *ADAJ* 41, 195-218.

41) Schluntz, E. L. 1997."The architectural sculpture of the Southern Temple at Petra, Jordan,"*AJA* 101, 339.

42) Twair, P. M. 1997. "Temple at Petra challenges veteran American archaeologist," *The Washington Report on Middle East Affairs Monthly*, 55. 98.

1998

43) Barrett, D. G. 1998a. "The lamps," in M. S. Joukowsky (ed.), *Great Temple,* vol. 1. 275-286.

44) Barrett, D. G. 1998b. "Other small finds," in M. S. Joukowsky (ed.), *Great Temple,* vol. 1, 287-315.

45) Barrett, D. G. 1998c."The coins," in M. S. Joukowsky (ed.), *Great Temple,* vol. 1, 317-324.

46) Basile, J. J. 1998. "The Lower Temenos," in M. S. Joukowsky (ed.), *Great Temple,* vol. 1, 188-208.

47) Bedal, L-A. 1998. "Neutron activatation analysis of pottery," in M. S. Joukowsky (ed.), *Great Temple,* vol. 1, 345-67.

48) Boucher, N. 1998. "Mystery in stone and sand," *BAM* 98, 3, 30-37.

49) Joukowsky, M. S. 1998a. "Re-discovering elephants at Petra!" in L. H. Lesko (ed.) *Ancient Egyptian and Mediterranean studies: in memory of William A. Ward.* Brown Univ. Dept. of Egyptology, Providence RI, 133-148.

50) Joukowsky, M. S. 1998b. "Brown University excavations in Jordan at the Petra Great Temple, 1988," *Occident and Orient,* Newsletter of the German Protestant Institut of Archaeology in Amman, Jordan, 10-11.

51) Joukowsky, M. S.1998c. "Petra: Brown University excavations of the Great (?) Temple," *ACORN* 48, 2, A-21.

52) Joukowsky, M. S.1998d. "The Great Temple at Petra," in "Archaeology in Jordan, 1997 Season," *AJA* 102. 3, 593-596.

53) Joukowsky, M. S.1998e. "The Petra Great Temple project, 1993-1995: a three year assessment," in J. Magness and S. Gitin (edd.), *HESED VE-EMET, studies in honor of Ernest S. Frerichs.* Brown Univ. Judaic Studies, Providence RI, 320, 291-312.

54) Joukowsky, M. S. 1998f. "Brown University1997 excavations at the Petra Great Temple," *ADAJ* 42. 293-318.

55) Joukowsky, M. S. (ed.) 1998g. *Great Temple,* vol. 1.

56) Joukowsky, M. S. 1998h. "Introduction," *Great Temple,* vol. 1, 1-46.

57) Joukowsky, M. S.1998i. "History of the Brown University excavations," *Great Temple,* vol. 1, 47-48.

58) Joukowsky, M. S.1998j. "Preface," *Great Temple,* vol. 1, xli-xlvi.

59) Joukowsky, M. S. and D. J. D'Agostino. 1998. "Artifact studies and databases," M. S. Joukowsky (ed.), *Great Temple,* vol. 1, 236-274.

60) Karz, S. G. 1998a. *The change in color of "colorless" glass at the Great Temple, Petra, Jordan.* Brown Univ. Dept. of Anthropology, Unpublished M. A. Thesis, Providence RI.

61) Karz, S. G. 1998b."The Roman and Byzantine glass," M. S. Joukowsky (ed.), *Great Temple,* vol. 1, 325-343.

62) Paradise, T. R. 1998. "Environmental setting and stone weathering," in M. S. Joukowsky (ed.), *Great Temple,* vol. 1, 150-166.

63) Payne, E. E. 1998. "Evidence for the Nabataean subterranean canalization system," in M. S. Joukowsky (ed.), *Great Temple,* vol. 1, 170-178.

64) Schluntz, E. L. 1998a."The Upper Temenos and the Great Temple," in M. S. Joukowsky (ed.), *Great Temple,* vol. 1, 209-224.

65) Schluntz, E. L. 1998b. "The architectural sculpture of the Great Temple," in M. S. Joukowsky (ed.), *Great Temple,* vol. 1, 225-234.

66) Tracy, S. V. 1998a. "The dedicatory inscription to Trajan at the 'metropolis' of Petra," in J. H. Humphrey (ed.), *The Roman and Byzantine Near East, some recent archaeological research.* JRA Suppl. 31, 2, 51-58.

67) Tracy, S. V. 1998b."An imperial inscription," in M. S. Joukowsky (ed.), *Great Temple,* vol. 1, 339-375.

68) Tracy, S. V. 1998c. "Inscribed finds," in M. S. Joukowsky (ed.), *Great Temple,* vol. 1, 376-379.

69) Tullis, T. E. and C. Worthington. 1998. "Ground penetrating radar study of the Petra Great Temple," in M. S. Joukowsky (ed.), *Great Temple,* vol. 1, 179-186.

70) Warnock, P. 1998. "Palynological analysis from the Great Temple," in M. S. Joukowsky (ed.), *Great Temple,* vol. 1, 167-168.

1999

71) Basile, J. J. 1999. "Preliminary report of the notes on the head of the goddess Tyche from Petra, Jordan," *ADAJ* 42, 223-226.

72) Bestock, L. D. 1999. "Nabataean pottery from the 'cistern:' some finds from the Brown University excavations at the Petra Great Temple," *ADAJ* 42, 241-248.

73) Corbeil, M-C. and K. Helwig. 1999. "Analysis of fresco fragments from the Petra Great Temple," *Analytical Research Laboratory. ARL Report 3779.* March 19. Institut Canadien De Conservation. (Ottawa).

74) Khuri, R. 1999. "Petra Great Temple excavations reveal massive, elaborate Nabataean complex," *Jordan Times,* December 6. (Amman), 7.

75) Joukowsky, M. S. 1999a."Petra: Brown University excavations of the Great Temple: questions about functional analysis," Seventh Int. Congress on the History and Archaeology of Jordan, "Jordan by the Millennia," *SHAJ* 7, 447-455.

76) Joukowsky, M. S. 1999b. "Petra, the Great Temple," in V. Egan and P. M. Bikai, (edd.), "Archaeology in Jordan, 1998 Season," *AJA,* 103. 3, 504-506.

77) Joukowsky, M. S. 1999c."The Petra Great Temple: Brown University excavations," *The First Conference on Nabataean Research and Studies. Conference Abstract*, German Protestant Institute, (Amman), 9-10.

78) Joukowsky, M. S. 1999d. "The water canalization system of the Petra Great Temple," *Men of dikes and canals: The archaeology of water in the Middle East.* Petra, Conference *Abstracts*, 15.

79) Joukowsky, M. S. 1999e. "Petra, Great Temple," in R. Ross Holloway (ed.), Brown Univ. *COWAA* 1988-89, 2-4.

80) Joukowsky, M. S. 1999f. "Petra: Great Temple," *ACORN,* 11.1, 9-10.

81) Joukowsky, M. S. 1999g. "The 1998 Brown University excavations at the Great Temple, Petra," *ADAJ* 43, 195-222.

82) Nehmé, L. and F. Villeneuve. 1999. *Pétra: métropole de l'Arabie antique.* (Paris) 81-86.

83) Schluntz, E. L. 1999. *From royal to public assembly space: the transformation of the "Great Temple" complex at Petra.* Ph.D. diss., Brown Univ., *COWAA* (Providence, RI).

84) Taylor, J. 1999. "The so-called 'Great Temple,'" in *Petra.* (London) 59-60.

2000

85) Acevedo, D, E. Vote, D. H. Laidlaw and M. S. Joukowsky. 2000. "ARCHAVE: a virtual environment for archaeological research," Work in progress report presented *IEEE Visualization 2000*, Salt Lake City, October. (pdf/ps/html).

86) Acevedo, D. and E. L. Vote. 2000. "ARCHAVE. immersive VR for scientific visualization: a progress report," in A. van Dam *et al.* (edd.), *IEEE Computer Graphics and Applications, IEEE Computer Society*, 20. 6.

87) Basile, J. J. 2000."When people lived at Petra," *Archaeology Odyssey*, 3.4, 14-31.

88) Bedal, L-A. 2000. "Paradise found: Petra's urban oasis," *Expedition*, 42.2, 23-36.

89) Bowersock, G. W. 2000. "La surprise du bouleutèrion," *Le Monde de la Bible*, 127, mai-juin , 60.

90) Hadingham, E. 2000. "Secrets of a desert metropolis: the hidden wonders of Petra's ancient engineers," in "Discovering archaeology," *Scientific American* 2.4, 70-77.

91) Khuri, R. 2000. "Volume on Great Temple at Petra targets specialists, general readers alike," *Jordan Times.* February 21 (Amman) 7.

92) Joukowsky, M. S. 2000a. "Brown University 1999 excavations at the Petra Great Temple," *Contexts: The Newsletter of the Friends of the Haffenreffer Museum of Anthropology*, Brown Univ., 28.1, 4-5.

93) Joukowsky, M. S.(ed.) 2000b. CD-ROM, *Great Temple excavations*, vol. 1, *Brown University Excavations 1993-1997*, (A. Brin, design). To accompany *Great Temple* vol. 1).

94) Joukowsky, M. S. 2000c. "Exploring the Great Temple at Petra: The Brown University excavations 1993-1995," in L. E. Stager, J. A. Greene and M. D. Coogan (edd.), *The archaeology of Jordan and beyond: essays in honor of James A. Sauer*. Semitic Museum, 221-234.

95) Joukowsky, M. S. 2000d. "Brown University 1999 excavations at the Petra Great Temple," *ADAJ* 44, 313-334.

96) Joukowsky, M. S. 2000e. "The center's research continues in old and new directions; prof. Martha Joukowsky kindly provided the following report of work at Petra in 2000," in R. R. Holloway (ed.) *Report of the Director 1999-2000*, Brown Univ. *COWAA*, 2-4.

97) Joukowsky, M. S. 2000f. "Petra, the Great Temple," in V. Egan, P. M. Bikai and K. Zamora (edd.) "Archaeology in Jordan, 1999 Season," *AJA* 104. 3, 582.

98) Joukowsky, M. S. 2000g. "Petra 2000: Brown University excavations of the Great Temple," *ASOR Annual Meeting Abstracts*, November 15-18, 5.

99) Joukowsky, M. S. 2000h. "Petra: Great Temple," *ACORN*, 12.1, 3-4.

100) Leymarie, F. F., D. B. Cooper, M. S. Joukowsky, B. B. Kimia, D. H. Laidlaw, D. Mumford and E. L. Vote. 2000. "The SHAPE lab: new technology and software for archaeologists," *Computer Applications in Archaeology*, 28th Annual Int. Conference, April 18-21, (Ljubljana, Slovenia), *BAR-IS*.

101) Romey, K. M. 2002. "Fourth in the field, celebrating home abroad," *Archaeology* 12-13. 53, 4.

102) Vote, E. L., D. Acevedo. D. Laidlaw and M. S. Joukowsky. 2000. "ARCHAVE: a virtual

environment for archaeological research," *Computer Applications in Archaeology, CAA 2000, 28th Annual Int. Conference* (Ljubljana, Slovenia).

103) Vote, E. L., D. Acevedo. D. Laidlaw and M. S. Joukowsky. 2000. "ARCHAVE: a three-dimensional GIS for a CAVE environment as applied to Petra's Great Temple Project)," November 15-18, *ASOR Annual Meeting Abstracts,* 4.

104) van Dam, A., A. S. Forsberg, D. H. Laidlaw, J. J. LaViola Jr. and R. M. Simpson. 2000. "Archave," in D. A. Feliz and E. L. Vote (edd.), "Immersive VR for scientific visualization: a progress report," *IEEE Computer Graphics and Applications.* November/December (pdf).

105) Vote, E. L, D. Acevedo, M. S. Joukowsky and D. Laidlaw. 2000."Virtual reality and scientific visualization in archaeological research," *Virtual Archaeology Conference between Scientific Research and Territorial Marketing* (Arezzo, Italy).

106) Vote, E. L. and M. S. Joukowsky. 2000. "Using desktop photogrammetry to document archaeological remains: the Great Temple at Petra, Jordan," *Proceedings of Computer Applications in Archaeology, 27th Annual Int. Conference.* Dublin Castle, April 1999, (Dublin).

107) Zimmerman, P. 2000. "Mapping Petra," *Expedition,* 42.2, 37-41.

2001

108) Acevedo, D. 2001. *Scientific archaeology vs. the Discovery Channel.* (S. Ginsberg, Advisor). Document in pdf, Brown Univ. MA thesis, (Providence).

109) D. Acevedo, D. Laidlaw and M. S. Joukowsky. 2001. "ARCHAVE: a virtual environment for archaeological research," in Z. Stancic and T. Veljanovski edd.) *CAA 2000 Proceedings: Computing Archaeology for Understanding the Past. BAR-IS* (Oxford) 931, 313-316.

110) Acevedo, D., E. L. Vote, D. H. Laidlaw and M. S. Joukowsky. 2001. "Archaeological data visualization in VR: analysis of lamp finds at the Great Temple of Petra, a case study," *Visualization 2001 Proceedings,* October. Winner, Best Case Study.

111) Cloke, C. 2001. Chris Cloke gets Petra-fied, *The College Hill Independent* 13. 3, 1-11.

112) Cooper, D. B., A. Willis, S. Andrews, J. Baker, Y. Cao, D. Han, K. Kang, W. Kong, F. F. Leymarie, X. Orriols, E. L. Vote, M. S. Joukowsky, B. B. Kimia, D. H. Laidlaw, D. Mumford and S. Velipasalar. 2001."Assembling virtual pots from 3D measurements of their fragments,"*VAST.*

113) Joukowsky, M. S. 2001a. "2000 Brown University excavations at the Great Temple of Petra, Jordan," in *AIA 102nd Annual Meeting Abstracts* 24. 57.

114) Joukowsky, M. S. 2001b. "2000 Brown University excavations at the Great Temple of Petra, Jordan," in 102nd Meeting of the Archaeological Institute of America, *AJA* 105.2, 273.

115) Joukowsky, M. S. 2001c. "Petra: Brown University excavations of the Great Temple: questions about functional analysis," *SHAJ* 7, 447-455.

116) Joukowsky, M. S. 2001d. Petra. "The Great Temple," in S. H. Savage, K. Zamora and D. R. Keller, (edd.), "The Archaeology of Jordan, 2000 Season" *AJA* 105.3, 451-453.

117) Joukowsky, M. S. 2001e. "Petra, The Great Temple," in A. Negev and S. Gibson (edd.), *Archaeological Encyclopedia of the Holy Land.* (New York) 384-388.

118) Joukowsky, M. S. (ed.), 2001f. *BASOR* 324. November.

119) Joukowsky, M. S. 2001g. "Nabataean Petra," *BASOR* 324, 1-4.

120) Joukowsky, M. S. 2001h. "A day of excavation at Petra: an archaeological experience," in J. L. Warner (ed.), *Cultural Horizons,* vol. 1. *A Festschrift in Honor of Talat S. Halman,* Yapi Kredi Yayinlari. (Syracuse) 240-246.

121) Joukowsky, M. S. 2000i. "Prof. Martha Sharp Joukowsky was on sabbatical leave during the second semester of the year, and has kindly offered the following account of her research," in R. R. Holloway (ed.), *Report of the Director, 2000-2001*, Brown Univ. *COWAA* 2-3.

122) Joukowsky, M. S. 2001j. "Petra: Great Temple excavations," *ACORN* 13.1, 5-6.

123) Joukowsky, M. S. 2001k. "Brown University excavations in Jordan at the Petra Great Temple, 2001," *BUFB,* October, 40-43.

124) Joukowsky, M. S. 2001l. "2001 Brown University excavations of the Great Temple of Petra, Jordan," *ASOR 2001 Annual Meeting Abstracts,* 2.

125) Joukowsky, M. S. 2001m. "Brown University 2000 excavations at the Petra Great Temple," *ADAJ* 45, 325-342.

126) Joukowsky, M. S. 2001n. "Petra: Brown University excavations of the Great Temple, questions about functional analysis," *SHAJ* 7, 447-455.

127) Joukowsky, M. S. and J. J. Basile. 2001. "More pieces in the Petra Great Temple puzzle," *BASOR* 324, 23-41.

128) Leymarie, F., D. Cooper, M. S. Joukowsky, B. Kimia, D. Laidlaw, D. Mumford and E. Vote. 2001. "The SHAPE lab: new technology and software for archaeologists," in Z. Stancic and T. Veljanovski (edd.), *The CAA 2000 Proceedings, Computing Archaeology for Understanding the Past - CAA 2000. BAR-IS* 931 (Oxford) 79-90.

129) Reid, S. K. 2001. "The 2001 season at the Petra Small Temple," *ASOR 2001 Annual Meeting Abstracts*, 34-35.

130) Taylor, J. 2001. *Petra and the lost kingdom of the Nabataeans*. (London/New York) 106-111.

131) Vote, E. L. 2001. *A new methodology for archaeological analysis: using visualization and interaction to explore spatial links in excavation data*. Ph.D. diss. Brown Univ. (Providence).

132) Vote, E. L. 2002b. "New archaeology analysis tools," *BUFB* October 2001, 44-45.

2002

133) Basile, J. J. 2002a. "Recently discovered relief sculptures from the Great Temple at Petra, Jordan," *ADAJ* 46, 331-346.

134) Basile, J. J. 2002b. "Petra rocks! tales from the ancient rock city," in M. S. Joukowsky (ed.), *dig* (an issue devoted to Petra) 5.

135) Basile, J. J. 2002c. "Two visual languages at Petra: aniconic and representational sculpture of the Great Temple," *NEA* 65. 4, 255-259.

136) Bodel, J. and S. K. Reid. 2002. "A dedicatory inscription to the emperor Trajan from the Small Temple at Petra, Jordan," *NEA* 65, 4, 249-250.

137) Egan, E. C. 2002a. "Stucco decoration from the South Corridor of the Petra Great Temple: discussion and interpretation," *ADAJ* 46, 347-361.

138) Egan, E. C. 2002b. *Putting the pieces together: an analysis and interpretation of the stucco finds recovered from the South Corridor of the Petra Great Temple, Petra, Jordan, during the 2001 excavation season.* Honors Thesis, Brown Univ. *COWAA* and Dept. of Classics (Providence).

139) Gilles, D. 2002. *Une nouvelle methode d'analyse archéologique: l'analyse du Petit Temple de Pétra assistée par une technique de visualisation en 3D.* Unpublished Mémoire de D.E.A, sous la direction de M. Le Professeur J. D. Forest, 2001-2002.

140) Gillespie, K. 2002. "Petra's Great Temple rises again 2,000 years later," *Jordan Times*, August 25 (Amman), 2.

141) Joukowsky, M. S. 2002a. "The Petra Great Temple elephant-headed capitals as a cultural artifact," *AIA 103rd Annual Meeting Abstracts*, January 3-6, Philadelphia, PA, 106-107.

142) Joukowsky, M. S. 2002b. "Petra. Great Temple," in S. H. Savage, K. Zamora and D. R. Keller (edd.), "Archaeology in Jordan, 2001 Season," *AJA* 106, 435-458.

143) Joukowsky, M. S. 2002c. "Technologies in use at the Brown University excavations of the Petra Great Temple," in *Conference Abstracts,* the Hashemite Univ., Zarqa, Jordan, for the Int. Conference on Science and Technology in Archaeology and Conservation; Under the Patronage of Her Majesty Queen Rania Al Abdullah of Jordan, with the Sponsorship of UNESCO, 38.

144) Joukowsky, M. S. 2002d. "Petra: Great Temple," *ACORN* 14.1, 10-11.

145) Joukowsky, M. S. 2002e. "The Brown University 2002 Petra Great Temple excavations offer more surprises," *ADAJ* 46, 315-330.

146) Joukowsky, M. S. 2002f. "The Petra Great Temple: a Nabataean architectural miracle," *NEA* 65, 4, 235-248.

147) Joukowsky, M. S. 2002g. "From the guest editor," *NEA* 65.4, 23, i.

148) Khalifeh, I. 2002. "The Petra Great Temple," *Ad-Dustour,* Daily Newspaper, [Arabic], July 20 (Amman), 5.

149) Lubell, S. 2002. "Virtually rebuilt, a ruin yields secrets," *New York Times,* May 2, 2002.

150) Mailé, F. 2002. *De la fouille à la modélisation animée 3D de vestiges de archéologiques: reconstitution du cryptoportique ouest de Grand Temple de Pétra, Jordanie,* vols. 1 & 2. Mémoire de DEA, sous la direction de MM. Les Professeurs J.- D. Forest and J.- P. Thalmann avec la participation de Mme. M. S. Joukowsky, Univ. de Paris I - Panthéon-Sorbonne UFR 03, en partenariat avec Division of Engineering/Shape Lab—Lems, Brown univ., Providence, RI, USA.

151) Reid, S. K. 2002. "Excavations at the Petra Small Temple 2000-2001," *ADAJ* 46, 363-379.

152) Ronay, V. 2002. *The Soul of Petra: Bedouin residents of a hidden city, Patterns The World,* n.p. 196-197.

153) Savvidou, M. 2002. "Petra—The magical city in Jordan ("ΠΕΤΡΑ—Της Μαριας Σαββιδου"), ΑΝΕΞΓΗΤΟ (*Anexigiton*)," November 17, Ευρϖ 44, 118-123 [Greek].

154) Seigne, J. 2002. "Compte rendu of M. Sharp JOUKOWSKY, *Petra Great Temple, volume I: Brown University Excavations 1993-1997*, Providence, Rhode Island (1998)," *Topoi*, 10.2, 507–516.

155) Shanks, H. 2002. "The state of the profession: few bright lights at annual meeting," *Archaeology Odyssey*, May/June, 5.3, 4.

156) Vote, E. L. 2002. "A virtual-reality application for post-excavation archaeological analysis," *IEEE Computer Graphics and Applications* (special issue on art history and archaeology).

157) Vote, E. L., D. A. Feliz, D. H. Laidlaw and M. S, Joukowsky. 2002. "Discovering Petra: archaeological analysis in VR," *IEEE Computer Graphics and Applications,* September/October, 38-49.

2003

158) Basile, J. J. 2003. "The relief sculpture program from the Great Temple at Petra, Jordan," The Near East in the Hellenistic and Roman Periods. *AIA, 104th Annual Meeting Abstracts,* (Philadelphia, PA), 61.

159) Borg, L. 2003. "At Brown, a virtual temple takes shape," *The Providence Journal*, April 15 (Providence) G 4.

160) Cloke, C. F. 2003. *Water in the desert: the water systems of the Petra Great Temple,* Honors Thesis 2003 Series, Brown Univ., (Providence).

161) Curtis, M. J. 2003. "Scientists and artists partner to create virtual Petra: digital technology electronically preserved the deteriorating temple and its artifacts," Liberal Arts: An Arts and Humanities Suppl. to the *George Street Journal*, February 28, 1-3.

162) Glouberman, N. 2003. "SHAPE, Higher Learning Technology Serving Education," http://www.teachmag.com/higher_learning.asp, 17-18.

163) Henry, A. 2003. "Out of school: unearthing the history of Petra with Brown University," *The Lawrentian*, Spring 2003, 67. 2, (Lawrenceville), 14-15.

164) "Higher learning: technology serving education. SHAPE," *Higher Learning* – Projects, May/June, 18-19.

165) Joukowsky, M. S. 2003a. "The unconventional Nabataeans: reflections from the Petra Great Temple," Cultural Relations in the Greco-Roman Near East, *AIA 104th Annual Meeting Abstracts,* (Philadelphia, PA) 119.

166) Joukowsky, M. S. 2003b. "Ten years of excavation at the Petra Great Temple: a retrospective," *ACORN* 14.2. 1-2.

167) Joukowsky, M. S. 2003c. "Petra. Great Temple," in S. H. Savage, K. Zamora and D. R. Keller (edd.) "Archaeology in Jordan, 2002 Season." *AJA* 107, 466-468.

168) Joukowsky, M. S. 2003d. "Portal to Petra," *Natural History.* 112.9, 40-43.

169) Joukowsky, M. S. 2003e. "Ten years of excavation at the Petra Great Temple: another retrospective," in *O Qui Complexus et Gaudia Quanta Fuerunt: Essays Presented to Michael C. J. Putnam by his Brown colleagues on the occasion of his 70th birthday*, Brown Univ., (Providence).

170) Joukowsky, M. S. 2003f. "The Great Temple," in G. Markoe, (ed.), *Petra rediscovered: lost city of the Nabataeans.* (New York), 214-222.

171) Joukowsky, M. S. 2003g. "A decade of Brown University excavations at the Petra Great Temple," *ASOR Annual Meeting Abstracts*, November, 16-17.

172) Joukowsky, M. S. 2003h. "Excavations at the Petra Great Temple: the eleventh campaign," *ACORN* 15. 2, 6.

173) Joukowsky, M. S. 2003i. "More treasure and Nabataean traditions at the Petra Great Temple: the Brown University 10th campaign, 2002," *ADAJ* 47, 389-406.

174) Mayercik, V. 2003. "Virtual archaeology—can you dig It?" *The Catalyst,* 10.1, Brown Univ., (Providence), 20-21.

175) Nelson, L. 2003. "Documentary on Petra debuts at Brown after two years spent in the making," in "Academic Watch," *Brown Daily Herald*, 138. 52, 6, 9.

176) Netzer, E. 2003. "Die tempel der Nabatäer: der grosse (Süd-)Tempel," in *Nabatäische architektur: inbesondere gräber und tempel.* (Mainz) 72-81.

177) Reid, S. K. 2003a. "Excavations at the Small Temple of Petra, Jordan," in the Near East in the Hellenistic and Roman Periods. *AIA 104th Annual Meeting Abstracts* (Philadelphia, PA) 61.

178) Reid, S. K. 2003b. "Excavations at the Small Temple of Petra," *ASOR Annual Meeting Abstracts,* 17.

179) Rossner, T. 2003. "Hats off!" in *Old Time Almanack, Eastside Marketplace,* (Providence), 8.

180) Villeneuvre, E. 2003. "La chamber baroque," *Le Monde de la Bible*, 150.9, 51.

2004

181) Barrett, D. G. 2004. *The ceramic oil lamp as an indicator of cultural change within Nabataean society in Petra and its environs circa CE 106.* Ph.D. diss. Brown Univ. Dept. of Anthropology, (Providence).

182) Curtis, M. J. 2004. "Joukowsky's work on exhibit at American Museum of Natural History,"*George Street Journal*, March, (Providence), 8.

183) DeKeukelarere, L. 2004. "Piecing the past: an algorithm quickly fits together: potsherds," *Scientific American*. (September) 30.

184) Egan, E. C. 2004. "Petra's wealth," *Archaeology,* 57.2, 60.

185) Joukowsky, M. S. 2004a. "The Petra Great Temple's water strategy," *The 9th Int. Conference on the History and Archaeology of Jordan, Abstracts.* Cultural Interaction Through the Ages. Jordanian Ministry of Tourism and Antiquities, Dept. of Antiquities and Al-Hussein Bin Talal Univ., under the patronage of His Majesty King Abdullah II of Jordan. Petra, May 25 (Amman), 23-27.

186) Joukowsky, M. S. 2004b. "Petra, the Great Temple," in S. H. Savage, K. A. Zamora and D. R. Keller (edd.), "Archaeology in Jordan, 2003 Season," *AJA* 108.3, 441-443.

187) Joukowsky, M. S. 2004c. "The 2004 Brown University Excavations at the Petra Great Temple," *ASOR 2004 Annual Meeting, Abstracts.* (San Antonio) 44.

188) Joukowsky, M. S. 2004d. "Brown University 2003 excavations at the Petra Great Temple: the eleventh field campaign," *ADAJ* 48,155-170.

189) Joukowsky, M. S. 2004e. "The water installations of the Petra Great Temple," in H.-D. Bienert and J. Häser (edd.), *Men of Dikes and Canals: The Archaeology of Water in the Middle East.* Int. Sym. held at Petra, Wadi Musa, June 1999. Deutsches Archäologisches Institut Orient-Abteilung, Orient-Archäologie 13.123-141.

190) Joukowsky, M. S. 2004f. Review. *Petra and the Nabataeans: A Bibliography*. By Gregory A. Crawford. ATLA Bibliography Series, vol. 49. 2003. (Lanham, MD), xxii + 275, *JAOS* 124. 2, 407.

191) Joukowsky, M. S. 2004g. Review. *Petra Ez Zantur II: ergebnisse der Schweizerisch-Liechtensteinischen ausgrabungen*. By S. G. Schmid and B. Kolb. Pt. 1: *Die feinkeramik der Nabatäer*; Pt. 2: *Die spätantiken Wohnbauten*. Terra Archaeologica, vol. 4, Mainz, 2000. Pp. xvii + 311, plates, plans. *JAOS* 124.2, 350-351.

192) Kansa, S. 2004. "Food and religion in the Petra region: a zooarchaeological study of two Nabataean temples," *ASOR 2004 Annual Meeting Abstracts*. (San Antonio), 35.

193) Reid, S. K. 2004. *The Small Temple: a Roman imperial cult building in Petra, Jordan.* Ph.D. diss. Brown Univ., Dept. of Anthropology, (Providence).

2005

194) 2005. "Lecture sheds light on different uses of Great Temple of Petra: functions include place of worship, fortress and market place," *The Daily Star* (May 6, Beirut), 11.688,12.

195) Abou-Assaly, E. K. 2005. "Conférence du professeur Martha Sharq Joukowsly au Musée de l'AUB: Le Grand Temple de Pétra: récente découverte archéologique," *La Revue du Liban et de l'Orient Arabe* (May, Beirut), 54.

196) Dergham, O. 2005. "Martha Sharp Joukowsky gives a lecture at the AUB [The American Univ. of Beirut]: The discovery of the PETRA GREAT TEMPLE: The city of history is a never ending series of surprises," [Arabic], *An-Nahar*, (5 May (Beirut), 21.

197) Ho, T. 2005. "Archaeology team's excavation of Petra Great Temple heading into its final year," *The Brown Daily Herald*, November 2, 101. 5, 6.

198) Jacobson, M. 2005. "Melanie Jacobson takes us on a backstage tour of the Great Temple excavation conducted by the Brown University archaeological team," *The Jordan Times*, August 11 (Amman), 30.9051, 4-5.

199) Joukowsky, M. S. 2005a. "Excavating a priceless heritage: scientific and other applications used by the Brown University explorations of the Petra Great Temple," in J. Pollini (ed.), *Terra marique: studies in art history and marine archaeology in honor of Anna Marguerite McCann on the receipt of the Gold Medal of the Archaeological Institute of America.* (Oxford/New York), 40-55, pl. 2-4.

200) Joukowsky, M. S. 2005b. "Petra Great Temple," *ACORN* 17.1, 4-5.

201) Joukowsky, M. S. "Brown University archaeological research at the Petra Great Temple, 2004," *ADAJ* 49, 147-165.

202) Saidi, L. 2005. "Recent discoveries at the Petra Great Temple," *American University of Beirut Archaeological Museum NEWSLETTER* (Beirut), 21.2, 10-15

203) Seeley, N. 2005. "Picking up the pieces," *JO Magazine*. July(Amman), 46-51.

2006

204) Joukowsky, M. S. 2006a. "Petra: The Great Temple," in S. H. Savage and D. R. Keller (edd.), "Archaeology in Jordan, 2005 Season," *AJA*, 110, 478-481.

205) Joukowsky, M. S. 2006b. "Brown University's 2005-2006 excavations at the Petra Great Temple," *ASOR 2006 Annual Meeting Abstracts*, Washington DC, 58-59.

206) Joukowsky, M. S. 2006c. "The Petra Great Temple: a final chapter," *ACORN* 18.1, 1-2.

207) Joukowsky, M. S. 2006d. "Challenges in the field: the Brown University 2005 Petra Great Temple excavations," *ADAJ* 50, 351-372.

208) Levintova, H. 2006. "Joukowsky to stop work on Jordanian dig after 14 years," *The Brown Daily Herald*. (September)1.

209) Macaulay-Lewis, E. R. 2006. "Planting pots at Petra: a preliminary study of *ollae perforatae* at the Petra Garden-Pool Complex and at the 'Great Temple,'" *Levant* 38, 159-170.

210) Perry, M. A. and M. S. Joukowsky. 2006. "An infant jar burial from the Petra Great Temple," *ADAJ* 50, 169-177.

211) Praeger, M. 2006. "In a land of kings, these relics are awesome, like their setting," *Boston Sunday Globe*, March 19, (Boston), M1, M12, travel section.

212) Reid, S. K. 2006. *The Small Temple: a Roman imperial cult building in Petra, Jordan.* Near Eastern Studies: GD 20, NES 7, (Piscataway, NJ).

213) Shao, W. 2006. *Animating Autonomous Pedestrians*. (D. Terzopoulos, Advisor). Ph.D. diss., New York Univ. Dept. of Computer Science, Courant Institute of Mathematical Sciences.

2007

214) Lawler, A. 2007. "Reconstructing Petra," *Smithsonian Magazine*, 38. 3, 42-49.

215) Joukowsky, M. S. 2007a. "Surprises at the Great Temple from 1993 to 2006," in T. E. Levy, M. P. M. Daviau, R. W. Younker and M. Shaer (edd.), *Crossing Jordan: North American contributions to the archaeology of Jordan*, (London & CT), 385-392.

216) Joukowsky, M. S. 2007b. "More surprises at the Petra Great Temple," 10th Int. *Conference on the History and Archaeology of Jordan, Abstracts*, Washington DC, (Amman), 38.

217) Joukowsky, M. S. 2007c. "Petra: the Great Temple," in S. H. Savage and D. R. Keller (edd.), "Archaeology in Jordan, 2006 Season," *AJA* 111, 542-544.

218) Joukowsky, M. S. 2007d. 2006. "Brown University excavations at the Petra Great Temple," *ASOR Annual Meeting Abstracts*, San Diego, 54.

219) Joukowsky, M. S. 2007e. *Petra Great Temple,* vol. 2.

220) Joukowsky, M. S. 2007f. "Exciting developments: The Brown University 2006 Petra Great Temple excavations," *ADAJ* 51, 81-102.

221) Joukowsky, M. S. and C. F. Cloke. 2007. "The Petra Great Temple's water strategy," *SHAJ*, 9, 431-437.

222) Kansa, E., S. A. Kansa and M. S. Joukowsky. 2007. "Petra, open city: an online publication of digital content from Brown University's excavations at the Great Temple," *ASOR Annual Meeting Abstracts*, San Diego, 54-55.

223) Power, E. A. 2007. *The Roman-Byzantine bath complex at the Petra Great Temple in Jordan.* Honors Thesis, Joukowsky Institute for Archaeology and the Ancient World, Brown Univ. (Providence).

2008

224) Barrett, D. G. 2008. *The ceramic oil lamp as an indicator of cultural change within Nabataean society in Petra and its environs circa CE 106.* Near Eastern Studies, diss. 32, (Piscataway, NJ).

225) Joukowsky, M. S. 2008a. "Common name: poppy; habitat: Nabataean sculpture, The Petra Great Temple," in S. E. Thompson and P. Der Manuelian (edd.) *Egypt and beyond, essays presented to Leonard H. Lesko upon his retirement from the Wilbour Chair of Egyptology at Brown University, June 2005*. Brown Univ. Dept. of Egyptology and Ancient Western Asian Studies (Providence), 197-208.

226) Joukowsky, M. S. 2008b. "Petra: The Great Temple," in S. H. Savage, D. R. Keller and C. A. Tuttle (edd.), "Archaeology in Jordan, 2007 Season," *AJA* 112, 524-525.

227) Joukowsky, M. S. 2008c. Review. *The Petra Siq, Nabataean hydrology uncovered*. I. Rubin, (ed.), *AJA* 112, 369-370.

228) Joukowsky, M. S. 2008c. "Into the land of research: 2007 Brown University Petra Great Temple documentation," *ADAJ* 52, 279-293.

229) Joukowsky, M. S. 2008d. *Petra Great Temple, Brown University excavations.* (Brochure) Brown University Petra Exploration Fund (Providence).

230) Tuttle, C. A. 2008. *The Nabataean coroplastic arts: a new approach for studying figurines, plaques, vessels, and other clay objects*. Ph.D. diss., Brown Univ., Joukowsky Institute for Archaeology and the Ancient World (Providence).

231) Rozenberg, S. 2008. "The Great Southern Temple," in Hasmonean and Herodian palaces at Jericho/ 4, The decoration of Herod's third palace at Jericho (Jerusalem), 389-391, Ill. 677.

2009

232) Gagos, T. 2009. "New inscriptional evidence and Petra's rôle in the province of Arabia," *JRS* 22, 381-389.

233) James, J. 2009. "The power of Petra: a lost civilization's 'rose-red city half as old as time,'" *The Wall Street Journal*, April 11-12, New York), W2.

234) Joukowsky, M. S. 2009a. "Surprises at the Petra Great Temple: a retrospective," *SHAJ* 10, 291-310.

235) Joukowsky, M. S. 2009b. "Highlights of the Brown University excavations at the Petra Great Temple, 1993-2006," in D. B. Counts and A. S. Tuck, (edd.), *KOINE: Mediterranean studies in honor of R. Ross Holloway*. (Oxford and Oakville), 166-186.

236) Joukowsky, M. S. 2009c. "Extraordinary revelations from the 2008 Brown University Petra excavations," *ADAJ* 53, 211-228.

2010

237) Joukowsky, M. S. 2010. "Petra," in M. Gagarin (ed.), *The Oxford Encyclopedia of Ancient Greece and Rome.* (New York, Oxford) 5. 232-234.

2012

238) Joukowsky, M. S. 2013. "Der 'Grosse Tempel' in Petra," in S. G. Schmid (ed.), *Petra, Wunder in der Wüste. Auf den Spuren von J.L. Burckhardt alias 'Scheich Ibrahim', 1812-2012.* Begleitbuch zur Ausstellung, Antikenmuseums Basel und Sammlung Ludwig in Zusammenarbeit mit dem Ministry of Tourism and Antiquities/ Department of Antiquities of Jordan und dem Jordan Museum, Amman, Antikenmuseum Basel und Sammlung Ludwig, 23 Oktober 212 bis 17. März 2013, exh. cat. (Basel). *1812-2012.* exh. cat. (Basel), 157-161.

2015

239) Joukowsky, M.S. 2015."An Architectural Marvel: The Petra Great Temple," in Z. Weiss (ed.), *Ehud Netzer Volume.* Eretz-Israel: Archaeological, Historical and Geographical Studies vol. 31, Israel Exploration Society (Jerusalem) 69-78.

Research in Progress

Dimitrov, Z. 2012-2013. Analysis of Nabataean models in cult architecture: Elephant-headed capitals from the Great Temple in Petra—unique Nabataean contributions to the architectural decoration in the east Mediterranean region during antiquity," in the Nabataean Conf. Proc., Univ. of Jordan, May 5, 2012. (Amman).

Joukowsky, M. S. 2012. Simpson, E. and S. German (edd.), "The Rôle of the Petra Great Temple in the Context of Nabataean Archaeology," in *The Adventure of the Illustrious Scholar: Papers Presented to Oscar White Muscarella.* (Leiden).

Joukowsky, M. S. "Rediscovering the Petra Great Temple," in *Festschrift, Leila Badre*, American University of Beirut (Beirut).

Joukowsky, M. S The Petra Great Temple Roman-Byzantine baths," in M.-F. Boussac, J.-P. Pascual and J.-F. Salles (edd.). *Bains et hammams de l'outre-Jourdain*, deuxième colloque. *Baths and Hammams of Jordan,* Int. Conference (May 21-24, 2008, Amman, Jordan). (Ifpo et Direction des Antiquités de Jordanie, Comité d'Histoire du Bilâd al-Shâm de l'Univ. de Jordanie. Balnéorient series.

Joukowsky, M. S. 2010. "The Petra Great Temple: a triumph of conservation, restoration and preservation," 11th Int. Conference on the History and Archaeology of Jordan, *ICHAJ* 11, Under the Patronage of HRH Prince El Hassan bin Talal. Changes and Challenges. Paris, June 7-14 (Amman).

Online Databases in Open Context

Open Context. < http://www.opencontext.org>. The Petra Great Temple data sets include aerial photographs of the site by year, 1993-2006 site plans of trenches excavated, 1998-2006 *ADAJ* reports, 1993-2006 catalog, coin catalog, architectural fragment and Grosso Modo databases, phasing charts of every trench and locus, architectural and artifact drawings, and trench reports.

The Full Citations for the OPEN CONTEXT Data Tables

Open Context. < http://www.opencontext.org>. The Petra Great Temple data sets include aerial photographs of the site by year, 1993-2006 site plans of trenches excavated, 1998-2006 *ADAJ* reports, 1993-2006 catalog, coin catalog, architectural fragment and Grosso Modo databases, phasing charts of every trench and locus, architectural and artifact drawings, and trench reports.

(These include the California Digital Library permanent archive identification numbers.)

Petra Great Temple Coin Analysis:

Augé, Christian, Deirdre Barrett, Emma Susan Libonati, Mary Prendergast, Martha Sharp Joukowsky, KM, Eleanor A. Power, Leigh-Ann Bedal, Christopher A. Tuttle, José I. Fusté, 71 Others (2010) "Petra Great Temple Coin Analysis" From projects: *Petra Great Temple Excavations.* Led by: Martha Sharp Joukowsky. Table generated by: Guest. Open Context. <http://opencontext.org/tables/eae25741c5277febf98ea584bd3e6989> California Digital Library Archival Identifier, <ark:/28722/k2h41jm0q>

Petra Great Temple Faunal Analysis:

Kansa, Sarah W. (2010) "Petra Great Temple Animal Bones" From projects: *Petra Great Temple Excavations.* Led by: Martha Sharp Joukowsky. Table generated by: Open Context Editors. Open Context.. <http://opencontext.org/tables/0dfc42274ae780c7f55ea45c05941557> California Digial Library Archival Identifier, <ark:/28722/k2mw28d4j>

Petra Great Temple Glass Analysis:

O'Hea, Margaret (2010) "Petra Great Temple Glass Analysis" From projects: *Petra Great Temple Excavations.* Led by: Martha Sharp Joukowsky. Table generated by: Open Context Editors. Open Context. <http://opencontext.org/tables/7e1f65e7cce475785211cf5518662c3d> California Digial Library Archival Identifier, <ark:/28722/k2cc0ts6z>

Petra Great Temple, Upper Temenos Small Finds:

Joukowsky, Martha Sharp, 41 Others (2010) "Petra Great Temple, Upper Temenos Small Finds [9 tables]" From projects: *Petra Great Temple Excavations.* Led by: Martha Sharp Joukowsky. Table generated by: Open Context Editors. Open Context. <http://opencontext.org/tables/f83076ff715703b6e501ec5ec3760da4> California Digial Library Archival Identifier, <ark:/28722/k27p8tc50>

<http://opencontext.org/tables/f83076ff715703b6e501ec5ec3760da4/2> California Digial Library Archival Identifier, <ark:/28722/k23x83k17>

<http://opencontext.org/tables/f83076ff715703b6e501ec5ec3760da4/3> California Digial Library Archival Identifier, <ark:/28722/k2057cr7s>

<http://opencontext.org/tables/f83076ff715703b6e501ec5ec3760da4/4> California Digial Library Archival Identifier, <ark:/28722/k2vd6p42t>

<http://opencontext.org/tables/f83076ff715703b6e501ec5ec3760da4/5> California Digial Library Archival Identifier, <ark:/28722/k2qn5z982>

<http://opencontext.org/tables/f83076ff715703b6e501ec5ec3760da4/6> California Digial Library Archival Identifier, <ark:/28722/k2kw57h49>

<http://opencontext.org/tables/f83076ff715703b6e501ec5ec3760da4/7> California Digial Library Archival Identifier, <ark:/28722/k2g44hq0g>

<http://opencontext.org/tables/f83076ff715703b6e501ec5ec3760da4/8> California Digial Library Archival Identifier, <ark:/28722/k2bg2h89f>

<http://opencontext.org/tables/f83076ff715703b6e501ec5ec3760da4/9> California Digial Library Archival Identifier, <ark:/28722/k26q1sg59>

Petra Great Temple, Lower Temenos Small Finds:
Joukowsky, Martha Sharp, 50 Others (2010) "Petra Great Temple, Lower Temenos Small Finds [5 tables]" From projects: *Petra Great Temple Excavations*. Led by: Martha Sharp Joukowsky. Table generated by: Open Context Editors. Open Context. <http://opencontext.org/tables/4bc5bef131fe4bf2c8204e5306464c23> California Digial Library Archival Identifier, <ark:/28722/k22z12p1j>

<http://opencontext.org/tables/4bc5bef131fe4bf2c8204e5306464c23/2> California Digial Library Archival Identifier, <ark:/28722/k2z60c168>

<http://opencontext.org/tables/4bc5bef131fe4bf2c8204e5306464c23/3> California Digial Library Archival Identifier, <ark:/28722/k2td9n72k>

<http://opencontext.org/tables/4bc5bef131fe4bf2c8204e5306464c23/4> California Digial Library Archival Identifier, <ark:/28722/k2pn8xd8t>

<http://opencontext.org/tables/4bc5bef131fe4bf2c8204e5306464c23/5> California Digial Library Archival Identifier, <ark:/28722/k2jw86m42>

Petra Gre*at Temple, Small Finds from Temple, Propylaeum, Surface and Unprovenienced Contexts:*

Joukowsky, Martha Sharp, 48 Others (2010) "Petra Great Temple, Small Finds from Temple, Propylaeum, Surface and Unprovenienced Contexts [4 tables]" From projects: *Petra Great Temple Excavations*. Led by: Martha Sharp Joukowsky. Table generated by: Open Context Editors. Open Context. <http://opencontext.org/tables/bb4ec1c3bafeaa9fc512bbddc06dad6b> California Digial Library Archival Identifier, <ark:/28722/k2f76663z>

<http://opencontext.org/tables/bb4ec1c3bafeaa9fc512bbddc06dad6b/2> California Digial Library Archival Identifier, <ark:/28722/k29g5gc96>

<http://opencontext.org/tables/bb4ec1c3bafeaa9fc512bbddc06dad6b/3> California Digial Library Archival Identifier, <ark:/28722/k25q4rk52>

<http://opencontext.org/tables/bb4ec1c3bafeaa9fc512bbddc06dad6b/4> California Digial Library Archival Identifier, <ark:/28722/k21z41s19>

Petra Great Temple Pottery:

Saunders, Shari L. (2010) "Petra Great Temple Pottery" From projects: *Petra Great Temple Excavations*. Led by: Martha Sharp Joukowsky. Table generated by: Open Context Editors. Open Context. <http://opencontext.org/tables/341853c35844195860d3e0cf731f0702> California Digial Library Archival Identifier, <ark:/28722/k2x63b461>

Petra Great Temple Descriptions of Architectural Elements:

Joukowsky, Martha Sharp, Eleanor A. Power, Christopher A. Tuttle, Marshall C. Agnew, Joseph J. Basile, Tarek M. Khanachet, Emma Susan Libonati, Shari L. Saunders, 73 Others (2010) "Petra Great Temple Descriptions of Architectural Elements [4 tables]" From projects: *Petra Great Temple Excavations*. Led by: Martha Sharp Joukowsky. Table generated by: Open Context Editors. Open Context. <http://opencontext.org/tables/dd3c06e3cc75ba631e4bff3fd2795e83> California Digial Library Archival Identifier, <ark:/28722/k20z70w12>

<http://opencontext.org/tables/dd3c06e3cc75ba631e4bff3fd2795e83/2> California Digial Library Archival Identifier, <ark:/28722/k2w66976s>

<http://opencontext.org/tables/dd3c06e3cc75ba631e4bff3fd2795e83/3> California Digial Library Archival Identifier, <ark:/28722/k2rf5kf2n>

<http://opencontext.org/tables/dd3c06e3cc75ba631e4bff3fd2795e83/4> California Digial Library Archival Identifier, <ark:/28722/k2ms3k117>

Petra Great Temple Excavation Trenches:

Joukowsky, Martha Sharp, Margaret O'Hea, Christian Augé, 1 Other (2010) "Petra Great Temple Excavation Trenches" From projects: *Petra Great Temple Excavations*. Led by: Martha Sharp Joukowsky. Table generated by: Open Context Editors. Open Context. <http://opencontext.org/tables/716b44e4f104bbb8a4fae802bba46ca2> California Digial Library Archival Identifier, <ark:/28722/k28g8fg9z>

Petra Great Temple Loci:

Joukowsky, Martha Sharp, Emma Susan Libonati, Joseph J. Basile, 59 Others (2010) "Petra Great Temple Loci" From projects: *Petra Great Temple Excavations*. Led by: Martha Sharp Joukowsky. Table generated by: Open Context Editors. Open Context. <http://opencontext.org/tables/4b46f90858e0c6e75fe9fd74ef25fbee> California Digital Library Archival Identifier, <ark:/28722/k24q7qp5t>

Links to the Data Tables:

Petra Great Temple Coin Analysis:

http://opencontext.org/tables/eae25741c5277febf98ea584bd3e6989

Petra Great Temple Faunal Analysis:

http://opencontext.org/tables/0dfc42274ae780c7f55ea45c05941557

Petra Great Temple Glass Analysis:

http://opencontext.org/tables/7e1f65e7cce475785211cf5518662c3d

Petra Great Temple, Upper Temenos Small Finds (9 tables):

Table 1 of 9: http://opencontext.org/tables/f83076ff715703b6e501ec5ec3760da4
Table 2 of 9: http://opencontext.org/tables/f83076ff715703b6e501ec5ec3760da4/2
Table 3 of 9: http://opencontext.org/tables/f83076ff715703b6e501ec5ec3760da4/3
Table 4 of 9: http://opencontext.org/tables/f83076ff715703b6e501ec5ec3760da4/4
Table 5 of 9: http://opencontext.org/tables/f83076ff715703b6e501ec5ec3760da4/5
Table 6 of 9: http://opencontext.org/tables/f83076ff715703b6e501ec5ec3760da4/6
Table 7 of 9: http://opencontext.org/tables/f83076ff715703b6e501ec5ec3760da4/7
Table 8 of 9: http://opencontext.org/tables/f83076ff715703b6e501ec5ec3760da4/8
Table 9 of 9: http://opencontext.org/tables/f83076ff715703b6e501ec5ec3760da4/9

Petra Great Temple, Lower Temenos Small Finds (5 tables):

Table 1 of 5: http://opencontext.org/tables/4bc5bef131fe4bf2c8204e5306464c23
Table 2 of 5: http://opencontext.org/tables/4bc5bef131fe4bf2c8204e5306464c23/2
Table 3 of 5: http://opencontext.org/tables/4bc5bef131fe4bf2c8204e5306464c23/3
Table 4 of 5: http://opencontext.org/tables/4bc5bef131fe4bf2c8204e5306464c23/4
Table 5 of 5: http://opencontext.org/tables/4bc5bef131fe4bf2c8204e5306464c23/5

Petra Great Temple, Small Finds from Temple, Propylaeum, Surface and Unprovenienced Contexts (4 tables):
Table 1 of 4: http://opencontext.org/tables/bb4ec1c3bafeaa9fc512bbddc06dad6b
Table 2 of 4: http://opencontext.org/tables/bb4ec1c3bafeaa9fc512bbddc06dad6b/2
Table 3 of 4: http://opencontext.org/tables/bb4ec1c3bafeaa9fc512bbddc06dad6b/3
Table 4 of 4: http://opencontext.org/tables/bb4ec1c3bafeaa9fc512bbddc06dad6b/4

Petra Great Temple Pottery:
http://opencontext.org/tables/341853c35844195860d3e0cf731f0702

Petra Great Temple Descriptions of Architectural Elements (4 tables):
Table 1 of 4: http://opencontext.org/tables/dd3c06e3cc75ba631e4bff3fd2795e83
Table 2 of 4: http://opencontext.org/tables/dd3c06e3cc75ba631e4bff3fd2795e83/2
Table 3 of 4: http://opencontext.org/tables/dd3c06e3cc75ba631e4bff3fd2795e83/3
Table 4 of 4: http://opencontext.org/tables/dd3c06e3cc75ba631e4bff3fd2795e83/4

Petra Great Temple Excavation Trenches:
http://opencontext.org/tables/716b44e4f104bbb8a4fae802bba46ca2

Petra Great Temple Loci:
http://opencontext.org/tables/4b46f90858e0c6e75fe9fd74ef25fbee

Media and Video

2013. *Petra: the lost city and its Great Temple.* A 2 hr. documentary.

2005-2007 (Web pages for digital videos and 3D images) The Joukowsky Institute Workplace>The Petra Great Temple Database Project or http://proteus.brown.edu/PGTdata/Home or http://lems.brown.edu/

2003 *Petra Great Temple.* A 54 minute film of the Brown University Excavations, Amedia Production by Michael Udris and David Udris © Martha Sharp Joukowsky. 124 Washington St. Providence, RI 02903 (401 523 4222), <www.udris.com>.

Petra and the Nabataeans, Trade, Intercultural Contacts and Associations, Influence of Hellenism, Crossroads of Occidental and Oriental Worlds, The Great Temple, City Planning, Hydrological Engineering. Open Curriculum, *Mariners of Greece International Education Program,* Video Roundtable with schools in Amman Jordan, Athens Greece, Copenhagen Denmark and New York City, USA. George Newman, ed., Technology Applications Research LLC. (May). Can be accessed at <www.oneplaneteducation.com> Webcast Segment II.

ARCHAVE. A Virtual Environment for Archaeological Research. June 14, 2000. Brown University Department of Computer Science. D. Acevedo, E. Vote, D. Laidlaw and M. S. Joukowsky (Providence RI).

Television

1996. Search. *Archaeology 101*, North Carolina State University. Short appearance as Brown University's Director, Petra 'Great' Temple Excavations.

1995. *Ancient Mysteries* Arts and Entertainment (Arts and Entertainment Network Series) documentary film produced by Bram Rose et. al., *Petra.* 52 minutes, color program, narrated by Kathleen Turner.

1995-1994. Archaeology series. Petra, City in the Sand. *Learning Channel*, New Dominion Films, narrated by John Rhys Davies. (Re-aired many times).

1995. Video Lecture on Petra 'Great' Southern Temple. *St. Louis Society Archaeological Institute of America*. M. S. Joukowsky, October 17, 1995.

Web Pages

1997, 1999-2007. (updated), "The Petra Great Temple." <http://www.brown.edu/Departments/Joukowsky_institute/Petra>. <http://www.brown.edu/Departments/Anthropology/Petra/>

2005-2007 (Web pages and for digital videos and 3D images) <The Joukowsky Institute Workplace> The Petra Great Temple Database Project or <http://proteus.brown.edu/PGTdata/Home> or <http://lems.brown.edu/>

2003. <http://www.lems.brown.edu/shape/#news>

2003 May/June issue of Higher Learning. *Higher Learning* pp. 18-19 <http://www.teachmag.com/higher-learning.html> Published by *TEACH Magazine*, 258 Wallace Ave. Ste 206 Toronto, Ontario, M6P 3M9, Canada.

Bazin, P. L. and A. Henry 2003. Wall Drawer: A Simple Solution to Traditional Drawing and Photographic Recording of Archaeological Features. <http://www.lwms.brown.edu/ basin/Research/WallDrawer.html>

1995 Southern Temple Excavations at Petra, Jordan, Brown University. <petra@stg.brown.edu>

1996 Petra. *ASOR Digs 96*, The American Schools of Oriental Research, Committee on Archaeological Policy: Reports of Affiliated Projects. <http://www.cobb.msstate.edu/asordigs.html>

Other

2006 National Canadian Radio, Petra Interview at the Canadian National Museum of Civilization, Ottawa, September 29, 2006.

2001 *Inaugural Faculty Program at Brown University for President Ruth J, Simmons*, Simulation and Visualization in the Petra Project, with D. Laidlaw, Computer Science, M. S. Joukowsky, Old World Art and Archaeology and Department of Anthropology, with E. Vote and D. Acevedo, Computer Science.

1997.Mannis, A. Coins of the 'Great' Southern Temple, Petra, The Digital Archive Project. (CD ROM), Honors Thesis at Brown Univ. *COWAA*. (Providence).

Illustration Credits

PHOTOGRAPH CREDITS

All photographs can be credited to Artemis W. Joukowsky unless otherwise noted.

Other credits are D. G. Barrett: Figures 10.1–12, 8.2, 12.9–12.26; C. F. Cloke: Figures 4.3, 4.6, 4.7, 4.8; E. E. and W. B. Myers: Figure 1.18; S. M. Rababeh: Figures 3.1–18; Elephant headed capital in porphyry from the Vatican Museum (Musei Vaticani), Courtesy of the Vatican Museum, Rome; Gilbert Design Associates: Figure 7B.19. R. Frederiksen: Figures 8.2–8.5, 8.7, 8.8, 8.10–8.13, 8.21, 8.24, 8.31, 8. 32; C. A. Tuttle: Figure 13.11; C. A. Tuttle and Q. Tweissi: Figures 13.1, 13.1b, 13.2, 13.4, 13.6–13.10, 13.13–13.15, 13.17, 13.19–13.20, 13.22, 13-25–26, 13.28, 13.30, 13.33–13.37, 13.39–14.40; M. O'Hea: Figures 15.2, 15.4–8, 15.12, 15.15, 15.18; S. F. Larsen: Chapter 15, complete; M. S. Joukowsky: Figures 18B.1–18B.5; 18C.1–18C.4; 19.1–20.23; and S. K. Reid: Figure 20.9.

PLAN CREDITS

Overall credits for Great Temple Plans—M. C. Agnew, C. F. Cloke, T. Tullis, E. A. Power, P. C. Zimmerman, and B. A. Brown: Figure 4.1; M. C. Agnew and F. R. Ishakat: Figures 1.3, 1.9; F. R. Ishakat: Figures 2.1, 2.2, 2.4; M. C. Agnew and E. A. Power: Figures 1.4, 1.5, 1.6, 12.1, 21.2; P. C. Zimmerman, B. A. Brown, C. F. Cloke, M. C. Agnew and E. A. Power: Figures 1.5, 1.6, 1.11, 1.16, 2.5, 2.6, 2.7, 7A.1, 7A.2, 7B.2, 7B.4; M. C. Agnew and E. A. Power: Figures 1.4, 1.5, 1.6, 4.14, 4.4, 9.1, 9.2, 9.7, 9.9, 9.13, 21.1 and 21.6 (drafted by M. S. Joukowsky); R. Frederiksen and M. Alepi: Figures 8.1, 8.29; R. Frederiksen and J. J. Basile: Figure 8.12; P. C. Zimmerman, B. A. Brown, C. F. Cloke, M. C. Agnew, E. A. Power, and F. R. Ishakat: Figures 2.6, 2.7. 3.1.

CHART CREDITS

D. G. Barrett: Figure 12.26, 12.27; R. Ceron-Carrasco: Figures 17B.1–17B.3; R. Frederiksen: Figures 8.15, 8.16, 8.17; F. R. Ishakat: Figures 2.3, 2.4; M. S. Joukowsky: Figures 1.23, 11.1–11.36; A. Murock Hussein: Figures 7A.12, 7A.13; S. W. Kansa: Figures 17A.1–17A.23; M. O'Hea: Figures 15.3, 15.10; and E. A. Power: Figure 1.7. M. S. Joukowsky: Appendices 1–4.1–7.5; Appendix 4.1–4.9 and Appendix 5.

DRAWING AND DRAFTING CREDITS

D. G. Barrett: Figure 13 (front); J. J. Basile: Figures 6.17, 6.31;U. Bellwald: Figures 5.3, 5.13; L. Braddock: Figures 6.21, 6.25; E. C. Egan: Figures 4.9, 5.4, 5.8, 5.9, 12.2–4, 19A.5, 19A.6; 19B.6, 19.B.7; E. C. Egan and M. S. Joukowsky: Figure 6.29; A. Grey: Figure 7A.10, 7A.11, 7A.19; J. P. Hagen: Figures 7B.9, 7B.11a-b, 7B.16a-b; M. S. Joukowsky: Figure 21.6; N. MacDonald, November/December 2006, Courtesy of *Saudi Aramco World*, Figures 7B.14, 7B.15; M. O'Hea: Figures 14.1, 14.9, 14.11, 14.13–14.14, 14.16–15.17; K. O'Meara: Figure 6.19; S. L. Saunders: Figures 11.2–11.4; and S. M. Sullivan: Figure 6.2; S. M. Sullivan and J. J. Basile: Figures 6.7, 6.9; S. M. Sullivan and K. O'Meara: Figures 6.4, 6.12, 6.15, 6.23; S. B. Tillack: Figure 7A.7; Q. Twessi: Figures 13.1a, 13.3, 13.5, 13.12, 13.16, 13.18, 13.21, 13.23, 13.24, 13.27, 13.29, 13.31, 13.32, 13.38; and E. L. Vote: Figures 1.8, 1.9, 1.10, 1.12, 1.13, 1.14, 1.15, 1.17.

SCULPTURE RECONSTRUCTIONS

D. Qublan, Figure 7B.18; R. Fishman: Figure 7B.19.

ON-LINE *OPEN CONTEXT*

Pottery, 58 Figures of ceramics, divided into 12 vessel classes, drawn by S. L. Saunders, Drafted by E. C. Egan and M.S. Joukowsky.

Lamps

D. G. Barrett: Figure 12.28. Great Temple Hellenistic and Miscellaneous Lamps; Figure 12.29. Great Temple Nabataean Lamps; Figure 12.30. Great Temple Roman Lamps; Figure 12.31, Great Temple Byzantine Lamps; Figure 12.32; and Great Temple Islamic Lamp. All lamp photographs reworked by Tyler Parker.

Great Temple Vol. III: Index

B